Nahj al-Balāghah

"People! We live in a challenging age and a difficult time …". This is one of the many statements that still ring true, and it is not surprising that *Nahj al-balāghah* (*The Way of Eloquence*) has remained one of the most revered Arabic texts among both Sunni and Shi'i Muslims. These speeches, letters, and sayings attributed to 'Alī ibn Abī Ṭālib, cousin and son-in-law of the Prophet Muḥammad, one of the key figures in Islamic history and considered an outstanding orator, were compiled around CE 1000. This volume, with Tahera Qutbuddin's splendid scholarly edition and masterly translation, is a major achievement.
– *Geert Jan van Gelder, Laudian Professor of Arabic Emeritus, University of Oxford*

Translating the sermons and sayings of Imam 'Ali, "the gate to the city of knowledge," is a momentous task. Dr. Qutbuddin has not only encapsulated the thoughts and ideas of Imam 'Ali accurately, but she has also beautifully preserved the fluency, flow and tempo of *Nahj al-Balāghah's* sermons and sayings in English through her selective choice of words and flowing structure. I strongly recommend this translation to the specialist and casual reader alike.
– *Syed Muhammad Rizvi, Principal Director, Shi'a Research Institute, Toronto, and Head, Council of Shi'a Muslim Scholars of North America*

Few works in Arabic contain the depth of wisdom and eloquence found in *Nahj al-Balāghah*, the fourth-century AH collection of the statements of Imam 'Ali b. Abi Talib. My journey with the text—published and lauded by the Egyptian reformer Muhammad Abduh—began more than fifty years ago at the Beirut Religious Seminary where I was required to memorize sections to hone my speaking skills; later, at al-Azhar University in Cairo, my professor Dr. Abd al-Halim Mahmoud made me recite from a sermon for my oral exams. This new edition of *Nahj al-Balāghah*, edited by a scholar of Arabic rhetoric, utilizes the oldest and most reliable manuscripts and includes an erudite and in-depth introduction, ensuring its place as a core reference for scholars and researchers. I congratulate Professor Qutbuddin on this outstanding academic achievement.
– *Ridwan al-Sayyid, Dean of the College of Postgraduate Studies and Research, Mohamed Bin Zayed University for Humanities, Abu Dhabi*

"Below the speech of the Creator but above the speech of created beings"—this is how commentator Ibn Abī al-Ḥadīd (d. ca. 1258) famously described *Nahj al-Balāghah*, recognizing this collection as the pinnacle of eloquence in the Arabic language. Tahera Qutbuddin presents in this volume a painstaking new edition of this monument of Arabic literature, based on the oldest and most reliable manuscripts and thorough consideration of the commentarial tradition. Her brilliant translation is faithful to the original text, precise, and elegant, capturing the force of pithy aphorisms, the cadence of Arabic oratory, and contemplative reflection on the trials and tribulations of human experience, the ethical quandaries of social and political life, and the wonders of the natural world.
– *Devin J. Stewart, Samuel Candler Dobbs Professor of Arabic and Middle Eastern Studies, and Chair of the Department of Middle Eastern and South Asian Studies, Emory University*

مِنْ كَلَامِ أَمِيرِ ٱلْمُؤْمِنِينَ عَلِيّ بْنِ أَبِي طَالِبٍ صَلَوَاتُ ٱللَّهِ عَلَيْهِ

لِلشَّرِيفِ ٱلرَّضِيّ مُحَمَّدِ بْنِ ٱلْحُسَيْنِ بْنِ مُوسَى

(تُوُفِّيَ سَنَةَ ٤٠٦هـ / ١٠١٥م)

Nahj al-Balāghah

The Wisdom and Eloquence of ʿAlī
A Parallel English-Arabic Text

Compiled by

al-Sharīf al-Raḍī (d. 406/1015)

Edited and translated by

Tahera Qutbuddin

BRILL

LEIDEN | BOSTON

Originally published in hardback in 2024 as Volume 15 in the series Islamic Translation Series.

Free E-Book (PDF) download is sponsored by the Shi'a Research Institute Open Access Grant (Toronto), https://shiaresearch.ca

Cover illustration: Nahj al-Balāghah ("The Way of Eloquence"). Cover calligraphy by Nihad Nadam, 2025.

The Library of Congress Cataloging-in-Publication Data is available online at https://catalog.loc.gov
LC record of the hardback edition available at https://lccn.loc.gov/2023054675

Typeface for the Latin, Greek, and Cyrillic scripts: "Brill". See and download: brill.com/brill-typeface.

ISBN 978-90-04-75960-2 (paperback, 2026)
ISBN 978-90-04-68259-7 (hardback)
ISBN 978-90-04-68260-3 (e-book)
DOI 10.1163/9789004682603

قال عليّ أمير المؤمنين عليه السلام
«العلماء باقون ما بقي الدهر أعيانهم مفقودة وأمثالهم في القلوب موجودة»

Dedicated
with deepest gratitude
to my revered father,
Syedna Khuzaima Qutbuddin,
and to his successor, my revered brother
Syedna Taher Fakhruddin,
Dāʿīs of Amīr al-Muʾminīn and disseminators
of his pure knowledge.

⁝

Contents

Acknowledgments   XI
Abbreviations   XIII

Introduction   1

Note on the Edition and Translation: Manuscripts and Methodology   28

Detailed Contents   56

TEXT AND TRANSLATION
Nahj al-Balāghah: The Eloquence and Wisdom of ʿAlī

Raḍī's Introduction   98

1 Orations   106

2 Letters   530

3 Sayings   678
       Section on Rare Words   752
       (cont. Sayings)   760

Raḍī's Conclusion   824

Glossary of Names, Places, and Terms   827
Appendix of Sources for the Texts of *Nahj al-Balāghah*   863
Bibliography   914
Index of Names and Places   944
Index of Terms   952
Index of Qurʾan, Hadith, Poetry, and Proverbs   970
فهرس المفاهيم الدينيّة والأخلاقيّة (Index of Religious and Ethical
   Concepts)   994

Acknowledgments

I first encountered Ali's wisdom and eloquence in classes I took as a child with my learned father, Syedna Khuzaima Qutbuddin. In early morning "sabaq" sessions in Mumbai, and during community trips to various towns and villages in India and worldwide, my siblings and I would memorize a saying and he would explain its life lessons, العلم وراثة كريمة، أغنى الغنى العقل، المؤمن هشّ بشّ، القناعة مال لا ينفد، and many more. These texts and lessons sparked an enduring passion, and I began academic work with *Nahj al-Balāghah* at Ain Shams University in Cairo, where I wrote my MA thesis with Professor Ahmad El Naggar on its ethical and historical themes. Then in my first year in Harvard's PhD program, Professor Roy Mottahedeh showed me a facsimile edition of a 5th/11th-century manuscript owned by the Marʿashi library in Qum. I wrote, they generously sent me a copy, and that was the beginning of my *Nahj al-Balāghah* manuscript collection. I also had enriching conversations about the text with my distinguished Doktorvater, Professor Wolfhart Heinrichs, and I contemplated writing my dissertation on Imam Ali's life and teachings before realizing that I needed to go slowly in approaching such a complex topic. Over the years, I published studies, critical editions, and translations of Ali's words, including *A Treasury of Virtues: Sayings, Sermons, and Teachings of ʿAli, with the One Hundred Proverbs*, and I continued to gather manuscripts. Finally in the past decade, I focused on editing and translating *Nahj al-Balāghah*.

Throughout my journey, the guidance and blessings of my revered father, Syedna Khuzaima Qutbuddin, and his eminent son and successor, Syedna Taher Fakhruddin, have been my source of strength. The prayers showered by my beloved mother, Sakina busaheba, sustained my courage. My dearest husband, Abduz-Zahir Mohyuddin, gave caring support and excellent advice, and Hyder, my darling son, supplied love and technological help. My wonderful and learned Qutbuddin family—especially Syedi Dr Abdeali bhaisaheb, Syedi Dr Husain bhaisaheb, Dr Aziz bhaisaheb, and Dr Bazat-Saifiyah behensaheba—offered insightful ideas.

In the project's final stages, numerous scholars provided generous assistance: Professor Devin Stewart gave detailed feedback on the full document, Dr Tynan Kelly spent several hundred hours helping to prepare the Appendix of Sources, my meticulous copy editor Dr Linda S. George waved her magic wand over my prose, and Dr Hasan Ansari shared ideas and manuscripts. Many individuals and institutions facilitated the acquisition of manuscripts from world libraries, including University of Chicago Librarian Dr Marlis Saleh, Dr Ayse Polat, Professor Robert Gleave, Mr Reza Hemyari, Dr Ali Haider, Professor Bilal Orfali, the Library of Arabic Literature at NYU-Abu Dhabi, and the London Alulbayt Foundation. Dr Mahdi Mojtahedi of the Amir al-Muminin Ali a.s. Specialized Library in Mashhad shared a PDF of Dr Qays Bahjat Attar's edition with his permission, and Mr Muhammed Sabbaghi brought me a physical copy from Iran. Professors Ridwan El Sayyed, James Montgomery, Shawkat Toorawa, and Muhammed Rustom gave constructive advice, Hatim Zakiyuddin saheb shared various Ali-related Tayyibi manuscripts, and my brilliant and enthusiastic *Nahj al-Balāghah* seminar students at the University of Chicago offered perceptive suggestions. Several colleagues answered queries about the text's dissemination, and I note their contribution in the Introduction's relevant footnotes.

At Brill, senior acquisitions editor Mr Abdurraouf Oueslati steered the project through its various stages with perfect kindness and expertise. I am also grateful to Brill's anonymous reviewer for their positive endorsement, Islamic Translations series editor Professor Ayman Shihadeh and Brill's Middle East acquisition editors for accepting my book, Dr Aisha Moussa who paginated the indexes, Pieter te Velde and Brill's excellent production and marketing teams, and the Shi'a Research Institute of Toronto who enabled free download of the e-book PDF by sponsoring Open Access.

To all who helped with this project, which is so dear to my heart, I offer heartfelt thanks.

جزا كم الله خيرًا

28 March, 2024
19 Ramadan, 1445

Abbreviations

A (آ)	Sulaymaniye Aya Sofya manuscript
ʿA	ʿAbduh's commentary
B	Baḥrānī's commentary
Ch (ج)	Chester Beatty manuscript
D (د)	Imam Reza Mashhad manuscript
EIr	*Encyclopaedia Iranica*
EI[2]	*Encyclopaedia of Islam*, 2nd edition
EI[3]	*Encyclopaedia of Islam*, 3rd edition
F	Ibn Funduq's commentary
fol.	folio
Gh	Mughniyyah's commentary
H (ه)	Rampur Raza manuscript
Ḥ	Ibn Abī al-Ḥadīd's commentary
K (ك)	Sulaymaniye Reisulkuttab manuscript 2
L (ل)	Mumtaz ul Ulama Lucknow manuscript
Q (ق)	Iraqi National Museum manuscript
M (م)	Marʿashī manuscript
MS, MSS	manuscript, manuscripts
N (ن)	Naṣīrī manuscript
r	recto
R	Rāwandī's commentary
S (س)	Sulaymaniye Reisulkuttab manuscript 1
Sh (ش)	Shahrastānī manuscript
T (ت)	Topkapi manuscript
v	verso
Y (ي)	Yaʿqūbī Tehran University manuscript
Z (ز)	Maulana Azad Aligarh manuscript

Introduction

دون كلام الخالق وفوق كلام المخلوقين

"Below the words of the creator and above the words of his creatures"

The eminent Sunni commentator Ibn Abī al-Ḥadīd (d. ca. 656/1258) endorsing a common line of praise for ʿAlī's words.[1]

Over fourteen centuries, across five continents, and among many faith denominations, scholars and laypeople alike have drawn on the deep wisdom stored in the eloquent words of ʿAlī ibn Abī Ṭālib (d. 40/661).[2] Cousin, son-in-law, and ward of the Prophet Muḥammad, ʿAlī was the first male to accept Islam, the first Shiʿi Imam, and the fourth Sunni Caliph. Revered as a sage and religious authority, he is also lauded as Islam's master orator. ʿAlī's words—including first and foremost his dazzling orations, as well as his pithy sayings and magisterial letters—span a wide spectrum of preaching, philosophy, and government. They offer profound reflections on the majesty of the creator, fervent warnings on the transience of this world, and urgent exhortations to prepare for the imminent hereafter. They encompass pious sermons counseling virtue, earnest directives to cultivate the intellect, and reverent praise for the Prophet Muḥammad. They animate rousing battle and political speeches, passionately maintaining righteousness. They instruct in strict dispatches to tax-collectors, urging compassion. They inscribe erudite letters to governors, demanding justice. And they contain a host of timeless maxims offering religious, pragmatic, and character-building wisdom. All these themes and more are articulated in

---

1   Ibn Abī al-Ḥadīd, *Sharḥ Nahj al-balāghah*, 1:24; the same laudation, with some variation in language, is offered by Rāwandī (d. 573/1177, Shiʿi), *Minhāj al-barāʿah*, 1:4: "below the words of God and his Messenger, and above the words of humans" (دون كلام الله ورسوله وفوق كلام البشر); and Muḥammad ʿAbduh (d. 1905, Sunni), *Sharḥ Nahj al-balāghah*, 1:6: "the most noble and eloquent of words after the words of God and the words of his Prophet" (أشرف الكلام وأبلغه بعد كلام الله تعالى وكلام نبيّه).

2   The attribution to ʿAlī, here and throughout, is to be understood in light of complexities discussed in the next section, "Collection of ʿAlī's Words: Orality, Authenticity, Written Sources, and Influence on Litterateurs": viz., many of the texts attributed to ʿAlī are probably genuine remnants, some with modifications, some even verbatim, but interpolations, modifications, and texts of later provenance are also likely to be in the mix. To determine probable authenticity, we must assess individual texts—rather than the compilation as a whole—based on early and wide provenance and compatibility with the literary and historical milieu of ʿAlī's time.

pulsating oral rhythms and vibrant desert-and-camel images within the pages of the present volume of ʿAlī's words, *Nahj al-Balāghah: The Wisdom and Eloquence of ʿAlī*, compiled by the eminent Twelver Shiʿi Baghdadi scholar, al-Sharīf al-Raḍī (d. 406/1015).

Accolades for ʿAlī's words and wisdom would fill volumes,[3] but suffice it to say that friend and foe alike have paid them homage: ʿAlī's follower Ḍirār ibn Ḍamrah (fl. 1st/7th c.), for example, declared that "wisdom spoke upon his tongue."[4] The chancery head of the intensely anti-ʿAlid Umayyads, ʿAbd al-Ḥamīd al-Kātib (d. 132/750), who is venerated as the father of Arabic prose, credited his training in the art of eloquence to "memorizing the orations of ʿAlī."[5] The ultimate tribute is paid in the lines I have cited in the epigraph above, in which ʿAlī's words are extolled as being "below the words of the creator and above the words of his creatures."

Nahj al-Balāghah is the most celebrated compilation of ʿAlī's words, and one of the most influential texts of the Arabic Islamic literary heritage. Widely acclaimed as a masterpiece of Arabic literature and font of Islamic wisdom, it has been avidly cited, studied, commented on, and memorized across the Islamic world continually for more than a thousand years. In this volume, I present a critical Arabic edition based on the earliest extant manuscripts, dating from the 5th/11th through the 7th/13th centuries, three of which were checked against a manuscript authorized by Raḍī himself, side-by-side with my carefully researched English translation. For the translation, I took a long, deep dive into the text, along with a careful reading of its major commentaries and a collation of the history and literature of the early Islamic period; all the while, I paid close attention to the graphic imagery that underpins the Arabic phrases and the parallelism of their pithy cadences. My hope is to have produced an accurate edition and a lucid translation that captures some of the depth and brilliance of the original.

---

3 See collected accolades by Ṭabāṭabāʾī, "Fī Riḥāb Nahj al-balāgha," part 4, *passim*; ʿAbd al-Zahrāʾ, *Maṣādir Nahj al-balāghah*, 1:87–99; ʿUṭāridī, "Introduction" to his edition of Kaydarī's commentary, 1:5–10, 52–53; Keizoghani and Nafchi, "The Greatness of *Nahj Al-Balagha*." Some laudatory statements are quoted later in the present Introduction.

4 (تنطق الحكمة على لسانه), with some variants: Nuʿmān, *Sharḥ al-akhbār*, 2:391–392; Qālī, *Amālī*, 2:147; Masʿūdī, *Murūj*, 2:415; Ibn ʿAsākir, *Tārīkh*, 24:402; Abū Nuʿaym al-Iṣfahānī, *Ḥilyat al-awliyāʾ*, 1:84–185; Ibn Ḥamdūn, *Tadhkirah*, 4:28; Ibn Abī al-Ḥadīd, *Sharḥ Nahj al-balāghah*, 18:225–226.

5 Ibn Abī al-Ḥadīd, *Sharḥ Nahj al-balāghah*, 1:24. The same report—with "words" instead of "orations"—is also cited by Jahshiyārī, *Wuzarāʾ*, 82; Thaʿālibī, *Thimār al-qulūb*, 165; Zamakhsharī, *Rabīʿ al-abrār*, 4:50; and Ṣafadī, *Wāfī*, 18:23.

1   ʿAlī ibn Abī Ṭālib (d. 40/661)

An appreciation of ʿAlī's renown is essential for understanding the resounding reception of his compiled words, just as his biography is essential to contextualizing their doctrinal and political content.[6] Since ʿAlī's words collected in the present volume directly speak to events in his life, a sketch of the main episodes and actors of his time will help the reader situate their consequence, and a summary of his legacy will help explain their dissemination.

ʿAlī ibn Abī Ṭālib ibn ʿAbd al-Muṭṭalib ibn Hāshim was born around 600 AD in Mecca, according to some reports, inside the Holy Kaaba, to the Hāshimite chieftain Abū Ṭālib and the Hāshimite noblewoman Fāṭimah bint Asad. When he was just an infant, his older cousin Muḥammad, an orphan whom ʿAlī's parents had raised, asked for his charge, and ʿAlī grew up in the care of the future Prophet of Islam. ʿAlī was approximately ten years old when Muḥammad began his call to the new religion, and he immediately accepted Islam. He prayed for two years alone with Muḥammad and Muḥammad's wife Khadījah before others joined the fold. Around twenty-three at the time of Muḥammad's migration to Medina, ʿAlī played a vital role in establishing Islam in its nascent stage. His valor in the battles of Badr, Uḥud, Khaybar, and Khandaq against the Meccans and their allies would become legendary, as would his sagacity and erudition. Both Sunni and Shiʿi Muslims recount numerous hadiths from the Prophet praising ʿAlī, among the most famous of which are the following: "I am the city of knowledge and ʿAlī is its gateway"; "ʿAlī is to me as Aaron was to Moses"; and "You, ʿAlī, are my brother in this world and the next."[7] Soon after Muḥammad settled in Medina, ʿAlī married Muḥammad's youngest daughter, Fāṭimah al-Zahrāʾ, and had four children with her: Ḥasan, Ḥusayn, Zaynab, and Umm Kulthūm. Muḥammad's line continued solely through them, and the line through Ḥusayn would become an important locus for the Shiʿi doctrine of the imamate. According to the Shiʿa, Muḥammad appointed ʿAlī as his successor on 18th Dhū al-Ḥijjah in the year 10/632, at the caravan stop of Ghadīr Khumm, enroute from Mecca to Medina after his last pilgrimage, uttering the

---

6 Western studies on ʿAlī's biography include Madelung, *The Succession to Muhammad*, 141–310; Gleave, "ʿAlī b. Abī Ṭālib," *EI*³; Manouchehri et al., "ʿAlī b. Abī Ṭālib," *Encyclopaedia Islamica*; Abbas, *The Prophet's Heir: The Life of ʿAlī ibn Abī Ṭālib*; Qutbuddin, "Ali ibn Abi Talib," *Dictionary of Literary Biography*.

7 (أَنتَ يا عليّ أخي في الدنيا والآخرة), (أنا مدينة العلم وعليّ بابها). Cited widely. Shiʿi sources include: Nuʿmān, *Sharḥ al-akhbār*, 1:89, 97. Sunni sources include: Tirmidhī, *Sunan*, §3720, §3725, §3730, §3731; Ibn Saʿd, *Ṭabaqāt*, 3:22; Ibn Mājah, *Sunan*, 145, §121.

famous line, "Whoever takes me as his master, 'Alī is his master."[8] The Sunnis also narrate this hadith, and they interpret the declaration as praise for 'Alī's high station, rather than a designation of succession.

Muḥammad died a few months later, in 11/632, and 'Alī led the burial preparations. Though upholding his right to the succession, he ceded command to the first three Sunni caliphs, Abū Bakr, 'Umar, and 'Uthmān. For the next twenty-five years, which saw the consolidation of the Muslim polity in the Arabian Peninsula and its expansion into Syria, Egypt, Iraq, and Iran, 'Alī retreated from direct involvement in governing. The history books recount that he spent those years collecting and collating the texts of the Qur'an and teaching Ḥasan and Ḥusayn.

In 35/656 in Medina, a group of irate Muslims assassinated 'Uthmān, accusing him of nepotism; in the turbulent aftermath and after repeated solicitations, 'Alī accepted the caliphal pledge of allegiance from the Muslim community in Medina and across most of the Islamic empire. He ruled until 40/661, when he, too, was assassinated. Most of 'Alī's recorded sermons, letters, and sayings are woven into the political and military fabric of those four difficult years. They articulate morality and conviction and champion justice and charity.

As caliph, 'Alī was forced to fight three groups of Muslims who rebelled against his strict ideas of equity and equality: the first two were armies brought against him by prominent individuals, who, in furtherance of their political ambitions, falsely accused him of complicity in 'Uthmān's murder; the third were rebels from his own army.

'Alī fought the first pitched battle of his caliphate just outside Basra, in Iraq, in 36/656, four months after he was proclaimed caliph. His challengers were the Prophet's widow 'Ā'ishah and the Quraysh Emigrants Ṭalḥah and Zubayr. Famed as the Battle of the Camel, it was named for the animal 'Ā'ishah rode onto the battlefield, serving as a metaphor for its rider. The so-called "associates

---

8 (من كنت مولاه فعلي مولاه). Sunni sources include: Ibn Mājah, *Sunan*, s.v. "*Faḍā'il aṣḥāb Rasūl Allāh*"; Ibn Ḥanbal, *Musnad*, s.v. "*al-Khulafā' al-rāshidūn*"; Tirmidhī, *Sunan*, s.v. "*Manāqib*"; Bayhaqī, *I'tiqād*, 354–357; Iskāfī, *Mi'yār*, 210–218; 'Abd al-Jabbār, *Mughnī*, 20.2:137; Ibn 'Abd Rabbih, *'Iqd*, 4:291; Zamakhsharī, *Rabī' al-abrār*, 1:69–70; Sibṭ, *Tadhkirah*, 29–34, 62; Ghazālī, *Sirr al-'ālamayn* 18, and in several other works; Dhahabī, *Siyar*, 8:335, classifying it as a "widely narrated" (*mutawātir*) hadith. Shi'a sources include: Ya'qūbī, *Tārīkh*, 2:112; Nu'mān, *Sharḥ al-akhbār*, 1:99, 104, 106; Nu'mān, *Da'ā'im al-Islām*, 1:15–19; Nu'mān, *al-Majālis wa-l-musāyarāt*, 327–329; Ṣadūq, *Ma'ānī*, 65–74; Ṣadūq, *Amālī*, 2, §1, 108, §26, 317–318, §56, 514, §84; 'Alī ibn Muḥammad, *Dāmigh al-bāṭil*, 2:112–113; Thaqafī, *Ghārāt*, 2:658–659; Ṭabrisī, *Iḥtijāj*, 1:55–67; Mufīd, *Irshād*, 1:174–177; idem, *Amālī*, 44; Fattāl, *Rawḍat al-wā'iẓīn*, 103, 350; Idrīs, *'Uyūn al-akhbār*, 1:480–487.

of the Camel" were recruited mostly among the Basrans, while 'Alī was supported by many from neighboring Kufa, a few groups from Basra, and several distinguished Emigrants and Allies, close Companions of the Prophet who had accompanied 'Alī from Medina. The battle ended swiftly in a clear victory for 'Alī. Ṭalḥah and Zubayr were killed, 'Ā'ishah was sent back to Medina, and their erstwhile supporters pledged allegiance to 'Alī.

'Alī stayed on in Iraq, with Kufa becoming his de facto capital, pressed to deal with the other grave challenger on the horizon, the Umayyad governor of Damascus, Mu'āwiyah. Mu'āwiyah was 'Uthmān's cousin, and son of one of Muḥammad's chief enemies, Abū Sufyān, many of whose pagan family members 'Alī had slain on the battlefield; he refused to accept 'Alī as caliph. 'Alī sent his associate Jarīr—earlier 'Uthmān's governor in Hamadhān—to Damascus to convince Mu'āwiyah to pledge allegiance. Mu'āwiyah responded with a call to arms. In 37/657, the two clashed at the Battle of Ṣiffīn, on the banks of the Euphrates at the border of Iraq and Syria. Mu'āwiyah was supported by his Umayyad clan and many tribesmen from Syria. His main advisor was 'Amr ibn al-'Āṣ, commander of the Muslim army that had conquered Egypt three decades earlier, recalled by 'Umar on charges of corruption. 'Alī's army consisted of several Companions of the Prophet from Medina, and many tribesmen from Iraq. 'Alī challenged Mu'āwiyah to a duel, but Mu'āwiyah, aware of 'Alī's reputation as an intrepid warrior, refused. Battle commenced and continued for ten days. 'Alī himself—then around sixty years of age—took up the sword. Tens of thousands were killed. Then, as the tide slowly turned in 'Alī's favor, Mu'āwiyah's army famously raised pages of the Qur'an on spears as an appeal for arbitration. 'Alī initially rejected the suggestion as a ruse. Ironically, many of his own Iraqi commanders insisted he accept, and he gave in, stipulating that the arbitrators must rule according to the Qur'an. 'Alī then attempted to appoint his cousin, the learned 'Abdallāh ibn al-'Abbās as arbitrator, but he was overruled, and, again ironically, his commanders insisted that he appoint the dismissed governor of Kufa, Abū Mūsā al-Ash'arī, who, in the lead-up to the Battle of the Camel, had publicly directed them not to support 'Alī. Mu'āwiyah appointed 'Amr. The two arbitrators met a few months later at Dūmat al-Jandal, in southern Syria. Their judgment—which, given their back-stories, was to be expected—had cataclysmic consequences: Abū Mūsā ruled against 'Alī. 'Amr ruled for Mu'āwiyah. The Syrians rejoiced. The Iraqis were thrown into disarray.

The rumblings of Iraqi dissatisfaction crescendoed in the renegade movement of the so-called Kharijites, "Seceders." Under the leadership of 'Abdallāh ibn Wahb, four thousand men "seceded" from Kufa and 'Alī's following. With the rallying cry, "No rule but God's!" they took up arms against him. 'Alī fought them at the Battle of Nahrawān in 38/658, on the banks of the Tigris River in

Iraq. A thousand Kharijites were persuaded to leave the battlefield before the fighting began, a few took flight during the battle, four hundred wounded were pardoned, and the rest, including their leader, were killed.

Having dealt with the immediate danger, 'Alī attempted to resume the fight against Mu'āwiyah. But the Iraqi tribesmen were tired, and 'Alī spent his final months urging them to mobilize. Meanwhile, Mu'āwiyah was gaining ground. He took over Egypt, where his ally 'Amr ibn al-'Āṣ tortured and killed 'Alī's ward and governor, Muḥammad ibn Abī Bakr. Mu'āwiyah also reportedly poisoned Mālik al-Ashtar, one of 'Alī's staunchest supporters, who had been enroute to Egypt to take over the governorship from Muḥammad. From Damascus, Mu'āwiyah sent raid after raid against the cities of Arabia and even to the heart of Iraq.

'Alī was praying in the Grand Mosque in Kufa at dawn on 19th Ramaḍān 40/661, when the Kharijite agent Ibn Muljam (or Ibn Muljim) struck him a deathblow. He lived for two more days, during which he counselled his followers to piety and appointed his son Ḥasan as his successor. He died on 21st Ramaḍān, at sixty-one years of age.

'Alī is a familiar figure in medieval Islamic histories. Chronicles refer to him frequently in their accounts of the Prophet's mission, the reigns of Abū Bakr, 'Umar, and 'Uthmān, and his own caliphate. Biographical works usually include a long entry on 'Alī, with chapters on his acceptance of Islam, his excellent character, the praise for him expressed by the Prophet, his juridical decisions, physical appearance, garments, seal and armor, marriages and children, death, elegies composed in his memory, and his sermons and sayings. Several monographs recount his battles, notably The Battle of Ṣiffīn (*Waq'at Ṣiffīn*) by the early author Naṣr ibn Muzāḥim al-Minqarī (d. 202/818). Martyrologies of 'Alī are also many, second in number only to those written about his son Ḥusayn, the martyr of Karbala; fourteen are listed by the Shi'i bibliographer Āghā Buzurg al-Tihrānī (d. 1970), including the lost martyrology of the early author Abū Mikhnaf (d. 157/773). Numerous medieval works are devoted to cataloging 'Alī's merits, including works by well-known Sunni hadith scholars: Nasā'ī (d. 303/915), Book of Virtues: The Excellence of 'Alī ibn Abī Ṭālib (*Kitāb al-Khaṣā'iṣ fī faḍl 'Alī ibn Abī Ṭālib*), Ibn al-Maghāzilī (d. 483/1090), Qualities of 'Alī ibn Abī Ṭālib (*Manāqib 'Alī ibn Abī Ṭālib*), Sibṭ Ibn al-Jawzī (d. 654/1256), Reminder for the Elite (*Tadhkirat al-khawāṣṣ*), and numerous others. 'Alī also figures prominently in devotional poetry composed through the centuries by Shi'i as well as Sunni poets.

Although events of 'Alī's life are portrayed in similar fashion by most historians, he is perceived differently by different denominations. For Sunnis, 'Alī is a pious and austere man, a close Companion of the Prophet, and the fourth

Rightly Guided caliph of Islam. His knowledge of Islamic doctrine and law, his love for Islam and his closeness to the Prophet Muḥammad, his heroic role in the early battles of the Muslims, and his principled and pious rule are all applauded. *Tafḍīlī* Sunnis ("Upholders of ʿAlī's Superiority"), who also revere the first three caliphs, believe that ʿAlī was the most excellent individual after the Prophet. For Sufi mystics, many of whom are *Tafḍīlī* Sunnis, ʿAlī is the first link after the Prophet in the chain of mystic masters, and they regularly quote his ethical and doctrinal statements in manuals of spiritual guidance. For the Shiʿa, ʿAlī is the spiritual and temporal successor of the Prophet, the infallible Imam, divinely guided and able to perform miracles. His descendants are believed to inherit this role, and allegiance to them is considered necessary for salvation. The Shiʿa—short for *Shīʿat ʿAlī*, or "followers of ʿAlī"—have branched out into several denominations, based on the line of succession they accept as legitimate. The majority in the present time are the Twelver Shiʿa—to whom our compiler, Raḍī, belonged—and they form the bulk of the population in Iran, Iraq, and Lebanon. The Fatimid-Ismāʿīlī Shiʿa ruled a large part of the Islamic empire from the 10th to the 12th centuries AD with their seat in Cairo and are now located primarily in South Asia, in the two main denominations, Ṭayyibīs and Nizārīs. The Zaydī Shiʿa—earlier also a large presence in the region of the Caspian Sea—are concentrated today in Yemen. Some smaller branches, such as the Nuṣayrī denomination, proclaim ʿAlī's divinity. Such groups are often termed Exaggerators (*Ghulāt*) in Islamic doctrinal works.

Muslims know ʿAlī by several titles that signify his preeminent stature. He is hailed by Shiʿa and Sunnis as "God's lion" (Arabic: *Asad Allāh*, Persian/Urdu: *Shēr-ē Khudā*), and "*Ḥaydar*" or "*Ḥaydarah*" a king among lions, stemming from his proverbial prowess in battle. He is petitioned as "Dispeller of hardships" (Persian/Urdu: *Mushkil kushā*). He is praised as "*Murtaḍā*," the one with whom God is pleased. He is lauded as the "*Waṣī*," the Prophet's legatee. And he is referenced as the "*Imām*," an authoritative religious leader. The Shiʿa also revere him as "*Sāqi-ye Kawthar*" (Cupbearer of the Pool of Kawthar in Paradise), "*Ṣid-dīq*" (Greatest Supporter of the Prophet), "*Mawlā*" (Master, a reference to the aforementioned Ghadīr Khumm hadith, "Whoever takes me as his master, ʿAlī is his master"), and "*Amīr al-muʾminīn*" (Commander of the Faithful). This last is the most used of his titles in Shiʿa circles; Sunnis apply the title to all Muslim caliphs, including ʿAlī.

ʿAlī's shrine in the city of Najaf, in southern Iraq, is visited annually by hundreds of thousands of pilgrims. His caliphate is upheld as a model for just rule, and his words and teachings are revered as repositories of inspired wisdom. ʿAlī had declared to his associate Kumayl, "Those who hoard wealth are dead even as they live, whereas the learned remain as long as the world remains—their persons may be lost, but their teachings live on in the hearts of men" (§ 3.133). ʿAlī's legacy lives on in the hearts of men.

2   Collection of ʿAlī's Words: Orality, Authenticity, Written Sources, and Influence on Litterateurs

ʿAlī lived in a world where the principal mode of production, transmission, and collection of words was oral. In his time, written Arabic texts were rare. Although ʿAlī himself served as one of the Prophet's scribes in Medina and wrote down Qurʾanic passages as they were revealed, written transcription by him and his few lettered compatriots was carried out with rudimentary instruments and limited to important documents. Most verbal materials from the early period were initially related and preserved for a century or more chiefly by means of oral transmission, until, after paper was introduced from China in the early 2nd/8th century, writing burgeoned and they were systematically transcribed in books.

It is fair to ask the question: Are ʿAlī's words as transcribed in the present volume genuine? The short answer is that substantial portions could be authentic, some in gist, and some—especially those with striking images and rhythmic lines—verbatim. ʿAlī was one of the most revered personages of early Islam, his eloquence was proverbial, and during the four years of his caliphate, he preached long and frequently to large, public audiences, and so it is likely that many recorded materials attributed to him are genuine. Moreover, given the consistent attribution to ʿAlī of certain Qurʾan-based themes and nature-oriented images, and given their compatibility with the historical and literary ambience of the time, it is likely that they represent a true picture of his teachings.

The longer, technical back-story to that assessment—based on detailed research grounded in empirical data and orality theory in my recent book, *Arabic Oration: Art and Function*—is as follows:[9] It is true that the extended period of oral transmission for early Arabic verbal materials meant that many inaccuracies entered the written corpus. It is also true that there were many drivers to false ascriptions, as well as instances of rhetorical "improvements."[10] Nevertheless, there is clear evidence for the existence of a genuine core of texts. As

---

9   Qutbuddin, "The Preservation of Orations: Mnemonics-Based Oral Transmission, Supplementary Writing, and the Question of Authenticity," in *Arabic Oration*, 21–63.
10   For example, the earliest manuscripts M, Sh, N, and H render the last sentence of ora-

scholars of orality theory have established, formal verbal productions of oral communities are rooted in "mnemonics"—i.e., memory aid techniques, such as intense rhythm and graphic imagery. In addition to producing beautiful language, these constitute a physiological aid to memorization. Neuroscientists explain memory formation through the propensity of the brain to organize information in patterns. The process is called "neuronal entrainment." Children today learn the ABCs, for example, through a melody. Imagine trying to memorize a random list of letters without that jingle! Rhythm is present even in writing societies. In an oral society, it is a primary characteristic. Like the Qurʾan, like orations and sayings by other leaders from this period, ʿAlī's words were rhythmic and visual. These rhetorical features—combined with the attested powerful memories of oral societies—ensured that many orations and sayings were captured. ʿAlī's family and close associates were the first narrators. Early transmitters narrated materials partly in substance and partly verbatim. This hybrid mode fell somewhere between the meaning-based transmission of historical reports and the near-literal transmission of the Qurʾan and poetry.[11]

Moreover, as Gregor Schoeler has convincingly demonstrated,[12] oral circulation in this society was increasingly supplemented by scholarly notetak-

---

tion §1.201 as (فقدّموا بعضًا يكن لكم ولا تخلّفوا كُلًّا فيكون عليكم), "Send ahead a part that will remain yours. Do not leave everything behind, for that will count against you." Whereas Y and many later manuscripts have (فقدّموا بعضًا يكن لكم قرضًا ولا تخلّفوا كُلًّا فيكون عليكم كَلًّا), which says basically the same thing, but has more elaborate parallelism and prose-rhyme. That latter reading is also added in the margins of M, Sh, and H.

11   Four reservations expressed by modern authors—e.g. Aḥmad Amīn, *Fajr al-Islām*, 1:148–149; and Ṣafāʾ Khulūṣī, *The Authenticity of Nahj al-Balagha*, 31–35—apply to a handful of *Nahj al-balāghah* texts, which, they say: contain (1) later philosophical terms such as "the where" (*al-ayn*) and "eternal-ness" (*al-azaliyyah*); (2) detailed descriptions, unusual for the period, of animals like the ant and the peacock; and (3) prophecies about future events, such as the Zanj rebellion. Also, (4) some sermons are long and would be difficult to memorize on the fly. The possibility of later provenance for some of these texts, or at least of modifications, remains high. As a caveat to the caveats, though, it is also possible that technical terms were inserted into original texts, and shorter pieces were later stitched together into lengthier scripts. And it could be argued that the prophecies are cryptically worded and plausible, and that copious descriptions of animals are also found in pre- and early Islamic poetry. As in all compilations of early Islamic materials, some parts are likely genuine, while others may be later additions or modifications. As mentioned earlier, we must examine individual pieces, rather than the compilation as a whole, to determine probable authenticity.

12   Schoeler (*Genesis of Literature*, 71–72, 77–78) discusses the composition of Ibn Isḥāq's *Maghāzī* as a teaching collection of notes. He also discusses an earlier work with the same name by ʿUrwah ibn Zubayr as a hypomnema notebook, collected by his students and used as a teaching aid (ibid., 17).

ing. Over the century following ʿAlī's death of primarily oral transmission, we see a steady increase of concurrent written transcription. Like the Prophet's hadith, a fraction of ʿAlī's words was probably transcribed during his lifetime or immediately afterward; we are told of a written collection titled *Khuṭab Amīr al-Muʾminīn ʿalā l-manābir fī l-jumaʿ wa-l-aʿyād wa-ghayrihā* (Orations of the Commander of the Faithful upon the Pulpit on Fridays, Eids, and Other Occasions) by Zayd ibn Wahb al-Juhanī (d. 96/715), who fought in ʿAlī's army at Ṣiffīn and Nahrawān.[13]

Through the following centuries, ʿAlī's words were recorded in books by major historians, litterateurs, and compilers.[14] From the late 2nd/8th and early 3rd/9th centuries, Kufan scholars—including Abū Mikhnaf Lūṭ ibn Yaḥyā (d. 157/773), Ibrāhīm ibn Ḥakam al-Fazārī (d. 177/793), Masʿadah ibn Ṣadaqah al-ʿAbdī (d. 183/799), and Ibn al-Kalbī (d. 206/820)—produced dedicated compilations of ʿAlī's words; this is as one would expect, given the presence of ʿAlī and his most loyal followers in Kufa. Scholars from Baghdad—including Wāqidī (d. 207/823), Minqarī (d. 212/827), and Madāʾinī (d. 224/829)—also compiled ʿAlī's words. All these works have been lost. The last three scholars, however, include many of ʿAlī's texts in their extant histories, as do other 3rd/9th- and 4th/10th-century historians from far-flung parts of the Muslim empire with disparate denominational affiliations: Ibn Hishām (d. 218/833, after Ibn Isḥāq, d. 151/768), Ibn Saʿd (d. 230/845), Balādhurī (d. 279/892), Abū Isḥāq al-Thaqafī of Isfahān (d. 283/896), Yaʿqūbī (d. 284/897), Ṭabarī (d. 310/923), Ibn Aʿtham (d. 314/926), al-Qāḍī al-Nuʿmān (d. 363/974), and many more. The above-mentioned Juhanī, who served in ʿAlī's army, is the chief source for Abū Mikhnaf's lost work on ʿAlī's battles, which is cited in turn by Ṭabarī in his celebrated History. Literary anthologists, including Jāḥiẓ (d. 255/868), Ibn Qutaybah (d. 276/889), Ibn ʿAbd Rabbih of Spain (d. 328/940), Masʿūdī (d. 345/956), and Ibn Shuʿbah of Ḥarrān (fl. 4th/10th c.), also include large numbers of ʿAlī's orations, and many praise them profusely. Jāḥiẓ is said—though this attribution is uncertain—to have produced a concise compilation of ʿAlī's maxims titled *Miʾat kalimah* (Hundred Proverbs), that I have edited and translated.[15] Jāḥiẓ also quoted ʿAlī abundantly in his accepted works and praised him as the archetypal paradigm of eloquence. Early Muʿtazilī thinkers such as Iskāfī (d. 240/854) record ʿAlī's orations on the unity of God. Chancery-manual

---

13   Ṭūsī, *Fihrist*, 130, after Minqarī (d. 212/827), on the authority of Abū Mikhnaf (d. 157/773).

14   See detailed list in ʿAbd al-Zahrāʾ, *Maṣādir*, 1:454–486.

15   Jāḥiẓ, *Miʾat kalimah*, ed. and trans. Qutbuddin, in Quḍāʿī, *A Treasury of Virtues: Sayings, Sermons, and Teachings of ʿAlī with the One Hundred Proverbs Attributed to al-Jāḥiẓ*, 219–233.

authors such as the Egyptian Naḥḥās (d. 338/950) present whole chapters on ʿAlī's orations as part of the scribe's curriculum. Twelver Shiʿi jurists such as Kulaynī (d. 329/941) and Ibn Bābawayh (d. 381/991) include numerous citations of ʿAlī's words in their works. The Shāfiʿī-Ashʿarī scholar Māmaṭīrī (d. ca. 360/971) compiled a large volume of ʿAlī's words and interactions.

In the 4th/10th, 5th/11th, and 6th/12th centuries, major independent collections of ʿAlī's words were compiled and are still extant. The earliest surviving compilation is the *Kitāb al-Tawḥīd* (The Book of God's Unity), compiled by the aforementioned Fatimid-Ismāʿīlī Shiʿi scholar al-Qāḍī al-Nuʿmān (d. 363/974), which contains two long sermons on God's oneness, titled The Pearl (*Durrah*) and The Unique Sermon (*Waḥīdah*), with Nuʿmān's commentary. Next is the present volume, compiled by Raḍī in 400/1010, *Nahj al-Balāghah* (The Way of Eloquence). Then came *Dustūr maʿālim al-ḥikam* (A Compendium of Signposts of Wisdom) by al-Qāḍī al-Quḍāʿī (d. 454/1062), which I have edited and translated;[16] Quḍāʿī's main source appears to have been Māmaṭīrī's *Nuzhat al-abṣār*. Subsequent compilations were dedicated to ʿAlī's aphorisms: *Nathr al-laʾālī* (Scattered Pearls) by Ṭabrisī (d. 548/1153), and *Ghurar al-ḥikam* (Radiant Maxims) by Āmidī (d. 550/1155). Kaydarī (d. after 576/1180), who also wrote a commentary on *Nahj al-Balāghah*, collected ʿAlī's verse into a *Dīwān* titled *Anwār al-ʿuqūl* (Lights for Intellects). Of less certain provenance, an anonymously compiled book of supplications titled *al-Ṣaḥīfah al-ʿAlawiyyah* (ʿAlī's Parchments) is also attributed to ʿAlī, as is a short compilation of Prophetic hadith titled *Ṣaḥīfat ʿAlī ibn Abī Ṭālib* (Scrolls of ʿAlī ibn Abī Ṭālib). Additionally, Twelver Shiʿis regularly recite a supplication ʿAlī is said to have taught his devotee Kumayl, known by the latter's name as *Duʿāʾ Kumayl* (The Kumayl Supplication). Finally, Fatimid Ṭayyibīs believe that ʿAlī composed *Kitāb al-ʿIlm* (The Book of Knowledge), which he bequeathed to his sons Ḥasan and Ḥusayn, and which is now with the Imam in seclusion.

In the emergent Islamic civilization, ʿAlī's words influenced major litterateurs and scholars of Islam across denominational boundaries. Among early orators, ʿAlī's words were favorite sources—memorized, alluded to, or quoted in full. Ibn Abī al-Ḥadīd compares ʿAlī's influence on orators to the influence of the preeminent pre-Islamic poet Imruʾ al-Qays on poets.[17] The pro-Umayyad ascetic preacher of Basra al-Ḥasan al-Baṣrī (d. 110/728) was guided by ʿAlī's pious themes and language, as was the Syrian preacher Ibn Nubātah al-Khaṭīb

---

16   Quḍāʿī, *Dustūr maʿālim al-ḥikam*, ed. and trans. Qutbuddin, *A Treasury of Virtues: Sayings, Sermons, and Teachings of ʿAlī*.

17   Ibn Abī al-Ḥadīd, *Sharḥ Nahj al-balāghah*, 2:83.

(d. 374/985), who had memorized a large number of ʿAlī's orations.[18] Among scribes, ʿAlī's words were equally effective. I have mentioned ʿAbd al-Ḥamīd's acknowledgment that he had "learned eloquence by memorizing the orations of ʿAlī," and Naḥḥās's allocation of four chapters of the Eloquence section in his chancery-manual to ʿAlī's words.[19] Tributes were also paid by early prose writers who recorded ʿAlī's words and praised them, and I have mentioned some of these litterateurs earlier. Masʿūdī, who recorded many of ʿAlī's texts, noted that scholars in his time had memorized more than 480 of ʿAlī's speeches, which they frequently quoted.[20] ʿAlī's orations had special resonance among those who held to the theological school of the Muʿtazilah, to whom Raḍī and several of his compilation's commentators belonged, and among whom Iskāfī was mentioned as having recorded ʿAlī's texts. These rationalist scholars acknowledged their debt to ʿAlī on the fundamental subject of God's unity.[21] And ʿAlī's influence was not limited to prose. Numerous wisdom-verses by the poet-prodigy Mutanabbī (d. 354/955)—who, it should be noted, grew up, as did ʿAbd al-Ḥamīd al-Kātib, in ʿAlī's capital, Kufa—are distilled from ʿAlī's words.[22]

3   Al-Sharīf al-Raḍī (d. 406/1015): Career and Works

Best known as compiler of *Nahj al-Balāghah*, al-Sharīf Abū al-Ḥasan Muḥammad ibn al-Ḥusayn al-Mūsawī al-Raḍī—in short, al-Sharīf al-Raḍī, or simply Raḍī—was an eminent Twelver Shiʿi Muʿtazilī thinker, a prominent political personage in the Abbasid-Būyid realm, and one of the most notable scholars of his time. He was born in 359/970 in Baghdad and was a lifelong resident of this city. His family was descended from the Prophet Muḥammad and ʿAlī, his grandfather being the great-grandson of Imam Jaʿfar al-Ṣādiq, and Raḍī was thus closely connected with the Shiʿi imamate. His father had held the post of Chief of the Prophet's Descendants (*Naqīb al-ashrāf*) in Baghdad; Raḍī was appointed aide to his father at the young age of twenty, and after him as *Naqīb* for the entire Abbasid realm. His extraordinary standing is illustrated by the

---

18   For al-Ḥasan al-Baṣrī, see Mourad, *Early Islam between Myth and History*, 85. For Ibn Nubātah, see Ibn Taghrībirdī, *al-Nujūm al-zāhirah*, 4:150.

19   Naḥḥās, *ʿUmdat al-kātib*, 304–310, 316–321.

20   Masʿūdī, *Murūj al-dhahab*, 3:172.

21   Ibn Abī al-Ḥadīd, *Sharḥ Nahj al-balāghah*, 1:17, cited later in the present Introduction. See more references and discussion in Qutbuddin, "Additional Categories: (2) Theology," in *Arabic Oration*, 372–377.

22   ʿAbd al-Zahrāʾ, *Miʾat shāhid wa-shāhid min maʿānī kalām al-Imām ʿAlī ʿalayhi l-salām fī shiʿr Abī al-Ṭayyib al-Mutanabbī*.

fact that he was given this high appointment ahead of his elder brother, al-Sharīf al-Murtaḍā, also a distinguished scholar, who would occupy the post after Raḍī's death. Additionally, Raḍī was put in charge of the annual Pilgrimage to Mecca and appointed Chief Judge over the Court of Petitions.

Raḍī studied various disciplines with famous scholars. His teachers included the grammarians Sīrāfī (d. 368/979), who died when Raḍī was nine, Fārisī (d. 377/987), and Ibn Jinnī (d. 392/1001), the aforementioned preacher Ibn Nubātah al-Fāriqī al-Khaṭīb (d. 374/984), the historian Marzubānī (d. 384/994), the Twelver Shiʿi hadith scholar Mufīd (d. 413/1022), and the Muʿtazilī theologian al-Qāḍī ʿAbd al-Jabbār (d. 415/1024). His students included the poet Mihyār al-Daylamī (d. 428/1037).

Raḍī enjoyed the patronage of the Buyid sultan Bahāʾ al-Dawla (r. 379–403/989–1012), who ruled in the name of the Abbasid caliph al-Qādir (r. 381–422/991–1031). Toward the end of his life, he had a showdown with Qādir regarding the Prophetic lineage of the rival Fatimid dynasty. Qādir was shown Raḍī's verses expressing his wish to live in the Fatimid realm,[23] and the caliph insisted he sign a manifesto denouncing the Fatimid lineage. Raḍī refused, and Qādir stripped him of his official positions. Most sources report the incident thus from Raḍī's colleague, the litterateur Hilāl al-Ṣābī (d. 448/1056), but a later report states that Raḍī submitted and signed; likely, his name was inserted after his death to lend credence to the Abbasid claim of legitimacy.[24] It is also reported that Raḍī believed himself worthier of the caliphate than the Abbasids and was poisoned by them.

Raḍī died in 406/1015 at the relatively young age of forty-seven. Attesting to his prominence and popularity, his funeral was attended by the grand vizier Fakhr al-Mulk, as well as judges, scholars, and other state dignitaries, and a large number of the people of Baghdad. Several elegies were composed in his memory.

Raḍī was an outstanding poet and scholar with sixteen substantial books to his name; high praise is recorded for his poetry and his prose from contemporaries as well as later scholars. His works include studies of the literary and grammatical features of the Qurʾan and hadith, works of history and biography, anthologies of poetry, and glosses on books of jurisprudence and grammar. Eight works are extant, listed here in chronological order of composition:

1.   *Dīwān* (Collected Poetry), 684 poems in about 10,000 verses, containing panegyric for ʿAlī and the family of the Prophet, as well as rulers and

---

23   Raḍī, *Dīwān*, 2:120.

24   Jiwa, "The Baghdad Manifesto," 42–43. Raḍī's brother Murtaḍā is also reported to have signed the document.

viziers, laments for Ḥusayn ibn ʿAlī and for the poet's family and friends, censure of the age, love, vaunt, and miscellaneous other themes, composed over Raḍī's lifetime, starting from 369/980, when he was ten years old.

2.   *Rasāʾil* (Letters), literary epistles exchanged with Hilāl al-Ṣābī, in about a thousand folios, of which only a small portion composed between 380/990 and 384/994 is extant.

3.   *Khaṣāʾiṣ al-aʾimmah: Khaṣāʾiṣ Amīr al-muʾminīn* (Qualities of the Imams: Qualities of the Commander of the Faithful), a compendium of ʿAlī's biography, virtues, and pithy sayings composed in 383/994. In his introduction, Raḍī explains that he planned to record the virtues of the Twelve Imams to refute an Abbasid detractor,[25] but was able to complete only the section on ʿAlī (82 pages in the 1986 Beirut edition). *Nahj al-Balāghah* is an expansion of the "sayings" section of this earlier work.

4.   *Nahj al-Balāghah* (The Way of Eloquence), a compilation of orations, letters, and sayings attributed to ʿAlī, composed in 400/1010 (the text of the present volume—more on this work below).

5.   *Majāzāt al-Qurʾan* or: *Majāz al-Qurʾan* (Figurative language of the Qurʾan), also titled *Talkhīṣ al-bayān fī majāzāt al-Qurʾān* (Summary Exposition of the Qurʾan's Figurative Concepts), composed in 401/1011, extant almost in full, with chapters arranged in the order of the Surahs.

6.   *Maʿānī al-Qurʾān* (Themes of the Qurʾan), also titled *Ḥaqāʾiq al-taʾwīl fī mutashābih al-tanzīl* (True Realities of Interpretation Regarding Ambiguous Verses of Revelation), a large multi-volume *tafsīr* work composed in 402/1011, of which only volume 5 (itself 376 pages in the Cairo edition) is extant, also with chapters arranged according to the order of the Surahs.

7.   *Al-Majāzāt al-nabawiyyah* (Figurative Language of Prophecy), also titled *Majāzāt al-āthār al-nabawiyyah* (Figurative Language of Prophetic Hadith), composed between 400/1010 and 406/1015, containing literary and theological commentary on 360 hadiths.

8.   *Amthāl* (Proverbial Verses), a compilation of unknown date, partially preserved in Ibn al-Ẓahīr al-Irbilī's (d. 677/1278) abridgment, *Mukhtaṣar Amthāl al-Sharīf al-Raḍī*.

The following eight works are lost:[26]

9.   *Al-Ziyādāt fī shiʿr Abī Tammām* (Additions to the Poetry of Abū Tammām).

10. *Al-Jayyid min shiʿr Ibn al-Ḥajjāj* (The Best Poems of [al-Ḥusayn ibn Aḥmad] Ibn al-Ḥajjāj).

---

25   Raḍī, *Khaṣāʾiṣ al-aʾimmah*, 36–38.
26   Najāshī, *Rijāl*, 398; Ṣafadī, *Wāfī*, 2:277.

11. *Al-Ziyādāt fī shiʿr Ibn al-Ḥajjāj* (Additions to Ibn al-Ḥajjāj's Poems).

12. *Mukhtār shiʿr Abī Isḥāq al-Ṣābī* (Selections from Abū Isḥāq [Ibrāhīm] al-Ṣābī's Poems).

13. *Taʿlīq Khilāf al-fuqahāʾ* (Annotation of "Jurists' Disagreements"), perhaps an annotation of the work better known as *Ikhtilāf al-fuqahāʾ* (Jurists' Differences) by Ṭabarī.

14. *Taʿlīq fī al-Īḍāḥ li-Abī ʿAlī* (Annotation of Abū ʿAlī [al-Fārisī's] "Elucidation"), on Arabic grammar.

15. *Sīrat wālidihi al-Ṭāhir* (Biography of [Raḍī's] Father, Ṭāhir).

16. *Akhbār quḍāt Baghdād* (Reports about Baghdad's Judges).

4   Nahj al-Balāghah: The Wisdom and Eloquence of ʿAlī

The full Arabic title of the present volume is *Nahj al-balāghah min kalām Amīr al-muʾminīn ʿAlī ibn Abī Ṭālib ṣalawāt Allāh ʿalayhi*, which translates literally as The Way (or: Well-Trodden Track, or: Clear Course) of Eloquence: Selections from the Words of the Commander of the Faithful ʿAlī ibn Abī Ṭālib, God's blessings on him. As Raḍī tells us in his Introduction, his main criterion for the selection of texts was eloquence, which is why he chose this title for his compilation. Sure enough, it includes some of the most beautiful and powerful expressions in the Arabic language. Compiled in 400/1010, its fame almost immediately took wing—within a few short decades, *Nahj al-Balāghah* had become one of the most celebrated texts of the Arabic Islamic heritage.

4.1   *Form and Organization*
Nahj al-Balāghah is a collection of texts—mostly excerpts, ranging roughly from a few lines to a page or two in most standard editions—divided into three genre-based sections: 232 orations (sing., *khuṭbah*), 78 letters (sing., *risālah* or *kitāb*), and 429 sayings (sing., *ḥikmah*), the latter containing aphorisms as well as slightly longer sayings.[27] Into these three sections are integrated texts from

---

27   Numbers vary slightly in different editions, depending on how an editor separates or amalgamates certain pieces. In a few cases, there is a difference of opinion as to the genre of the texts—Raḍī, for example, lists §30, §1.212, §1.215 as orations, whereas some other scholars list them as epistles (for details, see my notes for these texts). Raḍī also sometimes lists parts of a single text in different chapters: for example, he places §1.147, a text he identifies as ʿAlī's deathbed testament, under Orations, and what he says is another part of the same text, §2.23, under Letters. In what is probably a counterintuitive proposition for modern readers, a text could in some cases fall into both categories, oral and written. It could have been first delivered as an oration, then transcribed and disseminated as an

subsidiary genres, such as testaments (sing., *waṣiyyah* or *'ahd*), supplications (sing., *du'ā'*), questions and answers, responses to reports, and counsel to individuals. A subsection in the Sayings section contains nine lines with rare words (*gharīb*), followed by Raḍī's explications. The compilation is prefaced with Raḍī's introduction explaining the stimulus for his undertaking, his method of compiling, and the broad compass and immense value of the contents.

Within each section, the compilation's sequence is based on the order in which Raḍī happened to find his texts, rather than a methodical consideration of chronology or theme.[28] A handful of texts are followed by Raḍī's comments on their virtuosity. Most texts are prefaced by a phrase that goes something like "From an oration (or: letter, or: words) by him." A few texts are preceded by a line or two of context, but the circumstances are not systematically noted, in conformity with the practice of most literary anthologists of Raḍī's time.

4.2 *Sources*

Also consistent with the practice of other literary anthologists—such as Ibn 'Abd Rabbih (d. 328/940) and Tha'ālibī (d. 429/1039), for example—Raḍī does not systematically note the provenance of his texts. However, in the past fifty years or so, scholars including al-Khaṭīb 'Abd al-Zahrā' and Imtiyāz 'Arshī have meticulously listed extant early books in which the compilation's texts appear, sometimes with full or partial transmission chains (*isnād*); an updated list is provided as an Appendix of Sources to the present volume. Some of the earlier books could be Raḍī's actual sources,[29] but more work is needed to determine concrete lines of textual transmission. It is likely that Raḍī also sourced from early books and documents that are now lost.

For a handful of texts in *Nahj al-Balāghah*, Raḍī does furnish the name of a source. For orations, he notes 'Alī's associates Nawf al-Bikālī (§1.180) and Dhi'lib al-Yamānī (the latter through Aḥmad ibn Qutaybah, through 'Abdallāh ibn Mālik ibn Dajnah, §1.231). For letters, Raḍī mentions Wāqidī's *Kitāb al-Jamal* (Book of the Camel, §2.75), Iskāfī's *Kitāb al-Maqāmāt* (Book of Exhortations, §2.54), Sa'īd ibn Yaḥyā al-Umawī's (d. 249/863) *Maghāzī* (Expeditions, from the

---

epistle. It could also be that historians are unsure about the genre because excerpts from orations and epistles from the early period are stylistically quite similar. See discussion of this similarity in Qutbuddin, *Arabic Oration*, 416–419.

28 Themes may be located using the present volume's Detailed Contents and Indexes, and through published concordances, including Muḥammad, *al-Mu'jam al-mawḍū'ī li-Nahj al-balāghah*; Muḥammadī and Dashtī, *al-Mu'jam al-mufahras li-alfāẓ Nahj al-balāghah*; and Baydūn, *Taṣnīf Nahj al-balāghah*. Chronology—for the texts I was able to situate—is noted in the footnotes to the present volume's translation.

29 See a brief list of tentative sources in the introduction to the Appendix of Sources.

author's father, d. 184/809, after Ibn Isḥāq, § 2.78), and a copy in the hand of Ibn al-Kalbī (§ 2.74). For sayings, he cites ʿAlī's great-grandson Imam Muḥammad al-Bāqir (d. 117/735, § 3.79), Thaʿlab (d. 291/904, § 3.405), Abū ʿUbayd's (d. 224/838) *Gharīb al-ḥadīth* (Rare Words from the Hadith, § 3.248), and ʿAlī's associates, Nawf again (§ 3.95), and Kumayl ibn Ziyād al-Nakhaʿī (§ 3.133, § 3.242).

As a result of the early oral transmission of these materials, different sources offer assorted renderings of the same piece, and Raḍī sometimes includes more than one rendering in his compilation; aware of the phenomenon, he mentions it in his Introduction and flags texts that are repeated. Another consequence of the initial oral transmission is that a handful of texts attributed to ʿAlī in one source are attributed elsewhere to others, and Raḍī identifies some of these ascriptions as well.

4.3   *Contents: Contemporary History and Islamic Teachings*

The contents of *Nahj al-Balāghah* straddle two broad overlapping areas: contemporary history and Islamic teachings. Given the multipurpose function of oration, themes from each of these two areas intermingle and recur. Historical material in the volume is grounded in the final four-year period of ʿAlī's life, when he ruled as caliph of the Muslim empire. The texts depict the ethos of ʿAlī's time. They contain subtleties of event trajectories, particularly ʿAlī's accession to the caliphate and his battles. They offer nuanced portraits of historical personalities, above all, of ʿAlī himself, but also of influential individuals from his caliphate.[30] They portray his sons, Ḥasan, Ḥusayn, and Muḥammad (ibn al-Ḥanafiyyah), his brother ʿAqīl ibn Abī Ṭālib, his ward Muḥammad ibn Abī Bakr, and his cousin ʿAbdallāh ibn al-ʿAbbās. They praise staunch followers including Abū Dharr al-Ghifārī, ʿAmmār ibn Yāsir, Mālik al-Ashtar, and al-Ḥārith al-Hamdānī, and refer to various governors, commanders, judges, and tribal chieftains, some of whom he chastised, as he did al-Ashʿath ibn Qays. They describe adversaries, chiefly Muʿāwiyah and ʿAmr ibn al-ʿĀṣ, but also Ṭalḥah and Zubayr, as well as Muʿāwiyah's principal supporters and commanders. They present contextual shades in political and doctrinal positions, including proto-Shiʿi and proto-Sunni stances, as well as the evolution of the Kharijites. As mentioned above, most of the compilation's texts are from ʿAlī's caliphate, but several also refer to events and individuals earlier in his life, and they include copious praise for the Prophet Muḥammad and tribute to Muḥammad's first supporters. A few texts date from ʿAlī's pre-caliphate years, and these include a eulogy to his wife Fāṭimah, a letter to his close associate Salmān al-Fārisī, and interactions with and about the Sunni caliphs ʿUmar and ʿUthmān. In addition to actual data,

---

30   To locate names and themes within the volume, see Detailed Contents and Indexes.

the historical texts portray the personal struggle, bringing into relief the human aspect of ʿAlī's history and his impression of the events and persons therein.

ʿAlī's teachings, the second large content area of *Nahj al-Balāghah*, comprise facets of doctrine, philosophy, ethics, counsel, and practical wisdom. Growing up under Muḥammad's care, ʿAlī was continuously exposed to the Qurʾanic revelation. Permeated by its vocabulary and themes, his words urge worship of the creator, promote awareness of the transience of human life, and highlight the urgent need to prepare for the imminent hereafter.[31] Combining piety with virtue, they exhort truth, gratitude, and patience, and extol the benefits of living a modest and temperate life.[32] Taking the middle ground between secular humanism and insular faith, they advocate an inseparable blend of individual devotion and dynamic social engagement. Consistently, they highlight the eminence of reason and learning. Numerous texts feature a detailed parsing of God's transcendent oneness. Many describe the marvels of God's creation, mostly the heavens, the earth, and the human being, but also, in a couple of texts, the peacock, the bat, and the ant. Several texts laud the stature of the Prophet's family. Some contain down-to-earth instructions and acute observations of human behavior. Many portray the art of just leadership, predicating true justice on compassion, wisdom, integrity, pluralism, and accountability to God.[33] They advocate strongly for the socially disadvantaged. They preach kindness to animals. A few contain legal rulings, judgments pronounced by ʿAlī for actual cases. Yet others are supplications: some implore God's forgiveness and aid, one prays for rain, one at the start of battle beseeches God's protection and victory, and one, a daily morning prayer, contains thanks and entreaties.[34] Three texts of counsel are grounded in specific Qurʾanic verses.[35] In sum, the teachings of ʿAlī—a learned philosopher, a pious ascetic, a just leader, a governing caliph, a brave warrior, and an astute commander—bring together disparate elements of the human experience.

---

31   Qutbuddin, "ʿAlī's Contemplations on this World and the Hereafter in the Context of His Life and Times"; Qutbuddin, "The Sermons of ʿAlī ibn Abī Ṭālib: At the Confluence of the Core Islamic Teachings of the Qurʾan and the Oral, Nature-Based Cultural Ethos of Seventh Century Arabia."

32   Qutbuddin, "Piety and Virtue in Early Islam: Two Sermons by Imam Ali"; Qutbuddin, "Classical Islamic Oration's Art, Function, and Life-Altering Power of Persuasion: The Ultimate Response by Hammam to Ali's Sermon on Piety, and by Hurr to Husayn's Battle Oration in Karbala."

33   Qutbuddin, "Just Leadership in Early Islam: The Teachings and Practice of Imam Ali"; Shah-Kazemi, *Justice and Remembrance*, 73–133.

34   Supplications: general (§1.222, §1.224), for rain (§1.141), at the start of battle (§2.15), daily morning prayer (§1.213).

35   §1.218, §1.219, §1.220.

Some longer, thematically focused texts have special names. Five named orations are Ethereal Forms (*Ashbāḥ*), on the creation of the universe; The Crusher (*Qāṣiʿah*), which castigates Lucifer and factionalism; The Radiant (*Gharrāʾ*), which contemplates human mortality and counsels preparation for the imminent hereafter; The Roar of the Camel Stallion (*Shiqshiqiyyah*), on ʿAlī's right to the caliphate; and The Oration to Hammām: Description of the Pious (*Khuṭbat Hammām fī ṣifat al-muttaqīn*), which lists the myriad virtues of those who truly deserve the epithet pious. In the Letters section, two long texts are the Testament of Counsel for Ḥasan (*Waṣiyyat al-Ḥasan*), in which ʿAlī cataloged ethical and practical advice for his son, and the Letter of Appointment for Mālik al-Ashtar (*ʿAhd al-Ashtar*), in which he laid out for Ashtar, whom he was sending to govern Egypt, the moral backbone required for righteous rule. In the Sayings section, two are particularly lengthy and distinct: The Four Pillars of Faith (*Daʿāʾim al-īmān*) are parsed as forbearance, conviction, justice, and struggle against evil; Knowledge is Better than Wealth (*al-ʿIlmu khayrun mina l-māl*) is a text of advice to Kumayl al-Nakhaʿī.[36]

4.4   *Style: Oral Aesthetics of Rhythm and Imagery*

Rhythmically cadenced and stunningly visual, *Nahj al-Balāghah* reflects ʿAlī's oral milieu.[37] ʿAlī's orations and sayings, even his written letters, breathe the aesthetic of orality, articulated in mnemonics and metonymy. Mnemonics—memory aid techniques—manifest in intensely rhythmic prose with condensed sentences and balanced parallelisms, and graphic and often startling natural and lifeworld imagery, with extended verbal metaphors and gripping dramatization. Language is grounded in the features and movements of the camel and of other desert animals, lifeworld objects, and cosmic phenomena. Abstract concepts are made immediate and relevant through concrete physical images. Metonymy—evocation by association—manifests in skillful allusion to historical and literary context. Alongside emphatic grammar structures and rhetorical questions, these stylistic devices also served as audience-engagement techniques that invited the audience to participate in the speech act with internal response, and sometimes overt answers, comments, and

---

36   *Ashbāḥ*, §1.88; *Qāṣiʿah*, §1.190; *Gharrāʾ*, §1.80; *Shiqshiqiyyah*, §1.3; *Khuṭbat Hammām*, §1.191; *Waṣiyyat al-Ḥasan*, §2.31; *ʿAhd al-Ashtar*, §2.53; *Daʿāʾim al-īmān*, §3.26; *al-ʿIlmu khayrun mina l-māl*, §3.133.

37   For more detail, see Qutbuddin, "Style of the Oration," in *Arabic Oration*, 91–164; Qutbuddin, "A Sermon on Piety by Imam ʿAlī ibn Abī Ṭālib: How the Rhythm of the Classical Arabic Oration Tacitly Persuaded"; Qutbuddin, "The Sermons of ʿAlī ibn Abī Ṭālib: At the Confluence of the Core Islamic Teachings of the Qurʾan and the Oral, Nature-Based Cultural Ethos of Seventh Century Arabia."

actions. The texts are further characterized by fine-grained, condensed vocabulary and a high, dignified linguistic register.

Eloquence is a crucial component of preaching, and as scholars of literature have argued, it "tacitly persuades."[38] A brilliant exposition is more effective than a clumsy harangue, and beautiful language more likely to evoke a positive response than a plodding lecture. In combination with Qur'anic validation and rational argumentation, 'Alī attempted to stir the hearts and minds of his audience with verbal artistry. Moreover, there is a religious flavor, a focus on piety, in all modes of 'Alī's speech, undergirding even the material produced in a political or military context. At the same time, his words also have a distinctly local flavor, a cultural texture grounded in desert topography, tribal society, nomadic lifestyle, and the rich poetic tradition of the Arabian Peninsula.

4.5   *Commentaries and Response Works*

Nahj al-Balāghah has generated an extraordinary number of response-works, including commentaries, translations, supplements, and abridgments by Shi'i, Sunni, and Arab Christian scholars in medieval and modern times, as well as glosses, concordances, works on sources, and thematic essays by present-day scholars. In my rough estimate, the number of serious extant works in this category ranges around 500, many in multiple volumes.

Depending on the cataloger's range, the number of known commentaries on *Nahj al-Balāghah* lies somewhere between 81 and 210.[39] After the Qur'an, this is perhaps the largest number of commentaries generated by any Arabic work—compared with approximately 40 on Mutanabbī's *Dīwān*, 70 on Bukhārī's *Ṣaḥīḥ*, and 20 on Ḥarīrī's *Maqāmāt*, three of the best-known Arabic Islamic works. Most *Nahj al-Balāghah* commentaries are in Arabic; some are in Persian and other Islamic languages. Most comment on the full compilation; some comment on a specific longer text, and a few of these latter commentaries are in verse.

Some of the best-known full commentaries on *Nahj al-Balāghah* are the following (all in Arabic, except the three noted as Persian):
– Early Twelver Shi'i commentators include 'Alī ibn Nāṣir al-Sarakhsī (fl. 6th/ 12th c.), Quṭb al-Dīn al-Rāwandī (d. 573/1177), Quṭb al-Dīn al-Kaydarī (d. after 576/1180), and Ibn Maytham al-Baḥrānī (d. 679/1280).
– Early Sunni commentators include Ibn Funduq al-Bayhaqī (d. 565/1170) from Khurasan, who wrote one of the earliest commentaries, and relied on

---

38   See Lanham, *Analyzing Prose, passim.*

39   Amīnī, *Al-Ghadīr*, 4:257–272, lists 81; 'Abd al-Zahrā', *Maṣādir Nahj al-balāghah*, 1:202–254, lists 101; Lakhnawī, introduction to Rāwandī's commentary, 1:36–49, lists 112; and 'Āmilī, *Shurūḥ Nahj al-balāghah*, lists 210.

the lost, and possibly the first, *Nahj al-Balāghah* commentary of Aḥmad ibn Muḥammad al-Wabrī (fl. early 6th/12th c.), from Khwārazm. (Sarakhsī also quotes Wabrī). Prominent Sunni authors whose commentaries are lost include Fakhr al-Dīn al-Rāzī (d. 606/1209) and Saʿd al-Dīn al-Taftāzānī (d. 793/1390).

– Ibn Abī al-Ḥadīd al-Muʿtazilī (d. ca. 656/1258) is the best-known (early Sunni) commentator of all, whose celebrated commentary in 20 volumes itself generated numerous response works. Ibn Abī al-Ḥadīd—who also composed Seven Odes in Praise of ʿAlī—writes in his introduction that "the noblest branch of learning is knowledge of God … ʿAlī's words kindled that fire … the Muʿtazilah … masters of theology, from whom all others learned this skill, are ʿAlī's students and emulators."[40] He adds that ʿAlī is "leader of the eloquent and lord of the articulate … oratory and epistle-writing began with him."[41]

– The Yemeni Zaydī Shiʿi Imam al-Muʾayyad bi-llāh Yaḥyā ibn Ḥamzah (d. 749/1348) wrote a commentary in six volumes. He traced his license to teach the compilation back to Raḍī himself, by way of a sequence of licenses granted by Zaydī scholars.[42] Other Zaydī commentators are Fakhr al-Dīn ʿAbdallāh ibn al-Hādī (d. at the end of the 8th/14th c.) and Yaḥyā ibn Ibrāhīm al-Jaḥḥāf (d. 1102/1690).[43]

– Safavid-era Twelver Shiʿi Sufi scholars who wrote commentaries include Ilāhī-Ardabīlī (fl. ca. 9th/15th c., Persian), ʿAbd al-Bāqī Dānishmand (d. after 1039/1630), and Niẓām al-Dīn al-Jīlānī (d. 1053/1643).

– Commentaries by modern Egyptian-Sunni-Azharī scholars include the famed introduction-cum-wordlist by the Grand Mufti of Egypt Shaykh Muḥammad ʿAbduh (d. 1905), which was later expanded by Shaykh Ḥusayn al-Marṣafī (d. 1935) and then by Muḥammad Muḥyī al-Dīn ʿAbd al-Ḥamīd (d. 1972). In the introduction, ʿAbduh speaks of his first encounter with *Nahj al-Balāghah*, saying, "I felt I was witnessing a radiant intellect … which had detached itself from the divine procession and connected itself to the human soul." He goes on to declare that memorizing and studying the compilation "are essential to those who seek the precious gems of Arabic and wish to rise in its ranks."[44]

---

40 Ibn Abī al-Ḥadīd, *Sharḥ Nahj al-balāghah*, 1:17.

41 Ibn Abī al-Ḥadīd, *Sharḥ Nahj al-balāghah*, 1:24.

42 Muʾayyad Yaḥyā, *al-Dībāj al-waḍī*, 1:104–105.

43 Details of the latter two may be found in Ansari and Schmidtke, "The Literary-Religious Tradition among Seventh/Thirteenth-Century Yemeni Zaydīs (11): Appendix 11," 220.

44 ʿAbduh, *Sharḥ Nahj al-balāghah*, 1:4.

– Modern Iranian Twelver Shiʿi commentators include Muḥammad Taqī Na-
  qavī, Muḥammad Taqī al-Tustarī, Nawwāb Lāhījānī (d. ca. 1824), and the
  Grand Ayatollah Maḥmūd Ṭāliqānī, the last two writing in Persian. A modern
  Lebanese Twelver Shiʿi commentator is Muḥammad Jawād Mughniyyah.

The commentaries discuss lexical, grammatical, and rhetorical matters, and
sometimes provide historical context and transmission history. The longer
commentaries include extensive historical, doctrinal, thematic, and literary
annotation, as well as further texts attributed to ʿAlī and other historical fig-
ures. As we should expect, each commentator interprets ʿAlī's statements, both
historical and doctrinal, according to his own denominational approach.

Numerous abridgments of selections from *Nahj al-Balāghah* have been com-
piled:

– 3 medieval abridgments: Abū al-Saʿādāt al-Isfahānī's (d. 634/1237) published
  work, *Maṭlaʿ al-ṣabāḥatayn* (Two Suns Rising), transcribes the Sayings sec-
  tion from *Nahj al-Balāghah* alongside the ethical hadith of the Prophet
  Muḥammad compiled by Quḍāʿī (d. 454/1062) in *Kitāb al-Shihāb* (*Light in
  the Heavens*, which I have edited and translated).[45] Two further selection vol-
  umes are extant in manuscript form: *al-Nafāʾis* (Precious Words) by Niẓām
  al-Dīn al-Muṭahhar (fl. 8th/14th c., Sunni), and *al-Ṭarāʾif* (Marvelous Words)
  by an anonymous author.[46]
– More than 34 modern selections (called *mukhtārāt* or *muntakhabāt*).[47]
Nahj al-Balāghah has been translated into more than 15 languages:
– A medieval Persian translation by Fatḥallāh Kāshānī (d. 988/1580) titled *Tan-
  bīh al-ghāfilīn* (Waking the Heedless) is possibly the oldest translation.
– Numerous modern translations have been published in Persian, many in
  Urdu and Turkish, and several in other Asian languages, including Kazakh,
  Armenian, Chinese, and Thai, as well as a number of European languages,
  including English, French, German, Spanish, Russian, Italian, Romanian,
  Polish, and Croat. Many translations, including perhaps all the English trans-
  lations published to-date, have been rendered indirectly, via Persian.[48]

Also, many modern compilations style themselves as supplements (*musta-
drakāt*) to *Nahj al-Balāghah*, notably the 8-volume compilation by Muḥammad
Bāqir Maḥmūdī.

---

45   Quḍāʿī, *Kitāb al-Shihāb*, ed. and trans. Qutbuddin, *Light in the Heavens: Sayings of the
      Prophet Muhammad*.
46   Ṭabāṭabāʾī, "Fī Riḥāb," part 3, 49–50.
47   Ṭabāṭabāʾī, "Fī Riḥāb," part 3, 50–62.
48   Ṭabāṭabāʾī, "Fī Riḥāb," part 3, 63–89; Esḥāqī, "Manbaʿ-shināsī-yi tarjamah-hā-yi *Nahj al-
      balāghah*." Select list in present volume's Bibliography, under Raḍī, *Nahj al-balāghah*.

4.6   *Dissemination: Manuscripts, Study, Admiration, and Controversy*

In addition to the vast number of response works generated in the medieval Middle East by *Nahj al-Balāghah*, its immediate and wide circulation is evident in the hundreds of manuscripts produced in different parts of the Muslim world dating from as early as the 5th/11th century—many in Iraq and Iran, but also across the Islamic lands, from India (in later medieval times) in the East, through Khurasan in Central Asia, through Yemen in the Arabian Peninsula, toward the West to Turkey, Syria, and Egypt.[49] Of these, many manuscripts were produced in markedly Sunni communities, particularly in Khurasan—such as the manuscript of Yaʿqūb al-Naysābūrī (d. 474/1081), from which our manuscript Y was transcribed—from an early time.[50] And in the 9th/15th–10th/16th-century (Ḥanafī Sunni) Ottoman caliphate, compilations of ʿAlī's words were the centerpiece of the Topkapi Palace library's oration collection, used, among other things, to teach palace scribes.[51] Another example of the esteem with which Sunni scholars viewed the work is evidenced by the Ottoman scholar and head of the chancery (*Raʾīs al-kuttāb*) Ahmad Efendi Taşköprüzāde (d. 968/1561), who systematically cites ʿAlī's texts from *Nahj al-Balāghah*, alongside Qurʾan and hadith, in his commentary on Ījī's *Şerhu'l-Ahlaki'l-Adudiyye* (Book of Good Character);[52] he does not mention the *Nahj al-Balāghah* by name, though we know that he knew the text well—the Sulaymaniye library in Istanbul holds several manuscripts in its "Raʾīs al-kuttāb" collection, with ownership marks, including one with his name inscribed on the flyleaf in his own hand (MS "S" in the present volume; see also MS "K"). *Nahj al-Balāghah* entered China in the 19th and 20th centuries, when Chinese Muslims went to the Middle East and brought back religious texts, as well as Indonesia and Malaysia, where Muḥammad ʿAbduh's ideas were influential during that period.[53] Perhaps with some minor exceptions,[54] the two regions in the pre-

---

49   Ṭabāṭabāʾī lists 172 early manuscripts dating from the 5th/11th through the 12th/18th centuries in worldwide collections. Muttaqī lists 458 manuscripts through the early 14th/20th century. Details in Note on the Edition.

50   Ansari, "Tāzah-hā-yi darbāra-yi riwāyat *Nahj al-balāghah*." For details of our Y manuscript, see Note on the Edition in the present volume.

51   Qutbuddin, "Books on Arabic Philology and Literature," in *Treasures of Knowledge*, 607–623.

52   Taşköprüzāde, *Şerhu'l-Ahlak*, 37, 43, 49, 67, 69, 73, 75, 81, 83, 87, 89, 91, 93, 95, 97. I thank Sarah Aziz for this reference.

53   I thank Sachiko Murata and Wang Xi (Chinese Academy of Social Sciences, Beijing) for the information on China, and Karim Crow and Asna Husin for the information on Malaysia and Indonesia.

54   John Morrow notes two citations of ʿAlī's words—that do not, however, mention *Nahj al-balāghah* specifically—in Aljamiado traditions among Spanish Moriscos (Muslims who

modern Islamic world where *Nahj al-Balāghah* does not appear to have made inroads are Umayyad Spain and Umayyad-influenced (post-Fatimid) North Africa, which were both, for the most part, intensely anti-Shiʿi.[55] The dissemination question—which awaits more thorough exploration—is an important one and speaks to many aspects of religious, scholarly, literary, and political life in the premodern and modern Islamic world.

Study of *Nahj al-Balāghah* and admiration for the compilation are pronounced among all branches of the Shiʿa, as well as among Sunnis and Arab Christians, in medieval and modern times. A few quotations by the compilation's commentators have been cited earlier. The following snapshot of other authors who expressed high regard for the collection, with a few soundbites from their laudations, further underscores the esteem in which *Nahj al-Balāghah* was, and continues to be, held:

- Twelver Shiʿi reverence for *Nahj al-Balāghah* is well documented through the ages. In recent times, Āghā Buzurg al-Tihrānī (d. 1970) writes: "After divine revelation, no book has come into existence more bonded to God's word than *Nahj al-Balāghah*."[56] Among the Ṭayyibī Ismāʿīlī Shiʿa, the compilation is an integral part of the religious curriculum. It is quoted abundantly in sermons and works of history and doctrine, including the works of the Yemeni *Dāʿī*s Sayyidnā Ḥātim Muḥyī al-Dīn (d. 596/1199) and Sayyidnā Idrīs ʿImād al-Dīn (d. 872/1468), and the Indian *Dāʿī* Sayyidnā Ṭāhir Sayf al-Dīn (d. 1965); these authors also pronounce benedictions on Raḍī.[57] The latter quotes from *Nahj al-Balāghah* in a full 65 instances in his annual *Rasāʾil Ramaḍāniyyah* (Ramaḍān Treatises); in one instance, he prefaces the quotation with explicit reference to the compilation's title, saying: "Wisdom spoke on ʿAlī's tongue, and the *way of eloquence* (*nahj al-balāghah*) became clear through his exposition. Belief and conviction increase whenever a believer

---

were forcibly converted to Christianity) in the 16th century: § 38 in Morrow's "Sources" volume on divine decree, and § 41 on knowledge (Morrow, *Shiʿism in the Maghrib and al-Andalus*, 2:131–132 and 2:137) are the same as *Nahj al-balāghah*, § 3.273 and § 3.349. I thank Linda Jones for this reference.

55   There seem to be no manuscripts of *Nahj al-balāghah* from these two regions, no mention in scholarly curricula or biographies, and no citations in books. See the text's absence from Fierro's 8th–15th c. AD bio-bibliographical database, *History of the Authors and Transmitters of al-Andalus* (*HATA*- https://www.eea.csic.es/red/hata/). Ibn ʿAbd Rabbih however, as mentioned earlier, includes several orations attributed to ʿAlī in his anthology, *al-ʿIqd al-farīd*, which is mainly influenced by the Islamic East.

56   Tihrānī, *Dharīʿah*, 4:144.

57   Ḥātim, *al-Majālis al-Ḥātimiyyah*, Majlis § 110–130; Idrīs, *ʿUyūn al-akhbār*, 3:367; Ṭāhir Sayf al-Dīn, *Ḍawʾ nūr al-ḥaqq*, 98, *Masarrāt al-fatḥ*, 192.

hears his words."[58] Among the Nizārī Ismāʿīlī Shiʿa, quotations are found in early works of Khwājah Qāsim Tushtarī (died after 533/1139) and Naṣīr al-Dīn al-Ṭūsī (d. 672/1274).[59] Zaydī Shiʿi channels of transmissions to and within Yemen from the 7th/13th century onward have also been described recently in some detail.[60]

– In the past two centuries, distinguished Sunni Arab writers have continued to pay tribute.[61] The Iraqi Salafi al-Ālūsī (d. 1924) called *Nahj al-Balāghah* "an ember from the fire of God's speech, and a sun that radiates the Prophet's eloquence." The Egyptian Zakī Mubārak (d. 1952) wrote that it "bequeaths manliness, nobility, and loftiness of the soul, hailing from an indomitable spirit who faced danger with a lion's resolve." His fellow Egyptian scholar ʿAbbās Maḥmūd al-ʿAqqād (d. 1964) wrote a book on ʿAlī titled *ʿAbqariyyat al-Imām* (The Genius of the Imām)—assuming everyone would recognize that the quintessential Imām is ʿAlī—in which he declared that ʿAlī's words in *Nahj al-Balāghah* encompass "divine wisdom."

– *Nahj al-Balāghah* is also extolled broadly by Arab Christian scholars.[62] They include the Jordanian Rūkus ibn Zāʾid ʿUzayzī (b. 1903), the Syrian ʿAbd al-Masīḥ Anṭākī (d. 1923), and numerous Lebanese scholars, including Luwīs Maʿlūf (d. 1946), Būlus Salāmah (d. 1979), Amīn Nakhlah (d. 1976), Fuʾād Afrām al-Bustānī (d. 1994), and Ḥannā al-Fākhūrī (d. 2011). The Lebanese scholar Nāṣif al-Yāzijī (d. 1871) declared that anyone who wished to excel in eloquence "should memorize the Qurʾan and *Nahj al-Balāghah*."[63] Another Lebanese scholar, Jurj Jurdāq (d. 2014), memorized the collection by the age of thirteen, and engaged with it deeply in a five-volume work on ʿAlī that he titled *al-Imām ʿAlī: Ṣawt al-ʿadālah al-insāniyyah* (Imam ʿAlī: The Voice of Human Justice).

---

58   Sayf al-Dīn, *Zubdat al-burhān*, 31. Elsewhere, Sayf al-Dīn says: "Orations and sayings of the Commander of the Faithful ʿAlī ibn Abī Ṭālib are stairways to the True Realities. Their way is the heart-healing 'Way of Eloquence,' and their lines are lines of divine light" (*Dalw ghadīr ḥaqq*, 134).

59   Tushtarī, *Maʿrifat*, 253/260; Naṣīr al-Dīn al-Ṭūsī, *Rawḍah*, 41/44, 74/86, 79/93, 128/160; idem, *Maṭlūb*, 20/36; idem, *Āghāz*, 55/64–65.

60   Ansari and Schmidtke, "The Literary-Religious Tradition among Seventh/Thirteenth-Century Yemeni Zaydīs (11): Appendix 11," 220–230.

61   Quotes and references in ʿAbd al-Zahrāʾ, *Maṣādir*, 1:87–99; Ṭabāṭabāʾī, "Fī Riḥāb," part 4, *passim*.

62   Quotes and references in Keizoghani and Nafchi, "The Greatness of *Nahj Al-Balagha* and the Words of Imam Ali from the Perspective of Modern Christian Figures."

63   ʿAbd al-Zahrāʾ, *Maṣādir*, 1:91.

- *Nahj al-Balāghah* also continues to be admired in present-day India, where
  it forms a regular part of the curriculum in Shiʿi as well as many Sunni
  madrasas.[64]

I am not sure why, compared to other compilations of ʿAlī's words, *Nahj al-
Balāghah* has become the target of a certain amount of sectarian controversy.[65]
It is true that the volume includes the Shiqshiqiyyah oration (§1.3), in which
ʿAlī claims his right to Muḥammad's succession. But Jāḥiẓ, Ṭabarī, Ibn Hishām,
and Ibn ʿAbd Rabbih, for example—four famous and respected early Sunni
scholars—cite sermons, conversations, and letters by ʿAlī that contain similar
themes.[66] And large parts of the Shiqshiqiyyah itself are recorded much before
Raḍī by the early Sunni-Muʿtazilite author Abū al-Qāsim al-Balkhī (d. 319/931),
and the Sunni-Shāfiʿī-Ashʿarī scholar ʿAlī ibn Mahdī al-Ṭabarī al-Māmaṭīrī (d.
ca. 360/971).[67] The Testament of Ashtar (§2.53 in the present volume), too,
another unfairly maligned text (by, for example, Wadād al-Qāḍī, "An early
Fāṭimid political document"), is recorded not only in the Twelver Shiʿi Iraqi nar-
rative tradition by Ibn Shuʿbah al-Ḥarrānī (fl. 4th/10th c.) and Raḍī (d. 406/1015),
but also in a distinct Fatimid Ismāʿīlī Shiʿi Egyptian narrative tradition by
al-Qāḍī al-Nuʿmān (d. 363/974), and in a yet further and distinct Zaydi Shiʿi
Yemeni narrative tradition in an unpublished manuscript in the Ambrosiana
library in Milan.[68] It appears that it was almost three centuries after Raḍī,
when the Damascene historian Ibn Khallikān (d. 681/1282) first raised doubts
about the compilation's authenticity, that it began to be viewed in some quar-
ters as a "Shiʿi"—code for "seditious"—text. Several pro-Umayyad Damascus
authors—including, notably, Ibn Taymiyyah (d. 728/1328)—followed Ibn Khal-
likān's lead.[69] This limited group of detractors notwithstanding, *Nahj al-Balā-*

---

64   Kaur, *Madrasa Education in India*, 387.

65   See detailed analysis in Qutbuddin, "Is *Nahj al-balāghah* a Shiʿi Book? Insidious Labels
      and Academia's Myth of Objectivity."

66   E.g., Ibn Hishām, *Sīrah*, 2:489–490; Jahiz, *Bayān*, 2:50–52; Ṭabarī, *Tārīkh*, 4:231–233, 5:7–8;
      Ibn ʿAbd Rabbih, *ʿIqd*, 4:63, 68; more in Madelung, *Succession to Muhammad*, 28–33, 141,
      and *passim*.

67   Quotation of Shiqshiqiyyah oration in Balkhī's now lost books cited by Ibn Abī al-Ḥadīd (Ḥ
      1:205/206); Māmaṭīrī, *Nuzhat al-Abṣār*, 255 (several biographers say Māmaṭīrī was a Sunni
      Shāfiʿī Ashʿarī, a few say he was a Shiʿi Zaydi; details in editor's introduction, ibid., 15–23).

68   Nuʿmān, *Daʿāʾim*, 1:353–367; see details of Zaydi Ambrosiana manuscript (catalog no.
      H 129, fol. 167ᵛ ff.) in Anṣārī, "Majmūʿah-ye dīgar az nuskhah-hā-ye khaṭṭī Ambrosiana."
      See also Anṣārī, "Riwāyat wa-nuskha-i jadīd az ʿahdnāmah-ye Mālik-e Ashtar."

69   Ibn Taymiyyah (d. 728/1328), *Minhāj al-sunnah*, 8:55–56; Dhahabī (d. 748/1347), *Mīzān
      al-iʿtidāl*, 3:124; Ibn Ḥajar al-ʿAsqalānī (d. 852/1448), *Lisān al-mīzān*, 5:529. The following
      are their three main critiques: (1) *Nahj al-balāghah*'s materials are not found in earlier
      sources—which is simply incorrect; see, for example, Appendix of Sources in the present

ghah continues to be memorized, studied, and cited avidly across wide reaches of the Islamic world. This brilliant ecumenical text rightly belongs to the collective heritage of Islam, the communal legacy of Arabic, and the shared inheritance of humanity.

5   Concluding Remarks

Of the numerous compilations of ʿAlī's words, *Nahj al-Balāghah* towers above the rest in its fame. With a winning combination of brilliant prose and deep wisdom, it has enjoyed unprecedented currency through the centuries, being widely read and highly acclaimed throughout the Islamic world. On the one hand, the collection has become a benchmark for high style, the exemplar par excellence for those who would follow the Arabic "way of eloquence." On the other hand, ʿAlī's wise teachings have resonated with Muslims throughout the past fourteen centuries, and they continue to hold immense consequence today. As a system of values, they promote a just and compassionate vision of Islam. In strife-torn Muslim-majority lands, they could unify Shiʿis and Sunnis in their common faith. The divide between Shiʿism and Sunnism, to put the issue in simplistic terms, is largely based on the perception of ʿAlī's role as first Imam versus fourth Caliph. His own words and his example can and should be used not to create divisions between groups but to bring people together, to heal. As universal teachings of ethics, moreover, ʿAlī's words transcend time, place, and affiliation. They embody the best values we all possess. They teach harmonious relations with all humans—for, as ʿAlī reminds us, people are "are either our brothers in faith or our peers in creation."

–––––––––––––

volume, and the list of earlier sources in which *Nahj al-balāghah* texts are found in ʿAbd al-Zahrāʾ, *Maṣādir Nahj al-balāghah, passim*; ʿArshī, *Istinād Nahj al-balāghah, passim*; Dashtī, *Ravish-i taḥqīq, passim*. (2) Raḍī does not cite his sources—mostly correct, but, as mentioned earlier, he followed the norm for literary compilations of his time, and modern scholars have filled the breach. (3) The book contains insults (*sabb*) directed at the first three Sunni caliphs—a more complicated issue, but in essence, the charge is false. Only a handful of texts reference Abū Bakr and ʿUmar at all, and they say nothing directly critical. Even regarding ʿUthmān, whose administration many Muslims censured, *Nahj al-balāghah* texts contain no overt reproach. Abundant castigations, however, are directed at Muʿāwiyah and ʿAmr ibn al-ʿĀṣ, and, to a lesser extent, Ṭalḥah and Zubayr—individuals who brought armies to fight ʿAlī. ʿĀʾishah, another lead player in the Battle of the Camel, is not referenced directly, presumably for reasons of decorum. See further details of critiques and responses in Sultan, *Étude sur Nahj al-Balâgha, passim*; Hassan, *A Critical Study of Nahj al-balāgha*, 25–58; Djebli, *Encore à propos de l'authenticité du Nahj al-Balagha, passim*; ʿAbd al-Zahrāʾ, *Maṣādir*, 1:100–199; Jalālī, *Dirāsah ḥawl Nahj al-balāghah*, 52–75; summarized in Qutbuddin, "Nahj al-balāgha," *EI*³; and Qutbuddin, "Is *Nahj al-balāghah* a Shiʿi Book?"

Note on the Edition and Translation: Manuscripts and Methodology

The manuscripts and methodology used to prepare the present volume are described in the following pages. My hope is to have produced a highly accurate critical edition and translation of *Nahj al-Balāghah*, based on the earliest and most important extant manuscripts, and on a carefully constructed stemma.

1 Manuscripts

As can be expected for a text of such fame, several hundred manuscripts are extant in collections in the Middle East and worldwide,[1] some dating from the 5th/11th century just decades after Raḍī finished his compilation in 400/1010. To prepare my edition, I have consulted fourteen of the earliest manuscripts, dating from the 5th/11th through the 7th/13th centuries,[2] some examined for the first time in modern scholarship. These manuscripts are valuable not only because of their early provenance, but also because of their eminent genealogies: eight are copied or corrected by renowned scholars, and three even trace their lineage to Raḍī's own autograph manuscript.

1.1 *Summary List of Manuscripts*

The following is a summary list of the manuscripts—five primary and nine secondary—consulted for the present edition:

---

1   In a series of articles from 1986/1987 to 1992, ʿAbd al-ʿAzīz Ṭabāṭabāʾī listed and described 172 manuscripts from the 5th/11th through the 12th/18th centuries: Ṭabāṭabāʾī, "Al-Mutabaqqī min makhṭūṭāt *Nahj al-balāghah*," 62–102, MSS §1–86; Ṭabāṭabāʾī, "Mā tabaqqā min makhṭūṭāt *Nahj al-balāghah*," 13–36, MSS §87–147; Ṭabāṭabāʾī, "Fī Riḥāb *Nahj al-Balāghah: Makhṭūṭātuhu*," 3:7–20, MSS §148–172. In a 2016 online article, Ḥusayn Muttaqī listed 458 manuscripts from the 5th/11th through the early 14th/ late 19th centuries: *Iṭlālah ʿalā makhṭūṭāt Nahj al-balāghah fī al-maktabāt al-ʿālamiyyah*, http://manuscripts.ir/fa/90/اطلاعات-بانک-news/العالمية-المكتبات-في-البلاغة-نهج-مخطوطات-على-إطلالة-3835/مقالات; also listed and further manuscripts added in his 2019 publication, *Muʿjam al-Āthār al-makhṭūṭah fī al-Imām ʿAlī*, pp. 374–386.

2   I collected copies of eleven additional early manuscripts dating from the 7th–9th/13th–15th centuries, located in Iranian and Turkish libraries; I eventually decided not to consult them for the present edition, realizing that they would clutter the apparatus without adding anything new. All the manuscripts are relevant, however, to the text's reception history, which awaits detailed study.

TABLE 1   Primary manuscripts

Sigla	Date	Library	Location	Catalog number	Special Merit
M م	469/1077	Marʿashī	Qum, Iran	3827	Checked against manuscript read out to Raḍī
Sh ش	5th/11th c.	Shahrastānī	Baghdad, Iraq	–	Perhaps earliest manuscript, 406/1015 or 1016
N ن	494/1101	Naṣīrī	Tehran, Iran	–	Early manuscript
H ه	553/1158	Rampur Raza	Rampur, India	1190	Copied from Faḍlallāh al-Rāwandī's 511/1158 MS, which was checked against Raḍī's autograph copy
Y ي	608/1212	Tehran University	Tehran, Iran	1782	Copied from Yaʿqūbī's 474/1081 MS, which was checked against Raḍī's autograph copy

TABLE 2   Secondary manuscripts

Sigla	Date	Library	Location	Catalog number
L ل	510/1116	Mumtaz ul Ulama	Lucknow, India	—
Z ز	538/1144	Maulana Azad, AMU	Aligarh, India	485
D د	544/1149	Imam Reza	Mashhad, Iran	13847
Q ق	565/1170	Iraqi National Museum	Baghdad, Iraq	356
S س	567/1171	Sulaymaniye	Istanbul, Turkey	REISULKUT-TAB 942
Ch ج	588/1192	Chester Beatty	Dublin, Ireland	5451
A ا	598/1202	Sulaymaniye	Istanbul, Turkey	AYASOFYA 4344
T ت	615/1218	Topkapi Palace	Istanbul, Turkey	Aḥmad III 2556
K ك	684/1285	Sulaymaniye	Istanbul, Turkey	REISULKUT-TAB 943

1.2   *The Manuscripts' Contents*

The manuscript evidence shows that Raḍī's original *Nahj al-Balāghah* consists
of three main sections of ʿAlī's words: 232 orations, 78 letters, and 429 sayings,
including 9 sayings in a subsection on rare words; some texts are followed by

Raḍī's brief commentary. The anthology is bookended by Raḍī's introduction and brief conclusion.

Two ancillary aspects of the manuscripts' contents are as follows:

SEQUENCE OF ORATIONS: A set of eight orations—§1.183–190—are arranged in two different sequences:

Sequence 1 is the one followed in the present edition. It is found in primary manuscripts M and Sh, and secondary manuscripts Z, S, Ch, A, T, and K.

Sequence 2 is as follows: Oration §1.182 is followed by §1.191–232. Orations §1.183–190 come after §1.232, the final oration in Sequence 1; §190 (*Qāṣiʿah*) is the final oration in Sequence 2. Sequence 2 is found in primary manuscripts N, Y, and H, and secondary manuscripts L, D, and Q.

ADDENDA: A number of manuscripts contain the following post-Raḍī addenda (details are noted in the individual manuscript descriptions that follow this section):

Additional texts: Several manuscripts contain extra texts attributed to ʿAlī— six orations (§1.233–238), one letter (§2.79), and seventeen sayings (§3.430– 446)—that are inserted at the end of each of the three sections. The insertions are early, perhaps from Raḍī's lifetime and perhaps with his approval, but they were not part of his original compilation.[3] Other than K and Ch, all manuscripts signal the inserted sayings as additions (*ziyādah*), and earlier scholarship has noted their insertion. Y, H, and L also signal the added orations, and H and L the added letter—in modern scholarship, the present edition is the first to identify their insertion.

Supplements: Some manuscripts contain up to four supplements inserted right after Raḍī's conclusion (and others contain further ad hoc supplements):
- Three sets of verses in praise of *Nahj al-Balāghah* by: (1) Abū Yūsuf Yaʿqūb ibn Aḥmad al-Naysābūrī (d. 474/1081, who also penned an important lost manu- script of *Nahj al-Balāghah* consulted by some of our manuscripts); (2) his son Abū Bakr al-Ḥasan ibn Yaʿqūb (d. 517/1123); and (3) the grammarian ʿAlī ibn Aḥmad al-Fanjkurdī (d. 513/1119).
- Inscriptions of ʿAlī's signet-rings (*nuqūsh khawātimihi*).

Marginalia: All manuscripts contain a larger or smaller number of study notices, marginalia, and stamps of ownership.

---

3   According to Ibn Abī al-Ḥadīd (H 20:180) and Baḥrānī (B 1029), whose comments are cited at the end of the present edition's notes. As Raḍī mentions in his conclusion, he left spaces at the end of each of his three sections for himself or others to write in additional texts, and scholars appear to have done so.

I have transcribed the additional texts in the edition and translation notes, but not the supplements or marginalia.

1.3 *Primary Manuscripts*

For the present edition, I have relied primarily on five precious manuscripts, all probably originating in Iraq and Iran. The first three—M, Sh, and N—are each claimed by specialists, as detailed below, to be the oldest known manuscript of the work. They were transcribed in the 5th/11th century by scholars either contemporaneous to the compiler, Raḍī (d. 406/1015), or a generation or two after him; Sh may even be from as early as 406/1015 or 1016. M is especially valuable because it is said to have been checked against a manuscript corrected by Raḍī, but the other two manuscripts also go back to Raḍī's original: of the others making up the five primary manuscript sources, H was transcribed from the early 6th/12th manuscript of the scholar Faḍlallāh al-Rāwandī, and Y from the manuscript of the aforementioned 5th/11th-century scholar-poet Yaʿqūb al-Naysābūrī, both parent manuscripts said to have been copied from Raḍī's manuscript. In terms of preservation, manuscript Y is complete, while M, Sh, N, and H are nearly complete, missing only the first few folios and a few inner ones.

The following are details of my primary manuscripts, in approximate chronological order:

[م] or [M]: **Marʿashī Manuscript:** Iranian manuscript dated 469/1077,[4] located in the library of Ayatollah al-Marʿashī, Qum, catalog no. 3827, in two parts,[5] published in a single-volume facsimile edition titled *Nahj al-balāghah: Muṣawwarah min nuskhah makhṭūṭah nādirah min al-qarn al-khāmis*, edited by Maḥmūd al-Marʿashī (Qum: Maktabat Ayatollah al-Najafī al-Marʿashī, 1406/1986); the full manuscript is available online.[6] Mīrzā ʿAbdallāh Afandī, an 11th/17th-century historian who once owned the manuscript, writes that it was "checked against a manuscript read out [in a study session] to the compiler, Raḍī."[7] The eminent

---

4 The final folio 171ᵛ (p. 335 of facsim. ed.) contains a mostly undotted date: (سنة ـع وتس وارـماـه) that can be read as *"sanata tisʿin* [or: *sabʿin] wa-sittīna wa-arbaʿi-miʾah* (in the year nine [or: seven] and sixty and four hundred)." Afandī (*Riyāḍ al-ʿulamāʾ*, 49) confirms the 469 AH dating.

5 Part 1—fols. 1ʳ–91ᵛ (pp. 1–174 of facsim. ed.)—includes Raḍī's introduction and orations §1.1 to §1.186. Part 2—fols. 92ᵛ–171ᵛ (pp. 176–335 of facsim. ed.)—begins with oration §1.187 and goes to the end of the compilation.

6 http://arabic.balaghah.net/sites/default/files/book/1164/1.pdf.

7 Afandī, *Riyāḍ al-ʿulamāʾ*, 2:87, in his biography of the copyist, Ibn al-Muʾaddib. Afandī adds that Ibn al-Muʾaddib received a license to transmit the text from his teacher, Jaʿfar ibn

Nahj al-Balāghah scholar ʿAbd al-ʿAzīz Ṭabāṭabāʾī calls it "one of the oldest and most valuable manuscripts" of *Nahj al-Balāghah*, "perhaps even the most valuable of them all."[8]

- The copyist is the well-known scholar Abū ʿAbdallāh al-Ḥasan ibn al-Ḥusayn al-Muʾaddib al-Qummī (d. early 6th/12th c.). Place is not mentioned.

- The manuscript is almost complete in 171 folios, numbered in the facsimile edition in 335 pages.[9] The opening folios (Raḍī's introduction, orations § 1.1–18), and folio 24ʳ (orations § 1.55–59) are missing, and the facsimile edition inserts folios from later manuscripts to complete the text—in the present edition, I do not consult the inserted folios. The Sayings section is also missing a substantial portion (§ 3.132–355, § 3.429). A few sayings are in a different sequence than in some other manuscripts.

- The manuscript is written in clear Naskh script, though cramped in some places and difficult to read, fully dotted and vocalized. Numerous study notices, corrections, variant readings, and lexical explanations are provided in different hands in the margins.

- The added orations are transcribed without signaling the insertion. The added letter is transcribed by a later hand in the margin without flagging the insertion. The added sayings are not included.

- Oration texts are arranged in Sequence 1.

- Blessings for the Prophet Muḥammad are invoked throughout with the formula, "God's blessings and peace on him and his descendants" (*ṣalla llāhu ʿalayhi wa-ālihi*). Blessings for ʿAlī are invoked with the formula "peace on him" (*ʿalayhi al-salām*).

- Raḍī's explanatory remarks are not prefaced by the copyist's added phrase found in several other manuscripts, viz., "The Sayyid [al-Raḍī] said."

[ش] or [Sh]: Shahrastānī Manuscript: Early 5th/11th-century manuscript, possibly dated 406/1015 or 1016,[10] located in the private library of Ayatollah Hibatal-

---

Muḥammad ibn al-ʿAbbās al-Dūrīstī, and that the well-known early commentator of the text Quṭb al-Dīn al-Rāwandī (d. 573/1177) transmitted in turn from him (ibid., 2:79); see more on Ibn al-Muʾaddib in ibid., 2:43, 49.

8   Ṭabāṭabāʾī, "al-Mutabaqqī," 5:62, MS § 1.

9   There are two cases of misnumbering in the facsim. ed.: (1) Fol. 42ʳᵛ (pp. 75–76) and fol. 43ʳ (p. 77) are incorrectly numbered and switched around; the editor is mistaken in noting that three folios after fol. 43 are missing. (2) The numbering jumps from fol. 109 to fol. 111—there is no fol. 110—but no text is missing.

10 The date is transcribed on the penultimate folio as "the month of Rajab, in the [Hijri] year four hundred and [undotted number]." An entry on a prefatory folio clarifies the undotted number as six, saying, "This manuscript was written in Rajab, 406 AH [1015 or 1016 AD]."

lāh al-Shahrastānī in al-Kāẓimiyyah, Baghdad, Iraq;[11] beautiful facsimile print-
ing by Alulbayt Foundation (London: Mu'assasat Āl al-Bayt li-Iḥyā' al-Turāth,
2013). *Majallat al-Murshid al-Baghdādiyyah* (vol. 2, no. 2, 1927, p. 75) deems it
the oldest known manuscript; and a notation on the final folio states that the
esteemed Iraqi scholar Hibat al-Dīn al-Ḥusaynī al-Shahrastānī (d. 1967) has cer-
tified it as the oldest extant manuscript.

- Place is not mentioned, and the copyist's name is unreadable.
- The manuscript is almost complete in 175 folios. The first three folios of
  Raḍī's introduction are missing,[12] and there is some water damage through-
  out, especially on the last folios. The manuscript is written in clear Naskh
  script with Kufic undertones, the latter also suggesting early provenance.
  It is fully dotted and vocalized, with headings in red. The same red is used
  for some corrections in the margins and the text. Other corrections, variant
  readings, and lexical explanations are provided in several different hands, in
  black, in the margins.
- Oration texts are arranged in Sequence 1.
- The original manuscript contains the fuller blessings formula throughout for
  the Prophet Muḥammad as "God's blessings on him and his descendants"
  (*ṣallā llāhu 'alayhi wa-ālihi*). The phrase "and his descendants" (*wa-ālihi*),
  has been brushed out in most (though not all) places and overwritten with
  "and grant him peace" (*wa-sallam*), possibly signaling a "correction" by an
  overzealous Sunni reader. Blessings for 'Alī are invoked with the formula
  "peace on him" (*'alayhi al-salām*).
- The added orations are transcribed in the margin in a different hand. The
  added letter is transcribed in the original without flagging. The added say-
  ings are transcribed in the original and flagged in red with the line, "Extra
  texts added from a manuscript written in the lifetime of the compiler"
  (*ziyādah min nuskhah kutibat fī 'ahd al-muṣannif*).
- The final folios transcribe Ya'qūb's and Ḥasan's verses in praise of *Nahj al-
  Balāghah*, which would appear to be a later addition.
- Raḍī's explanatory remarks are prefaced with the line, "The Sayyid [al-Raḍī]
  said."

To complicate matters, though, the final folio contains verses of praise for the work by
Ya'qūb, who died in 474 AH, and his son Ḥasan, who died in 517 AH, with blessings for the
deceased invoked for both—if the manuscript date of 406 AH is correct, as it appears to
be, the verses must be a later addition.

11   Listed by Ṭabāṭabā'ī, "Fī Riḥāb," 29:8 MS §148.

12   Also, folios containing oration §1.80.6 (from: *sataraḥā 'ankum*) to §1.88.7 (to: *aw sā'in
hāfid*) are misplaced in the facsimile edition, where they are transcribed within §1.104.

[ن] or [N]: Naṣīrī Manuscript: Manuscript dated 494/1101, located in the library of Muṣṭafā Ṣadr al-Afāḍil Dānish Naṣīrī al-Amīnī al-Shīrāzī, Tehran;[13] facsimile printing by Madrasat Chihil Sutūn in the Grand Mosque of Tehran, titled *Nahjul Balagha of Hazrat Ali*, edited by Ḥasan Saʿīd (Tehran: Maṭbaʿat Gulshan, 1981; Library of Congress MLCMN 2001/01154). The copyist had likely consulted Yaʿqūb's manuscript.[14]

– The copyist is Faḍlallāh ibn Ṭāhir ibn al-Muṭahhar al-Ḥusaynī. The date is transcribed as 494/1101.[15] Place is not mentioned.

– The manuscript is almost complete in 162 folios, numbered in the facsimile edition in 324 pages, with the first 15 or so folios missing: the manuscript begins at §1.32.[16] The manuscript is written in clear Naskh script, fully dotted and vocalized. Numerous corrections, variant readings, and lexical explanations are provided in different hands in the margins. The orthography is archaic—e.g., عثمن with no *alif* after *mīm*.

– Oration texts are arranged in Sequence 2.

– Blessings for the Prophet Muḥammad are invoked with the formula, "God's blessings and peace on him" (*ṣallā llāhu ʿalayhi wa-sallam*), consistently leaving off the phrase "and his descendants" (*wa-ālihi*), probably signaling Sunni affiliation—notably, a few pious epithets present in most other manuscripts are also omitted, such as "the queen of all women" (*sayyidat al-nisāʾ*) for the Prophet's daughter and ʿAlī's wife, Fāṭimah (§1.200). Blessings for ʿAlī are invoked with the formula "peace on him" (*ʿalayhi al-salām*).

– The added orations are not included. The added letter is transcribed without flagging it as an insertion. The added sayings are transcribed and titled in red with the line, "Extra texts added from an excellent Iraqi manuscript" (*ziyādah kutibat min nuskhah sariyyah ʿIrāqiyyah*).

– The final folios transcribe Yaʿqūb's, Ḥasan's, and Fanjkurdī's verses in praise of *Nahj al-Balāghah*, probably a later addition.

– Raḍī's explanatory remarks are prefaced with the line, "The Sayyid [al-Raḍī] said."

---

13   Listed by Ṭabāṭabāʾī, "Al-Mutabaqqī," 5:64, MS §3.

14   Faḍlallāh transcribes Yaʿqūb's verses (p. 316) and says they "were written by Yaʿqūb in his own hand in his manuscript of this work," perhaps indicating that he had seen the verses in Yaʿqūb's manuscript and thus, presumably, the rest of the manuscript too.

15   The 494/1101 dating is corroborated by the fact that the final folios contain Yaʿqūb's and Ḥasan's verses in praise of *Nahj al-Balāghah* and the copyist pronounces the formula of blessings for the deceased for the former, and a prayer for the long life of the latter—thus confirming the dating of the manuscript between the deaths of the two men, in 474/1081 and 517/1123 respectively.

16   The facsim. ed. has inserted folios from a later manuscript to fill this lacuna—those are not consulted in the present edition.

[ھ] or [H]: Rampur Raza Manuscript. Manuscript dated 553/1158, located in the Rampur Raza Library in Rampur, Uttar Pradesh, India, catalog no. 1190,[17] in two parts.[18] A beautiful single-volume facsimile edition has been published under the auspices of the Government of India's Ministry of Culture, with an introduction in English, Arabic, Farsi, Urdu, and Hindi by the Library's director, S.M. Azizuddin Husain (Rampur: Rampur Raza Library Publication Series, 1433/2012). A microfilm is owned by the Central Library of Tehran University, catalog no. 5046. The manuscript is copied from an earlier manuscript dated 511/1117, transcribed by the eminent scholar Faḍlallāh al-Kāshānī al-Rāwandī (d. 571/1175, author of a lost commentary on *Nahj al-Balāghah*), which was copied directly from Raḍī's own manuscript. Presumably copying from Rāwandī's manuscript, moreover, the copyist of our manuscript transcribes in a colophon on the saying at § 3.354 (fol. 164ʳ) Raḍī's contextualizing comments, prefaced with the words, "[Perused] in Raḍī's copy (*fī nuskhat al-Raḍī*)."

- The copyist is ʿAbd al-Jabbār ibn al-Ḥusayn bin Abī al-Qāsim al-Farāhānī. He transcribed the manuscript in Jawsaqān near Rāwand, in Isfahan.
- The manuscript is almost complete in 169 folios: The first folio of Raḍī's introduction is missing, as are a couple of folios from the first part of volume two, from the beginning of oration § 1.191 to just before the beginning of oration § 1.192. There is water damage on the lower end of the first few folios.
- The manuscript is written in clear Naskh script, fully dotted, and vocalized, and has some corrections and annotations in the margins.
- Oration texts are arranged in Sequence 2.
- The added orations, letter, and sayings are transcribed,[19] and all three sets are flagged by a line that states, "Additional texts added from a manuscript written in the lifetime of the compiler."
- Yaʿqūb's and his son's verses are not present in the facsimile edition, though they may be present in the original manuscript.

---

17   Listed by Ṭabāṭabāʾī, "Al-Mutabaqqī," 5:71, MS § 17.

18   The first part contains Raḍī's introduction to the end of oration § 1.182, with a tag saying it is the end of part one. The second part contains oration § 1.183–190, followed by the chapter on letters, etc., to the end of the book.

19   The sequence of added orations in MS H is different than their sequence in the other manuscripts, and the same as MS Y, viz., § 1.238, 1.237, 1.233, 1.236, 1.234. These are followed by the phrase, "end of additional texts" (*intahat al-ziyādah*), then another phrase, "[another] additional [oration] from a Baghdad manuscript" (*ziyādah min nuskhah Baghdādiyyah*), followed by the added oration § 1.235.

- Blessings for the Prophet Muḥammad are invoked throughout with the formula, "God's blessings on him and his descendants" (*ṣallā llāhu ʿalayhi wa-ālihi*). Blessings for ʿAlī are invoked with the formula "peace on him" (*ʿalayhi l-salām*).
- Raḍī's explanatory remarks are prefaced with the line, "The Sayyid [al-Raḍī] said."

[ي] or [Y]: "Yaʿqūbī" Tehran University Manuscript. Manuscript dated 608/1212, located in the Central Library (al-Maktabah al-Markaziyyah) of Tehran University, catalog no. 1782.[20] A facsimile copy is preserved in the library of the Ṭabāṭabāʾī Foundation (Bunyād-i Muḥaqqiq Ṭabāṭabāʾī) in Qum, catalog no. M/214. The manuscript was copied from Yaʿqūb al-Naysābūrī's (d. 474/1081) manuscript,[21] which was copied from or checked against Raḍī's original manuscript.[22]

- The copyist is ʿAlī ibn Ṭāhir ibn Abī Saʿd. Place is not noted, but since the manuscript derives from Yaʿqūb al-Naysābūrī's manuscript, it too could be from Nishapur.
- The manuscript is complete in 193 folios, also numbered as 386 pages.[23] It is written in a rough but clear hand and is fully dotted and vocalized. The orthography is archaic. It contains numerous variants and lengthy annotations in the margins that appear to be in the original copyist's hand.
- In the Sayings section, the introductory phrase in most manuscripts preceding each text—viz., "'Alī, peace be on him, said" (*wa-qāla ʿalayhi l-salām*)—is mostly, though not always, absent.
- Oration texts are arranged in Sequence 2.
- The added letter is transcribed without flagging it as an insertion, but the added orations and sayings, which are also transcribed, are flagged by a line that states, "Additional texts added from a manuscript written in the lifetime of the compiler."[24] As for the added sayings, the copyist states (p. 384) that he copied them from Yaʿqūb's manuscript.

---

20   Listed by Ṭabāṭabāʾī, "Al-Mutabaqqī," 5:77, MS § 33.

21   As seen from the colophon on p. 2.

22   Another colophon states that "Raḍī wrote in his own hand here on the margin of his [original] manuscript" a lexical explanation for a word transcribed in saying § 3.436 (p. 383). There is a similar colophon for saying § 3.355 (p. 359). Ṭabāṭabāʾī ("Al-Mutabaqqī," 5:77) says, "it appears that [Yaʿqūb] copied his manuscript from al-Sharīf al-Raḍī's original manuscript in his own hand."

23   The facsimile edition's sequence of folios containing orations § 1.88–111 is jumbled.

24   The added orations are in a different order than several other manuscripts, presented in two parts: The "Additional texts" title is followed by five added orations (§ 1.238, 237, 233,

- Though copied from Yaʿqūb's manuscript, the manuscript does not appear to contain Yaʿqūb's or his son's verses—perhaps the folios that contained them are lost.
- Blessings for the Prophet Muḥammad are invoked throughout with the formula, "God's blessings on him and his descendants" (*ṣallā llāhu ʿalayhi wa-ālihi*), and sometimes, "Peace upon him" (*ʿalayhi l-salām*). Blessings for ʿAlī are invoked with the formula "peace on him" (*ʿalayhi al-salām*). The pious epithet for Fāṭimah, dropped from §1.200 of manuscript N, is also dropped from Y.
- Raḍī's explanatory remarks are prefaced with the line, "The Sayyid [al-Raḍī] said."

1.4 *Secondary Manuscripts*

I have consulted nine further manuscripts from the 6th/12th and 7th/13th centuries in order to transcribe the initial few folios that are missing from all but Y of the primary manuscripts, and for a further check of substantive variants throughout. These manuscripts also have important scholarly pedigrees. Among them, K was copied from the manuscript of the famous premodern editor of texts ʿAlī ibn Muḥammad ibn al-Sakūn (or: Sukūn, d. ca. 600/1204).[25]

The following are details of my secondary manuscripts in chronological order:

[ل] or [L]: **Mumtaz ul Ulama Lucknow Manuscript**. Manuscript dated 510/1116, located in the Mumtaz ul Ulama Library in Lucknow, India.[26] A facsimile copy is located in the library of the Theology Faculty (Dāneshkadeh-yi Ilahiyyāt), Ferdowsi University, Mashhad, catalog no. 77.

- Copyist and place are not noted. The date is written in a different hand on the margin of the final folio.
- The manuscript is almost complete in 158 unpaginated folios; the last lines of letter §2.11 to the middle of §2.31.11 appear to be missing, while parts of the

---

236, 234, in this order), followed by a line stating, "End of extra texts" (*intahat al-ziyādah*), followed by another line stating, "In a Baghdadi manuscript there is an addition from an oration by [ʿAlī] in which he speaks of Muḥammad's family," followed by oration §1.235.

25 Ibn al-Sakūn was born in Ḥillah, and lived in Baghdad, Medina, and Damascus. His biography is transcribed from Muḥibb al-Dīn Ibn al-Najjār, Mīrzā Afandī, Yāqūt al-Ḥamawī, and other medieval scholars by ʿAṭṭār in the Introduction (pp. 10–13) of his 2016 ed. of Ibn al-Sakūn's *Nahj al-Balāghah* manuscript.

26 Listed cursorily by Ṭabāṭabāʾī, "Al-Mutabaqqī," 5:67, MS §11; listed also by Waseem and Naqavi, *Nahjul Balagha*, 30.

first folios, and most of the final eight folios, have water damage. It is written in mostly clear Naskh script, fully dotted and partially vocalized, with some annotations and corrections in the margins. The first line of Raḍī's brief conclusion is transcribed as it appears in the other manuscripts, but the next two lines, which are blurred, appear to contain a different prayer formula.
- Oration texts are arranged in Sequence 2.
- The added orations, letter, and sayings are transcribed, and all three sets are flagged by a line that states, "Additional texts added from a manuscript written in the lifetime of the compiler."
- Seven lines of verse by an unnamed poet in praise of ʿAlī's words, in the same hand, are appended after Raḍī's conclusion.

[ز] or [Z]: **Maulana Azad Aligarh Manuscript.** Manuscript dated 538/1144, located in Maulana Azad Library, Aligarh Muslim University, Aligarh, India, catalog no. 485,[27] in two parts.[28] A beautiful facsimile edition has been published by Maulana Azad Library, Aligarh, and the Cultural Center of the Iranian Embassy in New Delhi, 2011. A microfilm is owned by Imam Reza Library in Mashhad.
- The copyist is ʿAlī ibn Abī al-Qāsim ibn ʿAlī al-Ḥajj. Place is not noted.
- The manuscript is complete in 173 folios. It is written in clear Naskh script, fully dotted and vocalized, with some corrections and annotations in the margins.
- A colophon on the final folio notes that the manuscript was checked against the copy of a scholar named Afḍal al-Dīn Ḥasan ibn Fādār al-Qummī. Several ownership marks are found at the beginning and end of each of the two parts.
- Oration texts are arranged in Sequence 1.
- The added orations, letter, and sayings are included but not flagged as insertions.

[د] or [D]: **Imam Reza Mashhad Manuscript.** Iranian manuscript dated 544/1149, located in the Imam Reza Library in Mashhad, catalog no. 13847, from the *Waqf* endowment of the library of Fāḍil Khān al-Khurāsānī al-Tūnī (d. 1060/

---

27   Listed by Ṭabāṭabāʾī, "Al-Mutabaqqī," 5:69, MS §15; listed also by Waseem and Naqavi, *Nahjul Balagha*, 30.

28   Part 1 contains Raḍī's introduction to the end of oration §1.190, with a line stating it is the end of part one. Part 2 contains oration §1.191 to the end of the book.

1650).[29] A facsimile copy is preserved in the library of the Ṭabāṭabā'ī Foundation in Qum, catalog no. M/203, and a microfilm in the Central Library of Tehran University, catalog no. 2134.

- The copyist is Muḥammad ibn Muḥammad ibn Aḥmad al-Naqīb, who finished writing the manuscript in Sabzevar (previously known as Bayhaq, in NE Iran, near Mashhad).
- The manuscript is almost complete in 183 folios, numbered in a later hand in 366 pages, with the first folio of Raḍī's introduction missing. A couple of folios from within the first oration (§1.1.2–1.1.7) and sayings §3.195–332 are also missing.[30]
- The manuscript is written in clear Naskh script, fully dotted, and mostly vocalized, and it has some corrections and annotations in the margins.
- Oration texts are arranged in Sequence 2.
- The added orations are not included. The added letter is transcribed without flagging it as an insertion. The added sayings are transcribed and titled in red, "Additional texts added from a manuscript written in the lifetime of the compiler."
- The final folios transcribe Yaʿqūb's and Ḥasan's verses in praise of *Nahj al-Balāghah*.

[ق] or [Q]: Iraqi National Museum Manuscript. Manuscript dated 565/ 1170, located in the Library of the Iraqi National Museum in Baghdad, catalog no. 356.[31]

- The copyist is Muḥammad ibn Saʿīd ibn al-Ḥusayn al-ʿĀmirī. Place is not noted.
- The manuscript is complete in 243 folios,[32] written in clear Naskh script, fully dotted and vocalized, with one- or two-word lexical and grammatical annotations in somewhat blurred red, in the margins or between the lines.
- Oration texts are arranged in Sequence 2.
- The added orations are not included. The added letter is transcribed without flagging. The added sayings are transcribed and titled in red, "Additional texts added from a manuscript written in the lifetime of the compiler."
- The final folios transcribe Fanjkurdī's verses in praise of *Nahj al-Balāghah*.

---

29   Listed by Ṭabāṭabā'ī, "Al-Mutabaqqī," 5:69–70, MS §16.

30   Ṭabāṭabā'ī ("Al-Mutabaqqī," 5:70) incorrectly states that the last folios containing sayings §210–350 are also missing.

31   Listed by Ṭabāṭabā'ī, "Al-Mutabaqqī," 5:71, MS §18.

32   Two folios—containing sayings §3.345 to the middle of §3.352—are misplaced, and come at the end of the volume, after the copyist's name and Fanjkurdī's verses.

[س] or [S]: **Sulaymaniye Raʾīs al-Kuttāb Manuscript 1.** Manuscript dated 567/1171, located in the Sulaymaniye Library in Istanbul, catalog no. REISUL-KUTTAB 942.[33] The manuscript was part of the collection of Raʾīs al-kuttāb Aḥmad ibn Muṣṭafā ibn Khalīl (Ṭāshkubrīzādah, d. 968/1561) whose ownership mark is on the cover folio, along with his name in his own hand.

- The copyist is ʿAlī ibn Muḥammad ibn Abī Saʿīd ibn Manṣūr. Place is not noted.
- The manuscript is complete in 172 folios, written in clear Naskh script, fully dotted and partially vocalized, with some annotations and corrections in the margins.
- Oration texts are arranged in Sequence 1.
- The first three of the six added orations are transcribed, and the first fifteen of the seventeen added sayings, without noting for either set that they are insertions. The added letter is also transcribed without flagging.

[ح] or [Ch]: **Chester Beatty Manuscript.** Manuscript dated 588/1192, located in the Chester Beatty library in Dublin, catalog no. 5451.[34]

- The copyist is Aḥmad ibn al-Muʾayyad ibn ʿAbd al-Jalīl ibn Muḥammad. The place is not noted. An ownership notice on the cover folio with the name Sadīd al-Dīn Yūsuf ibn Muṭahhar Ḥillī [= al-ʿAllāmah al-Ḥillī (d. 726/1325)] is written in Persian, with the mark of a library whose name is blotted out, also in Persian.
- The manuscript is complete in 169 folios. It is written in clear Naskh script, fully dotted and vocalized, and has numerous marginal variants and annotations.
- Oration texts are arranged in Sequence 1.
- The added orations are transcribed, as are the first fifteen of the seventeen added sayings, without noting for either set that they are additions. The added letter is also transcribed without flagging.

[آ] or [A]: **Aya Sofya Manuscript.** Manuscript dated 598/1202, located in the Sulaymaniye Library in Istanbul, catalog no. AYASOFYA 4344.[35]

- The copyist is Muḥammad ibn Aḥmad ibn ʿAbd al-Raḥīm al-Fāmī al-Harawī. Place is not noted.

---

33   Listed by Ṭabāṭabāʾī, "Al-Mutabaqqī," 5:72, MS §20.

34   Listed by Ṭabāṭabāʾī, "Al-Mutabaqqī," 5:73, MS §22. The Chester Beatty catalog incorrectly attributes it (à la Ibn Khallikān) to al-Sharīf al-Murtaḍā.

35   Not listed by Ṭabāṭabāʾī, "Al-Mutabaqqī."

- The manuscript is complete in 187 folios, written in clear Naskh script, fully dotted and vocalized, with headings of new orations, etc., in red. It contains numerous marginal variants and explications in the same red.
- Oration texts are arranged in Sequence 1.
- The six added orations are not included.[36] The added letter is transcribed without flagging. The added sayings are transcribed and titled in red, "Extra texts added from a manuscript written in the lifetime of the compiler."
- Raḍī's conclusion is followed by: the text of ʿAlī's seal rings; a further added oration (the *alif*-less oration titled *Badīhah* or The Spontaneous), reported by Muḥammad ibn al-Sāʾib al-Kalbī from Abū Ṣāliḥ (fols. 183ᵛ–185ᵛ); and Yaʿqūb's, Ḥasan's, and Fanjkurdī's verses in praise of *Nahj al-Balāghah*.

[ت] or [T]: Topkapi Manuscript. Manuscript dated 615/1218, located in the Topkapi Palace Library in Istanbul, catalog no. Aḥmad III 2556.[37]
- The copyist is ʿAbd al-Ghafūr ibn ʿAbd al-Ghaffār ibn Aḥmad ibn Marzawayh al-Kātib. Place is not noted.
- The manuscript is complete in 357 folios, with no lacunae, but the copyist has left out Raḍī's final texts in each section: the manuscript ends at oration §1.224 (missing eight texts, §1.225–232), at letter §2.72 (missing five texts, §2.73–78), and at saying §3.407 (missing twenty-one texts, §3.408–429). The added orations, letter, and sayings are also not included.
- Oration texts are arranged in Sequence 1.
- The manuscript appears to be either a special display copy or one used sparingly by Ottoman royalty: It is written in clear, handsome Naskh script, fully dotted and vocalized. Chapter headings are decorated with extensive gold illumination. Phrases introducing individual pieces are centered and sized larger. Only two variants, written in the margin in a different hand, are noted in the entire manuscript.

[ك] or [K]: Sulaymaniye Raʾīs al-Kuttāb Manuscript 2. Manuscript dated 684/ 1285, located in the Sulaymaniye Library in Istanbul, catalog no. REISULKUT-TAB 943.[38] The manuscript is copied from the manuscript of the aforementioned scholar Ibn al-Sakūn (d. ca. 600/1204). Like S, this manuscript was also part of the collection of Raʾīs al-kuttāb Ṭāshkubrīzādah (d. 968/1561).

---

36   Oration §1.231 is also missing, and §1.177 is (mis)placed between §1.230 and §1.232.
37   Listed by Ṭabāṭabāʾī, "Al-Mutabaqqī," 5:77, MS §34.
38   Not listed by Ṭabāṭabāʾī, "Al-Mutabaqqī." Used by ʿAṭṭār (he calls it MS "S-T") in his 2016 edition of Ibn al-Sakūn's copy of *Nahj al-Balāghah* (see his description of the manuscript in ibid., 38–43).

- Place is not noted, and a gold-bordered rectangle after the date which may have contained the copyist's name is pasted over with a blank piece of paper.
- The manuscript is almost complete in 225 folios, with just a few folios missing in the middle (folio 85, oration §1.163–172). It is written in beautiful and clear Naskh script, fully dotted and vocalized, with red rondelles separating the phrases, up to the end of folio 187. There are many corrections and variants in the margins in different hands, annotations in Arabic, Persian, and Ottoman Turkish. The title folio has numerous ownership marks, Waqf notices, and hadith praising ʿAlī. The title folio and final folio contain verses in the genre of renunciation of worldliness. The final folio also contains, after the sign-off, additional texts attributed to ʿAlī.
- Oration texts are arranged in Sequence 1.
- The added orations, letter, and sayings are transcribed, without noting that they are insertions.
- An earlier unreadable form of pious invocation attached to ʿAlī's name in the manuscript has been systematically erased and replaced with "May God be pleased with him (*raḍiya llāhu ʿanhu*)," presumably changed from a Shiʿite formula to a Sunni one.

1.5   *Manuscript Family Tree*

Based on four classification matrixes that will be discussed shortly, I have constructed the following family tree to show the relationships between my fourteen manuscripts. In conjunction with the matrixes, the relative chronology in the stemma provides a visual of possible parentage and sibling relationships. Some of the later manuscripts could derive from the earlier ones, or from manuscripts related to the earlier ones.

MANUSCRIPT GROUPS: The manuscripts may be divided into two broad groups:

Group 1:   primary manuscripts M and Y, and secondary manuscripts Z, S, Ch, T, and K.

Group 2:   primary manuscripts Sh and N, and secondary manuscripts D, Q, and A.

N.B.:   primary manuscript H and secondary manuscript L possess features from both groups.

CLASSIFICATION MATRIXES: Four matrixes have been used to construct the stemma, weighted in the following order: (1) the principal matrix is variants in wording, then (2) sequence of texts, then (3) presence or absence of added

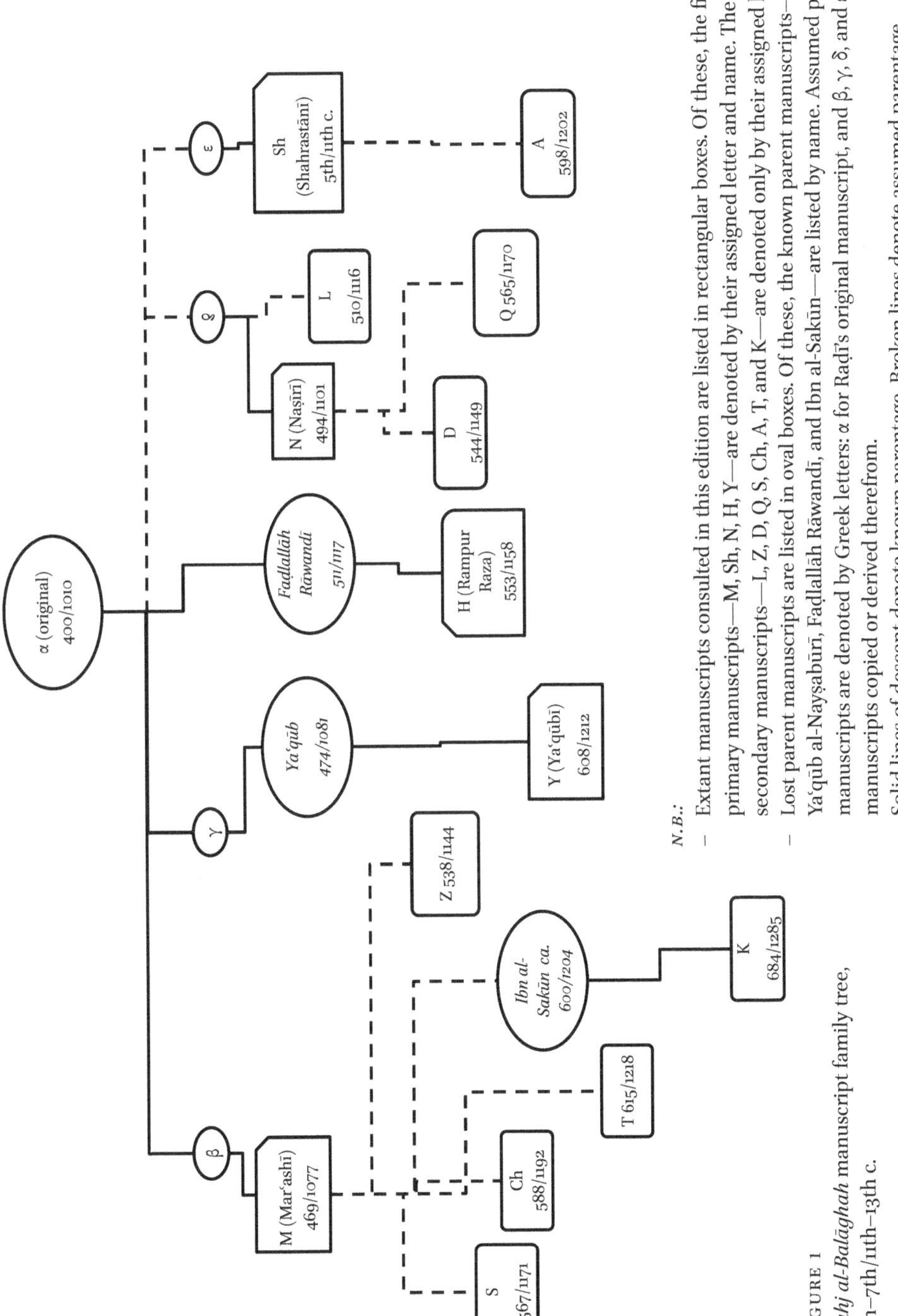

N.B.:

– Extant manuscripts consulted in this edition are listed in rectangular boxes. Of these, the five primary manuscripts—M, Sh, N, H, Y—are denoted by their assigned letter and name. The nine secondary manuscripts—L, Z, D, Q, S, Ch, A, T, and K—are denoted only by their assigned letter.

– Lost parent manuscripts are listed in oval boxes. Of these, the known parent manuscripts—Yaʿqūb al-Nayṣabūrī, Fadlallāh Rāwandī, and Ibn al-Sakūn—are listed by name. Assumed parent manuscripts are denoted by Greek letters: α for Raḍī's original manuscript, and β, γ, δ, and ε for manuscripts copied or derived therefrom.

– Solid lines of descent denote known parentage. Broken lines denote assumed parentage.

FIGURE 1
Nahj al-Balāghah manuscript family tree,
5th–7th/11th–13th c.

orations, and/or (4) supplements. The place where a manuscript was copied would also have been a useful matrix but unfortunately this data is mostly not available. Raḍī, as we know, compiled *Nahj al-Balāghah* in Baghdad, Iraq. Among our fourteen manuscripts, only two name the place where they were written: near Rāwand, in Isfahan, for H, and Sabzevar, in NE Iran, for D. Also, M's copyist was from Qum, Iran, so it may have originated there; and Yaʿqūb (whose manuscript is the parent of Y) lived in Nishapur, so his manuscript probably originated there. It should be noted, moreover, that the manuscript genealogy is not always clear cut, and a handful of apparently contradictory positionings—discussed briefly below—complicate stemma relationships.

TABLE 3   Matrixes of manuscript family tree

Matrix	*Group 1*	*Group 2*
1. Variants of words	M Y {H} / {L} Z S Ch T K	Sh N {H} / {L} D Q A
2. Sequence of orations	followed in present edition: M [Sh] / Z S Ch [A] T K	Sequence 2: N [Y] {H} / {L} D Q
3. Added orations	present: M Y {H} / {L} Z S Ch K	absent: Sh N / D Q A [T]
4. Yaʿqūb and Ḥasan verses	absent: M Y H / {L} Z [Q] S Ch T K	present: Sh N / D A

N.B.:

- Manuscripts in this table are listed in chronological order: primary manuscripts are listed first and followed by a slash; secondary manuscripts are listed after the slash.
- Square brackets signal manuscripts that in that particular matrix are not with their variant-matrix group.
- Curly brackets are used for the Mixed Group manuscripts, H and L.

Matrix 1: Variants of Words

Based on the variant matrix, manuscripts are clustered in the two groups listed in Table 3 above.[39] A sample list of seventeen substantive variants within the *Nahj al-Balāghah* text, and variant-based manuscript distribution, is provided in Table 4:

---

39   Note that H and L contain almost an equal number of variants from both groups. A—which is categorized in Group 2—contains three variants from Group 1.

TABLE 4 *Nahj al-Balāghah* manuscript variants

Text no.	M	Sh	N	H	Y	L	Z	D	Q	S	Ch	A	T	K	Variants
1.27	الإسهاب	الأسداد	×	الإسهاب	الإسهاب	الأسداد	الإسهاب	الأسداد	الأسداد	الأسداد	الأسداد	الأسداد	الإسهاب	الإسهاب	بالإسهاب / بالأسداد
1.27	ذمًّا	سدمًا	×	ذمًّا	ذمًّا	ذمًّا	ذمًّا	سدمًا	سدمًا	ذمًّا	ذمًّا	سدمًا	ذمًّا	ذمًّا	ذمًّا / سدمًا
1.80.11	دفاقًا	دهاقًا	دهاقًا	دهاقًا	دهاقًا	دفاقًا	دهاقًا	دفاقًا	دهاقًا	دفاقًا	دهاقًا	دهاقًا	دهاقًا	دهاقًا	دفاقًا / دهاقًا
1.102.2	يبكي	يشكي	يشكي	يبكي	يبكي	يشكي	يبكي	يشكي	يشكي	يبكي	يبكي	يشكي	يبكي	يبكي	يبكي / يشكي
1.161.1	بدية	أبدية	أبدية	أبدية	بدية	أبدية	أبدية	أبدية	أبدية	بدية	أبدية	أبدية؟	بدية	بدية	بدية / أبدية
1.166	أعرابكم	أغراركم	أغراركم	أغراركم	أعرابكم	أعرابكم	أعرابكم	أغراركم	أغراركم	أعرابكم	أعرابكم	أغراركم	أعرابكم	×	أعرابكم / أغراركم
1.170.2	هبّ	بُهِت	بُهِت	بُهِت	هبّ	بُهِت	هبّ	بُهِت	بُهِت	هبّ	بُهِت	بُهِت	هبّ	×	بُهِت / هبّ
1.171.2	أعلمهم	أعلمهم	أعلمهم	أعلمهم	أعلمهم	أعلمهم	أعلمهم	أعلمهم	أعلمهم	أعلمهم	غير واضح	أعلمهم	أعلمهم	×	أعلمهم / أعلمهم
1.183.2	صبّت	ضنّت	ضنّت	ضنّت	صبّت	ضنّت	صبّت	صبّت	ضنّت	صبّت	صبّت	صبّت	صبّت	صبّت	صبّت / ضنّت

TABLE 4 *Nahj al-Balāghah* manuscript variants (*cont.*)

Text no.	M	Sh	N	H	Y	L	Z	D	Q	S	Ch	A	T	K	Variants
1.183.2	النحلة	النحلة	النحلة	النحلة	النحلة	النحلة	النحلة	النحلة	النحلة	النحلة	النحلة	النحلة	النحلة	النحلة	النخلة / النحلة
1.196	آكام	إمام	إمام	إمام	آكام	إمام	آكام	إمام	إمام	آكام	إمام	آكام	آكام	آكام	آكام / إمام
2.10	مِجَنّ	مُنِج	مُنِج	مِجَنّ	مِجَنّ	مُنِج	مُنِج	مِجَنّ	مُنِج	مِجَنّ	مُنِج	مُنِج	مِجَنّ	مِجَنّ	مِجَنّ / مُنِج
2.28.2	جاهليّتكم	جاهليّتنا	جاهليّتنا	جاهليّتنا	جاهليّتكم	×	جاهليّتنا	جاهليّتنا	جاهليّتنا	جاهليّتنا	جاهليّتكم	جاهليّتنا	جاهليّتنا	جاهليّتنا	جاهليّتكم / جاهليّتنا
2.45.4	كالصنو	كالضوء	كالصنو	كالصنو	كالصنو	كالصنو	كالصنو	كالصنو	كالصنو	كالضوء	كالصنو	كالصنو	كالصنو	كالضوء	كالضوء من الضوء / كالصنو من الصنو
3.33	الفاجر	العاجز	العاجز	الفاجر	الفاجر	الفاجر	العاجز	العاجز	الفاجر	الفاجر	الفاجر	الفاجر	الفاجر	الفاجر	الفاجر / العاجز
3.137	×	أمر	أمرئ	أمرئ	أمرئ	أمرئ	أمرئ	أمرئ	أمر	أمرئ	أمرئ	أمر	أمر	أمر	أمر / أمرئ
3.237	×	الإمامة	الإمامة	الإمامة	الإمامة	الإمامة	الإمامة	×	الإمامة	الأمانة	الأمانة	الإمامة	الإمامة	الإمامة	الإمامة / الأمانة

Matrix 2: Sequence of Orations

Our manuscripts transcribe *Nahj al-Balāghah*'s orations in two different sequences, and these have been described earlier as Sequence 1, which is followed in the present edition, and Sequence 2, which is not.

Matrix 3: Added Orations

The six orations inserted into Raḍī's original (§ 1.233–238) are found in all manuscripts in Group 1, except T (which is missing all end texts anyway), and they are also found in H from the Mixed Group. The added letter (§ 2.79) is transcribed in all our manuscripts and is thus not particularly useful as a matrix for mapping the family tree. Similarly, the added sayings (§ 3.430–446) are also present in all our manuscripts except M and T. Two manuscripts, S and Ch, include only fifteen out of seventeen added sayings, and they may be more closely related to each other than to others in their group.

Matrix 4: Yaʿqūb's and Ḥasan's verses

Yaʿqūb's and Ḥasan's verses in praise of *Nahj al-Balāghah* are found in all manuscripts of Group 2, except Q.[40] In Sh and N, though, these are presumably later additions, as these manuscripts predate the poets. Further supplementary materials are also found in some Group 2 manuscripts:

– Fanjkurdī's verses in praise of *Nahj al-Balāghah* are transcribed in N, Q, and A. In N, this is presumably a later addition, as the manuscript predates the poet.
– Inscriptions of ʿAlī's signet rings are transcribed in D and A.

NB: Lost Parent Manuscripts

Some of our manuscripts derive from three lost parent manuscripts transcribed by the following scholars:

– Yaʿqūb al-Naysābūrī (d. 474/1081), who copied his manuscript from, or checked it against, Raḍī's original. Our manuscript Y is copied from it, N's copyist consulted it, and the copyists of D and A—because they contain Yaʿqūb's verses—may have consulted it or a manuscript derived from it.
– Faḍlallāh al-Rāwandī (d. 571/1175), who copied his manuscript in 511/1117 from Raḍī's original. Our manuscript H is copied from it.
– Ibn al-Sakūn (d. ca. 600/1204). Our manuscript K is copied from it.

---

40   Surprisingly, Group 1's manuscript Y—said to be copied from Yaʿqūb's own manuscript—does not contain Yaʿqūb's verses. Perhaps they were present in the original Y, and in H, and the end folios containing them are lost.

2　Previous Editions

From the late 1800s onward, *Nahj al-Balāghah* has been printed numerous times, including the printing with Muḥammad ʿAbduh's commentary, first published by al-Maṭbaʿah al-Adabiyyah in Beirut in 1885. Most *Nahj al-Balāghah* printings are trade editions which do not mention any manuscripts at all, and their texts contain unflagged insertions of headings and words, as well as numerous errors.

Two mistranscriptions are egregious and stem from anti-Shiʿi bias:

- §3.174: The original, transcribed thus in all the early manuscripts that I consulted and all the medieval commentaries that I looked at,[41] is as follows: "How strange! So, the caliphate can be justified through the Prophet's companionship, but not through companionship and kinship together?" (واعجباه أتكون الخلافة بالصحابة ولا تكون بالصحابة والقرابة). In the print editions, this is changed by dropping a few words in the middle—ولا تكون بالصحابة—to mean something quite different: "How strange that the caliphate is justified through companionship and kinship!" (واعجباه أتكون الخلافة بالصحابة والقرابة).[42]

- §3.237: The original, transcribed thus in all my primary manuscripts, and all except S and Ch of the secondary manuscripts, is as follows: … فرض الله الإمامة نظامًا للأُمّة (God has mandated the imamate as a system of governance for the community.) In modern printings, deriving perhaps from the later manuscript tradition (cf. S and Ch, just mentioned), the word *imāmah* (imamate) is changed to *amānah* (trustworthiness), by replacing the letter "M" with "N."[43]

Modern critical editions have been published by two scholars:

- Hāshim Mīlānī, Najaf: Maktabat al-Rawḍah al-Ḥaydariyyah, 2009. Mīlānī consulted the manuscripts I have labelled M and D, and two more from the 6th/12th century located in Iranian libraries.

- Qays Bahjat ʿAṭṭār, Qum: Muʾassasat al-Rāfid, 2010. ʿAṭṭār consulted the 5th/11th century manuscripts I have labelled M and N, and two more partial, undated ones, presumably from the 6th/12th or 7th/13th century. In a different edition (Najaf: al-ʿAtabah al-ʿAlawiyyah al-Muqaddasah, 2016), in which he focused on establishing Ibn al-Sakūn's vocalization of *Nahj al-Balāghah*,

---

41　E.g., Ibn Abī al-Ḥadīd, *Sharḥ Nahj al-balāghah*, 18:416, §185.

42　E.g., ʿAbduh, *Sharḥ Nahj al-balāghah*, 502, §190.

43　E.g., ʿAbduh, *Sharḥ Nahj al-balāghah*, 512, §252. The original Ibn Abī al-Ḥadīd commentary appears to have transcribed *imāmah*, and the later manuscript tradition appears to have changed it to *amānah*: the text before the commentary has *amānah* (Ḥ 19:86, §249), but the explanation (Ḥ 19:90) has retained the original *imāmah*.

ʿAṭṭār consulted two manuscripts derived from Ibn al-Sakūn's original manu-
script, including the manuscript I have labelled K, and another, also from the
7th/13th century.

Although these are welcome and relatively accurate editions, Mīlānī and ʿAṭṭār
do not use my primary manuscripts Sh, Y, or H, nor my secondary manuscripts
L, Z, Q, S, Ch, A, and T. Neither scholar flags the added orations or letter as
insertions. Neither constructs a manuscript stemma or lays out a concerted
methodology. Furthermore, they do not note the substantive variants in an
efficient manner: Mīlānī notes only some substantive variants; his focus is on
providing meanings of difficult words. ʿAṭṭār in his 2010 edition—an otherwise
excellent edition and remarkably free of typographical errors—lists all differ-
ences in vocalization. This is a redundant, or, at best, a secondary exercise, and
it has come at a cost: the profusion of vocalization differences in the notes
obscures the fewer, scattered substantive variants. The original vocalization is
not ascertainable in any case, for there is no evidence to suggest that Raḍī vocal-
ized his compilation let alone to establish the exact vowels that ʿAlī used in his
oral deliveries. ʿAṭṭār also lists all variants noted in the manuscripts' margins—
this adds to the reception data (albeit sketchily, because we don't know for the
most part when these variants were added to the margins or by who), but it fur-
ther obscures the manuscripts' text collation. These editions are also not easily
available.

3   This Edition

In formulating a new critical edition of *Nahj al-Balāghah*, I have relied princi-
pally on my five primary manuscripts: the three earliest extant 5th/11th-century
manuscripts of *Nahj al-Balāghah*, M, Sh, and N, as well as Y, which was copied
from a 5th/11th-century manuscript, and H, which was copied from an early
6th/12th-century manuscript. As noted earlier, M is believed to have been
copied from a manuscript authorized by Raḍī, and the parent manuscripts of
H and Y are said to have been copied from Raḍī's own manuscript. Substantial
variants among these primary manuscripts are relatively few in number.

The manuscript history of the text is extremely complicated, and each of the
manuscripts passed through many hands, so—despite best efforts to untan-
gle study notices and colophons—it is extremely difficult to fully tease out
what corrections were made, when they were made, by whom they were made,
and which other manuscripts or resources were used to make them. Also, it
is sometimes difficult to ascertain the original transcription from a later cor-
rection. Despite recourse to these precious early manuscripts, then, it is still
not possible to definitively determine the entirety of Raḍī's original text (or,

for that matter, his sequence of orations). In the case of some textual variants, the early manuscripts often present two choices that appear equally plausible in the historical, grammatical, and rhetorical context. Indeed, oftentimes the copyists themselves offer two possible readings, marked with the word *maʿa* (both), meaning both readings, according to them, are equally plausible. However, using the method described below, I believe I have constructed the close-to-best version we can hope to attain—barring somebody finding Raḍī's autograph manuscript!

3.1   *Substantive Features of this Edition*

- The present edition relies principally on the five primary manuscripts M, Sh, N, H, and Y. Of these, there is no one manuscript, and no one group, which consistently gives an indisputably better reading. Although some scholars have claimed one or the other of these as the best manuscript, I do not agree that there is a clear frontrunner. So, where the primary manuscripts differ, I use my best judgment: where they are strongly weighted toward one reading, I prioritize that majority reading; where they are nearly equally distributed, I choose the reading I deem most appropriate to the literary and historical context.
- I footnote all substantial variants occurring in my primary manuscripts. The secondary manuscripts from the 6th/12th and 7th/13th centuries are invoked only for variants in the first folios that are missing from the primary manuscripts, and for the substantive variants listed in Table 4 above.
- The manuscripts contain numerous variations in minor components such as conjunctions, prepositions, orthography, number, tense, and gender within ʿAlī's texts, and more so within Raḍī's headers and explanations. For these minor variations, I mostly follow M. I do not footnote these variants except in the few cases where they make a substantive difference to the meaning, for this would obscure the significant variants while not adding to our understanding of the material. ʿAṭṭār in his 2010 edition has listed all minor variations and the interested reader can find them there.
- In sequencing orations, I follow the primary manuscripts M, Sh, and others described earlier as Sequence 1.
- I transcribe the inserted orations, letter, and sayings following each of the three main chapters, under the sub-heading زيادة على الأصل, set apart from the original text by the sub-heading and a smaller font.

3.2   *Formal Features of this Edition*

- Except for lines from the Qurʾan and poetry, which are fully vocalized, I vocalize only those parts of the text where the meaning and correct vocalization may not be obvious to an educated reader of classical Arabic.

- For accessibility, I number the texts, divide them into paragraphs, and add minimal punctuation.
- I present ʿAlī's words in a larger font, and Raḍī's occasional comments in a smaller font, to further distinguish between the two.
- I follow standard rather than archaic orthography (e.g., إسحاق versus إسحق).
- Manuscripts differ in rendering pious formulae attached to the name of God and exalted personages in Islam (details were provided earlier for the primary manuscripts). I follow the majority reading, which, I believe, would follow Raḍī's original rendering. Note, however, that some formulae may be copyist additions or modifications.
- A few lines of poetry are cited in the text, and I identify their meters in the footnotes.
- Section headings are original from the manuscripts, and I retain them. The titles provided in most *Nahj al-Balāghah* printings are later copyist additions that are not found in the earliest manuscripts, and I do not transcribe those.
- I have used ❨ ❩ for quotations from the Qurʾan, and ⟨ ⟩ for hadith, proverbs, and half-lines of poetry. I have used ⟨ ⟩ also for citation of phrases from the text that Raḍī is explaining in his subsequent commentary, and for variants in my footnotes.

4 Previous Translations

Beginning in the middle of the twentieth century, several English translations of *Nahj al-Balāghah*, full or partial, were published in Iran and South Asia, most of them produced via a previous Persian translation. They render some lines effectively, but, for the most part, there is room for improvement: they are inaccurate in places and their English is frequently pedantic.[44] Two partial translations—selections from the sayings translated by Thomas Cleary (1996),[45] and the Testament of al-Ashtar (§ 2.53) translated by William Chittick (1981)[46]—are fairly accurate and idiomatic.

---

44   E.g., § 1.88: *Ashbāḥ*, the name of an oration which speaks of the creation of sky and angels, in my translation, "Ethereal Forms," which several prior translators have incorrectly rendered as "Skeletons" (https://www.al-islam.org/nahjul-balagha-part-1-sermons/sermon-91 -praise-belongs-god-who, accessed May 18, 2023).

45   Cleary, *Living and Dying with Grace: Counsels of Hadrat Ali.*

46   Chittick, *A Shiʿite Anthology*, 67–89.

5   This Translation

Translating *Nahj al-Balāghah* has been a supremely daunting task. The oceans of meaning infused into its lines cannot be fully plumbed, for a translation loses native implications and associations, while at the same time adding foreign ones. Neither can the eloquence of the Arabic be matched, for the texture of the language and its rhythms and metaphors cannot be reproduced. What I have attempted to do—given that any who set out on this path, no matter how careful and prepared they may be, can only fall short—is to come as close to the original as I can, both in meaning and in beauty.

Two guiding principles drive my methodology: First—to quote Aristotle—the whole is greater than the sum of its parts, and word-by-word translation fails to capture the clear simplicity of ʿAlī's expositions. Au contraire, it can lead to a meaningless conglomeration of high-sounding words, as has happened in prior renditions. Instead, it is important for the translator to read each original Arabic sentence as a single unit, to understand ʿAlī's concepts, with all their rich nuances, as best as she can, then render them forcefully into cogent English. Another aspect of this first principle is to bear in mind the context—historical, political, religious, cultural, and literary, among others—which is crucial for accurate translation. Accordingly, I have consulted the major *Nahj al-Balāghah* commentaries for lexical, contextual, and idiomatic insights, the major premodern lexicons for early usages of Arabic words, and historical and literary works, as well as books from various other genres from the classical Arabic library, for both the specific and the larger milieu of each text. Yet another aspect of this principle is maintaining the formal register. The Arabic of *Nahj al-Balāghah* is different than more informal conversations reported from ʿAlī's time, or even the more formal narrative prose of early histories; nowhere is the tone colloquial or chatty. Its texts deal with the serious subjects of salvation, succession, and war, and the translation attempts to maintain that gravitas. Yet, it is also important to bear in mind that ʿAlī's orations and letters were meant to be understood by their contemporary addressees. Since the audience was usually large and public, accessible vocabulary was presumably chosen, and, with some exceptions, rare words were avoided. Although the lexicon seems archaic to us now, that was not the case in its time. Keeping my translation in line with what I believe was the author's intent of clarity, I endeavor to render the text into lucid, modern English.

My second principle—which is particular to literary translation—is to maintain, as far as possible, the aesthetic spirit of the original. The first aspect of this principle is to preserve where possible the rhythm, especially the parallelism and pithy cadences, of the Arabic words. The second aspect is to keep the culture-specific imagery intact where possible, and not substitute it with foreign or anachronistic renderings. The third and most difficult aspect is to bring out the desert-and-camel metaphors that underpin the vocabulary, especially the verbs, which most prior translations have erased. An especially complicated example in which a heap of camel imagery is infused into a single verb, *fawwaqa*, is §1.74: إِنَّ بَنِي أُمَيَّة لَيُفَوِّقُونِي تُرَاثَ مُحَمَّد تَفْوِيقًا. I have translated this line with some (warranted, I think) prolixity as "The Umayyads stingily throw at me my share of Muḥammad's inheritance, piece by piece, like those who allow a camel-calf to suckle its mother only lightly, at intervals." Others have expunged the imagery to translate the line as, "The Umayyads are allowing me the inheritance of Muḥammad bit (by bit)." Yet another challenging line is §1.80.4: وَالْجُمَ الْعَرَق which I have translated as "Throats choke on sweat like a camel chokes on its bridle-straps." Others have removed the underpinning animal image to translate the line as, "Sweat would choke the throat." Bringing in the underlying metaphorical associations of the Arabic words, while preserving the clarity and vigor of the English, has called for a delicate—and highly challenging!—balance.

Additionally in this translation, I have:

- Added words to unpack the dense Arabic, but only minimally, preserving apparently deliberate ambiguities.
- Modified syntax and morphology for an idiomatic English rendering,
- Replaced pronouns with names, and added the name of fame, where needed for clarity.
- Changed some pronouns for idiomatic English rendering, sometimes changing third grammatical person to first, or singular to plural, when denoting generic humans, plural to singular when primarily denoting the speaker, ʿAlī, and so on.
- Translated a single Arabic word differently in different places, depending on context—e.g., *ʿāmil* is translated variously as "governor," "agent," "administrator," or "tax-collector"; *ḥaqq* is sometimes rendered as "truth," and sometimes as "right," while its opposite, *bāṭil*, is sometimes rendered as "falsehood" and sometimes as "wrong."
- Where the referent is clear, used lowercase for pronouns and adjectives referring to God.
- Used my own translations of Qurʾanic verses, to maintain consistency and to highlight a given verse's meaning in its context.
- Omitted pious invocations attached to the name of God, and of the Prophet

Muḥammad, ʿAlī, and other revered figures, for a smoother reading (these are preserved in the Arabic text).

– Replaced "Commander of the Faithful" in a few places with "ʿAlī."
– Retained the masculine gender in generic references to humans, following classical Arabic practice.
– Translated some technical religious terms differently from their conventional English rendering, to better reflect the spirit of the word: e.g. I translate "Islam" as "commitment to God's will" (rather than "submission"); *taqwā* as "piety" or being "conscious of God" or "godfearing" (rather than "fear of God"); *zuhd* as "rejection of worldliness" or "indifference to the world" (rather than "rejection of the world" or "asceticism"); and *bidʿah* as "heresy" or "heretical innovation" and not simply "innovation."
– Sometimes used the neutral form 'it' for pronouns referring to the world (*dunyā*), while at other times, when the context is clearly playing to the metaphor of the world as temptress, the feminine 'she' (note that the word *dunyā* is feminine in Arabic).
– Translated the standard post-benedictions phrase, *ammā baʿdu* (lit. "As for what comes after"), as "And now to the matter at hand." I have removed the phrase whenever it occurs at the beginning of a text, and sometimes also after the beginning "from" line (it is retained in the Arabic).
– Removed the prefacing words, "ʿAlī said," from most places in the Sayings section (they are retained in the Arabic).
– As in the edition, presented the text of ʿAlī's words in a larger font, and Raḍī's occasional prefaces and comments to ʿAlī's text in a smaller font.
– Used « » for quotations from the Qurʾan, and ⟨ ⟩ for hadith, proverbs, and half-lines of poetry.
– I have varied between the more formal "do not" and the less formal "don't"— and done the same for other contractions—to best fit the register of each text.
– To identify Raḍī's occasional comments, I preface them with his name followed by a colon, viz., "Raḍī:". The notation appears in some manuscripts too, in some places with the first-person pronoun ("I say"), but more frequently as "The Sayyid [al-Raḍī] said (*wa-qāla al-sayyid*)," where the use of the honorific "*al-sayyid*" indicates a copyist addition.
– As in the Edition, I have transcribed the additional orations, letter, and sayings, following each of the three main chapters, under the sub-heading "Additional Orations" (or: Letter, or: Sayings), set apart from the original text by the sub-heading and a smaller font.

Where available from the commentaries and historical sources, I have provided in a note for each text, its context, date, and place; I have also identified unnamed individuals therein.[47] Further details of people, places, and terms are provided in the Glossary. Additionally, I have provided notes to unpack cryptic lines, but minimally, since this is a translation and not a commentary. A modern English commentary—particularly on the pithy sayings—would be a wonderful addition to the *Nahj al-Balāghah* library, but that is a project for another time!

---

47 When a text is dated to ʿAlī's caliphate without a specific year, I have transcribed the dates of his full reign, 35–40/656–661, in order to avoid confusion. It should be noted however that ʿAlī was pledged allegiance in the last month of 35 AH, and most of the texts from his caliphate are from early 36 AH onward. ʿAbd al-Zahrāʾ, *Maṣādir Nahj al-balāghah*, contains further context for some texts, accompanied by primary source quotes.

Detailed Contents

NAHJ AL-BALĀGHAH: THE WISDOM AND ELOQUENCE OF ʿALĪ

Raḍī's Introduction   p. 98

SECTION 1: ORATIONS: Chapter containing selections from the Commander of the Faithful's orations and directives, including selections from his addresses that may be likened to orations, spoken in charged gatherings, famous battles, and times of danger

1.1   Creation of sky, earth, angels, Adam, and prophets, and the hajj[1]
"I praise God. Yet no speaker can articulate his praise"
(الحمد لله الذي لا يبلغ مدحته القائلون)   p. 106

1.2   Following Ṣiffīn, state of the people before Muḥammad, praise for the Prophet's family
"I praise God, seeking the completion of his favor"
(أحمده آستتمامًا لنعمته)   p. 114

1.3   "The Roar of the Camel Stallion" (*Shiqshiqiyyah*), on the caliphate
"By God, that man donned its cloak knowing that I am the pivot to its grinding stone"
(أما والله لقد تقمّصها آبن أبي فلان وإنّه ليعلم أنّ محلّي منها محلّ القطب من الرحا)   p. 118

1.4   Following the Battle of the Camel
"Through us you received guidance in the dark night"
(بنا آهتديتم في الظلماء)   p. 122

1.5   To ʿAbbās and Abū Sufyān following the Prophet's death, regarding the succession
"People! Cut through the waves of rebellion by boarding the ark of salvation"
(أيّها الناس شقّوا أمواج الفتن بسفن النجاة)   p. 124

---

1   The majority of *Nahj al-Balāghah* texts do not have titles. The descriptors here are thus my own, drawing on the content of the text, on Raḍī's remarks if there are any, and context from the history books. For each piece, I have also added the first line of both the translation and the Arabic.

1.6   When advised not to fight Ṭalḥah and Zubayr
"By God, I shall not behave like the hyena that, sleeping through a prolonged
barrage of pebbles, is captured"
(والله لا أكون كالضَّبُع تنام على طول اللَّدْم)   p. 124

1.7   Censuring a group of his challengers
"They made Satan master of their affairs and he made them his partners"
(اتّخذوا الشيطان لأمرهم مِلاكًا واتَّخذهم له أشراكًا)   p. 126

1.8   Before the Battle of the Camel, about Zubayr
"He declares that he pledged allegiance with his hand but not his heart"
(يزعم أنّه قد بايع بيده ولم يبايع بقلبه)   p. 126

1.9   Before the Battle of the Camel, in response to a speech by Talḥah
"They thundered and blazed but that is the way of cowards"
(وقد أرعدوا وأبرقوا ومع هذين الأمرين الفشل)   p. 126

1.10   During one of his battles
"Hark! Satan has mustered his host and armed his cavalry and infantry"
(ألا وإنّ الشيطان قد جمع حزبه واستجلب خيله ورجله)   p. 126

1.11   Instructions to Ibn al-Ḥanafiyyah at the Battle of the Camel, charging
him with the banner
"Mountains may move, but you should not"
(تزول الجبال ولا تزل)   p. 128

1.12   Following victory at the Battle of the Camel
"... Our fight has been witnessed by a mighty host in the loins of men"
(.. ولقد شهدنا فى عسكرنا هذا قوم في أصلاب الرجال)   p. 128

1.13   Following the Battle of the Camel, criticizing Basra and rebuking its
people
"You fought for the woman and followed the camel"
(كنتم جند المرأة وأتباع البهيمة)   p. 128

1.14   In Basra, following the Battle of the Camel
"Your land is close to the sea and far from the sky"
(أرضكم قريبة من الماء بعيدة من السماء)   p. 130

1.15   In Medina after he became caliph, on returning ʿUthmān's land grants
to the treasury
"By God, even if the money had been spent to wed women"
(والله لو وجدته قد تُزُوِّج به النساء)   p. 130

1.16   In Medina, when he became caliph
        "I guarantee the truth of what I say and stand as surety for my pledge"
        (ذمّتي بما أقول رهينة وأنا به زعيم)   p. 130

1.17   Censuring self-styled authorities
        "The most hateful creatures in God's eyes are of two kinds"
        (إنّ أبغض الخلائق إلى الله رجلان)   p. 132

1.18   Censuring scholars who follow their whims
        "When a case comes to one of them, he passes judgment based on his capri-
        cious opinion"
        (ترد على أحدهم القضيّة ... فيحكم فيها برأيه)   p. 134

1.19   When Ashʿath challenged him on the pulpit
        "What do you know about what goes against me"
        (وما يدريك ما عليّ)   p. 136

1.20   What comes after death
        "If you saw what the dead see"
        (فإنّكم لو عاينتم ما قد عاين من مات منكم)   p. 136

1.21   The swift passage of life
        "The end is ahead of you and the dreaded hour drives your caravan to the
        waterhole"
        (فإنّ الغاية أمامكم وإنّ وراء كم الساعة تحدوكم)   p. 136

1.22   Before the Battle of the Camel, on his opponents' responsibility for
        ʿUthmān's killing
        "Hear me! Satan has roared to his followers"
        (ألا وإنّ الشيطان قد ذمر حزبه)   p. 138

1.23   Unimportance of wealth, value of kin
        "God's command descends from the sky to the earth like raindrops"
        (فإنّ الأمر ينزل من السماء إلى الأرض كقطر المطر)   p. 138

1.24   Urging followers to fight for truth
        "By my life, no softness or weakness shall hold me back from fighting those who
        challenge the truth"
        (ولعمري ما عليّ من قتال من خالف الحقّ ... من إدهان ولا إيهان)   p. 142

1.25   Censuring followers for not fighting in the cause of truth
        "I only have you, Kufa"
        (ما هي إلّا الكوفة)   p. 142

1.26 The Arabs before Islam, ʿAlī's situation when Muḥammad died, ʿAmr ibn al-ʿĀṣ's corrupt deal with Muʿāwiyah
"God sent Muhammad as a warner to all peoples"
(إنّ الله بعث محمّدًا نذيرًا للعالمين) p. 144

1.27 Censuring followers for not fighting Muʿāwiyah, after Sufyān al-Ghāmidī's attack on Anbar
"Jihad is a door to heaven that God has opened for his special devotees"
(فإنّ الجهاد باب من أبواب الجنّة فتحه الله لخاصّة أوليائه) p. 146

1.28 Eid sermon containing pious counsel
"The world has shown its back and proclaimed its farewell"
(فإنّ الدنيا قد أدبرت وآذنت بوداع) p. 148

1.29 Censuring his followers, after Ḍaḥḥāk's attack on pilgrims at Thaʿlabiyyah
"People! You are together in body but divided in aspiration"
(أيّها الناس المجتمعة أبدانهم المختلفة أهواؤهم) p. 150

1.30 About ʿUthmān and his assassination
"If I had commanded it I would be a killer"
(لو أمرت به لكنت قاتلًا) p. 152

1.31 Instructions to ʿAbdallāh ibn al-ʿAbbās before the Battle of the Camel, to speak with Zubayr, not Ṭalḥah
"Don't speak with Ṭalḥah, for you will find him a bull with twisted horns"
(لا تلقينّ طلحة فإنّك إن تلقه تجده كالثور عاقصًا قرنه) p. 152

1.32 Four categories of men who seek to rule, pious counsel
"People! We live in a challenging age"
(أيّها الناس إنّا قد أصبحنا في دهر عنود) p. 154

1.33 At Dhū Qār, before the Battle of the Camel
"God sent Muhammad when no Arab read scripture"
(إنّ الله سبحانه بعث محمّدًا صلّى الله عليه وآله وليس أحد من العرب يقرأ كتابًا) p. 156

1.34 After the Battle of Nahrawān, urging followers to fight Muʿāwiyah
"Shame! I am tired of rebuking you!"
(أفٍّ لكم قد سئمت عتابكم) p. 158

1.35 After the arbitration
"I praise God even though this age has brought a great calamity"
(الحمد لله وإن أتى الدهر بالخطب الفادح) p. 158

1.36   Before the Battle of Nahrawān, warning the Kharijites
"I warn you! Take heed or you will soon be corpses strewn at the bend of this river"
(فأنا نذيرٌ لكم أن تصبحوا صرعى بأثناء هذا النهر)   p. 160

1.37   After the Battle of Nahrawān, describing his precedence in Islam, and his situation after the Prophet's death
"I answered Muḥammad's call when others held back"
(فقمتُ بالأمر حين فشلوا)   p. 162

1.38   On doubt's resemblance to truth
"Doubt is called doubt because it resembles truth"
(وإنّما سمّيت الشبهة شبهة لأنّها تشبه الحقّ)   p. 162

1.39   Censuring followers for not fighting, after the attack on ʿAyn al-Tamr
"I am tested with followers who do not obey my command"
(مُنيتُ بمن لا يطيع إذا أمرت)   p. 164

1.40   About the Kharijites' statement, "No rule save God's!"
"The statement is true, but the intent is false"
(كلمة حقّ يراد بها باطل)   p. 164

1.41   ʿAlī and his enemy
"Loyalty is honesty's twin"
(إنّ الوفاء توأم الصدق)   p. 166

1.42   In Basra, following the Battle of the Camel, pious counsel
"People! I fear most for you two things"
(أيّها الناس إنّ أخوف ما أخاف عليكم اثنتان)   p. 166

1.43   When advised to hasten in attacking Muʿāwiyah
"If I prepared to battle the Syrians while Jarīr is still with them, I would close the door to reconciliation"
(إنّ استعدادي لحرب أهل الشام وجرير عندهم إغلاق للشام)   p. 168

1.44   Following Maṣqalah's defection to Muʿāwiyah, after the Banū Nājiyah incident
"May God strike Maṣqalah with shame!"
(قبّح الله مصقلة)   p. 168

1.45   Eid sermon with pious counsel
"I praise God, never uncertain of his mercy"
(الحمد لله غير مقنوط من رحمته)   p. 170

1.46   Supplication when marching on Syria
"God, protect me from the hardships of travel"
(اللهمّ إنّي أعوذ بك من وعثاء السفر)   p. 170

1.47   Prophecy about Kufa
"I see you, Kufa, stretched like raw leather on display at the Market of 'Ukāẓ"
(كأنّي بك يا كوفة تُمَدِّينَ مدّ الأديم العكاظيّ)   p. 170

1.48   Informing of his instructions to his vanguard, when commencing the march on Syria
"I praise God whenever night spreads and darkens"
(الحمد لله كلّما وقب ليل وغسق)   p. 172

1.49   God's transcendence
"Praise God, who is concealed in unseen mysteries"
(الحمد لله الذي بطن خفيّاتِ الأمور)   p. 172

1.50   After the arbitration
"Revolt begins with the indulgence of whims"
(إنّما بدء وقوع الفتن أهواء تُتَّبَعَ)   p. 172

1.51   Urging his army to fight at Ṣiffīn, when Muʿāwiyah blocked access to water
"By this act, they beg to be fed the victuals of war"
(قد استطعموكم القتال)   p. 174

1.52   Eid of Sacrifice sermon with pious counsel, sacrificial animal
"Harken! The world has severed its rope"
(ألا وإنّ الدنيا قد تصرّمت)   p. 174

1.53   The Medinans' eagerness to pledge allegiance to him as caliph, reasons to fight the Syrians
"They crowded me like parched camels jostling at the waterhole"
(فتداكّوا عليّ تَداكَّ الإبل الهِيم يوم ورودها)   p. 176

1.54   To troops at Ṣiffīn, allaying their impatience to begin fighting
"You taunt, 'All these excuses to avoid death!'"
(أمّا قولكم أكلّ ذلك كراهية الموت)   p. 176

1.55   At or after the Battle of Ṣiffīn, describing Muḥammad's Companions' sincerity and courage
"We fought in support of God's Messenger and killed our fathers"
(ولقد كنّا مع رسول الله نقتل آباءنا)   p. 178

1.56   Prophecy and instructions for the future
"After me, you will be ruled by a man with a large maw and a massive belly"
(أما إنّه سيظهر عليكم بعدي رجل رَحْب البُلعُوم)   p. 178

1.57   To the Kharijites at Nahrawān
"May you be wiped out by sandstorms!"
(أصابكم حاصب)   p. 180

1.58   Before the Battle of Nahrawān, when told that the Kharijites had escaped
"Their deaths are written on this side of the clear water"
(مصارعهم دون النطفة)   p. 182

1.59   When warned about Ibn Muljam's intent to assassinate him
"I am protected by God's shield"
(وإنّ عَلَيَّ من الله جُنّة حصينة)   p. 182

1.60   Censure of this world
"Hear me! The world is an abode from which you cannot be saved except within it"
(ألا وإنّ الدنيا دار لا يُسلَم منها إلّا فيها)   p. 184

1.61   Counsel to consciousness of God
"Be conscious of God, O servants of God, and outrace your imminent end with good deeds"
(واتّقوا الله عباد الله وبادروا آجالكم بأعمالكم)   p. 184

1.62   God's transcendence
"No state for God precedes another state"
(الذي لم تَسبق له حال حالًا)   p. 186

1.63   Instructions to troops at Ṣiffīn
"Muslims! Sheathe yourselves in God's awe ... bite down hard on your back teeth"
(معاشر المسلمين اُستشعروا الخشية ... وعضّوا على النواجذ)   p. 186

1.64   Following the Prophet's death, response to report about the Assembly at the Portico
"Did you not remind them of the Messenger's directive"
(فهلّا احتجتم عليهم بأنّ رسول الله وصّى)   p. 188

1.65   When Muḥammad ibn Abī Bakr was killed, and the Umayyads took over Egypt
"My own choice for governor of Egypt was Hāshim ibn ʿUtbah"
(وقد أردت تولية مصر هاشم بن عتبة)   p. 190

1.66   Censuring followers for not fighting, after Ibn Bashīr's attack on ʿAyn al-Tamr
"How long should I coax you and blandish you? How long must I handle you gingerly as a young camel whose hump a heavy load would crush?"
(كم أداريكم كما تدارى البِكار العَمِدة)   p. 190

1.67   In the predawn hour of the day in which he was struck his death-blow
"Sleep overtook me as I sat, and the Messenger appeared before my eyes"
(ملكتني عيني وأنا جالس فسنح لي رسول الله)   p. 192

1.68   Following Ṣiffīn, censuring followers for agreeing to a truce on the verge of victory
"Iraqis! You are like a pregnant woman who, at full term, delivers a stillborn child"
(يا أهل العراق فإنّما أنتم كالمرأة الحامل حملت فلمّا أتمّت أملصت ومات قيّمها)   p. 192

1.69   Invoking blessings on the Prophet and praising him
"God, unfolder of lands unfolded"
(اللهمّ داحي المدحوّات)   p. 192

1.70   About Marwān, when he offered the pledge to ʿAlī after the Battle of the Camel
"Did he not pledge allegiance to me right after ʿUthmān was killed?"
(أفلم يبايعني بعد قتل عثمان)   p. 194

1.71   To the Shūrā Council, when they resolved to install ʿUthmān as caliph
"You know full well that I have more right to the caliphate than anyone else"
(لقد علمتم أنّي أحقّ الناس بها من غيري)   p. 196

1.72   When the Umayyads accused him of complicity in ʿUthmān's killing
"Is the Umayyads' own knowledge of my character not enough to stop them from injuring me?"
(أولم ينه بني أميّة علمها بي عن قَرَفي)   p. 196

1.73   Pious counsel
"May God have mercy on the man who listens to wisdom and retains"
(رحم الله عبدًا سمع حُكًا فوعى)   p. 198

1.74   Response to a gift sent by Saʿīd ibn al-ʿĀṣ, ʿUthmān's governor in Kufa
"The Umayyads stingily throw at me my share of Muḥammad's inheritance, piece by piece"
(إنّ بني أميّة ليُفَوِّقونني تراث محمّد تفويقًا)   p. 198

1.75   A frequent supplication
"God, forgive my sins—you know more about them than I do"
(اللّهمّ اغفر لي ما أنت أعلم به منّي)   p. 200

1.76   To an associate who cited astrological portents and warned him
against marching on the Kharijites
*"Do you presume to guide me to the hour in which those who advance are
shielded from injury?"*
(أتزعم أنّك تهدي إلى الساعة التي من سار فيها صرف عنه السوء)   p. 200

1.77   To the Basran army following their defeat at the Battle of the Camel,
oblique censure of ʿĀʾishah
"People! Women are deficient in faith"
(معاشر الناس إنّ النساء نواقص الإيمان)   p. 202

1.78   Pious counsel
"People! To reject worldliness is to desire little"
(أيّها الناس الزهادة قِصَر الأمل)   p. 202

1.79   Censure of the world
"How do I describe a world that begins in weariness and ends in death"
(ما أصف من دار أوّلها عناء وآخرها فناء)   p. 202

1.80   The Radiant Oration (*Gharrāʾ*), lengthy pious counsel
"Praise God, exalted in his might and near through his grace"
(الحمد لله الذي على بحوله ودنا بطوله)   p. 204

1.81   ʿAmr ibn al-ʿĀṣ's hypocrisy and ʿAlī's virtue
*"How strange! The Harlot's son tells the Syrians that I have a streak of foolish-
ness"*
(عجبًا لابن النابغة يزعم لأهل الشام أنّ فيَّ دُعابة)   p. 214

1.82   God's transcendence, paradise, pious counsel
*"I bear witness that there is no god but God, who has no partner. He is the first,
for there was nothing before him"*
(وأشهد أن لا إله إلّا الله لا شريك له الأوّل لا شيء قبله)   p. 214

1.83   Pious counsel
"God knows your thoughts and discerns your feelings"
(قد علم السرائر وخبر الضمائر)   p. 216

1.84   Pious versus immoral scholars, the Prophet's family
*"Servants of God! The most beloved of his servants … keeps his passions under
control"*
(عباد الله إنّ من أحبّ عباد الله إليه عبدًا أعانه الله على نفسه)   p. 218

1.85 In Medina, early in ʿAlī's caliphate, describing the errant
"God has not crushed tyrants of any era except after a long respite"
(فإنّ الله لم يقصم جبّاري دهر قطّ إلّا بعد تمهيل) p. 222

1.86 On the Prophet's mission
"God sent Muḥammad when an age had gone by without prophets"
(أرسله على حين قترة من الرسل) p. 222

1.87 God's transcendence, pious counsel
"God is recognized without being seen"
(المعروف من غير رؤية) p. 224

1.88 The Oration on Ethereal Forms (*Ashbāḥ*), on God's transcendence,
his creation of skies, angels, the earth, and prayer
"Praise God, whom withholding does not make richer"
(الحمد لله الذي لا يَفِرُه المنع) p. 226

1.89 After ʿUthmān's death, when entreated to assume the caliphate
"Leave me and seek another"
(دعوني وٱلتمسوا غيري) p. 242

1.90 ʿAlī's virtue, prophecy of the Umayyads' harsh governance after him
"People! I have gouged out the eyes of revolt"
(أيّها الناس فأنا فَقَأْتُ عين الفتنة) p. 242

1.91 God's transcendence, the Prophet's ancestry, pious counsel
"Blessed is God! Vaunting aspirations cannot attain him"
(فتبارك الله الذي لا يبلغه بعد الهمم) p. 246

1.92 Muḥammad's mission
*"At the time when God sent Muḥammad as a prophet, people wandered in
confusion"*
(بعثه والناس ضلّال في حيرة) p. 246

1.93 God's transcendence, the Prophet's ancestry and mission
"Praise God! He is the first—there was nothing before him"
(الحمد لله الأوّل فلا شيء قبله) p. 248

1.94 After the arbitration, chastising followers for disobedience, compar-
ing them unfavorably to the Prophet's Companions
*"God may have granted the tyrant a reprieve, but he will surely apprehend
him"*
(ولئن أمهل الله الظالم فلن يفوت أخذه) p. 248

1.95   At Ṣiffīn, censuring the Umayyads
"By God, they will continue thus until they commit every forbidden act"
(والله لا يزالون حتّى لا يَدَعُوا لله مُحَرَّمًا إلّا ٱستحلّوه)   p. 252

1.96   Friday sermon early in ʿAlī's caliphate, pious counsel
"We praise him for favors past and seek his help for what is to come"
(نحمده على ما كان ونستعينه من أمرنا على ما يكون)   p. 252

1.97   Muḥammad and his family
"Praise God who extended his grace to all creatures"
(الحمد لله الناشر في الخلق فضله)   p. 254

1.98   God's transcendence, prophesy of an epic battle
"He is the first before every first"
(الأوّل قبل كلّ أوّل)   p. 254

1.99   Judgment day, prophecy of coming seditions
"On that day, God will assemble all who went before and all who came after"
(وذلك يوم يجمع الله فيه الأوّلين والآخرين)   p. 256

1.100   Pious counsel, praise of the learned, prophecy of difficult times to come
"Look at the world with the eyes of those who have little interest in her"
(انظروا إلى الدنيا نظر الزاهدين فيها)   p. 258

1.101   ʿAlī's support of the Prophet's mission
"God sent Muḥammad as a prophet when no Arab read scripture"
(فإنّ الله سبحانه بعث محمّدًا صلّى الله عليه وآله وليس أحد من العرب يقرأ كتابًا)   p. 260

1.102   In Medina early in ʿAlī's caliphate, a leader's accountability to God, pious counsel
"God sent Muḥammad as a witness, a herald, and a warner"
(حتّى بعث الله محمّدًا شهيدًا وبشيرًا ونذيرًا)   p. 262

1.103   Islam and its Prophet
"Praise God who paved the path of Islam"
(الحمد لله الذي شرع الإسلام)   p. 264

1.104   At Ṣiffīn, praising the right wing's return to battle
"I saw you turn away from your battle lines and fall back"
(وقد رأيت جولتكم وٱنحيازكم عن صفوفكم)   p. 266

1.105   God's majesty, the Prophet as a physician healing hearts, censure of
followers for errant ways, warning of evil times
"Praise God, who appears to his creation through his creation"
(الحمد لله المتجلّي لخلقه بخلقه)   p. 268

1.106   God as creator and sustainer, angels, humans' blind love for the
world, imminence and horrors of death, praise for the Prophet and
his family
"Everything bows to him, and everything exists through him"
(كلّ شيء خاشع له وكلّ شيء قائم به)   p. 270

1.107   Worship rites and God's remembrance
"The deeds that bring you closest to God are the following"
(إنّ أفضل ما توسّل به المتوسّلون إلى الله)   p. 276

1.108   Censure of the world
*"I warn you against this world, for it is sweet and lush and surrounded by temp-
tations"*
(فإنّي أحذّركم الدنيا فإنّها حلوة خضرة حُفّت بالشهوات)   p. 278

1.109   Angel of death
"Do you sense his presence when he enters a home"
(هل تحسّ به إذا دخل منزلًا)   p. 282

1.110   Warning of life's transience, censure of followers
"I warn you of this world: it is a home from which you will be uprooted"
(وأحذّركم الدنيا فإنّها منزل قُلعة)   p. 282

1.111   God's favors, pious counsel, and this world
"Praise God who has linked praise with favors and favors with thanks"
(الحمد لله الواصل الحمد بالنعم والنعم بالشكر)   p. 284

1.112   Supplication for rain
"God, our mountains are parched, and our plains have filled with dust"
(اللهمّ قد أنصاحت جبالنا وأغبرّت أرضنا)   p. 288

1.113   The Prophet, followers' reluctance to fight, warning of a despot to
come
"God sent Muḥammad to call toward truth and bear witness to people"
(أرسله داعيًا إلى الحقّ وشاهدًا على الخلق)   p. 290

1.114   Wealthy who fail to help the needy
"You don't spend your wealth for the one who has provided it"
(فلا أموالَ بذلتموها للذي رزَقَها)   p. 292

1.115   Praise of supporters, following the Battle of the Camel
"You are my supporters in the cause of truth and my brothers in faith"
(أنتم الأنصار على الحقّ والإخوان في الدين)   p. 292

1.116   Chastising supporters for apathy in the wake of a Syrian raid
"What is wrong with you? What you propose is not the right course or the proper way!"
(ما لكم لا سُدّدتم لرشد ولا هديتم لقصد)   p. 294

1.117   ʿAlī's virtues, pious counsel
"By God! I have been taught the transmission of God's messages"
(تالله لقد علّمت تبليغ الرسالات)   p. 294

1.118   After the arbitration, to the emerging Kharijite faction
"This is how one who relinquishes a sound position is rewarded!"
(هذا جزاء من ترك العقدة)   p. 296

1.119   Reminding the Kharijites of their push for the arbitration, ʿAlī's service to Islam
"When the Syrians raised leaves from the Qurʾan on spears—using trickery"
(ألم تقولوا عند رفعهم المصاحف حيلةً)   p. 298

1.120   Instructions to troops ahead of Ṣiffīn
"If any of you finds composure in his heart when meeting the enemy"
(وأيّ امرئ منكم أحسّ من نفسه رباطة جأش عند اللقاء)   p. 298

1.121   Chastising followers for refusing to fight, presumably after Ṣiffīn
"I see you now, scuttling away like a group of thorn-tailed lizards"
(وكأنّي أنظر إليكم تكشّون كشيش الضِّباب)   p. 300

1.122   Instructions to troops during Ṣiffīn, exhortation to fight for God's cause
"Place the armor-clad in front and the unprotected behind"
(فقدّموا الدارع وأخّروا الحاسر)   p. 300

1.123   To the Kharijites, saying arbitration was sought from the Qurʾan
"I did not appoint men to arbitrate—I sought arbitration from the Qurʾan"
(إنّا لم نحكّم الرجال وإنّما حكّمنا القرآن)   p. 302

1.124   Response to complaints when ʿAlī levelled treasury stipends
"Do you urge me to seek victory by oppressing the people I rule?"
(أتأمروني أن أطلب النصر بالجور فيمن وليت عليه)   p. 304

1.125   To the Kharijites
"*Even if you insist—and you do so wrongly—on believing that I have sinned and erred*"
(فإن أبيتم إلّا أن تزعموا أنّي أخطأت)   p. 304

1.126   To Aḥnaf, foretelling epic fighting in Basra, interpreted as the Zanj revolt
"*Listen, Aḥnaf! I see him marching with troops that raise no dust*"
(يا أحنف كأنّي به وقد سار بالجيش الذي لا يكون له غُبار)   p. 306

1.127   Transience of life, corrupt trade practices
"*Servants of God! You, with all that you desire of this world, are lodgers with fixed timespans*"
(عباد الله إنّكم وما تأملون من هذه الدنيا أَثْوِياء مُؤَجَّلون)   p. 308

1.128   To Abū Dharr al-Ghifārī when ʿUthmān exiled him to Rabadhah
"*Abū Dharr, you were roused to anger in God's cause*"
(يا أبا ذرّ إنّك غضبت لله)   p. 310

1.129   Chastising followers for disobedience, ʿAlī's righteousness
"*You divided souls and fragmented hearts!*"
(أيّها النفوس المختلفة والقلوب المتشتّتة)   p. 310

1.130   Pious counsel
"*I give praise to God for what he has taken away and what he has granted*"
(نحمده على ما أخذ وأعطى)   p. 312

1.131   God's omnipotence, the Qur'an's guidance, Muḥammad's mission, censure of this world
"*This world and the hereafter have submitted their reins to God*"
(وانقادت له الدنيا والآخرة بأزمّتها)   p. 314

1.132   Response to ʿUmar's query on personally marching against the Byzantines
"*God has guaranteed to followers of this faith that he will protect their land*"
(وقد توكّل الله لأهل هذا الدين بإعزاز الحوزة)   p. 316

1.133   To Mughīrah ibn al-Akhnas, who offered to ʿUthmān that he would handle ʿAlī
"*You son of a barren, cursed father*"
(يا ابن اللّعين الأبتر)   p. 316

1.134   Early in ʿAlī's caliphate, on the Medinans sitting out the conflict
"Your oath of allegiance to me was not sworn on an impulse"
(لم تكن بيعتكم إيّاي فلْتة)   p. 318

1.135   Preceding the Battle of the Camel, censure of Ṭalḥah and Zubayr, reminder of entreaties to ʿAlī to assume the caliphate after ʿUthmān's death
"By God, they have no cause to fault me"
(والله ما أنكروا منكرًا)   p. 318

1.136   Prophesy of epic fighting in Iraq
"He will bend passion to conform to guidance"
(يعطف الهوى على الهدى)   p. 320

1.137   During the Shūrā Council
"No one will outpace me in calling to the truth"
(لن يسرع أحد قبلي إلى دعوة حقّ)   p. 322

1.138   Forbidding the shaming of people for their sins
"It befits those who are protected … to show compassion to sinners"
(فإنّما ينبغي لأهل العصمة ... أن يرحموا أهل الذنوب)   p. 322

1.139   Forbidding giving ear to rumors
"People! Whoever knows his brother to have strong faith and good ways should not give ear to the rumors men spread about him"
(أيّها الناس من عرف من أخيه وثيقة دين وسداد طريق فلا يسمعنّ فيه أقاويل الرجال)
p. 324

1.140   Urging giving to the needy and forbidding gifts to the undeserving
"A person who distributes gifts in unsuitable quarters … earns only the praise of the immoral"
(وليس لواضع المعروف في غير حقّه ... من الحظّ فيما أتى إلّا محمدة اللئام)   p. 324

1.141   Supplication for rain
"Hark! The earth that carries you"
(ألا وإنّ الأرض التي تحملكم)   p. 324

1.142   Praise of prophets and Muḥammad's family, censure of enemies
"God singled out messengers and sent them bearing the revelation"
(بعث رسله بما خصّهم به من وحيه)   p. 326

1.143   The world's vicissitudes, heretical innovations
"People! You are targets in this world at which the fates shoot their arrows"
(أيّها الناس إنّما أنتم في هذه الدنيا غرض تنتضل فيه المنايا)   p. 328

1.144 Response to ʿUmar's query on personally marching against the Persians
"In this matter, victory or defeat will not hinge on how large the number of troops is or how small"
(إنّ هذا الأمر لم يكن نَصرُه ولا خِذلانه بكثرة ولا بقلّة) p. 330

1.145 Muḥammad's mission, warning of difficult times
"God sent Muḥammad to turn his servants away from worship of idols"
(فبعث محمّدًا بالحقّ ليخرج عباده من عبادة الأوثان) p. 332

1.146 Before the Battle of the Camel, criticizing Ṭalḥah and Zubayr
"Each of the two wants the caliphate"
(كلّ واحد منهما يرجو الأمر له) p. 334

1.147 Pious counsel, just before ʿAlī's death
"People! Each person shall meet what he flees as he flees"
(أيّها الناس كلّ امرئ لاقٍ ما يفرّ منه في فراره) p. 336

1.148 Sedition-mongers
"Those others went right and left, travelling the paths of error"
(وأخذوا يمينًا وشمالًا ظعنًا في مسالك الغيّ) p. 336

1.149 Pious counsel, coming seditions
"I ask him for aid against Satan's expulsions and evictions"
(وأستعينه على مَداحِر الشيطان ومَزاجره) p. 340

1.150 In Medina early in ʿAlī's caliphate, God's transcendence, God's religion
"Praise God, who demonstrated his existence through his creatures"
(الحمد لله الدالّ على وجوده بخلقه) p. 342

1.151 Enroute from Medina before the Battle of the Camel, pious counsel
"Such men, during the respite granted them by God, fall into error"
(وهو في مُهلة من الله يهوي مع الغافلين) p. 344

1.152 The family of the Prophet
"An intelligent person possesses a keen heart"
(وناظرُ قلب اللبيب به يبصر أمده) p. 346

1.153 Marvelous creation of the bat
"Praise God! Descriptions are too feeble to plumb his core"
(الحمد لله الذي انحسرت الأوصاف عن كنه معرفته) p. 350

1.154   To the people of Basra after the Battle of the Camel, his righteousness, oblique criticism of ʿĀʾishah, on sedition, and pious counsel
"At that time, whoever is able to bind himself totally to God should do so"
(فمن ٱستطاع عند ذلك أن يعتقل نفسه على الله فليفعل)   p. 352

1.155   Pious counsel
"Praise God, who made praise the key to his remembrance"
(الحمد لله الذي جعل الحمد مفتاحًا لذكره)   p. 354

1.156   The Prophet, the Umayyads, prophesy of a quick end to their rule
"God sent Muḥammad after a period without prophets"
(أرسله على حين فترة من الرسل)   p. 356

1.157   ʿAlī's forbearance and care for the people
"I protected you well and strove to keep you safe"
(ولقد أحسنت جواركم وأحطت بجهدي من ورائكم)   p. 358

1.158   Placing hope in God, Muḥammad, Moses, David, and Jesus
"His command constitutes judgment and wisdom"
(أمره قضاء وحكمة)   p. 358

1.159   The Prophet, pious counsel, life's transience
"God sent Muḥammad with brilliant light"
(ابتعثه بالنور المضيّ)   p. 364

1.160   Response when asked: How is it that your tribe has driven you away from this station?
"You man of Asad! Your mount's girth is loose, and you fire without aim"
(يا أخا بني أسد إنّك لقلِق الوضِين تُرسِل في غير سَدَد)   p. 366

1.161   God's transcendence, human creation
"Praise God, who created his servants"
(الحمد لله خالق العباد)   p. 368

1.162   Advice to ʿUthmān, a little before his death
"People have gathered behind me, and they have sent me to negotiate"
(إنّ الناس ورائي وقد ٱستسفروني بينك وبينهم)   p. 370

1.163   The marvelous creation of birds, especially the peacock, marvels of paradise
"God created wondrous creatures"
(ابتدعهم خَلقًا عجيبًا)   p. 374

1.164   Censuring the Umayyads, chastising followers for weakness and stray-
        ing
        "Let your young emulate your elders, let your elders nurture your young"
        (لِيَتَأَسَّ صغيرُكم بكبيرِكم وَلْيَرْؤُفْ كبيرُكم بصغيرِكم)   p. 380

1.165   Pious counsel, injunctions to care for the earth and animals
        "God has revealed a book to guide you"
        (إنّ الله سبحانه أنزل كتابًا هاديًا)   p. 382

1.166   When urged to punish ʿUthmān's assailants
        *"Brothers, I am not unmindful of what you know, but how do I enforce retribu-
        tion"*
        (يا إخوتاه إني لست أجهل ما تعلمون ولكن كيف لي بقوّة)   p. 382

1.167   Before the Battle of the Camel, ʿAlī's righteousness, his challengers'
        iniquity
        "God sent a messenger, a guide, with a book that speaks"
        (إنّ الله بعث رسولًا هاديًا بكتاب ناطق)   p. 384

1.168   Injunction to a Basran to pledge allegiance
        *"If the people you represent had sent you as a scout to find out where the rains
        are falling"*
        (أرأيت لو أنّ الذين وراءك بعثوك رائدًا تبتغي لهم مساقط الغيث)   p. 384

1.169   Prayer and address just before the Battle of Ṣiffīn
        "God, O Lord of the lofty sky and layers of air"
        (اللّهمّ ربّ السقف المرفوع والجوّ المكفوف)   p. 386

1.170   Criticizing associates of the Camel, defending his right to the
        caliphate
        "Praise God, from whom one sky does not conceal another"
        (الحمد لله الذي لا تُواري عنه سماءٌ سماءً)   p. 388

1.171   Criticizing associates of the Camel, defending ʿAlī's right to the
        caliphate, pious counsel
        "Muḥammad was the trustee of God's revelation"
        (أمين وحيه)   p. 390

1.172   In Medina when associates of the Camel revolted, Ṭalḥah's complicity
        in ʿUthmān's killing
        "I have never been one to be shaken by threats of battle"
        (قد كنت وما أُهَدَّد بالحرب)   p. 392

1.173 'Alī's closeness to the Prophet, censure of followers for moving away from God
"O heedless people who go not unheeded!"
(أيُّها الغافلون غير المغفول عنهم) p. 394

1.174 Urging godliness, adherence to the Qur'an, good deeds, and the licit
"Profit from God's revelation"
(انتفعوا ببيان الله) p. 394

1.175 Criticizing the arbitrators
"Your majority opinion settled on choosing two arbitrators"
(فأجمع رأيُ ملائكم على أن اختاروا رجلين) p. 400

1.176 In Medina early in 'Alī's caliphate, God's transcendence, pious counsel, past events
"No matter can preoccupy him, no time can alter him"
(لا يشغله شان ولا يغيّره زمان) p. 402

1.177 On God's transcendence, in response to Dhiʿlib's question: "Have you seen your Lord?"
"Eyes do not see him through physical observation"
(لا تدركه العيون بمشاهدة العيان) p. 402

1.178 Censuring associates for disobedience and apathy, condemning Muʿāwiyah and 'Amr
"I offer praise to God for the affairs he has ordained"
(أحمد الله على ما قضى من أمر) p. 404

1.179 Condemnation of faction who left Kufa to join the Kharijites
"«Away with» them, «as the Thamūd were done away with!»"
(بُعْدًا لهم كَمَا بَعِدَتْ ثَمُودُ) p. 406

1.180 God's transcendence and creation, *ubi sunt* questions, God's proof, martyrs of Ṣiffīn, call to jihad
"Praise God, to whom all creation arrives"
(الحمد الله الذي إليه مصائر الخلق) p. 406

1.181 Praise of God, the Qur'an's guidance, pious counsel
"Praise be to God, recognized without being seen"
(الحمد الله المعروف من غير رؤية) p. 412

1.182 To the Kharijite Burj ibn Mus'hir, who shouted, "No rule save God's!"
"Silence! May God disfigure you, you toothless driveller!"
(أَسْكُتْ قبّحك الله يا أَثْرَم) p. 418

1.183 God's transcendence, the Prophet, God's marvelous creation, including the ant and the locust
"Praise God! Senses do not grasp him"
(الحمد لله الذي لا تدركه الشواهد) p. 418

1.184 God's transcendence and creation
"Those who assign him a form have not acknowledged his oneness"
(ما وحّده من كَيَّفَه) p. 422

1.185 Praise of those "whose names are recognized in the heavens but remain unknown on earth," prophesy of difficult times
"I would offer my father and mother as ransom for that host"
(ألا بأبي وأمّي هم من عدّة) p. 428

1.186 Piety, imminence of death
"People! I counsel you to be conscious of God and to give abundant thanks for his bounties to you"
(أوصيكم أيّها الناس بتقوى الله وكثرة حمده على آلائه إليكم) p. 430

1.187 Kinds of belief, migration, ʿAlī's deep knowledge, urging people to learn from him before the arrival of sedition
"Some people's hearts are firm and steadfast in belief"
(فمن الإيمان ما يكون ثابتًا مستقرًّا في القلوب) p. 430

1.188 Describing the pious and urging piety, recognition of God, God's messenger, and his family
"I offer praise to God in thanks for his blessings"
(أحمده شكرًا لإنعامه) p. 432

1.189 Urging piety and preparation for the hereafter
"Praise God, whose praise is pervasive"
(الحمد الله الفاشي حمدُه) p. 436

1.190 The Crushing Oration (*Qāṣiʿah*) containing censure of Lucifer, tribal factionalism, and pride, on lessons provided by past nations who incurred exemplary punishments, Moses' and Adam's humility, placement of God's Sacred House in a barren land, *ubi sunt*, chastisement of Muslims for straying from the path of truth, and description of ʿAlī's closeness to the Prophet
"Praise God, who donned robes of might and pride"
(الحمد لله الذي لبس العزّ والكبرياء) p. 438

1.191 Oration to Hammām, describing the truly pious
"When God created people ... The pious in this world are people of virtue"
(فالمتّقون فيها هم أهل الفضائل) p. 460

1.192   Hypocrites who feign faith
"We praise God for having guided us toward obedience"
(نحمده على ما وَفّق له من الطاعة)   p. 466

1.193   Pious counsel
"Praise God! He has revealed traces of his authority"
(الحمد لله الذي أظهر من آثار سلطانه)   p. 466

1.194   The Prophet's mission, pious counsel
"God sent Muḥammad when no waymark was raised"
(بعثه حين لا علم قائم)   p. 468

1.195   ʿAlī's loyalty and special closeness to the Prophet
"Muḥammad's true companions know"
(ولقد علم المستحفظون من أصحاب محمّد)   p. 470

1.196   Urging piety, God's knowledge, Islam, Muḥammad's mission, the
        Qurʾan
"He knows the bellowing of beasts in the forest"
(يعلم عَجيج الوحوش في الفَلَوات)   p. 470

1.197   Ritual prayer, the alms-levy, and upholding trust
"Be diligent in the matter of the ritual prayer"
(تعاهدوا أمر الصلاة وحافظوا عليها)   p. 476

1.198   Condemning Muʿāwiyah, declaring his own uprightness
"By God, Muʿāwiyah is not more astute than I, but he deceives and lies"
(والله ما معاوية بأدهى منّي ولكنّه يغدر ويفجر)   p. 478

1.199   Dissociating from evil people, Thamūd's slaughter of God's camel
        mare
*"People! Do not be nervous about following the path of guidance because its
followers are few"*
(أيّها الناس لا تستوحشوا في طريق الهدى لقلّة أهله)   p. 478

1.200   Address to the Prophet at his graveside, after the death of Fāṭimah
*"Salutations to you, Messenger of God, from me and from your daughter who
has come to stay with you"*
(السلام عليك يا رسول الله عنّي وعن ابنتك النازلة في جوارك)   p. 478

1.201   Pious counsel, preparation for the hereafter
"People! The world is a passage and the hereafter your permanent home"
(أيّها الناس إنّما الدنيا دار مجاز والآخرة دار قرار)   p. 480

1.202   Pious counsel, nearness of death
"Gather your supplies—May God have mercy on you!—for the call has come to depart"
(تجهّزوا رحمكم الله فقد نودي فيكم بالرحيل)   p. 480

1.203   To Ṭalḥah and Zubayr, who rebuked ʿAlī for levelling stipends
"You rebuke me for a small matter"
(لقد نقمتما يسيرًا)   p. 480

1.204   To supporters at Ṣiffīn who cursed the Syrians
"I don't like you to curse! Rather, describe their deeds"
(إنّي أكره لكم أن تكونوا سبّابين)   p. 482

1.205   At Ṣiffīn, when Ḥasan rushed into the fray
"Help me! Restrain this lad!"
(امْلِكُوا عنّي هذا الغلام)   p. 484

1.206   At Ṣiffīn, when ʿAlī's army insisted on accepting Muʿāwiyah's call for arbitration
"People! You have followed my command … but now warfare has worn you out"
(أيّها الناس إنّه لم يزل أمري معكم على ما أحبّ حتّى نَهِكَتْكُم الحرب)   p. 484

1.207   ʿAlāʾ al-Ḥārithī's lavish house, his brother ʿĀṣim's self-denial
"What will you do with this large house here in this world?"
(ما كنت تصنع بسعة هذه الدار في الدنيا)   p. 484

1.208   Four kinds of hadith reporters
"Reports current among people today include both the right and the wrong"
(إنّ في أيدي الناس حقًّا وباطلًا)   p. 486

1.209   God's sublime craftsmanship
"Through his supreme power and sublime and wondrous craftsmanship, God produced dry, solid earth from the raging, crashing, ocean masses"
(وكان من أقتدار جبروته وبديع لطائف صنعته أن جعل من ماء اليّم الزاخر المتراكِم المتقاصِف)
(يَبَسًا جامدًا)   p. 488

1.210   For God to bear witness against those who were holding back from fighting for the truth
"God! I ask you, O greatest witness, to bear witness over any of your servants who hear my words"
(اللّهمّ أيُّما عبد من عبادك سمع مقالتنا العادلة)   p. 490

1.211 God's transcendence, praise of the Prophet
"Praise God—exalted beyond comparisons to created beings"
(الحمد لله العليّ عن شبه المخلوقين)
p. 490

1.212 Praise for those entrusted with preserving God's knowledge
"I testify that God is the fount of justice"
(وأشهد أنّه عَدْلٌ عَدَل)
p. 492

1.213 'Alī's frequent supplication
"Praise God who brought me to this morning alive and healthy"
(الحمد الله الذي لم يصبح بي ميّتًا ولا سقيمًا)
p. 492

1.214 At Ṣiffīn, describing 'Alī's and his subjects' rights, forbidding flattery
"God has given me rights over you … you have rights over me"
(فقد جعل الله لي عليكم حقًّا ... ولكم عليّ من الحقّ مثل الذي عليكم)
p. 494

1.215 After the Battle of the Camel, describing opponents' crimes in Basra
"God! I ask your help against the Quraysh! They have severed my kinship"
(اللّهمّ إنّي أستعديك على قريش فإنّهم قد قطعوا رحمي)
p. 498

1.216 After the Battle of the Camel, while passing corpses of Ṭalḥah and 'Abd al-Raḥmān ibn 'Attāb
"Abū Muḥammad sleeps here this morning, an exile from his home!"
(لقد أصبح أبو محمّد بهذا المكان غريبًا)
p. 500

1.217 A pious man
"This man resuscitated his intellect and killed his sentient soul"
(قد أحيا عقله وأمات نفسه)
p. 500

1.218 Horrors of death, reciting Q Takāthur 102:1–2: «You are obsessed with gathering more and more until you visit your graves.»
"What a goal, and how distant!"
(ياله مَرامًا ما أبعده)
p. 500

1.219 Those who remember God, reciting Q Nūr 24:37: «They are men whom neither commerce nor trade distract from God's remembrance.»
"God has made his remembrance the burnish for your hearts"
(إنّ الله سبحانه جعل الذكر جلاء للقلوب)
p. 506

1.220 Arrogant humans, reciting Q Infiṭār 82:6: «O human, what has deceived you into neglecting your Generous Lord?»
"Of all who could be questioned, you have the most unstable arguments"
(أَدْحَضُ مسؤولٍ حجّة)
p. 508

1.221   ʿAlī's refusal to give treasury funds to ʿAqīl, or to accept Ashʿath's inappropriate gift
"By God! I would prefer to lie on a bed of three-pronged Saʿdān thorns"
(والله لأن أبيت على حَسَك السعدان)   p. 512

1.222   Supplication for honest wealth
"God! Protect my countenance through prosperity"
(اللّهمّ صنْ وجهي باليسار)   p. 514

1.223   Censure of this world
"This is a residence encircled by trials and renowned for deceit"
(دار بالبلاء محفوفة وبالغدر معروفة)   p. 514

1.224   Supplication for comfort and guidance
"God! You are the greatest comforter for those who love you"
(اللّهمّ إنّك آنس الآنسين لأوليائك)   p. 516

1.225   An upright Companion
"May God cherish the land that produced that man!"
(لله بلاد فلان)   p. 516

1.226   The fervor of the pledge to him as caliph
"You pulled my hand toward you, and I resisted"
(وبسطتم يدي فكففتها)   p. 516

1.227   Consciousness of God, approaching death, and renunciants
"Consciousness of God is the key to righteousness"
(فإنّ تقوى الله مفتاح سداد)   p. 518

1.228   At Dhū Qār before the Battle of the Camel, praising the Prophet
"God's Messenger proclaimed what he had been commanded to proclaim"
(فصدع بما أمر به)   p. 520

1.229   To ʿAbdallāh ibn Zamaʿah who asked for money from the treasury
"These funds do not belong to me, and they do not belong to you"
(إنّ هذا المال ليس لي ولا لك)   p. 520

1.230   The Prophet's family, people of ʿAlī's age
"Hark! The tongue is but an instrument wielded by men"
(ألا إنّ اللسان بَضْعَة من الإنسان)   p. 520

1.231   Differences among people according to the clay from which they are
        fashioned
        "What differentiates them is the source of their clay"
        (إنّما فرّق بينهم مبادئ طينهم)   p. 522

1.232   Address to the Prophet while preparing his body for burial
        *"May my father and mother give their lives for you! Your death has cut short
        what the death of no other has"*
        (بأبي أنت وأمّي لقد انقطع بموتك ما لم ينقطع بموت غيرك)   p. 522

Additional Orations   p. 524

SECTION 2: LETTERS: Chapter containing selections from the Commander of
the Faithful's dispatches and letters to his enemies and his regional governors,
including selections from instructions to his tax-collectors and testaments to
his family and companions

2.1   To the people of Kufa, as ʿAlī marched on Iraq from Medina, on events
        preceding and after ʿUthmān's death
        "I write to inform you of what happened to ʿUthmān"
        (فإنّي أخبركم عن أمر عثمان)   p. 530

2.2   To the people of Kufa, after the victory at the Battle of the Camel at
        Basra
        "Residents of Kufa, may God reward you on behalf of your Prophet's family!"
        (وجزاكم الله من أهل مصر عن أهل بيت نبيّكم)   p. 532

2.3   To his judge, Shurayḥ, who had just bought a large house: a "contract"
        *"Shurayḥ, soon there will come to you one who will not look at your written con-
        tract"*
        (يا شريح أما إنّه سيأتيك من لا ينظر في كتابك)   p. 532

2.4   To Ibn Ḥunayf, governor of Basra, when Ṭalḥah, Zubayr, and ʿĀʾishah
        marched there, and many residents turned against ʿAlī
        "If they reenter the canopy of obedience, then that is what we desire"
        (فإن عادوا إلى ظلّ الطاعة فذاك الذي نحبّ)   p. 534

2.5   To Ashʿath, governor of Azerbaijan, who had embezzled treasury funds
        "Your governorship is not a meal for you to devour"
        (وإنّ عملك ليس لك بطُعمة)   p. 534

2.6 Sent with Jarīr following the Battle of the Camel, to Muʿāwiyah, persuading him to pledge allegiance
"The same people who pledged allegiance to Abū Bakr, ʿUmar, and ʿUthmān pledged allegiance to me"
(إنّه بايعني القوم الذين بايعوا أبا بكر وعمر وعثمان) p. 536

2.7 To Muʿāwiyah, toward the end of the Battle of Ṣiffīn
"I have received from you a string of advice, enclosed in an embroidered epistle"
(فقد أتتني منك موعظة مُوَصَّلة ورسالة محبَّرة) p. 536

2.8 To Jarīr, emissary to Muʿāwiyah, before the Battle of Ṣiffīn, pressing for a decision
"When you receive my letter, tell Muʿāwiyah that he must take a final decision"
(فإذا أتاك كتابي فاحمل معاوية على الفصل) p. 538

2.9 Before the Battle of Ṣiffīn to Muʿāwiyah, who had accused ʿAlī of envying the earlier caliphs
"Our tribe decided to kill our Prophet and extirpate our root"
(فأراد قومنا قتل نبيّنا واجتياح أصلنا) p. 538

2.10 To Muʿāwiyah, just before marching to Ṣiffīn
"How will you fare when the robes with which this world adorns herself … are stripped off?"
(وكيف أنت صانع إذا تكشّفت عنك جلابيب ما أنت فيه من دنيا قد تبهّجت بزينتها) p. 540

2.11 Instructions sent from ʿAlī's camp at Nukhaylah to Ziyād ibn al-Naḍr and Shurayḥ, commanders of his vanguard to Syria
"When you reach the enemy, or when they reach you, set up camp just before the high ground"
(فإذا نزلتم بعدوّ أو نزل بكم فليكن معسكركم في قُبُل الأشراف) p. 542

2.12 Instructions sent from Kufa to Maʿqil, commander of troops who were likely sent against the Kharijite Ḥurayth in Ramhormoz
"Fear God, whom you must meet … and fight only those who fight you"
(اتق الله الذي لا بُدَّ لك من لقائه … ولا تقاتلنّ إلّا من قاتلك) p. 542

2.13 To Ziyād ibn al-Naḍr and Shurayḥ, commanders of the vanguard to Syria, appointing Ashtar over them
"I have appointed Mālik ibn al-Ḥārith al-Ashtar over both of you"
(وقد أمّرت عليكما … مالك بن الحارث الأشتر) p. 544

2.14 Instructions to the army just before the Battle of Ṣiffīn
"Don't attack them unless they attack you first"
(لا تقاتلوهم حتّى يبدؤوكم) p. 544

2.15   Battlefield supplication
        "God, it is to you that our hearts flow"
        (اللّٰهمّ إليك أَفْضَتِ القلوب)   p. 544

2.16   Instructions to the army at the Battle of Ṣiffīn
        "Don't hesitate to retreat then assail, to withdraw then attack"
        (لا تَشْتَدَّنَّ عليكم فرّةٌ فرَّةً بعدها كَرَّة)   p. 546

2.17   To Muʿāwiyah at Ṣiffīn, refusing to make him governor of Syria, deny-
        ing that they were peers
        *"You demand Syria, but I'm not about to give you today what I refused you yes-
        terday"*
        (فأمّا طلبك إليَّ الشامَ فإنّي لم أكن لأُعطيك اليوم ما منعتُك أمس)   p. 546

2.18   After the Battle of the Camel to ʿAbdallāh ibn al-ʿAbbās, governor of
        Basra, instructing kindness to Tamīm tribesmen
        "Know that Basra is where Iblīs landed after his fall from grace"
        (واعلم أنّ البصرة مَهبط إبليس)   p. 548

2.19   To ʿAmr ibn Salamah, governor of Isfahan, in rebuke for harshness to
        the populace
        "The Dihqān landowners in your province have complained of your harshness"
        (فإنّ دَهَاقين أهل بلدك شَكَوْا منك غلظة)   p. 548

2.20   To Ziyād, deputy governor of Basra, warning against misappropriating
        treasury funds
        "I swear this by God, in all truth: If I hear that you have misappropriated funds"
        (وإنّي أقسم بالله قسمًا صادقًا لئن بلغني أنّك خُنْتَ من فَيْء المسلمين)   p. 550

2.21   To Ziyād, deputy governor of Basra, warning against extravagance
        "Turn from extravagance to moderation"
        (فدَع الإسراف مقتصدًا)   p. 550

2.22   To ʿAbdallāh ibn al-ʿAbbās in Mecca, following his misappropriation of
        treasury funds, counselling focus on the hereafter
        "A man is gladdened by obtaining a thing that he was not going to lose"
        (فإنّ المرء يسرّه دَرَك ما لم يكن ليفوته ويسوءه فوت ما لم يكن ليدركه)   p. 550

2.23   Testament to family and close associates after the death blow
        "This is my testament to you: Do not assign partners to God"
        (وصيّتي لكم ألّا تشركوا بالله شيئًا)   p. 552

2.24   'Alī's will, written after Ṣiffīn, regarding distribution of properties
*"This is what I—God's servant, 'Alī ibn Abī Ṭālib, Commander of the Faithful—
have directed with regard to my property in the pursuance of God's pleasure"*
(هذا ما أمر به عبد الله عليّ بن أبي طالب أمير المؤمنين في ماله ٱبتغاء وجه الله)   p. 552

2.25   Instructions to tax collectors about compassion to subjects when
assessing their herds, and care while bringing animals to the trea-
sury
"Set out in consciousness of God"
(انطلق على تقوى الله)   p. 554

2.26   To Mikhnaf, sent to collect taxes, warning against abusing subjects or
misappropriating funds
*"'Alī commands his tax collector to be conscious of God in private affairs and
hidden acts"*
(أمره بتقوى الله في سرائر أمره وخفيّات أعماله)   p. 558

2.27   To Muḥammad ibn Abī Bakr on his appointment as governor of Egypt,
instructing piety, fairness, and kindness
"Lower your wing over them"
(فٱخفض لهم جناحك)   p. 558

2.28   Before the Battle of Ṣiffīn to Muʿāwiyah, who again accused 'Alī of envy
toward the first three caliphs, virtues of the Prophet's family, iniquities
of Muʿāwiyah's clan
*"I received your letter in which you speak of how God selected Muḥam-
mad"*
(فقد أتاني كتابك تذكر فيه ٱصطفاء الله محمّدًا)   p. 562

2.29   To the people of Basra, following Muʿāwiyah's seizure of Egypt, when
Muʿāwiyah sent Ibn al-Ḥaḍramī to foment dissent in Basra, and 'Alī's
commander Jāriyah defeated and killed him
*"You know this well: You severed your rope of allegiance earlier and seceded from
the community"*
(وقد كان من ٱنتشار حبلكم وشقاقكم)   p. 570

2.30   To Muʿāwiyah, presumably before the Battle of Ṣiffīn, persuading him
to obedience
"Fear God in all that you do"
(فٱتّق الله فيما لديك)   p. 572

2.31   The Testament of Ḥasan, written on the way back from Ṣiffīn, contain-
       ing lengthy pious counsel
       "From a father who admits the power of time"
       (من الوالد الفان المقرّ للزمان)
                                                                    p. 572

2.32   To Muʿāwiyah, presumably in the lead-up to Ṣiffīn
       "You have destroyed a whole generation of people"
       (وأردّيت جيلًا من الناس)
                                                                    p. 594

2.33   To Qutham, governor of Mecca, a few months before ʿAlī's death, warn-
       ing of Muʿāwiyah's agents fomenting dissent during the hajj
       *"My agent in the west has written to inform me that a group of Syrians ... are
       being sent to Mecca this hajj season"*
       (فإنّ عيني بالمغرب كتب إليّ يعلمني أنّه وُجّه على الموسم أناسٌ من أهل الشام)   p. 596

2.34   To Muḥammad ibn Abī Bakr, governor of Egypt, extolling Ashtar and
       explaining ʿAlī's reasons for sending him to take over
       *"I have learned that you are distressed at my sending Ashtar to take charge of
       your region"*
       (وقد بلغني مَوْجِدتك من تَسريح الأشتر إلى عملك)
                                                                    p. 596

2.35   To ʿAbdallāh ibn al-ʿAbbās, praising Muḥammad ibn Abī Bakr, who had
       been killed in Egypt, and describing ʿAlī's unsuccessful efforts to send
       aid
       *"Egypt has been conquered, and Muḥammad ibn Abī Bakr—may God have
       mercy on him!—has gained martyrdom"*
       (فإنّ مصر قد اُفتُتحت ومحمّد بن أبي بكر رحمه الله قد اَستُشهد)
                                                                    p. 598

2.36   To ʿAqīl in Medina, describing Ḥujr's fight against Ḍaḥḥāk, who had
       raided Iraq, condemning the Quraysh and declaring ʿAlī's resolve to
       continue fighting in the path of truth
       "I dispatched a large army of Muslims to fight him"
       (فسرّحت إليه جيشًا كثيفًا من المسلمين)
                                                                    p. 598

2.37   To Muʿāwiyah, before the Battle of Ṣiffīn, accusing him of using ʿUth-
       mān's killing for his own benefit, and of abandoning him earlier, when
       asked to aid him
       "Great God! How fervently you cling to your outlandish passions"
       (فسبحان الله ما أشدّ لزومك للأهواء المبتدِعة)
                                                                    p. 600

2.38   To the people of Egypt, when appointing Ashtar as governor
       *"... I have sent you one of God's own servants, who neither sleeps during the days
       of danger"*
       (...فقد بعثتُ إليكم عبدًا من عباد الله لا ينام أيّام الخوف)
                                                                    p. 602

2.39   Warning to ʿAmr ibn al-ʿĀṣ before marching on Ṣiffīn
"You have subordinated your faith to the worldly gain promised to you by a man whose deceit is plain"
(فإنّك جعلت دينك تبعًا لدنيا امرئ ظاهرٍ غَيّه)   p. 602

2.40   To a governor, possibly ʿAbdallāh ibn al-ʿAbbās, who had misappropriated funds
"I am informed that you have done something, which, if you have done it, means you have angered your Lord"
(فقد بلغني عنك أمر إن كنت فعلته فقد أسخطت ربّك)   p. 604

2.41   Sent shortly before ʿAlī's death, possibly to ʿAbdallāh ibn al-ʿAbbās in Mecca, rebuking him for misappropriation of funds
"I had shared my charge with you"
(فإنّي كنت أشركتك في أمانتي)   p. 604

2.42   To ʿUmar ibn Abī Salamah, governor of Bahrain, recalling him to participate in the march on Syria, and replacing him with al-Nuʿmān ibn ʿAjlān
"I have appointed al-Nuʿmān ibn ʿAjlān over Bahrain"
(فإنّي قد وليّت النعمان بن عجلان على البحرين)   p. 606

2.43   To Maṣqalah, governor of Ardashīr, rebuking him for misappropriation of treasury funds
"I am informed that you have done something, which, if you have done it, means that you have angered your Lord"
(بلغني عنك أمر إن كنت فعلته فقد أسخطت إلهك)   p. 608

2.44   To Ziyād, warning against Muʿāwiyah's blandishments
"I have learned that Muʿāwiyah wrote to you in an attempt to befuddle your mind and dull your blade"
(وقد عرفت أنّ معاوية كتب إليك يستزلّ لُبّك ويستفلّ غَرْبك)   p. 608

2.45   To Ibn Ḥunayf, governor of Basra, rebuking him for favoring the wealthy, Fadak, which was taken from his family, his own renunciant ways and compassionate governance, censure of the world, pious counsel
"Ibn Ḥunayf, I am informed that one of Basra's grandees invited you to a feast and you rushed to go"
(فقد بلغني أنّ رجلًا من فِتية أهل البصرة دعاك إلى مأدُبة فأسرعت إليها)   p. 610

2.46   To Ashtar, governor of Naṣībīn, recalling him after the arbitration,
        sending him to Egypt
        "You are one of those whose support I rely on to establish our religion"
        (فإنّك مّمن أستظهر به على إقامة الدين)   p. 616

2.47   Testament of counsel for Ḥasan and Ḥusayn after the death blow, and
        for ʿAlī's family, urging restraint in blood retaliation
        *"I counsel you both to remain conscious of God. Do not seek this world even if it
        seeks you"*
        (أوصيكما بتقوى الله وأن لا تبغيا الدنيا وإن بغتكما)   p. 616

2.48   To Muʿāwiyah at Ṣiffīn, reluctantly accepting arbitration, warning him
        against treachery, and underscoring ʿAlī's submission to the ruling of
        the Qurʾan
        "Treachery and lies kill a man's faith and ruin his worldly affairs"
        (وإنّ البغي والزور يُوتِغانِ بالمرء في دينه ودنياه)   p. 618

2.49   Warning to ʿAmr ibn al-ʿĀṣ, sent from Nukhaylah, just before the march
        on Syria
        "This world distracts you from the next"
        (فإنّ الدنيا مَشْغَلة عن غيرها)   p. 620

2.50   To his commanders, declaring his principled policies and offering
        pious counsel
        "It befits those in authority"
        (فإنّ حقًّا على الوالي)   p. 620

2.51   To tax collectors, instructing justice and compassion, and warning
        against unfair seizure of property from subjects, whether Muslim,
        Christian, or Jew
        *"Whoever fails to care about his end, fails to safeguard himself by advancing
        provisions for his soul"*
        (فإنّ من لم يحذر ما هو صائرٌ إليه لم يقدّم لنفسه ما يُحرزها)   p. 620

2.52   To governors on timings of the ritual prayers
        "Pray the noon prayer when the sun casts a shadow equal to a squatting goat"
        (فصلّوا بالناس الظهر حين تَفيء الشمس مثل مَرْبِض العَنْز)   p. 622

2.53   The Testament of Ashtar (*'Ahd al-Ashtar*) on his appointment as governor of Egypt, lengthy instructions on fair, kind, and astute governance, pious counsel
"This is what God's servant, 'Alī, Commander of the Faithful, commands Mālik ibn al-Ḥārith al-Ashtar, in the epistle he writes appointing him governor of Egypt"
(هذا ما أمر به عبد الله عليّ أمير المؤمنين مالك بن الحارث الأشتر في عهده إليه حين ولّاه مصر)
p. 624

2.54   To Ṭalḥah and Zubayr, preceding the Battle of the Camel, urging them to return to the fold
"Although you deny this now, you know that I did not approach the people"
(فقد علمتما وإن كَتَمْتما أنّي لم أُرِد الناس)
p. 646

2.55   To Muʿāwiyah in the lead-up to the Battle of Ṣiffīn, urging him to return to the path of truth
"God created this world for the hereafter"
(فإنّ الله سبحانه جعل الدنيا لما بعدها)
p. 648

2.56   To Shurayḥ, when appointing him commander of the vanguard to Syria, pious counsel
"Be conscious of God every morning and every night"
(اتّق الله في كلّ صباح ومساء)
p. 650

2.57   Sent from Dhū Qār to the people of Kufa, urging them to join 'Alī in fighting the associates of the Camel at Basra
"I have marched from my hometown as either oppressor or oppressed"
(فإنّي خرجت عن حَيّي هذا إمّا ظالمًا وإمّا مظلومًا)
p. 650

2.58   To the garrison towns, describing the Battle of Ṣiffīn
"Events began thus: We and the Syrians faced off"
(وكان بدء أمرنا أنّا ألتقينا والقوم من أهل الشام)
p. 650

2.59   To Aswad ibn Quṭbah, commander of Ḥulwān, pious counsel
"A ruler's passions, if they lean in one direction"
(فإنّ الوالي إذا ٱختلف هواه)
p. 652

2.60   To administrators through whose lands 'Alī's army was marching
"I have dispatched troops who, God willing, will pass through your lands"
(فإنّي قد سيّرت جنودًا هي مارّة بكم إن شاء الله)
p. 652

2.61   To Kumayl, governor of Hīt, rebuking him for failing to defend against Sufyān ibn ʿAwf's attack
"A man's neglect of what he has been charged with"
(فإنّ تضييع المرء ما وُلّي)
p. 654

2.62 To the people of Egypt, sent with the newly appointed governor Ashtar, on events after the Prophet's death, ʿAlī's righteousness, the Umayyads, urging the Egyptians to fight for the truth
"God sent Muḥammad as warner for the world"
(فإنّ الله سبحانه بعث محمّدًا نذيرًا للعالمين) p. 654

2.63 To Abū Mūsā, governor of Kufa, when he urged the people not to support ʿAlī in the Battle of the Camel, rebuking and dismissing him from his post
"I am told that you have spoken words that go both for you and against you"
(فقد بلغني عنك قول هو لك وعليك) p. 658

2.64 To Muʿāwiyah, presumably in the lead-up to the Battle of Ṣiffīn, who had written accusations and demands
"Yes, my clan and yours were on terms of affection and unity, as you say"
(فإنّا كّا نحن وأنتم على ما ذكرت من الألفة والجماعة) p. 658

2.65 After the Battle of Nahrawān, to Muʿāwiyah, who had demanded that ʿAlī appoint him successor
"This is the time for you to understand fully the affairs swiftly unfolding before your eyes"
(فقد آن لك أن تنتفع باللّمح الباصر من عيان الأمور) p. 662

2.66 To ʿAbdallāh ibn al-ʿAbbās, likely sent from Kufa to Mecca, shortly before ʿAlī's death
"A man is overjoyed by gaining a thing he was not going to lose"
(فإنّ العبد لَيَفْرَح بالشيء الذي لم يكن لِيَفُوته) p. 664

2.67 To Qutham, governor of Mecca, on leading the hajj, teaching the pilgrims, and disbursing charity
"Lead the hajj among the people and remind them to revere these, God's special days"
(فأقم للناس الحجّ وذكِّرهم بأيّام الله) p. 664

2.68 To Salmān, before ʿAlī's caliphate, pious counsel
"This world is like a snake"
(فإنّ مَثَل الدنيا مَثَل الحَيَّة) p. 664

2.69 To Ḥārith, pious counsel
"Hold fast to the Qurʾan and embrace its counsel"
(وتمسّك بحبل القرآن وأنتصحه) p. 666

2.70 To Sahl, governor of Medina, telling him not to grieve over defectors
"I have learned that men from your town are stealing out to join Muʿāwiyah"
(فقد بلغني أنّ رجالًا ممّن قَبَلَك يتسلّلون إلى معاوية) p. 668

2.71 To Mundhir, governor of Iṣṭakhr, chastising him for misappropriation of treasury funds
"I was deceived about you by your father's piety"
(فإنّ صلاح أبيك غَرَّني منك) p. 668

2.72 To ʿAbdallāh ibn al-ʿAbbās in Mecca, containing pious counsel
"You will not exceed your lifespan or be granted sustenance that is not yours"
(فإنّك لست بسابق أجلك ولا مرزوق ما ليس لك) p. 670

2.73 To Muʿāwiyah, possibly after the arbitration, rejecting his demands to make him successor
"I attribute to weak judgment … the fact that I exchanged letters with you"
(فإنّي على التردّد في جوابك ... لَمُوهِنٌ رأيي) p. 670

2.74 Treaty between the tribes of Yemen and Rabīʿah
"This is what the people of Yemen … have agreed upon"
(هذا ما أجتمع عليه أهل اليمن) p. 672

2.75 From Medina early in ʿAlī's caliphate to Muʿāwiyah, explaining recent events and instructing him to take the pledge of the caliphate for ʿAlī in Syria
"… You know that I was justified both in my efforts for your clan and in turning away from them"
(...فقد علمت إعذاري فيكم وإعراضي عنكم) p. 672

2.76 To ʿAbdallāh ibn al-ʿAbbās, while appointing him governor of Basra after the Battle of the Camel
"Be generous with your attention"
(سَع الناس بوجهك) p. 674

2.77 To ʿAbdallāh ibn al-ʿAbbās, sent to debate the Kharijites
"Don't argue with them on the basis of the Qurʾan"
(لا تخاصمهم بالقرآن) p. 674

2.78 To Abū Mūsā in the lead-up to the arbitration
"The state of the people is such that many have bartered away most of their allotted share"
(فإنّ الناس قد تغيّر كثير منهم عن كثير مِن حَظّهم) p. 674

Additional Letter p. 676

SECTION 3: SAYINGS: Chapter containing selections from the Commander of the Faithful's wise sayings and words of counsel, including selections from his answers to questions and short texts from all genres of his literary production [Includes aphorisms and short texts not listed here, and the following longer pieces]:

3.1   First aphorism in Sayings chapter
"In times of sedition, be like a young camel buck"
(كن في الفتنة كابن اللَّبُون)   p. 678

3.26   Four pillars of faith, four pillars of unbelief, four branches of doubt
"Faith stands on four pillars: forbearance, conviction, justice, and struggle against evil"
(الإيمان على أربع دعائم على الصبر واليقين والعدل والجهاد)   p. 684

3.33   Warning to Ḥasan about whom not to befriend
"My dear son, remember four things from me"
(يا بُنَيَّ احفظ عنّي أربعًا)   p. 688

3.69   Addressing this world, Ḍirār's report
"World, O world, get away from me!"
(يا دنيا يا دنيا إليك عنّي)   p. 696

3.70   Destiny and the march on Syria
"Woe! Perhaps you think destiny is final"
(وَيْحَك لعلّك ظننت قضاء لازمًا)   p. 696

3.73   Five traits of character
"I counsel you to five traits so precious it is only right that you should whip your camels to reach them"
(أوصيكم بخمس لو ضربتم إليها آباط الإبل لكانت لذلك أهلًا)   p. 698

3.95   To Nawf al-Bikālī, pious counsel, David and Jesus as exemplars
"Nawf, blessed are those who reject worldliness"
(يا نوف طُوبى للزاهدين في الدنيا)   p. 704

3.99   Vagaries of the heart
"There is a piece of flesh attached to the jugular vein"
(لقد عُلِّق بنِيَاط هذا الإنسان بَضْعةٌ)   p. 706

3.110   Clans of Quraysh, Hāshim
"Makhzūm are the sweet blossoms of Quraysh"
(أمّا بنو مخزوم فريحانة قريش)   p. 710

3.112　When a man laughed while following a funeral procession
"We behave as though death were decreed for everyone other than our-selves"
(كَأَنَّ الموت فيها على غيرنا كُتِب)　　　　　　　　　　　p. 712

3.119　Address to residents of graves
"O people of desolate abodes"
(يا أهل الديار الموحشة)　　　　　　　　　　　p. 714

3.120　To a man who criticized this world
"You who reproach this world—do you choose to be deceived by her yet censure her?"
(أَيُّها الذامّ للدنيا أتغترّ بالدنيا ثمّ تذمّها)　　　　　　　　　　　p. 714

3.124　The Qur'an's promise
"Whoever is granted four gifts will not be refused four others"
(من أُعْطِي أربعًا لم يُحْرَم أربعًا)　　　　　　　　　　　p. 718

3.133　To Kumayl on the virtues of knowledge, vaunt of his own knowledge, and the continuity of God's proof through one who upholds it in all ages
"Kumayl, these hearts are like vessels, and the best are those that best receive and store"
(يا كميل بن زياد إنّ هذه القلوب أوعية نخيرها أوعاها)　　　　　　　　　　　p. 720

3.136　Pious counsel in Kufa after the Battle of Nahrawān
"Do not be one of those who expect the hereafter without work"
(لا تكن ممّن يرجو الآخرة بغير العمل)　　　　　　　　　　　p. 722

3.237　Reasons for the Shariʿah laws
"God has mandated belief to purify you from polytheism"
(فرض الله الإيمان تطهيرًا من الشرك)　　　　　　　　　　　p. 746

3.245–253 Section on Rare Words: A selection from ʿAlī's sayings that need lexical explanations

3.245　First aphorism in Rare Words Section
"When that happens, religion's queen bee will rest its abdomen on the ground"
(فإذا كان ذلك ضَرَبَ يَعْسوبُ الدين بذَنَبه)　　　　　　　　　　　p. 752

3.263   The Ka'bah's ornaments
"At the time when the Qur'an was revealed to the Prophet, there were four kinds of property"
(إنّ القرآن أُنزل على النبيّ والأموالُ أربعة)   p. 764

3.275   The Prophet
"In a time now past, I had a brother whom I loved in God's name"
(كان لي فيما مضى أخٌ في الله)   p. 768

3.277   Condolence to Ash'ath on the death of his son
"Ash'ath, it is fitting that you mourn your son"
(يا أشعث إن تحزن على ابنك)   p. 770

3.319   A believer
"A believer shows his joy in his face and hides his sorrow in his heart"
(المؤمن بِشْرُه في وجهه وحزنه في قلبه)   p. 782

3.327   Pious counsel
"Words are remembered, intentions are tested, and «every soul is mortgaged to what it has earned.»"
(الأقاويل محفوظة والسرائر مَبْلُوّة وكلُّ نَفْسٍ بِمَا كَسَبَتْ رَهِينَةٌ)   p. 784

3.350   Pious counsel
"People! The stuff of this world is like rotten grass"
(يا أيّها الناس مَتاع الدنيا حُطام مُوبِئ)   p. 790

3.353   Counsel to Jābir
"The world is sustained by four types of people"
(قِوام الدنيا بأربعة)   p. 794

3.358   On sustenance being decreed and the need for contentment
"Sustenance is of two types"
(الرزق رزقان)   p. 796

3.367   How to apportion time
"The believer divides his time into three parts"
(للمؤمن ثلاث ساعات)   p. 800

3.387   Spending wealth for good
"My dear son, do not leave your wealth for others to inherit"
(يا بُنَيَّ لا تُخَلِّفَنَّ وراءك شيئًا من الدنيا)   p. 804

3.388   How to seek God's forgiveness
"May your mother be bereaved! Do you know what it means to beg God's forgiveness?"
(ثَكِلَتْكَ أُمُّك أتدري ما الاستغفار)   p. 806

3.403   God's special devotees
        "God's special devotees are those who perceive the world's reality"
        (إنّ أولياء الله هم الذين نظروا إلى باطن الدنيا)   p. 810

3.429   Last aphorism in Sayings chapter
        "Many are seduced by praise"
        (رُبَّ مَفتون بحسن القول فيه)   p. 816

Additional Sayings   p. 818

Raḍī's Conclusion   p. 824

Text and Translation

Nahj al-Balāghah

The Wisdom and Eloquence of ʿAlī

Compiled by al-Sharīf al-Raḍī
(d. 406/1015)

بسم الله الرحمٰن الرحيم

٠.١ أمّا بعد حمد الله الذي جعل الحمد ثمنًا لنعمائه ومعاذًا من بلائه ووسيلًا إلى جنانه وسببًا لزيادة إحسانه. والصلاة على رسوله نبيّ الرحمة وإمام الأئمّة وسراج الأمّة المنتخب١ من طينة الكرم وسلالة المجد الأقدم ومغرس الفخار المعرق وفرع العلاء المثمر المورق. وعلى أهل بيته مصابيح الظلم وعصم الأمم ومنار الدين الواضحة ومثاقيل الفضل الراجحة. صلّى الله عليهم أجمعين صلاة تكون إزاء لفضلهم ومكافاة لعملهم وكفاء لطيب فرعهم وأصلهم ما أنار فجر ساطع وخوى نجم طالع.

٠.٢ فإنّي كنت في عنفوان السنّ وغضاضة الغصن ابتدأت بتأليف كتاب في خصائص الأئمة عليهم السلام يشتمل على محاسن أخبارهم وجواهر كلامهم حداني عليه غرض ذكرته في صدر الكتاب وجعلته أمام الكلام. وفرغت من الخصائص التّي تخصّ أمير المؤمنين عليًّا عليه السلام وعاقت عن إتمام بقيّة الكتاب محاجزات الأيّام ومماطلات الزمان. وكنت قد بوّبت ما خرج من ذلك أبوابًا وفصّلته فصولًا فجاء في آخرها فصل يتضمّن محاسن ما نقل عنه عليه السلام من الكلام القصير في المواعظ والحكم والأمثال والأدب دون الخطب الطويلة والكتب المبسوطة.

٠.٣ فاستحسن جماعة من الأصدقاء ما اشتمل عليه الفصل المقدّم ذكره معجبين ببدائعه ومتعجّبين من نواصعه وسألوني عند ذلك أن أبدأ بتأليف كتاب يحتوي على مختار كلام أمير المؤمنين٢ عليه السلام في جميع فنونه ومتشعّبات غصونه من خطب وكتب ومواعظ وأدب علمًا أنّ ذلك يتضمّن من عجائب البلاغة وغرائب الفصاحة وجواهر العربيّة وثواقب الكلم الدينيّة والدنيويّة ما لا يوجد مجتمعًا في كلام ولا مجموع

<hr>

١ز، س، ج، ك، آ: كذا. ل، ت: ⟨المنتجب⟩. ي: معًا.   ٢تبدأ مخطوطة هـ من هنا.

Raḍī's Introduction

In the Name of God, the Compassionate, the Merciful

0.1 I praise God, who made praise the return for his favors, the refuge from his trials, the way to his garden, and the means to obtain yet more of his beneficence. May God shower blessings on his Messenger—the Prophet of mercy, the Imam of all Imams, lantern for the community, the one fashioned from the clay of honor, the scion of ancient nobility, the deep-rooted tree of glory, and the leafy, fruit-bearing bough of grandeur. May God shower blessings on the people of his house. They are lamps in the darkness, protectors of the nations, brilliant beacons of faith, and weighted scales of virtue. May God shower them with blessings that equal their virtue, requite their endeavors, and match the bouquet of their fragrant bough and root, for as long as the morning gleams bright and the stars rise and set.

0.2 In the days of my eager youth, motivated by a goal that I described in its introduction,[1] I began compiling a book about the qualities of the Imams that included their beautiful sayings and bejeweled maxims. I finished transcribing the qualities of the Commander of the Faithful, 'Alī, but fate put obstructions in my path and destiny cast delays, such that I was prevented from finishing the rest. I had divided the part I had already written into chapters and sections, and, at its end, I had placed a section on short sayings narrated from 'Alī, including words of counsel, aphorisms, maxims, and directions for refined behavior; I had excluded the longer orations and more expansive letters.[2]

0.3 A group of my friends were especially enthralled with this section. Astonished by the marvels of the Commander of the Faithful's words and amazed by their limpid clarity, they asked me to compile a book that would offer a selection in all its manifold categories and branches, including orations, letters, statements of counsel, and directions for refined behavior. They knew full well that these pieces offered wonderful eloquence and rare expressions, jewels of Arabic, and gems of earthly wisdom and spiritual sayings, which are assembled

---

1 Raḍī, *Khaṣā'iṣ al-a'immah*, 36–38. As noted in the present volume's Introduction, Raḍī's purpose in writing it was to refute an Abbasid (presumably Sunni) detractor.

2 Raḍī, *Khaṣā'iṣ al-a'immah, passim*. The section on 'Alī includes details of his appointment (*naṣṣ*) by the Prophet, some of his celebrated miracles, poetry in his praise and poetry describing his appointment at Ghadīr Khumm, the events of his caliphate, the grace enjoyed by those who visit his shrine, and a selection from his sayings and sermons.

الأطراف في كتاب. إذ كان مولانا أميرالمؤمنين عليه السلام مشرع الفصاحة وموردها ومنشأ البلاغة ومولدها ومنه عليه السلام ظهر مكنونها وعنه أخذت قوانينها وعلى أمثلته حذا كلّ قائل خطيب وبكلامه ٱستعان كلّ واعظ بليغ. ومع ذلك فقد سبق وقصّروا وتقدّم وتأخّروا لأنّ كلامه عليه السلام الكلام الذي عليه مَسحة من العلم الإلهيّ وفيه عَبقة من الكلام النبويّ.

٤.٥ فأجبتهم إلى الابتداء بذلك عالمًا بما فيه من عظيم النفع ومنشور الذكر ومذخور الأجر. وٱعتمدت به أن أبيّن عن عظيم قدر أمير المؤمنين عليه السلام في هذه الفضيلة مضافة إلى المحاسن الدثرة والفضائل الجمّة وأنّه عليه السلام ٱنفرد ببلوغ غايتها من جميع السلف الأوّلين الذين إنّما يؤثر عنهم منها القليل النادر والشاذّ الشارد فأمّا كلامه عليه السلام فهو البحر الذي لا يساجل والجمّ الذي لا يحافل. وأردت أن يسوغ لي التمثّل في الإفتخار به صلّى الله عليه بقول الفرزدق رحمة الله عليه[1]

أُولئِكَ آبائِي فَجِئنِي بِمِثلِهِـــمْ   إِذَا جَمَعَتنَا يَا جَرِيرُ المَجَامِعُ

٥.٥ ورأيت كلامه صلّى الله عليه يدور على أقطاب ثلاثة أوّلها الخطب والأوامر وثانيها الكتب والرسائل وثالثها الحكم والمواعظ. فأجمعت بتوفيق الله على الابتداء بٱختيار محاسن الخطب ثم محاسن الكتب ثم محاسن الحكم والأدب مفردًا لكلّ صنف من ذلك بابًا ومفضّلًا فيه أوراقًا لتكون مقدّمة لٱستدراك ما عساه يشذّ عنّي عاجلًا ويقع إليّ آجلًا. وإذا جاء شيء من كلامه عليه السلام الخارج في أثناء حوار أو جواب سؤال أو غرض آخر من الأغراض في غير الأنحاء التي ذكرتها وقرّرت القاعدة عليها نسبته إلى أليق الأبواب به وأشدّها ملاحمة[2] لغرضه. وربّما جاء فيما أختاره من ذلك فصول غير متّسقة ومحاسن كلم غير منتظمة لأنّني أورد النكت واللمع ولا أقصد التتالي والنسق.

---

[1] البحر: الطويل.   [2] چ، آ، ت، ك، س، ونسخة في ي: كذا. هـ، ل، ق، وأصل ي: ‹ملاحظة›.

nowhere else, neither in spoken words nor in written books. Indeed, the Commander of the Faithful is the fountainhead of elocution and its wellspring, the cradle of eloquence and its birthplace. It is from him that its secrets became known, and its rules were learned. He is the model for every articulate orator, his the words used by every persuasive preacher. Moreover, he was the first, while they came trailing, he forged ahead, while they lagged behind. His words were anointed with divine knowledge and perfumed by prophetic discourse.

0.4   I answered my friends' appeal and began the book, knowing it would bring me great benefit, redolent fame, and lasting reward. My purpose was to demonstrate the Commander of the Faithful's lofty station in this particular virtue, in addition to his numerous other qualities and abundant merits, and to highlight his singular attainment among the earliest Muslims. Of their words, we find a few sporadic pieces and occasional lines, while his are a bottomless ocean, an overwhelming torrent. With great pride in my own descent from him, I beg your leave to cite here a testimonial verse by Farazdaq:[1]

> These are my ancestors, Jarīr, bring on yours!
> Who will be your boast in our gatherings?

0.5   'Alī's verbal heritage, I have found, revolves around three poles: orations and directives; letters and epistles; and sayings and counsels. I have, with God's guidance, selected and transcribed his most beautiful orations, then his most beautiful letters, then his most beautiful sayings and directions for refined behavior. For each of these categories, I have dedicated its own separate chapter. In each chapter, I have left several pages blank, in case I have missed something that I might discover later. Whenever I have come across material from his oeuvre that was spoken in a conversation, or in answer to a question, or that belongs to a genre different than the ones around which I have structured my compilation, I have placed it in the chapter to which it is most suited, the one closest to it in form. Some sections therefore may not be fully harmonious in their coordination and some sayings may not be systematically arranged. My goal is to transcribe pithy sayings and dazzling expressions; consistent and methodical recording is not my intention.

---

1   Farazdaq, *Dīwān*, 360, from a poem beginning (مِنّا الذي أُختيرَ الرِجالِ سَماحةً). Farazdaq (d. ca. 110/728) was a famous Umayyad-era poet best, known for his satirical exchanges (*naqāʾiḍ*) with another eminent poet, Jarīr (also d. 110/728). Both were from the tribe of Tamīm, Farazdaq from the sub-tribe of Mujāshiʿ of the Dārim clan, Jarīr from the clan of Kulayb ibn Yarbūʿ. Farazdaq also composed praise poetry for the Umayyad caliphs, as well as for the Shiʿi Imam, 'Alī's grandson and namesake, ʿAlī Zayn al-ʿĀbidīn.

0.6   ومن عجائبه عليه السلام التي اّنفرد بها وأمن المشاركة فيها أنّ كلامه الوارد في الزهد والمواعظ والتذكير والزواجر إذا تأمّله المتأمّل وفكّر فيه المفكّر وخلع من قلبه أنّه كلام مثله ممّن عظم قدره ونفذ أمره وأحاط بالرقاب ملكه لم يعترضه الشكّ في أنه من كلام من لا حظّ له في غير الزهادة ولا شغل له بغير العبادة قد قبع في كِسر بيت أو اّنقطع في سفح جبل لا يسمع إلّا حسّه ولا يرى إلّا نفسه. ولا يكاد يوقن بأنّه كلام من ينغمس في الحرب مصلتًا سيفه فيقُطَّ الرقاب ويجدّل الأبطال ويعود به ينطف دمًا ويقطر مُهَجًا وهو مع تلك الحال زاهد الزهّاد وبدل الأبدال[1] وهذه من فضائله العجيبة وخصائصه اللطيفة التي جمع بها بين الأضداد وألّف بين الأشتات وكثيرًا ما أذاكر الإخوان بها وأستخرج عجبهم منها وهي موضع للعبرة بها والفكرة فيها.

0.7   وربّما جاء في أثناء هذا الاختيار اللفظ المردّد والمعنى المكرّر والعذر في ذلك أن روايات كلامه عليه السلام تختلف اّختلافًا شديدًا فربّما اّتفق الكلام المختار في رواية فنقل على وجهه ثمّ وجد بعد ذلك في رواية أخرى موضوعًا غير وضعه الأوّل إمّا بزيادة مختارة أو لفظ أحسن عبارة فتقتضي الحال أن يعاد اّستظهارًا للاختيار وغيرة على عقائل الكلام وربّما بعد العهد أيضًا بما اّختير أوّلًا فأعيد بعضه سهوًا ونسيانًا لا قصدًا واّعتمادًا. ولا أدّعي مع ذلك أنّني أحيط بأقطار جميع كلامه عليه السلام حتّى لا يشذّ عنّي منه شاذّ ولا يندّ نادّ بل لا أبعّد أن يكون القاصر عنّي فوق الواقع إليّ والحاصل في ربقتي دون الخارج من يديّ وما عليّ إلّا بذل الجهد وبلاغ الوسع وعلى الله سبحانه نهج السبيل ورشاد الدليل إن شاء الله تعالى.

---

[1] تبدأ مخطوطة ش من هنا.

0.6 Among the marvels unique to ʿAlī that no one else shares with him is the following: if a person were to ponder his words of renunciation, counsel, remembrance, or admonition, if he were to parse them thoroughly—while putting aside the knowledge that they were spoken by a man of lofty stature whose commands people followed and who ruled over a multitude—he would have no doubt that these are the words of one who knows nothing but renunciation, whose sole occupation is worship, who has withdrawn to a lonely corner or leads a solitary life at the foot of a mountain, hearing no other voice and seeing no other person. He would never imagine that they could have been spoken by a man who rushed into the fray of battle brandishing his sword, striking off men's heads and cutting down warriors, then returning with it dripping blood and gore. Yet, ʿAlī was also the most pious of renunciants and the greatest of God's deputies.[1] This—his combination of opposites and conjunction of contraries—is one of his most marvelous virtues and sublime characteristics. I often remind my companions of this quality and they are moved to wonder, for it offers lessons and provokes contemplation.

0.7 In my selection of material, it is possible that some words repeat and certain themes recur; the redundancy is occasioned by the strong variation in different narrations of ʿAlī's words. It could be that I have transcribed a piece as I found it in one narrative, then I came across it in another, somewhat different from the first, either in having a choice supplement, or a more eloquent turn of phrase, which led me to repeat it, to shore up my compilation and preserve these wondrously wise novelties. Or it could be that some time had gone by since my first selection and I repeated a text, not deliberately and intentionally, but in error or forgetfulness. Even so, I do not claim that I have gathered all the prominent pieces of ʿAlī's words such that no stray escaped my lasso and no breakaway absconded. Indeed, it is likely that the pieces I have missed are more numerous than the ones I found, and the examples I have tracked down are fewer than the ones that slipped from my grasp. The most I can do is to endeavor to the best of my ability. It is God—if he wills—who shows the path and guides aright.

---

1 Lit. "of the substitutes," (*abdāl*, sing. *badal*), refers to "certain righteous persons, of whom the world is never destitute; when one dies, God substitutes another in his place" (Lane, *Lexicon*, s.v. "B-D-L").

0.8 ورأيت من بعدُ تسمية هذا الكتاب بنهج البلاغة إذ كان يفتح للناظر فيه أبوابها ويقرّب عليه طِلابها وفيه حاجة العالم والمتعلّم وبغية البليغ والزاهد ويمضي في أثنائه من عجيب الكلام في التوحيد والعدل وتنزيه الله سبحانه عن شبه الخلق ما هو بلال كلّ غلّة وشفاء كلّ علّة وجلاء كلّ شبهة.

0.9 ومن الله سبحانه أستمدّ التوفيق والعصمة وأتنجّز التسديد والمعونة وأستعيذه من خطأ الجنان قبل خطأ اللسان ومن زلّة الكلم قبل زلّة القدم وهو حسبي ونعم الوكيل.

0.8 I have decided to name this book *Nahj al-Balāghah* (The Way of Eloquence), for it opens doors of eloquence for its readers and helps them acquire its tools. In it, both scholar and student can find something that speaks to them, and through it, both orator and renunciant can fulfill their desires. Within its pages, you will see marvelous expositions on God's unity and justice, on stripping God of attributes that would render him like his creatures,[1] and expositions that assuage thirst, cure sickness, and dispel doubt.

0.9 I ask God for guidance and protection. I appeal to him for direction and aid. I ask him to protect my heart before my tongue errs, and my tongue before my foot slips. God is my sufficiency and the best guardian.

---

1 Raḍī's mention of "God's unity and justice" and his words about "stripping God of attributes" speak to his Muʿtazilī beliefs.

باب المختار من خطب أمير المؤمنين صلّى الله عليه وأوامره ويدخل في ذلك المختار من كلامه الجاري مجرى الخطب في المقامات المحضورة والمواقف المذكورة والخطوب الواردة

1.1 فمن خطبة له عليه السلام يذكر فيها ابتداء خلق السماوات والأرض وخلق آدم عليه السلام

1.1.1 الحمد لله الذي لا يبلغ مدحته القائلون ولا يحصي نعمه[1] العادّون ولا يؤدّي حقّه المجتهدون الذي لا يدركه بعد الهمم ولا يناله غوص الفطن الذي ليس لصفته حدّ محدود ولا نعت موجود ولا وقت معدود ولا أجل ممدود فطر الخلائق بقدرته ونشر الرياح برحمته ووتّد بالصخور ميَدان أرضه. أوّل الدين معرفته وكمال معرفته التصديق به وكمال التصديق به توحيده وكمال توحيده الإخلاص له وكمال الإخلاص له نفي الصفات عنه لشهادة كلّ صفة أنّها غير الموصوف وشهادة كلّ موصوف أنّه غير الصفة. فمن وصف الله سبحانه فقد قرنه ومن قرنه فقد ثنّاه ومن ثنّاه فقد جزّأه ومن جزّأه فقد جهله ومن جهله فقد أشار إليه ومن أشار إليه فقد حدّه ومن حدّه فقد عدّه ومن قال فيمَ فقد ضمّنه ومن قال علامَ فقد أخلى منه. كائن لا عن حدث موجود لا عن عدم مع كلّ شيء لا بمقارنة وغير كلّ شيء لا بمزايلة فاعل لا بمعنى الحركات والآلة بصير إذ لا منظور إليه من خلقه متوحّد إذ لا سكن يستأنس به ولا يستوحش لفقده.

<hr>

١ ش: كذا. ه، ونسخة في ش: ﴿نعماءه﴾. ي: ﴿بقاه﴾.

Orations

Chapter containing selections from the Commander of the Faithful's orations and directives, including selections from his addresses that may be likened to orations, spoken in charged gatherings, famous battles, and times of danger

1.1 From an oration by ʿAlī, in which he spoke of the creation of sky and earth, and the creation of Adam:[1]

1.1.1 I praise God. Yet no speaker can articulate his praise, no reckoner can count his favors, and the most diligent cannot give him his due. Soaring thoughts cannot reach him and deep minds cannot fathom him. He cannot be described, for he is beyond the limits of demarcated boundaries, existing depictions, tallied times, and protracted lifespans. His power created the universe and his mercy sent forth rain-bearing winds. Then, to curb its oscillation, he pegged the earth with massive rocks. The first part of religion is knowledge of God. Knowledge of him is perfected by belief in him. Belief in him is perfected by the declaration of his oneness. Declaration of his oneness is perfected by sincere allegiance to him. Sincere allegiance to him is achieved by negating all attributes ascribed to him, by the testimony of every attribute that it is separate from the thing described, and by the testimony of each thing described that it is separate from the attribute.[2] To describe God is to ascribe associates to him. To ascribe associates to him is to ascribe duality to him. To ascribe duality to him is to divide him. To divide him is to undervalue him. To undervalue him is to depict him. To depict him is to circumscribe him. To circumscribe him is to quantify him. To ask, "In what?" is to confine him. To ask, "On what?" is to make another space empty of him. God is a being but not by coming into being. He is existent but not after non-existence. He is with all things but not by association. He is other than all things but not by detachment. He is an agent but not by movement or instrument. He was all-seeing when there was no creature to be seen. He existed in solitude when there was no friend in whose familiarity he could take comfort, or by whose absence he would be distraught.

---

1 The first section (§1.1.1) is from ʿAlī's oration to the Kufans, urging them to regroup to fight Muʿāwiyah, after the Battle of Nahrawān in 38/658. Kulaynī, *Kāfī*, 1:134.

2 I.e., the attribute and the thing described are two separate things, they are part of a pair and have "two-ness," and, as such, neither label can be applied to God, who is one.

1.1.2 أنشأ الخلق إنشاءً وابتدأه ابتداءً بلا رويّة أجالها ولا تجربة استفادها ولا حركة أحدثها ولا هَمامة نفس اضطرب فيها أحال الأشياء لأوقاتها ولأم بين مختلفاتها وغرّز غرائزها وألزمها أشباحها عالمًا بها قبل ابتدائها محيطًا بحدودها وانتهائها عارفًا بقرائنها وأحنائها. ثمّ أنشأ سبحانه فتق الأجواء وشقّ الأرجاء وسكائك الهواء فأجرى فيها ماءً متلاطمًا تيّاره متراكمًا زخّاره حمله على متن الريح العاصفة والزعزع القاصفة فأمرها بردّه وسلّطها على شدّه وقرنها إلى حدّه الهواء من تحتها فتيق والماء من فوقها دفيق ثمّ أنشأ سبحانه ريحًا اعتقم مهبّها وأدام مربّها وأعصف مجراها وأبعد منشاها فأمرها بتصفيق الماء الزخّار وإثارة موج البحار فمخضته مخض السِّقاء وعصفت به عصفها بالفضاء تردّ أوّله على آخره وساجيه على مائره حتّى عبّ عبابه ورمى بالزبد ركامه فرفعه في هواء منفتق وجوّ منفهق فسوّى منه سبع سموات جعل سفلاهنّ موجًا مكفوفًا وعلياهنّ سقفًا محفوظًا وسمكًا مرفوعًا بغير عمد يدعمها ولا دِسار ينتظمها ثمّ زيّنها بزينة الكواكب وضياء الثواقب وأجرى فيها سراجًا مستطيرًا وقمرًا منيرًا في فلك دائر وسقف سائر ورقيم مائر.

1.1.3 ثمّ فتق ما بين السموات العلى فملأهنّ أطوارًا من ملائكته منهم سجود لا يركعون وركوع لا ينتصبون وصافّون لا يتزايلون ومسبّحون لا يسأمون لا يغشاهم نوم العيون ولا سهو العقول ولا فترة الأبدان ولا غفلة النسيان ومنهم أمناء على وحيه وألسنة الى رسله ومختلفون بقضائه وأمره ومنهم الحفظة لعباده والسدنة لأبواب جنانه ومنهم الثابتة في الأرضين السفلى أقدامهم والمارقة من السماء العليا أعناقهم والخارجة من الأقطار أركانهم والمناسبة لقوائم العرش أكتافهم ناكسة دونه أبصارهم متلفّعون تحته بأجنحتهم مضروبة بينهم وبين من دونهم حجب العزّة وأستار القدرة لا يتوهّمون ربّهم بالتصوير ولا يجرون عليه صفات المصنوعين ولا يحدّونه بالأماكن ولا يشيرون إليه بالنظائر.

1.1.2 God created the world and gave it a beginning. He did this without long mulling, prior experience, generated movement, or stirring aspiration. He made all things in their proper time and combined their parts. He accorded them a particular nature and gave them a specific form. He knew them before he gave them a beginning, cognizant of their limits and consequences, and aware of their connections and complexities. Then he rent the ether, tore up the sky and air, and unleashed a torrent roiling with crashing waves. He placed the torrent on the back of a stormy wind, a raging tempest. He ordered the wind to hold the torrent in check, dispatched it to fetter the flood, and compelled it to restrict the advancing surf. Below, the air was vast and empty. The water gushed above. Then, he created a barren wind, its control permanent, its current tempestuous, and its perfume wafting. He commanded it to whip up the rolling waters and bring forth mighty waves. The wind churned up the water like cream in a churning skin and tossed it about in the sky, flipping it end over end and mixing the still and the shifting, until it frothed and bubbled and threw up a mountain of foam. Raising the frothy mixture in the expansive layers of air, in the vast ether, God molded seven skies—the lowest of them a frozen wave, and the loftiest a well-preserved canopy, an elevated firmament— with no pillar for support, and no nails or ropes to bind. Then he ornamented the sky with beautiful stars and bright lights. He set therein a radiant sun and a glowing moon, gliding in that spinning sphere, that moving sky, that flowing, studded expanse.

1.1.3 Then God rent the lofty skies and filled them with ranks of his angels: some continually prostrate, never bowing, others bow, never standing straight, yet others stand in rows, never quitting that position, and yet more chant litanies of his praise, never tiring. Drowsy eyes do not impede them, nor wandering minds, exhausted bodies, or forgetfulness occasioned by lack of heed. Among them, too, are angels God has entrusted with his revelation. Constituting God's tongues to his apostles, they come and go with his decrees and commands. Some are charged with protecting his servants, others are gatekeepers at the doors of his Garden. Yet others have feet firmly fixed in the nethermost regions of the earth, while their necks extend beyond the highest heaven, their flanks stretch beyond the land mass, and their shoulders reach the posts of God's throne. They lower their gaze before him and spread interlocked wings underneath, separated from those below by veils of might and cloaks of power. They do not attempt to picture their Lord through imagination, or apply to him the attributes of created beings, or demarcate him within a location, or depict him with comparisons.

1.1.4 منها في صفة خلق آدم عليه السلام

ثمّ جمع سبحانه من حزن الأرض وسهلها وعذبها وسبخها تربة سنّها بالماء حتّى خلصت ولاطها بالبلّة حتّى لزبت فجبل منها صورة ذات أحناء ووصول وأعضاء وفصول أجمدها حتّى اَستمسكت وأصلدها حتّى صلصلت لوقت معدود وأجل معلوم ثمّ نفخ فيها من روحه فمثلت إنسانًا ذا أذهان يجيلها وفكر يتصرّف بها وجوارح يختدمها وأدوات يقلّبها[1] ومعرفة يفرّق بها بين الحقّ والباطل[2] والأذواق والمشامّ والألوان والأجناس معجونًا بطينة الأكوان[3] المختلفة والأشباه المؤتلفة والأضداد المتعادية والأخلاط المتباينة من الحرّ والبرد والبلّة والجمود والمَساءة والسرور.

1.1.5 واَستأدى الله سبحانه الملائكة وديعته لديهم وعهد وصيّته إليهم في الإذعان بالسجود له والخنوع لتكرمته فقال ﴿اُسْجُدُواْ لِآدَمَ فَسَجَدُواْ إِلَّا إِبْلِيسَ﴾ وقبيله اَعترتهم الحميّة وغلبت عليهم الشقوة وتعزّزوا بخلقة النار واَستوهنوا خلق الصلصال فأعطاه الله النظرة اَستحقاقًا للسخطة واَستتمامًا للبليّة وإنجازًا للعدة فقال ﴿إِنَّكَ مِنَ الْمُنْظَرِينَ إِلَىٰ يَوْمِ الْوَقْتِ الْمَعْلُومِ﴾. ثمّ أسكن سبحانه آدم دارًا أرغد فيها عيشه وآمن فيها محلّته وحذّره إبليس وعداوته فأغترّه إبليس نفاسة عليه بدار المقام ومرافقة الأبرار فباع اليقين بشكّه والعزيمة بوهنه واَستبدل بالجذل وجلًا وبالاغترار ندمًا ثمّ بسط الله سبحانه له في توبته ولقّاه كلمة رحمته ووعده المردّ إلى جنّته فأهبطه إلى دار البليّة وتناسل الذرّيّة.

1.1.6 واَصطفى سبحانه من ولده أنبياء أخذ على الوحي ميثاقهم وعلى تبليغ الرسالة أمانتهم لمّا بدّل أكثرُ خلقه عهد الله إليهم فجهلوا حقّه واَتّخذوا الأنداد معه واَجتالتهم الشياطين عن معرفته واَقتطعتهم عن عبادته فبعث فيهم رسله وواتر إليهم أنبياءه ليستأدوهم ميثاق فطرته ويذكّروهم منسيّ نعمته ويحتجّوا عليهم بالتبليغ ويثيروا لهم

---

[1] ش، ه: كذا. ي: ⟨يستعملها⟩. [2] ش، وأضيفت في ه مع علامة الصحّة: كذا. ي، وأصل ه: سقطت ⟨الحقّ والباطل⟩. [3] ش، مصحّحة في ه: كذا. ي، وأصل ه: ⟨الألوان⟩.

1.1.4 From the same oration, describing the creation of Adam:
God gathered soil by sifting coarse earth and fine, sweet earth and salty. He rinsed it with water until it became pure and clean, and moistened and kneaded it until it was smooth and malleable. With this mixture, he molded a form with curves, joints, limbs, and nodes. He let it dry until it hardened, setting it aside for a fixed period of time, until it became firm. Then he breathed into it of his spirit, and it stood before him as a human being. This being had faculties it could harness, a mind it could engage, limbs it could yoke to its service, parts it could use as instruments, and perception with which it could differentiate between right and wrong, tastes and smells, colors, and species. Its clay was a blend of disparate entities, assembled forms, warring opposites, and dissimilar mixtures: hot and cold, wet and dry, painful and joyous.

1.1.5 Then God commanded his angels to fulfill the trust with which he had charged them and discharge the covenant he had enjoined—to prostrate humbly, deferentially, before Adam, in recognition of the honor he had received from God. God said, «Prostrate before Adam, and they all prostrated except Iblīs»[1] and Iblīs's tribe. Pride held them back and wretchedness took over when they boasted of their creation from fire and scorned the creation of clay. God gave Iblīs a respite so that he could earn yet more of God's wrath, to complete the trial and fulfill the pledge. He said, «You have been placed among those who have been granted respite until the day of destiny.»[2] As for Adam, God gave him a home, with a good life therein and a safe dwelling. He warned him of Iblīs and of Iblīs's enmity. Iblīs misled Adam, for he was jealous of Adam's heavenly abode and pious companions. Adam was deceived—he exchanged certainty for doubt and resolve for weakness, his bliss was replaced by fear, his deception was followed by regret. Afterward, God accepted his plea for forgiveness, spoke words of mercy, and promised him a return to paradise, but he nevertheless cast Adam into the abode of tribulation, where his descendants would multiply for generations.

1.1.6 From Adam's descendants, God selected prophets, exacting a pledge from them to convey his revelation, and entrusting them with delivering his message. As time passed, most people altered God's covenant, denied what they owed him, and ascribed partners to him. The devils had driven them away from their earlier recognition of him, stopping them from his worship altogether. God dispatched messengers and a succession of prophets to restore people to their

---

1   Qur'an, Baqarah 2:34, Ṭāhā 20:116, Isrāʾ 17:61. Iblīs refers to Lucifer.
2   Qur'an, Ḥijr 15:37–38, Ṣād 38:80–81.

دفائن العقول ويُروهم آيات المقدرة من سقف فوقهم مرفوع ومهاد تحتهم موضوع ومعايش تحييهم وآجال تفنيهم وأوصاب تُهرمهم وأحداث تتابع عليهم. ولم يُخْل الله سبحانه خلقه من نبيّ مرسل أو كتاب منزل أو حجّة لازمة أو محجّة قائمة. رسل لا تقصر بهم قلّة عددهم ولا كثرة المكذّبين لهم. من سابق سمّي له من بعده أو غابر عرّفه من قبله. على ذلك نسلت القرون ومضت الدهور وسلفت الآباء وخلفت الأبناء.

١.١.٧ إلى أن بعث الله سبحانه محمّدًا صلّى الله عليه لإنجاز عدته وتمام نبوّته مأخوذًا على النبيّين ميثاقه مشهورة سماته كريمًا ميلاده وأهل الأرض يومئذ ملل متفرّقة وأهواء منتشرة وطرائق متشتّتة بين مشبّه لله بخلقه أو ملحد في اسمه أو مشير إلى غيره فهداهم به من الضلالة وأنقذهم به١ من الجهالة. ثمّ اختار الله سبحانه لمحمّد صلّى الله عليه وآله لقاءه ورضي له ما عنده وأكرمه عن دار الدنيا ورغب به عن مقام البلوى فقبضه إليه كريمًا صلّى الله عليه وعلى آله وخلّف فيكم ما خلّفت الأنبياء لأممها إذ لم يتركوهم هَمَلًا بغير طريق واضح ولا عَلَم قائم كتاب ربكم مبيّنًا حلاله وحرامه وفضائله وفرائضه وناسخه ومنسوخه ورخصه وعزائمه وخاصّه وعامّه وعبره وأمثاله ومرسله ومحدوده ومحكمه ومتشابهه مفسّرًا جمله مبيّنًا غوامضه بين مأخوذ ميثاق علمه وموسّع على العباد في جهله وبين مثبت في الكتاب فرضه معلوم في السنّة نسخه وواجب في السنّة أخذه مرخّص في الكتاب تركه وبين واجب بوقته وزائل في مستقبله ومباين بين محارمه من كبير أوعد عليه نيرانه أو صغير أرصد له غفرانه وبين مقبول في أدناه وموسّع في أقصاه.

<hr>

١ م: كذا. ي: ⟨بمكانه⟩. ش: سقطت من المتن ⟨هداهم ... الجهالة⟩. ه: هذه العبارة مع بضعة أسطر أخرى محيت.

original pledge. He directed his prophets to remind people of the divine favors they had forgotten, establish the truth by conveying his message, and revive their numbed intellects. He instructed his prophets to show people the signs of his power: the sky raised above, and the earth spread below, livelihoods that sustained life, and lifespans that ended in death, suffering that made people age, and relentless calamities. Never in all this time did God allow his creation to be left without a prophet, a revealed scripture, a sure proof, or a clear path. The scanty number who answered did not stop God's messengers, nor the multitudes of their repudiators. Each messenger had his successor named for him, each successor was identified by his predecessor. In this manner, generations went by, and ages passed. Fathers died, and sons took their place.

1.1.7   So it was, until God sent Muḥammad to fulfill his promise and complete the line of prophecy. All earlier prophets had been made to affirm Muḥammad, whose qualities had been made known to them, with a binding oath. His birth, when it came, brought auspicious blessings. At that time, the earth's inhabitants were divided into numerous faiths with different notions and divergent views. One group likened God to his creatures, another rejected his name, and a third looked to a separate deity. Through Muḥammad, God saved the people from their errant ways. Because of his eminence, he delivered them from ignorance. Then God summoned Muḥammad to meet with him and desired for him the blessings to be enjoyed at his side. Raising him from the vileness of this worldly abode and lifting him from this place of tribulation, God brought him into his presence, honored and esteemed. For you, he left you what earlier prophets left their communities, they did not abandon their followers without guidance, without a clear path or a signpost. Muḥammad, too, left you your Lord's Book, and he fully elucidated its contents: the licit versus the illicit, recommended virtues versus required mandates, abrogating verses versus abrogated ones, licenses versus decrees, specifics versus generalities, lessons versus parables, free verses versus restricted ones, and clear verses versus ambiguous ones. He explained the Book's subtleties and clarified what was obscure, including things whose knowledge is required for all God's servants, versus others, ignorance of which is excused; things whose mandate is established in the Book while their abrogation is shown in the Sunnah, versus others whose practice is commanded in the Sunnah while vacating them is permitted in the Book; and things that were compulsory in their time, versus others whose directive subsequently ceased. He differentiated among the Book's prohibitions of grave sins which incur the punishment of the Fire, versus smaller transgressions which hold the prospect of God's forgiveness; of acts acceptable in minimal form, versus those that earn maximum reward.

1.1.8 منها

وفرض عليكم حجّ بيته الذي جعله قبلة للأنام يردونه ورود الأنعام ويألهون إليه ولوه الحمام جعله سبحانه علامة لتواضعهم لعظمته وإذعانهم لعزّته وآختار من خلقه سُمّاعًا أجابوا إليه دعوته وصدّقوا كلمته ووقفوا مواقف أنبيائه وتشبّهوا بملائكته المطيفين بعرشه يحرزون الأرباح في متجر عبادته ويتبادرون عنده موعد مغفرته. جعله سبحانه للإسلام علمًا وللعائذين حرمًا فرض حجّه وأوجب حقّه وكتب عليكم وفادته فقال سبحانه ﴿وَلِلّٰهِ عَلَى ٱلنَّاسِ حِجُّ ٱلْبَيْتِ مَنِ ٱسْتَطَاعَ إِلَيْهِ سَبِيلًا وَمَنْ كَفَرَ فَإِنَّ ٱللّٰهَ غَنِيٌّ عَنِ ٱلْعٰلَمِينَ﴾.

1.2 ومن خطبة له عليه السلام بعد آنصرافه من صفّين

1.2.1 أحمده آستتمامًا لنعمته وآستسلامًا لعزّته وآستعصامًا من معصيته وأستعينه فاقة إلى كفايته إنّه لا يضلّ من هداه ولا يئل من عاداه ولا يفتقر من كفاه فإنّه أرجح ما وُزِن وأفضل ما خُزِن. وأشهد أن لا إله إلّا الله¹ شهادة ممتحنًا إخلاصها معتقدًا مُصاصها نتمسّك بها أبدًا ما أبقانا ونذّخرها لأهاويل ما يلقانا فإنّها عزيمة الإيمان وفاتحة الإحسان ومرضاة الرحمان ومَدحرة الشيطان. وأشهد أنّ محمّدًا عبده ورسوله أرسله بالدين المشهور والعلم المأثور والكتاب المسطور والنور الساطع والضياء اللامع والأمر الصادع إزاحة للشبهات وآحتجاجًا بالبيّنات وتحذيرًا بالآيات وتخويفًا بالمثُلات. والناس في فتن آنجذم

---

¹ ش، ي: كذا. ه: أضيفت ﴿وحده لا شريك له﴾.

1.1.8 From the same oration:

God mandated the rite of pilgrimage to his House, which he commanded you to face in prayer. He directed you to race to the House like cattle to water, like doves to seed, demonstrating your prostration before his greatness and your submission to his power. He selected true listeners to answer his call, believe in his word, stand in the stations of the prophets, and follow the example of angels who circumambulate his throne. These pilgrims obtain abundant profit through their worship of him, and they speedily secure his forgiveness. God characterized his House as Islam's lofty banner and made it a sanctuary for all who seek shelter. Mandating pilgrimage to it, he commanded you to submit its due and come to it, and he decreed, «Pilgrimage to the House is compulsory for all who are able to find a path. As for those who disbelieve, they should know that God has need of no one from all the worlds.»[1]

1.2 From an oration given by ʿAlī during his return from Ṣiffīn:[2]

1.2.1 I praise God, seeking the completion of his favor, submitting to his might, and entreating his protection against sin. I beseech him, needing only his all-sufficing aid. Whomsoever God guides never goes astray, whomsoever he abhors never endures, and whomsoever he suffices never wants. His praise is the weightiest commodity placed on the celestial scales, and the best treasure one can hoard. I testify that there is no god but God—I render this testimony with firm sincerity and true belief. We, all of us, shall cling to it for as long as God gives us life, relying on it to dispel the terrors we must face, for it is the requirement of our faith and the key to God's gifts, it pleases the Merciful and banishes Satan. I testify that Muḥammad is God's servant and messenger and acknowledge that God sent Muḥammad with a celebrated religion, a legacy of knowledge,[3] a transcribed scripture, brilliant light, gleaming radiance, and clear command. All this, in order to remove doubts, establish proofs, caution with portentous signs, and warn against God's punishments. When Muḥam-

---

1 Qurʾan, Āl ʿImrān 3:97. God's House (Bayt Allāh) is the Kaʿbah in Mecca.

2 In 37/657. Alternatively, Ibn Abī al-Ḥadīd (H 1:143) states that the last line of §1.2.2, which speaks of truth being restored to its owners, cannot be placed at the time of ʿAlī's leaving Ṣiffīn but has to have been spoken early in his caliphate, immediately after the pledge of allegiance to him in 35/656.

3 Reading ʿilm. Or, reading ʿalam, "a time-honored banner."

فيها حبل الدين وتزعزعت[1] سواري اليقين وٱختلف النجر وتشتّت الأمر وضاق المخرج وعمي المصدر فالهدى خامل والعمى شامل عُصي الرحمان ونصر الشيطان وخذل الإيمان فٱنهارت دعائمه وتنكّرت معالمه ودرست سبله وعفت شُرُكه. أطاعوا الشيطان فسلكوا مسالكه ووردوا مناهله بهم سارت أعلامه وقام لواؤه[2] في فتن داستهم بأخفافها ووطئتهم بأظلافها وقامت على سنابكها[3] فهم فيها تائهون حائرون جاهلون مفتونون في خير دار وشرّ جيران نومهم سهود وكحلهم دموع بأرض عالمها ملجم وجاهلها مكرم.

1.2.2 ومنها يعني آل النبيّ صلّى الله عليه وعلى آله
هم موضع سرّه ولَجَأُ أمره وعيبة علمه وموئل حكمه وكهوف كتبه وجبال دينه بهم أقام ٱنحناء ظهره وأذهب ٱرتعاد فرائصه.

منها في المنافقين
زرعوا الفجور وسقوه الغرور وحصدوا الثبور.
لا يقاس بآل محمّد صلّى الله عليه وسلّم من هذه الأمّة أحد ولا يسوّى بهم من جرت نعمتهم عليه أبدًا هم أساس الدين وعماد اليقين إليهم يفيء الغالي وبهم يلحق التالي ولهم خصائص حقّ الولاية وفيهم الوصيّة والوراثة الآن إذ رجع الحقّ إلى أهله ونُقل إلى منتقله.

____

١ي، هـ، ومصحّحة في ش: كذا. وأصل ش، ونسخة في ي: ﴿تزحزحت﴾.   ٢هـ، وأضيفت في ي: كذا. ش، وأصل ي: سقطت ﴿أطاعوا الشيطان ... وقام لواؤه﴾.   ٣هـ، وأضيفت في ي: كذا. ش، أصل ي: سقطت ﴿وقامت على سنابكها﴾.

mad arrived,[1] people were embroiled in seditions. Religion's rope was severed, conviction's foundations were shaken, principles were scattered, the community was shattered, the egress had narrowed, and a way out could not be seen. Right guidance was not recognized, and the blindness was total. The Merciful Lord was disobeyed, Satan was abetted, and faith had no support. Its pillars had come crashing down, its features were distorted, its paths had fallen into disrepair, and its trails had worn away. In obedience to Satan, people had followed his ways and alighted at his watering hole. With their support, his banners were raised high, and his pennants were unfurled. This was a time when sedition was ascendant, when people were crushed by its steeds and trampled under its hooves. Enmeshed in its throes, they were in a state of convulsion, lost, confused, and ignorant. They lived in the best of abodes but with the worst of neighbors. They lived in a land where the learned were demeaned and the ignorant esteemed. Here, slumber had turned into insomnia and kohl had been replaced by tears.

1.2.2 From the same oration, referring to the Prophet's family:
They are the embodiments of God's mystery, the foundations of his creed, the vessels of his knowledge, the harbors for his wisdom, the havens for his scriptures, and the peaks of his religion. Through them, he straightens religion's back when it becomes crooked, and calms its limbs when it trembles.

From the same oration, referring to the hypocrites:
They sowed immorality, watered it with arrogance, and reaped perdition.

No one from this community may be compared to Muḥammad's family, and no one blessed by God's favors may be equated with them in this regard. They are the pillar of religion and the column of certainty. The exaggerator must return to their position, and the laggard must join up with it. Theirs is the right of allegiance, theirs the Prophet's testament and inheritance. Now, in this moment, truth has been restored to its owners and returned to its home.

---

1   After Ḥ 1:137. These lines, from "*fī fitanin*," to the end of the section, have alternatively been read as a reference to the seditions in ʿAlī's time.

1.3   ومن خطبته المعروفة بالشِّقْشِقيّة[1]

1.3.1   أما والله لقد تقمّصها ٱبن أبي فلان[2] وإنّه ليعلم أنّ محلّي منها محلّ القطب من الرحا ينحدر عنّي السيل ولا يرقى إليّ الطير. فسدلت دونها ثوبًا وطويت عنها كشحًا وطفقت أرتإي بين أن أصول بيد جذّاء أو أصبر على طخية عمياء يهرم فيها الكبير ويشبّ[3] فيها الصغير ويكدح فيها مؤمن حتّى يلقى فيها ربّه. فرأيت أنّ الصبر على هاتا أحجى فصبرت وفي العين قذى وفي الحلق شجى أرى تراثي نهبًا.

1.3.2   حتّى مضى الأوّل لسبيله فأدلى بها إلى فلان بعده.

ثمّ تمثّل عليه السلام[4]

شَتَّانَ مَا يَوْمِي عَلٰى كُورِهَا   وَيَوْمُ حَيَّانٍ أَخِي أَخِي جَابِرِ

فيا عجبًا بينا هو يستقيلها في حياته إذ عقدها لآخر بعد وفاته. لشدّ ما تشطّرا ضرعيها. فصيّرها في حوزة خشناء يغلظ كَلْمها ويخشن مسّها ويكثر العثار والاعتذار منها.

---

[1] ش، ي: كذا. ﻫ: أضيفت ﴿والمقمّصة﴾.   [2] ش: كذا، وكلمة ﴿فلان﴾ مثبتة مكان كلمة مُحيت لعلّها ﴿قحافة﴾. ﻫ: سقطت ﴿ٱبن أبي﴾، ولكن قبل لفظة ﴿فلان﴾ بياض ربّما حيث مُحيت ﴿ٱبن أبي﴾. ي: سقطت ﴿ٱبن أبي﴾، وأضيفت فوق لفظة "فلان" ﴿ٱبن أبي قحافة﴾.   [3] ش، ﻫ، مع علامة الصحّة، ويبدو أصل ي: كذا. ومصحّحة في ي، ونسخة في ش: ﴿يشيب﴾.   [4] البحر السريع. ش، ي: كذا. ﻫ: أضيفت ﴿بقول الأعشى﴾.

1.3 From an oration by ʿAlī known as *Shiqshiqiyyah*—"The Roar of the Camel Stallion":[1]

1.3.1 By God, that man donned its cloak knowing that I am the pivot to its grinding stone—its stream flows from my summit and no soaring bird can reach my heights. I draped a curtain across it and turned my face away. I weighed two options: strike with an amputated hand or endure a blind darkness that renders adults infirm and children old, in which believers continue to brave toil and turmoil until they meet their Lord. I saw that forbearance was the judicious choice. So I endured—but my eyes filled with dust and my throat choked as I saw my inheritance looted.

1.3.2 Thus it was, until the first went on his way, tossing it to another after him.

Then ʿAlī recited a testimonial verse:[2]

O how different my days today, always in the saddle,
and the days of Jābir's brother, Ḥayyān!

How strange that he should wish to give it up during his lifetime yet secure it for another after his death! The two divided the milk from its udders between them! This next one corralled it to a stony field, where any who ventured sustained deep wounds and experienced rough passage. How often did people stumble in this terrain, and how often did they make excuses for stumbling!

---

1 Delivered in Raḥbah, south of Kufa, toward the end of ʿAlī's caliphate, in response to Ibn ʿAbbās's query about the Prophet's succession, according to Mufīd (*Irshād*, 287). Sibṭ (*Tadhkirah*, 124) states it was delivered on the pulpit of the Prophet's Mosque in Medina in 35/656, soon after ʿAlī was pledged allegiance as caliph, in response to a person calling out to him, "What kept you back until now?", but this earlier dating is unlikely given the reference in the final section (§1.3.4) to the three groups who rebelled against him. "It" in the first line is the caliphate, and "that man" (lit. *Ibn Abī fulān*, "son of so-and-so") is Abū Bakr, the first historical caliph. The second individual (§1.3.2) is Umar, and "the third" (§1.3.3) is ʿUthmān; "his clan" refers to the Umayyads. This oration is controversial because of its political content, but it is not so different from materials recorded by the earliest historians: Ibn Hishām (*Sīrah*, 2:489–490), Ṭabarī (*Tārīkh*, 4:231–233, 5:7–8), Yaʿqūbī (*Tārīkh*, 2:126), and Ibn Qutaybah (*Imāmah*, 1:28–33), all note ʿAlī's refusal to accept Abū Bakr as caliph until forced to do so. They also record ʿAlī's declarations about his right to the caliphate immediately after Muhammad's death, and during the deliberations of ʿUmar's Shūrā council. For details of this issue and further primary sources, see Madelung, *The Succession to Muḥammad*, 28–33, 141, and *passim*; and Madelung, "Shīʿa," *EI²*. The Shiʿi commentators read the oration as proof of ʿAlī's imamate, while the Sunni commentators read it as an articulation of ʿAlī's superiority over all other Companions of the Prophet. B 153–155; R 1:122; Ḥ 1:156–159; ʿA 565.

2 By the pre-Islamic poet Aʿshā Maymūn (d. ca. 7/629), *Dīwān al-Aʿshā*, 147, §18, verse 57.

فصاحبها كراكب الصعبة إن أشنق لها خرم وإن أسلس لها تقحّم فُني الناس لعمر الله بخبط وشِماس وتلوّن واعتراض. فصبرت على طول المدّة وشدّة المحنة.

1.3.3 حتّى إذا مضى لسبيله جعلها في جماعة زعم أنّي أحدهم فيا لله وللشورى متى اعترض الريب فيّ مع الأوّل منهم حتّى صرت أقرن إلى هذه النظائر لكنّي أسففت إذ أسفّوا وطرت إذ طاروا فصغى رجل منهم لضغنه ومال الآخر لصهره مع هنٍ وهنٍ إلى أن قام ثالث القوم نافجاً حضنيه بين نثيله ومعتلفه وقام معه بنو أبيه يخضمون مال الله تعالى خضم الإبل نبتة الربيع.

1.3.4 إلى أن انتكث عليه فتله وأجهز عليه عمله وكبت به بطنته. فما راعني إلّا والناس إليّ كعُرف الضبع ينثالون عليّ من كل جانب[1] حتّى لقد وُطِىء الحسنان وشقّ عطافي مجتمعين حولي كربيضة الغنم. فلمّا نهضت بالأمر نكثت طائفة ومرقت أخرى وفسق آخرون كأنّهم لم يسمعوا الله سبحانه يقول ﴿تِلْكَ ٱلدَّارُ ٱلْآخِرَةُ نَجْعَلُهَا لِلَّذِينَ لَا يُرِيدُونَ عُلُوًّا فِي ٱلْأَرْضِ وَلَا فَسَادًا وَٱلْعَاقِبَةُ لِلْمُتَّقِينَ﴾. بلى والله لقد سمعوها ووعوها ولكنّهم حليت الدنيا في أعينهم وراقهم زبرجها. أما والذي فلق الحبّة وبرأ النسمة لولا حضور الحاضر وقيام الحجّة بوجود الناصر وما أخذ الله على العلماء ألّا يقارّوا على كِظّة ظالم ولا سغب مظلوم لألقيت حبلها على غاربها ولسقيت آخرها بكأس أوّلها ولألفيتم دنياكم هذه أزهد عندي من عفطة عنز.

<hr>

١ ش، ونسخة في ي: كذا. هـ، وأصل ي: ﴿وجه﴾.

Any who traversed it rode a bucking camel—tighten its rein and slit its nose or loosen the ropes and be thrown. By God, the community was struck by kicking feet and rearing hooves and tormented with caprice and obstruction. I endured—but it was a long time and a harsh affliction.

1.3.3 Thus it was, until, when he went on his way, he handed it over to a group of people he supposed I belonged with. Dear God, what a Council! Was there doubt regarding my stature, even in comparison with the first of them, that I was now being equated with these laggards! But I moved with them, falling when they fell and flying when they flew. Even so, one of them turned away from me because of an old grudge,[1] another inclined toward someone else because he was related to him by marriage,[2] along with this one and that one, until the third stood up, bosom swelling with pride, amid his dung and fodder. His clan stood up with him, munching on God's property like a herd of camels munching on spring grass.

1.3.4 Thus it was, until its strands came apart in his hands and his own actions delivered the death blow. It was greed that brought him to the ground. Then suddenly, people were flocking to me, thick as a hyena's mane, trampling Ḥasan and Ḥusayn and rending my own shirt, pressing in on me from every side like a surging herd of sheep.[3] But when I rose to undertake its charge, one group of rebels broke their pledge, another deserted the faith, and a third went astray. Had they never heard God's words, «We shall reserve the hereafter for those who do not seek to exalt themselves on the earth or spread corruption. The good end is for the godfearing»?[4] Yes, by God, they heard and understood it, but the world appeared bejeweled to their eyes and her ornaments dazzled them. I swear by him who split open the seed, the one who created living beings—were it not for those who appealed to me in that time, if the presence of supporters had not made it my binding duty, if God had not taken a pledge from the learned that they would not permit tyrants to ravage or the subjugated to starve, I would have flung the caliphate's reins onto its shoulders and offered the same cup to its latest emissary that I had offered to its earliest one. If not for this, you would have seen that your world means less to me than the sneeze of a goat.

---

1   Saʿd ibn Abī Waqqāṣ. R 1:122; Ḥ 1:184, 189.
2   ʿAbd al-Raḥmān ibn ʿAwf. Ḥ 1:189.
3   Similar lines in §1.53, §1.135.2, §1.226.
4   Qurʾan, Qaṣaṣ 28:83.

1.3.5 قالوا وقام اليه رجل من أهل السواد عند بلوغه إلى هذا الموضع من خطبته فناوله كتابًا فأقبل ينظر فيه. فلمّا فرغ من قراءته قال له ٱبن عبّاس رحمة الله عليه يا أمير المؤمنين لو ٱطّردت مقالتك من حيث أفضيت فقال هيهات يا ٱبن عبّاس تلك شقشقة هدرت ثمّ قرّت قال ٱبن عبّاس فوالله ما أسفت على كلام قطّ كأسفي على ذلك الكلام ألّا يكون أمير المؤمنين عليه السلام بلغ منه حيث أراد.

1.3.6 قوله عليه السلام في هذه الخطبة ﴿ كراكب الصعبة إن أشنق لها خرم وإن أسلس لها تقحّم﴾ يريد أنّه إذا شدّد عليها في جذب الزمام وهي تنازعه رأسها خرم أنفها وإن أرخى لها شيئًا مع صعوبتها تقحّمت به فلم يملكها. يقال ﴿أشنق الناقة﴾ إذا جذب رأسها بالزمام فرفعه و﴿شنقها﴾ أيضًا. ذكر ذلك ٱبن السكّيت في إصلاح المنطق. وإنّما قال ﴿أشنق لها﴾ ولم يقل ﴿أشنقها﴾ لأنّه جعلها في مقابلة قوله ﴿أسلس لها﴾ فكأنّه عليه السلام قال ﴿إن رفع لها رأسها بالزمام﴾ بمعنى أمسكه عليها.

1.4 ومن خطبة له عليه السلام

بنا ٱهتديتم في الظلماء وتسنّمتم العلياء وبنا ٱنفجرتم عن السِّرار. وُقِر سمع لم يفقه الواعية كيف يراعي النبأة من أصمّته الصيحة رُبط جنان لم يفارقه الخفقان. ما زلت أنتظر بكم عواقب الغدر وأتوسّمكم بحلية المغترّين سترني عنكم جلباب الدين وبصّرنيكم صدق النيّة أقمت لكم على سنن الحقّ في جوادّ المضلّة حيث تلتقون ولا دليل وتحتفرون ولا تُميهون. اليوم أنطق لكم العجماء ذات البيان عزب رأي ٱمرئ تخلّف عنّي ما شككت في الحقّ

1.3.5 When ʿAlī reached this point in his oration, a visitor from the countryside handed him a petition, and he paused to look at it. When he had finished reading, Ibn ʿAbbās asked, "Commander of the Faithful, will you not continue your speech where you left off?" "No, Ibn ʿAbbās," ʿAlī replied, "that was the roar of a camel stallion that burst out then subsided." Ibn ʿAbbās remarked, "By God, I have never regretted the loss of any words as much as I regret the loss of these—if only the Commander of the Faithful had completed what he began!"

1.3.6 Raḍī: ʿAlī's words in this oration: "Any who traversed it rode a bucking camel— tighten its rein and slit its nose, or loosen it and be thrown," mean that if the rider were to pull strongly on the reins of a bucking came while it pulled the other way, he would slit its nose, but if he were to slacken them a little, then that, coupled with the camel's recalcitrance, would mean that the camel would throw him off, for he would be unable to control it. It is said, "He tightened the reins of the camel mare" (*ashnaqa l-nāqata*), when someone pulls back the camel's muzzle with the nose-rein and lifts it up; the basic form of the verb (*shanaqa*) is also used—Ibn al-Sikkīt mentions this in *Iṣlāḥ al-manṭiq* (Correcting Speech). ʿAlī said, "He tightened for it its reins (*ashnaqa lahā*)" (using the preposition *li-*),[1] rather than "He tightened its reins (*ashnaqahā*)" (with the camel as direct object), because he wanted to preserve the parallelism with "if he loosened them (*aslasa lahā*)," where he also used the preposition *li-*. It is as though ʿAlī said, "if he raised the camel's head upward with the nose-rein," meaning that he held the camel tightly by means of it.

1.4 From an oration by ʿAlī:[2]

Through us you received guidance in the dark night, mounted the camel's lofty hump, and emerged from a moonless night into the light of dawn. How deaf are the ears that don't hear the mourners' wails! Can people whom a clap of thunder fails to awaken be expected to heed a gentle voice? How calm is the heart that shudders in fear of God! I knew you would be treacherous, for I saw you donning seduction's garb. But I wear the robe of religion, and it has prevented me from harming you, though my righteous spirit showed me clearly what you were. I stood up to guide you back to the trodden path of truth, from all those trails where you had wandered without a guide, where you had dug for water but found none. Today I have made mute signs, eloquent ones, speak to you. Those who held back from me have strayed. I never doubted the truth since it

---

1 *Li-* is the usual form of this preposition, but it changes to *la-* before pronominals, as it has here and a few lines below.

2 After the Battle of the Camel in 36/656, posthumously addressing Ṭalḥah and Zubayr, and their defeated followers. R 136, after Miskawayh; Ḥ 1:209; B 164.

مذ أريته لم يوجس موسى خيفة على نفسه أشفق من غلبة الجهّال ودول الضلّال اليوم تواقفنا على سبيل الحقّ والباطل من وثق بماء لم يظمأ.

1.5 ومن كلام له عليه السلام لمّا قبض رسول الله صلّى الله عليه وآله وخاطبه العبّاس وأبو سفيان ٱبن حرب في أن يبايعاه بالخلافة

أيّها الناس شقّوا أمواج الفتن بسفن النجاة وعرّجوا عن طريق المنافرة وضعوا تيجان المفاخرة. أفلح من نهض بجناح أو ٱستلسم فأراح. ماء آجن ولقمة يغصّ بها آكلها ومجتني الثمرة لغير وقت إيناعها كالزارع بغير أرضه فإن أقل يقولوا حرص على الملك وإن أسكت يقولوا جزع من الموت هيهات ‹بعد اللتيا والتي› والله لٱبن أبي طالب آنس بالموت من الطفل بثدي أمّه بل ٱندمجت على مكنون علم لو بُحْتُ به لٱضطربتم ٱضطراب الأرشية في الطويّ البعيدة.

1.6 ومن كلام له عليه السلام لمّا أشير عليه بألّا يتّبع طلحة والزبير ولا يرصد لهما القتال

والله لا أكون كالضَّبُع تنام على طول اللَّدْم حتّى يصل إليها طالبها ويختلها راصدها

was shown to me. Moses was not fearful for his life—what he feared was the dominance of the ignorant and the control of the errant.[1] Today, we faced off on the battlefield, one on the side of right, the other on the side of wrong. A man who knows he will find water does not feel thirst.

1.5 An address ʿAlī delivered when God's Messenger passed away, and ʿAbbās and Abū Sufyān came to him offering the pledge of caliphal allegiance:[2]

People! Cut through the waves of rebellion by boarding the ark of salvation. Leave the path of dissension and cast off the crown of pride. Success comes to those who rise when they have support, or yield and let people be. This affair resembles murky water, or a morsel that chokes those who swallow it. One who plucks before his time gains as little as one who plants in another's field. If I say something now, they will respond, "He covets power." If I remain silent, they will cry, "He is afraid of being killed!" No, indeed, ⟨not after the small calamity and the large one⟩![3] By God, Abū Ṭālib's son is more comfortable with death than an infant at his mother's breast! But I hold knowledge of mysteries. Were I to reveal them to you, you would tremble like ropes hanging down deep wells.

1.6 From an address ʿAlī delivered when advised not to pursue Ṭalḥah and Zubayr or make preparations to fight them:[4]

By God, I shall not behave like the hyena that, sleeping through a prolonged barrage of pebbles, is captured by the stealthy hunter.[5] I call on men who have

---

1   Refers to the Qurʾanic story of Moses (Qurʾan, Hūd 11:70, Ṭāhā 20:67), and compares ʿAlī's story to it.

2   In 11/632, in Medina. Ṭabrisī (*Iḥtijāj*, 1:127) cites the first three lines as part of a note ʿAlī wrote to Abū Bakr, after he had denied Fāṭimah her right to inherit the orchards of Fadak. ʿAbbās ibn ʿAbd al-Muṭṭalib was ʿAlī and Muḥammad's uncle. Abū Sufyān was Muʿāwiyah's father and Muḥammad's arch foe, before he converted to Islam following the Prophet's conquest of Mecca. The two—ʿAbbās and Abū Sufyān—were close associates.

3   Proverb signifying all sorts of calamities (etiology in Maydānī, *Majmaʿ*, 1:92), signifying that ʿAlī has faced death on the battlefield throughout his life.

4   In Rabadhah, near Medina, in 36/656, enroute to Iraq in the lead-up to the Battle of the Camel (Ṭabarī, *Tārīkh*, 4:455–456), or in Dhū Qār, soon after arriving in Iraq (ibid., 4:457–458); ʿAlī's son Ḥasan is named as his interlocutor.

5   See similar phraseology in §1.146. The signification of the simile is being naively unaware of danger despite ample warning. In medieval Arab lore, the hyena (*ḍabuʿ*) is reputed to be a stupid animal. Easily tricked by the hunter who throws pebbles to draw it out, it emerges from its den, thinking to find prey, and is killed. Hyenas were apparently hunted as food; their meat is considered licit in the Shāfiʿī and Ḥanbalī schools of law, and a delicacy in present-day Saudi Arabia (Osborne, "Hyena Burger?"). B 170; R 149; Ḥ 224; Ibn Manẓūr, *Lisān*, s.v. "L-D-Gh"; Jāḥiẓ, *Ḥayawān*, 6:38, 7:48; Damīrī, *Ḥayāt al-ḥayawān*, 2:206. For further details and sources, see Viré, "Ḍabuʿ," *EI*[2].

ولكنّي أضرب بالمقبل إلى الحقّ المدبر عنه وبالسامع المطيع العاصي المريب أبدًا حتّى يأتي عليّ يومي. فوالله ما زلت مدفوعًا عن حقّي مستأثرًا عليّ منذ قبض الله نبيّه صلّى الله عليه حتّى يوم الناس هذا.

١.٧   ومن خطبة له عليه السلام

اتّخذوا الشيطان لأمرهم ملاكًا واتّخذهم له أشراكًا فباض وفرّخ في صدورهم ودبّ ودرج في حجورهم فنظر بأعينهم ونطق بألسنتهم فركب بهم الزلل وزيّن لهم الخطل فعل من قد شركه الشيطان في سلطانه ونطق بالباطل على لسانه.

١.٨   ومن كلام له عليه السلام يعني به الزبير

يزعم أنّه قد بايع بيده ولم يبايع بقلبه فقد أقرّ بالبيعة وادّعى الوليجة فليأت عليها بأمر يعرف وإلّا فليدخل فيما خرج منه.

١.٩   ومن كلام له عليه السلام

وقد أرعدوا وأبرقوا ومع هٰذين الأمرين الفشل ولسنا نرعد حتى نوقع ولا نسيل حتّى نمطر.

١.١٠   ومن خطبة له عليه السلام

ألا وإنّ الشيطان قد جمع حزبه واستجلب خيله ورجله وإنّ بصيرتي لمعي٢ ما لبّست على نفسي ولا لبّس عليّ وايم الله لأفرطنّ لهم حوضًا أنا ماتحه لا يصدرون عنه ولا يعودون إليه.

١ش، ي: كذا. هـ: ﴿مالكًا﴾.   ٢ش، ي: كذا. هـ: ﴿وإنّ معي لبصيرتي﴾.

accepted the truth to attack those who have turned away. I call on those who hear and obey to fight those doubters who have disobeyed. I shall continue to call on you until my appointed time arrives. By God! From the day God took his Messenger unto him until this day, I have been continually driven away from this thing that is mine by right and passed over for another.

1.7   From an oration by ʿAlī:[1]
They made Satan master of their affairs and he made them his partners. He laid eggs in their breasts and hatched chicks. He frolicked in their laps and romped. He watched with their eyes and spoke with their tongues. He incited them to error and lured them to treachery. Their actions are the actions of people whose rule Satan shares and on whose tongues he utters his falsehoods.

1.8   From an address ʿAlī delivered about Zubayr:[2]
He declares that he pledged allegiance with his hand but not his heart. So he admits his pledge, although he claims he withheld intent. Let him bring tangible proof of that, or else return to the pledge he has forsaken.

1.9   From an address ʿAlī delivered:[3]
They thundered and blazed but that is the way of cowards. My thunder always strikes, and my torrent is always propelled by rain.

1.10   From an oration by ʿAlī:[4]
Hark! Satan has mustered his host and armed his cavalry and infantry. But my conviction has not deserted me, I have never deceived nor been deceived. By God, I shall fill the waterhole for them as only I can—they shall not leave sated or return.[5]

---

1   Presumably referring to ʿAlī's challengers at the battles of the Camel, Ṣiffīn, or Nahrawān. The referents are described by Rāwandī as "the errant leaders" (*aʾimmat al-ḍalāl*), but neither he nor the other major commentators specify names. Ḥ 1:228; B 170–171; R 1:151–152.
2   Responding just before the Battle of the Camel, in 36/656, to a speech by Zubayr's son ʿAbdallāh, in which he stated his father's claim. Mufīd, *Jamal*, 175, after Wāqidī.
3   Refers to ʿAlī's challengers at the Battle of the Camel in 36/656 (R 1:154, B 173). The lines are from an oration ʿAlī delivered in response to a speech by Ṭalḥah, just before battle commenced. Mufīd, *Jamal*, 177, after Wāqidī.
4   Delivered at Dhū Qār, thus in 36/656, en route to Basra (B 172), referring to ʿAlī's challengers at the Battle of the Camel. Alternatively, delivered at an unspecified time, and referring to Muʿāwiyah (Ḥ 1:240; R 1:155). See similar lines in §1.22 and §1.135.
5   The "waterhole" here refers to battle, and by saying he will fill it as only he can, ʿAlī refers to his prowess in combat. Ḥ 1:240; R 155.

1.11   ومن كلامه عليه السلام لابنه محمّد بن الحنفيّة لمّا أعطاه الراية يوم الجمل

تزول الجبال ولا تزل عضّ على ناجذك أعِر الله جمجمتك تِدْ في الأرض قدمك ارم ببصرك أقصى القوم وغضّ بصرك واعلم أنّ النصر من عند الله سبحانه.

1.12   ومن كلام له عليه السلام لمّا ظفر بأصحاب الجمل وقد قال له بعض أصحابه وددت أنّ أخي[1] كان شاهدًا ليرى ما نصرك الله به على أعدائك فقال أهَوى معنا أخيك فقال نعم قال فقد شهدنا. ولقد شهدنا في عسكرنا هذا قوم في أصلاب الرجال وأرحام النساء سيرعف بهم الزمان ويقوى بهم الإيمان.

1.13   ومن كلام له عليه السلام في ذمّ البصرة وأهلها

كنتم جند المرأة وأتباع البهيمة رغا فأجبتم وعُقر فهربتم أخلاقكم دقاق وعهدكم شقاق ودينكم نفاق وماؤكم زُعاق المقيم بين أظهركم مرتهن بذنبه والشاخص عنكم متدارك برحمة من ربّه. كأنّي بمسجدكم كجؤجؤ سفينة قد بعث الله عليها العذاب من فوقها ومن تحتها وغرّق من في ضمنها.

وفي رواية أخرى

وايم الله لتغرقنّ بلدتكم حتّى كأنّي أنظر إلى مسجدها كجؤجؤ سفينة أو نَعامة جاثمة.

ويروى

كجؤجؤ طير في لُجّة بحر.

---

[1] ش: كذا. ي، هـ: أضيفت ﴿فلانًا﴾.

1.11 From an address ʿAlī delivered to his son Muḥammad ibn al-Ḥanafiyyah, while entrusting him with the banner at the Battle of the Camel:[1]

Mountains may move, but you should not. Clench your teeth. Lend God your skull.[2] Dig your feet into the earth. Keep an eye on your farthest foes but focus on those who are close. Above all, know this: Victory comes from Almighty God.

1.12 From an address by ʿAlī, after his victory at the Battle of the Camel. One of his supporters said to him, "I wish my brother were present to witness the victory God has granted you over your enemies." ʿAlī asked, "Does your brother's loyalty lie with us?" The man replied, "Yes," and ʿAlī declared:[3]

Then he has witnessed us. Indeed, our fight has been witnessed by a mighty host in the loins of men and the wombs of women. Time will bring them forth and faith will gain strength.

1.13 An address ʿAlī delivered criticizing Basra and rebuking its people:[4]

You fought for the woman and followed the camel—when it bellowed, you answered, when it was killed, you fled. Your character is base, your custom is dissent, your faith is hypocrisy, and your water is bitter. Whoever resides with you is ensnared in sin, whoever leaves you is saved by God's mercy. I can see your mosque now, the prow of a ship enveloped by God's punishment from above and below. All on board will drown.

A variant narrative:

I swear by God, your city will drown! I see your mosque like a ship's prow, or a squatting ostrich.

It is also narrated as:

Like a bird's breast rising above the swells of the sea.

---

1 Basra, 36/656.

2 The commentators decode the metaphor as putting one's life on the line to defend God's religion; they also say the word "lend" (*aʿir*), (rather than "give"), denotes a promise that Ibn al-Ḥanafiyyah would not be killed in this battle. R 158–159, B 173, Ḥ 1:242.

3 According to Baḥrānī (B 174), this and the next texts (presumably § 1.13–1.14) are from a single oration ʿAlī delivered in Basra three days after the Battle of the Camel in Basra, in 36/656. He had criers call out for the people to gather, and when they had assembled, he stepped into the mosque, prayed the morning prayer, stood on the right side of the prayer niche with his back against the wall, and gave this speech. The lines are also placed at Nahrawān, following the battle there in 38/658. Barqī, *Maḥāsin*, 1:262.

4 See note to § 1.12. The reference in the first line is to ʿĀʾishah and the camel she rode onto the battlefield at the Battle of the Camel. B 175; Ḥ 1:252.

1.14 ومن كلام له في مثل ذلك

أرضكم قريبة من الماء بعيدة من السماء. خفّت عقولكم وسفهت حلومكم فأنتم غرض لنابل وأكلة لآكل وفريسة لصائل.[1]

1.15 ومن كلام له عليه السلام فيما ردّه على المسلمين من قطائع عثمان

والله لو وجدته قد تُزوّج به النساء ومُلك به الإماء لرددته فإنّ في العدل سعة ومن ضاق عليه العدل فالجور عليه أضيق.

1.16 من كلام له عليه السلام لمّا بويع بالمدينة

ذمّتي بما أقول رهينة وأنا به زعيم إنّ من صرّحت له العبر عمّا بين يديه من المثلات حجزه التقوى عن تقحّم الشبهات ألا وإنّ بليّتكم قد عادت كهيئتها يوم بعث الله نبيّه والذي بعثه بالحقّ لتبلبلنّ بلبلة ولتغربلنّ غربلة ولتساطنّ سوط القدر حتّى يعود أسفلكم أعلاكم وأعلاكم أسفلكم وليسبقنّ سابقون كانوا قصّروا وليقصّرنّ سبّاقون كانوا سبقوا. والله ما كتمت وشمة ولا كذبت كذبة ولقد نبّئت بهذا المقام وهذا اليوم. ألا وإنّ الخطايا خيل شمس حمل عليها أهلها وخلعت لجمها فتقحّمت بهم في النار ألا وإنّ التقوى مطايا ذلل حمل عليها أهلها وأعطوا أزمّتها فأوردهم الجنّة. حقّ وباطل ولكلّ أهل فلئن أمِر الباطل لقديماً فعل ولئن قلّ الحقّ لربّما ولعلّ ولقلّما أدبر شيء فأقبل. شغل من الجنّة والنار أمامه. ساعٍ سريع نجا وطالب بطيء رجا ومقصّر في النار. اليمين والشمال مضلّة

---

[1] ش، ي: كذا. هـ: ﴿لصائد﴾.

1.14 From a similar address delivered by ʿAlī:[1]

Your land is close to the sea and far from the sky. Your wits are feeble and your minds are weak. You are targets for the archer, morsels for the greedy, and easy prey for all who would attack.

1.15 ʿAlī's address defending his restoration of ʿUthmān's land grants to the public treasury:[2]

By God, even if the money had been spent to wed women or buy slave-girls, I would still have required its return. Justice has a wide scope—whoever finds it narrow should know that oppression is even more limiting.

1.16 From an address ʿAlī delivered when the pledge of allegiance was sworn to him in Medina:[3]

I guarantee the truth of what I say and stand as surety for my pledge. To be cautioned by history's lessons is to be protected by piety from galloping headlong into the abyss of doubt. Hark my words! You are being tested today, just as you were on the day God sent his Prophet. I swear by the one who sent him with the truth that you will be tossed hither and thither, sifted as in a sieve, and mixed and mingled as if in a boiling cauldron. Lowly folk will rise, and others in high positions will fall. Stragglers will race to the front, and others who are ahead will fall behind. By God, I have never held back a true word or spoken a single lie, and I was told of the arrival of this place and day. Hark my words! Sins are recalcitrant steeds, charging unreined with their riders into the Fire. Hear me! Piety is a docile mount that carries its riders, reins firm in their hands, steadily to paradise. There is truth and there is falsehood, and each has its people— what is new if falsehood prevails? Truth has few followers, and those who turn away rarely return. Those who see paradise or hellfire ahead have enough to occupy them. The swift runner is saved, the man who is tardy has hope, but the delinquent will end in the Fire. The right and the left lead to error, the middle

---

1   See note to §1.12. Wāqidī, cited in Mufīd, *Jamal*, 218, also places this oration on the battlefield immediately after the Battle of the Camel.

2   Lit. "to the Muslims." ʿAlī delivered this oration in Medina in 35/656, soon after allegiance was pledged to him as caliph (B 178; Nuʿmān, *Daʿāʾim*, 1:396). The second sentence also forms part of ʿAlī's address to Marwān et al. when they refused to pledge him allegiance (Yaʿqūbī, *Tārīkh*, 2:179).

3   First oration after assuming the caliphate in Medina in 35/656, delivered on the pulpit in the mosque; one of ʿAlī's most widely narrated orations (Jāḥiẓ, *Bayān*, 3:50–52, who adds a section on the excellence of the Prophet's family, narrated by Jaʿfar al-Ṣādiq). Yaʿqūbī (*Tārīkh*, 2:211) states that the oration was prompted by a man who criticized ʿAlī's judgment in a case he had brought before him.

والطريق الوسطى هي الجادّة عليها باقي الكتاب وآثار النبوّة ومنها منفذ السنّة وإليها مصير العاقبة. هلك من ادّعى و﴿خَابَ مَنِ ٱفْتَرَىٰ﴾ من أبدى صفحته للحقّ هلك عند جهلة الناس. وكفى بالمرء جهلًا ألّا يعرف قدره. لا يهلك على التقوى سنخ أصل ولا يظمأ عليه زرع قوم. فاستتروا ببيوتكم وأصلحوا ذات بينكم والتوبة من ورائكم. ولا يحمد حامد إلّا ربّه ولا يلم لائم إلّا نفسه.

وأقول إنّ في هذا الكلام من مواقع الإحسان ما لا تبلغه مواقع الاستحسان وإنّ حظّ العَجَب منه أكثر من حظّ العُجب به وفيه مع الحال التي وصفنا زوائد من الفصاحة لا يقوم بها لسان ولا يطّلع كنهها إنسان ولا يعرف ما أقوله إلّا من ضرب في هذه الصناعة بحقّ وجرى فيها على عرق وما يعقلها إلّا العالمون.

1.17 ومن كلام له عليه السلام في صفة من يتصدّى للحكم بين الأمّة وليس لذلك بأهل إنّ أبغض الخلائق إلى الله رجلان. رجل وكّله الله إلى نفسه فهو جائر عن قصد السبيل مشغوف بكلام بدعة ودعاء ضلالة فهو فتنة لمن افتتن به ضالٌّ عن هدى من كان قبله مضلّ لمن اقتدى به في حياته وبعد وفاته حمّال خطايا غيره رهن بخطيئته. ورجل قَمَشَ جهلًا مُوضِعٌ في جهّال الأمّة غارٍ في أغباش الفتنة عمٍ بما في عقد الهدنة قد سمّاه أشباه الناس عالمًا وليس به بكّر فاستكثر من جمع ما قلّ منه خير ممّا كثر حتّى إذا ارتوى من آجن وأكثر من غير طائل جلس بين الناس قاضيًا ضامنًا لتخليص ما التبس على غيره فإن نزلت به إحدى المبهمات هيّأ لها حشوًا رثًّا من رأيه ثمّ قطع به. فهو من لبس الشبهات في مثل نسج العنكبوت لا يدري أصاب أم أخطأ إن أصاب خاف أن يكون

way is the straight road, upon it you will find the remnants of scripture and the traces of prophecy, from it emerged the Sunnah, to it the people shall return. False claimants will perish and «those who lie will fail.»[1] Those who side with the truth will suffer at the hands of the ignorant. It is manifest ignorance for a man not to know his own worth! But fields sown by the pious will not wither. Roots planted by them will not shrivel. People, maintain the privacy of your homes and resolve your differences, and you will be forgiven. Praise only your Lord and blame only yourselves.

Raḍī: No admiration can encompass the beauty in these words; the awe they inspire exceeds any expression of appreciation. They have so much linguistic brilliance that no tongue can do them justice and no human can plumb their deep ravine. Only expert knowledge of this craft and an innate disposition for it can comprehend what I allude to. Only the learned can grasp the full meaning of this oration.

1.17 From an address ʿAlī delivered describing men who set themselves up as judges for the community when they are far from qualified:[2]

The most hateful creatures in God's eyes are of two kinds: The first is a man whom God has given up on and left to his own devices. Straying from the straight path, enamored of heretical innovation and errant agitation, he ensnares many. Having lost his predecessors' path of right guidance, he leads people astray in his lifetime and continues his misguidance after his death. Surely, he will bear the burden of their sins, while remaining hostage to his own. The second collects scraps of ignorance and engages with the community's dolts. Heedless of the black beasts of mutiny, he is blind to the benefits of peace. His comrades call him a scholar, but he is not. He is hasty to amass things of which less is better than more. When he has drunk his fill of stagnant water and increased his store without profit, he sits down to dispense judgment, to elucidate what has perplexed others. When faced with an impenetrable case, he stitches together a jumble of rags concocted from his own capricious opinions, then passes judgment. Yet, he remains entangled in a web of doubt,[3] not

---

1 Qurʾan, Ṭāhā 20:61.
2 Māmaṭīrī (*Nuzhah*, 317–319), Abū Ṭālib al-Makkī (*Qūt al-qulūb*, 1:246), and Hārūnī (*Taysīr*, 259) connect this oration to the previous one, viz., ʿAlī's accession speech, §1.16. Yaʿqūbī (*Tārīkh*, 2:211) also connects it, but he places the oration in a different context; see note at §1.16.
3 Echoes Qurʾan, ʿAnkabūt 29:41.

قد أخطأ وإن أخطأ رجا أن يكون قد أصاب. جاهل خبّاط جهالات عاشٍ ركّاب عشوات لم يعضّ على العلم بضرس قاطع يذري الروايات إذراء الريح الهشيم لا ملي‌ء والله بإصدار ما ورد عليه لا يحسب العلم في شي‌ء ممّا أنكره ولا يرى أنّ من وراء ما بلغ منه مذهبًا لغيره وإن أظلم عليه أمر أكتتم به لما يعلم من جهل نفسه. تصرخ من جور قضائه الدماء وتعجّ منه المواريث. إلى الله أشكو من معشر يعيشون جهّالًا ويموتون ضلّالًا ليس فيهم سلعة أبور من الكتّاب إذا تلي حقّ تلاوته ولا سلعة أنفق بيعًا ولا أغلى ثمنًا من الكتّاب إذا حرّف عن مواضعه ولا عندهم أنكر من المعروف ولا أعرف من المنكر.

1.18 ومن كلام له عليه السلام في ذمّ آختلاف العلماء في الفتيا

ترد على أحدهم القضيّة في حكم من الأحكام فيحكم فيها برأيه ثمّ ترد تلك القضيّة بعينها على غيره فيحكم فيها بخلاف قوله ثمّ تجتمع القضاة بذلك عند إمامهم الذي آستقضاهم فيصوّب آراءهم جميعًا. وإلههم واحد وكتابهم واحد ونبيّهم واحد. أفأمرهم الله تعالى بالاختلاف فأطاعوه أم نهاهم عنه فعصوه أم أنزل الله دينًا ناقصًا فآستعان بهم على إتمامه أم كانوا شركاء له فلهم[1] أن يقولوا وعليه أن يرضى أم أنزل الله سبحانه دينًا تامًّا فقصّر الرسول صلّى الله عليه وآله عن تبليغه وأدائه والله سبحانه يقول ﴿مَا فَرَّطْنَا فِي ٱلْكِتَابِ مِن شَيْءٍ﴾ وفيه تبيان كلّ شي‌ء. وذكر أنّ الكتّاب يصدّق بعضه بعضًا وأنّه لا آختلاف فيه فقال سبحانه ﴿وَلَوْ كَانَ مِنْ عِندِ غَيْرِ ٱللَّهِ لَوَجَدُوا فِيهِ ٱخْتِلَافًا كَثِيرًا﴾ وإنّ القرآن ظاهره أنيق وباطنه عميق لا تفنى عجائبه ولا تنقضي غرائبه ولا تكشف الظلمات إلّا به.

---

[1] تبدأ مخطوطة م من هنا.

knowing whether he has judged correctly or erred. When correct, he is afraid he may have erred. When errant, he hopes he judged correctly. A total ignoramus, he stumbles about in his ignorance like the night-blind riding the steeds of darkness. Never biting into knowledge with strong teeth, he flings around hadith reports as the wind scatters dry leaves.[1] By God, he is not qualified to judge the cases that come to his waterhole. He dismisses whatever is beyond his understanding, not realizing that others have found a path. When a case is too obscure for him to grasp, he hides the fact, for he knows he lacks knowledge. The blood of the executed screams from his oppression, and inheritances cry out from his injustice. God, I complain to you of men who live in ignorance and die in error! No commodity is less profitable to them than the Qur'an when explained correctly, no commodity more profitable or more valuable than that same Qur'an with its meanings corrupted. Nothing for them is worse than good, nothing better than evil.

1.18 From an address 'Alī delivered censuring disagreement among jurists:[2]
When a case comes to one of them, he passes judgment based on his capricious opinion. Then the same case is brought before someone else, who gives a different judgment. Then all the judges congregate before the leader who appointed them, and he confirms all their judgments. This, when their God is one, their Book is one, and their Prophet is one! Did God command them to disagree such that they are simply obeying him? Rather, did he not forbid it and they disobeyed? Did God send down an imperfect religion and seek their help to complete it? Or did he make them his partners such that he must accept their whims? Or, yet again, did he actually send a perfect religion, and it was the Messenger who fell short in conveying and delivering it? God says, «We have omitted nothing from the Book.»[3] It contains clarification of all things. He declares that one part of the Book supports the other without contradiction, saying, «If it had come from someone other than God, they would have found it to have many inconsistencies.»[4] The Qur'an's form is elegant, and its content is deep. Its marvels never fade, and its wonders never run out. Only through the Qur'an can darkness be dispelled.

---

1   Modified quote from Qur'an, Kahf 18:45.
2   Ibn Ṭalḥah (*Maṭālib*, 118) presents this oration as a continuation of the previous one §1.17.
3   Qur'an, Anʿām 6:38.
4   Qur'an, Nisāʾ 4:82.

1.19   ومن كلام له عليه السلام قاله للأشعث بن قيس وهو على منبر الكوفة يخطب فمضى في بعض كلامه شيء اعترضه الأشعث فقال يا أمير المؤمنين هذه عليك لا لك. فخفض عليه السلام إليه بصره ثمّ قال

وما يدريك ما عليّ ممّا لي عليك لعنة الله ولعنة اللاعنين حائك ابن حائك منافق ابن كافر والله لقد أسرك الكفر مرّة والإسلام أخرى فما فداك من واحدة منهما مالك ولا حسبك وإنّ امرأً دلّ على قومه السيف وساق إليهم الحتف لحريّ أن يمقته الأقرب ولا يأمنه الأبعد.

يريد أنّه أسر في الكفر مرّة وفي الإسلام مرّة. وأمّا قوله ⟨دلّ على قومه السيف⟩ فأراد به حديثًا كان للأشعث مع خالد بن الوليد باليمامة غرّ فيه قومه ومكر بهم حتّى أوقع خالد بهم وكان قومه بعد ذلك يسمّونه عُرف النار وهو اسم للغادر عندهم.

1.20   ومن خطبة له عليه السلام

فإنّكم لو عاينتم ما قد عاين من مات منكم لجزعتم ووهلتم وسمعتم وأطعتم ولكن محجوب عنكم ما عاينوا وقريب ما يُطرح الحجاب ولقد بُصّرتم إن أبصرتم وأُسمعتم إن سمعتم وهديتم إن اهتديتم. بحقّ أقول لكم لقد جاهرتكم العبر وزجرتم بما فيه مزدجر وما يبلّغ عن الله بعد رسل السماء إلّا البشر.

1.21   ومن خطبة له عليه السلام

فإنّ الغاية أمامكم وإنّ وراء كم الساعة تحدوكم تخفّفوا تلحقوا فإنّما يُنتظر بأوّلكم آخرُكم.

1.19 From words 'Alī spoke to al-Ashʿath ibn Qays while orating on the pulpit of Kufa. Ashʿath objected to something in 'Alī's speech, interjecting, "Commander of the Faithful, this point goes against you, it doesn't count in your favor," and 'Alī looked at him and exclaimed:[1]

What do you know about what goes against me or counts in my favor? God's curse upon you—weaver, son of a weaver,[2] hypocrite, son of an infidel—and the curse of all who curse! By God, unbelief captured you once, and Islam another time, and on neither occasion did your wealth or ancestry serve as ransom! If a man lifts the sword against his own tribe and brings death to them, he deserves to be hated by kin and feared by strangers.

Raḍī: 'Alī means that Ashʿath was taken captive once as an unbeliever and once as a Muslim. Regarding his words, "lifts the sword against his own tribe," he is alluding to a conversation between Ashʿath and Khālid ibn al-Walīd in Yamāmah, in which Ashʿath deceived his tribe and plotted against them, leading to Khālid's attack and defeat of them. After this incident, Ashʿath's kinsfolk named him "Cockscomb-of-the-Fire," a name they used for traitors.

1.20 From an oration by 'Alī:

If you saw what the dead see, you would be stricken with grief and fear, and would listen and obey. What they see is veiled from you, but soon the veil will be cast aside. The fact is, you have been given the capacity to see if you would but look, to hear if you would but listen, to be guided if you would but follow! I say this to you in truth: the world's deathly lessons have called out to you and given you harsh warning. After God's messengers who descend from the sky, who else but humans convey his message?

1.21 From an oration by 'Alī:[3]

The end is before you and the dreaded hour drives your caravan to the waterhole. Lighten your burden and catch up, for those who have gone ahead await those who remain behind.

---

1   After the Battle of Nahrawān in 38/658; 'Alī spoke of the arbitration, and Ashʿath sided with the Kharijite position. Ḥ 1:296.

2   This is a generic insult about weaving as a lowly trade, and not a remark about Ashʿath's or his father's actual trade. The commentators explain that 'Alī is (1) using Ashʿath's own worldly criteria to denigrate him (Ḥ 1:296–297; R 184–185), or (2) alluding to the assumption that weavers are not astute about affairs of war and government (B 193).

3   Excerpt from §1.165, from the early part of 'Alī's caliphate in Medina in 35/656, perhaps his first oration (Ṭabarī, *Tārīkh*, 4:436). "Your burden" is explained as sin.

وأقول إنّ هذا الكلام لو وزن بعد كلام الله سبحانه وكلام رسول الله صلّى الله عليه وآله بكلّ
كلام لمال به راجحًا وبرّز عليه سابقًا. فأمّا قوله عليه السلام ⟨تخفّفوا تلحقوا⟩ فما سمع كلام أقلّ
منه مسموعًا ولا أكثر محصولًا وما أبعد غورها من كلمة وأنقع نطفتها من حكمة. وقد نبّهنا في
كتاب الخصائص على عظم قدرها وشرف جوهرها.

1.22 ومن خطبة له عليه السلام

ألا وإنّ الشيطان قد ذمر حزبه واستجلب جلبه ليعود الجور إلى أوطانه ويرجع الباطل
إلى نصابه. والله ما أنكروا عليّ منكرًا ولا جعلوا بيني وبينهم نصفًا وإنّهم ليطلبون حقًّا
تركوه ودمًا هم سفكوه. فإن كنت شريكهم فيه فإنّ لهم لنصيبهم منه ولئن كانوا ولوه
دوني فما التبعة إلّا عندهم وإنّ أعظم حجّتهم لعلى أنفسهم. يرتضعون أُمًّا قد فطمت
ويحيون بدعة قد أميتت يا خيبة الداعي من دعا وإلى ما أجيب وإنّي لراضٍ بحجّة الله
عليهم وعلمه فيهم فإن أبوا أعطيتهم حدّ السيف وكفى به شافيًا من الباطل وناصرًا للحقّ.
ومن العجب بعثهم إليّ أن أبرز للطعان وأن أصبر للجلاد هبلتهم الهبول لقد كنت وما
أهدّد بالحرب ولا أرهّب بالضرب وإنّي لعلى يقين من ربّي وغير شبهة من ديني.¹

1.23 ومن خطبة له عليه السلام

<hr>

¹ش، م، ه، ونسخة في ي: كذا. أصل ي: كذا. أصل ي، ونسخة في ه: ⟨أمري⟩.

Raḍī: If these words were weighed against any other, barring the words of God and the words of his Messenger, they would outweigh and outstrip them all. Regarding ʿAlī's statement, "Lighten your burden and catch up," no pithier or weightier words have ever been heard. How deep the meaning of this maxim, how pure its font of wisdom! I have further discussed its tremendous value and noble essence in The Book of Special Attributes (*Kitāb al-Khaṣāʾiṣ*).[1]

1.22 From an oration by ʿAlī:[2]

Hear me! Satan has roared to his followers and herded his camels in order to return oppression to its homeland and restore evil to its roost. By God, they have no cause to fault me or seek redress. Rather, they demand from me a right they abandoned and vengeance for blood they spilt. If I had been their partner in this affair, they would still have their share of culpability. But if they have undertaken it on their own—which they have, without me—then they keep all the blame and their main allegation rebounds to them. In truth, they suckle at the breast of a woman who has weaned her young,[3] and resurrect a heresy that has been put to death. Losers, every one of them, the issuers of this call! Who is it, pray, who calls, and to what purpose do they expect me to answer? I am satisfied with God's proof against them and his knowledge of their deeds! If they persist, I will consign them to my blade—that will cure wrong and instate right! Is it not strange that they challenge me to face their spears and threaten me with sharpened swords? May their mothers mourn! I have never been intimidated by threats of battle or panicked by an impending attack. I have ever trusted my Lord and never doubted my faith.

1.23 From an oration by ʿAlī:[4]

---

1 Raḍī, *Khaṣāʾiṣ*, 112.

2 In the lead-up to the Battle of the Camel in Basra in 36/656: After ʿAlī's emissaries returned from speaking with Ṭalḥah, Zubayr, and ʿĀʾishah and informed him that they were adamant about confronting him on the battlefield (R 1:188; B 198; Ḥ 305–306). According to a minority opinion, the text refers to Muʿāwiyah (R 1:188–189). See similar lines in §1.10 and §1.135. The penultimate line of this oration is similar to the first line of §1.172.

3 I.e., they suckle a woman who has no more milk, a metaphor for the emptiness of their claim.

4 Various contexts are given for this oration: (1) Māmaṭīrī (*Nuzhah*, 228–229) transcribes the first paragraph as ʿAlī's answer in an oration in the Basra mosque a few days after the Battle of the Camel in 36/656; part of the same oration and answers are (in this order in ibid., 221–233): §1.103.1, §1.154.2, §3.26, §3.354.2, §1.170.4, §1.23, §1.208, §1.154.4. (2) Yaʿqūbī (*Tārīkh*, 2:207) transcribes it as part of an oration in which ʿAlī preceded these lines by reciting the Qurʾanic verse, «Indeed, it is I who brings the dead to life. I write down all that they have brought forth and note all their deeds. All things I have encompassed in a clear Imam» (Qurʾan, Yāsīn 36:12). (3) Minqarī (*Waqʿat Ṣiffīn*, 10) transcribes the second paragraph, the line of prayer, as part of ʿAlī's habitual Friday sermon in Kufa and Medina.

أمّا بعد. فإنّ الأمر ينزل من السماء إلى الأرض كقطر المطر إلى كلّ نفس بما قسّم لها من زيادة أو نقصان. فإذا رأى أحدكم لأخيه غفيرة في أهل أو مال أو نفس فلا تكونّ له فتنة. فإنّ المرء المسلم ما لم يغش دناءة تظهر فيخشع لها إذا ذكرت وتغرى بها لئام الناس كان كالفالج الياسر الذي ينتظر أوّل فوزة من قداحه توجب له المغنم ويرفع عنه بها المغرم. وكذلك المرء المسلم البريء من الخيانة ينتظر من الله إحدى الحسنيين إمّا داعي الله فما عند الله خير له وإمّا رزق الله فإذا هو ذو أهل ومال ومعه دينه وحسبه. إنّ المال والبنين حرث الدنيا والعمل الصالح حرث الآخرة وقد يجمعهما الله لأقوام. فاحذروا من الله ما حذّركم من نفسه واخشوه خشية ليست بتعذير واعملوا في غير رياء ولا سمعة فإنّه من يعمل لغير الله يكله الله إلى من عمل له. نسأل الله منازل الشهداء ومعايشة السعداء ومرافقة الأنبياء. أيّها الناس إنّه لا يستغني الرجل وإن كان ذا مال عن عشيرته ودفاعهم عنه بأيديهم وألسنتهم وهم أعظم الناس حيطة من ورائه وألهم لشعثه وأعطفهم عليه عند نازلة إذا نزلت به ولسان الصدق يجعله الله للمرء في الناس خير له من المال يورّثه غيره.

منها

ألا لا يعدلنّ أحدكم عن القرابة يرى بها الخصاصة أن يسدّها بالذي لا يزيده إن أمسكه ولا ينقصه إن أهلكه ومن يقبض يده عن عشيرته فإنّما تقبض منه عنهم يد واحدة وتقبض منهم عنه أيدٍ كثيرة. ومن تلن حاشيته يستدم من قومه المودّة.

God's command descends from the sky to the earth like raindrops, bringing to each soul what is decreed for it, be it plenty or dearth. Don't be envious if you see your brother in possession of family, health, and wealth. As long as a Muslim does not commit an outrage that would shame him if disclosed and embolden the rabble, he is like the adventurer whose first drawn arrow wins him the prize and pays off his debts.[1] Similarly, a Muslim who is innocent of treachery awaits one of two beautiful outcomes:[2] either he will receive God's call—and reward in God's presence is the best blessing anyone can obtain— or God's sustenance will come to him in this world, so he will have family and wealth, while also keeping his faith and character. Wealth and children are the harvest of this world, while good deeds are the harvest of the hereafter,[3] and God may certainly bless a man with both. Beware the punishment that God has warned you of and do not fall short in fearing him. Perform deeds with sincerity, not to show off or gather praise, for whoever performs deeds for any reason other than to please God will be handed over to the person he performed them for. We beseech God to grant us the station of the martyrs, the companionship of the blissful, and the fellowship of the prophets. People! Even the wealthy man needs his kin, and he needs them to defend him with hand and tongue. Their backing is his best protection, and their support gives strength to his shaky affairs. When a calamity hits him, they show him the most compassion. A true tongue granted by God to a man among his people brings him more benefit than the wealth he leaves for another.[4]

From the same oration:
Harken to my words! Let none of you turn away from an impoverished relative. Your wealth will not increase if you withhold your largesse or decrease if you provide. The man who is close-fisted with kin will find that his closed fist will be countered with many closed fists. The man who possesses gentleness will keep his people's affection.[5]

---

1   The metaphor is based on the pre-Islamic practice of drawing arrows (called *maysir*) to determine division of a slaughtered camel's meat. The man who draws the tallest arrow wins the choicest part. B 203; R 1:193–194.
2   Reference to Qur'an, Tawbah 9:52.
3   Reference to Qur'an, Shūrā 42:20.
4   Reference to Qur'an, Maryam 19:50, Shuʿarā' 26:84. "A true tongue" (*lisān ṣidq*) is the superior reputation he leaves behind, or the true teachings he imparts that continue to benefit after his death. B 205; R 1:195; Asad, *The Message of the Qur'ān*, commentary on Qur'an, Maryam 19:50.
5   "Who possesses gentleness"—lit. "whose intestines are soft."

وما أحسن المعنى الذي أراده عليه السلام بقوله ﴿ومن يقبض يده عن عشيرته﴾ إلى تمام الكلام فإنّ الممسك خيره عن عشيرته إنّما يمسك نفع يد واحدة فإذا احتاج إلى نصرتهم واضطرّ إلى مرافدتهم قعدوا عن نصره وتثاقلوا عن صوته فمنع ترافد الأيدي الكثيرة وتناهض الأقدام الجمّة.

1.24 ومن خطبة له عليه السلام

ولعمري ما عليّ من قتال من خالف الحقّ وخابط الغيّ من إدهان ولا إيهان. فاتّقوا الله عباد الله وفرّوا إلى الله من الله وامضوا في الذي نهجه لكم وقوموا بما عصبه بكم فعليٌّ ضامن لفُلْجكم آجلًا وإن لم تمنحوه عاجلًا.

1.25 ومن خطبة له عليه السلام وقد تواترت عليه الأخبار باستيلاء أصحاب معاوية على البلاد وقدم عليه عاملاه على اليمن وهما عبيد الله بن العباس وسعيد بن نمران لمّا غلب عليها بُسْر بن أبي أرطأة فقام عليه السلام إلى المنبر ضجرًا بتثاقل أصحابه عن الجهاد ومخالفتهم له في الرأي وقال عليه السلام

ما هي إلّا الكوفة أقبضها وأبسطها إن لم تكوني إلّا أنت تهبّ أعاصيرك فقبّحك الله.

وتمثّل[1]

لَعَمْرُ أَبِيكَ الخَيْرِ يَا عَمْرُو إِنَّنِي   عَلَى وَضَرٍ مِنْ ذَا الْإِنَاءِ قَلِيلِ

ثمّ قال عليه السلام

أنبئت بسرًا قد اطّلع اليمن وإنّي والله لأظنّ هؤلاء القوم سيُدالون منكم باجتماعهم على باطلهم وتفرّقكم عن حقّكم وبمعصيتكم إمامكم في الحقّ وطاعتهم إمامهم في الباطل وبأدائهم الأمانة إلى صاحبهم وخيانتكم وبصلاحهم في بلادهم وإفسادكم. فلو ائتمنت أحدكم على قعب لخشيت أن يذهب بعلاقته. اللهمّ إنّي قد مللتهم وملّوني وسئمتهم

______

[1] البحر: الطويل.

Raḍī: What a beautiful motif ʿAlī expounded when he said, "The man who is close-fisted with kin," and so on, till the end of the piece. For the man who withholds generosity from kin withholds the benefit he can bestow with one hand, whereas when he needs their aid and craves their support, they will hesitate to help him and be slow to answer his call, denying him the support of many hands and a host of marching feet.

1.24 From an oration by ʿAlī:
By my life, no softness or weakness shall hold me back from fighting those who challenge the truth and follow the way of error. Servants of God, fear God, and flee to God's reward from God's wrath.[1] Walk the path that he paved for you, fulfill the duties to which he bound you, and ʿAlī guarantees your success in the hereafter, even if victory is not granted you in the here and now.

1.25 From an oration by ʿAlī. Widespread reports reached ʿAlī that Muʿāwiyah's commanders had occupied his territories. When Busr ibn Abī Arṭāt seized Yemen, ʿAlī's governors, ʿUbaydallāh ibn al-ʿAbbās and Saʿīd ibn Nimrān, fled and returned to Kufa. Angered by his followers' apathy in rising to fight and their opposition to his commands, ʿAlī ascended the pulpit and exclaimed:[2]
I have only you, Kufa, to hold or relinquish; only you, with your dry winds that raise pillars of dust! May God render you foul!

He then recited a testimonial verse:

> By the life of your virtuous father, I swear:
> My pot has nothing but smudges of fat.[3]

He continued:
I am informed that Busr has ascended the Yemeni highlands. By God, I fear this group will vanquish you, for they are united in their false claim, while you, despite your truth, are divided. You disobey your leader in his call to the truth, while they obey theirs in his call to falsehood. They are loyal to their master, while you are treacherous. Their lands adhere to a proper state of affairs, while you are corrupt and dishonest—if I entrusted one of you with a wooden cup, he would make off with its palm-fronded handle! God, I am tired of these

---

1 Lit. "Flee to God from God." I have added the words "reward" and "wrath" for clarity.

2 One of ʿAlī's final orations, delivered in Kufa in 40/660. Ḥ 1:348. See details of Busr's attack in Ḥ 2:3–18; B 208.

3 The commenters explain the verse but do not identify the poet and I have not found an identification elsewhere. B 210; R 1:201.

وسئموني فأبدلني بهم خيرًا منهم وأبدلهم بي شرًّا منّي. اللهمّ مِثْ قلوبهم كما يماث الملح في الماء. أما والله لوددت أنّ لي بكم ألف فارس من بني فراس بن غَنم[1]

هُنَالِكَ لَوْ دَعَوْتَ أَتَاكَ مِنْهُمْ   رِجَالٌ مِثْلُ أَرْمِيَةِ الْحَمِيمْ

ثمّ نزل من المنبر عليه السلام.

قلت أنا و﴿الأرمية﴾ جمع ﴿رمي﴾ وهو السحاب. و﴿الحميم﴾ في هذا الموضع وقت الصيف. وإنّما خصّ الشاعر سحاب الصيف بالذكر لأنّه أشدّ جفولًا وأسرع خفوفًا لأنّه لا ماء فيه. وإنّما يكون السحاب ثقيل السير لامتلائه بالماء وذلك لا يكون في الأكثر إلّا في أزمان الشتاء. وإنّما أراد الشاعر وصفهم بالسرعة إذا دعوا والإغاثة إذا استغيثوا. والدليل على ذلك قوله ﴿هنالك لو دعوت أتاك منهم﴾.

1.26 ومن خطبة له عليه السلام

1.26.1 إنّ الله بعث محمّدًا صلّى الله عليه وآله نذيرًا للعالمين وأمينًا على التنزيل وأنتم معشر العرب على شرّ دين وفي شرّ دار مُنيخون بين حجارة خشن وحيّات صمّ تشربون الكدر وتأكلون الجشب وتسفكون دماءكم وتقطعون أرحامكم الأصنام فيكم منصوبة والآثام بكم معصوبة.

1.26.2 منها

فنظرت فإذا ليس لي معين إلّا أهل بيتي فضننت بهم عن الموت وأغضيت على القذى وشربت على الشجى وصبرت على أخذ الكظم وعلى أمرّ من طعم العلقم.

---

[1] البحر: السريع.

people, and they are tired of me. I am weary of them, and they are weary of me. So give me better and give them worse. Crush their hearts like salt dissolving in water. By God, would that I had a thousand tribesmen from Firās ibn Ghanam instead of the lot of you!

> When you call out
> Their men rush to you
> Like the hot summer cloud.[1]

Then he descended from the pulpit.

Raḍī: *Armiyah*, pl. *ramī*, is a cloud. *Ḥamīm* here means the heat of summer. The poet singles out summer clouds because they are blown along more swiftly and are light and fast moving. Clouds move heavily when they are full of water, and this is true mostly in winter. The poet wished to describe the warriors as swift to answer the call and as assisting as soon as they are asked. My interpretation is endorsed by his line, ⟨When you call out / Their men rush to you.⟩

1.26 From an oration by ʿAlī:[2]

1.26.1 God sent Muḥammad as a warner to all peoples and a trustee of his revelation at a time when you Arabs followed a foul religion and lived in a foul abode: You unloaded your camels between rough boulders and deadly adders, drank muddy water, ate coarse food, randomly spilt blood, and recklessly severed ties of kinship. Idols were ensconced in your lands, and sins were bound to your necks.

1.26.2 From the same oration:[3]
I looked around me, and when I saw that my family was my only support, I chose to save them from certain death. But I blinked down dust, choked when I drank, suffered harsh throttling, and endured a state more bitter than colocynth.

---

1 The verse is by the pre-Islamic poet Abū Jundub al-Hudhalī al-Mashʾūm, and is cited in Sukkarī, *Sharḥ Ashʿār al-Hudhaliyyīn*, 363; Ibn Manẓūr, *Lisān*, s.v. "R-M-Y"; Azharī, *Tahdhīb*, s.v. "R-M-Y." Ḥ 1:348; R 1:203–204.

2 ʿAlī delivered this oration in Kufa in 38/658 after ʿAmr ibn al-ʿĀṣ had conquered Egypt for Muʿāwiyah and killed ʿAlī's ward and governor, Muḥammad ibn Abī Bakr. Details in Ḥ 2:61–73.

3 This section refers to the pledge of allegiance to Abū Bakr after the Prophet's death. Details in Ḥ 2:21–60. Similar lines in §1.215.3.

1.26.3 منها

ولم يبايع حتّى شرط أن يؤتيه على البيعة ثمنًا فلا ظفرت يد المبايع وخزيت أمانة المبتاع. خذوا للحرب أهبتها وأعدّوا لها عدّتها فقد شبّ لظاها وعلا سناها.

1.27 ومن خطبة له عليه السلام

أمّا بعد. فإنّ الجهاد باب من أبواب الجنّة فتحه الله لخاصّة أوليائه وهو لباس التقوى ودرع الله الحصينة وجُنّته الوثيقة فمن تركه ألبسه الله ثوب الذلّ وشمله البلاء ودُيّث بالصغار والقماء وضرب على قلبه بالإسهاب[1] وأديل الحقّ منه بتضييع الجهاد وسِيمَ الخسف ومُنع النصف. ألا وإنّي قد دعوتكم إلى حرب هؤلاء القوم ليلًا ونهارًا وسرًّا وإعلانًا وقلت لكم اغزوهم قبل أن يغزوكم فوالله ما غزي قوم قطّ في عقر دارهم إلّا ذلّوا فتواكلتم وتخاذلتم حتّى شُنّت عليكم الغارات ومُلِكت عليكم الأوطان. هذا أخو غامد قد وردت خيله الأنبار وقد قتل حسّان بن حسّان البكريّ وأزال خيلكم عن مسالحها. ولقد بلغني أنّ الرجل منهم كان يدخل على المرأة المسلمة والأخرى المعاهدة فينتزع حِجْلها وقُلْبها وقلائدها ورِعاثها ما تمتنع منه إلّا بالاسترجاع والاسترحام ثمّ انصرفوا وافرين ما نال رجلًا منهم كَلْم ولا أريق له دم. فلو أنّ امرأً مسلمًا مات من بعد هذا أسفًا ما كان به ملومًا بل كان به عندي جديرًا. فيا عجبًا عجبًا والله يميت القلب ويجلب الهمّ من اجتماع هؤلاء القوم على باطلهم وتفرّقكم عن حقّكم فقبحًا لكم وترحًا حين قد صرتم غرضًا يُرمى يغار عليكم ولا تغيرون وتُغزَون ولا تغزُون ويعصى الله

---

^١ م، ي، هـ: كذا. ش: ﴿بالأسداد﴾.

1.26.3 From the same oration:[1]

ʿAmr pledged allegiance to Muʿāwiyah only after he had stipulated a price—may the pledger's hand stay empty, and the pledgee's charge be betrayed! Men, prepare for battle and ready your weapons! The fires of war have been stoked and their blaze has flared high.

1.27 From an oration by ʿAlī:[2]

Jihad is a door to heaven that God has opened for his special devotees. It is piety's robe,[3] God's own protective armor, and his trusty shield. Those who spurn it will be clothed in dishonor, engulfed by calamities, and whipped into compliance. Chaos will destroy their minds. If they forsake jihad, righteousness will cease, shame will consume, and justice will be denied. Listen to me! Day and night, in private and in public, I urged you to fight this group. I exhorted you to attack them before they attacked you, for, by God, a group attacked in its heartland is sure to be routed! But you looked at one another and abandoned your fellows until you were raided, time and again, and your homelands were overrun. So now the Ghāmidī man's horses have raided Anbar. He has killed Ḥassān ibn Ḥassān al-Bakrī and driven your cavalry from their fortifications. I have heard that their men forced their way into homes and ripped anklets, bracelets, necklaces, and earrings from our women, Muslim and non-Muslim,[4] who had no way to save themselves except to beg for mercy, and to cry out that all must return to God.[5] The horsemen then left unscathed, not a single individual injured, not a drop of their blood spilt. Who would blame a Muslim if, after this, he were to die in shame? I would say that his death is fully justified! O how incomprehensible your behavior! I am baffled at how that group unites behind their false claim, while you squabble among yourselves and refuse to fight for your right. It stabs my heart and gives me deep anguish. May you feel squalor and grief! You sit as a target for enemy arrows, you are

---

1 I have replaced the pronouns in the section with names, taken from the commentaries, which also provide details of ʿAmr's arrangement with Muʿāwiyah. Ḥ 2:61–73; B 214; R 1:204–205.

2 ʿAlī delivered this oration in the wake of an attack on Anbar in 39/660 by a cavalry troop led by Muʿāwiyah's commander Sufyān ibn ʿAwf al-Ghāmidī, who killed ʿAlī's governor Ḥassān ibn Ḥassān al-Bakrī and pillaged the town. In response to ʿAlī's oration, two men came up to him to offer support; ʿAlī prayed for them, and sighed, "But what can two men do?" (§ 3.254). R 1:214–215; B 215–216; Ḥ 2:75–76, 85–90.

3 Reference to Qurʾan, Aʿrāf 7:26.

4 Lit. *muʿāhadah*, "a woman protected by a covenant," referring to Christians and Jews.

5 Reference to Qurʾan, Baqarah 2:156: «We belong to God, and to him we return» a verse typically voiced in times of great distress.

وترضون. فإذا أمرتكم بالسير إليهم في أيّام الحرّ قلتم هذه حَمارّة القَيظ أمهلنا يسبّخ عنّا الحرّ وإذا أمرتكم بالسير إليهم في الشتاء قلتم هذه صَبارّة القُرّ أمهلنا ينسلخ عنّا البرد كلّ هذا فرارًا من الحرّ والقرّ فإذا كنتم من الحرّ والقرّ تفرّون فأنتم والله من السيف أفرّ. يا أشباه الرجال ولا رجال حلوم الأطفال وعقول ربّات الحِجال. لوددت أنّي لم أركم ولم أعرفكم معرفة والله جرّت ندمًا وأعقبت ذمًّا. قاتلكم الله لقد ملأتم قلبي قيحًا وشحنتم صدري غيظًا وجرّعتموني نُغَب التَّهمام أنفاسًا وأفسدتم عليّ رأيي بالعصيان والخذلان حتّى قالت قريش إنّ ابن أبي طالب رجل شجاع ولكن لا علم له بالحرب لله أبوهم وهل أحد منهم أشدّ لها مِراسًا وأقدم فيها مقامًا منّي. لقد نهضت فيها وما بلغت العشرين وها أنا ذا قد ذرّفت على الستّين. ولكنّه لا رأي لمن لا يطاع.

1.28 ومن خطبة له عليه السلام

أمّا بعد. فإنّ الدنيا قد أدبرت وآذنت بوداع وإنّ الآخرة قد أقبلت وأشرفت بِاطّلاع ألا وإنّ اليوم المِضمار وغدًا السِّباق والسُّبقة الجنّة والغاية النار. أفلا تائب من خطيئته قبل منيّته ألا عامل لنفسه قبل يوم بؤسه. ألا وإنّكم في أيّام أمل من ورائه أجل فمن عمل في أيّام أمله قبل حضور أجله نفعه عمله ولم يضرره أجله ومن قصّر في أيّام أمله قبل حضور أجله فقد خسر عمله وضرّه أجله ألا فاعملوا في الرغبة كما تعملون في الرهبة ألا وإنّي لم أر كالجنّة نام طالبها ولا كالنار نام هاربها ألا وإنّه من لا ينفعه الحقّ يضرره الباطل ومن لا يستقم به الهدى يجرّ به الضلال إلى الردى ألا وإنّكم قد أمرتم بالظعن

---

raided but do not raid, you are attacked but do not attack, God is disobeyed and you sit content. Earlier, when I commanded you to mobilize in the days of heat, you replied, "It is the swelter of midsummer—spare us until the heat lessens." When I commanded you to mobilize in wintertime, you replied, "It is the freeze of midwinter—spare us until the cold departs." All this, just to avoid heat and cold! By God, if you flee thus from heat and cold, you will flee in greater panic from the sword! Semblances of men, not men, with minds of children and wits of cloistered women! I wish I had never seen you! I wish I had never known you! By God, knowing you has brought me only regret, only defamation! May God attack you! You have filled my heart with pus and weighted my breast with ire. With every breath I take, you have poured me draughts of sorrow. You have ruined my strategy with your disobedience and opposition, such that the Quraysh tribesmen say, "Abū Ṭālib's son may be a brave man, but he has no knowledge of war." Good God![1] Is there anyone more familiar with its harshness, or who experienced it at a younger age? I knew war intimately before I turned twenty, and now I am past sixty! But there can be no strategy without obedience.

1.28 From an oration by ʿAlī:[2]

The world has shown its back and proclaimed its farewell. The hereafter has approached and announced its arrival. Hark my words! Today is the day of training and tomorrow the race: its goal is paradise, or its end hellfire. Will you not repent of your sins before your death? Will you not perform deeds for your soul before your day of adversity? Hark my words! These are your days of hope and coming up right behind them is death. Those who perform deeds during their days of hope, before the arrival of death, will benefit from their deeds, and death will cause no harm. Those who fall short in performing deeds during their days of hope, before the arrival of death, will have squandered their deeds, and death will cause them harm. Hark my words! Perform deeds from hope, just as you perform them from fear. Hark my words! I have never seen any who seek paradise or flee hellfire in heedless slumber. Hark my words! Those not helped by right are harmed by wrong. Those not placed on the path

---

1   Lit. "To God, purely, is attributable (the excellence of) their father" (*lillāhi abūhum*). It is an expression of wonder, praise, or incredulity. Lane, *Lexicon*, s.v. "A-B-W."

2   This is part of §1.45, which begins "I praise God, never uncertain of his mercy." B 221. §1.28 is also cited in a slightly different recension as §1.52. All these are parts of a sermon delivered on ʿĪd al-Fiṭr or ʿĪd al-Adḥā, presumably in Kufa during ʿAlī's caliphate. Details in note at §1.45. (Some lines are also similar in §1.42). On this oration, see Qutbuddin, "A Sermon on Piety by Imam ʿAlī ibn Abī Ṭālib: How the Rhythm of the Classical Arabic Oration Tacitly Persuaded."

ودُللتم على الزاد وإنّ أخوف ما أخاف عليكم اتّباع الهوى وطول الأمل تزوّدوا في الدنيا من الدنيا ما تحوزون به أنفسكم غدًا.

وأقول إنّه لو كان كلام يأخذ بالأعناق إلى الزهد في الدنيا ويضطرّ إلى عمل الآخرة لكان هذا الكلام وكفى به قاطعًا لعلائق الآمال وقادحًا زناد الاتّعاظ والازدجار. ومن أعجبه قوله عليه السلام ﴿ألا وإنّ المضمار اليوم وغدًا السباق والسبقة الجنّة والغاية النار﴾ فإنّ فيه مع نخامة اللفظ وعظم قدر المعنى وصادق التمثيل وواقع التشبيه سرًّا عجيبًا ومعنى لطيفًا وهو قوله عليه السلام ﴿والسبقة الجنّة والغاية النار﴾ نخالف بين اللفظين لاختلاف المعنيين ولم يقل ﴿والسبقة النار﴾ كما قال ﴿والسبقة الجنّة﴾ لأنّ الاستباق إنّما يكون إلى أمر محبوب وغرض مطلوب وهذه صفة الجنّة وليس هذا المعنى موجودًا في النار نعوذ بالله منها فلم يجز أن يقول ﴿والسبقة النار﴾ بل قال ﴿والغاية النار﴾ لأنّ الغاية قد ينتهي إليها من لا يسرّه الانتهاء ومن يسرّه ذلك فصلح أن يعبّر بها عن الأمرين معًا فهي في هذا الموضع كالمصير والمآل قال الله عزّ وجلّ ﴿قُلْ تَمَتَّعُوا فَإِنَّ مَصِيرَكُمْ إِلَى ٱلنَّارِ﴾ ولا يجوز في هذا الموضع أن يقال ﴿فإنّ سبقتكم إلى النار﴾. فتأمّل ذلك فباطنه عجيب وغوره بعيد وكذلك أكثر كلامه عليه السلام.

1.29 ومن خطبة له عليه السلام

أيّها الناس المجتمعة أبدانهم المختلفة أهواؤهم كلامكم يوهي الصمّ الصلاب وفعلكم يطمع فيكم الأعداء تقولون في المجالس كَيْتَ وكَيْتَ فإذا جاء القتال قلتم حِيدِي حَيادِ. ما عزّت دعوة من دعاكم ولا استراح قلب من قاساكم أعاليل بأضاليل دفاع ذي الدَّين المطول. لا يمنع الضيم الذليل ولا يدرك الحقّ إلّا بالجِدّ أيّ دار بعد داركم تمنعون ومع أيّ إمام بعدي تقاتلون المغرور والله من غررتموه ومن فاز بكم فاز بالسهم الأخيب ومن رمى بكم فقد رمى بأفْوَقِ ناصل أصبحت والله لا أصدّق قولكم ولا

by guidance are dragged by error to perdition. Hark my words! You have been commanded to journey and directed to provision. What I fear most for you is the pursuit of desire and lengthy yearnings. Take provisions in this world, from this world, to nourish your souls tomorrow.

Raḍī: If ever words grabbed you by the neck and compelled you to renounce the world and perform deeds for the hereafter, it would be these words, which cut the cords of false hope and ignite the flint of counsel and warning. Among their most wondrous lines are, "Today is the day of training and tomorrow the race: its goal is paradise, or its end hellfire." For in addition to majestic vocabulary, exalted themes, clear analogies, and effective metaphors, they enfold a wondrous secret and sublime significance in the line, "its goal (*subqah*) is paradise, or its end (*ghāyah*) hellfire." Here, ʿAlī differentiates between the two words because they have different significations. He does not say "its goal is hellfire" as he says "its goal is paradise" because one races towards something one wants, to a prize one hopes to win, and that is the description of paradise. But this significance does not apply to hellfire—may God protect us from it!—so it would be impermissible to say, "its goal is hellfire." Rather, ʿAlī says, "its end is hellfire," because an end is reached by those who are not pleased to reach it as well as by those who are pleased to reach it; it conveys both situations. In the context of this sermon, the word "end" indicates the last stop, the place of final return, as in God's words, «Say: Take pleasure if you wish! Your last stop is hellfire.»[1] It would be impermissible to say here, "your goal is hellfire." Reflect on ʿAlī's words, for the signification of this saying is wondrous, its well deep. And this is true for the entirety of ʿAlī's speech.

1.29 From an oration by ʿAlī:[2]
People! You are together in body but divided in aspiration. Your words would shatter mighty rocks, but your actions embolden the enemy. In your gatherings you say this and that, but when battle approaches, you yell, "Be gone! Get away!" A mission that depends on you never succeeds. A heart that is subjected to you is never at ease. Excuses and falsehoods! You keep asking for a delay, like debtors who put off and refuse to pay! Men without honor cannot fight injustice. Rights cannot be won except through earnest effort. Tell me—which home will you defend when this one is taken? Under which leader will you fight when I am gone? By God, whoever believes in you is deluded! Whoever wins you as his share wins the losing arrow! Whoever has you in his bow shoots a broken-

---

1 Qurʾan, Ibrāhīm 14:30.
2 ʿAlī delivered this oration in Kufa, following a raid by Muʿāwiyah's commander al-Ḍaḥḥāk ibn Qays al-Fihrī in 39/660 on pilgrims encamped at Thaʿlabiyyah. Ḥ 2:113–117, B 225. Nuʿmān (*Daʿāʾim*, 1:391) identifies it as a Friday sermon.

أطمع في نصركم ولا أوعد العدوّ بكم ما بالكم ما دواؤكم ما طبّكم القوم رجال أمثالكم أقَوْلًا بغير علم وغفلة من غير ورع وطمعًا في غير حقّ.

1.30   من كلام له عليه السلام في معنى قتل عثمان

لو أمرت به لكنت قاتلًا أو نهيت عنه لكنت ناصرًا غير أنّ من نصره لا يستطيع أن يقول خذله من أنا خير منه ومن خذله لا يستطيع أن يقول نصره من هو خير منّي. وأنا جامع لكم أمره ٱستأثر فأساء الأثرة وجزعتم فأسأتم الجزع ولله حكم واقع في المستأثر والجازع.

1.31   ومن كلام له عليه السلام لمّا أنفذ عبد الله بن العبّاس رحمه الله إلى الزبير قبل وقوع الحرب يوم الجمل يستفيئه إلى طاعته. قال له عليه السلام

لا تلقينّ طلحة فإنّك إن تلقه تجده كالثور عاقصًا قرنه يركب الصعب ويقول هو الذلول ولكن ٱلق الزبير فإنّه ألين عريكة فقل له يقول لك ٱبن خالك عرفتني بالحجاز وأنكرتني بالعراق فما عدا ممّا بدا.

وهو عليه السلام أوّل من سمعت منه هذه الكلمة أعني ﴿فما عدا ممّا بدا﴾.

nocked arrow with a dull point!¹ By God, I woke this morning not trusting anything you say, not expecting your support, not threatening the enemy with your strength. What is wrong with you? What is your cure? What is your remedy? They are but men like you! So much talk and no comprehension, so much rashness and no piety, so much greed for things that don't belong to you!

1.30 From words ʿAlī spoke about ʿUthmān's assassination:²

If I had commanded it, I would be a killer. If I had forbidden it, I would be a supporter. In truth, the supporter cannot claim that he is more righteous than the detractor, while the detractor would not be correct in saying that the supporter is more righteous than he is.³ Let me summarize the situation for you: ʿUthmān misappropriated, and that was wrong. You responded with violence, and that was also wrong. Both the one who misappropriated and the one who responded with violence will face God's judgment.

1.31 From words ʿAlī spoke just before the fighting began at the Battle of the Camel, when he sent ʿAbdallāh ibn al-ʿAbbās to urge Zubayr to return to the fold of obedience. ʿAlī said:⁴

Don't speak with Ṭalḥah, for you will find him a bull with twisted horns, a man who rides a refractory beast and swears it is docile. Speak instead with Zubayr, whose hump is softer, and say to him: Your cousin ʿAlī says to you: You acknowledged me in Medina and rejected me in Iraq—what turned you from what you deemed good?

Raḍī: ʿAlī was the first to use the expression, "What turned you from what you deemed good?" (*mā ʿadā mimmā badā*).

---

1   "Broken-nocked," (*fūq*, used here in the elative form, *afwaq*), is a notch at the end of an arrow into which the bowstring fits.

2   On the events leading up to ʿUthmān's killing in Medina in 35/656, see Ḥ 1:129–161. Raḍī transcribes this text among ʿAlī's orations, but Ibn Ṭāwūs (*Kashf*, 174, 180) cites it as part of a lengthy epistle ʿAlī wrote after Muḥammad ibn Abī Bakr was killed in 38/658, which ʿAlī gave to al-Aṣbagh ibn Nubātah et al., instructing them to have Ibn Abī Rāfiʿ read it out every Friday in the Kufa mosque. The Sunni commentators are at pains to point out that although ʿAlī did not pick up a sword to defend ʿUthmān, he spoke out against his murder, even sending his sons Ḥasan and Ḥusayn to guard ʿUthmān's door. Ḥ 2:126; ʿA 98 n. 1.

3   "The supporter" could be a reference to Marwān ibn al-Ḥakam, and "the detractor" to ʿAbdallāh ibn Masʿūd. R 1:224.

4   Basra, 36/656. On details of the conversation between ʿAbdallāh ibn al-ʿAbbās and Zubayr, and related events at the Battle of the Camel, see Ḥ 2:166–170. Zubayr was the son of ʿAlī's paternal aunt, Ṣafiyyah bint ʿAbd al-Muṭṭalib.

1.32 ومن خطبة له عليه السلام[1]

أيّها الناس إنّا قد أصبحنا في دهر عنود وزمن شديد[2] يعدّ فيه المحسن مسيئًا ويزداد الظالم فيه عتوًّا لا ننتفع بما علمنا ولا نسأل عمّا جهلنا ولا نتخوّف قارعة حتّى تحلّ بنا. فالناس على أربعة أصناف. منهم من لا يمنعه الفسادَ في الأرض إلّا مهانةُ نفسه وكلالة حدّه ونضيض وفره. ومنهم المصلت بسيفه والمعلن بسرّه[3] والمجلب بخيله ورَجله قد أشرط نفسه وأوبق دينه لحطام ينتهزه أو مِقنب يقوده أو منبر يفرعه. ولبئس المتجر أن ترى الدنيا لنفسك ثمنًا وممّا لك عند الله عوضًا. ومنهم من يطلب الدنيا بعمل الآخرة ولا يطلب الآخرة بعمل الدنيا قد طامن من شخصه وقارب من خطوه وشمّر من ثوبه وزخرف من نفسه للأمانة واتّخذ ستر الله ذريعة إلى المعصية. ومنهم من أقعده عن طلب الملك ضؤولة نفسه وانقطاع سببه فقصرته الحال على حاله فتحلّى باسم القناعة وتزيّن بلباس أهل الزهادة وليس من ذلك في مراح ولا مغدى. وبقي رجال غضّ أبصارهم ذكر المرجع وأراق دموعهم خوف المحشر. فهم بين شريد نادٍّ وخائف مقموع وساكت مكعوم وداعٍ مخلص وثكلان موجَع قد أخملتهم التقيّة وشملتهم الذلّة فهم في بحر أجاج أفواههم ضامزة وقلوبهم قرحة قد وعظوا حتّى ملّوا وقُهروا حتّى ذلّوا وقُتلوا حتّى قلّوا. فلتكن الدنيا أصغر في أعينكم من حُثالة القَرَظ وقُراضة الجَلَم واتّعظوا بمن كان قبلكم قبل أن يتّعظ بكم من بعدكم وارفضوها ذميمة فإنّها قد رفضت من كان أشغف بها منكم.

وهذه الخطبة ربّما نسبها من لا علم له إلى معاوية وهي من كلام أمير المؤمنين عليه السلام الذي لا شكّ فيه وأين الذهب من الرغام والعذب من الأجاج وقد دلّ على ذلك الدليل

---

[1] تبدأ مخطوطه ن من هنا.   [2] م، ش، ي، هـ: كذا. ن، ونسخة في م: ﴿كنود﴾.   [3] م، ي، ونسخة في هـ: كذا. ن، وأصل هـ: ﴿بشره﴾. ش: معًا.

1.32 From an oration by ʿAlī:[1]

People! We live in a challenging age and a difficult time, when the good are deemed evil, and oppressors grow ever more brutal. We neither benefit from what we have learnt, nor ask about what we don't know—we ignore calamities until they set up camp in our homes. Men today fall into one of four categories: One is prevented from spreading corruption on earth by the weakness of his person, the dullness of his blade, and the sparseness of his wealth. Another unsheathes his sword, announces his intention, and assembles foot soldiers and cavalry, selling his soul and forfeiting his religion to amass baubles, lead an army, or ascend a pulpit—what a terrible transaction, when you deem the world an equitable price for your soul, a fair exchange for heavenly reward! A third seeks worldly gain by performing the deeds of the hereafter, rather than seeking the hereafter by performing good deeds in this world; he appears calm in his person, walks with slow steps, tucks up his garments, and presents himself as a trustworthy man, taking advantage of the concealment offered by God's veil to sin. A fourth is only prevented from seeking power by his own servility and lack of support—these are what keeps him in his place. He wears the mark of contentment and dons the garment of renunciants, but neither his haunts in the daytime nor his retreats in the night are anything like theirs. Only a few men remain—their eyes are wet with remembrance of the return to God, and their tears flow from fear of the resurrection. One is a solitary fugitive, another is curbed by fear, a third is shushed and muzzled, a fourth, sincere, prays, and a fifth is bereaved and grieving. They are weakened by terror and humiliated on all sides; they drink from a bitter sea, tongues silenced, hearts wounded. They gave counsel until exhausted, now they are beaten down; almost all have been killed off, only a few remain. People, let this world be smaller in your eyes than fibers of a spiny acacia pod, or fluffs of wool floating off a pair of shears. Learn from the fate of those who came before, let not those who come later have occasion to learn from yours. Reject this world and censure her, for she has rejected many who were far more enamored of her than you.

Raḍī: Some individuals who lack any knowledge attribute this oration to Muʿāwiyah, when it is unquestionably the speech of the Commander of the Faithful. Can one compare dirt to gold, or the bitter to the sweet? Indeed, an experienced guide has shown

---

1   ʿAlī delivered this oration in the Grand Mosque of Kufa, during his caliphate, 35–40/656–661, in the presence of the community's leaders. Ibn Ṭalḥah, *Maṭālib*, 176.

الحِرّيت ونقده الناقد البصير عمرو بن بحر الجاحظ فإنّه ذكر هذه الخطبة في كتابه البيان والتبيُّن[1] وذكر من نسبها إلى معاوية ثمّ تكلّم من بعدها بكلام في معناها بجملته أنّه قال وهذا الكلام بكلام عليّ عليه السلام أشبه وبمذهبه في تصنيف الناس وفي الإخبار عمّا هم عليه من القهر والإذلال ومن التقيّة والخوف أليق. ومتى وجدنا معاوية في حال من الأحوال يسلك في كلامه مسلك الزهّاد ومذاهب العبّاد.

1.33 ومن خطبة له عليه السلام عند مسيره لقتال أهل البصرة. قال عبد الله بن العبّاس رضي الله عنه دخلت على أمير المؤمنين صلوات الله عليه بذي قار وهو يخصف نعله فقال لي ما قيمة هذه النعل فقلت لا قيمة لها قال والله لهي أحبّ إليّ من إمرتكم إلّا أن أقيم حقًّا أو أدفع باطلًا ثمّ خرج عليه السلام نخطب الناس فقال

إنّ الله سبحانه بعث محمّدًا صلّى الله عليه وآله وليس أحد من العرب يقرأ كتابًا ولا يدّعي نبوّة فساق الناس حتّى بوّأهم محلّتهم وبلّغهم منجاتهم فاستقامت قناتهم واطمأنّت صَفاتهم. أما والله إن كنت لفي ساقتها حتّى تولّت بحذافيرها ما عجزت ولا جبنت وإنّ مسيري هذا لمثلها فلأنقبنّ الباطل حتّى يخرج الحقّ من جنبه. مالي ولقريش والله لقد قاتلتهم كافرين ولأقاتلنّهم مفتونين وإنّي لصاحبهم بالأمس كما أنا صاحبهم اليوم.

---

[1] جميع المخطوطات الرئيسيّة: كذا. والأشهر: ⟨كتاب البيان والتبيين⟩.

us the way, a discerning assayer has scrutinized it and pronounced judgment: ʿAmr ibn Baḥr al-Jāḥiẓ, in his book, Eloquence and Exposition (*al-Bayān wa-l-tabyīn*), mentions that certain people attribute this oration to Muʿāwiyah, then he discusses the issue at some length. This is the gist of Jāḥiẓ's comments: "These words resemble the words of ʿAlī. They are closer to his style in categorizing people and providing information about their state, describing them as beaten, humiliated, fearful, and terrified. In contrast, when did we ever see Muʿāwiyah's speech follow the path of the renunciants and the way of the worshippers!"[1]

1.33 From an oration by ʿAlī, when he marched on the people of Basra. ʿAbdallāh ibn al-ʿAbbās narrated: I entered the Commander of the Faithful's tent at Dhū Qār and found him mending his sandal. He asked me, "What's the value of this sandal?" and, when I replied, "It's worth nothing," he responded, "By God, it's worth more to me than command over you! That I undertake only to establish truth and fight falsehood!" Then he went out and addressed the people in the following oration:[2]

God sent Muḥammad when no Arab read scripture or claimed prophecy. He shepherded them until he had brought them to a safe encampment, a place of refuge, where their lances were straightened and the ground under them made firm. By God, I always fought in the front, always battled until the enemy's battalions were repulsed and defeated, never holding back from weakness or cowardice. This march is the same. I shall impale the demon of falsehood until truth breaks out from its side. Heavens, why do the Quraysh hate me so? By God, I fought them when they were unbelievers, and I shall fight them now in this revolt. I brought them to their knees then and shall do so again.

---

1 Jāḥiẓ, *Bayān*, 2:59–61. Attributed to Muʿāwiyah in Ibn ʿAbd Rabbih, *ʿIqd*, 4:176. ʿAbd al-Zahrāʾ (*Maṣādir*, 1:418) argues in favor of the attribution to ʿAlī, based on Raḍī's and Jāḥiẓ's remarks, and on the fact that the individual who supposedly narrated the oration from Muʿāwiyah, Shuʿayb ibn Ṣafwān, is considered an untrustworthy narrator (after Abū Ḥātim al-Rāzī and Ibn ʿAdī).

2 The march culminated in the Battle of the Camel near Basra in 36/656—between the Caliph ʿAlī on one side, and the Prophet's widow ʿĀʾishah, and the Prophet's Companions Ṭalḥah and Zubayr on the other—in which ʿAlī won a decisive victory. This oration is also narrated in a variant version, §1.101. Dhū Qār was a caravan stop east of Kufa, in the direction of Wāsiṭ, where ʿAlī camped—on events there, see Ḥ 2:187–188—en route to the Battle of the Camel at Basra. Alternatively, Mufīd (*Irshād*, 247) places the oration at Rabadhah, where hajj pilgrims were also in the audience.

1.34 ومن خطبة له عليه السلام في ٱستنفار الناس إلى الشام

أُفٍّ لكم قد سئمت عتابكم أرضيتم بالحياة الدنيا من الآخرة عوضًا وبالذلّ من العزّ خلفًا إذًا دعوتكم إلى جهاد عدوّكم دارت أعينكم كأنّكم من الموت في غمرة ومن الذهول في سكرة يُرتَجُ عليكم حواري فتعمهون فكأنّ قلوبكم مألوسة فأنتم لا تعقلون. ما أنتم لي بثقة سَجِيسَ الليالي وما أنتم بركن يمال بكم ولا زوافر عزٍّ يفتقر إليكم ما أنتم إلّا كإبل ضلّ رعاتها فكلّما جمعت من جانب ٱنتشرت من آخر لبئس لعمر الله سُعُر نار الحرب أنتم تُكادُون ولا تكيدون وتنتقص أطرافكم فلا تمتعضون لا يُنام عنكم وأنتم في غفلة ساهون غُلُب والله المتخاذلون وآيم الله إنّي لأظنّ بكم أن لو حَمِس الوغى وٱستحرّ الموت قد ٱنفرجتم عن ٱبن أبي طالب ٱنفراج الرأس عن البدن. والله إنّ ٱمرأً يمكّن عدوّه من نفسه يعرق لحمه ويهشم عظمه ويفري جلده لعظيمٌ عَجزُه ضعيفٌ ما ضُمّت عليه جوانحُ صدره. أنت فكن ذاك إن شئت فأمّا أنا فوالله دون أن أعطي ذاك ضربٌ بالمشرفيّة تطير منه فراش الهام وتطيح السواعد والأقدام ويفعل الله بعد ذلك ما يشاء. أيّها الناس إنّ لي عليكم حقًّا ولكم عليّ حقّ. فأمّا حقّكم عليّ فالنصيحة لكم وتوفير فيئكم عليكم وتعليمكم كيلا تجهلوا وتأديبكم كيما تعلموا. وأمّا حقّي عليكم فالوفاء بالبيعة والنصيحة في المشهد والمغيب والإجابة حين أدعوكم والطاعة حين آمركم.

1.35 ومن خطبة له عليه السلام بعد التحكيم

1.34   From an oration by ʿAlī, as he mobilized his followers to fight the Syrians:[1]
Shame! I am tired of rebuking you! Is it that you are satisfied with this world
in exchange for the hereafter? Is it that you are happy with humiliation after
having known strength and might? When I call you to fight your enemy, you
roll your eyes as though in the throes of death, as if numb with strong drink.
You struggle to find words and appear mystified by what I say, pretending that
your minds are addled and that you grasped nothing. To the end of the long
nights, never will you be supporters in whom I can trust, or a column on which
I can lean, or allies on whom I can depend! You are like camels whose herder
is at his wits end—each time he gathers them from one side, they scatter from
another. God's life! What cowards you are when faced with the flames of war!
Your enemies conspire but you do not respond, your boundaries contract but
you feel no anger, your enemies never sleep but you remain merrily oblivious.
By God, the slothful will be crushed! By God, I know that when battle blazes
and death burns, you will split from Abū Ṭālib's son as cleanly as a head sliced
off a body. By God, how powerless the man who lets his enemy eat his flesh,
pound his bones, and flay his skin! His ribs conceal a feeble heart! You be that
person if you wish. I, by God, shall strike a blow with my Mashrafī sword that
will crush skulls and sever limbs. Then God may do with me as he wills! People!
You have rights over me, and I have rights over you. I owe you sincere coun-
sel, generous stipends, teaching that dispels ignorance, and lessons that make
you better. You owe me fulfilment of your pledge and sincere support in my
presence and my absence. You must answer when I call and obey when I com-
mand.

1.35   From an oration by ʿAlī after the arbitration:[2]

---

1   ʿAlī delivered this oration in Kufa, shortly after defeating the Kharijites at Nahrawān. Ṭabarī,
    Tārīkh, 5:90–91. It is his fourth post-Nahrawān oration attempting to muster his followers
    against Muʿāwiyah—the first was at Nahrawān itself, the second at Nukhaylah, near Kufa,
    the third immediately after reaching Kufa, and this, the fourth, after a few days had passed in
    Kufa. Details of his followers' responses at each of these events in B 239; Ḥ 2:193–197. ʿAbd al-
    Zahrāʾ (*Maṣādir*, 2:192) argues that this is part of the same oration as § 1.94 which ʿAlī delivered
    after Nahrawān, when the Kufans held back from marching on Muʿāwiyah.
2   Refers to the arbitration (*taḥkīm*) between ʿAlī and Muʿāwiyah, after the Battle of Ṣiffīn, at the
    hands of Abū Mūsā al-Ashʿarī and ʿAmr ibn al-ʿĀṣ at Dūmat al-Jandal, in 37/658 (on the arbi-
    tration, see Ḥ 2:206–264). This oration by ʿAlī was delivered soon thereafter in Kufa, before the
    Battle of Nahrawān. Ṭabarī, *Tārīkh*, 5:77; Ḥ 2:206; B 242–243 (includes an additional section).

الحمد لله وإن أتى الدهر بالخطب الفادح والحدث الجليل وأشهد أن لا إله إلّا الله ليس معه إله غيره وأنّ محمدًا عبده ورسوله صلّى الله عليه وآله. أمّا بعد.

فإنّ معصية الناصح الشفيق العالم المجرّب تورث الحسرة وتعقب الندامة وقد كنت أمرتكم في هذه الحكومة أمري ونخلت لكم مخزون رأيي ﴿لو كان يطاع لقُصيرٍ أمرٌ﴾ فأبيتم عليّ إباء المخالفين الجفاة والمنابذين العصاة حتى ارتاب الناصح بنصحه وضنّ الزند بقدحه فكنت أنا وإيّاكم كما قال أخو هوازن[1]

$$\text{أَمَرْتُكُمُ أَمْـرِي بِمُنْعَـرَجِ اللِّوٰى} \qquad \text{فَلَمْ تَسْتَبِينُوا النُّصْحَ إِلَّا ضُحَى الْغَدِ}$$

1.36 ومن خطبة له عليه السلام في تخويف أهل النهروان

فأنا نذير لكم أن تصبحوا صرعى بأثناء هذا النهر وبأهضام هذا الغائط على غير بيّنة من ربّكم ولا سلطان مبين معكم قد طوّحت بكم الدار واحتبلكم المقدار وقد كنت نهيتكم عن هذه الحكومة فأبيتم عليّ إباء المخالفين الجفاة والمنابذين العصاة[2] حتّى صرفتُ رأيي إلى هواكم وأنتم معاشر أخفّاء الهام سفهاء الأحلام ولم آت لا أبا لكم بُجرًا ولا أردت بكم ضرًّا.

---

[1] البحر: الطويل. [2] م، ي: كذا. ش، ن، ه: ﴿المخالفين المنابذين﴾.

I praise God even though this age has brought a great calamity and dealt a mighty blow. I testify that there is no god but God—there is no god other than he. I testify that Muḥammad is his servant and messenger—may God bless him and his descendants. And now to the matter at hand:[1]

Disobeying a kind, learned, and experienced counselor yields only regret and remorse. I gave you my considered opinion regarding this arbitration, ⟨O if only Qaṣīr's command had been obeyed!⟩[2] With rebellious defiance you rejected my warnings, enough to make a counsellor doubt his own counsel and a flint hold back its spark! In this, you and I may be likened to the Hawāzin poet's lines:[3]

> I gave you my considered opinion
> At the place of the winding sands
> But you heeded not my counsel
> Till forenoon the next day.

1.36 From an oration by ʿAlī warning the people of Nahrawān:[4]

I warn you! Take heed or you will soon be corpses strewn at the bend of this river in the hollows of this plain, holding no mandate from your Lord or proof of righteousness, cast out by your lands, and enmeshed in fate's deadly snare. I forbade you from engaging in arbitration, but you challenged me with defiance and insolence until I gave in to your reckless dictates. Lightheaded fools, the lot of you! May you be deprived of fathers! I'm not the one who has brought calamity on you, nor have I ever intended you harm.

---

1 "And now to the matter at hand" (lit. "As for what comes after," *ammā baʿdu*), is a standard phrase in the early Arabic oration, inserted between the praise-and-benedictions formula and the body of the oration.

2 Proverb referring to the treacherous death of the pre-Islamic Iraqi Azdī king Jadhīmah ("the leper") ibn Mālik ibn Naṣr (fl. 3rd c. AD)—at the hands of the Queen of Palmyra, Zenobia, whose father he had killed and whom he had set out to wed—and the unheeded warnings of his wise counsellor Qaṣīr ibn Saʿd al-Lakhmī. For details of the incident, see Maydānī, *Majmaʿ al-amthāl*, 1:570–575 (under "*khaṭb yasīr fī khaṭb kabīr*"); R 1:243; B 243–244; Kawar, "Djadhīma al-Abrash or al-Waḍḍāḥ," *EI*²; and Shahid, "al-Zabbāʾ," *EI*².

3 Often cited proverbially, the verse is by Durayd ibn al-Ṣimmah (*Dīwān*, 61) of the Hawāzin tribe, a famous poet and warrior who lived mostly in the pre-Islamic period and is said to have been killed at the age of a hundred fighting against Muḥammad in the Battle of Ḥunayn in 8/630. The verse is from a poem lamenting Durayd's deceased brother ʿAbdallāh, which begins: (أَرَثَّ جَدِيدُ الحَبْلِ مِن أُمِّ مَعْبَدِ). R 1:243–244; B 244–245.

4 Nahrawān, east of the Tigris River in Iraq, is the location and name of a pitched battle between ʿAlī and the Kharijites, and this oration was delivered in 38/658 before the battle (Ṭabarī, *Tārīkh*, 5:84, 91, includes full oration text). For details on the Kharijites and the Battle of Nahrawān, see B 245–246; Ḥ 2:265–283.

1.37 ومن كلام له عليه السلام يجري مجرى الخطبة

فقمت بالأمر حين فشلوا وتطلّعت حين تعتعوا ومضيت بنور الله حين وقفوا وكنت أخفضهم صوتًا وأعلاهم فوتًا فطرت بعنانها وٱستبددت بِرِهانها كالجبل لا تحرّكه القواصف ولا تزيله العواصف لم يكن لأحد فيّ مهمز ولا لقائل فيّ مغمز الذليل عندي عزيز حتّى آخذ الحقّ له والقويّ عندي ضعيف حتّى آخذ الحقّ منه رضينا عن الله قضاه وسلّمنا لله أمره. أُتراني أكذب على رسول الله صلّى الله عليه وآله والله لأنا أوّل من صدّقه فلا أكون أوّل من كذب عليه فنظرت في أمري فإذا طاعتي قد سبقت بيعتي وإذا الميثاق في عنقي لغيري.

1.38 ومن خطبة له عليه السلام

1.38.1 وإنّما سمّيت الشبهة شبهة لأنّها تشبه الحقّ.

1.38.2 فأمّا أولياء الله فضياؤهم فيها اليقين ودليلهم سمت الهدى وأمّا أعداء الله فدعاؤهم الضلال ودليلهم العمى فماينجو من الموت من خافه ولا يعطى البقاء من أحبّه.

1.37 From an address by ʿAlī that resembles an oration:[1]
I answered Muḥammad's call when others held back, sped forward when others dragged their feet, and welcomed God's light when others hesitated. The humblest in speech, I outpaced all in action. With the reins of religion firmly in my hands, I flew like the wind, staking everything I possessed, like a mountain that no gales could shake, no storms could budge. No one can find fault or speak ill of me in any of this. In my eyes, the weak were mighty as I strove to restore their rights, the mighty were weak as I wrested from them the rights of the weak. I accepted God's decree and bowed to his command. Do you think I would lie regarding God's Messenger when I was the first to support him? I shall not be the first to lie about him! But when I paused to reflect on my situation, I found that my obedience had preceded my oath of allegiance, and my pledge was a shackle around my neck.[2]

1.38 From an oration by ʿAlī:

1.38.1 Doubt is called doubt because it resembles truth.[3]

1.38.2 Certainty illumines the way for those who place their faith in God, and the path of right guidance carries them forward, while the call of God's enemies is the embodiment of error, and their guide is blindness itself. You will not escape death just because you fear it. You will not remain in this world just because you want to.[4]

---

1 The address was delivered following the Battle of Nahrawān against the Kharijites in Ṣafar 38/658. Ḥ 1:284. Kulaynī (*Kāfī*, 1:454–456) narrates the first paragraph as a posthumous address in the second grammatical person, by an anonymous speaker to ʿAlī, just after he died.

2 Multiple pronouns make this an ambiguous statement. The majority interpretation is this: ʿAlī is saying that he was obliged to obey the wishes of the Messenger who had commanded him to refrain from raising his sword to seek his right. He was thus forced to give an oath of allegiance to the earlier caliphs, for his pledge to the Messenger was a shackle around his neck that stopped him from fighting for his right (Ḥ 2:296; B 249; Gh 1:242). A second interpretation is this: ʿAlī is saying that the people had been commanded to render him obedience, a mandate that preceded their actual oath of allegiance to him; their pledge to him was a shackle around his neck, and he could not refuse to lead them (B 249).

3 The line plays on the paronomasia (*jinās*) between "doubt" (*shubhah*), and "resemble" (*tushbih*), both deriving from the root letters "Sh-B-H."

4 Some sources attribute the last two lines to ʿAlī's associate Mālik al-Ashtar in the lead-up to the Battle of Ṣiffīn, in a speech he gave following ʿAlī's speech, calling on the people to march on Muʿāwiyah. Minqarī, *Waqʿat Ṣiffīn*, 95; Iskāfī, *Miʿyār*, 126; Abū Ḥanīfah al-Dīnawarī, *Akhbār*, 164.

1.39 ومن خطبة له عليه السلام

مُنيتُ بمن لا يطيع إذا أمرت ولا يجيب إذا دعوت لا أبا لكم ما تنتظرون بنصركم ربّكم.
أما دين يجمعكم ولا حميّة تحمشكم. أقوم فيكم مستصرخًا وأناديكم متغوّثًا فلا تسمعون لي
قولًا ولا تطيعون لي أمرًا حتّى تكشّف الأمور عن عواقب المساءة فما يدرك بكم ثأر
ولا يبلغ بكم مرام. دعوتكم إلى نصر إخوانكم فجرجرتم جرجرة الجمل الأَسَرّ وتثاقلتم تثاقل
النَّضْو الأُدبر ثمّ خرج إليّ منكم جنيد متذائب ضعيف ﴿كَأَنَّمَا يُسَاقُونَ إِلَى ٱلْمَوْتِ وَهُمْ
يَنظُرُونَ﴾.

قوله عليه السلام ⟨متذائب⟩ أي مضطرب من قولهم ⟨تذاءبت الريح⟩ اي اضطرب هبوبها ومنه
سمّي الذئب لاضطراب مشيته.

1.40 ومن كلام له عليه السلام في معنى الخوارج لمّا سمع قولهم ⟨لا حكم إلّا لله⟩. قال
كلمة حقّ يراد بها باطل. نعم إنّه لا حكم إلّا لله ولكن هؤلاء يقولون لا إمرة وإنّه لا
بدّ للناس من أمير برّ أو فاجر يعمل في إمرته المؤمن ويستمتع فيها الكافر ويبلّغ الله فيها
الأجل ويجمع به الفيء ويقاتل به العدوّ وتأمن به السبل ويؤخذ به للضعيف من القويّ
حتّى يستريح برّ ويستراح من فاجر.

1.39 From an oration by ʿAlī:[1]

I am tested with followers who do not obey my command or answer my call. May you be deprived of fathers! What are you waiting for? Why do you not fight and serve your Lord? Does no religion unite you, no outraged honor goad you to action? I stand among you shouting till I'm hoarse, appealing to you for succor, but you hear not a word, not a single command. These events are the result of your despicable behavior. No requital can be sought with you at my side, no purpose achieved. When I summoned you to come to your brothers' aid, you growled like a sullen camel with sores on its chest, you plodded like a scraggy beast with lesions on its rump. The few who came forward came limp and dithering, «as though driven to a death they could see in front of their eyes.»[2]

Raḍī: By "dithering (*mutadhāʾib*)," ʿAlī means: "jerkily," from the commonly used phrase, "the wind dithered (*tadhāʾabat al-rīḥ*)," meaning, "it blew jerkily." It is from this meaning—the jerkiness of its walk—that the wolf (*dhiʾb*) is named.

1.40 From an address by ʿAlī when he heard the Kharijites shout, ⟨No rule save God's!⟩:[3]

The statement is true, but the intent is false. Yes, there is no authority save God's, but these people are claiming that there should be no other ruler. In truth, the community must have a ruler, whether pious or wicked, under whose jurisdiction believers do good and disbelievers make merry, till God brings each period to its destined conclusion. Taxes need to be collected, enemies repudiated, highways protected, and rights wrested from the mighty for the weak—all this, until the pious ruler goes to his rest, or the wicked ruler's death allows the community to rest.

---

1   ʿAlī delivered this address in Kufa following the raid by Muʿāwiyah's commander, Nuʿmān ibn Bashīr al-Anṣārī, on ʿAyn al-Tamr, west of the Euphrates, on the frontier between Syria and Iraq, in 39/659 (Ḥ 1:301; B 250; see events of the raid in Ḥ 1:301–306; Zetterstéen, "al-Nuʿmān b. Bashīr," *EI*[2]; see also §1.66, delivered at around the same time). Some lines are transcribed by Ṭabarī (*Tārīkh*, 5:107) within an oration ʿAlī delivered chastising the Kufans for not responding to his call to mobilize in aid of Muḥammad ibn Abī Bakr, who was killed by ʿAmr ibn al-ʿĀṣ in Egypt in 38/658.

2   Qurʾan, Anfāl 8:6.

3   Ar. *Lā ḥukma illā li-llāh.* ʿAlī was preaching in the mosque in Kufa, in 37/657, soon after the Battle of Ṣiffīn, when he was interrupted by a group of Kharijites shouting this slogan, and he responded with the words at hand (Balādhurī, *Ansāb*, 2:404; Shāfiʿī, *Umm*, 4:229; Ṭabarī, *Tārīkh*, 5:72–73; see the events surrounding the Kharijites' use of this slogan, and ʿAlī's attempts to conciliate them before the Battle of Nahrawān, in Ḥ 2:310–312). The first Kharijite to utter the slogan was Burak (or al-Ḥajjāj) ibn ʿAbdallāh al-Tamīmī, who later conspired with the Kharijites Ibn Muljam and ʿAmr ibn Bakr to assassinate ʿAlī, Muʿāwiyah, and ʿAmr ibn al-ʿĀṣ; Ibn Muljam killed ʿAlī, but the other two attempts failed, and all three conspirators were immediately executed (R 1:252). See also §1.182 and §3.182.

وفي رواية أخرى أنّه عليه السلام لمّا سمع تحكيمهم قال
حكم الله أنتظر فيكم.

وقال
أمّا الإمرة البرّة فيعمل فيها التقيّ وأمّا الإمرة الفاجرة فيتمتّع فيها الشقيّ إلى أن تنقطع
مدّته وتدركه منيّته.

1.41 ومن خطبة له عليه السلام
إنّ الوفاء توأم الصدق ولا أعلم جُنّة أوقى منه وما يغدر من علم كيف المرجع ولقد
أصبحنا في زمان قد اتّخذ أكثر أهله الغدر كَيْسًا ونسبهم أهل الجهل فيه إلى حسن
الحيلة. ما لهم قاتلهم الله قد يَرَى الحُوَّلُ القُلَّبُ وجهَ الحيلة ودونها مانع من أمر الله ونهيه
فيدعها رأي عين بعد القدرة عليها وينتهز فرصتها من لا حريجة له في الدين.

1.42 ومن خطبة له عليه السلام
أيّها الناس إنّ أخوف ما أخاف عليكم اثنتان اتّباع الهوى وطول الأمل فأمّا اتّباع الهوى
فيصدّ عن الحقّ وأمّا طول الأمل فينسي الآخرة ألا وإنّ الدنيا قد ولّت حذّاء فلم يبق
منها إلّا صُبابة كصبابة الإناء اصطبّها صابّها ألا وإنّ الآخرة قد أقبلت ولكلّ منهما بنون
فكونوا من أبناء الآخرة ولا تكونوا من أبناء الدنيا فإنّ كلّ ولد سيلحق بأمّه يوم القيامة
وإنّ اليوم عمل ولا حساب وغدًا حساب ولا عمل.

In another version of the report, ʿAlī said the following when he heard their declaration about authority:
It's the manifestation of God's authority in you that I'm waiting for!

In a third version, he said:
Under the rule of the pious, the virtuous perform good deeds. Under the rule of the wicked, the wretched make merry till their time runs out and death overtakes them.

1.41 From an oration by ʿAlī:[1]
Loyalty is honesty's twin. I know of no better shield from hellfire, and those who believe they will return to God never betray. We have entered an age when the public equates betrayal with intelligence and the ignorant view duplicitous liars as clever strategists. What is wrong with them? May God punish them! The man of discernment also knows how to practice cunning, but he is checked by God's commands and prohibitions. Although he sees the option and has the capability, he chooses to refrain. It is the man who has no religion or scruple who exploits the opportunity to deceive.

1.42 From an oration by ʿAlī:[2]
People! I fear most for you two things: pursuit of desire and lengthy yearnings. Pursuit of desire stops you from seeing the truth, while lengthy yearnings make you forget the hereafter. Take heed! The world is retreating in haste! Only a small residue remains, like dregs in an emptied vessel. Take heed! The hereafter is at hand! And each of the two has children. Be children of the hereafter, be not children of the world, for children will be returned to their mothers on the day of resurrection. Today is the day for deeds, not reckoning. Tomorrow is the day of reckoning, not deeds.

---

1   The commentators do not provide context, but Ibn Abī al-Ḥadīd narrates examples of ʿAlī's honorable actions in war, including his allowing Muʿāwiyah's army to access the river, even after they had earlier denied it to him. Ḥ 2:313–314. The "man of discernment" is ʿAlī himself.

2   ʿAlī delivered this oration in the Grand Mosque in Kufa immediately following his arrival after the Battle of the Camel in Rajab 36/656. Minqarī, *Waqʿat Ṣiffīn*, 3–4 (with this text, and further sections of the oration containing political themes). Some lines are similar in §1.28 and §1.45. Kulaynī (*Kāfī*, 8:58) transcribes it as the earlier part of §1.50, which is placed by Yaʿqūbī (*Tārīkh*, 2:191) after the arbitration in 37/658. Māmaṭīrī (*Nuzhah*, 211) attributes the oration to the Prophet, via ʿAlī.

1.43   ومن كلام له عليه السلام وقد أشار عليه أصحابه بالاستعداد للحرب بعد إرساله جرير بن عبد الله إلى معاوية

إنّ ٱستعدادي لحرب أهل الشام وجرير عندهم إغلاق للشام وصرف لأهله عن خير إن أرادوه ولكن قد وقَّتُ لجرير وقتًا لا يقيم بعده إلّا مخدوعًا أو عاصيًا والرأي مع الأناة فأرْوِدوا ولا أكره لكم الإعداد. ولقد ضربت أنف هذا الأمر وعينه وقلَّبت ظهره وبطنه فلم أر لي إلّا القتال أو الكفر إنّه قد كان على الأمّة والٍ أحدث أحداثًا وأوجد الناس مقالًا فقالوا ثمّ نقموا فغيّروا.

1.44   ومن كلام له عليه السلام لمّا هرب مصقلة بن هبيرة الشيبانيّ إلى معاوية وكان قد ٱبتاع سبي بني ناجية من عامل أمير المؤمنين عليه السلام وأعتقهم فلمّا طالبه بالمال خاسَ به وهرب إلى الشام. فقال

قبّح الله مصقلة فعَل فِعْل السادة وفرّ فرار العبيد فما أنطق مادحه حتّى أسكته ولا صدّق واصفه حتّى بكّته ولو أقام لأخذنا ميسوره وٱنتظرنا بماله وفوره.

1.43 From 'Alī's reply to his associates who, soon after he had sent Jarīr ibn 'Abdallāh as envoy to Mu'āwiyah, were urging him to make preparations for battle:[1]

If I prepared to battle the Syrians while Jarīr is still with them, I would close the door to reconciliation and eliminate the chance, were they to wish it, of a peaceful outcome. I have given Jarīr a limit for his return, which he should adhere to unless he is deceived or disobedient. I think we must wait, so go slowly, although I too am not against preparing. I've examined the eyes and nose of this affair, and flipped it over, back to belly, and the only alternative I see to fighting is to forsake Islam. Our community had a leader who instituted unwarranted practices, and he gave people the opportunity to rebuke him.[2] They rebuked him, then turned hostile, and took it upon themselves to effect change.

1.44 From an address by 'Alī after Maṣqalah ibn Hubayrah al-Shaybānī defected to Mu'āwiyah. Maṣqalah had purchased captive slaves of the Banū Nājiyah from 'Alī's commander in order to free them. When the commander asked for payment, he reneged and fled to Syria.[3]

May God strike Maṣqalah with shame! He behaved like a chieftain then fled like a slave! No sooner had he prompted his admirers to utter his praises before he shut their mouths, no sooner had he confirmed his extollers' commendations before he turned round and rebuked them. Had he remained in Iraq, I would have shown leniency and allowed him to postpone payment until his fortunes improved.

---

1 'Alī delivered this address in Kufa, shortly after the Battle of the Camel in 36/656. Jarīr had been 'Uthmān's governor in Hamadān, and, when 'Alī dismissed him, he came to 'Alī in Kufa and pledged allegiance. According to the sources, however, he remained pro-Umayyad. Details of Jarīr's embassy to Mu'āwiyah in Damascus as 'Alī's envoy, and related events and epistles, in Ḥ 3:74–91. See also Jarīr's background with 'Alī in Ḥ 3:70–74.

2 Refers to the third caliph, 'Uthmān (d. 35/656), who was killed in Medina by a group of Muslims from Kufa and Egypt decrying his nepotism and other shortcomings. Ḥ 2:323–333, 3:1–69 (with details of these events and the people's grievances); B 257–258.

3 This event took place after the arbitration, in the early months of 38/658, and 'Alī's oration was delivered in Kufa. Maṣqalah was then 'Alī's governor in Ardashīr. The commander from whom he had purchased the freedom of the Banū Nājiyah captives was Ma'qil ibn Qays al-Riyāḥī. When Maṣqalah fled to Syria, Mu'āwiyah appointed him to several important posts. Details of these events and people in Ḥ 3:120–151; R 1:258–261; B 258; Balādhurī, *Ansāb*, 2:417–418; Ṭabarī, *Tārīkh*, 5:113–132 ("The Banū Nājiyah Episode"), 5:128–131; Pellat, "al-Khirrīt," *EI²*. See also 'Alī's earlier epistles to Maṣqalah chastising him for misappropriating treasury funds, §2.39 and §2.44.

1.45 ومن خطبة له عليه السلام

الحمد لله غير مقنوط من رحمته ولا مخلوّ من نعمته ولا مأيوس من مغفرته ولا مستنكف عن عبادته الذي لا تبرح منه رحمة ولا تفقد له نعمة.

والدنيا دار مُني لها الفناء ولأهلها منها الجلاء وهي حلوة خضرة قد عُجّلت للطالب والتبست بقلب الناظر فارتحلوا منها بأحسن ما بحضرتكم من الزاد ولا تسألوا فيها فوق الكفاف ولا تطلبوا منها أكثر من البلاغ.

1.46 ومن كلام له عليه السلام عند عزمه على المسير إلى الشام

اللهمّ إنّي أعوذ بك من وعثاء السفر وكآبة المنقلب وسوء المنظر في الأهل والمال والولد.[1] اللهمّ أنت الصاحب في السفر وأنت الخليفة في الأهل ولا يجمعهما غيرك لأنّ المستخلف لا يكون مستصحبًا والمستصحب لا يكون مستخلفًا.

وابتداء هذا الكلام مرويّ عن رسول الله صلّى الله عليه وآله وقد قفّاه عليه السلام بأبلغ كلام وتمّمه بأحسن تمام من قوله ﴿ولا يجمعهما غيرك﴾ إلى آخر الفصل.

1.47 ومن كلام له عليه السلام في ذكر الكوفة

كأنّي بك يا كوفة تُمَدّينَ مدّ الأديم العكاظيّ وتُعرَكين بالنوازل وتُركبين بالزلازل وإنّي لأعلم أنّه ما أراد بك جبّار سوءًا إلّا ابتلاه الله بشاغل ورماه بقاتل.

---

[1] كذا. م: ﴿في الأهل والمال﴾. ن، ش: ﴿في النفس والأهل والمال﴾. هـ: ﴿في النفس والأهل والمال والولد﴾. وأضيفت في هامش م، ش: ﴿والولد﴾.

1.45 From an oration by ʿAlī:[1]
I praise God, never uncertain of his mercy, never empty of his favors, never doubtful of his forgiveness, never grudging in his worship. His mercy never ends, his favors never cease.

The world is an abode whose edifice awaits destruction and whose people await eviction. Sweet and green, she appears to the seeker as a gift and ensnares the viewer's heart. People! Leave her with the best provisions you can find. In life, do not ask of her more than you need, or seek from her more than you require.

1.46 From ʿAlī's supplication when he began the march to Syria:[2]
God, protect me from the hardships of travel, a sorrowful end, and the grief of seeing my family, children, and property in ruin. God, you are my companion in this journey and the guardian I leave behind with my family. Only you can do both, for a man who is left behind cannot travel as a companion, and a man who travels as a companion cannot be left behind.

Raḍī: The opening lines of this supplication have also been narrated from God's Messenger.[3] Beautifully completing the Prophet's, ʿAlī added his own eloquent lines: "Only you can do both," to the end of the piece.

1.47 From an address by ʿAlī about Kufa:[4]
I see you, Kufa, stretched like raw leather on display at the Market of ʿUkāẓ, beset by calamities and plagued with tremors. But I also know that should a tyrant intend you harm, God will engulf him in misfortune, then send a man to kill him.

---

1 Two unconnected excerpts from ʿAlī's sermon on ʿĪd al-Fiṭr or ʿĪd al-Aḍḥā, presumably delivered in Kufa in one of the four years of his caliphate between 36/656 and 40/661. Also part of this sermon is §1.28 (and its variant recension, §1.52). B 221, 259. Baḥrānī (B 259) says it is an ʿĪd al-Fiṭr sermon, but, if it is part of §1.52, and since §1.52.3 mentions the sacrificial animal, it was more likely delivered on ʿĪd al-Aḍḥā.

2 ʿAlī intoned this prayer "when he placed his foot in the stirrup," as he was leaving from his home in Kufa to fight Muʿāwiyah in Syria. Before praying it, he intoned the name of God and the Qurʾanic verse, «Glorious is the one who subjugated this (mount) to our use, otherwise we would not have been capable» (Qurʾan, Zukhruf 43:13: سبحان الذي سخّر لنا هذا وما كنّا له مقرنين). Ḥ 3:166–169 (with further prayers by ʿAlī during this march); Minqarī, Waqʿat Ṣiffīn, 132–133.

3 See, e.g., Muslim, Ṣaḥīḥ, 2:979 (§1343).

4 For examples of "tyrants" killed in Kufa in the early Umayyad period, see B 262. On sayings of the Prophet's family regarding "virtues of Kufa," see Ḥ 3:198–199.

1.48 ومن خطبة له عليه السلام عند المسير إلى الشام

الحمد لله كلّما وقب ليل وغسق والحمد لله كلّما لاح نجم وخفق والحمد لله غير مفقود الإنعام ولا مكافأ الإفضال. أمّا بعد.

فقد بعثت مقدّمتي وأمرتهم بلزوم هذا المِلْطاط حتّى يأتيهم أمري وقد رأيت أن أقطع هذه النطفة إلى شرذمة منكم موطّنين أكناف دجلة فأنهضهم معكم إلى عدوّكم وأجعلهم من أمداد القوّة لكم.

يعني عليه السلام بـ﴿الملطاط﴾ هاهنا السمت الذي أمرهم بلزومه وهو شاطئ الفرات ويقال ذلك أيضًا لشاطئ البحر وأصله ما آستوى من الأرض. ويعني بـ﴿النطفة﴾ ماء الفرات وهو من غريب العبارات وعجيبها.

1.49 ومن خطبة له عليه السلام

الحمد لله الذي بطن خفيّاتِ الأمور ودلّت عليه أعلام الظهور وآمتنع على عين البصير فلا عينُ مَن لم يره تُنكره ولا قلب من أثبته يبصره. سبق في العلوّ فلا شيء أعلى منه وقرب في الدنوّ فلا شيء أقرب منه فلا آستعلاؤه باعده عن شيء من خلقه ولا قربه ساواهم في المكان به. لم يطلع العقول على تحديد صفته ولم يحجبها عن واجب معرفته فهو الذي تشهد له أعلام الوجود على إقرار قلب ذي الجحود تعالى الله عمّا يقول المشبّهون به والجاحدون له علوًّا كبيرًا.

1.50 ومن خطبة له عليه السلام

إنّما بدء وقوع الفتن أهواء تُتّبع وأحكام تُبتدع يخالف فيها كتاب الله ويتولّى عليها رجال رجالًا على غير دين الله فلو أنّ الباطل خلص من مزاج الحقّ لم يخفَ على المرتادين ولو أنّ الحقّ خلص من لبس الباطل آنقطعت عنه ألسن المعاندين ولكن يؤخذ من هذا ضغث ومن هذا ضغث فيمزجان فيهنالك يستولي الشيطان على أوليائه وينجو ﴿ٱلَّذِينَ سَبَقَتْ لَهُم﴾ من الله ﴿ٱلْحُسْنَىٰ﴾.

1.48 From an oration by ʿAlī when he marched on Syria:[1]
I praise God whenever night spreads and darkens. I praise God whenever stars rise and set. I praise God whose favors are never deficient and whose gifts can never be repaid. And now to the matter at hand:

I have dispatched my vanguard and commanded them to stay close to the high bank until I send further orders. I intend to cross this clear water and make contact with the tribesmen who live in the lee of the Tigris. I will recruit them to fight your enemy and increase your strength and numbers.

Raḍī: By "high bank (*milṭāṭ*)," ʿAlī means the path he has commanded them to follow along the banks of the Euphrates. The word is also used for the seashore, and its original meaning is level ground. By "clear water (*nuṭfah*)" he means the water of the Euphrates, and it is a strange and marvelous expression.

1.49 From an oration by ʿAlī:
Praise God, who is concealed in unseen mysteries but confirmed by clear signs. He is hidden from the keenest observer, yet the eye that does not see him cannot deny his existence, while the heart that acknowledges him cannot comprehend him. He is lofty and nothing is loftier than he, he is near and nothing is nearer than he, yet his loftiness does not distance him from his creatures, while his nearness does not place him with them. He has not revealed to intellects his true description, but neither has he veiled them from recognizing him, which they must do. Creation bears witness to the creator and compels the denier to acknowledge him in his heart, but his reality is exalted above whatever is said about him by those who liken him to his creation, or those who deny his existence.

1.50 From an oration by ʿAlī:[2]
Revolt begins with the indulgence of whims and the prescription of heresies, whereby God's Book is disobeyed, and men follow men in defiance of God's religion. If falsehood had no trace of truth, its evil would not be concealed from observers, and if truth had no shadow of falsehood, its enemies' tongues would be silenced. But a bit is taken from here, a bit is taken from there, they are mixed together, and lo and behold, Satan gains mastery over his followers! Only «those for whom» God's «blessings have been decreed» are saved.[3]

---

1   ʿAlī delivered this oration on 5 Shawwāl 37 AH (Wednesday, March 17, 658 AD) at Nukhaylah, just outside Kufa, en route to Ṣiffīn. Minqarī, *Waqʿat Ṣiffīn*, 131–132; B 263 (includes a summary of the vanguard's commanders and numbers, and of ensuing events); Ḥ 3:201 (further lines from the oration), Ḥ 3:202–215 (details of the events).

2   ʿAlī delivered this oration in Kufa after the arbitration in 37/658. Yaʿqūbī, *Tārīkh*, 2:191.

3   Qurʾan, Anbiyāʾ 21:101.

1.51 ومن كلامه عليه السلام لمّا غلب أصحاب معاوية أصحابه على شريعة الفرات بصفّين ومنعوهم من الماء

قد ٱستطعموكم القتال فأقرّوا على مذلّة وتأخير محلّة أو روّوا السيوف من الدماء تَرْوَوا من الماء فالموت في حياتكم مقهورين والحياة في موتكم قاهرين ألا وإنّ معاوية قاد لُمَةً من الغواة وعمّس عليهم الخبر حتّى جعلوا نحورهم أغراض المنيّة.

1.52 ومن خطبة له عليه السلام. قد تقدّم مختارها برواية ونذكرها ههنا برواية أخرى لتغاير الروايتين

1.52.1 ألا وإنّ الدنيا قد تصرّمت وآذنت بٱنقضاء وتنكّر معروفها وأدبرت حذّاء فهي تحفز بالفناء سكّانها وتحدو بالموت جيرانها وقد أمرّ فيها ما كان حلواً وكدر منها ما كان صفواً فلم يبق منها إلّا سَمَلة كسملة الإداوة أو جرعة كجرعة المَقْلة لو تمزّزها الصديان لم ينقع.

1.52.2 فأزمعوا عباد الله الرحيل عن هذه الدار المقدور على أهلها الزوال ولا يغلبنّكم فيها الأمل ولا يطولنّ عليكم الأمد فوالله لو حننتم حنين الوُلّه العِجال ودعوتم بهَديل الحمام وجأرتم جُؤار متبتّلي الرهبان وخرجتم إلى الله من الأموال والأولاد ٱلتماس القربة إليه في ٱرتفاع درجة عنده أو غفران سيّئة أحصتها كتبه وحفظها رسله لكان قليلًا فيما

1.51 From ʿAlī's address when Muʿāwiyah's army prevailed over his by the Euphrates, and blocked their access to water:[1]

By this act, they beg to be fed the victuals of war. You can either accept defeat and retreat, or quench your swords' thirst for blood and your thirst for water. Death to a life that accepts defeat! Life, in reality, is in a fighter's death! Hark my words! Muʿāwiyah leads a band of fools and imbeciles. By muddying reports of what happened,[2] he has deceived them into exposing their throats to fate's arrows.

1.52 From an oration by ʿAlī, parts of which were cited earlier in a different transmission. We record it again in this transmission because of the variance between the two:[3]

1.52.1 Harken! The world has severed its rope and announced its end, its favors have become strangers and it turns away in speed, it spurs its residents to annihilation and drives its neighbors toward death, its sweetness has turned bitter and its clarity has become turbid, all that remains of it is the last few drops in the jug, the last mouthfuls apportioned with a pebble.[4] The thirsty man sucks on it in desperation, but it does not even wet his throat.

1.52.2 Servants of God, make ready to quit this abode, for its residents are fated to die. Let not hopes of its permanence take hold, nor suppose your time in it to be long. By God, if you were to moan like bereaved camel mares, supplicate like cooing doves, and intone like praying hermits, or if you forsook property and children to attain nearness to God, to achieve a high station near him, or forgiveness for the sins that are recorded in his accounts and noted by his

---

1 When the two armies arrived at Ṣiffīn in Dhū al-Ḥijjah 36/June 657, Muʿāwiyah's troops took control of the riverbank and blocked ʿAlī's troops from the water. ʿAlī fought and prevailed. Against the urgings of his supporters to requite like for like, ʿAlī allowed Muʿāwiyah's troops unfettered access to drink. Minqarī, *Waqʿat Ṣiffīn*, 156–162; Ḥ 3:312–331; Gh 1:287.

2 I.e., by falsely accusing ʿAlī of ʿUthmān's murder.

3 ʿĪd al-Aḍḥā sermon, as evidenced by its reference to the sacrificial animal (§1.52.3). See also the opening lines of this sermon—in Ṣadūq, *Man lā yaḥḍuruhu*, 1:518; Ṭūsī, *Miṣbāḥ*, 663—which includes the "God is great" peroration typical of an Eid sermon. The "earlier citation" was §1.28 (which is also said to be part of §1.45: B 221, 259); the opening lines of §1.28 and §1.52.1 are similar.

4 The reference is to a pebble (*maqlah*) placed in a vessel to ration water among a group of travelers; for each person, water was dripped until it covered the pebble, then he sucked those drops from the pebble. Ḥ 3:333; R 1:273; Gh 1:289.

أرجو لكم من ثوابه وأخاف عليكم من عقابه. وتالله لو أنماثت قلوبكم أنمياثا وسالت عيونكم من رغبة إليه ورهبة منه دمًا ثم عمّرتم في الدنيا ما الدنيا باقية ما جزت أعمالكم ولو لم تبقوا شيئًا من جهدكم أنعمه عليكم العظام وهداه إيّاكم للإيمان.

١.٥٢.٣ ومنها في ذكر يوم النحر وصفة الأضحيّة

ومن تمام الأضحيّة استشراف أذنها وسلامة عينها فإذا سلمت الأذن والعين سلمت الأضحيّة وتمّت ولو كانت عضباء القرن تجرّ رجلها إلى المنسك.

١.٥٣ ومن كلام له عليه السلام

فتداكّوا عليّ تداكّ الإبل الهيم يوم ورودها قد أرسلها راعيها وخُلعت مثانيها حتّى ظننت أنّهم قاتليّ أو بعضهم قاتل بعض لديّ.

وقد قلّبت هذا الأمر بطنه وظهره حتّى منعني النوم فما وجدتُني يسعني إلّا قتالهم أو الجحود بما جاء به محمّد صلّى الله عليه وآله. فكانت معالجة القتال أهون عليّ من معالجة العقاب وموتات الدنيا أهون عليّ من موتات الآخرة.

١.٥٤ ومن كلام له عليه السلام وقد استبطأ أصحابُه إذنَه لهم في القتال بصفّين

angels—all this would be little compared with the reward I hope for you and the punishment I fear. By God, if your hearts were to dissolve like salt, if your eyes shed blood in fear and hope, and if you were permitted to live in this world for as long as it continues to exist, your deeds—even with supreme toil and labor—would not repay God's immense favors, or his guidance of you to faith.

1.52.3 From the same oration, referring to the Eid of Sacrifice, and describing the requirements of a sacrificial animal:
The sacrificial animal is considered intact if its ears are whole and its eyes are sound.[1] If the ears and eyes are sound, then the sacrificial animal is considered sound and intact. This is true even if a horn is broken and the animal drags its foot to the slaughterhouse.

1.53 From an address by ʿAlī:[2]
They crowded me like parched camels jostling at the waterhole when the herder unfastens their hobbling ropes and sets them loose. I feared they would crush me or each other to death.[3]

I have turned over this matter in my mind through many sleepless nights and concluded that I can either fight the rebels or repudiate Muḥammad's religion, and braving war with men sits lighter on me than braving God's punishment, facing death in this world sits lighter on me than facing death in eternity.

1.54 From ʿAlī's address to his troops at Ṣiffīn when they expressed impatience at his reluctance to commence battle:[4]

---

1   Lit. "if its ears stand up" (*istishrāf udhunihā*), denoting an animal whose ears are neither slit nor defective. B 271.
2   Referring to the Medinans' pledge of allegiance to ʿAlī as caliph, after ʿUthmān's death, and to the breaking of that pledge, either by Ṭalḥah and Zubayr (H 4:6–11), or by Muʿāwiyah and the Syrians (R 1:275; B 272–273), or by both groups (Gh 1:297–298). Rāwandī and Baḥrānī add that ʿAlī refers here also to his initial delay in granting his army permission to fight the Syrians, explicitly mentioned next in §1.54. Ibn Qutaybah (*Imāmah*, 1:174) and Ibn Ṭāwūs (*Kashf*, 174, 180) cite it as part of a lengthy epistle ʿAlī wrote after Muḥammad ibn Abī Bakr's killing in 38/658. They include §1.30 in this epistle; see more details in note there.
3   Similar lines in §1.3.4, §1.135.2, §1.226.
4   37/657. Details of ʿAlī's efforts at reconciliation in H 4:13–32. Ibn ʿAbd Rabbih (*ʿIqd*, 1:95) and Māmaṭīrī (*Nuzhah*, 376) narrate the line (By God, I care not ... confront me!) as a response to associates who warned him, saying, "Do you fight the Syrians in the morning, then come out in the evening wearing only a waist-cloth and cloak?"

أمّا قولكم أكلّ ذلك كراهية الموت فوالله ما أبالي دخلت إلى الموت أو خرج الموت إليّ وأمّا قولكم شكًّا في أهل الشام فوالله ما دفعت الحرب يومًا إلّا وأنا أطمع أن تلحق بي طائفة فتهتدي بي وتعشو إلى ضوئي أحبّ إليّ من أن أقتلها على ضلالها وإن كانت تبوء بآثامها.

1.55 ومن كلام له عليه السلام

ولقد كنّا مع رسول الله صلّى الله عليه وآله نقتل آباءنا وأبناءنا وإخواننا وأعمامنا ما يزيدنا ذلك إلّا إيمانًا وتسليمًا ومضيًّا على اللَّقَم وصبرًا على مَضَض الألم وجدًّا على جهاد العدوّ ولقد كان الرجل منّا والآخر من عدوّنا يتصاولان تصاول الفحلين يتخالسان أنفسهما أيّهما يسقي صاحبه كأس المنون فمرّة لنا من عدوّنا ومرّة لعدوّنا منّا فلمّا رأى الله صدقنا أنزل بعدوّنا الكبت وأنزل علينا النصر حتّى استقرّ الإسلام ملقيًا جرانه ومتبوّئًا أوطانه. ولعمري لو كنّا نأتي ما أتيتم ما قام للدين عمود ولا اخضرّ للإيمان عود وأيم الله لتحتلبنّها دمًا ولتتبعنّها ندمًا.

1.56 ومن كلام له عليه السلام لأصحابه

You taunt, "All these excuses to avoid death!" By God, I care not whether I confront death or death confronts me! You mock, "Or perhaps you hesitate to fight the Syrians?" By God, I would not delay battle even by a day, were it not for the hope that a few may yet return, to be guided by me, and—although their sight is weak!—to discern my light. This would please me more than killing them for their errant ways, notwithstanding they would die yoked to their sins.

1.55 From an address by ʿAlī:[1]

We fought in support of God's Messenger and killed our fathers, our sons, our brothers, and our uncles,[2] all the while increasing in faith and acceptance, commitment to the true path, endurance in the face of stinging pain, and intensity in fighting the enemy. A warrior from our side and another from the enemy would clash like two stallions to the death, each attempting to steal the other's life, each offering the other fate's cup.[3] Ours would win in one combat, theirs would prevail in another. When God saw our true courage, he crushed our enemy in defeat and sent us triumphant victory. So was Islam founded. Thus did it rest its withers and settle into its stall. I swear on my life! If we had behaved like you, religion would never have been established, belief would never have blossomed. I swear God's oath! You shall squeeze calamity's udders and find blood in your pail.[4] You shall be dogged forever by regret.

1.56 From ʿAlī's address to his followers:[5]

---

1   ʿAlī gave this address to his followers, either at Ṣiffīn in 37/657, when many of his troops, despite being close to winning, pressed him to accept Muʿāwiyah's truce (B 273), or a year later in Kufa, when Muʿāwiyah's commander ʿAbdallāh ibn al-Ḥaḍramī attacked neighboring Basra (H 4:34–53). It is also possible that he spoke similar lines on more than one occasion.

2   In the Battle of Badr, for example, Ḥamzah ibn ʿAbd al-Muṭṭalib fought and killed Muʿāwiyah's paternal cousin, who was also from Ḥamzah's tribe, Shaybah ibn Rabīʿah, and ʿUmar ibn al-Khaṭṭāb fought and killed his own maternal uncle Hishām ibn al-Mughīrah. H 4:34.

3   In various early battles, for example, ʿAlī singlehandedly fought and killed the known warriors Walīd ibn ʿUtbah, Ṭalḥah ibn Abī Ṭalḥah, and ʿAmr ibn ʿAbd Wadd. H 4:34.

4   "Milking blood" is a metaphor for the painful results of the failure of ʿAlī's supporters to answer his call. B 274; Gh 1:305.

5   "The man with a large maw" is probably Muʿāwiyah, who was a glutton, or, less likely, Ziyād ibn Abīhi, Ḥajjāj ibn Yūsuf, or al-Mughīrah ibn Shuʿbah (R 1:276–277; B 275; H 4:54). The full text is narrated by Nuʿaym (*Fitan*, 1:164) from the Prophet via ʿAlī, and it names the man as Muʿāwiyah. The second half is placed by Kulaynī (*Kāfī*, 2:219) on the pulpit of the Kufa mosque, while it is transcribed by Kūfī (*Manāqib*, 2:64) as a tag to a response to a merchant from whom ʿAlī had purchased a shirt.

أما إنّه سيظهر عليكم بعدي رجل رحب البُلعوم منداحق البطن يأكل ما يجد ويطلب ما لا يجد فاقتلوه ولن تقتلوه ألا وإنّه سيأمركم بسبّي والبراءة منّي فأمّا السبّ فسبُّوني فإنّه لي زكاة ولكم نجاة وأمّا البراءة فلا تتبرّأوا منّي فإنّي ولدت على الفطرة وسبقت إلى الإيمان والهجرة.

1.57   ومن كلام له عليه السلام كلّم به الخوارج

أصابكم حاصب ولا بقي منكم آبر أبعد إيماني بالله وجهادي مع رسول الله أشهد على نفسي بالكفر لـ﴿قَدْ ضَلَلْتُ إِذًا وَمَا أَنَا مِنَ الْمُهْتَدِينَ﴾ فأوبوا شرّ مآب وارجعوا على أثر الأعقاب أما إنّكم ستلقون بعدي ذلًّا شاملًا وسيفًا قاطعًا وأثرة يتّخذها الظالمون فيكم سنّة.

قوله ﴿ولا بقي منكم آبر﴾ يروى بالراء من قولهم ﴿آبر﴾ للذي يأبر النخل أي يصلحه. ويروى ﴿آثر﴾ وهو الذي يأثر الحديث أي يحكيه ويرويه وهو أصحّ الوجوه عندي كأنّه قال ﴿لا بقي منكم مخبر﴾. ويروى ﴿آبز﴾ بالزاي معجمة وهو الواثب والهالك أيضًا يقال له آبز.

After me, you will be ruled by a man with a large maw and a massive belly who swallows all that is in front of him and demands everything else besides. Kill him! But no, you won't. Listen to me! He will command you to curse me with vile names and disassociate from me.[1] Call me names if you must—it will be a purge for me and save your life. But never disassociate from me, for I was born in a pure state of nature,[2] and was the first to believe and migrate.[3]

1.57 From ʿAlī's address to the Kharijites:[4]
May you be wiped out by sandstorms! May your date palms wither untended! Are you saying I should testify against myself and confess unbelief? This, after believing in God and fighting alongside his messenger! «I should stray from the path if so, no longer among the guided.»[5] Return to the hole that you came from! Turn on your heels and retreat! After me, you face complete humiliation and a cutting sword. Indeed, despots will make it their custom to attack you and plunder.[6]

Raḍī: In his line, "May your date palms wither untended (*wa-lā baqiya minkum ābir*)," the word *ābir*, when transmitted with an R, refers to a person who tends (*yaʾburu*) date palms, i.e., cultivates them. Another transmission is "one who narrates a tale (*āthir*)," i.e., recounts and transmits it. The latter, in my opinion, is the most viable option. Accordingly, ʿAlī is saying, "May not one of you remain to carry forward your report." Yet another transmission is "one who jumps (*ābiz*)" with a Z,[7] meaning someone who leaps. A dying man is also called *ābiz*.

---

1   Ibn Abī al-Ḥadīd discusses the Umayyads' commanding people to curse ʿAlī, often on penalty of death, in three full chapters. Ḥ 4:56–114; see also B 275–276. For additional reports and references, see Qutbuddin, *Arabic Oration*, 85–86.

2   Ar. *ʿalā l-fiṭrah*, meaning he was born Muslim. The usage derives from the Prophetic hadith, "Every child is born in the natural form (كلّ مولود يولد على الفطرة)—it is his parents who raise him Christian or Jewish." ʿAlī was "raised by the Prophet in the light of Islam." Ḥ 4:114–116; R 1:277–278; B 275–276.

3   Muslims consider early conversion and migration a source of honor, indicating dedication to the Prophet, and participation in setting up the nascent religion. On ʿAlī being the first male to accept Islam and to migrate with the Prophet from Mecca to Medina, see Ḥ 4:116–128.

4   In Nahrawān, 38/658 (Ṭabarī, *Tārīkh*, 5:84). Yaʿqūbī (*Tārīkh*, 2:193) places these lines in an oration ʿAlī delivered immediately upon his return to Kufa after Nahrawān, addressing his supporters.

5   Qurʾan, Anʿām 6:56.

6   Details of Umayyad-era Kharijite leaders and battles in Ḥ 4:132–278, 5:80–129.

7   Both Z and R have the same shape in Arabic orthography, but Z (ز) has a dot on top, and R (ر) is undotted.

1.58

1.58.1 وقال عليه السلام لمّا عزم على حرب الخوارج وقيل له إنّ القوم قد عبروا جسر النهروان مصارعهم دون النطفة والله لا يفلت منهم عشرة ولا يهلك منكم عشرة.

يعني بالنطفة ماء النهر وهي أفصح كناية عن الماء وإن كان كثيرًا جمًّا.

1.58.2 وقال لمّا قتلهم فقيل هلك القوم بأجمعهم كلّا والله إنّهم نطف في أصلاب الرجال وقرارات النساء كلّما نجم منهم قرن قطع حتّى يكون آخرهم لصوصًا سلّابين.

1.58.3 وقال عليه السلام فيهم لا تقتلوا الخوارج بعدي فليس من طلب الحقّ فأخطأه كمن طلب الباطل فأدركه.

يعني معاوية وأصحابه.

1.59 ومن كلام له عليه السلام لمّا خُوّف من الغيلة وإنّ عليَّ من الله جُنّة حصينة فإذا جاء يومي انفرجت عنّي وأسلمتني فحينئذ لا يطيش السهم ولا يبرأ الكَلْم.

1.58

1.58.1 When ʿAlī expressed his resolve to fight the Kharijites, he was told, "They have already crossed the river at Jisr al-Nahrawān," and he declared:[1]
Their deaths are written on this side of the clear water. By God, not ten of them will survive, and not ten of you will be killed.

Raḍī: By "clear water (*nuṭfah*)," he means the water of the river, an eloquent metaphor for water, even in large quantities.

1.58.2 Following the battle with the Kharijites, ʿAlī was told, "Every man among them has been killed," and he declared:
No, by God! They hide in the loins of men and the wombs of women. But whenever a horn protrudes from their head, it will be cut off,[2] and the last of them will be thieves and brigands.

1.58.3 ʿAlī also said about them:[3]
Do not fight the Kharijites after me, for those who seek right but miss it are not like those who seek wrong and find it.

Raḍī: He means Muʿāwiyah and his associates.

1.59 From ʿAlī's address, when warned of assassination:[4]
I am protected by God's shield. When my day comes, it will leave and hand me over. Then, the arrow will not miss, and the wound will not heal.

---

1 *Jisr al-Nahrawān* (The Bridge of Nahrawān) is the same as Nahrawān (present-day Sifwah), a town east of the Tigris River in Iraq, the location of the Battle of Nahrawān between ʿAlī and the Kharijites in 38/658. For details of the place and the battle, see Morony, "al-Nahrawān," *EI*².

2 "Horn" (*qarn*) is interpreted as leader, and a horn protruding is a metaphor for the emergence of a leader. B 277; R 1:283; Ḥ 5:73.

3 ʿAlī spoke these words after the Battle of Nahrawān in 38/658. Ṣadūq, *ʿIlal*, 218.

4 It is narrated that Ibn Muljam, the Kharijite who would shortly assassinate ʿAlī, had revealed his intention in Kufa. When people urged ʿAlī to act, he refused, saying that Ibn Muljam had not yet perpetrated the crime; then he spoke the words in the text at hand, thus, in Kufa, in 40/661. B 278–279.

1.60 ومن خطبة له عليه السلام

ألا وإنّ الدنيا دار لا يُسلَم منها إلّا فيها ولا يُنجَى بشيء كان لها أُبتلي الناس بها فتنة فما أخذوه منها لها أُخرجوا منه وحوسبوا عليه وما أخذوه منها لغيرها قَدموا عليه وأقاموا فيه وإنّها عند ذوي العقول كفيء الظلّ بَيْنا تراه سابغًا حتّى قلص وزائدًا حتّى نقص.

1.61 ومن خطبة له عليه السلام

1.61.1 واتّقوا الله عباد الله وبادروا آجالكم بأعمالكم وابتاعوا ما يبقى لكم بما يزول عنكم وترحّلوا فقد جُدَّ بكم واستعدّوا للموت فقد أظلّكم وكونوا قومًا صيح بهم فأنتبهوا وعلموا أنّ الدنيا ليست لهم بدار فاستبدلوا فإنّ الله لم يخلقكم عبثًا ولم يتركّكم سدى. وما بين أحدكم وبين الجنّة أو النار إلّا الموت أن ينزل به وإنّ غاية تنقصها اللحظة وتهدمها الساعة لجديرة بقصر المدّة وإنّ غائبًا يحدوه الجديدان الليل والنهار لحريّ بسرعة الأوبة وإنّ قادمًا يقدم بالفوز أو الشقوة لمستحقّ بأفضل العدّة.

1.61.2 فتزوّدوا في الدنيا من الدنيا ما تحرزون به نفوسكم غدًا.[1] فاتّقى عبد ربّه نصح نفسه قَدّم توبته غلب شهوته فإنّ أجله مستور عنه وأمله خادع له والشيطان موكّل به يزيّن له المعصية ليركبها ويمنّيه التوبة ليسوّفها حتّى تهجم منيّته عليه أغفل ما يكون عنها. فيا لها حسرة على كلّ ذي غفلة أن يكون عمره عليه حجّة وأن تؤدّيه أيّامه إلى الشقوة.

1.61.3 نسأل الله سبحانه أن يجعلنا وإيّاكم ممّن لا تبطره نعمة ولا تقصر به عن طاعة ربّه غاية ولا تحلّ به بعد الموت ندامة ولا كآبة.

ام، ه، وأضيفت في ش، ي: كذا. ن، وأصل ش، ي: سقطت ﴿فتزوّدوا ... غدًا﴾.

1.60 From an oration by ʿAlī:

Hear me! The world is an abode from which you cannot be saved except within it, yet no tribute you offer it will grant you passage beyond its rim. The world tests people with gifts: Whatever they take from it for worldly benefit they must leave behind and account for. Whatever they take from it for the next abode will stay with them forever. To the intelligent, the world is a shifting shadow—one moment you see it spreading and the next it has narrowed to a shard, one moment you see it growing and the next it has disappeared.

1.61 From an oration by ʿAlī:[1]

1.61.1 Be conscious of God, O servants of God, and outrace your imminent end with good deeds. Trade transient benefits for everlasting gain, prepare to depart, for the call has been given, and brace for death, for it hovers overhead. Be those who wake when shaken, who, knowing that the world is not their home, seek a better abode. God has not created you in vain, nor left you without direction.[2] Nothing stands between you and paradise or hellfire but the arrival of death. Diminished by each passing moment, demolished by each pressing hour, your time to the goalpost is short. That traveler, death, whose camels are steered by Night after Day and by Day after Night will soon be here. Prepare well for this visitor who will bring you immortal triumph or unending misery.

1.61.2 Gather provisions in this world from this world to sustain your souls tomorrow. A servant should fear his Master and be true to his soul, he should hasten to repent and conquer his passions, for his lifespan is veiled from him, his long hopes are false, and he is turned over to Satan, who adorns and encourages him to ride the steed of sin, while coaxing him to delay repentance. When he least expects it, fate will attack. O what agony for the heedless man! His life will testify against him, and his days will hand him over to unending misery.

1.61.3 We beseech Almighty God to include us among those who are not made insolent by his bounty, fall short in his obedience, or are seized in death by grief and regret.

---

1 Additional parts recorded in Sibṭ, *Tadhkirah*, 145. Some lines are similar in §1.202; see note on context there.

2 Modified quotes from Qurʾan, Muʾminūn 23:115, Qiyāmah 75:36.

1.62   ومن خطبة له عليه السلام

1.62.1   الذي لم تسبق له حال حالًا فيكون أوّلًا قبل أن يكون آخرًا ويكون ظاهرًا قبل أن يكون باطنًا. كلّ مسمّى بالوحدة غيره قليل وكلّ عزيز غيره ذليل وكلّ قويّ غيره ضعيف وكلّ مالك غيره مملوك وكلّ عالم غيره متعلّم وكلّ قادر غيره يقدر ويعجز وكلّ سميع غيره يَصَمّ عن لطيف الأصوات ويُصِمّه كبيرها ويذهب عنه ما بَعُدَ منها وكلّ بصير غيره يعمى عن خفيّ الألوان ولطيف الأجسام وكلّ ظاهر غيره غير باطن وكلّ باطن غيره غير ظاهر.

1.62.2   لم يخلق ما خلقه لتشديد سلطان ولا تخوّف من عواقب زمان ولا استعانة على نِدّ مثاور ولا شريك مكاثر ولا ضدّ منافر ولكن خلائق مربوبون وعباد داخرون لم يحلل في الأشياء فيقال هو فيها كائن ولم ينأَ عنها فيقال هو منها بائن لم يؤُدْه خلق ما ابتدأ ولا تدبير ما ذرأ ولا وقف به عجز عمّا خلق ولا ولجت عليه شبهة فيما قضى وقدّر بل قضاء متقن وعلم محكم وأمر مبرم المأمول مع النقم المرهوب مع النعم.

1.63   ومن كلام له عليه السلام يقوله لأصحابه في بعض أيّام صفّين

معاشر المسلمين استشعروا الخشية وتجلببوا السكينة وعضّوا على النواجذ فإنّه أنبا للسيوف عن الهام وأكملوا اللامة وقلقلوا السيوف في أغمادها قبل سلّها والحظوا الخزر واطعنوا الشزر ونافحوا بالظبى وصلوا السيوف بالخطى. واعلموا أنّكم بعين الله ومع ابن عمّ

1.62 From an oration by ʿAlī:[1]

1.62.1 No state for God precedes another state: he is neither first before he is last nor visible before he is hidden. Other than him, nothing can be described as one.[2] Other than him, the mighty are humble, the strong are weak, masters are slaves, the learned are students, and the powerful can fail. Other than him, all observers are blind to subtle colors and ethereal bodies, and all listeners strain to hear faint sounds, are deafened by loud noises, and miss distant echoes. Other than him, nothing that is visible is hidden, and nothing that is hidden is visible.

1.62.2 God did not create us to strengthen his authority or prevent time's blows, nor for help against an equal's attack, a partner's multitudes, or a malicious adversary. Far from it! We are but subservient mortals and humble servants. He does not enter into things, so we cannot say that he exists therein, nor is he distant from them, so we cannot say that he lives apart. Creating did not tire him, nor directing the universe. Weakness did not delay his design, nor doubt enter into his decree. His judgment is perfect, his knowledge exact, his command irrevocable. He is entreated in times of distress and venerated in times of bounty.

1.63 From ʿAlī's address to his followers on one of the battle days of Ṣiffīn:[3]
Muslims! Sheathe yourselves in God's awe and envelop your bodies with calm. Bite down hard on your back teeth, for that will deflect the blades that strike at your heads. Wear full armor and rattle your swords inside their sheaths before you draw them out. Stare down the enemy and launch your spears from the right and the left. Fight with your swords and leap into the thrust so that they

---

1   Ibn ʿAbd Rabbih (*ʿIqd*, 4:163–164) narrates lines from §1.62.2 as part of ʿAlī's Radiant Oration (*Gharrāʾ*), §1.80. Ṣadūq (*Tawḥīd*, 41, 43) places it in Kufa, after the arbitration in 37/658, as the praise opening for an oration urging supporters to rally against Muʿāwiyah.

2   Ar. *qalīl*, translation after R 1:290, Ḥ 5:155. Alternatively explained as anything understandable in terms of number, unlike God from whom any attribution is to be removed (B 285); or weak (M 1:330).

3   Narrated by ʿAbdallāh ibn al-ʿAbbās, who said, "I saw ʿAlī on the battle day of Ṣiffīn, a white turban on his head, his eyes like two glowing lamps, urging his followers to fight." (Māmaṭīrī, *Nuzhah*, 416). Either on the day of the first skirmish in Ṣiffīn, or, more likely, on the penultimate battle-day that preceded the final Night of Clamor (*laylat al-harīr*), Thursday-Friday 7–8 Ṣafar 37/27–28 July 657. B 289. Further orations in Ṣiffīn by ʿAlī and others, and poems and events, are recorded in Ḥ 5:175–258.

رسول الله صلّى الله عليه وآله فعاودوا الكرّ وٱستحيوا من الفرّ فإنّه عار في الأعقاب ونار يوم الحساب. وطيبوا عن أنفسكم نفسًا وٱمشوا إلى الموت مشيًا سُجُحًا. وعليكم بهذا السواد الأعظم والرِّواق المطنّب فٱضربوا ثَبَجه فإنّ الشيطان كامن في كِسره قد قدّم للوَثْبة يدًا وأخّر للنكوص رِجلًا. فصمدًا صمدًا حتّى ينجلي لكم عمود الحقّ ﴿وَأَنتُمُ ٱلْأَعْلَوْنَ وَٱللَّهُ مَعَكُمْ وَلَن يَتِرَكُمْ أَعْمَالَكُمْ﴾.

1.64 ومن كلام له عليه السلام في معنى الأنصار. قالوا لمّا ٱنتهت إلى أمير المؤمنين عليه السلام أنباء السقيفة بعد وفاة رسول الله صلّى الله عليه وآله قال عليه السلام

ما قالت الأنصار؟

قالوا
قالت منّا أمير ومنكم أمير.

قال عليه السلام
فهلّا ٱحتججتم عليهم بأنّ رسول الله صلّى الله عليه وآله وصّى بأن يُحسَن إلى محسنهم ويتجاوز عن مسيئهم.

قالوا
وما في هذا من الحجّة عليهم؟

فقال عليه السلام
لو كانت الإمارة فيهم لم تكن الوصيّة بهم.

ثمّ قال
فما ذا قالت قريش؟

pierce your foe. Know this: you fight under God's watch, and alongside his Messenger's cousin. Charge forward in attack. Do not flee the battlefield, for that would dishonor your line for generations and repay you with hellfire on judgment day. Be generous with your lives and approach death with gentle courage. Aim for the black mass and the pitched tent. Cut down its center pole, for Satan is hiding in its flap. He has one hand in front, ready to attack, and one foot at the back, ready to flee. Charge! Charge! Fight till the pillar of truth shines bright. «You shall overcome. God is with you, and he will not let your deeds go to waste.»[1]

1.64 From observations by ʿAlī regarding the Allies. After the death of God's Messenger, when reports of the Assembly at the Banū Sāʿidah Portico reached the Commander of the Faithful, he asked:[2]
What did the Allies say?

Those who had brought the report replied:
The Allies proposed: A commander from our side and another from yours.

ʿAlī responded:
Did you not remind them of the Messenger's directive to recompense those who do good among them and pardon those who transgress?

Those reporting asked:
How is that evidence against their claim?

ʿAlī replied:
The instruction would not be about them if they had the right to command.

Then he asked:
How did the Quraysh respond?

---

1 Qurʾan, Muḥammad 47:35.
2 ʿAlī spoke these lines in Medina, following the death of the Prophet in 11/632, as mentioned in Raḍī's comments. At this Assembly, immediately after the Prophet Muḥammad's death, some of his Companions gathered at the Portico (*Saqīfah*) of the Banū Sāʿidah and pledged allegiance to Abū Bakr as his successor. Neither ʿAlī nor anyone else from the Prophet's family was present; they were preparing for the Prophet's burial. See a summary of these events in B 292–293; Lecomte, "al-Saḳīfa," *EI*[2]; a more detailed version in Ḥ 1:21–61, 6:5–17, and events immediately following in Ḥ 5:17–52. See also ʿAlī's rebuke to Muʿāwiyah regarding this event in *Nahj al-Balāghah*, § 2.28.2.

قالوا

اَحتجّت بأنّها شجرة الرسول صلّى الله عليه وآله.

فقال عليه السلام

اَحتجّوا بالشجرة وأضاعوا الثمرة.

1.65   ومن كلام له عليه السلام لمّا قلّد محمّد بن أبي بكر مصر فملكت عليه وقُتل

وقد أردت تولية مصر هاشم بن عتبة ولو ولّيته إيّاها لما خلّى لهم العَرصة ولا أنهزهم

الفرصة بلا ذمّ لمحمّد فقد كان إليّ حبيباً وكان لي ربيباً.

1.66   ومن كلام له عليه السلام في ذمّ أصحابه

كم أداريكم كما تدارى البِكار العَمِدة والثِياب المتداعية كلّما حيصت من جانب تهتّكت

من آخر أ كلّما أطلّ[1] عليكم مَنسِر من مناسر أهل الشام أغلق كلّ رجل منكم بابه وانجحر

انجحار الضبّة في جحرها والضبع في وجارها الذليل والله من نصرتموه ومن رمى بكم

فقد رمى بأَفْوَق ناصل وإنّكم والله لكثير في الباحات قليل تحت الرايات وإنّي لعالم بما

يصلحكم ويقيم أَوَدَكم ولكنّي والله لا أرى إصلاحكم بإفساد نفسي أضرع الله خدودكم

وأتعس جدودكم لا تعرفون الحقّ كمعرفتكم الباطل ولا تبطلون الباطل كإبطالكم الحقّ.

اش، ن، ي: كذا. م، ه، ونسخة في ي: ⟨أظلّ⟩.

The reporters answered:
They argued that they are the Messenger's tree.

'Alī exclaimed:
They argue for the tree but forget about its fruit!

1.65 From an address by 'Alī when his recently appointed governor, Muḥammad ibn Abī Bakr, was killed, and Egypt was lost to the Umayyads:[1]
My own choice for governor of Egypt was Hāshim ibn 'Utbah. Hāshim would not have left a gap for them to enter or an opportunity to attack. I say this without criticizing Muḥammad, whom I loved and reared.[2]

1.66 From an address by 'Alī admonishing his supporters:[3]
How long should I coax you and blandish you? How long must I handle you gingerly as a young camel whose hump a heavy load would crush, or as a worn garment, patched in one place, and falling apart in another? How is it that each man among you locks your door when a Syrian squadron approaches, and holes up in his home like a lizard in its burrow or a hyena in its den? By God, to gain you as supporters is to lose! To shoot with you in my longbow is to shoot an arrow with a broken nock and no arrowhead! By God, you throng the square, but only a few stand firm under war's banners. I know well what would lick you into shape and straighten your crookedness—but, by God, I shall not do this at the cost of demeaning my soul. May God begrime your faces and destroy your fortunes! You embrace not truth but falsehood! You reject not falsehood but truth!

---

1 I have added the words, "to the Umayyads," for clarity. Muḥammad ibn Abī Bakr was killed in 38/658, after the arbitration, when 'Amr ibn al-'Āṣ took over Egypt for Mu'āwiyah. 'Alī delivered this address in Kufa (Ṭabarī, *Tārīkh*, 5:109–110). On the events mentioned in the address, see B 294 (summary); Ḥ 6:57–94 (details), Ḥ 6:94–100 (text of 'Alī's full oration following Muḥammad ibn Abī Bakr's death).

2 Muḥammad was the son of Abū Bakr, the first Sunni caliph, and Asmā' bint 'Umays. His father died when he was a child, and 'Alī, who married Asmā', raised him. R 1:294–295; Hawting, "Muḥammad b. Abī Bakr," *EI²*.

3 Among a number of orations (including §1.39) that 'Alī delivered in the wake of Nu'mān ibn Bashīr's raid on 'Ayn al-Tamr in 39/659 (Ya'qūbī, *Tārīkh*, 2:195–196; Ṭabarī, *Tārīkh*, 5:133–134). He admonishes them for their reluctance to muster to fight Mu'āwiyah (B 295).

1.67 وقال عليه السلام في سحرة اليوم الذي ضُرب فيه
ملكتني عيني وأنا جالس فسنح لي رسول الله صلّى الله عليه وآله فقلت يا رسول الله
ماذا لقيت من أُمّتك من الأَوَد واللدد فقال اُدع عليهم فقلت أبدلني الله بهم خيراً لي
منهم وأبدلهم بي شرًّا لهم منّي.

يعني عليه السلام بـ﴿الأَوَد﴾ الاعوجاج وبـ﴿اللدد﴾ الخصام وهذا من أفصح الكلام.

1.68 ومن كلام له عليه السلام في ذمّ أهل العراق
أمّا بعد. يا أهل العراق فإنّما أنتم كالمرأة الحامل حملت فلمّا أتمّت أملصت ومات قيّمها
وطال تأيّمها وورثها أبعدها. أما والله ما أتيتكم اختياراً ولكنّي جئت إليكم سوقًا ولقد
بلغني أنّكم تقولون يكذب قاتلكم الله فعلى مَن أكذب أعلى الله فأنا أوّل من آمن به أم
على نبيّه فأنا أوّل من صدّقه كلّا والله ولكنّها لهجة غبتم عنها ولم تكونوا من أهلها ويل
اُمّه كيلًا بغير ثمن لو كان له وعاء ﴿ولتعلمنّ نبأه بعد حين﴾.

1.69 ومن خطبة له عليه السلام علّم فيها الناس الصلاة على النبيّ صلّى الله عليه وآله

1.67 'Alī spoke these words in the predawn hour of the day in which he was struck his deathblow:[1]

Sleep overtook me as I sat, and the Messenger appeared before my eyes. "Messenger of God," I exclaimed, "what treachery I have encountered from your community, what hate!" He replied, "Invoke maledictions on them!" so I prayed, "God, give me better associates than they, and give them a worse leader than I!"

Raḍī: By "treachery (*awad*)" he means deceit and by "hate (*ladad*)" he means enmity. These are some of the most expressive words ever spoken.

1.68 From an address by 'Alī censuring the Iraqis:[2]

Iraqis! You are like a pregnant woman who, at full term, delivers a stillborn child, then her husband dies, and she lives for a long time as a widow—she dies alone, with only distant relatives as her inheritors. By God, I did not choose to come to you! I was forced come to you! I am told that you mutter behind my back, "He lies!" May God fight you! Who do you accuse me of lying about? God? I was the first to believe in him! The Prophet? I was the first to accept his message! Never would I lie about them! But my words are beyond your comprehension, and you are not worthy to hear them.[3] Woe to your mothers! I gave you a full measure, free of charge. If only there were vessels to hold it! «You shall surely learn the truth of its report, but only after a while.»[4]

1.69 From an oration by 'Alī in which he taught his companions how to invoke blessings on the Prophet:[5]

---

1 Kufa, 40/661. Nuʿmān (*Sharḥ al-akhbār*, 2:432) names the addressee as al-Ḥasan ibn 'Alī, along with some unnamed associates. For details about 'Alī's assassination, see Ḥ 6:113–126.

2 Excerpt from an oration 'Alī delivered after Ṣiffīn in 37/657, presumably in Kufa, chastising his Iraqi fighters who had agreed to a truce, when, after a hard-fought battle, they were on the verge of victory. See detailed parsing of the oration's 'pregnant woman' metaphor in light of these events in B 297; R 1:301; Ḥ 6:127–129.

3 According to the commentators, 'Alī's "manner of speaking that is beyond the addressees' comprehension" refers to his prophecies about future events (B 297; Ḥ 6:128–134). It could also refer to his orations explicating the mysteries of theology and metaphysics.

4 Qurʾan, Ṣād 38:88.

5 Ibn Abī Shaybah (*Muṣannaf*, 6:66) prefaces the prayer with the tag, "'Alī used to recite this supplication," meaning it was 'Alī's habitual prayer. Variant rendering in §1.103.3 (see details of context there; §1.103 is part of a larger oration that also includes §3.26, on the four pillars of belief, and §3.259).

اللّهمّ داحي المدحوّات وداعم المسموكات وجابل القلوب على فطرتها شقيّها وسعيدها. اجعل شرائف صلواتك ونوامي بركاتك على محمّد عبدك ورسولك الخاتم لما سبق والفاتح لما أنغلق والمعلن الحقّ بالحقّ والدافع جيشات الأباطيل والدامغ صولات الأضاليل كما حُمّل فاضطلع قائمًا بأمرك مستوفزًا في مرضاتك غير ناكل عن قُدم ولا واهٍ في عزم واعيًا لوحيك حافظًا لعهدك ماضيًا على نفاذ أمرك حتّى أورى قبس القابس وأضاء الطريق للخابط وهديت به القلوب بعد خوضات الفتن[1] وأقام موضحات الأعلام ونيّرات الأحكام فهو أمينك المأمون وخازن علمك المخزون وشهيدك يوم الدين وبعيثك بالحقّ ورسولك إلى الخلق. اللّهمّ آفسح له مفسحًا في ظلّك واجزه مضاعفات الخير من فضلك. اللّهمّ أعل على بناء البانين بناءه وأكرم لديك منزله وأتمم له نوره واجزه من ابتعاثك له مقبول الشهادة مرضيّ المقالة ذا منطق عدل وخطّة فصل. اللّهمّ أجمع بيننا وبينه في برد العيش وقرار النعمة ومنى الشهوات وأهواء اللذّات ورخاء الدعة ومنتهى الطمأنينة وتحف الكرامة.

1.70 ومن كلام له عليه السلام لمروان بن الحكَم بالبصرة. قالوا أخذ مروان بن الحكَم أسيرًا يوم الجمل فاستشفع الحسن والحسين عليهما السلام إلى أمير المؤمنين عليه السلام فكلّماه فيه نخلّى سبيله فقالا له يبايعك يا أمير المؤمنين فقال عليه السلام

---

[1] ش، ن، م: كذا. ي، هـ، وهامش م: أضيفت ‹والإثم›.

God, unfolder of lands unfolded, creator of skies elevated, infuser of hearts with their dispositions, blissful or wretched—Shower your noblest blessings, your manifold graces, on Muḥammad, your servant and messenger, the seal on what had come before, opener of all things locked, announcer of the truth in truth, repeller of the forces of evil, and crusher of the onslaught of error, doing all this as he was charged to do. He undertook your command and rose to serve your pleasure, with unfettered boldness and unfaltering resolve. He comprehended your revelation, safeguarded your compact, and executed your command, until he had ignited the flame of truth for those who sought its fire, and illuminated the road for those who stumbled. Through Muḥammad, hearts were guided after having been enmeshed in mutiny. He erected clear waymarks and luminous rules. He is the trustee whom you entrusted with your message, the custodian of your treasure of knowledge, your witness on judgment day, your emissary dispatched with the truth, and your messenger to the world. God, grant him a spacious home in your shade and a good reward multiplied by your generosity. God, let his palace soar above all others, give honor to his station at your side, and perfect his light.[1] Reward him for being an exemplary messenger, one whose testimonial was accepted and whose words convinced, who spoke justly and took decisive action. God, unite us with him in a peaceful afterlife in a blessed abode, every desire satisfied, every pleasure granted, in ease, gentleness, and serenity, welcomed with your gifts of honor.

1.70 From ʿAlī's address to Marwān ibn al-Ḥakam in Basra. It is reported that when Marwān was taken prisoner at the Battle of the Camel, he begged Ḥasan and Ḥusayn to intercede for his release with the Commander of the Faithful. They spoke with their father, who answered that he could go free. They then added, "Commander of the Faithful, he wishes to pledge allegiance to you," and he replied:[2]

---

1 Modified quote from Qurʾan, Taḥrīm 66:8.
2 36/656. On Marwān and his dealings with ʿAlī, see Ḥ 6:148–165. See also § 3.141.

أفلم يبايعني بعد قتل عثمان لا حاجة لي في بيعته إنّها كفّ يهوديّة لو بايعني بيده لغدر بسَبَّته أما إنّ له إمرة كلَعْقة الكلب أَنْفَه وهو أبو الأَكبُش الأربعة وستلقى الأُمّة منه ومن ولده يومًا أحمر.

١.٧١ ومن كلام له عليه السلام لمّا عزموا على بيعة عثمان

لقد علمتم أنّي أحقّ الناس بها من غيري والله لأُسلمنّ ما سلمت أمور المسلمين ولم يكن فيها جور إلّا عليّ خاصّة التماسًا لأجر ذلك وفضله وزهدًا فيما تنافستموه من زخرفه وزبرجه.

١.٧٢ ومن كلام له عليه السلام لمّا بلغه اتّهام بني أميّة له بالمشاركة في دم عثمان

Did he not pledge allegiance to me right after ʿUthmān was killed? I have no need of his pledge now. His is a Jewish hand![1] If he were to pledge allegiance to me with his hand, he would break it the next moment with wind from his arse.[2] One day, he will rule, but his rule will only last for as long as it takes a dog to lick its snout.[3] He will also father four rams.[4] At his hand and theirs, Muslims will encounter bloody death!

1.71 From ʿAlī's address to the Shūrā Council when they resolved to pledge allegiance to ʿUthmān as the next caliph:[5]

You know full well that I have more right to the caliphate than anyone else. I will concede—but, by God, I will continue to do so only for as long as the concerns of the Muslims remain unharmed, as long as the injustice is directed solely at me. I do so in the hope of God's reward and recompense and in distaste for the adornments and splendors for which you vie.

1.72 From ʿAlī's address when he heard reports that the Umayyads were accusing him of complicity in ʿUthmān's killing:

---

1   The hand is singled out for mention because a handclasp in that society sealed one's pledge of allegiance to a ruler. "A Jewish hand" presumably refers to the pledge given to the Prophet and then broken by the Medinan Jewish tribes. For a summary of Jews in the Qurʾan and early traditional Muslim historical works, see Stillman, "Yahūd," *EI*².

2   Lit. "he would deceive with his arse" (*la-ghadara bi-sabbatihi*). The commentators generally read this phrase metaphorically to denote strong censure and derision, but some also read it literally: Ibn Abī al-Ḥadīd says it was common practice among the Arabs for a man to break wind upon resolving to break a pledge (!), and Rāwandī notes that "to insult" (*sabbaḥū*) literally means to pierce in the buttocks with a spear. Ḥ 6:147; B 302; R 1:302.

3   Marwān (r. 64–65/684–685) became caliph after the last Sufyanid-Umayyad caliph, Muʿāwiyah II, and his reign lasted between six and ten months. Cf. Bosworth, "Marwān I b. al-Ḥakam," *EI*².

4   The "four rams" are said to be either (1) Marwān's sons: ʿAbd al-Malik (caliph, r. 65–86/685–705), and ʿAbd al-ʿAzīz, Bishr, and Muḥammad, who ruled respectively as governors of Egypt, Iraq, and the Arabian Peninsula; or (2) Marwān's grandsons through ʿAbd al-Malik, the only four brothers to rule as caliph: Walīd (r. 86–96/705–715), Sulaymān (r. 96–99/715–717), Yazīd (r. 101–105/720–724), and Hishām (r. 105–125/724–723). B 302; R 1:306–307; Ḥ 6:147–148.

5   ʿAlī delivered this address in Medina following ʿUmar's death in 23/644; I have added the words "the Shūrā Council" for clarity. Ibn Abī al-Ḥadīd also notes ʿAlī's citation at this time of several well-known hadith, including, ⟨For whomsoever I am master, ʿAlī is his master⟩, ⟨You are to me as Aaron was to Moses⟩, ⟨You are my brother in this world and the next⟩— the Shiʿa consider these hadith proof of the Prophet's appointment of ʿAlī as his successor. Ḥ 6:167–168.

أولم ينه بني أميّة علمها بي عن قَرَفي أوما وَزَع الجهّالَ سابقتي عن تهمتي ولَمّا وعظهم الله به أبلغ من لساني أنا هجيج المارقين وخصيم المرتابين. على كتاب الله تُعرض الأمثال وبما في الصدور تجازى العباد.

1.73 ومن خطبة له عليه السلام

رحم الله عبدًا سمع حُكمًا فوعى ودُعي إلى رشاد فدنا وأخذ بحُجزة هادٍ فنجا راقب ربّه وخاف ذنبه قدّم خالصًا وعمل صالحاً اكتسب مذخورًا واجتنب محذورًا رمى غرضًا وأحرز عوضًا كابر هواه وكذّب مناه جعل الصبر مطيّة نجاته والتقوى عدّة وفاته ركب الطريقة الغرّاء ولزم المحجّة البيضاء اغتنم المهل وبادر الأجل وتزوّد من العمل.

1.74 ومن كلام له عليه السلام

إنّ بني أميّة ليفوّقوني تراث محمّد تفويقًا والله لئن بقيت لهم لأنفضنّهم نفض اللحّام الوِذام التَرِبة.

ويروى ⟨التراب الوَذِمة⟩ وهو على القلب. قوله عليه السلام ⟨ليفوّقوني⟩ أي يعطوني من المال قليلًا قليلًا كفواق الناقة وهو الحلبة الواحدة من لبنها. و⟨الوذام⟩ جمع وَذمة وهي الحُزّة من الكَرِش أو الكبد تقع في التراب فتنفض.

Is the Umayyads' own knowledge of my character not enough to stop them from injuring me? Is my precedence in Islam not enough to curb those imbeciles from accusing me? In truth, God's admonitions are more stirring that any my tongue can produce![1] I shall confront those who desert the faith and challenge those who doubt. The Book of God resolves disputes, and the contents of hearts determine recompense.

1.73 From an oration by ʿAlī:

May God have mercy on the man who listens to wisdom and retains, who is called to guidance and follows, who clutches the hem of a guide and is saved, who is mindful of his Lord and fears sin, who carries out acts of purity and performs good, who earns something to put by and avoids hazardous terrain, who aims at a target and guards his treasure, who overcomes his passions and gives the lie to his desires, who makes forbearance the steed of his salvation and piety the provision for his passing, who rides on the illuminated path and keeps to the brightened road, who takes advantage of the respite and hastens to assemble provisions of good deeds before his life ends.

1.74 From an address by ʿAlī:[2]

The Umayyads stingily throw at me my share of Muḥammad's inheritance, piece by piece, like those who allow a camel calf to suckle its mother only lightly, at intervals. By God, if I live to show them, I will shake them up like a butcher shaking dirt off an animal's innards.

Raḍī: The phrase (*al-widhām al-taribah*), lit. "dirt-coated innards" is also narrated—in an instance of grammatical inversion—as "innards-coated dirt (*al-turāb al-wadhimah*)." By saying, "they treat me in the manner of a camel calf allowed to suckle its mother only lightly at intervals (*la-yufawwiqūnanī*)" ʿAlī means: "they give me the money bit by bit like the *fuwāq* of a she-camel, which is the quantity from a single milking." "*Widhām* (innards)," the plural of *wadhamah*, is a piece of the ruminant's stomach or liver; if it falls in the dirt, it must be shaken clean.

---

1   I.e., the Qurʾan's warnings against false accusations (Qurʾan, Aḥzāb 33:58), and its comparison of backbiting to «eating the flesh of one's dead brother» (Qurʾan, Ḥujurāt 49:12). B 303–304; Ḥ 6:170.

2   ʿAlī spoke these terse lines in Medina in response to a gift sent to him by Saʿīd ibn al-ʿĀṣ, who was governor of Kufa in the latter part of ʿUthmān's reign from 29–34/649–655. This is because Saʿīd, in an accompanying letter, had written to ʿAlī that he had not sent so much to any other except the caliph himself. B 306; Ḥ 6:174.

1.75 ومن كلمات كان عليه السلام يدعو بها

اللّهمّ ٱغفر لي ما أنت أعلم به منّي فإن عدت فعد لي بالمغفرة. اللّهمّ ٱغفر لي ما وأيت من نفسي ولم تجد له وفاء عندي. اللّهمّ ٱغفر لي ما تقرّبت به إليك ثمّ خالفه قلبي. اللّهمّ ٱغفر لي رمزات الألحاظ وسقطات الألفاظ وشهوات الجنان وهفوات اللسان.

1.76 ومن كلام له عليه السلام قاله لبعض أصحابه لمّا عزم على المسير إلى الخوارج فقال له يا أمير المؤمنين إن سرت في هذا الوقت خشيت ألّا تظفر بمرادك من طريق علم النجوم. فقال عليه السلام

أتزعم أنّك تهدي إلى الساعة التي من سار فيها صرف عنه السوء وتخوّف الساعة التي من سار فيها حاق به الضرّ فمن صدّقك بهذا فقد كذّب القرآن وٱستغنى عن الاستعانة بالله في نيل المحبوب ودفع المكروه وينبغي في قولك للعامل بأمرك أن يوليك الحمد دون ربّه لأنّك بزعمك أنت هديته إلى الساعة التي نال فيها النفع وأمن الضرّ.

ثمّ أقبل عليه السلام على الناس فقال

أيّها الناس إيّاكم وتعلّم النجوم إلّا ما يهتدى به في برّ أو بحر فإنّها تدعو إلى الكهانة. المنجّم كالكاهن والكاهن كالساحر والساحر كالكافر والكافر في النار. سيروا على ٱسم الله.

1.75 An excerpt from lines ʿAlī used to intone in supplication:[1]

God, forgive my sins—you know more about them than I do—and if I turn back to them, turn to me with forgiveness. God, forgive the promises I made to myself that you know I have broken. God, forgive the deeds by which I sought closeness to you that my passions then stopped me from doing. God, forgive the lapses of my eyes, the blunders in my words, the errors of my heart, and the slips of my tongue.

1.76 An address by ʿAlī in response to one of his associates who, when ʿAlī had resolved to march on the Kharijites, said to him: Commander of the Faithful, I fear you will not realize your goal if you march at this time—I know this through my knowledge of the stars.[2]

Do you presume to guide me to the hour in which those who advance are shielded from injury? Do you presume to warn me of the hour in which those who advance are attacked by harm? He who believes you challenges the Qurʾan, he relies on your help to achieve his wishes and repel his fears, instead of God's. You may as well instruct him to glorify you and not his Lord, for in your belief, you are the one who guides him to the hour in which he will gain benefit and avert harm.

ʿAlī then turned to the people and spoke:

People! Beware of studying the stars except to navigate on land and sea, for it leads to soothsaying. An astrologer is like a soothsayer, a soothsayer is like a magician, a magician is like an unbeliever, and an unbeliever will be cast into the Fire. March forward in God's name!

---

1   Kulaynī (*Kāfī*, 4:432–433) writes that this was ʿAlī's frequent supplication at the Kaʿbah, perhaps during the hajj pilgrimage, when pilgrims would perform the rite of walking between Ṣafā and Marwah: "Whenever the Commander of the Faithful climbed atop (the hill of) Ṣafā, he would face the Kaʿbah, lift up his hands, and intone (the supplication text)." For further prayers attributed to ʿAlī, see Ḥ 6:178–196 (also includes prayers by Muḥammad and Jesus), ʿAlī, "Prayers and Supplications," in Quḍāʿī, *Dustūr*, 176–197; ʿAlī, *al-Ṣaḥīfah al-ʿAlawiyyah, passim*.

2   ʿAlī spoke these words in Kufa, just before the Battle of Nahrawān in 38/658 (Māmaṭīrī, *Nuzhah*, 437–438; R 1:315, B 308). According to the commentators, the "associate" is ʿAfīf ibn Qays, brother of the infamous al-Ashʿath ibn Qays (R 1:315, B 308). On theological and legal aspects of the moratorium on astrology, see Ḥ 6:200–213; B 308–312. Ibn Ṭāwūs (*Faraj* 1:58) says the speaker was not ʿAfīf, but an unnamed landowner from Madāʾin.

1.77 ومن كلام له عليه السلام بعد فراغه من حرب الجمل في ذمّ النساء

معاشر الناس إنّ النساء نواقص الإيمان نواقص الحظوظ نواقص العقول فأمّا نقصان إيمانهنّ فقعودهنّ عن الصلاة والصيام في أيّام حيضهنّ وأمّا نقصان عقولهنّ فشهادة امرأتين منهنّ كشهادة الرجل الواحد وأمّا نقصان حظوظهنّ فمواريثهنّ على الأنصاف من مواريث الرجال فاتّقوا شرار النساء وكونوا من خيارهنّ على حذر ولا تطيعوهنّ في المعروف حتّى لا يطمعن في المنكر.

1.78 ومن كلام له عليه السلام

أيّها الناس الزهادة قصر الأمل والشكر عند النعم والورع عن المحارم فإن عزب ذلك عليكم فلا يغلب الحرام صبركم ولا تنسوا عند النعم شكركم فقد أعذر الله إليكم بحجج مسفرة ظاهرة وكتب بارزة العذر واضحة.

1.79 ومن كلام له عليه السلام في صفة الدنيا

ما أصف من دار أوّلها عناء وآخرها فناء في حلالها حساب وفي حرامها عقاب¹ من استغنى فيها فتن ومن افتقر فيها حزن ومن ساعاها فاتته ومن قعد عنها واتّته² ومن أبصر بها بصّرته ومن أبصر إليها أعمته.

---

¹م، ي، ه، ومصحّحة في ش: كذا. ن، وأصل ش، ونسخة في ه: ﴿حلالُها حساب وحرامُها عقاب﴾. ٢ش، ي، ن، ه: كذا. م، ونسخة في ه: ﴿آتته﴾.

1.77 From an address by ʿAlī following the Battle of the Camel, in censure of women:[1]
People! Women are deficient in faith, deficient in fortune, and deficient in mind. Their faith is deficient because they must abstain during menstruation from the rites of prayer and fasting. Their mind is deficient because the testimony of two women counts as the testimony of one man. Their fortune is deficient because their inheritance is half that of men. Beware of evil women and be cautious when dealing with those who are good. Don't obey them even when they propose a righteous action, so that they don't presume to influence you to do wrong.

1.78 From an address by ʿAlī:
People! To reject worldliness is to desire little, render thanks for favors, and restrain oneself from what is forbidden. If that is too much for you, then at least make sure that illicit temptations do not overwhelm your resistance or forget to render thanks when you receive favors. God has given you reason enough to obey him, with bright and clear proofs, and books with plainly defined arguments.

1.79 From an address by ʿAlī describing the world:[2]
How do I describe a world that begins in weariness and ends in death, where you are held accountable for approaching what is lawful and punished for consuming what is unlawful, where the wealthy are seduced and the poor grieve? The world eludes those who try to catch her while she comes willingly to those who pay her no heed. She instructs those who view her with discernment and blinds those who look at her with longing.

---

1   Excerpt from an oration ʿAlī delivered in Basra immediately after the Battle of the Camel in 36/656 (Sibṭ, *Tadhkirah*, 85). Though denigrating women in general terms, it refers particularly to ʿĀʾishah, who had the central role in raising opposition against ʿAlī, then led an army against him at this battle. Baḥrānī, while emphasizing the ʿĀʾishah-Camel connection, also deems this statement to apply to women generally. Ibn Abī al-Ḥadīd adds that the Muʿtazilites believe ʿĀʾishah repented and therefore earned a place in paradise (B 312; R 1:316–317; H 6:214–221, 224–229, includes the events relating to ʿĀʾishah and the Battle of the Camel, and her oration). The rulings regarding women mentioned in the text have their basis in the Qurʾan (Baqarah 2:282, Nisāʾ 4:11) and Sunnah. Amina Inloes, "Was Imam ʿAlī a Misogynist? The Portrayal of Women in Nahj al-Balaghah and Kitab Sulaym ibn Qays," argues that this and similar words attributed to ʿAlī denigrating women are later insertions.

2   Response to a man who asked ʿAlī, while he was orating, to describe the world. Ibn ʿAbd Rabbih, *ʿIqd*, 3:119; Karājikī, *Kanz*, 160.

وإذا تأمّل المتأمّل قوله عليه السلام ﴿من أبصر بها بصّرته﴾ وجد تحته من المعنى العجيب والغرض البعيد ما لا تبلغ غايته ولا يدرك غوره ولا سيّما إذا قرن إليه قوله ﴿ومن أبصر إليها أعمته﴾ فإنّه يجد الفرق بين ﴿أبصر بها﴾ و﴿أبصر إليها﴾ واضحًا نيّرًا وعجيبًا باهرًا.

1.80 ومن خطبة له عليه السلام وهي من الخطب العجيبة تسمّى الغرّاء

1.80.1 الحمد لله الذي علا بحوله ودنا بطوله مانح كلّ غنيمة وفضل وكاشف كلّ عظيمة وأزل أحمده على عواطف كرمه وسوابغ نعمه وأومن به أوّلًا باديًا وأستهديه قريبًا هاديًا وأستعينه قاهرًا قادرًا وأتوكّل عليه كافيًا ناصرًا. وأشهد أنّ محمّدًا صلّى الله عليه وآله عبده ورسوله أرسله لإنفاذ أمره وإنهاء عذره وتقديم نذره.

1.80.2 أوصيكم عباد الله بتقوى الله الذي[1] ضرب لكم الأمثال ووقّت لكم الآجال وألبسكم الرياش وأرفغ لكم المعاش وأحاط بكم الإحصاء وأرصد لكم الجزاء وآثركم بالنعم السوابغ والرفد الروافغ وأنذركم بالحجج البوالغ فأحصاكم عددًا ووظّف لكم مددًا في قرار خبرة ودار عبرة أنتم مختبرون فيها ومحاسبون عليها.

1.80.3 فإنّ الدنيا رنق مشربها ردغ مشرعها يونق منظرها ويوبق مخبرها غرور حائل وضوء آفل وظلّ زائل وسناد مائل حتّى إذا أنس نافرها واطمأنّ ناكرها قمصت بأرجلها وقنصت بأحبلها وأقصدت بأسهمها وأعلقت المرء أوهاق المنيّة قائدة له إلى ضنك المضجع ووحشة المرجع ومعاينة المحلّ وثواب العمل وكذلك الخلف بعقب السلف لا

____

[1] م، ي، ه، وأضيفت في ش: كذا. ن، وأصل ش: سقطت ﴿وتقديم نذره أوصيكم عباد الله بتقوى الله الذي﴾.

Raḍī: If a person were to ponder ʿAlī's words, "She instructs those who view her with discernment (*man abṣara bihā baṣṣarathu*)," he would find therein a wondrous meaning and a far-reaching aim whose end he can never attain and whose depths he can never plumb, especially if he reads them alongside ʿAlī's next words, "She blinds those who look at her with longing (*abṣara ilayhā aʿmathu*)." He will find the difference between "view her with discernment" and "look at her with longing" (with the same verb, *abṣara*, but a different prepositional phrase in each, *bihā* vs *ilayhā*) splendid and luminous, wondrous and dazzling.

1.80 From an oration by ʿAlī that is among his most marvelous, known as *Gharrāʾ*—"The Radiant Oration":[1]

1.80.1 Praise God, exalted in his might and near through his grace, bestower of gifts and favors and dispeller of calamities and hardships. I praise him for his ceaseless favors and perfect blessings. I believe in him—he is the first and the manifest. I seek his guidance—he is close to me, and he is my guide. I ask him for aid—he is the vanquisher, the all-powerful lord. I place my trust in him—he suffices and gives victory. I bear witness that Muḥammad is his servant and messenger, whom he sent to execute his command, vindicate his claim, and deliver his warning.

1.80.2 Servants of God, I counsel you to be conscious of God, who has taught you parables and decreed your lifespans, clothed you in finery and given you a good life, encompassed you in his reckoning and ordained recompense for your deeds, graced you with perfect favors and marvelous gifts, and warned you with convincing arguments. He has reckoned your numbers and appointed your time in this house of trial and abode of instruction—here you are tested and held accountable for what you do.

1.80.3 The world's water is murky and the path to her waterhole thick with mud. Her beauty dazzles but her reality kills. She is a fleeting deception, a fading light, an ephemeral shadow, and an unsteady support. When the man who shies away from her becomes familiar, when he who is wary relaxes, she gallops away at full stretch, traps him in her snares, targets him with her arrows, and entangles him in the noose of death. She leads him to a narrow bed and a place filled with terror, to live in his new home and be paid back for his deeds. In this

---

1 Abū Nuʿaym (*Ḥilyat*, 1:77–79) records §1.80.2, 6, 7, 9 and §1.82.2 as part of an oration ʿAlī declaimed after accompanying a funeral bier.

تقلع المنيّة ٱختِرامًا ولا يرعوي الباقون ٱجتِرامًا يحتذون مثالًا ويمضون أرسالًا إلى غاية الانتهاء وصيّور الفناء.

١،٨٠،٤ حتّى إذا تصرّمت الأمور وتقضّت الدهور وأَزِفَ النشور أخرجهم من ضرائح القبور وأوكار الطيور وأوجرة السباع ومطارح المهالك سِراعًا إلى أمره مهطعين إلى معاده رعيلًا صموتًا قيامًا صفوفًا ينفذهم البصر ويسمعهم الداعي عليهم لبوس الاستكانة وضرع الاستسلام والذلّة قد ضلّت الحيل وٱنقطع الأمل وهوت الأفئدة كاظمة وخشعت الأصوات مهينمة وألجم العرق وعظم الشفق وأرعدت الأسماع لزَبْرة الداعي إلى فصل الخطاب ومقايضة الجزاء ونكال العقاب ونوال الثواب.

١،٨٠،٥ عباد مخلوقون ٱقتدارًا ومربوبون ٱقتِسارًا ومقبوضون ٱحتضارًا ومضمّنون أجداثًا وكائنون رفاتًا ومبعوثون أفرادًا ومدينون جزاء ومميّزون حسابًا قد أمهلوا في طلب المخرج وهدوا سبيل المنهج وعمّروا مهل المستعتب وكشفت عنهم سدف الريب وخلّوا لمضمار الجياد وروِيّة الارتياد وأناة المقتبس المرتاد في مدّة الأجل ومضطرب المهل.

١،٨٠،٦ فيا لها أمثالًا صائبة ومواعظ شافية لو صادفت قلوبًا زاكية وأسماعًا واعية وآراء عازمة وألبابًا حازمة. فٱتّقوا الله تقيّة من سمع فخشع وٱقترف فٱعترف ووجل فعمل وحاذر فبادر وأيقن فأحسن وعُبِّر فٱعتبر وحُذِّر فٱزدجر وأجاب فأناب وراجع فتاب وٱقتدى فٱحتذى وأُري فرآى فأسرع طالبًا ونجا هاربًا فأفاد ذخيرة وأطاب سريرة وعمر معادًا وٱستظهر زادًا ليوم رحيله ووجه سبيله وحال حاجته وموطن فاقته وقدّم أمامه لدار مقامه. فٱتّقوا الله عباد الله جهة ما خلقكم له وٱحذروا منه كُنْه ما حذّركم من نفسه وٱستحِقّوا منه ما أعدّ لكم بالتنجّز لصدق ميعاده والحذر من هول معاده.

way, sons follow fathers. Death keeps cutting off lives, and people keep sinning. They follow the example of those who went before and advance, one herd after another, to the final end—the threshold of annihilation.

1.80.4 Then, when affairs conclude, eons run their course, and the resurrection draws near, God plucks people from the recesses of graves, from the nests of birds and the dens of beasts, and from every pit death has cast them into, and they hasten to answer his command. They rush to him in silent troops, standing upright in straight rows, the eye pierces them and the caller forces them to heed his call, clad in garments of submission, suckling the unholy milk of humiliation and shame. Ruses have vanished, hope is lost, hearts are gripped by terror, voices are hushed and mute, throats choke on sweat like a camel chokes on its bridle-straps, dread pervades, and ears are deafened by the thunderous call to judgment, to the payment for past deeds, be it punishment or reward.

1.80.5 All are God's servants, created by his power and ruled by his might. They will be seized by death, thrown into graves, transformed into dry bones, and resurrected alone, they will be held accountable for their deeds and singled out for the reckoning. They were given time to seek a way out and were guided to the beaten path, they had a lifetime to take warning and were led out from the shadows of doubt, they were left free to train for the race and contemplate their purpose, to seek a lighted torch and the promised goal. All this they could have done in their allotted time, in the respite granted for action.

1.80.6 What striking parables, what healing counsels! If only they fell on attentive ears, pure hearts, resolute minds, and mature intellects! People, be conscious of God in the manner of one who, when he hears the call, prostrates; if he sins, he confesses; because he fears, he does good; because he dreads, he hastens; attaining certainty, he is virtuous; given lessons, he takes heed; when warned, he recoils; in answering, he returns; if he regresses, he repents; when he emulates, he perseveres; and when shown the way, he perceives. In doing so, he races when he seeks and is saved when he flees. Thus, he amasses a treasure, purifies his heart, prepares for the return, and gathers provisions for his day of departure, his time on the road, his moment of need, and his state of want. He readies stocks for his final abode. Servants of God! Be conscious of him and attend to the purpose he created you for. Be afraid of him with regard to the thing he warned you to fear him for. Deserve the fulfilment of his promise. Beware the terror of the return.

1.80.7 منها

جعل لكم أسماعًا لتعي ما عناها وأبصارًا لتجلو عن عشاها وأشلاء جامعة لأعضائها ملائمة لأحنائها في تركيب صورها ومُدُد عُمُرها بأبدان قائمة بأرفاقها وقلوب رائدة لأرزاقها في مجلّلات نعمه وموجبات مننه وحواجز عافيته.[1] وقدّر لكم أعمارًا سترها عنكم وخلّف لكم عبرًا من آثار الماضين قبلكم من مستمتع خلاقهم ومستفسح خناقهم أرهقتهم المنايا دون الآمال وشذّبهم عنها تخرّم الآجال لم يمهدوا في سلامة الأبدان ولم يعتبروا في أُنُف الأوان. فهل ينتظر أهل بَضاضة الشباب إلّا حَواني الهرم وأهل غضارة الصحّة إلّا نوازل السقم وأهل مدّة البقاء إلّا آونة الفناء مع قرب الزِّيال وأزوف الانتقال وعلَز القلق وألم المضض وغصص الجرض وتلفّت الاستغاثة بنصرة الحفدة والأقرباء والأعزّة والقرناء.

1.80.8 فهل دفعت الأقارب أو نفعت النواحب وقد غودر في محلّة الأموات رهينًا وفي ضيق المضجع وحيدًا قد هتكت الهوامّ جلدته وأبلت النواهك جدّته وعفت العواصف آثاره ومحا الحدثان معالمه وصارت الأجساد شحبة بعد بَضّتها والعظام نخِرة بعد قوّتها والأرواح مرتهنة بثقل أعبائها موقنة بغيب أنبائها لا تستزاد من صالح عملها ولا تستعتب من سيّء زللها. أولستم أبناء القوم والآباء وإخوانهم والأقرباء تحتذون أمثلتهم وتركبون قِدّتهم[2] وتطؤون جادّتهم فالقلوب قاسية عن حظّها لاهية عن رشدها سالكة في غير مضمارها كأنّ المعنيّ سواها وكأنّ الرشد في إحراز دنياها.

1.80.9 واعلموا أنّ مجازكم على الصراط ومزالق دحضه وأهاويل زلله وتارات أهواله فاتّقوا الله تقيّة ذي لبّ شغل التفكّر قلبه وأنصب الخوف بدنه وأسهر التهجّد غِرار نومه وأظمأ الرجاء هواجر يومه وظلف الزهد شهواته وأوجف الذكر بلسانه وقدّم الخوف

---

[1] م، ن، ونسخة في ش: كذا. نسخة في م: ﴾بليّته﴿. أصل ش: ﴾وجوايز عافيته﴿، وفي الهامش مع علامة التصحيح ﴾وحواجز بليّته﴿. ي: ﴾وحواجز بليّته وجوائز عافيته﴿. هـ: ﴾وحوائز عافيته وحواجز بليّته﴿. [2] م، ن، هـ: كذا. ش، ي: كذا. ش، ي، ومصحّحة في هـ: ﴾قَذّتهم﴿.

1.80.7 From the same oration:

God has given you ears to hear what they should, eyes to dispel blindness, and a torso that encloses organs and is molded onto ribs; he has divided your forms—for use through a long life—into bodies that can attend to their needs, and hearts that can seek out their sustenance; he has given you these and many more splendid blessings, binding favors, and shelters of health and well-being; he has fixed your lifespans and concealed their duration. All the while, he has presented you with lessons in the tales of the people who went before you, who enjoyed good fortune and roamed with loosened halters, until fate overtook them and cut off their false hopes, and the termination of their lifespan drove them from their desires, who neglected to provide for themselves when their bodies were sound, nor heed life's lessons while there was time to choose. Think: Can the youth with rosy skin expect anything but the bowed back of old age? The man of fresh health anything but the hard blows of sickness? The living anything but the moment of perdition, the imminence of separation, the approach of dislocation, the insomnia of anxiety, the pain of burning grief, the throttle of the death rattle, and the futile appeal for help to grandchildren and relatives, friends and colleagues?

1.80.8 Can relatives ward off the ordeal, or wailing women avail, when the deceased are pledged to the dead man's quarter, when they lie alone in the grave? Maggots tear into their skin and the elements corrode their freshness. Storms erase their traces and routines obliterate their signs. Bodies once rosy of skin decay, and bones once strong desiccate. Souls, mortgaged to their burdens, now see the reality of the unseen. But the time to stock deeds is past, or to atone for transgressions. Are you not the children of the dead, their fathers, their brothers, their relatives? Do you not follow in their footsteps? Do you not walk their road and tread their path? But your hardened hearts cannot absorb a share of belief. You run in the wrong race, too preoccupied to discern. You behave as though someone else is the next target, as though wisdom lies in amassing wealth.

1.80.9 But know this: You too must cross the bridge of death, with its slippery surface, horrifying stumbles, and repeated terrors. So be conscious of God in the manner of a sage whose heart is deep in thought and whose body is emaciated by fear; whose snatches of sleep in the watches of night are interrupted by prayer, and whose hope for reward makes him choose thirst in the scorching hours of the day; whose passions renunciation dampens, whose tongue remembrance spurs on, and who fears God as he should, in order to obtain God's shelter; who shuns deviation from the straight path, and traverses the middle

لأمانه وتنكّب المخالج عن وَضَح السبيل وسلك أقصد المسالك إلى النهج المطلوب ولم تَفتِله فاتلات الغرور ولم تَعْمَ عليه مشتبهات الأمور ظافرًا بفرحة البشرى وراحة النعمى في أنعم نومه وآمن يومه قد عبر معبر العاجلة حميدًا وقدّم زاد الآجلة سعيدًا وبادر من وجل وأكمش في مهل ورغب في طلب وذهب عن هرب وراقب في يومه غده ونظر قُدُمًا أمامه. فكفى بالجنّة ثوابًا ونوالًا وكفى بالنار عقابًا ووبالًا وكفى بالله منتقمًا ونصيرًا وكفى بالكتاب حجيجًا وخصيمًا.

1.80.10 أوصيكم بتقوى الله الذي أعذر بما أنذر واحتجّ بما نهج وحذّركم عدوًّا نفذ في الصدور خفيًّا ونفث في الآذان نجيًّا فأضلّ وأردى ووعد فمنّى وزيّن سيّئات الجرائم وهوّن موبقات العظائم حتّى إذا استدرج قرينته واستغلق رهينته أنكر ما زيّن واستعظم ما هوّن وحذّر ما آمن.

1.80.11 منها في صفة خلق الإنسان
أم هذا الذي أنشأه في ظلمات الأرحام وشغف الأستار نطفة دِهاقًا وعلقة مُحاقًا وجنينًا وراضعًا ووليدًا ويافعًا ثمّ منحه قلبًا حافظًا ولسانًا لافظًا وبصرًا لاحظًا ليفهم معتبرًا ويقصر مزدجرًا حتّى إذا قام اعتداله واستوى مثاله نفر مستكبرًا وخبط سادرًا ماتحًا في غرب هواه كادحًا سعيًا لدنياه في لذّات طربه وبدوات أربه لا يحتسب رزيّة ولا يخشع تقيّة.

1.80.12 فات في فتنته غريرًا وعاش في هفوته يسيرًا لم يفد عوضًا ولم يقض مفترضًا دهمته فَجَعات المنيّة في غُبَّر جِماحه وسَنن مَراحه فظلّ سادرًا وبات ساهرًا في غمرات الآلام وطوارق الأوجاع والأسقام بين أخ شقيق ووالد شفيق وداعية بالويل جزعًا ولادمة للصدر قلقًا. والمرء في سكرة ملهية وغمرة كارثة وأنّة موجعة وجذبة مكربة وسوقة

***

road to reach his goal; whom delusion's snares do not entangle and dubious affairs do not blind. Such a man wins promised delights and blessed repose, a tranquil sleep, and a day of safety. He has crossed the bridge exemplarily, and arriving at the provisions he had sent on, he exults. Because he feared, he hastened; when given a chance, he labored; seeking, he hoped; fleeing, he dodged; in his present, he was mindful of the morrow; with courage, he looked ahead. O people, take heed: paradise suffices as reward and recompense, hellfire as punishment and penalty. God suffices as avenger and bestower of victory, his Book as interlocutor and adversary.

1.80.10 I counsel you to be conscious of God, who alerted when he cautioned, and justified his claim when he showed you the way. He warned you against the enemy who steals into breasts with stealth, and whispers into ears in secret; who misguides and leads into hell, and promises with vows that are false; who makes the evilest of crimes look attractive, and trivializes terrible sins—then, when he has deceived your soul and secured your collateral, he pronounces repulsive what he had bedecked and grave what he had dismissed, and he threatens you with the very things from which he had promised safety.

1.80.11 From the same oration, describing the creation of humans:
Look at this human, whom God created in the darkness of the womb, in layers of coverings, whom he transformed from a drop of gushing semen to a formless blood-clot, then to a fetus, a suckling babe, a child, and a youth. God bestowed on the human a heart that can remember, a tongue that can speak, and eyes that can see, so that he may learn when taught and refrain when admonished. But then, when he attained a balanced figure and his body stood up straight, he turned away in arrogance and bucked like a sun-struck camel, toiling only for worldly gain, and drawing up huge buckets from the deep wells of his passions. Seeking only ecstatic pleasures and wishful fancies, he neither heeded the approaching menace nor humbled himself before God.

1.80.12 And so he died pursuing pleasure, having lived for a moment, jolly in his sins, then leaving without fulfilling obligations or earning reward. Sudden fate attacked him as he galloped headstrong in his merry path. That day, he collapsed like a sun-struck camel, that night, he lay tortured by agonies of pain and convulsions of illness. Onlookers—a blood brother, a doting father, one woman crying woe, another beating her chest—stood by. Then he was seized by consuming paroxysms, intense distress, and painful groans, in an excruciating extraction and a most severe end. Then he was wrapped in the cloths of a shroud and moved hither and thither, passive at all times and submissive. Then

متعبة ثم أدرج في أكفانه مُبلَسًا وجُذب منقادًا سلسًا ثم ألقي على الأعواد رجيع وَصَب ونِضْو سقم تحمله حفدة الولدان وحشدة الإخوان إلى دار غربته ومنقطع زورته حتّى إذا انصرف المشيّع ورجع المتفجّع أقعد في حفرته نجيًّا لَبْتَة السؤال وعثرة الامتحان. وأعظم ما هنالك بليّة نزل الحميم وتصلية الجحيم وفورات السعير لا فترة مريحة ولا دعة مزيحة ولا قوّة حاجزة ولا موتة ناجزة ولا سِنة مسلية بين أطوار الموتات وعذاب الساعات ﴿إِنَّا لِلّهِ وَإِنَّا إِلَيْهِ رَاجِعُونَ﴾[1] إنّا بالله عائذون.

1.80.13   عباد الله الذين عُمّروا فنعموا وعُلّموا ففهموا وأنظروا فلَهُوا وسلموا فنسوا أُمهلوا طويلًا ومنحوا جميلًا وحذّروا أليمًا ووعدوا جسيمًا. احذروا الذنوب المورّطة والعيوب المسخطة أولي الأبصار والأسماع والعافية والمتاع هل من مَناص أو خلاص أو معاذ أو ملاذ أو فرار[2] أو محارٍ أم لا. ﴿فَأَنَّىٰ تُؤْفَكُونَ﴾ أم أين تصرفون أم بماذا تغتّرون وإنّما حظّ أحدكم من الأرض ذات الطول والعرض قِيْدُ قَدّه منعفراً على خدّه. الآن عباد الله والخناق مهمل والروح مرسل في فَيْنة الإرشاد وراحة الأجساد ومَهَل البقيّة وأُنُف المشيّة وإنظار التوبة وانفساح الحوبة قبل الضنك والمضيق والروع والزهوق وقبل قدوم الغائب المنتظر وأخذة العزيز المقتدر.

1.80.14   وفي الخبر أنّه عليه السلام لمّا خطب بهذه الخطبة اقشعرّت لها الجلود وبكت العيون ورجفت القلوب. ومن الناس من يسمّي هذه الخطبة الغرّاء.

---

[1] وأضيفت في ش: كذا. ه: ﴿إنّا بالله عائذون و﴿إِنَّا لِلّهِ وَإِنَّا إِلَيْهِ رَاجِعُونَ﴾﴾. ن، ي: سقطت الآية القرآنيّة.   [2] ن، ي، ش، ه: كذا. م: أضيفت ﴿أو مجان﴾.

his body, emaciated by disease and destroyed by illness, was tossed on a plank, and carried by his sons' children and his brothers' attendants to the house of exile and the state of separation. Finally, when those who had come to bury him had turned back and the grieving mourners had gone away, he was made to sit up alone in his tomb to face a frightening interrogation and a terrible ordeal. People, know that the afterworld's greatest torment is the Pit-of-Boiling-Liquid, the Blaze-of-Hellfire, the Conflagration-of-the Inferno.[1] It allows no period of rest, no alleviating respite, no shielding force, no soothing sleep, and no relief in a final death. This is all there is: death after death and hour after hour of torture. «Indeed, we belong to God, and to him we shall return.»[2] Truly, in God we seek refuge.

1.80.13 Servants of God! You were given long lives that you enjoyed, knowledge that helped you understand, respite that you squandered in play, and security that made you careless. You were given a long reprieve and beautiful gifts, warned of punishments, and promised rewards. Bearers of eyes and ears, health and wealth, beware of sins that hurl into the abyss, and transgressions that incur God's wrath! Do you see escape, deliverance, refuge, shelter, retreat, or return? No? Well, then, «how are you deluded,»[3] where are you directed, and what is deceiving you? Your share of the world, in all its length and breadth, is but the measure of your body as it lies with cheek in the dust! Servants of God! Take heed now, this very moment, while halters remain loosened and spirits untethered, while you have time to seek guidance and a body that is sound, with a remainder in your respite, the freedom to choose, a chance to repent, and room to move. Take heed before the calamity descends and straits narrow, before fear prevails and destruction sets in, before the arrival of that visitor who will surely arrive, and before you are seized by the Powerful, Almighty Lord.

1.80.14 Raḍī: The report goes on to state that when ʿAlī delivered this oration, bodies shuddered, eyes wept, and hearts trembled. Some people name this *Gharrāʾ*, "The Radiant Oration."

---

1 Modified quote from Qurʾan, Wāqiʿah 56:93–94.
2 Qurʾan, Baqarah 2:156.
3 Qurʾan, Anʿām 6:95, Yūnus 10:34, Fāṭir 35:3, Ghāfir 40:62.

1.81   ومن كلام له عليه السلام في ذكر عمرو بن العاص

عجبًا لابن النابغة يزعم لأهل الشام أنّ فيّ دُعابة وأنّي امرؤٌ تِلْعابة أعافس وأمارس لقد قال باطلًا ونطق آثمًا أما وشرّ القول الكذب إنّه ليقول فيكذب ويعد فيخلف ويَسأل فيُلحف ويُسأل فيبخل ويخون العهد ويقطع الإلّ فإذا كان عند الحرب فأيّ زاجر وآمر هو ما لم تأخذ السيوف مآخذها فإذا كان ذلك كان أكبر[1] مكيدته أن يمنح القوم سَبّته. أما والله إنّي ليمنعني من اللعب ذكر الموت وإنّه ليمنعه من قول الحقّ نسيان الآخرة إنّه لم يبايع معاوية حتّى شرط له أن يؤتيه أتيّة ويرضخ له على ترك الدين رضيخة.

1.82   ومن خطبة له عليه السلام

1.82.1   وأشهد أن لا إله إلّا الله وحده لا شريك له الأوّل لا شيء قبله والآخر لا غاية له لا تقع الأوهام له على صفة ولا تعقد القلوب منه على كيفيّة ولا تناله التجزئة والتبعيض ولا تحيط به الأبصار والقلوب.

1.82.2   منها

فاتّعظوا عباد الله بالعبر النوافع واعتبروا بالآي السواطع وازدجروا بالنذر البوالغ وانتفعوا بالذكر والمواعظ فكأن قد علقتكم مخالب المنيّة وانقطعت منكم علائق الأمنيّة

ام، ي: كذا. ن، ش، هـ: ﴿أكثر﴾.

1.81 From ʿAlī's address about ʿAmr ibn al-ʿĀṣ:[1]

How strange! The Harlot's son tells the Syrians that I have a streak of foolishness, that I am a joker interested only in frolics and flirtation! He speaks untruth and gives voice to sin, for lies are the evilest of words. When he speaks, he lies, when he promises, he breaks his promise, when he solicits, he badgers—but when he himself is solicited, he is stingy, he betrays his pledge and disowns his kin. When battle approaches, how boldly he chides and commands!—but only before swords reap their harvest, then, his best strategy is to show people his arse![2] By God, the thought of death stops me from indulging in frivolities, while disregard for the hereafter stops him from speaking the truth. In fact, he pledged allegiance to Muʿāwiyah only after he had elicited from him a promise of payment—a paltry bribe of baubles in exchange for abandoning the faith.

1.82 From an oration by ʿAlī:[3]

1.82.1 I bear witness that there is no god but God, who has no partner. He is the first, for there was nothing before him, and the last, for he has no end. Minds cannot find a way to describe him, hearts cannot comprehend his nature, dissecting or deconstructing cannot grasp him, and eyes and hearts cannot take him in.

1.82.2 From the same oration:

Servants of God! Take counsel from valuable lessons, warning from blazing signs, caution from powerful warnings, and benefit from reminders and counsels! Imagine that death's talons have pierced you and hope's threads are severed, that calamitous events have crushed you, and fate has driven you to the waterhole that is common to all. «Each soul is accompanied by its driver and

---

1   Thaqafī (*Ghārāt*, 2:513) states that this oration was delivered on the pulpit. Nuʿmān (*Manāqib*, 273) places the text in Iraq. ʿAmr's mother was infamous in the pre-Islamic period as "The Harlot" (*nābighah*, lit. "the woman who shows herself," B 335; Gh 1:415). During the month in which she conceived ʿAmr, it is reported that she had lain with five men—Abū Lahab ibn ʿAbd al-Muṭṭalib, Umayyah ibn Khalaf al-Jumaḥī, Hishām ibn al-Mughīrah al-Makhzūmī, Abū Sufyān ibn Ḥarb, and al-ʿĀṣ ibn Wāʾil al-Sahmī—and each of them claimed him as his son. She chose ʿĀṣ as the father because he supported her financially, although ʿAmr resembled Abū Sufyān more (Ḥ 6:283; Gh 1:415). ʿAmr's words about ʿAlī having "a streak of foolishness" (*duʿābah*) echoed a criticism earlier voiced by ʿUmar (Ḥ 6:326–330).

2   In one of the battle days of Ṣiffīn, ʿAmr came face to face with ʿAlī, and when ʿAlī was about to strike him, he exposed his private parts, and ʿAlī turned away. Idrīs, *ʿUyūn*, 3:244–246.

3   § 1.82.2 (also § 1.80.2, 6, 7, 9) are recorded by Abū Nuʿaym (*Ḥilyat* 1:77–79) as part of an oration ʿAlī declaimed after accompanying a funeral bier.

ودهمتكم مفظعات الأمور والسياقة إلى الورد المورود و﴿كُلُّ نَفْسٍ مَّعَهَا سَآئِقٌ وَشَهِيدٌ﴾ سائق يسوقها إلى محشرها وشاهد يشهد عليها بعملها.

1.82.3   منها في صفة الجنّة

درجات متفاضلات ومنازل متفاوتات لا ينقطع نعيمها ولا يظعن مقيمها ولا يهرم خالدها ولا ييأس ساكنها.

1.83   ومن خطبة له عليه السلام

1.83.1   قد علم السرائر وخبر الضمائر له الاحاطة بكلّ شيء والغلبة لكلّ شيء والقوّة على كلّ شيء.

1.83.2   فليعمل العامل منكم في أيّام مهله قبل إرهاق أجله وفي فراغه قبل أوان شغله وفي متنفّسه قبل أن يؤخذ بكظمه وليمهّد لنفسه وقدمه وليتزوّد من دار ظعنه لدار إقامته.

1.83.3   فالله الله أيّها الناس فيما استحفظكم من كتابه واستودعكم من حقوقه فإنّ الله سبحانه لم يخلقكم عبثًا ولم يتركّكم سدى ولم يدعكم في جهالة ولا عمى قد سمّى آثاركم وعلم أعمالكم وكتب آجالكم وأنزل عليكم الكتاب تبيانًا وعمّر فيكم نبيّه أزمانًا حتّى أكمل له ولكم فيما أنزل من كتابه الذي رضي لنفسه وأنهى إليكم على لسانه محابّه من الأعمال ومكارهه ونواهيه وأوامره فألقى إليكم المعذرة واتّخذ عليكم الحجّة وقدّم إليكم بالوعيد وأنذركم بين يدي عذاب شديد. فاستدركوا بقيّة أيّامكم واصبروا لها أنفسكم فإنّها قليل في كثير الأيّام التي تكون منكم فيها الغفلة والتشاغل عن الموعظة ولا ترخّصوا لأنفسكم فتذهب بكم الرخص مذاهب الظلمة ولا تداهنوا فيهجم بكم الإدهان على المعصية.

its witness»[1]—a driver who steers it to the place of accounting, and a witness who testifies to its deeds.

1.82.3 From the same oration describing paradise:
It has distinct ranks and diverse stations. Its blessings never end, its residents never leave, its occupants never age, and its inhabitants never want.

1.83 From an oration by ʿAlī:[2]

1.83.1 God knows your thoughts and discerns your feelings, he encompasses all things, subjugates all things, and controls all things.

1.83.2 Do good in your time of respite before the end of your lifespan, in your time of leisure before other things preoccupy you, in the time you draw breath before your throat chokes. Provide for your soul and secure it a high rank. Take provisions from the home you will leave for the home you will reside in forever.

1.83.3 People! Fear God in this: guard his Book, which he has asked you to preserve, and uphold his rights, which he has asked you to hold in trust. He has not created you in vain, nor left you without direction,[3] nor ignorant and blind. He records your acts and knows what you do, and he has decreed what your lifespan will be. Sending you the Book with its clear exposition,[4] God let his Prophet live among you through numerous seasons, until, by what he revealed in his Book, he perfected for him and for you the faith he was pleased to call his own.[5] Expressing approvals and disapprovals on his Prophet's tongue, as well as prohibitions and commands, God justified his claim to you, placed his proof before you, advanced his warning to you, and cautioned you of imminent and harsh chastisement. People, use your remaining days to rectify your wrongs and devote yourselves to that task, for your remaining days are few compared to the many you have squandered carelessly and in total neglect of admonition. Don't give yourselves undue license for that will lead you down the path of tyrants, don't be duplicitous for that will steer you into sin.

---

1 Qurʾan, Qāf 50:21.
2 §1.83.3 (and §1.171.2) are recorded by Minqarī (*Waqʿat Ṣiffīn*, 10) and Abū Ḥanīfah al-Dīnawarī (*Akhbār*, 152–153) as part of ʿAlī's first Friday sermon in Kufa (36/656). §1.83.4 is recorded by Ḥarrānī (*Tuḥaf*, 150) as part of "The Brocade (*Dībāj*) Oration," also recorded in §1.107; Mufīd (*Amālī*, 206) prefaces this section with "ʿAlī used to say."
3 Modified quotes from Qurʾan, Muʾminūn 23:115, Qiyāmah 75:36.
4 Modified quote from Qurʾan, Naḥl 16:89.
5 Modified quote from Qurʾan, Māʾidah 5:3. I have added the word "faith" (Ar. *dīn*) from the Qurʾanic verse to clarify the reference and meaning.

1.83.4 عباد الله إنّ أنصح الناس لنفسه أطوعهم لربّه وإنّ أغشّهم لنفسه أعصاهم لربّه والمغبون من غبن نفسه والمغبوط من سلم له دينه والسعيد من وُعظ بغيره والشقيّ من اَنخدع لهواه وغروره. واَعلموا أنّ يسير الرياء شرك ومجالسة أهل الهوى منساة للإيمان ومحضرة للشيطان. جانبوا الكذب فإنّه مجانب للإيمان الصادق على شفا منجاة وكرامة والكاذب على شرف مهواة ومهانة لا تحاسدوا فإنّ الحسد يأكل الإيمان كما تأكل النار الحطب ولا تباغضوا فإنّها الحالقة. واَعلموا أنّ الأمل يسهي العقل وينسي الذكر فأكذبوا الأمل فإنّه غرور وصاحبه مغرور.

1.84 ومن خطبة له عليه السلام

1.84.1 عباد الله إنّ من أحبّ عباد الله إليه عبدًا أعانه الله على نفسه فاَستشعر الحزن وتجلبب الخوف فزهر مصباح الهدى في قلبه وأعدّ القِرى ليومه النازل به فقرّب على نفسه البعيد وهوّن الشديد نظر فأبصر وذكر فاَستكثر واَرتوى من عذب فرات سهلت له موارده فشرب نهلًا وسلك سبيلًا جددًا قد خلع سرابيل الشهوات وتخلّى من الهموم إلّا همًّا واحدًا اَنفرد به نخرج من صفة العمى ومشاركة أهل الهوى وصار من مفاتيح أبواب الهدى ومغاليق أبواب الردى. قد أبصر طريقه وسلك سبيله وعرف مناره وقطع غماره واَستمسك من العرى بأوثقها ومن الحبال بأمتنها فهو من اليقين على مثل ضوء

1.83.4 Servants of God! He who counsels himself best, best obeys his Lord, while he who deceives himself most, most disobeys his Lord. He who cheats himself is truly cheated, he whose faith is safe is truly joyful, he who learns from the example of others is truly fortunate, and he who is misled by desire and conceit is truly wretched. Know this: If you do good to show off even a little, you assign partners to God, and when you keep company with the dissolute, you forget your faith and summon Satan. Stay away from lies for they weaken faith. The truthful stand on the threshold of salvation and honor, while liars stand at the rim of the abyss and the edge of abasement. Don't envy one another, for envy consumes faith just as fire consumes kindling. Don't hate one another, for hate destroys.[1] Know this: false hope diverts the mind and causes you to forget God.[2] Don't place your faith in it for it is nothing but deception and its friend is wholly deceived.

1.84 From an oration by ʿAlī:[3]

1.84.1 Servants of God! The most beloved of his servants in God's eyes is the man who, with his help, keeps his passions under control.[4] By wearing the shirt of grief and donning the robe of fear, this man illumines his heart with the lamp of guidance. Putting by stores for the day that will come, for that guest who will soon be here, he brings the future close and dismisses the present's tribulations. He looks and discerns, he learns and gains, and he slakes his thirst with sweet water. His track to the waterhole has become smooth, so he walks its beaten path and drinks his fill. Discarding desire's mantle and divesting from all aspirations, he holds on to just one. He escapes in this way from blindness and from the passion-driven rabble, and becomes a key to the door of guidance, a lock on the door of perdition. He sees his way, walks his path, recognizes his beacon, and crosses the deep seas. He grasps the firmest handle and the strongest rope, and so attains the certainty of one who sees the light of the

---

1   Lit. "[Hate] is the Shaver (*innahā al-ḥāliqah*)," an opaque metaphor interpreted variously to mean that hate (1) erases all good and blessings (ʿA 595); (2) cuts people off from one another (B 344); (3) harms faith (M 1:428); and (4) destroys society (R 1:359; Ḥ 6:357).

2   The usual rendering of *amal* (translated here as "false hope") is simply "hope." In the Arabic oratorical tradition, though, particularly in ʿAlī's sermons, the word invariably refers to the false hope that you will live forever, while it is the word *rajāʾ* that usually denotes positive hope. The phrase translated as "causes you to forget God" (*yunsī al-dhikr*) literally means, "makes you forget the remembrance," here, of God (B 344), and the hereafter.

3   Ḥ 6:382–383 records two additional passages from this oration.

4   The word translated as "passions" is *nafs* (lit. "soul," or "self"), in the Qurʾanic sense of «the [base faculty of the] soul that incites [its owner] to do evil» Qurʾan, Yūsuf 12:53.

الشمس قد نصب نفسه لله سبحانه في أرفع الأمور من إصدار كلّ وارد عليه وتصيير كلّ فرع إلى أصله مصباح ظلمات كشّاف غشوات مفتاح مبهمات دفّاع معضلات دليل فلوات يقول فيفهم ويسكت فيسلم قد أخلص لله فاستخلصه فهو من معادن دينه وأوتاد أرضه قد ألزم نفسه العدل فكان أوّل عدله نفي الهوى عن نفسه. يصف الحقّ ويعمل به لا يدع للخير غاية إلّا أمّها ولا مظنّة إلّا قصدها قد أمكن الكتاب من زمامه فهو قائده وإمامه يحلّ حيث حلّ ثقله وينزل حيث كان منزله.

1.84.2 وآخر قد تسمّى عالـمًا وليس به فاقتبس جهائل من جهّال وأضاليل من ضلّال ونصب للناس أشراكًا من حبال غرور وقول زور قد حمل الكتاب على آرائه وعطف الحقّ على أهوائه يؤمن من العظائم ويهوّن كبير الجرائم يقول أقف عند الشبهات وفيها وقع ويقول أعتزل البدع وبينها اضطجع فالصورة صورة إنسان والقلب قلب حيوان لا يعرف باب الهدى فيتبعه ولا باب العمى فيصدّ عنه فذلك ميّت الأحياء.

﴿فَأَيْنَ تَذْهَبُونَ﴾ و﴿أَنَّىٰ تُؤْفَكُونَ﴾ والأعلام قائمة والآيات واضحة والمنائر منصوبة فأين يتاه بكم بل كيف تعمهون وبينكم عترة نبيّكم وهم أزمّة الحقّ وألسنة الصدق فأنزلوهم بأحسن منازل القرآن وِردُوهم ورود الهيم العطاش. أيّها الناس خذوها عن خاتم النبيّين صلّى الله عليه وآله ﴿إنّه يموت من مات منّا وليس بميّت ويبلى من بلي منّا وليس ببال﴾. فلا تقولوا بما لا تعرفون فإنّ أكثر الحقّ فيما تنكرون واعذروا من لا حجّة لكم عليه وأنا هو. ألم أعمل فيكم بالثَّقَل الأكبر وأترك فيكم الثقل الأصغر

sun. He deputes for God in the loftiest matters, providing all comers with water, tracing each branch to its root. He is a lamp in the darkness, a dispeller of obscurities, a key to elucidation, a defender against calamities, and a guide in the wilderness. When he speaks, people can understand, and when silent, he protects himself from erring. He is sincere in his devotion to God, so God singles him out for himself. He is thus a repository of God's faith, a mountain that pegs God's earth. He enjoins his soul to justice, and his first act of justice is to banish all passions from his soul. He preaches the truth and practices it. He strives continually for good, with no avenue unexplored, no location untracked. He entrusts his reins to God's Book, which becomes his driver and leader. He settles where it unloads its wares and encamps where it sets up camp.

1.84.2 Then there is another kind: this man calls himself learned when he is not. He collects scraps of ignorance from the ignorant and bits of error from the errant, and traps people with deceptive snares and false reports. He interprets the Book to his fancies and bends the truth to his passions, he promises protection from punishment and trivializes major sins. He crows, "I pause if I have doubt," when he has fallen into its pit. He boasts, "I stay away from heresy," when he has made it his bedfellow. His form is human, but his heart is the heart of a beast. He does not recognize let alone follow guidance, he cannot identify let alone repel blindness. He is the living dead.

«So where do you go,»[1] «and how are you deluded,»[2] when banners are raised, waymarks are clear, and beacons are lit? Indeed, whereto do you stray, and how is it you are lost, when you have among you the Prophet's descendants, who are guide ropes of right and tongues of truth? Accord them the high regard you accord the Qur'an,[3] and race like parched camels to drink at their waterhole. People! Take this from the Seal of the Prophets, who said, ⟨When one of us dies, he is not dead. When his body disintegrates in the ground, it has not disintegrated.⟩[4] Don't speak of what you don't know, for what you deny is the truth. Absolve the man against whom you have no claim, and that is I! Have I not led you in accordance with the Greater Treasure and given you the Smaller

---

1   Qur'an, Takwīr 81:26.

2   Qur'an, Anʿām 6:95, Yūnus 10:34, Fāṭir 35:3, Ghāfir 40:62.

3   I.e., revere them and obey their commands, as you revere and obey the Qur'an. B 351; Ḥ 6:376; R 1:364.

4   Refers to the Qur'anic verse, «Do not think that those who die striving in the path of God are dead: They are alive, sustained by the side of their Lord.» Qur'an, Āl ʿImrān 3:169; B 351. The "Seal of the Prophets" is Muḥammad.

وركزت فيكم راية الإيمان ووقفتكم على حدود الحلال والحرام وألبستكم العافية من عدلي وفرشتكم المعروف من قولي وفعلي وأريتكم كرائم الأخلاق من نفسي فلا تستعملوا الرأي فيما لا يدرك قعره البصر ولا يتغلغل إليه الفكر.

1.84.3 منها

حتّى يظنّ الظانّ أنّ الدنيا معقولة على بني أميّة تمنحهم درّها وتوردهم صفوها ولا يُرفع عن هذه الأمّة سوطها ولا سيفها وكذب الظانّ لذلك بل هي مجّة من لذيذ العيش يتطعّمونها برهة ثم يلفظونها جملة.

1.85 ومن خطبة له عليه السلام

أمّا بعد. فإنّ الله لم يقصم جبّاري دهر قطّ إلّا بعد تمهيل ورخاء ولم يجبر عظم أحد من الأمم إلّا بعد أزْل وبلاء وفي دون ما استقبلتم من خطب واستدبرتم من خطب معتبر وما كلّ ذي قلب بلبيب ولا كلّ ذي سمع بسميع ولا كلّ ذي ناظر ببصير. فيا عجبًا ومالي لا أعجب من خطأ هذه الفرق على اختلاف حججها في دينها لا يقتصّون أثر نبيّ ولا يقتدون بعمل وصيّ ولا يؤمنون بغيب ولا يعفّون عن عيب يعملون في الشبهات ويسيرون في الشهوات المعروف فيهم ما عرفوا والمنكر عندهم ما أنكروا مفزعهم في المعضلات إلى أنفسهم وتعويلهم في المبهمات على آرائهم كأنّ كلّ امرئ منهم إمام نفسه قد أخذ منها فيما يرى بعرى ثقات وأسباب محكمات.

1.86 ومن خطبة له عليه السلام

One?[1] Have I not raised for you the banner of faith, shown you the boundaries between licit and illicit, clothed you through my justice in the garment of security, unfurled for you with my words and deeds the carpet of good, and exemplified for you with my behavior a virtuous character? So do not exercise your fancy in areas whose depths your eyes cannot plumb, or your minds penetrate!

1.84.3 From the same oration:
A man may well believe that the world is a camel tied up in the Umayyads' pen, giving them sweet milk and leading them to pure water, and that their whip and sword will never be lifted from the community's neck—but he would be wrong. This is but a delicious drink they will sip for a short while and then spit out all at once.

1.85 From an oration by ʿAlī:[2]
God has not crushed tyrants of any era except after a long respite and an abundant share of fortune, nor has he mended the bones of any community except after a period of anguish and trial. Lessons can be gleaned from lesser things than the calamities you have experienced, yet not every heart discerns, not every ear listens, and not every eye perceives. I am amazed—and how could I not be!—at the errors committed by these groups who produce such dissenting claims in faith. They neither follow the footsteps of a prophet nor emulate the actions of a legatee, they do not believe in the mystery or refrain from debauchery, rather, they base their actions on doubts and tread the path of passions. Good to them is what they find pleasing, and evil is what they find foul. When faced with obscurities, they rely on their own judgment, and when faced with ambiguities, they rely on their own caprice. Each of them is his own leader who—misguidedly, in his own view—has a firm grip on sturdy handles and strong ropes.

1.86 From an oration by ʿAlī:[3]

---

1   The reference is to the Prophet's hadith: ⟨I leave among you two weighty, or precious, things (*thaqalayn*—translated here as the Greater Treasure and the Smaller One), God's Book and my descendants, my family. They will never be separated and will come to me together at the pools of paradise.⟩ B 352; R 1:364; Ḥ 6:380.

2   Kulaynī (*Kāfī*, 8:64) and Mufīd (*Irshād*, 1:291) say ʿAlī delivered this oration in Medina, presumably at the beginning of his caliphate in 35/656. Baḥrānī (B 353) says the "tyrant" (*jabbār*) in the oration refers to Muʿāwiyah, but if the oration is early in ʿAlī's caliphate as Kulaynī states (*Kāfī*, 8:64), it would refer more generally to Muʿāwiyah's Umayyad clan.

3   The first three lines are the same in §1.156.1.

أرسله على حين فترة من الرسل وطول هجعة من الأمم وآعترام[1] من الفتن وآنتشار من الأمور وتلظٍّ من الحروب والدنيا كاسفة النور ظاهرة الغرور على حين آصفرار من ورقها وإياسٍ من ثمرها وآغورار من مائها قد درست أعلام الهدى وظهرت أعلام الردى فهي متجهّمة لأهلها عابسة في وجه طالبها ثمرها الفتنة وطعامها الجيفة وشعارها الخوف ودثارها السيف. فآعتبروا عباد الله وآذكروا تِلكَ التي آباؤكم وإخوانكم بها مرتهنون وعليها محاسبون ولعمري ما تقادمت بكم ولا بهم العهود ولا خلت فيما بينكم وبينهم الأحقاب والقرون[2] وما أنتم اليوم من يوم كنتم في أصلابهم ببعيد. والله ما أسمعهم الرسول شيئًا إلّا وها أنا ذا اليوم مسمعكموه وما أسماعكم اليوم بدون أسماعهم[3] بالأمس ولا شقّت لهم الأبصار وجعلت لهم الأفئدة في ذلك الأوان إلّا وقد أعطيتم مثلها في هذا الزمان ووالله ما بصّرتم بعدهم شيئًا جهلوه ولا أُصفيتم به وحُرموه ولقد نزلت بكم البليّة جائلًا خِطامها رِخْوًا بطانها فلا يغرنّكم ما أصبح فيه أهل الغرور فإنّما هو ظلّ ممدود إلى أجل معدود.

1.87 ومن خطبة له عليه السلام

المعروف من غير رؤية الخالق من غير رويّة الذي لم يزل قائمًا دائمًا إذ لا سماء ذات أبراج ولا حجب ذات أرتاج ولا ليل داجٍ ولا بحر ساجٍ ولا جبل ذو فِجاج ولا فجٌّ ذو آعوجاج ولا أرض ذات مهاد ولا خلق ذو آعتماد ذلك مبتدع الخلق ووارثه وإله الخلق ورازقه والشمس والقمر دائبان في مرضاته يُبليان كلّ جديد ويقرّبان كلّ بعيد. قسم أرزاقهم وأحصى آثارهم وأعمالهم وعدّد أنفاسهم وخائنة أعينهم وما تخفي صدورهم من الضمير ومستقرّهم ومستودعهم من الأرحام والظهور إلى أن تتناهى بهم الغايات. هو الذي آشتدّت نقمته على أعدائه في سعة رحمته وآتّسعت رحمته لأوليائه في شدّة نقمته قاهر مَن عازّه ومدمّر من شاقّه ومذلّ من ناواه وغالب من عاداه من توكّل عليه كفاه ومن

God sent Muḥammad when an age had gone by without prophets, when people had long been in slumber, when steeds of revolt were bucking, affairs were in disarray, and battles were aflame. The world was devoid of light, her deceit was shining bright, her leaves had yellowed and browned, her fruits could not be found, and her water had sunk underground. The waymarks of guidance had crumbled, the waymarks of hell were erected. The world glared at her tenants and scowled in the face of her seekers. Mutiny was her harvest, cadavers her preferred food, fear was her garment, and the sword her daily robe. Servants of God, take heed! Remember the deeds to which your fathers and brothers remain pledged, and for which they must account. I swear on my life and say this: No great time has passed between their years and yours, no eons separate their seasons and yours, you are not so far today from the day you were in their loins. By God! Everything God's Messenger told them, I reiterate to you today, for your hearing is no less keen today than theirs was yesterday. Just as they were given eyes to see, just as they were given hearts to comprehend, so too have you, in your generation, been given. And neither, by God, are you shown something they were ignorant of, or privileged with knowledge they were not. The calamity that has attacked you has a slackened nose-rein and a loosened belly-strap,[1] so do not be deceived by the ascendance of these men of deceit. Their spreading shade is fleeting.

1.87 From an oration by ʿAlī:

God is recognized without being seen, a creator who did not need to deliberate. He was existent and present from eternity, when there were no mansion-filled skies,[2] no inaccessible veils,[3] no dark nights, no tranquil seas, no craggy gorges, no twisting ravines, no outspread earth, and no legged creatures. God is the originator of all creation and its inheritor, the maker of all creation and its sustainer. The sun and the moon strive for his pleasure as they wear out the old and bring near the far. He apportions our sustenance and reckons our traces and deeds. He enumerates our breaths and our glances, the secrets our bosoms hide, and our places of rest and passage in wombs and loins until our final end. His punishment crushes his enemies, despite the vastness of his mercy, while his mercy enfolds his devotees, despite the harshness of his punishment. He subjugates his challengers, destroys those who defy him, humbles his opponents, and overthrows his foes. He suffices those who trust him, he gives to those who beseech him, he repays with favors those who extend him a loan of

---

1   I.e., its rider could fall off at any moment. Ḥ 6:390; B 357; R 1:372.
2   Reference to the signs of the zodiac, Qurʾan, Burūj 85:1.
3   Refers to "inaccessible veils of divine light," Ḥ 6:394; R 1:372–373.

سأله أعطاه ومن أقرضه قضاه ومن شكره جزاه. عباد الله زِنوا أنفسكم من قبل أن توزنوا وحاسبوها من قبل أن تحاسبوا وتنفّسوا قبل ضيق الخناق وانقادوا قبل عنف السياق واعلموا أنّه من لم يُعَن على نفسه حتّى يكون له منها واعظ وزاجر لم يكن له من غيرها زاجر ولا واعظ.

1.88 ومن خطبة له عليه السلام تعرف بخطبة الأشباح وهي من جلائل الخطب. روى مَسعدة بن صدقة عن الصادق جعفر بن محمّد عليهما السلام أنّه قال خطب أمير المؤمنين عليه السلام والصلاة بهذه الخطبة على منبر الكوفة وذلك أنّ رجلًا أتاه فقال له يا أمير المؤمنين صف لنا ربّنا لنزداد له حبًّا وبه معرفة فغضب عليه السلام ونادى ﴿الصلاة جامعة﴾ فاجتمع الناس حتّى غضّ المسجد بأهله فصعد المنبر وهو مغضب متغيّر اللون. فحمد الله سبحانه وصلّى على النبيّ صلّى الله عليه وآله ثمّ قال[1]

1.88.1 الحمد لله الذي لا يَفِرُه المنع ولا يُكديه الإعطاء والجود إذ كلّ معطٍ منتقص سواه وكلّ مانع مذموم ما خلاه وهو المنّان بفوائد النعم وعوائد المزيد والقِسَم. عياله الخلائق ضمن أرزاقهم وقدّر أقواتهم ونهج سبيل الراغبين إليه والطالبين ما لديه وليس بما سئل بأجود منه بما لم يسأل. الأوّل الذي لم يكن له قبل فيكون شيء قبله والآخر الذي ليس له بعد فيكون شيء بعده والرادع أناسيّ الأبصار عن أن تناله أو تدركه ما اختلف عليه دهر فتختلف منه الحال ولا كان في مكان فيجوز عليه الانتقال. ولو وهب ما تنفّست عنه معادن الجبال وضحكت عنه أصداف البحار من فِلِزّ[2] اللُّجين والعِقيان

<hr>

[1] م، ي، هـ: كذا. ن، ش: ﴿وكان سائل سأله أن يصف الله له حتّى كأنّه يراه عيانًا فغضب لذلك﴾.   [2] ن، ش، ي، هـ مع علامة الصحّة: كذا. م: ﴿فِلَق﴾.

their deeds, and rewards those who thank him. Servants of God! Weigh yourselves before you are weighed, judge yourselves before you are judged, breathe before your throats constrict, go meekly before you are shoved. Finally, know this: if a man is not guided to combat his own passions, if he cannot counsel and admonish himself, no other counselor, no other admonisher, will avail.

1.88 From an oration by ʿAlī known as *Ashbāḥ*, "Ethereal Forms," one of the most marvelous of orations. Masʿadah ibn Ṣadaqah narrated the following from Jaʿfar ibn Muḥammad al-Ṣādiq, who said: The Commander of the Faithful delivered this oration on the pulpit of Kufa, when a man approached him and asked, Commander of the Faithful, describe for us what our Lord looks like exactly so that our love and knowledge may increase. ʿAlī, outraged at the blasphemy, called loudly, ⟨Gather for the ritual prayer!⟩ and when the people crammed into the mosque, ʿAlī ascended the pulpit, pale with anger. He praised God, pronounced benedictions on the Prophet, then said:[1]

1.88.1 Praise God, whom withholding does not make richer nor munificence and generosity impoverish, for giving depletes every giver's store except God's, and every withholder is blameworthy except him. He is the Munificent Giver who bestows increasing favors and manifold gifts, and all creatures are his children—he guarantees the sustenance they receive, ordains the food they eat, and paves the way for people to petition him and seek his bounty. In fact, he is as generous in granting what they do not ask for as he is in granting what they do. He is the first, with no before, so nothing could exist before him, he is the last, with no after, so nothing will exist after him. He prevents the pupils of our eyes from capturing or grasping his image. Time never changes for him, so his condition will never change, nor is he in a place, so his location will never change. If he distributed all that mountain depths yield and smiling seashells emit, from nuggets of silver and native gold to forests of coral and fistfuls of

---

1   This introduction is from manuscripts M and Y, and is also found in Ṣadūq, *Tawḥīd*, 48. Manuscript N and Rāwandī's commentary (R 1:374) have the following version: "The oration was delivered in response to a man who asked ʿAlī to describe God for him in a way such that he could almost see him with his eyes. Angered, ʿAlī said [the text of the oration]." The commentaries of Baḥrānī (B 361) and Ibn Abī al-Ḥadīd (H 6:398) amalgamate both versions. I have added the words "at the blasphemy" for clarity; ʿAlī's anger, as it becomes clear from this alternative preface and from the oration text, is at the anthropomorphic views implicit in the man's question. ⟨Gather for the ritual prayer!⟩ is a dictum pronounced in early Islam to gather people for a momentous announcement. On its origin and early usage, see Qutbuddin, *Arabic Oration*, 202.

ونُثارة الدرّ وحصيد المرجان ما أثّر ذلك في جوده ولا أنفد سعة ما عنده ولكان عنده من ذخائر الإنعام ما لا تنفده مطالب الأنام لأنّه الجواد الذي لا يغيضه سؤال السائلين ولا يبخّله إلحاح الملحّين.

1.88.2 فأنظر أيّها السائل فما دلّك القرآن عليه من صفته فأئتمّ به واستضئ بنور هدايته وما كلّفك الشيطان علمه ممّا ليس في الكتاب عليك فرضه ولا في سنّة النبيّ صلّى الله عليه وآله وأئمّة الهدى أثرُه فكِلْ علمه إلى الله سبحانه فإنّ ذلك منتهى حقّ الله عليك. واعلمْ أنّ الراسخين في العلم هم الذين أغناهم عن اقتحام السُّدد المضروبة دون الغيوب الإقرار بجملة ما جهلوا تفسيرَه من الغيب المحجوب. فمدح الله اعترافهم بالعجز عن تناول ما لم يحيطوا به علمًا وسمّى تركهم التعمّق فيما لم يكلّفهم البحث عن كنهه رسوخًا. فاقتصر على ذلك ولا تقدّر عظمة الله سبحانه على قدر عقلك فتكون من الهالكين. هو القادر الذي إذا ارتمت الأوهام لتدرك منقطع قدرته وحاول الفكر المبرّأ من خطر الوساوس أن يقع عليه في عميقات غيوب ملكوته وتولّهت القلوب إليه لتجري في كيفيّة صفاته وغمضت مداخل العقول في حيث لا تبلغه الصفات لتنال علم ذاته ردعها وهي تجوب مهاوي سُدَف الغيوب متخلّصة إليه سبحانه فرجعت إذ جُبهت معترفة بأنّه لا يُنال بجور الاعتساف كنهُ معرفته ولا تخطر ببال أولي الرويّات خاطرة من تقدير جلال عزّته. الذي ابتدع الخلق على غير مثال أمتثله ولا مقدار احتذى عليه من خالق معبود كان قبله. وأرانا من ملكوت قدرته وعجائب ما نطقت به آثار حكمته واعتراف الحاجة من الخلق إلى أن يقيمها بمَساكِ قوّته ما دلّنا باضطرار قيام الحجّة له على معرفته وظهرت في البدائع التي أحدثها آثار صنعته وأعلام حكمته فصار كلّ ما خلق حجّة له ودليلًا عليه وإن كان خلقًا صامتًا فحجّته بالتدبير ناطقة ودلالته على المبدع قائمة.

<hr>

ان، ش، ي، ه، ونسخة في م: كذا. وأصل م، ونسخة في ش، ه: ﴿بمسلك﴾. ونسخة أخرى في ش، ه: ﴿بمسكِ﴾.

pearl, this would not affect his generosity or deplete his vast possessions. The appeals of all the people in the world do not exhaust his treasure. He is the Generous Giver. Supplications do not empty his wellsprings and persistence does not make him withhold.

1.88.2 See it this way, O seeker: Accept what the Qur'an tells you about God and seek light from its radiant guidance. As for the questions that Satan burdens you with, questions not mandated for you by the Book or reported in the Prophet's Sunnah and the Imams' guidance, consign their knowledge to God. That is God's ultimate right over you. Know this: Men rooted in knowledge do not attempt to force themselves through fortified barricades but accept the veiled mysteries whose details they lack as they are presented to them. They admit their inability to grasp things beyond their compass, which God praises them for, and he calls their abstention—the abstention from delving into things whose essence he has not burdened them with investigating— deep knowledge.[1] You, too, limit yourself to this boundary, and do not measure God's greatness by the measure of your intellect—if you venture there, you will perish. He is the All-Powerful Being. If the imagination sends scouts to survey the extent of his power, if minds free of Satan's whisperings attempt to penetrate the deep mysteries of his kingdom, if bewildered, yearning hearts walk in the way of his attributes, and if sharp intellects whose descriptions fail to capture him attempt to open the door to his essence, he repels them, one and all. They wander the deep and dark ravines of his mysteries to find a way to him, but, knocked hard on their foreheads, they are made to turn back, admitting that no aggression will plumb his core,[2] and no reflection will glimpse the magnitude of his might. He created the world with no model, no plan measured by a creator worshipped prior to him. He showed us his powerful kingdom, the wonders articulated in the traces of his wisdom, and the world's frank admission that it needs his strong grip to remain standing— thereby he provided the proof that compels us to acknowledge him. Traces of his artisanship and signs of his wisdom can be seen in the marvels he made. Everything he created offers proof of his existence and guides us to him, even silent objects, for their design speaks of that proof, and it guides us toward their creator.

---

1 Ar. *rusūkh*, echoes Qur'an, Āl ʿImrān 3:7, «Men rooted in knowledge» (*al-rāsikhūna fī al-ʿilm*).

2 "Aggression" (*jawr al-iʿtisāf*), is also interpreted as "turning away from the main road" (Ḥ 6:409; R 1:383), or "extreme wanderings in those stations" (B 369).

1.88.3 فأشهد أنّ من شبّهك بتباين أعضاء خلقك وتلاحم حِقاق مفاصلهم المحتجبة لتدبير حكمتك لم يعقد غيب ضميره على معرفتك ولم يباشر قلبه اليقين بأنّه لا نِدّ لك فكأنّه لم يسمع تبرّي التابعين من المتبوعين إذ يقولون ﴿تَٱللّٰهِ إِن كُنَّا لَفِي ضَلَالٍ مُّبِينٍ إِذْ نُسَوِّيكُم بِرَبِّ ٱلْعَالَمِينَ﴾. كذب العادلون بك إذ شبّهوك بأصنامهم ونحلوك حلية المخلوقين بأوهامهم وجزّؤوك تجزئة المجسّمات بخواطرهم وقدّروك على الخِلقة المختلفة القوى بقرائح عقولهم. فأشهد أنّ من ساواك بشيء من خلقك فقد عدل بك والعادل كافر بما تنزّلت به محكمات آياتك ونطقت عنه شواهد حجج بيّناتك فإنّك أنت الله الذي لم تتناه في العقول فتكون في مهبّ فكرها مكيّفًا ولا في رويّات خواطرها فتكون محدودًا مصرّفًا.

1.88.4 منها

قدّر ما خلق فأحكم تقديره ودبّره فألطف تدبيره ووجّهه لوجهته فلم يتعدّ حدود منزلته ولم يقصر دون الانتهاء إلى غايته ولم يستصعب إذ أُمر بالمضيّ على إرادته وكيف وإنّما صدرت الأمور عن مشيئته. المنشئ أصناف الأشياء بلا رويّة فكرٍ آلَ إليها ولا قريحة غريزة أضمر عليها ولا تجربة أفادها من حوادث الدهور ولا شريك أعانه على ٱبتداع عجائب الأمور. فتمّ خلقه وأذعن لطاعته وأجاب إلى دعوته لم يعترض دونه ريث المبطئ ولا أناة المتلكّئ فأقام من الأشياء أوَدها ونهج حدودها ولاءم بقدرته بين متضادّها ووصل أسباب قرائنها وفرّقها أجناسًا مختلفات في الحدود والأقدار[1] والغرائز والهيئات. بدايا خلائق أحكم صنعها وفطرها على ما أراد وٱبتدعها.

1.88.5 ومنها في صفة السماء

ونظم بلا تعليق رهوات فُرَجها ولا حَمَ صدوع أنفراجها ووشّج بينها وبين أزواجها وذلّل للهابطين بأمره والصاعدين بأعمال خلقه حُزونة معراجها وناداها بعد إذ هي دخان[2]

1.88.3 I bear witness that anyone who likens you to the disparate limbs of your creatures, or to their bonded joints that your clever design has concealed, has erred. His inner self has not recognized you, and his heart is not certain that you have no peer. He does not appear to have heard of followers disowning those they followed, saying, «By God, we were clearly misguided when we equated you with the Lord of the worlds!»[1] They lie who compare you! They lie when they liken you to their idols, when their imagination adorns you with the ornaments of your creatures, their notions divide you into physical parts, and their intellects measure you against the multiplicity of your creatures' faculties. I bear witness that to equate you with any of your creatures is to compare you, and to compare you is to profess unbelief in the clear verses you have revealed, in the witness provided by your eloquent signs. For you are God. Intellects with their penetrating thoughts cannot analyze your totality, nor hearts with their reflections limit or position you.

1.88.4 From this oration:
He planned the things he created with precision, arranged them with elegance, and led them in a certain direction, where they do not transgress the limits of their station, fall short of their goal, or pull back when commanded to proceed. How could they, pray, when all affairs transpire according to his will? He generated categories of things without relying on cogitation, engaging an inner disposition, drawing on experience obtained from the rise and fall of eons, or using a partner's help to originate his wondrous affairs. His creation was thus completed, and it bowed to him in obedience, and answered his call, unhindered by sluggish delay or laggardly indolence. He straightened out what was crooked, laid out its boundaries, harmonized its contrasting parts, bound the cords of linked entities, and distributed all into various species with distinct parameters, values, dispositions, and forms. Such was the beginning of God's creatures, each crafted with exquisite precision, produced and originated by his will.

1.88.5 From the same oration, describing the sky:
When God created the sky, he hung its spaces together without ropes, soldered the gaps in its parts, and connected them closely, each with the other.[2] He smoothed its knobby ladder for beings who descend with his command, and ascend with his creatures' deeds.[3] He called out to it while it was entirely

---

1 Qur'an, Shuʿarāʾ 26:97–98.
2 Ar. *azwāj*, interpreted as its "analogs" (R 1:377; Ḥ 1:419), "other celestial objects" (ʿA 600), or "the angels" (B 373).
3 Those who descend and ascend are the angels. B 373–374; R 1:388.

فَالْتحمت عُرى أشراجها وفتق بعد الارتتاق صوامت أبوابها وأقام رصدًا من الشهب الثواقب على نقابها وأمسكها من أن تمور في خرق الهواء بأَيْدِه وأمرها أن تقف مستسلمة لأمره وجعل شمسها آية مبصرة لنهارها وقمرها آية ممحوّة من ليلها وأجراهما في مناقل مجراهما وقدّر مسيرهما في مدارج درجهما ليميز بهما بين الليل والنهار بهما وليعلم ﴿عَدَدَ السِّنِينَ وَالْحِسَابَ﴾ بمقاديرهما ثمّ علّق في جوّها فلكها وناط بها زينتها من خفيّات دراريها ومصابيح كواكبها ورمى مسترقي السمع بثواقب شهبها وأجراها على أذلال تسخيرها من ثبات ثابتها ومسير سائرها وهبوطها وصعودها ونحوسها وسعودها.

1.88.6 ومنها في صفة الملائكة

ثمّ خلق سبحانه لإسكان سماواته وعمارة الصفيح الأعلى من ملكوته خلقًا بديعًا من ملائكته ملأ بهم فروج فجاجها وحشا بهم فتوق أجوائها. وبين فجوات تلك الفروج زجل المسبّحين منهم في حظائر القدس وسترات الحجب وسرادقات المجد ووراء ذلك الرجيج الذي تستكّ منه الأسماع سبحات نور تردع الأبصار عن بلوغها فتقف خاسئة على حدودها. أنشأهم على صور مختلفات وأقدار متفاوتات ﴿أُولِي أَجْنِحَةٍ﴾[1] تُسبّح جلال عزّته لا ينتحلون ما ظهر في الخلق من صنعه ولا يدّعون أنّهم يخلقون شيئًا معه ممّا انفرد به ﴿بَلْ عِبَادٌ مُّكْرَمُونَ لَا يَسْبِقُونَهُ بِالْقَوْلِ وَهُم بِأَمْرِهِ يَعْمَلُونَ﴾. جعلهم فيما هنالك أهل الأمانة على وحيه وحمّلهم إلى المرسلين ودائع أمره ونهيه وعصمهم من ريب الشبهات فما منهم زائغ عن سبيل مرضاته وأمدّهم بفوائد المعونة وأشعر قلوبهم تواضع إخبات السكينة وفتح لهم أبوابًا ذللًا إلى تماجيده ونصب لهم منارًا واضحة على أعلام توحيده لم تثقلهم موصرات الآثام ولم ترتحلهم عُقَب الليالي والأيّام ولم ترم الشكوك بنوازعها عزيمة إيمانهم ولم تعترك الظنون على معاقد يقينهم

---

[1] ن، ش، ي، ه: كذا. م: أُضيفت ﴿مَّثْنَىٰ وَثُلَاثَ﴾.

smoke,[1] and its crevices became sealed. He cracked its locked doors open and set blazing sentinels in the gaps, restraining them with his own hands from falling through breaks in the firmament and commanding them to remain where they were. He made the sun a sign that brightens the day and the moon a sign that wanes through the nights.[2] He set the two in motion within their orbits and ordained their passage within their tracks. By their movements, he distinguished night from day, and by their measure, he showed the «reckoning and calculation of years.»[3] Then he suspended the sky's sphere in the ether, hung ornaments of starry clusters and bright lamps,[4] used blazing meteors to strike down spying demons,[5] and launched the stars according to their stations: fixed versus moving, falling versus rising, and ominous versus lucky.

1.88.6 From the same oration, describing the angels:
Then God created wondrous angels to populate his skies and inhabit his kingdom's highest planes. With them he filled the gaps in its rifts and the fissures in its ether, and in those gaps, in that sacred enclosure, in veils of concealment and canopies of glory, their thunderous chanting of his praise rings out. Behind the roar that deafens the ear shines the majesty of light that dazzles the eye, and the eye is driven back at this boundary. He fashioned them in different forms, in diverse ranks, each «with sets of wings».[6] They chant litanies of praise for his glorious power, never claiming that they helped shape his creatures, nor professing to have created, alongside him, a single, solitary thing. In this, he has no peer. «Rather, they are his honored servants, they speak when he has spoken, and act on his command.»[7] He entrusts them with his revelation and sends them to his messengers bearing his commands and prohibitions. He shields them from doubt and uncertainty, so not one strays from the path of his pleasure. He equips them with aid and assistance, and infuses their hearts with deference, with humility, peace, and calm. He eases their path to glorifying him and erects beacons to illumine for them the signs of his unity. They are never weighed down by sins, or loaded, like camels, by the calamities brought by nights and days. Suspicion's arrows don't penetrate the robust frame of their belief, presumptions' rasps don't fray the strong cords of their convictions, the

---

1 Reference to Qur'an, Dukhān 44:10.
2 Reference to Qur'an, Isrā' 17:12.
3 Qur'an, Yūnus 10:5.
4 Reference to Qur'an, Ṣāffāt 37:6.
5 Reference to Qur'an, Ḥijr 15:18. I have specified the word "demons" based on the previous verse (Qur'an, Ḥijr 15:17): «We protected it from every cursed demon.»
6 Qur'an, Fāṭir 35:1.
7 Qur'an, Anbiyā' 21:26–27.

ولا قدحت قادحة الإحَن فيما بينهم ولا سلبتهم الحيرة ما لاقَ من معرفته بضمائرهم وسكن من عظمته وهيبة جلاله في أثناء صدورهم ولم تطمع فيهم الوساوس فتقترع[1] بريبها على فكرهم.

1.88.7 منهم من هو في خلق الغمام الدلّح وفي عظم الجبال الشمّخ وفي قترة الظلام الأيْهم ومنهم من خرقت أقدامهم تُخوم الأرض السفلى فهي كرايات بيض قد نفذت في مخارق الهواء وتحتها ريح هفّافة تحبسها على حيث أنتهت من الحدود المتناهية. قد أستفرغتهم أشغال عبادته ووسّلت حقائق الإيمان بينهم وبين معرفته وقطعهم الإيقان به إلى الوله إليه ولم تجاوز رغباتهم ما عنده إلى ما عند غيره. قد ذاقوا حلاوة معرفته وشربوا بالكأس الرويّة من محبّته وتمكّنت من سويداء قلوبهم وشيجة خيفته فخنَوا بطول الطاعة أعتدال ظهورهم ولم ينفد طول الرغبة إليه مادّة تضرّعهم ولا أطلق عنهم عظيم الزلفة ربق خشوعهم ولم يتولّهم الإعجاب فيستكثروا ما سلف منهم ولا تركت لهم أستكانة الإجلال نصيباً في تعظيم حسناتهم ولم تجر الفترات فيهم على طول دؤوبهم ولم تَغِض[2] رغباتهم فيخالفوا عن رجاء ربّهم ولم تجفّ لطول المناجاة أسَلات ألسنتهم ولا ملكتهم الأشغال فتنقطع بهمس الخبر إليه أصواتهم ولم تختلف في مقاوم الطاعة مناكبهم ولم يثنوا إلى راحة التقصير في أمره رقابهم ولا تعدو على عزيمة جدّهم بلادة الغفلات ولا تنتضل في هممهم خدائع[3] الشهوات. قد أتّخذوا ذا العرش ذخيرة ليوم فاقتهم ويمّموه عند أنقطاع الخلق إلى المخلوقين برغبتهم لا يقطعون أمد غاية عبادته ولا يرجع بهم الاستهتار بلزوم طاعته إلّا إلى موادّ من قلوبهم غير منقطعة من رجائه ومخافته لم تنقطع أسباب الشفقة منهم فينُوا في جدّهم ولم تأسرهم الأطماع فيؤثروا وشيك السعي على أجتهادهم ولم يستعظموا ما مضى من أعمالهم ولو أستعظموا

***

<hr>

١ن، م، ش، هـ: كذا. ي، ونسخة في م، ومصحّحة في ش: ‹فتفترع›. ٢م، ن، ش، هـ: كذا. ي، ونسخة في م: ‹تغص›، ويبدو أن التنقيط سقط من الحرفين الأخيرين. نسختان في م: ‹تنقص› و‹تفض›. ٣ن، ش، ي، هـ، ونسخة في م: كذا. أصل م: ‹بدائع›.

fever of malice doesn't burn their bonds, perplexity doesn't pillage recognition of God from their hearts or plunder veneration of God and awe for his grandeur from their breasts, and the devils with their whisperings don't dare to sow doubts or cast lots for controlling their thoughts.

1.88.7 Among them are angels created as heavy clouds, or with the massive dimensions of lofty mountains, or as dark as the starless night, angels whose feet pierce the nethermost regions of the earth and look like white banners protruding in the air. A gentle breeze below confines them inside the farthest limits they can reach. God's worship is their sole occupation, faith's realities provide them with the means to recognize him, and certainty in his existence severs them from all else save yearning for him. Their desires seek what he bestows, never crossing to seek another's favors. They taste the sweetness of his recognition and drink from the full cup of his love. His fear is rooted deep in their hearts, so they bend their backs in protracted worship. Lengthy petitions do not exhaust the store of their entreaties, and closeness to him does not loosen the cord of their submissiveness. No vanity aggrandizes for them their prior acts, while the humility generated in them by glorifying God leaves them no room to glorify their own deeds. No intervals of languor interrupt their protracted efforts, and no diminishing expectations make them question the hopes they have placed in their Lord. Long prayers do not parch their tongues, nor preoccupations weaken their raised voices. Their shoulders do not sag as they worship, standing in ranks, nor do they relax their necks and so fall short in carrying out his command. No dullness or disregard vanquishes their resolve, no deceiving passions vie to shoot down their high aspirations. They choose the Lord of the Throne to be the treasure they put by for their day of need, and they go to him with petitions when others go to his creatures. Their journey to perfect his worship never ends, and their passion for embracing his obedience stems from their hearts' inner substance, which is ever infused by hope in him and fear. No severance of the cord of dread makes them lessen their labors, no ensnaring greed makes them favor flighty acts over serious effort. They do not aggrandize their past deeds, else complacent hope would have expelled their palpitating trepidations. No Satanic dominion puts them at variance among themselves concerning their Lord: no evil sundering of ties divides them, no rancor caused by mutual envy takes hold, no calamitous doubts separate them, and no contrary aspirations—like a horse with one blue eye and one

ذلك لنسخ الرجاء منهم شفقات وجلهم ولم يختلفوا في ربّهم بٱستحواذ الشيطان عليهم ولم يفرّقهم سوء التقاطع ولا تولّاهم غلّ التحاسد ولا تشعّبتهم مصارف الريب ولا ٱقتسمتهم أخياف[1] الهمم فهم أسراء إيمان لم يفكّهم من ربقته زيغ ولا عدول ولا ونًى ولا فتور وليس في أطباق السماوات موضع إهاب إلّا وعليه ملك ساجد أو ساعٍ حافد يزدادون على طول الطاعة بربّهم علمًا وتزداد عزّة ربّهم في قلوبهم عظمًا.

1.88.8 ومنها في صفة الأرض ودَحْوها على الماء

كَبَسَ الأرض على مَور أمواج مستفحلة ولجج بحار زاخرة تلتطم أواذيّ أمواجها وتصطفق متقاذفات أثباجها وترغو زبدًا كالفحول عند هياجها. فخضع جماح الماء المتلاطم لثقل حملها وسكن هيج أرتمائه إذ وطئته بكلكلها وذلّ مستخذياً إذ تمعّكت عليه بكواهلها. فأصبح بعد ٱصطخاب أمواجه ساجياً مقهورًا وفي حكَمة الذلّ منقادًا أسيرًا وسكنت الأرض مدحوّة في لجّة تيّاره وردّت من نخوة بأْوه وٱعتلائه وشموخ أنفه وسموّ غُلَوائه وكَعَمَته على كِظّة جِريته فهمد بعد نزقاته وبعد زَيَفان وثباته. فلمّا سكن هَيج الماء من تحت أكتافها وحمل شواهق الجبال البُذّخ على أكتافها فجّر ينابيع العيون من عرانين أنوفها وفرّقها في سُهوب بيدها وأخاديدها وعدّل حركاتها بالراسيات من جلاميدها وذوات الشناخيب الشمّ من صياخيدها فسكنت من الميدان برسوب الجبال في قِطَع أديمها وتغلغلها متسرّبة في جَوبات خياشيمها وركوبها أعناق سهول الأرضين وجراثيمها وفسح بين الجوّ وبينها وأعدّ الهواء متنسَّمًا لساكنها وأخرج إليها أهلها على تمام مرافقها. ثمّ لم يدع جُرُز الأرض التي تقصر مياه العيون عن رَوابيها ولا تجد جداول الأنهار[2] ذريعة إلى بلوغها حتّى أنشأ لها ناشئة سحاب تحيي مواتها وتستخرج نباتها ألّف غمامها بعد ٱفتراق لُمَعه وتباين قَزَعه حتّى إذا تمخّضت لجّة المزن فيه وٱلتمع برقه في كِفَفه ولم يَنَمّ وميضه في كَنَهْوَر رَبابه ومترا كم سحابه سحًّا متداركًا قد أسفّ هيدَبه

---

[1] ن، م، ي، ومصحّحة في ه، ونسخة في ش: كذا. أصل ش: ﴿ٱختلاف﴾. أصل ه: ﴿أخلاف﴾.
[2] م، ي، ونسخة في ش: كذا. ن، ه، وأصل ش: ﴿الأرض﴾.

black—fragment them.[1] Captives of faith, no deviation, deflection, exhaustion, or lassitude frees them from its lasso. In all the skies' layers, there exists no place, not even the width of a strip of rawhide, that does not contain a prostrating angel or a swift messenger. Their long worship continually increases their knowledge of their Lord, and the grandeur of their Lord's might ever increases in their hearts.

1.88.8 From the same oration, describing the earth and how he laid it out over water: God poured earth into the mighty, heaving waves and the deep, swollen seas, where waves towered and clashed, and waters raced and crashed, as they grunted and frothed like a camel stallion in arousal. Weighed down by the earth's mass their recalcitrant gallop became tractable, crushed by the earth's torso their tumultuous tossing subsided, and dragged along by the earth's withers they submitted with docility. After their earlier clamor, the waves grew still and were conquered. Tamed with the curb of servility, they were herded in defeat and captivity. The earth ensconced itself then, spreading in the depths of the flowing current, repelling its pride, haughtiness, disdain, and excess of energy, and muzzling its overabundant flow. After much vaulting and supercilious assault, the waters abated. When the water's tumult had grown still under the earth's wings, under the weight of the soaring, lofty mountains placed on its shoulders, God made springs of pure water gush from the towering massifs and channeled them into outstretched wastelands and undulating furrows. He anchored the earth's movements with massive rocks and high-topped, stony crags. Sunk deep beneath its surface, rupturing the smooth hollows of its crust, and straddling the backs of its plains and compacted soils, the mountains caused the earth's heaving to still. He opened wide the space between the earth and the ether, and made the air fit for the earth's residents to breathe. Then, with all preparations complete, he extracted from it and introduced to it its living inhabitants. In all of this, he did not neglect those barren tracts too high for springs and beyond the reach of rivers. He created swollen clouds to bring life to those bare stretches and coax out their vegetation. Piecing together wispy swirls and scattered puffs, he shaped a thick, enveloping cloud. Then—when its deep waters roiled, when lightning flickered from its hands, when flashes in the massed white-and-black cloudbanks and the heaped rainclouds awoke from their slumber—he let it loose in one continuous downpour. The cloud

---

1 Ar. *akhyāf*, said of people who are "different, one from another, in their states or conditions, or in their forms, shapes or semblances;" from *khayafa*, which means, "having one of the eyes blue, the other black; said of a horse, or any animal." Brothers who are *akhyāf* are "sons of one mother but different fathers." Lane, *Lexicon*, s.v. "Kh-Y-F."

تَمْريه الجَنوب دِرَر أهاضيبه ودُفَع شآبيبه. فلمّا ألقت السحاب بَرْكَ بوانيها وبَعاع ما اُستقلّت به من العِبْء المحمول عليها أخرج به من هوامد الأرض النبات ومن زُعْر الجبال الأعشاب فهي تبهج بزينة رياضها وتزدهي بما ألبسته من رَيط أزاهيرها وحِلية ما سُمّطت١ به من ناضر أنوارها وجعل ذلك بلاغًا للأنام ورزقًا للأنعام وخرق الفجاج في آفاقها وأقام المنار للسالكين على جوادّ طرقها.

1.88.9 فلمّا مهّد أرضه وأنفذ أمره اختار آدم عليه السلام خِيَرةً من خلقه وجعله أوّل جبلّته وأسكنه جنّته وأرغد فيها أكله وأوعز إليه فيما نهاه عنه وأعلمه أنّ في الإقدام عليه التعرّض لمعصيته والمخاطرة بمنزلته فأقدم على ما نهاه عنه موافاة لسابق علمه فأهبطه بعد التوبة ليعمر أرضه بنسله وليقيم الحجّة به على عباده. ولم يخلهم بعد أن قبضه ممّا يؤكّد عليهم حجّة ربوبيّته ويصل بينهم وبين معرفته بل تعاهدهم بالحجج على ألسن الخِيَرة من أنبيائه ومتحمّلي ودائع رسالاته قرنًا فقرنًا حتّى تمّت بنبيّنا محمّد صلّى الله عليه وآله حجّته وبلغ المقطع عذره ونذره. وقدّر الأرزاق فكثّرها وقلّلها وقسّمها على الضيق والسعة فعدل فيها ليبتلي من أراد بميسورها ومعسورها وليختبر بذلك الشكر والصبر من غنيّها وفقيرها ثمّ قرن بسعتها عَقابيل فاقتها وبسلامتها طوارق آفاتها وبفُرَج أفراحها غُصَص أتراحها. وخلق الآجال فأطالها وقصّرها وقدّمها وأخّرها ووصل بالموت أسبابها وجعله خالجًا لأشطانها وقاطعًا لمرائر أقرانها.

1.88.10 عالم السرّ من ضمائر المضمرين ونجوى المتخافتين وخواطر رَجْم الظنون وعُقَد عزيمات اليقين ومسارق إيماض الجفون وما ضمنته أكنان القلوب وغيابات

<hr>

١م، ه مع علامة الصحّة: كذا. ن: ﴿شمطت﴾. ش، ي: معًا.

hung low and hugged the earth, and the South Wind milked its teats to yield torrents and spills. When the cloud had settled its limbs on the ground, when it had dropped all the water it had drawn and carried, he brought forth plants from the barren ground and herbage from the bare mountains. The earth now rejoiced in the beauty of its meadows, it flaunted its garments of delicate blossoms and its necklaces of fresh flowers. All this he created to sustain humans and nourish cattle. He then hewed passes in remote regions and erected beacons for those who would walk the open roads.

1.88.9 When God had primed the earth and executed his will, he singled out Adam from among his creatures and made him the first human.[1] He lodged him in paradise and offered him all manner of delectable foods but warned him to keep away from the forbidden tree.[2] He cautioned him that if he came near it, he would be committing a sin and jeopardizing his rank. Adam—as God had known he would—approached the tree God had forbidden to him. After he repented, however, God sent him down to populate the earth with his descendants and serve as God's proof for his servants. Then, when God took him back, he did not void them of the clear proof of his majesty or the means to his recognition. He sent them his proof on the tongues of his chosen prophets, who carried his entrusted messages to them, generation after generation, until he completed his message to his creatures through our own Prophet Muḥammad, and his advocacy and warnings reached their climax. God decreed sustenance, giving some people much and others little, distributing constricted shares to some and ample ones to others. In all this, he was just. He tested those he wished with prosperity and those he wished with poverty to assess the gratitude of the rich and the patience of the poor. He also paired abundance with sores of destitution, wellbeing with calamities that creep up in the night, and joys that gladden with sorrows that choke. He ordained lifespans to be long or short, swift or tardy, and he handed their reins to death. Death pulls in their long ropes and cuts through the tight plait of their fastenings.

1.88.10 God knows all secrets. He knows the thoughts of those who conceal what they are thinking, the clandestine conversations of those who whisper, stray notions generated by wild conjectures, secured resolutions arising from certainty, stolen glances flashed by drooping eyelids, veiled matters of the

---

1   Lit. "natural disposition" (Ar. *jibillah*). B 390 explains it as "human."

2   Lit. "that which God had forbidden to him." I have replaced the phrase, here and in the next line, with the word "tree," echoing the Qurʾan, Baqarah 2:35: «God said to Adam ... do not approach this tree.»

240 TEXT AND TRANSLATION

الغيوب وما أصغت لاَسْتراقه مصائخ الأسماع ومصائف الذَّر ومشاتي الهوامّ ورجع الحنين من المولّهات وهمس الأقدام ومنفسح الثمرة من ولائج غلف الأكمام ومنقمع الوحوش من غِيران الجبال وأوديتها ومختبأ البَعوض بين سُوق الأشجار وألحيتها ومغرِز الأوراق من الأفنان ومحطّ الأمشاج من مسارب الأصلاب وناشئة الغيوم ومتلاحمها ودرور قطر السحاب في متراكمها وما تَسفي الأعاصير بذيولها وتعفو الأمطار بسيولها وعَوم¹ نبات² الأرض في كثبان الرمال ومستقرّ ذوات الأجنحة بذُرى شناخيب الجبال وتغريد ذوات المنطق في دياجير الأوكار وما أوعته³ الأصداف وحضنت عليه أمواج البحار وما غشيته سُدفة ليل أو ذرَّ عليه شارق نهار وما اَعتقبت عليه أطباق الدياجير وسُبحات النور وأثر كلّ خطوة وحسّ كلّ حركة ورجع كلّ كلمة وتحريك كلّ شَفة ومستقرّ كلّ نسمة ومثقال كلّ ذرّة وهَماهم كلّ نفس هامّة وما عليها من ثمر شجرة أو ساقط ورقة أو قرارة نطفة أو نُقَاعة دم ومضغة أو ناشئة خَلْق وسلالة. لم تلحقه في ذلك كلفة ولا اَعترضته في حفظ ما اَبتدع من خلقه عارضة ولا اَعتورته في تنفيذ الأمور وتدابير المخلوقين ملالة ولا فترة بل نفذهم علمه وأحصاهم عدده⁴ ووسعهم عدله وغمرهم فضله مع تقصيرهم عن كنه ما هو أهله.

1.88.11 اللّهمّ أنت أهل الوصف الجميل والتَّعداد الكثير إن تؤمَّل نخير مأمول وإن تُرْجَ نخير مرجوّ. اللّهمّ وقد بسطت لي فيما لا أمدح به غيرك ولا أُثني به على أحد سواك ولا أوجّهه إلى معادن الخيبة ومواضع الريبة وعدلتَ بلساني عن مدائح الآدميّين والثناء على المربوبين المخلوقين. اللّهمّ ولكلّ مُثنٍ على من أثنى عليه مثوبة من جزاء أو عارفة من عطاء وقد رجوتك دليلًا على ذخائر الرحمة وكنوز المغفرة. اللّهمّ وهذا مقام من أفردك

<hr>

¹ م، ه، ونسخة في ش: كذا. ن، وأصل ش، ونسخة في ه: ﴿عموم﴾.   ² م، ن، ي، ش، ونسخة في ه: كذا. ي، وأصل ه، ونسخة في ش: ﴿بنات﴾.   ³ ش، ن، وشرح الراونديّ، ومصحّحة في ه: كذا. م: ﴿وعته﴾. أصل ه، ونسخة في ي: ﴿أودعته﴾.   ⁴ م، ي، ومصحّحة في ه: كذا. ن، ش: ﴿كتابه﴾. أصل ه، ونسخة في ش ﴿عدّه﴾.

heart, deep-welled mysteries, the sounds to which ears stealthily hearken, the summer nests of tiny ants, the winter habitats of mites, the repeated wails of mourning women, the sound of faint footsteps, the place hidden within the innermost sepal where fruit begins to grow, the concealed spaces in mountain hollows and riverbeds where wild beasts hole up, the cracks between the boles and bark of trees in which gnats hide away, the node on a branch from which a leaf sprouts, the basin where semen is deposited after flowing through the waterways of men's loins, the forming of the new clouds and their thick amassing, the abundant flow of raindrops from towering cloudbanks, what the whirlwinds stir up with their kicking gusts, what the rains erase with their flood water, how tumbleweeds are swept by the wind over dunes of sand, the resting places of birds atop the high mountain peaks, the warbling of birds in the dimness of their nests, what seashells store and waves on the deep water envelop, what a black night conceals and bright daybreak reveals, what is prevailed on in alternation by layers of darkness and splendors of radiance, the trace of every footstep, the sensation of every movement, the echo of every word, the motion of every lip, the resting place of every creature that breathes, the weight of every tiny particle, the sobbing of every grieving heart, and whatever is on the earth,[1] including the fruit growing on a tree, a falling leaf, the resting place of a drop of semen, the place where blood gathers in pools and where an embryonic clump of flesh congeals, and the emergence of creatures and offspring. In all this, God suffers no toil, no obstacle obstructs him from guarding his creation, and no stupor or apathy impedes him from executing his affairs or governing his creatures. Far from it! His knowledge penetrates them, his reckoning comprehends, his justice encompasses, and his favors engulf. All this, despite how short they fall in offering his due.

1.88.11   God, to you belong the loveliest epithets and the largest armies. When solicited, you are the best repository of hope, and when petitioned, you are the best receptacle of trust. God, you stretch out your hand to me with such favors that I can praise none but you, extol none but you, I do not direct my praise toward those who are founts of disappointment or sites of suspicion, for you have diverted my tongue from praising the children of Adam, from extolling your creatures and subjects. God, every extoller deserves a reward that compensates, a gift freely bestowed by the one he extolls: I beseech you to guide me to the treasures of your mercy and the riches of your forgiveness. God, here I stand before you. I have singled you out with the proclamation of unity that

---

1   Lit. "on it," explained in the commentaries as "on earth." Ḥ 7:30; B 392; R 1:418.

بالتوحيد الذي هو لك ولم ير مستحقًّا لهذه المحامد والممادح غيرك وبي فاقة إليك لا يجبر مسكنتها إلّا فضلك ولا ينعش من خلّتها إلّا منّك وجودك فهب لنا في هذا المقام رضاك وأغننا عن مدّ الأيدي إلى من سواك إنّك على ما تشاء قدير.[1]

1.89 ومن كلام له عليه السلام لمّا أراده الناس على البيعة بعد قتل عثمان

دعوني وٱلتمسوا غيري فإنّا مستقبلون أمرًا له وجوه وألوان لا تقوم له القلوب ولا تثبت عليه العقول وإنّ الآفاق قد أغامت والمحجّة قد تنكّرت. وٱعلموا أنّي إن أجبتكم ركبت بكم ما أعلم ولم أُصغِ إلى قول القائل وعَتْب العاتب وإن تركتموني فأنا كأحدكم ولعلّي أسمعكم وأطوعكم لمن ولّيتموه أمركم وأنا لكم وزيرًا خير لكم منّي أميرًا.

1.90 ومن خطبة له عليه السلام

1.90.1 أمّا بعد. أيّها الناس فأنا فقأتُ عين الفتنة ولم يكن ليجترئ عليها أحد غيري بعد أن ماجَ غَيهَبها وٱشتدّ كَلَبها.

1.90.2 فٱسألوني قبل أن تفقدوني فوالذي نفسي بيده لا تسألوني عن شيء فيما بينكم وبين الساعة ولا عن فئة تهدي مائة وتضلّ مائة إلّا نبّأتكم بناعقها وقائدها وسائقها ومُناخ ركابها ومحطّ رحالها ومن يُقتل من أهلها قتلًا ومن يموت منهم موتًا.

---

[1] م، ي: كذا. ش، ن: ﴿إِنَّكَ عَلَىٰ كُلِّ شَيْءٍ قَدِيرٌ﴾. ه: ﴿إنّك على ما تشاء وكلّ شيء قدير﴾.

is your due, and I see no one worthy of these tributes and praises but you. My need of you is urgent. Nothing but your kindness can heal my destitution's broken bones, nothing but your beneficence and generosity can raise me from my lowly state of privation. So grant us your acceptance now as we stand before you, and free us from spreading our hands before any but you. You are powerful over all that you will.[1]

1.89 From an address by ʿAlī, when, after ʿUthmān's killing, the people rushed to him to pledge allegiance:[2]

Leave me and seek another! We are looking at a thing with many faces and shades, in which hearts will not remain steady or minds stable, for the skies are overcast and the road is obscure. Know this: If I accept your pledge, I shall drive you on the path I know to be right, without caring about your chiding or rebuke. If you leave me be, however, I will be as one of you—in fact, I will be the most attentive and obedient among you toward the man you entrust with your rule. You will find me a better counselor than commander.

1.90 From an oration by ʿAlī:[3]

1.90.1 People! I have gouged out the eyes of revolt. None other would have dared to challenge it when its darkness had spread so far, when its madness had become so rabid.

1.90.2 Ask me before I am lost to you! By the one who holds my life in his hand, I swear this: If you ask me about what will happen between now and the last hour, about any group who will guide a hundred aright or lead a hundred astray, I shall inform you of who will call out and direct that herd, who will lead in the front and who will drive from the rear, where their camels will kneel and where they will set down their gear, who will be killed in battle and who will die a natural death.

---

1 Reference to Qurʾan, Āl ʿImrān 3:26, Taḥrīm 66:8.

2 In Medina, 35/656. Ṭabarī, *Tārīkh*, 4:434.

3 The commentators agree that §1.90.1 refers to ʿAlī's battles, but they differ on which ones: (1) Ḥ 7:57–58 (citing early, unnamed historical sources, and transcribing further sections of the oration) says the oration was delivered soon after Nahrawān, i.e., either in Nahrawān or Kufa in 38/658, presumably meaning it refers to this battle; Yaʿqūbī (*Tārīkh*, 2:193) places it in Kufa, just after Nahrawān. (2) R 1:424–425 says it refers to the Battle of the Camel and the Battle of Ṣiffīn. (3) B 395 says it refers to the Camel, Ṣiffīn, and Nahrawān.

1.90.3 ولو قد فقدتموني ونزلت كرائه الأمور وحوازب الخطوب لأطرق كثير من السائلين وفشل كثير من المسؤولين وذلك إذا قلّصت حربكم وشمّرت[1] عن ساق وضاقت الدنيا عليكم ضيقًا تستطيلون أيّام البلاء عليكم حتّى يفتح الله لبقيّة الأبرار منكم إنّ الفتن إذا أقبلت شبّهت وإذا أدبرت نبّهت يُنكَرن مقبلات ويعرفن مدبرات يَحُمْنَ حَوم الرياح يصبن بلدًا ويخطئن بلدًا.

1.90.4 ألا إنّ أخوف الفتن عندي عليكم فتنة بني أميّة فإنّها فتنة عمياء مظلمة عمّت خطّتها وخصّت بليّتها وأصاب البلاء من أبصر فيها وأخطأ البلاء من عمي عنها وأيم الله لتجدُنّ بني أميّة لكم أرباب سوء بعدي كالناب الضروس تَعذِم بفيها وتخبط بيدها وتَزْبِن برجلها وتمنع دَرّها لا يزالون بكم حتّى لا يتركوا منكم إلّا نافعًا لهم أو غير ضائر ولا يزال بلاؤهم حتّى لا يكون ٱنتصار أحدكم منهم إلّا مثل ٱنتصار العبد من ربّه والصاحب من مستصحبه ترد عليكم فتنتهم شوهاء مخشيّة وقِطَعًا جاهليّة ليس فيها منار هدى ولا عَلَم يُرى نحن أهلَ البيت منها بنجاة ولسنا فيها بدعاة.

1.90.5 ثمّ يفرّجها الله عنكم كتفريج الأديم بمن يسومهم خسفًا ويسوقهم عنفًا ويسقيهم بكأس مصبّرة لا يعطيهم إلّا السيف ولا يحلسهم[2] إلّا الخوف فعند ذلك تودّ قريش بالدنيا وما فيها لو يرونني مقامًا واحدًا ولو قدر جزر جَزور لأقبل منهم ما أطلب اليوم بعضه فلا يعطوننيه.

---

[1] م، ه، ومصحّحة في ش: كذا. ن، وأصل ش: ⟨إذا قلّصت حربكم عن ساق⟩ بسقوط ⟨وشمّرت⟩. ي: ⟨إذا قامت حربكم على ساق⟩، ونسختان في الهامش ⟨وشمّرت عن ساق⟩ و⟨إذا قلّصت⟩.   [2] ش، ن، ي، ه، ومصحّحة في م: كذا. أصل م: ⟨يجلسهم⟩.

1.90.3 After you lose me, when calamities strike you and devastation decimates, many who want to ask will cast down their eyes and many who are asked will fail to answer. When war tucks up its garments and girds its loincloth, when the world presses down on you and you have nowhere to turn, you will find the days of trial long, until, at last, God grants victory to the heirs of the righteous. When mutinies advance, they confuse, and as they turn away, they warn. Unrecognized in approach, they are identified only when they leave. They twist and turn like gusts of wind, striking one town and passing by another.

1.90.4 Hark! Of all seditions, the one I fear most for you is the Umayyads'. A blind and dark insurrection, its tyranny will range wide, yet its blows will target individuals, striking those who know it for what it is, but passing over those who choose to be blind. God's oath! You will find the Umayyads harsh overlords after I am gone, like a timeworn, quick-to-bite camel cow, that, jaws snapping, forelegs stamping, and hind feet kicking, refuses to be milked. They will oppress you all, until only those who bring them benefit remain standing, or those don't do them harm. Their tyranny will be so fierce that if you dare to seek retribution, you will be as ineffective as a slave seeking retribution against his master, or a minion against his ruler.[1] Ugly, frightening, a battalion from the Age of Ignorance,[2] their insurrection will leave you with no beacon that guides, no signpost to follow. In all this, we, the people of the Prophet's house, will remain quietly on the side. We will never take part in their mission.

1.90.5 Then God will strip their tyranny from you, as a hide is stripped from a carcass, at the hands of a man who will inflict them with humiliation, drive them with brute force, pour them bitter aloes, strike them with the sword, and shroud them in fear.[3] When that happens, the Quraysh will ache to see me—they would trade the world and all that it contains to have me beside them for one last stand, even if only for the swift instant it takes to butcher a camel, to accept from them in full what I ask for a scrap of today, and which they refuse to give.

---

1   I have added the word "ineffective" after Ḥ 7:55; B 397.

2   Ar. *jāhiliyyah*, referring to the pre-Islamic period and its pagan people's "ignorance" of the one God. The term *jahl*—from which the term *jāhiliyyah* derives—also means "foolish judgment." Lane, *Lexicon*, s.v. "J-H-L."

3   The commentators' interpretation that this is a prediction about the end of the Umayyad regime at the hands of the rising Abbasid power (Ḥ 7:57–60; B 397) seems unlikely, because the Abbasids, like the Umayyads, were also from the Quraysh tribe.

1.91 ومن خطبة له عليه السلام

1.91.1 فتبارك الله الذي لا يبلغه بعد الهمم ولا يناله حَدس١ الفطن الأوّل الذي لا غاية له فينتهي ولا آخر له فينقضي.

1.91.2 منها

فاستودعهم في أفضل مستودع وأقرّهم في خير مستقرّ تناسختهم كرائم الأصلاب إلى مطهّرات الأرحام كلّما مضى سلف قام منهم بدين الله خلف حتّى أفضت كرامة الله سبحانه إلى محمّد صلّى الله عليه وآله فأخرجه من أفضل المعادن مَنْبِتاً٢ وأعزّ الأرومات مغرسًا من الشجرة التي صدع منها أنبياءه وانتجب منها أمناءه عترته خير العتر وأسرته خير الأُسر وشجرته خير الشجر نبتت في حرم وبسقت في كرم لها فروع طوال وثمر لا يُنال فهو إمام من اتّقى وبصيرة من اهتدى سراج لمع ضوءه وشهاب سطع نوره وزَنْد برق لمعه سيرته القصد وسنّته الرشد وكلامه الفصل وحكمه العدل أرسله على حين فترة من الرسل وهفوة عن العمل وغَباوة من الأمم.

1.91.3 اعملوا رحمكم الله على أعلام بيّنة فالطريق نهجٌ يدعو إلى دار السلام وأنتم في دارِ مستعتَب على مَهَل وفراغ والصحف منشورة والأقلام جارية والأبدان صحيحة والألسن مطلقة والتوبة مسموعة والأعمال مقبولة.

1.92 ومن خطبة له عليه السلام

بعثه والناس ضلّال في حيرة وحابطون٣ في فتنة قد استهوتهم الأهواء واستزلّتهم الكبرياء واستخفّتهم الجاهليّة الجهلاء حيارى في زلزال من الأمر وبلاء من الجهل فبالغ صلّى الله عليه وآله في النصيحة ومضى على الطريقة ودعا إلى ﴿الْحِكْمَةِ وَالْمَوْعِظَةِ﴾.

١م، ي، هـ، ونسخة في ش، ن: كذا. أصل ش، ن: ﴿حسن﴾. ٢ش، ن، هـ، ونسخة في م: كذا. أصل م: ﴿منصباً﴾. ٣م، ش، ن، ومصحّحة في هـ: كذا. ي، وأصل هـ: ﴿خابطون﴾.

1.91 From an oration by ʿAlī:[1]

1.91.1 Blessed is God! Vaunting aspirations cannot attain him, swift intellects cannot find him, he has no limit and will not expire, he has no boundary and will not cease to be.

1.91.2 From the same oration:
God placed them in the finest depository and the choicest repository. Patrician loins conveyed them to chaste wombs. Each time a forebear passed, his successor stood up to establish God's religion, until this divine honor came to Muḥammad. God extracted him from the most precious of mines to be quarried, the most venerated of roots from which to grow, from the very same tree from which God brought forth his prophets and chose his trustees. Muḥammad's line is the best line, his family is the best family, his tree is the best tree. Rooted in the sacred enclave, it rises high in its fertile soil, with tall branches and matchless fruits. Muḥammad is the leader of the pious and a source of sight for those who follow the path, a shining lamp, a blazing star, and a sparking flint. His way is the middle way, his practice gives direction, his words are final, and his judgment is the embodiment of justice. God sent Muḥammad after a period had passed without prophets, when people had stopped doing good, and nations' minds had dulled.

1.91.3 Do good—May God have mercy on you!—and follow its clear waymarks, for its road is wide and leads to the Abode of Safety. Beware, for you live in the abode of those who have been warned, where you have been given a brief respite and a little time. Registers are still open, pens still run with ink, bodies are still healthy, tongues are still unfettered, repentance is still received, and deeds are still accepted.

1.92 From an oration by ʿAlī:
At the time when God sent Muḥammad as a prophet, people wandered in confusion and attempted to gather their firewood in the darkness of sedition. Passions had seduced them, arrogance had caused them to slip, gross ignorance had rendered them witless, and they stood confounded in the face of tumultuous affairs and painful folly. Muḥammad did his utmost to offer them sincere advice. He trod the true path and called to «wisdom and counsel.»[2]

---

1 Excerpt from a famous long oration that ʿAlī delivered in Kufa after the arbitration in 37/658, urging his followers to regroup and fight Muʿāwiyah (Ṣadūq, *Tawḥīd*, 41, 72). Iskāfī (*Miʿyār*, 255) says it is part of the Luminous Oration (*Zahrāʾ*), which also includes § 1.106 and § 1.158.
2 Qurʾan, Naḥl 16:125.

1.93 ومن خطبة له عليه السلام

الحمد لله الأوّل فلا شيء قبله والآخر فلا شيء بعده والظاهر فلا شيء فوقه والباطن فلا شيء دونه.

منها في ذكر رسول الله صلّى الله عليه وآله

مستقرّه خير مستقرّ ومنبته أشرف منبت[1] في معادن الكرامة ومَماهد السلامة قد صُرفت نحوه أفئدة الأبرار وثُنيت إليه أزمّة الأبصار. دَفن به الضغائن وأطفأ به النوائر ألّف به إخوانًا وفرّق به أقرانًا أعزّ به الذلّة وأذلّ به العزّة كلامه بيان وصمتُه لسانٌ.

1.94 ومن كلام له عليه السلام

1.94.1 ولئن أمهل الله الظالم[2] فلن يفوت أخذه وهو له بالمرصاد على مجاز طريقه وبموضع الشجا من مساغ ريقه. أما والذي نفسي بيده ليظهرنّ هؤلاء القوم عليكم ليس لأنّهم أولى بالحقّ منكم ولكن لإسراعهم إلى باطل صاحبهم[3] وإبطائكم عن حقّي. ولقد أصبحت الأمم تخاف ظلم رعاتها وأصبحت أخاف ظلم رعيّتي أستنفرتكم للجهاد فلم تنفروا وأسمعتكم فلم تسمعوا ودعوتكم سرًّا وجهرًا فلم تستجيبوا ونصحت لكم فلم تقبلوا. شهود؛ كغيّاب وعبيد كأرباب أتلو عليكم الحِكَم فتنفرون منها وأعظكم بالموعظة البالغة فتتفرّقون عنها وأحثّكم على جهاد أهل البغي فما آتي على آخر قولي حتّى أراكم ﴿متفرّقين

١ش، ن، ي، ه، ونسخة في م: كذا. أصل م: ﴿ومنصبه ... منصب﴾.   ٢ش، ن، م، ه: كذا. ي: ﴿الباطل﴾.   ٣م، ي، ه، ومصحّحة في ش: كذا. ن، وأصل ش: ﴿لإسراعهم إلى باطلهم﴾. ٤م، ن: كذا. ش، ي، ه: بإضافة همزة قبلها ﴿أشهود﴾.

1.93 From an oration by ʿAlī:
Praise God! He is the first—there was nothing before him. He is the last—there is nothing after him. He is the manifest—there is nothing above him. He is the hidden—there is nothing below him.

From the same oration describing God's Messenger:
Muḥammad came from the worthiest repository and the noblest roots, from the mine of honor and the cradle of soundness. Virtuous hearts inclined to him, and discerning eyes were drawn. Rancorous intentions were buried because of him, and burning flames were doused. Brothers were reconciled and peers were separated, servility was converted to might and might was rendered servile. His words were the epitome of elucidation, his very silence was eloquent.

1.94 From an address by ʿAlī:[1]

1.94.1 God may have granted the tyrant a reprieve, but he will surely apprehend him. He lies in wait on the road along which the tyrant must pass, in the place where his saliva, dripping into his throat, will choke him. By the one who holds my life in his hand, I swear that this faction will overpower you—not because they have a greater right, but because they hasten to support their leader's unrighteous claim,[2] while you hold back from supporting my right! Other communities fear tyranny from their rulers, while I have come to fear tyranny from my subjects! I urge you to fight, but you don't respond, I speak to you, but you don't listen, I call on you in private and in public, but you don't answer, I counsel you, but you don't accept my counsel. Those present among you are like those absent, and servants behave like masters. I recite litanies of wisdom to you but you bolt from them, I counsel you with profound advice but you scatter in its wake, I urge you to fight these treacherous people, but before I reach the end of my speech you ⟨disperse like the hands of Sabā⟩[3]—you

---

1   In Nukhaylah, just outside Kufa, after the arbitration in 37/658. A few lines are repeated in §3.254, that specifies the location. Mufīd (*Irshād*, 277) cites it as part of an oration which begins "O people of Kufa, start preparations for fighting your enemy Muʿāwiyah and his supporters." ʿAbd al-Zahrāʾ (*Maṣādir*, 2:192) argues that this text is part of §1.34, delivered after Nahrawān when the Kufans held back from marching on Muʿāwiyah.

2   The reference is to the Syrians, the Umayyads, and Muʿāwiyah. Ḥ 7:72; B 403; R 1:431.

3   The reference is to the proverb, ⟨They dispersed like the hands of Saba (Sheba)⟩ (*tafarraqū aydiya Sabā*), i.e., they dispersed never to be reunited again. Sabā was a pre-Islamic man from Yemen. His hands are a metaphor for his sons who, warned by a sybil of the Maʾrib dam's imminent rupture and flooding, dispersed widely across the Arabian Peninsula. Maydānī, *Majmaʿ al-amthāl*, 2:6–8; Ḥ 7:74–75; B 403; R 1:432.

أيَادِيَ سَبَا﴾ ترجعون إلى مجالسكم وتخادعون عن مواعظكم أقوّمكم غدوة وترجعون إليّ عشيّة كظهر الحنيّة. عجز المقوِّم وأعضل المقوَّم.

1.94.2 أيّها الشاهدة أبدانهم الغائبة عنهم عقولهم المختلفة أهواؤهم المبتلى بهم أمراؤهم صاحبكم يطيع الله وأنتم تعصونه وصاحب أهل الشام يعصي الله وهم يطيعونه لوددت والله أنّ معاوية صارفني بكم صرف الدينار بالدرهم فأخذ منّي عشرة منكم وأعطاني رجلًا منهم.

1.94.3 يا أهل الكوفة مُنيت منكم بثلاث واثنتين صمّ ذوو أسماع وبكم ذوو كلام وعمي ذوو أبصار لا أحرار صدق عند اللقاء ولا إخوان ثقة عند البلاء تَرِبَت أيديكم. يا أشباه الإبل غاب عنها رعاتها كلّما جمعت من جانب تفرّقت من آخر. والله لكأنّي بكم فيما إخالُ لو حمس الوغى وحمي الضراب قد انفرجتم عن ابن أبي طالب انفراج المرأة عن قُبُلها إنّي لعلى بيّنة من ربّي ومنهاج من نبيّي وإنّي لعلى الطريق الواضح ألقطُه لَقطًا. انظروا أهل بيت نبيّكم فالزموا سمتهم واتّبعوا أثرهم فلن يخرجوكم من هدى ولن يعيدوكم في ردى فإن لَبَدُوا فالْبُدُوا وإن نهضوا فانهضوا ولا تسبقوهم فتضلّوا ولا تتأخّروا عنهم فتهلكوا.

1.94.4 لقد رأيت أصحاب محمّد صلّى الله عليه وآله فما أرى أحدًا منكم يشبههم لقد كانوا يصبحون شُعثًا غُبرًا قد باتوا سجّدًا وقيامًا يراوحون بين جباههم وخدودهم ويقفون على مثل الجمر من ذكر معادهم كأنّ بين أعينهم رُكَبُ المِعزى من طول سجودهم إذا ذكر الله هملت أعينهم حتّى تبُلّ جيوبهم ومادُوا كما يميد الشجر يوم الريح العاصف خوفًا من العقاب ورجاء للثواب.

____

ام، ي، ومصحّحة في ش، ه: كذا. ن، وأصل ش، ه: ﴿جانب﴾.

return to your assemblies and incite one another not to heed the counsel you have heard. I straighten you out in the morning, but you come to me in the evening, crooked as a bow. The one who would straighten has given up, for the one who needs straightening cannot be cured!

1.94.2 You people! Your bodies are present, but your minds are gone, your ambitions are divided so your commanders suffer,[1] your ruler obeys God, yet you disobey him, and the Syrians' ruler disobeys God, yet they obey him. By God, how I wish Muʿāwiyah would trade me dirham for dinar, taking ten of you and giving me one of them!

1.94.3 Kufans! I have been tested by three things in you, and two more: you have ears but are deaf, you have speech but are dumb, you have eyes but are blind, you are not courageous in battle as free men ought to be, nor trustworthy brothers in times of trial. May your hands be filled with dirt! You people, you resemble camels whose herdsmen have disappeared—gathered together on one side, you scatter from the other. I see you, by God, when war clamors and fighting heats up, running away from Abū Ṭālib's son and leaving the way to him open like a woman with her legs spread wide, her front part exposed.[2] I stake my claim on a clear proof from my Lord,[3] and follow a path laid out by my Prophet. I walk with purpose on the clear road.[4] Look to your Prophet's family, stay on their course, and follow their trace, for they will never steer you from the path of guidance or return you to the path of destruction. Sit if they sit and stand if they stand, don't get ahead of them or you will stray, don't hold back from them or you will perish.

1.94.4 I have seen Muḥammad's Companions and none of you resembles them! The morning would find them disheveled and covered in dust, having spent the night in prostration and prayer, pressing foreheads and cheeks to the ground, yearning for the return as though walking on live coals, the skin of their brows gnarly from long prostrations like the knees of a goat. Their eyes would stream at the mention of God's name until their bosoms were soaked. They would shudder from fear of punishment and hope of reward like trees in a gale.

---

1   These first lines echo the opening lines of §1.29.

2   "Abū Ṭālib's son" is ʿAlī. "A woman with her legs spread wide, her front part exposed" (*infirāj al-marʾati ʿan qubulihā*) is an idiom that refers to a woman giving birth. Ḥ 7:76; B 404.

3   Reference to Qurʾan, Anʿām 6:57.

4   Ar. *alquṭuhu laqṭan*, explained as I have translated it by Rāwandī and Ibn Abī al-Ḥadīd (R 1:432. Ḥ 7:76). Baḥrānī (B 404) says it means "I pick my way through it," adding that it means "I pick out right from wrong." Lane (*Lexicon*, s.v. "L-Q-Ṭ") supports both meanings.

1.95   ومن كلام له عليه السلام

والله لا يزالون حتّى لا يَدَعُوا لله مُحَرَّمًا إلّا ٱستحلّوه ولا عَقْدًا إلّا حلّوه وحتّى لا يبقى بيت مدر ولا وبر إلّا دخله ظلمهم ونبَا به سوء رَعْيِهِم وحتّى يقوم الباكيان يبكيان باكٍ يبكي لدينه وباكٍ يبكي لدنياه وحتّى تكون نصرة أحدكم من أحدهم كنصرة العبد من سيّده إذا شهد أطاعه وإذا غاب ٱغتابه وحتّى يكون أعظمكم فيها غناء أحسنكم بالله ظنًّا فإن أتاكم الله بعافية فٱقبلوا وإن ٱبتليتم فٱصبروا فـ﴿إِنَّ ٱلْعَاقِبَةَ لِلْمُتَّقِينَ﴾ .

1.96   ومن خطبة له عليه السلام

نحمده على ما كان ونستعينه من أمرنا على ما يكون ونسأله المعافاة في الأديان كما نسأله المعافاة في الأبدان. أوصيكم بالرفض لهذه الدنيا التاركة لكم وإن لم تحبّوا تركها والمبلية لأجسامكم وإن كنتم تحبّون تجديدها. فإنّما مثلكم ومثلها كسفَرٍ سلكوا سبيلًا فكأنّهم قد قطعوه وأمّوا عَلَمًا فكأنّهم قد بلغوه وكم عسى المجري إلى الغاية أن يجري إليها حتّى يبلغها وما عسى أن يكون بقاءُ من له يوم لا يَعدوه وطالبُ حثيثٌ يحدوه في الدنيا حتّى يفارقها. فلا تنافسوا في عزّ الدنيا ونخرها ولا تَعجبوا بزينتها ونعيمها ولا تجزعوا من ضرّائها وبؤسها فإنّ عزّها ونخرها إلى ٱنقطاع وزينتها ونعيمها إلى زوال وضرّاءها وبؤسها إلى نفاد وكلّ مدّة فيها إلى ٱنتهاء وكلّ حيّ فيها إلى فناء. أوليس لكم في آثار الأوّلين وفي آبائكم الماضين تبصرة ومعتبر إن كنتم تعقلون. أوَلَم تروا إلى الماضين منكم لا

1.95 From an address by ʿAlī:[1]

By God, they will continue thus until they commit every forbidden act and untie every knot, until not one brick house and not one goat-hair tent remains unpenetrated by their tyranny or uprooted by their corrupt herding, until two weepers stand up to weep, one weeping over his religion, another weeping over his possessions, and until, if one of you seeks vengeance on one of them, he will be a slave seeking vengeance upon his master,[2] obeying if present and slandering if absent. The richest of you will be the person who places his trust entirely in God. Remember this: If God grants you his protection accept it, and if he tests you be patient, for «the best outcome is reserved for the pious.»[3]

1.96 From an oration by ʿAlī:[4]

We praise him for favors past and seek his help for what is to come. We ask him to grant us vigor in our faith, just as we ask him to grant us vigor in our bodies. I counsel you to reject the world, for she will reject you despite your dislike of leaving her and cause your bodies to decay despite your wish for renewal. You and she are like a band of travelers who seem already to have crossed the path they traverse, who seem already to have reached the mountain they are headed for. How likely it is that if you race your steed toward a goal, you will soon attain it! How likely it is that your life today will not continue into tomorrow! For you are driven on by a pursuer who will not relent until he makes you leave the world. Don't compete for the world's might and glories, don't be captivated by her beauty and delights or shaken by her injuries and sorrows, for her might and glories will be cut off, her beauty and delights will cease, and her injuries and sorrows will end. Each period of her time will end, and every being living in her will perish. Doesn't the evidence of earlier peoples and the example of your own ancestors alarm and enlighten you? If you would only reflect!

---

1   Excerpt from an oration—preceded, according to Ibn Qutaybah (*Imāmah*, 1:174), by § 1.124, and including § 1.140—delivered at Ṣiffīn (in 37/657), when some of ʿAlī's associates told him about how Muʿāwiyah lavishly rewarded his supporters and urged him to do the same (Ḥarrānī, *Tuḥaf*, 185). This section concerns the Umayyads' tyranny and corruption (B 405; Ḥ 7:78–79).

2   Similar language in § 1.90.4, also about the Umayyads, interpreted as ineffectiveness against them. Ḥ 7:55; B 397.

3   Qurʾan, Hūd 11:49.

4   Friday sermon delivered early in ʿAlī's caliphate, presumably in Medina in 35/656. R 1:438. Iskāfī (*Miʿyār*, 271) cites some lines in a passage that he says "ʿAlī used to call out every night in a raised voice." The last paragraph is also cited as part of an oration (of which § 1.202 is another part) in the mosque in Basra, a few days after the Battle of the Camel in 36/656 (Māmaṭīrī, *Nuzhah*, 235).

يرجعون وإلى الخلف الباقي لا يبقون أَوَلستم ترون أهل الدنيا يمسون ويصبحون على أحوال شتّى فميّت يُبكى وآخر يُعزّى وصريع مبتلى وعائد يعود وآخر بنفسه يجود وطالب للدنيا والموت يطلبه وغافل وليس بمغفول عنه وعلى أثر الماضي ما يمضي الباقي. ألا فاَذكروا هادم اللذات ومنغّص الشهوات وقاطع الأمنيّات عند المساورة للأعمال القبيحة واَستعينوا الله على أداء واجب حقّه وما لا يحصى من أعداد نعمه وإحسانه.

1.97 ومن خطبة له عليه السلام

الحمد لله الناشر في الخلق فضله والباسط فيهم بالجود يده. نحمده في جميع أموره ونستعينه على رعاية حقوقه. ونشهد أن لا إله غيره[1] وأنّ محمّدًا عبده ورسوله أرسله بأمره صادعًا وبذكره ناطقًا فأدّى أمينًا ومضى رشيدًا وخلّف فينا راية الحقّ من تقدّمها مَرَقَ ومن تخلّف عنها زَهَقَ ومن لزمها لَحِقَ دليلها مكيث الكلام بطيء القيام سريع إذا قام فإذا أنتم أَلَّتمُ له رقابكم وأشرتم إليه بأصابعكم جاءه الموت فذهب به فلبثتم بعده ما شاء الله حتّى يطلع الله لكم من يجمعكم ويضمّ نشركم. فلا تطمعوا في غير مقبل ولا تيأسوا من مدبر فإنّ المدبر عسى أن تزلّ إحدى قائمتيه وتثبت الأخرى فترجعا حتّى تثبتا جميعًا. ألا إنّ مثل آل محمّد صلّى الله عليه وآله وسلّم كمثل نجوم السماء إذا خوى نجم طلع نجم. فكأنّكم قد تكاملت من الله فيكم الصنائع وأراكم ما كنتم تأملون.

1.98 ومن خطبة له عليه السلام وهي من خطبه التي تشتمل على ذكر الملاحم

----

[1] ش، ن، ي، ه، ي، ونسخة في م: كذا. وأصل م: ﴿غير الله﴾.

Haven't you seen that those who pass away don't return, and that you, their heirs, will not remain forever? Don't you see the people of this world, at dusk and at dawn, in disparate states? One dead and lamented, another bereaved, one struck and afflicted, another giving up the ghost, one who seeks this world when death seeks him, another heedless who goes not unheeded? In truth, those who remain walk in the traces of those who have passed. Hark! Before you rush to do evil, remember the destroyer of pleasures, the slasher of passions, and the slayer of hopes. Seek God's help in offering him what you owe for his incalculable blessings and abundant favors.

1.97 From an oration by ʿAlī:[1]

Praise God who extended his grace to all creatures and stretched out his hand to them with generous gifts. We praise him in all his affairs and seek his help in guarding his rights. We bear witness that there is no god other than he, and that Muḥammad is his servant and messenger, whom he sent to transmit his command and express his remembrance. He discharged the trust with honor, and died having guided us, having bequeathed to us the banner of truth; whoever gets ahead of it strays, whoever holds back from it perishes, and whoever remains beneath it catches up with those who have gone ahead. The guide who carries it is deliberate when speaking, measured when rising, and swift once risen,[2] but when you have bent your necks to him fully and pointed toward him with your fingers,[3] death will come to him, and he will be taken away. You will remain after him in this manner for as long as God wills, until he brings to you one who will unite you again and gather your scattered fragments. So do not keep hoping for a man to step up who is not going to, but do not despair of one who has turned away. Though he may have turned away because one foot slipped, the other could be stable, and both feet could once again stand firm. Hark! Muḥammad's descendants are like stars in the firmament: if one sets, another rises. The time is near and has almost arrived—the time when God's blessings will reach perfection, and when he will show you what you hope to see.

1.98 From one of ʿAlī's orations containing narratives of epic fighting:[4]

---

1 ʿAlī's third Friday sermon delivered after becoming caliph, presumably in Medina, 35/656. Ḥ 7:93.

2 Referring to himself. Ḥ 7:85; B 408.

3 The commentaries state that "pointing with fingers" means that "people recognized ʿAlī as ruler." Ḥ 7:94; B 408.

4 Part of an oration—that includes §1.99 and §1.126—which ʿAlī delivered in Basra immediately after the Battle of the Camel in 36/656. B 480; ʿAbd al-Zahrāʾ, *Maṣādir*, 2:202, 203, 288.

1.98.1 الأوّل قبل كلّ أوّل والآخر بعد كلّ آخر بأوّليته وجب أن لا أوّل له وبآخريّته وجب أن لا آخر له وأشهد أن لا إلٰه إلّا الله شهادة يوافق فيها السرّ الإعلان والقلب اللسان.

1.98.2 أيّها الناس ﴿لَا يَجْرِمَنَّكُمْ شِقَاقِي﴾ ولا يستهوينّكم عصياني ولا تتراموا بالأبصار عندما تسمعونه منّي فوالذي فلق الحبّة وبرأ النسمة إنّ الذي أنبّئكم به عن النبيّ صلّى الله عليه وآله. ما كذب المبلّغ ولا جهل السامع.

1.98.3 لكأنّي أنظر إلى ضِلّيل قد نَعَقَ بالشام وفحص براياته في ضواحي كوفان فإذا فَغَرَتْ فاغرته واشتدّت شكيمته وثقلت في الأرض وطأته عضّت الفتنة أبناءها بأنيابها وماجت الحرب بأمواجها وبدا من الأيّام كُلوحُها ومن الليالي كُدوحُها فإذا يَنَعَ زرعه وقام على يَنعِه وهدرت شقاشقه وبرقت بوارقه عُقدت رايات الفتن المعضلة وأقبلن كالليل المظلم والبحر الملتطم. هذا وكم يخرق الكوفة من قاصف ويمرّ عليها من عاصف وعن قليل تلتفّ القرون بالقرون ويُحصَد القائم ويُحطَم المحصود.

1.99 *ومن خطبة له عليه السلام تجري هذا المجرى*

1.99.1 وذلك يوم يجمع الله فيه الأوّلين والآخرين لنقاش الحساب وجزاء الأعمال خضوعًا قيامًا قد أَلجَمهم العرق ورجفت بهم الأرض فأحسنهم حالًا من وجد لقدميه موضعًا ولنفسه متّسعًا.

1.98.1 He is the first before every first and the last after every last, his firstness dictates that he has no beginning, and his lastness dictates that he has no end. I bear witness that there is no god but God; my thoughts match my declaration, my heart matches my tongue.

1.98.2 People! «Let not your enmity of me drive you to accuse me of lies»[1] or seduce you into disobeying me—and do not look at one another so when you hear me speak these words! I swear by him who split open the seed and created the living being that what I say to you comes from the Prophet—that speaker did not lie, and this listener did not forget.

1.98.3 A wicked man will call out to his flock in Syria and scrapes the ground for his banners to roost in the hinterlands of Kufa—I can almost see him![2] When his maw has opened wide, his defiance has become strong, and he stamps his feet with violence, sedition will sink its fangs into the city's children, waves of war will swell, the days will scowl, and the nights will maim. Then, with sedition's fruit fully ripened, its thunderclaps booming and its lightning flashing, its obdurate banners will become ranged in tight ranks and march like the dark night, like the surging sea. All this will happen. How many winds will sweep into Kufa! How many storms will lash into her! Soon, very soon, horn will lock with horn. All who stand will be harvested, and all that is harvested will be crushed.

1.99 From an oration by ʿAlī with similar content:[3]

1.99.1 On that day, God will assemble all who went before and all who came after, standing, necks bowed, to be interrogated for the judgment and receive payback for their deeds. Sweat will streak their cheeks like straps of a bridle, and the ground beneath them will tremble. The best any man can hope for is space for his feet and room for his frame.[4]

---

1 Qurʾan, Hūd 11:89.

2 The commentators state that this prophecy refers most likely to the fifth Umayyad caliph ʿAbd al-Malik ibn Marwān (r. 65–86/685–705), or perhaps to Muʿāwiyah, or the Antichrist. B 401, Ḥ 7:99–100. The first few lines are similar to §1.136.3.

3 Part of an oration—that includes §1.98 and §1.126—which ʿAlī delivered in Basra immediately after the Battle of the Camel in 36/656. B 480; ʿAbd al-Zahrāʾ, *Maṣādir*, 2:202, 203, 288.

4 Ar. *nafs*, translated here as "frame," also means "life," "person," and "soul." Differently vocalized as *nafas*, it can also mean "breath" (Ibn Manẓūr, *Lisān*, s.v. "N-F-S"). My translation is based on Ḥ 7:102; B 411.

١.٩٩.٢ منها

فتن كقطع الليل المظلم لا تقوم لها قائمة ولا تُردّ لها راية تأتيكم مزمومة مرحولة يحفزها قائدها ويجهدها راكبها أهلها قوم شديد كَلَبُهم قليل سَلَبُهم يجاهدهم في الله قوم أذلّة عند المتكبّرين في الأرض مجهولون وفي السماء معروفون فويلٌ لك يا بصرة عند ذلك من جيش من نقم الله لا رَهَجَ له ولا حسّ وسيبتلى أهلك بالموت الأحمر والجوع الأغبر.

١.١٠٠ ومن خطبة له عليه السلام

١.١٠٠.١ انظروا إلى الدنيا نظر الزاهدين فيها الصادفين عنها فإنّها والله عمّا قليل تزيل الثاوي الساكن وتفجع المترف الآمن لا يرجع ما تولّى منها فأدبر ولا يُدرى ما هو آتٍ منها فيُنتظر سرورها مشوب بالحزن وجَلَد الرجال فيها إلى الضعف والوهن فلا تغرنّكم كثرة ما يعجبكم فيها لقلّة ما يصحبكم منها. رحم الله اَمرأً تفكّر فاَعتبر واَعتبر فأبصر فكأنّ ما هو كائن من الدنيا عن قليل لم يكن وكأنّ ما هو كائن من الآخرة عمّا قليل لم يزل وكلّ معدود منقَضٍ وكلّ متوقّع آتٍ وكلّ آتٍ قريب دانٍ.

١.١٠٠.٢ منها

العالم من عرف قدره وكفى بالمرء جهلًا ألّا يعرف قدره وإنّ من أبغض الرجال إلى الله لعبد وكّله الله إلى نفسه جائر عن قصد السبيل سائر بغير دليل إن دعي إلى حرث الدنيا عمل أو إلى حرث الآخرة كسل كأنّ ما عمل له واجب عليه وكأنّ ما وَنى فيه ساقط عنه.

1.99.2 From the same oration:[1]
Seditions will approach like hosts of darkness—no horse will be able to withstand them, and no banner of theirs will be repelled. Advancing like bridled and saddled warhorses, they will be urged on by their drivers, and pushed hard by their riders, a rabid group with little appetite for stopping at plunder. Those who fight them for God will be a force deemed lowly by the arrogant, unrecognized on earth but eminent in the hereafter. Basra, you will be afflicted at that time with an army that brings God's chastisement, an army that neither raises dust nor makes any sound. Your inhabitants will be stricken with red death and black hunger.

1.100 From an oration by ʿAlī:[2]

1.100.1 Look at the world with the eyes of those who have little interest in her and who turn away from her. By God, she will soon evict her tenants and afflict the complacent and secure. That part which turns away and leaves never returns, while that part which you think is approaching is not guaranteed to arrive. Her happiness is blemished with grief, and men's strength, as they continue to live in her bosom, deteriorates into weakness and incapacity. Do not be beguiled by her many beauties, for her companionship is short-lived. May God have mercy on the man who reflects and takes heed, and who, taking heed, discerns! In a short while, it will be as though this world never was, as if the hereafter has already come. All that is tallied will run out, all that is expected will be, and all that will be is at hand.

1.100.2 From the same oration:
The learned man knows his worth—suffice it as a mark of ignorance when a man does not know his worth. Among the most hateful of men in God's eyes is a person whom God has given up on, a person he has left to his own devices, who strays from the straight path, and wanders without a guide. If called on to cultivate the fields of this world, he works hard, but if called on to cultivate the fields of the hereafter, he is lazy. He behaves as though the things he works for are mandatory, but the things in which he is remiss are an unpleasant burden that he is not required to carry.

---

1   The commentators state that this section prophesies either (1) end-of-time apocalyptic events (Ḥ 7:104), or (2) the Zanj Rebellion (B 411–412). Led by the "Chief of the Zanj," ʿAlī b. Muḥammad, this 15-year rebellion in southern Iraq (255–270/869–883) caused "innumerable material losses and tens of thousands of lives." Popovic, "*al-Zandj*: (ii) The *Zandj* revolts in ʿIrāk," *EI*².

2   Kulaynī (*Kāfī*, 8:17) cites §1.100.1 in a set of lines with which "the Commander of the Faithful used to counsel his supporters."

1.100.3 منها

وذلك زمان لا ينجو فيه إلّا كلّ مؤمن نُومَة إن شهد لم يُعرَف وإن غاب لم يُفتقَد أولئك مصابيح الهدى وأعلام السُّرى ليسوا بالمَساييح ولا المَذاييع البُذُر أولئك يفتح الله لهم أبواب رحمته ويكشف عنهم ضرّاء نقمته. أيّها الناس سيأتي عليكم زمان يُكفَأ فيه الإسلام كما يُكفَأ الإناء بما فيه. أيّها الناس إنّ الله قد أعاذكم من أن يجور عليكم ولم يعذكم من أن يبتليكم وقد قال جلّ من قائل ﴿إِنَّ فِي ذٰلِكَ لَآيَاتٍ وَإِن كُنَّا لَمُبْتَلِينَ﴾.

1.100.4 أمّا قوله عليه السلام ⟨كلّ مؤمن نومة⟩ فإنّما أراد به الخامل الذكر القليل الشرّ. و⟨المساييح⟩ جمع مِسْياح وهو الذي يسيح بين الناس بالفساد والنمائم. و⟨المذاييع⟩ جمع مِذْياع وهو الذي إذا سمع لغيره بفاحشة أذاعها ونوَّهَ بها. و⟨البُذُر⟩ جمع بَذُور وهو الذي يكثر سَفَهُهُ ويَلْغُو منطقه.

1.101 ومن خطبة له عليه السلام وقد تقدّم مختارها بخلاف هذه الرواية أمّا بعد. فإنّ الله سبحانه بعث محمّدًا صلّى الله عليه وآله وليس أحد من العرب يقرأ كتابًا ولا يدّعي نبوّة ولا وحيًا فقاتل بمن أطاعه من عصاه يسوقهم إلى منجاتهم ويبادر بهم الساعة أن تنزل بهم يَحْسَر الحسير ويقف الكسير فيقيم عليه حتّى يلحقه غايته إلّا هالكًا لا خير فيه حتّى أراهم منجاتهم وبوّأهم محلّتهم فاستدارت رحاهم واستقامت قناتهم. وايم الله لقد كنت من ساقتها حتّى تولّت بحذافيرها واستوسقتُ في قيادها ما ضعفتُ ولا جبنت ولا خنت ولا وهنت. وايم الله لأَبْقُرَنَّ الباطل حتّى أخرج الحقّ من خاصرته.

1.100.3 From the same oration:

A time will come when only humble believers are safe,[1] not recognized if present and not missed when absent. They are lamps of guidance and waymarks for travelers, never gossipmongers or blabbering slanderers. God will open the gates of his mercy for them and offer protection from the blows of his punishment. People! A time will come upon you when Islam is overturned, just as a vessel is overturned, with its water poured away. People! God has promised to protect you against his injustice, but he has not promised to protect you against his trials. He, the most glorious of speakers, has said: «Truly there are signs in that, truly we shall put you to the test.»[2]

1.100.4 Raḍī: By the words, "every humble believer (*kullu muʾminin nūmah*)," ʿAlī meant a person whom no one mentions and who does no one harm. "*Masāyīḥ* (gossipmongers)" is the plural of *misyāḥ*, one who goes around spreading discord and defamation. "*Madhāyīʿ* (slanderers)" is the plural of *midhyāʿ*, one who, whenever he hears of a person having committed an immoral act, circulates and disseminates it. "*Budhur* (blabberers)" is the plural of *badhūr*, one whose levity is excessive and whose speech is nonsensical.

1.101 From an oration by ʿAlī of which some parts have previously been cited in a variant form:[3]

God sent Muḥammad as a prophet when no Arab read scripture or claimed revelation and prophecy. Mustering those who obeyed him, he fought those who disobeyed, herding all to their place of refuge and hastening to set them on the right path before the final hour arrived. He raised the weary and nurtured the broken, until, except for those bereft of any good who perished, he had guided them all to their goal, shown them their refuge, and brought them into a safe enclosure, where their handmills spun and their lances straightened. By God, I was one of those who fought the Age of Ignorance until its battalions fled and Islam's forces were corralled,[4] never holding back out of weakness, cowardice, disloyalty, or impotence. By God, I shall impale falsehood's torso until truth emerges from its flank.

---

1 Ar. *nūmah*, translated here as "humble," is alternatively vocalized as *nuwamah*, "those who sleep a lot." B 414.

2 Qurʾan, Muʾminūn 23:30.

3 This oration is a variant of §1.33, specified there as delivered "when ʿAlī marched on the people of Basra." See also Mufīd, *Irshād*, 247.

4 This line contains only pronouns, which I have replaced based on the commentaries: "Age of Ignorance" for "the earlier age," and "Islam's forces" for "our forces." Ḥ 7:116; B 415; R 339; Gh 2:108.

1.102 ومن خطبة له عليه السلام

1.102.1 حتّى بعث الله محمّدًا صلّى الله عليه وآله وسلّم شهيدًا وبشيرًا ونذيرًا خير البريّة طفلًا وأنجبها كهلًا أطهر المطهّرين شيمة وأجود المستمطرين ديمة. فما أحلولت لكم الدنيا في لذّتها ولا تمكّنتم من رَضاع أخلافها إلّا من بعده.١ صادفتموها جائلًا خطامها قلقًا وضينها قد صار حرامًا عند أقوام بمنزلة السدر المخضود وحلالها بعيدًا غير موجود وصادفتموها والله ظلًّا ممدودًا إلى أجل معدود فالأرض لكم شاغرة وأيديكم فيها مبسوطة وأيدي القادة عنكم مكفوفة وسيوفكم عليهم مسلّطة وسيوفهم عنكم مقبوضة. ألا إنّ لكلّ دم ثائرًا ولكلّ حقّ طالبًا وإنّ الثائر في دمائنا كالحاكم في حقّ نفسه وهو الله الذي لا يعجزه مَن طلب ولا يفوته من هرب. فأُقسم بالله يا بني أميّة عمّا قليل لتعرفنّها في أيدي غيركم وفي دار عدوّكم ألا وإنّ أبصر الأبصار ما نفذ في الخير طرفه ألا إنّ أسمع الأسماع ما وَعى التذكير وقَبِلَه.

1.102.2 أيّها الناس استصبحوا من شعلة مصباح واعظ متّعظ وامتاحوا من صفو عين قد رُوّقت من الكدر. عباد الله لا تركنوا إلى جهالتكم ولا تنقادوا لأهوائكم فإنّ النازل بهذا المنزل نازل بـ«شَفَا جُرُفٍ هَارٍ» ينقل الردى على ظهره من موضع إلى موضع لرأي يحدثه بعد رأي يريد أن يلصق ما لا يلتصق ويقرّب ما لا يتقارب. فاللَّهَ اللَّهَ أن تشكوا إلى من لا يبكي٢ شَجْوَكم ولا ينقض برأيه ما قد أبرم لكم. إنّه ليس على الإمام إلّا ما حمّل من أمر ربّه الإبلاغ في الموعظة والاجتهاد في النصيحة والإحياء

١م، ش، ن، ي، هـ مع علامة الصحّة: كذا. مصحّحة في ش، م: ﴿بعد ما﴾.   ٢م، ي، هـ، ونسخة في ش: كذا. ن، وأصل ش، ونسخة في م، هـ: ﴿يشكي﴾.

1.102   From an oration by ʿAlī:[1]

1.102.1   God sent Muḥammad as a witness, a herald, and a warner.[2] As a child, he was the best of the entire world, as a man, the most noble, purest of the pure in character, the most generous of all rainclouds. Until he came,[3] you had neither tasted the world's sweetness nor succeeded in milking its teats. But afterward, when its halter was loose and its girth slack,[4] some of you turned what he had forbidden into a «laden lote tree»,[5] and what he had made lawful into a distant fancy. You found the world to be a cool, spreading shade: the earth defenseless before your aggression, your hands reaching out to grab it and the hands of just leaders restrained, your swords on their necks, their swords forcibly sheathed. Be warned! For every life taken vengeance will be sought, for every right abused redress will be pursued. Our avenger is none other than God, who will be both petitioner and judge. No one he seeks eludes him, no one who flees escapes. By God, Umayyads! Soon you will see rule in the hands of another, in the house of your enemy. Listen now! For the keenest eye kens good and the sharpest ear heeds counsel.

1.102.2   People! Light your lamp from the flame of one who gives counsel and heeds it, draw your water from a spring that is unmuddied and pure.[6] Servants of God! Do not rest on your ignorance or follow your caprice for that camper encamps at «the lip of a crumbling cliff».[7] As he moves from place to place, as he innovates one heresy then another, as he tries to glue two things that cannot bond, as he works to join two things that are far apart, he carries his doom on his back. Fear God, and do not take your complaints to one who does not feel your pain, who cannot undo with his makeshift ruling a mandated rule. A leader's duties are those with which God has charged him: he must counsel the people

---

1   ʿAlī delivered this oration in Medina in 35/656, five days after allegiance was pledged to him as caliph. ʿAlī ibn Ibrāhīm al-Qummī, *Tafsīr*, 1:384.

2   Modified quote from Qurʾan, Aḥzāb 33:45. The Arabic begins with *ḥattā* ("until"), presumably connecting from an earlier section on the condition of people just before the coming of Islam.

3   Ar. *min baʿdihi*: "until he came," addressing the early Muslims (H 7:119); or: "until he had gone," addressing the Umayyads (B 105). Or, if reading the text as *min baʿdi mā*, as in some manuscripts, the sentence would connect to the next word and read as "You did not taste ... until after you had earlier found the world to have a loose halter."

4   I.e., difficult to ride, referring to the upheavals in the leadership of the Muslim empire after Muḥammad. H 7:119.

5   Ar. *sidr makhḍūd*. Qurʾan, Wāqiʿah 56:28; H 7:119; R 1:449; B 417.

6   Referring to himself. H 7:168; B 418.

7   Qurʾan, Tawbah 9:109.

للسنّة وإقامة الحدود على مستحقّيها وإصدار السُّهْمان على أهلها. فبادروا العلم من قبل تصويح نبته ومن قبل أن تشغلوا بأنفسكم عن مستثار العلم من عند أهله وانهوا عن المنكر وتناهوا عنه فإنّما أمرتم بالنهي بعد التناهي.

1.103 ومن خطبة له عليه السلام

1.103.1 الحمد لله الذي شرع الإسلام فسهّل شرائعه لمن ورده وأعزّ أركانه على من غالبه فجعله أمنًا لمن عَلِقَه وسلمًا لمن دخله وبرهانًا لمن تكلّم به وشاهدًا لمن خاصم به ونورًا لمن استضاء به وفهمًا لمن عقل ولبًّا لمن تدبّر وآية لمن توسّم وتبصرة لمن عزم وعبرة لمن اتّعظ ونجاة لمن صدّق وثقة لمن توكّل وراحة لمن فوّض وجنّة لمن صبر. فهو أبلج المناهج واضح الولائج مشرف المنار مشرق الجوادّ مضيء المصابيح كريم المضمار رفيع الغاية جامع الحَلْبة متنافس السَّبْقة شريف الفرسان. التصديق منهاجه والصالحات مناره والموت غايته والدنيا مضماره والقيامة حَلْبَته والجنّة سَبْقته.

1.103.2 منها في ذكر النبيّ صلّى الله عليه وآله

to good purpose, exert effort in giving advice, keep alive the Sunnah, punish those who commit crimes, and distribute treasury stipends fairly. People, hasten to pluck knowledge before its plant withers, seek to acquire knowledge from its keepers before preoccupations distract, forbid evil and desist from it, for you have been commanded to desist before forbidding others.

1.103 From an oration by ʿAlī:[1]

1.103.1 Praise God who paved the path of Islam, made it smooth for those who come to its waterholes, and protected its ramparts from attackers. He made it a source of security for those who cling to it, a place of safety for those who enter it, a proof for those who argue by it, a witness for those who litigate with it, a light for those who seek illumination by it, comprehension for those who understand, reason for those who ponder, a sign for those who search for pasture,[2] perception for those who resolve to advance, a lesson for those who take heed, salvation for those who believe, support for those who trust, comfort for those who submit, and a shield for those who endure. Islam's paths are lit, its trails marked,[3] its beacons high, its highway bright, its lamps aglow, its arena honorable, its goal elevated, its racehorses numerous, its prize sought, and its champions noble. Its path is faith, its road good deeds, its end death, its racecourse the world, its track the day of resurrection, and its prize paradise.

1.103.2 From the same oration in praise of the Prophet:[4]

1　Excerpt from an oration that ʿAlī delivered in his home, either in Medina or Kufa, additional parts of which are recorded as §1.69, and sayings §3.26 (about the four pillars of belief) and §3.259 (ʿAbd al-Zahrāʾ, *Maṣādir*, 4:214–216). It is related that ʿAlī was asked by an associate to describe belief (*īmān*), and ʿAlī instructed him to come back the next day, so that others could hear it too. He did return, presumably with others. ʿAlī then delivered this oration and instructed that it be written down and read out to the public (Kulaynī, *Kāfī*, 2:49). Kulaynī (ibid.) names the associate as ʿAbdallāh ibn al-Kawwāʾ, while Ghazālī (*Iḥyāʾ*, 4:60) names him as ʿAmmār ibn Yāsir (if so, the oration would have been delivered before Ṣiffīn, in 37/657, when ʿAmmār was killed). Alternatively, §1.103.1 is also cited as an answer given during an oration in the mosque in Basra, a few days after the Battle of the Camel in 36/656 (Māmaṭīrī, *Nuzhah*, 224–225). Other parts of the same oration in ibid., 221–233 are listed in note to §1.23. §1.103.1 is similar to §1.154.2.

2　Or, for those who perceive hidden things (*tafarrasa*). B 420; R 1:455; Ḥ 7:122.

3　Or, its inner workings are clear. B 420.

4　Ibn Abī al-Ḥadīd (Ḥ 7:174–175) remarks that none of the Prophet's Companions praised the Prophet and prayed for him after his death as passionately as ʿAlī did, just as no one aided and served the Prophet during his lifetime as sincerely as ʿAlī and his family did.

حتّى أَوْرى قبسًا لقابس وأنار عَلَمًا لحابس فهو أمينك المأمون وشهيدك يوم الدين
وبعيثك نعمة ورسولك بالحقّ رحمة. اللّهمّ أقسم له مقسمًا من عدلك وأجزه مضعّفات
الخير من فضلك. اللّهمّ أَعْلِ على بناء البانين بناءه وأكرم لديك نُزُله وشرّف عندك
منزله وآته الوسيلة وأعطه السناء والفضيلة وأحشرنا في زمرته غير خزايا ولا نادمين ولا
ناكبين ولا ناكثين ولا ضالّين ولا مفتونين.

وقد مضى هذا الكلام فيما تقدّم إلّا أنّنا كرّرناه هٰهنا لما في الروايتين من الاختلاف.

١٠٣.٣.١ منها في خطاب أصحابه

وقد بلغتم من كرامة الله لكم منزلة تكرم بها إماؤكم وتوصل بها جيرانكم ويعظّمكم من لا
فضل لكم عليه ولا يَدَ لكم عنده ويهابكم من لا يخاف لكم سطوة ولا لكم عليه إمرة.
وقد ترون عهود الله منقوضة فلا تغضبون وأنتم لنقض ذمم آبائكم تأنفون. وكانت أمور
الله عليكم ترد وعنكم تصدر وإليكم ترجع فكّنتم الظَّلَمة من منزلتكم وألقيتم إليهم أزمّتكم
وأسلمتم أمور الله في أيديهم يعملون بالشبهات ويسيرون[1] في الشهوات. وايم الله لو فرّقكم
تحت كلّ كوكب لجمعكم الله لشرّ يوم لهم.

١٠٤.١ ومن خطبة له عليه السلام في بعض أيّام صفّين

وقد رأيت جولتكم وانحيازكم عن صفوفكم تحوزكم الجفاة الطغام وأعراب أهل الشام
وأنتم لهاميم العرب ويآفيخ الشرف والأنف المقدّم والسنام الأعظم. ولقد شفى

―――――

[1] ش، ن، ي، ه: كذا. م: ﴿تعملون ... تسيرون﴾.

He ignited the flame of truth for any who sought a burning brand and lit torches on the road to paradise for those who had tied up their camels not knowing where to go. He is the trustee whom you, God, entrusted with your message, your witness on judgment day, your emissary sent as a blessing, and your messenger dispatched with the truth as the embodiment of mercy. God, bestow on him a bounteous share of your justice, and reward him with a munificent recompense, multiplied manifold by your generosity. God, let his palace tower high above all others, provide him a noble place near you, honor his station at your side, bestow him the right of intercession, grant him radiance and excellence, and resurrect us in his company—let us not be people of dishonor, remorse, deviation, violation, or error, or those who succumb to sedition.

Raḍī: This passage was narrated earlier.[1] I have repeated it here because the two reports vary in some of their language.

1.103.3 From the same oration addressing his associates:
It is through God's bounty that you have attained this high standing, in which your slave girls are honored, and your neighbors receive gifts, where you are revered by people to whom you have given no special favors or grants, while others stand in your awe who have no reason to fear your attack and over whom you have no command. Yet here you see God's compacts broken and are not roused to anger, while when your ancestors' traditions are rent, you profess outrage. God's affairs used to frequent your waterhole, but you have relinquished your station to tyrants, and entrusted your guide ropes to them. You have surrendered God's affairs into their hands, as they implement their dubious actions and walk in the path of their passions. But, by God, even if they strew you beneath every distant star, God will reunite you, on an evil day for them.

1.104 From an oration ʿAlī delivered during one of the battle-days of Ṣiffīn:[2]
I saw you turn away from your battle lines and fall back, pushed away by the rough rabble and common Bedouins of Syria, you, the aristocracy of the Arabs, the summit of nobility, the bridge of its nose, and its lofty hump! But my racing heart was calmed when later I saw you push them back as they had pushed

---

1 §1.69.
2 Ṣiffīn, 37/657. At one point during the battle, ʿAlī's right wing fell back. Ashtar, prompted by ʿAlī, addressed them with a rousing oration, and they returned to fight and routed the Syrians. ʿAlī then addressed them with the oration at hand. Ṭabarī, *Tārīkh*, 5:19–25; Iskāfī, *Miʿyār*, 149.

وَحاوِحَ صدري أن رأيتكم بأُخَرَة تحوزونهم كما حازوكم وتزيلونهم عن مواقفهم كما أزالوكم حَسًّا بالنصال وشَجرًا بالرماح تَرَكب أولاهم أخراهم كالإبل الهيم المطرودة ترمى عن حياضها وتذاد عن مواردها.

1.105 ومن خطبة له عليه السلام وهي من خطب الملاحم

1.105.1 الحمد لله المتجلّي لخلقه بخلقه والظاهر لقلوبهم بحجّته خلق الخلق من غير رويّة إذ كانت الرويّات لا تليق إلّا بذوي الضمائر وليس بذي ضمير في نفسه خرق علمه باطن غيب السترات وأحاط بغموض عقائد السريرات.

1.105.2 منها في ذكر النبيّ صلّى الله عليه وآله
اختاره من شجرة الأنبياء ومشكاة الضياء وذُؤابة العلياء وسُرّة البطحاء ومصابيح الظلمة وينابيع الحكمة.

منها

طبيبٌ دوّار بطبّه قد أحكم مَراهمه وأحمى١ مواسمه يضع ذلك حيث الحاجة إليه من قلوب عمي وآذان صمّ وألسنة بُكْم متتبّع بدوائه مواضع الغفلة ومواطن الحيرة لم يستضيئوا بأضواء الحكمة ولم يقدحوا بزناد العلوم الثاقبة فهم في ذلك كالأنعام السائمة والصخور القاسية قد اَنجابت السرائر لأهل البصائر ووضحت محجّة الحقّ لخابطها٢ وأسفرت الساعة عن وجهها وظهرت العلامة لمتوسّمها. مالي أراكم أشباحًا بلا أرواح وأرواحًا بلا أشباح ونسّاكًا بلا صلاح وتجّارًا بلا أرباح وأيقاظًا نُوَّمًا وشهودًا غيّبًا وناظرة عميًا وسامعة صمًّا وناطقة بُكْمًا. راية ضلالة قد قامت على قطبها وتفرّقت بشعبها.

١ش، ن، ي، هـ، ومصحّحة في م: كذا. أصل م: ⟨وأمضى⟩.   ٢ش، ن، ي، هـ، ونسخة في م: كذا. أصل م: ⟨لأهلها⟩.

you earlier, forcing them from their positions as they had forced you earlier, striking them with arrows and thrusting at them with spears, shoving the men in their front rows bodily onto the heads and chests of the men in the rows behind them, like parched camels driven from the waterhole and pushed away from drink.

1.105   From an oration by ʿAlī with prophecies of future calamities:

1.105.1   Praise God, who appears to his creation through his creation and manifests himself to their hearts through his proof. He created without cogitation or thought, for cogitation and thought only come from those who have an inner disposition—and God does not possess an inner disposition in his self. His knowledge rends the hidden veils of mystery and encompasses beliefs stored in the innermost recesses of peoples' hearts.

1.105.2   From the same oration in praise of the Prophet:
God selected him from the tree of prophets, the lamp-niche of illumination, the forelock of majesty, and the navel of Baṭḥāʾ,[1] from the lamps in the darkness, and the wellsprings of wisdom.

From the same oration:
He was a physician who carried his medicine from place to place.[2] He had prepared ointments and heated his cauteries, and he used them to heal the hearts of the blind, the ears of the deaf, and the tongues of the dumb, as called for by their needs. He sought out for his medicine places of heedlessness and locales of perplexity never illumined by the light of wisdom or sparked by the flints of glinting erudition. They had been like untended cattle and hard rocks, but then secret purposes became plain for the perceptive, the road of truth became clear for those who had been stumbling in the dark, the imminent hour unveiled its face, and fluttering banners came into sight for those looking for signs. Why is it that I see you as bodies without souls and souls without bodies, ascetics without piety and merchants without profit, awake yet asleep and present yet absent, seeing yet blind, hearing yet deaf, and speaking yet dumb? There will rise a banner of error, entrenched in its socket, spreading its streamers, measuring you with its yardstick, and striking you with outstretched hand, and its leader will be a man who has forsaken the faith to establish his errant claim.

---

1   Baṭḥāʾ—lit. "the flatland"—is another name for Mecca.
2   Or, "I am a physician …" B 425. The pronoun is implied, not explicit, and the physician could be a reference to the Prophet or to ʿAlī himself.

تَكِيلُكم بصاعها وتخبطكم بباعها. قائدها' خارج من الملّة قائم على الضّلّة. فلا يبقى يومئذ منكم إلّا ثفالة كثفالة القِدْر أو نُفاضة كنفاضة العِكْم تَعْرُككم عَرْك الأديم وتدوسكم دَوْس الحصيد وتستخلص المؤمنَ من بينكم ٱستخلاص الطير الحبّة البطينة من بين هَزيل الحبّ. أين تذهب بكم المذاهب وتتيه بكم الغياهب وتخدعكم الكواذب ومن أين تؤتَون و﴿أَنَّىٰ تُؤْفَكُونَ﴾. و﴿لِكُلِّ أَجَلٍ كِتَابٌ﴾ ولكلّ غيبة إياب.

1.105.3   فٱسمعوا من ربّانيّكم وأحضروه قلوبكم وٱستيقظوا إن هتف بكم وليصدق رائد أهله وليجمع شمله وليحضر ذهنه فلقد فلق لكم الأمر فَلْقَ الخَرَزة وقرفه قرف الصَّمْغة فعند ذلك أخذ الباطل مآخذه وركب الجهل مراكبه وعظمت الطاغية وقلّت الداعية وصال الدهر صِيال السَّبُع العقور وهدر فَنيق الباطل بعد كُظوم وتواخى الناس على الفجور وتهاجروا على الدين وتحابّوا على الكَذب وتباغضوا على الصدق فإذا كان ذلك كان الولد غَيظًا والمطر قَيظًا وتفيض اللئام فيضًا وتغيض الكرام غيضًا وكان٢ أهل ذلك الزمان ذئابًا وسلاطينه سباعًا وأوساطه أُكّالًا وفقراؤه أمواتًا وغار٣ الصدق وفاض الكَذب وٱستُعملت المودّة باللسان وتشاجر الناس بالقلوب وصار الفسوق نسبًا والعفاف عجبًا ولبس الإسلام لُبْس الفَرْو مقلوبًا.

1.106   ومن خطبة له عليه السلام

1.106.1   كلّ شيء خاشع له وكلّ شيء قائم به غنى كلّ فقير وعزّ كلّ ذليل وقوّة كلّ ضعيف ومفزع كلّ ملهوف من تكلّم سمع نطقه ومن سكت علم سرّه ومن عاش فعليه رزقه ومن مات فإليه منقلبه. لم تَرَكَ العيونُ فتخبرَ عنك بل كنت قبل الواصفين من

١ش، ن، ه، ومصحّحة في م: كذا. أصل م: ﴿قائمها﴾.   ٢ش، ن، ي، ه: كذا. م: ﴿عاد﴾.   ٣ش، ن، ي، ه، ومصحّحة في م: كذا. أصل م: ﴿غاض﴾.

On that day, those of you who remain standing will be as sediments in a cooking pot, or fluffs of wool after bales are packed. The sedition will scrape you like tanned leather, stamp you like harvested grain, picking out the believers among you as a bird picks out plump kernels from a dried-up heap of grain. So tell me, where are these paths taking you, these shadows leading you, these lies tempting you? How is it you have been deceived, «how is it you have been duped?»[1] But «each term is written»[2] and every absence is followed by a return.

1.105.3 Listen to your godly leader, listen to him with your hearts, and pay attention when he speaks! A scout must tell his people the truth, gather them together, and remain alert.[3] But this one has indeed exposed the affair for you and split it open like a cowrie shell,[4] he has peeled it clear like gum from tree bark. The time will come when evil ensconces itself in its cradle, ignorance mounts its steeds, tyranny grows strong, callers to truth dwindle, time attacks like a rapacious carnivore, and evil's camel stallion, gagged for a time, roars. People will become brothers in debauchery, deserters from religion, best friends in their mutual lying, and fierce enemies in the face of truth. When this happens, the son will bring his parents utter despair, the rain will bring scorching heat, the wicked will brim like a flood, and the noble will be depleted like an exhausted wellspring. The people of that time will be wolves, its rulers will be predators, its commoners will be gluttons, and its poor will be dead. Truth will collapse and falsehood spread, tongues will profess affection while hearts will conceal malice, adultery will be the source of kinship while chastity will be a thing of wonder, and Islam will be worn as a fur turned inside out.

1.106 From an oration by 'Alī:[5]

1.106.1 Everything bows to him, and everything exists through him. He is the wealth of the poor, the might of the humble, the strength of the weak, and the refuge of the desperate. If someone speaks, he hears, if someone stays silent, he knows their secret, while someone lives, he provides them sustenance, and when someone dies, it is to him they return. God, eyes cannot see you, so they

---

1 Qurʾan, Ghāfir 40:62.
2 Qurʾan, Raʿd 13:38.
3 The "scout" refers to ʿAlī himself.
4 Or, a glass bead.
5 Ibn ʿAbd Rabbih (*ʿIqd*, 4:166–169) says this is ʿAlī's "Luminous Oration" (*Zahrāʾ*), which also includes §1.91 and §1.158.

خلقك لم تخلق الخلق لوحشة ولا ٱستعملتهم لمنفعة ولا يسبقك من طلبت ولا يفلتك من أخذت ولا ينقص سلطانك من عصاك ولا يزيد في ملكك من أطاعك ولا يردّ أمرك من سخط قضاءك ولا يستغني عنك من تولّى عن أمرك كلّ سرّ عندك علانية وكلّ غيب عندك شهادة. أنت الأبد[1] لا أمد لك وأنت المنتهى لا محيص عنك وأنت الموعد لا منجا منك[2] بيدك ناصية كلّ دابّة وإليك مصير كلّ نسمة. سبحانك ما أعظم ما نرى من خلقك وما أصغر عظيمه في جنب قدرتك وما أهول ما نرى من ملكوتك وما أحقر ذلك فيما غاب عنّا من سلطانك وما أسبغ نعمك في الدنيا وما أصغرها في نعم الآخرة.

١.١٠٦.٢ منها

من ملائكة أسكنتهم سمواتك ورفعتهم عن أرضك هم أعلم خلقك بك وأخوفهم لك وأقربهم منك لم يسكنوا الأصلاب ولم يضمّنوا الأرحام ولم يخلقوا من ماء مهين ولم يشعّبهم ريب المنون وإنّهم على مكانهم منك ومنزلتهم عندك وٱستجماع أهوائهم فيك وكثرة طاعتهم لك وقلّة غفلتهم عن أمرك لو عاينوا كنه ما خفي عليهم منك لحقّروا أعمالهم ولَزَرَوا على أنفسهم ولعرفوا أنّهم لم يعبدوك حقّ عبادتك ولم يطيعوك حقّ طاعتك.

١.١٠٦.٣ سبحانك خالقًا ومعبودًا بحسن بلائك عند خلقك خلقت دارًا وجعلت فيها مأدبة مشربًا ومطعمًا وأزواجًا وخدمًا وقصورًا وأنهارًا وزروعًا وثمارًا. ثمّ أرسلت داعيًا يدعو إليها فلا الداعي أجابوا ولا فيما رغّبت فيه رغبوا ولا إلى ما شوّقت إليه ٱشتاقوا أقبلوا على جيفة قد ٱفتضحوا بأكلها وٱصطلحوا على حبّها. ومن عشق شيئًا أعشى بصره وأمرض قلبه فهو ينظر بعين غير صحيحة ويسمع بأذن غير سميعة قد خرقت الشهوات عقله وأماتت الدنيا قلبه وولهت عليها نفسه فهو عبد لها ولمن

---

[1] ش، ن، ي، ه: كذا. م: ⟨الأمد⟩.   [2] ن، ه، م، ش: كذا. ي: كذا. ش: ومصحّحة في م، ش: أضيفت ⟨إلّا إليك⟩.

cannot inform about you. Indeed, you existed before any of your creatures who could describe you. You did not create them because you felt lonely or because they would bring you benefit. Those you pursue cannot outrun you, those you seize cannot escape. Those who disobey you do not lessen your authority, those who obey you do not bolster your kingdom, those who are unhappy with your decree cannot deflect your command, and those who turn away from your command still need you. For you, all secrets are open, all mysteries evident. You are eternal without end, the terminus from where there is nowhere to flee. Yours is the promised meeting from which there is no escape, your hand holds the forelock of every four-footed beast, to you returns every living being. Glory to you! How wondrous the marvels we see of your creation, yet how small its greatness alongside your power! How grand what we see of your kingdom, yet how humble in comparison with what is hidden from us of your might! How perfect your blessings for us in this world, yet how small against the blessings of the hereafter!

1.106.2 From the same oration:
You created angels, whom you lodged in your skies and raised above your earth. Of all your creatures, they know you best, fear you most, and are closest to you. They were never housed inside loins, enveloped in wombs, created from a lowly drop of sperm, or dispersed by fate's calamity. But despite their station near you and their position by your side, despite the absorption of their desires in you, the scale of their obedience for you, and their absence of inattention to your command—if they were to plumb your hidden depths, they would deem their deeds trivial and reprimand themselves. They would know that they have not worshipped you as they ought or obeyed you as you deserve.

1.106.3 Glory to you, revered creator whom we worship! Bestowing a great favor on your creatures, you created a dwelling and placed therein a banquet of food and drink, spouses, servants, palaces, streams, grain, and fruit. Then you sent someone to invite people in—but they did not answer the call, show interest in what you encouraged them to do, or evince passion for what you enthused about. Instead, they fell upon a rotten carcass, and, to their deepest shame, they devoured it and fell in love with it.[1] Love blinds the eye and makes the heart ill—the lover sees with blurry eyes and listens with deaf ears, passions ravage his mind, and the world, his beloved, kills his heart and con-

---

1 The house is paradise (see descriptions of paradise in the Qur'an, e.g., Baqarah 2:25, Āl ʿImrān 3:15, Furqān 25:10), the caller is Muḥammad, and more generally, each prophet, and the carcass is this world (B 434; Ḥ 7:206–207).

في يده شيء منها حيثما زالت زال إليها وحيثما أقبلت أقبل عليها لا ينزجر من الله بزاجر ولا يتّعظ منه بواعظ وهو يرى المأخوذين على الغِرّة حيث لا إقالة ولا رجعة كيف نزل بهم ما كانوا يجهلون وجاءهم من فراق الدنيا ما كانوا يأمنون وقدموا من الآخرة على ما كانوا يوعدون.

فغير موصوف ما نزل بهم اْجتمعت عليهم سكرة الموت وحسرة الفوت ففترت لها أطرافهم وتغيّرت لها ألوانهم. ثمّ اْزداد الموت فيهم ولوجًا فحيل بين أحدهم وبين منطقه وإنّه لبين أهله ينظر ببصره ويسمع بأذنه على صحّة من عقله وبقاء من لبّه يفكّر فِيم َأفنى عمره وفيم أذهب دهره ويتذكّر أموالًا جمعها أغمض في مطالبها وأخذها من مصرّحاتها ومشتبهاتها قد لزمته تبعات جمعها وأشرف على فراقها تبقى لمن وراءه ينعمون فيها ويتمتّعون بها فيكون المَهْنأ لغيره والعِبْء على ظهره. والمرء قد غلقت رهونه بها فهو يعَضُّ يده ندامة على ما أصحر له عند الموت من أمره ويزهد فيما كان يرغب فيه أيّام عمره ويتمنّى أنّ الذي كان يغبطه بها ويحسده عليها قد حازها دونه. فلم يزل الموت يبالغ في جسده حتّى خالط سمعه فصار بين أهله لا ينطق بلسانه ولا يسمع بسمعه يردّد طرفه بالنظر في وجوههم يرى حركات ألسنتهم ولا يسمع[1] رجع كلامهم. ثمّ اْزداد الموت اْلتياطًا به فقبض بصره كما قبض سمعه وخرجت الروح من جسده فصار جيفة بين أهله قد أوحشوا من جانبه وتباعدوا من قربه لا يُسعد باكيًا ولا يجيب داعيًا. ثمّ حملوه إلى مَخَطّ في الأرض فأسلموه فيه إلى عمله وانقطعوا عن زَورته.

1.106.4 حتّى إذا بلغ الكتاب أجله والأمر مقاديره وألحق آخر الخلق بأوّله وجاء من أمر الله ما يريده من تجديد خلقه أماد السماء وفطرها وأرجّ الأرض وأرجفها وقلع جبالها ونسفها ودكّ بعضها بعضًا من هيبة جلالته ومخوف سطوته وأخرج من فيها فجدّدهم بعد إخلاقهم وجمعهم بعد تفريقهم ثمّ ميّزهم لما يريد من مُسائلتهم عن الأعمال

---

[1] ش، ن، ي، هـ، ومصحّحة في م: كذا. أصل م، ونسخة في ش: ⟨يستطيع⟩.

sumes his soul. He thus becomes a slave to the world and to all who possess any-thing of her, wherever she goes he follows, and wherever she turns he turns. He pays no heed to God's warning and takes no counsel from God's lessons. All the while, he sees the heedless abruptly taken from her to a place from which there is no return, and he sees the terror they had denied descend upon them. He sees them leave the world in which they had taken comfort, and move to the afterlife as they had been warned.

The horror that descends upon the dying person is beyond words. As the anguished convulsions of death and the remorseful pangs of loss together bear down upon him, his extremities begin to lose feeling, and his color changes. Then, death penetrates further and prevents him from speech. He lies among his family, seeing them with his eyes, hearing them with his ears, still able to discern, still able to understand. He can think only about his wasted life and squandered time. He remembers the wealth he has amassed, both licit and illicit, from honest and dubious sources. The sins he has gathered now weigh him down, now, when he is about to leave everything behind. The people who survive him will enjoy his wealth. Its gratification will belong to another, while the burden will weigh down his back. His debt has come due for payment. He bites on his knuckles, regretting the misdeeds that are now clear to him, caring little for the things he craved all the days of his life. He wishes that the person who envied him his wealth and coveted his property had taken it all! Mean-while, death continues to penetrate his body and it pierces his hearing. Now he lies among his family, his tongue unable to speak, his ears unable to hear. His eyes go from face to face, he sees their tongues moving but cannot hear their words. Then death tightens its grip. His sight is taken away, just as his hearing had been earlier, and his soul leaves his body. He becomes a corpse lying amid his family, and they recoil from him in fear and back away—he cannot console those who weep or answer those who call out. Then they carry him to a grave marked with lines in the earth. They give him over to his deeds and cease to visit.

1.106.4 Until destiny reaches its term and the affair approaches its ordained hour, when the last of creation has caught up with the first and God's command arrives to renew his creation, he shakes the sky and splits it, convulses the earth and agitates it, plucks out each mountain and uproots it, and, terrified by his majesty and cowed by his power, each crushes the other. He extracts all who are on earth, renewing them after their decay, gathering them after their sepa-ration. Then he stands them, each in his place, to be interrogated about deeds and secret acts. He divides them into two groups, blessing the one and punish-ing the other. He rewards the obedient with nearness to his divine self and with

وخبايا الأفعال وجعلهم فريقين أنعم على هؤلاء وٱنتقم من أولاء١ فأمّا أهل الطاعة
فأثابهم بجواره وخلّدهم في داره حيث لا يظعن النُّزّال ولا يتغيّر بهم الحال ولا تنوبهم
الأفزاع ولا تنالهم الأسقام ولا تعرض لهم الأخطار ولا تشخصهم الأسفار وأمّا أهل
المعصية فأنزلهم شرّ دار وغَلَّ الأيدي إلى الأعناق وقرن النواصي بالأقدام وألبسهم
سرابيل القَطِران ومقطّعات النيران في عذاب قد ٱشتدّ حرّه وباب قد أُطبق على أهله
في نارها كَلَب ولَجَب ولَهَب ساطع وقصيف هائل لا يظعن مقيمها ولا يفادى أسيرها
ولا تقصم٢ كُبولها لا مدّة للدار فتفنى ولا أجل للقوم فيُقضى.

١.١٠٦.٥　منها في ذكر النبيّ صلّى الله عليه وآله

قد حقّر الدنيا وصغّرها وأهون بها وهوّنها وعلم أنّ الله زواها عنه ٱختيارًا وبسطها لغيره
ٱحتقارًا فأعرض عن الدنيا بقلبه وأمات ذكرها من نفسه وأحبّ أن تغيب زينتها عن
عينه لكيلا يتّخذ منها رياشًا أو يرجو فيها مقامًا. بلّغ عن ربّه معذرًا ونصح لأمّته منذرًا
ودعا إلى الجنّة مبشّرًا.

نحن شجرة النبوّة ومحطّ الرسالة ومختلَف الملائكة ومعادن العلم وينابيع الحِكَم. ناصرنا
ومحبّنا ينتظر الرحمة وعدوّنا ومبغضنا ينتظر السطوة.

١.١٠٧　ومن خطبة له عليه السلام

إنّ أفضل ما توسّل به المتوسّلون إلى الله سبحانه الإيمان به وبرسوله والجهاد في سبيله
فإنّه ذروة الإسلام وكلمة الإخلاص فإنّها الفطرة وإقام الصلاة فإنّها الملّة وإيتاء الزكاة
فإنّها فريضة واجبة وصوم شهر رمضان فإنّه جنّة من العقاب وحجّ البيت وٱعتماره

١ش، ن، ه، ونسخة في ي: كذا. م، ي، ونسخة في ه: ﴿هؤلاء﴾.　٢ش، ن: كذا. م، ي: ﴿يفصم﴾.

eternal life in his abode, which its inhabitants never leave, where their condition never changes, misfortunes never befall, illness never takes hold, dangers never approach, and journeys never displace. He locks up the disobedient in the abode of horrors. He shackles their hands to their necks, binds their forelocks to their feet, clothes them in garments of pitch, and dresses them in robes of fire. He throws them into the chamber of torture, whose heat endlessly sears, whose door remains bolted, and whose blaze rages with rabid hunger, clamorous tumult, sheets of flame, and terrifying thunder. Its resident never leaves, its captive is never ransomed, its shackles are never broken. This abode has no limit, so it never ceases to be. Its people have no lifespan, so the terror never ends.

1.106.5 From the same oration in praise of the Prophet:
He viewed the world with contempt, demeaned it, disparaged it, and deemed it lowly. He recognized that God had deliberately turned the world away from him while allowing it ungrudgingly to many, so he turned his heart away from it and drove all thoughts of it from his mind. He preferred that its ornaments be absent from his eyes, so he would not be tempted to don its splendid garments or long for it to be his permanent residence. He conveyed his Lord's message and proved his claim, instructed his community and gave them warning, and called them to paradise with glad tidings of its bliss.

We are the tree of prophecy, the station of God's message, and the place where angels alight. We are mines of knowledge and springs of wisdom. Whoever supports and loves us should expect God's mercy. Whoever bears us enmity or malice should expect God's assault.

1.107 From an oration by ʿAlī:[1]
The deeds that bring you closest to God are the following: belief in him and his messenger; jihad in his path, for it is Islam's summit; the testament of sincerity—⟨There is no god but God⟩—for it is the natural state; performing the ritual prayer, for it is the way of truth; offering the alms levy, for it is a man-

---

1   Excerpt from one of ʿAlī's famous sermons, named in several sources as "The Brocade (*Dībāj*)
Oration" that begins with the line, "Praise to God, creator of the world" (الحمد لله فاطر الخلق),
of which another part is §1.83.4 (Ḥarrānī, *Tuḥaf*, 149–150). The first paragraph is attributed
to the Prophet Muḥammad in Yaʿqūbī, *Tārīkh*, 2:96–97. "The testament of sincerity" (*kalimat
al-ikhlāṣ*) is ⟨There is no god but God⟩ (*Lā ilāha illā Allāh*), the central creed of Islam, which
I have added in the translation for clarity. The "natural state" (*fiṭrah*) is to believe in God,
according to the prophetic hadith stating that each human child at the time of birth is Muslim.

فإنّهما ينفيان الفقر ويرحضان الذنب وصلة الرحم فإنّها مَثْراة في المال ومنساة في الأجل وصدقة السرّ فإنّها تكفّر الخطيئة وصدقة العلانية فإنّها تدفع ميتة السوء وصنائع المعروف فإنّها تقي مصارع الهوان.

أفيضوا في ذكر الله فإنّه أحسن الذكر وأرغبوا فيما وعد المتّقين فإنّ وعده أصدق الوعد واقتدوا بهدي نبيّكم فإنّه أفضل الهدي واستنّوا بسنّته فإنّها أهدى السنن وتعلّموا القرآن فإنّه ربيع القلوب واستشفوا بنوره فإنّه شفاء الصدور وأحسنوا تلاوته فإنّه أنفع القصص. وإنّ العالم العامل بغير علمه كالجاهل الحائر الذي لا يستفيق من جهله بل الحجّة عليه أعظم والحسرة له ألزم وهو عند الله أَلْوَم.

1.108   ومن خطبة له عليه السلام

1.108.1   أمّا بعد. فإنّي أحذّركم الدنيا فإنّها حلوة خضرة حُفّت بالشهوات وتحبّبت بالعاجلة وراقت بالقليل وتحلّت بالآمال وتزيّنت بالغرور لا تدوم حَبرتها ولا تؤمن فجعتها غرّارة ضرّارة حائلة زائلة نافدة بائدة أكّالة غوّالة لا تعدو إذا تناهت إلى أمنيّة أهل الرغبة فيها والرضى بها أن تكون كما قال الله سبحانه ﴿كَمَاءٍ أَنزَلْنَاهُ مِنَ ٱلسَّمَاءِ فَٱخْتَلَطَ بِهِ نَبَاتُ ٱلْأَرْضِ فَأَصْبَحَ هَشِيماً تَذْرُوهُ ٱلرِّيَاحُ وَكَانَ ٱللَّهُ عَلَىٰ كُلِّ شَيْءٍ مُّقْتَدِراً﴾. لم يكن امرؤ منها في حبرة إلّا أعقبته بعدها عبرة ولم يَلْقَ من سرّائها بطناً إلّا منحته من ضرّائها ظهراً ولم تطلّه فيها ديمة رخاء إلّا هتنت عليه مزنة بلاء وحريّ إذا أصبحت له منتصرة أن تمسي له متنكّرة وإن جانب منها أعذوذب وأحلولى أمرّ منها جانب فأوبى لا ينال امرؤ من غضارتها رَغَباً إلّا أرهقته من نوائبها تعباً ولا يمسي منها في جناح أمن إلّا أصبح على قوادم خوف. غرّارة غرور ما فيها فانية فانٍ من عليها لا خير في شيء من أزوادها إلّا التقوى من أقلّ منها استكثر ممّا يؤمنه ومن استكثر منها استكثر ممّا يوبقه وزال عمّا قليل عنه كم من واثق بها فجعته وذي طمأنينة إليها

dated obligation; fasting in the month of Ramadan, for it is a shield from God's punishment; performing the hajj and the ʿumrah pilgrimage to Mecca, for they dispel poverty and wash away sins; fostering close ties with kin, for it increases wealth and prolongs life; giving alms in secret, for it expiates transgressions; disbursing alms in public, for it wards off horrible forms of death; and acts of charity, for they protect you from dishonor and shame.

Fill yourself with God's remembrance for it is the best remembrance. Wish for everything he promised the pious, for his promise is the truest of promises. Follow the guidance of your Prophet, for it is the best guidance. Follow his Sunnah, for it is the most righteous of practices. Learn the Qurʾan, for it is the heart's springtime. Heal yourselves by its light, for it is a cure for souls. And recite it beautifully, for it is the most beneficial exhortation. A learned man who acts contrary to his learning is as bad as the ignorant and perplexed man who never wakes from his stupor. In fact, the case against him is stronger, his anguish more binding, and his culpability greater before God.

1.108 From an oration by ʿAlī:[1]

1.108.1 I warn you against this world, for it is sweet and lush and surrounded by temptations. It breeds love for the here and now and excites wonder with its trifles, it is adorned with false hopes and embellished with deceptions, its joy does not last and its trauma is relentless. A ghoulish devourer, it deceives, harms, changes, ceases, wanes, perishes, and consumes. At the very moment that it fulfills your dearest hopes, it becomes—as God Most High has said—«like water that we sent down from the sky: the earth's vegetation drew from it, then became dry straw, and was scattered by the winds. God has power over all things.»[2] The world never gives a man joy without following it with tears, it never bestows happiness without following it with harm, it never sprinkles soft ease without following it with a cloudburst of calamity. If it braces him in the morning it rejects him in the evening, if one of its aspects is sweet and sugary the other is bitter and pestilential, if it bestows fresh bounties it oppresses later with oppressive misfortunes; a man does not pass the night sheltered under its wing without waking up under its pinion of fear. The world deceives and all in it is deception. The world will perish and all upon it will perish. There is no good in any of its provisions save piety. Those who take little from the world gather stores of protection, while those who amass its wares hoard that which will destroy, whose benefit will soon cease.

---

1 On the pulpit in Basra, immediately after the Battle of the Camel in 36/356. Kulaynī, *Kāfī*, 8:256.

2 Qurʾan, Kahf 18:45.

قد صرعته وذي أُبَّهَة قد جعلته حقيرًا وذي نَخوة قد ردّته ذليلًا سلطانها دُوَل وعيشها رَنِق وعذبها أجاج وحلوها صَبِر وغذاؤها سِمام وأسبابها رِمام حيّها بعَرَض موت وصحيحها بعرض سقم ملكها مسلوب وعزيزها مغلوب وموفورها منكوب وجارها محروب.

١٠٨.٢.١ ألستم في مساكن من كان قبلكم أطول أعمارًا وأبقى آثارًا وأبعد آمالًا وأعدّ عديدًا وأكثف جنودًا تعبّدوا للدنيا أيَّ تعبّد وآثروها أيَّ إيثار ثمّ ظعنوا عنها بغير زاد مبلّغ ولا ظهر قاطع. فهل بلغكم أنّ الدنيا سخت لهم نفسًا بفدية أو أعانتهم بمعونة أو أحسنت لهم صحبة بل أرهقتهم بالفوادح وأوهنتهم بالقوارع وضعضعتهم بالنوائب وعفّرتهم للمناخر ووطئتهم بالمناسم وأعانت عليهم ريب المنون. فقد رأيتم تنكّرها لمن دان لها وآثرها وأخلد إليها حتّى ظعنوا عنها لفراق الأبد هل زوّدتهم إلّا السَغَب أو أحلّتهم إلّا الضَّنْك أو نوّرت لهم إلّا الظلمة أو أعقبتهم إلّا الندامة أفهذه تؤثرون أم إليها تطمئنّون أم عليها تحرصون فبئست الدار لمن لم يتّهمها ولم يكن فيها على وجل منها.

١٠٨.٣.١ فاعلموا وأنتم تعلمون بأنّكم تاركوها وظاعنون عنها واتّعظوا فيها بالذين ﴿قَالُوٱ مَنْ أَشَدُّ مِنَّا قُوَّةً﴾ حُملوا إلى قبورهم فلا يُدعَون ركبانًا وأُنزلوا فلا يدعون ضِيفانًا وجعل لهم من الصفيح أجنان ومن التراب أكفان ومن الرُّفات جيران فهم جِيرة لا يجيبون داعيًا ولا يمنعون ضَيمًا ولا يبالون مَنْدَبة إن جيدوا لم يفرحوا وإن قُحطوا لم يقنطوا جميع وهم آحاد وجِيرة وهم أبعاد متدانُون لا يتزاورون وقريبون لا يتقاربون حلماء قد ذهبت أضغانهم وجهلاء قد ماتت أحقادهم لا يُخشى فَجْعهم ولا يرجى دفعهم

The world strikes those who trust it and fells those who place in it their faith. How many grandees has it humbled! How many arrogant men has it debased! Its power goes around in turns, its life is turbid, its water is brackish, its sweets are filled with bitter juice, its nourishment is poison, its ropes are decayed, its living are targets for death, its healthy are targets for illness, its kingdom will be pillaged, its mighty will be vanquished, its wealthy will be afflicted, and its neighbors will be plundered.

1.108.2 Do you not dwell in the abodes of those who came before you and enjoyed longer lives, who left behind more lasting monuments, had lengthier aspirations, were more profuse in number, and led vaster armies? They worshipped the world abjectly, they gave it preference, fully and truly, but they left it without sufficient provisions for the journey, or even a mount to carry them on its back. Have you ever heard that the world in its generosity let a single soul escape in lieu of ransom, or that it gave them any form of help, or offered to accompany them? No. It crushed them with catastrophes, weakened them with calamities, shook them with misfortunes, ground their noses in the dust, trampled them under its hooves, and equipped fate to bring them down. You have seen how it rejected those who bowed before it, gave it preference, and offered it loyalty. Their departure is an eternal separation. Did the world supply them with anything other than thirst, house them in anything other than narrow graves, give them anything other than dark gloom, or requite them with anything other than regret? Is this the same world that you too favor above all else, put your faith in, covet? What a wretched abode for those who do not view it with suspicion, who are not on their guard!

1.108.3 Know this—and you do—that you too will leave the world, you too will depart. Take lessons from the fate of those who «said: is anyone mightier than we are?»[1] They have been carried to their graves but cannot be called wayfarers, they have been laid there to rest but cannot be called guests, they have been covered in dirt and shrouded by earth. Decaying bones are their neighbors—neighbors who cannot answer those who call out to them, offer protection from attackers, or care about their mourners' wails. If they get rain they do not rejoice, if they encounter drought they do not despair. They are together yet each is alone, neighbors yet so far distant from one another, so close yet they do not visit, so near yet they cannot meet, senior commanders whose hostilities are a thing of the past, rash youths whose hate and rancor

---

1   Qurʾan, Fuṣṣilat 41:15.

آستبدلوا بظهر الأرض بطنًا وبالسعة ضيقًا وبالأهل غربة وبالنور ظلمة بجاءوها كما
فارقوها حفاة عراة قد ظعنوا عنها بأعمالهم إلى الحياة الدائمة والدار الباقية كما قال سبحانه
﴿كَمَا بَدَأْنَا أَوَّلَ خَلْقٍ نُعِيدُهُ وَعْداً عَلَيْنَا إِنَّا كُنَّا فَاعِلِينَ﴾ .

١٠٩.١ ومن خطبة له عليه السلام ذكر فيها ملك الموت وتوفّيه الأنفس

هل تحسّ به إذا دخل منزلًا أم هل تراه إذا توفّى أحدًا بل كيف يتوفّى الجنين في بطن
أمّه أيلج عليه من بعض جوارحها أم الروح أجابته بإذن ربّها أم هو ساكن معه في
أحشائها. كيف يصف إلهَه من يعجز عن صفة مخلوق مثله.

١١٠.١ ومن خطبة له عليه السلام

وأحذّركم الدنيا فإنّها منزل قُلعة وليست بدار نُجعة قد تزيّنت بغرورها وغرّت بزينتها
دار هانت على ربّها فخلط حلالها بحرامها وخيرها بشرّها وحياتها بموتها وحلوها بمرّها.
لم يُصَفِّها الله لأوليائه ولم يضنّ بها على أعدائه خيرها زهيد وشرّها عتيد وجمعها ينفد
وملكها يسلب وعامرها يخرب فما خير دار تنقض نقض البناء وعمر يفنى فناء الزاد
ومدّة تنقطع انقطاع السير. اجعلوا ما افترض الله عليكم من طلبتكم واسألوه من أداء
حقّه ما سألكم وأسمعوا دعوة الموت آذانكم قبل أن يدعى بكم. إنّ الزاهدين في الدنيا
تبكي قلوبهم وإن ضحكوا ويشتدّ حزنهم وإن فرحوا ويكثر مقتهم أنفسهم وإن اغتبطوا بما
رزقوا قد غاب عن قلوبكم ذكر الآجال وحضرتكم كواذب الآمال فصارت الدنيا أملك
بكم من الآخرة والعاجلة أذهب بكم من الآجلة. وإنّما أنتم إخوان على دين الله ما فرّق

have been swept away, their blows no longer feared, their protection no longer sought. They surrendered the back of the earth for its belly, a vast space for narrow straits, family for exile, and light for darkness. They left the world as they had come, barefoot and naked, departing with their deeds to eternal life and the everlasting abode. For, as God says, «as I brought the first creation into being, so I shall bring it forth anew—this is my pledge, and I shall bring it to pass.»[1]

1.109 From an oration by ʿAlī in which he spoke of the Angel of Death and the manner in which he takes souls:[2]

Do you sense his presence when he enters a home, or see him when he takes someone away? In fact, do you know how he takes the life of a fetus from inside its mother's womb? Does he enter through one of her limbs, or does its spirit answer the angel with God's permission, or is he residing with it already inside the mother? How can we who are incapable of describing a creature like us aspire to describe our creator?

1.110 From an oration by ʿAlī:

I warn you of this world: it is a home from which you will be uprooted, not an abode where you own the right to pasture, a dwelling adorned in deception, deceiving with its adornments. It is worth nothing in the eyes of its Lord, which is why he has intertwined the lawful in it with the unlawful, the good with the bad, life with death, and sweet with bitter. God has not made the world pure for his friends to enjoy, nor begrudged it to his enemies, for its good is meager, its evil ever present, its goods are temporary, its realm awaits pillage, and its habitations anticipate ruin. What good is a house that will crumble as a timeworn edifice, a life that will be exhausted like provisions, and a timespan that will be completed like a journey? When you supplicate God, include a prayer for his help in undertaking his mandates and ask him to aid you in giving him his due. Bend your ears to death's summons before your name is called. True renunciants live thus: their hearts weep even when they laugh, their grief is intense even when they are joyful, and their self-condemnation is great even though they are delighted with what they have been given. But your hearts have lost awareness of your imminent end and are filled with false hopes; the world controls you to the detriment of the hereafter; the here-and-now has distanced you from the afterlife. You are brethren in God's religion, but foul intentions and evil

---

1 Qurʾan, Anbiyāʾ 21:104.
2 Excerpt from a long oration on God's unity (*tawḥīd*). B 448.

بينكم إلّا خبث السرائر وسوء الضمائر فلا توازرون ولا تناصحون ولا تباذلون ولا
توادّون ما لكم! تفرحون باليسير من الدنيا تدركونه ولا يحزنكم الكثير من الآخرة
تُحرَمونه ويقلقكم اليسير من الدنيا يفوتكم حتّى يتبيّن ذلك في وجوهكم وقلّة صبركم عمّا
زوي منها عنكم كأنّها دار مقامكم وكأنّ متاعها باقٍ عليكم. وما يمنع أحدكم أن يستقبل
أخاه بما يخاف من عيبه إلّا مخافة أن يستقبله بمثله قد تصافيتم على رفض الآجل وحبّ
العاجل وصار دين أحدكم لُعْقَة على لسانه صنيع من قد فرغ من عمله وأحرز رضى سيّده.

1.111 ومن خطبة له عليه السلام

1.111.1 الحمد لله الواصل الحمد بالنعم والنعم بالشكر. نحمده على آلائه كما نحمده على بلائه.
ونستعينه على هذه النفوس البِطاء عمّا أمرت به السراع إلى ما نهيت عنه. ونستغفره ممّا
أحاط به علمه وأحصاه كتابه علم غير قاصر وكتاب غير مغادر. ونؤمن به إيمان من عاين
الغيوب ووقف على الموعود إيمانًا نفى إخلاصه الشرك ويقينه الشكّ. ونشهد أن لا إله
إلّا الله وحده لا شريك له وأنّ محمّدًا عبده ورسوله شهادتين تصعدان القول وترفعان
العمل لا يخفّ ميزان توضعان فيه ولا يثقل ميزان ترفعان عنه.

1.111.2 أوصيكم عباد الله بتقوى الله التي هي الزاد وبها المعاد زاد مبلّغ ومعاد منجح
دعا إليها أسمعُ داعٍ ووعاها خير واعٍ فأسمع داعيها وفاز واعيها. عباد الله إنّ تقوى الله
حمت أولياء الله محارمه وألزمت قلوبهم مخافته حتّى أسهرت لياليهم وأظمأت هواجرهم

اش، ن، ه: كذا. م: ﴿ما بالكم﴾.

purposes have divided you—you have stopped supporting one another, counseling one another, giving to one another, or bearing one another affection. Why are you so overjoyed when you win the world's baubles, yet not grieved when deprived of the hereafter's bounty? How are you so exasperated by the loss of these trifles that your anger, your frustration, is plain on your face? You act as though you will always live here, as though this wealth will always remain yours! The only thing that stops you from confronting your brother or disclosing his failings is your fear that he will do the same. You have both rejected the afterlife and devoted yourselves to the present. Religion to you has become a dollop for your tongue to lick up, as though you had already completed your work and satisfied your master.

1.111 From an oration by ʿAlī:[1]

1.111.1 Praise God who has linked praise with favors and favors with thanks. We praise him for his blessings, as we praise him for his trials. We ask him to rally our hearts, which are slow to undertake his command and quick to rush into what he has forbidden. We ask his forgiveness for everything we have done that his knowledge encompasses and his inventory includes—that knowledge never falls short, and that inventory never omits. We believe in him, as though we have already seen the deep mysteries and attained the promised reward—our sincerity refuses to assign partners to him, and our certainty rejects all doubt. We bear witness that there is no god but God, he has no partner, and Muḥammad is his servant and messenger, a testimony that assures our prayers' and our deeds' ascent to God—no scale on which it is placed is light, no scale from which it is absent has weight.

1.111.2 Servants of God, I counsel you to be conscious of him, to be pious. Piety is the best provision for the journey and the best means of return, for it is the provision that will get you to your destination and the return it promises is assured. A perfect caller has called toward it and a perfect listener has taken it to heart—that caller was effective, and that listener will win entry to paradise. Servants of God, his consciousness has protected his chosen ones from trans-

---

1   Ṭūsī (*Amālī*, 443) prefaces § 1.111.2 by saying, "The Commander of the Faithful would say," indicating that the theme and words were frequent in ʿAlī's oration; Naḥḥās (*ʿUmdah*, 1:353) cites it in an oration attributed to Zayd ibn ʿAlī.

فأخذوا الراحة بالنصب والرِّيّ بالظمأ واستقربوا الأجل فبادروا العمل وكذّبوا الأمل فلا حظوا الأجل. ثمّ إنّ الدنيا دار فناء وعناء وغِيَر وعبر فمن الفناء أنّ الدهر مُوتِر قوسه لا تخطئ سهامه ولا توسى جراحه يرمي الحيّ بالموت والصحيح بالسقم والناجي بالعطب آكل لا يشبع وشارب لا ينقع ومن العناء أنّ المرء يجمع ما لا يأكل و يبني ما لا يسكن ثمّ يخرج إلى الله لا مالًا حمل ولا بناء نقل ومن غيرها أنّك ترى المرحوم مغبوطًا والمغبوط مرحومًا ليس ذلك إلّا نعيمًا زلّ وبؤسًا نزل ومن عبرها أنّ المرء يشرف على أمله فيقطعه حضور أجله فلا أمل يُدرَك ولا مؤمّل يترك. فسبحان الله ما أغرّ سرورها وأظمأ ريّها وأضحى فَيْئَها لا جاءٍ يردّ ولا ماضٍ يرتدّ. فسبحان الله ما أقرب الحيّ من الميّت للحاقه به وأبعد الميّت من الحيّ لأنقطاعه عنه.

١.١١١.٣   إنّه ليس شيء بشرّ من الشرّ إلّا عقابه وليس شيء بخير من الخير إلّا ثوابه. وكلّ شيء من الدنيا سماعه أعظم من عيانه وكلّ شيء من الآخرة عيانه أعظم من سماعه فليكفكم من العيان السماع ومن الغيب الخبر. واعلموا أنّ ما نقص من الدنيا وزاد في الآخرة خير ممّا نقص من الآخرة وزاد في الدنيا فكم من منقوص رابح ومزيد خاسر إنّ الذي أمرتم به أوسع من الذي نهيتم عنه وما أحلّ لكم أكثر ممّا حرّم عليكم فذَروا ما قلّ لما كثر وما ضاق لما اتّسع. قد تُكُفِّل لكم بالرزق وأمرتم بالعمل فلا يكونَنّ المضمون لكم طلبه أولى بكم من المفروض عليكم عمله مع أنّه والله لقد اعترض الشكّ ودُخِل اليقين حتّى كأنّ الذي ضمن لكم قد فرض عليكم وكأنّ الذي فرض عليكم قد وضع عنكم. فبادروا العمل وخافوا بغتة الأجل فإنّه لا يرجى من رجعة العمر ما يرجى من

gressing, and infused their hearts with fear, it has made their nights wakeful and filled their days with thirst, so that they find comfort in toil and satiety in thirst. Aware of approaching death, they hasten to do good. Denying false hopes, they keep death in front of their eyes. Next, know that the world is a place of perishing, weariness, vicissitudes, and instruction. Perishing is this: fate stands stretching his bow, his arrows do not miss, their wounds do not heal; he strikes the living with death, the healthy with illness, and the one who flees with destruction; an eater whose appetite is never satiated, a drinker whose thirst is never quenched. Weariness is this: a man gathers food he will not eat and builds edifices he will not inhabit; he leaves the world and returns to God with no property to carry, no edifice to transport. Vicissitudes are these: you see the pitied become the object of envy, and the envied become the object of pity, simply because of a blessing that has disappeared or a misfortune that has arrived. Lessons are these: a man is about to see his aspirations fulfilled when they are severed by the ending of his life; no aspiration is attained, no aspirer is left alive. Praise God! How deceptive are the world's pleasures! How parching its drink! How scorching its shade! No one who arrives is turned back, while no one who leaves can return. Praise God! How close are the living to the dead, for they will soon be with them, but how far the dead from the living, for they have been cut off from them forever!

1.111.3 There is nothing worse than evil except its punishment, and nothing better than good except its reward. Everything in the world that you hear about is greater than what you see, while everything in the hereafter that you will see is greater than what you hear. Hearing should suffice you, there is no need to see. Reports should suffice you, even without direct witness. Know that a thing that decreases your share of the world but increases your share of the hereafter is better than a thing that decreases your share of the hereafter while increasing your share of the world. Many a person with a decreased share of the world earns good profit, while many a person with an increased share of the world loses everything. What you are commanded to do is more capacious than what you are prohibited from, and the things that are lawful for you are more numerous than the things that are unlawful, so abandon the little for the large, the narrow for the wide. God has guaranteed your sustenance and commanded you to do good, so let not the thing that is guaranteed deserve more effort from you than what is mandated upon you. But, by God, doubt has appeared in your midst, your conviction has become tainted; you act as though seeking the sustenance guaranteed for you is a mandatory act of worship, while the worship that is actually mandated is no longer required! Hasten to do good and fear the sudden arrival of death. There is no hope for return of life, while there is always

رجعة الرزق ما فات اليوم من الرزق رُجي غدًا زيادته وما فات أمس من العمر لم يُرجَ اليوم رجعته الرجاء مع الجائي واليأس مع الماضي فـ﴿اتَّقوا اللهَ حَقَّ تُقاتِهِ وَلا تَمُوتُنَّ إلّا وأنتم مُسْلِمُونَ﴾.

^{1.112} ومن خطبة له عيه السلام في الاستسقاء

اللّهمّ قد انصاحت جبالنا واغبرّت أرضنا وهامت دوابّنا وتحيّرت في مرابضها وعجّت عجيج الثَّكالى على أولادها وملّت التردّد في مراتعها والحنين إلى مواردها.[1] اللّهمّ فارحم حيرتها في مذاهبها وأنينها في موالجها. اللّهمّ خرجنا إليك حين اعتكرت علينا حدابير السنين وأخلفتنا مخايل الجَوْد فكنت الرجاء للمبتئس والبلاغ للملتمس ندعوك حين قنط الأنام ومنع الغمام وهلك السوام أن لا تؤاخذنا بأعمالنا ولا تأخذنا بذنوبنا وانشر علينا رحمتك بالسحاب المنبعق والربيع المغدق والنبات المونق سحًّا وابلًا تحيي به ما قد مات وتردّ به ما قد فات. اللّهمّ سُقْيَا منك محيية تامّة عامّة طيّبة مباركة هنيئة مريعة[2] زاكيًا نبتُها ثامرًا فرعها ناضرًا ورقها[3] تنعش بها الضعيف من عبادك وتحيي بها الميّت من بلادك. اللّهمّ سُقْيَا منك تعشب بها نجادُنا وتَجري بها وِهادنا ويخصب بها جنابنا وتزكو[4] بها ثمارنا وتعيش بها مواشينا وتندى بها أقاصينا وتستعين بها ضواحينا من بركاتك الواسعة وعطاياك الجزيلة على بريّتك المُرملة ووحشك المُهمَلة. وأنزل علينا سماء مُخضَلّة مِدْرارًا هاطلة يدافع الوَدْقُ منها الودق ويحفز القطر منها القطر غير خُلَّب برقها ولا جَهام عارضها ولا قَزَع رَبابها ولا شَفّان ذِهابها حتّى يخصب لإمراعها المجدبون ويحيى ببركتها المُسنِتون فإنّك تنزل الغيث من بعد ما قنطوا وتنشر رحمتك وأنت الوليّ الحميد.

---

[1] ن، م، ش: كذا. ي، ه، وفي هامش م، ش: أضيفت ﴿اللّهمّ فارحم أنين الآنّة وحنين الحانّة﴾. [2] م، ن، ش، ه: كذا. ي: أضيفت قبلها ﴿مريئة﴾. نسخة في ش، ه: ﴿مريئة﴾. [3] م، ن، ش، ومصحّحة في ه: كذا. ي، وأصل ه: أضيفت ﴿غامرًا أرزاقها﴾. [4] ش، ه، وأضيفت في ن: كذا. م، ي، ونسخة في ش، ه: ﴿وتقبِل﴾. أصل ن: ﴿تعشب بها مواشينا﴾ حيث سقطت ﴿نجادنا ... وتعيش بها﴾.

hope for return of sustenance; what is lost today of your sustenance may come back increased tomorrow, but what was lost yesterday of your time will never, ever return. Hope lies in the future, despair inhabits the past, so «be conscious of God as you should, and make sure you die submitting to him.»[1]

1.112   From an oration by ʿAlī beseeching God for rain:

God, our mountains are parched, and our plains have filled with dust. Our sheep have gone mad with thirst and stand dazed in their pens.[2] They moan like bereaved mothers, too exhausted to look for pasture or search out waterholes. God, have mercy on their panic when they head out, and their sad cries when they return! God, we have come to you in this open space because lean years of drought, like emaciated camels, have hemmed us in, and clouds that promised rain approached but turned away. You alone are the sufferer's hope and the petitioner's provider. We call out to you in this time when people have lost heart, when rainclouds have withheld their bounty, and grazing animals have perished. Do not hold us hostage to our deeds or punish us for our sins. Unfold your mercy for us with torrential clouds, abundant herbage, and wondrous vegetation. Send us rain in a heavy downpour that revives what had died and restores what was lost. God, we beseech you for water that is reviving, quenching, perfect, universal, fragrant, blessed, wholesome, and fertile. Let it bring forth plants that flourish, trees full of fruit, and leaves fresh and green. Let it revive your weak servants and renew your barren lands. God, we beseech you for water that makes our highlands verdant, our lowlands lush, our countryside fertile, our fruits grow, and our sheep thrive. Let it irrigate our farthest lands and soak our nearby areas. Shower your vast grace and rich blessings on us, your destitute human creatures, and your forsaken beasts. Send us a soaking, gushing, drenching sky in which one deluge drives away another and raindrops jostle for space—a sky whose lightning does not deceive, whose clouds do not disappoint, whose puffs do not dissipate, and whose drizzle does not usher in cold, barren winds. Let its fertility irrigate the lands struck by famine, let its felicity revive the people hit by drought. You are the one who sends rain after all hope is gone, you are the one who pours down your mercy, you are the protector, the one worthy of all praise![3]

---

1   Qurʾan, Āl ʿImrān 3:102.

2   Ar. *dawābbunā*, lit. livestock, or pack animals. The use of the term *marābiḍ*, which are pens for sheep, rather than *mawāṭin*, which are pens for camels (Ḥ 7:264), appears to specify sheep.

3   The last two lines are modified from Qurʾan, Shūrā 42:28.

تفسير ما في هذه الخطبة من الغريب قوله عليه السلام ﴿أنصاحت جبالنا﴾ أي تشقّقت من المحول. يقال ﴿أنصاح الثوب﴾ إذا أنشقّ ويقال أيضًا ﴿أنصاح النبت﴾ وصاح وصوّح إذ جفّ ويبس. وقوله ﴿هامت دوابّنا﴾ أي عطشت والهُيام العطش. وقوله ﴿حدابير السنين﴾ جمع حِدْبار وهي الناقة التي أنضاها السير فشبّه بها السنة التي فشا فيها الجدب. قال ذو الرمّة١

حَدَابِيرُ مَا تَنْفَكُّ إِلَّا مُنَاخَةً   عَلَى الْخَسْفِ أَوْ نَرْمِي بِهَا بَلَدًا قَفْرَا

وقوله ﴿ولا قزع ربابها﴾ القزع القِطَع الصغار المتفرّقة من السحاب. وقوله ﴿ولا شفّان ذهابها﴾ فإنّ تقديره ﴿ولا ذات شفّان ذهابها﴾. والشَّفّان الريح الباردة والذِّهاب الأمطار اللّينة فحذف ذات لعلم السامع به.

١١٣.١ ومن خطبة له عليه السلام

١١٣.١.١ أرسله داعيًا إلى الحقّ وشاهدًا على الخلق فبلّغ رسالات ربّه غير وانٍ ولا مقصّر وجاهد في الله أعداءه غير واهن ولا معذّر إمام من أتّقى وبصر من اهتدى.

١١٣.١.٢ ولو تعلمون ما أعلم ممّا طُوي عنكم غيبه إذًا لخرجتم إلى الصُّعُدات تبكون على أعمالكم وتلتدمون على أنفسكم ولتركتم أموالكم لا حارس لها ولا خالف عليها ولهمّت كلّ امرئ منكم نفسه لا يلتفت إلى غيرها ولكنّكم نسيتم ما ذُكّرتم وأمنتم ما حُذّرتم فتاهَ عنكم رأيكم وتشتّت عليكم أمركم. لوددت أنّ الله فرّق بيني وبينكم وألحقني بمن هو أحقّ بي منكم قوم والله ميامين الرأي مراجيح الحلم مقاويل بالحقّ متاريكُ للبغي مضوا قُدُمًا على الطريقة وأوجفوا على المحجّة فظفروا بالعقبى الدائمة والكرامة

―――――
١ البحر: الطويل.

Raḍī: An explanation of the rare words in the oration: ʿAlī's saying "our mountain meadows are parched (*inṣāḥat*)" means they have cracked from the effects of the drought; the Arabs use the same verb for a garment if it is torn, and a plant if it dries up and withers. ʿAlī's saying "our sheep have gone mad with thirst (*hāmat*)" means they are thirsty; *huyām* means thirst. ʿAlī's saying "emaciated camels of drought (*ḥadābīr*)" uses the plural of *ḥidbār*, a female camel made gaunt by hard travel, to which he compared a drought-stricken year. Dhū al-Rummah said:

> Emaciated camels (*ḥadābīr*)
> fodderless in the night when they kneel down to rest,
> or ridden hard into the desert wastes.

In the phrase "whose puffs (*qazaʿ*) do not dissipate," *qazaʿ* are small and scattered wisps of cloud. The phrase "whose drizzle does not usher in barren, cold winds (*shaffānin dhihābuhā*)" actually means "whose drizzle is not a bearer of cold, barren winds"; *shaffān* is a cold, barren wind, and *dhihāb* are light showers of rain; the word "bearer (*dhāt*)" is elided because the hearer would know it is implied.

1.113 From an oration by ʿAlī:[1]

1.113.1 God sent Muḥammad to call toward truth and bear witness to people. He conveyed his Lord's messages, untiring and unstinting. He battled God's enemies, unflagging and unfaltering. He is the leader of the pious and the eyes of the righteous.

1.113.2 If you knew what I know of the mysteries hidden from you, you would run out into the wilderness, weeping over your deeds, and striking your breasts, leaving your property without guard or protector. Every man would be absorbed in his own apprehensions and not spare a single thought for anyone else. But no! You have forgotten what you were told and become complacent about what you were warned. You have gone astray and fallen into total chaos. O, how I wish that God would deliver me from you and unite me with those who deserve my companionship! They, by God, were people of felicitous vision, grave maturity, and truthful speech, people who shunned treachery, advanced on the path, and raced on the road, who won everlasting life and gracious bounty. By God,

---

1   Excerpt from a Kufa oration in which ʿAlī attempted to muster his supporters against the Syrians (B 456). Azharī (*Tahdhīb*, s.v. "Kh-Ḍ-R") says it was delivered during ʿAlī's final days, thus in 40/661. Ṭūsī (*Miṣbāḥ*, 380–381) describes it as a Friday sermon.

الباردة. أما والله ليسلّطنّ عليكم غلام ثقيف الذيّال الميّال يأكل خضرتكم ويذيب شَحمتكم. إيهٍ أبا وَذَحة.

و﴿الوذحة﴾ الخُنفساء. وهذا القول يومئ به إلى الحجّاج وله مع الوذحة حديث ليس هذا موضع ذكره.

1.114　ومن كلام له عليه السلام

فلا أموالَ بذلتموها للذي رَزقها ولا أنفُسَ خاطرتُم بها للذي خلقها تَكرُمون بالله على عباده ولا تُكرِمون اللهَ في عباده فاعتبروا بنزولكم منازل من كان قبلكم وانقطاعكم عن أصل إخوانكم.

1.115　ومن كلام له عليه السلام

أنتم الأنصار على الحقّ والإخوان في الدين والجُنَن يوم البأس والبِطانة دون الناس بكم أضرب المدبر وأرجو طاعة المقبل فأعينوني بمناصحة جليّة[1] من الغِشّ سليمة من الريب فوالله إنّي لأولى الناس بالناس.

---

١ م، ي، ومصحّحة في هـ: كذا. ش، ن، وأصل هـ: ﴿خليّة﴾.

a swaggering, despotic youth from Thaqīf will take control over you. He will devour your green grass and melt down your fat-tail. Come on, then, you piece of dung on a sheep's butt![1]

Raḍī: The phrase "you piece of dung on a sheep's butt" refers to the black beetle, and by this ʿAlī means Ḥajjāj: there is a long story about him and a beetle, but this is not the place to tell it.[2]

1.114 From an address by ʿAlī:
You don't spend your wealth for the one who has provided it or risk your lives as you should for the one who has created you. You claim honor in God's name from his servants, yet you don't honor God in your treatment of his servants. Be warned! You reside in the homes of those who went before you. Your rope is severed from them, the source that connected you with your brethren.

1.115 From an address by ʿAlī:[3]
You are my supporters in the cause of truth and my brothers in faith, my shields on the day of combat and my closest associates. Through you, I strike those who turn away, and hope for the obedience of those who come forward. Give me sincere counsel, then, which is pure of deceit, and free of doubt, for, by God, I am the worthiest of the people to lead them.

---

1 Or: "… you beetle-man!" (*abā waḍhaḥah*), lit. "O father of—(meaning one who has some close association with)—a *waḍhaḥah*." The dictionary meaning of *waḍhaḥah* is "a piece of dry dung and urine sticking to the wool of a sheep's butt" (Ibn Manẓūr, *Lisān al-ʿArab*, s.v. "W-Dh-Ḥ"). Raḍī says *waḍhaḥah* denotes *khunfusāʾ* (black- or dung-beetle), a denotation, as Ibn Abī al-Ḥadīd mentions, not found in the lexicons. Baḥrānī says the term "piece of dung" here indicates the "dung beetle," due to their similarity in shape and size. These two commentators and Rāwandī agree that the prophecy is about the Umayyad governor of Iraq, Ḥajjāj ibn Yūsuf al-Thaqafī (d. 95/714), explaining the characterization through Ḥajjāj's phobia of black beetles, or, apparently, his use of those insects to scratch his butt (!) (Ḥ 7:279–281; R 2:22; B 457–458). Mughniyyah (Gh 2:203) says the attribution is due to Ḥajjāj's swarthy coloring, and his small physical and moral stature.
2 For the story, see the previous note.
3 Excerpt from an address by ʿAlī to supporters immediately after the Battle of the Camel, presumably in Basra or Kufa, in 36/656 (Ḥ 7:284, after Madāʾinī and Wāqidī). Ṭabarī (*Tārīkh*, 5:79) places the oration in 37/658 after the arbitration, with ʿAlī urging his followers to regroup to fight Muʿāwiyah, but the relatively hopeful tone fits better with ʿAlī's other orations in the former context.

1.116 ومن كلام له عليه السلام وقد جمع الناس وحضّهم على الجهاد فسكتوا مليًّا فقال ما بالكم أَمُخْرَسون أنتم فقال قوم منهم يا أمير المؤمنين إن سرت سرنا معك فقال عليه السلام ما لكم لا سُدّدتم لرشد ولا هديتم لقصد أفي مثل هذا ينبغي لي أن أخرج إنّما يخرج في مثل هذا رجل ممّن أرضاه من شجعائكم وذوي بأسكم ولا ينبغي لي أن أدع الجند والمصر وبيت المال وجباية الأرض والقضاء بين المسلمين والنظر في حقوق المطالبين ثمّ أخرج في كتيبة أتبع أخرى أتقلقل تقلقل القدح في الجفير الفارغ وإنّما أنا قطب الرحى تدور عليّ وأنا بمكاني فإذا فارقته اْستحار مدارها واْضطرب ثفالها. هذا لعمر الله الرأي السوء. والله لولا رجائي الشهادة عند لقاء العدوّ لو قد حُمَّ لي لقاؤه لقرّبت ركابي ثمّ شخصت عنكم فلا أطلبكم ما اْختلفت جَنوب وشَمال.

1.117 ومن كلام له عليه السلام

تالله لقد عُلّمت تبليغ الرسالات وإتمام العِدات وتمام الكلمات وعندنا أهل البيت أبواب الحكم وضياء الأمر ألا وإنّ شرائع الدين واحدة وسبله قاصدة من أخذ بها لَحِقَ وغَنِم ومن وقف عنها ضلّ ونَدِم. اعملوا اليوم تُذخر له الذخائر وتبلى فيه السرائر ومن لا ينفعه

1.116 From an address by ʿAlī. ʿAlī instructed the people to assemble and urged them to fight, and they all fell silent. "What is wrong with you? Have you been struck dumb?" he exclaimed angrily. Some people answered, "Commander of the Faithful, if you march, we will march with you," whereupon ʿAlī thundered:[1]

What is wrong with you? What you propose is not the right course or the proper way! Is it fitting in this situation for me to take to the field? The one who should set out is a warrior I choose from your bravest and strongest. I should not abandon the main army, the capital city, the public treasury, collection of revenues, dispensation of justice, or oversight of petitioners' rights! I should not ride in one battalion to chase another, shaken about like an arrow shaft in an empty quiver! I am the pivot in the grinding stone. It rotates around me while I remain in my place. If I were to abandon it, it would spin out of control and its base would shudder and break. God's life! This is a terrible proposition! By God, again! Were it not for my hope of earning a martyr's death when I encounter the enemy—an encounter that is preordained!—I would fetch my camel and ride away. I would not seek you out then for as long as the north and the south winds blow.

1.117 From an address by ʿAlī:

By God! I have been taught the transmission of God's messages, the fulfillment of his pledges, and the full meaning of his words.[2] We—the people of his Prophet's house—possess the keys to wisdom and the light of command. Hark! All trodden paths of religion are as one, its roads lead to the same destination. Whoever traverses them catches up with those who went before and wins God's favors, and whoever stays back strays from the path and earns regret. Set aside deeds for the day for which all provisions are hoarded, in which all hearts will be tested. If your intelligence does not benefit you now, that which is farther from you is even more out of your reach, and that which is absent is even less accessible.[3] Protect yourself from a fire whose heat is intense, whose pit is deep, and

---

1 Excerpt from an address by ʿAlī in Kufa to supporters, castigating their apathy, in the wake of a Syrian raid on an Iraqi town after the Battle of Nahrawān in 38/658. Ḥ 7:287.

2 The first part of the sentence may also be read as "I know about …" (ʿalimtu, vs. ʿullimtu). The sentence's referents are as follows: "messages" refers to the Shariʿah; "pledges" refers to either God's pledges to his prophets and humankind, or Muḥammad's pledges that ʿAlī fulfilled on his behalf; and "full meanings of his words" refers to the Qurʾan's inner meaning (taʾwīl). Ḥ 7:288–289; R 2:25; B 458–459.

3 Two interpretations: (1) Whoever is not benefitted by his own rationality that is present in him is incapable of being helped by the wits of another who is separate from him and unable to benefit from the mind of a person who is absent from him (Ḥ 7:289–290). (2) One who does not benefit now from the presence of his intelligence, will not benefit from it when it leaves him when death arrives, or afterward, when he faces the conditions of the hereafter (B 459).

حاضر لبّه فعازبه عنه أعجز وغائبه أعوز وأتّقوا نارًا حرّها شديد وقعرها بعيد وحِليتها حديد
ألا وإنّ اللسان الصالح يجعله الله للمرء في الناس خيرٌ له من المال يورثه من لا يحمده.

1.118 ومن كلام له عليه السلام وقد قام رجل من أصحابه فقال نهيتنا عن الحكومة ثم أمرتنا
بها فما ندري أيّ الأمرين أرشد فصفق عليه السلام إحدى يديه على الأخرى ثمّ قال
هذا جزاء من ترك العقدة أما والله لو أنّي حين أمرتكم بما أمرتكم به حملتكم على المكروه
الذي يجعل الله فيه خيرًا فإن استقمتم هديتكم وإن اعوججتم قوّمتكم وإن أبيتم تداركتكم
لكانت الوثقى ولكن بِمَن وإلى مَن. أريد أن أداوي بكم وأنتم دائي كـ⟨ناقش الشوكة
بالشوكة وهو يعلم أنّ ضَلْعها معها⟩. اللهمّ قد ملّت أطبّاء هذا الداء الدويّ وكلّت النزعة
بأشطان الرَّكيّ. أين القوم الذين دُعوا إلى الإسلام فقبلوه وقرأوا القرآن فأحكموه
وهِيجوا إلى الجهاد فولّهوا اللّقاحَ أولادها وسلبوا السيوف أغمادها وأخذوا بأطراف
الأرض زحفًا زحفًا وصفًّا صفًّا. بعضٌ هلك وبعض نجا لا يبشّرون بالأحياء ولا
يعزّون عن القتلى[1] مُرْهُ العيون من البكاء خُمْص البطون من الصيام ذُبْل الشِّفاه من
الدعاء صُفْر الألوان من السهر على وجوههم غبرة الخاشعين أولئك إخواني الذاهبون
فحقّ لنا أن نظمأ إليهم ونعضّ الأيدي على فراقهم. إنّ الشيطان يُسَنّي لكم طرقه ويريد
أن يحلّ دينكم عقدة عقدة ويعطيكم بالجماعة الفرقة[2] فاصدفوا عن نزغاته ونفثاته وأقبلوا
النصيحة ممّن أهداها إليكم واعقلوها على أنفسكم.

---

[1] م، ي، ومصحّحة في ش، هـ: كذا. ن، وأصل ش، هـ: ⟨الموتى⟩.   [2] ش، ن، م، ومصحّحة في هـ: كذا. ي، وأصل هـ، وهامش م: أضيفت ⟨وبالفرقة الفتنة⟩.

whose ornaments are chains of iron. Listen to me! A pious reputation, one that God sustains through people's tongues, is better for a person than any wealth he may leave behind for his ungrateful heirs.

1.118 From an address by ʿAlī, when one of his associates stood up and confronted him, saying, "You forbade us to enter into arbitration then commanded us to enter it, and we don't really know which of the two was the more reasonable course." ʿAlī clapped one hand over the other in frustration and anger, then spoke:[1]

This is how one who relinquishes a sound position is rewarded! By God! Had I forced you—when I commanded you what I did—to follow the hard course in which God has ordained good, that sound position would have been established. Then, if you had stayed resolute, I would have guided you, if you had deviated, I would have straightened you, and if you had balked, I would have set you right. But with whom, and through whom! I apply you as the cure when you are my disease, like ⟨a person who extracts a thorn with a thorn, knowing that the one inclines toward the other!⟩[2] O God! How weary the physician treating this vicious disease! How tired the water-drawer hauling up these well ropes! O where are the people who were called to Islam and accepted it, who recited the Qurʾan and acted on it, who were urged to fight and raced to it? They tore camels from nurslings, snatched swords from their sheaths, and set out to the far regions of the earth, marching steadily, row by row. Some perished, and some survived, neither gladdened by their living nor saddened by their dead, their eyes raw from weeping, their stomachs lean from fasting, their lips withered from praying, their color pale from wakeful nights, and their faces dusty from long prostration. Those were my departed brothers! It is only right that I should thirst for them, that I should wring my hands at their separation! Satan has smoothed his paths for you. He wants to undo your religion, knot by knot, and replace your unity with dissent. Reject his incitements and whisperings! Accept your benefactor's counsel and guard it with care!

---

1   I have added the words "in frustration and anger" for clarity. The confronter is a member of the newly emerging Kharijite group in Kufa, following the Battle of Ṣiffīn in 37/657, challenging ʿAlī for his acceptance of the arbitration. Details in Ḥ 7:294, R 2:31, B 460. Iskāfī (*Miʿyār*, 241) places the latter lines of the second paragraph as an answer to a group who claimed to be his followers, while ʿAlī denied that they were, for they did not possess the pious qualities outlined here.

2   Proverb denoting a person who seeks aid against his enemy from his enemy's kin. Ḥ 7:292–294; R 2:30; B 460; ʿA 620.

١٫١١٩ ومن كلام له عليه السلام قاله للخوارج وقد خرج إلى معسكرهم وهم مقيمون على إنكار الحكومة فقال عليه السلام أكلّكم شهد معنا صفّين فقالوا منّا من شهد ومنّا من لم يشهد قال فأمتازوا فرقتين فليكن من شهد صفّين فرقة ومن لم يشهدها فرقة حتّى أكلّم كلًّا بكلامه. ونادى الناس فقال أمسكوا عن الكلام وأنصتوا لقولي وأقبلوا بأفئدتكم إليّ فمن نشدناه شهادة فليقل بعلمه فيها ثمّ كلّمهم عليه السلام بكلام طويل من جملته أن قال

ألم تقولوا عند رفعهم المصاحف حيلةً وغيلةً ومكرًا وخديعةً إخوانُنا وأهلُ دعوتنا اَستقالونا واَستراحوا إلى كتاب الله سبحانه فالرأي القبول منهم والتنفيس عنهم فقلت لكم هذا أمر ظاهره إيمان وباطنه عدوان وأوّله رحمة وآخره ندامة فأقيموا على شأنكم وألزموا طريقتكم وعضّوا على الجهاد بنواجذكم ولا تلتفتوا إلى ناعق نعق إن أجيب أضلَّ وإن تُرك ذلّ. فلقد كنّا مع رسول الله صلّى الله عليه وآله وإنّ القتل ليدورُ بين الآباء والأبناء والإخوان والقرابات فما نزداد على كلّ مصيبة وشدّة إلّا إيمانًا ومُضيًّا على الحقّ وتسليمًا للأمر وصبرًا على مضض الجراح. ولكنّا إنّما أصبحنا نقاتل إخواننا في الإسلام على ما دخل فيه من الزيغ والاعوجاج والشبهة والتأويل فإذا طمعنا في خصلة يَلُمّ الله بها شَعَثَنا ونتدانى بها إلى البقيّة فيما بيننا رغبنا فيها وأمسكنّا عمّا سواها.

١٫١٢٠ ومن كلام له عليه السلام قاله لأصحابه في وقت الحرب

وأيّ اَمرئ منكم أحسّ من نفسه رباطة جأش عند اللقاء ورأى من أحد من إخوانه فشلًا فليذبّ عن أخيه بفضل نجدته التي فُضّل بها عليه كما يذبّ عن نفسه فلو شاء الله لجعله مثله إنّ الموت طالب حثيث لا يفوته المقيم ولا يُعجزه الهارب إنّ أكرم الموت القتل والذي نفس اَبن أبي طالب بيده لأَلْف ضربة بالسيف أهون من مِيتة على الفراش.[١]

___

١ ش، ن، م، ومصحّحة في ه: كذا. ي، وأصل ه: أضيفت ﴿في غير طاعة الله﴾.

1.119 This is from ʿAlī's address to the Kharijites—who condemned his acceptance of the arbitration—after he had marched to their encampment.[1] He first asked, "Were all of you present with me at Ṣiffīn?" "Some among us were, and others were not," they replied. He then instructed, "Separate into two groups, those present at Ṣiffīn and those not, so I can address each group according to their position." He then called out in a raised voice, "Stop your talk, listen to my words, and attend with your hearts, and if I ask a person to testify about a point, let him say what he knows about it." After this, he spoke with them at length, and this is some of what he said:

When the Syrians raised leaves from the Qurʾan on spears—using trickery, deception, cunning, and lies—wasn't it you who said, "These are our brothers and people of our faith who beg us to cease fighting and take refuge in the Book of God—we should accept what they offer and deliver them from calamity"? I said to you then, "This is an affair whose facade is faith but whose reality is pure malice, its beginning is mercy, but its end is regret. So keep to your positions and stay steady on your path, bite down with your back teeth and fight, and do not heed this errant bleater. If you accept his call, he will lead you astray, if you don't, we will defeat him." When we were with God's Messenger, we stood by him when fighting raged between fathers, sons, brothers, and kin. Calamities and hardships only increased our faith, our steadfastness in truth, our acceptance of God's command, and our fortitude in the face of painful wounds. But here, today, we have had to fight our brothers in Islam over their deviations, deviances, doubts, and false interpretations. When I thought there could be a way in which God may yet bring order to our scattered nation, and by which we may yet draw closer and conciliate, I was hopeful, and so I desisted from the other course.

1.120 From an address by ʿAlī to his supporters before the start of a battle:[2]

If any of you finds composure in his heart when meeting the enemy, and if he senses fear in one of his brothers, he should use his courage to defend him just as he defends himself. Had God wished it, he would have created them both the same. Death is an assiduous seeker. No one who stays home escapes it, and no one who flees battle eludes it. The most honorable death is on the battlefield. By the one who holds the soul of Abū Ṭālib's son in his hand, a thousand sword strikes are easier to bear than dying on your bed!

---

1 Presumably, leading up to or just before the Battle of Nahrawān, in Kufa or Nahrawān, in 37/657 or 38/658. I have added the words "his acceptance of" for clarity.

2 The second paragraph is placed by Yaʿqūbī (*Tārīkh*, 2:209) at the Battle of the Camel in 36/656. However, according to MS N, the next two texts—§1.121 and §1.122—are part of the same oration, and §1.122, according to Ḥ 8:9, is from the Battle of Ṣiffīn in 37/657. It is possible that ʿAlī may have given similar counsel before both battles.

1.121 ومن كلام له عليه السلام

وكأنّي أنظر إليكم تكِشّون كشيش الضِّباب لا تأخذون حقًّا ولا تمنعون ضَيمًا قد خُلّيتم
والطريقَ فالنجاة للمقتحِم والهلكة للمتلوّم.

1.122 ومن كلام له عليه السلام في حضّ أصحابه على القتال

1.122.1 فقدّموا الدارع وأخّروا الحاسر وعضّوا على الأضراس فإنّه أنبى للسيوف عن
الهام والْتَوُوا في أطراف الرماح فإنّه أَمْوَر للأسنّة وغُضّوا الأبصار فإنّه أربط للجأش
وأسكن للقلوب وأميتوا الأصوات فإنّه أطرد للفشل. ورايتَكم فلا تُميلوها ولا تخلّوها
ولا تجعلوها إلّا بأيدي شجعانكم١ والمانعين الذِّمار منكم فإنّ الصابرين على نزول الحقائق
هم الذين يَحُفّون براياتهم ويكتنفونها حفافَيها ووراءها وأمامها لا يتأخّرون عنها فيُسلموها
ولا يتقدّمون عليها فيفردوها. أجزَأَ امرؤٌ قِرنَه وآسى أخاه بنفسه ولم يكِلْ قرنه إلى أخيه
فيجتمع عليه قرنه وقرن أخيه.

1.122.2 وايم الله لئن فررتم من سيف العاجلة لا تسلموا من سيف الآخرة. وأنتم لَهاميم
العرب والسنام الأعظم إنّ في الفرار مَوجِدةَ الله والذلّ اللازم والعار الباقي وإنّ الفارّ
غير مزيد في عمره ولا محجوز بينه وبين يومه مَن رائحٌ إلى الله كالظمآن يرد الماء الجنّة
تحت أطراف العوالي اليوم تُبلى الأخبار.٢ اللّهمّ فإن رَدّوا الحقّ فأفضض جماعتهم
وشتّت كلمتهم وأبسِلْهم بخطاياهم إنّهم لن يزولوا عن مواقفهم دون طعنٍ دِراكٍ
يخرج منه النسيم وضربٍ يفلق الهام ويطيح العظام ويُندر السواعد والأقدام وحتّى

١ن، ي، ش، ه: كذا. م، ومصحّحة في ش: ﴿شُجعائكم﴾.   ٢م، ن، ش: كذا. ي، ه، ونسخة
في ش مع علامة معًا: ﴿الأخيار﴾. وأُضيفت في ي، وفي هامش ه: ﴿والله لأنا أشوق إلى لقائهم
منهم إلى ديارهم﴾.

1.121 From an address by ʿAlī:[1]

I see you now, scuttling away like a group of thorn-tailed lizards, neither demanding your rights, nor defending against attackers. But you are free to choose your path! Those who brave danger will be saved, those who hold back will perish.

1.122 From an address by ʿAlī urging his followers to fight:[2]

1.122.1 Place the armor-clad in front and the unprotected behind. Bite down on your back teeth, for that will blunt the blades that strike at your heads. Twist when facing lances, for that will make spearheads glance off your body. Focus your eyes low, for that will calm your hearts. Kill idle talk, for that will boost your courage. Don't let your banner list, or leave it unprotected, or give it to any but your bravest warriors who are staunch in defending honor. Indeed, those who are valiant in the face of death will guard it and surround it from both sides and from front and back, neither falling back and surrendering it, nor rushing ahead and leaving it unguarded. Each man should tackle his own opponent and also come to his brother's aid. He should never leave his own opponent for his brother to face, such that both his and his brother's opponents join forces against his brother.

1.122.2 By God, if you are successful in fleeing the sword of this world you will still not be safe from the sword of the hereafter. This, when you are chieftains of the Arabs and the lofty crest of the camel's hump! Fleeing from the battlefield earns God's wrath, eternal dishonor, and lasting shame, and anyway, the absconder cannot increase his lifespan—nothing will protect him when his day arrives. Who among you will return to God in the evening like a thirsty man coming to a waterhole? Paradise lies beneath the points of tall spears! This is the day when resolutions will be tested—O God, scatter the enemy if they challenge the truth, divide their views, and destroy them for their sins! They will be dislodged from their positions only when sharp spears leave gaping wounds on their torsos, and cutting swords split skulls, slice bones, and sever arms and legs,

---

1 Presumably also delivered at the Battle of Ṣiffīn in 37/657. As mentioned, according to MS N, this text and the one after it—§ 1.121 and 1.122—are a continuation of § 1.120.

2 Delivered just before the Battle of Ṣiffīn in 37/657 (Ṭabarī, *Tārīkh*, 5:16–17; Ḥ 8:9). As mentioned, according to MS N, this text and the one before it—§ 1.121 and 1.122—are a continuation of § 1.120.

يُرَمَوا بالمناسر تتبعها المناسر ويُرجَموا بالكتائب تقفوها الجلائب[1] حتّى يُجَرَّ ببلادهم الخميس يتلوه الخميس وحتّى تَدعَق الخيول في نواحر أرضهم وبأعنان مساربهم[2] ومسارحهم.

⟨الدَّعْق⟩ الدَّقّ أي تدقّ الخيول بحوافرها أرضهم. ⟨نواحر أرضهم⟩ متقابلاتها. يقال ⟨منازل بني فلان تتناحر⟩ أي تتقابل.

1.123 ومن كلام له عليه السلام في معنى الخوارج لمّا أنكروا تحكيم الرجال ويذمّ فيه أصحابه قال عليه السلام

إنّا لم نحكّم الرجال وإنّما حكّمنا القرآن وهذا القرآن إنّما هو خطّ مسطور بين الدفّتين لا ينطق بلسان ولا بدّ له من ترجمان وإنّما ينطق عنه الرجال. ولمّا دعانا القوم إلى أن نحكّم بيننا القرآن لم نكن الفريق المتولّي عن كتاب الله وقال الله سبحانه ﴿فَإِن تَنَازَعْتُمْ فِي شَيْءٍ فَرُدُّوهُ إِلَى اللَّهِ وَالرَّسُولِ﴾ فردّه إلى الله أن نحكم بكتابه وردّه إلى الرسول أن نأخذ بسنّته فإذا حُكم بالصدق في كتاب الله فنحن أحقّ الناس به وإن حكم بسنّة رسول الله فنحن أولاهم به. وأمّا قولكم لِمَ جعلت بينك وبينهم أجلًا في التحكيم فإنّما فعلت ذلك ليتبيّن الجاهل ويتثبّت العالم ولعلّ الله أن يصلح في هذه الهدنة أمر هذه الأمّة ولا يؤخذ بأكظامها فتعجّل عن تبيّن الحقّ وتنقاد لأوّل الغيّ. إنّ أفضل الناس عند الله من كان العمل بالحقّ أحبّ إليه وإن نقصه وكَرَّثَه من الباطل وإن جرّ إليه فائدة وزاده فأين يُتاهُ بكم ومن أين أُتيتم. استعدّوا للمسير إلى قوم حَيارى عن الحقّ لا يبصرونه وموزَعين بالجور لا يعدلون به جفاة عن الكتاب نُكُب عن الطريق ما أنتم بوثيقة يُعلق بها ولا زوافر يعتصم إليها لبئس حُشّاش نار الحرب أنتم أُفٍّ لكم لقد لقيت منكم بَرَحًا يومًا أناديكم ويومًا أناجيكم فلا أحرارُ عند النداء ولا إخوان ثقة عند النجاء.

<hr>

١ن، ش، ي، ه: كذا. م: ⟨الحلائب⟩. ٢م، ن، ي، ه: كذا. ش: ⟨مشاربهم⟩.

when they are attacked by column after column and battered by battalions and cavalry, when their lands are attacked by army upon army, when the interlocking arteries of their terrain and the open vistas of their trails and pastures are trampled by squadrons of cavalry.

Raḍī: "Trample (*daʿq*)" means pounding, i.e., squadrons of cavalry pounding the terrain with their horses' hooves. "Interlocked arteries of their terrain (*nawāḥir arḍihim*)" are separate sections that face one another. It is said "the campsites of such-and-such tribe are as interlocked necks (*manāzilu banī fulānin tatanāḥaru*)," meaning they face one another.

1.123 From ʿAlī's address censuring the Kharijites when they condemned his appointment of men to arbitrate:[1]

I did not appoint men to arbitrate—I sought arbitration from the Qurʾan. But yes, this Qurʾan is a set of written lines enclosed by two covers; it does not speak with a tongue and thus has need of an interpreter, and those who speak on its behalf are men. When the Syrians proposed to have the Qurʾan arbitrate between us, I did not turn away from God's Book, for he has said «If you disagree about something, refer it to God and his Messenger.»[2] To refer it to God is to rule by his Book, and to refer it to the Messenger is to follow the Messenger's Sunnah. Had the arbitration been executed by the Book of God, I would have been found to be the person most worthy of the caliphate. If it had been executed according to the Sunnah of God's Messenger, I would have been established as the most deserving. You object, "Why did you allow them an interval to decide the arbitration?" I did so in order that the ignorant might see the light and the informed might gain strength. I hoped that in the interim of truce God would stabilize the community, so it would not be grabbed by the throat and rushed back into error before the truth was became clear. The best man in God's eyes holds right dearer than wrong, no matter how hard or painful it is to act on, and no matter how much gain or benefit it brings. Pray, then, whereto do you stray, what corrupted you? Prepare to march against that confounded group of men who cannot see the truth! Seduced by tyranny, they cling to it; uneasy with the Book, they stray from its path. But you are also not a sturdy rope to cling to, or mighty lions who defend! What courage have the likes of you to ignite the blaze of combat? Shame! All you give me is pain! One day I rally you in public, the next I urge you in private, but your response to a call to muster is not that of the free and brave, or, when approached in confidence, of brothers I can trust.

---

1 Delivered at the Kharijites' camp outside Kufa after the arbitration in 37/658. B 465; Ṭabarī, *Tārīkh*, 5:66.

2 Qurʾan, Nisāʾ 4:59.

1.124 ومن كلام له عليه السلام لمّا عوتب على تصييره الناس أسوة في العطاء من غير تفضيل
أولي السابقات والشرف قال

أتأمروني أن أطلب النصر بالجور فيمن وليت عليه والله ما أُطورُ به ما أَطَّ
نجم في السماء نجمًا لو كان المال لي لسوّيت بينهم فكيف وإنّما المال لهم.[1]

ثمّ قال عليه السلام

ألا وإنّ إعطاء المال في غير حقّه تبذير وإسراف وهو يرفع صاحبه في الدنيا ويضعه في
الآخرة ويكرمه في الناس ويهينه عند الله ولم يضع اَمرؤ ماله في غير حقّه وعند غير أهله
إلّا حرمه الله شكرهم وودّهم وكان لغيره فإن زلّت به النعل يومًا فاحتاج إلى معونتهم
فشرُّ خدين وأَلأَمُ خليل.

1.125 ومن كلام له عليه السلام للخوارج أيضًا

فإن أبيتم إلّا أن تزعموا أنّي أخطأت وضللت فلِمَ تُضلّلون عامّة أمّة محمّد صلّى الله عليه
وآله بضلالي وتأخذونهم بخطأي وتكفّرونهم بذنوبي. سيوفكم على عواتقكم تضعونها
مواضع البراءة والسقم وتخلطون من أذنب بمن لم يذنب. وقد علمتم أنّ رسول الله
صلّى الله عليه وآله رجم الزاني ثمّ صلّى عليه ثمّ ورّثه أهله وقتل القاتل وورّث ميراثه
أهله وقطع السارق وجلد الزاني غير المحصَن ثمّ قسم عليهما من الفيء ونكحا المسلمات.
فأخذهم رسول الله بذنوبهم وأقام حقّ الله فيهم ولم يمنعهم سهمهم من الإسلام
ولم يُخرج أسماءهم من بين أهله ثمّ أنتم شِرار الناس ومن رمى به الشيطان مراميه
وضرب به تِيهَه. وسيهلك فيَّ صنفان محبّ مفرط يذهب به الحبّ إلى غير الحقّ ومبغض

<hr>

[1] م، ن، ش، ي، ه: كذا. مصحّحة في ن، ش، ه: ﴿إنّما المال مال الله﴾.

1.124 From an address by ʿAlī responding to the outpouring of complaints when he standardized treasury stipends with no privilege for precedence or nobility:[1]
Do you urge me to seek victory by oppressing the people I rule? By God, no, I will never do so, not as long as the night-watch is kept or while one star follows another in the heavens! If the funds had been mine, I would still have distributed them equally. How, then, when they belong to the people?

Then he said:
Listen to me! Awarding funds from the treasury to those who have no right to them counts as waste and squandering. It elevates the provider on earth but lowers his worth in the hereafter, it ennobles him among people but belittles him in the eyes of God. When a man gives money for unrighteous ends to undeserving recipients, God deprives him of their gratitude and veers their loyalty toward another. Then, if one day his foot slips and he needs their help, his previous act will reveal itself to be his worst bedfellow and most sordid friend.

1.125 From another address by ʿAlī to the Kharijites:[2]
Even if you insist—and you do so wrongly—on believing that I have sinned and erred, then why do you hold the whole of Muḥammad's community errant because of my supposed error?[3] Why do you hold them responsible for my sin and label them unbelievers because of my transgression? You strap swords to your shoulders and use them equally against the sound and the sick, placing the sinner with those who have not sinned. You know that the Messenger stoned the fornicator then prayed over him and allowed his family to inherit. He executed the murderer then distributed his property to his family. He cut the hand of the thief and flogged the unmarried fornicator yet continued to give them a share of the war booty and allowed them to marry Muslim women. The Messenger punished these sinners for their sins and carried out God's mandated penalties, yet he did not deprive them of their share of Islam's benefits, nor did he remove their names from the roster of Muslims. But you! You are the worst of people! In you, Satan has struck his target. Through you, he has accomplished his mission of obfusca-

---

1   Excerpt from an oration—followed, according to Ibn Qutaybah (*Imāmah*, 1:174), by §1.95, and also including §1.140—delivered at Ṣiffīn (37/657), when some of ʿAlī's associates told him about Muʿāwiyah's lavish rewarding of his supporters and urged him to do the same (Ḥarrānī, *Tuḥaf*, 185; similar context in §1.203). For a brief discussion of this issue, and further primary source references, see Qutbuddin, "ʿAlī's Contemplations on this World and the Hereafter in the Context of His Life and Times," 339–340.

2   In Nahrawān, just before the battle, 38/658. Ṭabarī, *Tārīkh*, 5:85.

3   The Kharijites claimed that ʿAlī and his followers had left Islam because they had agreed to human arbitration, and thus they held their blood licit. On the Kharijite doctrine declaring those who commit a 'major sin' to have apostatized, see Ḥ 8:113–118.

مفرط يذهب به البغض إلى غير الحقّ وخير الناس فيّ حالًا النمط الأوسط فألزموه
وٱلزموا السواد الأعظم فإنّ يد الله على الجماعة وإيّاكم والفرقة فإنّ الشاذّ من الناس
للشيطان كما أنّ الشاذّة من الغنم للذئب ألا من دعا إلى هذا الشعار فٱقتلوه ولو كان تحت
عمامتي هذه. فإنّما حُكِّمَ الحَكَمان ليحييا ما أحيا القرآن ويميتا ما أمات القرآن وإحياؤه
الاجتماع عليه وإماته الافتراق عنه فإن جرّنا القرآن إليهم ٱتّبعناهم وإن جرّهم إلينا
ٱتّبعونا. فلم آتِ لا أبا لكم بُجْرًا ولا خَتَلْتُكم عن أمركم ولا لبّسته عليكم إنّما ٱجتمع رأي
مَلَئِكم على ٱختيار رجلين أخذنا عليهما أن لا يتعدّيا القرآن فتاها عنه وتركا الحقّ وهما
يُبصرانه وكان الجور هواهُما فَضَيا عليه وقد سبق ٱستثناؤنا عليهما في الحكومة بالعدل
والصَّمْد للحقّ سوءَ رأيهما وجورَ حكمهما.

1.126   ومن كلام له عليه السلام فيما يخبر به عن الملاحم بالبصرة

يا أحنف كأنّي به وقد سار بالجيش الذي لا يكون له غُبار ولا لَجَب ولا قعقعة لُجُم
ولا حمحمة خيل يثيرون الأرض بأقدامهم كأنّها أقدام النعام.

يومئ بذلك إلى صاحب الزنج. ثمّ قال عليه السلام

ويل لِسكَككُم العامرة ودُوركم المزخرفة التي لها أجنحة كأجنحة النسور وخراطيم
كخراطيم الفِيَلة من أولئك الذين لا يُندَب قتيلُهم ولا يفقد غائبهم. أنا كابُّ الدنيا لوجهها
وقادرها بقَدْرها وناظرها بعينها.

tion. Two types of people—with regard to their relationship with me—will perish: one who loves to excess, whose love crosses the boundary of right, and one who hates, whose hate crosses the boundary of right.[1] The best of people—with regard to their relationship with me—are the ones who keep to the middle road,[2] so keep to it! Keep to the assembled group, for God's hand guides the congregation. Beware of division, for the isolated individual is hunted by Satan, just as the lone sheep is hunted by the wolf. Kill any person who calls to that evil banner, even if that man were me, the man wearing this turban! The arbitrators' charge was to revive what revives the Qurʾan and to kill what kills the Qurʾan. To revive the Qurʾan is to unite around it, and to kill it is to splinter from it. The mandate was that if the Qurʾan drew us to them, we would follow them, and if it drew them to us, they would follow us. I have committed no wrong—may you have no fathers! I did not deceive you or muddy your affair. It was you, the majority of you, who chose these two men. I made them pledge that they would not transgress the Qurʾan, but they strayed from it and abandoned the truth, while seeing it all the while in front of them. Their intent was to oppress, and they did. I had made their arbitration contingent upon justice and truth—by their corrupt judgment and unjust ruling they have invalidated it.

1.126 From an address by ʿAlī foretelling epic fighting in Basra:[3]
Listen, Aḥnaf! I see him marching with troops that raise no dust, that make no sound, with no clanking of irons or neighing of horses, their feet silently pounding the earth like swift ostriches.

Raḍī: In these lines, ʿAlī predicted the uprising of the Chief of the Zanj.[4] Then he said:
Grief to your flourishing quarters and beautiful homes, with their eagle wings and elephant trunks,[5] from an army whose dead will go unmourned and whose missing will go unnoticed! As for me, I hurl the world on its face, I measure it for what it is worth, I view it with its own eyes!

---

1 On the so-called Exaggerators (*ghulāt*), who attributed divinity to ʿAlī, see Ḥ 8:119–122; Asatryan, *Controversies in Formative Shiʿi Islam*; Halm, *Die islamische Gnosis*; Halm, "Golāt," *EIr*. On the 'haters,' usually taken to mean the Umayyads and the Kharijites, see Husayn, *Opposing the Imām: The Legacy of the* Nawāṣib *in Islamic Literature*.

2 Reference to Qurʾan, Baqarah 2:143.

3 Part of an oration—that includes § 1.98 and § 1.99—which ʿAlī delivered in Basra immediately after the Battle of the Camel in 36/656. B 480; ʿAbd al-Zahrāʾ, *Maṣādir*, 2:202, 203, 288.

4 The Chief of the Zanj was ʿAlī ibn Muḥammad al-Zanjī (d. 270/883), who led the 15-year rebellion that ravaged southern Iraq from 255/869 to 270/883. For details, see Ḥ 8:126–214 (includes excerpts from Ṭabarī, Masʿūdī, and other early historical sources); Ṭabarī, *History*, vol. 17: *The Revolt of the Zanj*; Popovic, "al-Zandj, 2. The Zandj revolts in ʿIrāk," *EI*².

5 "Eagle wings (*ajniḥah*)" of houses refer to overhanging wooden dormers, and "elephant trunks (*kharāṭīm*)" refer to waterspouts snaking down from the roof (Ḥ 8:125; B 480; ʿA 623). Or, to the houses' detailed decorations, and their height (R 2:44).

ومنه ويومئ به إلى وصف الأتراك

كأنّي أراهم١ قومًا كأنّ وجوههم المجانّ المطرّقة يلبسون السَّرَق والديباج ويعتقبون الخيل العِتاق ويكون هناك اِستحرار قتل حتّى يمشي المجروح على المقتول ويكون المفلت أقلّ من المأسور.

فقال له بعض أصحابه لقد أعطيت يا أمير المؤمنين علم الغيب فضحك عليه السلام وقال للرجل وكان كلبيًّا

يا أخا كلب ليس هو بعلم غيب وإنّما هو تعلّم من ذي علم وإنّما علم الغيب علم الساعة وما عدّده الله بقوله ﴿إِنَّ اللّٰهَ عِندَهُ عِلْمُ السَّاعَةِ وَيُنَزِّلُ الْغَيْثَ وَيَعْلَمُ مَا فِي الْأَرْحَامِ وَمَا تَدْرِي نَفْسٌ مَّاذَا تَكْسِبُ غَدًا وَمَا تَدْرِي نَفْسٌ بِأَيِّ أَرْضٍ تَمُوتُ إِنَّ اللّٰهَ عَلِيمٌ خَبِيرٌ﴾ فيعلم سبحانه ما في الأرحام من ذكر أو أنثى وقبيح أو جميل وسخيّ أو بخيل وشقيّ أو سعيد ومن يكون في النار حَطَبًا أو في الجنان للنبيّين مرافقًا. فهذا علم الغيب الذي لا يعلمه أحد إلّا الله وما سوى ذلك فعلم علّمه الله نبيّه صلّى الله عليه وآله فعلّمنيه ودعا لي بأن يَعِيه صدري وتضطمّ عليه جوانحي.

1.127   ومن خطبة له عليه السلام في ذكر المكاييل والموازين

عباد الله إنّكم وما تأملون من هذه الدنيا أثْوِياء مُؤَجّلون ومَدينون مُقتضَون. أجل منقوص وعمل محفوظ فربّ دائب مضيّع وربّ كادح خاسر. قد أصبحتم في زمن لا يزداد الخير فيه إلّا إدبارًا والشرّ إلّا إقبالًا والشيطان في هلاك الناس إلّا طمعًا فهذا أوان قويت عُدّته وعمّت مكيدته وأمكنت فريسته. اضرب بطرفك حيث شئت من الناس فهل تبصر٢ إلّا فقيرًا يكابد فقرًا أو غنيًّا بدّل نعمة الله كفرًا أو بخيلًا اِتّخذ البخل بحقّ الله وفرًا أو متمرّدًا كأنّ بأذنه عن سمع المواعظ وقرًا. أين خياركم وصلحاؤكم وأين أحراركم وسمحاؤكم وأين المتورّعون في مكاسبهم والمتنزّهون في مذاهبهم أليس قد ظعنوا جميعًا عن

From the same address, foretelling the coming of the Turks:[1]
I see them before me now, their craggy faces latticed shields, their robes silk and brocade, their mounts purebred steeds. I see violent fighting, the wounded trampling the slain, hardly any escaping and a host being captured.

At that, one of ʿAlī's associates exclaimed, "You have knowledge of the mysteries, Commander of the Faithful!" ʿAlī laughed and said to the man, who was from the tribe of Kalb:
This is not knowledge of the mysteries, O Kalbite, but what I have learned from one who had true knowledge.[2] Knowledge of the mysteries constitutes knowing the coming hour and the things God has enumerated in his words, «God has knowledge of the coming hour, he sends down rain, and knows what is in wombs. No man knows what he will earn tomorrow, and no man knows the land in which he will die, but God is all-knowing, all-aware.»[3] God knows what is in wombs, male or female, ugly or beautiful, generous or stingy, wretched or blissful. He knows who will go to hell and who will enjoy the company of the prophets in paradise. This is the knowledge of mysteries that God alone possesses. All else is knowledge that God taught to his Prophet, who taught it to me, and he prayed for my heart to preserve it and my breast to keep it safe.

1.127   From an oration by ʿAlī about measures and weights:[4]
Servants of God! You, with all that you desire of this world, are lodgers with fixed timespans and debtors whose reckoning is coming due. The term approaches and deeds are preserved. Some who strive still squander and some who work still lose. You live in an era when good retreats, evil advances, and Satan is greedy for people he can throw into hell. This is that time: his army is strong, his plots commonplace, and his victims easy prey. Look at the people, look where you like! All you will see is paupers who suffer, rich men who repay God's blessings with ingratitude, misers who withhold God's due, and rebels whose ears are deaf to counsel. Where are the virtuous and the pious, where are the free and the generous, where are the honest earners and the people of scru-

---

1   The commentators explain this prophecy as foretelling the Mongol attack on the Muslim heartlands in the 7th/13th century initially under Chingiz Khan and culminating in the sack of Baghdad under Chingiz's grandson Hülegü in 656/1258. For details, see Ḥ 8:218–243; Jackson, "Hülegü b. Toluy b. Chinggis Khān," *EI*³; Biran, "Chinggis Khān," *EI*³; Morgan, "Mongols," *EI*².

2   The reference is to the Prophet Muḥammad.

3   Qurʾan, Luqmān 31:34.

4   Although this text does not mention measures or weights, presumably ʿAlī is condemning his addressees for marketplace cheating.

هذه الدنيا الدنيّة والعاجلة المنغّصة وهل خلّفتم إلّا في حُثالة لا تلتقي بذمّهم الشفتان
آستصغارًا لقدرهم وذهابًا عن ذكرهم فـ﴿إِنَّا لِلَّهِ وَإِنَّا إِلَيْهِ رَاجِعُون﴾ ظهر الفساد فلا
منكرٌ مغيّر ولا زاجر مزدجر أفبهذا تريدون أن تجاوروا الله في دار قدسه وتكونوا أعزّ
أوليائه عنده هيهات لا يُخْدَع الله عن جنّته ولا تنال مرضاته إلّا بطاعته. لعن الله
الآمرين بالمعروف التاركين له والناهين عن المنكر العاملين به.

1.128 ومن كلامه عليه السلام لأبي ذرّ رحمه الله لمّا أُخرج إلى الربذة

يا أبا ذرّ إنّك غضبت لله فآرجُ من غضبت له إنّ القوم خافوك على دنياهم وخفتهم
على دينك فآترك في أيديهم ما خافوك عليه وآهرب منهم بما خفتهم عليه فما أحوجهم
إلى ما منعتهم وأغناك عمّا منعوك وستعلم مَنِ الرابح غدًا والأكثر حسدًا.[1] ولو أنّ
السماوات والأرض[2] كانتا على عبد رَتْقًا ثم آتّقى الله لجعل الله له منهما مخرجًا ولا
يؤنسنّك إلّا الحقّ ولا يوحشنّك إلّا الباطل فلو قبلت دنياهم لأحبّوك ولو قرضت منها
لآمنوك.

1.129 ومن كلام له عليه السلام

أيّتها النفوس المختلفة والقلوب المتشتّتة الشاهدة أبدانهم والغائبة عنهم عقولهم أظأَرُكم
على الحقّ وأنتم تنفرون عنه نفور المِعْزى من وَعْوَعة الأسد. هيهات أن أطلع بكم سِرار

<hr>

[1] ن، ش، م، ه، ونسخة في ي: كذا. أصل ي، ونسخة في م، ش: ﴿خسرًا﴾. [2] ن، ش، ي، ه:
كذا. م، ومصحّحة في ه: ﴿والأرضين﴾.

ple? They have departed this vicious, murky world, leaving you insignificant scum, you, whose very censure lips disdain to utter, whose slightest mention they spurn! «Truly, to God we belong, and to him we return!»[1] Corruption is everywhere, but no one condemns or changes it, no one censures or disapproves. Is this how you earn lodging in God's sacred abode and seek to become his dearest friends? Perish the thought! God cannot be tricked into giving you paradise, his pleasure is earned only by obedience. God's curse on those who command good yet don't perform, who forbid evil yet don't renounce!

1.128 From an address by ʿAlī to Abū Dharr when he was exiled to Rabadhah:[2]
Abū Dharr, you were roused to anger in God's cause, so place your trust in the one in whose cause you were roused to anger. Your adversaries fear you with regard to their worldly gain, while you fear them because of your pious beliefs. Leave in their hands the thing they fear you will seize, and flee from them, taking with you the thing you fear they will take. How desperately they need the thing you forbid them, and how little you need the thing they forbid you! They will learn on the morrow who has the most profit, who is the most envied. Even if skies and earth close in on a true servant of God, God will show him a way to escape, if he remains conscious of him. Let truth be your comfort, and don't be afraid of anything except keeping company with falsehood. If you had accepted their proposals for worldly gain, they would have been on your side. If you had partaken of their offers, they would have offered you full protection.

1.129 From an address by ʿAlī:[3]
You divided souls and fragmented hearts, present in body but absent in mind! I urge you toward truth, but you bolt from it like goats from a lion's snarl! How impossible a task to brighten through your help this night of obscured justice,[4]

---

1 Qurʾan, Baqarah 2:156.

2 ʿAlī delivered this address to Abū Dharr al-Ghifārī on the outskirts of Medina; it was reportedly committed to memory by Dhakwān, freedman of ʿAlī's sister Umm Hānī, who was present. I have not located the date in the sources, but it is presumably shortly before 32/652, which is when Abū Dharr died. Abū Dharr was one of Muḥammad's prominent and pious companions and an early convert to Islam. ʿUthmān exiled him to Rabadhah, two hundred kilometers northeast of Medina, because he was an outspoken supporter of ʿAlī and openly condemned the Umayyads, and he died there. For details, see Ḥ 8:252–262; B 473–474; Afsaruddin, "Abū Dharr al-Ghifārī," *EI*[3].

3 Part of an oration ʿAlī delivered during his caliphate on the pulpit of Kufa (Sibṭ, *Tadhkirah*, 120), presumably, based on the opening line, after the arbitration in 37/658, when he was urging his supporters to regroup to fight Muʿāwiyah.

4 Ar. *sirār al-ʿadl*; the commentators give different explanations for *sirār*: (1) the last (moonless) night of the month (R 2:51; Ḥ 8:264); (2) a concealed thing (B 475); (3) shining lines on someone's forehead (Ḥ 8:264). They agree on the general meaning of the phrase that contains the word.

العدل أو أقيم ٱعوجاج الحقّ. اللّهمّ إنّك تعلم أنه لم يكن الذي كان منّا منافسة في سلطان ولا ٱلتماس شيء من فضول الحُطام ولكن لنردّ المعالم من دينك ونظهر الإصلاح في بلادك فيأمن المظلومون من عبادك وتقام المعطّلة من حدودك. اللّهمّ إنّي أوّل من أناب وسمع وأجاب لم يسبقني إلّا رسول الله صلّى الله عليه وآله بالصلاة. وقد علمتم أنّه لا ينبغي أن يكون على الفروج والدماء والمغانم والأحكام وإمامة المسلمين البخيل فتكون في أموالهم نَهْمَته ولا الجاهل فيضلّهم بجهله ولا الجافي فيقطعهم بجفائه ولا الجانف[1] للدول فيتّخذ قومًا دون قوم ولا المرتشي في الحكم فيذهب بالحقوق ويقف بها دون المقاطع ولا المعطّل للسنّة فيهلك الأمّة.

1.130   ومن خطبة له عليه السلام

1.130.1   نحمده على ما أخذ وأعطى وعلى ما أبلى وٱبتلى الباطن لكلّ خفيّة الحاضر لكلّ سريرة العالم بما تُكِنّ الصدور وما تخون العيون ونشهد أن لا إلٰه غيره وأنّ محمّدًا نجيبه وبعيثه شهادة يوافق فيها السرّ الإعلان والقلب اللسان.

1.130.2   منها

فإنّه والله الجدّ لا اللعب والحقّ لا الكذب وما هو إلّا الموت أَسْمَعَ داعيه وأَعجل حاديه فلا يغرّنّك سواد الناس من نفسك فقد رأيت من كان قبلك مّمن جمع المال وحذر الإقلال وأمن العواقب طول أمل وٱستبعاد أجل كيف نزل به الموت فأزعجه عن وطنه وأخذه من مأمنه محمولًا على أعواد المنايا يتعاطى به الرجالُ الرجالَ حملًا على المناكب وإمساكًا بالأنامل. أما رأيتم الذين يأملون بعيدًا ويبنون مشيدًا ويجمعون كثيرًا أصبحت بيوتهم قبورًا وما جمعوا بورًا وصارت أموالهم للوارثين وأزواجهم لقوم آخرين لا في حسنة يزيدون ولا من سيّئة يستعتبون. فمن أشعر التقوى قلبه برّز مَهَله وفاز عمله

<hr />

[1] ن، ش، ه: كذا. م، ي، ونسخة في ه: ﴿الخائف﴾. شرح ٱبن أبي الحديد والراونديّ والبحرانيّ، وأضيف في ه مع لفظة معًا: ﴿الحائف﴾.

or to straighten out the distorted truth! God! You know my intent was not to vie for power or seek this world's fleeting possessions. I did what I did in order to restore the waymarks of your religion and reform your lands, so your oppressed servants would find security and your forsaken mandates be once more upheld. God! I am the first who turned to you, who heard and answered your call. No one except your Messenger preceded me in the prayer of Islam. O people, you know that one who is in charge of marriage contracts, penalties for murder, distribution of war gains, legal rulings, and leadership of the Muslims should not be a miser or his greed would target their property, he should not be ignorant or he would lead them astray, he should not be harsh or he would alienate them, he should not be a tyrant or he would favor one group over another, he should not be corrupt or he would squander rights and be unjust in the distribution of stipends, and he should not be a person who obstructs the Sunnah or the community would perish.

1.130   From an oration by ʿAlī:

1.130.1   I give praise to God for what he has taken away and what he has granted, for what he has gifted to us and what he has tested us with. He is aware of all that is hidden and present with all that is concealed, he knows all that hearts cover and all that eyes disclose. Thus, with my thoughts the same as my declaration, and my heart in accord with my tongue, I testify that there is no god other than he, and that Muḥammad is his chosen messenger.

1.130.2   From this same oration:
By God, it is seriousness, no jest, all truth, no lies—there is nothing before you but death. Its caller has made its voice heard, and its driver has quickened the caravan, so don't let the recklessness of the masses distract you from your soul. You have seen the people who went before who amassed wealth and dreaded destitution, who were complacent about retribution because they cherished long hopes and ignored their shrinking lifespans. You saw death alight at each one's door, shove him out of his homeland, and seize him from his place of safety. He was carried out on fate's wooden planks, one group of men handing him on to another, transporting him on their shoulders and gripping him by their fingers. Have you not seen those who cherished long hopes, raised edifices with strong mortar, and amassed abundant wealth? Their houses have become graves, what they gathered is in ruin, their property has gone to their heirs, their wives to other men. They are no longer asked to do good or to repent of earlier sins. It is those who robe their hearts in piety, who outrace their peers, whose deeds win the day. Work hard for this. Perform the deeds required to win par-

فٱهتبِلوا هَبَلها وٱعملوا للجنّة عملها فإنّ الدنيا لم تخلق لكم دار مُقام بل دار مُقام لكم خلقت بل دار مُقام لكم مجازًا لتزوّدوا منها الأعمال إلى دار القرار فكونوا منها على أوفاز وقرّبوا الظهور للزِّيال.

1.131 ومن خطبة له عليه السلام

1.131.1 وٱنقادت له الدنيا والآخرة بأزمّتها وقذفت إليه السماوات والأرضون مقاليدها وسجدت له بالغدوّ والآصال الأشجار الناضرة وقدحت له من قضبانها النيران المضيئة وآتت أكلها[1] بكلماته الثمار اليانعة.

1.131.2 منها

وكتاب الله بين أظهركم ناطق لا يَعْيا لسانه وبيت لا تهدم أركانه وعزّ لا تهزم أعوانه.

1.131.3 منها

أرسله على حين فترة من الرسل وتنازع من الألسن فقفّى به الرسل وختم به الوحي فجاهد في الله المدبرين عنه والعادلين به.

1.131.4 منها

وإنّما الدنيا منتهى بصر الأعمى لا يبصر ممّا وراءها شيئًا والبصير ينفُذها بصره ويعلم أنّ الدار وراءها فالبصير منها شاخص والأعمى إليها شاخص والبصير منها متزوّد والأعمى لها متزوّد.

1.131.5 منها

وٱعلموا أنّه ليس من شيء إلّا ويكاد صاحبه يشبع منه ويملّه إلّا الحياة فإنّه لا يجد له في الموت راحة وإنّما ذلك بمنزلة الحكمة التي هي حياة للقلب الميّت وبصر للعين العمياء وسمع للأذن الصمّاء وريّ للظمآن وفيها الغنى كلّه والسلامة.

---

[1] م، ي، هـ، ومصحّحة في ش: كذا. ن، وأصل ش: سقطت ⟨أكلها⟩.

adise. This world has not been created for you as a home, it has been created for you as a passage on which to gather provisions for the final residence. Make haste to leave it. Make ready the backs of your camels for the journey.

1.131 From an oration by ʿAlī:

1.131.1 This world and the hereafter have submitted their reins to God, the skies and the earth have handed him their keys, and the blossoming trees prostrate to him at dawn and at dusk. From their branches, his luminous flames are kindled, and in response to his words, they bring forth their harvest of fruit.[1]

1.131.2 From the same oration:
The Book of God is in front of you. It is a speaker whose tongue does not stutter, a house whose pillars do not collapse, and a force whose supporters are never crushed.

1.131.3 From the same oration:
God sent Muḥammad—when prophecy had lagged, and tongues fiercely quarreled—to follow his messengers and seal his revelation. Muḥammad fought in God's path against those who had turned away from him or who assigned him peers.

1.131.4 From the same oration:
The blind see only this world. They cannot see past it, whereas the sighted penetrate it to see what is beyond, and they know their home is yonder. The sighted are waiting to leave it, whereas the blind are moving toward it. The sighted gather provisions from it, whereas the blind gather provisions for it.

1.131.5 From the same oration:[2]
Know this: there is almost nothing its possessor doesn't weary of except life— no one ever takes comfort in death. This knowledge is the wisdom that brings life to the dead heart, sight to the blind eye, sound to the deaf ear, and water to the parched throat.[3] It gives you all the counsel you need, and total safety.

---

1 References in this section are to Qurʾan, Ḥajj 22:18, Yāsīn 36:80, Baqarah 2:265.

2 The next three paragraphs are thematically unconnected excerpts from different orations (Ḥ 8:288).

3 This "wisdom" refers to (1) the Qurʾan (R 2:54); (2) the Prophet's words (Ḥ 8:293); and (3) knowledge of the hereafter (B 480).

كتاب الله تبصرون به وتنطقون به وتسمعون به وينطق بعضه ببعض ويشهد بعضه
على بعض لا يختلف في الله ولا يخالف بصاحبه عن الله.

قد اصطلحتم على الغلّ فيما بينكم ونبَت المرعى على دِمَنكم وتصافيتم على حبّ الآمال
وتعاديتم في كسب الأموال لقد استهام بكم الخبيث وتاهَ بكم الغَرور والله المستعان على
نفسي وأنفسكم.

1.132   ومن كلام له عليه السلام وقد شاوره عمر في الخروج إلى الروم

وقد توكّل الله لأهل هذا الدين بإعزاز الحوزة وستر العورة والذي نصرهم وهم قليل
لا ينتصرون ومنعهم وهم قليل لا يمتنعون حيّ لا يموت. إنّك متى تَسِرْ إلى هذا العدوّ
بنفسك فتلْقَهم فتُنكَب لا تكن للمسلمين كانفة دون أقصى بلادهم ليس بعدك من
جمع يرجعون إليه فابعث إليهم رجلًا محربًا واحفز معه أهل البلاء والنصيحة فإن أظهر
الله فذاك ما تحبّ وإن تكن الأخرى كنت رِدْءًا للناس ومثابة للمسلمين.

1.133   ومن كلام له عليه السلام وقد وقعت مشاجرة بينه وبين عثمان. فقال المغيرة بن
الأخنس لعثمان أنا أكفيكه فقال أمير المؤمنين صلوات الله عليه للمغيرة

يا ابن اللعين الأبتر والشجرة التي لا أصل لها ولا فرع أنت تكفيني٢ فوالله ما أعزّ الله من
أنت ناصره ولا قام من أنت مُنهِضه اخرج عنّا أبعد الله نَوْأَك ثمّ أبلغ جهدك فلا أبقى
الله عليك إن أبقيتَ.

By God's Book you see and perceive, through it you speak with reason, and from it you hear the truth. One part of the Qur'an supports the other—it contains no contradictions about God, and never leads its reader away from him.

Although you hate one another, you band together to cultivate the refuse dump of malice, clasping hands for worldly gain, while fighting one another in the pursuit of wealth. Surely, the evil one has caught you in his spell and arrogance has led you astray! I seek God's help to fight my passions and yours.

1.132 From an address by 'Alī responding to 'Umar's request for advice on whether he should lead the expedition against the Byzantines:[1]

God has guaranteed to followers of this faith that he will protect their land and guard their honor. He was the one who gave victory to their small band when they struggled to gain the upper hand, and he protected them when they could not protect themselves. He is the everliving who never dies. When you lead the expedition against the enemy, if you engage them and are pushed back, our fighters will have no stronghold to give them refuge and will flee to distant lands. If you are gone, they will have no community to which to return. Instead, dispatch a seasoned fighter accompanied by an experienced and intelligent group of warriors. If God grants them victory, then you have achieved your goal. If the outcome is otherwise, then you will still be here to harbor our people and provide a haven to which our warriors can return.

1.133 From an address by 'Alī. 'Alī and 'Uthmān exchanged words, whereupon al-Mughīrah ibn al-Akhnas said to 'Uthmān, "I will take care of him for you." 'Alī thundered at Mughīrah:[2]

You son of a barren, cursed father, of a tree without root or branch, you will see to me? By God, no man you support will ever obtain God's aid, no man you prop up will remain standing! Be gone, may God starve you of rain, and do your worst! And if you do, may God see to you!

---

1 In Medina, in 15/636, just before 'Umar, the second Sunni caliph, participated in the march to Palestine. For details of this episode and the conquest of Syro-Palestine see Ḥ 8:298–300; B 481; Ṭabarī, *Tārīkh*, 3:608. Similar context and language in §1.144, re 'Umar's march against the Persians.

2 The incident took place in Medina soon after Abū Dharr's death in exile in Rabadhah in 32/652, when 'Uthmān resolved to also send 'Ammār into exile. 'Alī objected, and Mughīrah— a close associate of 'Uthmān's who would be killed alongside him—came, along with Zayd ibn Thābit, as 'Uthmān's emissary, to remonstrate with and threaten 'Alī (Ibn A'tham, *Futūḥ*, 2:380). Al-Mughīrah ibn al-Akhnas—whose brother, Abū al-Ḥakam, 'Alī had killed at the Battle of Uḥud (details in Ḥ 8:301–303)—was 'Alī's keen enemy. On disagreements between 'Alī and 'Uthmān during the latter's caliphate, see Ḥ 9:3–30.

1.134 ومن كلام له عليه السلام

لم تكن بيعتكم إيّاي فَلْتة وليس أمري وأمركم واحدًا إنّي أريدكم لله وأنتم تريدونني لأنفسكم. أيّها الناس أعينوني على أنفسكم وايم الله لأنصفنّ المظلوم ولأقودنّ الظالم بخَزامته حتّى أورده منهل الحقّ وإن كان كارهًا.

1.135 ومن كلام له عليه السلام في معنى طلحة والزبير

1.135.1 والله ما أنكروا منكرًا ولا جعلوا بيني وبينهم نِصْفًا وإنهم ليطلبون حقًّا[1] تركوه ودمًا هم سفكوه فإن كنت شريكهم فيه فإنّ لهم نصيبهم منه وإن كانوا وَلُوه دوني فا الطَّلبة إلّا قِبَلهم وإنّ أوّل عدلهم للحكم على أنفسهم. وإنّ معي لبصيرتي ما لَبَست ولا لُبَّس عليّ وإنّها لَلفئة الباغية فيها الحمأ والحُمة والشبهة المغدفة وإنّ الأمر لواضح وقد زاح الباطل عن نصابه وانقطع لسانه عن شَغَبه وايم الله لأفرطنّ لهم حوضًا أنا ماتحه لا يصدرون عنه بِرِيّ ولا يَعُبّون بعده في حِسْي.

1.135.2 منه

<hr>

١م، ش، ن، ه: كذا.ي: أضيفت ﴿هم﴾.

1.134   From an address by ʿAlī:[1]

Your oath of allegiance to me was not sworn on an impulse,[2] and, furthermore, our intentions are not the same: I pursue you for the sake of God, while you pursue me for your own ends. People, help me to make you better! By God, I shall bring justice to the oppressed! I shall drag the oppressor by his nose-ring until I bring him kicking and screaming to the waterhole of truth!

1.135   From an address by ʿAlī regarding Ṭalḥah and Zubayr:[3]

1.135.1   By God, they have no cause to fault me, nor is the dispute they raise a fair one. They demand from me a right they abandoned and vengeance for blood they spilt. If I had been their partner in this affair, they would still have their share of culpability. But if they have undertaken it on their own—which they have—then they should be the target of vengeance, and the first justice they mete out should be against themselves. But my conviction has not deserted me, and I have never deceived nor been deceived! They are the treacherous faction![4] Their insides are filled with dark slime, scorpion venom, and black suspicions.[5] But the truth has become clear. Falsehood's grinding mill has been pushed out of its pivot, and its tongue has been curbed from inciting evil. By God, I shall fill the waterhole for them as only I can—they shall neither leave it sated nor ever drink again from a smooth-bottomed pond!

1.135.2   From the same address:[6]

---

1   From ʿAlī's oration in Medina, soon after his accession to the caliphate in 35/656, referring to ʿAbdallāh ibn ʿUmar ibn al-Khaṭṭāb, Saʿd ibn Abī Waqqāṣ, Muḥammad ibn Maslamah, Ḥassān ibn Thābit, and Usāmah ibn Zayd, who refused to pledge allegiance to him and decided to sit out the ongoing conflict. Mufīd, *Irshād*, 1:243, which also includes earlier lines from this oration.

2   Refers to ʿUmar's statement, "The oath of allegiance to Abū Bakr was driven by an impulse (*faltah*), but God protected the community from its evil. Whoever repeats such an action must be killed" (Ḥ 9:31; B 482), narrated widely in both Shiʿi and Sunni sources.

3   From ʿAlī's oration in Dhū Qār just before he left for Basra to fight his challengers at the Battle of the Camel, in 36/656 (Mufīd, *Irshād*, 1:251). See similar lines in §1.10 and §1.22.

4   The commentators state that the definite article "*al-*" in *al-fiʾah al-bāghiyah* (*the* treacherous faction) indicates ʿAlī's prior knowledge of this group based on a portent from the Prophet. B 483; Ḥ 9:37.

5   "Dark slime" (*hamaʾ*) is a metaphor for deceit and corruption (B 483); some say it refers to the Qurʾanic verse in Ḥijr 15:26, which says humans were made from *hamaʾ* (Ḥ 9:34). The variant reading "relative" (*hamā*) is a reference to Zubayr, who was the son of Muḥammad's, and ʿAlī's, paternal aunt (ibid.).

6   Refers to the Muslims in Medina—including Ṭalḥah and Zubayr—who rushed to ʿAlī after ʿUthmān's death, insisting that he accept their oath of allegiance (*bayʿah*). First lines are similar to §1.3.4 (*Shiqshiqiyyah*), §1.53, §1.226.

فأقبلتم إليّ إقبال العُوذ المَطافيل على أولادها تقولون البيعةَ البيعةَ قبضت كفّي فبسطتموها ونازعتكم يدي بجاذبتموها. اللّهمّ إنّهما قطعاني وظلماني ونكثا بيعتي وألّبَا الناس عليّ فأحلل ما عقدا ولا تحكم لهما ما أبرما وأرِهما المَساءة فيما أمّلا وعملا. ولقد ٱسْتَثْبَتُّهما قبل القتال وٱستأنيت بهما أمام الوقاع فغَمَطا النعمة ورَدّا العافية.

1.136   ومن خطبة له عليه السلام في ذكر الملاحم

1.136.1   يعطف الهوى على الهدى إذا عطفوا الهدى على الهوى ويعطف الرأي على القرآن إذا عطفوا القرآن على الرأي.

1.136.2   منها

حتّى تقوم الحرب بكم على ساق باديًا نواجذُها مملوءة أخلافها حلوًا رضاعها علقمًا عاقبتها ألا وفي غدٍ وسيأتي غدٌ بما لا تعرفون يأخذ الوالي من غيرها عمّالها على مساوي أعمالها وتخرج له الأرض أفاليذ كبدها وتلقي إليه سلمًا مقاليدها فيريكم كيف[1] عدل السيرة ويحيي ميّت الكتاب والسنّة.

1.136.3   منها

___

[1] ن، ش، م، ه: كذا. ي، ومصحّحة في ش: أضيفت ﴿يكون﴾.

Shouting "the oath! the oath!" you crowded around me like camel mares snuggling their newborn calves. I closed my palm shut, but you forced it open. I snatched my hand away, but you pulled it toward you. I beseech you, O God: Ṭalḥah and Zubayr have severed my ties of kinship, they have wronged me, they have broken their pledge of allegiance, and incited people to march against me. Undo the knots they have tied, unravel the ropes they have twisted, and show them the opposite of what they wish and strive for! Before beginning the fight, I asked them to return to their pledge; before commencing battle, I gave them a second chance; but they have scorned my kindness and rejected my offer of safety.

1.136 From an oration by ʿAlī containing narratives of epic battles:[1]

1.136.1 He will bend passion to conform to guidance, where others have bent guidance to conform to passion. He will bend caprice to conform to the Qurʾan, where others have bent the Qurʾan to conform to caprice.

1.136.2 From the same oration:
War will stand fierce among you, baring its teeth, with full udders that are sweet to suckle but leave a bitter aftertaste of gourd.[2] Be wary of the morrow which will bring you the unknown. A new sovereign will arrive who will punish governors for their injustice. The earth will reveal to him her inner treasures,[3] and offer him submissively the keys to her fortress. He will make you walk the path of justice and resurrect what you have killed of the Book and the Sunnah.

1.136.3 From the same oration, about an unjust ruler:[4]

---

1   Part of ʿAlī's oration in Basra a few days after the Battle of the Camel in 36/656 (Ṭabrisī, *Iḥti-jāj*, 1:289–290). The commentators state that the reference in §1.136.1 and §1.136.2 is to the Messiah, who will come at the end of time. Ḥ 9:40; B 484, R 2:62.

2   The Arabic sentence begins with *ḥattā* ("until"), connecting to the previous part of the text which is not transcribed.

3   Lit. "The earth will reveal the pieces of its liver (*afālīdh kabidihā*)." Translation after Ḥ 9:46; B 485; R 2:62.

4   The commentators state that this prophecy refers to the Umayyad caliph ʿAbd al-Malik (r. 65–86/685–705) (Ḥ 9:47; B 486), or—unlikely, I think, because of the more immediate context of the lines following—to "a rebel toward the end of time like Sufyānī" (R 2:63), and also because the first few lines are similar to §1.98.3, which also, according to them, refers to ʿAbd al-Malik. Based on the context, I have added the phrase, "about an unjust ruler," to differentiate the paragraph from the one before.

كأنّي به قد نَعَقَ بالشام وفحص براياته في ضَواحي كوفان فعطف عليها عطف الضَّروس وفرش الأرض بالرؤوس قد فَغَرت فاغرته وثقلت في الأرض وطأته بعيدَ الجولة عظيم الصولة والله لَيُشَرِّدَنَّكم في أطراف الأرض حتّى لا يبقى منكم إلّا قليل كالكحل في العين فلا تزالون كذلك حتّى تؤوب إلى العرب عوازب أحلامها فألزموا السنن القائمة والآثار البيّنة والعهد القريب الذي عليه باقي النبوّة واعلموا أنّ الشيطان إنّما يُسَنّي لكم طرقه لتتّبعوا عقبه.

1.137 ومن كلام له عليه السلام في وقت الشورى

لن يسرع أحد قبلي إلى دعوة حقّ وصلة رحم وعائدة كرم فاسمعوا قولي وَعُوا منطقي عسى أن تروا هذا الأمر من بعد هذا اليوم تُنتضى فيه السيوف وتُخان فيه العهود حتّى يكون بعضكم أئمّة لأهل الضلالة وشيعة لأهل الجهالة:

1.138 ومن كلام له عليه السلام في النهي عن عيب[1] الناس

فإنّما ينبغي لأهل العصمة والمصنوع إليهم في السلامة أن يرحموا أهل الذنوب والمعصية ويكون الشكر هو الغالب عليهم والحاجز لهم عنهم. فكيف بالعائب الذي عاب أخاه وعيّره ببلواه أما ذكر موضع ستر الله عليه من ذنوبه ما هو أعظم من الذنب الذي عابه به وكيف يذمّه بذنب قد ركب مثله فإن لم يكن ركب ذلك الذنب بعينه فقد عصى الله فيما سواه ممّا هو أعظم منه وايم الله لئن لم يكن عصاه في الكبير وعصاه في الصغير لَجَراتُه على عيب الناس أكبر يا عبد الله لا تعجل في عيب عبد[2] بذنبه فلعلّه مغفور له ولا تأمن على نفسك صغير معصية فلعلّك معذّب عليه فليكفف مَن علم منكم عيب غيره لما يعلم من عيب نفسه. وليكن الشكر شاغلًا له على معافاته ممّا ابتلي به غيره.

---

[1] م، ي، ومصحّحة في ش، ه: كذا. ن، وأصل ش، ه: ﴿غِيبة﴾.   [2] م، ي، ومصحّحة في ه: كذا. ن، ش، وأصل ه: ﴿أحد﴾.

I can almost see him now as he calls to his flock in Syria and scrapes the ground for his banners to roost in the hinterlands of Kufa. Like an ill-tempered camel mare, he snaps and nips at your townspeople. He carpets its earth with decapitated heads. His jaws wide open, he stamps violently, he ranges far, and his onslaughts are brutal. By God, he will scatter you to the ends of the earth until few remain, as specks of kohl in the eye. You will continue thus until the Arabs' long-departed reason returns home. During that difficult time, hold fast to established practices and clear traces. Look to your recent era that was stamped by the Prophet's mark.[1] Know that Satan smooths his pathways to lure you into treading in his steps.

1.137 From an address by ʿAlī during the Shūrā Council:[2]
No one will outpace me in calling to the truth, fostering kinship, or acting with kindness, so listen to my words and pay attention to what I say. You will see swords drawn over this matter after today, and pledges broken; some of you will become leaders of the errant, others, followers of reckless fools.

1.138 From an address by ʿAlī in which he forbade his followers from exposing people's sins:
It befits those who are protected by good character and blessed with sound judgment to show compassion to sinners and transgressors. Gratitude should be their dominant trait, and it should stop them from pointing fingers. Doesn't the faultfinder who censures his brother and shames him for his trials remember the times when God concealed his own sins, sins that were far graver than the ones he censures his brother for? How can he condemn his brother for a sin he himself has also committed? Even if he has not committed the exact same crime, he has still disobeyed God in other things, some of which were perhaps more severe. By God, even if he has committed no mortal sin, even if has transgressed only in minor ways, his insolence in shaming others is worse than anything else. O servant of God, don't rush to expose your fellow man's offence, perchance God may have forgiven it! Don't think your small transgression trivial, perchance God may punish you for it! Any man who recognizes that he too has committed shameful acts should refrain from shaming another. Thanksgiving for being spared the other man's trials should give him occupation enough.

---

1 Refers to ʿAlī's own caliphate. Ḥ 9:48.
2 In Medina, 23/644. Ṭabarī, *Tārīkh*, 4:236; Ḥ 9:49–58; details of Shūrā Council that appointed ʿUthmān in both.

1.139 ومن كلام له عليه السلام

أيّها الناس من عرف من أخيه وثيقة دين وسداد طريق فلا يسمعنّ فيه أقاويل الرجال١ أما إنّه قد يرمي الرامي وتخطئ السهام ويَحيكُ الكلام وباطل ذلك يبور والله سميع وشهيد أما إنّه ليس بين الحقّ والباطل إلّا أربع أصابع.

فسئل عليه السلام عن معنى قوله هذا بجمع أصابعه ووضعها بين أذنه وعينه ثمّ قال الباطل أن تقول سمعت والحقّ أن تقول رأيت.

1.140 ومن كلام له عليه السلام

وليس لواضع المعروف في غير حقّه وعند غير أهله من الحظّ فيما أتى إلّا محمدة اللئام وثناء الأشرار ومقالة الجهّال ما دام منعمًا عليهم ما أجود يده وهو عن ذات الله بخيل فمن آتاه الله مالًا فليصل به القرابة وليحسن منه الضيافة وليفكّ به الأسير والعاني وليعط منه الفقير والغارم وليصبر نفسه على الحقوق والنوائب ابتغاء الثواب فإنّ فوزًا بهذه الخصال شرف مكارم الدنيا ودرك فضائل الآخرة.٢

1.141 ومن خطبة له عليه السلام في الاستسقاء

1.141.1 ألا وإنّ الأرض التي تحملكم والسماء التي تظلّكم مطيعتان لربّكم وما أصبحتا تجودان لكم ببركتهما توجّعًا لكم ولا زلفة إليكم ولا لخير ترجوانه منكم ولكن أُمِرتا بمنافعكم فأطاعتا وأقيمتا على حدود مصالحكم فقامتا إنّ الله يبتلي عباده عند الأعمال

<hr>

١م، ي، ومصحّحة في ش، ه: كذا.ن، وأصل ش، ه: ﴿الناس﴾. ٢م، ن، ي، ه، ومصحّحة في ش: كذا. أصل ش، وزيادة في م: أضيفت ﴿إن شاء الله﴾.

1.139 From an address by ʿAlī:[1]

People! Whoever knows his brother to have strong faith and good ways should not give ear to the rumors men spread about him. An archer may shoot, and his arrows may stray, but words always wound, and unjust words bring perdition, for God is listening and witnessing. The span of four fingers separates truth from falsehood.

ʿAlī was asked about the meaning of this statement, upon which he lined up his fingers and placed them between his ear and his eye, then said:

"I heard," is false. "I saw," is true.

1.140 From an address by ʿAlī:[2]

A person who distributes gifts in unsuitable quarters and makes presents to undeserving people earns only the praise of the immoral, the tribute of the wicked, and the commendation of the ignorant. As long as he continues to show favor, these churls exclaim, "What a generous hand he possesses!" Yet, when called to spend in God's name, he is tightfisted. If God has granted a person wealth, he should use it to help kin, feed the guest, free the captive and the hostage,[3] and give to the mendicant and the debtor. Even when difficult, he should pay his dues and endure adversities to earn God's reward. These virtues, if won, bring honor in this world and merit in the next.

1.141 From an oration by ʿAlī in which he supplicated God for rain:

1.141.1 Hark! The earth that carries you and the sky that shades you obey their Lord. They favor you with their generous blessings not because they pity you, or seek to endear themselves to you, or hope for your reward, rather, they have been commanded to provide you with benefit and they obey, they have been appointed to ensure your welfare and they comply. Hear me! When God's servants do evil things, he tests them by reducing fruits, curtailing blessings,

---

1   The "span of four fingers" line is included in the following report by al-Aṣbagh ibn Nubātah: The Byzantine Emperor wrote ten questions to Muʿāwiyah, who could not answer, and sent a rider to ʿAlī with the questions. Among the questions was this one, "What is the distance between truth and falsehood?" (Thaqafī, *Ghārāt*, 1:187–188). Presumably in Kufa, toward the end of ʿAlī's life in 40/661.

2   Excerpt from an oration—including § 1.95 and § 1.124—delivered at Ṣiffīn (37/657), when ʿAlī's associates informed him of Muʿāwiyah's lavish rewards and urged him to do the same. Ḥarrānī, *Tuḥaf*, 185; Minqarī, *Waqʿat Ṣiffīn*, 235.

3   Ar. *ānī*, lit. "the exhausted," is translated here as "the hostage," based on the interpretation of the word as synonymous to "the captive" (*asīr*). Ḥ 9:74; B 490; R 2:63.

السيّئة بنقص الثمرات وحبس البركات وإغلاق خزائن الخيرات ليتوب تائب ويُقلع مقلع ويتذكّر متذكّر ويزدجر مزدجر وقد جعل الله سبحانه الاستغفار سبباً لدرور الرزق ورحمة للخلق فقال ﴿ٱسْتَغْفِرُوا رَبَّكُمْ إِنَّهُ كَانَ غَفَّارًا يُرْسِلِ السَّمَاءَ عَلَيْكُم مِّدْرَارًا وَيُمْدِدْكُمْ بِأَمْوَالٍ وَبَنِينَ﴾[1] فرحم الله امرأ ٱستقبل توبته وٱستقال خطيئته وبادر منيّته.

1.141.2 اللّهمّ إنّا خرجنا إليك من تحت الأستار والأكنان وبعد عجيج البهائم والولدان راغبين في رحمتك وراجين فضل نعمتك وخائفين من عذابك ونقمتك. اللّهمّ فٱسقنا غيثك ولا تجعلنا من القانطين ولا تهلكنا بالسنين ولا تؤاخذنا بما فعل السفهاء منّا يا أرحم الراحمين. اللّهمّ إنّا خرجنا إليك نشكو إليك ما لا يخفى عليك حين ألجأتنا المضايق الوَعِرة وأجاءتنا المقاحط المجدبة وأعيتنا المطالب المتعسّرة وتلاحمت علينا الفتن المستصعبة. اللّهمّ إنّا نسألك ألّا تردّنا خائبين ولا تَقلبنا واجمين ولا تخاطبنا بذنوبنا ولا تقايسنا بأعمالنا. اللّهمّ ٱنشر علينا غيثك وبركتك ورزقك ورحمتك وٱسقنا سقيًا نافعة مُروية معشبة تُنبت بها ما قد فات وتحيي بها ما قد مات ناقعة الحيا كثيرة المجتنى تُروي بها القيعان وتُسيل البُطنان وتستورق الأشجار وترخّص الأسعار إنّك على ما تشاء قدير.

1.142 ومن خطبة له عليه السلام

1.142.1 بعث رسله بما خصّهم به من وحيه وجعلهم حجّة له على خلقه لئلّا تجب الحجّة لهم بترك الإعذار إليهم فدعاهم بلسان الصدق إلى سبيل الحقّ ألا إنّ الله قد كشف

---

and locking away treasures, so that any who are stirred to repent, to stop sinning, to listen to reminders, and to heed reproach, may do so. God has made a man's quest for forgiveness the cord that releases sustenance, and his mercy for the world, and he instructs, «Ask your Lord for forgiveness, for he is ever forgiving—he will make the sky pour rain and provide you with wealth and children.»[1] May God show mercy to the person who hastens to repent, renounces sin, and races against death!

1.141.2 God, we have ventured out to you from under shades and shelters, prompted by the heartrending groans of our cattle and our children. We seek your compassion, implore your abundant blessings, and fear your punishment and retribution. God, give us water to drink, send us rain! Do not place us among the disheartened, do not destroy us with years of drought,[2] do not take us to task for what the foolish among us have done,[3] O most compassionate one! God, we have ventured out under the sky to complain of things that are not hidden from you: rough constrictions have made us desperate, ruinous droughts have caused us anguish, extreme indigence has made us weak, and severe trials have banded against us. God, we beseech you, do not turn us away with empty hands! Do not send us back battered by grief! Do not chastise us for our sins! Do not measure us by our deeds! God, spread over us your rainclouds, your grace, your sustenance, and your compassion. Give us water, beneficial, quenching, and refreshing. Let it cause to grow what has withered and revive what has died. Give us drenching rain that yields abundant, ripe fruit. Let it quench plains, make pools overflow, urge trees to leaf and food prices to come down. Doubtless, you are powerful over all that you will.

1.142 From an oration by ʿAlī:

1.142.1 God singled out messengers and sent them bearing his revelation, making them his proof against the people and giving them no cause to say he had stopped providing them with signs—thus, he continually called them to the path of right with the tongue of truth. Hark! God surveils all people, not because he is ignorant of the guarded secrets and the innermost thoughts they conceal,

---

1 Qurʾan, Nūḥ 71:10–12.

2 Lit. "Do not destroy us with those years." Reference to Qurʾan, Aʿrāf 7:130, where Pharaoh's people are seized with years of drought.

3 Reference to Qurʾan, Aʿrāf 7:155, where Moses's people beg forgiveness for having worshipped the Golden Calf.

الخلق كشفة لا أنّه جَهِلَ ما أخفوه من مَصون أسرارهم ومكنون ضمائرهم ولكن ليبلوهم ﴿أَيُّهُمْ أَحْسَنُ عَمَلًا﴾ فيكون الثواب جزاء والعقاب بواء.

أين الذين زعموا أنّهم ﴿الرَّاسِخُونَ فِي الْعِلْمِ﴾ دوننا كذباً وبغياً علينا أن رفعنا الله ووضعهم وأعطانا وحرمهم وأدخلنا وأخرجهم. بنا يستعطى الهدى ويستجلى العمى إنّ الأئمّة من قريش غُرِسوا في هذا البطن من هاشم لا تصلح على سواهم ولا تصلح الولاة من غيرهم.

1.142.2 منها

آثروا عاجلًا وأخّروا آجلًا وتركوا صافياً وشربوا آجنًا. كأنّي أنظر إلى فاسقهم وقد صحب المنكر فألِفَه وبَسِئ به ووافقه حتّى شابت عليه مفارقه وصبغت به خلائقه ثمّ أقبل مُزبدًا كالتيّار لا يبالي ما غرّق أو كوقع النار في الهشيم لا يحفل ما حرّق. أين العقول المستصبحة بمصابيح الهدى والأبصار اللامحة إلى منار التقوى أين القلوب التي وُهبت لله وعوقدت على طاعة الله. ازدحموا على الحُطام وتَشاحّوا على الحرام ورُفع لهم علَم الجنّة والنار فصرفوا عن الجنّة وجوههم وأقبلوا إلى النار بأعمالهم دعاهم ربّهم فنفروا وولّوا ودعاهم الشيطان فاستجابوا وأقبلوا.

1.143 ومن خطبة له عليه السلام

1.143.1 أيّها الناس إنّما أنتم في هذه الدنيا غرَض تنتضل فيه المنايا مع كلّ جُرعة شَرَقٌ وفي كلّ أُكلة غَصَصٌ لا تنالون منها نعمة إلّا بفراق أخرى ولا يعمّر معمّر منكم يوماً من

but because he wishes to test them, to see «who among them performs the best deeds.»[1] His reward is just recompense, and his punishment is equitable retaliation.

Where are the people who claim that they, not we, are the ones «firmly rooted in knowledge»?[2] Their claim is false and treacherous, for God has raised us and lowered them, favored us and deprived them, admitted us and excluded them. It is from us that guidance is to be sought and blindness cured. The Imams of Quraysh sprout from the seedbed of Hāshim. No others are fit for the Imamate. No others are fit to rule.[3]

1.142.2 From the same oration:
They prioritized the present and put off the hereafter, rejected what is pure and drank what is foul. I can almost see their libertines as they go about befriending sin, growing familiar and intimate with it, and staying with it till their hair turns grey, till its dye stains their character; then they step forward, like a foaming torrent that cares not whom it drowns, or like sparks of fire falling on straw that care not what they burn. Where are the minds illumined by lamps of guidance, the eyes that looked to piety's beacon? Where are the hearts that gave themselves to God and bound themselves to his obedience? These people here crowded around worldly baubles and quarreled over forbidden things. Banners for both paradise and hellfire were raised before them, but they averted their faces from paradise and set out to earn hellfire. When their Lord called to them, they turned and bolted. When Satan called to them, they answered him and rushed forward.

1.143 From an oration by ʿAlī:[4]

1.143.1 People! You are targets in this world at which the fates shoot their arrows. With every sip you choke, with every bite you gag. You obtain no blessing without giving up another. No one lives for a day without erasing a day from his allotted time, he consumes nothing without depleting his apportioned sus-

---

1 Qurʾan, Kahf 18:7.

2 Qurʾan, Āl ʿImrān 3:7.

3 ⟨The Imamate is vested in Quraysh⟩ (*al-imāmatu fī l-Quraysh*) is a hadith attributed to the Prophet Muḥammad. The Shiʿi commentator takes ʿAlī's lines about it being confined to the clan of Hāshim, as confirmation that the Imamate is vested solely in the Prophet's family (B 494). The Sunni commentator—who acknowledges that if ʿAlī said this then it must be true—takes it as an optimal, but not required, state of affairs (Ḥ 9:88).

4 In Ḥarrānī, *Tuḥaf*, 98, §1.143.1 is an excerpt from a longer, aphoristic oration titled The Intercessor (*Wasīlah*). Other excerpts are §3.29, §3.99, §3.103, §3.175, and §3.195.

عمره إلّا بهدم آخر من أجله ولا تجدّد له زيادة في أكله إلّا بنفاد ما قبلها من رزقه ولا يحيا له أثر إلّا مات ولا يتجدّد له أثر ولا يخلق له جديد إلّا بعد أن يخلق له جديد ولا تقوم له نابتة إلّا وتسقط منه محصودة.١ وقد مضت أصول نحن فروعها فما بقاء فرع بعد ذهاب أصله.

١.١٤٣.٢   منها

وما أحدثت بدعة إلّا تُرك بها سنّة فاتّقوا البدع والزموا المَهْيَع إنّ عوازم الأمور أفضلها وإنّ محدثاتها شِرارها.

١.١٤٤   ومن كلام له عليه السلام وقد استشاره عمر بن الخطّاب في الشخوص لقتال الفرس بنفسه

إنّ هذا الأمر لم يكن نصره ولا خذلانه بكثرة ولا بقلّة وهو دين الله الذي أظهره وجنده الذي أعدّه وأمدّه حتّى بلغ ما بلغ وطلع حيث طلع ونحن على موعود من الله والله منجز وعده وناصر جنده. ومكانُ القَيِّم بالأمر مكانُ النِّظام من الخَرَز يجمعه ويضمّه فإن انقطع النظام تفرّق وذهب ثمّ لم يجتمع بحَذافيره أبدًا. والعرب اليوم وإن كانوا قليلًا فهم كثيرون بالإسلام عزيزون بالاجتماع فكن قطبًا واستَدِر الرَّحا بالعرب وأصلِهم دونك نار الحرب فإنّك إن شخصت من هذه الأرض انتقضت عليك العرب من أطرافها وأقطارها حتّى يكون ما تدع وراءك من العورات أهمّ إليك ممّا بين يديك. إنّ الأعاجم إن ينظروا إليك غدًا يقولوا هذا أصل العرب فإذا اقتطعتموه استرحتم فيكون ذلك أشدّ لكَلَبِهم عليك وطمعهم فيك فأمّا ما ذكرت من مسير القوم إلى قتال المسلمين فإنّ الله سبحانه هو أكره لمسيرهم منك وهو أقدر على تغيير ما يكره وأمّا ما ذكرت من عددهم فإنّا لم نكن نقاتل فيما مضى بالكثرة وإنّما كنّا نقاتل بالنصر والمعونة.

---

١ م، ش، ي، ه: كذا. ن: ⟨محصودة⟩، ومصحّحة في ش: ⟨محضودة⟩.

tenance, no sign of him is revitalized without another dying out, no new clothes are given to him except after the earlier ones have worn out, and no new shoots grow except after the dead wood is cut down. The roots have gone, and we are their branches—how long can a branch survive after its root has died?

1.143.2 From the same oration:
No heresy is innovated without an accepted practice being abandoned, so fear innovations and keep to the highway. The ancient ways are best, the newfangled ones are evil.

1.144 From an address by ʿAlī to ʿUmar ibn al-Khaṭṭāb responding to his request for advice on whether he should lead the expedition to fight the Persians:[1]
In this matter, victory or defeat will not hinge on how large the number of troops is or how small. This is God's faith that he has made victorious, and his army that he has prepared and equipped, until it reached what it has, and spread where it has. We await the fulfilment of God's pledge—God will fulfil his pledge and grant his victory to his army.[2] The custodian of the caliphate is like a string to beads, it gathers them and holds them together. If the string breaks, they scatter and disperse and are never whole again. The Arabs, though few today, are many by virtue of Islam, and mighty because they are united. You should be the pivot that spins them like grain in your mill. Have them brave the fires of war instead of you. If you leave the region, the Bedouins will swoop in from all sides and from the peripheries until the unguarded areas you leave behind will give you far more cause for concern than the ones that lie before you. If the Persians see you tomorrow, they will say, "Here is the Arab's tree trunk, cut him down, and you can sit back!" Their rage against you will become rabid, and their hunger to get you intensify. Yes, as you say, they march to fight the Muslims. But God detests their expedition more than you do, and he has more power to change what he detests. As for what you say about their numbers, we didn't fight in the past on the strength of superior numbers. We fought on the strength of God's support and aid.

---

1 Madāʾinī (*Futūḥ*, lost, cited by Ibn Abī al-Ḥadīd) places this address before the Battle of Qādisiyyah in ca. 16/637, and Ṭabarī (*Tārīkh*, 4:124) before the Battle of Nahāwand in 21/642, both against the Persians—details from both works are transcribed in Ḥ 9:96–102; B 497. Similar context and language in §1.132 re ʿUmar's march against the Byzantines.

2 Reference to Prophet Muḥammad's hadith (الحمد لله الذي أنجز وعده ونصر عبده وهزم الأحزاب وحده), narrated in, e.g., Ibn Ḥanbal, *Musnad*, §4907.

1.145 ومن خطبة له عليه السلام

1.145.1 فبعث محمّدًا بالحقّ ليخرج عباده من عبادة الأوثان إلى عبادته ومن طاعة الشيطان إلى طاعته بقرآن قد بيّنه وأحكمه ليَعلم العبادُ ربَّهم إذ جهلوه وليُقرّوا به بعد إذ جحدوه وليُثبتوه بعد إذ أنكروه فتجلّى سبحانه لهم في غير أن يكونوا رأوه بما أراهم من قدرته وخوّفهم من سطوته وكيف محَقَ مَن محق بالمَثُلات واحتصد من احتصد بالنّقمات.

1.145.2 وإنّه سيأتي عليكم من بعدي زمان ليس فيه شيء أخفى من الحقّ ولا أظهر من الباطل ولا أكثر من الكذب على الله ورسوله وليس عند أهل ذلك الزمان سِلْعَة أَبْوَر من الكتاب إذا تُلي حقّ تلاوته ولا أنفق منه إذا حُرّف عن مواضعه ولا في البلاد شيء أنكر من المعروف ولا أعرف من المنكر. فقد نَبَذَ الكتاب حَمَلَتُه وتناساه حفظته فالكتاب يومئذ وأهله مَنفيّان طريدان وصاحبان مصطحبان في طريق واحد لا يؤويهما مُؤْوٍ. فالكتاب وأهله في ذلك الزمان في الناس وليسا فيهم ومعهم وليسا معهم لأنّ الضلالة لا توافق الهدى وإن اجتمعا واجتمع القوم على الفرقة وافترقوا عن الجماعة كأنّهم أَئمَّة الكتاب وليس الكتاب إمامهم فلم يبق عندهم منه إلّا اسمه ولا يعرفون إلّا خطّه وزَبْره. ومن قبل ما مَثّلوا بالصالحين كلّ مُثلة وسمّوا صدقهم على الله فِرية وجعلوا في الحسنة العقوبة[1] السيئة. وإنّما هلك من كان قبلكم بطول آمالهم وتغيّب آجالهم حتّى نزل بهم الموعود الذي تُردّ عنه المعذرة وترفع عنه التوبة وتحلّ معه القارعة والنقمة.

1.145.3 أيّها الناس إنّه من استنصح الله وُفِّق ومن اتّخذ قوله دليلًا هدي ﴿لِلَّتِي هِيَ أَقْوَمُ﴾ فإنّ جار الله آمِنٌ وعدوّه خائف وإنّه لا ينبغي لمن عرف عظمة الله أن يتعظّم

1.145   From an oration by ʿAlī:[1]

1.145.1   God sent Muḥammad to turn his servants from worship of idols to his worship, from obeying Satan to his obedience. He sent him with the truth, with a clear and comprehensive Qurʾan, so his servants may know how to recognize their Lord after their earlier ignorance of him, that they may acknowledge him after prior repudiation, and accept him after previous denial. He, the Most Luminous, unveiled to them in his Book without their ever seeing him, by showing them his power, warning them of his rule, and reminding them that he had destroyed nations with his strong reckoning and reaped lives in harsh punishment.

1.145.2   After I am gone, you will see a time when there will be nothing more suppressed than right, nothing more dominant than wrong, and nothing more prevalent than false attributions to God and his Messenger. No commodity will be worth less than the Book's proper recitation or valued more than its blatant corruption. Nothing anywhere will be less familiar than good or more prominent than evil. Those who had upheld the Book will have cast it away, and those who had memorized it will pretend they remember nothing. On that day, the Book and its Companions will be banished into exile, two friends walking together whom no one is willing to shelter. In that age, the Book and its Companions will be among the people yet not among them, they will be with the people yet not with them, for error is not compatible with righteousness, even if they come together in one place. People will unite in their dissension, they will splinter from the congregation, they will think themselves to be imams who rule the Book rather than realizing that the Book is the Imam who rules them. Nothing of the Book will remain with them except its name, they will know nothing of it but its script and scrolls. In all this time, they will continue to inflict torture on the pious, mislabel their truths as lies against God, and requite their good with evil. You should know that those who lived before you perished because they harbored long hopes and neglected their diminishing lifespans. The end befell them as promised—a time when all excuses are rejected, all opportunity to repent removed, and calamity and punishment come home to roost.

1.145.3   People! Those who seek God's counsel receive direction, those who take his word as guide are led to «the path that is straightest»,[2] and those whom

---

1   From ʿAlī's oration at Dhū Qār, just before the Battle of the Camel at Basra in 36/656. Kulaynī, *Kāfī*, 8:386–391.
2   Qurʾan, Isrāʾ 17:9.

فإنّ رفعة الذين يعلمون ما عظمته أن يتواضعوا له وسلامة الذين يعلمون ما قدرته أن يستسلموا له فلا تنفروا من الحقّ نفار الصحيح من الأجرب والباريّ من ذي السقم. واعلموا أنّكم لن تعرفوا الرشد حتّى تعرفوا الذي تركه ولن تأخذوا بميثاق الكتاب حتّى تعرفوا الذي نقضه ولن تمسّكوا به حتّى تعرفوا الذي نبذه فالتمسوا ذلك من عند أهله فإنّهم عيش العلم وموت الجهل هم الذين يخبركم حكمهم[1] عن علمهم وصمتهم عن منطقهم وظاهرهم عن باطنهم لا يخالفون الدين ولا يختلفون فيه فهو بينهم شاهد صادق وصامت ناطق.

1.146 ومن خطبة له عليه السلام في ذكر أهل البصرة

كلّ واحد منهما يرجو الأمر له ويعطفه عليه دون صاحبه لا يمتّان إلى الله بحبل ولا يمدّان إليه بسبب كلّ واحد منهما حاملُ ضَبٍّ لصاحبه وعمّا قليل يكشف قناعه به والله لئن أصابوا الذي يريدون لينتزعنّ هذا نفس هذا وليأتينّ هذا على هذا. قد قامت الفئة الباغية فأين المحتسبون قد سُنّت لهم السنن وقُدّم لهم الخبر ولكلّ ضَلّة علّة ولكلّ ناكث شبهة والله لا أكون كمستمع اللَّدْم يَسمع الناعي ويحضر الباكي ثمّ لا يعتبر.[2]

---

[1] م، ي، ه، ونسخة في ش: كذا. ن، وأصل ش: ‹حلمهم›.   [2] ن، ش: كذا. م، ي، ه: سقطت ‹ثمّ لا يعتبر›.

God protects are safe, while those who challenge him are fearful. All who recognizes God's greatness should avoid self-glorification, for real exaltation comes from humility before God, just as the security of those who know God's power comes from their submission to him. So shy not away from the truth, like the healthy from the mangy, or the sound from the sick. Know this: you will not recognize guidance until you know who has abandoned it, you will not abide by your pledge to the Book until you know who has broken it, you will not hold fast to it until you know who has cast it aside. Seek the truth from the people of truth. They are the life of knowledge and the death of ignorance. Their judgments reveal to you their knowledge, their silence tells you of their reason, and their outward aspect shows you their inner being. They never violate religion or diverge from its laws—it is always among them as a truthful witness and a silent speaker.

1.146 From an oration by ʿAlī about the people of Basra:[1]
Each of the two wants the caliphate, he maneuvers it toward himself and away from the other, with no rope in this affair connecting them to God, no cord attaching them to him. Each of the two harbors the malice of a treacherous, spiny-tailed lizard against his companion,[2] and before long, he will remove his mask. By God, if they got what they wanted, each would assault the other, each would threaten the other's life. Behold! The treacherous faction has risen! Are there any among you who would seek God's reward? Clear paths have been laid out for you and you have warnings from the past. Every error has a trigger, and every breach is prompted by doubt. By God, I shall not be like the hyena listening meekly to the sound of pebbles being thrown,[3] nor yet like the person who hears a death proclaimed and sees the mourners but pays no heed.[4]

---

1   The "people of Basra" refers to those who fought ʿAlī in the Battle of the Camel, outside Basra in 36/656; the oration is from the lead-up to the battle, and "the two" refers to two of his three chief adversaries in the battle, Ṭalḥah and Zubayr (the third was ʿĀʾishah, who is not mentioned), (Ḥ 9:109; B 502; R 2:75). Details of the battle in Ḥ 9:111–115.

2   Lit. ⟨he carries a spiny-tailed lizard⟩ (*ḥāmil ḍabb*), a proverb that signifies betrayal; the spiny-tailed lizard is said to devour its young. B 502.

3   Lit. "the one who listens to the sound of pebbles hitting the ground" (*ka-mustamiʿ al-ladm*). My translation, with the insertion of the word "hyena," is based on Ḥ 9:109–110; R 2:75–76. The same simile, with an explicit mention of the word hyena, is used in §1.6: see note there for details. Other commentators explain the phrase non-zoologically, connecting it with events alluded to in the next two phrases, as "the sound of hitting and weeping as a sign of danger," B 502, and, in a similar vein, "slapping on the face and chest as an act of mourning," ʿA 627.

4   Refers to Ṭalḥah and his companions' killing of Ḥakīm ibn Jabalah and his followers in Basra before the Battle of the Camel, 36/656. Ḥ 9:110.

1.147   ومن كلامه له عليه السلام قبل موته

أيّها الناس كلُّ امرئٍ لاقٍ ما يفرّ منه في فراره والأجل مَساقُ النفس والهرب منه مُوافاته كم اطّردتُ الأيّامَ أبْحَثُها عن مكنون هذا الأمر فأبى الله إلّا إخفاءه هيهات علم مخزون. أمّا وصيّتي فالله لا تشركوا به شيئًا ومحمّد فلا تضيّعوا سنّته. أقيموا هذين العمودين وأوقدوا هذين المصباحين وخَلاكم ذمّ ما لم تَشرُدوا. حُمّل كلُّ امرئٍ مجهودَه وخُفّف عن الجهلة. رَبٌّ رحيم ودين قويم وإمام عليم. أنا بالأمس صاحبكم وأنا اليوم عبرة لكم وغدًا مفارقكم غفر الله لي ولكم إن تثبت الوطأة في هذه المزلّة فذاك وإن تدحَض القدم فإنّا كنّا في أفْياء أغصان ومَهابّ رياح وتحت ظلّ غمام اضمحلّ في الجوّ مُتلفّقُها وعَفا في الأرض مَخَطُّها. وإنّما كنت جارًا جاوركم بدني أيّامًا وستعقُبون منّي جُثّةً خلاءً ساكنةً بعد حراك وصامتة بعد نُطوق ليعظكم هُدوّي وخُفوت إطراقي وسكون أطرافي فإنّه أوعظ للمعتبرين من المنطق البليغ والقول المسموع. ودَاعيكم وداعُ امرئ مُرصد للتلاقي غدًا ترون أيّامي ويُكشف لكم عن سرائري وتعرفوني بعد خلوّ مكاني وقيام غيري مقامي.

1.148   ومن خطبة له عليه السلام في الملاحم

1.148.1   وأخذوا يمينًا وشمالًا ظعنًا في مسالك الغيّ وتركًا لمذاهب الرشد فلا تستعجلوا ما هو كائن مُرصَد ولا تستبطئوا ما يجيء به الغد فكم من مستعجل بما إن أدركه ودَّ أنّه لم يدركه وما أقرب اليوم من تباشير غد. يا قوم هذا إبّانُ ورود كلّ موعود ودنوّ من طلعة ما لا تعرفون ألا وإنّ من أدركها منّا يسري فيها بسراج منير ويحذو فيها على

---

١ ن، ش، ويبدو في ي، ونسخة في ه: كذا. م، وأصل ه: ﴿طعنًا﴾.

1.147 From an address by ʿAlī just before his death:[1]
People! Each person shall meet what he flees as he flees,[2] for death is the place toward which the soul is driven and running away only brings it closer. How many days I wasted searching for the answer to this mystery, but God would not allow it to be revealed! Far from it! A guarded piece of knowledge! My testament is this: Hold fast to God and do not assign him partners. Hold fast to Muḥammad and do not squander his Sunnah. Erect these two pillars, kindle these two lamps, and, as long as you do not bolt from their stable, no blame will attach to you. Each person is made to carry his own burden, although the ignorant masses are given a lighter load. Your Lord is compassionate, your religion is strong, and your Imam is endowed with knowledge. Yesterday I was your companion, today I am a lesson for you to heed, and tomorrow I shall leave you. May God pardon both you and me. If my foot regains its balance on this slippery ground, then that was meant to be. But if it slips, then know that the shade of the tree of life is intermittent, winds come and go, clouds that cast shadows are soon dispersed, and signs are quick to vanish. For a while I was your companion, my body your neighbor. Soon you will see my empty corpse, motionless after having movement, silent after possessing speech. Let the quiet of my pose, the closing of my eyes, the stillness of my limbs, teach you a lesson, a lesson more effective than eloquent speech and loud words. I bid you farewell, eager for my meeting with God! Tomorrow, when you will look back on my life, my worth will be revealed to you. You will know me then, when my seat is empty, and someone else has taken my place.

1.148 From an oration by ʿAlī containing accounts of epic events:

1.148.1 Those others went right and left, travelling the paths of error and forsaking the roads of guidance. People, don't be impatient for the arrival of an anticipated event or deem slow tomorrow's child! Many's the person impatient for a thing that, were he to attain it, would wish he never had. How close is today to the glimmer of tomorrow! This is the moment when all that is promised begins. The dawn of a time you will not recognize is come. Hark! A man from our family will witness this time, and he will traverse the night with a bright lamp.[3] He will follow the example of the pious, loosen that which is bound,

---

1 Part of a testament—that includes § 2.23—delivered in his home in Kufa in 40/661, where he was carried after the deathblow. Kulaynī, *Kāfī*, 1:299.

2 Reference to Qurʾan, Jumʿah 62:8.

3 Interpreted as referring to the "Rightly Guided" Messiah from the family of the Prophet, "Mahdī," who will come at the end of time (Ḥ 9:128–129; B 506; R 2:82). I have added the word "family" for clarity; the Arabic is more cryptic, "a man from among us."

مثال الصالحين ليحلّ فيها رِبْقًا ويُعتِق رِقًّا ويصدع شَعْبًا ويَشعَب صَدْعًا في سترة عن الناس لا يبصر القائف أثره ولو تابع نظره ثمّ لَيُشحَذنّ فيها قومٌ شَحْذَ القَينِ النصلَ يُجْلى بالتنزيل أبصارهم ويرمى بالتفسير في مسامعهم ويُغبَقون كأس الحكمة بعد الصَّبوح.

1.148.2 منها

وطال الأمد بهم ليستكملوا الخزي ويستوجبوا الغِيَر حتّى إذا اخلولق الأجل واستراح قوم إلى الفتن واشتالوا عن لَقاح حربهم لم يمنّوا على الله بالصبر ولم يستعظموا بذل أنفسهم في الحقّ حتّى إذا وافق وارد القضاء انقطاع مدّة البلاء حملوا بصائرهم على أسيافهم ودانوا لربّهم بأمر واعظهم.

1.148.3 حتّى إذا قبض الله رسوله صلّى الله عليه وآله رجع قوم على الأعقاب وغالتهم السبل واتّكلوا على الولائج ووصلوا غير الرحم وهجروا السبب الذي أمروا بمودّته ونقلوا البناء عن رَصّ أساسه فبنوه في غير موضعه معادن كل خطيّة وأبواب كل ضارب في غمرة قد ماروا في الحيرة وذَهَلوا في السكرة على سنّةٍ من آل فرعون من منقطع إلى الدنيا راكن أو مفارق للدين مباين.

free those who are in bondage, sunder those who share a bond, and unite those who are dispersed. In all this, he will remain concealed from the people; no tracker will uncover his traces no matter how keenly he scans the ground. Then, a group will rise with resolve sharpened like a whetted sword.[1] Their eyes will be opened by the Revealed Book, their ears will be filled with its interpretation, and they will be served the cup of wisdom morning and night.

1.148.2 From the same oration:
Their term was prolonged so they could finish their shameful deeds and deserve to be struck with cataclysms.[2] Then, when that era's fabric frayed,[3] while one group became comfortable with sedition and refused to impregnate war's camel, another group endured without thinking that in laying down their lives for truth, they were doing God a favor, or anything more that they should. Finally, when the period of tribulation ended as ordained, they unsheathed their swords to spread their beliefs and drew close to their Lord at their guide's command.

1.148.3 Then, when God took back his Messenger, one group turned on their heels, and followed roads that tempted them into the waterless waste.[4] They relied on treachery,[5] cultivated other people but not the Prophet's family,[6] and abandoned his kin, whom they had been commanded to love.[7] Uprooting the edifice from its fortified foundation, they erected it in the wrong location. These people are mother lodes of every sin and entry ways for those who set out on dangerous waters. In the manner of Pharaoh's family, they drifted without comprehension, intoxicated and confounded. Some devoted themselves to the world and inclined toward it, others deserted and discarded the faith.

---

1   Lit. "a group will rise sharpened like a whetted sword." I have added "with resolve" based on Ḥ 9:128; alternatively, "with minds" (B 506).
2   Interpreted as referring to an errant faction who usurped rule (Ḥ 9:130; B 507); enemies of the family of the Prophet (R 2:82).
3   Ar. *ikhlawlaqa*, translation based on R 2:82; B 507. Or, "became ready to rain down," said of a cloud, or "were razed to the ground," said of a house. Ḥ 9:130.
4   This segment may follow from the previous one (R 2:85), or it is a new segment (B 507). Ṭabarī-Āmulī (*Mustarshid*, 401) prefaces §1.48.3 by saying that a group of people had harbored malice against ʿAlī since the time of the Prophet, and after his death, their enmity came into the open. He cites the full address.
5   Ar. *walāʾij*, translated as "treachery" after R 2:85; or "partisans," B 508.
6   Lit. "not the family"; translation based on Ḥ 9:132; B 508.
7   Interpreted as a reference to Qurʾan, Shūrā 42:23: «Say, I do not ask of you any recompense except love for (my) kin.» Ḥ 9:133; B 508.

1.149   ومن خطبة له عليه السلام

1.149.1   وأستعينه على مَداحر الشيطان ومَزاجره والاعتصام من حبائله ومَخاتله. وأُشهد أنّ محمّدًا عبده ورسوله ونجيبه وصفوته لا يوازى فضله ولا يجبر فقده أضاءت به البلاد بعد الضلالة المظلمة والجهالة الغالبة والجفوة الجافية والناس يستحلّون الحريم ويستذلّون الحكيم يحيَون على فترة ويموتون على كَفْرة.

1.149.2   ثمّ إنّكم معشر العرب أغراض بلايا قد اقتربت فاتّقوا سكرات النعمة واحذروا بوائق النقمة وتثبّتوا في قَتام العشوة واعوجاج الفتنة عند طلوع جنينها وظهور كَمينها وانتصاب قطبها ومَدار رَحاها. تبدأ في مدارج خفيّة وتؤول إلى فظاعة جليّة. شِبابها كشِباب الغلام وآثارها كآثار السِّلام تتوارثها الظلمة بالعهود أوّلهم قائد لآخرهم وآخرهم مقتدٍ بأوّلهم يتنافسون في دنيا دنيّة ويتكالبون على جيفة مريحة وعن قليل يتبرّأ التابع من المتبوع والقائد من المقود فيتزايلون بالبغضاء ويتلاعنون عند اللقاء.

1.149.3   ثمّ يأتي بعد ذلك طالع الفتنة الرَّجوف والقاصمة الزَّحوف فتزيغ قلوب بعد استقامة وتضلّ رجال بعد سلامة وتختلف الأهواء عند هجومها وتلتبس الآراء عند نجومها من أشرف لها قصمته ومن سعى فيها حطمته يتكادمون فيها تكادم الحُمُر في العانَة قد اضطرب معقود الحبل وعمي وجه الأمر تغيض فيها الحكمة وتنطق فيها الظلمة

1.149 From an oration by ʿAlī:

1.149.1 I ask him for aid against Satan's expulsions and evictions.[1] I seek his protection against Satan's snares and ambushes. I bear witness that Muḥammad is his servant and messenger, his chosen one and his elect. His virtues cannot be matched, and the heartbreak caused by his loss cannot be mended.[2] The land became illuminated with Muḥammad's light after a time of black error, intense ignorance and uncouth ways, a time when people had made the unlawful legal and demeaned the wise, when they were living in a state of stupor,[3] and dying as unbelievers.

1.149.2 You, Arabs, are targets for approaching calamities, so be fearful lest your blessings intoxicate you and beware the blows of God's punishment. Remain firm when dust storms darken, when sedition begins to twist and turn, when its fetus is born, and its secret made manifest, when its pivot becomes entrenched, and its mill begins to turn. Sedition begins on hidden paths and soon reaches the status of clear atrocity. It dances around like a young boy, but its footprints are like wounds made by stoning. Tyrants inherit it, one from the other, through mutual agreement, the first among them impelling the last, and the last among them emulating the first. They compete fiercely for this vile world and fight like dogs over its stinking carcass. Soon the follower will dissociate from the one he followed, and the driver from those he steered. They will disown one another in enmity when they meet face to face, each will curse the other.

1.149.3 After the first, a second seismic sedition, a crushing, relentless sedition, will march. Hearts once steadfast will falter, men once righteous will stray, tempestuous passions will bolt in every direction, and capricious opinions will appear in every quarter and lead to total confusion; this sedition will crush all who rise to face it and shatter all who attempt to withstand; people will nip and bite at one another like a herd of wild asses; knots will be undone and direction will be obscured; wisdom will recede and tyrants will speak out; sedition's iron

---

1 The line could also be translated as, "I ask God for aid in expelling Satan and driving him out" (R 2:85), where the subject of the expulsion is the speaker and the object is Satan, rather than the other way around. In either case, the speaker is asking God for aid in withstanding Satan. Some commentaries offer both readings (B 509; H 9:138).

2 Lit. "cannot be splinted (*yujbaru*)," referring to the joining of broken bones, a metaphor for coming to terms with a death or other painful event.

3 Ar. *fatrah*. Or, "living during the interval between prophets." H 9:139; B 510; R 2:85; A 628, citing Qurʾan, Māʾidah 5:19.

342	TEXT AND TRANSLATION

وتدُقّ أهل البدو وبِمِسحَلها وتَرُضّهم بكلكلها يضيع في غبارها الوُحدان ويهلك في طريقها الرُكبان ترد بمرّ القضاء وتحلب عَبيط الدماء وتثلِم منار الدين وتنقض عُقَد اليقين تهرب منها الأكياس وتدبّرها الأرجاس مِرعادٌ مِبراقٌ كاشفة عن ساق تُقطع فيها الأرحام ويفارَق عليها الإسلام بريئها سقيم وظاعنها مقيم.

1.149.4	منها

بين قتيل مطلول وخائف مستجير يَختِلون بعَقْد الأيمان وبغرور الإيمان فلا تكونوا أنصاب الفتن وأعلام البدع والزموا ما عقد عليه حبل الجماعة وبنيت عليه أركان الطاعة وأقدموا على الله مظلومين ولا تقدّموا عليه ظالمين واتّقوا مدارج الشيطان ومهابط العدوان ولا تدخلوا بطونكم لُعَق الحرام فإنّكم بعين من حرّم عليكم المعصية وسهّل لكم سبيل الطاعة.[1]

1.150	ومن خطبة له عليه السلام

1.150.1	الحمد لله الدالّ على وجوده بخلقه وبمُحدَث خلقه على أزليّته وباشتباههم على أن لا شِبْه له لا تَستلمه المشاعر ولا تحجبه السواتر لأفتراق الصانع والمصنوع والحادّ والمحدود والربّ والمربوب الأحد لا بتأويل عدد والخالق لا بمعنى حركة ونصب والسميع لا بأداة والبصير لا بتفريق آلة والشاهد لا بمماسّة والبائن لا بتراخي مسافة والظاهر لا برؤية والباطن لا بلطافة بانَ من الأشياء بالقهر لها والقدرة عليها وبانت الأشياء منه بالخضوع له والرجوع إليه من وصفه فقد حدّه ومن حدّه فقد عدّه ومن عدّه فقد أبطل أزَلَه ومن قال كيف فقد أستوصفه ومن قال أين فقد حَيَّزَه. عالم إذ لا معلوم وربّ إذ لا مربوب وقادر إذ لا مقدور.

---

bridle will bruise the Bedouins and its looming torso will crush them; individuals will be lost in its dust and riders will perish in its path; it will come bearing bitter fate, and when milked, it will yield fresh blood; it will extinguish the beacon of faith, and undo the bonds of certainty; the intelligent will flee, while the degenerate will be mesmerized; it will hurl bolts of thunder and lightning and bare its shanks;[1] kinship ties will be cut, and Islam will be forsaken; the unscathed will be afflicted, and the shirker will not escape.

1.149.4 From the same oration:
Some will be killed, their blood unavenged, others, desperately afraid, will seek asylum, and people everywhere will be taken in by false oaths and the pretense of faith. Be watchful, all of you, that you don't turn into temples of sedition or waymarks of heresy. Stay with the true belief to which the community's rope is bound, and on which the pillars of obedience are raised. Go forward to God as victims of oppression, not inflictors. Beware the ways of Satan, beware the abyss of rancor. Don't fill your stomachs with unlawful morsels. Remember! You are watched by the one who has forbidden sin and smoothed the path of obedience.

1.150 From an oration by ʿAlī:[2]

1.150.1 Praise God, who demonstrated his existence through his creatures, his eternity through their temporality, and his singularity through their resemblance to one another. But although veils cannot conceal him, neither can senses grasp him, for the craftsman and the handicraft, the delimiter and the delimited, the master and the servant, are mutually distinct. He is one but not in the sense of numbers, the creator but not through movement and effort, the hearer but not with an appendage, the seer but not through an organ, the witness but not by being present, the separate but not through distance, the manifest but not through vision, and the hidden but not because he is transparent. He is separate from all things, for he subjugates and wields power over them, and all things are separate from him, for they bow and return to him. To describe him is to circumscribe him, to circumscribe him is to quantify him, and to quantify him is to deny his eternity. To ask "How?" is to seek a description of him, to ask "Where?" is to confine him. He was knowledgeable when there was nothing to be known, Lord when there was no one to be Lord over, and powerful when there was nothing over which to wield power.

---

1 Ar. *kāshifatun ʿan sāq*, echoes Qurʾan, Qalam 68:42; it connotes severe hardship (Ḥ 9:145), or girding for an attack (B 511).
2 From the beginning of ʿAlī's caliphate in Medina, in 35/656. Ḥ 9:153; R 2:91; B 515.

1.150.2 مِنها

قد طلع طالع ولمع لامع ولاح لائح وَاعتدل مائل وَاستبدل الله بقوم قومًا وبيوم يومًا
وَانتظرنا الغِيَرَ اَنتظار المُجدِب المطر وإنّما الأئمّة قوّام الله على خلقه وعرفاؤه على عباده
لا يدخل الجنّة إلّا من عرفهم وعرفوه ولا يدخل النار إلّا من أنكرهم وأنكروه. إنّ الله
خصّكم بالإسلام وَاستخصلكم له وذلك لأنّه اَسم سلامة وبِجماع كرامة اَصطفى الله
تعالى منهجه وبيّن حججه من ظاهر علم وباطن حكم لا تفنى غرائبه ولا تنقضي عجائبه
فيه مرابيع النعم ومصابيح الظلم لا تفتح الخيرات إلّا بمفاتحه ولا تكشف الظلمات إلّا
بمصابحه قد أحمى حماه وأرعى مرعاه فيه شفاء المشتفي وكفاية المكتفي.

1.151 ومن خطبة له عليه السلام

1.151.1 وهو في مُهلة من الله يهوي مع الغافلين ويغدو مع المذنبين بلا سبيل قاصد ولا
إمام قائد.

1.151.2 مِنها

حتّى إذا كَشف لهم عن جزاء معصيتهم وَاستخرجهم من جلابيب غفلتهم اَستقبلوا
مدبرًا وَاستدبروا مقبلًا فلم ينتفعوا بما أدركوا من طَلبتهم ولا بما قضوا من وَطرهم. فإنّي
أحذّركم ونفسي هذه المنزلة فلينتفع اَمرؤ بنفسه فإنّما البصير من سمع فتفكّر ونظر فأبصر
وَانتفع بالعبر ثمّ سلك جَدَدًا واضحًا يتجنّب فيه الصَّرْعة في المهاوي والضلال في المغاوي
ولا يعين على نفسه الغواة بتعسّف في حقّ أو تحريف في نطق أو تخوّف من صدق

____

١ ن، م، ش، ه: كذا. ي: كذا، ومصحّحة في ه: ﴿حلم﴾.

1.150.2 From the same oration:

What was going to rise has risen, what was going to shine forth has shone, what was going to emerge has emerged, and what had listed to one side has straightened. God has replaced one group with another, one day with another, a change we awaited as the drought-stricken wait for rain. Hear me! The Imam is God's caretaker over his creatures and the leader he has appointed over his servants: no one will enter paradise except those he recognizes and who recognize him, no one will enter hellfire except those he denies and who deny him.[1] God has privileged and blessed you with Islam: its name denotes safety and it is the aggregate of honor; its way is chosen by God, and its proofs are explained by him, both its manifest knowledge and its concealed wisdom;[2] its wonders never cease, its marvels never end; it boasts verdant blessings and lamps that dispel darkness; its keys open goodness, its lamps dispel the dark; God has strengthened its fortifications and permitted grazing in its pastures; it heals those who seek healing and suffices those who seek sufficiency.

1.151 From an oration by ʿAlī:[3]

1.151.1 Such men, during the respite granted them by God, fall into error with the heedless, and set out every morning with sinners, with no path to follow, no Imam to guide them.

1.151.2 From the same oration:

Then, when God reveals the payback for their disobedience and tears off their garments of negligence, they must face what they ignored and leave what they loved, benefitting not at all from desires they slaked or passions they gratified. I warn you—and myself—don't reach this station! Let each man save himself! The discerning listens and contemplates, he sees and understands, he learns from exemplary lessons, follows the clear road, and avoids twisting ravines and perilous canyons, he does not give ammunition to his deceivers by dismiss-

---

1   Reference to Qurʾan, Aʿrāf 7:46–49. The word *ʿurafāʾ* (leaders) is explained through the root meaning of *ʿarafa* (to recognize); the name of the Surah—Aʿrāf—is also derived from the same root, "ʿ-R-F."

2   "Manifest knowledge and concealed wisdom" refer to the Qurʾan. Ḥ 9:156; R 2:91; B 517.

3   Delivered en route from Medina to Basra in 36/656, before the Battle of the Camel (Ḥ 9:162; B 521). §1.151.1 refers to individuals who refused to support ʿAlī and sat out the Battle of the Camel (R 2:92), or to all errant humans (Ḥ 9:157; B 518). §1.151.3 refers to the leaders in the Battle of the Camel, ʿĀʾishah, Ṭalḥah, and Zubayr (Ḥ 9:161–162; B 521).

فَأَفِقْ أَيّها السامع من سكرتك وٱستيقظ من غفلتك وٱختصر من عجلتك وأَنْعِم الفكر فيما
جاءك على لسان النبيّ الأُمّيّ صلّى الله عليه وآله ممّا لا بدّ منه ولا محيص عنه وخالِفْ مَن
خالَفَ ذلك إلى غيره ودَعْهُ وما رضي لنفسه وضَعْ نخرك وٱحطط كبرك وٱذكر قبرك
فإنّ عليه ممرّك وكما تَدين تُدان وكما تزرع تحصد وما قدّمت اليوم تَقْدَمُ عليه غدًا فأمهد
لِقَدَمِك وقدّم ليومك فالحذرَ الحذرَ أيّها المستمع والجِدَّ الجِدَّ أيّها الغافل ﴿وَلَا يُنَبِّئُكَ
مِثْلُ خَبِيرٍ﴾.

1.151.3 إنّ من عزائم[1] الله في الذكر الحكيم التي عليها يثيب ويعاقب ولها يرضى ويسخط
أنّه لا ينفع عبدًا وإن أجهد نفسه وأخلص فعله أن يخرج من الدنيا لاقيًا ربّه بخصلة من
هذه الخصال لم يتب منها أن يشرك بالله فيما ٱفترض عليه من عبادته أو يشفي غيظه
بهلاك نفس[2] أو يقرّ بأمرٍ فعله غيره أو يستنجح حاجة إلى الناس بإظهار بدعة في دينه
أو يلقى الناس بوجهين أو يمشي فيهم بلسانين. اعقل ذلك فإنّ المثل دليل على شِبْهه إنّ
البهائم همّها بطونها وإنّ السباع همّها العدوان على غيرها وإنّ النساء همّهنّ زينة الحياة
الدنيا والفساد فيها إنّ المؤمنين مستكينون إنّ المؤمنين مشفقون إنّ المؤمنين خائفون.

1.152 ومن خطبة له عليه السلام

---

١ ش، ن، ي، ه، ومصحّحة في م: كذا. وأصل م: كذا. ٢ ش، ن، ي: ﴿كرائم﴾.   ٢ ش، ن، ه: كذا.
م، ي: ﴿نفسه﴾.

ing truth, distorting speech, or dodging battle.[1] Emerge, O listener, from your intoxication, awake from your slumber, and temper your haste for worldly gain! Ponder the warning that has come to you on the Meccan Prophet's tongue about the inexorable, inescapable end.[2] Resist anyone who resists this view, reject him and his errant ways. Discard your pride, abandon your arrogance, and remember the grave, for your path leads straight to it. As you treat others, so shall you be treated, as you sow, so shall you reap, the deeds you perform today shall you come to in the morrow—prepare for your arrival and provide for that day. Beware, O listener, beware! Heed, reckless one, heed! Indeed, «no one informs you as well as one who is fully aware.»[3]

1.151.3 One of the resolutions that God has transcribed in the Wise Remembrance[4]—and these are the resolutions on whose basis he rewards or punishes, accepts or rebukes—is that he will not show favor to the man who leaves the world to meet him, even one who has expended effort and performed sincere acts, if he comes unrepentant with the following sins: having assigned partners to God in worship, slaked his rage with murder, accused someone of a crime another has committed, sought gain by innovating a heresy, or displayed two faces and spoken with two tongues. Understand this, for one example sheds light on all similar cases. Cattle care only about their stomachs, predators care only about attacking, and women care only about worldly adornments and sowing discord.[5] Believers are humble, believers are compassionate, believers fear God!

1.152 From an oration by ʿAlī:

---

1   Ar. *aw takhawwufin min ṣidq*: *ṣidq*—translated here as "battle"—means "truth" in common parlance, but in the context of battle, it denotes "courage in fighting for the truth." Discussion and examples in Qutbuddin, *Arabic Oration*, 318–320.

2   The word *ummī* in the Qurʾan's designation of Muḥammad as "the *ummī* Prophet" (*al-nabī al-ummī*, Qurʾan, Aʿrāf 7:157) has differing interpretations. One is "the Meccan Prophet," as I have translated here (following R 3:248, commentary on §3.41), which signals Muḥammad's birth affiliation to "the mother of all cities" (*Umm al-qurā*), Mecca. Other interpretations for *ummī* are "unlettered," or "belonging to a community (*ummah*)" of earlier prophets.

3   Qurʾan, Fāṭir 35:14.

4   The Wise Remembrance (*al-Dhikr al-ḥakīm*) is the Qurʾan.

5   The reference about women is to ʿĀʾishah, who was at the head of the coalition challenging ʿAlī's caliphate. See also text and note at §1.154.1, §2.1.

348 TEXT AND TRANSLATION

١.١٥٢.١ وناظرُ قلب اللبيب به يبصر أمده ويعرف غَوره ونَجْده داعٍ دعا وراعٍ رعا فاستجيبوا للداعي واتّبعوا الراعي قد خاضوا بحار الفتن وأخذوا بالبدع دون السنن وأُرِزَ المؤمنون ونطق الضالّون المكذّبون.

١.١٥٢.٢ نحن الشعار والأصحاب والخزنة والأبواب لا تؤتى البيوت إلّا من أبوابها فمن أتاها من غير أبوابها سمّي سارقًا.

منها

فيهم كرائم الإيمان[١] وهم كنوز الرحمن إن نطقوا صدقوا وإن صمتوا لم يُسبَقوا. فليَصدُق رائد أهله وليحضر عقله وليكن من أبناء الآخرة فإنّه منها قدم وإليها ينقلب فالناظر بالقلب العامل بالبصر يكون مبتدأ عمله أن يعلم أعمله عليه أم له فإن كان له مضى فيه وإن كان عليه وقف عنه وإنّ العامل بغير علم كالسابل[٢] على غير طريق فلا يزيده بعده عن الطريق إلّا بعدًا من حاجته والعامل بالعلم كالسائر على الطريق الواضح فلينظر ناظر أسائر هو أم راجع واعلم أنّ لكلّ ظاهر باطنًا على مثاله فما طاب ظاهره طاب باطنه وما خبث ظاهره خبث باطنه وقد قال الرسول الصادق صلّى الله عليه وآله ﴿إنّ الله يحبّ العبد ويبغض عمله ويحبّ العمل ويبغض بَدَنه﴾. واعلم أنّ كلّ عمل نبات وكلّ نبات لا غنى به عن الماء والمياه مختلفة فما طاب سقيه طاب غرسه وحَلَتْ ثمرته وما خبث سقيه خبث غرسه وأمرّت ثمرته.

—————
[١] م، ي، ونسخة في ه: كذا. ش، ن، وأصل ه: ﴿القرآن﴾.   [٢] م، ي: كذا. ش، ن، ه: ﴿كالساير﴾. ومصحّحة في ي، ه: ﴿كالسايل﴾.

1.152.1 An intelligent person possesses a keen heart with which he perceives his goal and distinguishes high ground from low. The caller has called, and the shepherd has gathered his herd, so answer the caller and follow the shepherd! Those people plunged into seas of revolt and followed heretical innovations instead of established practice. Believers cowered, while those who had strayed, who were calling the truth a lie, spoke loudly.

1.152.2 We are its vestments and companions, its vault-keepers and doors, and homes should be entered only through doors—whoever enters any other way will be called a thief![1]

From the same oration:
We are religion's jewels, the Merciful Lord's treasure; when we speak, we speak the truth, when we stay silent, no one outpaces us.[2] Let the scout be true to his people and stay alert![3] Let him be a child of the hereafter from where he has come and to where he will return! The person who perceives with his heart and would act with discernment should first determine, will his deed count for or against him? If it will count for him, he should proceed, if it will count against him, he should desist. A person who acts without knowledge is like someone who loses his way—the further he strays from the road, the further he strays from his goal; the person who acts with knowledge is like someone who travels on the clear road. Let each individual assess for himself, should he go forward, or should he turn back? Know that every outward aspect has a corresponding inner one—whatever is pure in its outward aspect is pure in its inner one, and whatever is foul in its outward aspect is foul in its inner one. The truthful messenger has said, ⟨God can love a servant and yet hate his deeds or love his deeds and yet hate his being⟩. Know further that every deed is a plant, every plant requires water, and all water is not the same. A plant watered with pure water yields pure shoots and sweet fruit. A plant watered with foul water yields foul shoots and bitter fruit.

---

1   "It" refers to the Imamate. "We" (here and in the next section) refers to the family of the Prophet. The simile of the "door" echoes the Prophet's hadith, ⟨I am the city of knowledge and ʿAlī is its gateway⟩ and the Qurʾan verse, «Enter homes through their doorways and fear God» (Qurʾan, Baqarah 2:189). "Vestments" (*shiʿār*), more specifically, "inner garments," denotes closeness to the Prophet. Ḥ 9:165–166, 176; B 522–523; R 2:94. See twenty-four hadiths in praise of ʿAlī, and their references, in Ḥ 9:166–175.

2   "No one outpaces us (*lam yusbaqū*)" means that (1) our silence is not due to incapacity, we are still the incumbents of the Imamate; and/or (2) no one dares to speak until we do; they stay silent out of respect and awe. Ḥ 9:177.

3   Refers to the proverb, ⟨The scout does not lie to his people⟩ (الرائد لا يكذب أهله). Ḥ 9:177; B 523.

1.153   ومن خطبة له عليه السلام يذكر فيها بديع خلقة الخُفَّاش

1.153.1   الحمد لله الذي ٱنحسرت الأوصاف عن كنه معرفته وردعت عظمته العقول فلم تجد مَساغًا إلى بلوغ غاية ملكوته هو الله الحقّ المبين أحقّ وأبين ممّا ترى العيون لم تبلغه العقول بتحديد فيكون مشبّهًا ولم تقع عليه الأوهام بتقدير فيكون ممثَّلًا خلق الخلق على غير تمثيل ولا مشورة مشير ولا معونة معين فتمّ خلقه بأمره وأذعن لطاعته فأجاب ولم يدافع وٱنقاد ولم ينازع.

1.153.2   ومن لطائف صنعته وعجائب خلقته ما أرانا من غوامض الحكمة في هذه الخفافيش التي يقبضها الضياء الباسط لكلّ شيء ويبسطها الظلام القابض لكلّ حيّ وكيف عَشِيَتْ أعينها عن أن تستمدّ من الشمس المضيئة نورًا تهتدي به في مذاهبها وتتّصل بعلانية برهان الشمس إلى معارفها وردعها بتلألؤ ضيائها عن المضيّ في سُبُحات إشراقها وأكَنّها في مكامنها عن الذهاب في بلَج ٱئتلاقها فهي مُسدلة الجفون بالنهار على حِداقها وجاعلة الليل سراجًا تستدلّ به في ٱلتماس أرزاقها فلا يَرُدّ أبصارها إسدافُ ظلمته ولا تمتنع من المُضيّ فيه لغسق دُجنّته فإذا ألقت الشمس قناعها وبدت أوضاح نهارها ودخل من إشراق نورها على الضِباب في وِجارها أطبقت الأجفان على مآقيها وتبلّغت بما ٱكتسبته من المعاش في ظلم ليلها. فسبحان من جعل الليل لها نهارًا ومعاشًا والنهار سكنًا وقرارًا وجعل لها أجنحة من لحمها تعرج بها عند الحاجة إلى الطيران كأنّها شظايا الآذان غير ذوات ريش ولا قَصَب إلّا أنّك ترى مواضع العروق بيّنة أعلامًا جناحان لمّا يرِقّا فينشقّا ولم يغلظا فيثقلا. تطير وولدها لاصق بها لاجئ إليها يقع إذا وقعت ويرتفع إذا ٱرتفعت لا يفارقها حتّى تشتدّ أركانه ويحمله للنهوض جناحه ويعرف مذاهب عيشه ومصالح نفسه. فسبحان الباري لكلّ شيء على غير مثال خلا من غيره.

1.153 From an oration by ʿAlī in which he describes the wondrous creation of the bat:

1.153.1 Praise God! Descriptions are too feeble to plumb his core, for his majesty curbs intellects from reaching the limits of his kingdom. He is God, real and clear, too real, too clear, for eyes to see. Intellects cannot delineate his boundaries—he can never be likened to another. Imaginations cannot capture him—he can never be pictured as another. He created without paradigm, advice, or help. His command brought forth a perfect creation, which bowed to him in obedience, responded without defiance, and submitted without fighting.

1.153.2 Among the sublimities of his craftsmanship and the marvels of his creation are the profound mysteries he has shown us in these bats. They are constricted by light which causes other creatures to emerge, and drawn out by darkness, which causes other beings to seek shelter. See how he caused their eyes to be dazzled by the sun's brilliance, instead of using the sun to guide their movements, or harnessing its light to visit their haunts. See how he curbed them with the sun's very brilliance from flitting about in its majestic gleams, how he restrained them in their caverns from setting out in its intense glare. They let their eyelids droop during the day over their pupils and use the night as a lamp to guide them toward sustenance. The darkening gloom does not impede their sight, its black obscurity does not hinder their movement. But as the sun removes its veil and the morning glimmers, as its bright rays penetrate the lizard in its hole, the bats shut their eyelids and settle down with the food they were able to collect in the shadows of the night. Glory to him who made night for them as daylight hours, as the time to gather food, and daylight hours the time for rest and tranquility! Glory to him who created their wings from flesh! Wings they use to propel themselves in flight, that look like bow-shaped ears and have no feathers or quills, but in which you can see their clearly marked fingers;[1] two wings, not so thin as to tear, but not so thick either that they would weigh down their bodies. When bats fly, their pups cling to them for shelter, swooping and rising with their mothers when their mothers swoop and rise. They do not fly off until their limbs are strong, and their wings can support them, until they can find their own way to food and safety. Glory to the creator of all things, who created without following another's paradigm!

---

1 Ar. *ʿurūq* (sing. *ʿirq*), lit. "roots" or "veins," translated as "fingers" based on modern zoology.

١.١٥٤   ومن كلام له عليه السلام خاطب به أهل البصرة على جهة ٱقتصاص الملاحم

١.١٥٤.١   فمن ٱستطاع عند ذلك أن يعتقل نفسه على الله فليفعل. وإن أطعتموني فإنّي حاملكم إن شاء الله على سبيل الجنّة وإن كان ذا مشقّة شديدة ومَذاقة مَريرة. وأمّا فلانة فأدركها رأي النساء وضِغْنٌ غَلا في صدرها كِمرْجَل القَيْن ولو دعيتْ لتنال من غيري ما أتت إليّ لم تفعل ولها بعدُ حرمتُها الأولى والحساب على الله.

١.١٥٤.٢   منه

سبيل أبلج المِنهاج أنور السراج فبالإيمان يُستدلّ على الصالحات وبالصالحات يستدلّ على الإيمان وبالإيمان يعمر العلم وبالعلم يرهب الموت وبالموت تختم الدنيا وبالدنيا تحرز الآخرة. وإنّ الخلق لا مَقْصَر لهم عن القيامة مُرقِلين في مِضمارها إلى الغاية القصوى.

١.١٥٤.٣   منه

قد شخصوا من مستقرّ الأجداث وصاروا إلى مصاير الغايات لكلّ دار أهلها لا يستبدلون بها ولا ينقلون عنها وإنّ الأمر بالمعروف والنهي عن المنكر لَخُلُقان من خلق الله سبحانه وإنّهما لا يقرّبان من أجل ولا ينقصان من رزق. وعليكم بكتاب الله فإنّه الحبل المتين والنور المبين والشفاء النافع والرّيّ الناقع والعصمة للمتمسّك والنجاة للمتعلّق لا يَعْوَجّ فيُقام ولا يزيغ فيستعتب ولا يُخلقه كثرة الردّ وولوج السمع من قال به صدق ومن عمل به سبق.

١.١٥٤.٤   وقام إليه رجل فقال يا أمير المؤمنين أخبرنا عن الفتنة وهل سألت عنها رسول الله صلّى الله عليه وآله فقال عليه السلام

1.154 From an address by ʿAlī to the people of Basra, foretelling calamities:[1]

1.154.1 At that time, whoever is able to bind himself totally to God should do so. If you obey me, I shall, God willing, drive you on the path to the celestial garden, even when it brings severe hardships and bitter trials. As for that woman, the suppositions of women overtook her and malice simmered in her breast like a dyer's boiling cauldron.[2] If she had been invited to malign anyone else with the aggression she used against me, she would not have done so. No matter. Let her retain her state of spousal sanctity.[3] Her reckoning is in God's hands.

1.154.2 From the same address:
It is a road whose track is clear and whose lamp is bright. Through faith you are guided to deeds, through deeds you are guided to faith. Through faith you enliven knowledge, through knowledge you fear death, through death your life in the world ends, and through life in the world you attain the hereafter. There is no place where you can hide from the resurrection. In its arena, all race to the final post.

1.154.3 Emerging from the repose of graves, they set off for their destined end;[4] each abode receives its residents, and they are never removed from it, or given another, forever after. Commanding good and forbidding evil are traits of divinity, they will not hasten your death or decrease your sustenance. Hold fast to God's Book: it is the strong rope, the clear light, the effectual cure, the quencher of thirst, the adherent's protection, and the devotee's salvation; it never becomes crooked and needs straightening, or deviates and needs to be forced back; it is not worn out by the tongue's recitation or frayed by the ear's audition—whoever affirms it speaks the truth, whoever acts upon it wins.

1.154.4 At that time, a man stood up and said, "Commander of the Faithful, tell us about this sedition—did you ask God's Messenger about it?" and ʿAlī responded:

---

1   In Basra, immediately after the Battle of the Camel in 36/656 (Ṭūsī, *Talkhīṣ al-Shāfī*, vol. 1 pt. 2, 274–275). §1.154.2 and §1.154.4 are cited as answers given during an oration in the mosque in Basra, a few days after the Battle of the Camel in 36/656 (Māmaṭīrī, *Nuzhah*, 224–225, 230). Other parts of the same oration in ibid., 221–233, are listed in note to §1.23. Also, §1.154.2 is similar to §1.103.1.

2   Refers to ʿĀʾishah, who brought an army to fight ʿAlī in the Battle of the Camel outside Basra in 36/656. Details of her conflicts with ʿAlī and Fāṭimah in Ḥ 9:190–200; B 527. "Dyer's boiling cauldron" after R 2:101; or, "a cauldron made by a blacksmith" (Ḥ 9:189).

3   As the Prophet Muḥammad's wife. B 527; Ḥ 9:199.

4   I.e., paradise or hellfire.

لمّا أنزل الله سبحانه قوله ﴿الٓمٓ أَحَسِبَ النَّاسُ أَن يُتْرَكُوا أَن يَقُولُوا آمَنَّا وَهُمْ لَا يُفْتَنُونَ﴾ علمت أنّ الفتنة لا تنزل بنا ورسول الله صلّى الله عليه وآله بين أظهرنا فقلت يا رسول الله ما هذه الفتنة التي أخبرك الله بها فقال ﴿يا عليّ إنّ أمّتي سيفتنون من بعدي﴾ فقلت يا رسول الله أوليس قد قلت لي يوم أُحُد حيث اُستشهد من اُستشهد من المسلمين وحيزت عنّي الشهادة فشقّ ذلك عليّ فقلت لي أَبْشِرْ فإنّ الشهادة من ورائك فقال لي إنّ ذلك لكذلك فكيف صبرك إذًا فقلت يا رسول الله ليس هذا من مواطن الصبر ولكن من مواطن البشرى والشكر وقال ﴿يا عليّ إنّ القوم سيفتنون بأموالهم ويمنّون بدينهم على ربّهم ويتمنّون رحمته ويأمنون سطوته ويستحلّون حرامه بالشبهات الكاذبة والأهواء الساهية فيستحلّون الخمر بالنبيذ والسحت بالهديّة والربا بالبيع﴾ فقلت يا رسول الله فبأيّ المنازل أُنزلهم عند ذلك أبمنزلة رِدّة أم بمنزلة فتنة فقال بمنزلة فتنة.

1.155 ومن خطبة له عليه السلام

1.155.1 الحمد لله الذي جعل الحمد مفتاحًا لذكره وسببًا للمزيد من فضله ودليلًا على آلائه وعظمته. عباد الله إنّ الدهر يجري بالباقين كجَرْيِه بالماضين لا يعود ما قد ولّى منه ولا يبقى سرمدًا ما فيه. آخر فعاله كأوّله متسابقةً أمورُه متظاهرة أعلامه فكأنّكم بالساعة تحدوكم حَدْوَ الزاجر بشَوله. فمن شغل نفسه بغير نفسه تحيّر في الظلمات وأرتبك في

When the Almighty revealed the verses, «*Alif Lām Mīm*. Do people think they can claim, "we believe," without being tested»?[1] I knew that sedition would not befall us while the Messenger remained among us, so I asked, "Messenger of God, what is this sedition that God has informed you about and when will it come to pass?" He replied, ⟨ʿAlī, my community will be thrown into turmoil when I die.⟩ I probed, "Messenger of God, did you not say to me at the Battle of Uḥud—when some were martyred and I was sad that I was denied the honor—'Be happy, for you shall win martyrdom too'?" He said, "Yes, that is correct. What will your acceptance look like then?" and I replied, "Messenger of God, it will not be an occasion for acceptance, but for immense joy and gratitude!" The Prophet also told me, ⟨ʿAlī, people will be tested with regard to wealth—thinking their support of Islam a favor to their Lord,[2] they will feel entitled to his mercy and believe themselves secure against his punishment. By raising false suspicions and wayward passions, they will legalize the things he has forbidden—they will drink wine, calling it date juice, take bribes, calling it gift-giving, and practice usury, calling it trade.⟩ I asked him then, "Messenger of God, which category will they fall in at that time, apostasy or sedition?" and he answered, "Sedition."

1.155   From an oration by ʿAlī:[3]

1.155.1   Praise God, who made praise the key to his remembrance,[4] the means to increasing his bounty,[5] and a sign of his blessings and glory. Servants of God! Time's river flows on with those who are alive, just as it swept away those who are now gone. The part that has gone will never return, and the part that is present will not remain. The last of its actions are like the first, its affairs outrace each other, its banners reinforce each other, and the final hour pushes you forward as a rough herdsman drives his thirsty camels to the waterhole. Whoever occupies himself with anything other than his soul stumbles in darkness and

---

1   Qurʾan, ʿAnkabūt 29:1–2. The first verse—«*Alif Lām Mīm*»—consists of three letters of the Arabic alphabet that many exegetes explain as an allusion to angels or prophets by whom God swears an oath, after which he makes the declaration that follows in the second verse.

2   Refers to Qurʾan, Ḥujurāt 49:17.

3   Oration delivered in the mosque of Basra, a few days after the Battle of the Camel in 36/656 (Māmaṭīrī, *Nuzhah*, 233–235).

4   "The Remembrance (*Dhikr*)" is also one of the names of the Qurʾan, the first Surah of which begins, "Praise God, Lord of all the worlds," Qurʾan, Ḥamd/Fātiḥah 1:1. Ḥ 9:210; R 2:106–107.

5   The Arabic word for "praise," *ḥamd*, also includes the meaning of "thanks," and this is what is intended here, as a reference to the Qurʾanic verse, "If you give thanks, we shall increase your blessings." Qurʾan, Ibrāhīm 14:7; B 531; Ḥ 9:211; R 2:107.

الهلكات ومَدّت به شياطينه في طغيانه وزيّنت له سيّئ أعماله فالجنّة غاية السابقين والنار

غاية المفرطين اعلموا عباد الله أنّ التقوى دار حصن عزيز والفجور دار حصن ذليل

لا يمنع أهله ولا يحرز من لجأ إليه ألا وبالتقوى تُقطع حُمة الخطايا وباليقين تدرك الغاية

القصوى.

١.١٥٥.٢ عباد الله الله الله في أعزّ الأنفس عليكم وأحبّها إليكم فإنّ الله قد أوضح سبيل

الحقّ وأنار طرقه فشقوة لازمة أو سعادة دائمة فتزوّدوا في أيّام الفناء لأيّام البقاء فقد

دللتم على الزاد وأمرتم بالظعن وحثثتم على المسير[١] فإنّما أنتم كركب وقوف لا تدرون

متى تؤمرون بالسير[١] ألا فما يصنع بالدنيا مَن خُلِقَ للآخرة وما يصنع بالمال من عمّا قليل

يُسلبه وتبقى عليه تَبِعتُه وحسابه عباد الله إنّه ليس لما وعد الله من الخير مَتْرَك ولا فيما

نهى عنه من الشرّ مَرْغَب عباد الله احذروا يومًا تفحص فيه الأعمال ويكثر فيه الزلزال

وتشيب فيه الأطفال. اعلموا عباد الله أنّ عليكم رَصَدًا من أنفسكم وعيونًا من جوارحكم

وحُفّاظ صدق يحفظون أعمالكم وعدد أنفاسكم لا تستركم منهم ظلمة ليل داج ولا يُكنّكم

منهم باب ذو رِتاج. وإنّ غدًا من اليوم قريب يذهب اليوم بما فيه ويجيء الغد لاحقًا به

فكأنّ كلّ امرئ منكم قد بلغ من الأرض منزل وحدته ومخطّ حفرته فياله من بيت

وحدة ومنزل وحشة ومَفْرَد غربة وكأنّ الصيحة قد أتتكم والساعة قد غشيتكم وبرزتم

لفصل القضاء قد زاحت عنكم الأباطيل واضمحلّت عنكم العلل واستحقّت بكم الحقائق

وصدرت بكم الأمور مصادرها فاتّعظوا بالعبر واعتبروا بالغِيَر وانتفعوا بالنُّذُر.

١.١٥٦ ومن خطبة له عليه السلام

<hr>

[١] ن، ش، ي، ه: كذا. م، ومصحّحة في ش: ﴿المسير﴾.

is ensnared in catastrophe, he is incited by his devils to persist in depravity and to pile on the evil deeds they adorn in his eyes. Paradise is the destination of those who are quick to believe, hellfire the destination of malefactors. Servants of God! Know that piety's fortress is mighty, while immorality's citadel is easily breached—it neither protects its people nor shields those who seek its refuge. Listen to me! Piety heals the scorpion-sting of sin. Certainty carries you to the ultimate goal.

1.155.2 Servants of God! Fear God and look to the direction of your own soul, the one most precious to you and beloved, for God has shown you the path of truth and illumined its course: the end is either unshakable wretchedness, or eternal bliss. Stock up in the days that will expire for the days that will endure, for you have been shown where to find provisions, commanded to load up, and encouraged to set out. Yours is a halted caravan unsure of when it will be instructed to resume. Harken and listen! What does someone created for the hereafter want with this world? What does someone whose possessions will soon be plundered—indeed, while its burden and reckoning will remain— want with gold and livestock?[1] Servants of God! There is no reason you should refrain from the good for which God has promised reward or seek the evils he has forbidden! Servants of God! Fear the day when deeds will be examined, earthquakes will intensify, and infants' locks will turn white. Servants of God, know this: Your own self surveils you, your own limbs spy on you, and truthful chroniclers record your deeds and count your breaths. Dark nights cannot veil you from them, nor locked doors keep you concealed. Tomorrow is close to today. Today, with all that is in it, will soon pass, and tomorrow will follow. It is as though each one of you has already reached his place of solitude inside the earth, that pit marked with lines. What a lonely residence! What a menacing domicile! What a forlorn exile! Imagine that the thunderclap has already pealed, the last hour has already come, and that you have already emerged for the final judgment, falsehoods uncovered, excuses obliterated, truths come to the fore, and matters having taken their course. Learn from exemplary lessons, benefit from warnings, beware the conversion of blessings into punishment!

1.156 From an oration by ʿAlī:[2]

---

1   Ar. *māl*, which signifies movable wealth, including gold and silver, livestock, and grain.
2   Opening lines same in §1.86.

1.156.1 أرسله على حين فترة من الرسل وطول هَجْعة من الأمم وأنتقاض من المُبْرَم جاءهم بتصديق الذي بين يديه والنور المقتدى به. ذلك القرآن فأستنطقوه ولن ينطق ولكن أُخبركم عنه ألا إنّ فيه علم ما يأتي والحديث عن الماضي ودواء دائكم ونَظْم ما بينكم.

1.156.2 منها

فعند ذلك لا يبقى بيت مَدَر ولا وَبَر إلّا وأدخله الظلمة تَرْحة وأولجوا فيه نقمة فيومئذ لا يبقى لهم في السماء عاذر ولا في الأرض ناصر. أصفيتم بالأمر غير أهله وأوردتموه غير وِرْده وسينتقم الله ممّن ظلم مأكلًا بمأكل ومشربًا بمشرب من مطاعم العلقم ومشارب الصَّبِر والمَقِر ولباس شعار الخوف ودِثار السيف وإنّما هم مَطايا الخطيئات وزوامل الآثام. فأُقسم ثمّ أُقسم لتَنَخَّمَنَّها أميّة من بعدي كما تُلفَظ النُّخامة ثمّ لا تذوقها ولا تتطعم بطعمها أبدًا ما كَرَّ الجديدان.

1.157 ومن خطبة له عليه السلام

ولقد أحسنت جواركم وأحطت بجهدي من ورائكم وأعتقتكم من رِبَق الذلّ وحَلَق الضيم شكرًا منّي للبرّ القليل وإطراقًا عمّا أدركه البصر وشهده البدن من المنكَر الكثير.

1.158 ومن خطبة له عليه السلام

1.158.1 أمره قضاء وحكمة ورضاه أمان ورحمة يقضي بعلم ويعفو١ بحلم.

اللهمّ لك الحمد على ما تأخذ وتعطي وعلى ما تعافي وتبتلي حمدًا يكون أرضى الحمد لك وأحبّ الحمد إليك وأفضل الحمد عندك حمدًا يملأ ما خلقت ويبلغ ما أردت حمدًا لا

____
١م، ي، ومصحَّحة في ه: كذا. ش، ن، وأصل ه: ﴿يغفر﴾.

1.156.1 God sent Muḥammad after a period without prophets, when people had long been in slumber and bonds had frayed. Muḥammad brought them confirmation of earlier revelations and light for them to follow—the Qur'an. Ask it to speak to you, then! It cannot, but I can tell you about it, so listen to me! The Qur'an contains knowledge of the future and reports of the past. It is the cure for your illness and the benchmark for regulating your affairs.

1.156.2 From the same oration:
That day, when there remains no house of brick or goat-hair tent that the tyrants have not steeped in grief or invaded with cruelty, no one in the sky will grant the oppressors pardon and no one on earth will offer them shelter. You offered the caliphate to those who have no right to it,[1] gave them access to a waterhole that is not theirs, but God will exact revenge from the despots, exchanging one food for another, one drink for another. Then they will swallow bitter morsels of colocynth and gulp acid drafts of aloes and vinegar, they will wear the garment of fear and their vestments will be the striking of swords. What are they but beasts carrying sin and camels laden with wickedness! I swear—and again I swear—that the Umayyads will spit out the caliphate after me like a man spits out phlegm and mucus! After that time, they will never get to savor it or enjoy its taste for as long as day follows night and night follows day.

1.157 From an oration by ʿAlī:
I protected you well and strove to keep you safe. I freed you from the tethers of degradation and the fetters of tyranny. All this in gratitude for small favors, while staying silent about the great wrongs my eyes had seen and my body had suffered!

1.158 From an oration by ʿAlī:[2]

1.158.1 His command constitutes judgment and wisdom, his acceptance constitutes safety and mercy, he judges with knowledge and forgives with clemency.

God, we offer you praise for what you grant and what you take back, for what you heal and what you inflict. We offer the praise most acceptable to you, the praise most liked by you, the praise most excellent in your eyes. We offer you praise that fills the bounds of your creation and attains the limits that you will

---

1   Ar. *al-amr*, lit. "the matter," translated here as "the caliphate"; "those who have no right to it" are the Umayyads. Ḥ 9:218–219.

2   Iskāfī (*Miʿyār*, 257) and Ibn ʿAbd Rabbih (*ʿIqd*, 4:167) state that §1.158 is part of the Luminous Oration (*Zahrāʾ*), which also includes §1.91 and §1.106.

يُحجب عنك ولا يقصر دونك حمدًا لا ينقطع عدده ولا يفنى مَدده. فلسنا نعلم كُنْهَ
عظمتك إلّا أنّا نعلم أنّك حيّ قيّوم لا تأخذك سنة ولا نوم لم ينته إليك نظر ولم يدركك
بصر أدركت الأبصار وأحصيت الأعمار[1] وأخذت بالنواصي والأقدام وما الذي نرى
من خلقك ونعجب له من قدرتك ونصفه من عظيم سلطانك[2] وما تغيّب عنّا منه
وقصرت أبصارنا عنه وانتهت عقولنا دونه وحالت سواتر الغيوب بيننا وبينه أعظم. فمن
فرّغ قلبه وأعمل فكره ليعلم كيف أقمت عرشك وكيف ذرأت خلقك وكيف علّقت في
الهواء سماواتك وكيف مددت على مَوْر الماء أرضك رجع طرفه حسيرًا وعقله مبهورًا
وسمعه والِهًا وفكره حائرًا.

1.158.2   منها

يدّعي بزعمه أنّه يرجو الله كَذَبَ والعظيم ما باله لا يتبيّن رجاؤه في عمله وكلّ من رجا
عُرف رجاؤه في عمله إلّا رجاءَ الله فإنّه مدخول وكلّ خوف محقَّق إلّا خوف الله فإنّه
معلول يرجو الله في الكبير ويرجو العباد في الصغير فيعطي العبد ما لا يعطي الربّ فما
بال الله جلّ ثناؤه يقصَّر به عمّا يصنع بعباده. أتخاف أن تكون في رجائك له كاذبًا أو
تكون لا تراه للرجاء موضعًا وكذلك إن هو خافَ عبدًا من عبيده أعطاه من خوفه ما
لا يعطي ربّه بجعل خوفه من العباد نقدًا وخوفه من خالقهم ضِمارًا ووعدًا وكذلك من
عظمت الدنيا في عينه وكبر موقعها من قلبه آثرها على الله فانقطع إليها وصار عبدًا لها.

1.158.3   ولقد كان في رسول الله صلّى الله عليه وآله كافٍ لك في الأسوة ودليل لك
على ذمّ الدنيا وعيبها وكثرة مخَازيها ومساويها إذ قُبضت عنه أطرافها ووطّئت لغيره

---

[1]ش، ن، ي، ه: كذا. م: ﴿الأعمال﴾.   [2]ش، ن، ي، ه، ونسخة في م: كذا. أصل م: ﴿شانك﴾.

it to attain. We offer you praise that is neither veiled from you nor falls short in reaching you. We offer you praise in sums that never end and gifts that never run out. We do not know the essence of your majesty. All we know is that you are alive, existent, neither slumber overtakes you nor sleep,[1] neither glances perceive you nor eyes. You see all eyes, you reckon all lifespans, you seize people by forelocks and feet.[2] How little we understand of your creation, how inadequately we marvel at your strength, how feebly we describe your great power! That which is hidden from us, which our eyes fall short of, which our intellects fail to attain, which the veils of mystery prevent us from discerning—that is far greater. Anyone who clears his heart and applies his mind to comprehend how you established your throne, originated your creation, suspended the skies in the air, and spread the earth on heaving water will have his glances befuddled, his intellect bedazzled, his ears bewildered, and his reason bemused.

1.158.2 From the same oration:
You claim that you place your hopes in God. Great God, what lies! What is it with you! These hopes do not show in your actions! When you place your hopes in anyone, your hopes show in your actions, except for the hopes you say you place in God, which are insincere. Every fear you feel is real except your fear of God, which is a sham. You expect from God what is great, and from God's servants what is small, but you offer to God's servants what you don't offer to your Lord! How is it that your actions for God—may his praise be exalted!— fall short, when you do so much for God's servants? Are you afraid that you may be making a mistake in relying on God, are you worried he may not be the right place in which to lodge your hopes? Likewise, when you fear one of God's servants, you render to him the awe born of fear that you don't render to your Lord—you render your fear to God's servants in ready cash, while you make your fear for God a deferred promise. Indeed, those whose eyes find the world grand, whose hearts find it imposing, give it preference over God. When this happens, they become its devotees and servants.

1.158.3 The Messenger of God should suffice you as exemplar, as proof of the world's wickedness and its flaws, its many disgraces and evils. The world's hands refused the Messenger their largesse, even though its wings were lowered for others; he, in contrast, was weaned off its milk, and shoved away from its orna-

---

1 Modified quote from Qur'an, Baqarah 2:255.
2 Modified quote from Qur'an, Raḥmān 55:41.

أكّافها وفُطم من رَضاعها وزُوي عن زخارفها. وإن شئت ثنّيت بموسى كليم الله صلّى الله عليه وآله إذ يقول ﴿رَبِّ إِنِّي لِمَا أَنزَلْتَ إِلَيَّ مِنْ خَيْرٍ فَقِيرٌ﴾ والله ما سأله إلّا خبْزًا يأكله لأنّه كان يأكل بقْلة الأرض ولقد كانت خضرة البقْل تُرى من شفيف صِفاق بطنه لهُزاله وتشذّب لحمه. وإن شئت ثلّثت بداود عليه السلام صاحب المزامير وقارئ أهل الجنّة فلقد كان يعمل سَفائف الخُوص بيده ويقول لجلسائه أيّكم يكفيني بيعها ويأكل قرص الشعير من ثمنها. وإن شئت قلت في عيسى بن مريم عليهما السلام فلقد كان يتوسّد الحجر ويلبس الخشن وكان إدامه الجوع وسراجه بالليل القمر وظلاله في الشتاء مشارق الأرض ومغاربها وفاكهته وريحانه ما تنبت الأرض للبهائم ولم تكن له زوجة تفتنه ولا ولد يحزنه ولا مال يلفته ولا طمع يذلّه دابّته رجلاه وخادمه يداه.

1.158.4   فتأسَّ بنبيّك الأطيب الأطهر صلّى الله عليه وآله فإنّ فيه إسوة لمن تأسّى وعزاء لمن تعزّى وأحبّ العباد إلى الله المتأسّي بنبيّه والمقتصّ لأثره قضَم الدنيا قضمًا ولم يُعِرْها طرْفًا أهْضَمُ أهل الدنيا كَشحًا وأخمصهم من الدنيا بطنًا عُرضت عليه الدنيا فأبى أن يقبلها وعلم أن الله أبغض شيئًا فأبغضه وحقر شيئًا فحقره وصغّر شيئًا فصغّره ولو لم يكن فينا إلّا حبّنا ما أبغض الله وتعظيمنا ما صغّر الله لكفى به شقاقًا لله ومُحادّة عن أمر الله. ولقد كان صلّى الله عليه يأكل على الأرض ويجلس جِلسة العبد ويخصف بيده نعله ويرقع بيده ثوبه ويركب الحمار العاري ويُردف خلفه. ويكون السِّتر على باب بيته فتكون فيه التصاوير فيقول ﴿يا فلانة﴾ لإحدى أزواجه ﴿غيّبيه عنّي فإنّي إذا نظرت إليه ذكرت الدنيا وزخارفها﴾. فأعرض عن الدنيا بقلبه وأمات ذكرها من نفسه وأحبّ أن

ments. If you wish, I will give you a second example, that of Moses, he to whom God spoke. Moses beseeched, «My Lord, I am in dire need of whatever you may bestow!»[1] By God, Moses asked God for nothing more than a piece of bread, for he had only wild plants to eat. He was so thin, his flesh so pared, that the green of the plants he had eaten shone through the translucent skin of his stomach. If you wish, I will give you a third example, that of David, he with the Psalms, reciter for the people of paradise. David would plait palm fronds with his own two hands and say to his associates, "Who will sell these for me?" then he would eat a coarse loaf of barley purchased with its sale. And if you wish, I will also tell you about Jesus, son of Mary. Jesus would use a rock for a pillow and wear rough garments. His food was hunger, his lamp at night the moon, his shelter in the winter the sun's rays from East and West, his fruit and his fragrance the plants grown by the earth for the beasts. He had no wife to distract him, no son to grieve him, no wealth to occupy him, no greed to bring him low. His mount was his own two feet, his servant his own two hands.

1.158.4   People, follow the example of your own virtuous and pure Prophet. Any who look for an exemplar can find one in him. Any who look for consolation can find it in him. Of all his servants, God loves most the one who follows the example of his Prophet, who walks in his footsteps. The Prophet took the smallest morsel from the world, he never gave the world a full glance. His waist was the most emaciated, his stomach the emptiest of worldly things. The world was offered to him, but he refused. He knew that God hated it, so he hated it too. He knew that God considered it wretched, so he considered it wretched too. He knew that God considered it of little worth, so he considered it of little worth too. People, if our only faults are love for what God hates and exaltation of what he considers paltry, they would be sufficient to count as opposition to God and challenge to his command! The Prophet used to eat on the ground and sit like a servant. He used to mend his sandals with his own hands. He used to patch his garments with his own hands. He used to ride an unsaddled donkey, not even alone, but with someone often sitting behind him. A curtain with images was hung on the door of his home, and he said to one of his wives, ⟨Remove it from my sight—it reminds me of the world and its ornaments!⟩ He turned his heart away from the world, he suppressed its mention in his heart, he preferred that its adornments be removed from his eyes, so that he would not to be seduced by its soft luxuries or led to view it as a lasting home or permanent residence. He drove it from his spirit, banished it from his heart, and removed it

---

1   Qur'an, Qaṣaṣ 28:24.

تغيب زينتها عن عينه لكيلا يتّخذ منها رياشًا ولا يعتقدها قرارًا ولا يرجو فيها مقامًا فأخرجها من النفس وأشخصها عن القلب وغيّبها عن البصر وكذلك من أبغض شيئًا أبغض أن ينظر إليه وأن يُذكر عنده. ولقد كان في رسول الله صلّى الله عليه وآله ما يدلّك على مساوي الدنيا وعيوبها إذ جاع فيها مع خاصّته وزويت عنه زخارفها مع عظيم زلفته. فلينظر ناظر بعقله أَكْرَمَ الله محمّدًا بذلك أم أهانه فإن قال أهانه فقد كذب والعظيمِ وإن قال أكرمه فليعلم أنّ الله قد أهان غيره حيث بسط الدنيا له وزواها عن أقرب الناس منه. فتأسّى متأسٍّ بنبيّه وأقتصّ أثره وولج مَوْلِجه وإلّا فلا تأمن الهلكة فإنّ الله جعل محمّدًا صلّى الله عليه وآله عَلَمًا للساعة ومبشّرًا بالجنّة ومنذرًا بالعقوبة. خرج من الدنيا خميصًا وورد الآخرة سليمًا لم يضع حَجَرًا على حجر حتّى مضى لسبيله[1] وأجاب داعي ربّه فما أعظم منّة الله عندنا حين أنعم علينا به سلفًا نتّبعه وقائدًا نطأ عقبه.

والله لقد رقعتُ مِدْرَعتي هذه حتّى أستحييت من راقعها. ولقد قال لي قائل ألا تَنْبِذُها فقلت أغرب عنّي ف﴿عِنْدَ الصَّبَاحِ يَحْمَدُ القَوْمُ السُّرى﴾.

1.159 ومن خطبة له عليه السلام

ابتعثه بالنور المضيّ والبرهان الجليّ والمنهاج البادي والكّتاب الهادي أُسرته خير أُسرة وشجرته خير شجرة أغصانها معتدلة وثمارها متهدّلة مولده بمكّة وهجرته بطَيْبة علا بها ذكره وآمتدّ منها صوته أرسله بحجّة كافية وموعظة شافية ودعوة متلافية أظهر به الشرائع المجهولة وقمع به البدع المدخولة وبيّن به الأحكام المفصولة. ف﴿مَن يَبْتَغِ غَيْرَ الْإِسْلَامِ

---

[1] م، وأُضيفت في هامش هـ مع علامة الصحّة: كذا. ش، ن، وأصل هـ: سقطت ﴿لسبيله﴾.

from his sight; for those who hate a thing hate to look at it, and they hate to have it mentioned. The Messenger's story teaches you about the evils of the world and its flaws. He faced hunger and his loved ones did too. Its ornaments were kept from him despite his closeness to God. Let the discerning mind think: Did God honor Muḥammad by this or demean him? If he answers, "God demeaned him," then, by God, he lies! If he answers, "God honored him," then that person should know that God, in fact, demeaned others to whom he gave worldly chattels, while turning them away from the one closest to him. Any who seek an exemplar should follow God's Prophet, walk in his footsteps, and enter through his door, else he will face perdition. God has made Muḥammad the banner for the coming hour, the herald of paradise, the warner ahead of the decisive punishment. Leaving the world empty-bellied, he entered the hereafter in sound health. Never once did he build a grand house, or place stone upon stone, until at last he answered his Lord's call and went on to his final abode. What a great favor God has granted us, having blessed us with Muḥammad as an exemplar to follow, a commander in whose footsteps to walk.

By God, I too have patched my rough cloak so often that I am embarrassed to have it mended. Someone said to me, "Why don't you throw it away?" and I replied, "Get away from me! ⟨When morning comes, the night-traveler will be praised!⟩"[1]

1.159 From an oration by ʿAlī:
God sent Muḥammad with brilliant light, clear proof, a distinct path, and a book of guidance. His family is the best family, his tree is the best tree, its branches straight and tall, its fruits hanging low. His birth was in Mecca, his migration was to Ṭaybah,[2] from there his fame rose high, and his voice spread far and wide. God sent Muḥammad with ample evidence, healing counsel, and an enlivening faith,[3] through him, he revived abandoned laws,[4] crushed newfangled heresies, and explained decreed rules. Indeed, «whoever seeks a religion other than Islam»[5] will find his wretchedness real, his support bro-

---

1 A line of *rajaz* by the pre-Islamic poet Jumayḥ ibn al-Sharīd al-Taghlibī, used proverbially to mean that fortitude begets a praiseworthy result. F 270; Abū Hilāl, *Jamharah*, 2:32, 2:42; Bakrī, *Faṣl al-maqāl*, 254, 334; Maydānī, 2:3, § 2382; Jāḥiẓ, *Ḥayawān*, 6:508.
2 Earlier Yathrib, Ṭaybah—"The Pure (City)"—is the name given by Muḥammad to his new hometown. After Muḥammad's migration, people began referring to it as "The City of the Prophet" (*Madīnat al-nabī*) in short, Medina, which is how it is best known.
3 Ar. *daʿwah*, lit. call.
4 Ar. *sharāʾiʿ* sing., *sharīʿah*, lit. paths, potentially referring to the laws of earlier prophets.
5 Qurʾan, Āl ʿImrān 3:85. The verse may also be translated, «… other than commitment (*islām*) to God's will».

دِينًا﴾ تتحقّق شقوته وتنفصم عروته وتعظم كبوته ويكن مآبه إلى الحزن الطويل والعذاب الوبيل. وأتوكّل على الله توكّل الإنابة إليه وأسترشده السبيل المؤدّية إلى جنّته القاصدة إلى محلّ رغبته. أوصيكم عباد الله بتقوى الله وطاعته فإنّها النجاة غدًا والمنجاة أبدًا. رهّب فأبلغ ورغّب فأسبغ ووصف لكم الدنيا وأنقطاعها وزوالها وأنتقالها فأعرضوا عمّا يعجبكم فيها لقلّة ما يصحبكم منها أقرب دار من سخط الله وأبعدها من رضوان الله فغُضّوا عنكم عباد الله غمومها وأشغالها لما قد أيقنتم به من فراقها وتصرّف حالاتها فأحذروها حذر الشفيق الناصح والمُجِدّ الكادح وأعتبروا بما قد رأيتم من مصارع القرون قبلكم قد تزايلت أوصالهم وزالت أسماعهم وأبصارهم وذهب شرفهم وعزّهم وأنقطع سرورهم ونعيمهم. فبدّلوا بقرب الأولاد فقْدها وبصحبة الأزواج مفارقتها لا يتفاخرون ولا يتناسلون ولا يتزاورون ولا يتجاورون. فأحذروا عباد الله حذر الغالب لنفسه المانع لشهوته الناظر٢ بعقله فإنّ الأمر واضح والعَلَم قائم والطريق جَدَد والسبيل قصد.

1.160 ومن كلامه عليه السلام لبعض أصحابه وقد سأله كيف دفعكم قومكم عن هذا المقام وأنتم أحقّ به فقال

يا أخا بني أسد إنّك لَقَلِقُ الوَضين تُرسِل في غير سَدَد ولك بعدُ ذمامة الصِّهر وحقّ المسألة وقد ٱستعلمت فٱعلم. أمّا الاستبداد علينا بهذا المقام ونحن الأعلَون نسبًا والأشدُّون بالرسول نَوْطًا فإنّها كانت أَثَرَة شَحَّت عليها نفوس قوم وسخت عنها نفوس آخرين والحَكَمُ

---

١ م، ش، ي، هـ، ومصحّحة في ن: كذا. أصل ن، ونسخة في ش: ﴿بُعدها﴾.   ٢ش، ن، ي، هـ، ونسخة في م: كذا. أصل م: ﴿الناطق﴾.

ken, and his tread unsteady. His final return will be to long-lasting grief and painful punishment. I place my trust in God and turn to him. I seek his guidance in finding the path that will lead to his Garden and direct me to his pleasure. Servants of God! I counsel you to be conscious of him and obey him, for that will bring you salvation on the morrow and eternal deliverance. He cautioned you to beware and gave full warning. He directed you to earn reward and gave complete measure. He described the world to you and told you of its severance, its transience, its departure. People, turn away from everything in it that excite your wonder, because it will not be with you for long. This world is the domicile that is closest to God's anger and farthest from his pleasure. Servants of God, be certain of its separation and mutability, turn your eyes away from its griefs and occupations, be true to your soul and work hard for it, fear the world's dealings, and learn from the generations before you that you have seen die. Their limbs fell asunder, their ears and eyes ceased to function, their grandeur and might were lost, their happiness and joys were severed. In place of proximity to their children they were given loss, in place of the companionship of spouses they were given isolation. They no longer boast, or procreate, or visit, or associate. Servants of God, beware! Control your passions, restrain your desires, and use your intellect! The matter is clear, the banner is erect, the road is compact, and the path is straightforward.

1.160 From an address by ʿAlī, to one of his associates who asked him, "How is it that your tribe has driven you away from this position when you are worthier?" ʿAlī answered:[1]

You man of Asad! Your girth is loose, and you fire without aim![2] Still, you possess kinship through marriage, and have the right to ask.[3] You want to know, so I will give you an answer: The injustice done to us concerning this position—when we are loftier in lineage and our kinship with the Messenger is closer—was an act of amoral appropriation. Some hearts coveted it, other

---

1   Ṣadūq (*Amālī*, 716–717) places this address at Ṣiffīn in 37/657; the speaker is a man from the Dūdān clan of Asad. "This position" (*hādhā l-maqām*), refers to the caliphate; Sunni commentators (Ḥ 2:243; also mentioned in B 543) interpret the referent as the Shūrā Council who elected ʿUthmān, while Shiʿi commentators (B 543; R 2:125) interpret the referent as ʿUthmān in particular, but also Abū Bakr and ʿUmar.

2   Refers to the man's lack of discernment and his speaking out of turn. R 2:122; Ḥ 9:242; B 543; F 271.

3   ʿAlī's kinship to the Asad tribe was through one of the following Asadī women: (1) ʿAlī's wife Laylā bint Masʿūd ibn Khālid (F 271–272); (2) an unnamed wife of ʿAlī (R 2:123); (3) the Prophet's wife Zaynab bint Jaḥsh (Ḥ 9:242–243; Ibn Abī al-Ḥadīd says ʿAlī himself never married into Asad).

اللهِ والمَعود إليه القيامةُ. ﴿وَدَعْ عَنْكَ نَهْبًا صِيحَ فِي حَجَرَاتِهِ﴾[1] وهَلُمَّ الخَطْب في ٱبن أبي سفيان فلقد أضحكني الدهر بعد إبكائه ولا غَرْوَ واللهِ فيا له خطبًا يستفرغ العجب ويُكثر الأَوَد حاول القوم إطفاء نور اللهِ من مصباحه وسَدَّ فوَّارُه من يَنبوعه وجدَحوا بيني وبينهم شِرْبًا وبيئًا. فإن ترتفع عنّا وعنهم محن البلوى أحملهم من الحقّ على محضه وإن تكن الأخرى ﴿فَلَا تَذْهَبْ نَفْسُكَ عَلَيْهِمْ حَسَرَاتٍ إِنَّ اللهَ عَلِيمٌ بِمَا يَصْنَعُونَ﴾.

1.161   ومن خطبة له عليه السلام

1.161.1   الحمد للهِ خالق العباد وساطح المهاد ومسيّل الوِهاد ومخصب النِّجاد ليس لأَوَّليّته ٱبتداء ولا لأزليّته ٱنقضاء هو الأوّل لم يزل والباقي بلا أجل خرّت له الجِباه ووَحَّدته الشِّفاه حَدَّ الأشياءَ عند خلقه لها إبانة له[2] من شبهها لا تقدِّره الأوهام بالحدود والحركات ولا بالجوارح والأدوات لا يقال له متى ولا يضرب له أمد بحتّى الظاهر لا يقال مِمَّا والباطن لا يقال فيما لا شَبَحُ فيُتقضَّى ولا محجوب فيُحوى لم يقرب من الأشياء بٱلتصاق ولم يبعد عنها بٱفتراق لا يخفى عليه من عباده شخوص لحظة

---

[1] البحر: الطويل.   [2] م، ي: كذا. ش، ه: ﴿لها﴾. ن: سقطت عن المتن، وفي الهامش ﴿لها له﴾.

hearts relinquished it, and God is the judge, the resurrection the time of return. But ⟨forget about the looting that caused screams in the neighborhood⟩ and call out the crime of Abū Sufyān's son![1] Time has made me weep and then laugh![2] No wonder, by God! What a calamity, what astonishment, what toil! These people seek to extinguish the light of God's lamp and block the water that gushes from his wellspring. They pour pestilence into the water between them and us. If these calamitous trials are lifted, I shall drive them on the course of unadulterated truth. If the opposite, well, «do not grieve over their actions, for God knows all that they do!»[3]

1.161 From an oration by ʿAlī:[4]

1.161.1 Praise God, who created his servants, unfurled the earth, filled valleys with streams, and covered highlands with green. His primacy has no beginning, and his perpetuity never concludes, he is first without ceasing, and eternal without end, foreheads touch the ground before him, and lips declare his oneness. He demarcated all the entities he created to differentiate between their likeness and him.[5] Imaginations cannot evaluate him with perimeters and movements, nor with limbs and instruments. It cannot be asked of him, "When?" nor can a limit be set for him by saying, "Until." He is the manifest about whom no one can ask, "From what?" and the hidden, about whom no one can ask, "In what?" He is neither a form that can be destroyed, nor is he veiled and thus encompassed. He is neither near to things by adherence nor remote from them by separation. An unblinking gaze, an echoing word, an approach to a hilltop, a lengthening of step—none of his servants' actions are hidden from

---

1 The quotation is the first hemistich of a proverbial verse by the pre-Islamic poet Imruʾ al-Qays (Imruʾ al-Qays, *Dīwān*, 140; Maydānī, *Majmaʿ al-amthāl*, s.v. "D-ʿ"), said to mean the following: Forget about the previous looting, viz., by the first three Sunni caliphs, or, by the Shūrā Council. The second hemistich, which would also be evoked for the audience and the real point of the citation, is (ولكنّ حديثًا ما حديثُ الرواحلِ): "but the real story is the story of the riding camels," interpreted as: At this moment, we should worry about more immediate events, viz., "the crime of Abū Sufyān's son," who is Muʿāwiyah ibn Abī Sufyān, governor of Damascus, who fought ʿAlī at the Battle of Ṣiffīn, and later became the first Umayyad caliph (B 544; Ḥ 9:243–246; R 2:124; F 272; Māmaṭīrī, *Nuzhah*, 426).

2 The laughter is in disbelief and astonishment. Ḥ 9:246–247; B 544.

3 Qurʾan, Fāṭir 35:8.

4 Delivered in the Grand Mosque of Kufa, presumably during ʿAlī's caliphate 35–40/656–661, in response to an unnamed Jewish man from Yemen who asked him to describe the Lord (Ṣadūq, *Tawḥīd*, 78–79).

5 Thus, if read as *lahū* (MS M, Y, commentaries Ḥ 9:252, B 544, ʿA 634). If read as *lahā* (MS Sh, H, and commentaries Kaydarī, 2:126, F 273): "to differentiate them from each other."

ولا كرور لفظة ولا ازدلاف ربوة ولا انبساط خطوة في ليل داجٍ ولا غسق ساجٍ يتفيّأ عليه القمر المنير وتعقبه الشمس ذات النور في الكرور والأفول والأفول وتقليب الأزمنة والدهور من إقبال ليل مقبل وإدبار نهار مدبر. قبل كلّ غاية ومدّة وكلّ إحصاء وعدّة تعالى عمّا ينحله المحدّدون من صفات الأقدار ونهايات الأقطار وتأثّل المساكن وتمكّن الأماكن فالحدّ لخلقه مضروب وإلى غيره منسوب. لم يخلق الأشياء من أصول أزليّة ولا من أوائل بَديّة[1] بل خلق ما خلق فأقام حدّه وصوّر ما صوّر فأحسن صورته ليس لشيء منه امتناع ولا له بطاعة شيء انتفاع علمه بالأموات الماضين كعلمه بالأحياء الباقين وعلمه بما في السماوات العلى كعلمه بما في الأرضين السفلى.

1.161.2 منها

أيّها المخلوق السويّ والمنشأ المرعيّ في ظلمات الأرحام ومضاعفات الأستار بُديت ﴿مِن سُلَالَةٍ مِّن طِينٍ﴾ ووضعت ﴿فِي قَرَارٍ مَّكِينٍ إِلَىٰ قَدَرٍ مَّعْلُومٍ﴾ وأجل مقسوم تمور في بطن أمّك جنيناً لا تُحير دعاء ولا تسمع نداء ثمّ أُخرجتَ من مقرّك إلى دار لم تشهدها ولم تعرف سبل منافعها فمن هداك لاجترار[2] الغذاء من ثدي أمّك وعرّفك[3] عند الحاجة مواضع طلبك وإرادتك. هيهات إنّ من يعجز عن صفات ذي الهيئة والأدوات فهو عن صفات خالقه أعجز ومن تناوله بحدود المخلوقين أبعد.

1.162 ومن كلام له عليه السلام لمّا اجتمع الناس إليه وشكوا ما نقموه على عثمان وسألوه مخاطبته عنهم واستعتابه لهم فدخل على عثمان فقال

---

١ م، ي: كذا. ش، ن، هـ، ونسخة في ي: ﴿أبديّة﴾.   ٢ ش، ن، ي، هـ: كذا. م: ﴿لاحتراز﴾.   ٣ ش، ن، ي، هـ: كذا. م، ونسخة في هـ: ﴿وحرّك﴾.

him, even in the darkest night, even in motionless dusk. The moon shines above the darkness, and the blazing sun follows, rising and setting in the rotation of eras and eons, with nights advancing and days in retreat. He is before every end and term, every reckoning and calculation. He is exalted above every description ascribed to him: attributes of quantity, terminal points in space, location in dwellings, and fixedness in place. Limits are specified for his creation—they relate only to beings other than him. He did not create things from eternal fundamentals or timeless principles. Rather, he created what he created and established its limit, he shaped what he shaped and made it beautiful. No one can withstand his power, just as no one can seek to benefit him by obeying him. His knowledge of the dead equals his knowledge of the living, his knowledge of what is in the lofty skies equals his knowledge of what is in the nethermost regions of the earth.

1.161.2 From the same oration:

O you who have been created with harmonious proportions, carefully nurtured in the darkness of wombs and the multiplicity of veils. You began as «an extraction of clay»[1] and were placed in «a safe abode for a known term»[2] and an ordained duration. You quickened in your mother's belly as a fetus, never answering a call or hearing a shout. Then you were brought out of your dwelling to an abode you had not witnessed, and whose benefits you did not know how to attain. Who guided you then to suckle from your mother's breast? Who showed you in your time of need the place where you could obtain what you sought and wished for? One who is incapable of describing a being with form and appendages is even more incapable of describing the creator, far from it! He is even further from being able to grasp the creator through the definitions of created beings.

1.162 From an address by ʿAlī, when people gathered around him to complain of wrongs ʿUthmān had committed and asked ʿAlī to remonstrate with him on their behalf and rebuke him. ʿAlī went to ʿUthmān and said:[3]

---

1 Qurʾan, Muʾminūn 23:12.

2 Qurʾan, Mursalāt 77:21–22.

3 In Medina, in 35/656, toward the end of ʿUthmān's caliphate. Ṭabarī, *Tārīkh*, 4:336–337. Ibn Abī Quḥāfah is the first Sunni caliph, Abū Bakr. Ibn al-Khaṭṭāb is the second Sunni caliph, ʿUmar.

1.162.1 إنّ الناس ورائي وقد استسفروني بينك وبينهم ووالله ما أدري ما أقول لك ما أعرف شيئًا تجهله ولا أدلّك على أمر لا تعرفه إنّك لتعلم ما نعلم ما سبقناك إلى شيء فنخبرك عنه ولا خلونا بشيء فنبلّغكه وقد رأيت كما رأينا وسمعت كما سمعنا وصحبت رسول الله صلّى الله عليه وآله كما صحبنا وما ابن أبي قحافة ولا ابن الخطّاب بأولى بعمل الحقّ منك وأنت أقرب إلى رسول الله صلّى الله عليه وآله وَشِيجةَ رَحِمٍ منهما وقد نلت من صهره ما لم ينالا. فاللهَ اللهَ في نفسك فإنّك والله ما تُبصَّر من عمى ولا تُعلَّم من جهل وإن الطرق لواضحة وإنّ أعلام الدين لقائمة.

1.162.2 فاعلم أنّ أفضل عباد الله عند الله إمام عادل هُدي وهَدى فأقام سنّة معلومة وأمات بدعة مجهولة وإنّ السنن لنيّرة لها أعلام وإنّ البدع لظاهرة لها أعلام وإنّ شرّ الناس عند الله إمام جائر ضَلّ وضُلّ به فأمات سنّة مأخوذة وأحيا بدعة متروكة وإنّي سمعت رسول الله صلّى الله عليه وآله يقول ﴿يؤتى يوم القيامة بالإمام الجائر وليس معه نصير ولا عاذرٰ١ فيلقى في جهنّم فيدور فيها كما تدور الرحى ثمّ يرتبط في قعرها﴾. وإنّي أنشدك الله أن تكون إمام هذه الأمّة المقتول فإنّه كان يقال ﴿يُقتل في هذه الأمّة إمام يفتح عليها القتل والقتال إلى يوم القيامة﴾ ويَلبِس أمورَها عليها ويَبثّ الفتن فيها فلا يبصرون الحقّ من الباطل يموجون فيها موجًا ويمرُجون فيها مَرْجًا. فلا تكوننّ لمروان سَيِّقة يسوقك حيث شاء بعد جلال السنّ وتقضّي العمر.

1.162.3 فقال له عثمان
كَلِّم الناس في أن يؤجّلوني حتّى أخْرُج إليهم من مظالمهم.

---

١ ش، ن، ي، ه، ومصحّحة في م: كذا. أصل م: سقطت من الجملة بعض الألفاظ فجاء ﴿يؤتى بالإمام الجائر وليس معه عاذر﴾.

1.162.1 People have gathered behind me, and they have sent me to negotiate. By God, I don't know what to say! There is nothing I know that you don't, no path I can guide you to that you are not familiar with already. You know what we know, we have not preceded you to something that we can tell you about, nor privately learned something we can share. You have seen what we saw, you have associated with God's Messenger as we did. In truth, Ibn Abī Quḥāfah and Ibn al-Khaṭṭāb were not worthier of doing what is right than you! You are closer to the Messenger in kinship, and you, not they, have the honor of being his son-in-law. Fear God for the sake of your soul! By God, you do not need to be given sight as though you were blind, or knowledge as though you were ignorant! The roads are clear, and faith's banners stand high.

1.162.2 Know that the best of his servants in God's eyes is a just leader who is rightly guided and guides aright, who establishes time-honored practices and puts to death unacceptable heresies. The paths of the Sunnah are brightly illumined and have their banners. Innovations are also clearly visible, and they too have their banners. The worst of people in God's eyes is an unjust leader who goes astray and leads people astray, who puts to death time-honored practices and revives abandoned heresies. I have heard the Messenger of God say, ⟨On the day of resurrection, the unjust leader will be brought for judgment, and he will not have a single person to help him or speak on his behalf. He will be thrown into the Pit of Gehenna and spin there like a millstone, then he will be tethered in its lowest point.⟩ I ask you in God's name, do not be the slain leader of this community, for it has been said that "a leader will be slain in this community who will open unto it the door of killing and assault till the resurrection." The community's affairs will slide into chaos and seditions will become widespread, such that people will stop distinguishing right from wrong. They will heave in agitated waves, disordered and confused. At your advanced age, having neared the end of your life, don't become a camel driven by Marwān's whim![1]

1.162.3 ʿUthmān responded to ʿAlī:
Talk to the people and ask them to give me time to address their grievances.

---

1 Marwān ibn al-Ḥakam, who had earlier been exiled along with his father from Medina by the Prophet, was a member of the Umayyad clan and one of ʿUthmān's chief advisors during his caliphate. Later, he fought against ʿAlī at the Battle of the Camel but reluctantly pledged allegiance to him in defeat. After the death of Muʿāwiyah's grandson Muʿāwiyah II, Marwān became the first caliph of the Marwānid branch of the Umayyads.

فقال عليه السلام

ما كان بالمدينة فلا أجل فيه وما غاب فأجله وصول أمرك إليه.

١.١٦٣ ومن خطبة له عليه السلام يذكر فيها عجيب خلقة الطاووس

١.١٦٣.١ ابتدعهم خَلْقًا عجيبًا من حيوان وموات وساكن وذي حركات وأقام من شواهد البيّنات على لطيف صنعته وعظيم قدرته ما أنقادت له العقول معترفة به ومسلّمة له ونَعَقَتْ في أسماعنا دلائله على وحدانيّته وما ذَرَأَ من مختلف صور الأطيار التي أسكنها أخاديد الأرض وخروق فِجاجها ورواسي أعلامها من ذوات أجنحة مختلفة وهيئات متباينة مصرّفة في زمام التسخير ومرفرِفة بأجنحتها في مخارق الجوّ المنفسح والفضاء المنفرج. كَوَّنها بعد إذ لم تكن في عجائب صور ظاهرة وركّبها في حِقاق مفاصل محتجبة ومنع بعضها بعَبالة خلقه أن يسمو في السماء١ خفوفًا وجعله يدِفّ دفيفًا ونسقها على اختلافها في الأصابيغ بلطيف قدرته ودقيق صنعته فمنها مغموس في قالب لون لا يشوبه غير لون ما غُمِس فيه ومنها مغموس في لون صِبْغٍ قد طُرّق٢ بخلاف ما صبغ به.

١.١٦٣.٢ ومن أعجبها خلقًا الطاووس الذي أقامه في أحكم تعديل ونضّد ألوانه في أحسن تنضيد بجناح أسرج٣ قصبه وذَنَب أطال مسحبه إذا درج إلى الأنثى نشره من طَيّه وسما به مُطِلًّا على رأسه كأنّه قلع داريّ عنجه نوتيّه يختال بألوانه ويميس بزَيَفانه يفضي كإفضاء الدِّيَكة ويؤرّ بملاقحة. أحيلك من ذلك على معاينة لا كمن يحيل على ضعيف إسناده. ولو كان كزعم من يزعم أنّه يُلقح بدمعة تسفحها٤ مدامعه فتقف ضَفّتي

<hr>

١ ش، ن، ي، ه: كذا. م، ونسخة في ي: ﴿الهواء﴾.   ٢ ش، ن، ه: كذا. م، ي، ونسخة في ش، ه: ﴿طوّق﴾.   ٣ ش، ن: كذا. م، ي، ه، ونسخة في ش: ﴿أشرج﴾.   ٤ ش، ن، ي، ه: كذا. م، ونسخة في ن، ي، ه: ﴿تنشجها﴾. ونسختان في ش: ﴿تسحّها﴾ و﴿تنجسها﴾.

'Alī replied:

For grievances within Medina, there can be no reprieve. For those from other places, you can have only as much time as it takes for your orders to get there.

1.163 From 'Alī's oration in which he describes the wondrous creation of the peacock:

1.163.1 God created wondrous creatures, living beings, inanimate bodies, still objects, and things that move, and he set up clear testimonies to his sublime craftsmanship and great power, impelling intellects to recognize and submit to him. Proofs of his oneness cry out to our ears, including the birds that he created in a multitude of forms, that he lodged in the furrows of the earth and in the crevices of its mountain passes and mighty crags. Possessing many kinds of wings and different shapes, all are controlled by the rein of subjugation, yet soar in spaces within the vastness of the ether and the wide-open skies. He brought them from non-being into being in marvelous forms. He fitted joints to sockets and covered them with flesh. He made some birds bulky, preventing them from rising easily into the sky, and causing them to flutter and flap on the ground. He fashioned them all differently, in diverse hues, with his sublime power and precise craftsmanship. Some he gave a single unadulterated color, others he dyed with a color iridescent with the sheen of a second hue.

1.163.2 The most marvelous of birds in the manner of its creation is the peacock, which is formed by the creator in the most congruent harmony, with its colors arrayed in the best possible way, with wings of interlacing, golden feather-shafts, and a tail with a lengthened train. When it approaches the hen, the peacock spreads out the folds of its tail and lifts it high over its head, like a Dārī sail hoisted by a boatman.[1] It struts haughtily in its many colors and swaggers dragging its train. It mates in the manner of the cockerel, leaping onto the female and inseminating it. I relate this to you from observation, not as one whose narrations are based on weak attribution.[2] Even if it were the case, as some believe, that the peacock inseminates through a teardrop emitted by its tear ducts and poised on the edge of its eyelids, and that the female imbibes it

---

1   Dārī is a relative adjective from Dārīn, the name of the main settlement on an island near Qaṭīf, on the eastern coast of present-day Saudi Arabia. In pre-Islamic and early Islamic times, Dārīn was the main port of Bahrain, through which musk was imported from India. Yāqūt, *Muʿjam al-buldān*, 2:432, s.v. "Dārīn"; B 549; Ḥ 9:268.

2   Although not native to the Arabian Peninsula, peacocks were common in the Persian empire, and the commentators state that 'Alī would have seen them in Kufa. Ḥ 9:270; Jāḥiẓ, *Ḥayawān* 7:170, 186.

جفنُه وأنّ أنثاه تطعم ذلك ثمّ تبيض لا من لقاح فحل سوى الدمع المنبجس لمّا كان ذلك بأعجب من مطاعمة الغراب.

تخال قَصَبه مَداري من فضّة وما أنبت عليها من عجيب داراته وشموسه خالص العِقيان وفِلَذ الزَّبَرجَد فإن شبّهته بما أنبتت الأرض قلت جَنيّ جُنِي من زهرة كلّ ربيع وإن ضاهيته بالملابس فهو كمَوشِيّ الحُلَل أو مُونق عَصب اليمن وإن شاكلته بالحلي فهو كفصوص ذات ألوان قد نُطّقت بالجُين المكلَّل. يمشي مشي المَرح المختال ويتصفّح ذنبه وجناحه فيُقَهقِهُ ضاحكًا لجمال سرباله وأصابيغ وِشاحه فإذا رمى ببصره إلى قوائمه زَقا مُعْوِلًا بصوت يكاد يُبين عن استغاثته ويشهد بصادق توجّعه لأنّ قوائمه حُمْشٌ كقوائم الديكة الخِلاسيّة وقد نجمت من ظُنبوب ساقه صيصِيّة خفيّة وله في موضع العُرف قُنزُعة خضراء مُوشّاة ومخرج عنقه كالإبريق ومغرزها إلى حيث بطنه كصبغ الوَسْمة اليمانيّة أو كحريرةٍ مُلبَسة مرآةً ذاتَ صِقال وكأنّه متلفّع بمِعْجَرٍ[1] أَسْحَم إلّا أنّه يخيّل لكثرة مائه وشدّة بريقه أنّ الخضرة الناضرة ممتزجة به. ومع فتق سمعه خطٌّ كمُستدقّ القلم في لون الأُقْحُوان أبيض يَقَقٌ فهو ببياضه في سواد ما هنالك يأتلق. وقلّ صبغ إلّا وقد أخذ منه بقسط وعلاه بكثرة صِقاله وبريقه وبصيص ديباجه ورونقه فهو كالأزاهير المبثوثة لم تُرَبِّها أمطار ربيع ولا شموس قَيظ. وقد ينخسر من ريشه ويَعرى من لباسه فيسقط تَتْرى وينبت تِباعًا فينحتّ من قصبه انحتاتَ أوراق الأغصان ثمّ يتلاحق ناميًا حتّى يعود كهيئته قبل سقوطه لا يخالف سائرُ[2] ألوانه ولا يقع لون في غير مكانه وإذا تصفّحتَ شعرة من شعرات قصبه أرَتْكَ حمرة ورديّة وتارة خضرة زَبَرجَديّة وأحيانًا صفرة عَسجَديّة وكيف تصل إلى صفة هذا

<hr>

[1] م، ي، ونسخة في ش: كذا. ش، ن، ه: ﴾متقنّع﴿. [2] ش، ن، ي، ه: كذا. م، ونسخة في ي: ﴾سالف﴿.

then lays eggs,[1] rather than through insemination by a male with a fluid other than his teardrop, that would not be more marvelous than the mating of crows through mutual feeding.[2]

You would think the shafts of the peacock's feathers silver combs and the astonishing halos and suns that sprout from them coins of pure gold and shards of green emerald! If you were to compare them to the earth's produce, you would call it a bouquet of spring flowers. If you were to liken them to garments, you would say they are an embroidered robe, or a beautiful Yemeni turban. If you were to equate them with jewelry, they would be bezelled gemstones of different colors rimmed with studs of silver. The peacock struts, haughty and exultant, it fans its tail and wings and laughs out loud, relishing its beautiful dress and its many-hued scarf. But when it looks at its legs, it cries out in pain with a voice that reveals its need for help and testifies to its real suffering, for its legs are scrawny, like the legs of a drab cockerel, and a small spur juts out from its shinbone. In its crest, though, it has a beautiful crown of green feathers, while the curve of its neck is shaped like the mouth of a water-jug, and underneath, its belly is like the cobalt-blue dye of Yemen, or like silk cloth draped on a polished mirror. It appears wrapped in a veil of purest black, except that its luster is so intense and its sheen so bright that it is as if fresh green is mixed in with the black. At the slit of its earhole, there is a line like the fine edge of a reed-pen, snowy white in color like the chamomile flower, and its whiteness gleams against the blackness that prevails there. There is hardly a color it does not have a share of, and that has not been enhanced further by a unique polish, gleam, sheen, and radiance. It looks like scattered flowers untouched by spring showers or full summer suns. Sometimes, it sheds its feathers, as if stripping off its clothes; they fall off, one by one, then grow back altogether. They fall from their shaft-roots like leaves from a branch, then grow and connect, until they come back the way they were before; the new colors are no different, and not a single color appears in the wrong place. If you examine just one of the plumules growing from the shaft, it will display the red of a rose, the green of an emerald, and even at times the yellow of pure gold. Not even the deepest of minds and the most gifted of intellects can find a way to describe this creature, so how

---

1   In Hindu mythology, peahens self-impregnate by drinking the tears of peacocks, which are celibate (*brahmachārī*), and to laud ascetics, Lord Krishna wears a peacock feather in his crown.

2   In ancient Arab folklore, crows mate by exchanging inseminating fluid through their beaks, and their proverb says, ⟨more hidden than the mating of a crow⟩. Details and caveats in Ḥ 9:270; Jāḥiẓ, *Ḥayawān*, 3:177, 3:464, 7:244. I have added "mating" in the translation to clarify this context.

عمائق الفطن أو تبلغه قرائح العقول أو تستنظم وصفه أقوال الواصفين وأقلّ أجزائه قد

أعجز الأوهام أن تدركه والألسنة أن تصفه فسبحان الذي بهر العقول عن وصف خلق

جلاه للعيون فأدركته محدودًا مكوّنًا ومؤلّفًا ملوّنًا وأعجز الألسن عن تلخيص صفته

وقعد بها عن تأدية نعته[1] وسبحان من أدمج قوائم الذرّة والهَمَجة إلى ما فوقهما من خلق

الحيتان والأفْيِلة ووأى على نفسه ألّا يضطرب شَبَح ممّا أولج فيه الروح إلّا وجعل الحِمام

موعده والفناء غايته.

1.163.3 منها في صفة الجنة

فلو رميت ببصر قلبك نحو ما يوصف لك منها لَعَزَفَتْ نفسك عن بدائع ما أخرج إلى

الدنيا من شهواتها ولذّاتها وزخارف مناظرها ولذهلت بالفكر في اصطفاق أشجار غُيّبت

عُروقها في كُثْبان المِسْك على سواحل أنهارها وفي تعليق كبائس اللؤلؤ الرَّطب في

عَساليجها وأفنانها وطلوع تلك الثمار مختلفة في غُلُف أكمامها تجنى من غير تكلّف فتأتي على

مُنية مجتنيها ويطاف على نزّالها في أفنية قصورها بالأعسال المصفّقة والخمور المروّقة قوم

لم تزل الكرامة تتمادى بهم حتّى حلّوا دار القرار وأمنوا نقلة الأسفار فلو شغلت قلبك

أيّها المستمع بالوصول إلى ما يهجم عليك من تلك المناظر المونقة لزهقت نفسك شوقًا

إليها ولتحمّلت من مجلسي هذا إلى مجاورة أهل القبور استعجالًا بها. جعلنا الله وإيّاكم

ممّن يسعى بقلبه إلى منازل الأبرار برحمته.

1.163.4 تفسير بعض ما في هذه الخطبة من الغريب قوله عليه السلام ﴿ويؤرّ بملاقّحة﴾ الأَرّ

كناية عن النكاح يقال ﴿أرّ المرأة يؤرّها﴾ إذا نكحها. وقوله ﴿كأنّه قلع داريّ عنجه نوتيّه﴾ القلع

شراع السفينة وداريّ منسوب إلى دَارِيْن وهي بلدة على البحر يُجلب منها الطيب وعنجه أي

عطفه يقال ﴿عنجت الناقة أعنِجها عَنجًا﴾ إذا عطفتها والنوتيّ الملّاح. وقوله ﴿ضفّتي جفونه﴾

أراد جانبي جفونه والضفّتان الجانبان. وقوله ﴿وفلذ الزبرجد﴾ الفلذ جمع فلذة وهي القطعة.

وقوله ﴿كبائس اللؤلؤ الرطب﴾ الكِبَاسة العِذْق والعساليج الغصون واحدها عسلوج.

اش، ن، م، ه: كذا. ي: ﴿حقّه﴾.

can words be mustered to illustrate it? Even the smallest of its parts is so splendid that it exceeds the grasp of imagination and surpasses the descriptions of tongues. Glory to the one who has dazzled intellects, who has rendered them incapable of describing a creature that he placed in the open, where eyes could perceive its outline, shape, structure, and color! He made tongues incapable of describing it succinctly and rendered them too weak to give its depiction full due. Glory to the one who gave strong structures to all creatures, from ants and gnats to whales and elephants, and who pledged to himself that no form he has infused with spirit shall move, without death being its end, and destruction its goal!

1.163.3 From the same oration, describing the celestial garden:
If you gaze with your heart's eye at the wonders described for you of paradise, your soul will loathe the marvels of this world, its sensualities, pleasures, and gilded landscapes. You will lose yourself in heaven's rustling trees whose roots are buried in dunes of musk on the banks of its rivers, in the clusters of brilliant pearls that hang from their branches, in the fruits that burst from their sepals that can be gathered without effort and delight the gatherer. You will see the residents of heaven's pavilions and arcades, who are served pure honey and rich wine; they lived in this world nobly until, at last, they settled in a permanent home, with no further need of travels and journeys. If you were to task your heart truly, O listener, with reaching these wondrous landscapes, your longing soul would leave your body right now, and you would hasten from this assembly here to the company of the people of the grave! May God, in his mercy, place us among those whose hearts strive to reach the abode of the pious!

1.163.4 Raḍī: Explanation of some of the rare words in this oration: As for ʿAlī's words, "it leaps on the female and inseminates it (*wa-yaʾurru bi-mulāqaḥah*)," "leaping on" alludes to copulation; it is said, "he leaped on the woman, he leaps on her," if he copulates with her. As for ʿAlī's words, "as though it were a Dārī sail hoisted by a boatman (*ka-annahū qalʿu Dāriyyin ʿanajahu nūṭiyyuhu*)," *qalʿ* is a ship's canvas sheet, and Dārī is related to Dārīn, a sea town through which perfumes are imported; "hoisted (*ʿanaja*)" means he made it turn; it is said "I hoisted the female camel;" "I hoist it a hoisting," if I make it turn; *nūṭī* is a seaman. As for ʿAlī's words, "*ḍaffah* of its eyelids," he meant the sides of its eyelids; *ḍaffah* means side. As for ʿAlī's words, "bits (*filadh*) of green emerald," *filadh* is the plural of *fildhah*, which means piece. As for ʿAlī's words, "clusters of brilliant pearls (*kabāʾis al-luʾluʾ al-raṭb*)," *kibāsah* (clusters) means bunch, *ʿasālīj* (branches) are tree limbs; the singular is *uslūj*.

1.164 ومن خطبة له عليه السلام

1.164.1 لِيَتَأَسَّ صغيركم بكبيركم وَلْيَرْؤُفْ كبيركم بصغيركم ولا تكونوا كَجُفاة الجاهليّة لا في الدين يتفقّهون ولا عن الله تعقلون. كقَيْضِ بَيْضٍ في أَداجٍ يكون كَسرها وِزرًا ويُخرج حِضانُها شرًّا.

1.164.2 منها

افترقوا بعد أُلْفَتِهم وتشتّتوا عن أصلهم فمنهم آخذ بغصن أينما مال مال معه على أنّ الله سيجمعهم لشرّ يوم لبني أميّة كما تجتمع قَزَع الخريف يؤلّف الله بينهم ثمّ يجعلهم رُكامًا كركام السحاب ثمّ يفتح لهم أبوابًا يسيلون من مستثارهم كسيل الجنّتين حيث لم تسلم عليه قارة ولم تثبت له أَكَمة ولم يردّ سَنَنه رَصّ طود ولا حِداب أرض يذعذعهم الله في بطون أوديته ثمّ يسلكهم ﴿يَنَابِيعَ فِي الْأَرْضِ﴾ يأخذ بهم من قوم حقوق قوم ويمكّن لقوم في ديار قوم. وأيم الله ليذوبنّ ما في أيديهم بعد العلوّ والتمكين كما تذوب الأَلْية على النار.

1.164.3 أيّها الناس لو لم تتخاذلوا عن نصر الحقّ ولم تهنوا عن توهين الباطل لم يطمع فيكم مَن ليس مثلكم ولم يَقْوَ من قوي عليكم لكنّكم تِهْتُم مَتاهَ بني إسرائيل ولعمري لَيُضْعفَنّ

1.164 From an oration by ʿAlī:[1]

1.164.1 Let your young emulate your elders, let your elders nurture your young. Don't be like churls from the Age of Ignorance who have no understanding of religion and no comprehension of God's commands. Dealing with you is like crushing a nest of eggs in the sand—breaking them is a sin but brooding them produces vipers![2]

1.164.2 From the same oration:
They scattered after having come together and moved away from the tree trunk, but some will continue to hold fast to the main branch—wherever it bends, they will bend too.[3] Later, God will bring them together, mustering them like wisps of autumn clouds, on an evil day for the Umayyads. God will assemble them, then pile them up like winter cloudbanks, then open their doors, and they will gush out from their source like the flood of the Two Gardens,[4] no knoll will be safe, and no hillock withstand, neither strong cliff nor high rock will stem their current. God will send them into the bellies of the earth's valleys, then make them «flow out in streams».[5] Through them, he will wrest from one group the rights they had usurped from another, he will settle one group in the abodes of another. By God, after their time of might and establishment, all that is in Umayyad hands will melt away as a fat-tail melts on the fire!

1.164.3 People! If you had not held back from supporting right, if you had not shown weakness in upending wrong,[6] these challengers who are not nearly your match would not have become emboldened against you, and those who overpowered you would have failed. But you strayed as the Israelites did. By my life, when I am gone, you will stray more and more. You turned away from what

---

1   §1.164.2 is said to have been declaimed as part of an oration ʿAlī delivered in Medina, presumably in 35/656 at the beginning of his caliphate (Kulaynī, *Kāfī*, 8:63–65). §1.164.3 is said to have been declaimed as part of an oration ʿAlī delivered in Kufa, presumably during his caliphate 35–40/656–661 (Mufīd, *Irshād*, 1:290).
2   Lit. "brooding them produces evil." I.e., if you crush them before they have done wrong, you incur sin; if you leave them be, they may hatch vipers. F 287; Ḥ 9:282; B 553; R 2:146–147.
3   The trunk (lit. root, *aṣl*) refers to ʿAlī, the branch to his son and successor, Ḥasan. Ḥ 9:284; B 553.
4   The flood of the Two Gardens is a Qurʾanic reference to the devastating flood of the Maʾrib dam in Yemen that submerged the Gardens of Sheba. Qurʾan, Sabaʾ 34:15–16; Ḥ 9:285; B 554; R 2:149–150.
5   Qurʾan, Zumar 39:21.
6   Reference to Qurʾan, Āl ʿImrān 3:139.

لكم التِّيه من بعدي أضعافًا خلَّفتم الحقّ وراء ظهوركم وقطعتمِ الأدنى ووصلتم الأبعد وٱعلموا أنّكم إن ٱتبعتم الداعي لكم سلك بكم منهاج الرسول وكُفيتم مؤونة الاعتساف ونبذتم الثقل الفادح عن الأعناق.

1.165 ومن خطبة له عليه السلام في أوّل خلافته

إنّ الله سبحانه أنزل كتابًا هاديًا بيّن فيه الخير والشرّ نخذوا نهج الخير تهتدوا وٱصدِفوا عن سَمْت الشرّ تقصدوا. الفرائضَ الفرائضَ أدّوها إلى الله تُؤَدِّ كم إلى الجنّة إنّ الله حرّم حرامًا غير مجهول وفضّل حرمة المسلم على الحُرَم كلّها وشدّ بالإخلاص والتوحيد حقوق المسلمين في معاقدها ف﴿المسلم مَن سَلِمَ المسلمون من لسانه ويده﴾ إلّا بالحقّ ولا يحلّ أذى المسلم إلّا بما يجب. بادروا أمر العامّة وخاصّة أحدكم وهو الموت فإنّ الناس أمامكم وإنّ الساعة تحدوكم من خلفكم تَخَفَّفوا تلْحَقوا فإنّما يُنتظر بأوّلكم آخرُكم اتّقوا الله في عباده وبلاده فإنّكم مسؤولون حتّى عن البِقاع والبهائم أطيعوا الله ولا تعصوه وإذا رأيتم الخير نخذوا به وإذا رأيتم الشرّ فأعرِضوا عنه.

1.166 ومن كلام له عليه السلام بعد ما بويع بالخلافة وقد قال له قوم من الصحابة لو عاقبتَ قومًا ممّن أجلب على عثمان فقال

يا إخوتاه إني لست أجهل ما تعلمون ولكن كيف لي بقوّة والقوم المجلبون على حدّ شوكتهم يملكوننا ولا نملكهم وهاهُمْ هؤلاء قد ثارت معهم عِبدانكم وٱلتفّت إليهم

was right, severed your bonds of kinship from the person who was close, and forged them with the person who was distant. Know this: If you follow him who calls you,[1] he will lead you on the Messenger's path—you will be spared the weight of deviation and cast this crushing yoke from your necks.

1.165 From an oration by ʿAlī at the beginning of his caliphate:[2]
God has revealed a book to guide you and explained in it the difference between good and evil. Follow the path of good and you shall be rightly guided. Shun the path of evil and you shall you remain on the high road. The mandated rites must be performed; offer them to God, and they will take you to paradise. God has made certain things illicit, and these are known. He has placed the sanctity of Muslims above all sanctities; through their devotion and declaration of his oneness, he has bound them, and their rights, together. A Muslim is someone from whose tongue and hand all other Muslims are safe,[3] except when it is lawfully required to punish; it is unlawful to injure a Muslim, except with just cause. People, hasten to accept death! Death is common to all, yet particular to each individual. Generations have preceded you, and the dreaded hour now drives you forward. Lighten your burden of sin, so that you may be quick to catch up—those who have gone ahead await the arrival of those who are yet to come. Fear God, and do not injure his servants or his lands. You are answerable for your actions, even those relating to the earth and to cattle. Obey God and do not sin. If you see an opportunity to do good, take it. If you see a chance to do evil, shun it.

1.166 From an address by ʿAlī following the people's pledge to him as caliph, responding to some of the Prophet's Companions who urged, "You should punish the people who conspired to kill ʿUthmān." ʿAlī answered:[4]
Brothers, I am not unmindful of what you know, but how do I enforce retribution when the people who conspired to kill ʿUthmān are so powerful? They control us, we don't control them! Here they are now, your own slaves having risen up with them, as well as the Bedouins. They are mixed in among you and impose their will. Do you see a way to carry out any part of your plan?

---

1   Refers to ʿAlī himself. F 281.
2   35/656, in Medina. Ṭabarī (*Tārīkh*, 4:436) says this was ʿAlī's first oration as caliph.
3   Hadith attributed to the Prophet in Quḍāʿī, *Shihāb*, §1.134.
4   Delivered in 35/656 in Medina (Ṭabarī, *Tārīkh*, 4:437). It is reported that ʿAlī assembled the people and said, "Let ʿUthmān's killers stand up," and most people stood up in solidarity with the assaulters. (B 556). On ʿAlī's initial dealings with ʿUthmān's killers, see Ḥ 9:293–294.

أعرابكم١ وهم خلالكم يسومونكم ما شاؤوا وهل ترون موضعًا لقدرة على شيء تريدونه إنّ هذا الأمر أمرُ جاهليّةٍ وإنّ لهؤلاء القوم مادّة إنّ الناس من هذا الأمر إذا حُرّك على أمور فرقةٌ ترى ما ترون وفرقة ترى ما لا ترون وفرقة لا ترى هذا ولا هذا فاصبروا حتّى يهدأ الناس وتقع القلوب مواقعها وتؤخذ الحقوق مُسْمَحة فاهدأوا عنّي وانظروا ماذا يأتيكم به أمري ولا تفعلوا فَعْلة تُضعضع قوّة وتُسقط منّة وتورث وَهْنًا وذلّة. وسأمسك الأمر ما اسْتمسك وإذا لم أجد بُدًّا فـ﴿آخِرِ الداء الكَيّ﴾.

1.167 ومن خطبة له عليه السلام عند مسير أصحاب الجمل إلى البصرة

إنّ الله بعث رسولًا هاديًا بكتاب ناطق وأمر قائم لا يهلك عنه إلّا هالك وإنّ المبتدَعات المشبّهات هنّ المهلِكات إلّا ما حفظ٢ الله منها وإنّ في سلطان الله عصمة لأمركم٣ فأعطوه طاعتكم غير مَلومة ولا مُستكرَهٍ بها والله لتفعلُنّ أو لينقُلَنّ الله عنكم سلطان الإسلام ثمّ لا ينقله إليكم أبدًا حتّى يأرِزَ الأمر إلى غيركم. إنّ هؤلاء قد تَمَالَؤوا على سَخْطة إمارتي وسأصبر ما لم أخف على جماعتكم فإنّهم إن تمّموا على فيالة هذا الرأي انقطع نظام المسلمين وإنّما طلبوا هذه الدنيا حسدًا لمن أفاءها الله عليه فأرادوا ردّ الأمور على أدبارها. ولكم علينا العمل بكتاب الله وسيرة رسوله والقيام بحقّه والنَّعْش لسنّته.

1.168 ومن كلام له عليه السلام كلّم به بعض العرب وقد أرسله قوم من أهل البصرة لمّا قرب عليه السلام منها يعلم لهم منه حقيقة حاله مع أصحاب الجمل لتزول الشبهة من نفوسهم. فبيّن

١م، ي، ونسخة في ش، ه: كذا. ش، ن، ه: ﴿أغراركم﴾. ٢ش، ن، ي، ه، ونسخة في م: كذا. أصل م: ﴿عصم﴾. ٣ش، ن، ي، ه، ونسخة في م: كذا. أصل م: ﴿لربّكم﴾.

'Uthmān's killing is an act from the Age of Ignorance and its perpetrators have strong support. If an order were given now, you would see the people divide into three groups: one would agree with you, another would think the opposite, and a third would see neither the one nor the other. Be patient, let the people calm down and hearts settle, then justice can be exacted more easily. Step back and see what my rule brings—don't be impulsive in doing something that will wreck your power, ruin your force, and bequeath weakness and humiliation. I will hold things together as long as they will stay together. If I am left with no alternative, then, when afflicted by an incurable disease, ⟨cauterizing is the last resort⟩.[1]

1.167 From an oration by 'Alī in the lead-up to the Battle of the Camel, when his opponents marched on Basra:[2]

God sent a Messenger, a guide, with a book that speaks and an established religion.[3] Whoever dies having strayed from them will perish, for dubious and heretical innovations bring perdition, except when God protects from their harm. Submitting to God's authority safeguards your religion. Render him obedience, then, without blame or force. By God, you must do this, else he will remove Islam's authority from your control and never give it back, and rule will pass to another group! These individuals have banded to condemn my command, and I will be patient for as long as I don't fear for your concord—if they continue to pursue this errant course, the Muslims' stability will crumble. They seek this world and envy those to whom God has awarded it, they wish to turn these affairs back on their heels. My promise to you is this: I shall act on the Book of God and the practice of his Messenger. I shall uphold his right and revive his Sunnah.

1.168 From 'Alī's address to an Arab sent by a group of Basrans when he approached their city, in the lead-up to the Battle of the Camel, to find out the truth of 'Alī's dealings with his opponents, because they were unsure of who was in the right. When 'Alī explained what had transpired, the man accepted that he, 'Alī, was in the right. 'Alī

---

1   Ar. *ākhir al-dā' al-kayy*, proverb referring to battle as the final option; also rendered: *ākhir al-dawā' al-kayy*, ⟨the final medicine is cauterization⟩, or *ākhir al-ṭibb al-kayy*, ⟨the final treatment is cauterization⟩. Etiology in F 283–284; Ibn Manẓūr, *Lisān*, s.v. "K-W-Y."

2   Delivered in Medina in 36/656, while preparing to march to Iraq, urging the Medinans to mobilize. Ṭabarī, *Tārīkh*, 4:445–446.

3   Ar. *amr*, translated here as "religion," lit. "affair," used twice more in this passage, once in the plural *umūr*. In addition to the faith of Islam, the word also simultaneously denotes its political entity; I have used "caliphate" to translate the second instance, and "affairs" to bring together both meanings in the third instance.

له عليه السلام من أمره معهم ما علم به أنّه على الحقّ ثمّ قال له بايع فقال إنّي رسول قومي ولا
أحدث حدثًا دونهم حتّى أرجع إليهم فقال عليه السلام١

أرأيت لو أنّ الذين وراءك بعثوك رائدًا تبتغي لهم مساقط الغيث فرجعت إليهم وأخبرتهم
عن الكَلَأ والماء فخالفوا إلى المعاطش والمجادب والمجادب ما كنت صانعًا.

قال كنت تاركهم ومخالفهم إلى الكلأ والماء. فقال له عليه السلام فأمدد إذًا يدك. فقال الرجل
فوالله ما ٱستطعت أن أمتنع عند قيام الحجّة عليّ فبايعته عليه السلام. والرجل يعرف بكُليب
الجَرْميّ.

١.١٦٩ ومن كلامه عليه السلام لمّا عزم على لقاء القوم بصفّين

اللهمّ ربّ السقف المرفوع والجوّ المكفوف الذي جعلته مَغيضًا لليل والنّهار ومجرى
للشمس والقمر ومختلَفًا للنجوم السيّارة وجعلت سكّانه سِبْطًا من ملائكتك لا يَسأمون
من عبادتك وربَّ هذه الأرض التي جعلتها قرارًا للأنام ومَدْرَجًا للهَوامّ والأنعام وما
لا يحصى ممّا يُرى وما لا يرى وربَّ الجبال الرواسي التي جعلتها للأرض أوتادًا وللخلق
ٱعتمادًا إن أظهرتَنا على عدوّنا فجنّبنا البغي وسدّدنا للحقّ وإن أظهرتهم علينا فٱرزقنا
الشهادة وٱعصمنا من الفتنة.

أين المانع للذِّمار والغائر عند نزول الحقائق من أهل الحِفاظ. العارُ وراء كم والجنّة
أمامكم.

<hr>

١ م، وأصل ش: كذا. ن، ي، ﻫ: ﴿ومن كلامه عليه السلام لمّا قال لكليب الجرميّ قبل الجمل
بايع. فقال إنّي رسول قومي ولا أحدث حدثًا دونهم﴾.

then said to him, "Pledge the oath of allegiance!" to which he replied, "I am my people's emissary, and can do nothing on my own; I have to first return to them." ʿAlī then said:[1] If the people you represent had sent you as a scout to find out where the rains are falling, and, if, when you told them where to find grass and water, they went against your recommendation and headed for parched, drought-hit lands, what would you do then?

The man replied, "I would leave them and proceed to where there was grass and water." ʿAlī declared, "In that case, extend your hand!" The man said later, "By God, I was not able to refuse when the case was so clearly proven, and I pledged him allegiance." The man's name was Kulayb al-Jarmī.

1.169 From ʿAlī's prayer when he had resolved to fight the enemy at Ṣiffīn:[2]
God! O Lord of the lofty sky and layers of air, you made the sky and air the marshland into which night and day are absorbed, the course where the sun and moon orbit, and the space through which the moving planets sail. You populated it with tribes of your angels, who never tire of your worship. O Lord of this earth, you made the earth a home for humans, a place for insects to crawl and cattle to roam, and a habitat for countless other creatures, seen and unseen. O Lord of the mighty mountains, you made the mountains anchors for the earth and a refuge for your creatures. Hear our prayer: If you grant us victory over our enemy, then hold us back from treachery and direct us to follow the truth. If you grant them victory over us, then honor us with martyrdom and save us from sedition.

People, where are your doughty fighters who would defend honor and guard families with zeal when the blows of war descend? Behind you lies shame! Before you is paradise!

---

1   This event took place a little before the Battle of the Camel, after Ṭalḥah and Zubayr had entered Basra, and ʿAlī, on his way to confront them in Basra, was encamped nearby in Dhū Qār. Mufīd, *Jamal*, 156, after Wāqidī; full account in Ṭabarī, *Tārīkh*, 4:490–492.
2   Intoned just before the battle at Ṣiffīn, 37/657. Minqarī, *Waqʿat Ṣiffīn*, 232; Ṭabarī, *Tārīkh*, 5:14–15.

1.170   ومن خطبة له عليه السلام

1.170.1   الحمد لله الذي لا تُواري عنه سماءٌ سماءً ولا أرضٌ أرضًا.

1.170.2   منها

وقال لي قائل إنّك على هذا الأمر يا ابن أبي طالب لحريص فقلت بل أنتم والله أحرص وأبعد وأنا أخصّ وأقرب وإنّما طلبت حقًّا لي وأنتم تحولون بيني وبينه وتضربون وجهي دونه. فلمّا قَرَعتُ بالحجّة في الملأ الحاضرين هَبّ[1] لا يدري ما يجيبني به.

1.170.3   اللّهمّ إنّي أستعديك على قريش ومن أعانهم فإنّهم قطعوا رحمي وصغّروا عظيم منزلتي وأجمعوا على منازعتي أمرًا هو لي ثمّ قالوا ألا إنّ في الحقّ أن تأخذه وفي الحقّ أن تتركه.

1.170.4   منها في ذكر أصحاب الجمل

نخرجوا يَجُرّون حرمة رسول الله صلّى الله عليه وآله كما تُجَرّ الأَمَة عند شِرائها متوجّهين بها إلى البصرة فحَبَسا نساءهما في بيوتهما وأبرزا حَبيس رسول الله لهما ولغيرهما في جيش ما منهم رجل إلّا وقد أعطاني الطاعة وسمح لي بالبيعة طائعًا غير مُكرَهٍ. فقدموا على عاملي بها وخزّان بيت مال المسلمين وغيرهم من أهلها فقتلوا طائفة صبرًا وطائفة غدرًا. فوالله لو لم

1.170 From an oration by ʿAlī:[1]

1.170.1 Praise God, from whose vision one sky does not conceal another, one earth does not conceal another.

1.170.2 From the same oration:
Someone said to me, "How you covet the caliphate, son of Abū Ṭālib!" I retorted, "No, by God, you are more covetous and farther away from it, while I am closer and more worthy! What I seek is my right, and you are blocking me from it, you are hitting me in the face and pushing me away!" When I struck him with this clear argument in front of the whole group, he was dumbstruck and could find no answer.

1.170.3 God, I ask your help against Quraysh and their supporters. They have severed the bonds of my kinship, demeaned my lofty station, and banded together to wrest my right from me. Then they say, "A right may be taken, a right may also be abandoned."[2]

1.170.4 From the same oration describing ʿAlī's opponents at the Battle of the Camel:[3] They marched toward Basra dragging the Messenger's wife with them like a slave-girl dragged for sale, having veiled their own women to their homes, while exposing the Messenger's wife to their eyes and the eyes of others in their army. There was not a single individual in that army, moreover, who had not sworn obedience to me, who had willingly, without coercion, pledged allegiance to me. They advanced against my governor in Basra, as well as the custodians of the public treasury and other townspeople, and they killed a number after capturing them, and several more whom they tricked with their treachery. By God, if they had purposefully killed even a single Muslim without a crime to justify

---

1   In Basra, in 36/656, soon after the Battle of the Camel (reference to the battle in §1.170.4). §1.170.4 is cited as an answer given during an oration in the mosque in Basra, a few days after the battle (Māmaṭīrī, *Nuzhah*, 228); other parts of the oration as cited in ibid., 221–233, are listed in the note to §1.23. The reference in §1.170.2–3 is to the Shūrā Council that elected ʿUthmān in 23/644. Ḥ 9:305.

2   Similar lines in §1.215.1.

3   "They" are Ṭalḥah and Zubayr, "the Messenger's wife" is ʿĀʾishah. For context of the Battle of the Camel and ʿĀʾishah's role, see Ḥ 9:310–327; B 561–564; F 288–289. ʿAlī's governor in Basra was ʿUthmān ibn Ḥunayf, a Companion of the Prophet. Similar lines in §1.215.2.

يصيبوا من المسلمين إلّا رجلًا واحدًا معتمدين لقتله بلا جرمٍ جرّه لَحَلَّ لي قتل ذلك الجيش كلّه إذ حضروه، فلم ينكروا ولم يدفعوا عنه بلسان ولا يد. دع ما أنّهم قد قتلوا من المسلمين مثل العدّة التي دخلوا بها عليهم.

1.171 ومن خطبة له عليه السلام

1.171.1 أمين وحيه وخاتم رسله وبشير رحمته ونذير نقمته.

1.171.2 أيّها الناس إنّ أحقّ الناس بهذا الأمر أقواهم عليه وأعلمهم[1] بأمر الله فيه فإن شغب شاغب ٱستعتب فإن أبى قوتل. ولعمري لئن كانت الإمامة لا تنعقد حتّى يحضرها عامّة الناس ما إلى ذلك سبيل ولكنّ أهلها يحكمون على من غاب عنها ثمّ ليس للشاهد أن يرجع ولا للغائب أن يختار. ألا وإنّي أقاتل رجلين رجلًا ٱدّعى ما ليس له وآخر منع الذي عليه. أوصيكم بتقوى الله فإنّها خير ما تواصى العباد به وخير عواقب الأمور عند الله. وقد فُتح باب الحرب بينكم وبين أهل القبلة ولا يحمل هذا العلم إلّا أهل البصر والصبر والعلم بمواضع الحقّ فَٱمضوا لما تؤمرون به وقفوا عندما تنهون عنه ولا تعجلوا في أمر حتّى تتبيّنوا فإنّ لنا مع كلّ أمر تنكرونه غِيَرًا.

---

[1] ش، ن، ي، ه: كذا. م: كذا، ونسخة في ه: ﴿أعلمهم﴾.

his killing, it would be lawful for me to execute their whole army, for they all stood by without protest. They failed to defend any of the innocent victims with their hands or even with their tongues! But, in fact, they have not just killed one—they have killed a great many Muslims, as many as the numbers with which they themselves entered the city.

1.171   From an oration by ʿAlī:[1]

1.171.1   Muḥammad was the trustee of God's revelation, the seal of his prophets, the herald of his mercy, and the warner ahead of his punishment.

1.171.2   People! The individual most worthy to assume the mantle of leadership is the one who is most capable of carrying its trust, most knowledgeable about God's command. After the pledge, if a rebel revolts, he is to be persuaded to return to the fold, and if he refuses, he is to be fought. By my life, if you are saying that the imamate can be pledged only with the whole populace in attendance, there is no way to do this! Instead, the leaders decide on behalf of the absent,[2] and afterward, those who were present have no right to rescind their pledge, while the absent have no right to choose another. Hark! I shall fight two kinds of men, the man who claims what does not belong to him, and another who refuses to render his due. I counsel you to be conscious of God—this is the best counsel his servants can give one another, and the way that obtains the best outcome before God. Hear me! War has commenced between you and people of the Qiblah,[3] and our banner can be carried only by people of perception and fortitude, those who know where truth resides. Enact what you are commanded, then, and desist from what you are forbidden. Do not hasten to an action until you have clarity, for anything you discover to be wrong I will change.[4]

---

1   Likely delivered just before or soon after the Battle of the Camel in 36/656: § 1.171.3 is included by Ḥarrānī (*Tuḥaf*, 183–184) in an oration that he says ʿAlī delivered "when some people expressed unhappiness at his levelling of stipends among the people," which fits with what the sources say of Ṭalḥah's and Zubayr's source of dissatisfaction with ʿAlī's rule. § 1.171.2 (and § 1.83.3) are recorded by Minqarī (*Waqʿat Ṣiffīn*, 10) and Abū Ḥanīfah al-Dīnawarī (*Akhbār* 152–153) as part of ʿAlī's first Friday sermon in Kufa.

2   Ar. *ahlahā*, lit. "its people"; my translation, "their leaders," is based on B 566; Ḥ 9:329, which interpret the phrase as "the people of loosening and binding" (*ahl al-ḥall wa-l-ʿaqd*) and "scholars" (*ʿulamāʾ*).

3   I.e., fellow Muslims. The Qiblah is the direction of the Kaʿbah in Mecca that all Muslims face in ritual prayer.

4   The context for this last statement is ʿUthmān's unwillingness to make changes in his administration, even when its wrongs were brought to his notice. B 566.

1.171.3 ألا وإنّ هذه الدنيا التي أصبحتم تتمنّونها وترغبون فيها وأصبحت تغضبكم وترضيكم ليست بداركم ولا منزلكم الذي خلقتم له ولا الذي دعيتم إليه ألا وإنّها ليست بباقية لكم ولا تبقون عليها وهي وإن غرّتكم منها فقد حذّرتكم شرّها فدَعُوا غرورها لتحذيرها وإطماعها لتخويفها وسابقوا فيها إلى الدار التي دعيتم إليها وانصرفوا بقلوبكم عنها ولا يَخِنّنّ أحدكم خَنين الأُمّة على ما زوي عنه منها واستتمّوا نعمة الله عليكم بالصبر على طاعة الله والمحافظة على ما استحفظكم من كتابه. ألا وإنّه لا يضرّكم تضييع شيء من دنياكم بعد حفظكم قائمة دينكم ألا وإنّه لا ينفعكم بعد تضييع دينكم شيء حافظتم عليه من أمر دنياكم. أخذ الله بقلوبنا وقلوبكم إلى الحقّ وألهمنا وإيّاكم الصبر.

1.172 ومن كلام له عليه السلام في معنى طلحة بن عبيد الله

قد كنت وما أُهَدَّد بالحرب ولا أرهَّب بالضرب وأنا على ما وعدني ربّي من النصر والله ما استعجل متجرّدًا للطلب بدم عثمان إلّا خوفًا من أن يطالَب بدمه لأنّه مَظِنّته ولم يكن في القوم أحرص عليه منه فأراد أن يُغالط بما أجلب فيه ليلبس الأمر ويقع الشكّ. ووالله ما صنع في أمر عثمان واحدة من ثلاث لئن كان ابن عفّان ظالمًا كما كان يزعم لقد كان ينبغي له أن يوازر قاتليه أوٰ ينابذ ناصريه ولئن كان مظلومًا لقد كان ينبغي له أن يكون من المنهنِين عنه والمعذّرين فيه ولئن كان في شكّ من الخصلتين لقد كان ينبغي له أن يعتزله ويركد جانبًا ويدع الناس معه فما فعل واحدة من الثلاث وجاء بأمر لم يعرف بابه ولم تسلم معاذيره.

ا ش، ن، ي، هـ: كذا. م: كذا، ومصحّحة في ش: ﴿وأن﴾.

1.171.3 Hark my words! This world that you covet and desire, that causes you anger and pleasure, is not your home, it is not the residence for which you have been created or to which you have been called. Listen to me! It will not remain for you, nor will you remain in it. While it tempts you with its allures, it also warns you of its evil, so heed its warnings and threats, and shun its temptations and enticements. Turn your heart away and race to the home to which you are called. Let no one among you sniffle like a young slave-girl over anything he has lost of this world! Instead, seek the completion of God's blessings by being patient in the path of his obedience and holding fast to God's Book. Hark and listen! Nothing you surrender of this world will harm you if you secure the principles of your faith! Hark again! Nothing you secure of your worldly affairs will benefit you if you surrender your faith! May God guide our hearts toward the truth. May he grant us patience in adversity.

1.172 From an address by ʿAlī about Ṭalḥah ibn ʿUbaydallāh:[1]
I have never been one to be shaken by threats of battle or panicked by notices of attack. I await the victory my Lord has promised me. By God, Ṭalḥah only hastened to draw his sword and demand vengeance for ʿUthmān's blood because he feared that the same call was going to be made against him! He is implicated in this matter, for none among the people was more avid for it than he—he wishes to create confusion and has raised a tumult about it only in order to muddy the issue and raise doubt. By God, he took none of the three proper courses in the crisis around ʿUthmān: If Ibn ʿAffān was an oppressor, as Ṭalḥah believed, he should have backed those who killed him or at least rebuffed his supporters. If ʿUthmān was a victim, Ṭalḥah should have been among those who defended him and pleaded his cause. And if he was in doubt about both choices, he should have dissociated from ʿUthmān and remained on the sidelines, leaving the people to do their will. But he did none of this—he followed a path whose entryway was unsanctioned and whose justifications were unsound.

---

1   In Medina in 36/656, soon after ʿAlī's accession to the caliphate, when news arrived that Ṭalḥah and Zubayr were on their way to Basra to recruit an army to fight him (B 567; on Ṭalḥah's misconduct with ʿUthmān, see Ḥ 10:5–9; B 568). Kulaynī (*Kāfī*, 5:53) quotes the first few lines in an oration at the Battle of the Camel outside Basra in 36/656. The first line is similar to the penultimate line of §1.22.

1.173 ومن خطبة له عليه السلام

أيّها الغافلون غير المغفول عنهم والتاركون والمأخوذ منهم ما لي أراكم عن الله ذاهبين
وإلى غيره راغبين كأنّكم نَعَمٌ أراح بها سائم إلى مرعًى وبيّ ومشرب دويّ إنّما هي
كالمعلوفة للهُدى لا تعرف ماذا يراد بها إذا أحسن إليها تحسب يومها دهرها وشِبَعها
أمرها. والله لو شئت أن أخبر كلّ رجل منكم بمخرجه ومَولِجه وجميع شأنه لفعلت ولكن
أخاف أن تكفروا فيَّ برسول الله صلّى الله عليه وآله ألا وإنّي مُفضيه إلى الخاصّة مّن
يؤمَن ذلك منه والذي بعثه بالحقّ واصطفاه على الخلق ما أنطق إلّا صادقًا وقد عهد
إليَّ بذلك كلّه وبمهلك من يهلك ومنجى من ينجو ومآل هذا الأمر وما أبقى شيئًا يمرّ
على رأسي إلّا أفرغه في أذنيّ وأفضى به إليّ. أيّها الناس إنّي والله ما أحثّكم على طاعة إلّا
وأسبقكم إليها ولا أنهاكم عن معصية إلّا وأتناهى قبلكم عنها.

1.174 ومن خطبة له عليه السلام

1.174.1 انتفعوا ببيان الله واتّعظوا بمواعظ الله واقبلوا نصيحة الله فإنّ الله قد أعذر إليكم
بالجليّة واتّخذ عليكم الحجّة وبيّن لكم مَحابّه من الأعمال ومكارهه لتتّبعوا هذه وتجتنبوا هذه
فإنّ رسول الله صلّى الله عليه وآله كان يقول ﴿إنّ الجنّة حُجبت بالمكاره وإنّ النار حُفّت
بالشهوات﴾. واعلموا أنّه ما من طاعة الله شيء إلّا يأتي في كرهٍ وما من معصية الله شيء
إلّا يأتي في شهوة فرحم الله رجلًا نزع[1] عن شهوته وقمع هوى نفسه فإنّ هذه النفس أبعد
شيءٍ مَنزَعًا وإنّها لا تزال تنزع إلى معصية في هوى. واعلموا عباد الله أنّ المؤمن لا يصبح
ولا يمسي إلّا ونفسه ظَنون عنده فلا يزال زاريًا عليها ومستزيدًا لها. فكونوا كالسابقين
قبلكم والماضين أمامكم قَوَّضوا من الدنيا تقويض الراحل وطَوَوها طَيّ المنازل.

---

[1] ش، ن، ي، هـ: كذا. م: ﴿...في شهوة فنزع رجل﴾.

1.173 From an oration by ʿAlī:

O heedless people who go not unheeded! Spurners of good who will soon be brought to account! How is it that I see you moving away from God and placing your hopes in another? As though you were a herd of sheep driven to a plague-ridden pasture and contaminated water! Or beasts fattened for the knife, who have no idea what lies in store for them, who, if treated well, think the remainder of their days to be as long as an age, and that all they must do is fill their bellies! By God, if I wished to inform each of you about his exit, his entry, and all that he will encounter, I would do so, but I fear that you will abandon God's Messenger for me. Harken to me! I shall pass on its knowledge to individuals who are to be trusted in this regard. I swear by the one who sent Muḥammad with truth and placed him above all people, I never speak anything but the truth! Muḥammad bequeathed me this knowledge and told me about the perishing of all who will perish, the saving of all who will be saved, and the end result of this affair. He left no question that might occur to me without pouring its secrets into my ear and communicating to me its mysteries. People! By God, I do not urge you to an act of obedience without preceding you to it! I do not forbid you from an act of disobedience without staying away from it myself!

1.174 From an oration by ʿAlī:[1]

1.174.1 Profit from God's revelation, heed God's counsels, and accept God's direction, for God has cautioned you with clear guidance and brought you convincing proofs. He has shown you what he likes and what he dislikes so that you may follow the former and shun the latter. His Messenger used to say, ⟨Paradise is veiled by torments, while the Fire is surrounded by delights.⟩[2] Know that every act of obedience to God is achieved with toil, while every act of disobedience to God comes in the guise of pleasure. May God have mercy on the man who roots out his desires and crushes the passions of his appetitive soul.[3] This appetite ranges far, and, urged on by its desires, it never stops urging you to acts of disobedience. Servants of God! Know that a believer wakes up every morning and sleeps every night wary of his gluttonous soul, continually rebuking it and seeking to provision himself for the hereafter. Be like those who preceded you, who died before you. They pulled up their tent-pegs from this world as those striking camp and traversed through it as in the successive stages of a journey.

---

1 One of ʿAlī's first orations after becoming caliph, delivered in Medina in 35/656. B 573.

2 Quḍāʿī, *Shihāb*, § 3.1.

3 Ar. *nafs*, lit. "soul" or "self," translated here as "appetitive soul," refers to the base, animal faculty of the human soul, «Indeed, the soul urges one to evil.» Qurʾan, Yūsuf 12:53.

1.174.2 وٱعلموا أنّ هذا القرآن هو الناصح ٱلذي لا يَغُشّ والهادي الذي لا يُضِلّ والمحدّث الذي لا يَكذب وما جالَسَ هذا القرآن أحد إلّا قام عنه بزيادة أو نقصان زيادةٍ في هدى أو نقصان من عمى. وٱعلموا أنّه ليس على أحد بعد القرآن من فاقة ولا لأحد قبل القرآن من غنى فٱستشفوه من أدوائكم وٱستعينوا به على لَأوائكم فإنّ فيه شفاء من أكبر الداء وهو الكفر والنفاق والغيّ والضلال فٱسألوا الله به وتوجّهوا إليه بحبّه ولا تَسألوا به خلقه إنّه ما توجّه العباد إلى الله بمثله. وٱعلموا أنّه شافع مشفَّع وقائلٌ مصدَّق وأنّه من شفع له القرآن يوم القيامة شُفِّع فيه ومن مَحَلَ به القرآن يوم القيامة صُدِّق عليه فإنّه ينادي منادٍ يوم القيامة ألا إنّ كلّ حارث مبتلى في حرثه وعاقبة عمله غيرَ حَرَثة القرآن فكونوا من حرثته وأتباعه وٱستدلّوه على ربّكم وٱستنصحوه على أنفسكم وٱتّهموا عليه آراءكم وٱستغِشّوا فيه أهواءكم.

1.174.3 العملَ العملَ ثمّ النهايةَ النهايةَ والاستقامةَ الاستقامةَ ثمّ الصبرَ الصبرَ والورعَ الورعَ. إنّ لكم نهاية فأنتهوا إلى نهايتكم وإنّ لكم عَلَمًا فٱهتدوا بعَلَمكم وإنّ للإسلام غاية فٱنتهوا إلى غايته وٱخرجوا إلى الله ممّا ٱفترض عليكم من حقّه وبين لكم من وظائفه. أنا شاهد لكم وحَجِيج يوم القيامة عنكم.

1.174.4 ألا وإنّ القَدَر السابق قد وقع والقضاء الماضي قد تورّد وإنّي متكلّم بعدة الله وحجّته قال الله تعالى ﴿إِنَّ الَّذِينَ قَالُوا رَبُّنَا اللهُ ثُمَّ ٱسْتَقَامُوا تَتَنَزَّلُ عَلَيْهِمُ الْمَلَائِكَةُ أَلَّا تَخَافُوا وَلَا تَحْزَنُوا وَأَبْشِرُوا بِالْجَنَّةِ الَّتِي كُنتُمْ تُوعَدُونَ﴾ وقد قلتم ﴿رَبُّنَا اللَّهُ﴾ فٱستقيموا على كتابه وعلى منهاج أمره وعلى الطريقة الصالحة من عبادته. ثمّ لا تَمرُقوا منها ولا تبتدعوا فيها ولا تخالفوا عنها فإنّ أهل المُروق منقطع بهم عند الله يوم القيامة.

1.174.2 Know also that the Qurʾan is a counselor that never deceives, a guide that never leads astray, and a speaker that never lies. Whoever sits down with this Qurʾan gets up with either an increase or a decrease: an increase of guidance or a decrease of blindness. Know, furthermore, that no person will remain poor after accepting the Qurʾan and that no person will be wealthy before accepting it. Seek its cure for your ailments and its support against your hardships, for it holds the cure for the greatest ailments of all—unbelief, hypocrisy, gross error, and miscreance. Beseech God through its sanctity and turn to him through your love for it. Do not misuse it to seek favors from God's creatures. Nothing equals the Qurʾan in helping you to turn to God. Know, too, that the Qurʾan is an intercessor that is heeded and a speaker that is believed. Those for whom it intercedes on judgment day will have their plea accepted, while those it accuses on judgment day will have the claim against them upheld. Indeed, a crier will cry out on judgment day: "Hark! Every tiller's crop and all the fruits of his labor have been destroyed, except that of the tillers of the Qurʾan!" Be, therefore, among the Qurʾan's tillers and followers! Secure it as the guide to your Lord, accept it as a counselor who restrains your appetites, and distrust any of your opinions that contradict its teachings. Learn from the Qurʾan and know that your passions deceive.

1.174.3 Deeds, deeds! Goals, goals! Rectitude, rectitude! Endurance, endurance! Ethics, ethics! Truly, you have a goal, so proceed toward it! You have been given a signpost, so be guided by it! Islam has an objective, so race toward it! Stand before God having cleared the dues he has mandated, having performed the duties he has required. Do this, and I shall bear witness on your behalf and plead your cause on judgment day.

1.174.4 Hark! The preordained commandment has come to pass, and the predestined event has arrived at its waterhole. Let me tell you of God's promise and his proof, for he has said, «as for those who proclaim that "Our Lord is God," and then remain upright, angels come to them, saying, "do not fear and do not grieve, but rejoice, for paradise, as promised, is yours!"»[1] You have proclaimed, «Our Lord is God.» Now remain upright in the manner shown by his Book. Follow the straight path of his command and the pious road of his worship. Do not abandon the faith, do not introduce heresies, and do not transgress, for those who abandon the faith will be severed from God on judgment day.

---

1 Qurʾan, Fuṣṣilat 41:30.

1.174.5 ثمّ إيّاكم وتهزيعَ الأخلاق وتصريفها وٱجعلوا اللسان واحدًا وَلْيَخْتَزِن الرجل لسانه فإنّ هذا اللسان جَموح بصاحبه والله ما أرى عبدًا يتّقي تقوى تنفعه حتّى يختزن لسانه فإنّ لسان المؤمن من وراء قلبه وإنّ قلب المنافق من وراء لسانه لأنّ المؤمن إذا أراد أن يتكلّم بكلام تدبّره في نفسه فإن كان خيرًا أبداه وإن كان شرًّا واراه وإنّ المنافق يتكلّم بما أتى على لسانه ماذا له وماذا عليه. وقد قال رسول الله صلّى الله عليه وآله ﴿لا يستقيم إيمان عبد حتّى يستقيم قلبه ولا يستقيم قلبه حتّى يستقيم لسانه﴾. فمن ٱستطاع منكم أن يلقى الله سبحانه وهو نقيّ الراحة من دماء المسلمين وأموالهم سليم اللسان من أعراضهم فليفعل.

1.174.6 وٱعلموا عباد الله أنّ المؤمن يستحلّ العام ما ٱستحلّ عامًا أوّلَ ويحرّم العام ما حرّم عامًا أوّل وأنّ ما أحدث الناس لا يُحِلّ لكم شيئًا مّا حُرّم عليكم ولكنّ الحلال ما أحلّ الله والحرام ما حرّم الله. فقد جرّبتم الأمور وضَرّستموها ووُعظتم بمن كان قبلكم وضربت الأمثال لكم ودعيتم إلى الأمر الواضح فلا يَصَمُّ عن ذلك إلّا أَصَمُّ ولا يَعمى عن ذلك إلّا أعمى ومن لم ينفعه الله بالبلاء والتجارب لم ينتفع بشيء من العظة وأتاه التقصيرُ[1] من أمامه حتّى يعرف ما أنكر وينكر ما عرف. وإنّما الناس رجلان مُتبعٌ شِرعةً ومبتدع بدعة ليس معه من الله سبحانه برهان سنّة ولا ضياء حجّة.

1.174.7 وإنّ الله سبحانه لم يعظ أحدًا بمثل هذا القرآن فإنّه حبل الله المتين وسببه[2] الأمين وفيه ربيع القلب وينابيع العلم وما للقلب جلاء غيره مع أنّه قد ذهب المتذكّرون وبقي الناسون والمتناسون. فإذا رأيتم خيرًا فأعينوا عليه وإذا رأيتم شرًّا فٱذهبوا عنه فإنّ رسول الله صلّى الله عليه وآله كان يقول ﴿يا ٱبن آدم ٱعمل الخير ودع الشرّ فإذا أنت جوادُ قاصد﴾.

---

١ ش، ن، ي، هـ، ونسخة في م: كذا. أصل م: ﴿النقض﴾.   ٢ ش، ن، ي، هـ، ونسخة في م: كذا. أصل م، ونسخة في ش: ﴿سننه﴾.

1.174.5 Beware of marring your morals and shifting your mores—speak with a single tongue. Let every man safeguard his tongue, for the tongue can bolt and carry off its master. By God, I see no godfearing person profiting from his piety until he safeguards his tongue. A believer's tongue is found behind his heart and a hypocrite's heart is found behind his tongue. When a believer intends to say something, he first mulls in his heart the words he will say. Then, if he finds them to be good, he voices them, and if he finds them to be wicked, he buries them. A hypocrite, on the other hand, says whatever comes to his tongue without knowing what is for and what against him. God's Messenger has said, ⟨A person's belief is right only when his heart is right, and his heart is right only when his tongue is righteous.⟩[1] Let those of you who can, meet the Almighty with hands unsullied by Muslim blood or property, and tongue unblemished by defiling their honor.

1.174.6 Servants of God! Know that a believer considers licit this year what he had considered licit the year before. He considers illicit this year what he had considered illicit the year before. The innovations of men do not make the illicit licit for you. What God has made licit is licit, and what God has made illicit is illicit. You have experienced many affairs and bitten down on them with strong teeth, you have been forewarned by the example of those who lived before you, parables have been drawn for you, and you have been called to the clear way. Only the truly deaf remain deaf to the call, only the truly blind remain blind. Those whom God does not benefit through their own trials and experiences will not benefit from homilies and counsel. It is when their own sins confront them that they will accept as good what they had thought to be bad, and as bad what they had thought to be good. People are of two kinds: one follows a clear path, while another introduces heresies with no proof of established practice nor gleam of evidence from God.

1.174.7 The Almighty's best counsel is found in this Qurʾan. It is God's strong rope, it is his firm cord, it is the heart's springtime, it is the wellspring of wisdom. Nothing burnishes the heart like the Qurʾan. But all who were mindful have disappeared, only those who have forgotten it, or pretend to have forgotten, remain. People, when you know something to be good, lend it support. When you know something to be evil, distance yourself. The Messenger used to say, ⟨Son of Adam, do good and avoid evil, and you will race ahead like a thoroughbred!⟩

---

1 Quḍāʿī, *Shihāb*, § 6.41.

١.١٧٤.٨ ألا وإنّ الظلم ثلاثة فظلم لا يُغفر وظلم لا يترك وظلم مغفور لا يطلب فأمّا الظلم
الذي لا يغفر فالشرك بالله قال الله سبحانه ﴿إِنَّ اللهَ لَا يَغْفِرُ أَن يُشْرَكَ بِهِ﴾ وأمّا الظلم
الذي يغفر فظلم العبد نفسه عند بعض الهَنات وأمّا الظلم الذي لا يترك فظلم العباد
بعضهم بعضًا. القصاص هناك شديد ليس هو جَرْحًا بالمُدى ولا ضربًا بالسِّياط ولكنّه
ما يُستصغر ذلك معه. فإيّاكم والتلوُّن في دين الله فإنّ جماعةً فيما تكرهون من الحقّ خير
من فُرقة فيما تحبّون من الباطل وإنّ الله سبحانه لم يعط أحدًا بفرقة خيرًا ممّن مضى ولا
ممّن بقي.

١.١٧٤.٩ يا أيّها الناس طوبى لمن شغله عيبه عن عيوب الناس وطوبى لمن لزم بيته وأكل
قوته وٱشتغل بطاعة ربّه١ وبكى على خطيئته فكان من نفسه في شغل والناس منه في
راحة.

١.١٧٥ ومن كلام له عليه السلام في معنى الحكمين
فأجمع رأيُ ملائكم على أن ٱختاروا رجلين فأخذنا عليهما أن يُجَعجِعا عند القرآن ولا
يجاوزاه ويكون ألسنتهما معه وقلوبهما تبَعَه فتاها عنه وتركا الحقّ وهما يبصرانه وكان
الجور هَواهما والاعوجاج دأبُهما وقد سبق ٱستثناؤنا عليهما في الحكم بالعدل والعمل
بالحقّ سوءَ رأيِهما وجور حكمهما. والثقة في أيدينا لأنفسنا حين خالفا سبيل الحقّ وأتيا
بما لا يُعرف من معكوس الحكم.

---

١ ش، ن، ي، ه: كذا. م: كذا، ونسخة في ه: ﴿بطاعته﴾.

1.174.8   Harken to me! Wrongs are of three kinds: a wrong that will not be forgiven, one that will not be left unrequited, and a third that will be forgiven and not pursued. The wrong that will not be forgiven is assigning partners to God, for the Almighty has said, «God does not forgive being assigned partners.»[1] The wrong that will be forgiven is the wrong a person incurs against himself when committing small sins. The wrong that will not be left unrequited is the wrong people commit against one another, and retribution in this instance will be severe. It will not consist of being stabbed with a knife or struck with a whip, but these will seem slight in comparison. Beware of capricious change in God's religion. Uniting to face a challenge in the cause of right is far better than dividing the community to attain wrong. The Almighty has never granted anyone anything good through dissent, not among those who are gone, nor among those who remain.

1.174.9   People! Blessed are those whose faults distract them from the faults of others.[2] Blessed are those who remain in their homes, eat their food, occupy themselves with acts of obedience for their Lord, weep for their sins, and weary themselves by constant chiding, while never causing others unease.

1.175   From an address by ʿAlī regarding the arbitrators:[3]
Your majority opinion settled on choosing two arbitrators. I made them pledge that they would kneel before the Qurʾan and not transgress its command, that their tongues would speak according to its guidance and their hearts follow it. But they strayed from the Qurʾan and abandoned the truth, despite seeing it before their eyes—discrimination was their desire and crookedness their practice! I had declared at the outset that my acceptance of their ruling would be contingent on their implementing justice and truth, and that stipulation excluded any ruling at which they might arrive at through corrupt views or unjust dictates. Since they have strayed from the path of truth and produced a contrary ruling, authority remains in my hands.

---

1   Qurʾan, Nisāʾ 4:48, 116.
2   Attributed to the Prophet in Quḍāʿī, *Shihāb*, §3.35.
3   ʿAlī addressed this oration to the Kharijites after news of the arbitrators' ruling—against him and in Muʿāwiyah's favor—arrived in Kufa in 37/658 (B 578; Ṭabarī, *Tārīkh*, 5:85). The arbitrators were ʿAmr ibn al-ʿĀṣ on Muʿāwiyah's side, and Abū Mūsā al-Ashʿarī on ʿAlī's. ʿAlī signals here his own reservations about the choice of arbitrators, and the fact that it was the Kufan army that had forced his hand. On details of the arbitrators' injustice, see F 295. On verses attributed to ʿAmr, boasting of deceiving Abū Mūsā, see Ḥ 10:56–57.

1.176 ‏ومن خطبة له عليه السلام

1.176.1 ‏لا يشغله شان ولا يغيّره زمان ولا يحويه مكان ولا يصفه لسان ولا يعزُب عنه عدد قطر الماء ولا نجوم السماء ولا سَوافي الريح في الهواء ولا دبيب النمل على الصفا ولا مَقيل الذرّ في الليلة الظلماء يعلم مساقط الأوراق وخفيّ طَرْف الأحداق. وأشهد أن لا إله إلّا الله غير معدول به ولا مشكوك فيه ولا مكفورٍ دينه ولا مجحود تكوينه شهادة مَن صدقت نيّته وصفت دخلَته وخلص يقينه وثقلت موازينه. وأشهد أنّ محمّدًا عبده ورسوله المجتبى من خلائقه والمُعتام لشرح حقائقه والمختصّ بعقائل كراماته والمصطفى لكرائمِ¹ رسالاته والموضّحةُ به أشراطُ الهدى والمجلوُّ به غِرِبيبُ العمى.

1.176.2 ‏أيّها الناس إنّ الدنيا تَغُرّ المؤمّل لها والمُخلد إليها ولا تَنْفَس بمن نافس فيها وتغلب من غلب عليها. وأيم الله ما كان قوم قطّ في غَضّ نعمة من عيش فزال عنهم إلّا بذنوب أجترحوها لـ﴿أَنَّ اللَّهَ لَيْسَ بِظَلَّامٍ لِّلْعَبِيدِ﴾. ولو أنّ الناس حين تنزل بهم النقم وتزول عنهم النعم فزعوا إلى ربّهم بصدق من نيّاتهم وولَهٍ من قلوبهم لَرَدَّ عليهم كلّ شارد وأصلح لهم كلّ فاسد وإنّي لأخشى عليكم أن تكونوا في فترة وقد كانت أمور مضت ملتُم فيها مَيلةً كنتم فيها عندي غير محمودين ولئن رُدّ عليكم أمرُكم إنّكم لسعداء وما عليّ إلّا الجهد ولو أشاء أن أقول لقلت عفا الله عمّا سلف.

1.177 ‏ومن كلام له عليه السلام وقد سأله ذِعْلِب اليمانيّ فقال هل رأيت ربّك يا أمير المؤمنين فقال عليه السلام أفأعبد ما لا أرى قال وكيف تراه قال

___

‏¹ ش، ن، ي، هـ: كذا. م: ونسخة في ش: ﴿لمكارم﴾.

1.176 From an oration by ʿAlī:[1]

1.176.1 No matter can preoccupy him, no time can alter him, no place can encompass him, and no tongue can describe him. Nothing escapes his reach— not the droplets in water, nor the stars in the sky, not the dust-raising winds in the air, not the crawling of ants on rocks, not the sleeping of insects in the dark night. He knows the falling of leaves and the blinking of eyes. I bear witness that there is no god but God. I do not equate him with another, or doubt him, or reject his religion, or deny his creation. This testimony comes from one whose intention is true, whose motives are pure, whose certainty is limpid, and whose scales are heavy. I bear witness that Muḥammad is God's servant and messenger, the one chosen from among all his creation, the one selected to explain his truths, the one singled out for his exquisite glories, the one designated to convey his precious message, the one who clarifies signs of guidance, the one through whom dark blindness is dispelled.

1.176.2 People! The world deceives those who desire her and incline toward her. Cherishing not those who compete for her, she conquers those who try to conquer her. By God, no group who are given life's delightful bounties have them taken away except due to their sins, for «God is not unjust to his servants.»[2] When calamities swarm and bounties cease, if people turned to their Lord with sincere intent and heartfelt longing, he would recover their runaway camels and heal what was corrupted. I fear you are in a state of ignorance. Events happened in the past during which you deviated, and your behavior was less than admirable. If matters reverted to what they were before, you would attain happiness, and I can try to make that happen. If I so wished, I could also say: May God forgive the past.

1.177 From an address by ʿAlī when Dhiʿlib, the Yemenite, asked him, "Commander of the Faithful, have you seen your Lord?" ʿAlī replied, "Would I worship what I do not see?" Dhiʿlib asked, "How do you see him, then?" ʿAlī answered:[3]

---

1 After ʿUthmān's assassination, at the beginning of ʿAlī's caliphate, in 35/656, in Medina. B 579; Ḥ 10:62; Ibn ʿAbd Rabbih, *ʿIqd*, 4:157.

2 Qurʾan, Anfāl 8:51.

3 Early in ʿAlī's caliphate in Medina, 36/656: ʿAlī ascended the pulpit of the Prophet's mosque wearing the Prophet's mantle and sword, and said to the people, "Ask me before you lose me" (§ 1.187). Dhiʿlib, a renowned and audacious orator, stepped forward with this question, hoping to dumbfound him. ʿAlī answered with these lines, and Dhiʿlib, repentant, fell in a swoon. Ṣadūq, *Amālī*, 423, § 55.

لا تدركه^١ العيون بمشاهدة العِيان ولكن تدركه القلوب بحقائق الإيمان قريب من الأشياء غيرُ ملامِس بعيد منها غير مباينٍ متكلّم بلا رويّة مريد بلا همّة صانع لا بجارحة لطيف لا يوصف باللطفا كبير لا يوصف بالجفا بصير لا يوصف بالحاسّة رحيم لا يوصف بالرقّة تعنو الوجوه لعظمته وتَوجل^٢ القلوب من مخافته.

1.178 ومن كلام له عليه السلام في ذمّ أصحابه

أحمد الله على ما قضى من أمر وقدّر من فعل وعلى ٱبتلائي بكم أيّتها الفرقة التي إذا أمرت لم تطع وإذا دعوت لم تجب إن أهملتم^٣ خُضتم وإن حوربتم خُرتم وإن ٱجتمع الناس على إمام طعنتم وإن أُجبتم إلى مُشاقّة نكصتم. لا أبا لغيركم ما تنتظرون بنصركم والجهاد على حقّكم الموت أو الذلّ لكم فوالله لئن جاء يومي ولَيأتينّي ليفرّقنّ بيني وبينكم وأنا لصحبتكم قالٍ وبكم غير كثير. لله أنتم أما دينٌ يجمعكم ولا حَميّة تَشحَذكم أوليس عجيباً أنّ معاوية يدعو الجفاة الطغام فيتّبعونه على غير معونة ولا عطاء وأنا أدعوكم وأنتم تَريكة الإسلام وبقيّة الناس إلى المعونة أو طائفة من العطاء فتَفرّقون عنّي وتختلفون عليّ. إنّه لا يخرج إليكم من أمري رضى فترضونه ولا سخط فتجتمعون عليه. وإنّ أحبّ ما أنا لاقٍ إليَّ الموت قد دارستُكم الكتاب وفاتحتكم الحِجاج وعرّفتكم ما أنكرتم وسوّغتكم ما مَجَجْتم لو كان الأعمى يلحظ أو النائم يستيقظ. وأقْرِبْ بقوم من الجهل بالله قائدُهم معاوية ومؤدّبهم ٱبن النابغة.

Eyes do not see him through physical observation, but hearts perceive him with true belief. He is near to all things without touching them, yet far from them without being apart. He speaks without the need to reflect, wills without the need to aspire, and crafts without the need for hands. He is sublime but cannot be described as concealed. He is mighty but cannot be described as harsh. He is all-seeing but cannot be described as having eyes. He is merciful but cannot be described as having compassion. All faces bow to his majesty. All hearts tremble in awe.

1.178 From an address by ʿAlī censuring his associates:[1]

I offer praise to God for the affairs he has ordained and the events he has destined, and even for afflicting me with you, the faction who don't obey when I command, or answer when I call! In times of peace, you speak boldly, but when attacked, you bleat like lambs.[2] When people unite behind a leader, you challenge him, and if you answer a call to fight, you soon retreat. May you not be deprived of fathers! What are you waiting for? Why do you sit back, why do you not fight for your rights? This way, you will only find death or dishonor! By God, when my day comes—and it is coming—and when it takes me from you, I will leave you as one who detests your company, and who, when he has you on his side, has nothing. My God, what manner of men are you! Does no religion unite you, no zealous honor sharpen your resolve? Is it not astonishing that when Muʿāwiyah calls to his uncouth riffraff they follow him, even without wages or stipend, and when I call out to you—you, who are the legacy of Islam and sons of the first Muslims,[3] and even though I promise you wages and stipend—you dissent, you oppose my command! Everything I propose, you reject, and everything I reject, you band together to promote. O how I long to meet death! I instructed you in the Book and showed you its proofs, I dispelled your ignorance and taught you to swallow the dribble from your flaccid mouths—but the blind can't see, and the sleeping don't wake! O how close to unbelief is that faction whose caravan is led by Muʿāwiyah, and whose instructor in morals is the Harlot's son![4]

---

1 ʿAlī delivered this oration in Kufa in 38/658, urging his followers to march in support of Muḥammad ibn Abī Bakr, his governor in Egypt, who had been besieged by Muʿāwiyah's commander ʿAmr ibn al-ʿĀṣ. Ṭabarī, *Tārīkh*, 5:107. Thaqafī, *Ghārāt*, 1:291.

2 Ar. *khurtum*. Or, "you show weakness."

3 "Legacy of Islam," lit. "broken ostrich shells (*tarīkah*) of Islam." "Sons of the first Muslims," lit. "remainder of the people."

4 Referring to ʿAmr ibn al-ʿĀṣ, whose mother was infamous in the pre-Islamic period as "The Harlot" (*nābighah*, lit. "the woman who shows herself"). Details in note at §1.81.

1.179 ومن كلام له عليه السلام وقد أرسل رجلًا من أصحابه يَعْلَم له عِلمَ قوم من جند الكوفة هَمّوا باللحاق بالخوارج وكانوا على خوف منه عليه السلام فلمّا عاد إليه الرجل قال له أَأَمِنوا فَقَطنوا أم جَبُنوا فظَعنوا.

فقال الرجل بل ظعنوا يا أمير المؤمنين فقال عليه السلام ﴿بُعْدًا لـ﴾ـهم ﴿كَمَا بَعِدَتْ ثَمُودُ﴾ أما لو أُشرعت الأسِنّة إليهم وصُبّت السيوف على هاماتهم لقد ندموا على ما كان منهم إنّ الشيطان اليوم قد اُستقلّهم وهو غدًا متبرّئ منهم ومخلٍّ عنهم. فحسبهم بخروجهم من الهدى وارتكاسهم في الضلال والعمى وصدّهم عن الحقّ وجِماحهم في التيه.

1.180 ومن خطبة له عليه السلام. روي عن نَوف البِكاليّ قال خطبنا بهذه الخطبة أمير المؤمنين عليّ عليه السلام بالكوفة وهو قائم على جِجارة نصبها له جَعدة بن هُبيرة المخزوميّ وعليه مِدْرَعة من صوف وحمائل سيفه ليفٌ وفي رجليه نعلان من ليف وكأنّ جبينه ثَفِنة بَعِير فقال

1.180.1 الحمد الله الذي إليه مصائر الخلق وعواقب الأمر نحمده على عظيم إحسانه ونيّر برهانه ونوامي فضله وآمتنانه حمدًا يكون لحقّه قضاء ولشكره أداء وإلى ثوابه مقرّبًا ولحسن مزيده موجبًا. ونستعين به آستعانة راج لفضله مؤمّل لنفعه واثق بدفعه معترف له بالطَّول مذعن له بالعمل والقول. ونؤمن بهٍ إيمان من رجاه موقنًا وأناب إليه مؤمنًا وخنع له مذعنًا وأخلص له موحّدًا وعظّمه ممجّدًا ولاذَ به راغبًا مجتهدًا.

1.179 From an address by ʿAlī. ʿAlī had sent one of his men to bring news of a group from his Kufan army who were tempted to join the Kharijites and were fearful of ʿAlī's retribution. When the man came back, ʿAlī asked him:
Did they feel secure enough to stay, or did they become cowards and run?

The man answered: They're gone, Commander of the Faithful. ʿAlī then said:[1]
«Away with» them, «as the Thamūd were done away with!»[2] If spears had been hurled at them and swords had rained on their heads, they would have regretted what they have done! Satan has found them small pickings today, and tomorrow he will discard them and disown them completely. Enough that they have left the home of guidance and lapsed into error and blindness. Enough that they have challenged right and bolted into the waterless wastes.

1.180 From an oration by ʿAlī. Nawf al-Bikālī reported: The Commander of the Faithful addressed us in Kufa, standing on a rock placed for him by Jaʿdah ibn Hubayrah al-Makhzūmī. He was wearing a simple wool garment, his sword-belt was plaited from palm fronds, he wore palm-frond sandals on his feet, and his forehead looked like the calloused knee of a camel stallion. He orated:[3]

1.180.1 Praise God, to whom all creation arrives, and all affairs return! We praise him for his great blessings, his lucent proof, and his abundant favor and bounty. We praise him to repay his due, render him thanks, draw closer to his reward, and deserve more of his beautiful favors. We ask his aid, hoping for his favor, wishing for his profit, trusting in his protection, acknowledging his gift, and submitting to him with deed and word. We believe in him, placing our hopes in him with certainty, turning to him as believers, bowing to him in submission, proclaiming his unity with sincerity, glorifying his greatness, and seeking his protection through our hopes and efforts.

---

1   The group ʿAlī refers to in this text are the Banū Nājiyah, a Christian tribe, who, under their leader al-Khirrīt ibn Rāshid al-Nājī, deserted from ʿAlī's army after the arbitration, in the early months of 38/658. ʿAlī sent his commander Maʿqil ibn Qays al-Riyāḥī with troops to fight them, and Khirrīt and many of his warriors were killed in the ensuing battle. Details in Ḥ 3:120–151 (text at 130). The rest were made captive, and Maṣqalah ibn Hubayrah—ʿAlī's governor in Ardashīr—purchased them from Maʿqil and freed them. Maṣqalah, after paying only a fraction of the price, defected to Muʿāwiyah (see §1.44 and the accompanying note).

2   Qurʾan, Hūd 11:95. Thamūd were the tribe who challenged the Arabian Prophet Ṣāliḥ and were destroyed.

3   Said to be the last oration that ʿAlī delivered standing, before he was struck the death blow, in Kufa, in 40/661. Ḥ 10:112. Possibly a Friday sermon, based on Nawf's mention of "the next Friday" in §1.180.7. "His forehead looked like the calloused knee of a camel stallion" from long prostrations in prayer.

1.180.2 لم يولد سبحانه فيكونَ في العزّ مشارَكًا ولم يلد فيكون موروثًا هالكًا ولم يتقدّمه وقت ولا زمان ولم يَتعاوَرْه زيادة ولا نقصان بل ظهر للعقول بما أرانا من علامات التدبير المتقن والقضاء المبرم. فمن شواهد خلقه خلق السماوات موطَّدات بلا عمد قائمات بلا سند دعاهنّ فأجبن طائعات مذعنات غير متلكّئات ولا مبطئات ولولا إقرارهن له بالربوبيّة وإذعانهنّ بالطَّواعية لما جعلهنّ موضعًا لعرشه ولا مسكًا لملائكته ولا مَصعَدًا للكَلِم الطيّب والعمل الصالح من خلقه. جعل نجومها أعلامًا يَستدلّ بها الحيران في مختلَف بِجاج الأقطار لم يمنع ضوء نورها أدلْهمام سُجُف الليل المظلم ولا أستطاعت جَلابيب سواد الحَنادِس أن تردّ ما شاع في السماوات من تلألؤ نور القمر. فسبحان من لا يخفى عليه سواد غسق داج ولا ليل ساج في بِقاع الأرضين المتطأطئات ولا في يَفاع السُّفْع المتجاورات وما يتجلجل به الرعد في أفق السماء وما تلاشت عنه بروق الغمام وما تَسقط من ورقة تزيلها عن مسقطها عواصف الأنواء وأنهطال السماء. ويعلم مسقط القطرة ومقرّها ومَسحَب الذرّة ومجَرّها وما يكفي البَعوضة من قوتها وما تحمل من أنثى في بطنها.

1.180.3 والحمد لله الكائن قبل أن يكون كرسيٌّ أو عرش أو سماء أو أرض أو جانّ أو إنس. لا يدرك بوهم ولا يقدّر بفهم ولا يشغله سائل ولا ينقصه نائل ولا يبصر¹ بعين ولا يُحَدَّ بِأين ولا يوصف بالأزواج ولا يَخلق بعِلاج ولا يدرك بالحواسّ ولا يقاس بالناس. الذي كلّم موسى تكليمًا وأراه من آياته عظيمًا بلا جوارح ولا أدوات ولا نطق ولا لَهوات بل إن كنت صادقًا أيّها المتكلّف لوصف ربّك فصِفْ جبريل أو ميكائيل وجنود الملائكة المقرّبين في حُجُرات القدس مُرِجَحِنّين مُتولّهة عقولهم أن يَحُدّوا وأحسن

1.180.2 Never begotten, he has no partner in might, never begetting, he has no heir, for he will never die.[1] Time and age have not preceded him, increase and decrease have not affected him. Rather, he appeared before our intellects through the signs he showed us of his perfect planning and his irrevocable decree. Among the testaments of his creation is the creation of the skies, anchored without columns and standing without supports. He called out to them, and they answered, obedient and submissive, neither hesitant nor slow. If not for their acknowledgment of his sovereignty and their submission to him in obedience, he would not have made them the home for his throne, the habitation of his angels, or the place to which the pure word and the pious deed ascends from his creation.[2] He made its stars waymarks through which those lost in the myriad valleys of the earth's provinces are guided. The darkening of the dusky night does not veil their glow, and the swathes of intense black do not block the gleam of the moon from spreading in the skies. Glory to the one from whom nothing is hidden! Not the blackness of spreading obscurity or tranquil night in the earth's low regions and its rust-colored mountain ranges, not the crash of thunder in the sky's far horizons and the momentary brilliance of lightning bolts in the clouds, not the falling of a leaf that is then blown away by stormy winds and pouring skies! He knows where each raindrop falls and pools, where each ant trails and drags its food, what foodstuffs suffice the gnat, and what every female carries in her belly.

1.180.3 Praise God, who existed before stool, or throne, or sky, or earth, or jinn, or human. He cannot be grasped by the imagination or measured by perception. No suppliant distracts him from responding, no gift diminishes his treasures. No eye can see him, no "where" can limit him, he cannot be described as being one of a pair, he need not toil to create, he cannot be grasped with the senses, he cannot be compared to people. He spoke to Moses and showed him his majestic signs without limbs, or implements, or speech, or mouth.[3] If you are sincere—O you who take on the burden of describing your Lord!—then first describe the archangels Gabriel and Michael, or the legions of cherubim in the vaults of the holy heavens, who bend low in humility, whose intellects bewilderment hinders from constraining the best of creators! Only entities with forms and appendages, entities that run their course and perish when

---

1 Reference to Qurʾan, Ikhlāṣ 112:3.
2 Modified quote of Qurʾan, Fāṭir 35:10.
3 Ar. *lahawāt*, lit. "uvulas," translated as "mouths." God's speaking to Moses is a modified quote from Qurʾan, Nisāʾ 4:164.

الخالقين وإنّما يدرك بالصفات ذوو الهيئة والأدوات ومن ينقضي إذا بلغ أمدَ حدّه بالفناء. فلا إله إلّا هو أضاء بنوره كلّ ظلام وأظلم بظلمته كلّ نور.

1.180.4 أوصيكم عباد الله بتقوى الله الذي ألبسكم الرياش وأسبغ عليكم المعاش. ولو أنّ أحدًا يجد إلى البقاء سُلَّمًا أو لدفع الموت سبيلًا لكان ذلك سليمان بن داود عليهما السلام الذي سُخِّر له ملك الجنّ والإنس مع النبوّة وعظيم الزلفة فلمّا اَستوفى طُعْمَته واَستكمل مدّته رمته قِسيّ الفناء بنبال الموت وأصبحت الديار منه خالية والمساكن معطّلة ورثها قوم آخرون وإنّ لكم في القرون السالفة لعبرة. أين العَمالقة وأبناء العمالقة أين الفراعنة وأبناء الفراعنة أين أصحاب مدائن الرَّسّ الذين قتلوا النبيّين وأطفأوا سنن المرسلين وأحيوا سِيَرَ الجبّارين وأين الذين ساروا بالجيوش وهزموا الألوف وعسكروا العساكرَ ومَدَّنوا المدائن.

1.180.5 ومنها

قد لبس للحكمة جُنّتها وأخذها بجميع أدبها من الإقبال عليها والمعرفة بها والتفرّغ لها فهي عند نفسه ضالّتُه التي يطلبها وحاجته التي يسأل عنها فهو مغترب إذا اَغترب الإسلام وضرب بِعَسيب ذَنَبه وأَلْصَقَ الأرض بِجِرانه بقيّة من بقايا حجّته خليفة من خلائف أنبيائه.

1.180.6 ثمّ قال عليه السلام

أيّها الناس إنّي قد بثثت لكم المواعظ التي وعظ بها الأنبياء أممهم وأدّيت إليكم ما أدّت الأوصياء إلى من بعدهم وأدّبتكم بسوطي فلم تستقيموا وحدَوتكم بالزواجر فلم تستوسقوا. لله أنتم أتتوقّعون إمامًا غيري يطأ بكم الطريق ويرشدكم السبيل. ألا إنّه قد أدبر من الدنيا ما كان مقبلًا وأقبل منها ما كان مدبرًا وأزمَعَ التَّرحالَ عبادُ الله الأخيار وباعوا قليلًا من الدنيا لا يبقى بكثير من الآخرة لا يفنى. ما ضرّ إخواننا الذين سفكت دماؤهم بصفّين

___
ش، ن، ي: كذا. م، ونسخة في ش: ﴿سنن﴾.

they have reached their limit, can be grasped through a description of their attributes. Understand that there is no God but he. Every darkness brightens with his light, every light darkens with his darkness.

1.180.4 Servants of God, I counsel you to be conscious of God, who clothed you in finery and gave you a life of plenty. If ever there was one who could have found a ladder to eternity or a path to repel death, it would have been Solomon, son of David, who was given dominion over the kingdom of jinn and humans, along with prophecy and intimacy with God. But when he had received his fill of the world and completed his time, annihilation felled him with the arrow of death. Abodes became empty of him and habitations vacant. They were inherited by others. Truly, you have been given lessons in the passage of generations! Where are the Amalekites and the descendants of the Amalekites? Where are the Pharaohs and the descendants of the Pharaohs? Where are the people of the cities of Rass, who killed their prophets, extinguished the practice of God's emissaries, and revived the ways of tyrants?[1] Where are those who marched at the head of armies, defeating thousands, mobilizing troops, and building great cities?

1.180.5 From the same oration:
He will come bearing the shield of wisdom, having seized it with all its requirements—attention, recognition, and devotion. For him, wisdom is his own lost camel that he seeks, his own missing saddlebags about which he inquires. Whenever Islam is exiled, tail down like a camel and neck flat on the earth, he too hides in exile. He is God's remaining proof, the successor of his prophets.

1.180.6 Then he said:
People! I have given you the counsel with which prophets guided their nations and conveyed to you what their legatees conveyed to the subsequent generation. I have disciplined you with my whip, but you have not stayed upright. I have steered you with admonitions, but your flock has not kept together. O God, what manner of men are you? Are you waiting for another leader to walk you on the path and guide you to the way? Listen to me! That portion of the world which had approached has turned back, and that which had turned back now approaches. God's pious servants have resolved to depart on their journey. They have sold the paltry ephemera of the world for the permanent abundance of the hereafter. Our brothers whose blood was spilt in Ṣiffīn have lost noth-

---

1   The people of Rass are mentioned in Qurʾan, Furqān 25:38, Qāf 50:12.

أَلَّا يكونوا اليوم أحياء يُسيغون الغَصَص ويشربون الرَّنَق قد والله لقوا الله فوقّاهم
أجورهم وأحلّهم دار الأمن بعد خوفهم. أين إخواني الذين ركبوا الطريق ومضوا على
الحقّ أين عمّار وأين اٰبن التَّيِّهان وأين ذو الشهادتين وأين نظراؤهم من إخوانهم الذين
تعاقدوا على المنيّة وأُبرِدَ برؤوسهم إلى الفجرة.

ثمّ ضرب عليه السلام بيده إلى لحيته فأطال البكاء ثمّ قال
أَوِّه على إخواني الذين تلوا القرآن فأحكموه وتدبّروا الفرض فأقاموه أحيوا السنّة وأماتوا
البدعة دُعوا للجهاد فأجابوا ووثقوا بالقائد فاتّبعوا.

1.180.7 ثمّ نادى بأعلى صوته
الجهادَ الجهادَ عباد الله. ألا وإنّي معسكر في يومي هذا فمن أراد الرواح إلى الله فليخرج

قال نوف وعقد للحسين عليه السلام في عشرة آلاف ولقيس بن سعد في عشرة آلاف ولأبي
أيّوب الأنصاريّ في عشرة آلاف ولغيرهم على أعداد أُخَر وهويريد الرجعة إلى صفّين. فا
دارت الجمعة حتّى ضربه الملعون اٰبن ملجم لعنه الله فتراجعت العساكر فكّاً كالأغنام فقدت
راعيها تختطفها الذئاب من كلّ مكان.

1.181 ومن خطبة له عليه السلام

1.181.1 الحمد لله المعروف من غير رؤية والخالق من غير مَنْصَبَة خلق الخلائق بقدرته
واٰستعبد الأرباب بعزّته وساد العظماء بجوده. وهو الذي أسكن الدنيا خلقه وبعث
إلى الجنّ والإنس رسله ليكشفوا لهم عن غطائها وليحذّروهم من ضرّائها وليضربوا لهم
أمثالها وليبصّروهم عيوبها وليهجموا عليهم بمعتبر من تصرّف مَصاحِّها وأسقامها وحلالها
وحرامها وما أعدّ سبحانه للمطيعين منهم والعصاة من جنّة ونار وكرامة وهوان. أحمده إلى

ing by not being alive today. They no longer choke on morsels of food or drink muddy water. By God, they have returned to him, and he has given them their full reward, housing them in a place of safety after their earlier trepidations! O where are my brothers who rode on the high road and trod the track of right? Where is ʿAmmār, where is Ibn al-Tayyihān, where is Dhū al-Shahādatayn?[1] Where are their peers, their brothers, who pledged to fight to the death, and whose decapitated heads the dispatch carried to the depraved?

Upon saying these words, ʿAlī placed his hand on his beard and wept long and hard, then he continued:
Alas for my brothers who recited the Qurʾan and recited it well, who reflected on their duty and undertook it! They revived the Sunnah and killed heresy, they were called to jihad and answered the call, they trusted in their commander and followed him.

1.180.7 Then ʿAlī called out in a raised voice:
Servants of God! Jihad, jihad! Harken to me! I will set up camp today! All who wish to return to God should muster!

Raḍī: Nawf said: In planning the return to Ṣiffīn, ʿAlī appointed Ḥusayn commander over ten thousand troops, Qays ibn Saʿd commander over ten thousand, Abū Ayyūb al-Anṣārī commander over ten thousand, and different commanders over varying numbers of troops. But no sooner had the next Friday come around than the cursed Ibn Muljam struck him his deathblow, and the troops pulled back. We were like sheep who had lost their shepherd, snatched by wolves from every side.

1.181 From an oration by ʿAlī:

1.181.1 Praise be to God, recognized without being seen, and creator without toil. He created all things with his power, subjugated kings with his might, and dominated grandees with his generosity. It was he who lodged his creatures in the world, and he sent messengers to jinn and humans to lift her veils, warn of her harm, explain her ciphers, and highlight her faults, to offer lessons in her cycles of illness and health and her bounds of licit and illicit, and to show them what God has prepared for those who obey or disobey—paradise versus hell-

---

1 The three are the Prophet's venerable Companions, ʿAmmār ibn Yāsir, Ibn al-Tayyihān al-Anṣārī, and Khuzaymah ibn al-Thābit, Dhū al-Shahādatayn, "The-Twice-Martyred," who were killed fighting for ʿAlī at the Battle of Ṣiffīn in 37/657.

نفسه كما اَستحمد إلى خلقه ﴿جَعَلَ اللّٰهُ لِكُلِّ شَيْءٍ قَدْرًا﴾ ولكلّ قدر أجلًا و﴿لِكُلِّ أَجَلٍ كِتَابٌ﴾ اً.

1.181.2 منها في ذكر القرآن

فالقرآن آمر زاجر وصامت ناطق حجّة الله على خلقه أخذ عليه ميثاقهم[1] وأرتهن عليه أنفسهم أتمّ نوره وأكرم به دينه وقبض نبيّه صلّى الله عليه وآله وقد فرغ إلى الخلق من أحكام الهدى به. فعظّموا منه سبحانه ما عظّم من نفسه فإنّه لم يُخْفِ عنكم شيئًا من دينه ولم يترك شيئًا رضيه أو كرهه إلّا وجعل له عَلَمًا باديًا وآية محكمة تزجر عنه أو تدعو إليه فرضاه فيما بقي واحد وسخطه فيما بقي واحد. وأعلموا أنّه لن يرضى عنكم بشيء سخطه على من كان قبلكم ولن يسخط عليكم بشيء رضيه ممّن كان قبلكم وإنّما تسيرون في أثر بيّن وتتكلّمون بِرَجْع قول قد قاله الرجال من قبلكم. قد كفاكم مؤونة دنياكم وحثّكم على الشكر وأقترض من ألسنتكم الذكر.

1.181.3 وأوصاكم بالتقوى وجعلها منتهى رضاه وحاجته من خلقه فأتّقوا الله الذي أنتم بعينه ونَواصيكم بيده وتقلّبكم في قبضته إن أسررتم علمه وإن أعلنتم كتبه قد وكّل بذلك حفظة كرامًا لا يسقطون حقًّا ولا يُثبتون باطلًا وأعلموا أنّه ﴿مَنْ يَتَّقِ اللّٰهَ يَجْعَلْ لَهُ مَخْرَجًا﴾ من الفتن ونورًا من الظُّلَم ويخلّده فيما اَشتهت نفسه وينزله منزل الكرامة عنده في دار اَصطنعها لنفسه ظلّها عرشُه ونورها بهجته وزوّارها ملائكته ورفقاؤها رسله. فبادروا المعاد وسابقوا الآجال فإنّ الناس يوشِك أن ينقطع بهم الأمل ويرهقهم الأجل ويسدّ عنهم باب التوبة فقد أصبحتم في مثل ما سأل إليه الرجعة من كان قبلكم

---

[1] م، هـ: كذا. ش، ن، ي: ﴿عليهم ميثاقه﴾.

fire, honor versus shame. I offer him praise in the full measure he deserves from his creatures. «God has appointed for each thing a measure,» for each measure a timespan, and «for each timespan a prescribed end.»[1]

1.181.2 From the same oration about the Qur'an:
The Qur'an commands and forbids, it is silent and yet it speaks, it is God's proof against his creatures. He required them to offer the Qur'an their oaths and pledge their souls. He perfected its light, honored his religion through it, and recalled his Prophet only after he had fully conveyed the guidance of its rulings. Glorify God, then, in all the glories that he has shown you, for he has not concealed from you any part of his religion. He has left nothing that he likes or dislikes without setting up a shining banner and a clear sign that either forbids a thing or calls toward it. His likes for future generations are the same, and his dislikes for them are also identical, so you should know that he will not be pleased with something you do that displeased him from the generations before you, while he will also not be displeased with you for doing something that pleased him from them. You follow clear footsteps, and your speech echoes the words of men who walked before. In all this, God has provided you with enough provisions for your life in this world—he has urged you to give thanks and claimed tribute from your tongues.

1.181.3 God has counseled you to piety and made it the ultimate way to earn his pleasure and fulfil what he requires of his creatures. Be conscious of God, then, for you are always before his eyes, your forelocks are in his hand, and your fortunes are in his grip. If you hide something, he knows it, and if you disclose something, he writes it down. He has appointed noble guardians over you who never miss something or transcribe something in error.[2] Know that «God shows the God-conscious a way out»[3] from seditions, and he grants them light after darkness and eternal life with everything their hearts desire.[4] He houses the pious with honor near him, in the home he has prepared for himself which is shaded by his throne, whose light is from his splendor, whose visitors are his angels, and whose companions are his messengers. Hasten to return to God, and race against your lifespans! The time is near when your hopes will be cut off, death will overtake you, and the door of repentance will be shut in your face. This morning, you are still in the place to which your deceased ancestors

---

1 Qur'an, Ṭalāq 65:3, Raʿd 13:38.
2 Reference to Qur'an, Infiṭār 82:10–11.
3 Qur'an, Ṭalāq 65:2.
4 Reference to Qur'an, Anbiyāʾ 21:102.

وأنتم بنو سبيل على سفر من دار ليست بداركم قد أوذنتم منها بالارتحال وأمرتم فيها بالزاد. واعلموا أنّه ليس لهذا الجِلْد الرقيق صبر على النار فأرحموا نفوسكم فإنّكم قد جرّبتموها في مصائب الدنيا فرأيتم جزع أحدكم من الشوكة تصيبه والعثرة تُدْميه والرَّمْضاء تحرقه فكيف إذا كان بين طابقين من نار ضجيع حجر وقرين شيطان أعلمتم أنّ مالكًا إذا غضب على النار حطم بعضها بعضًا لغضبه وإذا زجرها توثّبت بين أبوابها جزعًا من زجرته.

أيّها اليَفَن الكبير الذي قد لَهَزَه القَتير كيف أنت إذا التحمت أطواق النار بعظام الأعناق ونَشِبت الجوامع حتّى أكلت لحوم السواعد. فاللهَ اللهَ معشر العباد وأنتم سالمون في الصحّة قبل السقم وفي الفسحة قبل الضيق فاسعوا في فكاك رقابكم من قبل أن تغلق رهائنها أَسهِروا عيونكم وأضمروا بطونكم واستعملوا أقدامكم وأنفقوا أموالكم وخذوا من أجسادكم تجودوا بها على أنفسكم ولا تبخلوا بها عنها. فقد قال الله سبحانه ﴿إِنْ تَنصُرُوا اللّهَ يَنصُرْكُمْ وَيُثَبِّتْ أَقْدَامَكُمْ﴾ وقال ﴿مَن ذَا الذي يُقْرِضُ اللّهَ قَرْضًا حَسَنًا فيُضَاعِفَهُ لهُ ولَهُ أَجْرٌ كَرِيمٌ﴾. فلم يستنصركم من ذلّ ولم يستقرضكم من قلّ استنصركم وله ﴿جُنُودُ السَّمَاوَاتِ وَالْأَرْضِ﴾ ﴿وَهُوَ الْعَزِيزُ الْحَكِيمُ﴾ واستقرضكم وله ﴿خَزَائِنُ السَّمَاوَاتِ وَالْأَرْضِ﴾ و﴿هُوَ الْغَنِيُّ الْحَمِيدُ﴾. وإنّما أراد أن ﴿يَبْلُوَكُمْ أَيُّكُمْ أَحْسَنُ عَمَلًا﴾. فبادروا بأعمالكم تكونوا مع جيران الله في داره رَافَقَ بهم رسله وأزَارَهم ملائكته وأكرم أسماعهم أن تسمع حسيس نار أبدًا وصان أجسادهم أن تلقى لُغوبًا ونصَبًا ﴿ذَلِكَ فَضْلُ اللّهِ يُؤْتِيهِ مَن يَشَاءُ واللّهُ ذُو الْفَضْلِ الْعَظِيمِ﴾.

pleaded to be allowed to return.[1] You are travelers soon to leave this abode, which is not your home—you have heard the announcement to depart and the command to gather your provisions. Know that your delicate skin cannot bear the torture of the Fire and take pity on your souls, for you have seen how they crumbled when faced with the hurts of this world. You know how each of you dreads the prick of a thorn, a fall that draws blood, the heat of burning sands. How, then, will you endure being crushed between two sheets of fire with a stone for bedmate and a devil for companion![2] Don't you know that when the angel Mālik vents his anger upon the Fire, one part devours another in terror, and when he shouts at it, its flames shoot in panic from locked door to locked door![3]

O decrepit, timeworn man whose hair is flecked with white! What will you do when shackles of fire choke you and fuse with the bones of your neck, when fetters eat into the flesh of your arms? O assembly of God's servants, fear God, fear God, while you are still sound, while you have health before illness strikes, while you have room before your straits constrict! Strive to free your necks before their release from bondage is forfeit! Keep the night-vigil, starve your bellies, make use of your feet, spend your wealth, put your bodies to work, and exert them for the benefit of your souls. Do not be stingy in this, for God has promised, «If you help God, he will help you and give you a firm foothold.»[4] God has also invited you, «Who will offer God a beautiful loan of deeds, that he may multiply it for him, and give him a generous recompense?»[5] God does not ask you for help out of weakness, nor for a loan because he is poor. He asks you for help while possessing «the legions of the skies and the earth», «and he is mighty and wise».[6] He asks you for a loan while possessing «the treasures of the skies and the earth», and «he is rich and praised».[7] In truth, he wishes to «put you to the test, to see who among you performs the best of deeds».[8] Hasten to perform good deeds, then, and you shall be among God's neighbors in his abode, with his messengers for companions, his angels for visitors, your ears protected from the Fire's frightening roar, and your bodies safe from fatigue or weakness.[9] «That is God's bounty, which he bestows on whom he wills—great is God's bounty!»[10]

---

1   Reference to Qur'an, Mu'minūn 23:99–100.

2   Reference to Qur'an, Baqarah 2:24, Qāf 50:23.

3   Mālik is the angel in charge of hell.

4   Qur'an, Muḥammad 47:7.

5   Qur'an, Ḥadīd 57:11. I have added the words "of deeds" for clarity.

6   Qur'an, Fatḥ 48:7, Ibrāhīm 14:4.

7   Qur'an, Munāfiqūn 63:7, Ḥajj 22:64.

8   Qur'an, Hūd 11:7.

9   Reference to Qur'an, Nisā' 4:69, Fāṭir 35:35.

10   Qur'an, Jum'ah 62:4; Ḥadīd 57:21.

أقول ما تسمعون والله المستعان على نفسي وأنفسكم وهو حسبنا ونعم الوكيل.

1.182 ومن كلام له عليه السلام قاله للبرْج بن مُسْهِر الطائيّ وقد قال بحيث يسمعه ‹لا حكم إلّا لله› وكان من الخوارج

أُسْكُتْ قبّحك الله يا أَثْرَم فوالله لقد ظهر الحقّ فكنتَ فيه ضئيلًا شخصُك خفيًّا صوتُك حتّى إذا نَعَرَ الباطل نجمت نجوم قرن الماعز.

1.183 ومن خطبة له عليه السلام[1]

1.183.1 الحمد الله الذي لا تدركه الشواهد ولا تحويه المشاهد ولا تراه النواظر ولا تحجبه السواتر الدالّ على قدمه بحدوث خلقه وبحدوث خلقه على وجوده وبأشباههم على أن لا شِبْه له الذي صدق في ميعاده وأرتفع عن ظلم عباده وقام بالقسط في خلقه وعدل عليهم في حكمه مستشهد بحدوث الأشياء على أزليّته وبما وسمها به من العجز على قدرته وبما أضطرّها إليه من الفناء على دوامه واحد لا بعدد ودائم لا بأمد وقائم لا بعمد تتلقّاه الأذهان لا بمشاعِرة وتشهد له المَرائي لا بمحاضرة لم تحط به الأوهام بل تجلّى لها بها[2] وبها أمتنع منها وإليها حاكمها ليس بذي كبر أمتدّت به النهايات فكبّرته تجسيمًا ولا بذي عظم تناهت به الغايات فعظّمته تجسيدًا بل كبر شأنًا وعظم سلطانًا.

وأشهد أنّ محمّدًا عبده[3] الصفيّ وأمينه الرضيّ[4] صلّى الله عليه وآله أرسله بوجوب الحجج وظهور الفُلْج وإيضاح المنهج فبلّغ الرسالة صادعًا بها وحمل على المحجّة دالًّا عليها وأقام أعلام الاهتداء ومنار الضياء وجعل أمراس الإسلام متينة وعُرى الإيمان وثيقة.

I say what you hear and ask God's aid against my passions and yours. He suffices us and he is the best trustee.[1]

1.182 From an address by ʿAlī to Burj ibn Mus'hir al-Ṭāʾī, one of the Kharijites, when he called out in ʿAlī's hearing, ⟨No rule save God's!⟩:[2]
Silence! May God disfigure you, you toothless driveller! By God, when right showed itself, your arms offered feeble support and your voice could not be heard, but when wrong snorted, you emerged like the horns of a goat!

1.183 From an oration by ʿAlī:[3]

1.183.1 Praise God! Senses do not grasp him, places do not hold him, eyes do not see him, and veils do not hide him. He proves his antiquity by the newness of his creatures. By the newness of his creatures, he proves his existence, and by their similarities, he proves that he has no peer. He is true to his promise, rises above any wrong to his servants, upholds equity among his creatures, and is just when he commands. The newness of all things testifies to his eternity, the incapacity he has marked them with testifies to his power, and the annihilation he has subjugated them to testifies to his permanence. He is one without number, permanent without end, standing without need of support. The mind receives him without touching him, all that we see testifies to his existence without entering his presence. The imagination cannot encompass him: rather, he shows his light to it and in it, while he renders himself inaccessible to it and by it, and he also summons it for judgment to it. He possesses greatness, but not in the sense of flexible perimeters that make him massive in body. He possesses might, but not in the sense of expanding limits that make him grand in form. Rather, he is great in majesty and mighty in power.

I testify that Muḥammad is God's chosen servant and his faithful trustee, whom he sent with compelling arguments, clear direction, and triumphant victory. He conveyed God's message and announced it to all, showed people the straight road and led them to it, raised banners of guidance and beacons of light, fastened Islam's ropes and strengthened faith's bonds.

---

1 Modified quote from Qurʾan, Āl ʿImrān 3:173.
2 Presumably in Kufa, after the arbitration in 37/658. See similar materials in §1.140 and §3.182.
3 Hārūnī (*Taysīr*, 273) places §1.183.1 in Kufa, sometime during his caliphate 35–40/656–661, at the beginning of an oration he calls The Radiant Oration (*Gharrāʾ*; Raḍī calls §1.80 in the present volume by that name).

1.183.2   منها في صفة عجيب خلق أصناف من الحيوان

ولو فكّروا في عظيم القدرة وجسيم النعمة لرجعوا إلى الطريق وخافوا عذاب الحريق ولكنّ القلوب عليلة والأبصار مدخولة. ألا ينظرون إلى صغير ما خلق كيف أحكم خلقه وأتقن تركيبه وفلق له السمع والبصر وسوّى له العَظْم والبَشَر. انظروا إلى النملة في صغر جُثّتها ولطافة هيئتها لا تكاد تنال بلحظ النظر١ ولا بمستدرك الفكر كيف دبّت على أرضها وصُبّت٢ على رزقها تنقل الحبّة إلى جُحرها وتعُدّها في مستقرّها تجمع في حرّها لبردها وفي ورودها لصَدَرها مكفول برزقها مرزوقة بوفْقها٣ لا يغفلها المنّان ولا يحرمها الديّان ولو في الصَّفا اليابس والحجر الجامس ولو فكّرت في مجاري أكلها في علوّها وسفلها وما في الجوف من شَراسيف بطنها وما في الرأس من عينها وأذنها لقضيت من خلقها عجبًا ولقيت من وصفها تعبًا فتعالى الذي أقامها على قوائمها وبناها على دعائمها لم يشركه في فطرتها فاطر ولم يعنه على خلقها قادر. ولو ضربت في مذاهب فكرك لتبلغ غاياته٤ ما دلّتك الدلالة إلّا أنّ فاطر النملة هو فاطر النحلة٥ لدقيق تفصيل كلّ شيء وغامض اختلاف كلّ حيّ وما الجليل واللطيف والثقيل والخفيف والقويّ والضعيف في خلقه إلّا سواء.

1.183.3   كذلك السماء والهواء والرياح والماء فأنظر إلى الشمس والقمر والنبات والشجر والماء والحجر واختلاف هذا الليل والنهار وتفجّر هذه البحار وكثرة هذه الجبال وطول هذه القلال وتفرّق هذه اللغات والألسن المختلفات. فالويل لمن بحد المقدّر وأنكر المدبّر زعموا أنّهم كالنبات ما لهم زارع ولا لاختلاف صورهم صانع ولم يلجأوا إلى حجّة فيما ادّعوا ولا تحقيق لما أوْعَوْا وهل يكون بناء من غير بانٍ أو جناية من غير جانٍ.

---

١ ش، ن، ي، ه: كذا. م: كذا، ونسخة في ه: ﴿البصر﴾.   ٢ م، ي، ونسخة في ه مع علامة الصحّة: كذا. ش، ن، وأصل ه: ﴿ضنّت﴾.   ٣ ش، ن، م، ه: كذا. ي: ﴿بوقتها﴾.   ٤ ش، م، ي، ومصحّحة في ه: كذا. ن، وأصل ه، ونسخة في ش: ﴿غاياتك﴾.   ٥ ش، ن، ه: كذا. م، ونسخة مع لفظة معًا في ه: ﴿النخلة﴾.

1.183.2 From the same oration, describing the wondrous creation of many species of animals:

Had they contemplated the greatness of his power and the vastness of his bounty, they would have returned to the Path, and feared the punishment of the Fire. But hearts are sickly and eyes diseased. Do they not observe the smallest of things he has created, how he has perfected its creation, refined its form, provided orifices for hearing and sight, and fashioned bones and skin? Observe the ant in its tiny frame and delicate shape! It can hardly be spotted by the eye or grasped by the mind, yet see how it crawls on the earth and guards its food, transporting a single seed to its nest and stashing it in its lair! It gathers in the hot season for the cold, in the time of abundance for the time of dearth, its sustenance is guaranteed, and its provisions are made to suit. The Great Benefactor does not ignore it and the Great Rewarder does not deprive it, even when it lives on dry rock and barren stone. And if you were to contemplate the tracts through which its food passes inside its parts, high and low, the membranes of its stomach within its abdomen, and all that its head contains, eyes, ears, and everything else, you would marvel at its creation and be hard pressed to describe it. Exalted be the one who righted it upon its legs and set it on its limbs! No partner assisted him to make it, no power helped him in its creation! And if you were to follow the path of your thought to its logical end, you would infer that the maker of the ant is also the maker of the honeybee.[1] Every creature has subtle particulars, and every living being has imperceptible variances, but with regard to their being created, the large, the slight, the heavy, the light, the strong, the weak, all are the same—all are God's creatures.

1.183.3 The case of sky, air, wind, and water is similar. Observe the sun, moon, plants, trees, water, and rocks. Observe the alternation of night and day, the roiling of the seas, the majesty of the mountains, the loftiness of the massifs, the diversity of languages, and the variety of tongues. Woe to those who deny the Great Ordainer, who reject the Great Planner! They claim they are like plants without a cultivator, that there is no artisan who crafted their different forms, but they have no proof for their claim and no justification for their belief. Can there ever be a building without a builder, an act without an actor?[2]

---

1 Ar. *naḥlah*; Or, per MSS M "the date-palm (*nakhlah*)."

2 Lit. "Can there be a crime without a perpetrator?"; my translation is in the generic sense of action, following Ḥ 13:65.

1.183.4 وإن شئت قلت في الجرادة إذ خلق لها عينين حَمْراوين وأسرج لها حَدَقتين قَمْراوَين وجعل لها السمع الخفيّ وفتح لها الفم السويّ وجعل لها الحسّ القويّ ونابين بهما تقرض ومنجلَين بهما تقبض يرهبها الزُّرّاع في زرعهم ولا يستطيعون ذَبَها ولو أجلبوا بجمعهم حتّى ترد الحرث في نزواتها وتقضي منه شهواتها وخلقها كلّه لا يكون إصبعًا مستدقّة فتبارك الذي يسجد له ﴿مَن في السَّمَاوَاتِ وَالْأَرْضِ طَوعًا وَكَرْهًا﴾ ويعفِر له خدًّا ووجهًا ويلقي بالطاعة إليه سلمًا وضعفًا ويعطي القياد رهبة وخوفًا.

فالطير مسخّرة لأمره أحصى عدد الريش منها والنفَس وأرسى قوائمها على الندى واليَبَس قدّر أقواتها وأحصى أجناسها فهذا غُراب وهذا عُقاب وهذا حَمام وهذا نَعام. دعا كلّ طائر باسمه وكفل له برزقه وأنشأ السحاب الثقال فأهطل دِيَمها وعدّد قِسَمها فبَلَّ الأرض بعد جفوفها وأخرج نبتها بعد جُدوبها.

1.184 ومن خطبة له عليه السلام في التوحيد وتجمع هذه الخطبة من أصول العلوم ما لا تجمعه خطبة

1.184.1 ما وحّده مَن كَيَّفَه ولا حقيقته أصاب من مَثَّلَه ولا إيّاه عنى من شبّهه ولا صَمَده من أشار إليه وتوهّمه كلّ معروف بنفسه مصنوع وكلّ قائم في سواه معلول فاعل لا باضطراب آلة مقدّر لا بجَوَل فكرة غنيّ لا باستفادة لا تصحبه الأوقات ولا تَرفده الأدوات سبق الأوقات كونه والعدم وجوده والابتداء أزله بتشعيره المشاعر عُرف ألّا مشعر له وبمُضادّته بين الأمور عرف ألّا ضدّ له وبمقارنته بين الأشياء عرف ألّا قرين له ضادَّ النور بالظلمة والوضوح بالبُهمة والجمود بالبَلَل والحَرور بالصَّرَد. مؤلّف بين متعادياتها مقارن بين متبايناتها مقرّب بين متباعداتها مفرّق بين متدانياتها لا يُشمل

1.183.4 If you wish, I can also speak of the locust. God gave it two red eyes and within them he suspended two pupils, two moon-like orbs. He fashioned for it minute ears and an opening for a mouth, gave it keen senses, two fang-like teeth with which to cut, and two scythe-like forelegs with which to grip. Farmers dread their ravages—even if they join forces, they can't drive the locusts away until they've inflicted their violence on the crops and satisfied their hunger, yet all the while each one measures no more than a tiny finger! Blessed is he before whom «all who are in the skies and the earth, obedient or unwilling,»[1] fall prostrate! They press their cheeks and faces to the earth, throw down their weapons in a vulnerable plea for amnesty, and offer their reins to him in awe and fear!

The birds are also subject to his command. He reckons the number of their feathers and their breaths, keeps their feet firm on wet land and dry, ordains their food, and knows their innumerable species. This one is a crow, that an eagle, this one a pigeon, that an ostrich. He calls each bird by its name, and he guarantees its sustenance. Quickening heavy clouds,[2] drawing forth pouring rain, and enumerating appointed bounties, he drenches the land after it was parched and prompts it to germinate after it was barren.

1.184 From an oration by ʿAlī on God's oneness that brings together principles of knowledge like no other:

1.184.1 Those who assign him a form have not acknowledged his oneness, those who liken him have not hit upon his reality, those who compare him have not denoted him, those who point to him or imagine him have not directed themselves to him. Each entity that is known in its essence is constructed, and each entity that stands with another's support is a result. God acts without implements, he ordains without thought, he is wealthy without acquisition. Time does not accompany him, and appendages do not attend him. His being precedes time, his existence precedes non-existence, and his eternity precedes the beginning. By his forming of the senses, we know that he has no senses, by his creation of opposites, we know that he has no rival, by his design of similarities, we know that he has no peer. He made light the opposite of darkness, clarity the opposite of gloom, dry the opposite of wet, and heat the opposite of cold. He joined what was disparate, gathered what was distinct, brought close the things that were far, and separated those that were near. He cannot be confined

---

1 Qurʾan, Raʿd 13:15.
2 Modified quote from Qurʾan, Raʿd 13:12.

بحدّ ولا يحسب بعَدّ وإنّما تَحُدّ الأدوات أنفسها وتشير الآلات إلى نظائرها. منعتها منذ القِدْمة وحمتها قَدُ الأزليّة وجنّبتها لولا التكملة. بها تجلّى صانعها للعقول وبها امتنع عن نظر العيون. لا يجري عليه السكون والحركة وكيف يجري عليه ما هو أجراه ويعود فيه ما هو أبداه ويحدث فيه ما هو أحدثه إذًا لتفاوتت ذاته ولتجزّأ كنهه ولامتنع من الأزل معناه ولكان له وراءٌ إذ وجد له أمامٌ ولالتمس التمام إذ لزمه النقصان وإذا لقامت آية المصنوع فيه ولتحوّل دليلًا بعد أن كان مدلولًا عليه وخرج بسلطان الامتناع من أن يؤثّر فيه ما يؤثّر في غيره.

1.184.2   الذي لا يحول ولا يزول ولا يجوز عليه الأفول لم يلد فيكون مولودًا ولم يولد فيصير محدودًا جلّ عن اتّخاذ الأبناء وطهر عن ملامسة النساء لا تناله الأوهام فتقدّره ولا تتوهّمه الفطن فتصوّره ولا تدركه الحواسّ فتُحسّه ولا تلمسه الأيدي فتمسّه لا يتغيّر بحال ولا يتبدّل في الأحوال ولا تبليه الليالي والأيّام ولا يغيّره الضياء والظلام ولا يوصف بشيء من الأجزاء ولا بالجوارح والأعضاء ولا بعرض من الأعراض ولا بالغيريّة والأبعاض. ولا يقال له حدّ ولا نهاية ولا انقطاع ولا غاية ولا أنّ الأشياء تحويه فتُقلّه أو تُهويه أو أنّ شيئًا يحمله فيميله أويعدله. ليس في الأشياء بوالِج ولا عنها بخارج يخبر لا بلسان ولهوات ويسمع لا بخروق وأدوات يقول ولا يلفظ ويحفظ ولا يتحفّظ ويريد ولا يضمر يحبّ ويرضى من غير رقّة ويبغض ويغضب من غير مشقّة. يقول لما أراد كونه ﴿كُنْ فَيَكُونُ﴾ لا بصوت يقرع ولا نداء يسمع وإنّما كلامه سبحانه فعل

ام، ي، ومصحَّحة في هـ، ونسخة في ش: كذا. ن، وأصل ش، هـ: ﴿فيكون﴾.

by a limit or reckoned by counting, for instruments can only limit other instruments, and implements can only indicate similar things. "Since" prevents them from antiquity, "just" precludes them from eternity, and "if not for" drives them from perfection.[1] Through these things, the artisan who crafted them displays his light to intellects, yet because of these things, it is impossible for eyes to see him. Stillness and motion do not apply to him. How can something he set forth apply to him? How can something he originated become part of him? How can something he made happen, happen to him? If that were the case, his being would have contrasting modes, his essence would be divided into parts, and it would be impossible for his reality to be eternal. If he had a front, he would also have a back, if he were incomplete, he would need completing, and if that were the case, the mark of craftsmanship would appear in him. He would become a sign instead of something to which all signs point. But—through the utter impossibility of that being the case—nothing that affects his creatures affects God.

1.184.2 He is the one who never changes, never ceases, never sets. He has not begotten, else he himself would be like one born, he was not begotten, else he would be constrained.[2] His glory precludes begetting sons, his purity precludes intimacy with women. The imagination cannot attain or measure him, the intellect cannot imagine or picture him, our senses cannot grasp or sense him, our hands cannot touch or feel him. No situation causes him to change, no conditions cause him to alter. The passage of night and day do not cause him to decay, light and dark do not cause him to transform. He cannot be described as possessing parts, or limbs and organs, or segments, or accidental qualities that can change, or the trait of being other than something, or comprised of sections. It cannot be said of him that he has limit, end, termination, conclusion, or that things control him so as to raise or lower him, or that things carry him so as to balance him or cause him to incline. He neither enters into things nor exits them. He informs without tongue or mouth. He hears without ears or any other organ. He speaks without uttering, remembers without memorizing, and wills without pondering. He loves and is pleased without sentiment, he hates and is angry without toil. For anything whose being he wills, he says «"Be!"— and it is,»[3] without emitting a sound that strikes the ear, or a call that can be

---

1 Ar. *mundhu*, *qad*, and *law-lā*. These words distinguish creatures from the creator, to whom none of these terms apply, for they imply coming into existence, being newly created, and imperfection.

2 Reference to Qurʾan, Ikhlāṣ 112:3.

3 Qurʾan, Baqarah 2:117.

منه أنشأه ومثّله لم يكن من قبل ذلك كائنًا ولو كان قديمًا لكان إلهًا ثانيًا. لا يقال كان بعد أن لم يكن فتُجرى عليه الصفات المحدثات ولا يكون بينها وبينه فصل ولا له عليها فضل فيستوي الصانع والمصنوع ويتكافأ المبتدع والبديع.

1.184.3 خلق الخلائق على غير مثال خلا من غيره ولم يستعن على خلقها بأحد من خلقه وأنشأ الأرض فأمسكها من غير اشتغال وأرساها على غير قرار وأقامها بغير قوائم ورفعها بغير دعائم وحصّنها من الأَوَد والاعوجاج ومنعها من التهافت والانفراج. أرسى أوتادها وضرب أسدادها واستفاض عيونها وخَدَّ أوديتها فلم يَهُن ما بناه ولا ضعف ما قوّاه هو الظاهر عليها بسلطانه وعظمته وهو الباطن لها بعلمه ومعرفته والعالي على كلّ شيء منها بجلاله وعزّته لا يعجزه شيء منها طلبه ولا يمتنع عليه فيغلبه ولا يفوته السريع منها فيسبقه ولا يحتاج إلى ذي مال فيرزقه. خضعت الأشياء له وذلّت مستكينة لعظمته لا تستطيع الهرب من سلطانه إلى غيره فتمتنع من نفعه وضرّه. ولا كفو له فيكافيه ولا نظير له فيساويه.

1.184.4 هو المفني لها بعد وجودها حتّى يصير موجودها كمفقودها وليس فناء الدنيا بعد ابتداعها بأعجب من إنشائها واختراعها وكيف ولو اجتمع جميع حَيَوانها من طيرها وبهائمها وما كان من مُراحها وسائمها وأصناف أسناخها وأجناسها ومتبلّدة أممها وأكياسها على إحداث بَعوضة ما قدرت على إحداثها ولا عرفت كيف السبيل إلى إيجادها ولتحيّرت عقولها في علم ذلك وتاهت وعجزت قواها وتناهت ورجعت خاسية حسيرة عارفة بأنّها مقهورة مقرّة بالعجز عن إنشائها مذعنة بالضعف عن إفنائها وأنّه يعود سبحانه بعد فناء الدنيا وحده لا شيء معه كما كان قبل ابتدائها كذلك يكون بعد فنائها بلا وقت ولا مكان ولا حين ولا زمان عُدمت عند ذلك الآجال والأوقات

heard. Rather, his speaking of words is itself an act that he created and formed. His words did not exist before, for if they had been present from antiquity, they would have constituted a second god. It cannot be said of him that he came into being after non-existence, or else the attributes of newly created beings would apply to him, there would be no difference then between him and them, nor would he possess any distinction over them. The craftsman and his craft would become the same, the initiator and the initiated would become equal.

1.184.3 He created his creation without using an earlier model, without seeking help from any of his creatures. Forming the earth, he held it firm without labor, anchored it without a seabed, erected it without supports, raised it without pillars, ensured it was safe from bending and buckling, and secured it from disintegration and rupture. He then set down its stakes, established its barriers, released its wellsprings, and furrowed its valleys. What he built never becomes unstable, what he strengthened never becomes weak. He is powerful over it through his authority and glory, he is concealed within it through his knowledge and recognition, he is lofty above all things through his magnificence and might. Nothing that he seeks eludes him, nothing can stand up against him or overpower him, no creature can outrun or outstrip him, he needs no wealthy benefactor to sustain him. All things bow to him and efface themselves before his majesty. No one can flee his power or be free of his benefit or harm. He has no equal to match him, no peer to rival him.

1.184.4 He will annihilate the world after its existence, until everything that existed in it will be lost. But the annihilation of the world after its creation is no more marvelous than its origination and formation. How could it not be so? For if all the world's living beings came together—its birds and its beasts, all its cattle in stables and pastures, all its many species in terms of their origins and types, the dullards among its nations and the clever—if they all came together to try to create a gnat, they could not, they would never find a way to bring it into existence. Their minds would be dazed by the attempt to know how, their faculties would be perplexed and incapacitated and would retreat, beaten and weary, recognizing defeat, conceding their incapacity to bring it into existence, and acknowledging that they are too weak even to cause its destruction. God will once again be alone after the annihilation of this world— nothing else will exist with him. As he was before its beginning, so will he be after its end, beyond season, place, moment, or time. Lifespans and seasons will become non-existent, years and hours will cease. Nothing will remain save the

وزالت السنون والساعات فلا شيء إلّا الواحد القهّار الذي إليه مصير جميع الأمور بلا قدرة منها كان ٱبتداء خلقها وبغير ٱمتناع منها كان فناؤها ولو قدرت على الامتناع لدام بقاؤها.

1.184.5   لم يتكاءَدْه صنع شيء منها إذ صنعه ولم يؤُدْه منها خلق ما برأه وخلقه ولم يكوّنها لتشديد سلطان ولا خوف من زوال ونقصان ولا للاستعانة بها على نِدّ مكاثر ولا للاحتراز بها من ضدّ مثاور ولا للازدياد بها في ملكه ولا لمكاثرة شريك في شركه ولا لوحشة كانت منه فأراد أن يستأنس إليها. ثمّ هو يفنيها بعد تكوينها لا لسأم دخل عليه في تصريفها وتدبيرها ولا لراحة واصلة إليه ولا لثقل شيء منها عليه لا يُمِلّه طول بقائها فيدعوَه إلى سرعة إفنائها لكنّه سبحانه دبّرها بلطفه وأمسكها بأمره وأتقنها بقدرته ثمّ يعيدها بعد الفناء من غير حاجة منه إليها ولا ٱستعانة بشيء منها عليه ولا لٱنصراف من حال وحشة إلى حال ٱستيناس ولا من حال جهل وعمى إلى علم وٱلتماس ولا من فقر وحاجة إلى غنى وكثرة ولا من ذلّ وضعة إلى عزّ وقدرة.

1.185   ومن خطبة له عليه السلام في الملاحم
ألا بأبي وأمّي هم من عدّة أسماؤهم في السماء معروفة وفي الأرض مجهولة. ألا فتوقّعوا ما يكون من إدبار أموركم وٱنقطاع وُصَلكم وٱستعمال صغاركم ذاك حيث تكون ضربة السيف على المؤمن أهون من الدرهم من حِلّه ذاك حيث يكون المعطى أعظم أجرًا من المعطي ذاك حيث تَسكرون من غير شراب بل من النَّعمة والنعيم وتُحلفون من غير ٱضطرار وتكذبون من غير إحراج ذاك إذا عضّكم البلاء كما يَعَضّ القَتَبُ غاربَ البعيرِ. ما أطول هذا العناء وأبعد هذا الرجاء. أيّها الناس ألقوا هذه الأزِمّة التي تَحمل ظهورها الأثقالَ من أيديكم ولا تصدّعوا على سلطانكم فتذمّوا غِبَّ فَعالكم ولا تقتحموا ما

one, the vanquisher, to whom all affairs return. The beginning of their creation took place without their volition, their annihilation too will come without them having the power to arrest its march. If they had been able to, they would have existed forever.

1.184.5 Crafting any part of what he crafted caused him no hardship. Creating what he created, what he formed, caused him no fatigue. He did not bring his creatures into being in order to consolidate his authority, or from fear of cessation or loss, or to bolster his worth against a wealthier peer, or to protect himself from an avenging enemy, or to expand his kingdom, or to boast of greater riches to a partner, or out of loneliness such that he wanted the comfort of their company. Now, after bringing the world into being, he will annihilate it, but not because he is wearied by planning and running it, or to seek rest, or because any of it weighs him down. Its long existence does not tire him and require him to annihilate it swiftly. He has planned it through his grace, upheld it with his command, and perfected it with his power. After annihilating it, he will bring it back again. This, too, without having a need for it, without seeking help from any creature to create it, or to emerge from a state of loneliness to a state of comfort, or from a state of ignorance and blindness to knowledge and attainment, or from poverty and destitution to wealth and abundance, or from shame and abjectness to might and power.

1.185 From an oration by ʿAlī prophesying a calamitous time:[1]
I would offer my father and mother as ransom for that host whose names are recognized in the heavens but remain unknown on earth. Hark, people, prepare for what is coming! Your affairs will soon turn topsy turvy, your ties will soon be severed. Only the rash among you will find employment. On that day, it will be easier for a believer to suffer the blow of a sword than to earn a single dirham through licit means. On that day, the receiver will be rewarded more than the giver.[2] On that day, you will become intoxicated, not from drink, but with luxury and affluence, you will swear gratuitous oaths and lie without scruple. On that day, calamity will bite like a packsaddle biting into a camel's withers. O how lengthy the hardship, how distant the hope! People! Stop driving beasts you have loaded with sin! Stop challenging your authorities, or you will

---

1 Excerpt from an oration ʿAlī delivered in Kufa after the Battle of Nahrawān in 38/658. Ḥ 6:134–135, after Madāʾinī (the preceding lines are also recorded).

2 Because those who give at this time will do so from illicit earnings, while those who receive will do so legitimately. Ḥ 13:96–97; B 712; F 350; R 2:440.

آستقبلتم من فَورِ نار الفتنة وأميطوا عن سَنَنِها وخلّوا قصد السبيل لها. فقد لعمري يهلك في لهبها المؤمن ويسلم فيها غير المسلم.

1.186   ومن خطبة له عليه السلام

أوصيكم أيّها الناس بتقوى الله وكثرة حمده على آلائه إليكم ونعمائه عليكم وبلائه لديكم فكم خصّكم بنعمة وتدارككم برحمة أعورتم له فستركم وتعرّضتم لأخذه فأمهلكم وأوصيكم بذكر الموت وإقلال الغفلة عنه وكيف غفلتكم عمّا ليس يُغفلكم وطمعكم فيمن ليس يمهلكم. فكفى واعظًا بموتى عاينتموهم حُملوا إلى قبورهم غير راكبين وأنزلوا فيها غير نازلين كأنّهم لم يكونوا للدنيا عُمّارًا وكأنّ الآخرة لم تزل لهم دارًا أوحشوا ما كانوا يوطِنون وأوطنوا ما كانوا يوحِشون وآشتغلوا بما فارقوا وأضاعوا ما إليه آنتقلوا لا عن قبيح يستطيعون آنتقالًا ولا في حسن يستطيعون آزديادًا أنسوا بالدنيا فغرّتهم ووثقوا بها فصرعتهم. فسابقوا رحمكم الله إلى منازلكم التي أمرتم أن تعمروها والتي رُغبتم فيها ودعيتم إليها وآستتمّوا نعم الله عليكم بالصبر على طاعته والمجانبة لمعصيته فإنّ غدًا من اليوم قريب ما أسرع الساعاتِ في اليوم وأسرع الأيّامَ في الشهر وأسرع الشهورَ في السنة وأسرع السنين في العمر.

1.187   ومن خطبة له عليه السلام

denounce the results of your action! Stop rushing into sedition's raging fire, stay away from its path, leave its road empty! By my life, I fear believers will perish in its flames, while non-Muslims will stay safe!

1.186 From an oration by ʿAlī:[1]
People! I counsel you to be conscious of God and to give abundant thanks for his bounties to you, his blessings on you, and his favors for you. How often has he singled you out for a blessing and rescued you with an act of mercy! You revealed your shame, and he concealed it, you put yourself in the way of his punishment, and he granted you reprieve. I counsel you to remember death and lessen your neglect! How can you forget something which will not forget you? How can you place your hopes in something which will not grant you reprieve? The dead whom you have seen with your own eyes are sufficient counselors. They are carried to their graves, not riding there, then placed inside without choosing to dismount, as though they had never lived merrily in the world, as though the hereafter had always been their home. Now, they recoil from their earlier abode, they make their home in that place from which they had earlier recoiled. Long did they occupy themselves with concerns they now have to leave behind! Long did they ignore the cares to which they are now transported![2] Now, they cannot run away from their vile deeds or increase their stock of good. They became familiar and comfortable with the world, and she deceived them. They trusted her, and she hurled them to the ground. People, race toward the home that you have been commanded to inhabit—may God have mercy on you!—the one to which you have been urged and invited. Seek the completion of God's blessings through obedience, do good and shun sin, for tomorrow is close to today. O how swift the passage of hours in a day! How swift the passage of days in a month! How swift the passage of months in a year! How swift the passage of years in a lifetime!

1.187 From an oration by ʿAlī:[3]

---

1   Excerpt from ʿAlī's oration soon after his accession to the caliphate in Medina, when he was informed that Ṭalḥah and Zubayr had rebelled. Iskāfī, *Miʿyār*, 109–111.

2   Or, "They are occupied with paying for the things they have had to leave behind, having squandered the opportunity to prepare for that to which they are now transported." Ḥ 13:100.

3   This could be an excerpt from an early oration in Medina in 35–36/356, since the penultimate line, "Ask me before you lose me," is said to be the prompt for Dhiʿlib's question about seeing God and ʿAlī's answer in §1.177 (Ṣadūq, *Amālī*, 423, Majlis no. 55; see note there), set in Medina. But, on the other hand, the line also occurs in §90.2, from the late Kufa period, ca. 38/658, and in another oration in Māmaṭīrī, *Nuzhah*, 145–147—the line appears to be a recurrent one in ʿAlī's orations, from the beginning of his caliphate to the end.

فمن الإيمان ما يكون ثابتًا مستقرًّا في القلوب ومنه ما يكون عَواريّ بين القلوب والصدور إلى أجل معلوم. فإذا كانت لكم براءة من أحد فقفوه حتّى يحضره الموت فعند ذلك يقع حدّ البراءة. والهجرة قائمة على حدّها الأوّل ما كان لله تعالى في أهل الأرض حاجة من مستسرّ الأمّة ومعلنها لا يقع ٱسم الهجرة على أحد إلّا بمعرفة الحُجّة في الأرض فمن عرفها وأقرّ بها فهو مهاجر ولا يقع ٱسم الاستضعاف على من بلغته الحُجّة فسمعتها أذنه ووعاها قلبه. إنّ أمرنا صعب مستصعَب لا يحتمله إلّا عبد ٱمتحن الله قلبه للإيمان[1] ولا يعي حديثنا إلّا صدور أمينة وأحلام رزينة. أيّها الناس سَلوني قبل أن تفقدوني فلَأَنا بطرق السماء أعلم منّي بطرق الأرض قبل أن تَشغَر برِجلها فتنة تطأ في خِطامها وتذهب بأحلام قومها.

1.188   ومن خطبة له عليه السلام

أحمده شكرًا لإنعامه وأستعينه على وظائف حقوقه عزيز الجند عظيم المجد. وأشهد أنّ محمّدًا عبده ورسوله دعا إلى طاعته وقاهر أعداءه جهادًا عن دينه لا يثنيه عن ذلك ٱجتماع على تكذيبه وٱلتماس لإطفاء نوره.

---

[1] ن، م، ش، ه: كذا. ي: ﴿لا تحمله إلّا ملك مقرّب أو نبيّ مرسل أو مؤمن ٱمتحن الله إلّا عبد ٱمتحن الله قلبه للإيمان﴾. وأضيفت في هامش ش: ﴿ملك مقرّب أو نبيّ مرسل أو مؤمن﴾.

Some people's hearts are firm and steadfast in belief, while for others belief is a temporary loan lodged between heart and breast. If you wish to dissociate from anyone, wait until death comes to him—that is the point at which dissociation becomes appropriate.[1] Migration continues to be required as it was when first mandated,[2] although God has no need of any of the earth's people, neither those who conceal their affiliation to this community, nor those who declare it publicly.[3] Moreover, the honor of migration is not earned by a person unless he recognizes God's proof on earth.[4] To recognize and acknowledge this proof is to be a true migrant. The phrase "too weak" does not apply to anyone whom God's proof reaches, that is, if his ears hear it and his heart preserves it.[5] Our affair is hard and challenging, and only a person whose heart God has tested with belief can bear it patiently. Our words are preserved only by trusted hearts and mature minds. People! Ask me before you lose me, for I know more about the pathways of the heavens than I do about the pathways of the earth! Do this before sedition rushes to attack, raising its hind-foot, trampling on its nose-rein, and destroying people's minds.

1.188   From an oration by ʿAlī:[6]

I offer praise to God in thanks for his blessings and ask his aid in upholding his rights. His army is mighty, and his nobility great. I bear testimony that Muḥammad is his servant and messenger, who called on people to obey God and vanquished his enemies, fighting tirelessly to defend his religion. They banded together to call him a liar and attempted to extinguish his light, but they could not turn him away from his purpose.

---

1   I.e., see whether the person dies a believer or an unbeliever before you cast him off.

2   Ar. *hijrah*. The first migration refers to the migration to Medina, the Prophet Muḥammad's city, following his own migration there from Mecca.

3   Translation based on reading *mā* as a negation and the two sentences as independent clauses, based on B 717; R 2:444–445. If we read *mā* to be the particle that means "as long as," the two lines would be combined into one clause (cf. Ḥ 13:103), and would translate quite differently as: "Migration continues to be required as it was when first mandated, *as long as* God has need of any of the earth's people, those who conceal their affiliation to this community and those who declare it publicly."

4   The Shiʿi commentators Baḥrānī (B 717–718) and Rāwandī (R 2:444–445) state that "God's proof" is the Imam. The Sunni Ibn Abī al-Ḥadīd (Ḥ 13:103–104) says this passage is about the "secrets of legatee-ship," and it refers to migration toward the Imam, ʿAlī himself. Both are effectively saying the same thing.

5   Reference to Qurʾan, Nisāʾ 4:97, which excuses people who are "too weak" from migrating to Medina.

6   Called one of ʿAlī's most eloquent orations, especially for the rhythmic and graphic description of hellfire; echoed later by Ibn Nubātah al-Khaṭīb (d. 374/985) (Ḥ 13:114; B 725). The last paragraph about standing fast is interpreted variously: ʿAlī is either (1) instructing his Kufan supporters not to be hasty in drawing swords against the Kharijites (Ḥ 13:113); or (2) directing his followers never to draw swords in the absence of the rightful Imam (B 725); possibly both.

فاعتصموا بتقوى الله فإنّ لها حبلًا وثيقًا عروته ومعقلًا منيعًا ذروته. وبادروا الموت وغمراته وأمهدوا له قبل حلوله وأعدّوا له قبل نزوله فإنّ الغاية القيامة وكفى بذلك واعظًا لمن عقل ومعتبرًا لمن جهل وقبل بلوغ الغاية ما تعلمون من ضيق الأرماس وشدّة الإبلاس وهول المُطَّلَع وروعات الفزع واختلاف الأضلاع واستِكاك الأسماع وظلمة اللحد وخيفة الوعد وغمّ الضريح ورَدْم الصفيح. فاللهَ اللهَ عباد الله فإنّ الدنيا ماضية بكم على سَنن وأنتم والساعة في قَرَن وكأنّها قد جاءت بأشراطها وأزِفَت بأفراطها ووقفت بكم على سِراطها[1] وكأنّها قد أشرفت بزلازلها وأناخت بكلاكلها وانصرمت[2] الدنيا بأهلها وأخرجتهم من حِضنها فكانت كيوم مضى وشهر انقضى وصار جديدها رَثًّا وسمينها غَثًّا في موقف ضَنك المقام وأمور مشتبهة عظام ونارٍ شديدٍ كَلَبُها عالٍ لَجَبها ساطع لَهَبها متغيّظ زفيرها متأجّج سعيرها بعيد خُمودها ذاكٍ وَقُودها مخوف وعيدها عَمٍ قرارها مظلمة أقطارها حامية قدورها فظيعة أمورها. ﴿وَسِيقَ الَّذِينَ اتَّقَوْا رَبَّهُمْ إِلَى الْجَنَّةِ زُمَرًا﴾ قد أُمن العذاب وانقطع العِتاب وزُحزحوا عن النار واطمأنّت بهم الدار ورضوا المثوى والقرار الذين كانت أعمالهم في الدنيا زاكية وأعينهم باكية وكان ليلهم في دنياهم نهارًا تخشّعًا واستغفارًا وكان نهارهم ليلًا توحّشًا وانقطاعًا فجعل الله لهم الجنّة ثوابًا ﴿وَكَانُوا أَحَقَّ بِهَا وَأَهْلَهَا﴾ في ملك دائم ونعيم قائم. فارعوا عباد الله ما برعايته يفوز فائزكم وبإضاعته يخسر مبطلكم وبادروا آجالكم بأعمالكم فإنّكم مرتهنون بما أسلفتم ومَدينون بما قدّمتم وكأن قد نزل بكم المخوف فلا رجعة تنالون ولا عثرة تُقالون. استعملنا الله وإيّاكم بطاعته وطاعة رسوله وعفا عنّا وعنكم بفضل رحمته.

١م، ن، ش: كذا. ي، ه: ﴾صراطها﴿. ٢ن، ه، ش، ونسخة في ي: كذا. م، وأصل ي، ونسخة في ش: ﴾وانصرفت﴿.

Take refuge, people, in consciousness of God, for its rope has a strong grip, and its refuge is on an impregnable height. Hasten to prepare for the engulfing pangs of death, make ready before it arrives. Know that the resurrection is the final end—enough counsel for the perceptive, enough lesson for the ignorant! But even before you arrive at that terminus, you know well what you will encounter: the narrow confines of earth-filled graves, the sheer abyss of despair, the terror of the prospect, the disintegration of ribs, the blocking of ears, the darkness of the tomb, the fear of the portent, and the horror of that crypt sealed with slabs of stone! Fear him, servants of God, fear him! The world, as is her wont, is sweeping you along, your rope tethered to her last hour, whose heralds are here and whose dawn glimmers. The hour has already stood you in readiness to meet it on its concourse. It will arrive any moment now. Imagine that its earthquakes are already here, as though its brutish chest is already crushing out your breath, as though the world has already cut her ties with you, her children, and hurled you from her lap! Indeed, your world is like a day that has already passed, and a month that has already ended, the new in her has worn out, the healthy are wasted and thin. All in her proceed to an assembly that is tight and narrow, to matters that are grave and dark. Ahead lies a fire of rabid thirst, whose roar is deafening, whose flames rise high, whose crackle rages, whose conflagration is fierce and slow to extinguish, whose inferno blazes, whose threat is terrifying, whose pit is unfathomable, whose sides are dark, whose cauldrons are iron-hot, and everything about it is horrific. But «those who were conscious of their Lord will be led in groups into paradise»,[1] secure from punishment, safe from reprimand, snatched from the clutches of hellfire. Paradise will delight in their arrival, and they will rejoice in their new dwelling, their permanent home. These are people whose deeds in this world were righteous, whose eyes were full of tears, whose nights were spent as daylight hours in humble entreaty to God for forgiveness, whose days were spent as nighttime vigils in alienation and separation from the world. God rewarded them with paradise—«and they were worthy of it and deserving!»[2]—with life in the eternal kingdom, in everlasting bliss. Servants of God, stay the course whose fulfilment will lead you to triumph, but whose squandering will hand you defeat. Outrace your lifespans with good deeds, for you remain mortgaged to your past actions and will be rewarded for what you advance. The time that you dread is almost upon you, when no return to the world can be availed, no fall can be averted. May God help us to obey him and his Messenger! May he forgive us with his kind mercy!

---

1 Qurʾan, Zumar 39:73.
2 Qurʾan, Fatḥ 48:26.

الزموا الأرض وأصبروا على البلاء ولا تحرّكوا بأيديكم وسيوفكم هوى ألسنتكم ولا تستعجلوا بما لم يعجّله الله لكم فإنّه من مات منكم على فراشه وهو على معرفة حقّ ربّه وحقّ رسوله وأهل بيته مات شهيدًا ووقع أجره على الله وأستوجب ثواب ما نوى من صالح عمله وقامت النيّة مقام إصلاحته بسيفه فإنّ لكلّ شيء مدّة وأجلًا.

1.189 ومن خطبة له عليه السلام

الحمد الله الفاشي حمدُه والغالب جنده والمتعالي جدّه أحمده على نعمه التّؤام[1] وآلائه العظام الذي عظم حلمه فعفا وعدل في كلّ ما قضى وعلم ما يمضي وما مضى مبتدع الخلائق بعلمه ومنشئهم بحكمه بلا اقتداء ولا تعليم ولا احتذاء لمثال صانع حكيم ولا إصابة خطأ ولا حضرة ملأ. وأشهد أنّ محمّدًا عبده ورسوله أبتعثه والناس يضربون في غمرة ويموجون في حيرة قد قادتهم أزمّة الحَين وأستغلقت على أفئدتهم أقفال الرَّين.

أوصيكم عباد الله بتقوى الله فإنّها حقّ الله عليكم والموجبة على الله حقّكم وأن تستعينوا عليها بالله وتستعينوا بها على الله. فإنّ التقوى في اليوم الحِرْز والجُنّة وفي غد الطريق إلى الجنّة مسلكها واضح وسالكها رابح ومستودَعها حافظ. لم تبرح عارضة نفسها على الأمم الماضين والغابرين لحاجتهم إليها غدًا إذا أعاد الله ما أبدا وأخذ ما أعطى وسأل عمّا أسدى فما أقلّ من قبلها وحملها حقّ حملها أولئك الأقلّون عددًا وهم أهل صفة الله سبحانه إذ يقول ﴿وَقَلِيلٌ مِنْ عِبَادِي الشَّكُورُ﴾. فأهطعوا[2] بأسماعكم إليها ووا كِظوا بجِدّكم عليها وأعتاضوها من كلّ سلف خلفًا ومن كلّ مخالف موافقًا أيقظوا بها نومكم وأقطعوا بها يومكم وأشعروها قلوبكم وأرحضوا بها ذنوبكم وداووا بها الأسقام وبادروا بها الحِمام وأعتبروا بمن أضاعها ولا يعتبرنّ بكم من أطاعها ألا وصونوها وتصونوا بها. وكونوا عن الدنيا نزّاهًا وإلى الآخرة ولّاهًا ولا تضعوا من رفعته التقوى ولا ترفعوا من رفعته

<hr>

[1] م، ش، ي، هـ: كذا. ن، ونسخة في م: ﴿التَّوامّ﴾.   [2] م، ي، ونسخة في ش: كذا. ن، هـ، وأصل ش: ﴿فأنقطعوا﴾.

People, stand fast in your land and be patient in the face of trial. Don't follow your hot tongues with drawn swords, don't rush into something that God has not urged you to. Know that if one of you dies in his bed, if he has recognized the right of his Lord, his Messenger, and the Messenger's family, he dies a martyr, and God guarantees his recompense. He has earned reward for his pious intention, and that intention is equal to him unsheathing his sword. Know that everything has a time and a term.

1.189 From an oration by ʿAlī:

Praise God, whose praise is pervasive, whose armies are victorious, whose greatness is exalted. I offer thanks for his multiplied blessings and immense favors: his clemency is vast, and he pardoned; he was just in all he ordained; he knows all that will happen and all that already has, he originated all creatures by his knowledge, he conceived them all through his wisdom—no imitation or instruction, no emulation of prior artisan, no mistake made, no advisors present. I bear witness that Muḥammad is his servant and messenger, dispatched when people were swamped in confusion, tossed on waves of deviation, led by reins of destruction, hearts clamped in padlocks of grime.

I counsel you to piety, to be conscious of God, O servants of God, for it is God's right that you owe to him, and it will earn you rights from God. I counsel you to seek God's help to become pious, and seek to become pious in order to please God. Piety is a refuge today and protection, and it is tomorrow's path to the celestial garden. Piety's way is clear, those who walk it profit, and he who guarantees your deposit of it is trustworthy. Piety presented itself to past nations and will do so to those that remain. They will have need of it tomorrow, when God recalls what he created, takes back what he gave, and asks for an account of his gifts. But how rare the people who were pious, how few who practiced it well! Those are the few in number, the people whom God has praised, when he said, «few among my servants are truly grateful.»[1] So dedicate your ears to piety's call and apply your efforts to responding. Exchange your past wrongs for it, make it your ally against foes. Use it to wake you from your sleep, get through your days with its help. Infuse your hearts with it, scrub off your sins with it, heal your maladies with it, outpace your death with it. Be warned by those who squandered it, let others not take warning from your terrible end. Hark and listen! Preserve it carefully, people, and thereby preserve yourselves. Free yourself from this world and focus your longings on the next. Don't scorn those elevated by piety, don't elevate those elevated by the world. Don't look

---

1   Qurʾan, Sabaʾ 34:13.

الدنيا ولا تَشيموا بارقها ولا تَسمعوا ناطقها ولا تُجيبوا ناعقها ولا تَستضيئوا بإشراقها ولا تُفتنوا بأعلاقها فإنّ برقها خالب ونطقها كاذب وأموالها محروبة وأعلاقها مسلوبة. ألا وهي المتصدّية العَنون والجامحة الحَرون والمائنة الخَؤون والجَحود الكَنود والعَنود الصَّدود والحَيود المَيود حالها اَنتقال¹ ووطأتها زَلزال وعزّها ذلّ وجِدّها هَزْل وعلْوُها سُفْل دار حرب وسلب ونهب وعطب أهلها على ساق وسياق ولَحاق وفراق قد تحيّرت مذاهبها وأعجزت مهاربها وخابت مطالبها فأسلمتهم المعاقل ولفظتهم المنازل وأعيتهم المحاول فمن ناجٍ معقور ولحم مجزور وشِلْوٍ مذبوح ودم مسفوح وعاضٍّ على يديه وصافق لكفّيه ومرتفق بخدّيه وزارٍ على رأيه وراجع عن عزمه وقد أدبرت الحيلة وأقبلت الغِيْلة ﴿وَلَاتَ حِينَ مَنَاصٍ﴾. هيهات هيهات قد فات ما فات وذهب ما ذهب ومضت الدنيا لحالٍ بالها ﴿فَمَا بَكَتْ عَلَيْهِمُ السَّمَاءُ وَالْأَرْضُ وَمَا كَانُوا مُنظَرِينَ﴾.

1.190 ومن خطبة له عليه السلام تسمّى القاصعة وهي طويلة وفيها ذمّ إبليس والعصبيّة²

1.190.1 الحمد لله الذي لبس العزّ والكبرياء واَختارهما لنفسه دون خلقه وجعلهما حِمى وحرمًا على غيره واَصطفاهما لجلاله وجعل اللعنة على من نازعه فيهما من عباده. ثمّ

---

¹ م، ي، ومصحّحة في ه: كذا. ن، ش، وأصل ه: ﴿اَفتعال﴾. ² ن، ي، ه: كذا. م، ش: ﴿ومن الناس من يسمّي هذه الخطبة القاصعة وهي تتضمّن ذمّ إبليس على اَستكباره وتركه السجود لآدم عليه السلام وأنّه أوّل من أظهر العصبيّة وتبع الحميّة وتحذير الناس من سلوك طريقته﴾.

for her rainclouds, don't attend her speakers, don't answer her callers, don't seek her glitter, don't fancy her jewels—for her flashes are empty, her speech is false, her wealth will be plundered, and her jewels will be looted. Hark! She is but a strumpet who will pull away, a bronco that will bolt, a liar who will betray, a churl who is ungrateful, a deviator who shuns, who strays. Her nature is to terminate, her step causes earthquakes, her might is equal to shame, her seriousness is equal to jest, and her elevation is equal to disgrace. She is an abode of plunder and pillage, of loot and ruin. Her people are in torment, in agony, they rush forward, they disperse, they are confused by her roads, enmeshed by her evils, frustrated by her tricks. Their fortresses do not protect them, their homes spit them out, and their ruses fail them. What are they but hamstrung fugitives, butchered meat, slaughtered limbs, and spilt blood! Some among them bite on their hands, strike with their palms, lean cheeks on elbows in regret. Others among them are beset by doubt and withdraw after resolve. But the time of scheming has passed, the hour of calamity has come, «and it is too late to escape.»[1] Far be it! Far be it! What is lost is lost, what has gone has gone, and the world has moved on with everything that it housed. «Then, neither the sky nor the earth weeps over them, and they are not granted a reprieve.»[2]

1.190 From an oration by ʿAlī known as *Qāṣiʿah*—"The Crusher." It is a long oration, containing censure of Iblīs,[3] and of arrogance and tribal factionalism.[4]

1.190.1 Praise God, who donned robes of might and pride, reserving them for himself and allowing them to no other, who made them a fortress and sanctuary that only he inhabits, selecting them for his own majesty and cursing all who attempt to challenge him for them. Then he tested his cherubim to see

---

1   Qurʾan, Ṣād 38:3.
2   Qurʾan, Dukhān 44:29.
3   Iblīs refers to Lucifer.
4   The oration was delivered in (a) Kufa in 38/658 during the episode with Muʿāwiyah's envoy Ibn al-Ḥaḍramī in Basra (see note at §2.29), with ʿAlī rebuking his followers, particularly certain individuals from the Tamīm and Azd tribes for bickering among themselves when they had a common enemy to fight (Thaqafī, *Ghārāt*, 2:394–396); or (b) sometime in the last few months of ʿAlī's caliphate, after the Battle of Nahrawān when there was tribal strife in Kufa, condemned in the oration (B 736; Ḥ 13:167–168, 198). The context of internal quarreling among ʿAlī's followers is a possible reason for the name assigned to the oration: *Qāṣiʿah*, "The Crusher," from: (1) *qaṣaʿa l-qamlah*, "he crushed the louse," i.e., the oration crushed Satan and his supporters; (2) *qaṣaʿat al-nāqah*, "the camel crushed its grain," referring to a camel chewing cud, because ʿAlī rode out to the tribes and delivered this oration from the back of his camel; or (3) *qaṣaʿa l-māʾu ʿaṭashahu*, "the water slaked his thirst," i.e., the oration breaks the false pride of those who heed its teachings (B 736; Ḥ 13:128; F 354).

اَختبر بذلك ملائكته المقرّبين ليميز المتواضعين منهم من المستكبرين فقال سبحانه وهو العالم بمُضمَرات القلوب ومحجوبات الغيوب ﴿إِنِّي خَالِقٌ بَشَرًا مِّن طِينٍ فَإِذَا سَوَّيتهُ وَنَفَخْتُ فِيهِ مِن رُوحِي فَقَعُوا لَهُ سَاجِدِينَ فَسَجَدَ الْمَلَائِكَةُ كُلُّهُمْ أَجْمَعُونَ إِلَّا إِبْلِيسَ﴾ اَعترضته الحميّة فاَفتخر على آدم بخلقه وتعصّب عليه لأصله فعدوُّ الله إمام المتعصّبين وسلف المستكبرين الذي وضع أساس العصبيّة ونازع الله رداء الجبريّة وآدّرع لباس التعزّز وخلع قِناع التذلّل ألا ترون كيف صغّره الله بتكبّره ووضعه بترفّعه فجعله في الدنيا مدحورًا وأعدّ له في الآخرة سعيرًا. ولو أراد سبحانه أن يخلق آدم من نورٍ يَخْطَف الأبصار ضياؤه ويَبهر العقول رُواؤه وطيبٍ يأخذ الأنفاس عَرفه لفعل ولو فعل لظلّت له الأعناق خاضعة ولخفّت البلوى فيه على الملائكة ولكنّ الله سبحانه يبتلي خلقه ببعض ما يجهلون أصله تمييزًا بالاختيار[1] لهم ونفيًا للاستكبار عنهم وإبعادًا للخُيَلَاء منهم. فاَعتبروا بما كان من فعل الله بإبليس إذا أحبط عمله الطويل وجهده الجهيد وقد كان عَبَدَ الله ستّة آلاف سنة لا يدرى أمِنْ سِنِي الدنيا أم سِنِي الآخرة عن كبر ساعة واحدة فمَن بعد إبليس يَسلَم على الله بمثل معصيته كلَّا ما كان الله سبحانه ليدخل الجنّة بشرًا بأمرٍ أخرج به منها مَلَكًا إنّ حكمه في أهل السماء وأهل الأرض لواحد وما بين الله وبين أحد من خلقه هَوادة في إباحة حِمًى حرّمه الله على العالمين.

1.190.2 فاَحذروا عدوّ[2] الله أن يُعديكم بدائه وأن يستفزّكم بخَيله ورجله فلعمري لقد فَوَّقَ لكم سهم الوعيد وأغرق لكم بالنزع الشديد ورماكم من مكان قريب و﴿قَالَ رَبِّ بِمَا أَغْوَيتَنِي لَأُزَيِّنَنَّ لَهُمْ فِي الْأَرْضِ وَلَأُغْوِيَنَّهُمْ أَجْمَعِينَ﴾ قذفًا بغيب بعيد ورجمًا بظنّ غير مصيب صدّقه به أبناء الحميّة وإخوان العصبيّة وفرسان الكبر والجاهليّة. حتّى إذا

---

who were humble and who arrogant. He said—while knowing all that was concealed in their hearts and their hidden secrets—«I shall create a human out of clay; when I have fashioned him in good proportion and breathed into him my spirit, bow before him in prostration. The angels prostrated, every one of them, except Iblīs»[1]—his pride prevented him, and he claimed superiority over Adam, citing his loftier creation and higher origin. Iblīs—God's enemy—is leader of the bigots and forebear of the arrogant, the one who laid the foundations of factionalism. He challenged God for his robe of haughtiness, donned garments of self-glorification and cast off the veil of humility. Do you not see how God diminished him because of his arrogance and debased him because of his pride? He banished him in this world and prepared for him a blazing fire in the hereafter! If the Almighty had wished to create Adam from light whose radiance dazzled the eye and whose brilliance stupefied the mind, and from fragrance whose perfume filled the senses, he would have done so; and had he done so, necks would have bowed to Adam in servility, and the trial of the angels would have had little weight. But God tests his creation through things whose reality they do not know, in order to differentiate them through their choices, dispel their arrogance, and repulse their vanity. Learn a lesson from God's punishment of Iblīs, whose long-standing worship and painstaking efforts he obliterated for a single hour of pride! Iblīs had worshipped God for six thousand years, either by the reckoning of years in this world or by the unknown reckoning of the hereafter. Who, then, is safe from God's retribution if he disobeys God as Iblīs did? No one! God will never allow a human to enter the celestial garden if he has committed a crime for which he evicted an angel. God's judgment among the inhabitants of the heavens and the inhabitants of the earth is one and the same. He will show no leniency in allowing anyone to enter a fortress he has forbidden to all the worlds.

1.190.2 Beware lest Iblīs infect you with his disease or intimidate you with his cavalry and infantry.[2] By my life, he has fitted the arrow of threat to his longbow, pulled the bowstring, aimed, and shot at you from close by. «He said: My Lord, because you caused me to stray, I shall place temptations before them on earth and lead them all astray.»[3] His was a farfetched idea and a wild supposition, but zealotry's offspring, factionalism's brothers, and men riding horses of pride and intolerance made his aspiration come true. Then the hidden secret turned into an open affair, when the recalcitrant among you became docile

---

1   Qurʾan, Ṣād 38:71–74.
2   Modified quote from Qurʾan, Isrāʾ 17:64.
3   Qurʾan, Ḥijr 15:39.

اَنقادت له الجامحة منكم وَاستَحكمت الطَّماعية منه فيكم فنجمت الحال من السرّ الخفيّ إلى الأمر الجليّ اَستفحل سلطانه عليكم ودَلَفَ بجنوده نحوكم فأقحموكم وَلَجات الذلّ وأحلوكم وَرَطات القتل وأوطؤوكم إثخان الجراحة طعنًا في عيونكم وحَزًّا في حلوقكم ودَقًّا لمناخركم وقصدًا لمقاتلكم وسَوْقًا بِخَزائم القهر إلى النار المُعَدّة لكم فأصبح أعظم في دينكم جَرْحًا وأورى في دنياكم قدحًا من الذين أصبحتم لهم مناصبين وعليهم متألّبين فأجعلوا عليه حدّكم وله جدّكم. فلعمر الله لقد نخر على أصلكم ووقع في حسبكم ودفع في نسبكم وأجلب بخَيله عليكم وقصد برَجْله سبيلكم يقتنصونكم بكلّ مكان ويضربون منكم كلّ بَنان لا تمتنعون بحيلة ولا تدفعون بعزيمة في حَوْمة ذلّ وحَلْقة ضيق وعَرْصة موت وجَوْلة بلاء. فأطفئوا ما كَمَنَ في قلوبكم من نيران العصبيّة وأحقاد الجاهليّة وإنّما تلك الحميّة تكون في المسلم من خطرات الشيطان ونَخَواته ونَزَغاته ونَفَثاته وَاعتمدوا وضع التذلّل على رؤوسكم وإلقاء التعزّز تحت أقدامكم وخلع التكبّر من أعناقكم وَاتَّخذوا التواضع مَسلَحة بينكم وبين عدوّكم إبليس وجنوده فإنّ له من كلّ أمّة جنودًا وأعوانًا ورجْلًا وفرسانًا. ولا تكونوا كالمتكبّر على اَبن أمّه من غيرِ ما فضلٍ جعله الله فيه سوى ما ألحقت العظمة بنفسه من عداوة الحسد وقدحت الحميّة في قلبه من نار الغضب ونفخ الشيطان في أنفه من ريح الكبر الذي أعقبه الله به الندامة وألزمه آثام القاتلين إلى يوم القيامة.

1.190.3   ألا وقد أمعنتم في البغي وأفسدتم في الأرض مُصارَحة لله بالمناصبة ومبارزة للمؤمنين بالمحاربة فالله الله في كبر الحميّة وفخر الجاهليّة فإنّه مَلاقِح الشَّنآن ومَنافِخ الشيطان

enough for him to lead, and his ambitions for you took firm hold. His power over you grew oppressive and he marched against you with his armies. They forced you into caverns of humiliation, hurled you into chasms of carnage, and trampled you causing terrible wounds, thrusting spears into your eyes, slashing your throats, smashing your noses, slashing your organs, and dragging you by the nose-rings of subjugation toward the Fire. Iblīs has maimed your religion and scorched your worldly affairs far more effectively than the people you took as adversaries and against whom you gathered your armies. Draw your swords against him and double your efforts in his face! By my life, he has boasted that his origin is better than yours, he has slandered your ancestors, and tarnished your lineage. He has attacked you with his cavalry and assaulted you with his infantry. They hunt you down wherever you hide and slice off each of your fingers,[1] while you cannot defend yourself through any stratagem or push back with any act of resolve. You are caught in the abyss of degradation, the nose-ring of compulsion, the arena of death, and the circle of affliction. Extinguish the fires of factionalism that lie concealed in your hearts and the resentments that belong to the Age of Ignorance! Factionalist zeal in a Muslim comes from Satan's incitements, from his goads, provocations, and splutterings. Resolve to adorn your head with modesty, trample self-glory beneath your feet, and cast the yoke of arrogance from your necks. Make humility the garrison that stands between you and your enemy, Iblīs, and his armies, for he has armies, infantry, cavalry, and spies in all nations. Don't be like Cain, who thought himself better than his brother, with no superior God-given virtue except the glory he attributed to himself, generated by hate and envy, and the supercilious zeal of his heart, kindled by the fire of anger![2] Satan breathed his own pride into Cain's nose.[3] Because of that pride, God bequeathed him eternal remorse, and will hold him responsible for the crimes of all who kill until the day of resurrection.

1.190.3 Hark! You have galloped on the course of treachery and caused mayhem on earth, openly challenging God and fighting his believers. Fear God, fear God! Stay away from the arrogant bigotry and boasting that characterized the Age of Ignorance! Those are rancor's pregnant camels and Satan's bellows! With them, he duped past nations and bygone generations, making them race

---

1   Modified quote from Qurʾan, Anfāl 8:12.

2   Lit. "Don't be like the one who ..." The reference is to Adam's sons Cain (Ar. Qābīl) and Abel (Ar. Hābīl), to Cain's killing of Abel at Iblīs's suggestion, and later, when it was too late, feeling remorse. Qurʾan, Māʾidah 5:27–31; Ḥ 13:145–146; B 747; F 358–359.

3   The nose symbolizes pride in Arab culture, in addition to being the organ of breathing.

اللاتي خدع بها الأمم الماضية والقرون الخالية حتّى أَعْنَقوا في حَنادِس جهالته ومهاوي ضلالته ذُلًّا عن سياقه سُلسًا في قياده أمرًا تشابهت القلوب فيه وتتابعت القرون عليه وكبرًا تضايقت الصدور به. ألا فالحذرَ الحذرَ من طاعة ساداتكم وكبرائكم الذين تكبّروا عن حسبهم وترفّعوا فوق نسبهم وألقوا الهَجينة على رَبّهم وجاحدوا الله ما صنع بهم مكابَرة لقضائه ومغالَبة لآلائه فإنّهم قواعد آساس العصبيّة ودعائم أركان الفتنة وسيوف اعتزاء الجاهليّة. فاتّقوا الله ولا تكونوا لنعمه عليكم أضدادًا ولا لفضله عندكم حُسّادًا ولا تطيعوا الأدعياء الذين شربتم بصفوكم كَدَرهم وخلطتم بصحّتكم مرضهم وأدخلتم في حقّكم باطلهم وهم آساس الفسوق وأحلاس العقوق اتّخذهم إبليس مطايا ضلال وجندًا بهم يصول على الناس وتراجمة ينطق على ألسنتهم استراقًا لعقولكم ودخولًا في عيونكم ونفْثًا في أسماعكم فجعلكم مَرْمى نبله وموطئ قدمه ومأخذ يده.

١.١٩٠.٤   فاعتبروا بما أصاب الأمم المستكبرين من قبلكم من بأس الله وصَولاته ووقائعه ومَثُلاته واتّعظوا بمثاوي خدودهم ومصارع جنوبهم واستعيذوا بالله من لَواقح الكبر كما تستعيذونه من طوارق الدهر. فلو رخّص الله في الكبر لأحد من عباده لرخّص فيه لخاصّة أنبيائه ولكنّه سبحانه كَرَّهَ إليهم التكابر[٢] ورضي لهم التواضع فألصقوا بالأرض خدودهم وعَفَرُوا في التراب وجوههم وخفضوا أجنحتهم للمؤمنين وكانوا أقوامًا مستضعفين. وقد اختبرهم الله بالمخْمَصة وابتلاهم بالمجْهَدة وامتحنهم بالمخاوف ومخَضَهم بالمكاره فلا تعتبروا الرضاء والسخط بالمال والولد جهلًا بمواقع الفتنة والاختبار في مواضع الغنى والإقتار.[٣] فقد قال سبحانه ﴿أَيَحْسَبُونَ أَنَّمَا نُمِدُّهُم بِهِ مِن مَّالٍ وَبَنِينَ نُسَارِعُ لَهُمْ فِي الْخَيْرَاتِ بَلْ لَا يَشْعُرُونَ﴾ فإنّ الله سبحانه يختبر عباده المستكبرين

١م، ي، ونسخة في ش، ه: كذا. ن، ش، ه، ونسخة في ي: ‹نثًّا›.   ٢ن، م، ي، ه، ومصحّحة في ش: كذا. أصل ش، ومصحّحة في م: ‹التكاثر›.   ٣م، ي، ومصحّحة في ه: كذا. ن، ش، وأصل ه، ونسخة في م: ‹الافتقار›.

into the dark night of his ignorance and the abyss of his error, docile under his direction and submissive under his reins. In Satan's grip, hearts resembled one another as generation followed generation. Pride ruled as breasts became straitened by its grip. Hark and beware! Beware of obeying these chieftains and elders,[1] who have magnified themselves above their stature and aggrandized themselves beyond their lineage, who have attributed vile deeds to their Lord and challenged his actions, scorning his decree and impugning his favors. They are pillars of factionalism, columns of sedition, and swords of ancestor boasts from the Age of Ignorance. Be conscious of God. Do not repulse his favors by acting in a contrary manner or repel his generosity by your envy. Don't obey false claimants whose muddy slime you have drunk instead of your pure water, whose diseases have infected your sound health, and whose wrong you have mixed in with your right. They are the foundations of vice, the constant companions of rebellion. Iblīs owns them—steeds of error and an army with which he assaults people. He has appointed them his interpreters. Speaking with their tongues, he weakens your minds, lends you his eyes, and whispers in your ears. In this manner, he targets you with his arrows, tramples you under his foot, and crushes you in his closed fist.

1.190.4 Learn lessons from what arrogant nations before you faced: God's crushing blows, his sudden attacks, his shocking onslaughts, and his exemplary punishments. Take counsel from knowing that their cheeks are now stuck inside the earth and their torsos are struck onto the ground. Seek refuge in God from the pregnant dangers of pride, just as you seek refuge in him from the battering calamities of the age. If God had permitted any of his servants pride, he would have permitted it to his select prophets, but he disliked them to be proud and preferred them to be humble. They placed their cheeks on the earth before him and pressed their faces to the dirt. They lowered their wings for believers and were a group that was widely scorned as weak.[2] He tested them with hunger, afflicted them with weariness, tried them with dangers, and ground them down with adversities. People, do not weigh God's pleasure and displeasure in terms of wealth and offspring, without knowing what tests and trials inhere in positions of wealth or poverty! God has said, «Do they think we supply them with wealth and sons in order to increase their comforts? No indeed, they have no idea!»[3] God tests people who are mighty in their own view, through his chosen ones, who are weak in their eyes. Moses, son of Amram,

---

1 Reference to Qur'an, Aḥzāb 33:67.
2 Reference to Qur'an, Ḥijr 15:88, Qaṣaṣ 28:4.
3 Qur'an, Mu'minūn 23:55–56.

في أنفسهم بأوليائه المستضعفين في أعينهم. ولقد دخل موسى بن عمران ومعه أخوه هارون عليهما السلام على فرعون وعليهما مَدارِعُ الصوف وبأيديهما العِصِيّ فشرطا له إن أسلم بقاء مِلكه ودوام عِزّه فقال ألا تعجبون من هذين يشرطان لي دوام العزّ وبقاء الملك وهما بما ترون من حال الفقر والذلّ فهَلّا أُلقِي عليهما أساورة من ذهب إعظامًا للذهب وجمعه واحتقارًا للصوف ولبسه ولو أراد الله سبحانه بأنبيائه حيث بعثهم أن يفتح لهم كنوز الذِّهْبان ومعادن العِقيان ومَغارِس الجِنان وأن يَحشر معهم طير السماء ووحوش الأرضين لفعل ولو فعل لسقط البلاء وبطل الجزاء واضمحلّ الأنباء ولما وجب للقابلين أجور المبتلين ولا استحقّ المؤمنون ثواب المحسنين ولا لزمت الأسماءُ معانيَها. ولكنّ الله سبحانه جعل رسله أولي قوّة في عزائمهم وضَعَفَة فيما ترى الأعين من حالاتهم مع قناعة تملأ القلوب والعيون غنًى وخَصاصة تملأ الأبصار والأسماع أذى. ولو كانت الأنبياء أهل قوّة لا تُرام وعزّة لا تُضام ومُلْك تُمَدّ نحوه أعناق الرجال وتُشَدّ إليه عُقَد الرِّحال لكان ذلك أهون على الخلق في الاعتبار وأبعد لهم من الاستكبار ولآمنوا عن رهبة قاهرة لهم أو رغبة مائلة بهم وكانت النيّات مشترَكة والحسنات مقتَسَمة. ولكنّ الله سبحانه أراد أن يكون الاتّباع لرسله والتصديق بكتبه والخشوع لوجهه والاستكانة لأمره والاستسلام لطاعته أمورًا له خاصّة لا يَشُوبها من غيرها شائبة وكلّما كانت البلوى والاختبار أعظم كانت المثوبة والجزاء أجزل.

5.190.1 ألا ترون أنّ الله سبحانه اختبر الأوّلين مِن لَدُن آدم صلّى الله عليه إلى الآخرين من هذا العالم بأحجار لا تضرّ ولا تنفع ولا تبصر ولا تسمع فجعلها بيته الحرام الذي جعله للناس قيامًا. ثمّ وضعه بأوعر بِقاع الأرض حجرًا وأقلّ نَتائق الدنيا مَدَرًا وأضيق بطون الأودية قُطْرًا بين جبال خَشِنة ورِمال دَمِثة وعيون وَشِلة وقُرًى منقطعة

and with him his brother Aaron, were admitted to Pharaoh wearing shifts of coarse wool and holding wooden staffs, and they offered him a guarantee—if he committed to God's will, his kingdom would last forever, and his might would persist. Pharaoh exclaimed, "Do you not wonder at these two? They promise me the continuation of my might and the perpetuation of my kingdom when, as you see, they are utterly poor and totally contemptible! How is it they are not adorned with bracelets of gold?" Pharaoh prized gold and the hoarding of it and mocked coarse wool and the wearing of it. If God, when he sent his prophets, had wished to open for them treasuries of gold, stores of bullion, and the granaries of the celestial garden, if he had wished to assemble in their legions the birds of the air and the beasts of the earth, he would have done so. And had he done so, the trial would have been nullified, recompense would have become invalid, and true reports would have dwindled. Those who accepted the prophets' message would not have deserved the reward of those who had been tested, believers would not have merited the reward of good deeds, and words would not have retained their meanings. But God sent his messengers strong in resolution, weak in terms of what eyes perceived. Their contentment filled hearts and eyes with riches, while their destitution filled eyes and ears with pain. If these prophets had possessed strength that could not be challenged, might that could not be diminished, and kingship toward which men's necks craned and saddles were fastened, these conditions would have relieved the weight of reflection for the people and broken their arrogance. People would have become believers either out of subjugation to fear or the pull of desire. Intentions would have been split and benefits would accordingly have been divided. But God willed that all pious acts—devotion to his messengers, acceptance of the truth of his books, self-effacement for his sake, humility before his command, and submission to him and obedience—all these things should be pure and for himself alone, untainted by any drop of insincerity. The greater the test and trial, the grander the reward and recompense.

1.190.5 Do you not see? Starting with Adam, God tested all who came before, up to the very last people in this world, with stones that neither harm nor benefit nor see nor hear, shaping them into his sacred house and designating it a place of worship for all humans. He placed this House in the most rugged, most rocky region of the earth, in the most barren place in the world, in the narrowest, steepest cleft of a valley, between rough mountains, tracts of porous sand, springs with slow-trickling water, and scattered habitations, where no hoofed animals—neither camels, nor mules, nor sheep—could feed or thrive. Then he commanded Adam and his children to turn their bodies toward it, making it the place to which they should return time after time to seek their journeys' bene-

لا يزكو بها خُفّ ولا حافر ولا ظِلْف. ثمّ أمر آدم وولده أن يَثنوا أعطافهم نحوه
فصار مَثابة لمُنتجَع أسفارهم وغاية لمُلْقى رحالهم تهوي إليه ثمار الأفئدة من مَفاوِز
قفار سحيقة ومَهاوي بِفِجاج عميقة وجزائر بحار منقطعة حتّى يهزّوا مناكبهم ذُلّلًا يهلّون
لله حوله ويرمُلون على أقدامهم شُعْثًا غُبرًا له قد نبذوا السرابيل وراء ظهورهم وشوّهوا
بإعفاء الشعور محاسن خلقهم أبتلاء عظيمًا وآمتحانًا شديدًا وآختبارًا مبينًا وتمحيصًا بليغًا
جعله الله سببًا لرحمته ووُصلة إلى جنّته. ولو أراد سبحانه أن يضع بيته الحرام ومشاعِره
العظام بين جنّات وأنهار وسهل وقرار جَمّ الأشجار داني الثمار مُلتَفّ البُنى متّصل القُرى
بين بُرّة سمراء وروضة خضراء وأرياف مُحدِقة وعِراص مغدقة وزروع ناضرة وطرق
عامرة لكان قد صغّر قدر الجزاء على حسب ضعف البلاء. ولو كانت الآساس المحمول
عليها والأحجار المرفوع بها بين[١] زُمُرُّدة خضراء وياقوتة حمراء ونور وضياء لخفّف ذلك
مُضارَعة الشكّ في الصدور ولوضع مُجاهَدة إبليس عن القلوب ولنفى مُعتلَج الريب
من الناس ولكنّ الله يختبر عباده بأنواع الشدائد ويتعبّدهم بألوان المجاهد ويبتليهم
بضروب المكاره إخراجًا للتكبّر من قلوبهم وإسكانًا للتذلّل في نفوسهم وليجعل ذلك
أبوابًا فُتحًا إلى فضله وأسبابًا ذُلُلًا لعفوه. فاللهَ اللهَ في عاجل البغي وآجل وَخامة الظلم
وسوء عاقبة الكبر فإنّها مَصيَدة إبليس العظمى ومَكيده الكبرى التي تُساور قلوب
الرجال مُساورة السموم القاتلة فما تُكدي أبدًا ولا تُشوي أحدًا لا عالمًا لعلمه ولا مُقلًّا في
طِمره.

١.١٩٠.٦ وعن ذلك ما حرس الله عباده المؤمنين بالصلوات والزكوات ومُجاهدة الصيام
في الأيّام المفروضات تسكينًا لأطرافهم وتخشيعًا لأبصارهم وتذليلًا لنفوسهم وتخفيضًا
لقلوبهم وإذهابًا للخُيَلاء عنهم لما في ذلك من تَعفير عَتائِق الوجوه بالتراب تواضعًا
وإلصاق كرائم الجوارح بالأرض تصاغرًا ولحوق البطون بالمتون من الصيام

---

fit,[1] and the final station where they should cast down their saddles. Sincere hearts rush toward it,[2] coming from remote, waterless deserts, deep, hidden ravines, and isolated islands in the sea. They come to it with their bodies shaking in awe, declaring God's oneness as they circumambulate and quicken their feet, disheveled and covered in dust, having cast off stitched clothing and tarnished the comeliness of their form by foregoing shaving or cutting their hair. This is truly a great trial, a harsh ordeal, a clear test—refinement by fire. God has made it the means to obtain his mercy and the path to reach his celestial garden. If he had placed his sacred house and sites of ceremonial rites among gardens and rivers and valleys and plains thick with trees and low-hanging fruits, densely packed with habitats, flourishing with sun-ripened wheat and bright green flowerbeds, with expansive pastures and well-watered plains, with freshly sprouted grain and well-worn paths, all this would have decreased the value of the reward, in keeping with the ease of the trial. Indeed, if the pillars that support the sacred house and the slabs that raise it had been made from green emerald and red ruby, from light and incandescence, this would have hindered doubt from entering into breasts, prevented Satan's attacks on hearts, and blocked uncertainty's waves from crashing down on people. No, indeed! God tests his servants with many kinds of hardship, urges them to worship him through many types of privation, and afflicts them with many different sufferings, in order to remove pride from their hearts and instill humility in their souls. These trials act as doors that open wide toward his generosity, as docile mounts that carry their riders toward his forgiveness. Fear God, people, fear God, and beware the imminent penalties of treachery, the unwholesome end of oppression, and the terrible outcome of pride! Pride is Iblīs's greatest snare and his principal scheme. He infiltrates men's hearts with its deadly poison. It is never ineffectual, and it misses no one—not the learned man with his knowledge, nor the beggar with his rags.

1.190.6 God has protected his believing servants from pride by prescribing the ritual prayer, the alms-levy, and the hardship of obligatory fasting on certain days, in order to quieten their limbs, lower their eyes, humble their souls, chasten their hearts, and repel their conceit. These actions prompt them to smear their precious faces with dust in self-effacement, prostrate their noble limbs upon the earth in humility, and join belly to back through fasting in

---

1 Reference to Qurʾan, Baqarah 2:125.
2 "Sincere hearts," Lit. "the fruit of hearts (*thimār al-afʾidah*)." Reference to Qurʾan, Ibrāhīm 14:37.

تذلّلًا مع ما في الزكاة من صرف ثمرات الأرض وغير ذلك إلى أهل المسكنة والفقر. انظروا إلى ما في هذه الأفعال من قَمْع نواجِم الفخر وقدع طوالع الكبر.

1.190.7 ولقد نظرت فما وجدت أحدًا من العالمين يتعصّب لشيء من الأشياء إلّا عن علّة تحتمل تَمويه الجهلاء أو حجّة تليط بعقول السفهاء غيرَكم فإنّكم تتعصّبون لأمر لا يعرف له سبب ولا مسّ يد علّة.[1] أمّا إبليس فتعصّب على آدم لأصله وطعن عليه في خلقته فقال أنا ناريٌّ وأنت طينيّ وأمّا الأغنياء من مُتْرَفة الأمم فتعصّبوا لآثار مواقع النعم فقالوا ﴿نَحْنُ أَكْثَرُ أَمْوَالًا وَأَوْلَادًا وَمَا نَحْنُ بِمُعَذَّبِينَ﴾. فإن كان لا بدّ من العصبيّة فليكن تعصّبكم لمكارم الخصال ومحامد الأفعال ومحاسن الأمور التي تفاضلت فيها المُجَداء والنُّجَداء من بُيوتات العرب ويَعاسِيب القبائل بالأخلاق الرغيبة والأحلام العظيمة والأخطار الجليلة والآثار المحمودة فتعصّبوا لخلال الحمد من الحفظ للجوار والوفاء بالذِّمام[2] والطاعة للبِرّ والمعصية للكبر والأخذ بالفضل والكفّ عن البغي والإعظام للقتل والإنصاف للخلق والكظم للغيظ واجتناب الفساد في الأرض.

1.190.8 واحذروا ما نزل بالأمم قبلكم من المثُلات بسوء الأفعال وذميم الأعمال فتذكّروا في الخير والشرّ أحوالهم واحذروا أن تكونوا أمثالهم فإذا تفكّرتم في تَفاوُت حالَيهم فآلزموا كلّ أمر لزمت العزّة به حالهم وزاحت الأعداء له عنهم ومَدّت العافية فيئَه بهم وانقادت النعمة له معهم ووصلت الكرامة عليه حبلهم من الاجتناب للفرقة واللزوم للأُلفة والتَّحاضِّ عليها والتَّواصي بها. واجتنبوا كلّ أمر كسر فقرتهم وأوهن مُنّتهم من تضاغن القلوب وتشاحن الصدور وتدابر النفوس وتخاذل الأيدي.

1.190.9 وتدبّروا أحوال الماضين من المؤمنين قبلكم كيف كانوا في حال التمحيص والبلاء ألم يكونوا أثقل الخلائق أعباء وأجهد العباد بلاء وأضيق أهل الدنيا حالًا

______
[1] ن، ش، ه: كذا. م، ي، ومصحّحة في ه: سقطت ﴿مسّ يد﴾. نسخة في ش: ﴿لا تُخشى له علّة﴾.
[2] ن، ش، ي، ه، ونسخة في م: كذا. أصل م، ونسخة في ش: ﴿الذمار﴾.

submission. In addition, the alms-levy procures the fruits of the earth and other commodities for the poor and destitute. See how these actions blast people's nascent shoots of self-importance and wither their budding sprouts of pride!

1.190.7 I looked around and found no one anywhere—other than you—who displays zealotry without a reason, any reason, that could possibly prompt the ignorant to confusion, or an argument, any argument, that could potentially appeal to the minds of the foolish. You show prejudice toward a matter whose reason is unknown, that is untouched by any hand of purpose. Iblīs felt himself superior to Adam because of his origin, and he defamed Adam's mode of creation when he said, "My origin is fire, while yours is clay." Scions of wealthy nations who were given enormous riches felt themselves superior because they had become used to luxury, and they said, «We have more wealth and more children; we shall never have to endure suffering.»[1] If you must feel superior, then save your pride for the noble qualities, praiseworthy acts, and beautiful deeds that the honorable and courageous Arabian clans and tribal chieftains strived for through their cultivation of desirable traits, great minds, kingly thoughts, and praiseworthy deeds.[2] Their zeal was for traits that earn praise—protection of neighbors, fulfillment of pledges, obeying good, desisting from pride, embrace of virtue, refraining from treachery, deeming killing to be a grave affair, dispensing of justice to all, suppression of anger, and abstention from wreaking havoc on earth.

1.190.8 Beware of exemplary punishments that befell earlier nations because of their evil acts and hateful deeds. Recall their conditions, the good and then the bad, and beware of becoming like them. Think about the change in their states. Hold fast to everything that gave them might, scattered their enemies, spread wellbeing among them, attracted beneficence to them, and bolstered the bonds of generosity—avoidance of division, holding fast to friendship, promoting harmony, and counselling one another to unite. Refrain from everything that broke their spine and weakened their strength—malice in the heart, rancor in the breast, turning one's back, and withholding one's hand.

1.190.9 Reflect on the condition of past believers. Think about how they lived through states of trial and testing. Were they not the most burdened of creatures, the most tested of God's servants, the most straitened among the world's

---

1 Qur'an, Sabaʾ 34:35.
2 "Chieftains," lit. "queen bees" (*yaʿāsīb*, sing. *yaʿsūb*).

اتّخذتهم الفراعنة عبيدًا فساموهم سوء[1] العذاب وجرّعوهم جُرَع المُرار فلم تبرح الحال بهم في ذلّ الهلكة وقهر الغلبة لا يجدون حيلة في امتناع ولا سبيلًا إلى دفاع. حتّى إذا رأى الله جِدّ الصبر منهم على الأذى في محبّته والاحتمال للمكروه من خوفه جعل لهم من مضايق البلاء فرجًا فأبدلهم العزّ مكان الذلّ والأمن مكان الخوف فصاروا ملوكًا حُكّامًا وأئمّة أعلامًا وبلغت الكرامة من الله لهم ما لم تذهب الآمال إليه بهم. فأنظروا كيف كانوا حيث كانت الأملاء مجتمعة والأهواء مؤتلفة والقلوب معتدلة والأيدي مترادفة والسيوف متناصرة والبصائر نافذة والعزائم واحدة ألم يكونوا أربابًا في أقطار الأرضين وملوكًا على رقاب العالمين فأنظروا إلى ما صاروا إليه في آخر أمورهم حين وقعت الفُرقة وتشتّتت الألفة واختلفت الكلمة والأفئدة وتشعّبوا مختلفين وتفرّقوا متحاربين.[2] قد خلع الله عنهم لباس كرامته وسلبهم غضارة نعمته وبقّى قصص أخبارهم فيكم عبرًا للمعتبرين منكم.

1.190.10 فاعتبروا بحال ولد إسماعيل وبني إسحاق وبني إسرائيل عليهم السلام فما أشدّ اعتدال الأحوال وأقرب اشتباه الأمثال. تأمّلوا أمرهم في حال تشتّتهم وتفرّقهم ليالي كانت الأكاسرة والقياصرة أربابًا لهم يحتازونهم عن رِيف الآفاق وبحر العراق وخضرة الدنيا إلى منابت الشيح ومهافي الريح ونَكَد المعاش فتركوهم عالة مساكين إخوان دَبَر ووَبَر[3] أذلّ الأمم دارًا وأجدبهم قرارًا لا يأوون إلى جناح دعوة يعتصمون بها ولا إلى ظلّ ألفة يعتمدون على عزّها. فالأحوال مضطربة والأيدي مختلفة والكثرة متفرّقة في بلاءٍ أزْلٍ وأطباق جهل من بنات مَوؤُودة وأصنام معبودة وأرحام مقطوعة وغارات مشنونة. فأنظروا إلى مواقع نعم الله عليهم حين بعث إليهم رسولًا فعقد بملّته طاعتهم وجمع على دعوته ألفتهم كيف نشرت النعمة عليهم جناح كرامتها وأسالت لهم

––––––––––

[1] ن، ش، ي، ه: كذا. م: ﴿سوم﴾.   [2] م، ي، ه: كذا. ن، ش: ﴿متحازبين﴾.   [3] ن، ش، ه: كذا. م، ومصحّحة في ه: ﴿دين ووت﴾. ي: ﴿دبر ووت﴾.

people? Various pharaohs enslaved them, inflicted on them the vilest of tortures, and forced them to drink from the bitterest of cups. Their condition continued thus in servile desperation and forceful subjugation with no means to repel and no way to defend, until God, seeing them endure suffering, out of their love for him, seeing them accept hardship, out of their fear of him, showed them a way out of the narrow straits of trial, giving them might in exchange for humiliation, security instead of fear. They became kings who ruled and leaders with great fame. They received gifts from God beyond their furthest hopes. Think! What was their state when factions were united, desires were in concert, hearts were balanced, hands were used to help, swords were drawn in assistance, perceptions were acute, and resolutions were one? Did they not become lords of all the realms, kings ruling over the necks of all peoples of the world? Again, think! How did their state change near the end, when division befell them, friendships shattered, words and hearts moved apart, when they split into opposing factions and separated into warring groups? God stripped them of his enveloping generosity and plundered them of his fresh bounty. Yes, and he ensured that their tales stayed alive among you as a lesson for all who would heed.

1.190.10 Take a lesson from the condition of the sons of Ishmael, the children of Isaac, and the children of Israel. How strongly their states harmonize, how closely their examples match! Think of their state during their time of division and disunity. Those were the nights in which the kings of Persia and the emperors of Byzantium were their overlords. They drove them out of their pasturelands from the river valleys of Iraq and the world's abundance of green herbage into tracts where bitter wormwood grew, where hot winds blew, and life was harsh. They left them poor and abject, camel-herders tending to their beasts' sores and harvesting their wool. They lived as the most wretched of nations, with the least fertile fields, with no mission under whose wing they could seek shelter, no column of unity on whose strength they could depend. Their situation was volatile, their hands discordant, their numbers scattered. They were trapped in a hard trial and crushed under rocks of ignorance: they buried baby girls alive,[1] worshipped idols, cut ties of kinship, and raided one another. Observe the abundance of God's blessings on them. He sent them a messenger, secured their obedience through his religion, and gathered their company within his mission. See how bounty spread the wings of her generosity over

---

1 Reference to Qurʾan, Takwīr 81:8. On female infanticide in pre-Islamic Arabia, see Ḥ 13:174–177; F 362–364; B 766–768.

جداول نعيمها والتفّت الملّة بهم في عوائد بركتها فأصبحوا في نعمتها غَرِقين وعن خضرة عيشها فَكِهين فكهين قد تربّعت الأمور بهم في ظلّ سلطان قاهر وآوَتْهم الحال إلى كنف عزّ غالب وتعطّفت الأمور عليهم في ذُرى مُلْك ثابت فهم حُكّام على العالمين وملوك في أطراف الأرضين يملكون الأمور على مَن كان يملكها عليهم ويُمضون الأحكام فيمن كان يمضيها فيهم لا تُغمَز لهم قَناة ولا تُقرَع لهم صَفاة.

1.190.11 ألا وإنّكم قد نفضتم أيديكم من حبل الطاعة وثَلَمتم حصن الله المضروب عليكم بأحكام الجاهليّة وإنّ الله سبحانه قد امْتَنّ على جماعة هذه الأمّة فيما عقد بينهم من حبل هذه الأُلفة التي يتنقّلون في ظلّها ويأوون إلى كنفها بنعمة لا يعرف أحد من المخلوقين لها قيمة لأنّها أرجح من كلّ ثمن وأجلّ من كلّ خطر. واعلموا أنّكم صرتم بعد الهجرة أعرابًا وبعد الموالاة أحزابًا ما تتعلّقون من الإسلام إلّا باسمه ولا تعرفون من الإيمان إلّا رسمه تقولون النار ولا العار وكأنّكم تريدون أن تُكفِئوا الإسلام على وجهه انتهاكًا لحريمه ونقضًا لميثاقه الذي وضعه الله لكم حرمًا في أرضه وأمنًا بين خلقه وإنّكم إن لجأتم إلى غيره حاربكم أهل الكفر ثمّ لا جبريلَ ولا ميكائيلَ ولا مهاجرين ولا أنصار ينصرونكم إلّا المُقارَعة بالسيف حتّى يحكم الله بينكم وإنّ عندكم الأمثال من بأس الله وقوارعه وأيّامه ووقائعه فلا تستبطئوا وعيده جهلًا بأخذه وتهاونًا ببطشه[1] ويأسًا من بأسه فإنّ الله سبحانه لم يلعن القرن الماضي بين أيديكم إلّا لتركهم الأمر بالمعروف والنهي عن المنكر فلعن السفهاء لركوب المعاصي والحلماء لترك التناهي. ألا وقد قطعتم قيد

____

[1] ن، م، ه، ومصحّحة في ش: كذا.ي، وأصل ش: ‹ببسطه›.

them and the wellsprings of her delights flowed. See how the new religion gathered them within the gifts of its grace. They were immersed in its bounty, joyful in the fresh greenness of its way of life. Their affairs reposed comfortably in the shade of powerful authority, events brought them under the aegis of victorious might, and affairs looked kindly upon them, as they lived in ease in the protection of an established empire. They became rulers of the world and kings over the far reaches of the earth, controlling the affairs of those who had controlled theirs, and issuing commands to those who had commanded them. ⟨Their spear became hard, their rock uncrushable.⟩[1]

1.190.11 Hark! Your hands have loosed the rope of allegiance and breached God's fortress by indulging in judgments from the Age of Ignorance. This, when God has blessed this congregation by binding them with bonds of affection, so they can move in its shade and take refuge in its shelter! No one can fathom the value of this favor; it exceeds any price and is grander than any eminence. Know this: After your migration to Muḥammad's city, you have reverted to living as rough Bedouins,[2] after loyal unison, you have again split into factions. You own nothing of Islam except its name, you recognize nothing of belief except its ritual. You say, "Flames rather than shame!" as though you wished to knock Islam over on its face, rending its holiness, and breaking the covenant by which God gave you a sanctuary upon his earth and a source of safety among the earth's people. If you seek any other refuge, unbelievers will wage war against you, and neither Gabriel nor Michael, neither Immigrants nor Allies, will come to your aid.[3] You will see only the clashing of swords until God rules between you once and for all. You have witnessed examples of God's might, of his blows, battle-days, and onslaughts. Do not ignore his chastisement, underestimate his assault, and undervalue his force, do not think his retribution will be slow in coming! God damned the generation just before you because they ceased to command good and forbid evil. He damned the immature because they mounted the steeds of sin and the mature because they ceased to forbid.

---

1 Arabic idioms. Lit. ⟨Their spear could never be squeezed (*lā tughmaz*), and their rock could never be crushed (*lā tuqraʿ*)⟩. For references in poetry re "squeezing" (*ghamz*) of a spear, see Ibn Manẓūr, *Lisān*, s.v. "Gh-M-Z." ⟨Their rock cannot be crushed⟩ (*lā tuqraʿu lahum ṣafāh*) is attributed to the Prophet in Nuwayrī, *Nihāyah*, s.v. "Ṣ-F-W."

2 Re the migration (*hijrah*), I have added the words "to Muḥammad's city" for clarity. Re Bedouins (*aʿrāb*), the line signifies that "after having accepted the refinements of Islam, you have reverted to the factional ways of pre-Islamic Arabians." B 768; Ḥ 13:18. Bedouins are chastised for hypocrisy in the Qurʾan, Tawbah 9:97, 99.

3 Gabriel and Michael are two archangels. Immigrants (*Muhājirūn*) are those who migrated to Muḥammad in Medina, and Allies (*Anṣār*) are the Medinans who supported him.

الإسلام وعطّلتم حدوده وأَمَتُّم أحكامه. ألا وقد أمرني الله بقتال أهل البغي والنكث والفساد في الأرض فأمّا الناكثون فقد قاتلت وأمّا القاسطون فقد جاهدت وأمّا المارقة فقد دوّخت وأمّا شيطان الرَّدْهة فقد كُفيته بصعقة سمعتُ لها وَجْبة قلبه ورَجّة صدره وبقي بقيّة من أهل البغي ولئن أذن الله في الكرّة عليهم لأُدِيلنّ منهم إلّا ما يتشذّر في أطراف الأرض تشذّرا.

1.190.12   أنا وضعت بكلكل العرب وكسرت نواجم قرون ربيعة ومضر وقد علمتم موضعي من رسول الله صلّى الله عليه وآله بالقرابة القريبة والمنزلة الخصيصة. وضعني في حَجْره وأنا وليد يضمّني إلى صدره ويكنفني في فراشه ويمسّني جسده ويُشمّني عَرْفه وكان يمضغ الشيء ثمّ يُلقمنيه وما وجد لي كَذْبة في قول ولا خَطْلة في فعل ولقد قرن الله به صلّى الله عليه وآله من لدن كان فطيمًا أعظم ملك من ملائكته يسلك به طريق المكارم ومحاسن أخلاق العالم ليله ونهاره ولقد كنت أتبعه اتّباع الفصيل أثرَ أمّه يرفع لي في كلّ يوم علمًا من أخلاقه ويأمرني بالاقتداء به ولقد كان يجاور في كلّ سنة بِحِراء

Hark! You have cut off Islam's restrictions, stripped off its constraints, and killed off its commands. Hark! God has commanded me to fight those who commit treachery, break their pledge, and cause mayhem on earth: I have fought those who broke their pledge, battled those who acted wrongfully, and subdued those who left the faith.[1] The Satan of the Stony Hollow was taken out by a thunderbolt that made his heart scream and his breast quake.[2] A small number of rebels remain: If God permits another attack, I shall most certainly prevail, except for the handful that escape, who will scatter to the corners of the realm.

1.190.12 It was I who felled the trunk of the Arabs and crushed the horns of Rabīʿah and Muḍar.[3] Besides, you all know my relationship with God's Messenger, our close kinship and special intimacy.[4] He took me to his bosom as a newborn, clasping me to his breast and covering me with his bedspread, his body touching mine and I inhaling his fragrance; he would chew a piece of food to soften it then place it in my mouth. He never found falseness in my words or foulness in my actions. Ever since the Messenger's own infancy, God had placed his greatest angel to guide him day and night on the path of virtue and the most beautiful traits. I would follow him as a camel calf follows its mother, and each day he would raise in front of me a banner displaying his virtuous character and command me to emulate. Every year he would retreat to Mount Ḥirāʾ for prayer, where no one but I saw him. In those days, not one home housed any supporters

---

1 The pledge-breakers (*nākithūn*) are said to be ʿAlī's opponents at the Battle of the Camel, the wrongdoers (*qāsiṭūn*) are Muʿāwiyah and his Syrian supporters, and those who left the faith (*māriqūn*) are the Kharijites, the three groups that ʿAlī fought in the Battles of the Camel, Ṣiffīn, and Nahrawān. Muḥammad's hadith, whose terminology ʿAlī echoes in his oration, is reported as, ⟨You [O ʿAlī] will battle the pledge-breakers, the wrongdoers, and the faith-leavers after me⟩. Ḥ 13:183–184; B 771–772; F 364–365.

2 The Satan of the Stony Hollow (*shayṭān al-radʾhah*) is a man known as *Dhū al-Thudayyah*, "The Man with the Breast," called thus because of a mass of flesh on his shoulder, a Kharijite whose death at Nahrawān ʿAlī said the Prophet had told him would signal his own imminent martyrdom. ʿAlī personally sought out Dhū al-Thudayyah's corpse among the dead at Nahrawān, and when he saw it, he exclaimed, "God is great! I have never lied, nor has [the Prophet] lied to me." Ḥ 13:183–184; B 771–772; F 364–365.

3 Refers to ʿAlī's slaying of famous pre-Islamic Arabian warriors in single combat during the early Muslims' battles, when he was only around twenty years of age, thereby playing a major role in Islam's military and political ascendancy. Muḍar is the eponymous ancestor of the Prophet's own tribe of Meccan Quraysh, who formed the largest bloc of his enemies, and ʿAlī slew several of their leaders in the Muslims' early battles. The Rabīʿah tribe was divided among ʿAlī and his opponents during the Battles of the Camel and Ṣiffīn, and ʿAlī slew several of their leaders who fought against him then. B 772; Ḥ 13:198.

4 Muḥammad had taken the infant ʿAlī as his ward, and ʿAlī grew up in Muḥammad's care. Details in Ḥ 13:198–212; B 772–776.

فأراه ولا يراه غيري ولم يجمع بيت واحد يومئذ في الإسلام غير رسول الله صلّى الله عليه وآله وخديجة وأنا ثالثهما أرى نور الوحي والرسالة وأشمّ ريح النبوّة. ولقد سمعت رنّة الشيطان حين نزل الوحي عليه صلّى الله عليه وآله فقلت يا رسول الله ما هذه الرنّة فقال هذا الشيطان قد أيس من عبادته إنّك تسمع ما أسمع وترى ما أرى إلّا أنّك لست بنبيّ وإنّك لوزير وإنّك لعلى خير.

ولقد كنت معه صلّى الله عليه وآله لمّا أتاه الملأ من قريش فقالوا له يا محمّد إنّك قد ادّعيت عظيمًا لم يَدَّعه آباؤك ولا أحد من بيتك ونحن نسألك أمرًا إن أجبتنا إليه وأريتناه علمنا أنّك نبيّ ورسول وإن لم تفعل علمنا أنّك ساحر كذّاب فقال لهم صلّى الله عليه وما تسألون قالوا تدعو لنا هذه الشجرة حتّى تنقلع بعروقها وتقف بين يديك فقال صلّى الله عليه وآله ﴿إِنَّ اللَّهَ عَلَىٰ كُلِّ شَيْءٍ قَدِيرٌ﴾ فإن فعل الله ذلك لكم أتؤمنون وتشهدون بالحقّ قالوا نعم قال فإنّي سأريكم ما تطلبون وإنّي لأعلم أنّكم لا تَفيئون إلى خير وأنّ فيكم من يُطرَح في القليب ومن يُحزِّب الأحزاب. ثمّ قال يا أيّتها الشجرة إن كنت تؤمنين بالله واليوم الآخر وتعلمين أنّي رسول الله فانقلعي بعروقك حتّى تقفي بين يديّ بإذن الله. فوالذي بعثه بالحقّ لأنقلعت بعروقها وجاءت ولها دَويّ شديد وقصف كقصف أجنحة الطير حتّى وقفت بين يدي رسول الله صلّى الله عليه وآله مرفرفة وألقت بغصنها الأعلى على رسول الله وببعض أغصانها على مَنكِبي وكنت عن يمينه عليه السلام فلمّا نظر القوم إلى ذلك قالوا علوًّا واستكبارًا فمُرْها فليأتك نصفُها

of Islam, it was just the Messenger and Khadījah, and I was the third. Throughout, I saw the light of revelation and messengerhood, and inhaled the fragrance of prophecy. I heard Satan's cry when revelation descended on the Messenger, and when I asked, "What is this cry?" he answered me, ⟨This is Satan, who now despairs of being worshipped. You see what I see and hear what I hear, ʿAlī, though you are not a prophet, but my vizier, and on the path of virtue.⟩

I was with the Messenger when a group of the Quraysh came to him and said, "Muḥammad, you have made a grand claim, one that none of your forebears or any of your house has ever made. We want to ask you to do something: If you are able to do it, if you are able to show it to us, we will be convinced that you are indeed a prophet and a messenger, but if you don't, then we will know that you are a magician and a liar." The Messenger responded, "What do you seek?" They answered, "Ask this tree to pull up its roots and come forward to stand before you."[1] The Messenger exclaimed, "«Truly, God is powerful over all things.»[2] If God does this for you, will you believe and testify to the truth?" They replied with one voice, "Yes, we will." The Messenger said to them, "All right, I will show you what you demand, although I know that you will not turn to virtue. I know that there are among you men who will be cast into the Well, and others who will convene the fated Confederacy."[3] Then he intoned, "O tree, if you believe in God and the last day, if you know that I am God's messenger, then, with God's permission, pull up your roots and come stand in front of me!" I swear by the one who sent Muḥammad with the truth that the tree pulled up its roots and came forward with a loud rumble and a fluttering like the fluttering of birds' wings. Boughs rustling, it came to stand before the Messenger and let its highest branches fall over him. Some branches brushed my shoulders—I was standing to his right. When the men from Quraysh saw this, they demanded with pride and arrogance, "Now command half of it to come to you, while the other half stays in its place." The Messenger commanded the tree to do this. Half of it came forward most wondrously and with an even louder

---

1   Recounts the Miracle of the Tree that Muslims believe Muḥammad performed in Mecca. B 776; Ḥ 13:214.

2   Qurʾan, Baqarah 2:20, 109, 148, Āl ʿImrān 3:165, Naḥl 16:77, Nūr 24:45, ʿAnkabūt 29:20, Fāṭir 35:1.

3   "Persons cast into the Well" is a prophecy about those of the Quraysh who would be killed fighting against Muḥammad at the Battle of Badr in 2/624 and were thrown into its wells, including ʿUtbah ibn Rabīʿah ibn ʿAbd Shams, Shaybah ibn Rabīʿah ibn ʿAbd Shams, Umayyah ibn ʿAbd Shams, Abū Jahl (ʿAmr ibn Hishām ibn al-Mughīrah), and Walīd ibn al-Mughīrah. "Others who will convene the fated Confederacy" is a prophecy about those of the Quraysh who would spearhead the Battle of the Confederates in 5/627, including Abū Sufyān Ṣakhr ibn Ḥarb ibn Umayyah, ʿAmr ibn ʿAbd Wadd, Ṣafwān ibn Umayyah, ʿIkrimah ibn Abī Jahl, and Suhayl ibn ʿAmr. B 776; Ḥ 13:214; F 365.

ويبقى نصفها فأمرها بذلك فأقبل إليه نصفها كأعجب إقبال وأشدّه دويًّا فكادت تلتفّ برسول الله صلّى الله عليه وآله فقالوا كفرًا وعُتوًّا فُرَّ هذا النصف فليرجع إلى نصفه كما كان فأمره عليه السلام فرجع فقلت أنا ⟨لا إله إلّا الله⟩ إنّي أوّل مؤمن بك يا رسول الله وأوّل من آمن بأنّ الشجرة فعلت ما فعلت بأمر الله تصديقًا لنبوّتك وإجلالًا لكلمتك فقال القوم كلّهم بل ساحر كذّاب عجيب السحر خفيف فيه وهل يصدّقك في أمرك إلّا مثل هذا يعنونني. وإنّي لمن قوم لا تأخذهم في الله لَومة لائم سيماهم سيما الصّدّيقين وكلامهم كلام الأبرار عُمّار الليل ومنار النهار متمسّكون بحبل[1] القرآن يحيون سُنن الله وسنن رسوله لا يستكبرون ولا يعلون[2] ولا يَغُلّون ولا يفسدون قلوبهم في الجنان وأجسادهم في العمل.

1.191   ومن خطبة له عليه السلام. روي أنّ صاحبًا له يقال له هَمّام كان رجلًا عابدًا فقال له يا أمير المؤمنين صف لي المتّقين كأنّي أنظر إليهم فتثاقل عن جوابه ثمّ قال يا همّام اتّق الله وأحسن فـ﴿إِنَّ اللّٰهَ مَعَ الَّذِينَ اتَّقَوا وَالَّذِينَ هُمْ مُحْسِنُونَ﴾ فلم يقنع همّام بذلك القول حتّى عزم عليه قال نحمد الله وأثنى عليه وصلّى على النبيّ صلّى الله عليه وآله ثمّ قال أمّا بعد. فإنّ الله سبحانه خلق الخلق حين خلقهم غنيًّا عن طاعتهم آمنًا بمعصيتهم لأنّه لا تضرّه معصية من عصاه ولا تنفعه طاعة من أطاعه. فقسم بينهم معايشهم ووضعهم من الدنيا مواضعهم.

---

١ ش، ن، ي، ه: كذا. م، ونسخة في ه: أضيفت ⟨الله⟩.   ٢ م، ي، ه: كذا. ش، ن: ⟨يغلون⟩.

rumble, and it almost wrapped itself around the Messenger. The group then cried out in rejection and insolence, "Command this half to go back to its other half as it was." The Messenger did so, and the tree went back. I spontaneously exclaimed, "⟨There is no god but God!⟩ I am the first to profess belief in you, O Messenger of God, the first to profess belief that the tree did what it did by God's command to prove the truth of your prophethood, the first to offer obeisance to your word!" That group, however, every one of them, sneered, "No, you are a magician and a liar! Your magic is quite something, and you are good at it. Only someone like this nobody—meaning me—would believe you to be a prophet." People, I belong to a group who care not if they are criticized when their actions are for the sake of God! Our mark is the mark of those who uphold the truth of God's word, our speech is the speech of the virtuous. We inhabit the night with prayer, we are beacons of light during the day. We hold fast to the Qur'an, keeping alive God's ways and the practices of his Messenger. We never behave with arrogance, never conduct ourselves with conceit, never cheat, are never corrupt. Our hearts are in paradise, while our bodies are occupied here with doing good.

1.191 From an oration by ʿAlī: It is reported that one of ʿAlī's companions, a man named Hammām, who was devoted to worship, said to him, "Commander of the Faithful, describe to me the pious, such that I see them before my eyes!" ʿAlī hesitated, then answered, "Hammām, be pious and do good, for «God is with those who are pious and do good.»[1] Hammām was not satisfied with this brief answer and persisted. The narrator continues that ʿAlī then thanked God, praised him, invoked blessings on the Prophet, and delivered the following oration:[2]

When God created people, he created them not needing their obedience, and untouched by their disobedience. The disobedience of those who disobey does not harm him, and the obedience of those who obey does not benefit him. He distributed sustenance among them and gave them various stations in this life.

---

1 Qurʾan, Naḥl 16:128.

2 Presumably in Kufa, during ʿAlī's caliphate 35–40/656–661, based on the context given by Ibn Ṭalḥah (*Maṭālib*, 269), in which a few individuals approached ʿAlī asking for a favor, presumably money; they would have been more likely to petition ʿAlī when he, as caliph, was in charge of the treasury. Ibn Ṭalḥah further narrates that they identified themselves as his followers, to which ʿAlī replied, "I don't see any signs of my true followers in you." At this time, Hammām asked ʿAlī to explain the signs of his true followers (*shīʿah*, rather than "the pious, *muttaqūn*," as per the present volume), and ʿAlī responded with the oration at hand. On this text, see Qutbuddin, "Piety and Virtue in Early Islam: Two Sermons by Imam Ali," and Qutbuddin, "Classical Islamic Oration's Art, Function, and Life-Altering Power of Persuasion: The Ultimate Response by Hammam to Ali's Sermon on Piety, and by Hurr to Husayn's Battle Oration in Karbala." Hammām (d. ca. 36/656), according to the commentators, is Hammām ibn Shurayḥ ibn Yazīd (Ḥ 10:134), or Hammām ibn ʿUbādah ibn Khuthaym (B 599).

فالمتّقون فيها هم أهل الفضائل منطقهم الصواب وملبسهم الاقتصاد ومشيهم التواضع غضّوا أبصارهم عمّا حرّم الله عليهم ووقفوا أسماعهم على العلم النافع لهم نزلت أنفسهم منهم في البلاء كالذي نزلت في الرخاء لولا الأجل الذي كتب الله لهم لم تستقرّ أرواحهم في أجسادهم طرفة عين شوقاً إلى الثواب وخوفاً من العقاب عظم الخالق في أنفسهم فصغر ما دونه في أعينهم. فهم والجنّة كمن قد رآها فهم فيها منعَّمون وهم والنار كمن قد رآها فهم فيها معذّبون قلوبهم محزونة وشرورهم مأمونة وأجسادهم نحيفة وحاجتهم خفيفة وأنفسهم عفيفة صبروا أيّامًا قصيرة أعقبتهم راحة طويلة تجارة مربحة يسّرها لهم ربّهم أرادتهم الدنيا ولم يريدوها وأسرتهم ففدوا أنفسهم منها.

أمّا الليل فصافّون أقدامهم تالُون لأجزاء القرآن يرتّلونها ترتيلًا يحزّنون به أنفسهم ويستثيرون به دواء دائهم فإذا مرّوا بآية فيها تشويق ركنوا إليها طمعًا وتطلّعت نفوسهم إليها شوقًا وظنّوا أنّها نَصْبَ أعينهم وإذا مرّوا بآية فيها تخويف أصغوا إليها مسامع قلوبهم وظنّوا أنّ زفير جهنم وشهيقها في أصول آذانهم فهم حانُونْ على أوساطهم مفترشون لجباههم وأكفّهم وركبهم وأطراف أقدامهم يطلبون إلى الله في فَكاك رقابهم. وأمّا النهار فحلماء علماء أبرار أتقياء قد بَراهم الخوف بَرْيَ القِداح ينظر إليهم الناظر فيحسبهم مرضى وما بالقوم من مرض ويقول قد خولطوا ولقد خالطهم أمر عظيم لا يرضون من أعمالهم القليل ولا يستكثرون الكثير فهم لأنفسهم متّهمون ومن أعمالهم مشفقون إذا زُكِّيَ أحد منهم خاف ممّا يقال له فيقول أنا أعلم بنفسي من غيري وربّي أعلم منّي بنفسي اللّهمّ لا تؤاخذني بما يقولون واجعلني أفضل ممّا يظنّون واغفر لي ما لا يعلمون.

فمن علامة أحدهم أنّك ترى له قوّة في دين وحزمًا في لين وإيمانًا في يقين وحرصًا في علم وعلمًا في حلم وقصدًا في غنى وخشوعًا في عبادة وتجمّلًا في فاقة وصبرًا في شدّة وطلبًا

The pious in this world are people of virtue. Their speech is rational, their garments simple, and their gait embodies humility. They lower their eyes, avoiding what God has forbidden them to see, and dedicate their ears to hearing words of wisdom that bring them benefit. Their hearts are at peace, both in times of tribulation, and in times of prosperity. If not for the lifespans decreed for them by God, their souls would not tarry in their bodies for the blink of an eye but, yearning for God's reward and fearing his punishment, they would instantly depart. The creator's majesty in their hearts makes all else paltry in their eyes. Paradise is before their eyes—they see it as clearly as though they were already enjoying its blessings. Hellfire too is before their eyes—they see it as clearly as though they were being tortured there. Their hearts are sorrowful, their malice never feared, their bodies emaciated, their needs few, and their persons chaste. They patiently endure their few days here in this world, awaiting the long comfort of the hereafter. Theirs is a profitable transaction bestowed in ease and security by their Lord. The world approached them, but they turned away. It shackled them, but they ransomed their souls and set themselves free.

In the night they stand in worship and recite sections of the Qur'an. They chant them in sweet melody, moving their own hearts to tears, and finding there the cure for their illness. If they come across a verse that rouses their yearning, they consume it hungrily, their hearts stretching out toward it in longing. They see its promised blessings before their eyes. If they come across a verse that stokes their fear, they incline their hearts toward its warning. The hiss and crackle of the inferno fills the innermost recesses of their ears. They bow their backs, laying their forehead, palms, knees, and toes on the ground, beseeching God to free their necks from the Fire. In the day, they are kind, wise, good, and pious. Fear has made them as thin as arrow shafts. The onlooker thinks them ailing, but they are not ill. He says, "They're crazy!" but they are crazed only by something immensely grave. They are not satisfied with a few deeds of goodness, nor do they consider their numerous endeavors too many. They constantly chide themselves and fear the consequence of their actions. If one of them is praised, he is apprehensive, and replies, "I know myself better than you know me, and my Lord knows me even better! Lord, do not hold me to what they say about me, but make me more virtuous than they think I am, and forgive those actions of which they do not know."[1]

Their hallmark is strength in faith, resolve with gentleness, belief with certainty, voracity for knowledge, knowledge with maturity, temperance in affluence, humility in worship, forbearance in indigence, patience in hardship, desire for the licit, enthusiasm in following guidance, and aversion to greed.

---

1   Final lines similar to § 3.90.

في حلال ونشاطًا في هدى وتحرّجًا عن طمع يعمل الأعمال الصالحة وهو على وجل
يمسي وهمّه الشكر ويصبح وهمّه الذكر يبيت حَذِرًا ويصبح فَرِحًا حذرًا لما حُذّر من الغفلة
وفَرِحًا بما أصاب من الفضل والرحمة إن اَستصعبت عليه نفسه فيما تكره لم يعطها سؤلها
فيما تحبّ قرّة عينه فيما لا يزول وزهادته فيما لا يبقى يمزج الحلم بالعلم والقول بالعمل.

تراه قريبًا أملُه قليلًا زللُه خاشعًا قلبه قانعة نفسه منزورًا أكله سهلًا أمره حريزًا دينه
ميّتة شهوته مكظومًا غيظه الخير منه مأمول والشرّ منه مأمون إن كان في الغافلين كُتب
في الذاكرين وإن كان في الذاكرين لم يكتب من الغافلين يعفو عمّن ظلمه ويعطي من
حرمه ويصل من قطعه بعيدًا فحشه لينًا قوله غائبًا منكره حاضرًا معروفه مقبلًا خيره
مدبرًا شرّه في الزلازل وقور وفي المكاره صبور وفي الرخاء شَكور لا يحيف على من
يبغض ولا يأثم فيمن يحبّ يعترف بالحقّ قبل أن يشهد عليه لا يضيع ما اَستُحفظ ولا
ينسى ما ذُكِّر ولا ينابز بالألقاب ولا يضارّ بالجار ولا يشمت بالمصائب ولا يدخل في
الباطل ولا يخرج من الحقّ. إن صمت لم يغمّه صمته وإن ضحك لم يعل صوته وإن بُغي
عليه صبر حتّى يكون الله هو الذي ينتقم له نفسه منه في عناء والناس منه في راحة
أتعب نفسه لآخرته وأراح الناس من نفسه بُعده عمّن تباعد عنه زهدٌ ونزاهة ودنوّه ممّن
دنا منه لين ورحمة ليس تباعده بكبر وعظمة ولا دنوّه بمكر وخديعة.

قال فصعق همّام صعقة كانت نَفْسُه فيها فقال أمير المؤمنين عليه السلام أما والله لقد كنت
أخافها عليه ثمّ قال هكذا تصنع المواعظ البالغة بأهلها. فقال له قائل فما بالك يا أمير المؤمنين
فقال وَيحَك إنّ لكلّ أجل وقتًا لا يعدوه وسببًا لا يتجاوزه فمهلًا لا تعد لمثلها فإنّما نفث الشيطان
على لسانك.

They do good while always being on guard. They spend the night thanking God and the morning praising him. They sleep vigilant and awake in joy, vigilant because they have been warned against neglect, and joyful because of the blessings and mercy they have gained. If their ego bucks against doing something it dislikes, they do not give it free rein to do what it desires. Their joy is centered on whatever brings lasting reward, while they care little for ephemeral baubles that will not remain. They combine maturity with learning and words with action.

You will see this—their needs are few, their slips are rare, their hearts are humble, their souls are content, their fare is meager, their manner is affable, their faith is secure, their appetite is dead, and their rage is held in check. Their goodness is always anticipated, their evil never feared. If they sit with the heedless, they are still numbered among the heedful, and if they sit with the heedful, they are not numbered among the heedless. They forgive those who oppress them, give to those who refuse them, and foster those who cut them off. Lewdness is far removed from their persons, gentleness imbues their words, and wrongdoing is absent from their actions. Their decency is ever present, their goodness always forthcoming, and their wickedness always distant. In calamities they remain dignified, in catastrophes they remain patient, in happy times they remain thankful. They never wrong an enemy or transgress to help loved ones. They acknowledge the dues they owe to others before testimony is given against them. They never squander what they have been given in trust, they never forget what they have been reminded of, they never call others vile names, they never harm a neighbor, they never gloat at another's misfortune, they never enter into wrongdoing or abandon the truth. If they are silent, their silence is not burdensome. If they laugh, they are not raucous. If attacked treacherously, they are patient—God himself avenges them. They weary themselves by constant chiding, while never causing others unease. They push themselves to prepare for the hereafter and never cause others harm. Chaste and upright, they stay away from those who distance themselves. Kind and merciful, they draw near to those who seek to come close. Their detachment is not out of arrogance or grandiosity, and their accessibility is not out of cunning or trickery.

Raḍī: The narrator said: Hammām fell as though struck by a thunderbolt and died then and there. The Commander of the Faithful exclaimed, "By God, I feared this effect on him!" Then he continued, "This is what strong counsel does to people who listen!" A man challenged ʿAlī, "Commander of the Faithful, how about you, then?" and ʿAlī replied angrily, "Good grief! Each lifespan has an allotted time that it does not transgress and a cause that it does not overstep. Slow down! Don't repeat this kind of talk again, for it was Satan who spoke with your tongue."

1.192 ومن خطبة له عليه السلام يصف فيها المنافقين

نحمده على ما وَفّق له من الطاعة وذادَ عنه من المعصية. ونسأله لمنّته تماماً وبحبله أعتصاماً.
ونشهد أنّ محمّداً عبده ورسوله خاض إلى رضوان الله كلّ غمرة وتجرّع فيه كلّ غصّة وقد
تلوّن له الأدنَون وتألّب عليه الأقصَون وخلعت إليه العرب أعنّتها وضربت الى محاربته
بطون رواحلها حتّى أنزلت بساحته عداوتها من أبعد الدار وأسحق المزار.

أوصيكم عباد الله بتقوى الله وأحذّركم أهل النفاق فإنّهم الضالّون المضلّون والزالّون
المزلّون يتلوّنون ألواناً ويفتنّون أفتناناً ويعمدونكم بكلّ عماد ويرصدونكم بكلّ مِرصاد
قلوبهم دويّة وصفاحهم نقيّة يمشون الخفاء ويدبّون الضرّاء وصفهم دواء وقولهم شفاء
وفعلهم الداء العَياء حسدة الرخاء ومؤكّدوا البلاء ومقنطوا الرجاء لهم بكلّ طريق
صريع وإلى كلّ قلب شفيع ولكلّ شجو دموع يتقارضون الثناء ويتراقبون الجزاء إن
سألوا ألحفوا وإن عذلوا كشفوا وإن حكموا أسرفوا قد أعدّوا لكلّ حقّ باطلاً ولكلّ
قائم مائلاً ولكلّ حيّ قاتلاً ولكلّ باب مفتاحاً ولكلّ ليل مصباحاً يتوصّلون إلى الطمع
باليأس ليقيموا به أسواقهم وينفّقوا به أعلاقهم يقولون فيشبّهون ويصفون فيموّهون قد
هيّبوا الطريق وأضلعوا المضيق فهم لُمة الشيطان وحُمة النيران ﴿أُولَٰئِكَ حِزْبُ الشَّيْطَانِ
أَلَا إِنَّ حِزْبَ الشَّيْطَانِ هُمُ الْخَاسِرُونَ﴾.

1.193 ومن خطبة له عليه السلام

الحمد لله الذي أظهر من آثار سلطانه وجلال كبريائه ما حيّر مُقَل العقول من عجائب
قدرته وردع خطرات هَمَاهِم النفوس عن عرفان كُنْه صفته. وأشهد أن لا إله إلّا الله
شهادة إيمان وإيقان وإخلاص وإذعان. وأشهد أنّ محمّداً عبده ورسوله أرسله وأعلام
الهدى دارسة ومناهج الدين طامسة فصدع بالحقّ ونصح للخلق وهدى إلى الرشد وأمر
بالقصد صلّى الله عليه وآله.

1.192 From an oration by ʿAlī in which he describes the hypocrites who feign faith:
We praise God for having guided us toward obedience and guarded us from disobedience. We ask him to perfect his blessings and help us hold fast to his rope. We testify that Muḥammad is his servant and messenger, who plunged into every swelling wave, and swallowed every choking morsel, to earn his pleasure. Close relatives showed their true colors and turned away, while distant kin banded against him; loosening their horses' reins and whipping the bellies of their camels, Arab tribesmen raced from the furthest, most distant abodes to fight him, until their rancor alighted in his courtyard.

Servants of God, I counsel you to remain conscious of him! I warn you against hypocrites, who, having strayed from the path, lead others astray, and having slipped, cause others to slip. Chameleon-like, they change color, change narratives; they aim at you from behind every pillar and lie in wait at every lookout. Their hearts are diseased while their faces look fresh, they walk with stealth and creep through the thicket, their words seem to heal but their actions bring chronic illness, they envy good fortune, magnify hardship, and destroy hope. In every path they leave a body felled, into every heart they find access, for every sad situation they produce false tears. They trade praises and expect material reward. When they solicit, they do not stop, when they turn away, they expose your shame, when they are given rule, they commit all kinds of excess. For every right, they have prepared an opposing wrong, for everything upright, something that will make it bend, for every living thing a killer, for every door a key, and for every night a lamp. They nourish their greed by creating desperation, in order to sustain their markets and sell their expensive wares; they speak to confuse and describe to delude; they frighten you from the path and create confusion in the narrow defile. They are Satan's host and hellfire's scorpion-sting. «These are Satan's faction. Hark! Satan's faction are losers.»[1]

1.193 From an oration by ʿAlī:
Praise God! He has revealed traces of his authority and the magnificence of his majesty—their mighty wonders dazzle the intellect's eyes and prevent the soul's flashing thoughts from plumbing the depths of his attributes. I testify with belief, certainty, sincerity, and humility that there is no god but God. I testify that Muḥammad is his servant and messenger, whom he sent when guidance's banners had frayed and religion's pathways had eroded to declare the truth, counsel the world, guide toward virtue, and command temperance. May God bless him and his descendants.

---

1 Qurʾan, Mujādalah 58:19.

واعلموا عباد الله أنّه لم يخلقكم عبثًا ولم يرسلكم هَمَلًا علم مبلغ نعمه عليكم وأحصى
إحسانه إليكم فاستفتحوه واستنجحوه واطلبوا إليه واستمنحوه فما قطعكم عنه حجاب ولا
أغلق عنكم دونه باب وإنّه لبكلّ مكان وفي كلّ حين وأوان ومع كلّ إنس وجانّ لا
يَثلِمه العطاء ولا ينقصه الحِباء ولا يستنفده سائل ولا يستقصيه نائل ولا يَلويه شخص
عن شخص ولا يُلهيه صوت عن صوت ولا تَحجُزه هِبة عن سلب ولا يشغله غضب
عن رحمة ولا تُولّهه رحمة عن عقاب ولا تُجِنّه البطون عن الظهور ولا تقطعه الظهور
عن البطون قرب فنأى وعلا فدنا وظهر فبطن وبطن فعلن ودَانَ ولم يُدَنْ لم يذرأ الخلق
باحتيال ولا استعان بهم لكَلال.

أوصيكم عباد الله بتقوى الله فإنّها الزِّمام والقِوام فتمسّكوا بوثائقها واعتصموا
بحقائقها تَؤُلْ بكم إلى أكنان الدعة وأوطان السعة ومعاقل الحرز ومنازل العزّ في ﴿يَوْمٍ
تَشْخَصُ فِيهِ الْأَبْصَارُ﴾ وتُظلِم له الأقطار وتعطّل فيه صُروم العِشار وينفخ في الصور
فتزهق كلّ مُهجة وتبكَم كلّ لَهجة وتذلّ الشمّ الشوامخ والصمّ الرواسخ فيصير صلْدها سرابًا
رَقرَقًا ومعهدها قاعًا سَمْلَقًا فلا شفيع يشفع ولا حميم يدفع ولا معذرة تنفع.

1.194 ومن خطبة له عليه السلام

بعثه حين لا علم قائم ولا منار ساطع ولا منهج واضح.
أوصيكم عباد الله بتقوى الله وأحذّركم الدنيا فإنّها دار شخوص ومحلّة تنغيص ساكنها
ظاعن وقاطنها بائن تميد بأهلها مَيَدان السفينة تصفّقها العواصف في لُجَج البحار فمنهم
الغَرِق الوَبِق ومنهم الناجي على متون الأمواج تَحفِزه الرياح بأذيالها وتحمله على أهوالها
فما غَرِق منها فليس بمستدرك وما نجا منها فإلى مَهلك. عباد الله الآن فاعملوا والألسن
مطلقة والأبدان صحيحة والأعضاء لَدْنة والمتقلّب فسيح والمجال عريض قبل إرهاق
الفوت وحلول الموت فحقّقوا عليكم نزوله ولا تنتظروا قدومه.

Servants of God! Know that God has not created you in jest, nor cut you loose without direction. He knows the extent of his blessings and keeps track of his bounties, so ask him to grant you victory and success, seek his favors and generosity. No veil separates you from his favors, nor is any door to him closed. He is present in every place, in each time and moment, with every human and jinn. Generosity does not deplete his possessions, charity does not decrease them, supplicants do not use them up, and gifts do not drain their depths. One person does not divert his attention from another, nor does one voice distract him from another. But giving also does not prevent him from taking away. Anger does not preoccupy him from mercy, nor does mercy confound him from punishing. The visible does not block him from the hidden, nor does the hidden separate him from the visible. He is close yet distant, transcendent yet near, manifest yet hidden, hidden yet open, and close yet utterly beyond reach. He did not create the world through artifice, nor did fatigue ever prompt him to solicit help.

Servants of God! I counsel you to be conscious of God! Piety is your harness and mainstay. Hold fast to its ropes and seek protection in its truths, for they will lead you to comfortable dwellings, expansive homelands, protective fortresses, and mighty abodes, on «the day when eyes stare fixedly in terror»,[1] the earth falls dark, camel mares in full term are abandoned, and the horn is blown.[2] At that time, spirits will perish, and tongues will be struck dumb. Lofty peaks and rugged rocks will crumble, their hardness will turn into a shifting mirage, their fastness will convert to bare, flat desert. In that moment, no intercessor will intercede, no kin will offer protection, no excuse will avail.

1.194 From an oration by ʿAlī:
God sent Muḥammad when no waymark was raised, no beacon shone, and there was no clear road.

Servants of God! I counsel you to be conscious of God! I warn you of this world, a habitation you must vacate, a quarter plagued by suffering; its tenants must depart, and its occupants must leave. It heaves—with its people—like a ship tossed by stormy winds on the swells of the deep sea; some drown and perish, while others are saved on waves whose strong currents carry them away and dash them into further dangers; those who drown cannot be saved, while those who are saved will still die. Servants of God, take heed now! Act while tongues are free, bodies are sound, limbs are pliant, the course is free, and the track is open. Act before this chance is gone and death arrives. Know that it will come upon you—don't delay until it is here.

---

1 Qurʾan, Ibrāhīm 14:42.
2 Reference to Qurʾan, Takwīr 81:4, Nabaʾ 78:18. Camel mares in full term would in normal times be the most carefully tended.

1.195 ومن خطبة له عليه السلام

ولقد علم المستحفظون من أصحاب محمّد صلّى الله عليه وآله أنّي لم أُرُدَّ على الله ولا على رسوله ساعة قطّ ولقد واسيته بنفسي في المواطن التي تنكص فيها الأبطال وتتأخّر فيها الأقدام نَجْدة أكرمني الله بها. ولقد قبِض رسول الله صلّى الله عليه وآله وإنّ رأسه لعلى صدري ولقد سالت نفسه في كفّي فأمررتها على وجهي ولقد وليت غسله والملائكة أعواني فضَجّت الدار والأفنية ملأٌ يهبط وملأٌ يعرج وما فارقت سمعي هَيْنَمةٌ منهم يصلّون عليه حتّى وارَيناه في ضريحه فمن ذا أحقّ به منّي حيًّا وميّتًا فأنفذوا على بصائركم ولتصدق نيّاتكم في جهاد عدوّكم فو الله الذي لا إلٰه إلّا هو وإنّي لعلى جادّة الحقّ وإنّهم لعلى مزلّة الباطل.

أقول ما تسمعون وأستغفر الله لي ولكم.

1.196 ومن خطبة له عليه السلام

1.196.1 يعلم عَجيج الوحوش في الفَلَوات ومعاصي العباد في الخلوات واختلاف النِّينان في البحار الغامرات وتلاطم الماء بالرياح العاصفات. وأشهد أنّ محمّدًا نجيب الله وسفير وحيه ورسول رحمته. أمّا بعد.

فإنّي أوصيكم بتقوى الله الذي ابتدأ خلقكم وإليه يكون معادكم وبه نجاح طَلِبتكم وإليه منتهى رغبتكم ونحوه قصد سبيلكم وإليه مرامي مفزعكم فإنّ تقوى الله دواء داء قلوبكم وبصر عمى أفئدتكم وشفاء مرض أجسادكم وصلاح فساد صدوركم وطهور دنس أنفسكم وجلاء عشا أبصاركم وأمن فزع جأشكم وضياء سواد ظلمتكم. فاجعلوا طاعة الله شعارًا دون دثاركم ودخيلًا دون شعاركم ولطيفًا بين أضلاعكم وأميرًا فوق أموركم ومنهلًا

<hr>

١ م، ي، ومصحّحة في ش، ونسخة في ه: كذا. ن، وأصل ش، ه: ﴿غشا﴾.

1.195 From an oration by ʿAlī:[1]

Muḥammad's true companions know that never, not in a single instance, have I ever renounced God or his Messenger. I laid down my life to protect him during times so fraught that champions hesitated, and all feet floundered—my courage was a gift from God. Moreover, the Messenger died with his head on my chest, and his spirit flowed out over my palm, and I put my palm to my face directly. I undertook his final ablution with angels as my helpers—the house and courtyard rang out as one group descended and another ascended, each praying over him, my ears hearing every soft invocation, until we buried him in his grave. Who is closer to him, alive or dead, than I? Act with perception, people, and fight your enemy with true courage! I swear by the God save whom there is no god, that I walk the firm path of right, they flounder on the slippery slope of wrong.

I say what you hear, and seek God's forgiveness for me and for you.

1.196 From an oration by ʿAlī:

1.196.1 He knows the bellowing of beasts in the forest, the sins his servants commit in private, the movements of fish in the deep oceans, and the crashing of waters tossed by stormy winds. I testify that Muḥammad is God's noble representative, the ambassador who conveyed his revelation, and the messenger who brought his mercy. And now to the matter at hand:

I counsel you to be conscious of God, who created you in the beginning, to whom you shall return. With him lies your petition's success, in him rests your hopes' realization. Your path leads to him, in him you will find protection. Consciousness of God is the remedy for your sick hearts, the bringer of sight to your blind spirits, the cure for your diseased bodies, the healing for your corrupt breasts, the purification of your begrimed souls, the luster for your impaired eyes, the safeguard for your fearful minds, and the light for your black darkness. Wear it as an undergarment, not just as an outer robe, wear it next to your skin, not simply as an undergarment. Make it the essence that

---

1 At Ṣiffīn in 37/657, in response to orations by Muʿāwiyah and ʿAmr ibn al-ʿĀṣ, in which they urged their Syrian army to fight ʿAlī and accused him of breaking his oath of allegiance and spilling blood unjustly (Minqarī, *Waqʿat Ṣiffīn*, 223–224). "Muḥammad's true companions," lit. "custodians (*mustaḥfaẓūn*) from among Muḥammad's Companions," are explained by commentators as being (1) the first three historical caliphs, Abū Bakr, ʿUmar, and ʿUthmān, or (2) the learned. The statement about ʿAlī's never having disobeyed the Prophet is an oblique criticism of ʿUmar's objections to Muḥammad's truce at Ḥudaybiyyah. Ḥ 10:179; R 2:292; B 612; details of Muḥammad's final moments and ʿAlī's performance of his ablutions are recounted in Ḥ 10:183–187; B 612–613.

لحين وِردكم وشفيعًا لدرك طلبتكم وجُنّةً ليوم فزعكم ومصابيح لبطون قبوركم وسكنًا لطول وحشتكم ونفَسًا لكرب مواطنكم فإنّ طاعة الله حرز من متالف مكتنفة ومخاوف متوقّعة وأُوارِ نيران موقدة. فمن أخذ بالتقوى عزبت عنه الشدائد بعد دنوّها وأحلولت له الأمور بعد مرارتها وأنفرجت عنه الأمواج بعد تراكمها وأسهلت له الصعاب بعد إنصابها وهطلت عليه الكرامة بعد قحوطها وتحدّبت عليه الرحمة بعد نفورها وتفجّرت عليه النعم بعد نضوبها ووبلت عليه البركة بعد إرذاذها فاتّقوا الله الذي نفعكم بموعظته ووعظكم برسالته وأمتنّ عليكم بنعمته فعَبّدوا أنفسكم لعبادته وأخرجوا إليه من حقّ طاعته.

1.196.2 ثمّ إنّ هذا الإسلام دين الله الذي اصطفاه لنفسه واصطنعه على عينه وأصفاه خِيرة خلقه وأقام دعائمه على محبّته أذلّ الأديان بعزّته ووضع الملل برفعه وأهان أعداءه بكرامته وخذل محادّيه بنصره وهدم أركان الضلالة بركنه وسقى مَن عطش من حياضه وأتأقَ الحياض بمواتحه. ثمّ جعله لا انفصام لعروته ولا فكّ لحلقته ولا انهدام لآساسه ولا زوال لدعائمه ولا انقلاع لشجرته ولا انقطاع لمدّته ولا عفاء لشرائعه ولا حَزّ لفروعه ولا ضنك لطرقه ولا وعوثة لسهولته ولا سواد لوَضَحه ولا عِوَج لانتصابه ولا عَصَل في عوده ولا وَعْث لفجّه ولا انطفاء لمصابيحه ولا مَرارة لحلاوته. فهو دعائم أساخَ في الحقّ أسناخها وثبت لها آساسها وينابيع غَزُرت عيونها ومصابيح شُبّت نيرانها ومنار اقتدى بها سُفّارها وأعلام قُصد بها فِجاجها ومناهل رَوِي بها وُرّادها. جعل الله فيه منتهى رضوانه وذروة دعائمه وسنام طاعته فهو عند الله وثيق الأركان رفيع البنيان منير

ام، ي: كذا. ن، ش، ه: ﴿جذّ﴾. ي: ﴿حدّ﴾. نسخة في ه: ﴿حذّ﴾.

penetrates your ribs, the commander who governs your affairs, the waterhole where you drink, the advocate for your petition, the shield that will protect you on the day of dread, the lamp in the hollow of your grave, the comforter during your long, lonely suffering, and the air that helps you breathe during the anguish of your battles. Obedience to God is an amulet that protects against encroaching dangers, looming perils, and blazing fires. Whoever is conscious of God finds troubles retreat after having approached, concerns sweeten after bitterness, waves recede after whipping up, hardships ease after exhaustion, generosity flow after drought, mercy come forward after having fled, favors gush out after draining away, and blessings pour down after scanty rain. Be conscious of God—he aided you with his guidance, counselled you with his message, and blessed you with his favors. Devote yourselves to his worship and discharge your duties of obedience to him.

1.196.2 Islam is God's religion that he chose for himself and fashioned in front of his eyes.[1] He bestowed it upon the best of his creation,[2] and raised its pillars upon his love. He humbled all religions by honoring it, lowered all nations by elevating it, shamed all enemies by giving it renown, chastened all challengers by giving it victory, razed error's columns by erecting its column, slaked the thirsty from its pools, and filled these pools through its watercarriers' efforts. He has made it such that its handle will never break, its links will never separate, its foundations will never be destroyed, its pillars will never cease to stand, its tree will never be uprooted, its time will never end, its ways will never be effaced, its branches will never be chopped, its paths will never become narrow, its ease will never change to harshness, its dawn will never dim, its straightness will never twist, its shaft will never warp, its canyon will never become rutted, its lamps will never be extinguished, and its sweetness will never turn bitter. It is built with columns whose bases are embedded in truth and whose pediments are strong, it has wellsprings whose water gushes, lamps whose flames rise high, beacons by which travelers are guided, waymarks by which mountain passes are indicated, and watering places where thirst is slaked. God is pleased with his religion.[3] He has made it the pinnacle of his pillars and the summit of obedience. It stands before God, column compact,

---

1   Reference to Qur'an, Ṭāhā 20:39.
2   The Shiʿi commentators interpret "the best of his creation" (*khayrata/khiyarata khalqihi*) as Muḥammad and his descendants (B 617; R 2:301–302), the Sunni commentators as (2) all Muslims (Ḥ 10:192).
3   Reference to Qur'an, Māʾidah 5:3, Āl ʿImrān 3:19.

البرهان مضيء النيران عزيز السلطان مشرف المنار مُعوِز المَثار فشرّفوه واتّبعوه وأدّوا إليه حقّه وضعوه مواضعه.

1.196.3 ثمّ إنّ الله سبحانه بعث محمّدًا صلّى الله عليه وآله بالحقّ حين دنا من الدنيا الانقطاع وأقبل من الآخرة الاطّلاع وأظلمت بهجتها بعد إشراق وقامت بأهلها على ساق وخشن منها مهاد وأَزِفَ منها قياد في اتقطاع من مدّتها واقتراب من أشراطها وتصرّم من أهلها وانفصام من حلقتها وانتشار من سببها وعَفاء من أعلامها وتكشّف من عوراتها وقِصَر من طولها. جعله الله سبحانه بلاغًا لرسالته وكرامة لأمّته وربيعًا لأهل زمانه ورفعة لأعوانه وشرفًا لأنصاره.

1.196.4 ثمّ أنزل عليه الكتاب نورًا لا تطفأ مصابيحه وسراجًا لا يخبو توقّده وبحرًا لا يدرك قعره ومنهاجًا لا يضلّ نهجه وشعاعًا لا يظلم ضوءه[1] وفرقانًا لا يخمد برهانه وبنيانًا لا تهدم أركانه وشفاء لا تخشى أسقامه وعزًّا لا تهزم أنصاره وحقًّا لا تخذل أعوانه. فهو معدن الإيمان وبُحبوحته وينابيع العلم وبحوره ورياض العدل وغُدْرانه وأثافيّ الإسلام وبنيانه وأودية الحقّ وغيطانه وبحر لا ينزفه المستنزفون وعيون لا يُنضبها الماتحون ومناهل لا يغيضها الواردون ومنازل لا يضلّ نهجها المسافرون وأعلام لا يعمى عنها السائرون وآكام لا يجوز عنها[2] القاصدون. جعله الله ريًّا لعطش العلماء وربيعًا لقلوب الفقهاء ومَحاجّ لطرق الصلحاء ودواءً ليس بعده داء ونورًا ليس معه ظلمة وحبلًا وثيقًا عروته ومعقلًا منيعًا ذروته وعزًّا لمن تولّاه وسلمًا لمن دخله وهدى لمن أتمّ به وعذرًا لمن انتحله وبرهانًا لمن تكلّم به وشاهدًا لمن خاصم به وفلْجًا لمن حاجّ به وحاملًا لمن حمله ومطيّة لمن أعمله وآية لمن توسم وجنّة لمن استلأم وعِلمًا لمن وعى وحديثًا لمن روى وحُكمًا لمن قضى.

---

edifice exalted, proof shining, fires burning, power mighty, and beacon raised, impossible to destroy.[1] So honor it, follow it, give it its due, and accord it the position it deserves.

1.196.3 God sent Muḥammad with the truth when the end of the world had drawn near and the next life had approached, when her splendor had dulled after long brightness, her people confronted attack, her bed had turned rough, and her reins had become slack. This was a time when the world's lifespan was drawing to a close, her signs were at hand, her people were mowed down, her ropes had frayed, her waymarks were effaced, her shame was manifest, and her long rope had been cut. God made Muḥammad the bearer of his message, honor for his community, springtime for his people, exaltation for his helpers, and distinction for his allies.

1.196.4 God revealed to him the Book—a light whose flame cannot be extinguished, a lamp whose glow cannot be hidden, a sea whose depths cannot be plumbed, a road whose course does not mislead, a ray whose brightness never darkens, a dawn whose proof is never extinguished, an edifice whose columns cannot be razed, a cure after which no disease is feared, might whose supporters are never vanquished, and truth whose proponents are never bested. It forms the mine and home of belief, the founts and seas of wisdom, the meadows and pools of justice, the frame and edifice of Islam, and the valleys and orchards of truth. It holds a mighty river that water-seekers cannot exhaust, wellsprings that water-drawers cannot deplete, waterholes that drinkers cannot drain, waystations that travelers cannot miss, waymarks to which wayfarers cannot remain blind, and highlands that travelers cannot circumvent. God has made it water to quench the thirst of the learned, springtime for the hearts of the wise, the high road for the pious to walk, a healing after which there is no illness, a light alongside which there is no darkness, a handle whose grip is strong, and a fortress whose ramparts are never stormed. It gives might to those who are loyal, peace to those who enter, guidance to those who follow, defense for those who adhere, proof to those who articulate, witness to those who argue, victory to those who fight, support for those who carry, steeds for those who ride, signs for those who foretell, shields for those who seek armor, knowledge for those who heed, truth for those who narrate, and discernment for those who judge.

---

1   Ar. *muʿwiz al-mathār*; translation based on Ḥ 10:193; R 2:303; or "difficult to excavate," referring to the treasures of its wisdom, based on B 619.

1.197 ومن كلام له عليه السلام كان يوصي به أصحابه

تعاهدوا أمر الصلاة وحافظوا عليها وَاستكثروا منها وتقرّبوا بها فإنّها ﴿كَانَتْ عَلَى الْمُؤْمِنِينَ كِتَابًا مَّوْقُوتًا﴾ ألا تسمعون إلى جواب أهل النار حين سئلوا ﴿مَا سَلَكَكُمْ فِي سَقَرَ قَالُوا لَمْ نَكُ مِنَ الْمُصَلِّينَ﴾ وإنّها لَتَحُتّ الذنوب حَتَّ الورق وتطلقها إطلاق الرِّبق وشبّهها رسول الله صلّى الله عليه بالحَمّة تكون على باب الرجل فهو يغتسل منها في اليوم والليلة خمس مرّات فما عسى أن يبقى عليه من الدَّرَن وقد عرف حقّها من المؤمنين الذين لا يشغلهم عنها زينة متاع ولا قرّة عين من ولد ولا مال يقول الله سبحانه ﴿رِجَالٌ لَّا تُلْهِيهِمْ تِجَارَةٌ وَلَا بَيْعٌ عَن ذِكْرِ اللهِ وَإِقَامِ الصَّلَاةِ وَإِيتَاءِ الزَّكَاةِ﴾ وكان رسول الله صلّى الله عليه وآله نَصِبًا بالصلاة بعد التبشير له بالجنّة لقول الله سبحانه ﴿وَأْمُرْ أَهْلَكَ بِالصَّلَاةِ وَاصْطَبِرْ عَلَيْهَا﴾ فكان يأمر بها أهله ويصبر عليها نفسه. ثمّ إنّ الزكاة جعلت مع الصلاة قربانًا لأهل الإسلام فمن أعطاها طيّب النفس بها فإنّها تجعل له كفّارة ومن النار حجازًا ووقاية فلا يتبعنّها أحد نفسه ولا يكثرنّ عليها لَهَفه وإنّ من أعطاها غير طيّب النفس بها يرجو بها ما هو أفضل منها فهو جاهل بالسنّة مغبون الأجر ضالّ العمل طويل الندم. ثمّ أداء الأمانة فقد خاب من ليس من أهلها إنّها عرضت على السموات المبنيّة والأرضين المَدحوّة والجبال ذات الطول المنصوبة فلا أطول ولا أعرض ولا أعلى ولا أعظم منها ولو امتنع شيء بطول أو عرض أو قوّة أو عزّ لَامتنعن ولكن أشفقن من العقوبة وعقلن ما جهل من هو أضعف منهنّ وهو ﴿الْإِنسَانُ إِنَّهُ كَانَ ظَلُومًا جَهُولًا﴾. إنّ الله سبحانه لا يخفى عليه ما العباد مقترفون في ليلهم ونهارهم لَطُفَ به خُبرًا وأحاط به علمًا أعضاؤكم شهوده وجوارحكم جنوده وضمائركم عيونه وخلواتكم عيانه.

1.197 From an address by ʿAlī with which he would counsel his associates:[1]
Be diligent in the matter of the ritual prayer—pray regularly and frequently, and seek to come closer to God through it, for it is «prescribed for believers at fixed times.»[2] Have you not heard the people of hell when they were asked, «"What led you into the Fire?" and they answered, "We were not among those who prayed"».[3] Prayer makes sins fall from you like leaves and loosens their bonds from your necks. God's Messenger compared it to a hot spring located at a man's doorstep, one that he can bathe in five times in one day and night—tell me, what grime will remain on his body then? Prayer's value is recognized by believers who are not diverted by gilded furniture or the gratifications of children and herds, believers God praises as «men whom neither trade nor commerce divert from remembering God, from performing the prayer, or submitting the alms-levy».[4] Even after being pledged paradise, the Messenger exerted himself to the utmost in prayer, for God instructed him, «command your family to pray, and adhere to it yourself»[5]—he thus commanded his family to pray, and adhered to it himself. Second, be assiduous in offering the alms-levy, which, alongside the ritual prayer, is a means for the followers of Islam to obtain closeness to God. Whoever gives it freely and happily will find that it serves as expiation for his sins and a barrier and shield against hellfire. Let no one yearn for it after giving it or mourn its loss! For whoever gives it unwillingly, hoping only for material benefit, is ignorant of the Sunnah and will be cheated of its reward; his deed will be lost and his regret will persist. Third, be careful to uphold trust—whoever does so will not fail. Indeed, the trust was offered to the lofty skies, the outspread earth, and the towering, deep-rooted mountains—there is nothing taller, or broader, or higher, or greater than they, and if anything could have borne it because of height, or breadth, or strength, or might it would have been they. But they feared the punishment and understood what was not recognized by a weaker being, «the human, for he was a tyrant, an ignoramus.»[6] The sins that God's servants commit at night or by day are not concealed from him. His awareness of them is total, his knowledge encompasses them fully: your limbs are his witnesses,[7] your bodies are his armies, your hearts are his spies, and your private conversations are open to him.

---

1 Kulaynī's report (*Kāfī*, 5;36) says ʿAlī would counsel his followers thus ahead of any battle— perhaps as a testament, in anticipation of his death.

2 Qurʾan, Nisāʾ 4:103.

3 Qurʾan, Muddaththir 74:42–43.

4 Qurʾan, Nūr 24:37.

5 Qurʾan, Ṭāhā 20:132.

6 Qurʾan, Aḥzāb 33:72; the lines leading up to it are a modified quote from the earlier part of the same verse.

7 Reference to Qurʾan, Nūr 24:24.

١.١٩٨ ومن كلام له عليه السلام

والله ما معاوية بأدهى منّي ولكنّه يغدر ويفجر ولولا كراهية الغدر لكنت من أدهى الناس ولكنّ كلّ غَدْرة فَجْرة وكلّ فَجْرة كَفْرة ولكلّ غادر لواء يُعرف به يوم القيامة. والله ما أُستَغفل بالمكيدة ولا أُستَغمز بالشديدة.

١.١٩٩ ومن كلام له عليه السلام

أَيّها الناس لا تَستوحشوا في طريق الهدى لقلّة أهله فإنّ الناس قد اجتمعوا على مائدة شِبَعُها قصير وجُوعها طويل. أيّها الناس إنّما يجمع الناس الرضاء والسخط وإنّما عقر ناقة ثمود رجل واحد فعمّهم الله بالعذاب لمّا عمّوه بالرضاء فقال سبحانه ﴿فَعَقَرُوهَا فَأَصْبَحُوا نَادِمِينَ﴾ فما كان إلّا أن خارت أرضهم بالخَسْفة خُوار السِّكّة المُحْمَاة في الأرض الخَوّارة. أيّها الناس من سلك الطريق الواضح ورد الماء ومن خالف وقع في التيه.

١.٢٠٠ ومن كلام له عليه السلام روي عنه أنّه قاله عند دفن سيّدة النساء فاطمة عليها السلام كالمناجي به رسول الله صلّى الله عليه وآله عند قبره

السلام عليك يا رسول الله عنّي وعن ابنتك النازلة في جوارك والسريعة اللّحاق بك. قَلّ يا رسول الله عن صفيّتك صبري ورقّ عنها تجلّدي إلّا أنّ لي في التأسّي بعظيم فُرقتك وفادح مصيبتك موضع تَعَزٍّ فلقد وَسَّدْتُك في ملحودة قبرك وفاضت بين نحري وصدري نفْسك ﴿إِنَّا لِلَّهِ وَإِنَّا إِلَيْهِ رَاجِعُونَ﴾ فلقد اسْتُرجعت الوديعة وأُخذت الرهينة أمّا حزني فسرمدٌ وأمّا ليلي فمُسهَّدٌ إلى أن يختار الله لي دارك التي أنت بها مقيم. وستنبّئك ابنتك فأَحْفِها السؤال واستخبرها الحال هذا ولم يَطُل العهد ولم يَخْلُ منك الذكر.

1.198 From an address by ʿAlī:[1]

By God, Muʿāwiyah is not more astute than I, but he deceives and lies. If I did not abhor deception, I would be the most cunning of people, but every act of deception is a lie, every lie is an act of unbelief, and every deceiver will be given a banner by which he shall be known on judgment day.[2] But, by God, I am not one to be taken unawares by a plot or found weak in the face of adversity!

1.199 From an address by ʿAlī:[3]

People! Do not be nervous about following the path of guidance because its followers are few. The public has gathered round a table where satiety is short, and hunger will be long. People! Approval and disapproval unite people. Only one man slaughtered Thamūd's camel mare, but God included them all in his punishment because they united in approving his act. God said, «They slaughtered the mare, and in the morning, they had cause to regret.»[4] For their land roared and was swallowed up with its inhabitants, like a fire-seared ploughshare hissing as it sinks into soft soil. People! Whoever follows the trodden path reaches water. Whoever strays dies in the scorching desert.

1.200 From words uttered by ʿAlī just after he had buried the queen of all women, Fāṭimah, at the graveside of God's Messenger:[5]

Salutations to you, Messenger of God, from me and from your daughter who has come to stay with you, who has joined you so swiftly. I have little strength to bear the loss of your cherished one, O Messenger of God! My endurance is broken! But I bore the anguish of your separation and the calamity of your passing and shall strive to endure this too. It was I who placed you in the hollow of your grave. You breathed your last with your head resting between my neck and chest. «Truly, to God we belong and to him we shall return!»[6] The deposit has been reclaimed and the loan has been repossessed, but my grief will remain forever, my nights will be wakeful evermore, until the time when God transports me to the home where you now reside. Your daughter will inform you, so press her to answer, and find out from her what has happened to us—so soon, when your memory was still fresh among the people! Salutations to you both from one who bids you farewell, but not because of aversion or fatigue. When I take

---

1 Delivered in the Grand Mosque in Kufa, presumably after the arbitration in 37/658 (Kulaynī, *Kāfī*, 2:338). On Muʿāwiyah's and ʿAlī's strategies of governance and warfare, see Ḥ 10:212–260; B 626–627.

2 Modified quote of the Prophet's hadith, Quḍāʿī, *Shihāb*, §1.162.

3 Delivered in the Grand Mosque in Kufa during ʿAlī's caliphate, presumably between 37/658 and 40/661. Ibn Abī Zaynab, *Ghaybah*, 37.

4 Qurʾan, Shuʿarāʾ 26:157.

5 Delivered in Medina in 11/632.

6 Qurʾan, Baqarah 2:156.

والسلام عليكم سلام مودِّع لا قالٍ ولا سَئِم فإن أنصرف فلا عن مَلالة وإن أُقم فلا عن سوء ظنّ بما وعد الله الصابرين.

1.201 ومن كلام له عليه السلام

أيّها الناس إنّما الدنيا دار مجاز والآخرة دار قرار نخذوا من ممرّكم لمقرّكم ولا تهتكوا أستاركم عند من يعلم أسراركم وأخرجوا من الدنيا قلوبكم من قبل أن تُخرَج منها أبدانكم ففيها اختبرتم ولغيرها خُلقتم. إنّ المرء إذا هلك قال الناس ما ترك وقالت الملائكة ما قدّم. لله آباؤكم فقدّموا بعضًا يكن لكم ولا تخلّفوا كُلًّا فيكون عليكم.¹

1.202 ومن كلام له عليه السلام كان كثيرًا ما ينادي به أصحابه

تجهّزوا رحمكم الله فقد نودي فيكم بالرحيل وأقلّوا العُرْجة على الدنيا وانقلبوا بصالح ما بحضرتكم من الزاد فإنّ أمامكم عَقَبة كَؤودًا ومنازل مَخوفة مَهولة لا بدّ من الورود عليها والوقوف عندها. واعلموا أنّ ملاحظ المنيّة نحوكم دائبة² وكأنّكم بمَخالبها وقد نَشبت فيكم وقد دهمتكم فيها مُفظعات الأمور ومُضلعات المحذور فقطّعوا علائق الدنيا واستظهروا بزاد التقوى.

وقد مضى شيء من هذا الكلام فيما تقدّم بخلاف هذه الرواية.

1.203 ومن كلام له عليه السلام كلّم به طلحة والزبير بعد بيعته بالخلافة وقد عتبا من ترك مشاورتهما والاستعانة في الأمور بهما

---

¹ ن، ش، م، ه: كذا. ي: كذا. وزيادة في هامش ش، م، ه: ⟨فقدّموا بعضًا يكن لكم قرضًا ولا تخلّفوا كُلًّا فيكون عليكم كَلًّا⟩. ² ن، ش، ي، ه: كذا. ونسخة في م: كذا. م، ونسخة في ش، ي: ⟨دانية⟩.

my leave, it is not because I wearied of grieving. When I stay, it is not from lack of faith in God's promise to the patient.

1.201 From an address by ʿAlī:

People! The world is a passage and the hereafter your permanent home. Gather supplies from your abode of transience for your abode of residence. Do not rend your veils before one who knows all your secrets. Remove your hearts from the world before your bodies are removed from it. Here you are tested, but you are created for another home. When a man dies, people ask, "What did he leave behind?" while the angels inquire, "What has he sent on ahead?" May God reward your fathers! Send ahead a portion that will remain yours. Do not leave everything behind, for that will count against you.

1.202 From words ʿAlī often addressed in oration to his associates:[1]

Gather your supplies—May God have mercy on you!—for the call has come to depart. Lessen your inclination toward the world and see that you leave your present life with provisions. A tough ascent lies ahead with fearsome and strange waystations through which you must pass and at which you must alight. Know this: Death homes in on you. Imagine that you are already trying to ward off its claws, that its horrors and fearsome calamities are already upon you. Cut off all ties to this world and prepare provisions of piety.

Raḍī: Similar lines have been recorded earlier in a different version.[2]

1.203 From an address by ʿAlī to Ṭalḥah and Zubayr when—after pledging allegiance to him as caliph—they reproached him for not consulting them or seeking their assistance in governing:[3]

---

1 Delivered regularly in the Grand Mosque in Kufa during ʿAlī's caliphate, 35–40/656–661. Ṣadūq (*Amālī*, 402–403, Majlis 75), says: "The Commander of the Faithful would pray the ʿishāʾ night-prayer, then call out thrice, so all the people in the mosque would hear him: (the text)." Similar tag in Mufīd, *Irshād*, 2:234. Māmaṭīrī (*Nuzhah*, 420), says: "The Commander of the Faithful would call out every night, in the face of the morning: (the text of the first half)." He cites the second half as part of an oration (of which §1.96 is another part) in the mosque in Basra, a few days after the Battle of the Camel in 36/656 (ibid., 236).

2 Possibly referring to §1.182.

3 Delivered in Medina in 35/656, soon after ʿAlī received the pledge. ʿAlī rescinded the earlier caliphs' practice of graded stipends and gave everyone an equal share from the state treasury (similar context in §1.124). Ṭalḥah and Zubayr were unhappy with this new arrangement and complained. When ʿAlī replied as he did in this address, they sought leave to go to Mecca, and once there, planned with ʿĀʾishah a revolt against him, which resulted in the Battle of the Camel. On the events leading up to this address, and the address itself, see Iskāfī, *Miʿyār*, 112–114. On Ṭalḥah's and Zubayr's pledge to ʿAlī and their subsequent breaking of it, see Ḥ 11:10–20. See also §3.186.

لقد نقمتما يسيرًا وأرجأتما كثيرًا. ألا تُخبِراني أيّ شيء لكما حقّ دفعتكما عنه أو أيّ
قسم اَستأثرت عليكما به أم أيّ حقّ رفعه إليّ أحد من المسلمين ضعفت عنه أم جهلته أم
أخطأت بابه. والله ما كانت لي في الخلافة رغبة ولا في الوِلاية إربة ولكنّكم دعوتموني
إليها وحملتموني عليها فلمّا أفضت إليّ نظرت إلى كتاب الله وما وضع لنا وأمرنا بالحكم به
فاَتّبعته وما اَستسنّ النبيّ صلّى الله عليه وآله فاَقتديته فلم أحتج في ذلك إلى رأيكما ولا
رأي غيركما ولم يقع حكم جهلته فأستشيركما وإخواني من المسلمين ولو كان ذلك لم أرغب
عنكما ولا عن غيركما. وأمّا ما ذكرتما من أمر الإسوة فإنّ ذلك أمر لم أحكم أنا فيه برأيي
ولا وليته هوًى منّي بل وجدت أنا وأنتما ما جاء به رسول الله صلّى الله عليه وآله قد فرغ
منه فلم أحتج إليكما فيما قد فرغ الله من قَسْمه وأمضى فيه حكمه فليس لكما والله عندي
ولا لغيركما في هذا عُتبى. أخذ الله بقلوبكم وقلوبنا إلى الحقّ وألهمنا وإيّاكم الصبر.

ثمّ قال عليه السلام
رحم الله رجلًا رأى حقًّا فأعان عليه أو رأى جورًا فردّه وكان عونًا بالحقّ على صاحبه.

1.204 ومن كلام له عليه السلام وقد سمع قومًا من أصحابه يسبّون أهل الشام أيّام حربهم
بصفّين
إنّي أكره لكم أن تكونوا سبّابين ولكنّكم لو وصفتم أعمالهم وذكرتم حالهم كان أصوب
في القول وأبلغ في العذر وقلتم مكان سبّكم إيّاهم اَللّهمّ اَحقن دماءنا ودماءهم وأصلح
ذات بيننا وبينهم واَهدهم من ضلالتهم حتّى يعرف الحقّ مَن جهله ويَرعوي عن الغيّ
والعدوان مَن لَهج به.

You rebuke me for a small matter and you're going to bring on much more besides. Tell me—which rights have I deprived you of, what share due to you have I withheld? Or which claim has been brought to me by any Muslim that I have been too weak to deal with, or proved to be ignorant about, or mistaken in handling? By God, I had no wish to assume the caliphate and no interest in ruling. It was you who urged me and pleaded with me to accept. And when the caliphate came to me, I looked to God's Book for guidance, and to its ordinances and commandments for governance, and followed its path. I looked to the Prophet's Sunnah and emulated his example. I had no need of your opinion or the opinion of any other, there was no ruling I was uncertain about such that I needed to consult you or any of my Muslim brethren. Had I needed advice, I would not have held back from you or anyone else. My equal distribution of treasury funds is a matter neither of personal decision nor whim, but I have found this—and you know it too—to be the ruling brought and decided by God's Messenger. I did not need your help in deciding the manner of distribution that God had already set forth, that he already ruled on. By God, neither you nor anyone else has grounds to reproach me! May God guide your hearts and mine to right and move me and you to have patience in adversity.

Then ʿAlī said:
May God have mercy on the man who supports right when he sees it and repudiates wrong when he sees it, who courageously supports right against those who promote wrong.

1.204 From an address by ʿAlī when he heard some of his supporters cursing the Syrians during the conflict at Ṣiffīn:[1]
I don't like you to curse! Rather, describe their deeds and define their situation, that is a more judicious way of speaking and more convincing. Instead of cursing, it's better for you to say this: "God, preserve our blood and theirs from being spilled, reconcile us, guide them out of their error until the ignorant recognize right and those enamored of deception and enmity retreat from their unrighteous ways."

---

[1] In 37/657, in Kufa, just before ʿAlī set out to fight the Syrians. The supporters are Ḥujr ibn ʿAdī and ʿAmr ibn al-Ḥamiq al-Khuzāʿī. Minqarī, *Waqʿat Ṣiffīn*, 102–103. Note that this event took place before the Battle of Ṣiffīn, when ʿAlī was still hopeful of persuading the Syrians to pledge allegiance to him; moreover, he is forbidding his followers from cursing the Syrians generally. As for Muʿāwiyah, ʿAmr ibn al-ʿĀṣ, and even his own disloyal arbiter, Abū Mūsā al-Ashʿarī, ʿAlī himself is later said to have regularly cursed them and four others of Muʿāwiyah's commanders after each prayer. Ibid., 552.

1.205 وقال عليه السلام في بعض أيّام صفّين وقد رأى الحسن عليه السلام يتسرّع إلى الحرب اِمْلِكُوا عنّي هذا الغلام لا يَهُدَّني فإنّي أَنْفَسُ بهٰذين (يعني الحسن والحسين عليهما السلام) على الموت لئلّا ينقطع بهما نسل رسول الله صلّى الله عليه وآله.

قوله عليه السلام ‹املكوا عنّي هذا الغلام› من أعلى الكلام وأفصحه.

1.206 ومن كلام له عليه السلام قاله لمّا اضطرب عليه أصحابه في أمر الحكومة أيّها الناس إنّه لم يزل أمري معكم على ما أحبّ حتّى نَهِكتكم الحرب لقد والله أخذت منكم وتركت وهي لعدوّكم أَنْهَك. لقد كنت أمس أميرًا فأصبحت اليوم مأمورًا وكنت أمس ناهيًا فأصبحت اليوم مَنهيًّا وقد أحببتم البقاء وليس لي أن أحملكم على ما تكرهون.

1.207 ومن كلام له عليه السلام بالبصرة وقد دخل على العلاء بن زياد الحارثيّ يعوده وهو من أصحابه فلمّا رأى سعة داره قال

1.207.1 ما كنت تصنع بسعة هذه الدار في الدنيا ما أنت إليها في الآخرة كنت أحوج وبَلٰى إن شئتَ بلغتَ بها الآخرة تَقري فيها الضيف وتصل فيها الرحم وتُطلع منها الحقوق مطالعها فإذا أنت قد بلغت بها الآخرة.

1.205 From an address by ʿAlī on one of the battle-days of Ṣiffīn, when he saw Ḥasan rushing into the fray:[1]

Help me! Restrain this lad! Don't let him crush my hopes! I am determined to protect both (meaning Ḥasan and Ḥusayn) from death, so that the Messenger's line doesn't end here!

Raḍī: ʿAlī's expression, "Help me! Restrain this lad! (*imlikū ʿannī hādhā l-ghulām*)" is among the most sublime and eloquent of words.

1.206 From an address ʿAlī delivered when his supporters disagreed with him in the matter of the arbitration:[2]

People! You have followed my command as I have wished thus far, but now warfare has worn you out. By God, it has indeed taken some and left some, but it has depleted your enemy more than you! Yesterday I was your commander, and today you command me. Yesterday I was the one who forbade you, and today you forbid me. You want to live, and I have no way of convincing you to do what you are dead set against.

1.207 From an address by ʿAlī in Basra. ʿAlī went to visit ʿAlāʾ ibn Ziyād al-Ḥārithī, one of his supporters who was ill; when ʿAlī saw the size of the house, he said:[3]

1.207.1 What will you do with this large house here in this world? You will have more need of it in the hereafter! And yes, if you wish, you can take it with you. Offer hospitality in it to guests, use it to foster ties with kin, and pay your dues on it as they accrue. If you do all this, you will take it with you to the hereafter.

---

1   In 36–37/657. For events before and after, see Minqarī, *Waqʿat Ṣiffīn*, 529–530.

2   This was at Ṣiffīn in 37/657. The battle was going in ʿAlī's favor when Muʿāwiyah—after earlier having rebuffed ʿAlī's efforts at negotiation—held aloft Qurʾan leaves attached to spears and asked for arbitration. ʿAlī believed this to be a ruse and urged his supporters to continue fighting, but there were many who insisted he accept. Some details in Ḥ 11:29–31; text and further context in Minqarī, *Waqʿat Ṣiffīn*, 484.

3   In 36/656, following the Battle of the Camel (Iskāfī, *Miʿyār*, 243). Ibn Abī al-Ḥadīd (Ḥ 11:37) says the man was named Rabīʿ ibn Ziyād al-Ḥārithī (cf. the same anecdote in Māmaṭīrī, *Nuzhah*, 384, which also has Rabīʿ), and that the name ʿAlāʾ is an error. Rabīʿ was a Companion of the Prophet, who was a commander during the conquest of Khurasan and served as governor of Bahrain during ʿUmar's caliphate. Ibn Abī al-Ḥadīd says this anecdote about Rabīʿ and ʿAlī is well known, while ʿAlāʾ is not mentioned elsewhere in the sources.

١.٢٠٧.٢ فقال له العلاء يا أمير المؤمنين أشكو إليك أخي عاصم بن زياد قال وما له قال لبس العباء وتخلّى من الدنيا قال علَيّ به. فلمّا جاء قال

يا عُدَيّ نفسه لقد آستهام بك الخبيث أما رحمتَ أهلك وولدك أترى الله أحلّ لك الطيّبات وهو يكره أن تأخذها أنت أهون على الله من ذلك.

قال يا أمير المؤمنين هذا أنت في خشونة ملبسك وجشوبة مأكلك. قال

وَيحَك إنّي لست كأنت إنّ الله فرض على أئمّة الحقّ١ أن يقدّروا أنفسهم بضَعَفة الناس كي لا يتبيّغ بالفقير فقره.

١.٢٠٨ ومن كلام له عليه السلام وقد سأله سائل عن أحاديث البِدَع وعمّا في أيدي الناس من آختلاف الخبر فقال

إنّ في أيدي الناس حقًّا وباطلًا وصدقًا وكذبًا وناسخًا ومنسوخًا وعامًّا وخاصًّا ومحكمًا ومتشابهًا وحفظًا ووهمًا وقد كُذب على رسول الله صلّى الله عليه وآله على عهده حتّى وإنّما أتاك بالحديث .﴿من كذب عليّ متعمّدًا فليتبوّأ مقعده من النار﴾ قام خطيبًا فقال رجل منافق مظهر للإيمان متصنّع بالإسلام لا يتأثّم ولا .أربعة رجال ليس لهم خامس يتحرّج يكذب على رسول الله صلّى الله عليه وآله متعمّدًا فلو علم الناس أنّه منافق كاذب لم يقبلوا منه ولم يصدّقوا قوله ولكنّهم قالوا صاحب رسول الله رآه وسمع منه ولَقِف عنه فيأخذون بقوله وقد أخبرك الله عن المنافقين بما أخبرك ووصفهم بما وصفهم به لك ثمّ

<hr>

١ن، ش، ي، ه، ونسخة في م: كذا. أصل م، ونسخة في ه: ﴿العدل﴾.

1.207.2 ʿAlāʾ then said to ʿAlī, "Commander of the Faithful, I have a complaint against my brother ʿĀṣim ibn Ziyād." ʿAlī asked, "What is your problem with him?" and ʿAlāʾ replied, "He has donned a striped cloak of haircloth and renounced the world." ʿAlī instructed, "Bring him to me!" and when ʿĀṣim was brought before him, ʿAlī berated him:

O self-hater, the evil one has befuddled you! Do you feel no compassion toward your wife and children? Do you think that God has made licit for you the good things of this world when he did not want you to partake of them? Are you so important to God that he should trouble with all that!

Raḍī: ʿĀṣim replied, "But, Commander of the Faithful, here you stand with your rough clothing and coarse food!" and ʿAlī exclaimed:

Good grief! Our situations are not the same. God has mandated for true leaders that they should measure themselves against the needy so that the poor are not crushed by their penury.

1.208 From an address by ʿAlī responding to a man who asked him about invented hadith and contrary reports current among people. He said:[1]

Reports current among people today include both the right and the wrong, the true and the false, the abrogating and the abrogated, the general and the specific, the clear and the ambiguous, and the accurate and the flawed. People attributed things falsely to the Messenger even when he was alive, until finally he stood up to orate and declared, ⟨Whoever deliberately misattributes something to me will take possession of a seat in hellfire⟩. There are four kinds of men who come to you with hadith, there is no fifth after them: The first is the hypocrite who makes a show of faith and pretends to be a Muslim. He neither fears sinning nor hesitates to commit an act of wickedness, and he deliberately misattributes words to God's Messenger. If people knew that he is a lying hypocrite, they would not accept the report from him or believe his words, but instead they say, "This is the Messenger's Companion, who saw him, heard from him, and took from him," and so they accept his words. You know what God has

---

1   Presumably in Kufa, during the years of ʿAlī's caliphate, 35–40/656–661. The man is said to be Sulaym ibn Qays, who prefaced his question to ʿAlī with the lines, "I have heard Salmān, Abū Dharr, and Miqdād speak of certain things regarding exegesis of the Qurʾan, and hadith and reports from God's Messenger, and I have heard you endorse those. But there are many hadith and reports in people's hands that contradict them ..." (text and context in Ḥarrānī, *Tuḥaf*, 193–196). On Sulaym, see Muḥammad Bāqir Anṣārī, "Lamḥah ʿan ḥayāt Sulaym wa-taʾrīkh kitābihi," in the introduction to his edition of *Kitāb Sulaym*, 1:41–84. Alternatively, the text is cited as an answer given during an oration in the mosque in Basra, a few days after the Battle of the Camel in 36/656 (Māmaṭīrī, *Nuzhah*, 229). Other parts of the same oration, as cited in ibid., 221–233, are listed in the note to §1.23.

بَقوا بعده عليه السلام فتقرّبوا إلى أئمّة الضلالة والدعاة إلى النار بالزور والبهتان فولّوهم الأعمال وجعلوهم على رقاب الناس وأكلوا بهم الدنيا وإنّما الناس مع الملوك والدنيا إلّا من عصم الله فهذا أحد الأربعة. ورجل سمع من رسول الله صلّى الله عليه وآله شيئًا لم يحفظه على وجهه فوَهِمَ فيه ولم يتعمّد كَذِبًا فهو في يديه يرويه ويعمل به ويقول أنا سمعته من رسول الله فلو علم المسلمون أنّه وَهِمَ فيه لم يقبلوه منه ولو علم هو أنّه كذلك لرفضه. ورجل ثالث سمع من رسول الله صلّى الله عليه وآله شيئًا يأمر به ثمّ نهى عنه وهو لا يعلم أو سمعه ينهى عن شيء ثمّ أمر به وهو لا يعلم فحفظ المنسوخ ولم يحفظ الناسخ فلو علم أنّه منسوخ لرفضه ولو علم المسلمون إذ سمعوه منه أنّه منسوخ لرفضوه. وآخر رابع لم يكذب على الله ولا على رسوله مبغض للكذب خوفًا لله وتعظيمًا لرسول الله ولم يهِمْ بل حفظ ما سمع على وجهه فجاء به على ما سمعه لم يزد فيه ولم ينقص منه وحفظ الناسخ فعمل به وحفظ المنسوخ فجنّب عنه وعرف الخاصّ والعامّ فوضع كلّ شيء موضعه وعرف المتشابه ومحكمه. وقد كان يكون من رسول الله صلّى الله عليه وآله الكلام له وجهان فكلام خاصّ وكلام عامّ فيسمعه من لا يعرف ما عنى الله به ولا ما عنى به رسول الله صلّى الله عليه وآله فيحمله السامع ويوجّهه على غير معرفة بمعناه وما قُصد به وما خَرج من أجله. وليس كلّ أصحاب رسول الله كان يسأله ويستفهمه حتّى إن كانوا ليحبّون أن يجيء الأعرابيّ أو الطارئ فيسأله عليه السلام حتّى يسمعوا. وكان لا يمرّ بي من ذلك شيء إلّا سألت عنه وحفظته. فهذه وجوه ما عليه الناس في اختلافهم وعللهم في رواياتهم.

1.209 ومن خطبة له عليه السلام

وكان من اقتدار جبروته وبديع لطائف صنعته أن جعل من ماء اليمّ الزاخر المتراكم المتقاصِف يَبَسًا جامدًا ثمّ فطر منه أطباقًا ففتقها سبع سماوات بعد ارتتاقها فاستمسكت

ام، ي، ومصحّحة في ه: كذا. ش، ن، وأصل ه: ﴿البحر﴾.

said to you about hypocrites, you know how God has described them! After the Messenger's death they persisted, seeking closeness with lies and fabrications to false leaders and hell's advocates who made them governors and gave them authority over people's necks—leaders who, in turn, amassed wealth through them. Except for those whom God protects, most people side with kings and choose the path of worldly benefit. This is one of the four. The second is a man who has heard something from the Messenger but has not retained it correctly, he errs but does not deliberately lie. The report as he remembers it is in his hands, and he narrates it and acts upon it, saying, "I heard this from God's Messenger." The Muslims would not accept it from him if they knew that he errs; he too would reject it if he knew. The third is a man who heard the Messenger ordain something that he later forbade but does not know this, or he heard the Messenger forbid something that he later ordained but does not know this, he thus preserves the abrogated, but not the abrogating, ruling. He himself would reject it if he knew it was abrogated; the Muslims would reject it too if they knew it was abrogated. The fourth is a man who never attributes words falsely to God or to his Messenger. He fears God and reveres God's Messenger, and he detests lies. He does not err and correctly preserves what he heard, relating the report as he heard it without addition or omission. He knows the abrogating ruling and acts upon it, and he knows the abrogated act and stays away from it. He knows the specific and the general and places everything in its proper place, he knows the ambiguous and the clear. Indeed, the words the Messenger spoke were of two kinds, the specific and the general. Many who heard them did not fully understand what God or his Messenger had meant. These people narrated and interpreted them in a particular way without understanding their real meaning, or what the Messenger had intended in uttering them, or the context in which he had spoken them. Not all the Messenger's Companions questioned him and sought clarity, in fact, they used to hope that a Bedouin or a stranger would turn up and inquire so that they could hear the explanation. I, on the other hand, asked the Messenger about all his utterances and remembered them correctly. These are the categories of disagreement among the people, and the reasons for their varied narrations.

1.209 From an oration by ʿAlī:
Through his supreme power and sublime and wondrous craftsmanship, God produced dry, solid earth from the raging, crashing, ocean masses.[1] He then divided the firmament into layers and separated its mass into seven skies that held together through his command and stood at the limit he had set. The skies

---

1 I have inserted the word "earth," following Ḥ 11:52; B 640; R 2:336–337.

بأمره وقامت على حدّه يحملها الأخضر المُثْعَنْجِر والقَمْقام المسخّر قد ذلّ لأمره وأذعن
لهيبته ووقف الجاري منه لخشيته وجَبَلَ جلاميدَها ونشوزَ متونها وأطوادَها فأرساها في
مَراسيها وألزمها قراراتها فمضت رؤوسها في الهواء ورَسَبَتْ‏١ أصولها في الماء فأنهد جبالها
عن سهولها وأساخَ قواعدها في متون أقطارها ومواضع أنصابها فأشهق قلالها وأطال
أنشازها وجعلها للأرض عمادًا وأَرَزَها فيها أوتادًا فسكنت على حركتها من أن تميد
بأهلها أو تَسيخ بحَملها أو تزول عن موضعها. فسبحان من أمسكها بعد مَوَجان مياهها
وأجمدها بعد رطوبة أكنافها بجعلها لخلقه مهادًا وبسطها لهم فراشًا فوق بحر لُجّيّ راكد
لا يجري وقائم لا يسري تُكَرِكره الرياح العواصف وتَمَخَضه الغمام الذوارف ﴿إنَّ في
ذٰلِكَ لَعِبْرَةً لِمَنْ يَخْشَى﴾ .

1.210 ومن خطبة له عليه السلام

اللّهمّ أيُّما عبد من عبادك سمع مقالتنا العادلة غير الجائرة والمُصلحة في الدين والدنيا
غير المفسدة فأبى بعد سمعه لها إلّا النكوص عن نصرتك والإبطاء عن إعزاز دينك
فإنّا نستشهدك عليه يا أكبر الشاهدين شهادة ونستشهد عليه جميع من أسكنته أرضك
وسماواتك. ثمّ أنت بعْدُ المُغني عن نصره والآخذ له بذنبه.

1.211 ومن خطبة له عليه السلام

الحمد لله العليّ عن شبه المخلوقين الغالب لمقال الواصفين الظاهر بعجائب تدبيره للناظرين
الباطن بجلال عزّته عن فكر المتوهّمين العالم بلا اكتساب ولا ازدياد ولا علم مستفاد
المقدّر لجميع الأمور بلا رويّة ولا ضمير الذي لا تغشاه الظلَم ولا يستضيء بالأنوار ولا
يرهقه ليل ولا يجري عليه نهار ليس إدراكه بالأبصار ولا علمه بالأخبار.‏٢

منها في ذكر النبيّ عليه السلام

‏١ م، ي، ومصحّحة في ش، ه: كذا. ن، وأصل ش، ه: ﴿ورَسَتْ﴾.   ‏٢ ش، ن، ي: بفتح الهمزة
وكسرها معًا في كلمتي ﴿ابصان﴾ و﴿اخبار﴾. ه: ﴿بالإخبار﴾، ونسخة ﴿بالاختبار﴾.

were borne by the aquamarine depths, and those vast seas that submitted to his command bowed in reverence and stilled their flow in awe. He formed the earth's rocky crags and towering ridges and peaks, anchoring and embedding them in the seabed until their summits rose high in the firmament and their roots sank deep below the water's surface. He elevated the mountains above its plains and sank its supports into the backs of its far-reaching regions and landmarks, summits lofty and pinnacles high, columns for the earth fixed inside it like pegs. The earth became still. It no longer heaved or tossed around its inhabitants, nor sank under their weight, nor shifted position. Glory to him who stopped its movement after its waters had surged in billows, who made it dry and solid after its regions had been covered in water! He made it a cradle for his creatures and unfurled it like a carpet. He settled it on still ocean depths that do not surge, a quiet sea that does not flow, though it is whipped by blustery winds, and churned by tempestuous clouds. «There is a lesson here for all who venerate God.»[1]

1.210   From an oration by ʿAlī:[2]

God! I ask you, O greatest witness, to bear witness over any of your servants who hear my words—words that are always just, never tyrannical, always righteous, never corrupt—and, after hearing them, refuses to support you and holds back from fighting for your religion. I ask all whom you have housed upon your earth and in your skies to bear witness over him. And God, I know that you will suffice me without his support and hold him accountable for his sin.

1.211   From an oration by ʿAlī:

Praise God—exalted beyond comparisons to created beings, greater than the utterances of those who describe, manifest through his wondrous planning to beholders, concealed in his majestic might from thinkers, all-knowing without acquisition, increase, or learning, ordainer of all affairs without reflection or thought. Darkness does not cover him, lights do not illumine him, nights do not torment him, and days do not fatigue him. His perception does not stem from vision, his knowledge does not stem from reports.

From the same oration in praise of the Prophet:

---

1   Qurʾan, Nāziʿāt 79:26.
2   Presumably in Kufa, between 37/658 and 40/661. B 640: "This is an excerpt from an oration with which ʿAlī frequently urged his associates to muster against the Syrians, delivered after most of them held back from supporting him in the fight."

أرسله بالضياء وقدّمه في الاصطفاء فرتَقَ به المَفاتق وساوَر به المُغالب وذلّل به الصعوبة وسهّل به الحُزونة حتّى سرّح الضلال عن يمين وشمال.

1.212   ومن خطبة له عليه السلام

وأشهد أنّه عدلٌ عَدَل وحَكَمٌ فصَل وأشهد أنّ محمّدًا عبده وسيّد عباده كلّما نسخ الله الخلق فرقتين جعله في خيرهما لم يُسهِم فيه عاهر ولا ضرب فيه فاجر. ألا وإنّ الله جعل للخير أهلًا وللحقّ دعائم وللطاعة عِصَمًا وإنّ لكم عند كلّ طاعة عونًا من الله يقول على الألسنة ويثبّت الأفئدة فيه كفاء لمكتفٍ وشفاء لمشتفٍ. واعلموا أنّ عباد الله المستحفَظين علمه يصونون مصونه ويفجّرون عيونه يتواصلون بالولاية ويتلاقَون بالمحبّة ويَتساقَون بكأس روية ويصدرون بِريَّة لا تَشوبهم الريبة ولا تَسرع فيهم الغيبة على ذلك عقد خلقهم وأخلاقهم فعليه يتحابُّون وبه يتواصلون فكانوا كتفاضل البَذر يُنتقى فيؤخذ منه ويلقى قد ميّزه التخليص وهذّبه التمحيص. فَلْيَقْبَلَ امرؤ كرامة بقبولها وليحذر قارعة قبل حلولها ولينظر امرؤ في قصير أيّامه وقليل مقامه في منزل حتّى يستبدل به منزلًا فليصنع لمتحوّله ومعارف منتقَله. فطوبى لذي قلب سليم أطاع من يهديه وتجنّب من يُرديه وأصاب سبيل السلامة ببصر من بصّره وطاعة هادٍ أمره وبادر الهدى قبل أن تغلق أبوابه وتقطع أسبابه واستفتح التوبة وأماط الحَوبة فقد أُقيم على الطريق وهدي نهج السبيل.

1.213   ومن دعائه عليه السلام

God sent him with light and precedence among his select. Through him, God repaired torn ties, fought off powerful enemies, made the unruly tractable, and smoothed rough ground—until he had dispelled error from the right and from the left.

1.212 From an oration by 'Alī:[1]

I testify that God is the fount of justice who always gives justice, the judge whose judgment is final. I testify that Muḥammad is his servant, and the chief among his servants. Whenever God divided a blood line into two, he placed Muḥammad in the best line; no fornicator ever had a share in producing him, nor an adulterer any part. Harken to me! God has created upholders of good, pillars of right, and guardians for acts of obedience. When you perform an act of obedience, you will find that God's aid speaks to you through people's tongues and makes your hearts steadfast—God's aid suffices those who rely on it and cures those who seek to be cured. Know this: Those whom God has entrusted with preserving his knowledge protect its fortifications, pour forth its streams, associate with each other in loyalty, meet each other with affection, offer each other refreshing cups, and leave the waterhole with their thirst quenched; doubts never plague them and backbiting never gains traction. God has bound their bodies and their character to this holy way of being, and they love each other and foster mutual regard. They are like high quality grain used for planting: first it is sorted, and the best—distinguished by purity and refined by fire—is picked out and sown into the ploughed earth. Let each man among you secure honor by adopting this counsel! Let him fear the great calamity before it descends! Let each man reflect on the shortness of his days, on the brevity of his stay, in this abode that he will soon exchange for another! Let him prepare for the journey and watch for the signs of the exodus! Blessed is the person who possesses a sound heart, obeys his guide, and shuns his destroyer, who finds the road to security through the sight bestowed on him by his teacher and obedience to the commands of his guide, who hastens to attain guidance before its doors close and its ropes sever, who knocks on the door of forgiveness and repulses sin! Such a person has been placed on the right path. He has been guided to the straight road.

1.213 From a supplication by 'Alī:

---

1 Raḍī transcribes this text among 'Alī's orations, but Ibn Ṭāwūs (*Kashf*, 189–192) cites it as part of a letter, which he says 'Alī "wrote to one of his eminent companions."

الحمد لله الذي لم يُصبح بي ميّتًا ولا سقيمًا ولا مضروبًا على عُروقي بسوء ولا مأخوذًا بأسوأ عملي ولا مقطوعًا دابري ولا مرتدًّا عن ديني ولا منكرًا لربّي ولا مستوحشًا من إيماني ولا ملتبسًا عقلي ولا معذَّبًا بعذاب الأمم من قبلي. أصبحت عبدًا مملوكًا ظالمًا لنفسي لك الحجّة عليّ ولا حجّة لي لا أستطيع أن آخذ إلّا ما أعطيتني ولا أتّقي إلّا ما وَقَيْتني. اللّهمّ إنّي أعوذ بك أن أفتقر في غناك أو أضلّ في هداك أو أُضام في سلطانك أو أُضطهد والأمرِ لك. اللّهمّ اجعل نفسي أوّل كريمة تنتزعها من كرائمي وأوّل وديعة ترتجعها من ودائع نعمك عندي. اللّهمّ إنّا نعوذ بك أن نذهب عن قولك أو نفتتن عن دينك أو تَتَايَعَ بنا أهواؤنا دون الهدى الذي جاء من عندك.

1.214 ومن خطبة له عليه السلام بصفّين

1.214.1 أمّا بعد. فقد جعل الله لي عليكم حقًّا بولاية أمرِكم ولكم عليّ من الحقّ مثل الذي عليكم فالحقّ أوسع الأشياء في التواصف وأضيقها في التناصف لا يجري لأحد إلّا جرى عليه ولا يجري عليه إلّا جرى له ولو كان لأحد أن يجري له ولا يجري عليه لكان ذلك خالصًا لله سبحانه دون خلقه لقدرته على عباده ولعدله في كلّ ما جرت عليه صروف قضائه ولكنّه جعل حقّه على العباد أن يطيعوه وجعل جزاءهم عليه مُضاعفة الثواب تفضّلًا منه وتوسّعًا بما هو من المزيد أهله.

ثمّ جعل سبحانه من حقوقه حقوقًا افترضها لبعض الناس على بعض فجعلها تتكافأ في وجوهها ويوجب بعضها بعضًا ولا يُستوجب بعضُها إلّا ببعض وأعظم ما افترض

Praise God who brought me to this morning alive and healthy with no leprosy in my veins,[1] not seized for my worst deeds, or with my line of descendants severed, or an apostate from my religion, or a denier of my Lord, or estranged from my faith, or with my mind confused, or punished with the punishment meted out to nations before me. God! I have come into this morning your servant and bondsman, one who has oppressed his own soul. You have established your case against me, while I have no case to offer you. I can take nothing except what you give me, I can protect myself against nothing except what you protect me against. God! I seek refuge in you! Let me not be poor when you possess riches. Let me not stray when you are the guide. Let me not be assaulted in the domain of your authority. Let me not be persecuted when you are the one who commands. God! Of all the precious faculties I possess, let my spirit be the first thing you wrest from me. Of all the blessings you have given me in trust, let it be the first deposit you ask to be returned. God! We seek refuge in you! Do not let us forsake your word or be lured away from your religion. Do not let our passions rush us headlong into evil, rather than being led by the guidance that has come from you.

1.214 From an oration by ʿAlī at Ṣiffīn:[2]

1.214.1 God has given me rights over you by placing me in charge of your affairs, and you have rights over me, just as I have over you. Rights are the broadest of things in the scope of their delineation, but the narrowest in terms of equitable application. They are never credited to any individual except that they can also be credited against him, and they are likewise never credited against him except that they can also be credited to him. If it were possible for any being to have rights credited to but not against him, that position would be reserved for Almighty God alone; it would not apply to any of his creatures because he is all-powerful over his servants and always just in enacting his decrees. But God made it his right over his servants that they obey him, while also making it incumbent upon himself to recompense them with manifold reward through the abundant generosity and expansive bounty only he can bestow.

Then, as part of God's own rights, he mandated rights for some people over others. He balanced these rights in their various aspects, making some entail others, and some not be entailed except by others. The greatest of his mandated rights are those of the ruler over his subjects and those of subjects over

---

1 Ar. *sūʾ*, lit. "with my veins being hit with evil," translation based on Ḥ 11:85, who says that "evil" was a euphemism for "leprosy" (*baraṣ*).

2 In 37/657.

سبحانه من تلك الحقوق حقّ الوالي على الرعيّة وحقّ الرعيّة على الوالي فريضة فرضها الله سبحانه لكلّ على كلّ بجعلها نظامًا لألفتهم وعزًّا لدينهم فليست تصلح الرعيّة إلّا بصلاح الولاة ولا تصلح الولاة إلّا بٱستقامة الرعيّة. فإذا أَدّت الرعيّة إلى الوالي حقّه وأَدّى الوالي إليها حقّها عزّ الحقّ بينهم وقامت مناهج الدين وٱعتدلت معالم العدل وجرت على أذلالها السنن فصلح بذلك الزمان وطُمع في بقاء الدولة ويَئست مطامع الأعداء. وإذا غلبت الرعيّة واليَها أو أجحف الوالي برعيّته ٱختلفت هنالك الكلمة وظهرت معالم الجور وكثرت الإدغال في الدين وتُركت مَحاجّ السنن فعُمل بالهوى وعُطّلت الأحكام وكثرت علل النفوس فلا يُستوحش لعظيم حقّ عُطّل ولا لعظيم باطل فُعل فهنالك تذلّ الأبرار وتعزّ الأشرار وتعظم تَبِعات الله عند العباد.

فعليكم بالتناصح في ذلك وحسن التعاون عليه فليس أحد وإن ٱشتدّ على رضى الله حرصه وطال في العمل ٱجتهاده ببالغ حقيقة ما الله أهله من الطاعة له ولكنّ من واجب حقوق الله على العباد النصيحة بمبلغ جهدهم والتعاون على إقامة الحقّ بينهم. وليس ٱمرؤ وإن عظمت في الحقّ منزلته وتقدّمت في الدين فضيلته بفَوقِ أن يعان على ما حمّله الله من حقّه ولا ٱمرؤ وإن صغّرته النفوس وٱقتحمته العيون بِدونِ أن يعين على ذلك أو يعان عليه.

1.214.2   فأجابه رجل من أصحابه بكلام طويل يكثر فيه الثناء عليه ويذكر سمعه وطاعته له فقال عليه السلام

إنّ من حقّ من عظم جلال الله في نفسه وجلّ موضعه من قلبه أن يصغر عنده لعظم ذلك كلّ ما سواه وإنّ أحقّ من كان كذلك لَمَنْ عظمت نعمة الله عليه ولطف إحسانه إليه فإنّه لم تعظم نعمة الله على أحد إلّا ٱزداد حقّ الله عليه عُظْمًا. وإنّ من أسخف حالات الولاة عند صالح الناس أن يُظَنّ بهم حبّ الفخر ويوضع أمرهم على الكبر وقد كرهتُ أن يكون جالَ في ظنّكم أنّي أحبّ الإطراء وٱستماع الثناء ولست بحمد الله كذلك ولو كنت أحبّ أن يقال ذلك لتركته ٱنحطاطًا لله سبحانه عن تناول

their ruler. This is a duty that God has mandated for everyone over everyone, in a system that generates mutual regard and strengthens Islam. For subjects will not be righteous except when their ruler is righteous, and a ruler will not be righteous except when his subjects are steadfast. If subjects render the ruler his rights and the ruler renders them theirs, truth will become strong, the ways of religion will be established, the waymarks of justice will be fixed, and the road of the Sunnah will become easy to follow. Thereby, the age will become virtuous, the state can be expected to remain stable, and its enemies' ambitions will be thwarted. But if subjects overpower their ruler, or if the ruler overburdens his subjects, voices will be divided, oppression will rage, religious corruption will increase, and the straight road will be abandoned. Then, passions will drive actions, rules will be forsaken, and hearts will become diseased. People will cease to be outraged even when essential rights are abandoned, or great injustices perpetrated. In that moment, the pious will be shamed and the evil honored, and God will afflict his servants with great punishments.

People, counsel one another in this matter and help one another as you should. No one, no matter how strong his wish to secure God's pleasure, or how far-reaching his efforts in doing good, is capable of rendering to God the obedience that is truly his due. God has mandated as a right for himself over his servants that they counsel one another as much as they are able, and help one another in establishing what is proper. No man, no matter how great his station in truth, or how superior his precedence in religion, is above needing help in establishing God's charge. And no man, no matter how servile people might think him, or how humble he may appear to their eyes, is too lowly to help in this, or to be helped.

1.214.2 One of ʿAlī's associates responded with a long speech, in which he praised ʿAlī profusely and declared that he would hear and obey,[1] to which ʿAlī countered:
Those who feel God's majesty in their souls and his grandeur in their hearts should find all else insignificant by comparison; those who have received his great blessings and sublime favors should be the most assiduous in this regard, for when God's blessings for a person increase, God's rights over him also increase. The pious would say that it is the most foolish rulers who crave acclaim and who ground their authority in pride, so I am mortified that you thought your adulation and praise would please me. But, by God's grace, I am not that man. Even if I had relished that kind of speech, I would have set it aside in submission to God, not daring to stretch my hand toward that greatness and

---

1 Text of the man's full speech reported by Kulaynī, *Kāfī*, 5:352.

ما هو أحقّ به من العظمة والكبرياء. وربّما ٱستحلى الناس الثناء بعد البلاء فلا تُثنوا
عليّ بجميل ثناء لإخراجي نفسي إلى الله وإليكم من البقيّة١ في حقوق لم أفرغ من أدائها
وفرائض لا بدّ من إمضائها. فلا تكلّموني بما تُكلّم به الجبابرة ولا تتحفّظوا منّي بمايُتحفّظ به
عند أهل البادرة ولا تخالطوني بالمُصانعة ولا تظنّوا بي ٱستثقالًا لحقّ قيل لي ولا ٱلتماس
إعظام لنفسي فإنّه من ٱستثقل الحقّ أن يقال له أو العدل أن يعرض عليه كان العمل
بهما عليه أثقل. فلا تكفّوا عن مقالة بحقّ أو مشورة بعدل فإنّي لست في نفسي بِفَوْقِ أن
أخطئ ولا آمن ذاك من فعلي إلّا أن يكفي الله من نفسي ما هو أملك به منّي. فإنّما أنا
وأنتم عبيد مملوكون لربّ لا ربّ غيره يملك منّا ما لا نملك من أنفسنا وأخرجنا ممّا كنّا
فيه إلى ما صلحنا عليه فأبدلنا بعد الضلالة بالهدى وأعطانا البصيرة بعد العمى.

1.215 ومن كلامه له عليه السلام

1.215.1 اللّهمّ إنّي أستعديك على قريش فإنّهم قد قطعوا رحمي وكَفَؤُوا إنائي وأجمعوا على
منازعتي حقًّا كنت أولى به من غيري وقالوا ألا إنّ في الحقّ أن تأخذه وفي الحقّ أن
تُمنعه فاصبر مغمومًا أو مُتْ متأسّفًا. فنظرتُ فإذا ليس لي رافد ولا ذابّ ولا مساعد
إلّا أهل بيتي فضننت بهم عن المنيّة فأغضيت على القذى وجرعت ريقي على الشجى
وصبرت من كظم الغيظ على أمَرّ من العَلْقَم وآلَم للقلب من حَزّ الشِّفار.

وقد مضى هذا الكلام في أثناء خطبة متقدّمة إلّا أنّي كرّرته هٰهنا لٱختلاف الروايتين.

١م، يي، ه، ومصحّحة في ش: كذا. ن، وأصل ش، ونسخة في ه: ⟨التقيّة⟩.

glory of which he is far worthier than I. It may be that some people do find praise sweet after achieving an intensely contested victory, but don't shower me with praise just yet for having fought in God's cause and yours—I still have many obligations to discharge and many requirements to fulfill. Don't address me as you would tyrants, don't be wary of me as you would those quick to anger, don't try to influence me with flattery. Don't think, moreover, that I should be pained by a word spoken to me in truth, or that I should think myself above it. Anyone who finds the truth painful to hear, who is angered when presented with a sound opinion, will find action even harder. Don't hold back from telling me the truth or offering good counsel, for I don't consider myself above error,[1] nor do I count myself safe in my actions, except that God, who has the power to do so, will save me, I know. You and I are his slaves and bondsmen, there is no Lord other than he—he owns us more surely than we own ourselves. He brought us out from where we were to a better place, replacing our error with guidance, and our blindness with sight.

1.215 From an address by ʿAlī:[2]

1.215.1 God! I ask your help against the Quraysh! They have severed my kinship, upended my vessels, and banded together to wrest from me a right that I have always been worthier of than any other. They mocked, "A right may be taken, and a right may also be denied, so bear your grief, or die lamenting!" I looked around and saw no supporter, no protector, no helper other than my own family, and I chose to save them from sure death. I closed my eyes tight against the dust, choked on my saliva, and swallowed my anger, in a state that was more bitter than colocynth and caused my heart more anguish than a knife wound.

Raḍī: These lines were seen in an earlier oration—I have repeated them here because some language is different.[3]

---

1   The Shiʿi commentators see this line as evidence of ʿAlī's humility (R 2:357; B 650). The Sunni commentator interprets it as an admission of fallibility (Ḥ 11:107–108).

2   Some sources transcribe this text as part of an epistle ʿAlī sent to be read out in public to his supporters following ʿAmr ibn al-ʿĀṣ's killing of Muḥammad ibn Abī Bakr in Egypt in 38/658 (Thaqafī, *Ghārāt*, 1:302, 308, 311; Ibn Ṭāwūs, *Kashf*, 174, 180). It refers to the succession after the Prophet's death in 11/632 and also to the Shūrā Council that appointed ʿUthmān in 23/644. The text could have been first delivered as an oration, then transcribed and disseminated as an epistle. It could also be that the historians are unsure about the genre because excerpts from orations and epistles from the early period are stylistically quite similar. See discussion of this similarity in Qutbuddin, *Arabic Oration*, 416–419.

3   First half of §1.215.1 in §1.170.3, second half in §1.26.2.

1.215.2 ومنه في ذكر السائرين إلى البصرة لحربه

فقدموا على عمّالي وخزّان مال المسلمين الذي في يدي وعلى أهل مصر كلّهم في طاعتي وعلى بيعتي فشتّتوا كلمتهم وأفسدوا عليّ جماعتهم ووَثَبوا على شيعتي فقتلوا طائفة منهم غدرًا وطائفة عضّوا على أسيافهم فضاربوا بها حتّى لقوا الله صادقين.

1.216 ومن كلام له عليه السلام لمّا مرّ بطلحة وعبد الرحمان بن عَتّاب بن أُسيد وهما قتيلان يوم الجمل

لقد أصبح أبو محمّد بهذا المكان غريبًا أما والله لقد كنت أكره أن تكون قريش قتلى تحت بطون الكواكب أدركت وِتري من بني عبد مناف وأفلتتني أعنان[1] بني جُمَح. لقد أَتْلَعوا أعناقهم إلى أمر لم يكونوا أهله فوُقِصوا دونه.

1.217 ومن كلام له عليه السلام

قد أحيا عقله وأمات نفسه حتّى دَقَّ جليله ولطف غليظه وبَرَق له لامع كثير البرق فأبان له الطريق وسلك به السبيل وتدافعته الأبواب إلى باب السلامة ودار الإقامة وثبتت رجلاه بطمأنينة بدنه في قرار الأمن والراحة بما اِستعمل قلبه وأرضى ربّه.

1.218 ومن كلام له عليه السلام بعد تلاوته ﴿أَلْهَاكُمُ التَّكَاثُرُ حَتَّى زُرْتُمُ الْمَقَابِرَ﴾

______

[1] ن، ش، ي، ومصحّحة في هـ: كذا. م، وأصل هـ، ومصحّحة في ش، ونسخة في ي مع تعليق معًا: ﴿أعيان﴾. ونسخة أخرى في هـ: ﴿أغيان﴾.

1.215.2 From the same address, describing those who marched to Basra to fight him:[1]
They advanced against my governors in Basra and the custodians of the public treasury under my jurisdiction, and against others among the townspeople—all bound to my obedience and pledged to my allegiance—creating division and fragmenting their unity. They attacked my followers, killing a group of them through treachery, while another group of loyalists gripped their swords and exchanged blows until they met God, having fought with true courage.

1.216 From words that ʿAlī spoke when he passed by the corpses of Ṭalḥah and ʿAbd al-Raḥmān ibn ʿAttāb ibn Asīd, who had been slain during the Battle of the Camel:[2]
Abū Muḥammad sleeps here this morning, an exile from his home! By God, I am grieved that the Quraysh should lie slain under the stars! The chieftains of Jumaḥ have escaped my grasp, but I have obtained my revenge against the clan of ʿAbd Manāf. Their necks strained after a position that did not belong to them and they were broken.

1.217 From an address by ʿAlī:
This man resuscitated his intellect and killed his sentient soul, until his body became emaciated and his frame became slight. Lightning shone in a brilliant flash that illuminated the road for him and showed the way. Doors opened before him, one after another, until they conveyed him to the door of safety and the abode of permanence. His feet stood firm, his body serene, in the stable earth of security and comfort. All this because he engaged his heart in good and pleased his Lord.

1.218 From an address by ʿAlī upon reciting, «You are obsessed with gathering more and more until you visit your graves.»[3]

---

1 Some lines of §1.215.2 also in §1.170.3.

2 Outside Basra, in 36/656. Abū Muḥammad is Ṭalḥah. ʿAbd Manāf—to which ʿAlī's and the Prophet Muḥammad's clan of Hāshim also belonged—was a sub-tribe of the Quraysh. At the Battle of the Camel, the ʿAbd Manāf clansmen killed fighting ʿAlī included ʿAbd al-Raḥmān ibn ʿAttāb, from the clan of Umayyah (Ḥ 11:123–124); Ṭalḥah and Zubayr—from the clans of Taym and Asad respectively—were also descended from ʿAbd Manāf on their mothers' side (B 652). Jumaḥ was another sub-tribe of Quraysh, and, although some of its chieftains were killed, others, including ʿAbdallāh ibn Ṣafwān and ʿAbd al-Raḥmān ibn Ṣafwān, fled; Marwān ibn Ḥakam, also from Jumaḥ, was captured and pardoned (B 652; Ḥ 11:125; see also §1.70).

3 Qurʾan, Takāthur 102:1–2.

1.218.1 ياله مَرامًا ما أبعده وزَوْرًا ما أغفله وخطرًا ما أفظعه لقد ٱستخلوا منهم أيّ مُذكّر وتناوشوهم من مكان بعيد أفبمصارع آبائهم يفخرون أم بعديد الهَلكى يتكاثرون يرتجعون منهم أجسادًا خَوَت وحركات سكنت ولأن يكونوا عِبَرًا أحقّ من أن يكونوا مُفتخَرًا ولأن يهبطوا بهم جناب ذلّة أحجى من أن يقوموا بهم مقام عزّة. لقد نظروا إليهم بأبصار العَشوة وضربوا منهم في غمرة جهالة[1] ولو ٱستنطقوا عنهم عَرَصات تلك الديار الخاوية والربوع[2] الخالية لقالت ذهبوا في الأرض ضُلّالًا وذهبتم في أعقابهم جهّالًا تطؤون في هامِهم وتَستنبتون[3] في أجسادهم وترتعون فيما لَفِظوا وتسكنون فيما خرّبوا وإنّما الأيّام بينكم وبينهم بواكٍ ونوائحُ عليكم.

1.218.2 أولئك سلف غايتكم وفُرّاط مناهلكم الذين كانت لهم مقاوم العزّ وحَلَبَات الفخر ملوكًا وسُوَقًا. سلكوا في بطون البَرزخ سبيلًا سُلّطت الأرض عليهم فيه فأكلت من لحومهم وشربت من دمائهم فأصبحوا في جَوات قبورهم جمادًا لا يَنمُون وضمارًا لا يوجدون لا يفزعهم ورود الأهوال ولا يحزنهم تنكّر الأحوال ولا يحفلون بالرواجف ولا يأذنون للقواصف غَيْبًا لا يُنتظرون وشهودًا لا يَحضرون وإنّما كانوا جميعًا فتشتّتوا وأُلّافًا فٱفترقوا. وما عن طول عهدهم ولا بعد محلّهم عميت أخبارهم وصَمّت ديارهم ولكنّهم سُقوا كأسًا بدّلتهم بالنطق خَرَسًا وبالسمع صممًا وبالحركات سكونًا فكأنّهم في ٱرتجال[4]؛ الصفة صرعى سُبات جيران لا يتأنّسون وأحبّاء لا يتزاورون بَلِيَت بينهم عُرى التعارف وٱنقطعت منهم أسباب الإخاء فكلّهم وحيد وهم جميع وهم بجانب الهجر وهم أخلّاء لا يتعارفون لليل صباحًا ولا لنهار مساء. أيّ الجديدين ظعنوا فيه كان عليهم سرمدًا شاهدوا من أخطار دارهم أفظع ممّا خافوا ورأوا من آياتها أعظم ممّا قدّروا فكِلا الغايتين مُدّت لهم إلى مَباءة فاتت مبالغ الخوف[5] والرجاء.

1.218.1 What a goal, and how distant! What a visitor, and how heedless! What a danger, and how terrible! You reckless people have emptied your minds of every lesson the dead could teach you but have seized on their ancient glories![1] Is it of the felling of your forebears that you boast? Or about the large numbers of their dead that you crow? You attempt to resurrect those spiritless corpses and stilled movements—they should be harsh lessons for you rather than a source of pride, more correctly denigrated to a place of shame than elevated to a position of honor! You view the deceased with night-blind eyes and plunge with them into the deep waters of ignorance. But if you were to ask their ruined homes and empty courtyards about them, they would answer: "They were laid in the earth in their error, and you follow in their footsteps in your ignorance. You trample on their skulls and grow crops in their corpses. You pasture on grass growing from their bodies and inhabit what they laid waste. The days will weep and wail over you, just as they wept and wailed over them."

1.218.2 They have preceded you to the destination that you too will reach. They are the early arrivals scouting out your watering hole. Rulers or subjects in this life, they grasped ploughshares of might and raced steeds of pride. Then they journeyed into the belly of the earth, where she took over, eating their flesh and drinking their blood. Morning dawned on them, inert in the clefts of their graves, a mortgage that could not be recovered. Now, the onset of dangers terrifies them no more, worsening conditions cause them no grief, they are neither shaken by earthquakes nor do they heed claps of thunder, they have vanished and are no longer awaited, they are present yet do not appear, they were all together, but now are fragmented, they were friends, but now they are separated. Their stories are forgotten and their homes silent, but not because of the time that has passed or the distance of their abodes. They have been given a cup to drink that has made their tongues dumb, their ears deaf, and their movements still—a passing observer would describe them as deep in slumber, but they are neighbors who do not give each other comfort, friends who no longer visit, the ropes of affection between them have frayed, the ties of brotherhood are severed, each of them is alone, though they are all together, each of them is forsaken, though they are all fellows. They do not recognize the morning after the night, or the evening after the day, whichever of the two they departed in, be it day or night, it stays with them forever—either they have found the dangers of their new abode far more terrifying than they had feared, or they have seen its blessed signs to be far greater than they had anticipated. Both destinations are a home whose reality surpasses all fear and all hope.

---

1 Reference to Qur'an, Saba' 34:52.

1.218.3 فلو كانوا ينطقون بها لَعَيّوا بصفة ما شاهدوا وما عاينوا ولئن عميت١ آثارهم وانقطعت أخبارهم لقد رجعت فيهم أبصار العبر وسمعت عنهم آذان العقول وتكلّموا من غير جهات النطق فقالوا كَلَحَت الوجوه النواضر وخَوَت الأجساد النواعم ولبسنا أهدام البِلى وتكاءَدَنا ضيق المضجع وتوارثنا الوحشة وتهكّمت علينا الربوع الصّموت فأَمّحت محاسن أجسادنا وتنكّرت معارف صورنا وطالت في مساكن الوحشة إقامتنا ولم نجد من كَرب فرجًا ولا من ضيق متّسعًا. فلو مثّلتهم بعقلك أو كشف عنهم محجوب الغطاء لك وقد ارتسخت أسماعهم بالهَوامّ فاستكّت واكتحلت أبصارهم بالتراب نخسفت وتقطّعت الألسنة في أفواههم بعد ذَلاقتها وهَمدت القلوب في صدورهم بعد يقظتها وعاث في كلّ جارحة منهم جديد بِلًى سَمّجها وسهّل طرق الآفة إليها مستسلمات فلا أيدٍ تدفع ولا قلوب تجزع لرأيت أشجان قلوب وأقذاء عيون. لهم في كلّ فظاعة صفة حال لا تنتقل وغمرة لا تنجلي.

1.218.4 فكم أكلت الأرض من عزيز جسد وأنيق لون كان في الدنيا غَذيّ تَرَف وربيب شرف يتعلّل بالسرور في ساعة حزنه ويفزع إلى السَّلوة إن مصيبة نزلت به ضِنًّا بغَضارة عيشه وشَحاحةً بلَهوِه ولعبه. فبينا هو يضحك إلى الدنيا وتضحك إليه في ظلّ عيش غَفول إذ وطئ الدهر به حَسكه ونقضت الأيّام قواه ونظرت إليه الحُتوف من كَثَب نخالطه بَثٌّ لا يعرفه ونجيّ همّ ما كان يجده وتولّدت فيه فترات علل آنس ما كان بصحّته ففزع إلى ما كان عوّده الأطبّاء من تسكين الحارّ بالقارّ وتحريك البارد بالحارّ فلم يطفئ ببارد إلّا ثَوّر حرارة ولا حرّك بحارٍّ إلّا هيّج برودة ولا اعتدل بممازج لتلك الطبائع إلّا أمدّ منها كلّ ذات داء حتّى فتر معلِّله وذهل ممرِّضه وتعايا أهلُه بصفة دائه وخرسوا عن جواب السائلين عنه وتنازعوا دونه شجى خبرٍ يكتمونه. فقائل هو لما به ومُمنٍّ لهم إياب عافيته ومُصبِّر لهم على فقده يذكِّرهم أسى الماضين من قبله. فبينا هو كذلك على

1.218.3 Had they been able to speak, they would have faltered in describing what they witnessed, what they saw. But even though their traces are effaced, and their stories erased, eyes that heed warnings can still see them, and ears of the intelligent can hear. For they speak to us, though without the instruments of speech, and this is what they have to say: "Our fresh faces have become foul, and our soft bodies putrid; we have donned the rags of decay, and the narrow walls of our bedchambers hem us in, we have inherited the desolate strip of the grave, and this silent bier mocks us—here the beauties of our bodies are erased, our defined features are unrecognizable. Long has been our stay in this desolate residence—we find no relief from our agony, no release from our fetters!" If you were to depict them in your imagination, or if the veil were removed and you could actually see them, this is what you would see: ears blocked up and crawling with scorpions, eyes burst open and dirt the kohl that smears them, tongues cut out after keen eloquence, hearts once vigilant fallen silent in breasts, decay, ever new, ravaging each of their limbs, making them hideous, and preparing the way for yet more calamities to attack. All this, while the dead lie submissive, hands unable to push anything away, hearts unable to recoil. You would see the real anguish in each of their hearts and the pus in each of their eyes. The abominations never move away. The pangs of horror never dissipate.

1.218.4 How completely has the earth eaten up that precious body, that elegant color that was nurtured in luxury and reared in grace! Whenever its owner was faced with grief, he would soothe himself with sensual pleasures, whenever a catastrophe descended, he would seek comforts, clinging to the freshness of his life and unwilling to give up his frolicsome play in the shade of his reckless life. But even as he smiled at the world, and even as she smiled back at him, time pierced him with its thorns, the days assaulted his senses, and death's eyes drew ever closer. Then, a new and alien sorrow infected him, and anxieties never felt before whispered in his ear. Earlier smugly complacent about his health, disease now birthed lassitude in his body. He rushed to physicians for treatments, suppressing hot with cold and expelling cold with hot, but his attempt to extinguish hot with cold only made the heat blaze, and his attempt to expel cold with hot only made the blast more frigid—his attempt to balance the mixtures of these elements only worsened his diseased organs. Eventually, his consolers grew tired and his attendants neglectful. His family were no longer able to describe his disease, and they stopped answering any who inquired about his condition. They argued among themselves about the gravity of his condition and concealed their thoughts from him. One said, "His disease will take him." Another spoke hopefully of recovery. A third urged the family to bear his loss with patience, reminding them of how generations had borne losses in the past.

جَناح من فراق الدنيا وترك الأحبّة إذ عرض له عارض من غُصصه فتحيّرت نوافذ فطنته ويبست رطوبة لسانه فكم من مهمّ من جوابه عرفه فعَيَّ عن ردّه ودعاءٍ مؤلم لقلبه سمعه فتَصامَّ عنه من كبير كان يعظّمه أو صغير كان يرحمه. وإنّ للموت لغمرات هي أفظع من أن تَستغرق بصفة أو تعتدل على عقول أهل الدنيا.

1.219 ومن كلام له عليه السلام عند تلاوته ﴿رِجَالٌ لَّا تُلْهِيهِمْ تِجَارَةٌ وَلَا بَيْعٌ عَن ذِكْرِ اللهِ﴾

1.219.1 إنّ الله سبحانه جعل الذكر جِلاءً للقلوب تسمع به بعد الوَقْرة وتبصر به بعد العَشوة وتَنقاد به بعد المُعاندة وما بَرِح لله عزّت آلاؤه في البُرهة بعد البرهة وفي أزمان الفترات عباد ناجاهم في فكرهم وكلّمهم في ذات عقولهم فاستصبحوا بنور يقظة في الأسماع والأبصار والأفئدة يذكِّرون بأيّام الله ويخوّفون مقامه بمنزلة الأدلّة في الفَلَوات من أخذ القصد حمدوا إليه طريقه وبشّروه بالنجاة ومن أخذ يميناً وشمالاً ذمّوا إليه الطريق وحذّروه من الهلكة وكانوا كذلك مصابيح تلك الظلمات وأدلّة تلك الشبهات. وإنّ للذكر لأهلاً أخذوه من الدنيا بدلاً فلم تشغلهم تجارة ولا بيع عنه يقطعون به أيّام الحياة ويهتفون بالزواجر عن محارم الله في أسماع الغافلين ويأمرون بالقسط ويأتمرون به وينهون عن المنكر ويتناهَون عنه فكأنّما قطعوا الدنيا إلى الآخرة وهم فيها فشاهدوا ما وراء ذلك وكأنّما اطّلعوا غيوب أهل البَرزخ في طول الإقامة فيه وحقّقت القيامة عليهم

While this man was thus perched on the wing of departure from the world and of separation from loved ones, a sudden obstruction choked his throat. His acumen turned to bewilderment and the saliva dried up on his tongue. How many an important answer he knew but was unable to give! How many an entreaty pained his heart, but he was forced to turn a deaf ear! A question coming from an elder whom he revered, an appeal from a young one whom he loved! Truly, the pangs of death are too terrible to be contained in any description, or to be grasped by the minds of the living.

1.219 From an address by ʿAlī upon reciting, «They are men whom neither commerce nor trade distracts from God's remembrance.»[1]

1.219.1 God has made his remembrance the burnish for your hearts[2]—with it, you can hear after your earlier deafness, see after your earlier night-blindness, and quieten after your earlier recalcitrance. Age after age, even in periods of dormancy, God communicates with certain servants whose minds he speaks to and whose intellects he engages, who kindle bright lamps of vigilance in people's ears, eyes, and hearts. God's gifts are precious! Guides in the wilderness, his chosen men remind the nations of his special days,[3] and warn them that their meeting with him is near. They praise those who keep to the middle road and give them tidings of salvation, they censure those who stray to the right and the left and caution them against damnation—in this way, they serve as lamps in times of darkness and guides in periods of doubt. Remembrance is the province of men who consider it fair exchange for worldly chattels, neither commerce nor trade distracts them from it. They traverse their days always remembering God, crying warnings against the illicit to the ears of the heedless, commanding justice and undertaking it, forbidding evil and staying away from it. You would think they have already cut through the world to the hereafter and are there now, as though they have already witnessed what is beyond the grave. You would think they were privy to the mysteries of the Barzakh from

---

1   Qurʾan, Nūr 24:37. On this oration, see Shah-Kazemi, *Justice and Remembrance*, 134–207.

2   "Remembrance" (*dhikr*) refers to (1) remembering God with the heart and with the tongue (Ḥ 11:178; R 2:381; ʿA 668); and, specifically, (2) the Qurʾan (B 658–659), among whose names is "The Wise Remembrance (*al-Dhikr al-ḥakīm*)," which reminds people of God.

3   Lit. "God's days" (*ayyām Allāh*), were either (1) days of calamity when retribution descended on past nations who defied God (R 2:382; B 659), or (2) days that God had consecrated for his worship.

عِداتها فكشفوا غطاء ذلك لأهل الدنيا حتّى كأنّهم يرون ما لا يرى الناس ويسمعون ما لا يسمعون.

1.219.2 فلو مثّلتهم لعقلك في مَقاوِمهم المحمودة ومجالسهم المشهودة وقد نشروا دواوين أعمالهم وفرغوا لمحاسبة أنفسهم على كلّ صغيرة وكبيرة أمِروا بها فقصّروا عنها أو نُهوا عنها ففرّطوا فيها وحَمَلوا ثقل أوزارهم ظهورهم فضعفوا عن الاستقلال بها فنشجوا نشيجًا وتجاوبوا نحيبًا يَعِجّون إلى ربّهم من مقام ندم واعتراف لرأيت أعلام هدى ومصابيح دُجى قد حفّت بهم الملائكة وتنزّلت عليهم السكينة وفُتحت لهم أبواب السماء وأعدّت لهم مقاعد الكرامات في مقام¹ اطّلع الله عليهم فيه فرضي سعيهم وحمد مقامهم يتنسّمون بدعائه روح التجاوز. رهائن فاقة إلى فضله وأسارى ذلّة لعظمته جرح طول الأسى قلوبهم وطول البكا عيونهم لكلّ باب رغبة إلى الله منهم يد قارعة يسألون من لا تضيق لديه المنادح ولا يخيب عليه الراغبون. فحاسب نفسك لنفسك فإنّ غيرها من الأنفس لها حسيب غيرك.

1.220 ومن كلام له عليه السلام قاله عند تلاوته ﴿يَا أَيُّهَا الْإِنسَانُ مَا غَرَّكَ بِرَبِّكَ الْكَرِيمِ﴾

1.220.1 أَدْحَضُ مسؤولٍ حجّةً وأقطع مغترّ معذرة لقد أبرح جهالة بنفسه. يا أيّها الإنسان ما جرّأك على ذنبك وما غرّك بربّك وما آنسك بهلكة نفسك أما من دائك بُلول أم ليس من نَوْمَتك يقظة أما ترحم من نفسك ما ترحم من غيرها فلربّما ترى الضاحي لحرّ الشمس فتظلّه أو ترى المبتلى بألم يُمِضّ جسده فتبكي رحمة له فما صبّرك على دائك

---

¹ م، ومصحّحة في ش، هـ: كذا. ن، ي، وأصل ش، هـ، ونسخة في م: ‹مقعد›.

long residence in it,[1] as though they have already seen the resurrection fulfilling its promise. These men draw back the veil for the living, until those who heed them see what most cannot see and hear what most cannot hear.

1.219.2 You will see the strength of their piety if you picture them in their praiseworthy standings and laudable sittings. You will see them as they unfold the registers of their deeds and apply themselves to reckoning their accounts; as they list every small and large deed they were commanded to perform but fell short in accomplishing, and note every one they were forbidden but transgressed; as they feel the weight of their sins on their backs, but find themselves too weak to bear the burden; as they sob then and choke with tears, and wail to one another, and cry out to their Lord from repentance and recognition. You will see that they are true banners of guidance and lamps in the darkness, shaded by angels, enveloped by gentle calm, awaited by heaven's open doors. There, they are promised seats of high honor near God—he will be pleased with their deeds and praise their efforts, and they will surely inhale the wafting fragrance of his pardon. In this world, they choose to remain hostage to his generosity and captives to his majesty. Long repentance has wounded their hearts and long weeping has wounded their eyes. Their hand knocks ceaselessly at every door of divine supplication—and surely, they petition the one whose generosity never fades, whose suppliants are never rebuffed. O listener, call yourself to account for your own soul! Other souls have a reckoner other than you.

1.220 From an address by ʿAlī upon reciting, «O human, what has deceived you into neglecting your Generous Lord?»[2]

1.220.1 Of all who could be questioned, you have the most unstable arguments and the most deficient excuses, your ignorance of yourself is extreme—O human, what has emboldened you to sin, what has deceived you into neglecting your Lord, what has made you complacent about the damnation of your soul? Will you not cure yourself of your disease, will you not wake from your slumber, will you not feel compassion for your own soul as you have compassion for others? You see a person burning in the hot sun, and you offer him shade. You see a person whose body is wracked with pain, and you weep for

---

1 "The Barzakh," lit., "a thing that intervenes between any two things," (Lane, *Lexicon*, s.v. "B-R-Z-Kh"), interpreted as the intermediary station between life on earth and the final end in hell or paradise.

2 Qurʾan, Infiṭār 82:6.

وجلّدك على مصابك وعزّاك عن البكاء على نفسك وهي أعزّ الأنفس عليك وكيف لا يوقظك خوف بَيات نقمة وقد تورّطت بمعاصيه مدارج سطواته. فتَداوَ من داء الفترة في قلبك بعزيمة ومن كَرى الغفلة في ناظرك بيقظة وكن لله مطيعًا وبذكره آنسًا وتمثّل في حال توليّك عنه إقباله عليك يدعوك إلى عفوه ويتغمّدك بفضله وأنت متولٍّ عنه إلى غيره.

1.220.2   فتعالى من قويّ ما أكرمه وتواضعتَ من ضعيف ما أجرأك على معصيته وأنت في كنف ستره مقيم وفي سعة فضله متقلّب فلم يمنعك فضله ولم يهتك عنك ستره بل لم تخل من لطفه مَطْرَفَ عين في نعمة يحدثها لك أو سيّئة يسترها عليك أو بليّة يصرفها عنك فما ظنّك به لو أطعته وأيم الله لو أنّ هذه الصفة كانت في مُتّفِقَيْنِ في القوّة متوازِيَين في القدرة لكنتَ أوّل حاكم على نفسك بذميم الأخلاق ومساوي الأعمال.

وحقًّا أقول ما الدنيا غرّتك ولكن بها اغتررت ولقد كاشفتك العظات وآذنتك على سواء وهي بما تعدك من نزول البلاء بجسمك والنقص¹ في قوّتك أصدق وأوفى من أن تكذبك أو تغرّك ولربّ ناصح لها عندك متّهم وصادق من خبرها مكذّب ولئن تعرّفتها في الديار الخاوية والربوع الخالية لتجدنّها من حسن تذكيرك وبلاغ موعظتك بمحلّة الشفيق عليك والشحيح بك ولنعم دار من لمريض بها دارًا ومحلّ من لم يوطّنها محلًّا وإنّ السعداء بالدنيا غدًا هم الهاربون منها اليوم إذا رجفت الراجفة وحقّت بجلائلها القيامة ولحق بكلّ منسك أهله وبكلّ معبود عبدته وبكلّ مطاع أهل طاعته. فلم يُجْزَ في عدله وقسطه يومئذ خرق بصر في الهواء ولا همس قدم في الأرض إلّا بحقّه فكم حجّة يوم ذاك داحضة وعلائق عذر منقطعة. فتَحَرَّ من أمرك ما يقوم به عذرك وتثبت به حجّتك وخذ ما يبقى لك ممّا لا تبقى له وتيسّر لسفرك وشِم برق النجاة وأرحل مطايا التشمير.

---

him. What has made you so stoic about your own disease, so forbearing in your own affliction, so resigned that you do not weep for your own soul? It is surely the most precious of all souls to you! How is it that fear of a sudden strike in the night does not keep you awake, when your sins have hurled you into the path of God's assaults? Renew your resolve and vigilance, O human, cure your heart of apathy and your eyes of slumber. Obey God and take comfort in his remembrance! While you are turning away from him, picture him turning to you, calling you to his forgiveness, covering you with his generosity, even as you turn from him to another.

1.220.2 How exalted is God, how strong, how generous! How lowly you are, how weak, how brazen! You continue to disobey him while you enjoy his shelter, while you live in the shade of his expansive generosity, yet he neither holds back his gifts nor rends the veil he has drawn. Never, even for the blink of any eye, are you deprived of his many kindnesses—here he bestows a favor, there he conceals a transgression, here again he turns a calamity away from you. How do you think he will treat you then if you obey him? By God, if this situation obtained among two individuals equal in strength and identical in power, you would be the first to condemn yourself for your immoral traits and wicked deeds!

I say this truly: The world has not deceived you, it is you who have chosen to be deceived. She, in fact, has given you open counsel and fair warning. In all that she promises—of affliction attacking your body and your strength waning— she is too true, too faithful to lie or deceive. How many counsellors she sent have you accused of falsehood? How many reports she recounted have you refused to believe? If you were to seek knowledge of her reality in her empty homes and abandoned courtyards, you would discover through these striking reminders and far-reaching counsel that the world feels only compassion for you and deep caring. O how good a home she is for those who don't want her as their home! How good an abode she is for those who don't adopt her as their native land! Those who flee from the world today are those to whom she will grant true happiness tomorrow. This, when the earth convulses at the blast of the trumpet, when the resurrection with its great calamities arrives, when all followers are given over to the rites they followed, all worshippers are given over to the deities they worshipped, and all who obeyed are given over to those they obeyed. That day, in the realm of God's fairness and justice, every glance of an eye, every tread of a foot, will be requited with its due. How many arguments will be refuted on that day, how many trailing excuses will be severed! Follow a course, then, that will support your account and prove your claim. Take provisions that will remain for you, from this place in which you will not remain. Prepare for your journey. Seek the rain-giving lightning of salvation. Saddle the steeds of readiness.

1.221 ومن كلامه له عليه السلام

1.221.1 والله لأن أبيت على حَسَكِ السعدان مسهّدًا وأُجَرّ في الأغلال مصفّدًا أحبّ إليّ من أن ألقى الله ورسوله يوم القيامة ظالمًا لبعض العباد وغاصبًا لشيء من الحُطام وكيف أظلم أحدًا لنفس يسرع إلى البِلى قفولها ويطول في الثرى حلولها.

1.221.2 والله لقد رأيت عقيلًا وقد أملق حتّى اَستماحني من بُرّكم صاعًا ورأيت صبيانه شُعْث الألوان من فقرهم كأنّما سوّدت وجوههم بالعِظلِم وعاودني مؤكّدًا وكرّر عليّ القول مرّددًا فأصغيت إليه سمعي فظنّ أنّي أبيعه ديني وأتّبع قياده مفارقًا طريقتي فأحميت له حديدة ثمّ أدنيتها من جسمه ليعتبر بها فضجّ ضجيج ذي دَنَف من ألمها وكاد أن يحترق¹ من مِيسمها. فقلت له ثكلتّكَ الثواكل يا عقيل أتئنّ من حديدة أحماها إنسانها للعبه وتجرّني إلى نار سجّرها جبّارها لغضبه أتئنّ من الأذى ولا أئنّ من لظى.

1.221.3 وأعجبُ من ذلك طارقٌ طرقنا بملفوفة في وعائها ومعجونة شَنِئتُها كأنّما عُجنت بريق حيّة أو قَيئها فقلت أصلة أم زكاة أم صدقة فذلك محرّم علينا أهلَ البيت فقال لا ذا ولا ذاك ولكنّها هديّة فقلت هَبِلَتْكَ الهُبول أعن دين الله أتيتني لتخدعني أمختبط أم ذو جِنّة أم تهجر. والله لو أُعطيت الأقاليم السبعة بما تحت أفلاكها على أن أعصي الله في نملة

---

¹ ش، ن، ه، ونسخة في م: كذا. م، ي: ﴿يحرق﴾. نسخة في ه: ﴿يخرق﴾.

1.221 From an address by ʿAlī:[1]

1.221.1 By God! I would prefer to lie on a bed of three-pronged Saʿdān thorns and be dragged along the ground in iron fetters than to meet God and his Messenger on the day of resurrection having oppressed any of his servants or having usurped any part of any person's property! How could I oppress someone to benefit a body that is part of a caravan speeding toward decay, which will long reside inside the belly of the earth!

1.221.2 By God! I saw ʿAqīl, in his dire poverty, begging me for a measure of wheat from the treasury, and I saw his children, ashen from destitution, as if their faces had been blackened with indigo.[2] He implored, he insisted, he entreated over and over, and since I listened, he assumed I would sell out my religion. He thought I'd be led by his rope and step off my path. I wanted him to understand. I heated an iron bar and brought it close to his body, and he screamed in pain, as if stabbed by the pangs of an excruciating illness. "May your women mourn you, ʿAqīl!" I cried, "How do you bawl so from the pain inflicted by an iron that a human has carelessly heated, while you drag me into the Fire of Wrath stoked by the All-Powerful Lord? How is it that you scream from this small injury and think I should not scream from the flames of hell?"

1.221.3 Even stranger is the case of the night visitor who brought me a gift wrapped in a box, a cake that I found as hateful as though it had been kneaded with the venom or bile of a snake.[3] "Is this an offering to curry favor, or the alms-levy, or charity?" I asked him, "for all those are forbidden to us, the Prophet's household." "It is none of those, but a free gift," he replied. I rebuked him then, "May your mother lose you! Have you come to lead me astray from God's religion? Has the devil touched you, or the jinn? Are you in a state of delirium?"[4] By God, if I were given the earth's seven climes and everything that lies below the celestial spheres in exchange for disobeying God in something as paltry as snatching the husk of a single grain of barley from the mouth

---

1 Presumably in Kufa after the arbitration in 37/658, since ʿAqīl (mentioned at §1.221.2) then went to Muʿāwiyah for help.
2 ʿAqīl ibn Abī Ṭālib was ʿAlī's brother. Details of ʿAlī's exchange with him are related in Ḥ 11:250–254; Māmaṭīrī, *Nuzhah*, 125–131.
3 The "night-visitor" is said to be the Kufan notable al-Ashʿath ibn Qays. Ḥ 11:247–248; B 667.
4 It is possible that ʿAlī's reply to Ashʿath continues to the end of the following line, "... I should not do so."

أسلبها جِلْبَ شَعيرة ما فعلته. وإنّ دنيا كم عندي لأهون من ورقة في فم جَرادة تَقضُمها. ما لعليّ ولنعيمٍ يفنى ولذّة لا تبقى. نعوذ بالله من سُبات العقل وقبح الزلل وبه نَستعين.

1.222 ومن دعاء له عليه السلام

اللّهمّ صُن وجهي باليسار ولا تبذل جاهي بالإقتار فأسترزقَ طالبي رزقِك[1] وأستعطفَ شِرار خلقك وأُبتلى بحمد من أعطاني وأُفتتَن بذمّ من منعني وأنت من وراء ذلك كُلّه وليّ الإعطاء والمنع ﴿إِنَّكَ عَلَى كُلِّ شَيْءٍ قَدِيرٌ﴾.

1.223 ومن خطبة له عليه السلام

دار بالبلاء محفوفة وبالغدر معروفة لا تدوم أحوالها ولا يسلم نزّالها أحوال مختلفة وتارات متصرّفة العيش فيها مذموم والأمان منها معدوم وإنّما أهلها فيها أغراض مستهدفة ترميهم بسهامها وتُفنيهم بحُمامها. واّعلموا عباد الله أنّكم وما أنتم فيه من هذه الدنيا على سبيل من قد مضى قبلكم ممّن كان أطول منكم أعمارًا وأعمر ديارًا وأبعد آثارًا أصبحت أصواتهم هامدة ورياحهم را كدة وأجسادهم بالية وديارهم خالية وآثارهم عافية فاّستبدلوا بالقصور المشيّدة والنّمارق الممهّدة الصخور والأحجار المسنّدة والقبور اللاطئة الملحدة التي قد بُني على الخراب فِناؤها وشيّد بالتراب بناؤها فمحلّها مقترب وساكنها مغترب بين أهل محلّة موحشين وأهل فراغ متشاغلين لا يستأنسون بالأوطان ولا يتواصلون تواصل الجيران على ما بينهم من قرب الجوار ودنوّ الدار وكيف يكون بينهم تزاور وقد طحنهم بِكَلكَلِه البِلى وأكلتهم الجَنَادل والثرى. وكأن قد صرتم إلى ما صاروا إليه وأرتهنكم ذلك المضجع وضمّكم ذلك المستودع فكيف بكم لو تناهت بكم

---

of a single ant, I should not do so. This world of yours is worth less to me than a leaf munched in the mouth of a locust. What would ʿAlī want with delights that will perish and pleasures that will not remain? We entreat God to protect our intelligence from dulling, and from terrible slips and falls. It is him we ask for aid.

1.222 From a supplication by ʿAlī:
God! Protect my countenance through prosperity, do not dissipate my dignity through poverty. Let me not importune seekers of your sustenance or beg kindness from your worst creatures. Let me not be afflicted with flattering those who give or provoked to reviling those who refuse. You—beyond them all—are the one who gives or refuses, «you are powerful over all things».[1]

1.223 From an oration by ʿAlī:[2]
This is a residence encircled by trials and renowned for deceit, its conditions are never stable, its residents are never safe, its states are changing, its times are unstable, its life is sordid, its security is nonexistent, and its people are targets for arrows that shoot to kill. Servants of God, know that you, along with the world you live in, tread the path of those who went before: they were longer lived than you, they had more flourishing homes than you, they had more lasting monuments than you, but their voices have fallen silent, their breath has stilled, their bodies have decomposed, their homes are abandoned, their monuments are gone. They have exchanged fortified palaces and cushioned thrones for immovable stones and rocks, for the crushing recess of graves whose courtyard is built on ruin and shored with dirt, whose dwelling is near, but whose residents are far away and out of reach. For they reside in a community who take no comfort from one another, who need not labor yet are preoccupied, who, though they live in proximity and their homes are near, find neither solace in their homeland nor visit their neighbors. But how would they visit? For decay has crushed them, like a massive camel with a heavy chest, and rocks and earth have consumed their bodies. People, imagine that you too have arrived at the place where they have gone, as though that same bed has claimed you, that

---

1 Qurʾan, Taḥrīm 66:8.

2 Sibṭ (*Tadhkirah*, 122–123) reports this as part of an oration he says is named The Attainer, or The Eloquent Oration (*Bālighah*). In his text, he includes lines also present in §1.42, delivered in Kufa immediately following ʿAlī's arrival there after the Battle of the Camel in Rajab 36/January–February 657.

الأمور وبُعثرت القبور ﴿هُنَالِكَ تَبْلُو كُلُّ نَفْسٍ مَّا أَسْلَفَت ورُدّوا إلَى اللهِ مَوْلَاهُمُ الْحَقِّ وَضَلَّ عَنْهُم مَّا كَانُوا يَفْتَرُونَ﴾.

1.224   ومن دعائه عليه السلام

اللّٰهمّ إنّك آنس الآنسين لأوليائك وأحضرهم بالكفاية للمتوكّلين عليك تشاهدهم في سرائرهم وتطّلع عليهم في ضمائرهم وتعلم مبلغ بصائرهم فأسرارهم لك مكشوفة وقلوبهم إليك ملهوفة. إن أوحشتهم الغربة آنسهم ذكرك وإن صبّت عليهم المصائب لجأوا إلى الاستجارة بك علمًا بأنّ أزِمّة الأمور بيدك ومصادرها عن قضائك. اللّٰهمّ إن فَهِهْتُ عن مسألتي أو عَمِهتُ١ عن طلبتي فدُلَّني على مصالحي وخذ بقلبي إلى مراشدي فليس ذاك بنُكْرٍ من هداياتك ولا ببِدْعٍ من كفاياتك. اللّٰهمّ احملني على عفوك ولا تحملني على عدلك.

1.225   ومن كلام له عليه السلام

لله بلادُ٢ فلان فقد قوّم الأَوَد وداوى العَمَد أقام السنّة وخلّف الفتنة ذهب نقيّ الثوب قليل العيب أصاب خيرها وسبق شرّها أدّى إلى الله طاعته واتّقاه بحقّه رحل وتركهم في طرق متشعّبة لا يهتدي فيها الضالّ ولا يستيقن المهتدي.

1.226   ومن كلام له عليه السلام في وصف بيعته بالخلافة وقد تقدّم مثله بألفاظ مختلفة

١م، ي، ونسخة في ش، هـ: كذا. ن، وأصل ش، هـ: ﴿عميت﴾.   ٢ش، ن، ي، هـ، ومصحّحة في م: كذا. أصل م، ونسخة في ي، هـ: ﴿بلاء﴾.

same dwelling has encased you! How will it be with you when affairs end, when graves are emptied?[1] «There, each soul will be tried for what it did in past times, and all creatures will be returned to God, their true master—their falsehoods will no longer avail.»[2]

1.224 From a supplication by ʿAlī:
God! You are the greatest comforter for those who love you, the readiest caregiver for those who trust you. You see their minds, view their thoughts, and know the strength of their perceptions, their secrets are open to you, and their hearts long for you. When loneliness makes them fearful, your remembrance gives them comfort, when calamities rain down, they seek refuge in your protection. They know that your hand holds the reins of all things, that your decree steers the course of all events. God, whenever I falter in asking, whenever I stray from my goal, guide me to my advantage and lead my heart to the right path, for that is not alien to your way of guidance or new to your way of care. God, mount me on the steed of your forgiveness, do not mount me on the steed of your justice.

1.225 From an address by ʿAlī:
May God cherish the land that produced that man![3] He straightened crooked backs and healed lesions that were hidden inside fatty humps, established tradition and shunned sedition, departed with clean garments and few faults, hit the target of good and raced away from evil, offered obedience to God and feared him as was his due. But he went on, leaving others to scatter in many different paths—paths in which the errant find no guidance, the guided no certainty.

1.226 From an address by ʿAlī describing the manner of the pledge to him as caliph. Similar lines have been recorded earlier in slightly different language:[4]

---

1 Reference to Qurʾan, Infiṭār 82:4.

2 Qurʾan, Yūnus 10:30.

3 This is an idiom used for commendation. "That man," lit. "So-and-So (*fulān*)," refers, according to the Shiʿi commentators, to an unnamed Companion (R 2:402; B 682). According to the Sunni commentators, the reference is to ʿUmar (H 12:3–5; Ṭabarī, *Tārīkh*, 4:218).

4 Delivered at Dhū Qār just before the march on Basra and the Battle of the Camel in 36/656; §1.228 is part of the same oration (Mufīd, *Jamal*, 143–144, citing Wāqidī). See details of the event in Iskāfī, *Miʿyār*, 49–50. Similar lines in §1.3.4 (*Shiqshiqiyyah*), §1.53, and §1.135.2.

وبسطتم يدي فكففتها ومددتموها فقبضتها ثمّ تداككتم عليّ تَداكَّ الإبل الهيم على حياضها يوم ورودها حتّى انقطعت النعل وسقط الرداء ووطئ الضعيف وبلغ من سرور الناس ببيعتهم إيّاي أن ابتهج بها الصغير وهَدَج إليها الكبير وتحامل نحوها العليل وحَسَرت إليها الكَعاب.

١.٢٢٧ ومن خطبة له عليه السلام

١.٢٢٧.١ فإنّ تقوى الله مفتاح سداد وذخيرة معاد بها ينجح الطالب وينجو الهارب وتُنال الرغائب فاعملوا والعمل يُرفع والتوبة تنفع والدعاء يسمع والحال هادية والأقلام جارية وبادروا بالأعمال عمرًا ناكسًا أو مرضًا حابسًا أو موتًا خالسًا فإنّ الموت هادم لَذّاتكم ومكدّر شهواتكم ومُباعد طِيّاتكم زائر غير محبوب وقِرْن غير مغلوب ووات غير مطلوب قد أعلقتكم حبائله وتكنّفتكم غوائله وأقصدتكم مَعابله وعظمت فيكم سطوته وتتابعت عليكم عَدوته وقلّت عنكم نَبْوَته فيوشِك أن تغشاكم دواجي ظلله واحتدام علله وحَنادس غمراته وغواشي سكراته وأليم إزهاقه[٢] ودُجُوّ إطباقه وجشوبة[٣] مَذاقه فكأن قد أتاكم بغتةً فأسكت نجيّكم وفرّق نديّكم وعفّى آثاركم وعطّل دياركم وبعث ورّاثكم يقتَسمون تراثكم بين حميم خاصّ لم ينفع وقريب محزون لم يمنع وآخر شامت لم يجزع.

١.٢٢٧.٢ فعليكم بالجدّ والاجتهاد والتأهّب والاستعداد والتزوّد في منزل الزاد ولا تغرنّكم الدنيا كما غرّت من كان قبلكم من الأمم الماضية والقرون الخالية الذين احتلبوا درّتها وأصابوا غِرّتها وأفنوا عِدّتها وأخلقوا جِدّتها أصبحت مساكنهم أجداثًا وأموالهم

____
[١] ش، ن، ي، هـ: كذا. م: ⟨تتايعت⟩.   [٢] ش، ن، ي: كذا. م، ونسخة في هـ: ⟨إرهاقه⟩.   [٣] ش، ن، ي، هـ: كذا. م: ⟨خشونة⟩.

You pulled my hand toward you, and I resisted. You forced it open, and I closed it shut. Then, like parched camels jostling each other at the waterhole on their allocated day, you crowded around me, your sandals tearing, your cloaks falling, the slow trampled underfoot. In your delight to pledge me allegiance, children sped rejoicing, the old and unsteady hurried, the sick asked to be carried, and young girls ran out without putting on a veil.

1.227   From an oration by ʿAlī:[1]

1.227.1   Consciousness of God is the key to righteousness and a store of treasure for the return. Because of it, one who seeks succeeds, one who flees escapes, and all wishes are obtained. People, act while deeds still ascend, repentance still benefits, supplications are still heard, affairs are still calm, and pens still flow with ink. Hasten to do good before your lifespan runs out, disease seizes you, and death snatches you away. Remember that death is the destroyer of pleasures, the roiler of passions, and the expeller of hopes, a visitor who is not loved, an adversary who is never vanquished, and a shedder of blood from whom no vengeance can be extracted. Already its snares have entrapped you, its misfortunes have encircled you, and its arrowheads fly toward you. Its assault is terrible, its attack is unremitting, and chances are small that its sword will glance off your skull. Soon you will be surrounded by its lowering clouds, its burning illnesses, its dark floods, its calamitous spasms, its painful piercing, its dusky folds, and its coarse rations. Imagine that death has already, abruptly, arrived, as though it has already silenced your conversations, scattered your assemblies, erased your footsteps, emptied your homes, and prompted your heirs to divide your inheritance. There you lie—among close relatives who cannot help you, and grieving kinsfolk who cannot push away death, and among others who gloat and feel no sorrow at your departure.

1.227.2   Expend effort, work hard, prepare stocks, ready supplies, and gather provisions in this waystation. Let not the world deceive you as she deceived those before you, ancient nations and past generations who milked her udders, hoarded her choice parts,[2] used up her days, and wore out her new clothes.

---

1   Ḥ 13:7: "This is one of ʿAlī's most beautiful orations—its rhetorical embellishments (*badīʿ*, referring here to parallelism, paronomasia, antithesis, and consonant-rhyme) are clearly visible to any who would look."

2   Ar. *aṣābū ghurratahā*. Or, "benefitted from her (temporary) carelessness (*ghirratahā*)," after R 2:404; ʿA 973.

ميراثًا لا يعرفون من أتاهم ولا يحفلون من بكاهم ولا يجيبون من دعاهم فآحذروا الدنيا فإنّها غرّارة خَدوع معطية مَنوع ملبسة نَزوع لا يدوم رخاؤها ولا ينقضي عناؤها ولا يركد بلاؤها.

1.227.3 منها في صفة الزهّاد

كانوا قومًا من أهل الدنيا وليسوا من أهلها فكانوا فيها كمن ليس منها عملوا فيها بما يبصرون وبادروا فيها ما يحذرون تُقلّب أبدانهم بين ظَهْرانَي أهل الآخرة يرون أهل الدنيا يعظّمون موت أجسادهم وهم أشدّ إعظامًا لموت قلوب أحيائهم.

1.228 ومن خطبة له عليه السلام خطبها بذي قار وهو متوجّه إلى البصرة ذكرها الواقديّ في كتاب الجمل

فصدع بما أُمر به وبلّغ رسالة ربّه فَلَمَّ الله به الصدع ورتق به الفتق وألّف به بين ذوي الأرحام بعد العداوة الواغرة في الصدور والضغائن القادحة في القلوب.

1.229 ومن كلام له عليه السلام كلّم به عبد الله بن زَمَعة وهو من شيعته وذلك أنّه قدم عليه في خلافته وطلب منه مالًا فقال عليه السلام

إنّ هذا المال ليس لي ولا لك وإنّما هو فَيء المسلمين وجَلَبُ أسيافهم فإن شركتَهم في حربهم كان لك مثل حظّهم وإلّا فجَناة أيديهم لا تكون لغير أفواههم.

1.230 ومن كلام له عليه السلام

Their homes have become sepulchers and their possessions have been inherited by others. They no longer recognize those who come to them, or heed those who weep over them, or answer those who call out to them. Beware of the world! She deceives and cheats, gives then denies, provides clothes then strips them away. Her ease does not last, her struggles do not end, and her trials never quieten.

1.227.3 From the same oration, in praise of renunciants:
They were of this world yet not of her. They lived in her as those who never truly belonged, enacting what they believed and outracing what they feared.[1] Their forms moved among the people of the hereafter: they saw men here fear the death of their bodies, but they were more afraid of the death of the hearts of the living.

1.228 From an oration by ʿAlī delivered at Dhū Qār, en route to Basra, related by Wāqidī in his book on the Battle of the Camel:[2]
God's Messenger proclaimed what he had been commanded to proclaim,[3] and communicated the messages of his Lord. Through him, God mended divisions and stitched rips and tears. Through him, God brought kinsfolk together after enmity had burned in their breasts and rancor had kindled in their hearts.

1.229 From an address by ʿAlī to ʿAbdallāh ibn Zamaʿah, one of his followers, who came during his caliphate to ask for money:[4]
These funds do not belong to me, and they do not belong to you. They are battle gains won by the Muslims and wealth procured by their swords. If you join in their warfare, you will get a similar share, otherwise, the harvest of their swords is for their mouths alone.

1.230 From an address by ʿAlī:[5]

---

1 I.e., death (Ḥ 13:8); or God's punishment (B 677).
2 In 36/656, before the Battle of the Camel. Part of the same oration as §1.226.
3 Reference to Qurʾan, Ḥijr 15:94.
4 Presumably in Kufa, between 36/656 and 40/661. ʿAbdallāh ibn Zamaʿah was from Quraysh, and one of ʿAlī's devoted followers.
5 Part of a long oration (presumably in Kufa, during his caliphate, 35–40/656–661) after Jaʿdah ibn Hubayrah al-Makhzūmī, ʿAlī's nephew, who had ascended the pulpit at his command to orate, stood there tongue-tied. The Abbasid commander who defeated the Umayyads, Abū Muslim al-Khurāsānī, re-used these lines by ʿAlī in one of his well-known orations. Ḥ 13:130; B 679.

ألا إنّ اللسان بَضْعَة من الإنسان فلا يُسعده القول إذا امتنع ولا يُمهله النطق إذا اتّسع. وإنّا لأمراء الكلام وفينا تنشّبت عروقه وعلينا تهدّلت غصونه.

وآعلموا رحمكم الله أنّكم في زمان القائل فيه بالحقّ قليل واللسان عن الصدق كليل واللازم للحقّ ذليل أهله معتكفون على العصيان مصطلحون على الإدهان فتاهم عارم وشائبهم آثم وعالمهم منافق وقارئهم مماذق لا يعظّم صغيرهم كبيرهم ولا يعول غنيّهم فقيرهم.

1.231 ومن كلام له عليه السلام في ذكر اختلاف الناس. روى اليمانيّ[1] عن أحمد بن قتيبة عن عبد الله بن يزيد عن مالك بن دَجْنة[2] قال كنّا عند أمير المؤمنين عليه السلام فقال وقد ذُكر عنده اختلاف الناس

إنّما فرّق بينهم مبادئ طينهم وذلك أنّهم كانوا فِلْقة من سَبَخ أرض وعذبها وحُزون تربة وسهلها. فهم على حسب قرب[3] أرضهم يتقاربون وعلى قدر اختلافهم يتفاوتون. فتامّ الرواء ناقص العقل ومادُّ القامة قصير الهمّة وزاكي العمل قبيح المنظر وقريب القعر بعيد السَّبْر ومعروف الضريبة منكر الجليبة وتائه القلب متفرّق اللبّ وطليق اللسان حديد الجنان.

1.232 ومن كلام له عليه السلام قاله وهو يلي غسل رسول الله صلّى الله عليه وآله وتجهيزه بأبي أنت وأمّي لقد انقطع بموتك ما لم ينقطع بموت غيرك من النبوّة والأنباء وأخبار السماء. خصصت حتّى صرت مسلّياً عمّن سواك وعممت حتّى صار الناس فيك سواء.

١ش: كذا. م: ﴿الثمالﻲّ﴾. ي: ﴿اليماميّ﴾. ن: سقط الاسم. تختلف مخطوطات شرح الراونديّ، حيث تثبت ﴿ذعلب اليمانيّ﴾ و﴿أبو محمد اليمانيّ﴾. شرح ابن أبي الحديد ﴿ذعلب اليمانيّ﴾. شرح البحرانيّ: ﴿أبو محمد ذعلب اليمانيّ﴾. ﻫ: سقط التعليق بتمامه.   ٢ش: كذا. م: ﴿دُجُنَّة﴾ مشكّلة هكذا بنون مشدّدة. ي: ﴿دِحْيَة﴾. ن، ﻫ: سقط الاسم.   ٣ش، ن، ﻫ مع علامة الصحّة: كذا. م: سقطت اللفظة. ي: ﴿قرار﴾.

Hark! The tongue is but an instrument wielded by men.[1] Words do not come to it when a man feels constrained, nor does it hesitate to produce speech when its owner feels at ease. Indeed, it is we, the Prophet's family, who are the princes of language.[2] It is in us that its roots are fixed, upon us that its branches dangle.

Know this, may God have mercy on you! You live in an age when upholders of right are few, tongues are blunted against truth, and champions of justice are shamed. People in this age practice incessant disobedience and shake hands on treason. Their youth are violent, their old are sinners, their scholars are hypocrites, and their Qur'an-readers are two-faced. Their young do not respect the old, their rich do not care for the poor.

1.231 From 'Alī's address explaining why people differ. Yamānī[3] narrated this report from Aḥmad ibn Qutaybah, who narrated it from 'Abdallāh ibn Mālik ibn Dajnah,[4] who said: We were with the Commander of the Faithful when the talk turned to differences among people, and he said:

What differentiates them is the source of their clay, for they are fragments from saline or sweet soil, and from hard or smooth earth. They resemble one another based on the closeness of their soil and diverge in accordance with its difference. A person may have perfect features but an imperfect mind, or be tall in stature but short in aspiration, or have beautiful deeds but an ugly appearance, or he may have little depth yet be able to sense a great deal, or his temper could be good while his traits are bad, or his heart could be lost while his wits are also scattered, or he could possess an eloquent tongue as well as a strong heart.

1.232 From an address 'Alī delivered as he conducted the Messenger's funeral ablutions and prepared his body for burial:[5]

May my father and mother give their lives for you! Your death has cut short what the death of no other has: prophecy, divine reports, and accounts of the heavens. You brought some of us so close that you comforted us against the loss of anyone else, yet you were there for all—all people were equal in your

---

1 Ar. *badʿah*, lit. "part" or "piece," translated here as "instrument," based on Ḥ 13:12; B 679.
2 I have added "the Prophet's family" based on context in B 679.
3 Or, "Yamāmī" (MS Y), or, "Thumālī" (MS M), or, "Dhiʿlib al-Yamānī" (Ḥ, and some MSS of R).
4 Or, "Dujunnah" (MS M), or, "Diḥyah" (MS Y).
5 In Medina, in 11/632.

ولولا أنّك أمرت بالصبر ونهيت عن الجزع لأنفدنا عليك ماء الشؤون ولكان الداء مماطلًا والكَمَد محالفًا وقَلًّا لك. ولكنّه ما لا يُملك ردّه ولا يستطاع دفعه. بأبي أنت وأمّي أذكرنا عند ربّك وأجعلنا من بالك.

زيادة على الاصل[1]

1.233   ومن كلام له عليه السلام اقتصّ فيه ذكر ما كان منه بعد هجرة النبيّ صلّى الله عليه وآله ثمّ لَحاقه به

فجعلتُ أتبع ما أخذ رسول الله صلّى الله عليه فأَطأ ذِكرَه حتّى انتهيت إلى العَرج

في حديث طويل فقوله عليه السلام ⟨فأطأ ذكره⟩ من الكلام الذي رمى به إلى غايتَي الفصاحة والإيجاز وأراد أنّني كنت أُعطى خبرَه عليه السلام من بدء خروجي إلى أن انتهيت إلى هذا الموضع فكَنى عن ذلك بهذه الكناية العجيبة.

1.234   ومن خطبة له عليه السلام في شأن الحكمين وذمّ أهل الشام

جُفاةٌ طَغام وعبيد أقْزام جُمِّعوا من كلّ أوْب وتلقّطوا من كلّ شَوب ممّن ينبغي أن يُفقَّه ويؤدَّب ويعلَّم ويدرَّب ويولَّى عليه ويؤخذ على يديه. ليسوا من المهاجرين والأنصار ولا الذين تبوّءوا الدار. ألا وإنّ القوم اختاروا لأنفسهم أقرب القوم ممّا يحبّون وأنّكم اخترتم لأنفسكم أقرب القوم ممّا تكرهون. وإنّما عهدُكم بعبد الله بن قيس بالأمس يقول إنّها فتنة فقَطِّعوا أوتاركم

---

[1] أُضيفت هنا في بعض المخطوطات زيادة على الأصل قديمة، وهي عبارة عن ستّ خطب أخرى لعليّ، مسبوقة في مخطوطة ي، ه‍، ل بسطر يشير الى أن الخطب زائدة على الأصل: ⟨زيادة من نسخة كتبت في عهد المصنّف⟩. والخطب الستّة الزائدة مثبتة أيضًا في م، ج، ك، وثلاث منها في س، ولكن بدون اشارة إلى أنّها زائدة. والزوائد ساقطة عن ش، ن، د، ق، ع، ت.

eyes.[1] If you had not commanded us to be patient in adversity or forbidden outpourings of grief, we would have used up all the tears in our eyes weeping over you, and our ailment would be chronic, our grief would endure—and yet both would be sorely inadequate! But enough! Death cannot be fended off or rebuffed. May my father and mother be your ransom, O Messenger! Remember us to your Lord and keep us in your thoughts.

Additional Orations[2]

1.233 From an address by ʿAlī in which he narrated what all he did after the Prophet's migration until he caught up with him:[3]
I began to follow the path taken by God's Messenger and continued to tread the footsteps of his reports until I reached ʿAraj.
Raḍī: This is a passage from a long address by ʿAlī. His words, "I continued to tread the footsteps of his reports (*aṭaʾu dhikrahu*)," strike the targets of eloquence and pithiness both. He means that "I kept receiving word of God's Messenger from when I started out until I reached this location." He expressed this meaning through this marvelous allusion.

1.234 From an oration by ʿAlī discussing the two arbitrators and censuring the Syrians:[4]
They are uncouth riffraff and vile bondsmen gathered from every shore and gleaned from every rabble, who need to be taught, disciplined, instructed, trained, supervised, and restricted in their doings. They belong neither to the Emigrants nor the Allies who made their homes in Medina. Hark and listen! The Syrians have selected the person who is closest to what they love, while you have selected the person who is closest to what you hate. You have experienced ʿAbdallāh ibn Qays (Abū Mūsā al-Ashʿarī)! Just yesterday, he was saying to you, "This is sedition—cut your bowstrings and sheathe your swords!" If he was right then, he is wrong in marching with us today, but if he was wrong then—and he was—he deserves to be viewed with suspicion. Strike ʿAmr ibn

---

1 I have translated this differently than Ibn Abī al-Ḥadīd and Baḥrānī (Ḥ 13:24–25; B 682), who state that "making special (*khaṣaṣta*)" and "making common (*ʿamamta*)" both refer to the grief of the Prophet's passing: with their interpretation, I find the next phrase—"that you comforted us against the loss of any other"—difficult to understand. Rāwandī (R 2:415) states that the two phrases refer to the manner of the Prophet's life and death.

2 An additional six orations—perhaps added by Raḍī, or by others—are transcribed in some of our primary and secondary manuscripts (further details in the Edition's footnotes, and in Note on the Edition and Translation)

3 Details of ʿAlī's role in Muḥammad's migration in B 778; Ḥ 13:303–306, after Ibn Isḥāq, *Maghāzī*.

4 Presumably in Ṣiffīn, in 37/657, after the Syrians asked for arbitration.

526 TEXT AND TRANSLATION

وشيموا سيوفكم. فإن كان صادقًا فقد أخطأ بمسيره غير مستكره وإن كان كاذبًا فقد لزمته التهمة. فٱدفعوا في صدر عمرو بن العاص بعبد الله بن العبّاس وخذوا مُهَل الأيّام وحوطوا قواصي الإسلام ألا ترون إلى بلادكم تُغزى وإلى صَفاتكم تُرمى.

1.235 ومن خطبة له عليه السلام يذكر فيها آل محمّد عليهم السلام

هم عيش العلم وموت الجهل يخبركم حلمهم عن علمهم وصمتهم عن حُكم منطقهم لا يخالفون الحقّ ولا يختلفون فيه. هم دعائم الإسلام وولائج الاعتصام بهم عاد الحقّ في نِصابه وٱنزاح الباطل عن مَقامه وٱنقطع لسانه من مَنبِته عقلوا الدين عقل وعاية ورعاية لا عقل سَماع ورواية. وإنّ رواة العلم كثير ورعاته قليل.

1.236 ومن خطبة له عليه السلام

فٱعملوا وأنتم في نفَس البقاء والصحفُ منشورةٌ والتوبة مبسوطة والمدبر يُدعى والمسيء يرجى قبل أن يَخمَد العمل وينقطع المهل وتنقضي المدّة ويسدّ باب التوبة وتصعد الملائكة. فأخذ ٱمرؤ من نفسه لنفسه وأخذ من حيّ لميّت ومن فانٍ لباقٍ ومن ذاهب لدائم. ٱمرؤ خاف الله وهو معمّر إلى أجله ومنظور إلى عمله. ٱمرؤ أَلْجَم نفسه بلِجامها وزَمَّها بزمامها فأمسكها بلجامها عن معاصي الله وقادها بزمامها إلى طاعة الله.

1.237 ومن كلام له عليه السلام يحثّ فيه أصحابه على الجهاد

واللهُ مُستأديكم شكرَه ومورثكم أمرَه ومهلكم في مِضمار ممدود لتتنازعوا سَبقَه فشُدّوا عُقَد المآزر وأوطِئوا (أو: وٱطْوُوا) فضول الخواصر. لا تجتمع عزيمة ووليمة. وما أنقض النوم لعزائم اليوم وأمحى الظلَم لتذاكير الهمم.

al-ʿĀṣ in the chest with ʿAbdallāh ibn al-ʿAbbās! Take advantage of the respite granted by these days and protect the borders of Islam! Don't you see your lands under attack, your ramparts under siege?

1.235   From an oration by ʿAlī in which he speaks of the Prophet's family:
They are the life of knowledge and the death of ignorance. Their forbearance stems from their knowledge, and their silence from the wisdom of their speech. They never go against what is right and never differ in it. They are the pillars of Islam and the doors to the halls of protection. It is through them that right has returned to its home, wrong has been displaced from its residence, and its tongue has been excised at the root. They have assimilated religion with understanding and mindful attention, not by rote learning and narration. There are many narrators of hadith,[1] but those who tend to it mindfully are rare.

1.236   From an oration by ʿAlī:
Act while you still possess the breath of life, while registers are open and repentance is extended, while one who turns away is invited back and one who sins is asked to desist, before action is extinguished, the respite is cut short, the interlude ends, the door of repentance is shut, and the angels ascend. Let each man gather provisions by himself, for himself, by the self that is living for the self that will soon be dead, by the self that will perish for the self that will remain, by the self that will depart, for the self that will abide. Such a man fears God during his allotted span, while he is given time to act. Such a man places a bridle and halter on his sentient soul. He curbs it with this bridle from acts of disobedience to God and leads it with the halter toward acts of obedience to God.

1.237   From an address by ʿAlī urging his supporters to jihad:[2]
God has required you to thank him, given you his command, and a lengthy respite to prepare for the race so that you may compete and win. Tighten your belts and lose your belly fat, for resolve and feasting never come together. How completely does sleep destroy resolutions made in the day! How completely does darkness erase the memory of high aspirations!

---

1   Lit. "knowledge," *ʿilm*; in early Islamic times, the word usually referred to religious knowledge, and often specifically to the Prophet Muḥammad's teachings.
2   Presumably in Kufa, after the arbitration in 37/658.

1.238   من كلام له عليه السلام قاله لعبد الله بن العبّاس رضي الله عنهما وقد جاءه برسالة من عثمان بن عفّان وهو محصور يسأله فيها الخروج إلى ماله بِيَنبُع ليقلّ هتف الناس بٱسمه للخلافة بعد أن كان سأله مثل ذلك من قبل. فقال عليه السلام

يا ٱبن عبّاس ما يريد عثمان أن يجعلني إلّا جملًا ناضحًا بالغرب أُقبِل وأُدبِر. بعث إليّ أن ٱخرج ثمّ بعث إليّ أن ٱقدم ثمّ هو الآن يبعث إليّ أن ٱخرج. والله لقد دفعت عنه حتّى خشيت أن أكون آثمًا.

آخر الخطب. ويتلوه المختار من كتبه ورسائله.[1]

---

[1] م: كذا. ش: ﴿تمّت المختارات من خطب أمير المؤمنين عليه السلام ويتلوه باب المختارات من كتبه وصلّى الله على محمّد وآله الطيّبين﴾. ن، ي، هـ: سقط التعليق.

1.238 From words ʿAlī spoke to ʿAbdallāh ibn al-ʿAbbās[1]—Ibn al-ʿAbbās had brought ʿAlī a missive from ʿUthmān ibn ʿAffān, who was under siege, asking him to depart for his estate in Yanbuʿ al-Nakhl, hoping this would stop people calling out ʿAlī's name for the caliphate; ʿUthmān had made the same demand of ʿAlī earlier. ʿAlī responded to Ibn al-ʿAbbās:

Ibn al-ʿAbbās! ʿUthmān wishes to make me a camel drawing water with a pulley, constantly going forward and back! He insisted that I leave, then sent for me to return, and now he has again sent you with instructions for me to leave! By God, I have defended him until I feared I was sinning!

This is the end of the section on orations. It is followed by selections from ʿAlī's letters and epistles.

---

1 In Medina, 35/656.

باب المختار من كتب أمير المؤمنين عليه السلام ورسائله إلى أعدائه وأمراء بلاده ويدخل في ذلك ما اختير من عهوده إلى عمّاله ووصاياه لأهله وأصحابه

2.1 من كتاب له عليه السلام إلى أهل الكوفة عند مسيره من المدينة إلى البصرة

من عبد الله عليّ أمير المؤمنين إلى أهل الكوفة جبهة الأنصار وسنام العرب. أمّا بعد. فإنّي أخبركم عن أمر عثمان حتّى يكون سمعه كعيانه. إنّ الناس طعنوا عليه فكنت رجلًا من المهاجرين أكثر استعتابه وأقلّ عتابه وكان طلحة والزبير أهوَن سَيرهما فيه الوجيف وأرفق حِدائهما العنيف وكان من عائشة فيه فَلتة غضب فأتيح له قوم فقتلوه وبايعني الناس غير مستكرهين ولا مُجبَرين بل طائعين مخيَّرين. واعلموا أنّ دار الهجرة قد

2

Letters

Chapter containing selections from the Commander of the Faithful's dispatches and letters to his enemies and his regional governors, including selections from instructions to his tax collectors and testaments to his family and companions

2.1 From ʿAlī's dispatch to the residents of Kufa, when he was about to march from Medina on Basra:[1]
From God's servant, ʿAlī, Commander of the Faithful, to the residents of Kufa—renowned face of the Allies, crest of the Arabs.[2] And now to the matter at hand:

I write to inform you of what happened to ʿUthmān, and when you hear my words,[3] you will see the events unfold before your eyes: The public censured ʿUthmān for his conduct, and the Emigrants each took their stand. I tried hard to reconcile and lower the heat, while Ṭalḥah and Zubayr galloped to escalate the affair, harshly driving the camels of castigation toward their destination, and ʿĀʾishah fired out an angry outburst.[4] A group, emboldened, killed ʿUthmān. The Muslims then pledged allegiance to me as their caliph, willingly and of their free choice, without any coercion or force. Kufans, know that Medina

---

1   Sent with Ḥasan and ʿAmmār in 36/656, from Rabadhah, 200 km to the NE of Medina, soon after ʿAlī's accession to the caliphate, on his way to confront ʿĀʾishah, Ṭalḥah, and Zubayr, who had rebelled and marched to Basra to garner military support (Mufīd, *Jamal*, 131–132). See also Ibn Abī al-Ḥadīd's (H 14:8–21) "Accounts of ʿAlī's march on Basra, and his letters to the residents of Kufa." See also comments on ʿĀʾishah's, Ṭalḥah's, and Zubayr's later repentance, according to this Sunni-Muʿtazilī account (H 14:24–25).

2   "Allies" (*Anṣār*) here refers either to (1) the Medinese Allies, of which there was a small but discrete section in Kufa in the earliest time of its settlement (cf. Ṭabarī, *Tārīkh*, 4:44–45); or (2) ʿAlī's allies more generally (H 14:6; R 3:12). "Crest," lit. "camel's hump (*sanām*)."

3   Note that ʿAlī writes, "When you *hear* my words." At this time, and for some centuries thereafter, official state letters and proclamations were read out to the populace in the mosque or other public space. Similarly, in § 2.73.

4   When ʿUthmān stood up in the mosque trying to appease the public, ʿĀʾishah reportedly spoke harshly from behind a curtain, and she displayed a pair of the Prophet's slippers, shouting that ʿUthmān had "changed the Prophet's religion, when the Prophet's slippers had not even worn out" (B 785). ʿĀʾishah reportedly called out to the people of Medina to "Kill the Long-beard (*naʿthal*)!" ʿUthmān's nickname (R 3:13). Unusually, ʿAlī calls her out by name in this letter, presumably due to the very real and imminent danger she posed in that moment. In the aftermath of the battle, he used the generic "woman/women" to allude to her: § 1.13, § 1.77, § 1.151.3, § 1.154.1.

قَلَعَتْ بأهلها وقُلِعوا بها وجاشت جيش المِرجل وقامت الفتنة على القطب فأسرعوا إلى أميركم وبادروا جهاد عدوّ كم إن شاء الله.

٢.٢ ومن كتاب له عليه السلام إليهم بعد فتح البصرة

وجزاكم الله من أهل مصرٍ عن أهل[1] بيت نبيّكم أحسن ما يجزي العاملين بطاعته والشاكرين لنعمته فقد سمعتم وأطعتم ودعيتم فأجبتم.

٢.٣ ومن كتاب كتبه عليه السلام لشُرَيح بن الحارث قاضيه. روي أنّ شريح بن الحارث قاضي أمير المؤمنين اشترى على عهده دارًا بثمانين دينارًا فبلغه عليه السلام ذلك فاستدعى شريحًا وقال له بلغني أنّك ابتعت دارًا بثمانين دينارًا وكتبت كتابًا وأشهدت شهودًا. فقال شريح قد كان ذلك يا أمير المؤمنين. قال فنظر إليه نظر مُغضَب ثمّ قال له

يا شريح أما إنّه سيأتيك من لا ينظر في كتابك ولا يسألك عن بيّنتك حتّى يُخرِجك منها شاخصًا ويسلّمك إلى قبرك خالصًا. فانظر يا شريح لا تكون ابتعت هذه الدار من غير مالِكَ أو نقدت الثمن من غير حِلٍّ لك[2] فإذا أنت قد خسرت دار الدنيا ودار الآخرة. أما إنّك لو كنت أتيتني عند شرائك ما اشتريت لكتبت لك كتابًا على هذه النسخة فلم ترغب في شراء هذه الدار بدرهم فما فوقه.

والنسخة

هذا ما اشترى عبد ذليل من ميّت قد أُزعِج للرحيل اشترى منه دارًا من دار الغرور من جانب الفانين وخِطّة الهالكين. وتجمع هذه الدار حدودٌ أربعة الحدّ الأوّل ينتهي إلى دواعي الآفات والحدّ الثاني ينتهي إلى دواعي المصيبات والحدّ الثالث ينتهي إلى الهوى المردي والحدّ الرابع ينتهي إلى الشيطان المغوي وفيه يُشرَع باب هذه الدار. اشترى هذا

____

[1] م، ي، ومصحّحة في ش، ه: كذا. ن، وأصل ش، ه: سقطت ⟨أهل⟩. [2] م، ي، ومصحّحة في ش، ه: كذا. ن، وأصل ش، ه: ⟨من غير حلالك⟩.

reels, and its people reel with it.[1] It boils like a cauldron and revolt has raised its banner, so hasten to join your ruler and advance to fight your enemy! Battle, if that be God's will, looms ahead.

2.2 From 'Alī's dispatch to the residents of Kufa, after his victory at Basra:[2]
Residents of Kufa, may God reward you on behalf of your Prophet's family! May he bestow on you the reward he reserves for those who obey him through their actions and thank him for his favors! You heard and you obeyed, you were called, and you answered.

2.3 From a missive that 'Alī wrote to his judge, Shurayḥ ibn al-Ḥārith. It is related that during 'Alī's reign, Shurayḥ ibn al-Ḥārith, a judge appointed by the Commander of the Faithful, purchased a house for eighty gold dinars. The news reached 'Alī, who summoned Shurayḥ and said, "I'm told that you have bought a house for eighty gold dinars, and that you wrote up a contract and called witnesses to attest to the purchase." Shurayḥ responded, "That is correct, Commander of the Faithful." 'Alī looked at Shurayḥ with some anger, then said to him:[3]
Shurayḥ, soon there will come to you one who will not look at your written contract nor ask for your testimonials but will turn you out of your house and over to your grave. Take heed, Shurayḥ! You had better not have bought this house with money that doesn't belong to you or in coin gained from unlawful sources. If so, you will have lost the abode of this world and the abode of the hereafter. If you had come to me when you were about to buy the house, I would have written up a different kind of contract, in this manner. You would not then have wished to purchase this house for a single silver dirham, let alone for the sum you paid.

The transcript:
This is what a humble servant has bought from a soon-to-be-dead man whose departure from the world has already begun. The humble servant bought from the soon-to-be-dead man one of the houses of calamity located in the district of those soon-to-perish in the quarter of the dead. There are four borders to this house: The first extends to the summons of calamity, the second extends

---

1   "Medina," lit. "The Home of Migration" (*dār al-hijrah*; Ḥ 14:8; B 785; R 3:15). Rāwandī (R 3:15) states it could also refer to "Kufa, to which 'Alī migrated," which appears incorrect, as 'Alī settled there only after the Battle of the Camel.

2   In 36/656, in Basra, following the Battle of the Camel, sent with 'Amr ibn Salamah al-Hamdānī al-Arḥabī. The Kufans had been the mainstay of 'Alī's army. Full letter in Mufīd, *Jamal*, 216, after Wāqidī.

3   Shurayḥ served as judge in Kufa during 'Alī's reign, 35–40/656–661.

المغترّ بالأمل من هذا المُزَعِج بالأجل هذه الدار بالخروج من عزّ القناعة والدخول في ذلّ الطلب والضّراعة فما أدرك هذا المشتري فيما اشترى مِن دَرَك. فعلى مُبلبِل أجسام الملوك وسالب نفوس الجبابرة ومزيل ملك الفراعنة مثل كسرى وقيصر وتبّع وحِمْيَر ومن جمع المال على المال فأكثر ومن بنى وشيّد وزخرف ونجّد وآدّخر واعتقد ونظر بزعمه للولد إشخاصُهم جميعًا إلى موقف العرض والحساب وموضع الثواب والعقاب إذا وقع الأمر بفصل القضاء ﴿وَخَسِرَ هُنَالِكَ الْمُبْطِلُونَ﴾. شهد على ذلك العقل إذا خرج من أسر الهوى وسلم من علائق الدنيا.

٢.٤	ومن كتاب له عليه السلام إلى بعض أمراء جيشه

فإن عادوا إلى ظلّ الطاعة فذاك الذي نحبّ وإن توافت١ الأمور بالقوم إلى الشقاق والعصيان فأنهد بمن أطاعك إلى من عصاك واستغن بمن انقاد معك عمّن تقاعس عنك فإنّ المتكاره مَغيبه خير من مشهده وقعوده أغنى من نهوضه.

٢.٥	ومن كتاب له عليه السلام إلى الأشعث بن قيس وهو عامل أَذْرَبِيجان

وإنّ عملك ليس لك بطُعمة ولكنّه في عنقك أمانة وأنت مُسترعًى لمن فوقك ليس لك أن تَفتاتَ في رعيّة ولا تخاطر إلّا بوثيقة وفي يديك مال من مال الله عزّ وجلّ وأنت من خزّاني حتّى تسلّمه إليّ ولعلّي ألّا أكون شرّ ولاتك لك. والسلام.

---

to the summons of catastrophe, the third extends to destructive passions, and the fourth extends to Satan, the great deceiver. The door of this house opens from this side. This man, deceived by false hopes, has bought this house from that man, who is soon to be evicted by death. The buyer has left the protective might of contentment and entered the shameful condition of petition and entreaty—he has not purchased anything good. Might belongs to God, who decomposes the bodies of kings, snatches the souls of pharaohs, destroys the empire of despots such as Chosroes, Caesar, Tubbaʿ, and Ḥimyar, rulers who amassed wealth, who constructed, fortified, decorated, furnished, hoarded, and stockpiled, thinking they were providing for their children. When the command comes for the final judgment, all will be forced to the dock of review and reckoning, the station of reward and punishment, «and there shall the falsifiers lose everything.»[1] This contract has been witnessed by an intellect liberated from the shackles of passion and protected from worldly attachments.

2.4 From ʿAlī's dispatch to one of his army commanders:[2]
If they reenter the canopy of obedience, then that is what we desire. But if their affairs direct them to dissent and disobey, then rise up with those who obey you to fight those who disobey, make do with those who accept your leadership, without seeking the help of the recalcitrant. One who marches against his will is better absent than present. He is more helpful to us sitting than standing.

2.5 From ʿAlī's dispatch to al-Ashʿath ibn Qays, his governor in Azerbaijan:[3]
Your governorship is not a meal for you to devour but a trust to which your neck is shackled. You have been charged with taking care of it by a man who is superior to you in rank, and are not authorized to order your subjects around, or to imperil their funds—those must be secured. What you have in your hands is property belonging to God—you have been entrusted with safeguarding it and submitting it to me. Rest assured, however, that I shall be one of the kinder rulers you encounter.[4] Go in peace.

---

1 Qurʾan, Ghāfir 40:78.

2 Excerpt from dispatch to ʿUthmān ibn Ḥunayf, governor of Basra, when many residents had turned away from their sworn pledge to ʿAlī, after ʿĀʾishah, Ṭalḥah, and Zubayr marched there in the lead-up to the Battle of the Camel in 36/656. B 787.

3 Excerpt from letter to Ashʿath following the Battle of the Camel in 36/656, when Ashʿath seized 100,000 dirhams from the treasury. Minqarī, *Waqʿat Ṣiffīn*, 20; B 787; Ḥ 14:34, also records preceding lines of the text.

4 Lit. "I shall not be the worst of rulers you encounter." The line is meant to placate. B 787; Ḥ 14:34.

2.6 ومن كتاب له عليه السلام إلى معاوية

إنّه بايعني القوم الذين بايعوا أبا بكر وعمر وعثمان على ما بايعوهم عليه فلم يكن للشاهد أن يختار ولا للغائب أن يردّ وإنّما الشورى للمهاجرين والأنصار فإن اجتمعوا على رجل وسمّوه إمامًا كان ذلك لله رضًى فإن خرج من أمرهم خارج بطعن أو بدعة ردّوه إلى ما خرج منه فإن أبى قاتلوه على اتّباعه غير سبيل المؤمنين وولّاه الله ما تولّى. ولعمري يا معاوية لئن نظرت بعقلك دون هواك لتجدنّي أبرأ الناس من دم عثمان ولتعلمنّ أنّي كنت في عزلة عنه إلّا أن تتجنّى فتجنَّ ما بَدا لك. والسلام.

2.7 ومن كتاب له عليه السلام إليه أيضًا

أمّا بعد. فقد أتتني منك موعظة مُوصَّلة ورسالة محبّرة نَمَّقتَها بضلالك وأمضيتها بسوء رأيك. وكتاب امرئٍ ليس له بصر يهديه ولا قائد يرشده قد دعاه الهوى فأجابه وقاده الضلال فاتّبعه فهجر لاغطًا وضلّ خابطًا.

منه

لأنّها بيعة واحدة لا يثنّى فيها النظر ولا يُستأنَف فيها الخِيار الخارج منها طاعن والمُروّي فيها مُداهن.

2.6 From ʿAlī's letter to Muʿāwiyah:[1]
The same people who pledged allegiance to Abū Bakr, ʿUmar, and ʿUthmān pledged allegiance to me, and they did so on the same basis.[2] Those who were present did not have the right to choose, and those absent did not have the right to object—consultation is reserved for the Emigrants and Allies alone, and if they agree on someone and name him their leader, then that is God's will. Afterward, if a person secedes from the consensus with accusations and excuses, they should compel him to return. If he refuses, they should fight him, for he has strayed from the path of believers, and God will shun him for as long as he continues his recalcitrance. By my life, Muʿāwiyah, if you would look with your mind and not your passion, you would find me of all people to have the least share of blame in the matter of ʿUthmān's blood, you would know that I kept away from the fray. Unless you insist on making a patently false accusation—if so, then go ahead and accuse me of what you will! Go in peace.

2.7 From another letter sent by ʿAlī to Muʿāwiyah:[3]
I have received from you a string of advice, enclosed in an embroidered epistle, embellished with your misguidance, and dispatched by your specious views. It is the letter of a man with no perception to direct him and no guide to show him the way, a man who answered the call of his passions, who was led by the reins of misguidance, a delirious man who rambles and blunders from the path.

From the same letter:
The pledge of allegiance happens once. It is not open to reconsideration or a second round of selection. One who breaks the pledge is an aggressor, one who holds back and wavers is a traitor.

---

1 One of ʿAlī's earliest letters to Muʿāwiyah following the Battle of the Camel, sent from Kufa to Damascus in 36/656 with Jarīr ibn ʿAbdallāh al-Anṣārī. Full text and context in Minqarī, *Waqʿat Ṣiffīn*, 28–30. Further details of Jarīr's embassy to Muʿāwiyah in Damascus as ʿAlī's envoy, and related events and letters, in Ḥ 3:74–91; Jarīr's prior dealings with ʿAlī in Ḥ 3:70–74.

2 The Sunni Muʿtazilī commentator (Ḥ 14:35) takes these lines to endorse the validity of the people selecting a caliph. The Shiʿi commentators (B 787; R 3:18) say ʿAlī used this argument here, rather than citing the Prophet's designation (*naṣṣ*) of himself, because it was what his addressees were more likely to accept.

3 Excerpt from letter in response to Muʿāwiyah's, (1) sent from Kufa, while ʿAlī's envoy Jarīr was in Damascus in 36/656, persuading Muʿāwiyah to give the pledge of allegiance to ʿAlī (Minqarī, *Waqʿat Ṣiffīn*, 57–58; Māmaṭīrī, *Nuzhah*, 300–303); and/or (2) written in Ṣiffīn, toward the end of the battle, in 37/657 (Ḥ 14:42–43, includes text of Muʿāwiyah's letter, and ʿAlī's full response; B 788).

2.8   ومن كتاب له عليه السلام إلى جرير بن عبد الله البَجَليّ لمّا أرسله إلى معاوية

أمّا بعد. فإذا أتاك كتابي فاحمل معاوية على الفصل وخذه بالأمر الجَزْم ثمّ خيّره بين حرب مُجلية أو سِلم مُخزية فإن ٱختار الحرب فٱنبذ إليه وإن ٱختار السلم نخذ بيعته. والسلام.

2.9   ومن كتاب له عليه السلام إلى معاوية

فأراد قومنا قتل نبيّنا وٱجتياح أصلنا وهمّوا بنا الهموم وفعلوا بنا الأفاعيل ومنعونا العَذْب وأحلسونا الخوف وٱضطرّونا إلى جبل وَعْر وأوقدوا لنا نار الحرب فعزم الله لنا على الذبّ عن حوزته والرمي من وراء حرمته مؤمننا يبغي بذلك الأجر وكافرنا يحامي عن الأصل ومن أسلم من قريش خِلُوٌ ممّا نحن فيه بحلْف يمنعه أو عشيرة تقوم دونه فهم من القتل بمكان أمن. وكان رسول الله صلّى الله عليه وآله إذا ٱحمرّ البأس وأحجم الناس قدّم أهل بيته فوقى بهم أصحابه حرّ السيوف والأسنّة. فقُتل عبيدة بن الحارث يوم بدر وقتل حمزة يوم أحد وقتل جعفر يوم مؤتة وأراد من لو شئت ذكرت ٱسمه مثل الذي أرادوا من الشهادة ولكنّ آجالهم عجّلت ومنيّته أخّرت. فيا عجباً للدهر إذ صرت يقرن بي من لم يسع بقدمي ولم يكن له كسابقتي التي لا يدلي أحد بمثلها إلّا أن يدّعي مدّعٍ ما لا أعرفه ولا أظنّ الله يعرفه. والحمد لله على كلّ حال. وأمّا ما سألت من دفع قتلة عثمان إليك فإنّي نظرت في هذا الأمر

2.8 From ʿAlī's missive to Jarīr ibn ʿAbdallāh al-Bajalī, his emissary to Muʿāwiyah:[1] When you receive my letter, tell Muʿāwiyah that he must take a final decision and give a binding response. Then ask him to choose between a war that displaces or a settlement that disgraces. If he chooses war, then dissolve the covenant of peace and fling that threat at him. If he chooses to settle, then make him give me the pledge of allegiance. Go in peace.

2.9 From ʿAlī's letter to Muʿāwiyah:[2] Our tribe decided to kill our Prophet and extirpate our root. They came at us with evil intentions and spiteful actions, denying us the sweetness of life, throwing over us a blanket of fear, forcing us into the rugged mountains, and kindling the flames of war. But God willed that we should protect the enclosure of his religion and shield its sanctity from piercing arrows. Those of us who were believers did so in the hope of God's reward, and those who were unbelievers acted in defense of their kin. Muslims from other clans of Quraysh—protected by a pact or by kin—were not exposed to our hardships but were protected from lethal assault. Whenever red flames of battle blazed, moreover, whenever the Muslims drew back in fear, the Messenger would send men of his own family to the front, and, through them, he would shield his Companions from the heat of swords and spears. ʿUbaydah ibn al-Ḥārith was killed at the Battle of Badr, Ḥamzah was killed at the Battle of Uḥud, Jaʿfar was killed at the Battle of Muʾtah. Another man—and I could name him if I wished—sought to attain martyrdom just as they did, but their deaths were decreed early, while his was deferred.[3] What a strange age we live in, when I am placed on the same level as men who have not raced out in front, who do not possess my precedence! If any man were to make this, or any similar claim, they would be claiming a status I do not recognize, nor, I believe, does God. But God deserves praise in every situation. You demand that ʿUthmān's killers be handed over—I have looked

---

1 From Kufa to Damascus, 36/656, between the Battle of the Camel and Ṣiffīn. Minqarī, *Waqʿat Ṣiffīn*, 55.

2 In response to Muʿāwiyah's letter sent with Abū Muslim al-Khawlānī before the Battle of Ṣiffīn, in 36/656, in which Muʿāwiyah accused ʿAlī of envying the first three caliphs and treachery toward them (Minqarī, *Waqʿat Ṣiffīn*, 85–94; Ḥ 15:73–78, after Minqarī; includes text of Muʿāwiyah's letter, and ʿAlī's full response; a lengthy account of the historical events during the Prophet's lifetime is provided in this letter, particularly with regard to Muḥammad's years in Mecca and the actions of Quraysh against his family, as well as his major battles after the migration to Medina; these are recorded from the histories of Wāqidī, Ibn Isḥāq, and other sources in Ḥ 14:52–281, end, 15:3–78; see also F 368; B 789; R 3:26–31). § 2.28 is possibly another part of this letter (B 819).

3 Referring to himself. R 3:38; Ḥ 14:50; B 789.

فلم أره يسعني دفعهم إليك ولا إلى غيرك. ولعمري لئن لم تنزع عن غيّك وشقاقك لتعرفنّهم عن قليل يطلبونك لا يكلّفونك طلبهم في برّ ولا بحر ولا جبل ولا سهل إلّا أنّه طلب يسوءك وجدانه وزور لا يسرّك لُقيانه. والسلام لأهله.

2.10 ومن كتاب له عليه السلام إليه أيضًا

وكيف أنت صانع إذا تكشّفت عنك جلابيب ما أنت فيه من دنيا قد تبهّجت بزينتها وخدعت بلذّتها دعتك فأجبتها وقادتك فاتّبعتها وأمرتك فأطعتها وإنّه يوشِك أن يقفك واقف على ما لا يُنجيك منه مِجَنّ[1] فاقعس عن هذا الأمر وخذ أُهبة الحساب وشمّر لما قد نزل بك ولا تمكّن الغواة من سمعك وإلّا تفعل أعلمك ما أغفلت من نفسك فإنّك مُتَرَفٌ قد أخذ الشيطان منك مأخذه وبلغ فيك أمله وجرى منك مجرى الروح والدم. ومتى كنتم يا معاوية ساسة الرعيّة وولاة أمر الأمّة بغير قدم سابقٍ ولا شرف باسقٍ ونعوذ بالله من لزوم سوابق الشقاء. وأحذّرك[2] أن تكون متماديًا في غِرّة الأمنيّة مختلف العلانية والسريرة. وقد دعوت إلى الحرب فدع الناس جانبًا واخرج إليّ وأَعْفِ الفريقين من القتال لتعلم أيّنا المَرين على قلبه والمغطّى على بصره فأنا أبو حسن قاتل جدّك وخالك وأخيك شَدْخًا يوم بدر وذلك السيف معي وبذلك القلب ألقى عدوّي ما استبدلت دينًا ولا استحدثت نبيًّا. وإنّي لعلى المنهاج الذي تركتموه طائعين ودخلتم فيه مكرَهين. وزعمت أنّك جئت ثائرًا بعثمان ولقد علمت

<hr>

[1] م، ي، ه، ومصحّحة في ش: كذا. ن، وأصل ش، ونسخة في م، ه: ⟨مُنْجٍ⟩. [2] م، ي، ومصحّحة في ش، ه: كذا. ن، وأصل ش، ه: سقطت ⟨ومتى كنتم ... أن تكونَ⟩.

into the matter and have concluded that I am unable to hand them over to you, or to anyone else. By my life, if you do not desist in your deceit and dissent, you will very soon see those same men seeking you out, saving you the trouble of seeking them out on land, or sea, or mountains, or plains. Your search will end badly—these are visitors you will not enjoy meeting. Peace to the deserving.

2.10 From another letter sent by ʿAlī to Muʿāwiyah:[1]

How will you fare when the robes with which this world adorns herself, with whose beauty she has ensnared you, are stripped off? She called, and you answered, she led, and you followed, she commanded, and you obeyed. Very soon, you will face something no shield can protect you from. Stand down from this path, gather provisions for the final reckoning, roll up your sleeves to prepare for life's imminent end, and do not give ear to the wicked. Desist, or let me inform you about your own situation, a situation that you appear not to know: You live a life of excess. Satan has had his way with you, he has achieved his fullest hopes of you, and he now moves inside you as your own blood and spirit. When were your family ever rulers of the people, Muʿāwiyah, or guardians of the community's affairs? You can claim no high honor there, no winning horse! We should all seek refuge in God from clinging to the stakes of wretchedness! I give you warning: Cease to be deceived by false hopes. Cease to hide intentions that differ from your speech. You call me to war, do you? Leave the people out of this and take the field! Meet me yourself and spare our armies the killing! Let it be known to all which of us possesses a blinded heart and blindfolded eyes![2] I am Abū Ḥasan, who killed your grandfather, your uncle, and your brother in the Battle of Badr with the cutting blow of my sword—that same sword is with me today, and so too that same heart with which I shall meet my enemy![3] I have not changed my religion or adopted a new prophet. I walk the path that you abandoned so willingly, that you had joined only under com-

---

1 Excerpt from ʿAlī's letter to Muʿāwiyah from Kufa, in 37/657, after Jarīr's embassy had failed, just before ʿAlī set out with an army to Ṣiffīn—context, full text, and Muʿāwiyah's response in Minqarī, *Waqʿat Ṣiffīn*, 108–110; Ḥ 15:86–88; ʿAlī's opening paragraph in B 790. Similar lines in §2.64.

2 "Blinded heart" is a reference to Qurʾan, Muṭaffifūn 83:14.

3 Ar. *anā Abū Ḥasan* (I am Ḥasan's father), i.e., I am ʿAlī; it was common to refer to use a filionymic ("father of X") to address individuals; see also §2.18. At the Battle of Badr, ʿAlī had killed Muʿāwiyah's maternal grandfather, ʿUtbah ibn Rabīʿah, his maternal uncle Walīd ibn ʿUtbah, and his brother Ḥanẓalah ibn Abī Sufyān. B 792; R 3:31; F 369.

حيث وقع دم عثمان فاطلبه من هناك إن كنت طالبًا فكأنّي قد رأيتك تضجّ من الحرب إذا عضّتك ضبّيج الجمال بالأثقال وكأنّي بجماعتك تدعوني جزعًا من الضرب المتتابع والقضاء الواقع ومصارع بعد مصارع إلى كتاب الله وهي كافرة جاحدة أو مبايعة حائدة.

2.11   ومن وصيّة له وصّى بها عليه السلام جيشًا بعثه إلى العدوّ

فإذا نزلتم بعدوٍّ أو نزل بكم فليكن معسكركم في قُبُل الأشراف أو سِفاح الجبال أو أثناء الأنهار كيما تكون لكم رِدءًا ودونكم مَرَدًّا ولتكن مقاتلتكم من وجه أو اثنين واجعلوا لكم رقباء في صَياصي الجبال وبمناكب الهِضاب لئلّا يأتيكم العدوّ من مكان مخافة أو أمن واعلموا أنّ مقدّمة القوم عيونهم وعيون المقدّمة طلائعهم وإيّاكم والتفرّق فإذا نزلتم فانزلوا جميعًا وإذا ارتحلتم فارتحلوا جميعًا وإذا غشيكم الليل فاجعلوا الرماح كِفّة ولا تذوقوا النوم إلّا غِرارًا أو مضمضة.

2.12   ومن وصيّته عليه السلام لمَعْقِل بن قيس الرِّياحيّ حين أنفذه إلى الشام في ثلاثة آلاف مقدّمة له

اتّق الله الذي لا بدّ لك من لقائه ولا منتهى لك دونه ولا تقاتلنّ إلّا من قاتلك وسِر البَرْدَين وغَوِّر بالناس ورفِّه في السير ولا تسِر أوّل الليل فإنّ الله جعله سكنًا وقدّره مُقامًا لا ظعنًا فأرِح فيه بدنك وروِّح ظهرك فإذا وقفت[1] حين ينتطح[2] السحَر أو حين ينفجر

١ش، ن، ي، ه: كذا. م:﴿وافقت﴾. ٢م، ي، ونسخة في ث: كذا. ن، ه، وأصل ش:﴿ينبطح﴾.

pulsion.[1] You claim to seek vengeance for ʿUthmān—you know well who was responsible for shedding ʿUthmān's blood, so seek vengeance there if you wish! I can see you now, mauled by battle, screaming like a camel grumbling under a heavy load. I can see your faction panicked by unrelenting sword strikes, by the descent of fate, by death after death, inviting me, ironically, to follow the Qurʾan's judgment, while you yourselves are unbelieving deniers, or men who swore allegiance then broke the pledge![2]

2.11 From ʿAlī's instructions to a battalion he had dispatched against the enemy:[3] When you reach the enemy, or when they reach you, set up camp just before the high ground, or on the foothills of a mountain, or at the bend of a river, so these can serve as protection and barrier. Attack from a single side or from two at most. Place sentries on the horns of mountains and the shoulders of knolls—the enemy should not be able to take you by surprise, whether from a side you fear or even one you think is secure. Know that the eyes of the army are its vanguard, and the eyes of its vanguard are its scouts. Don't split up into separate groups—stay together when you set up camp and stay together when you set off. When night descends, place your spears in a circle around you and sip the cup of sleep only from time to time.

2.12 From ʿAlī's instructions to Maʿqil ibn Qays al-Riyāḥī, when he dispatched him to Syria at the head of a three-thousand-man vanguard:[4] Fear God, whom you must meet, and beyond whom you have no goal. Fight only those who fight you. March during the two cooler periods of the day, alight at noon so your men can rest, and drive your camels at a comfortable pace. Don't march in the first part of the night, for God has made it a time for repose and ordained it as a time of quiet and calm, not as a time for marching—so rest your body and your mounts. Then, when you rise at the spread of dawn, at the

---

1   The reference is to Muʿāwiyah and his clan, who waged war against the Prophet for years, then accepted Islam only after the Conquest of Mecca, in 8/630, when they had no choice.
2   Prophecy regarding the Battle of Ṣiffīn and how it would end. Ḥ 15:83.
3   Excerpt from a missive ʿAlī wrote in 36/657 from his army camp at Nukhaylah, near Kufa, to Ziyād ibn al-Naḍr al-Ḥārithī and Shurayḥ ibn Hānī, whom he had sent at the head of his vanguard to Syria. Ziyād was commander of the contingent. Shurayḥ was commander of a sub-contingent, and subordinate to Ziyād. B 793. Text of full letter in Minqarī, *Waqʿat Ṣiffīn*, 123–125. See also § 2.13 and § 2.56.
4   From Kufa in 36/657, in the lead-up to Ṣiffīn, when ʿAlī sent Maʿqil to Mosul from Madāʾin, both cities in Iraq, at the head of three thousand men, and asked him to go on from there to Raqqah, in Syria, where he, ʿAlī, and the main army would meet up with him. Minqarī, *Waqʿat Ṣiffīn*, 148–149; B 794.

الفجر فسِر على بركة الله. فإذا لقيت العدوّ فقف من أصحابك وسطًا ولا تَدْنُ من القوم دنوّ من يريد أن يُنشب الحرب ولا تباعد منهم تباعد من يهاب البأس حتّى يأتيك أمري. ولا يحملنّكم سِبابهم¹ على قتالهم قبل دعائهم والإعذار إليهم.

2.13 ومن كتاب له عليه السلام إلى أميرين من أمراء جيشه

وقد أمّرت عليكما وعلى من في حيّزكما مالك بن الحارث الأشتر فاسمعا له وأطيعا واجعلاه درعًا ومِجنًّا فإنّه ممّن لا يُخاف وهنه ولا سقطته ولا بطؤه عمّا الإسراع إليه أحزم ولا إسراعه إلى ما البُطْءُ عنه أمثل.

2.14 ومن وصيّته عليه السلام لعسكره قبل لقاء العدوّ بصفّين

لا تقاتلوهم حتّى يبدؤوكم فإنّكم بحمد الله على حجّة وترككم إيّاهم حتّى يبدؤوكم حجّة أخرى لكم عليهم فإذا كانت الهزيمة بإذن الله فلا تقتلوا مدبرًا ولا تصيبوا معورًا ولا تُجهزوا على جريح. ولا تَهيجوا النساء بأذًى وإن شَتَمْنَ أعراضكم وسببن أمراءكم فإنّهن ضعيفات القوى والأنفس والعقول إن كنّا لنؤمر بالكفّ عنهن وإنّهن لمشركات وإن كان الرجل ليتناول المرأة في الجاهليّة بالفِهر أو الهِراوة فيعَيَّر بها وعَقِبُه من بعده.

2.15 وكان عليه السلام يقول إذا لقي العدوّ محاربًا

اللّهمّ إليك أفضت القلوب ومُدّت الأعناق وشخصت الأبصار ونقلت الأقدام وأنضيت الأبدان. اللّهمّ قد صَرّح مكتوم² الشنآن وجاشت مَراجِل الأضغان. اللّهمّ إنّا

---

break of day, march forward with God's blessing. When you meet the enemy, stand at the center of your men. Don't allow your army to draw so near to the enemy that they fear you are on the verge of battle, but don't stay so far away from them that they think you fear their attack. Wait on my further orders. Don't let their insults incite you to begin the fight before you have called on them to make peace and exhausted your pleas.

2.13 From ʿAlī's missive to two of his army commanders:[1]
I have appointed Mālik ibn al-Ḥārith al-Ashtar over both of you and over all those under your command. Listen to him and obey his orders, consider him your armor and shield. He is a person from whom neither weakness nor error is to be feared—he will not delay when speed is of the essence, nor hasten when measured steps are called for.

2.14 From ʿAlī's instructions to his army just before confronting the enemy at Ṣiffīn:[2]
Don't attack them unless they attack you first. Praise God, you already possess proof of righteousness, and waiting until they begin the fighting will be yet another proof against them and in your favor. If we defeat the enemy— and with God's permission, we shall!—then don't kill those who flee, don't strike the unarmed, and don't bear down on the wounded. Don't threaten or hurt women, even if they insult your honor or abuse your leaders, for women are weak in strength, spirit, and mind, and we were commanded not to hurt them even when they were unbelievers. Even in the Age of Ignorance, if a man struck a woman with as much as a pebble or a small stick, he was held in shame for his act evermore, and so too were his descendants after him.

2.15 ʿAlī would offer this supplication whenever he met his enemy on the battlefield:[3]
God, it is to you that our hearts flow, our necks stretch, our eyes are raised, and our feet move. It is from the swiftness of our journey to you that our bodies have

---

1 The two commanders are Ziyād ibn al-Naḍr and Shurayḥ ibn Hānī, whom ʿAlī sent from Kufa, at the head of his 12,000-strong vanguard, to Syria in 36/657 (see also § 2.11 earlier, and § 2.56 later, addressed to them). En route, the vanguard encountered a Syrian contingent under Abū al-Aʿwar al-Sulamī. They wrote for help to ʿAlī, who responded by sending Mālik. Details of ʿAlī's instructions to Mālik and the incident in B 795; Minqarī, *Waqʿat Ṣiffīn*, 152–155; Ṭabarī, *Tārīkh*, 4:566–567 (letter at 567).
2 In 37/657, at Ṣiffīn. ʿAlī reportedly delivered this same battle-ethics speech ahead of any military conflict. B 795. Minqarī, *Waqʿat Ṣiffīn*, 203–204; Ṭabarī, *Tārīkh*, 5:10–11.
3 Prayer at Ṣiffīn, 37/657, and elsewhere, intoned when mounting his horse for battle. Minqarī, *Waqʿat Ṣiffīn*, 231. Full version of ʿAlī's battlefield supplication in B 796.

نشكو إليك غيبة نبيّنا وكثرة عدوّنا وتشتّت أهوائنا ﴿رَبَّنَا افْتَحْ بَيْنَنَا وَبَيْنَ قَوْمِنَا بِالْحَقِّ وَأَنتَ خَيْرُ الْفَاتِحِينَ﴾.

2.16   وكان يقول عليه السلام لأصحابه عند الحرب

لا تَشْتَدَّنَّ عليكم فَرَّةٌ بعدها كَرَّة ولا جَولة بعدها حملة. وأعطوا السيوف حقوقها ووَطِّنوا للجُنوب مصارعها وآذِمُروا أنفسكم على الطعن الدَّعْسيّ والضرب الطَّلَخْفيّ.[1] وأميتوا الأصوات فإنّه أطرد للفشل. والذي فلق الحبّة وبرأ النسمة ما أسلموا ولكن ٱستسلموا وأسرّوا الكفر فلمّا وجدوا أعوانًا عليه أظهروه.

2.17   ومن كتاب له عليه السلام إلى معاوية جوابًا عن كتاب منه

فأمّا طلبك إليّ الشام فإنّي لم أكن لأعطيك اليوم ما منعتك أمس.[2] وأمّا ٱستواؤنا في الحرب والرجال فلست بأمضى على الشكّ منّي على اليقين وليس أهل الشام بأحرص على الدنيا من أهل العراق على الآخرة. وأمّا قولك إنّا بنو عبد مناف فكذلك نحن وليس أميّة كهاشم ولا حَرْب كعبد المطّلب ولا أبو سفيان كأبي طالب ولا المهاجر كالطليق ولا الصريح كاللصيق ولا المحقّ كالمبطل ولا المؤمن كالمُدغِل. ولبئس الخلف خلف يتبع سلفًا هوى في نار جهنّم. وفي أيدينا بَعْدُ فضل النبوّة التي أذللنا بها العزيز ونعشنا بها الذليل. ولمّا أدخل الله العرب في دينه أفواجًا وأسلمت له هذه الأمّة

---

[1] جميع المخطوطات الرئيسيّة: كذا. شروح الراونديّ والبحرانيّ وٱبن ابي الحديد: ﴿الطلحفيّ﴾، والمعنى واحد.   [2] م، ش، ن: كذا. ي، هـ، وزيادة في هامش ش، م: أضيفت ﴿وأمّا قولك إنّ الحرب قد أكلت العرب إلّا حُشاشات أنفسٍ بقيت ألا ومَن أكله الحقّ فإلى الجنّة ومن أكله الباطل فإلى النار﴾.

become emaciated.[1] God, buried rancor has surfaced today, and cauldrons of malice simmer. God, we complain to you of our Prophet's death, our enemies' numbers, and our community's implosion. «Lord, decide between us and our tribesmen with truth, for you are the best conqueror.»[2]

2.16 'Alī would give his supporters these instructions ahead of battle:[3]
Don't hesitate to retreat then assail, to withdraw then attack. Give your swords their due. Think of the place where your body may fall as your home. Prepare your frames for piercing spear-throws and powerful sword-strikes. Deaden your voices, for this will drive out your fear. I swear by him who split the grain and created the soul—your enemies have never really accepted Islam! They had to surrender but concealed their unbelief. When they found supporters, they revealed it again.

2.17 From 'Alī's letter replying to Mu'āwiyah:[4]
You demand Syria, but I'm not about to give you today what I refused you yesterday. We are not equal in war and men—you in your state of doubt don't possess sharper perception than I do in my certainty, and the people of Syria don't covet this world more than the people of Iraq covet the hereafter. You say, "We are all sons of 'Abd Manāf"—yes, we are, but Umayyah is not the equal of Hāshim, Ḥarb is not the equal of 'Abd al-Muṭṭalib, Abū Sufyān is not the equal of Abū Ṭālib, the Emigrant is not like the Freedman,[5] the purebred is not like the adopted, the righteous is not like the falsifier, and the believer is not like the closet antagonist! The worst son is one who follows his forebears into the Fire of Gehenna! Our hands possess the honor of prophecy, with it we brought low the mighty and raised the humble. When God brought the Arabs in droves into

---

1 Lit. "It is to you that bodies become emaciated (*unḍiyat*)." I have inserted, "from swift journeying," based on the literary context, which evokes a journey in which the rider pushes his camel to swift and continuous travel, thereby emaciating it—in our text, the emaciated camel signifies the rider himself.

2 Qur'an, A'rāf 7:89.

3 At Ṣiffīn, 37/657. Minqarī, *Waqʿat Ṣiffīn*, 235–236.

4 On one of the battle-days at Ṣiffīn, 37/657. Mu'āwiyah wrote to 'Alī at Ṣiffīn, offering him the pledge in return for the governorship of Syria. Mu'āwiyah's letter and 'Alī's full reply in Minqarī, *Waqʿat Ṣiffīn*, 470–471; Māmaṭīrī, *Nuzhah*, 258–259; B 798; R 3:47; Ḥ 15:120–124, after Minqarī.

5 Freedman (*ṭalīq*, pl. *ṭulaqāʾ*) is a derogatory term referring to those of the Quraysh, including Mu'āwiyah's father, Abū Sufyān, who remained the Prophet's committed enemies until forced to capitulate upon the Muslim conquest of Mecca. On that day, instead of forcing them into captivity according to the standard practice, Muḥammad pardoned them and granted them their freedom, saying, "You are freedmen." Ibn Hishām, *Sīrah*, 4:35; Ṭabarī, *Tārīkh*, 3:61.

طوعًا وكرهًا كنتم ممّن دخل في الدين إمّا رغبةً وإمّا رهبةً على حين فازَا أهل السبق بسبقهم وذهب المهاجرون الأوّلون بفضلهم. فلا تجعلنّ للشيطان فيك نصيبًا ولا على نفسك سبيلًا.

2.18 ومن كتاب له عليه السلام إلى عبد الله بن العبّاس رحمهما الله وهو عامله على البصرة

وٱعلم أنّ البصرة مَهبِط إبليس ومغَرِس الفتن فحادِثْ أهلها بالإحسان إليهم وٱحلل عقدة الخوف عن قلوبهم. وقد بلغني تَنَمُّرُك لبني تميم وغلظتك عليهم وإنّ بني تميم لم يغب لهم نجم إلّا طلع لهم آخر وإنّهم لم يُسبقوا بوغْمٍ في جاهليّة ولا إسلام وإنّ لهم بنا رحمًا ماسّة وقرابة خاصّة نحن مأجورون على صلتها ومأزورون على قطيعتها. فأربعْ أبا العبّاس رحمك الله فيما جرى على يدك ولسانك من خير وشرّ فإنّا شريكان في ذلك وكن عند صالح ظنّي بك ولا يَفيلنّ رأيي فيك. والسلام.

2.19 ومن كتاب له عليه السلام إلى بعض عمّاله

أمّا بعد. فإنّ دَهاقين أهل بلدك شكوا منك غلظة وقسوة وٱحتقارًا وجفوة فنظرت فلم أَرهم أهلًا لأن يُدنَوا لشركهم ولا أن يُقصَوا ويُجفَوا لعهدهم فألبس لهم جِلبابًا من اللين تَشوبه بطرف من الشدّة وداوِل بهم بين القسوة والرأفة وٱمزِج لهم بين التقريب والإدناء والإبعاد والإقصاء إن شاء الله.

<hr>

ام، ي، ويبدو أصل ش، ومصحّحة في ه، ومصحّحة في ه: كذا. ن، وأصل هـ، ومصحّحة في ش، ونسخة في م: ‹فات›.

the fold of his religion, when this nation submitted to Islam, some willingly and some by force, you were among those who did so out of greed or fear. By that time, the true winners had already attained precedence, and the first Emigrants had already won distinction. Don't let Satan have a share in you, Muʿāwiyah, don't show him a way to control your soul.

2.18 From ʿAlī's missive to ʿAbdallāh ibn al-ʿAbbās, his governor in Basra:[1]
Know that Basra is where Iblīs landed after his fall from grace and where the trees of sedition have taken root, so tame its people with kindness and unravel from their heart the knot of fear. It has reached me that you have castigated the Tamīm tribesmen and spoken with them harshly. Know that no star of Tamīm has ever set except that another has risen in its place, and no one has dared to attack them either in the Age of Ignorance or since the coming of Islam. They are our intimate kin and our close relations—we shall be rewarded for fostering their bonds and incur sin if we sever them. Exercise restraint, Abū al-ʿAbbās[2]—may God have mercy on you!—in whatever flows from your hand or your tongue, be it good or bad, for we are partners in this endeavor. Behave as I hope you will behave, and don't make me change my opinion of you. Go in peace.

2.19 From ʿAlī's missive to one of his governors:[3]
The Dihqān landowners in your province have complained of your harshness, strictness, contempt, and ill-treatment.[4] I have looked into this matter, and although I find them unworthy of being your close associates because of their polytheism, yet they certainly do not deserve to be alienated or to be treated harshly, for they have entered into our compact. In dealing with them, wear a soft garment with an edge of toughness, and alternate between strictness and compassion. Mix intimacy and closeness with remoteness and reserve. You will do this, God willing.

---

1 Presumably from Kufa, soon after the Battle of the Camel in 36/656. During that battle, the loyalties of the Tamīm tribe of Basra had been divided, and many had fought against ʿAlī. Afterward, when ʿAlī appointed Ibn al-ʿAbbās governor of Basra, Ibn al-ʿAbbās was harsh with the Tamīm for this reason. Details and ʿAlī's full letter in B 801.

2 "Abū (father of) al-ʿAbbās," addressing ʿAbdallāh ibn al-ʿAbbās. Though commonly known as "Ibn (son of) al-ʿAbbās," ʿAbdallāh is referred to here in relation to his son, who, like ʿAbdallāh's father, is also named al-ʿAbbās. For another use of this form of nomenclature, see §2.10.

3 Presumably from Kufa between 37/658 and 40/661. Balādhurī (*Ansāb*, 2:161), Yaʿqūbī (*Tārīkh*, 2:203), and Māmaṭīrī (*Nuzhah*, 258) name the recipient as ʿAmr ibn Salamah al-Hamdānī al-Arḥabī, ʿAlī's governor in Isfahan.

4 Ar. *dihqān*, pl. *dahāqīn*, class of lesser nobles in early Muslim Iran. Most were Zoroastrians, while some in northern Mesopotamia were Christians. For details, see Paul, "Dihqān," *EI*[3]. Baḥrānī (B 801) says ʿAlī's missive refers to Zoroastrian (*Majūs*) landowners.

2.20 ومن كتاب له عليه السلام إلى زياد بن أبيه وهو خليفة عامله عبد الله بن العبّاس رحمة الله عليه على البصرة. وعبد الله عامل أمير المؤمنين عليه السلام يومئذ عليها وعلى كور الأهواز وفارس وكرمان

وإنّي أقسم بالله قسمًا صادقًا لئن بلغني أنّك خُنْتَ من فيء المسلمين شيئًا صغيرًا أو كبيرًا لأُشُدَّنَّ عليك شَدّةً تدعك قليل الوفر ثقيل الظهر ضئيل الأمر. والسلام.

2.21 ومن كتاب له عليه السلام إليه أيضًا

فدَع الإسراف مقتصدًا واذكر في اليوم غدًا وأمسك من المال بقدر ضرورتك وقدّم الفضل ليوم حاجتك أترجو أن يؤتيك١ الله أجر المتواضعين وأنت عنده من المتكبّرين وتطمع وأنت متمرّغ في النعيم تمنعه الضعيف والأرملة أن يوجب لك ثواب المتصدّقين وإنّما المرء مَجزِيّ بما سَلَف وقادم على ما قدّم. والسلام.

2.22 ومن كتاب له عليه السلام إلى عبد الله بن العبّاس. كان ابن عبّاس يقول ما انتفعت بكلام بعد كلام رسول الله صلّى الله عليه وآله كانتفاعي بهذا الكلام

١ن، ش، ي، ه: كذا. م، ونسخة في ش، ه: ﴿يعطيك﴾.

2.20 From 'Alī's missive to Ziyād ibn Abīhi, who was acting as deputy for 'Alī's governor 'Abdallāh ibn al-'Abbās in Basra. 'Abdallāh was then 'Alī's governor in Basra and he also had jurisdiction over the provinces of Ahwaz, Fars, and Kirman.[1]

I swear this by God, in all truth: If I hear that you have misappropriated funds from the Muslims' treasury, whether it be a small or a large amount, I shall inflict on you a harsh punishment that will leave you short of wealth, diminished in strength, and burdened with shame. Go in peace.

2.21 From another missive sent by 'Alī to Ziyād:[2]

Turn from extravagance to moderation, think today of tomorrow, and spend what you must, but put by the rest for your day of want. Do you expect God to remunerate you with the humble if he counts you among the arrogant? Do you think he will reward you with the charitable when you wallow in luxuries and refuse to help the weak and the widowed? A man is recompensed for the work he has accomplished. He advances to meet what he sent on. Go in peace.

2.22 From 'Alī's letter to 'Abdallāh ibn al-'Abbās. Ibn al-'Abbās used to say: After the words of the Prophet, I have benefited from no words as much as I have benefited from these:[3]

---

1   Presumably sent from Kufa to Fars sometime in 37–38/657–658: Yaʿqūbī (*Tārīkh*, 2:204) prefaces this missive with the words, "['Alī] wrote to Ziyād, his governor in Fars"; Ziyād was appointed as governor there after Ṣiffīn, which was in 37/657. This text is an escalation from the earlier, relatively milder reproof against corruption in § 2.21.

2   Presumably also from Kufa, but earlier than § 2.20, in 36/657, in the lead-up to the Battle of Ṣiffīn, when 'Abdallāh ibn al-'Abbās left his post to join 'Alī for preparations. 'Alī had dispatched his freedman Saʿd to Ziyād, instructing him to send funds to him in Kufa from the treasury of Basra; they argued, and, presumably, Ziyād did not send the funds, which is what prompted 'Alī's reply. Details of the context, 'Alī's full missive, and Ziyād's reply, in Balādhurī, *Ansāb*, 2:164–165; Ḥ 16:196–197, within the commentary on § 2.44.

3   Excerpt from a letter—of which § 2.66 is a variant rendering, and § 2.41 and § 2.72 are possibly other parts—likely sent from Kufa to Mecca in 40/661, a short while before 'Alī's death. 'Abdallāh ibn al-'Abbās, 'Alī's cousin and governor of Basra during 'Alī's reign, apparently took money for personal use from the Basra treasury, arguing that as a member of the Prophet's family, he had a right to the Qurʾanic "fifth" (*khums*) share. When 'Alī chastised him, he retracted his claim and returned the money. Text and context for § 2.22 and § 2.66 in Yaʿqūbī, *Tārīkh*, 2:205. The commentators also discuss the episode under § 2.41, which includes explicit mention of the affair: Ḥ 16:169–172; B 867, includes 'Abdallāh's reply, and 'Alī's further reply; details are also given in Balādhurī, *Ansāb*, 2:169–176; Rāwandī (R 3:134–135) argues—*contra* the other commentators—that the reference is more likely to 'Abdallāh's brother 'Ubaydallāh ibn al-'Abbās.

أمّا بعد. فإنّ المرء يسرّه دَرَك ما لم يكن ليفوته ويسوءه فوت ما لم يكن ليدركه فليكن سرورك بما نلت من آخرتك وليكن أسفك على ما فاتك منها وما نلت من دنياك فلا تكثر به فرحًا وما فاتك منها فلا تأسَ عليه جزعًا وليكن همّك فيما بعد الموت.

2.23 ومن كلام له عليه السلام قاله قبيل موته لمّا ضربه ابن ملجم على سبيل الوصيّة

وصيّتي لكم ألّا تشركوا بالله شيئًا ومحمّدٌ صلّى الله عليه وآله فلا تضيّعوا سنّته أقيموا هذين العمودين وخَلاكم ذمّ. أنا بالأمس صاحبكم واليوم عبرة لكم وغدًا مفارقكم. إن أبقَ فأنا وليّ دمي وإن أفنَ فالفناء ميعادي وإن أعفُ فالعفو لي قربة وهو لكم حسنة فاعفوا ﴿ألا تُحِبّونَ أن يَغْفِرَ اللَّهُ لَكُمْ﴾. والله ما فجِئَني من الموت وارد كرهتُه ولا طالع أنكرته وما كنت إلّا كقاربٍ ورد وطالب وجد ﴿وَمَا عِندَ اللَّهِ خَيرٌ لِلأبْرَارِ﴾.

وقد مضى بعض هذا الكلام فيما تقدّم من الخطب إلّا أنّ فيه هٰهنا زيادة أوجبت تكريره.

2.24 ومن وصيّة له عليه السلام بما يُعمل في أمواله كتبها بعد منصَرفه من صفّين

هذا ما أمر به عبد الله عليّ بن أبي طالب أمير المؤمنين في ماله ابتغاء وجه الله ليولجني به الجنّة ويعطيني الأمنة.

A man is gladdened by obtaining a thing he was not going to lose and saddened by the loss of a thing he was not going to obtain. Be glad for what you have achieved for the hereafter. Be sad for what you have lost of it. Whatever you achieve of this world, don't exult over it excessively. Whatever you may lose of it, don't grieve too much. Save your worries for what comes after death.

2.23 From ʿAlī's address after Ibn Muljam struck him with his sword, spoken as a testament just before ʿAlī's death:[1]

This is my testament to you: Do not assign partners to God or abandon the Sunnah of the Prophet—keep these two pillars upright, and you shall be free of blame. Yesterday I was your companion, today I serve as a plain lesson for you, and tomorrow I shall be gone from your midst. If I survive, I shall claim my own blood-wit,[2] and if I die, well, death is what we are promised. If I forgive, my action will gain me nearness to God, and if you do the same, you too will earn God's reward. Choose forgiveness—«Do you not wish that God should forgive you?»[3] By God, death has not surprised me as an unwelcome visitor, or as a sudden arrival that I find unpleasant. I am like a person who has arrived at the watering hole he sought, who found the object he pursued. «What God has prepared for people of virtue is the best!»[4]

Raḍī: Part of this address was previously recorded in the Orations section.[5] This version contains some additions, which is why I have found it necessary to repeat it here.

2.24 From a testament ʿAlī wrote after turning back from Ṣiffīn, regarding the distribution of his properties:[6]

This is what I—God's servant, ʿAlī ibn Abī Ṭālib, Commander of the Faithful—have directed with regard to my property in the pursuance of God's pleasure, in the hope that God will allow me entry into the celestial garden and grant me his protection.

---

1 Delivered as part of a testament in his home in Kufa, where he was carried after he was struck the deathblow, in 40/661. Kulaynī, *Kāfī*, 1:299.

2 Blood-wit and forgiveness are mentioned in the context of punishment for ʿAlī's killer, Ibn Muljam.

3 Qurʾan, Nūr 24:22.

4 Qurʾan, ʿĀl ʿImrān 3:198.

5 §1.147.

6 En route from Ṣiffīn to Kufa in 37/657. Full testament with list of transmitters and some details of ʿAlī's concubines in B 806–807. Some details of his properties in Ḥ 15:149. The testament starts out in the conventional third grammatical person, which I have changed to first person for clarity, since the final line in Arabic is in the first person.

منها

وإنّه يقوم بذلك الحسن بن عليّ يأكل منه بالمعروف وينفق منه في المعروف فإن حدث بحسن حدث وحسين حيّ قام بالأمر بعده وأصدره مصدره. وإنّ لابني فاطمة من صدقة عليّ مثل الذي لبني عليّ وإنّي إنّما جعلت القيام بذلك إلى ابني فاطمة ابتغاء وجه الله وقربة إلى رسول الله صلّى الله عليه وآله وتكريمًا لحرمته وتشريفًا لوصلته. ويَشتَرِط على الذي يجعله إليه أن يترك المال على أصوله وينفق من ثمره حيث أُمِر به وهدي له وأن لا يبيع من نخيل¹ هذه القرى وديّة حتّى تُشْكِل أرضُها غِراسًا. ومن كان من إمائي اللاتي أطوف عليهنّ لها ولد أو هي حامل فتُمسَك على ولدها وهي من حظّه فإن مات ولدها وهي حيّة فهي عتيقة قد أُفرِج عنها الرقّ وحرّرها العتق.

قوله عليه السلام في هذه الوصيّة ⟨وألّا يبيع من نخلها وديّة⟩ فإنّ الوديّة الفسيلة وجمعها وَدِيّ. وقوله ⟨حتّى تشكل أرضها غراسًا⟩ هو من أفصح الكلام والمراد به أنّ الأرض يكثر فيها غراس النخل حتّى يراها الناظر على غير تلك الصفة التي عرفها بها فيُشكِل عليه أمرها ويحسبها غيرها.

2.25 ومن وصيّة له عليه السلام كان يكتبها لمن يستعمله على الصدقات وإنّما ذكرنا منها جملًا هٰهنا ليعلم بها أنّه عليه السلام كان يقيم عماد الحقّ ويشرع أمثلة العدل في صغير الأمور وكبيرها ودقيقها وجليلها.

2.25.1 انطلق على تقوى الله وحده لا شريك له ولا تُرِوِّعَنّ مسلمًا ولا تجتازَنّ² عليه كارهًا ولا تأخذنّ منه أكثر من حقّ الله في ماله.

---

¹ ن، ش، ه‍: كذا. م، ي، ونسخة في ه‍: ⟨أولاد نخيل⟩.   ²م، ي، ه‍: كذا. ن، ش: ⟨تجتازنّ⟩.

From the same testament:

My property shall be administered by al-Ḥasan ibn ʿAlī.[1] He should use a portion from it in licit ways and disburse from it also in licit ways. If something happens to Ḥasan while Ḥusayn lives, Ḥusayn shall administer the property thereafter and in the same way. Fāṭimah's sons are both to have the same share from my trusts as my other sons, but I have selected them for the charge of administering my trusts in order to obtain God's pleasure, gain closeness to God's Messenger, honor his sanctity, and privilege his kinship. The administrator is to leave the property's principal in its original form and spend only from its fruits as he has been directed and instructed. He may not sell the estates' date-palm shoots until the entire land has ripened with them and become a fully green plantation. If any of my concubines with whom I cohabit has a child or is pregnant, then the cost of freeing her is to be deducted from her child's share. If her child dies and she lives, she is still free, for her bondage has already been removed, and my freeing her has certified her liberty.[2]

Raḍī: As for ʿAlī's words in this testament, "He may not sell the estates' date-palm shoots (*wadiyyah*)": *wadiyyah* are saplings, and the plural is *wadī*. His words: "until the land has ripened with them and become (*an tushkila*) a green plantation" is among the most eloquent of expressions. It means that date-palm plantings will grow with such abundance in that land that the beholder will think it a landscape different to the one before; he will be thrown into doubt (*ashkala*, which also means ripen) and will think it is a different piece of land altogether.

2.25 From a testament ʿAlī would customarily inscribe for tax collectors he appointed to oversee collection of the alms-levy. I have recorded some sections from it here to show how ʿAlī raised the pillar of right and followed the path of justice in matters small and large, and in affairs trivial and momentous:[3]

2.25.1 Set out in consciousness of God, who is one and has no partner. Don't threaten a Muslim, don't survey his property without his consent, and don't take from his possessions more than what is due to God.

---

1   This is ʿAlī's son Ḥasan from his wife Fāṭimah Zahrāʾ, daughter of the Prophet. Following convention for official documents, ʿAlī refers to him as "Ḥasan ibn (= son of) ʿAlī" rather than saying "my son Ḥasan."

2   Translation after Ḥ 15:150.

3   In Kufa, during his caliphate, 35–40/656–661, when he sent tax collectors to agricultural lands to collect the alms-levy (*ṣadaqāt*) annually required of Muslims. Thaqafī, *Ghārāt*, 1:126–131.

٢.٢٥.٢   فإذا قدمت على الحيّ فأنزل بمائهم من غير أن تخالط أبياتهم ثمّ أمض إليهم بالسكينة والوقار حتّى تقوم بينهم فتسلّم عليهم ولا تُخْدِج بالتحيّة لهم ثمّ تقول عباد الله أرسلني إليكم وليّ الله وخليفته لآخذ منكم حقّ الله في أموالكم فهل لله في أموالكم من حقّ فتؤدّوه إلى وليّه. فإن قال قائل لا فلا تراجعه وإن أنعم لك منعم فأنطلق معه من غير أن تخيفه أو توعده أو تَعَسفه أو تَرهَقه نخذ ما أعطاك من ذهب أو فضّة. فإن كانت له ماشية أو إبل فلا تدخلها إلّا بإذنه فإنّ أكثرها له فإذا أتيتها فلا تدخلها دخول متسلّط عليه ولا عنيف به ولا تُنفِّرَنَّ بهيمة ولا تُفزِّعَنَّها ولا تَسوءَنَّ صاحبها فيها. وأصْدَع المال صَدْعين ثمّ خَيِّره فإذا اختار فلا تَعرِضنّ لما اختار ثمّ اصدع الباقي صدعين ثمّ خيِّره فإذا اختار فلا تعرضنّ لما اختار فلا تزال بذلك حتّى يبقى ما فيه وفاء لحقّ الله في ماله فاقبض حقّ الله منه فإن استقالك فأقِلْهُ ثمّ أخلطهما ثمّ اصنع مثل الذي صنعت أوّلًا حتّى تأخذ حقّ الله في ماله. ولا تأخذنَّ عَودًا ولا هَرِمة ولا مكسورة ولا مهلوسة ولا ذات عَوار.

٢.٢٥.٣   ولا تأمننّ عليها إلّا من تثق بدينه رافقًا بمال المسلمين حتّى يوصله إلى وليّهم فيقسمه بينهم ولا توكّل بها إلّا ناصحًا شفيقًا وأمينًا حفيظًا غير مُعْنِف ولا مُجحف ولا مُلغب ولا متعب ثمّ احدُر إلينا ما اجتمع عندك نُصيِّره حيث أمر الله به. فإذا أخذها أمينك فأوْعِزْ إليه ألّا يحول بين ناقة وبين فصيلها ولا يَمصُر لبنها فيضرّ ذلك بولدها ولا يجهدنّها ركوبًا وليعدل بين صَواحباتها في ذلك وبينها وليُرفِّهْ على اللاغب وليَستأن بالنَّقِب والظالع[١] وليوردها ما تمرّ به من الغُدُر ولا يعدل بها عن نبت الأرض إلى جوادّ الطرق وليروّحها في الساعات وليمهلها عند النِّطاف والأعشاب حتّى تأتينا بإذن الله

____

١   ن، ش، ي: كذا. م، هـ: ﴿الضالع﴾.

2.25.2 When you arrive in the lands of a tribe, pitch your tent at their watering hole and don't enter their residential areas. Then walk toward them calmly and with dignity and stand in their midst. Then hail them in peace and don't stint with your greeting. Then say, "Servants of God, God's vicegerent, his caliph, has sent me to secure God's due from your property. Is there anything you owe God from your property that you should submit to his vicegerent?" If a person says no, don't ask him again. If a person is forthcoming, set out with him, but don't frighten, threaten, force, or oppress him—accept whatever gold or silver he submits to you freely. If he has goats or camels, don't enter their pens without his permission, for most of the animals belong to him. When you do enter, don't behave rudely or with violence. Don't frighten the animals or startle them, and don't cause the owner distress by maltreating them. Divide the animals into two groups and have the owner select one set. When he has made his selection, don't object. Then divide the remaining the animals again into two groups, and have the owner select one set. When he has made his selection, don't object. Keep doing this until God's due is fulfilled by the number of animals that remain in your share, then accept them as God's due from the owner. If, after that, he asks you to rescind the operation, rescind it. Then bring all the animals together once again and repeat what you had done earlier until you have secured his acceptance of God's due from his property. Make sure, however, that you don't accept animals that are old, decrepit, broken-boned, sickly, or defective.

2.25.3 Assign the animals only to the care of someone you know to be pious and who will be gentle with these flocks that belong to the Muslim community, until he delivers them to their leader, and that leader distributes the animals among them. Entrust the animals only to the care of someone who is kind and sincere, a vigilant custodian who won't treat them roughly, overburden them, fatigue them, or drive them too hard. Then hasten to send me all the animals that have been collected under your supervision so that I may distribute them in the manner commanded by God. When your deputy takes charge of them, instruct him not to separate a camel from her calf, or to milk her to the extent that it harms the calf, or to ride her so hard that she collapses. He should divide his riding evenly between her and her fellow mares. He should allow tired animals to rest and be unhurried in herding the animals with worn hooves or a limp. He should let them drink whenever they pass a pool of water and not force them from green shoots to the beaten road. He should let them have a respite every few hours and pause wherever there is water and grass. He should do this until he delivers the animals to me, with God's permission, healthy and fat with marrow, neither fatigued nor distressed, so that I may distribute them

بُدَّنًا مُنقِيات غير مُتعَبات ولا مجهودات لنقسمها على كتاب الله وسنّة نبيّه صلّى الله عليه وآله. فإنّ ذلك أعظم لأجرك وأقرب لرشدك إن شاء الله.

2.26 ومن عهد له عليه السلام في مثله إلى بعض عمّاله وقد بعثه على الصدقة

2.26.1 أمره بتقوى الله في سرائر أمره وخفيّات أعماله حيث لا شهيد غيره ولا وكيل دونه وأمره ألّا يعمل بشيء من طاعة الله فيما ظهر فيخالف إلى غيره فيما أسرّ ومن لم يختلف سرّه وعلانيته وفعله ومقالته فقد أدّى الأمانة وأخلص العبادة وأمره أن لا يَجبَههم ولا يَعْضَهَهم ولا يرغب عنهم تفضّلًا بالإمارة عليهم فإنّهم الإخوان في الدين والأعوان على اَستخراج الحقوق.

2.26.2 وإنّ لك في هذه الصدقة نصيبًا مفروضًا وحقًّا معلومًا وشركاء أهل مسكنة وضعفاء ذوي فاقة وإنّا مُوَفُّوك حقّك فوَفِّهم حقوقهم وإلّا فإنّك من أكثر الناس خصومًا يوم القيامة وبؤسًا لمن خصمه عند الله الفقراء والمساكين والسائلون والمدفوعون والغارم وابن السبيل ومن اَستهان بالأمانة ورتَعَ في الخيانة ولم ينزّه نفسه ودينه عنها فقد أحلّ بنفسه في الدنيا الخزي وهو في الآخرة أذلّ وأخزى. وإنّ أعظم الخيانة خيانة الأمّة وأفظع الغِشّ غشّ الأئمّة.

2.27 ومن عهد له عليه السلام إلى محمّد بن أبي بكر رحمه الله حين قلّده مصر

according to God's Book and the Prophet's Sunnah. Do this, and God willing, it will increase your reward and bring you closer to the way of guidance.

2.26 From ʿAlī's missive to one of his tax collectors whom he had sent to collect the alms-levy:[1]

2.26.1 ʿAlī commands his tax collector to be conscious of God in private affairs and hidden acts, for there is no true witness, and no real agent, other than God. ʿAlī commands his tax collector to make sure that while he shows obedience to God in public, he should never do the opposite in private. To discharge his trust and offer worship with sincerity, the tax collector's private and public life should not contradict, and his actions and words should not be in opposition. ʿAlī also commands him to make sure he never abuses or reviles his subjects. He should never raise himself above them because of his charge, for they are his brothers in faith and his helpers in the collection of dues.

2.26.2 You have a prescribed share, a recognized right, in this levy. You also have partners—the poor, the weak, and the destitute. I will give you your share in full, but you should leave them their full share, else you will be among those who face an army of adversaries on the day of resurrection. Woe to the man whose adversaries before God are the mendicant, the poor, the beggar, the helpless, the debtor, and the wayfarer![2] If you scorn your trust and forage in the pastures of embezzlement, if you don't keep your soul and your faith clean from its filth, you will secure shame for yourself in this world, and even greater shame and humiliation in the hereafter. The most dreadful embezzlement is embezzlement of property that belongs to the community. The most terrible deception is deceiving the Imam.

2.27 From ʿAlī's testament to Muḥammad ibn Abī Bakr, when he placed him in charge of Egypt:[3]

---

1 In Kufa during his caliphate, 35–40/656–661, when he sent Mikhnaf ibn Sulaym al-Azdī to collect the alms-levy (*ṣadaqah*). Nuʿmān, *Daʿāʾim*, 1:252.

2 These are among the eight categories of recipients for the alms-levy named in the Qurʾan, Tawbah 9:60. Discussion in B 811; Ḥ 15:161. The Arabic word *madfūʿūn*—translated here as "helpless" (after R 3:61; Ḥ 15:161, in the Qurʾanic category of "in the path of the God," *fī sabīl Allāh*)—could also be interpreted, pace Ḥ 15:161, as "weakly faithful," i.e., the category of those "whose hearts are reconciled" (*al-muʾallafati qulūbuhum*) to Islam.

3 Presumably written in Kufa between 36/656 and 38/658, in answer to questions Muḥammad ibn Abī Bakr posed to him in a letter. Thaqafī, *Ghārāt*, 1:235–248; Māmaṭīrī, *Nuzhah*, 264–281, Jurjānī, *Iʿtibār* 561–572 (Māmaṭīrī and Jurjānī include the text of ʿAlī's full letter, and Muḥammad's letter of request). These lines are similar to § 2.46.

2.27.1 فٱخفض لهم جناحك وأَلِنْ لهم جانبك وٱبسط لهم وجهك وآسِ بينهم في اللحظة والنظرة حتّى لا يطمع العظماء في حيفك لهم ولا ييأس الضعفاء من عدلك عليهم. وإنّ الله يسائلكم معشر عباده عن الصغيرة من أعمالكم والكبيرة والظاهرة والمستورة فإن يعذّب فإن يعذّب فأنتم أظلم وإن يَعف[1] فهو أكرم.

2.27.2 وٱعلموا عباد الله أنّ المتّقين ذهبوا بعاجل الدنيا وآجل الآخرة فشاركوا أهل الدنيا في دنياهم ولم يشاركهم أهل الدنيا في آخرتهم. سَكنوا الدنيا بأفضل ما سُكنت وأكلوها بأفضل ما أُكلت فحظوا من الدنيا بما حظي به المترَفون وأخذوا منها ما أخذه الجبابرة المتكبّرون ثمّ ٱنقلبوا عنها بالزاد المبلّغ والمتجر الرابح[2] أصابوا لذّة زهد الدنيا في دنياهم وتيقّنوا أنّهم جيران الله غدًا في آخرتهم لا يُرَدّ لهم دعوة ولا ينقص لهم نصيب من لذّة.

2.27.3 فٱحذروا عباد الله الموت وقربه وأعدّوا له عدّته فإنّه يأتي بأمر عظيم وخطب جليل بخير لا يكون معه شرّ أبدًا أو شرّ لا يكون معه خير أبدًا فمن أقرب إلى الجنّة من عاملها ومن أقرب إلى النار من عاملها وأنّكم طُرداء الموت إن أقمتم له أخذكم وإن فررتم منه أدرككم وهو ألزم لكم من ظِلّكم الموت معقود بنواصيكم والدنيا تُطوى من خلفكم فٱحذروا نارًا قعرها بعيد وحرّها شديد وعذابها جديد دار ليس فيها رحمة ولا تُسمع فيها دعوة ولا تفرّج فيها كربة. وإن ٱستطعتم أن يشتدّ خوفكم من الله وأن يحسن ظنّكم به فٱجمعوا بينهما فإنّ العبد إنّما يكون حسن ظنّه بربّه على قدر خوفه من ربّه وإنّ أحسن الناس ظنًّا بالله أشدّهم خوفًا لله.

2.27.4 وٱعلم يا محمّد بن أبي بكر أنّي قد ولّيتك أعظم أجنادي في نفسي أهل مصر فأنت محقوق أن تخالف على نفسك وأن تنافح عن دينك ولو لم يكن لك إلّا ساعة من الدهر

2.27.1 Lower your wing over them, offer them your softer side, show them your face, and give equal attention to all in glance and look, such that the powerful are not emboldened to expect unfair favors and the weak do not despair of getting justice. God will ask all his servants about small and large deeds, those open and those concealed. If he punishes, it is because you are the sinners. If he forgives, it is because he is the benefactor.

2.27.2 Servants of God! Know that the pious partake of the joys of this world and the next. They share the world with the worldly, but the worldly do not share the hereafter with them. In this world, they reside in the most splendid of residences and consume the finest of delicacies. They possess the opulent comforts of the wealthy and partake of the lavish luxuries of the mighty. Yet, when they depart, they leave with a full supply of provisions and a large profit. They enjoy the pleasures of this world without becoming immersed in worldliness, content in the certain knowledge that they will be God's neighbors in the next—no prayer rejected, no pleasure withheld.

2.27.3 Servants of God! Beware of death, for it is imminent! Ready your provisions, for death will bring a momentous affair, a fateful end—good with no evil attached to it forever after, or evil with no good attached to it forever after. Tell me: Who is closer to paradise than its seeker? Who is closer to hellfire than its seeker? Death stalks you. If you remain motionless, it will snatch you, if you flee, it will find you—it is more firmly attached to you than your shadow. Death is bound to your forelock while behind you the earth continues to be rolled up, like a scroll. Beware of the Fire whose pit is bottomless, whose heat is intense, and whose punishment is ever renewed! It is an abode where there is no mercy, no prayer is heard, no pain is healed. If you can fear God intensely and also place your hopes in him at the same time, then do so, combine the two. Indeed, a servant's hope in his Lord is only as strong as his fear of his Lord. Those who harbor the greatest hopes of God's bounty are the ones who fear him most.

2.27.4 Muḥammad ibn Abī Bakr! Know that I have placed you in charge of the region most important to me—Egypt. This is what is due from you: oppose your passions and defend your religion, even if you have only a single hour left in this world. Do not anger God in trying to please his creatures. God compensates for

ولا تُسخِط الله برضاء أحد من خلقه فإنّ في الله خلفًا من غيره وليس من الله خلف في غيره. صلِّ الصلاة لوقتها الموقّت لها ولا تعجّل وقتها لفراغ ولا تؤخّرها عن وقتها لاشتغال وآعلم أنّ كلّ شيء من عملك تبعٌ لصلاتك.

٢.٢٧.٥ ومنه

فإنّه لا سواء إمام الهدى وإمام الردى ووليّ النبيّ وعدوّ النبيّ ولقد قال لي رسول الله صلّى الله عليه وآله ﴿إنّي لا أخاف على أمّتي مؤمنًا ولا مشركًا أمّا المؤمن فيمنعه الله بإيمانه وأمّا المشرك فيقمعه الله بشركه ولكنّي أخاف عليكم كلّ منافق الجنان عالم اللسان يقول ما تعرفون ويفعل ما تنكرون﴾.

٢.٢٨ ومن كتاب له عليه السلام إلى معاوية جوابًا وهو من محاسن الكتب

٢.٢٨.١ أمّا بعد. فقد أتاني كتابك تذكر فيه آصطفاء الله محمّدًا صلّى الله عليه وآله لدينه وتأييده إيّاه بمن أيّده من أصحابه. فلقد خبّاً لنا الدهر منك عجبًا إذ طَفِقْتَ تُخبرنا ببلاء الله عندنا ونعمته علينا في نبيّنا فكنتَ في ذلك ﴿كناقل التمر إلى هَجَر﴾ أو داعي مسدّده إلى النِّضال. وزعمت أنّ أفضل الناس في الإسلام فلان وفلان فذكرت أمرًا إن تمّ آعتزلك كلّه وإن نقص لم يلحقك¹ ثَلْمه وما أنت والفاضل والمفضول والسائس والمَسوس

____
¹م، ي، ومصحّحة في ش: كذا. ن، ه، وأصل ش: ﴿ينقصك﴾.

the loss of others, but no one can compensate for the loss of God. Pray the ritual prayer at its appointed time. Do not pray it early just because you have time or delay it because you are occupied. Know that every single one of your duties is subordinate to prayer.

2.27.5 From the same testament:
They are not equal—an Imam who leads to guidance and an Imam who leads to perdition, a man who loves the Prophet and a man who hates the Prophet. God's Messenger said to me: ⟨I do not fear harm for my community from either believer or unbeliever. As for the believer, God holds him back because of his belief. As for the unbeliever, God thwarts him because of his unbelief. I fear harm for you from every man whose heart harbors hypocrisy while his tongue spouts knowledge, who says what you know to be good, but does what you know is evil.⟩[1]

2.28 From ʿAlī's reply to Muʿāwiyah. This is one of the most eloquent letters of all time:[2]

2.28.1 I received your letter in which you speak of how God selected Muḥammad to propagate his religion and aided him through his Companions. How astonishing the things time reveals about you! You presume to inform us about the bounties God has bestowed upon us and of the fact that he has blessed us with our Prophet—you are ⟨like the man who carried dates to sell in Hajar⟩, the motherlode of dates,[3] or the man who challenged his instructor to duel with bow and arrow! You allege that So-and-So and So-and-So are the most excellent Muslims.[4] If what you say is true, you have disqualified yourself from consideration, whereas if what you say is false, the breach is none of your concern. What have you to do with deciding who possesses more and who less excellence, who is to lead and who is to be led! How dare Freedmen and sons of

---

1 Hadith cited in Ṭabarānī, *al-Muʿjam al-awsaṭ*, 7:128; Muttaqī-Hindī, *Kanz*, 10:271.

2 In response to Muʿāwiyah's second letter in 36/656 before the Battle of Ṣiffīn—which Muʿāwiyah sent with Abū Umāmah al-Bāhilī—in which he again accused ʿAlī of envy of the first three caliphs and treachery towards them. Text of Muʿāwiyah's letter in Ḥ 15:185–187. Baḥrānī (B 819) says that § 2.28 is part of ʿAlī's reply to Muʿāwiyah, of which another part was transcribed earlier as § 2.9.

3 Ar. *ka-nāqili tamrin ilā Hajar*, lit. ⟨like one who carries dates to Hajar⟩, is an ancient proverb, also rendered, ⟨like one who carries dates to sell in Hajar⟩ (*ka-mustabḍiʿi tamrin ilā Hajar*), similar in meaning to the English idiom, ⟨carrying coal to Newcastle⟩. Hajar is a town near Bahrain famous for its dates. I have added "the motherlode of dates" in the translation for clarity. Proverb's explanation in Ḥ 15:188; B 819; F 372.

4 Abū Bakr and ʿUmar, the first two Sunni Caliphs. Ḥ 15:189.

وما للطلقاء وأبناء الطلقاء والتمييز بين المهاجرين الأوّلين وترتيب درجاتهم وتعريف طبقاتهم هيهات لقد ﴿حَنَّ قِدْحٌ لَيْسَ مِنْهَا﴾ وطَفِق يَحكُم فيها مَن عليه الحكم لها. ألا تَربَع أيّها الإنسان على ظِلْعك وتعرف قصور ذرعك وتتأخّر حيث أخّرك القَدَر فما عليك غلبة المغلوب ولا لك ظفر الظافر وإنّك لَذَهّاب في التيه رَوّاغ عن القصد.

2.28.2 ألا ترى غيرَ مُخبِرٍ لك لكن بنعمة الله أُحدِّث أنّ قومًا اَستُشهدوا في سبيل الله من المهاجرين ولكلٍّ فضلٌ حتّى إذا اَستشهد شهيدنا قيل سيّد الشهداء وخصّه رسول الله صلّى الله عليه وآله بسبعين تكبيرة عند صلاته عليه. أَوَلا ترى أنّ قومًا قُطعت أيديهم في سبيل الله ولكلٍّ فضل حتّى إذا فُعل بواحدنا ما فُعل بواحدهم قيل الطيّار في الجنّة وذو الجناحين. ولولا ما نهى الله عنه من تزكية المرء نفسه لَذَكر ذا كُرٌّ فضائل جمّة تعرفها قلوب المؤمنين ولا تَمُجّها آذان السامعين. فدَع عنك ﴿مَنْ مَالَتْ بِهِ الرَّمِيَّة﴾

Freedmen presume to draw distinctions between the first Emigrants, by classifying their stations and determining their ranks![1] Woe! ⟨An arrow has whirred that does not belong to the quiver!⟩[2] A person has passed judgment on a matter in which he should be the one judged, not the judge! You, man! Will you not pity your limping hoof, recognize the shortness of your stride, and retreat to where destiny has placed you? What have you to do with the defeat of the defeated or the victory of the victorious! You are plunging deep into the waterless desert and straying far from the right path!

2.28.2 Do you not see—and I say this not to give you information but to speak of God's blessings[3]—that many Emigrants were martyred in God's cause, and each one had merit, but when our martyr was killed, he was named the King of Martyrs, and God's Messenger singled him out by performing seventy supplications when he prayed over his body?[4] Do you not see that many warriors had their hands severed in God's cause, and each one had merit, but when the same injury was inflicted on one of us, he was named He-Who-Soars-in-Paradise and He-of-the-Two-Wings?[5] And if God had not forbidden men to praise themselves, I could mention someone else whose abundant virtues are known to believers' hearts and not rejected by the ears of them who listen![6] Leave off talking about ⟨one whose arrows pursued an animal that veered to one side⟩![7] We are beholden only to our Lord and all people are beholden to

---

1 On "Freedmen," see note at § 2.18.

2 Ancient Arabian proverb. B 820; Ḥ 15:191; F 373; R 3:72.

3 Reference to Qurʾan, Ḍuḥā 93:11.

4 The passage is about the excellence of the Prophet's and ʿAlī's clan of Hāshim. He compares their virtue and their service in the cause of Islam to the ignobility and anti-Islamic activities of Muʿāwiyah's Umayyad clan. The "King of Martyrs" (*Sayyid al-Shuhadāʾ*) is the Prophet's and ʿAlī's uncle Ḥamzah ibn ʿAbd al-Muṭṭalib, who was killed fighting for him at the Battle of Uḥud. Translated here as "supplications," the term *takbīr*, lit. "proclaiming that [God] is the greatest (*Allāhu akbar*)," is invoked during a funeral prayer, where it leads into a supplication for the deceased (*takbīr* is also used in other contexts); the usual number of supplications in a funeral prayer is five, and the seventy that the Prophet prayed over Ḥamzah were unprecedented and never repeated. Ḥ 15:193; B 820; F 373; R 3:73.

5 "He-Who-Soars-in-Paradise" (*Ṭayyār*), also called "He-of-the-Two-Wings" (*Dhū al-Janāḥayn*) is ʿAlī's brother and the Prophet's cousin, Jaʿfar ibn Abī Ṭālib, killed at the Battle of Muʾtah. Ḥ 15:193; B 821; F 373; R 3:73.

6 The one with "abundant virtues" is ʿAlī himself, who fought valiantly in the Muslims' early battles. Ḥ 15:193; B 820–821; R 3:74.

7 Ar. *mālat bihi l-ramiyyah*, lit. ⟨his arrows pursued an animal that veered to one side⟩, is a proverb denoting one who pursues the elusive prey of worldly gain. Ibn Abī al-Ḥadīd (Ḥ 15:194) says ʿAlī alludes here to ʿUthmān, who was from the clan of Umayyah. Baḥrānī (B 821) says the reference is to ʿAmr ibn al-Āṣ, and if so, the translation should be amended to "Leave off talking *with* (instead of: *about*) one whose arrows pursues an animal that veers to one side."

فإنّا صنائع ربّنا والناس بعد صنائع لنا لم يمنعنا قديم عزّنا وعاديّ طولنا على قومك أن خلطنا كم بأنفسنا فنكحنا وأنكحنا فعل الأكفاء ولستم هناك. وأنّى يكون ذلك كذلك ومنّا النبيّ ومنكم المكذِّب ومنّا أسد الله ومنكم أسد الأحلاف ومنّا سيّدا شباب أهل الجنّة ومنكم صبية النار ومنّا خير نساء العالمين ومنكم حمّالة الحطب في كثير ممّا لنا وعليكم. فإسلامنا قد سُمع وجاهليّتكم لا تُدفع وكتاب الله يجمع لنا ما شذّ عنّا وهو قوله ﴿وَأُولُو الْأَرْحَامِ بَعْضُهُمْ أَوْلَىٰ بِبَعْضٍ فِي كِتَابِ اللَّهِ﴾ وقوله تعالى ﴿إِنَّ أَوْلَى النَّاسِ بِإِبْرَاهِيمَ لَلَّذِينَ اتَّبَعُوهُ وَهَٰذَا النَّبِيُّ وَالَّذِينَ آمَنُوا وَاللَّهُ وَلِيُّ الْمُؤْمِنِينَ﴾ فنحن مرّة أولى بالقرابة وتارة أولى

ام، ي، ونسخة في ش: كذا. ن، هـ، وأصل ش، ونسخة في م: ﴿جاهليّتنا﴾.

us. We intermingled with you despite our time-honored might and our ancient superiority over your people. We married among you and let you marry among us as though we were peers—we are not.[1] How could we be equal when we have the Prophet and you have the Nay-Sayer,[2] when we have the Lion-of-God and you have the Lion-of-the-Alliances,[3] when we have the Chiefs-of-the-Youth-of-Paradise and you have the Boys-of-Hellfire,[4] when we have the Most-Virtuous-Woman-of-all-People and you have the Woman-Who-Carries-Firewood-to-Hell?[5] And there are many more things that speak for us and against you. Our noble deeds in Islam have been heard by all, and your Age-of-Ignorance misdeeds cannot be denied.[6] God's Book brings together for us what was taken from us, in his words, «Those who are from the same womb have more claim upon each other according to God's Book,»[7] with his words, «Those who have the most claim on Abraham are the ones who followed him, and this Prophet, and those who profess belief. God is the believers' master.»[8]

---

1   Marriages between the Hāshim and Umayyah clans discussed in Ḥ 15:195–196.

2   "The Prophet" (*Nabī*) is Muḥammad. "The Nay-Sayer" (*Mukadhdhib*) is the Umayyad Abū Jahl ibn Hishām, at the head of nine other men who fought Muḥammad at Badr (Qurʾan, Muzzammil 73:11; B 821; R 3:75; ʿA 681), or, less likely, Muʿāwiyah's father, Abū Sufyān ibn Ḥarb (Ḥ 15:196).

3   "The-Lion-of-God" (*Asad Allāh*) is Ḥamzah ibn ʿAbd al-Muṭṭalib (B 821; Ḥ 15:196; R 3:76; F 374, ʿA 681) and/or ʿAlī himself (again, F 374). "The Lion-of-the-Alliances" (*Asad al-Aḥlāf*) is one of several possible Umayyads, either from the pre-Islamic period (more likely)—ʿUtbah ibn Rabīʿah (Ḥ 15:196; F 374), or some other men who had the name "Asad," viz., Asad ibn ʿAbd al-ʿUzzā (B 821; R 3:76), Asad ibn Khuzaymah ibn Mudrikah ibn Ilyās (again, F 374), or Asad ibn Rabīʿah ibn Nizār (again, F 374)—or from the early Islamic period, viz., Abū Sufyān (ʿA 681). "The Alliances" refers to the so-called "Alliance of the Pure Ones" (*Ḥilf al-Muṭayyabīn*) between certain Quraysh clans in the pre-Islamic period, regarding the allocation of the ritual offices of the Kaʿbah (R 3:86; B 821); if the "Lion" is Abū Sufyān, it refers to the tribal alliance put together by the Quraysh against Muḥammad.

4   "The Chiefs-of-the-Youth-of-Paradise" (*Sayyidā Shabāb Ahl al-Jannah*) are Ḥasan and Ḥusayn, ʿAlī's sons with Fāṭimah, the Prophet's grandsons (R 3:77; F 77; Ḥ 15:197; B 822; ʿA 681). "The Boys-of-Hellfire" (*Ṣibyat al-Nār*) are the sons of the Umayyad ʿUqbah ibn Abī Muʿīṭ, who was killed fighting against the Muslims at the Battle of Badr (Ḥ 15:197; F 374; B 822), or the sons of Muʿāwiyah's second cousin Marwān ibn al-Ḥakam (R 3:77; again B 822; ʿA 681).

5   "The Most-Virtuous-Woman-of-all-People" (*Khayr Nisāʾ al-ʿĀlamīn*) is Fāṭimah al-Zahrāʾ, the Prophet's daughter and ʿAlī's wife (R 3:77; Ḥ 15:197; B 822; ʿA 681). "The Woman-Who-Carries-Firewood-to-Hell" (*Ḥammālat al-Ḥaṭab*; "to-Hell" is added in the translation from the Qurʾan-ic context) is Umm Jamīl bint Ḥarb, Muʿāwiyah's paternal aunt and wife of Abū Lahab (Reference to Qurʾan, Masad 111:4; Ḥ 15:197; B 822; R 3:77; F 374; ʿA 681).

6   In some manuscripts, the pronoun is "our" (*-nā*), which would read, "and our noble deeds in the Age of Ignorance (*jāhiliyyatunā*) cannot be denied." On the virtues of the Hāshim clan, see Ḥ 15:198–269. Refutation of virtues attributed to the Umayyads in Ḥ 15:270–295.

7   Qurʾan, Aḥzāb 33:6.

8   Qurʾan, Āl ʿImrān 3:68.

بالطاعة. ولمّا ٱحتجّ المهاجرون على الأنصار يوم السقيفة برسول الله صلّى الله عليه وآله فَلجوا عليهم فإن يكن الفُلْج به فالحقّ لنا دونكم وإن يكن بغيره فالأنصار على دعواهم.

2.28.3 وزعمتَ أنّي لكلّ الخلفاء حسدتُ وعلى كلّهم بَغَيت فإن يكن ذلك كذلك فليس الجِناية عليك فيكون العذر إليك ﴿وَتِلْكَ شَكَاةٌ ظَاهِرٌ عَنْكَ عَارُهَا﴾. وقلت إنّي كنت أُقاد كما يُقاد الجمل المخشوش حتّى أبايع ولَعَمْرُ الله لقد أردت أن تذمّ فمدحت وأن تفضح فٱفتَضحت وما على المسلم من غَضاضة في أن يكون مظلومًا ما لم يكن شاكًّا في دينه ولا مُرتابًا بيقينه. وهذه حجّتي إلى غيرك قصدها ولكنّي أطلقت لك منها بقدر ما سَنَح من ذكرها.

2.28.4 ثمّ ذكرتَ ما كان من أمري وأمر عثمان فلك أن تجاب عن هذه لرحمك منه. فأيّنا كان أعدى له وأهدى إلى مقاتله أمَن بذل له نصرته فٱستقعده وٱستكفّه أم من ٱستنصره فتراخى عنه وبثّ المَنون إليه حتّى أتى قَدَره عليه كلّا والله لقد علم ﴿اللَّهُ الْمُعَوِّقِينَ مِنكُمْ وَالْقَائِلِينَ لِإِخْوَانِهِمْ هَلُمَّ إِلَيْنَا وَلَا يَأْتُونَ الْبَأْسَ إِلَّا قَلِيلًا﴾. وما كنتُ لأعتذر من أنّي كنت أنقِم عليه أحداثًا فإن كان الذنب إليه إرشادي وهدايتي له فرُبَّ

We possess the higher claim—because of our kinship, yes, but also because of our obedience to God. When the Emigrants argued against the Allies on the Day of the Portico,[1] the Emigrants challenged the Allies' claim on the basis of their own kinship with God's Messenger. If the argument is based on kinship with the Messenger, then we, not they, possess the truer claim. If it is based on something else, then the Allies' claim stands.

2.28.3 You allege that I was envious of every caliph and disloyal to all. If that is true, then the crime was not committed against you, and you are due no justification. As the saying goes, ⟨that is a disease whose shame is external to you.⟩[2] You also say that I had to be dragged to give the pledge of allegiance, like a camel pulled by a wooden bit in its nose. God's life, you intended to revile but have offered praise instead, you intended to disgrace but are yourself disgraced! A Muslim is never shamed because he is a victim of oppression, as long as he does not doubt in his faith or falter in his certainty. The argument I have made here is intended for another, but I have set it before you to the extent that I thought necessary.

2.28.4 You recount what happened between me and ʿUthmān—you are due a response in this matter because of your kinship with him. So tell me, which of us was more wrong in our actions toward him and did more to bring about his assassination? Was it the one who offered him support, but who he insisted should stand back and desist? Or was it the one with whom he pleaded for help, who loosened the reins of his mount to slow it down and stalled in giving a response, who pushed death toward him until his fate overpowered him?[3] No, indeed! God knows the identity of «those among you who impede, who say to their brothers, "Come help us," while they themselves seldom enter the fray.»[4] I will not apologize for the fact that I chastised him for some of his actions. If my crime against him is my counsel and guidance, then how often are the

---

1 "The Day of the Portico" (*Yawm al-Saqīfah*) refers to the assembly, immediately after Muḥammad's death, when some of the Emigrants and Allies gathered in the covered assembly area of the Banū Sāʿidah clan, and which ended with the pledge for Abū Bakr. See ʿAlī's similar initial response (and references for further details) in §1.64 and my note there.

2 Second hemistich of a verse by the pre-Islamic poet Abū Dhuʾayb al-Hudhalī (*Dīwān al-Hudhaliyyīn*, 1:21), used as a proverb. The first half is (وَعَيَّرَهَا الْوَاشُونَ أَنِّي أُحِبُّهَا): ⟨Accusers shamed her, saying I was in love with her.⟩ F 373; R 3:79; B 822.

3 "The one who offered him support" is ʿAlī. "The one with whom he pleaded for help" is Muʿāwiyah. Details in B 823.

4 Qurʾan, Aḥzāb 33:18.

مَلُومٍ لا ذنب له ﴿وَقَدْ يَسْتَفِيدُ الظِّنَّةَ المُتَنَصِّحُ﴾. وما أردتُ ﴿إِلَّا الْإِصْلَاحَ مَا اسْتَطَعْتُ وَمَا تَوْفِيقِي إِلَّا بِاللَّهِ عَلَيْهِ تَوَكَّلْتُ﴾.

2.28.5 وذكرتَ أنّه ليس لي ولأصحابي عندك إلّا السيف فلقد أَضحكت بعد اَستعبار متى أُلْفِيَتْ بنو عبد المطّلب عن الأعداء ناكلين وبالسيوف مخوَّفين فـ﴿لَبِثْ قَلِيلًا يَلْحَقِ¹ الْهَيْجَا حَمَل﴾. فسيطلبك من تطلب ويقرب منك ما تستبعد وأنا مُرقِل نحوك في جَحْفَل من المهاجرين والأنصار والتابعين بإحسان شديد زِحامِهم ساطع قَتامِهم متَسربلين سرابيل الموت أحبّ اللقاء إليهم لقاء ربّهم قد صحبتهم ذرّيّة بدريّة وسيوف هاشميّة قد عرفتَ مواقع نِصالها في أخيك وخالك وجدّك وأهلك ﴿وَمَا هِيَ مِنَ الظَّالِمِينَ بِبَعِيدٍ﴾.

2.29 ومن كتاب له عليه السلام إلى أهل البصرة

وقد كان من اَنتشار حبلِكم وشقاقكم ما لم تَغْبَوْا عنه فعفوتُ عن مجرمكم ورفعت السيف عن مدبركم وقبلت من مقبلكم. فإن خَطَتْ بكم الأمور المُردية وسفَه الآراء الجائرة إلى

اش، ن، ي، ه، ونسخة في م: كذا. أصل م: ﴿يدرك﴾.

innocent blamed! ⟨Sometimes, the only benefit a well-wisher derives is suspicion!⟩[1] I intend «only to set things right as much as I can. My direction comes from God. In him I place my trust.»[2]

2.28.5 You also say that you have nothing to offer me and my supporters but the sword. My eyes were moist earlier and now you make me laugh! When have you ever found the sons of ʿAbd al-Muṭṭalib to shrink from enemies or fear the sword? ⟨Wait just a little—Ḥamal will soon join the fray!⟩[3] The one you seek shall soon seek you, and what you think is far will come close indeed! I shall ride to you swiftly, bringing a large army of Emigrants, Allies, and Followers-in-Virtue, pressing strongly, raising dust, clothed in robes of death, and longing to meet their Lord. They number children of the warriors of Badr, wielding the swords of Hāshim—you have experienced their strikes on your brother, your uncle, your grandfather, and your kinsmen![4] The blade «is never far from the wicked.»[5]

2.29 From ʿAlī's letter to the people of Basra:[6]
You know this well: You severed your rope of allegiance earlier and seceded from the community, but I pardoned those among you who had committed crimes, lifted the sword from those who had turned their backs, and accepted those who returned to me. If damning events and the immaturity of your

---

1 Second hemistich of a verse by an anonymous poet used as a proverb. The first half is (وَكَمْ
   نَصِيحَة مِنْ آثَارِهِمْ فِي سُقْتُ): ⟨How many camels of counsel did I drive toward them!⟩ F 375;
   B 824.
2 Qurʾan, Hūd 11:88.
3 First half of a verse by the pre-Islamic warrior Ḥamal ibn Badr (or: Ḥamal ibn Saʿd al-ʿAshīrah),
   in response to threats by Mālik ibn Zuhayr, used as a proverb. The second half is (مَا أَحْسَنَ
   نَزَل المَوْت إِذَا المَوْت): ⟨O how beautiful is death when death alights!⟩ F 374; R 3:82; B 824.
4 The Umayyad men slain by the Muslims in the Battle of Badr included Muʿāwiyah's brother
   Ḥanẓalah ibn Abī Sufyān, his maternal uncle Walīd ibn ʿUtbah, and his grandfather ʿUtbah
   ibn Rabīʿah. R 3:83; B 824.
5 Qurʾan, Hūd 11:83.
6 Excerpt from a letter to the Basrans in 38/658, during the Ibn al-Ḥaḍramī episode: After
   Muʿāwiyah took Egypt, he sent ʿAbdallāh ibn ʿĀmir ibn al-Ḥaḍramī to Basra to recruit its peo-
   ple, and many welcomed him. ʿAlī's governor, Ziyād ibn Abīhi, wrote for help, and ʿAlī sent the
   Basran Jāriyah ibn Qudāmah al-Saʿdī with fifty men from Kufa, and with this letter addressed
   to the Basrans. Jāriyah confronted Ibn al-Ḥaḍramī and killed him and his men. Details of Ibn
   al-Ḥaḍramī's attack in Thaqafī, *Ghārāt*, 2:383–412 (with full text of the letter at 2:403–404);
   Ṭabarī, *Tārīkh*, 5:110–112. See also oration §1.1.90 (*Qāṣiʿah*), which is said to have been deliv-
   ered at this time.

مُنابذتي وخلافي فها أنا ذا قد قرّبت جيادي ورحلت ركابي ولئن ألجأتموني إلى المسير إليكم لأُوقِعَنَّ بكم وقعة لا يكون يوم الجمل إليها إلّا كَلَعقَة لاعق. مع أنّي عارف لذي الطاعة منكم فضله ولذي النصيحة حقّه غير متجاوز مُتَّهَمًا إلى بريء ولا ناكًّا إلى وفيّ.

2.30   ومن كتاب له عليه السلام إلى معاوية

فاتّق الله فيما لديك وانظر في حقّه عليك وارجع إلى معرفة ما لا تُعذَر بجهالته فإنّ للطاعة أعلامًا واضحة وسبلًا نيّرة ومَحَجّة نَهْجة وغاية مُطَلَبة يَردها الأكياس ويخالفها الأنكاس من نَكَب عنها جارَ عن الحقّ وخَبَط في التيه وغَيَّر الله نعمته وأحلّ به نقمته. فنفسَك نفسَك فقد بيّن الله لك سبيلك وحيث تناهت بك أمورك فقد أجريت إلى غاية خسر ومحلّة كفر وإنّ نفسك قد أولَجَتك شرًّا وأقحمتك غَيًّا وأوردتك المهالك وأوعرت عليك المسالك.

2.31   ومن وصيّة للحسن بن عليّ عليهما السلام كتبها إليه بحاضرين عند انصرافه من صفّين

2.31.1   من الوالد الفانِ[2] المقرّ للزمان المدبر العمر المستسلم للدهر الذامّ للدنيا الساكن مساكن الموتى الظاعن عنها غدًا إلى المولود[3] المؤمّل ما لا يدرك السالك سبيل من قد هلك غرض الأسقام ورهينة الأيّام ورميّة المصائب وعبد الدنيا وتاجر الغرور وغريم المنايا وأسير الموت وحليف الهموم وقرين الأحزان ونَصْب الآفات وصريع الشهوات وخليفة الأموات.

<hr>

[1] ش، ن، ي، هـ، ونسخة في م: كذا. أصل م، ونسخة في ش: ﴿يؤدّيها﴾.   [2] م، ن، هـ، ونسخة في ش: كذا. ي، وأصل ش: ﴿الفانِي﴾.   [3] م، ن، ي، هـ، ونسخة في ش: كذا. أصل ش: ﴿الولد﴾.

despotic views now incite you to break your pledge again and challenge me, then beware! I have kept my steeds close, and my mounts saddled! If you force me to march, I shall charge against you in a battle that will make the thrashing you received at the Battle of the Camel seem like a romp in the meadow. I am also aware of the virtue of those of you who are obedient and the rights of those who are sincere. In punishing the guilty I shall not violate the innocent, in punishing those who break the pledge I shall not violate the faithful.

2.30 From ʿAlī's letter to Muʿāwiyah:[1]
Fear God in all that you do and reflect on what you owe him. Return to the path of obedience, for your ignorance of it will not be excused. Its waymarks are clear, its roads are bright, its thoroughfare is open, and its destination is the one you should seek. The intelligent traverse it to reach water, while the wretched turn away. Whoever deviates from it strays from the truth and is lost in the waterless desert—God overturns his blessings and afflicts him with harsh punishment. Look out for your soul, Muʿāwiyah, look out for your soul! God has shown you the grim reality of your current path and where your affairs will end. You speed inexorably toward the destination of utter loss and the resting-place of unbelief. Your passions have led you into evil, cast you into error, brought you to uncharted wastes, and made the road ahead of you steep and arduous.

2.31 From a testament of counsel that ʿAlī wrote to his son Ḥasan, at Ḥāḍirīn, on the return from Ṣiffīn:[2]

2.31.1 From a father who admits the power of time, bows to the supremacy of fate, censures this world below, lives in the abodes of the dead, and will depart from them tomorrow, to a son who hopes for what he cannot attain and walks the path of men long gone, a target for disease, a mortgage pledged to the passage of days, a quarry stalked by adversity, a slave of the world, a merchant trading in deception, a debtor bound to doom, a prisoner of death, a friend of sorrow, a companion of grief, a victim of calamity, a man felled by passion, and an heir to the dead.

---

1   Excerpt from a letter—presumably from Kufa, and, since there is no reference to a prior battle, before the Battle of Ṣiffīn in 37/657—in reply to a letter by Muʿāwiyah containing threats and accusations. Earlier part of ʿAlī's letter recorded in B 825; Ḥ 16:7–8.

2   In 37/657; in northern Syria. Ḥāḍirīn could be the name of a place, or the word could be *ḥāḍirayn*, sing. *ḥāḍir*, meaning "two urban spaces" (Ḥ 16:52). Addressed to Muḥammad ibn al-Ḥanafiyyah (rather than Ḥasan) in Māmaṭīrī, *Nuzhah*, 201. One of the most famous and widely narrated of ʿAlī's testaments.

2.31.2   أمّا بعد. فإنّ فيما تبيّنتُ من إدبار الدنيا عنّي وجُموح الدهر عليّ وإقبال الآخرة إليّ ما يزَعُني عن ذكر مَن سواي والاهتمام بما ورائي غيرَ أنّي حيث تفرّد بي دون هموم الناس همّ نفسي فصدفني رأيي وصرفني عن هواي وصرّح لي محض أمري فأفضى بي إلى جِدّ لا يكون فيه لعب وصدق لا يشوبه كذب. وجدتُك بعضي بل وجدتك كلّي حتّى كأنّ شيئًا لو أصابك أصابني وكأنّ الموت لو أتاك أتاني فعَناني من أمرك ما يعنيني من أمر نفسي فكتبت إليك كتابي هذا مستظهِرًا به إن أنا بقيت لك أو فنيت.

2.31.3   فإنّي أوصيك بتقوى الله أي بُنَيّ ولزوم أمره وعمارة قلبك بذكره والاعتصام بحبله وأيُّ سبب أوثق من سبب بينك وبين الله إن أنت أخذت به. أحِي قلبك بالموعظة وأمِتْه بالزهادة وقوِّه باليقين ونوّره بالحكمة[1] وذلّله بذكر الموت وقرّره بالفناء وبصّره بفجائع الدنيا وحذّره صولة الدهر وفحش تقلّب الليالي والأيّام وأعرِض عليه أخبار الماضين وذكّره بما أصاب من كان قبلك من الأوّلين وسِر في ديارهم وآثارهم فأنظر ما فعلوا وعمّا انتقلوا وأين حلّوا ونزلوا فإنّك تجدهم انتقلوا عن الأحبّة وحلّوا دار الغربة. وكأنّك عن قليل قد صرت كأحدهم فأصلح مثواك ولا تبَع آخرتك بدنياك ودَع القول فيما لا تعرف والخطاب فيما لا تكلّف وأمسك عن طريق إذا خفت ضلالته فإنّ الكفّ عند حيرة الضلال خير من ركوب الأهوال وأُمُرْ بالمعروف تكن من أهله وأنكِر المنكر بيدك ولسانك وباينْ مَن فعله بجُهدك وجاهد في الله حقّ جهاده ولا تأخذك في الله لومة لائم وخُض الغمرات للحقّ حيث كان وتَفَقَّه في الدين وعوّد نفسك الصبر على المكروه ونعم الخلق التصبّر وألجِئ نفسك في الأمور كلّها

―――――――

[1]ن، ي، ه: كذا. ش: ﴿ونجّده بالحكمة﴾. م: سقطت ﴿ونوّره بالحكمة﴾.

2.31.2 I have observed how the world has turned its back on me, how refractory fate has bolted with my affairs, and how the hereafter steadily approaches. This has restrained me from thinking about anyone else or from worrying about any circumstances I might leave behind—cares about myself have driven out cares about other people. My prudence has led me to rebuff and reject my passions, and my reality has become clear, impelling me to gravity untainted by frolic and truth untarnished by lies. Yet, I realize that you are part of me, nay, you are all of me. If something hurts you, it hurts me. If death comes to you, it comes to me. Your affairs are as important to me as my own, and for this reason, I write this testament for you. It will support you while I remain with you and after I am gone.

2.31.3 My dear son! I counsel you to be conscious of God. Obey his command, nourish your heart with his remembrance, and hold fast to his rope—if grasped tightly, can you imagine a stronger bond between you and God?[1] Revive your heart with pious counsel, kill its appetites through renunciation, strengthen it through certainty, and illuminate it with wisdom. Humble it by the remembrance of death, impress upon it the reality of annihilation, and make it aware of the world's sudden assaults. Give it warning of the violent attacks of fate and the horrible changes wrought by the passage of nights and days. Place before it reports of past peoples and remind it of the calamities that befell the ancients. Walk among their dwellings, their ruins, and reflect: What happened to them? What did they leave behind? Where did they take up residence? You will find that they left their loved ones and took residence in a strange land. Before long, you too will join them, so strive to build your permanent home and do not sell out the hereafter in exchange for this world. Leave off talking about what you do not know, or calling out people about things you are not charged with addressing; desist from any path that might lead you astray, for holding back when you fear error is far better than sailing the dread swells of the unknown; command good, and you will belong to its people; forbid evil with hand and tongue and strive hard to distance yourself from those who practice it; fight wickedness in the name of God, as is his due; do not be disheartened by any who might revile or shame you for anything you do for God; dive into the depths in the quest for truth, wherever or whenever you may have to do so; gain a good understanding of religion; and habituate yourself to patience—what a beautiful trait is patience! In all your affairs, seek support from God, for in him you seek the

---

1 "Hold fast to his rope," reference to Qurʾan, Āl ʿImrān 3:103. The Shiʿi commentator Rāwandī (R 3:93–94) narrates a hadith in which the Prophet named ʿAlī as the embodiment of God's rope.

إلى إلهك فإنّك تُلجِئُها إلى كهف حريز ومانع عزيز وأخلص في المسألة لربّك فإنّ بيده
العطاء والحرمان وأكثِرِ الاستخارة. وتفهّم وصيّتي ولا تذهبنّ صفحًا فإنّ خير القول ما
نفع واعلم أنّه لا خير في علم لا ينفع ولا ينتفع بعلم لا يحقّ تعلّمه.[1]

2.31.4 أي بنيّ إنّي لمّا رأيتُني[2] قد بلغتُ سنًّا ورأيتُني أزداد وهنًا بادرتُ بوصيّتي إليك
خصالًا منها أن يعجل[3] بي أجلي دون أن أفضي إليك بما في نفسي وأن أُنقَص في رأيي كما
نقصت في جسمي أو يسبقني إليك بعض غلبات الهوى وفتن الدنيا فتكون كالصَّعب
النَّفور. وإنّما قلب الحَدَث كالأرض الخالية ما أُلقِي فيها من شيء قبلته فبادرتك بالأدب
قبل أن يَقسُو قلبك ويشتغل لُبّك لتستقبل بجِدّ رأيك؛ من الأمور ما قد كفاك أهل
التجارب بُغْيَته وتجربته فتكون قد كُفِيتَ مؤونة الطَّلبة وعوفيت من علاج التجربة
فأتاك من ذلك ما قد كنّا نأتيه واستبان لك ما ربّما أظلم علينا منه.

2.31.5 أَيْ بُنَيَّ إنّي وإن لم أكن عمّرت عمر من كان قبلي فقد نظرت في أعمالهم
وفكّرت في أخبارهم وسرت في آثارهم حتّى عدت كأحدهم بل كأنّي بما انتهى إليّ من
أمورهم قد عُمّرت مع أوّلهم إلى آخرهم فعرفت صفو ذلك من كدره ونفعه من ضرره
فاستخلصت لك من كلّ أمر نَخِيلته۰ وتوخّيت لك جميله وصرفت عنك مجهوله. ورأيتُ
حيث عَنانِي من أمرك ما يعني الوالد الشفيق وأجمعت عليه من أدبك أن يكون ذلك
وأنت مقبل العمر ومقتبل الدهر ذو نيّة سليمة ونفس صافية وأن أبتدئك بتعليم كتاب
الله عزّ وجلّ وتأويله وشرائع الإسلام وأحكامه وحلاله وحرامه لا أجاوز ذلك بك

۱ن، ش، ي، ه، وأُضيفت في م: كذا. أصل م: سقطت ﴿وأخلص ... تعلّمه﴾.   ۲م، ش، ي،
ه: كذا. ن، ونسخة في ش: ﴿رأيتك﴾.   ۳م، ش، ه: كذا. ن، ي، وزيادة في ش، مع إضافة
بعض الألفاظ: ﴿بوصيّتي إليك أوردت خصالًا منها قبل أن يعجل﴾.   ٤م، ش: كذا. ن، ي:
﴿بجِدّ رأيك﴾. ه: معًا، وفيها نسخة مع علامة الصحّة: ﴿بحداثتك﴾.   ٥م، ي، ونسخة في ش، ه:
كذا. ن، وأصل ش، ه، ونسخة في ي: ﴿جليله﴾.

shelter of a deep cave and a mighty protector. Petition your Lord with a sincere heart, for his hand holds the power to give or refuse, ask him to help you choose what is good. Understand my testament and do not turn your face away, for the best words are those that bring benefit. Know this: There is no good in knowledge that brings no benefit, there is also no benefit in acquiring classes of knowledge that are not recommended for you to learn.[1]

2.31.4 My dear son! When I saw that I had lived to a full age, when I saw that I was growing weak, I hastened to prepare this testament for you and listed virtuous traits of character. I worried lest death overtake me before I could reveal to you what was in my heart, before weakness affected my mind as it has my body, and before forces of passion or the seductive powers of the world rushed to make you intractable and skittish. A young heart is like untilled land—it accepts whatever is sown. I have sought to refine your disposition before your heart hardens and before your mind becomes preoccupied. I hope that serious commitment will help you learn through the experiences of the experienced and save you from confrontation and investigation, and that it will spare you the hardship of pursuit and the bitter medicine of suffering. I hope that you learn from my experience, yet I further hope that even those things that may have remained obscure to me become clear to you.

2.31.5 My dear son! Although I have not lived as long as those before me, I have reflected upon their acts, pondered their histories, and walked among their ruins, until I am almost one of them. In fact, because of what I have learned of their affairs, I feel as though I have lived with the first of them all the way to the last of them. I have distinguished the pure from the impure and the beneficial from the harmful. From each of their affairs, I have extracted the essential points of benefit, sought out the most beautiful, and dispensed with those that are unproven. My concern for you is as a loving father, and my hope is to complete the refinement of your character. The time for this is now, while you are still young, with your life ahead of you, while your intentions are innocent and your soul pure. I wish to begin by teaching you the Book of God and its deep meanings, the laws of Islam and its commands, what it has made licit and what illicit. I want you to focus on these things and leave the rest aside.

---

1 The "classes of knowledge that are not recommended for you to learn" are interpreted as (1) any kind of knowledge that it is not required or recommended to learn (R 3:94); or (2) that constitutes arts prohibited in Islam, such as magic, soothsaying, and astrology (B 831); or (2) that does not bring benefit for the hereafter (F 375); specifically, (4) geometry, mathematics, or their like (!) (Ḥ 16:66).

إلى غيره. ثمّ أشفقت أن يلتبس عليك ما اختلف الناس فيه من أهوائهم وآرائهم مثل الذي التبس عليهم فكان إحكام ذلك على ما كرهت من تنبيهك أحبّ إليّ من إسلامك إلى أمر لا آمن عليك فيه الهلكة ورجوت أن يوفّقك الله فيه لرشدك وأن يهديك لقصدك فعهدت إليك وصيّتي هذه.

2.31.6   واعلم يا بنيّ أنّ أحبّ ما أنت آخذ به إليّ من وصيّتي تقوى الله والاقتصار على ما افترضه الله عليك والأخذ بما مضى عليه الأوّلون من آبائك والصالحون من أهل بيتك. فإنّهم لم يدعوا أن نظروا لأنفسهم كما أنت ناظر وفكّروا كما أنت مفكّر ثمّ ردّهم آخر ذلك إلى الأخذ بما عرفوا والإمساك عمّا لم يكلّفوا. فإن أبت نفسك أن تقبل ذلك دون أن تعلم كما علموا فليكن طلبك ذلك بتفهّم وتعلّم لا بتورّط الشبهات وعلوّ الخصومات. وابدأ قبل نظرك في ذلك بالاستعانة بإلهك عليه والرغبة إليه في توفيقك وترك كلّ شائبة أولجتك في شبهة أو أسلمتك إلى ضلالة فإذا أيقنت أن قد صفا قلبك فخشع وتمّ رأيك واجتمع وكان همّك في ذلك همًّا واحدًا فانظر فيما فسّرت لك وإن أنت لم يجتمع لك ما تحبّ من نفسك وفراغ نظرك وفكرك فاعلم أنّك إنّما تخبط العشواء وتتورّط الظلماء وليس طالب الدين من خبط ولا من خلّط والإمساك عن ذلك أمثل.

2.31.7   فتفهّم يا بنيّ وصيّتي واعلم أنّ مالك الموت هو مالك الحياة وأنّ الخالق هو المميت وأنّ المفني هو المعيد وأنّ المبتلي هو المعافي وأنّ الدنيا لم تكن لتستقرّ إلّا على ما جعلها الله عليه من النعماء والابتلاء والجزاء في المعاد أو ما شاء ممّا لا نعلم. فإن أشكل عليك شيء من ذلك فاحمله على جهالتك به فإنّك أوّل ما خُلِقتَ[1] جاهلًا ثمّ علمت وما أكثر ما تجهل من الأمر ويتحيّر فيه رأيك ويضلّ فيه بصرك ثمّ تبصره بعد ذلك. فاعتصم بالذي خلقك ورزقك وسوّاك وليكن له تعبّدك وإليه رغبتك ومنه شفقتك.

ا م، ي، ه: كذا. ن، ش: تكرّرت ⟨خلقت⟩.

I worry lest you should become confused, as others have, about issues on which people's interpretations and views differ. Although I am loath to alarm you, I prefer to strengthen you in advance, rather than leave you without caution about approaching times in which you could perish. I ask God to direct you to the right path and guide you toward your goal. Accordingly, I bequeath to you this testament.

2.31.6 My dear son! Know that the directives of my testament most dear to me, the ones to which I sincerely hope you will adhere, are the following: Remain conscious of God and do not overstep the boundaries of God's mandates for you. Adhere to the path followed by your forebears and your pious family. Like you, they never stopped caring for their souls or reflecting deeply on matters, so they carried out all that was good and refrained from all they had not been charged to undertake. If your heart refuses to accept their path without first learning what they learned, then commence your search with understanding and acumen, without hurtling down the precipice of doubt, or engaging in strident argumentation. Begin your exploration, moreover, by seeking aid from God and petitioning him for direction. Beware of lapses that could throw you into doubt or give you over to error. Once you have ensured that your heart has become pure and humble, your mind mature and composed, your aspiration resolute, begin reflecting on what I have explained. If you cannot achieve this, if you cannot compose your heart or clear your perception and thoughts, then—and this you should know too—you will stumble around heavily like a blind camel and be flung headlong down a dark precipice; and one who stumbles around heavily, one who is delirious, is no seeker of religion. In such a case, it is better to refrain altogether.

2.31.7 My dear son! Try to understand my testament. Know that the master of death is also the master of life, the creator is also the destroyer, the demolisher is also the restorer, the one who inflicts pain is also the one who bestows wellbeing. The world can be sustained only in the way of God's plan—with blessings and affliction, and repayment in the return to him, or other things that he wills that remain unknown to us. If any of this is difficult for you to grasp, attribute it to your ignorance. At the time of your creation, you were created ignorant, then you learned. How often it happens that you are ignorant of something, that your mind is perplexed about it and your perception leads you astray, but then afterward you perceive it clearly! Seek refuge in the one who created you, who sustained you, who molded you in harmonious form. Let your worship be for him, let your hope be in him, let your fear be of him.

2.31.8 وآعلم يا بنيّ أنّ أحدًا لم ينبئ عن الله سبحانه كما أنبأ عنه نبيّنا صلّى الله عليه وآله فآرتضَ به رائدًا وإلى النجاة قائدًا. فإنّي لم آلُكَ نصيحةً وإنّك لن تبلغ في النظر لنفسك وإن آجتهدت مبلغ نظري لك.

2.31.9 وآعلم يا بنيّ أنّه لو كان لربّك شريك لأتتك رسله ولرأيت آثار ملكه وسلطانه ولعرفت أفعاله وصفاته ولكنّه إلٰه واحد كما وصف نفسه لا يُضادُّه في ملكه أحد ولا يزول أبدًا ولم يزل أوّل قبل الأشياء بلا أوّلية وآخر بعد الأشياء بلا نهاية عظم عن أن تثبت ربوبيّته بإحاطة قلب أو بصر. فإذا عرفت ذلك فآفعل كما ينبغي لمثلك أن يفعله في صغر خطره وقلّة مقدرته وكثرة عجزه وعظيم حاجته إلى ربّه في طلب طاعته والرهبة من عقوبته والشفقة من سخطه فإنّه لم يأمرك إلّا بحسن ولم ينهك إلّا عن قبيح.

2.31.10 يا بُنيّ إنّي قد أنبأتك عن الدنيا وحالها وزوالها وآنتقالها وأنبأتك عن الآخرة وما أُعدّ لأهلها فيها وضربت لك فيهما الأمثال لتعتبر بها وتحذو عليها. إنّما مَثَل مَن خَبَرَ الدنيا كَمَثَل قوم سَفْر نَبا بهم منزل جديب فأمّوا منزلًا خصيبًا وجنابًا مَريعًا فآحتملوا وَعثاء الطريق وفراق الصديق وخشونة السفر وجشوبة المطعم ليأتوا سعة دارهم ومنزل قرارهم فليس يجدون لشيء من ذلك ألمًا ولا يرون نفقة مغرمًا ولا شيء أحبّ إليهم ممّا قرّبهم من منزلهم وأدناهم إلى محلّهم. ومثل من آغترّ بها كمثل قوم كانوا بمنزل خصيب فنبا بهم إلى منزل جديب فليس شيء أكره إليهم ولا أفظع عندهم من مفارقة ما كانوا فيه إلى ما يهجمون عليه ويصيرون إليه.

2.31.8 My dear son! Know that no one has brought God's message in the manner of our Prophet, so take joy in accepting him as your scout for salvation and your leader. I have never held back from giving you advice. Though you may strive hard, you will never look out for yourself as much as I look out for you.

2.31.9 My dear son! Know that if your Lord had a partner, his messengers would have come to you. You would have seen the evidence of that deity's kingship and power and recognized his actions and attributes. But there is only one God—he has described himself as one,[1] and no one can challenge him for his kingdom. As he has always been, so he will never cease to be. He is first before all things, yet without beginning, he is last after all things, yet without end. His majesty is too great to be encompassed by heart or eye. If you recognize this, do what someone like you should do, a human of little significance, of meager power, of complete incapacity, a human in great need of his Lord—seek to obey him, beware his punishment, and fear his wrath, for he only ever commands you to do what is right, and he only forbids you from doing what is wrong.

2.31.10 My dear son! I have told you about this world, about its condition, its imminent end, and its inexorable passing. I have told you about the hereafter and what has been prepared in it for its people. You have been given illustrations about both so that you may learn from them and act upon them. Those who have tested the world's reality are like a group of travelers who, finding it an unsatisfactory, drought-stricken abode, seek another that is fertile and rich in pasture. They patiently suffer the tribulations of the road, the separation from friends, the roughness of the journey, and the coarseness of their food, in order to arrive at the vast and lovely expanse of their new home, their permanent residence. They care nothing for the pain they must experience on the road, nor do they deem the expense they must incur an indemnity. Nothing pleases them more than the things that bring them closer to their permanent abode, that draw them nearer to their real home. In contrast, those who are taken in by the world's deceptions are like a group of people who live in a fertile pasture and leave it behind to travel to a place of drought. Nothing will bring them more grief or be more devastating for them than leaving the pleasures they enjoy, and arriving, suddenly, at the place to which they must come, and in which they must stay forever.

---

1   E.g., Qurʾan, Ikhlāṣ 112:1, Naḥl 16:51, Baqarah 2:163.

2.31.11 يا بنيّ ٱجعل نفسك ميزانًا فيما بينك وبين غيرك فأحبب لغيرك ما تحبّ لنفسك وٱكره له ما تكره لها ولا تظلم كما لا تحبّ أن تُظلم وأحسن كما تحبّ أن يحسن إليك وٱستقبح من نفسك ما تستقبح من غيرك وٱرضَ من الناس بما ترضاه لهم من نفسك ولا تقل ما لا تعلم وإن قلّ ما تعلم ولا تقل ما لا تحبّ أن يقال لك وٱعلم أنّ الإعجاب ضدّ الصواب وآفة الألباب فٱسْعَ في كَدْحِك ولا تكن خازنًا لغيرك وإذا أنت هُديت لقصدك فكن أخشع ما تكون لربّك.

2.31.12 وٱعلم أنّ أمامك طريقًا ذا مسافة بعيدة ومشقّة شديدة وأنّه لا غنى بك فيه عن حسن الارتياد وقدر بلاغك من الزاد مع خفّة الظهر فلا تحملنّ على ظهرك فوق طاقتك فيكون ثقل ذلك وبالًا عليك. وإذا وجدت من أهل الفاقة من يحمل لك زادك إلى يوم القيامة فيُوافيك به غدًا حيث تحتاج إليه فٱغتنمه وحَمِّله إيّاه وأكثر من تزويده وأنت قادر عليه فلعلّك تطلبه فلا تجده وٱغتنم من ٱستقرضك في حال غناك ليجعل قضاءه لك في يوم عسرتك. وٱعلم أنّ أمامك عَقبة كَؤودًا المُخَفّ فيها أحسن حالًا من المثقل والمبطئ عليها أقبح أمرًا[1] من المسرع وأنّ مَهبِطها بك لا محالة على جنّة أو على نار فٱرْتَدْ لنفسك قبل نزولك ووطّن[2] المنزل قبل حلولك فليس بعد الموت مُستعتَب ولا إلى الدنيا منصرَف.

2.31.13 وٱعلم أنّ الذي بيده خزائن السماوات والأرض قد أذن لك في الدعاء وتكفّل لك بالإجابة وأمرك أن تسأله ليعطيك وتسترحمه ليرحمك ولم يجعل بينك وبينه من يَحجُبك عنه ولم يُلجِئك إلى من يشفع لك إليه ولم يمنعك إن أسأت من التوبة ولم

---

١ م، ي: كذا. ش، ن، ه: ﴿حالًا﴾.   ٢ ن، ي، ومصحّحة في ش: كذا. م، ه، وأصل ش، ونسخة في ي: ﴿ووطّئ﴾.

2.31.11 My dear son! How you wish to be treated should be the measure with which you treat others. Choose for others what you would choose for yourself, and dislike for them what you dislike for yourself; do not oppress, just as you would not wish to be oppressed; be good, just as you would have others be good to you; consider ugly in yourself what you consider ugly in others; accept from others what you would have them accept from you; do not speak about things you do not know, even when there is not much that you do know; do not say things you would not wish to have said to you. Know that conceit is the enemy of good judgment and the bane of good minds. Toil hard but do not hoard your wealth for others to inherit. When you are guided to your purpose, humble yourself before your Lord.

2.31.12 Know that ahead of you lies a road whose route is long and whose hardships are severe. You must traverse it as well as you are able and take with you the provisions you will need. Keep your load light, and do not burden your back beyond its capacity, for a heavy load will cause a bad outcome.[1] Whenever you find a mendicant to carry your provisions for you till the day of resurrection, such that tomorrow, when you are in need of them, he can hand them over to you—take advantage of him, give him your cargo to carry, and load him up with as many provisions as you are able.[2] Do this while you have the opportunity, for it could happen that you go out to search for him but cannot find him. Take advantage, too, of any who ask you for a loan on your day of wealth and defer repayment for your day of hardship. Know that there is a tough climb before you in which it is better to travel light than to carry a heavy load, where it is much worse to go slowly than to go in speed. Know that you must dismount in either paradise or hell, so seek provisions for your soul before you are made to alight. Embrace your final home and make it ready before you take up residence. Remember: After death, there will be no way to please God, and no way to return to this world.

2.31.13 Know that he whose hands hold the treasures of the skies and the treasures of the earth has permitted you to petition him and promised to answer. He has commanded you to ask in order that he may give, he has commanded you to beseech his mercy in order that he may shower it upon you. He has not placed any veil between you and him, nor has he required you to seek refuge with anyone who will intercede for you. If you sin, he does not withhold his

---

1 The "heavy load" on your back is a metaphor for sins.

2 "Finding a mendicant to carry your provisions for you" is an injunction to charity, which will bring abundant rewards on judgment day.

يعاجلك بالنقمة ولم يفضحك حيث الفضيحة ولم يشدّد عليك في قبول الإنابة ولم يناقشك بالجريمة ولم يؤيِسك من الرحمة بل جعل نزوعك عن الذنب حسنة وحسب سيّئتك واحدة وحسب حسنتك عشرًا وفتح لك باب المتاب فإذا ناديته سمع نداك وإذا ناجيته علم نجواك فأفضيت إليه بحاجتك وأَبْثَثْته ذات نفسك وشكوت إليه همومك واَستكشفته كروبك واَستعنته على أمورك وسألته من خزائن رحمته ما لا يقدر على إعطائه غيره من زيادة الأعمار وصحّة الأبدان وسعة الأرزاق.

ثمّ جعل في يديك مفاتيح خزائنه بما أذن لك فيه من مسألته فمتى شئت اَستفتحت بالدعاء أبواب نعمته واَستمطرت شآبيب رحمته. فلا يُقنطنّك إبطاء إجابته فإنّ العطيّة على قدر النيّة وربّما أُخّرت عنك الإجابة ليكون ذلك أعظم لأجر السائل وأجزل لعطاء الآمل وربّما سألت الشيء فلا تؤتاه وأوتيت خيرًا منه عاجلًا أو آجلًا أو صرف عنك لما هو خير لك. فَلَرُبَّ أمرٍ قد طلبته فيه هلاك دينك لو أوتيته فلتكن مسألتك فيما يبقى لك جماله ويُنفى عنك وباله والمال لا يبقى لك ولا تبقى له.

٢.٣١.١٤ واَعلم أنّك إنّما خُلِقت للآخرة لا للدنيا وللفناء لا للبقاء وللموت لا للحياة وأنّك في منزل قُلعة ودار بُلغة وطريق إلى الآخرة وأنّك طريد الموت الذي لا ينجو منه هاربه ولا بدّ أنّه مدرككَ فكن منه على حذرٍ أن يدرككَ وأنت على حال سيّئة قد كنت تحدّث نفسك منها بالتوبة فيحول بينك وبين ذلك فإذا أنت قد أهلكت نفسك. يا بنيّ أكثر من ذكر الموت وذكر ما تَهجُم عليه وتُفضي بعد الموت إليه حتّى يأتيك وقد أخذت منه حِذْرك وشددت له أَزْرك ولا يأتيك بَغتةً فيُبهِرَك.

٢.٣١.١٥ وإيّاك أن تَغترّ بما ترى من إخلاد أهل الدنيا إليها وتكالُبِهم عليها. فقد نبّأك الله عنها ونعت لك نفسَها وتكشّفت لك عن مساويها فإنّما أهلها كِلابٌ عاوية وسباع

pardon, nor does he hasten to punish. He does not disgrace you even when you deserve shame. He does not rebuke while accepting your repentance. He does not chide you for your crimes or cause you to despair of his mercy. Rather, he counts it as a good deed when you shun sin. He reckons your bad deed as a single bad deed but multiplies your good deeds by ten. He has opened the door of repentance for you—if you call out to him, he hears your call, if you whisper to him, he knows your words—so open your heart and plead with him to take care of you. Divulge to him your inner self, tell him of your griefs, entreat him to dispel your sorrows, beseech him to help you in all that you do. Ask him for the treasures of his mercy, for that is something he alone can bestow. Ask him for a long life, a healthy body, and abundant providence.

God has placed in your hands the keys to his treasury, for he has permitted you to pray. Whenever you so desire, you can beseech him and unlock the doors of his favors. Whenever you so desire, you can supplicate him and receive the copious showers of his mercy. Do not despair if the answer is slow in coming, for the gift will be in proportion to the intent. Perhaps the answer has been delayed so that the petitioner may receive yet greater rewards, and the aspirant may obtain yet richer gifts. When you asked for a thing and it was not given to you, perhaps it was because you will be given something even better, either here or in the next world. Perhaps it was turned away for something better. It may so happen that a thing you requested would have ruined your faith if it were granted. Ask for things whose beauty you will always cherish and against whose harm you will be guarded. Wealth will not remain for you, nor will you remain for it.

2.31.14 Know that you have been created for the hereafter, not for this world, for annihilation, not existence, for death, not life. You are in a temporary home, a place for gathering provisions, a path to the hereafter. Death stalks you. No one who attempts to flee can escape, for it will inevitably overtake him. Be watchful lest it seize you in a state of sin. You tell yourself you will repent later, but death may get in the way—if that happens, you will have caused your soul to perish. My dear son! Think about death and do so often. Reflect on what you are rushing toward and where you may be pitched after death. Make sure death does not take you before you have taken the warning to heart or girded your loins. Let it not come upon you suddenly and dash you to the ground!

2.31.15 Beware! Do not be deceived by the world, do not become like the covetous who fight over her like wild dogs! God has informed you about her reality, she too has given you tidings of her own death, shown you her real evils. Are her people anything but howling dogs and savage predators? Yowling at each other,

ضارية يَهِرّ بعضُها بعضًا ويأكل عزيزها ذليلها ويقهر كبيرها صغيرها. نَعَمٌ مُعقّلة١ وأخرى مهملة قد أضلّت عقولها وركبت مجهولها. سُروحُ عاهةٍ بوادٍ وَعْثٍ ليس لها راعٍ يقيمها ولا مُسيمٌ يُسيمها سلكت بهم الدنيا طريق العمى وأخذت بأبصارهم عن منار الهدى فتاهوا في حيرتها وغرِقوا في نعمتها وٱتّخذوها ربًّا فلعبت بهم ولعبوا بها ونسوا ما وراءها. رُوَيدًا يُسفر الظلام كأن قد وردت الأظعان يوشِك مَن أسرع أن يَلحق وأعلم أنّ من كانت مطيّته الليل والنهار فإنّه يُسار به وإن كان واقفًا ويقطع المسافة وإن كان مقيمًا وادعًا.

2.31.16   وٱعلم يقينًا أنّك لن تبلغ أملك ولن تعدو أجلك وأنّك في سبيل من كان قبلك نخَفِّض في الطلب وأجمل في المكتسب فإنّه رُبّ طلب قد جرّ إلى حَرَب وليس كل طالب بمرزوق ولا كلّ مُجمِل بمحروم وأكرم نفسك عن كلّ دنيّة وإن ساقتك إلى الرغائب فإنّك لن تعتاض بما تبذل من نفسك عوضًا ولا تكن عبد غيرك وقد جعلك الله حرًّا وما خيرُ خيرٍ لا يُنال٢ إلّا بشرّ ويسر لا ينال إلّا بعسر وإيّاك أن توجِف بك مطايا الطمع فتُوردك مناهل الهلكة وإن ٱستطعت أن لا يكون بينك وبين الله ذو نعمة فٱفعل فإنّك مدرك قسْمك وآخذ سهمك وإنّ اليسير من الله أكرم وأعظم من الكثير من خلقه وإن كان كلٌّ منه.

2.31.17   وتَلافيك ما فرط من صمتك أيسر من إدراكك ما فات من منطقك.

وحفظ ما في الوعاء بِشَدّ الوِكاء.

وحفظ ما في يديك أحبّ إليّ من طلب ما في يد غيرك.

ومرارة اليأس خير من الطلب إلى الناس.

والحِرفة مع العفّة خير من الغنى مع الفجور.

١ن، ش، ي، ه، ومصحّحة في م: كذا. أصل م: ⟨مغفّلة⟩.   ٢م، ي، ومصحّحة في ه، ونسخة في ش: كذا. ن، وأصل ش، ه، ونسخة في م: ⟨لا يوجد⟩.

the strong devour the weak, the large attack the small. Herded and tended camels, some, but others gone loose, having slipped their ropes and run off in unknown directions. They graze now on foul weeds in stony valleys, no shepherd to watch them, no herdsman to lead them to grass. The world took them on the path of blindness and made them oblivious to their beacons of guidance, they drifted in her perplexities and drowned in her pleasures, they took her as their lord and master, she toyed with them, and they dallied with her, forgetting what was coming. But wait, go gently! Darkness will soon give way to morning. Travelers have already arrived at the watering hole, yet those who hasten may very well catch up. Know this: If your steeds are Day and Night, you are driven forward even when you stand still. You cut the distance to the destination even when you remain motionless and calm.

2.31.16 Know this with full certainty: Your path is the path of those before you, and you will not achieve your long hopes and surpass your allotted lifespan, so be moderate in your pursuits and restrained in what you seek. A pursuit often leads to deprivation: not every seeker finds sustenance, while not every person of restraint is denied. Honor yourself by rising above despicable acts, even when they lead to the fulfilment of your passions, for there is no adequate recompense for expended honor. Do not become a slave to another when God has created you free. What is the good of something good obtained through evil? Or of ease obtained through privation? Beware lest ambition's steeds run off with you and pitch you down at the station of destruction! If you can arrange things such that no benefactor stands between you and God, then do so. No matter what, you will attain your destiny and receive your share, and a little from God is both more in quantity and greater in worth than a lot from his creatures. Ultimately, everything comes from him.

2.31.17 Making up for too much silence is easier than retracting what escapes your lips.

Secure your sack by tightening the strap.

It is far better to guard your property than to covet another's.

It is far better to taste the bitterness of resignation than to importune people.

It is far better for you to combine poverty with restraint than to pair wealth with dissolution.

والمرء أحفظ لسرّه.

ورُبَّ ساعٍ فيما يضرّه.

من أكثر أهجر ومن تفكّر أبصر.

قارِنْ أهل الخير تكن منهم وباين أهل الشرّ تبِن عنهم.

بئس الطعام الحرام.

وظلم الضعيف أفحش الظلم.

إذا كان الرفق خُرْقًا كان الخرق رفقًا.

ربّما كان الدواء داء والداء دواء وربّما نصح غير الناصح وغَشّ المستنصح.

وإيّاك والاتّكال على المنى فإنّها بَضائع النَّوكى.

والعقل حفظ التجارب وخير ما جرّبت ما وعظك.

بادر الفرصة قبل أن تكون غُصّة.

ليس كلّ طالب يصيب ولا كلّ غائب يؤوب.

ومن الفساد إضاعة الزاد ومَفسدة المعاد.

ولكلّ أمر عاقبة.

سوف يأتيك ما قُدّر لك.

التاجر مخاطر.

ورُبَّ يسير أنمى من كثير.

لا خير في مُعين مَهين ولا في صديق ظَنين.

ساهِل الدهرَ ما ذَلّ لك قعوده.

ولا تخاطر بشيء رجاء أكثر منه.

وإيّاك أن تَجمح بك مطيّة اللجاج.

٢٦١٨،٢،٣١ احمل نفسك من أخيك عند صُرْمه على الصلة وعند صدوده على اللطف والمقاربة وعند جُموده على البذل وعند تباعده على الدنوّ وعند شدّته على اللين وعند

You protect your own secret best.

Often the very thing you strive for harms you when you get it.

Whoever talks too much, blathers.

Associate with good people, and you will be one of them. Stay away from evil people, and you will be separate from them.

How vile is forbidden food!

Oppressing the weak is the worst oppression.

If goodness is stupid, then stupidity is good.

Sometimes the cure becomes the disease.

A person who does not intend to often unwittingly gives counsel, while a well-wisher sometimes unwittingly deceives.

Beware of placing faith in worldly hopes—they are the property of fools.

Learning from experience is smart—the best experience gives good counsel.

Seize opportunities before they are lost.

Not every seeker gets what he wants, and not everyone who goes comes back.

To squander provisions and to spoil your return is to cause your own ruin.

Every affair has a consequence.

Your destiny will come to you.

A trader takes risks.

A little often produces more than a lot.

There is no good in a contemptible helper or a suspicious friend.

Fate is a camel. Loosen its reins and give it slack as long as it remains docile.

Don't risk what you have in hopes of getting more.

Beware lest a quarrel run away with you.

2.31.18 Maintain bonds of kinship with your brother, even when he is bent on cutting them. Perform kindnesses for him, even when he shuns you. Be generous to him, even when he is aloof and close-fisted. Stay close to him, even when he distances himself. Be kind to him, even when he is harsh. Placate him,

جرمه على العذر حتّى كأنّك له عبد وكأنّه ذو نعمة عليك وإيّاك أن تضع ذلك في غير موضعه أو أن تفعله بغير أهله.

لا تتّخذنّ عدوّ صديقك صديقًا فتعادي صديقك.

وامحَض أخاك النصيحة حسنة كانت أم قبيحة.

وتجرّع الغَيظ فإنّي لم أَرَ جُرعة أحلى منها عاقبة ولا ألذّ مَغبّة.

ولِنْ لمن غالظك فإنّه يوشِك أن يلين لك.

وخذ على عدوّك بالفضل فإنّه أحلى الظفرين.

وإن أردت قطيعة أخيك فاستبقِ له من نفسك بقيّة ترجع إليها إن بدا له ذلك يومًا ما.

ومن ظنّ بك خيرًا فصَدّق ظنّه.

ولا تضيّعنّ حقّ أخيك اتّكالًا على ما بينك وبينه فإنّه ليس لك بأخٍ من أضعت حقّه.

ولا يكن أهلك أشقى الخلق بك ولا ترغبنّ فيمن زهد فيك.

ولا يكوننّ أخوك أقوى على قطيعتك منك على صلته ولا يكوننّ على الإساءة أقوى[1] منك على الإحسان.

ولا يَكبُرنّ عليك ظلم من ظلمك فإنّه يسعى في مضرّته ونفعك وليس جزاء من سرّك أن تسوءه.

2.31.19 واعلم يا بنيّ أنّ الرزق رزقان رزق تطلبه ورزق يطلبك فإن أنت لم تأتِه أتاك.

ما أقبح الخضوع عند الحاجة والجفاء عند الغنى.

إنّما لك من دنياك ما أصلحت به مثواك وإن كنت جازعًا على ما تفَلّتَ من يديك فاجزع على كلّ ما لم يصل إليك.

اِسْتَدِلَّ على ما لم يكن بما قد كان فإنّ الأمور أشباه.

____
[1] ن، ش، ي، هـ، ونسخة في م: كذا. أصل م، ومصحّحة في ش: ﴿أقدر﴾.

even when he is cruel. Behave towards him as though you were a slave, and he a generous benefactor. But beware lest you do this where it is not fitting, or with people who are not worthy.

To befriend your friend's enemy is to spurn your friend.

Give your brother sincere advice, whether palatable or unpleasant.

Swallow your rage—no other drink leaves a sweeter taste or has a pleasanter effect.

Be kind to one who is harsh with you, perhaps, then, he will be kinder to you.

Be generous to your enemy—that is the sweetest of the two ways of celebrating victory.

If you must sever relations with your brother, save a small space in your heart for him, in case, one day, he wants to return.

If someone thinks you are good, prove them right.

Don't squander your brother's rights by taking the bond between you for granted. If you squander his rights, he is no longer your brother.

Don't give your family members the least share of you. Don't place your desires in those indifferent to you.

Don't let your brother be more capable of severing himself from you than you of associating with him. Don't let him be more capable of meanness than you are of being kind.

Don't be unduly troubled by an oppressor's oppression. Know that he harms himself and benefits you—don't reward someone who benefits you by doing him harm.

2.31.19 My dear son! Know that providence is of two types—the one you seek and the one that seeks you. If you don't find it, it will find you.

How loathsome is a show of humility in times of need, and aloofness in times of affluence!

Your greatest assets are the deeds you carry to the grave. If you would bewail the loss of what you once had, then bewail too the absence of things you never had.

ولا تكونَنّ ممّن لا تنفعه العظة إلّا إذا بالغتَ في إيلامه فإنّ العاقل يتّعظ بالآداب والبهائم لا تتّعظ إلّا بالضرب.

اطرح عنك واردات الهموم[1] بعزائم الصبر وحسن اليقين.

من ترك القصد جار.

الصاحب مناسب.

والصديق من صدق غَيبُهُ.

والهوى شريك العمى.

رُبّ بعيد أقرب من قريب وقريب أبعد من بعيد.

والغريب من لم يكن له حبيب.

من تعدّى الحقّ ضاق مذهبه.

ومن اقتصر على قَدْره كان أبقى له.

وأوثق سبب أخذت به سبب بينك وبين الله سبحانه.

من لم يُبالِك فهو عدوّك.

قد يكون اليأس إدراكًا إذا كان الطمع هلاكًا.

ليس كلّ عورة تظهر ولا كلّ فرصة تصاب.

وربّما أخطأ البصير قصده وأصاب الأعمى رشده.

أخِّر الشرّ فإنّك إذا شئت تعجّلته.

وقطيعة الجاهل تعدل صلة العاقل.

من أَمِنَ الزمان خانه ومن أعظمه أهانه.

ليس كلّ من رمى أصاب.

إذا تغيّر السلطان تغيّر الزمان.

سَلْ عن الرفيق قبل الطريق وعن الجار قبل الدار.

إيّاك أن تذكر من الكلام ما كان مضحكًا وإن حكيت ذلك عن غيرك.

____

[1] م، ش، ي، هـ، ونسخة في ن: كذا. ن، ونسخة في ش: ﴿الأمور﴾.

Expect what will happen by extrapolating from what has happened—history repeats.[1]

Don't heed counsel only when it haunts you and causes you pain. A rational person takes counsel from rebuke. Only cattle are counseled by the whip.

Cast off the fevers of anxiety with patient resolve and seemly conviction.

To leave the middle road is to deviate.

Friends are like kin.

A friend is true in your absence.

Passion blinds.

Those far are often closer than those close. Those close are often farther than those far.

The real exile is the person who has no one to love.

Whoever transgresses the truth finds his path closing in on him.

Whosoever limits himself to his capacity abides.

The sturdiest rope is the one that links you to God.

A person who doesn't care for your wellbeing is your enemy.

Accepting that hopes may not be realized could lead to their realization, whereas coveting them could lead to your destruction.

Not every gap in a fortress can be breached. Not every opportunity can be availed.

Sometimes the perceptive miss the target and the blind hit the mark.

Impede evil, else you may hasten its onset.

Dissociating from a fool is equal to befriending an intelligent man.

Trust the world and you will be deceived by it. Venerate the world and you will be reviled by it.

Not every arrow hits the mark.

New ruler, new age.

Before beginning a journey, inspect your fellow travelers. Before buying a house, inspect your neighbors.

Beware of cracking unseemly jokes, even when attributing them to another.

---

1   Ar. *inna l-umūra ashbāhun*, lit. "all things are the same."

2.31.20 وإيّاك ومُشاورة النساء فإنّ رأيهنّ إلى أَفْن وعزمهنّ إلى وَهن واكفف عليهنّ من أبصارهنّ بحجابك إيّاهنّ فإنّ شدّة الحجاب أبقى عليهنّ وليس خروجهنّ بأشدّ من إدخالك من لا يوثق به عليهنّ وإن اسطعت أن لا يعرفن غيرك فافعل. ولا تُمَلّك المرأة من أمرها ما جاوز نفسها فإنّ المرأة ريحانة وليست بقَهْرَمانة ولا تَعدُ بكرامتها نفسها ولا تُطمِعها أن تشفع لغيرها. وإيّاك والتغايُر في غير موضع غَيرة فإنّ ذلك يدعو الصحيحة إلى السقم والبريئة إلى الريب.

2.31.21 واجعل لكلّ إنسان من خَدَمك عملًا تأخذه به فإنّه أحرى أن لا يتواكلوا في خدمتك.

واكرم عشيرتك فإنّهم جناحك الذي به تطير وأصلك الذي إليه تصير ويدك التي بها تصول.

2.31.22 أستودع الله دينك ودنياك. وأساله خير القضاء لك في العاجلة والآجلة والدنيا والآخرة إن شاء الله.

2.32 ومن كتاب له عليه السلام إلى معاوية

وأرديت جيلًا من الناس كثيرًا خدعتهم بغيّك وألقيتهم في موج بحرك تغشاهم الظلمات وتتلاطم بهم الشبهات فجاروا عن وجهتهم ونكصوا على أعقابهم وتولّوا على أدبارهم وعوّلوا على أحسابهم إلّا من فاءَ من أهل البصائر فإنّهم فارقوك بعد معرفتك وهربوا إلى الله من مُوازرتك إذ حملتهم على الصعب وعدلت بهم عن القصد. فاتّق الله يا معاوية في نفسك وجاذِب الشيطان قيادك فإنّ الدنيا منقطعة عنك والآخرة قريبة منك. والسلام.

2.31.20 Beware of seeking advice from women, for their opinion can be weak and their resolve can waiver.[1] Employ the veil to shade their eyes, for strict veiling preserves modesty; also, private visits from untrustworthy men are as harmful as going out unveiled—if you can, make it so that they know only you. Don't allow a woman to govern affairs other than her own, for a woman is a fragrant flower, not a manager of affairs; don't allow your generosity to her extend beyond her to another, don't encourage her to intercede for others. Beware, on the other hand, of irrational jealousy, for jealousy leads the healthy wife to sickness and the innocent one to engage in suspicious behavior.

2.31.21 Make every individual under your command responsible for his own particular task. If you do, he will be less likely to slacken and point a finger.

Honor your kinsmen. They are the wings with which you fly, the tree on which you lean, and the hand with which you attack.

2.31.22 I place your religious and your worldly affairs in God's care. I beseech him to ordain for you everything good, now and later, both in this world and the hereafter, if he so wills, *Inshāʾallāh*!

2.32 From a letter by ʿAlī to Muʿāwiyah:[2]
You have destroyed a whole generation of people, deceiving them with your evil ways and pitching them into the waves of your turbulent sea, where they were engulfed in darkness and tossed hither and thither by doubt. Straying from the destination, they spun on their heels, turned their backs on religion, and placed their faith in ties of kinship—except for the few who were discerning. When you mounted the latter on refractory camels and led them off the straight path, they recognized your misguidance and fled, leaving your service to return to God. Fear God for your own sake, Muʿāwiyah, and wrench your halter out of Satan's hands. Very soon, the world will sever its rope from you. The hereafter has drawn near. Go in peace.

---

1 Some of these lines, alongside a few others in which women are referred to harshly in this volume, are usually read as an indirect rebuke of the Prophet's widow ʿĀʾishah, who led an army against ʿAlī at the Battle of the Camel (see also §1.77, §2.1, and accompanying notes).

2 Excerpt from a letter within a series of acrimonious exchanges, presumably in the lead-up to the Battle at Ṣiffīn in 37/657. Preceding part of ʿAlī's letter in B 859; Ḥ 16:133, and Muʿāwiyah's reply and the full exchange, in Ḥ 16:133–137.

2.33   ومن كِتاب له عليه السلام إلى قُثَم بن العبّاس وهو عامله على مكّة

أمّا بعد. فإنّ عيني بالمغرب كتب إليّ يعلمني أنّه وُجّه على الموسم أُناسٌ من أهل الشام العُمي القلوب الصمّ الأسماع الكُمه الأبصار الذين يلتمسون الحقّ بالباطل ويطيعون المخلوق في معصية الخالق ويحتلبون الدنيا دَرَّها بالدين ويشترون عاجلها بآجل الأبرار المتّقين ولن يفوز بالخير إلّا عامله ولا يُجزى جزاء الشرّ إلّا فاعله. فأقم على ما في يديك قيام الحازم الصليب والناصح اللبيب والتابع لسلطانه المطيع لإمامه و﴿إيّاك وما يُعتذَر منه﴾ ولا تكن عند النعماء بَطِرًا ولا عند البأساء فَشِلًا.

2.34   ومن كِتاب له عليه السلام إلى محمّد بن أبي بكر لمّا بلغه توجُّده من عزله بالأشتر عن مصر ثمّ توفّي[1] الأشتر في توجّهه إلى مصر قبل وصوله إليها

وقد بلغني مَوجِدتك من تَسريح الأشتر إلى عملك وإنّي لم أفعل ذلك ٱستبطاء لك في الجهد ولا ٱزديادًا لك في الجِدّ ولو نزعتُ ما تحت يدك من سلطانك لولّيتك ما هو أيسر عليك مؤونة وأعجب إليك وِلاية. إنّ الرجل الذي كنتُ ولّيته أمر مصر كان رجلًا لنا ناصحًا وعلى عدوّنا شديدًا ناقًّا فرحمه الله فلقد ٱستكمل أيّامه ولاقى حِمامه ونحن عنه راضون أوْلاه الله رضوانه وضاعف الثواب له. فأصحر لعدوّك وٱمضِ على بصيرتك[2] وشَمِّر لحرب من حاربك وٱدعُ إلى سبيل ربّك وأكثِر الاستعانة بالله يكفِك ما أهمّك ويُعِنك على ما ينزل بك إن شاء الله.

ـــــــــــــ
[1] ن، م، ي، ه، ومصحّحة في ش: كذا. أصل ش: ﴿سمّ﴾.   [2] ش، ن، ي، ه، ونسخة في م: كذا. أصل م: ﴿سيرتك﴾.

2.33 From ʿAlī's dispatch to Qutham ibn al-ʿAbbās, his governor in Mecca:[1]
My agent in the west has written to inform me that a group of Syrians—blind of heart, deaf of ear, and weak of eye—are being sent to Mecca this hajj season. They claim to establish a right through wrong means, obey a human, a creature, while disobeying the creator,[2] and attempt to milk the world's udders in the name of religion. They purchase the temporary benefits of this realm and sell off the reward promised to the pious and godfearing. But good will be won only by those who practice good, while the recompense of those who practice evil will be nothing but evil. Govern your city well—be astute, strong, sincere, and thoughtful, a man who follows his leader and obeys his Imam. ⟨Beware of an action you must justify.⟩[3] Do not exult in times of prosperity or despair in times of distress.

2.34 From ʿAlī's letter to Muḥammad ibn Abī Bakr, upon learning of Muḥammad's distress at being replaced by Ashtar as governor of Egypt (Ashtar died en route):[4]
I have learned that you are distressed at my sending Ashtar to take charge of your region. That was not because I found you remiss in your efforts or less diligent than I would have wished—although I retracted the authority I had placed in your hands, I had intended to replace it with a governorship that would have been easier for you to handle and more fulfilling. The man I sent as the new governor of Egypt—may God have mercy on him!—was sincere in his love for me and a fierce enemy to my foe. But he has finished his days and met his end. I am pleased with his deeds—may God too be pleased with him and multiply his reward. Now go out and confront your enemy. Be guided by your discerning mind, gird up to fight your attacker, call to the path of your Lord, and beseech God repeatedly for aid. He will dispel your grief and help you to combat the calamities that have come your way, if he so wills.

---

1 From Kufa, just prior to the hajj season, in Dhū al-Ḥijjah, 39/659, warning Qutham about the imminent arrival in Mecca of Muʿāwiyah's troops under Yazīd ibn Shajarah al-Rahāwī. B 859; Ḥ 16:138–139. Context and text in Thaqafī, *Ghārāt*, 2:504–510.

2 Echoes a well-known hadith, ⟨Do not obey humans if it means you will disobey God⟩ (لا طاعة لمخلوق في معصية الخالق). Quḍāʿī, *Shihāb*, §6.24.

3 Proverb. R 3:381.

4 From Kufa to Egypt in 38/658. Ṭabarī, *Tārīkh*, 5:87. See next text, §2.35, for ʿAlī's grief when Muḥammad ibn Abī Bakr too was killed. "Ashtar died" (*tuwuffiya al-Ashtar*), or, as per MS Sh, "Ashtar was poisoned" (*summa al-Ashtar*).

2.35 ومن كتاب له عليه السلام إلى عبد الله بن العبّاس بعد مقتل محمّد بن أبي بكر بمصر

أمّا بعد. فإنّ مصر قد اُفتُتحت ومحمّد بن أبي بكر رحمه الله قد اُستُشهد فعند الله نَحتسبه ولدًا ناصحًا وعاملًا كادحًا وسيفًا قاطعًا وركنًا دافعًا. وقد كنت حَثثْت الناس على لَحاقه وأمرتهم بغياثه قبل الوقعة ودعوتهم سرًّا وجهرًا وعَوْدًا وبدءًا فمنهم الآتي كارهًا ومنهم المُعتَلّ كاذبًا ومنهم القاعد خاذلًا أسأل الله أن يجعل لي منهم فرجًا عاجلًا فوالله لولا طمعي عند لقائي عدوّي في الشهادة وتوطيني نفسي على المنيّة لأحببت أن لا أبقى مع هؤلاء يومًا واحدًا ولا ألتقي بهم أبدًا.

2.36 ومن كتاب له عليه السلام في ذكر جيش أنفذه إلى بعض الأعداء وهو جواب كتاب كتبه إليه أخوه عقيل بن أبي طالب

فسرّحت إليه جيشًا كثيفًا من المسلمين فلمّا بلغه ذلك شمّر هاربًا ونكص نادمًا فلحقوه ببعض الطريق وقد طفّلت الشمس للإياب فاُقتتلوا شيئًا كَلا ولا. فما كان إلّا كموقف ساعة حتّى نَجا جريضًا بعد ما اُخذ منه بالمُخنّق ولم يبق معه غير الرَّمَق فلأْيًا بِلأْيٍ ما نَجا.

2.35 From ʿAlī's letter to ʿAbdallāh ibn al-ʿAbbās, after Muḥammad ibn Abī Bakr was killed in Egypt:[1]

Egypt has been conquered, and Muḥammad ibn Abī Bakr—may God have mercy on him!—has gained martyrdom. I seek God's recompense for enduring the pain of his death! He was a sincere son, a diligent governor, a cutting sword, and a pillar of support. I had urged people to succor him ahead of the skirmish and commanded them to come to his aid, and I pleaded with them early and often, in private and in public, but to no avail—a few reluctantly stood up, some gave insincere excuses, and others sat back and flatly refused.[2] I entreat God to grant me swift relief from their company! By God, were I not hoping for martyrdom when I meet the enemy in battle, had I not trained myself to face death in combat, I would prefer not to stay among these people for another day, I would wish never to see them again!

2.36 From ʿAlī's reply to a letter from his brother ʿAqīl ibn Abī Ṭālib, describing the movements of a military unit he had sent against one of his enemies:[3]

I dispatched a large army of Muslims to fight him. When he learned of its coming, he tucked up his garments and fled, regretting his incursion, and attempting to retreat. They caught up with him on a certain road just as the sun was about to set, and the two sides exchanged quick blows.[4] After a short hour's skirmish, in which he was personally grabbed by the throat and had his breath squeezed out of him, he escaped, choking on his spittle. He escaped, but only with terrible effort.

---

1   From Kufa to Basra in 38/658 (Ṭabarī, *Tārīkh*, 5:109). Muḥammad ibn Abī Bakr, ʿAlī's foster-son and ward, and his governor in Egypt, was tortured and killed by Muʿāwiyah's commander, ʿAmr ibn al-ʿĀṣ.

2   ʿAlī's public and private orations urging his supporters to mobilize and aid Muḥammad ibn Abī Bakr are recorded in Ṭabarī, *Tārīkh*, 5:107–108.

3   Excerpt from a post-Ṣiffīn reply from Kufa in 39/659 to ʿAqīl in Medina, describing the raids of Muʿāwiyah's commander Ḍaḥḥāk on Iraqi towns, and the actions of ʿAlī's commander Ḥujr ibn ʿAdī, at the head of four thousand men, against him. Details of events in Ḥ 2:113–125, ʿAqīl's letter to ʿAlī and ʿAlī's full reply in Māmaṭīrī, *Nuzhah*, 295–297; Ḥ 2:118–120.

4   Ar. *fa-qtatalū shayʾan ka-lā wa-lā*, lit. "They fought for a bit like no and no!" ⟨Like no and no⟩ (*ka-lā wa-lā*) is an idiom signifying something quick and fleeting, onomatopoeic for the staccato shortness of the repeated single-syllable *lā*. B 863; F 381; Ḥ 16:149.

فدَع عنك قريشًا وتَركاضَهم في الضلال وتَجوالهم في الشقاق وجِماحهم في التيه فإنّهم قد أجمعوا على حربي كإجماعهم على حرب رسول الله صلّى الله عليه وآله قبلي فجَزَت قريشًا عنّي الجوازي فقد قطعوا رحمي وسلبوني سلطان اّبن أمّي. وأمّا ما سألتَ عنه من رأيي في القتال فإنّ رأيي قتال المُحِلّين حتّى ألقى الله. لا يزيدني كثرة الناس حولي عزّة ولا تفرّقهم عنّي وحشة. ولا تحسبنّ اّبن أبيك ولو أسلمه الناس متضرّعًا متخشّعًا ولا مقرًّا للضيم واهنًا ولا سَلِس الزمام للقائد ولا وَطِئ الظهر للراكب المقتعد ولكنّه كما قال أخو بني سُليم[1]

فَإِنْ تَسْأَلِيني كَيْفَ أَنْتَ فَإِنَّني   صَبورُ عَلَى رَيْبِ الزَّمانِ صَلِيبُ

يَعِزُّ عَلَيَّ أَنْ تَرَى بِي كَآبَةً   فَيَشْمَتَ عَادٍ أَوْ يُسَاءُ حَبِيبُ

2.37   ومن كتاب له عليه السلام إلى معاوية

فسبحان الله ما أشدّ لزومك للأهواء المبتدعة والحيرة المتّبعة مع تضييع الحقائق واّطّراح الوثائق التي هي لله طلبة وعلى عباده حجّة. فأمّا إكثارك الحِجاج في عثمان وقتلته فإنّك إنّما نصرتَ عثمان حيث كان النصر لك وخذلته حيث كان النصر له. والسلام.

---

[1] البحر: الطويل.

Don't speak to me of Quraysh! They have raced into error, galloped into dissent, and bolted into the waterless waste. They have banded to fight me, just as they banded earlier to fight God's Messenger. May Quraysh be repaid as they deserve! They have cut the bonds of my kinship and looted the authority given to me by my brother, Muḥammad.[1] You have asked about my view on fighting—here it is: I shall continue to fight all who break their pledge of allegiance until I meet God. My might is not increased by large numbers, nor do I grow uneasy if they disperse. Don't think that I, your brother will be broken or humbled, even if I am abandoned by any and all! You will not find me weak in the face of oppression, like a docile camel, or one with a broad back on which a rider can sit in comfort. In the words of the Sulaym tribesman:[2]

> If you asked, "How do you fare?" I would answer:
> I am patient and I am strong in the face of fate's attacks.
> I do not allow myself to show distress,
> Lest my enemy gloat, and my friend grieve.

2.37 From a letter sent by ʿAlī to Muʿāwiyah:[3]
Great God! How fervently you cling to your outlandish passions and your obsessive machinations! How blatantly you disregard the facts and reject God's compacts that are proofs against his servants! You make repeated arguments in the matter of ʿUthmān and his killers, but the reality is that you are only coming forward to defend ʿUthmān now in order to help yourself. You abandoned him earlier, when you could have helped him. Go in peace.

---

1 Lit. "my mother's son" (*ibn ummī*), refers to ʿAlī's closeness to Muḥammad generally, and to the fact that he was raised by ʿAlī's parents. F 382; R 3:126–127; Ḥ 16:151; B 832. "Muḥammad" is added to the translation for clarity.
2 Attributed to ʿAbbās ibn Mirdās al-Sulamī, a pagan poet and warrior who converted to Islam after the Conquest of Mecca (d. bet. 18/639 and 36/656). B 863; Ḥ 16:152.
3 Presumably from Kufa to Damascus in 36/656, or at Ṣiffīn before the battle in 37/657. Earlier part in B 83; Ḥ 16:153–154; details of Muʿāwiyah's withholding of aid in the face of ʿUthmān's pleas in B 864; Ḥ 16:154, after Balādhurī.

2.38 ومن كتاب له عليه السلام إلى أهل مصر لمّا ولّى عليهم الأشتر رحمه الله

من عبد الله عليّ أمير المؤمنين إلى القوم الذين غضبوا لله حين عُصِي في أرضه وذُهِب بحقّه فضَرب الجور سُرادقه على البرّ والفاجر والمقيم والظاعن فلا معروف يُستراح إليه ولا منكر يتناهى عنه. أمّا بعد.

فقد بعثتُ إليكم عبدًا من عباد الله لا ينام أيّام الخوف ولا يَنْكَل عن الأعداء ساعات الرَّوع أشدّ على الفجّار من حريق النار وهو مالك بن الحارث أخو مَذْحِج. فاسمعوا له وأطيعوا أمره فيما طابَقَ الحقّ فإنّه سيف من سيوف الله لا كليلُ الظُّبة ولا نابي الضريبة فإن أمركم أن تنفروا فانفروا وإن أمركم أن تقيموا فأقيموا فإنّه لا يقدم ولا يحجم ولا يؤخّر ولا يقدّم إلّا عن أمري. وقد آثرتكم به على نفسي لنصيحته لكم وشدّة شكيمته على عدوّكم.

2.39 ومن كتاب له عليه السلام إلى عمرو بن العاص

فإنّك جعلت دينك تبعًا لدنيا امرئٍ ظاهرٍ غيّهُ مهتوك ستره يَشين الكريم بمجلسه ويُسَفّه الحليم بخُلطته فاتّبعتَ أثره وطلبت فضله اتّباع الكلب للضِّرغام يلوذ إلى مَخالبه وينتظر ما يلقى إليه من فضل فريسته فأذهبتَ دنياك وآخرتك ولو بالحقّ أخذت أدركت ما

2.38 From a letter sent by ʿAlī to the people of Egypt, when he sent Ashtar to them as their governor:[1]

From God's servant, ʿAlī, Commander of the Faithful, to the people who rose up in anger for the sake of God, when God was disobeyed on earth and his dues were flouted, when tyranny raised its canopy over pious and debauched, over resident and traveler, when good was no longer pursued, and evil was no longer hindered.[2]

I have sent you one of God's own servants, who neither sleeps during the days of danger, nor shrinks from confronting the enemy in the hours of terror. He is more ardent in attacking the wicked than a blazing fire. He is Mālik ibn al-Ḥārith, from the tribe of Madhḥij. Listen to him and obey his command in everything that accords with the truth, for he is one of God's own swords. His blade is far from blunt, his blow is never weak. March when he commands you to march, halt when he commands you to halt, for he advances and withdraws, delays and proceeds, only at my command. I would wish to keep him by my side, but have sent him to you instead, because he is sincere in his wish to guide you and unyielding in his severity toward your enemy.

2.39 From a letter sent by ʿAlī to ʿAmr ibn al-ʿĀṣ:[3]

You have subordinated your faith to the worldly gain promised to you by a man whose deceit is plain, whose dishonor is manifest, who uses his assemblies to slander the noble, and who transforms mature associates into fools. You follow in his footsteps and seek his favors like a dog trailing a lion, begging for largesse, and waiting for whatever scraps of prey it might toss your way. You

---

1   Kufa, 38/658. ʿAlī sent Ashtar to replace Muḥammad ibn Abī Bakr as governor of Egypt when a group there turned to Muʿāwiyah and Muḥammad was besieged. Ashtar was poisoned by Muʿāwiyah's agent en route. This letter was found among his belongings. Details in Ṭabarī, *Tārīkh*, 5:95–97; Yaʿqūbī, *Tārīkh*, 2:193–194; Māmaṭīrī, *Nuzhah*, 282–284 (text of letter, 283–284). Other relevant letters are § 2.53 and § 2.62.

2   The reference is to the Egyptians' displeasure with ʿUthmān's rule, which resulted in a delegation demanding reform or abdication. Ḥ 16:156–157 and B 864: ʿAlī was supportive of the Egyptians' grievances, but not of ʿUthmān's killing.

3   From Kufa to Damascus in 36/656, before leaving for Ṣiffīn. Text, context, and ʿAmr's reply, in Minqarī, *Waqʿat Ṣiffīn*, 110–111; Ṭabrisī, *Iḥtijāj*, 1:267. Earlier part of ʿAlī's letter in B 865; Ḥ 16:163. ʿAmr had agreed to support Muʿāwiyah against ʿAlī, in exchange for the governorship of Egypt. Ḥ 16:160–161. Earlier, ʿAmr had been in command of the Muslim army that had conquered Egypt during the caliphate of ʿUmar, who then dismissed him for corruption. "Whose dishonor is manifest," lit. "whose veil is rent" (*mahtūkin sitruhu*). "Abū Sufyān's son" is Muʿāwiyah.

طلبت. فإن يُمكِن الله منك ومن ٱبن أبي سفيان أَجْزِكما بما قدّمتما وإن تُعجِزا وتَبقيا فما أمامكما شرّ لكما. والسلام.

2.40 ومن كتاب له عليه السلام إلى بعض عمّاله

أمّا بعد. فقد بلغني عنك أمر إن كنت فعلته فقد أسخطت ربّك وعصيت إمامك وأخزيت أمانتك بلغني أنّك جَردتَ الأرض فأخذت ما تحت قدميك وأكلت ما تحت يديك فٱرفع إليّ حسابك وٱعلم أنّ حساب الله أعظم من حساب الناس.

2.41 ومن كتاب له عليه السلام إلى بعض عمّاله

أمّا بعد. فإنّي كنت أشركتك في أمانتي وجعلتك شِعاري وبِطانتي ولم يكن في أهلي رجل أوثق منك في نفسي لمُواساتي ومُوازرتي وأداء الأمانة إليّ. فلمّا رأيت الزمان على ٱبن عمّك قد كَلِب والعدوّ قد حَرِب وأمانة الناس قد خزيت وهذه الأمّة قد فُتنت[1] وشَغرت قَلَبتَ لٱبن عمّك ظهر المِجَنّ ففارقته مع المفارقين وخذلته مع الخاذلين وخُنته مع الخائنين فلا ٱبن عمّك آسَيت ولا الأمانة أدّيت وكأنّك لم تكن اللهَ تريد بجهادك وكأنّك لم تكن على بيّنة من ربّك وكأنّك إنّما كنت تكيد هذه الأمّة عن دنياهم وتنوي غِرّتهم عن فيئهم فلمّا أمكنتك الشدّة في خيانة الأمّة أسرعت الكرّة وعاجلت الوَثْبة وٱختطفت ما قدرت عليه من أموالهم المَصونة لأراملهم وأيتامهم ٱختطاف الذئب

_____

[1] ان، م، ه، ونسخة في ش: كذا. ي، وأصل ش، ونسخة في م: ⟨فتكت⟩.

have lost out in this world and in the hereafter, when you could have achieved your desires through rightful means. Beware! If God grants me victory over you and Abū Sufyān's son, I will requite you like for like. But should you elude me and manage to stay alive, beware: what lies ahead is much worse. Go in peace.

2.40 From a letter sent by ʿAlī to one of his governors:[1]
I am informed that you have done something, which, if you have done it, means you have angered your Lord, disobeyed your Imam, and betrayed your trust. I am informed that you stripped the land bare, devoured whatever was under your control, and consumed whatever you could lay your hands on. Send me your accounts, then, and know that God's accounting is more stringent than man's!

2.41 From a letter sent by ʿAlī to one of his governors:[2]
I had shared my charge with you and kept you as close to me as an intimate garment, I trusted none of my family to support and serve me, to stay true to his charge, more than I trusted you. But when you saw that the age had turned rabid against your cousin, the enemy was attacking with savage madness, the people were becoming increasingly corrupt, and the community had risen up in revolt and abandoned me, you turned your shield in your cousin's face.[3] You left me, along with all the others; you abandoned me, along with all the others; you betrayed me, along with all the others. You failed to support your cousin or fulfill your trust. When you fought beside me earlier, you appear to have had something other than God's cause in mind, to have never truly held a mandate from your Lord; you appear to have been deceiving this community in order to defraud them, as though, all along, you had intended to cheat them of their war gains. For when you saw the opportunity to swindle, you were swift to charge and quick to attack. You swooped and ran off with whatever money you could

---

1 The governor is ʿAbdallāh ibn al-ʿAbbās in Basra and ʿAlī's letter—sent from Kufa sometime after Nahrawān, in 38/658—was prompted by a complaint written to him by his treasurer there, Abū al-Aswad al-Duʾalī (Balādhurī, *Ansāb*, 2:170; Ibn ʿAbd Rabbih, *ʿIqd*, 5:103). § 2.43, ʿAlī's letter to Maṣqalah ibn Hubayrah, governor in Ardashīr, Fars, contains similar language.
2 Excerpt from a letter likely sent from Kufa to Mecca in 40/661 to ʿAbdallāh ibn al-ʿAbbās, a short while before ʿAlī's death; § 2.22, and its variant rendering, § 2.66, is possibly another part from the same letter (text and context in Yaʿqūbī, *Tārīkh*, 2:205), and perhaps also § 2.72. Details of event in note to § 2.22. Text of § 2.41 in Balādhurī, *Ansāb*, 2:175–176; Ibn al-ʿAbbās's reply, and ʿAlī's further reply in B 867.
3 An action usually taken in the face of an enemy, denotes disloyalty; cf. proverb: ⟨Turned the face of his shield⟩ (*qalaba ẓahr al-mijann*). Ḥ 16:169; ʿA 690; R 3:136–137; F 382.

الأَزَلّ داميةَ المِعزى الكسيرة فحملته إلى الحجاز رحيب الصدر بحمله غير متأثّم من أخذه كأنّك لا أبا لغيرك حَدَرْت إلى أهلك تراثًا من أبيك وأمّك. فسبحان الله أما تؤمن بالمعاد أو ما تخاف نِقاش الحساب. أيّها المعدود كان عندنا من ذوي الألباب كيف تَسيغ شرابًا وطعامًا وأنت تعلم أنّك تأكل حرامًا وتشرب حرامًا وتبتاع الإماء وتنكح النساء من مال اليتامى والمساكين والمؤمنين والمجاهدين الذين أفاء الله عليهم هذه الأموال وأحرز بهم هذه البلاد. فاتّق الله وأردد إلى هؤلاء القوم أموالهم فإنّك إن لم تفعل ثمّ أمكنني الله منك لأُعذرنّ إلى الله فيك ولأضربنّك بسيفي الذي ما ضربت به أحدًا إلّا دخل النار. ووالله لو أنّ الحسن والحسين فعلا مثل الذي فعلت ما كانت لهما عندي هَوادة ولا ظَفِرا منّي بإرادة حتّى آخذ الحقّ منهما وأزيح الباطل عن مَظلمتِهما. وأُقسم بالله ربّ العالمين ما يَسرّني أنّ ما أخذتَه من أموالهم حلال لي أتركه ميراثًا لمن بعدي فضَحِّ رُوَيْدًا فكأنّك قد بلغت المدى ودُفنت تحت الثرى وعُرِضت عليك أعمالك بالمحلّ الذي ينادي الظالم فيه بالحسرة ويتمنّى المضيّع الرجعة ﴿وَلَاتَ حِينَ مَنَاصٍ﴾. والسلام.

2.42   ومن كتاب له عليه السلام إلى عمر بن أبي سَلَمَة المخزوميّ وكان عامله على البحرين فعزله وّاستعمل النعمان بن عَجْلان الزُّرَقيّ مكانه

أمّا بعد. فإنّي قد ولّيت النعمان بن عجلان على البحرين ونزعت يدك بلا ذمّ لك ولا تثريب عليك فلقد أحسنت الوِلاية وأدّيت الأمانة فأقبل غير ظَنين ولا مَلوم ولا متّهَم

grab—money held in trust for their widows and orphans—like a lean-hipped wolf pouncing and snatching a bleeding, limping goat. You blithely carried it away to Mecca, without deeming your appropriation a crime, as though you—may other people be deprived of fathers!—were gifting to your family property inherited from your father and mother![1] Great God! Do you not believe in the return to him? Do you not fear interrogation at the reckoning? I counted you among the intelligent! How can you eat and drink when you know that what you eat and drink is illicit? How can you purchase slave-girls and marry women, using money that belongs to orphans and beggars, to believers, to warriors on whom God has bestowed these properties, and through whom God has protected these lands? Fear God and return their property! If you do not, and if God places you in my power, I shall redeem myself before him by punishing you appropriately. I shall strike you with my sword, a sword that has thrust every man it has struck into the Fire of Hell. By God, if Ḥasan and Ḥusayn had done what you have done, they would have met with no leniency from me, nor would they have gotten their way! I would have wrested from them what was due and redressed the injustice wrought by their actions. I swear this by God, Lord of all the peoples—I would not even wish to own lawfully what you have usurped of the community's property, or to leave it as inheritance for those who live after me. ⟨Pasture lightly in the forenoon!⟩[2] Think: how will it be when you reach the end of your path and are buried beneath the earth, when your deeds are laid before you in that abode where the tyrant cries out in despair and the wicked begs for a chance to return?[3] «But it will be too late then to escape!»[4]

2.42 From a missive sent by ʿAlī to ʿUmar ibn Abī Salamah al-Makhzūmī, his governor in Bahrain, discharging him and replacing him with al-Nuʿmān ibn ʿAjlān al-Zuraqī:[5] I have appointed al-Nuʿmān ibn ʿAjlān over Bahrain and discharged you without censure or reproach. You undertook your duties as governor admirably and fulfilled the trust I had placed in you. Come to me, then, without blame, liabil-

---

1 "To Mecca," lit. "to the Ḥijāz," western Arabia, where Mecca and Medina are located.
2 Ar. *ḍaḥḥi ruwaydan*, an idiom enjoining restraint. Two interpretations: (1) The verb *ḍaḥḥā* means to allow camels to pasture only very lightly in the forenoon (*ḍuḥā*), to ensure they can resume walking swiftly without needing to rest. Ḥ 16:169; B 868; R 3:138–139. (2) F 382 explains the idiom as "slaughter gently," from the verb *ḍaḥḥā*, meaning to sacrifice an animal, which, when followed by "gently" (*ruwaydan*), similarly denotes restraint.
3 Reference to Qurʾan, Sajdah 32:12.
4 Qurʾan, Ṣād 38:3.
5 From Kufa to Bahrain in 36/656, in the lead-up to the Battle of Ṣiffīn. ʿUmar ibn Abī Salamah was the Prophet's stepson and ward, son of his wife Umm Salamah from her previous marriage.

ولا مأثوم. فقد أردت المسير إلى ظَلَمَة أهل الشام وأحببت أن تشهد معي فإنّك ممّن أستظهر به على جهاد العدوّ وإقامة عمود الدين إن شاء الله.

2.43 ومن كتاب له عليه السلام إلى مَصْقَلة بن هُبيرة الشَّيبانيّ وهو عامله على أَرْدَشير خُرّة[1] بلغني عنك أم إن كنت فعلته فقد أسخطتَ إلٰهك وأغضبت إمامك أنّك تقسم فَيء المسلمين الذي حازته رماحهم وخيولهم وأُريقت عليه دماؤهم فيمن اعتامَك[2] من أعراب قومك فوالذي فلق الحبّة وبرأ النسمة لئن كان ذلك حقًّا لتجدنّ بك عليّ هوانًا ولتخفّنّ عندي ميزانًا. فلا تَستهن بحقّ ربّك ولا تصلح دنياك بمَحْق دينك فتكون من الأخسرين أعمالًا ألا وإن حقّ مَن قِبَلَك وقِبَلنا من المسلمين في قسمة هذا الفيء سواء يردون عندي عليه ويصدرون عنه. والسلام.

2.44 ومن كتاب له عليه السلام إلى زياد بن أبيه وقد بلغه أنّ معاوية كتب إليه يريد خديعته باستلحاقه

وقد عرفت أنّ معاوية كتب إليك يستزلّ لُبّك ويستفلّ غَرْبَك فاحذره فإنّما هو الشيطان يأتي المرأ من بين يديه ومن خلفه وعن يمينه وعن شماله ليقتحم غفلته ويستلب

---

١ م، ي، ونسخة في هـ: كذا. ن، ش: ﴿خَرْبِه﴾. أصل هـ: ﴿خُوَرَّة﴾   ٢ ن، ش، ونسخة في م: كذا. أصل م: ﴿أعماك﴾. ي، هـ: ﴿اعتماك﴾ وتبدو خطأ. أصل هـ: ﴿اعتمدك﴾.

ity, culpability, or guilt. I intend to march against the despots of Syria and want you beside me in the battle. You are one of those whose support I rely on to fight the enemy and erect the pillar of religion. We shall do so, God willing!

2.43 From a missive sent by ʿAlī to Maṣqalah ibn Hubayrah al-Shaybānī, his governor in Ardashīr-khurrah:[1]

I am informed that you have done something, which, if you have done it, means that you have angered your Lord and enraged your Imam. I am informed that you distribute among your ingratiating Bedouin tribesmen the war booty won by the Muslims' arms, their cavalry, and their blood. I swear by him who split the grain and created the soul—if this is true, you will be disgraced in my eyes and worthless in my scales! Don't make light of your obligations to your Lord, don't advance your worldly life by effacing your religion, else you will be among those who lose all their deeds. Hark! All Muslims—those who live in your jurisdiction and those who live in mine—have equal share in the war booty. They come to my watering hole to receive it, and leave, having drunk their fill. Go in peace.

2.44 From ʿAlī's missive to Ziyād ibn Abīhi, when he learned that Muʿāwiyah had written to Ziyād, enticing him to defect by connecting Ziyād's lineage to his own:[2]

I have learned that Muʿāwiyah wrote to you in an attempt to befuddle your mind and dull your blade. Beware of him! He is Satan, approaching a man from the front and the back, the right and the left,[3] storming in wherever he finds laxity, and plundering wherever he finds negligence. Once, during the reign of

---

1 Presumably sent from Kufa in or just before 38/658. The first line is similar to §2.40, and Maṣqalah is also castigated in §1.44 (details of event in notes there). Ardashīr-khurrah was a district in Fars.

2 Presumably from Kufa to Fars, between 38/658 and 40/661. The correspondence between Muʿāwiyah and Ziyād likely began when Maṣqalah defected to Muʿāwiyah in 38/658 (see Ibn ʿAsākir, *Tārīkh*, 58:269–270). Ziyād was ʿAlī's governor in Fars who, soon after ʿAlī's death, left ʿAlī's son Ḥasan and defected to Muʿāwiyah in 44/665. Muʿāwiyah won him over by officially declaring that Ziyād was his own (illegitimate half-)brother and appointing him governor in Iraq. The *Nahj al-Balāghah* text—like most primary sources—calls him "Ziyād ibn Abīhi," lit. "Ziyād, son of his father" (instead of "Ziyād, son of ʿAbīd," the name of his legal father) because of the uncertainty regarding his parentage; several candidates are mentioned in the sources, including Muʿāwiyah's father, Abū Sufyān. Ziyād's mother, Sumayyah, a slave, is characterized as promiscuous, and—this is the incident mentioned in ʿAlī's letter—Abū Sufyān had once boasted to ʿAlī that he, Abū Sufyān, had "placed Ziyād inside Sumayyah's womb." Details of these events, texts of the letters exchanged between Muʿāwiyah and Ziyād, and between ʿAlī and Ziyād, and Ziyād's orations, in Ḥ 16:179–204 (after Ibn ʿAbd al-Barr, Balādhurī, Wāqidī, Madāʾinī, and Ṭabarī); B 870–871; F 383–384; R 3:140–142.

3 Reference to Qurʾan, Aʿrāf 7:17.

غِرّته. وقد كان من أبي سفيان في زمن عمر بن الخطّاب فَلْتة من حديث النفس ونزغة من نزغات الشيطان لا يثبت بها نسب ولا يستحقّ بها إرث والمتعلّق بها كالواغل المدفَّع والنَّوط المُذبذَب.

فلمّا قرأ زياد الكتاب قال شهد بها وربِّ الكعبة. ولم يزل في نفسه حتّى ادّعاه معاوية.

قوله عليه السلام ﴿كالواغل المدفَّع﴾ الواغل هو الذي يهجم على الشرب ليشرب معهم وليس منهم فلا يزال مدفَّعًا محاجَزًا. و﴿النوط المذبذب﴾ هو ما يُناط برحل الراكب من قَعْب أو قدح أو ما أشبه ذلك فهو أبدًا يتقلقل إذا حثّ ظهره واستعجل سيره.

2.45   ومن كتاب له عليه السلام إلى عثمان بن حُنيف الأنصاريّ وكان عامله على البصرة وقد بلغه أنّه دُعي إلى وليمة قوم من أهلها فمضى إليهم

2.45.1   أمّا بعد يا ابن حنيف. فقد بلغني أنّ رجلًا من فتية أهل البصرة دعاك إلى مأدُبة فأسرعت إليها تُستطاب لك الألوان وتنقل عليك الجِفان وما ظننت أنّك تجيب إلى طعام قوم عائلهم مجفوّ وغنيّهم مدعوّ فأنظر إلى ما تَقضَمه من هذا المَقضَم فما اشتبه عليك علمه فألفِظه وما أيقنت بطيب وجوهه فنَل منه.

2.45.2   ألا وإنّ لكلّ مأموم إمامًا يقتدي به ويستضيء بنور علمه ألا وإنّ إمامكم قد اكتفى من دنياه بطِمرَيه ومن طعمه بقُرصَيه ألا وإنّكم لا تقدرون على ذلك ولكن أعينوني بورع واجتهاد فوالله ما كنزت من دنياكم تِبرًا ولا ادّخرت من غنائمها وفرًا ولا أعددت لبالي ثوبي طِمرًا.[1]

<hr>

[1] م، ن، ش، ه: كذا. وأضيفت في ش، ي: ﴿ولا حزت من أرضها شبرًا﴾. شروح ابن الحديد والبحرانيّ وبعض مخطوطات شرح الراونديّ: أضيفت ﴿ولا حزت من أرضها شبرا ولا أخذت منه إلّا كقوت أتان دبرة ولهي في عيني أوهى من عفصة مقرة﴾.

'Umar ibn al-Khaṭṭāb, Abū Sufyān admitted that he had lapsed, an immoral admission that Satan propelled from his mouth, one which establishes neither lineage nor inheritance. Whoever relies on it as evidence is like a gatecrasher who is thrown out, or like a cup dangling from a saddle that is tossed hither and thither.

When Ziyād read 'Alī's missive, he exclaimed, "By the Lord of the Ka'bah, he has testified to it!" And this stayed with him, until, eventually, Mu'āwiyah proclaimed him his brother.

Raḍī: 'Alī said, "like a gatecrasher who is thrown out (*ka-l-wāghil al-mudaffaʿ*)": a gatecrasher is someone who bursts in uninvited upon a group of drinkers in order to join them, but, since he is not one of them, he is repulsed. "A cup dangling from a saddle that is tossed hither and thither (*al-nawṭ al-mudhabdhab*)" is a cup or a bowl or something similar fastened to a rider's saddle, that rattles and jiggles whenever the rider urges his mount and quickens his pace.

2.45 From 'Alī's letter to 'Uthmān ibn Ḥunayf al-Anṣārī, his governor in Basra, when he heard that a certain group of people had invited Ibn Ḥunayf to a wedding banquet, and he had attended:[1]

2.45.1 Ibn Ḥunayf, I am informed that one of Basra's grandees invited you to a feast and you rushed to go—choice foods were presented to you there, and many dishes were served, but I would not have expected you to accept an invitation from people who are harsh to the needy and welcome only the rich! Look to the chickpeas you crunch up, and spit out anything you have misgivings about! Eat only what you know to be categorically clean.

2.45.2 Harken to me! Every follower has a leader he emulates, whose knowledge he seeks for illumination. Harken again! Your leader is satisfied for his share of the world with his two shabby garments and his two pieces of bread. And harken once more! You will not be able to do what I do—but help me by practicing restraint and striving for good. By God, I have never hoarded the gold of your world, nor amassed loads of riches, nor even laid aside an extra garment to replace my rags!

---

1 Presumably from Medina to Basra at the beginning of 'Alī's caliphate in 36/656, before the Battle of the Camel. A Companion of the Prophet, one of the Allies, Ibn Ḥunayf was 'Alī's first governor in Basra, and he was expelled by the Camel forces in the lead-up to the battle. He fought for 'Alī in that battle, then remained with him in Kufa, living there until his death in Mu'āwiyah's reign. Ṣadūq (*Amālī*, 604) states that the letter (§ 2.45.4) was to Sahl (not 'Uthmān) ibn Ḥunayf.

٣.٤٥.٢ بلى كانت في أيدينا فَدَكُ من كلّ ما أظلّته السماء فشحّت عليها نفوس قوم وسخَت عنها نفوس آخرين ونِعْمَ الحَكُمُ الله.١ وما أصنع بفدك وغير فدك والنفس مظانُّها في غدٍ جَدَثٌ تنقطع في ظلمته آثارها وتغيب أخبارها وحفرة لو زِيدَ في فسحتها وأوسعت يَدًا حافرها لأضغطها الحجر والمدر وسدّ فُرَجها التراب المتراكم. وإنّما هي نفسي أروضها بالتقوى لتأتي آمنة يوم الخوف الأكبر وتثبت على جوانب المَزلَق ولو شئتُ لاهتديت الطريق إلى مُصفّى هذا العسل ولُباب هذا القَمْح ونسائج هذا القَزّ ولكن هيهات أن يغلبني هواي ويقودني جَشَعي إلى تخيّر الأطعمة ولعلّ بالحجاز أو باليمامة من لا طمع له في القُرْص ولا عهد له بالشِّبَع أو أبيت مِبطانًا وحولي بُطون غَرثى وأكباد حَرّى أو أكون كما قال القائل٢

وَحَسْبُكَ دَاءً أَنْ تَبِيتَ بِبِطْنَةٍ   وَحَوْلَكَ أَكْبَادٌ تَحِنُّ إِلَى الْقَدّ١

٤.٤٥.٢ أأقنَعُ من نفسي بأن يقال أميرُ المؤمنين ولا أشاركهم في مكاره الدهر أو أكون أسوة لهم في جشوبة٣ العيش فما خُلقت ليشغلني أكل الطيّبات كالبهيمة المربوطة همّها عَلَفها أو المُرسَلة شغلها تَقَمُّمها تَكترِش من أعلافها وتلهو عمّا يراد بها أو أُترَك سُدًى أو أُهمَل عابثًا أو أجُرّ حبل الضلالة أو أعتسف طريق المَتاهة. وكأنّي بقائلكم يقول إذا كان هذا قوت ابن أبي طالب فقد قعد به الضعف عن قتال الأقران ومنازلة الشجعان ألا وإنّ الشجرة البَرّيّة أصلب عودًا والروائع الخضرة أرَقّ جلودًا والنباتات العَذِيّة أقوى وُقودًا وأبطأ خمودًا. وأنا من رسول الله صلّى الله عليه وآله كالضوء من الضوء٤

---

١ ش، ن، ي، ه: كذا. م: أضيفت ⟨ربّ العالمين⟩.   ٢ البحر: الطويل.   ٣ ش، ن، ه: كذا. م، ونسخة في ش: ⟨خشونة⟩. ي: معًا.   ٤ ش، س، ك، ومصحّحة في ق، وشروح ابن أبي الحديد والبحراني والراونديّ: كذا. ل، ز، ن، م، ي، ه، د، ج، آ، ت، وأصل ق، ومصحّحة في ش: ⟨كالصِّنو من الصِّنو⟩.

2.45.3 And yes, of all the lands under the sky, we possessed only Fadak.[1] But the hearts of one group coveted it, while the generous hearts of another group relinquished it—and God is the best judge! Yet, what should I do with Fadak, or with a land other than Fadak, when tomorrow every man will make his home in the grave? In that darkness, his features will be erased, his renown will fade. The tomb is a pit which, no matter how wide its hollow, how capaciously dug by the grave-digger's hands, is still crushed by stones and slabs, still sealed with piles of earth. As for my own soul, I train it to piety, so that I can come in full security to the day of great terror and have a firm foothold on the slippery edge of the abyss! If I had wished, I could have enjoyed the purest honey, the finest wheat, and lengths of woven silk. But far be it for passion to overpower me, for gluttony to make me partake of delicate foods, when perhaps in Yamāmah or the Ḥijāz there is someone with no hope of finding a piece of bread, no memory even of having eaten a full meal! Far be it for me to sleep with a full belly when I am surrounded by hungry stomachs and empty bellies! Far be it for me to be among those of whom the poet has said:[2]

> How sick you are! You sleep with a full belly
> Surrounded by hearts yearning for a mouthful of dry hide.

2.45.4 Should I be content to be hailed as Commander of the Believers without sharing in the hardships inflicted on them by fate, or without serving as an example for how to endure a rough life? I was not created in order to eat sumptuous foods, like a tethered beast who thinks only of fodder, or a pastured animal who merely looks to eat, an animal that fills its belly with grass, while remaining blithely unaware of what is intended for it! I was not created in order to be ignored and unheeded and left alone to frolic, to drag along the rope of error or to wander off into the wilderness! I can hear some of you saying that Abū Ṭālib's son's diet of uncooked food has made him too weak to fight his rivals or challenge warriors. Hark! A tree in the wilderness is made of stronger wood. Green shoots that are tended have soft surfaces, while plants watered only by rain produce tougher and longer-burning kindling. I am to God's Messenger as

---

1 Fadak was an estate near Khaybar, north of Medina, which the Prophet had bequeathed to his daughter, ʿAlī's wife, Fāṭimah. After the Prophet's death, Abū Bakr denied it to her, claiming that the community are heirs to the Prophet's property. Long discussion in Ḥ 16:209–286; B 874–876. Fāṭimah's oration in Abū Bakr's court, arguing for her right to Fadak, in Qutbuddin, *Arabic Oration*, 385–388 (text, translation, and analysis).

2 By the pre-Islamic poet Ḥātim al-Ṭāʾī, proverbial for his generosity. B 877; Ḥ 16:288.

والذراع من العضد. والله لو تظاهرت العرب على قتالي لما وليّت عنها ولو أمكنت الفُرَص من رقابها لسارعت إليها وسأجهد في أن أطهّر الأرض من هذا الشخص المعكوس والجسم المركوس حتّى تخرج المدرة من بين حبّ الحصيد.

‏2.45.5 إليك عنّي يا دنيا فحبلك على غاربك قد انسللتُ من مَخالبك وأفلَتُّ من حبائلك واجتنبت الذهاب في مَداحضك. أين القرون[1] الذين غررتهم بمَداعبك أين الأمم الذين فتنتهم بزخارفك هاهُم رهائن القبور ومضامين اللحود. والله لو كنتِ شَخصًا مرئيًّا وقالبًا حسّيًّا[2] لأقمت عليك حدود الله في عباد غررتهم بالأمانيّ وأمم ألقيتهم في المَهاوي وملوك أسلمتهم إلى التَّلَف وأوردتهم موارد البلاء إذ لا وِردَ ولا صَدَر. هيهات من وطىء دَحْضَك زَلِق ومن ركب لُجَّك غَرِق ومن آزوَرَّ عن حبالك وُفِّق والسالم منك لا يبالي أن[3] ضاق به مُناخه والدنيا عنده كيوم حان آنسلاخه. اغربي[4] عنّي فوالله لا أذلّ لك فتستذليني ولا أسلس لك فتقوديني وأيم الله يمينًا أستثني فيها بمشيّة الله لَأُروضَنّ نفسي رياضة تَهَشّ معها إلى القُرص إذا قدرت عليه مطعومًا وتقنع بالملح مأدومًا ولأَدَعَنّ مُقلتي كعين ماء نَضَب معينها مستفرَغة دموعها. أتمتلئ السائمة من رِعْيها فتبرُك وتشبع الربيضة من عُشْبها فتربِض ويأكل عليٌّ من زاده فيهجَع فيَهجَع قَرّت إذا عينه إذا اقتدى بعد السنين المتطاولة بالبهيمة الهاملة والسائمة المرعيّة. طوبى لنفس أدّت إلى ربّها فرضها وعَرَكت بجنبها بؤسَها وهجرت في الليل غُمْضَها حتّى إذا غلب الكَرى عليها افترشت أرضها وتوسّدت كفّها في معشر أسهر عيونهم خوف معادهم وتجافت عن مضاجعهم جنوبهم وهَمْهَمَت بذكر ربّهم شِفاههم وتقشّعت بطول استغفارهم ذنوبهم.

______

[1] م، ي، ومصحّحة في ش، ونسخة في ه: كذا. ن، وأصل ش، ه: ﴿القوم﴾.   [2] ن، ش، ه، ونسخة في م، ي: كذا. أصل م، ي، ونسخة في ش، ه: ﴿جنسيًّا﴾.   [3] م، ن، ه، ومصحّحة في ش، وأصل ش: كذا. ي، ومصحّحة في ش: كذا. ه، وأصل ش: ﴿إن﴾.   [4] م، ن، ي، ومصحّحة في ش: كذا. ه، وأصل ش، ونسخة في م: ﴿اعزبي﴾.

light issuing from light,[1] as the hand at the end of the arm. By God, even if all the Arabs came together to attack me, I would stand my ground. If the opportunity to strike off their heads were presented, I would rush forward alone. I shall do my best to cleanse the earth of this warped hulk, this grotesque carcass.[2] All dirt shall be removed from the harvested grain.

2.45.5 Keep away from me, world, go on your way, for I have cast your reins on your withers, evaded your claws, escaped your snares, and sidestepped your slippery paths! Where are the generations you enticed with your pandering, the nations you seduced with your jewels? Here they all are, pledged to their graves, enclosed in their tombs! By God, if you possessed a visible form, a sentient body, I would flog you for the multitudes you enticed with false hopes, for the nations you pitched into the abyss, for the kings you handed over to destruction and swept to their ruin, to a waterhole where no one drinks and no one leaves. Far be you from me! Whoever steps onto your slippery trail tumbles, whoever sails your swelling waves drowns, while whoever escapes your snares is well-directed! Those saved from your harm care not if their beds are narrow. To them, this world is but a day, and its end is near. Get away from me! By God, I shall never be submissive and let you steer me, I shall never be docile and let you lead me! God's oath, I shall train myself to delight in a piece of bread, should I be fortunate enough to obtain it, and be content with salt as my sauce—God willing, I shall do this! I shall let my eyes stream like a gushing spring until I exhaust all my tears. Camels fill their bellies with fodder and kneel to rest, sheep stuff their stomachs with grass and lie down—should ʿAlī also be content to eat his provisions and sleep? His eyes would close in prolonged torpor if—after many long years of life—he started to emulate the grazing beasts and the cattle of the fields! Blessed is the man who discharges his obligations toward his Lord, who endures the rough grip of calamities on his body, who resists closing his eyes at night in slumber, until, when sleep overpowers him, he stretches out on the earth with his palm for a pillow. He is among a devout group whose eyes stay awake in fear of the return to God, whose bodies renounce their beds, whose lips whisper the name of their Lord, and whose sins are sloughed off by long prayer.

---

1 Ar. *ka-l-ḍawʾi mina l-ḍawʾ*. The variant reading is "as brother to brother" (*ka-l-ṣinwi mina l-ṣinw*).

2 Refers to Muʿāwiyah, echoing Qurʾan, Nisāʾ 4:88, Mulk 67:22. R 3:152; Ḥ 16:291–292; B 878–879.

٢٫٤٦ ومن كتاب له عليه السلام إلى بعض عمّاله

أمّا بعد. فإنّك ممّن أستظهر به على إقامة الدين وأقمع به نَخْوَة الأثيم وأسدّ به لَهاة١ الثغر المَخوف. فاستعن بالله على ما أهمّك واخلِط الشدّة بضغث من اللين وارفُق ما كان الرفق أرفق واعتزم بالشدّة حين لا يغني عنك إلّا الشدّة واخفِض للرعيّة جناحك وألِن لهم جانبك وآسِ بينهم في اللحظة والنظرة والإشارة والتحيّة حتّى لا يطمع العظماء في حَيفك ولا يَأس الضعفاء من عدلك. والسلام.

٢٫٤٧ ومن وصيّة له للحسن والحسين عليهما السلام لمّا ضربه ابن ملجم

٢٫٤٧٫١ أوصيكما بتقوى الله وأن لا تبغيا الدنيا وإن بغتكما ولا تأسفا على شيء منها زُوي عنكما وقُولا بالحقّ واعملا للأجر وكُونا للظالم خصمًا وللمظلوم عونًا. أوصيكما وجميع ولدي وأهلي ومن بلغه كتابي بتقوى الله ونظم أمركم وصلاح ذات بينكم فإنّي سمعت جدّكما٢ صلّى الله عليه وآله يقول ﴿صلاح ذات البين أفضل من عامّة الصلاة والصيام﴾. الله الله في الأيتام فلا تُغِبّوا أفواههم ولا يَضيعوا بحضرتكم. والله الله في جيرانكم فإنّهم وصيّة نبيّكم ما زال يوصي بهم حتّى ظننّا أنّه سيورّثهم. والله الله في القرآن لا يسبقكم بالعمل به غيركم. والله الله في الصلاة فإنّها عَمود دينكم. والله الله في بيت ربّكم لا تُخلوه ما

____

١م، ي، ونسخة في ش، ه‍: كذا. ن، وأصل ش، ه‍: ﴿أفواه﴾. ٢ش، ن، ي، ه‍: كذا. م: ﴿سمعت من رسول الله﴾.

2.46 From a letter sent by ʿAlī to one of his governors:[1]
You are one of those whose support I rely on to establish our religion, break the rebel's false pride, and protect vulnerable gaps at the frontier.[2] Ask God for help in any matter that causes you anxiety. Mix your firmness with a hint of gentleness, be compassionate when compassion is called for, and be resolutely firm when only firmness will work. Lower your wing over your subjects in humility,[3] show them your softer side, and give equal attention to all in glance, look, gesture, and greeting, such that the powerful are not emboldened to expect unfair favors and the weak do not despair of receiving justice. Go in peace.

2.47 From ʿAlī's testament for Ḥasan and Ḥusayn, after Ibn Muljam had struck him the death blow:[4]

2.47.1 I counsel you both to remain conscious of God. Do not seek this world even if it seeks you, do not grieve over any of its benefits that are turned away from you. Speak the truth, strive to earn God's reward, be an enemy of the oppressor and a friend of the oppressed. I counsel you both, and all my children and family, as well as all who read my testament, to be conscious of God, to cooperate in common affairs, and to reconcile with kinsfolk. I have heard your grandfather, Muḥammad, say, ⟨To reconcile with kin is even better than to pray and to fast⟩.[5] Fear God, fear God, in the matter of orphans! Do not fill their mouths only every other day, do not let them be uncared for, for as long as you live. Fear God, fear God, in the matter of your neighbors! Your Prophet counseled you to be good to them, and he did this so often we thought he might actually give them a share of inheritance. Fear God, fear God, in the matter of the Qurʾan! Do not let others precede you in following its guidance. Fear God, fear God, in the matter of the ritual prayer! It is the foundation of your reli-

---

1 Excerpt from epistle sent from Kufa to Mālik al-Ashtar, then governor in Naṣībīn, in northern Iraq, after the arbitration in 37/658; by this letter, ʿAlī recalled Ashtar to Kufa, then sent him as governor to Egypt, to take over from Muḥammad ibn Abī Bakr, and Mālik died en route. Text and context in Thaqafī, *Ghārāt*, 1:257–258; Ṭabarī, *Tārīkh*, 5:94–96; Māmaṭīrī, *Nuzhah*, 282–283.
2 Lit. "protect the uvula (*lahāh*) of the frontier, [for whose safety we] fear." The image is of a weak barrier (the uvula) between the enemy and the heartland (the inside of the body, accessed through the mouth).
3 Reference to Qurʾan, Isrāʾ 17:24.
4 Kufa, 40/661. Fuller text and context in Ṭabarī, *Tārīkh*, 5:146–147; Abū al-Faraj, *Maqātil*, 51–53.
5 Hadith cited in Tirmidhī, *Sunan*, § 2501.

بقيتم فإنّه إن تُرك لم تُناظروا. والله الله في الجهاد بأموالكم وأنفسكم وألسنتكم في سبيل الله. وعليكم بالتواصل والتباذل وإيّاكم والتدابر والتقاطع. لا تتركوا الأمر بالمعروف والنهي عن المنكر فيولّى عليكم أشراركم ثمّ تدعون فلا يستجاب لكم.

2.47.2   ثمّ قال

يا بني عبد المطّلب لا أُلْفِيَنّكم تخوضون دماء المسلمين خَوضًا تقولون قُتل أمير المؤمنين قُتل أمير المؤمنين.[1] ألا لا يُقتَلَنّ بي إلّا قاتلي اُنظروا إذا أنا مُتّ من ضربته هذه فاضربوه ضربة بضربة ولا يُمثَّل بالرجل فإنّي سمعت رسول الله صلّى الله عليه وآله يقول ﴿إيّاكم والمَثُلة ولو بالكَلب العَقور﴾.

2.48   ومن كتاب له عليه السلام إلى معاوية

وإنّ البغي والزور يُوتِغانِ[2] بالمرء في دينه ودنياه ويبديان خلله عند من يعيبه. وقد علمتَ أنّك غير مدرِك ما قُضي فواته وقد رام أقوام أمرًا بغير الحقّ فتأوّلوا على الله فأكذبهم فاحذر يومًا يغتبط فيه من أحمد عاقبة عمله ويندم من أمكن الشيطان من قياده فلم يجاذبه. وقد دعوتنا إلى حكم القرآن ولستَ من أهله ولسنا إيّاك أجبنا ولكنّا أجبنا القرآن الى حكمه.

<hr>

[1] ش، ن، ه: كذا. م، ي: لم تكرّر ﴿قُتل أمير المؤمنين﴾.   [2] ن، ش، ي، ه: كذا. م، ونسخة في ه: ﴿يذيعان﴾.

gion. Fear God, fear God, in the matter of your Lord's House! Do not abandon it as long as you live, for if you forsake it, you will not be granted reprieve. Fear God, fear God, in the matter of jihad! Fight with your wealth, your lives, and your tongues in the path of God. Furthermore, foster bonds with family and help each other, never turn away from each other or sever relations, and never cease to command good or forbid evil, lest the wicked gain ascendancy. If that happens, your prayers will no longer be answered.

2.47.2 Then he said:

Sons of 'Abd al-Muṭṭalib! Let me not find you spilling the blood of Muslims, shouting, "The Commander of the Faithful has been killed, the Commander of the Faithful has been killed!" Listen to me! Only my killer should be killed in retaliation for my killing. Pay further attention! If I should die from his blow, then kill him with a single blow. Do not torture him, for I have heard the Messenger say, "Never torture, not even a rabid dog!"

2.48 From 'Alī's letter to Mu'āwiyah:[1]

Treachery and lies kill a man's faith and ruin his worldly affairs, and they expose his faults to those who know him to be shameful. You realize you will not attain what is destined to remain unattained![2] Certain people coveted a thing they had no right to, and they came up with false interpretations of God's words that God then proved false.[3] Beware the coming day! The man with good deeds will rejoice, the one who surrendered his reins to Satan will regret. You proposed that we should submit to the rule of the Qur'an, yet you are not a man who follows the Qur'an. It was not you I answered, but the Qur'an, whose judgment I agreed to follow.

---

1 Ṣiffīn, 37/657, after Mu'āwiyah raised pages from the Qur'an on spears and solicited arbitration, and 'Alī's army compelled 'Alī to accept. Fuller text and context in Minqarī, *Waq'at Ṣiffīn*, 489–494 (text at 493–494). Baḥrānī (B 884) places the letter following Mu'āwiyah's claim to the caliphate after the arbitration in 37/658; in his version, the letter would have been sent from Kufa to Damascus.

2 B 884; 'A 695: the line refers to Mu'āwiyah's call to avenge 'Uthmān in 35–36/656. My reading: the line refers to Mu'āwiyah's bid for the caliphate, based on the subsequent lines, re the proposal to submit to the Qur'an's judgment, which took place at the end of the Battle of Ṣiffīn in 37/657.

3 "A certain group" is Ṭalḥah, Zubayr, and 'Ā'ishah, who fought 'Alī in the Battle of the Camel on the same pretext as Mu'āwiyah at Ṣiffīn, namely, vengeance for 'Uthmān's killing. The "thing" is the caliphate, which they coveted for themselves. The line, "came up with false interpretations (*ta'awwalū*) of God's word," may alternatively be read, "swore they knew God's destiny," as per the variant reading (*ta'allahū*): F 386, citing the hadith, ⟨God proves wrong those who swear they know his judgments (*yata'alla*)⟩, (Quḍā'ī, *Shihāb*, § 2.3).

٢.٤٩ ومن كتاب له عليه السلام إلى غيره[1]

أمّا بعد. فإنّ الدنيا مَشغَلة عن غيرها ولم يصب صاحبها منها شيئًا إلّا فتحت له حرصًا عليها ولَهَجًا بها ولن يستغني صاحبها بما نال فيها عمّا لم يبلغه منها ومن وراء ذلك فراق ما جمع ونقض ما أبرم ولو اعتبرت بما مضى حفظت ما بقي. والسلام.

٢.٥٠ ومن كتاب له عليه السلام إلى أمرائه على الجيوش

من عبد الله عليّ أمير المؤمنين إلى أصحاب المسالح. أمّا بعد.

فإنّ حقًّا على الوالي أن لا يغيّره على رعيّته فضلٌ ناله ولا طَول خُصّ به وأن يزيده ما قسم الله له من نعمه دنوًّا من عباده وعطفًا على إخوانه. ألا وإنّ لكم عندي أن لا أحتجز دونكم سرًّا إلّا في حرب ولا أطوي دونكم أمرًا إلّا في حكم ولا أؤخّر لكم حقًّا عن محلّه ولا أقف به دون مقطعه وأن تكونوا عندي في الحقّ سواء. فإذا فعلت ذلك وجبت لله عليكم النعمة ولي عليكم الطاعة وأن لا تَنكُصوا عن دعوة ولا تفرّطوا في صلاح وأن تخوضوا الغمرات إلى الحقّ فإن أنتم لم تستقيموا على ذلك لم يكن أحد أهون عليّ ممّن اعوجّ منكم ثمّ أعظم له العقوبة ولا يجد عندي فيها رخصة نخذوا هذا من أمرائكم وأعطوهم من أنفسكم ما يصلح الله به أمركم.

٢.٥١ ومن كتاب له عليه السلام إلى عمّاله على الخراج

من عبد الله عليّ أمير المؤمنين إلى أصحاب الخراج. أمّا بعد.

---

[1] ن، ش، ي، ه: كذا. م، ونسخة في ي، ه: ﴿إليه﴾.

2.49 From ʿAlī's letter to someone else:[1]

This world distracts you from the next. When a worldly man obtains a bit of the world, it opens the door to further greed and craving. Never satisfied with what he has, he is always thinking of what he doesn't have. And the end? Separation from all he amassed and destruction of everything he built! If you heed lessons of the past, you will safeguard what remains. Go in peace.

2.50 From ʿAlī's letter to his military commanders:[2]

From God's servant, ʿAlī, Commander of the Faithful, to officers in charge of the garrisons.

It befits those in authority that the honor they have received and the favor for which they have been singled out do not change their behavior toward their subjects. Rather, God's blessings on them should prompt them to greater closeness with God's servants and greater kindness toward their brothers. Harken to my words! You can expect this from me: I shall not keep secrets from you except in war, I shall not hide matters from you except when I judge, I shall not delay in paying your stipends or obstruct disbursements, and all of you shall be equal before me in claiming your rights. If I fulfill my duty, you, in turn, are required to do the following: Give thanks to God for his bounty, offer me full obedience, do not hold back when called, do not shirk in doing good, and plunge into deep and dangerous waters for the sake of truth. If you do not remain upright, though, beware, for no one will fall more from my regard than those who deviate. I shall punish them harshly and they shall receive no leniency. Take this promise from me, your Commander, and give me yours. If you do, God will keep your affairs in good order.

2.51 From ʿAlī's epistle to his officers in charge of collecting the land tax:[3]

From God's servant, ʿAlī, Commander of the Faithful, to the officials in charge of collecting the land tax.

---

1 From Nukhaylah, just before ʿAlī set out for Syria, addressed, according to Minqarī (*Waqʿat Ṣiffīn*, 110–111), to ʿAmr ibn al-ʿĀṣ. Minqarī records the text and context, and ʿAmr's response, calling for ʿAlī to step down as caliph. Addressed to Muʿāwiyah, per the variant reading "to him again" (*ilayhi*) in some MSS and commentaries.

2 Minqarī (*Waqʿat Ṣiffīn*, 107) and Ṭūsī (*Amālī*, 222) place this letter in Kufa or Nukhaylah, just before setting out for Ṣiffīn, in 36/656.

3 Along with the previous text, Minqarī (*Waqʿat Ṣiffīn*, 108) appears to place this letter in Kufa or Nukhaylah, just before setting out for Ṣiffīn, in 36/656. "Land tax" (*kharāj*) is different from the alms-levy (*ṣadaqāt*) mentioned in §2.25.

فإنّ من لم يحذر ما هو صائر إليه لم يقدّم لنفسه ما يُحرزها وٱعلموا أنّ ما كلّفتم يسير وأنّ ثوابه كثير ولو لم يكن فيما نهى الله عنه من البغي والعدوان عقاب يُخاف لكان في ثواب ٱجتنابه ما لا عذر في ترك طلبه فأنصفوا الناس من أنفسكم وٱصبروا لحوائجهم فإنّكم خزّان الرعيّة ووكلاء الأمّة وسفراء الأئمّة ولا تُحشموا أحدًا عن حاجته ولا تحبسوه عن طلبته ولا تَبيعُنّ للناس في الخراج كسوة شتاء ولا صيف ولا دابّة يعتملون عليها ولا عبدًا ولا تَضرِبُنّ أحدًا سوطًا لمكان درهم ولا تَمَسُّنّ مال أحد من الناس مصلٍّ ولا معاهد إلّا أن تجدوا فرسًا أو سلاحًا يُعدى به على أهل الإسلام فإنّه لا ينبغي للمسلم أن يدع ذلك في أيدي أعداء الإسلام فيكون شوكة عليه. ولا تدّخروا أنفسكم نصيحة ولا الجند حسن سيرة ولا الرعيّة معونة ولا دين الله قوّة وأبلوا في سبيله ما ٱستوجب عليكم فإنّ الله سبحانه قد ٱصطنع عندنا وعندكم أن نشكره بجهدنا وأن ننصره بما بلغت قوّتنا ولا قوّة إلّا بالله.٢

2.52 ومن كتاب له عليه السلام إلى أمراء البلاد في معنى الصلاة

أمّا بعد. فصلّوا بالناس الظهر حين تفيء الشمس مثل مَربِض العَنز وصلّوا بهم العصر والشمس بيضاء حيّة في عُضو من النهار حين يُسار فيها فرسخان وصلّوا بهم المغرب حين يفطر الصائم ويدفع الحاجّ وصلّوا بهم العشاء حين يتوارى الشفَق إلى ثلث الليل وصلّوا بهم الغداة والرجل يعرف وجه صاحبه وصلّوا بهم صلاة أضعفهم ولا تكونوا فتّانين.

---

١ م، ي، ونسخة في هـ: كذا. ن، ش، هـ، ونسخة في م: ⟨تحسموا⟩.   ٢ م، ي، ومصحّحة في هـ: كذا. ن، ش، وأصل هـ: أضيفت ⟨العليّ⟩.

Whoever fails to care about his end, fails to safeguard himself by advancing provisions for his soul. Know that your obligations are small while their reward will be great. Even if you feared no punishment for breaking God's prohibitions against treachery and hostility, the reward promised for shunning them should leave you with no excuse. Treat people with justice and be patient in tending to their needs. You are the people's treasurers, the community's trustees, and the Imam's agents. Do not come between a man and his needs, do not restrain him from going about his business, do not force people to pay taxes by selling their winter garments, their summer clothes, the beasts they need for work, or their slaves, do not whip anyone for silver. Do not seize the property of a single individual, whether Muslim, Christian, or Jew,[1] except when you find a horse or weapon that could be used to attack the people of Islam, for a Muslim should not leave in the hands of Islam's enemies objects they could use to strengthen their attack. Do not hold back—give each other counsel, set an example for your troops, help your subjects, and support God's religion. Push yourself hard in God's way and fulfil your duties. God has blessed me with his immense favors, and he has blessed you. We must thank him through our actions and serve him with our full strength. All strength comes from God.

2.52 From ʿAlī's instructions to his governors regarding the ritual prayers:[2]
Pray the noon prayer when the sun casts a shadow equal to a squatting goat.[3] Pray the afternoon prayer while the sun burns intensely bright, when what remains of the day is enough to travel two leagues.[4] Pray the sunset prayer when a person would break fast, and a hajj pilgrim would make his descent.[5] Pray the night prayer when twilight ends and through the first third of the night. Pray the dawn prayer when a man can see his neighbor's face. Pray the prayer that suits the weakest among them and do not cause sedition.[6]

---

1   Lit. "whether he prays the ritual prayer [of Islam] (*muṣallin*) or is guaranteed protection by a covenant (*muʿāhid*)."

2   Presumably from Kufa sometime during ʿAlī's caliphate 35–40/656–661. Discussion on various legal opinions regarding prayer times in Ḥ 17:23–29.

3   I.e., when the sun's shadow reaches the length of a handspan. R 3:163; 17:23.

4   Lit. two *farsakh*s. A *farsakh* is a unit of distance between four to six miles.

5   From ʿArafāt to Muzdalifah, per the pilgrimage rites.

6   I.e., keep it short—do not pray long Surahs, or people will stop attending. B 888; R 3:164. Similar to § 2.53.16.

2.53   ومن عهد له عليه السلام كتبه للأَشْتَر النَّخَعيّ رحمه الله على مصر وأعمالها حين اضطرب

أمرُ أميره عليها محمّد بن أبي بكر رحمه الله. وهو أطول عهد كتبه وأجمعه للمحاسن

2.53.1   بسم الله الرحمٰن الرحيم

هذا ما أمرَ به عبد الله عليّ أمير المؤمنين مالك بن الحارث الأشتر في عهده إليه حين

ولّاه مصر جَبوة خراجها وجهاد عدوّها واستصلاح أهلها وعمارة بلادها. أمرَه بتقوى

الله وإيثار طاعته واتّباع ما أمر به في كتابه من فرائضه وسننه التي لا يسعد أحد إلّا

باتّباعها ولا يشقى إلّا مع جحودها وإضاعتها وأن ينصر الله سبحانه بيده وقلبه ولسانه

فإنّه جلّ اسمه قد تكفّل بنصر من نصره وإعزاز من أعزّه. وأمرَه أن يكسر نفسه عند

الشهوات ويزعها عند الجمحات ف﴿إِنَّ النَّفْسَ﴾ لَ﴿أَمَّارَةٌ بِالسُّوءِ إِلَّا مَا رَحِمَ﴾ الله.

2.53.2   ثمّ اعلم يا مالك أنّي قد وجّهتك إلى بلاد قد جرت عليها دُوَل قبلك من عدل

وجور وأنّ الناس ينظرون من أمورك في مثل ما كنت تنظر فيه من أمور الولاة قبلك

ويقولون فيك ما كنت تقول فيهم. وإنّما يُستَدَلّ على الصالحين بما يُجري الله لهم على

ألسن عباده فليكن أحبّ الذخائر إليك ذخيرة العمل الصالح فاملك هواك وشُحّ بنفسك

عمّا لا يحلّ لك فإنّ الشحّ بالنفس الإنصاف منها فيما أحبّت وكرهت.

2.53.3   وأشعر قلبك الرحمة للرعيّة والمحبّة لهم واللطف بهم ولا تكوننّ عليهم سَبُعًا

ضاريًا تغتنم أكلهم فإنّهم صنفان إمّا أخٌ لك في الدين وإمّا نظير لك في الخلق يَفرط

منهم الزلل وتعرض لهم العلل ويؤتى على أيديهم في العمد والخطأ فأعطهم من عفوك

وصفحك مثل الذي تحبّ أن يعطيك الله من عفوه وصفحه فإنّك فوقهم ووالي الأمر

عليك فوقك والله فوق من ولّاك وقد استكفاك أمرهم وابتلاك بهم. لا تنصبنّ نفسك

2.53 From ʿAlī's testament for Mālik al-Ashtar al-Nakhaʿī when he appointed him governor of Egypt and its provinces, to replace Muḥammad ibn Abī Bakr, whose control over the region had been severely challenged. It is ʿAlī's longest epistle and gathers within it the most beautiful aspects of language:[1]

2.53.1 In the name of God, the Compassionate, the Merciful.

This is what God's servant, ʿAlī, Commander of the Faithful, commands Mālik ibn al-Ḥārith al-Ashtar, in the epistle he writes appointing him governor of Egypt, with the charge to collect its land tax, fight its enemies, reconcile its people, and make its lands prosper: ʿAlī commands him to be conscious of God and prefer God's obedience above all; to follow what God has commanded in his Book, both the mandatory and the recommended acts, for only those who follow them attain happiness and only those who deny them and squander them fall into wretchedness; and to support God's cause with his hand, heart, and tongue, for God has promised to support those who support him, and to exalt those who exalt him. ʿAlī commands him to break the passions of his sentient soul and to rein them in when they become restive. For «the sentient soul commands vice unless God shows it mercy».[2]

2.53.2 Know, O Mālik, that I send you to a land where just and unjust rulers have ruled before you. Its people will watch what you do, as you watched the actions of earlier rulers, they will speak about you, as you spoke about those rulers. The pious are recognized through what God prompts his servants to say about them, so let praiseworthy deeds be your dearest treasure. Control your passions and restrain yourself from all that is illicit for you, holding yourself accountable in what you love and in what you hate.

2.53.3 Clothe your heart with compassion, love, and kindness toward your subjects. Do not be a ravening lion who devours their flesh.[3] People are of two kinds: they are either your brothers in faith or your peers in creation. They make mistakes, they are exposed to temptations, and their hands do wrong, be it deliberately or in error. Grant them your forgiveness and pardon, just as you wish for God to forgive and pardon you. You are above them in rank, but the one who appointed you is above you, and God is above him. God has required

---

1 In Kufa, 38/658. Ḥarrānī, *Tuḥaf*, 126. See also §2.38 and §2.62. On this oration, see Shah-Kazemi, *Justice and Remembrance*, 73–114; Qutbuddin, "Just Leadership in Early Islam: The Teachings and Practice of Imam Ali."

2 Qurʾan, Yūsuf 12:53.

3 Lit. "predatory beast (*sabuʿ ḍārī*)," usually used for a lion. R 3:172.

لحرب الله فإنّه لا يَدَيْ لك بنقمته ولا غنى بك عن عفوه ورحمته. ولا تَنْدَمَنّ على عفو ولا تَبْجَحَنّ بعقوبة ولا تُسرعنّ إلى بادرة وجدت عنها مَنْدوحة. ولا تقولنّ إنّي مؤمَّر آمُر فأُطاع فإنّ ذلك إدغال في القلب ومَنْهَكة للدين وتقرّب من الغِيَر. وإذا أحدث لك ما أنت فيه من سلطانك أُبَّهة أو مَخِيلة فانظر إلى عظم ملك الله فوقك وقدرته منك على ما لا تقدر عليه من نفسك. فإنّ ذلك يُطامِن إليك من طِماحك ويكفّ عنك من غَرْبك ويفيء إليك بما عَزَب عنك من عقلك. إيّاك ومُساماة الله في عظمته والتشبّه به في جبروته فإنّ الله يُذلّ كلّ جبّار ويُهِين كلّ مُختال.

2.53.4 أنصف الله وأنصف الناس من نفسك ومن خاصّة أهلك ومن لك فيه هوى من رعيّتك فإنّك إلّا تفعل تظلم ومن ظلم عباد الله كان الله خصمه دون عباده ومن خاصمه الله أدحض حجّته وكان لله حرباً حتّى ينزع ويتوب وليس شيء أدعى إلى تغيير نعمة الله وتعجيل نقمته من إقامة على ظلم.[1] وليكن أحبّ الأمور إليك أوسطها في الحقّ وأعمّها في العدل وأجمعها لرضى الرعيّة فإنّ سخط العامّة يُجحف برضى الخاصّة وإنّ سخط الخاصّة يُغتفر مع رضى العامّة وليس أحد من الرعيّة أثقل على الوالي مؤونة في الرخاء وأقلّ معونة له في البلاء وأكره للإنصاف وأسأل بالإلْحاف وأقلّ شكراً عند الإعطاء وأبطأ عذراً عند المنع وأضعف صبراً عند ملمّات الدهر من أهل الخاصّة. وإنّما عَمود الدين وجِماع المسلمين والعُدّة للأعداء العامّة من الأمّة فليكن صَغوُك لهم وميلك معهم.

2.53.5 وليكن أبعد رعيّتك منك وأشْنأهم عندك أطلَبهم لمعائب الناس فإنّ في الناس عيوبًا الوالي أحقّ من سترها فلا تكشفنّ عمّا غاب عنك منها فإنّما عليك تطهير ما ظهر لك والله يحكم على ما غاب عنك فاستر العورة ما استطعت يستر الله منك ما تحبّ ستره من رعيّتك. أطلق عن الناس عقدة كلّ حقد واقطع عنك سبب كلّ وِتر وتغابَ عن كلّ ما لا يصحّ لك ولا تعجلنّ إلى تصديق ساعٍ فإنّ الساعي غاشّ وإن تشبّه

---

[1] ان، ش، مي، ومصحّحة في ي، ه: كذا. أصل ي، ه: وفي هامش م: أضيفت ﴿فإنّ الله سميع دعوة المظلومين وهو للظالمين بالمرصاد﴾.

you to tend to their needs and tested you through them. Do not set yourself up to be at war with God, for your hands do not have the strength to repulse his punishment, while you have utter need of his forgiveness and compassion. Never regret having pardoned, never rejoice in punishing, and never hasten to act in a fit of passion when you can find a calmer way. Never say, "I have been given command—I command, and I shall be obeyed," for that will make hearts fester, weaken religion, and draw calamities close. If your sovereignty makes you haughty, then look to the greatness of God's kingdom above you, at his power over your own life, which is far beyond anything you possess. That will subdue your recalcitrance, restrain your sword, and bring you back to your senses. Beware of exalting yourself in the face of God's majesty or of imitating his power. God abases every tyrant and degrades all who show pride.

2.53.4 Render God justice and render people justice against yourself, your close family, and those whom you favor among your subjects. Otherwise, you will have oppressed. Whoever oppresses God's servants, God, not his servants, will be his adversary, and whoever has God for adversary will find his arguments void. He will find himself at war with God until he desists and repents—nothing calls more strongly for God's blessings to be rescinded and his punishment to be hastened than persistent oppression. Let the way most dear to you be the most moderate in truth, the most universal in justice, and the most far reaching in achieving your subjects' satisfaction. The people's dissatisfaction washes away the satisfaction of the elite, while the elites' dissatisfaction is not significant when the people are satisfied. In fact, there are none among a ruler's subjects more burdensome in times of ease, less helpful in times of trial, more opposed to equity, more importunate in demands, less grateful for gifts, more petulant when denied, and less patient in the face of calamities than the elite. The support of religion, the majority of Muslims, and the armies with which to combat enemies come from the common people of the community. Let your attention be focused on them, let your inclination be toward them.

2.53.5 Loathe and distance those who persist in exposing other people's shame. Everyone possesses faults, and it behooves the ruler, more than any other, to conceal them. Do not seek to unearth a shame that is hidden from you, for your charge is to cleanse what is exposed—it is for God to judge the hidden. Conceal people's shame as much as you are able, and God will conceal the things you wish to conceal about yourself from your subjects. Unbind the people from knots of rancor and sever yourself from ropes of vengeance. Close your eyes against things you should not inspect. Do not be hasty to uphold a slanderer, for the slanderer deceives, even when he comes in the guise of a well-

بالناصحين. ولا تدخلنّ في مشورتك بخيلًا يعدل بك عن الفضل ويعدك الفقر ولا جبانًا يضعّفك عن الأمور ولا حريصًا يزيّن لك الشَّرَه بالجور فإنّ البخل والجبن والحرص غرائز شتّى يجمعها سوء الظنّ بالله.

شرّ وزرائك من كان للأشرار قبلك وزيرًا ومَن شَرِكهم في الآثام فلا يكوننّ لك بِطانة فإنّهم أعوان الأَثَمة وإخوان الظَلَمة وأنت واجدٌ منهم خير الخلف ممّن له مثل آرائهم ونفاذهم وليس عليه مثل آصارهم وأوزارهم' ممّن لم يعاون ظالمًا على ظلمه ولا آثمًا على إثمه أولئك أخفّ عليك مؤونة وأحسن لك معونة وأحنى عليك عطفًا وأقلّ لغيرك إلفًا فاّتّخذ أولئك خاصّة لخلواتك وحفلاتك. ثمّ ليكن آثرُهم عندك أقوَلهم بمُرّ الحقّ لك وأقلّهم مساعدة فيما يكون منك ممّا كره الله لأوليائه واقعًا ذلك من هواك حيث وقع وأَلصق بأهل الورع والصدق ثمّ رُضْهم على أَلّا يُطروك ولا يبجّحوك بباطل لم تفعله فإنّ كثرة الإطراء تحدث الزّهْو وتُدني من العزّة. ولا يكوننّ المحسن والمسيء عندك بمنزلة سواء فإنّ في ذلك تزهيدًا لأهل الإحسان في الإحسان وتدريبًا لأهل الإساءة على الإساءة وأَلزم كلًّا منهم ما أَلزم نفسه.

٦.٥٣.٢ واّعلم أنّه ليس شيء بأدعى إلى حسن ظنّ والٍ برعيّته من إحسانه إليهم وتخفيفه المؤونات عنهم وترك اّستكراهه إيّاهم على ما ليس له قِبَلهم فليكن منك في ذلك أمرٌ يجتمع لك به حسن الظنّ برعيّتك فإنّ حسن الظنّ يقطع عنك نَصَبًا طويلًا وإنّ أحقّ من حسن ظنّك به لَمَنْ حسن بلاؤك عنده وإنّ أحقّ من ساء ظنّك به لمن ساء بلاؤك عنده. ولا تنقض سنّة صالحة عمل بها صدور هذه الأُمّة واّجتمعت بها الأُلفة وصلحت عليها الرعيّة ولا تُحدثنّ سنّة تضرّ بشيء من ماضي تلك السنن فيكون الأَجر لمن سَنَّها والوِزر عليك بما نقضت منها. وأَكثِر مُدارَسة العلماء ومُثافَنة الحكماء في تثبيت ما صلح عليه أمرُ بلادك وإقامة ما اّستقام به الناس قبلك.

<hr>

١ن، ش، ي، ه: كذا. م: أضيفت ⟨وآثامهم⟩.

wisher. Do not appoint as counsellor a miser who will stem your generosity, who will alarm you with the specter of poverty, or a coward who will weaken your resolve in the face of combat, or a glutton who will render attractive the tyranny of avarice. Miserliness, cowardice, and greed are diverse temperaments united by a common lack of trust in God.

The worst people you could choose to serve as your viziers are those who served as viziers for evil rulers before you, who were their partners in crime. Do not include them among your courtiers, for they are supporters of criminals and brothers to tyrants. You will find excellent choices among similarly astute and equally effective men who are not encumbered by wickedness and sin, who have never supported a tyrant in his tyranny or a criminal in his crime. They will be a lighter burden and a firmer support. They will be more inclined to feel affection for you and less inclined to feel esteem for another. Take them as your confidantes, keep them by your side in private assemblies and public gatherings. Favor above all the one who most often tells you bitter truths, who least often supports actions that God dislikes—especially from his chosen ones—and who does so without pandering to your wishes. Embrace people of restraint and truth. Train them never to flatter, never to lavish upon you undue praise. Too much praise generates vanity and propels the praised one toward pride. Do not give the good and the evil equal consequence. That would discourage the good from doing good and encourage the evil to do evil. Keep each person in the position that befits him.

2.53.6 Know that nothing helps build a stronger bond of trust between a ruler and his subjects than when he is good to them, lightens their burdens, and does not coerce them. You should endeavor to achieve a manner of governance that includes trust in your subjects, for trust will terminate longstanding apprehensions. It is also important to remember that the person whom you have tested and found trustworthy is the one who most deserves your trust. In contrast, the person whom you have tested and found untrustworthy is the one who most deserves your mistrust. Do not end any pious tradition enacted by leaders of this community that has created harmony among your subjects and helped them prosper. Do not introduce any new tradition that harms traditions of the past. If you do, those who established the earlier traditions will be rewarded for establishing them, and you will be punished for ending them. Devote time to understanding this aspect—study with scholars and converse with sages about consolidating the prosperity of your lands and perpetuating earlier practices that ensured success for the people.

٢.٥٣.٧ وٱعلم أنّ الرعيّة طبقات لا يصلح بعضها إلّا ببعض ولا غنى ببعضها عن بعض. فمنها جنود الله ومنها كتّاب العامّة والخاصّة ومنها قضاة العدل ومنها عمّال الإنصاف والرفق ومنها أهل الجزية والخراج من أهل الذمّة ومُسلِمة الناس ومنها التجّار وأهل الصناعات ومنها الطبقة السفلى من ذوي الحاجة والمسكنة. وكلّ قد سمّى الله سهمه ووضع على حدّه وفريضته في كتابه أو سنّة نبيّه صلّى الله عليه وآله عهدًا منه عندنا محفوظًا. فالجنود بإذن الله حصون الرعيّة وزين الولاة وعزّ الدين وسبل الأمن وليس تقوم الرعيّة إلّا بهم. ثمّ لا قِوام للجنود إلّا بما يخرج الله لهم من الخراج الذي يقوَون به في جهاد عدوّهم ويعتمدون عليه فيما أصلحهم ويكون من وراء حاجتهم. ثمّ لا قوام لهذين الصنفين إلّا بالصنف الثالث من القضاة والعمّال والكتّاب لما يُحكمون من المعاقد ويجمعون من المنافع ويؤتمنون عليه من خواصّ الأمور وعوامّها. ولا قوام لهم جميعًا إلّا بالتجّار وذوي الصناعات فيما يجتمعون عليه من مرافقهم ويقيمونه من أسواقهم ويكفُونهم من الترفّق بأيديهم ممّا لا يبلغه رفق غيرهم. ثمّ الطبقة السفلى من أهل الحاجة والمسكنة الذين يَحِقّ رِفدُهم ومعونتهم. وفي الله لكلّ سعة ولكلّ على الوالي حقّ بقدر ما يصلحه.

٢.٥٣.٨ فوَلِّ من جنودك أنصحهم في نفسك لله ولرسوله ولإمامك^١ جَيبًا وأفضلهم حلمًا ممّن يبطئ عن الغضب ويستريح إلى العذر ويرؤُف بالضعفاء وينبو على الأقوياء وممّن لا يثيره العنف ولا يقعد به الضعف. ثمّ ٱلصق بذوي الأحساب وأهل البيوتات الصالحة والسوابق الحسنة ثمّ أهل النجدة والشجاعة والسخاء والسماحة فإنّهم جِماعٌ من الكرم وشُعَبٌ من العُرْف. ثمّ تفقّد من أمورهم ما يتفقّده الوالدان من ولدهما ولا يَتفاقَمَنّ في نفسك شيء قوّيتهم به ولا تحقرنّ لطفًا تعاهدتهم به وإن قلّ فإنّه داعية لهم إلى بذل النصيحة لك وحسن الظنّ بك ولا تدع تفقُّد لطيف أمورهم ٱتّكالًا على

———

^١ م، ش، ن، ومصحّحة في ه: كذا. ي، وأصل ه: أضيفت ﴿وأنقاهم﴾. وهامش ن: أضيفت ﴿وأطهرهم﴾.

2.53.7 Know that the subject population consists of categories of people, each category sustained by the others and in need of the others. The categories are these: soldiers who fight in God's cause, scribes who write for the public or for the elite, judges who dispense justice, administrators who work with equity and compassion, members of the protected peoples and the conquered who have converted to Islam and who pay the poll tax and land tax, merchants and artisans, and the lowest category, the poor and needy. God has prescribed a role for each, drawing boundaries through the laws mandated in his Book and in the practice of his Prophet. This is a covenant from him, one that we preserve. Soldiers serve with God's permission as a fortress for the public, the ornament of the realm, the might of religion, and the path to security—the public can be sustained only through them. Soldiers, in turn, are sustained by the land tax that God has ordained to be used for their maintenance, through which they gain the strength to fight their enemy, and upon which they depend to improve their living conditions and fulfill their basic needs. These two groups are sustained by the third—judges, tax collectors, and administrators, who draw up careful contracts, collect taxes, and are entrusted with affairs of private and public utility. All these groups are sustained by the merchants and artisans who gather together the stuff of life, set up markets, and suffice the other groups in their daily needs with services that no one else can perform. Then comes the lowest category, the poor and needy, who merit help and aid. God's grace encompasses all. Each group has rights that the governor should uphold to the best of his ability.

2.53.8 Place in charge of your soldiers the man who, in the service of God, his Messenger, and your Imam, has kept his pockets clean,[1] who is the most forbearing, a man who is slow to anger, happy to pardon, compassionate with the weak, and harsh with the mighty, who is neither quick to violence nor restrained by weakness. Select for leadership people of noble lineage who belong to virtuous families and have performed many good deeds.[2] Look for people of valor, courage, generosity, and benevolence, for they are storehouses of nobility and wellsprings of honor. Afterward, keep an eye on their affairs as parents keep an eye on their children. Do not consider excessive the benefits you bestow on them in order to strengthen them. Do not consider trivial the little kindnesses you have habituated them to. All this motivates them to wish

---

1 Lit. "who is the sincerest of pocket" (*anṣaḥahum ... jayban*), where "sincere" refers to "clean," meaning trustworthy and not corrupt. R 3:172; B 898.
2 Lit. "make cling to" (*alṣiq*), i.e., "make" the leadership of the army "cling to" people who possess these attributes. B 900; H 17:53; R 3:180–181.

جسيمها فإنّ لليسير من لطفك موضعًا ينتفعون به وللجسيم موقعًا لا يستغنون عنه وليكن آثر رؤوس جندك عندك مَن واساهم في معونته وأفضلَ عليهم من جِدَته بما يَسَعهم ويسع مَن وراءهم مِن خُلوف أهليهم حتّى يكون همّهم همًّا واحدًا في جهاد العدوّ. فإنّ عطفك عليهم يعطف قلوبهم عليك ولا تصحّ نصيحتهم إلّا بحيطتهم على ولاة أمورهم وقلّة اُستثقال دُوَلهم وترك اُستبطاء اَنقطاع مدّتهم فاَفسح في آمالهم وواصل من حسن الثناء عليهم وتعديد ما أبلى ذوو البلاء منهم فإنّ كثرة الذكر لحسن فعَالهم يهزّ الشجاع ويحرّض النا كل إن شاء الله ثمّ اَعرف لكلّ اَمرئٍ منهم ما أبلى ولا تضمّن[1] بلاء اَمرئٍ إلى غيره ولا تُقصرنّ به دون غاية بلائه ولا يَدعُونّك شرف اَمرئٍ إلى أن تعظّم من بلائه ما كان صغيرًا ولا ضَعة اَمرئٍ إلى أن تَستصغر من بلائه ما كان عظيمًا.

وأردد إلى الله ورسوله ما يظلعك[2] من الخطوب ويشتبه عليك من الأمور فقد قال سبحانه لقوم أحبّ إرشادهم ﴿يَا أَيُّهَا الذينَ آمَنُوا أَطِيعُوا اللهَ وَأَطِيعُوا الرَّسُولَ وَأُولِي الْأَمْرِ مِنكُمْ فَإِن تَنَازَعْتُمْ فِي شَيْءٍ فَرُدُّوهُ إِلَى اللهِ وَالرَّسُولِ﴾. فالردّ إلى الله الأخذ بمحكم كتابه والردّ إلى الرسول الأخذ بسنّته الجامعة غير المفرّقة.

9.53.2 ثمّ اَختر للحكم بين الناس أفضل رعيّتك في نفسك ممّن لا تضيق به الأمور ولا تَمحكه الخصوم ولا يتمادى في الزلّة ولا يَحصُر من الفَيء إلى الحقّ إذا عرفه ولا تشرف نفسه على طمع ولا يكتفي بأدنى فهم دون أقصاه أوقفهم في الشبهات وآخذهم بالحجج وأقلّهم تبرّمًا بمراجعة الخصم وأصبرهم على تكشّف الأمور وأصرمهم عند إيضاح الحكم ممّن لا يَزدَهيه إطراء ولا يستميله إغراء وأولئك قليل. ثمّ أكثِر تعاهُد قضائه وأفسح

---

you well and place their trust in you. Do not be remiss in keeping an eye on their small affairs, relying solely on your inspection of greater ones. There are places where small kindnesses benefit, just as there are circumstances in which people cannot survive without more substantial support. Among the officers of your troops, give preference to those who give the troops steady assistance, and give your troops the means to sustain themselves and the families they leave behind. Do all this until their aspiration becomes as one—to fight the enemy. Your kindness will attract their hearts to you. Unless they are devoted to their commanders, unless they find their control not burdensome and their continuing tenure acceptable, they will not be sincere in service. Encourage their hopes, praise them profusely, and be generous in mentioning the great services of those who have rendered these services. God willing, your frequent praise of their deeds will encourage the bold and inspire the timid. Recognize each man's service, do not attribute one man's service to another, and do not fall short in articulating the extent of his service. A man's eminence should not prompt you to glorify his trifling service, and another's humble position should not prompt you to belittle his great deed.

Refer to God and his Messenger the problems that make you stop in your tracks, the matters that you find obscure. God has said to a people whom he wished to set right, «Believers, obey God, obey the Messenger, and the people in command among you. If you disagree over something, refer it to God and the Messenger.»[1] Referring something to God is to abide by the clear text of his Book. Referring something to the Messenger is to abide by his agreed upon Sunnah, keeping away from what is disputed.

2.53.9 Select the man you deem the most excellent among your subjects to judge between the people: a man who will not be overwhelmed by lawsuits or angered by litigants, who, upon recognizing the truth, will not persist in error or hesitate to revert to what is right, whose heart is not drawn to greed, who is not satisfied with superficial understanding but goes the full course, the most cautious when encountering points of doubt, the one who puts the most emphasis on evidence, the one who is least wearied by having to question litigants, who is the most patient in probing truths, and the most decisive in determining when the truth has become clear, the one who does not strut when he is praised, and is not seduced by temptations. Such men are rare. Once you have appointed a judge, moreover, exercise vigilance in checking his judgments. Pay him generously to remove his wants and to reduce his need to appeal to others. Give him

---

1 Qur'an, Nisā' 4:59.

له في البذل ما يزيح علّته وتقلّ معه حاجته إلى الناس وأعطه من المنزلة لديك ما لا يطمع فيه غيره من خاصّتك ليأمن بذلك ٱغتيال الرجال له عندك. فٱنظر في ذلك نظرًا بليغًا فإنّ هذا الدين قد كان أسيرًا في أيدي الأشرار يعمل فيه بالهوى وتطلب به الدنيا.

2.53.10 ثمّ ٱنظر في أمور عمّالك فٱستعملهم ٱختبارًا ولا تُوَلِّهِم مُحاباة وأَثَرَة فإنّهما جِماع من شُعَب الجور والخيانة. وتَوَخَّ منهم أهل التجربة والحياء من أهل البيوتات الصالحة والقَدَم في الإسلام المتقدّمة فإنّهم أكرم أخلاقًا وأصحّ أعراضًا وأقلّ في المطامع إسرافًا[1] وأبلغ في عواقب الأمور نظرًا. ثمّ أَسبغ عليهم الأرزاق فإنّ ذلك قوّة لهم على ٱستصلاح أنفسهم وغنى لهم عن تناول ما تحت أيديهم وحجّة عليهم إن خالفوا أمرك أو ثَلَموا أمانتك. ثمّ تفقّد أعمالهم وٱبعث العيون من أهل الصدق والوفاء عليهم فإنّ تعاهدك في السرّ لأمورهم حَدوة لهم على ٱستعمال الأمانة والرفق بالرعيّة. وتحفّظ من الأعوان فإن أحد منهم بسط يده إلى خيانة ٱجتمعت بها عليه عندك أخبار عيونك ٱكتفيت بذلك شاهدًا فبسطت عليه العقوبة في بدنه وأخذته بما أصاب من عمله ثمّ نصبته بمقام المذلّة ووَسَمته بالخيانة وقلّدته عار التهمة.

2.53.11 وتفقّد أمر الخراج بما يصلح أهله فإنّ في صلاحه وصلاحهم صلاحًا لمن سواهم ولا صلاح لمن سواهم إلّا بهم لأنّ الناس كلّهم عِيال على الخراج وأهله. وليكن نظرك في عمارة الأرض أبلغ من نظرك في ٱستجلاب الخراج لأنّ ذلك لا يدرك إلّا بالعمارة. ومن طلب الخراج بغير عمارة أخرب البلاد وأهلك العباد ولم يستقم أمره إلّا قليلًا. فإن شكوا ثقلًا أو علّة أو ٱنقطاع شِربٍ أو بالّةٍ أو إحالة أرض ٱغتمرها غرق أو أجحف بها عطش خفّفتَ عنهم ما ترجو أن يصلح به أمرهم. ولا يثقلنّ عليك

____
ن، ش، ي: كذا. م، ه: ﴿إشرافًا﴾.

a high station by your side, such that none of your associates dare to slander him and that he be secure against harm threatened him by prominent men. In sum, be vigilant in your inspection of the dispensation of justice. In recent times, our religion has become a prisoner in the hands of the wicked, who have abused it to further their passions, and who, through it, have sought worldly gain.[1]

2.53.10 Scrutinize the affairs of your administrators. Test people, then employ them. Do not make appointments based on caprice or nepotism, for these two attributes bring together all kinds of oppression and dishonesty. Seek individuals with experience and modesty from virtuous families who have precedence in Islam, for they possess nobler character and greater honor, are less prone to greed, and have keener anticipation of consequences. Award them a generous livelihood, for that will strengthen their prosperity and inhibit them from misappropriation. Moreover, that can also be used to shame them if they disobey your command or breach your trust. Exercise vigilance regarding their activities and send truthful and loyal observers to clandestinely observe what they do. If they know you are keeping an eye on them, this will encourage them to be honest and compassionate toward their subjects. Be watchful too with regard to your aides. If an administrator stretches his hands toward illicit gains, and if all your observers' reports concur, consider their testimony enough to indict. Subject the man to corporeal punishment and chastise him for abusing his authority. Degrade him, brand him as a thief, and garland him with shameful expulsion.

2.53.11 Exercise vigilance in the matter of the land tax and ensure that those who pay it prosper. In its prosperity and in theirs lies the prosperity of all other categories of people. In fact, no one prospers unless taxpayers prosper, for everyone's prosperity depends on the land tax and on those who pay it. Let your concern for the land to thrive be greater than your concern for collecting abundant land tax—the land tax can be collected only when the land thrives. A governor who seeks to collect the land tax without ensuring the land's productivity destroys the country and brings death to the people; moreover, his rule will not last. If the people complain that the tax burden is too heavy, if they complain of blight, or lack of irrigation, or insufficient rain, or if their lands have been inundated by floods, or ruined by drought, you should reduce their

---

1 Ḥ 17:60: the line about religion becoming a prisoner is a criticism of ʿUthmān's judges and governors; in the line, certain particles (*fa-inna … qad kāna*) grammatically denote a recent past.

شيء خفَّفت به المؤونة عنهم فإنّه ذخر يعودون به عليك في عمارة بلادك وتزيين وِلايتك مع ٱستجلابك حسن ثنائهم وتبجّحك بٱستفاضة العدل فيهم معتمدًا فضل قوّتهم بما ذَخَرْتَ عندهم من إجمامك لهم والثقة منهم بما عوّدتهم من عدلك عليهم في رفقك بهم. فربّما حدث من الأمور ما إذا عَوَّلْتَ فيه عليهم من بعد ٱحتملوه طيبة أنفسهم به فإنّ العُمران محتمل ما حمّلته. وإنّما يؤتى خراب الأرض من إعواز أهلها وإنّما يُعْوِزُ أهلها لإشراف أنفس الولاة على الجمع وسوء ظنّهم بالبقاء وقلّة ٱنتفاعهم بالعبر.

2.53.12   ثمّ ٱنظر في حال كتّابك فوَلِّ على أمورك خيرهم وٱخصص رسائلك التي تدخل فيها مكائدك وأسرارك بأجمعهم لوجود صالح الأخلاق ممّن لا تبطره الكرامة فيجترئ بها عليك في خلاف لك بحضرة ملأ ولا تقصّر به الغفلة عن إيراد مكاتبات عمّالك عليك وإصدار جواباتها على الصواب عنك وفيما يأخذ لك ويعطي منك ولا يضعّف عَقْدًا ٱعتقده لك ولا يعجز عن إطلاق ما عقد عليك ولا يجهل مبلغ قدر نفسه في الأمور فإنّ الجاهل بقدر نفسه يكون بقدر غيره أجهل. ثمّ لا يكن ٱختيارك إيّاهم على فِراستك وٱستنامتك وحسن الظنّ منك فإنّ الرجال يتعرّفون لفراسات الولاة بتصنّعهم وحسن خدمتهم ليس وراء ذلك من النصيحة والأمانة شيء ولكن ٱختبرهم بما وَلُوا للصالحين قبلك فٱعمد لأحسنهم كان في العامّة أثرًا وأعرفهم بالأمانة وجهًا فإنّ ذلك دليل على نصيحتك لله ولمن وَليت أمره. وٱجعل لرأس كلّ أمر من أمورك رأسًا منهم لا يقهره كبيرها ولا يتشتّت عليه كثيرها. ومهما كان في كتّابك من عيب فتغابَيتَ عنه أُلزِمتَه.

tax burden and improve their living conditions. Do not let the fact that you had to reduce taxes weigh you down—think of the lost monies as a loan that the farmers will repay manifold by cultivating your lands and enriching your governorate. Besides, you will earn their heartfelt praise and gain great joy yourself when you give them this full measure of justice. You will ensure enough rations for them by providing this relief, while gaining their trust by orienting them to your fairness and compassion. You may need to enlist their support later, and if that happens, they will willingly shoulder the weight—prosperity has the strength to carry whatever burden you load on its back. Conversely, the land is ruined when farmers become destitute, and farmers become destitute when tax collectors become obsessed with collection—this happens when tax collectors think they will live forever,[1] and do not learn from the exemplary lessons of past peoples.

2.53.12 Next: Inspect the abilities of your scribes and put the best of them in charge of your chancery. Entrust the writing of top-secret epistles in which you outline strategies and transcribe confidential information to the scribe who possesses the best character—choose one whom eminence does not embolden to oppose you in public, and whom negligence does not hinder from presenting to you administrative reports, or issuing appropriate responses, or receiving and disbursing funds on your behalf; choose one who does not undercut the agreements he draws up for you, or fail to take down clauses that go against you; choose one who is not ignorant of his own worth, for such a man is even more ignorant of the worth of others. Do not select scribes, moreover, based on casual impression, blind trust, or plain faith. Men deliberately give a certain impression of themselves to rulers by cunning and by ingratiating behavior that is not always supported by sincerity or honesty. Instead, examine the work they have done for virtuous rulers before you, and single out the scribe who has the best reputation among the common people, one whose countenance is recognized by all as trustworthy. If you take this course, you will prove your devotion to God and to the one who has appointed you to govern. Furthermore, appoint a head scribe to lead each of your chancery's operations, and choose someone who will not be overwhelmed by a large project or panic when more than a few matters need attention. Remember this: all of your scribes' faults that you ignore will be attributed to you.

---

1   Lit. "have doubts about remaining" (*sūʾ ẓannihim bi-l-baqāʾ*), translation based on R 3:187; Ḥ 17:73—I prefer this reading because it leads more naturally into the next line about exemplary lessons, which are in these texts a reference to the death of earlier peoples. Alternative translation, "they are afraid they will not remain long in their posts," based on Ḥ 17:73, who gives both explanations; B 903; F 389.

2.53.13 ثمّ آستوصِ بالتجّار وذوي الصناعات وأَوصِ بهم خيرًا المقيم منهم والمضطرب بماله والمترفّق ببدنه فإنّهم موادّ المنافع وأسباب المرافق وجلّابها من المباعد والمطارح في برّك وبحرك وسهلك وجبلك وحيث لا يلتئم الناس لمواضعها ولا يجترئون عليها فإنّهم سِلمٌ لا تُخاف بائقتُه وصلح لا تَخشى غائلته وتفقّد أمورهم بحضرتك وفي حواشي بلادك. وآعلم مع ذلك أنّ في كثير منهم ضيقًا فاحشًا وشُحًّا قبيحًا وآحتكارًا للمنافع وتحكّمًا في البياعات وذلك باب مضرّة للعامّة وعيب على الولاة فآمنع من الاحتكار فإنّ رسول الله صلّى الله عليه وآله منع منه. وليكن البيع بيعًا سَمْحًا بموازين عدل وأسعار لا تُجحِف بالفريقين من البائع والمُبتاع فمن قارف حُكرة بعد نهيك إيّاه فنكّل وعاقب في غير إسراف.

2.53.14 ثمّ اللهَ اللهَ في الطبقة السفلى من الذين لا حيلة لهم والمساكين والمحتاجين والبؤسى والزمنى فإنّ في هذه الطبقة قانعًا ومُعترًّا وآحفظ لله ما آستحفظك من حقّه فيهم وآجعل لهم قِسمًا من بيت مالك وقسمًا من غَلّات صوافي الإسلام في كلّ بلد فإنّ للأقصى منهم مثل الذي للأدنى وكلّ قد آسترعيت حقّه فلا يشغلنّك عنهم بَطَرُ فإنّك لا تُعذَر بتضييع التافه لإحكامك الكثير المهمّ. فلا تُشخِص همّك عنهم ولا تصعِّر خدّك لهم وتفقّد أمور من لا يصل إليك منهم ممّن تقتحمه العيون وتحقره الرجال ففرّغ لأولئك ثقتك من أهل الخشية والتواضع فليرفع إليك أمورهم ثمّ آعمل فيهم بالإعذار إلى الله سبحانه يوم تلقاه فإنّ هؤلاء من بين الرعيّة أحوج إلى الإنصاف من غيرهم وكلٌّ فأعذِر إلى الله تعالى في تأدية حقّه إليه. وتعهّد أهل اليُتم وذوي الرقّة في السنّ ممّن لا

2.53.13 Next: Be good to merchants and artisans and instruct your officers to be good to them as well, including those who reside in your towns, those who travel to sell their wares, and those who profit by physical labor. These workers increase everyone's benefits and provide them with goods. They procure merchandise from isolated and faraway places, from the land and the sea, from the plains and the mountains, from places where people never gather in large numbers and locations where others dare not go. They are peaceful folks from whom no attack is to be feared, docile people from whom no treachery is to be expected. Keep a watch on the prosperity of their affairs in your town as well as in the peripheries of your land. Know also, however, that many merchants can be excessively stingy and monstrously avaricious. They hoard grain and fix prices. These things harm the common people and stain the reputation of rulers. Forbid hoarding, for the Messenger forbade it. Ensure that trading is peaceful, scales are balanced, and prices are set at levels that harm neither buyer nor seller. If someone dares to hoard after you have publicly forbidden it, make an example of him and punish him, but here, too, not in excess.

2.53.14 Beware God's wrath, and never, ever forsake the people of the lowest strata who have no means—the poor, the destitute, the wretched, the suffering, and the disabled. In this category, too, are the beggar and the suppliant.[1] Protect their rights for the sake of God, for he has entrusted them to you. Set aside for them a share from the common treasury and, in every town, a share from the produce of public lands won in battle by the Muslim army. The indigent in far-off lands have the same right as those who live near you; you are responsible for securing the rights of all. Do not let any kind of pomp and ceremony distract you from attending to the needy. You will not be excused for neglecting small petitions, even if you attend assiduously to the large and important ones. Do not repudiate your solicitude for the poor or avert your face from them in contempt. Keep a check on the welfare of those who do not have direct access to you, people whom eyes disdain and men scorn. Appoint a trusted agent, a man who is godfearing and humble, to care for their needs particularly. Have him bring you their concerns and respond to them in a manner that will earn you God's pardon on the day you meet him. Of all your subjects, these are most in need of your justice. Render to each of your subjects his rights in a manner that will earn you God's pardon! Take care of the orphan and the elderly who have no means of support and cannot advocate for themselves.

---

1   Reference to Qur'an, Ḥajj 22:36.

حيلة له ولا يَنصِب للمسألة نفسه وذلك على الولاة ثقيل والحقّ كلّه ثقيل وقد يخفّفه الله على أقوام طلبوا العاقبة فصبروا وثقوا بصدق موعود الله لهم. واجعل لذوي الحاجات منك قِسمًا تُفرِّغ لهم فيه شخصك وتجلس لهم مجلسًا عامًّا فتتواضع فيه لله الذي خلقك وتقعد عنهم جندك وأعوانك من أحراسك وشُرَطك حتى يكلّمك مكلّمهم غير مُتعتِع فإنّي سمعت رسول الله صلّى الله عليه وسلّم يقول في غير موطن ‹لن تُقدَّس أمّة لا يؤخذ للضعيف فيها حقّه من القويّ غير متعتع›. ثمّ احتمل الخُرق منهم والعِيّ ونحِّ عنك الضيق والأنَف يبسط الله عليك بذلك أكناف رحمته ويوجب لك ثواب طاعته وأعط ما أعطيت هنيئًا وامنع في إجمال وإعذار.

2.53.15 ثمّ أمورٌ من أمورك لا بدّ لك من مباشرتها منها إجابة عمّالك بما يَعيا عنه كُتّابك ومنها إصدار حاجات الناس عند ورودها عليك ممّا تَحرَج به صدور أعوانك. وأمْضِ لكلّ يوم عمله فإنّ لكلّ يوم ما فيه.

2.53.16 واجعل لنفسك فيما بينك وبين الله تعالى أفضل تلك المواقيت وأجزل تلك الأقسام وإن كانت كلّها لله إذا صَلَحت فيها النيّة وسلمت منها الرعيّة. وليكن في خاصّة ما تخلص لله به دينك إقامة فرائضه التي هي له خاصّة فأعط الله من بدنك في ليلك ونهارك ووفِّ ما تقرّبت به إلى الله من ذلك كاملًا غير مَثلُوم ولا منقوص بالغًا من بدنك ما بلغ. وإذا قمت في صلاتك للناس فلا تكونن منفّرًا ولا مضيّعًا فإنّ في الناس من به العلّة وله الحاجة وقد سألت رسول الله صلّى الله عليه وآله حين وَجَّهني إلى اليمن كيف أصلّي بهم فقال ‹صَلِّ بهم كصلاة أضعفهم وكن بالمؤمنين رحيمًا›.

This responsibility weighs heavily on rulers, but fulfilling rights is no doubt a weighty responsibility—God lightens the burden for those who seek the hereafter, are patient in adversity, and trust in the truth of God's promise. Set aside a share of your time for petitioners. Attend to them in person, without distractions. Hold public audience and humble yourself therein before your creator. Keep your soldiers, aides, guards, and police officers at a distance, so that people may speak to you freely without anxiously stammering. I have heard the Messenger say on more than one occasion, ⟨A nation in which the weak are not given justice against the strong except by anxiously stammering will never be made holy.⟩[1] Be patient with their coarse language and faltering speech, put aside your prejudice and pride. In return, God will spread for you the wings of his mercy, and decree for you the reward of his obedience. Give whatever you give in a kind and agreeable manner and refuse when you must, with sympathy and apology.

2.53.15 Next: There are certain matters to which you must attend personally. Reply to your administrators when your scribes cannot find a solution. Respond directly to petitions if your aides find them challenging. Get through each day's work that very day—to each day its own tasks.

2.53.16 Next: Reserve the best of your hours, the choicest parts of your time, for your soul's communion with God. Indeed, all your hours and times are spent in devotion to God if your intention is sincere and your subjects secure from your harm. The most important acts of devotion you undertake for God's religion are the mandatory acts of worship, which are for God alone. Offer God your body's worship both night and day. When you offer this worship—the worship that you perform to gain nearness to God—offer it perfectly and completely, not damaged or flawed, and push your body to its limits. When you stand to lead the people in ritual prayer, you should neither disrespect the prayer nor repel the people, for among them there may be some who are ill or disabled.[2] I asked the Messenger when he sent me to Yemen, "How should I lead the prayer?" and he replied, ⟨Pray the prayer of the weakest among them—show compassion to all believers.⟩

---

1   Hadith cited in Abū Nuʿaym, *Ḥilyah*, 7:315.
2   I.e., pray at moderate speed. You should neither "disrespect (lit. 'squander') the prayer" by rushing and not performing the prayer rites as they ought, nor "repel the people" by praying so long that the "ill and disabled" stop coming. B 908; Ḥ 17:90. Similar to § 2.52.

2.53.17 وأمّا بعد هذا فلا تُطوّلَنّ اَحتجابك عن رعيّتك فإنّ اَحتجاب الولاة عن الرعيّة شُعبة من الضيق وقلّة علم بالأمور والاحتجاب منهم يقطع عنهم علم ما اَحتجبوا دونه فيصغر عندهم الكبير ويعظم الصغير ويقبح الحسن ويحسن القبيح ويُشاب الحقّ بالباطل. وإنّما الوالي بشر لا يعرف ما توارى عنه الناس به من الأمور وليست على الحقّ سمات تعرف بها ضروب الصدق من الكذب. وإنّما أنت أحد رجلين إمّا اَمرؤ سخت نفسك بالبذل في الحقّ ففيمَ اَحتجابك من واجب حقّ تعطيه أو فعل كريم تُسديه أو مبتلًى بالمنع فما أسرع كفّ الناس عن مسألتك إذا أيسوا من بَذلك. مع أنّ أكثر حاجات الناس إليك ما لا مؤونة فيه عليك من شَكاة مَظلَمة أو طلب إنصاف في معاملة.

2.53.18 ثمّ إنّ للوالي خاصّة وبطانة فيهم اَستئثار وتطاول وقلّة إنصاف فاَحْسِم مادّة[1] أولئك بقطع أسباب تلك الأحوال ولا تُقطعنّ لأحد من حاشيتك وحامّتك قطيعة ولا يطمعنّ منك في اَعتقاد عقدة تضرّ بمن يليها من الناس في شِرب أو عمل مشترك يحملون مؤونته على غيرهم فيكون مَهْنأ ذلك لهم دونك وعيبه عليك في الدنيا والآخرة. وألزم الحقّ مَن لزمه من القريب والبعيد وكن في ذلك صابرًا محتسبًا واقعًا ذلك من قرابتك وخاصّتك حيث وقع واَبتغ عاقبته بما يثقل عليك منه فإنّ مَغَبّة ذلك محمودة. وإن ظنّت الرعيّة بك حَيفًا فأصحر لهم بعذرك وأعدل عنك ظنونهم باِصحارك فإنّ في ذلك إعذارًا تبلغ فيه حاجتك من تقويمهم على الحقّ.

2.53.19 ولا تدفعنّ صلحًا دعاك إليه عدوّك ولله فيه رضى فإنّ في الصلح دَعَة لجنودك وراحة من همومك وأمنًا لبلادك ولكنّ الحذرَ كلّ الحذر من عدوّك بعد صلحه فإنّ العدوّ ربّما قارب ليتغفّل فخذ بالحزم واتّهم في ذلك حسن الظنّ. وإن عقدت بينك وبين عدوّ لك عقدة أو ألبسته منك ذمّة فحُطّ عهدك بالوفاء واَرْعَ ذمّتك بالأمانة واَجعل نفسك جُنّة دون ما أعطيت فإنّه ليس من فرائض الله شيء الناس أشدّ

2.53.17 And further: Do not withdraw from your subjects for long periods. A ruler's seclusion is a kind of constraint, and it leads to his receiving inadequate information about his subjects' affairs. Likewise, it cuts them off from getting correct information: they soon begin to deem the trivial great and the great trivial, to think the ugly beautiful and the beautiful ugly, and to mix right with wrong. A ruler is human; he does not know what people conceal from him of their affairs; no waymarks distinguish expressions of truth from falsehood so as to enable easy recognition of what is right. So, you can be one of two men: Either you can be someone who gives generously in the way of truth—and if so, why hold back from dispensing a valid right or carrying out an act of generosity in person? Or else you are afflicted with a stingy nature—if that, well, you will see just how soon people stop petitioning you, when they lose hope in your charity! Besides, most petitions do not impose a financial burden. In most cases, they consist of complaints against unfairness or appeals for justice in a transaction.

2.53.18 Next: A ruler has intimates and courtiers who often misappropriate, transgress, or commit acts of injustice. Check their rise by cutting off their access to such acts. Do not award land grants to any of your retinue or relatives. Do not raise their hopes for an estate, because in their exercise of ownership they might harm a neighboring estate's water supply, or there may be common services whose burden they pass on to others. If you award them such grants, the benefits will be theirs and the blame will be yours, in this world and the next. Compel all people to abide by what is right, whether they are near to you or distant. In this, be patient and seek God's reward, no matter how your relatives and intimates react. If any of this should weigh on you, look only to the goal, for its outcome will be admirable. If your subjects should suspect you of an injustice, be open and explain your reasons—deflect their suspicions through your candor. If you explain your reasons, you will attain your objective of keeping them on the path of truth.

2.53.19 Never reject a peace treaty when your enemy calls for peace, if it is a course that pleases God. A peace treaty brings relief to your troops, release from your worries, and security for your lands. But stay wary, utterly wary, of your enemy's treachery. He may have drawn near only because he hopes to make you careless. Act with prudence. Be cautious, not gullible. And if you draw up a truce with your enemy, or if you offer him a covenant of protection, then fulfill your pledge, abide by your pact, and scrupulously protect your agreement. There is nothing among all of God's mandated acts about which people are more united—despite their various leanings and divided views—

عليه اجتماعًا مع تفريق أهوائهم وتشتيت آرائهم من تعظيم الوفاء بالعهود وقد لزم ذلك المشركون فيما بينهم دون المسلمين لما اَستوبَلوا من عواقب الغدر فلا تغدرنّ بذمّتك ولا تخيسَنّ بعهدك ولا تَختِلَنّ عدوّك فإنّه لا يجترئ على الله إلّا جاهل شقيّ وقد جعل الله عهده وذمّته أمنًا أفضاه بين العباد برحمته وحريمًا يسكنون إلى مَنَعَته ويستفيضون إلى جواره فلا إدغال ولا مُدالسة ولا خِداع فيه. ولا تعقد عقدًا تجوز فيه العلل ولا تُعوِلَنّ على لَحن القول بعد التأكيد والتوثقة ولا يدعونّك ضيق أمرٍ لزمك فيه عهد الله إلى طلب اَنفساحه بغير الحقّ فإنّ صبرك على ضيق ترجو اَنفراجه وفضل عاقبته خير من غدرٍ[١] تخاف تبعته وأن تحيط بك من الله فيه طِلبة لا تستقيل فيها دنياك ولا آخرتك.

٢.٥٣.٢٠ إيّاك والدماء وسفكها بغير حِلّها فإنّه ليس شيء أدعى لنقمة ولا أعظم لتبعة ولا أحرى بزوال نعمة واَنقطاع مدّة من سفك الدماء بغير حقّها والله سبحانه مبتدئ بالحكم بين العباد فيما تسافكوا من الدماء يوم القيامة. فلا تقوّينّ سلطانك بسفك دم حرام فإنّ ذلك ممّا يُضعفه ويوهنه بل يزيله وينقله. ولا عذر لك عند الله ولا عندي في قتل العمد لأنّ فيه قَوَد البدن وإن اَبتُليت بخطأ وأفرط عليك سوطك أو يدك بعقوبة فإنّ في الوَكزة فما فوقها مَقتلة. فلا تطمحنّ بك نَخوة سلطانك عن أن تؤدّي إلى أولياء المقتول حقّهم.

٢.٥٣.٢١ وإيّاك والإعجاب بنفسك والثقة بما يعجبك منها وحبّ الإطراء فإنّ ذلك من أوثق فُرَص الشيطان في نفسه ليمحق ما يكون من إحسان المحسن. وإيّاك والمنّ على رعيّتك بإحسانك أو التزيّد فيما كان من فعلك أو أن تعدهم فتتبع موعودك بخلفك فإنّ المنّ يبطل الإحسان والتزيّد يذهب بنور الحقّ والخلُف يوجب المَقت عند الله والناس قال الله سبحانه ﴿كَبُرَ مَقْتًا عِندَ اللهِ أَن تَقُولُوا مَا لَا تَفْعَلُونَ﴾.

---

than the importance they attach to fulfilling a pledge. Not just the Muslims, even idolaters in the past adhered to compacts they had agreed on, because they knew the evil outcome of treachery. Never betray a pledge of protection, never break your covenant, never defraud your enemy. Only a wretched fool dares to transgress against God. God has made his covenant, his pledge of protection, a deed of safe conduct that he, in his mercy, has disseminated among his servants, a haven in whose unassailable strength they can find comfort, and within whose protective shelter they can gather. There should be no malice, no deceit, no treachery in the enaction of a covenant. Do not draw up an agreement and then, after you have concluded and confirmed it, claim loopholes, or rely on misinterpretations to retract. Even if you find the confines of an affair in which God's covenant binds you constricting, you cannot seek an unjust way out. Patience accompanied by hope for relief and a virtuous outcome is far better than deception accompanied by fear of the consequences, the fear of God's all-encompassing reckoning. You will not be able to disavow that deception in this world or the next.

2.53.20 Beware of spilling blood without legal cause. Nothing calls down God's punishment more swiftly, or has graver consequences, or causes God's blessings to be taken away faster, or cuts your allotted lifespan shorter, than spilling blood without legal cause. When God commences judgment among his servants on the day of resurrection, he will begin with cases of spilled blood. Do not attempt to strengthen your hand by spilling forbidden blood, for it will actually weaken and enfeeble your power, in fact, it will rout you and end your rule. You will find no excuse before God or me for willful killing—the punishment for that can be nothing but in-kind reprisal. If by sorry chance you kill someone involuntarily, if your whip or hand go too far when inflicting a punishment and cause death, the blood-wit for a blow with the fist or anything stronger is the one mandated for manslaughter. Do not let the might of your authority embolden you to shirk payment to the family of the man you have accidentally killed.

2.53.21 Beware of self-importance, pomposity, and love of flattery, for that is where Satan is most confident of his opportunity to erase the good deeds of a virtuous man. Beware of keeping tally of the favors you bestow on your subjects,[1] exaggerating your deeds, or making and then breaking a promise. Keeping tally nullifies favors, exaggeration extinguishes the light of truth, and breaking promises earns the outrage of God and men. God has said, «God deems it a great outrage when you say what you do not do.»[2]

---

1 Reference to Qur'an, Baqarah 2:264.
2 Qur'an, Ṣaff 61:3.

2.53.22   إِيَّاك والعَجَلة بالأمور قبل أوانها أو التساقط فيها عند إمكانها أو اللَّجاجة فيها إذا تنكّرت أو الوهن عنها إذا اسْتوضحت فضع كلّ أمر موضعه وأوْقِعْ كلّ عمل موقعه. وإيّاك والاستئثار بما الناس فيه إسوة والتغابي عمّا تعنى به ممّا قد وضح للعيون فإنّه مأخوذ منك لغيرك وعمّا قليل تنكشف عنك أغطية الأمور ويُنتَصف منك للمظلوم. اِملِكْ حَمِيَّة أنفك وسَورة حدّك وسطوة يدك وغَرْب لسانك واحترس من كلّ ذلك بكفّ البادرة وتأخير السطوة حتّى يسكن غضبك فتملك الاختيار ولن تُحكّم ذلك من نفسك حتّى تكثر همومك بذكر المعاد إلى ربّك.

2.53.23   والواجب عليك أن تتذكّر ما مضى لمن تقدّمك من حكومة عادلة أو سنّة فاضلة أو أثر عن نبيّنا صلّى الله عليه وآله أو فريضة في كتاب الله فتقتدي بما شاهدت ممّا عملنا به فيها وتجتهد لنفسك في اتّباع ما عهدت إليك في عهدي هذا واستوثقت به من الحجّة لنفسي عليك لكيلا تكون لك علّة عند تسرّع نفسك إلى هواها.[1]

2.53.24   ومن هذا العهد وهو آخره

وأنا أسأل الله بسعة رحمته وعظيم قدرته على إعطاء كلّ رغبة أن يوفّقني وإيّاك لما فيه رضاه من الإقامة على العذر الواضح إليه وإلى خلقه مع حسن الثناء في العباد وجميل الأثر في البلاد وتمام النعمة وتضعيف الكرامة وأن يختم لي ولك بالسعادة والشهادة إنّا إليه راغبون. والسلام على رسول الله كثيرًا.

2.54   ومن كتاب له عليه السلام إلى طلحة والزبير مع عمران بن الحُصين الخُزاعيّ وذكر هذا الكتاب أبو جعفر الإسكافيّ في كتاب المقامات

أمّا بعد. فقد علمتما وإن كتمتما أنّي لم أُرد الناس حتّى أرادوني ولم أبايعهم حتّى بايعوني

---

[1] م، ش، ن، ه: كذا. ي: كذا، وزيادة في م: أضيفت ﴿فلن يعصم من السوء ولا يوفّق للخير إلّا الله تبارك وتعالى وقد كان فيما عهد إليّ رسول الله صلّى الله عليه وآله في وصاياه تحضيضًا على الصلاة والزكاة وما ملكت أيمانكم. فبذلك أختم لك بما عهدت ولا قوّة إلّا بالله العليّ العظيم﴾.

2.53.22 Beware of rushing into things before their time, or hesitating at the opportune moment, of persistence in the face of ambiguity, or weakness in following through when the facts become clear—place each thing in its rightful place and perform every action in its rightful time. Beware of appropriating property to which the common people possess an equal right, or of feigning ignorance of problems you should handle when they are obvious and plain to see. If you transgress, what is in your hands will be taken away and given to another. Very soon, the veil will be removed, and those you have wronged will obtain justice. Control your prideful passion, your violent anger, your brutal hand, and your cutting tongue. Restrain the blade and delay the strike until your anger abates and you regain control and mastery of your will. Know this: You will not master yourself until you remember that you will return to your Lord.

2.53.23 You should study the methods of just governance used by those who preceded you, their virtuous practices, the traditions of our Prophet, and the mandates of God's Book. You have seen how I have put these principles into practice—emulate me in this. Strive hard to follow the path I have laid out for you in this testament. I trust that I have done my duty to guide you and that your heart has now no excuse to follow its passions.

2.53.24 From this same testament, the final section:
With full trust in God's vast mercy and his power to grant every wish, I beseech him to direct us to do what will please him, what he and his creatures deem good, what earns us praise among his servants and acclaim in his lands, what completes his blessings for us and multiplies his favors. I beseech him to end your days and mine in happiness and martyrdom. In God we place our hopes.[1]
I end with abundant greetings of peace to God's Messenger.

2.54 From 'Alī's letter to Ṭalḥah and Zubayr, sent with 'Imrān ibn al-Ḥusayn al-Khuzāʿī (Abū Jaʿfar al-Iskāfī records it in his Book of Exhortations, *Kitāb al-Maqāmāt*):[2]
Although you deny this now, you know that I did not approach the people until they approached me, you know well that I did not demand their pledge of allegiance until they offered it to me—the two of you were among them, among those who approached me and offered allegiance. You also know well

---

1   Reference to Qurʾan, Tawbah 9:59.
2   Sent just before the Battle of the Camel, outside Basra in 36/656. Text and context in Ibn Aʿtham, *Futūḥ*, 2:465. The full title of Iskāfī's book is *Kitāb al-Maqāmāt fī tafḍīl 'Alī* (The Book of Exhortations Regarding the Superiority of 'Alī). The book is mentioned by Dhahabī, *Siyar*, 10:51, but appears to be lost.

وأنّكما ممّن أرادني وبايعني وأنّ العامّة لم تبايعني لسلطان غاصب[1] ولا لحرص[2] حاضر. فإن كنتما بايعتماني طائعين فأرجعا وتوبا إلى الله من قريب وإن كنتما بايعتماني كارهين فقد جعلتما لي عليكما السبيل بإظهاركما الطاعة وإسراركما المعصية. ولعمري ما كنتما بأحقّ المهاجرين بالتقيّة والكتمان. وإنّ دفعكما هذا الأمر قبل أن تدخلا فيه كان أوسع عليكما من خروجكما منه بعد إقراركما به. وقد زعمتما أنّي قتلت عثمان فبيني وبينكما من تخلّف عنّي وعنكما من أهل المدينة ثمّ يلزم كلّ امرئ بقدر ما احتمل. فأرجعا أيّها الشيخان عن رأيكما فإنّ الآن أعظم أمركما العار من قبل أن يجتمع العار والنار. والسلام.

2.55 ومن كتاب له عليه السلام إلى معاوية

أمّا بعد. فإنّ الله سبحانه جعل الدنيا لما بعدها وابتلى فيها أهلها ليعلم أيّهم أحسن عملًا ولسنا للدنيا خُلِقنا ولا بالسعي فيها أمِرنا وإنّما وُضِعنا فيها لنُبتلى بها. وقد ابتلاني بك وابتلاك بي بجعل أحدنا حجّة على الآخر فعدوت على طلب الدنيا بتأويل القرآن فطلبتني بما لم تَجنِ يدي ولا لساني وعَصَبْتَه أنت وأهل الشام بي وألَّب عالمكم جاهلكم وقائمكم قاعدكم. فاتّق الله في نفسك ونازع الشيطان قيادك واصرف إلى الآخرة وجهك فهي طريقنا وطريقك واحذر أن يصيبك الله بعاجل قارعة تمسّ الأصل وتقطع الدابر فإنّي أولى لك بالله أليّةً غير فاجرة لئن جمعتني وإيّاك جوامع الأقدار لا أزال بباحتك ﴿حَتَّىٰ يَحْكُمَ ٱللَّهُ بَيْنَنَا وَهُوَ خَيْرُ ٱلْحَاكِمِينَ﴾.

---

[1] م، ي، ن، ش: كذا. ه: ﴿غالب﴾. [2] م، ي، ومصحّحة في ه: كذا. ش، ن، وأصل ه، ونسخة في م: ﴿لعرض﴾.

that every last one pledged without coercion or inducement. If the two of you pledged freely, then you must return to the fold and ask God's forgiveness, and you must do so directly. If you pledged unwillingly, then by pretending to obey while masking your intent to disobey, you have given me just cause to march against you. I swear by my life, you have no special rights over the other Emigrants that let your concealed thoughts justify your actions. It would have been far less grave if you had challenged my caliphate before giving the pledge, than doing this—giving the pledge and then breaking it. As for your claim that I killed ʿUthmān: There are men in Medina who have held back from supporting either of us—let those neutral individuals judge the matter between you and me, then, on the basis of their judgment, let each man among us be charged with what he perpetrated. Turn back from this path now, O sheikhs, while the greatest penalty you face is shame—turn back before shame combines with flames! Go in peace.

2.55 From a letter sent by ʿAlī to Muʿāwiyah:[1]
God created this world for the hereafter, and he tests its people to ascertain who among them performs the best of deeds. We have not been created to live in this world, we have not been commanded to strive for this world, we have been placed in it in order to be tested. God has tested me through you, he has tested you through me, and he has made one of us a rightful plaintiff against the other. You transgress in your pursuit of this world, relying on deliberate misinterpretation of the Qurʾan, and hold me responsible for something neither my hand nor my tongue has perpetrated. You and the people of Syria wrap its malicious turban around my head, the learned among you incite the ignorant, those standing incite those sitting.[2] Fear God, Muʿāwiyah, for the sake of your soul, and snatch your halter from Satan's hands! Turn your face to the hereafter, for it is my destination and yours. Beware, lest God strike you with a calamity that will eradicate you and sever your line! I am more worthy than you of swearing an honest oath: By God, if the will of the gathering fates joins us in battle, I shall encamp in your courtyard «until God judges between us—and he is the best of judges»![3]

---

1 Presumably in 36/656, in the lead-up to the Battle of Ṣiffīn, from Kufa to Damascus (see the threat in the last line).
2 "The learned" are Abū Hurayrah, Mughīrah ibn al-Shuʿbah, and others among the Prophet's Companions who supported Muʿāwiyah. "Those standing" are ʿAmr ibn al-ʿĀṣ and Marwān ibn al-Ḥakam. The "ignorant" and "the sitting" are the common people of Syria. F 391; ʿA 703.
3 Qurʾan, Aʿrāf 7:87.

ومن كلام وصّى به شُرَيح بن هاني لـمّا جعله على مقدّمته إلى الشام   2.56

اتّق الله في كلّ صباح ومساء وخَف على نفسك الدنيا الغَرور ولا تأمنها على حال واعلم
أنّك إن لم تَردَع نفسك عن كثير مـمّا تحبّ مخافة مكروهه سمت بك الأهواء إلى كثير من
الضرر فكن لنفسك مانعًا رادعًا ولنَزوَتك عند الحفيظة واقمًا قامعًا.

ومن كتاب له عليه السلام إلى أهل الكوفة عند مسيره من المدينة إلى البصرة   2.57

أمّا بعد. فإنّي خرجت عن حَيّي هذا إمّا ظالـمًا وإمّا مظلومًا وإمّا باغيًا وإمّا مَبغيًّا عليه.
وأنا أذكّر الله مَن بلغه كتابي هذا لـمّا نفر إليّ فإن كنت محسنًا أعانني وإن كنت مسيئًا
استعتبني.

ومن كتاب كتبه عليه السلام إلى أهل الأمصار يقتصّ فيه ما جرى بينه وبين أهل   2.58
صفّين

وكان بدء أمرنا أنّا التقينا والقوم من أهل الشام والظاهر أنّ ربّنا واحد ونبيّنا واحد
ودعوتنا في الإسلام واحدة لا نستزيدهم في الإيمان[1] بالله والتصديق برسوله صلّى الله
عليه وآله ولا يستزيدوننا. الأمر واحد إلّا ما اختلفنا فيه من دم عثمان ونحن منه بُراء
فقلنا تعالوا نداوي ما لا يدرك اليوم بإطفاء النائرة وتسكين العامّة حتّى يشتدّ الأمر
ويستجمع فنقوى على وضع الحقّ في مواضعه فقالوا بل نداويه بالمكابرة.[2] فأبوا حتّى

١ن، ش، ي، ه: كذا. م: ﴿في الإسلام والإيمان﴾.   ٢ن، ش، ي، ه: كذا. م: ﴿بالمكاثرة﴾.

2.56 From instructions ʿAlī gave to Shurayḥ ibn Hānī when he appointed him commander of the vanguard he sent ahead of his army to Syria:[1]

Be conscious of God every morning and every night, beware the snares of this treacherous world, don't trust her ever, at any time, and know that if you don't restrain yourself from many of the things you love, if you don't recognize the damage they can cause, your passions will lead you into terrible harm. Restrain your soul and forbid it from evil. Control your impulse to erupt when enraged and vanquish your fury.

2.57 From a letter by ʿAlī to the people of Kufa when he marched from Medina on Basra:[2]

I have marched from my hometown as either oppressor or oppressed, either treacherous or a target of treachery. I call out in God's name to all whom my letter reaches: Come to me! If I am in the right, support me. If I am in the wrong, berate me.

2.58 From an epistle ʿAlī wrote to the garrison towns, narrating what had taken place between him and those who fought against him at Ṣiffīn:[3]

Events began thus: We and the Syrians faced off, both sides believing in the same God, the same Prophet, and the same call to Islam. We were not attempting to increase their belief in God and his Messenger, and they were not attempting to increase ours, our beliefs were already one. What we differed on was the charge of ʿUthmān's blood, and we were innocent of it. We said to them, "Come, let us approach this objective—which we are not in a position to achieve today—with prudence. Let us first extinguish these burning fires and bring calm to the community. Once we have strengthened our control, we will have the power to disburse justice and put things where they belong." "No!"

---

1 In 36/657 at the camp at Nukhaylah, near Kufa. In Minqarī's version (*Waqʿat Ṣiffīn*, 121–122), the remarks are addressed jointly to Shurayḥ and his co-commander, Ziyād ibn al-Naḍr. § 2.11, § 2.13 are from the same event.

2 In the lead-up to the Battle of the Camel, sent from ʿAlī's camp close by, in Dhū Qār, in 36/656, with his son Ḥasan and ʿAmmār ibn Yāsir. Text and context in Ṭabarī, *Tārīkh*, 4:499–500.

3 From the content, the letter appears to have been written soon after the cessation of hostilities at Ṣiffīn in 37/657, before arbitration results were declared a few months later. The main Muslim garrison cities (*amṣār*, sing. *miṣr*) in ʿAlī's time were Kufa and Basra in Iraq, and Fusṭāṭ in Egypt. Additional cities in Iran and Central Asia could also have been addressed; they were set up to serve the early conquests and by his time had become permanent and important settled towns in the region.

جنحت الحرب وركدت ووقدت نيرانها وحَمِشت فلمّا ضرّستنا وإيّاهم ووضعت مَخالبها فينا وفيهم أجابوا عند ذلك إلى الذي دعوناهم إليه فأجبناهم إلى ما دعوا وسارعناهم إلى ما طلبوا حتّى اَستبانت عليهم الحجّة واَنقطعت منهم المعذرة. فَن تَمّ على ذلك منهم فهو الذي أنقذه الله من الهلكة ومن لَجَّ وتمادى فهو الراكس الذي رانَ الله على قلبه وصارت دائرة السوء على رأسه.

2.59 ومن كتاب له عليه السلام إلى الأسوَد بن قُطبة صاحب جند حُلوان

أمّا بعد. فإنّ الوالي إذا اَختلف هواه منعه ذلك كثيرًا من العدل فليكن أمر الناس عندك في الحقّ سواء فإنّه ليس في الجور عوض من العدل فاَجتنب ما تُنكِر أمثاله واَبتذل نفسك فيما اَفترض الله عليك راجيًا ثوابه ومتخوّفًا عقابه. واَعلم أنّ الدنيا دار بليّة لم يَفرُغ صاحبها قطّ فيها ساعة إلّا كانت فَرغَتُه عليه حسرة يوم القيامة وأنّه لن يغنيك عن الحقّ شيء أبدًا ومن الحقّ عليك حفظ نفسك والاَحتساب على الرعيّة بجهدك فإنّ الذي يصل إليك من ذلك أفضل من الذي يصل بك. والسلام.

2.60 ومن كتاب له عليه السلام إلى العمّال الذين يطأ عملَهم الجيش

they replied, "we shall decide it through combat!" and they refused to budge from this entrenched position, until war spread her wings and settled upon her brood, until her flames crackled and burned hot. When she had chewed both sides with her maw, when she had pierced both sides with her claws, then they came soliciting the course we had proposed earlier. We were nonetheless swift to respond and agreed to their proposal, in a way that made the rightfulness of our claim clear and left them bereft of excuse. God will save all who abide by this realization from perdition, but all who persevere in their wrongdoing will be driven back—God will corrode their hearts, and the wheel of evil fortune will descend on their heads.[1]

2.59 From ʿAlī's letter to al-Aswad ibn Quṭbah, commander of the garrison of Ḥulwān:[2]

A ruler's passions, if they lean in one direction, prevent him from dispensing justice. Let the rights of all people be equal in your eyes, for injustice is never defensible. Stay away from actions you would find deplorable if directed at you. Hope for God's reward and fear his punishment, and exert yourself to undertake his charge. Know that this world is a domain of trial—no man wastes an hour of his time here without regretting it on the day of resurrection. Remember: Nothing can release you from the obligation to do what is right, especially the charge to protect your soul, and to safeguard your subjects to the best of your ability. If you do, the benefit that will come to you is greater than the benefit that will come to them through you.

2.60 From ʿAlī's epistle to administrators whose lands his army would march through:[3]

---

1 Reference to Qurʾan, Nisāʾ 4:88, Muṭaffifūn 83:14, Fatḥ 48:6.

2 This letter could date from any time in ʿAlī's caliphate, 35–40/656–661, after his arrival in Kufa. The identity of the addressee, named here as al-Aswad ibn Quṭbah, is also uncertain. Ibn Abī al-Ḥadīd (Ḥ 17:145) says he was not able to ascertain a genealogy for him, and conjectures that the name may be a mistranscription for al-Aswad ibn Zayd ibn Quṭbah ibn Ghanam al-Anṣārī, from the ʿAdī tribe. Minqarī (*Waqʿat Ṣiffīn*, 106) names the recipient of this letter as al-Aswad ibn Quṭnah. Ibn Mākūlā (*Ikmāl*, 7:283), without any reference to ʿAlī or this letter, mentions a man named Abū Mufazziz al-Aswad ibn Quṭbah, who took part in the conquest of Iraq; Ḥulwān is located today in the Kermanshah province of Iran.

3 Presumably from the camp at Nukhaylah, outside Kufa, on the way to Ṣiffīn in 36/657. Minqarī's version (*Waqʿat Ṣiffīn*, 125) is transcribed by ʿAlī's scribe, Abū Tharwān. "Tax collectors," in the first line, lit., "collectors of the land tax (*kharāj*)."

من عبد الله عليّ أمير المؤمنين إلى من مرّ به الجيش من جُباة الخراج وعمّال البلاد. أمّا بعد.

فإنّي قد سيّرت جنودًا هي مارّة بكم إن شاء الله وقد أوصيتهم بما يجب لله عليهم من كفّ الأذى وصرف الشذى وأنا أبرأ إليكم وإلى ذمّتكم من مَعرّة الجيش إلّا من جوعة المضطرّ لا يجد عنها مذهبًا إلى شِبَعه. فنكّلوا من تناول منهم شيئًا ظلمًا عن ظلمهم وكُفّوا أيدي سفهائكم عن مُضادّتهم والتعرّض لهم فيما آستثنيناه منهم. وأنا بين أظهُر الجيش فآدفعوا إليّ مظالمكم وما عَرَاكم ممّا يغلبكم من أمرهم ولا تطيقون دفعه إلّا بالله وبي أغيّره بمعونة الله إن شاء الله.

2.61 ومن كتاب له عليه السلام إلى كُميل بن زياد النخعيّ وهو عامله على هِيت ينكر عليه تركه دفع من يجتاز به من جيش العدوّ طالبًا للغارة

أمّا بعد. فإنّ تضييع المرء ما وُلّي وتكلّفه ما كُفي لَعجز حاضر ورأي مُتبّر. وإنّ تعاطيك الغارة على أهل قَرقيسيا وتعطيلك مسالحك التي ولّيناك ليس بها من يمنعها ولا يَرُدّ الجيش عنها لَرأي شَعاع. فقد صرت جِسرًا لمن أراد الغارة من أعدائك على أوليائك غير شديد المَنكِب ولا مَهيب الجانب ولا سادٍّ ثُغرة ولا كاسر شوكة ولا مُغنٍ عن أهل مصره ولا مُجزٍ عن أميره.

2.62 ومن كتاب له عليه السلام إلى أهل مصر مع مالك الأشتر رحمه الله لمّا ولّاه إمارتها

2.62.1 أمّا بعد. فإنّ الله سبحانه بعث محمّدًا نذيرًا للعالمين ومهيمنًا على المرسلين فلمّا مضى صلّى الله عليه وآله تنازع المسلمون الأمر من بعده فوالله ما كان يُلقى في رُوعي ولا يخطر ببالي أنّ العرب تُزعِج هذا الأمر من بعده صلّى الله عليه وآله عن أهل بيته ولا أنّهم

From God's servant, ʿAlī, Commander of the Faithful, to the tax collectors and administrators whose lands my army will pass through.

I have dispatched troops who, God willing, will pass through your lands, and I have instructed them to observe what they owe to God, to refrain from causing destruction or any kind of harm. I repudiate before God and before our compact, any violations by the army except in times of hunger when they have no other way to curb its pangs. Punish anyone who seizes something he has no right to, but restrain too the hands of your rash fools from obstructing the troops or challenging them when they take what I have allowed. I am coming up right behind the army, so bring me any complaints of unjust behavior or hardships which you are not able to repel except through God and me. If God wills it and with his help, I shall correct the wrong.

2.61 From ʿAlī's letter to Kumayl ibn Ziyād al-Nakhaʿī, his governor in Hīt, rebuking him for setting out on a raid while failing to defend his own town from enemy forces:[1] A man's neglect of what he has been charged with and his zeal in pursuing what others were charged to do reflects palpable weakness and flawed judgment. Your decision to raid Qarqīsiyā, while leaving open the stronghold you are responsible for with no one to defend it or to repel enemy forces, was a rash decision. You opened the gates for enemies waiting to raid your people.[2] Out in the open, no longer strong shouldered or fearsome of mien, you were rendered powerless to repel a breach or crush an attack, unable to defend your townsfolk or to serve me, your Commander.

2.62 From an epistle ʿAlī sent to the people of Egypt with Mālik al-Ashtar, when he appointed him governor:[3]

2.62.1 God sent Muḥammad as warner for the world and witness to the truth of the Messengers. When he died, the Muslims quarreled over who was to succeed—by God, the thought had never entered my heart, never crossed my mind, that the Arabs would uproot the caliphate from Muḥammad's family,

---

1   From Kufa to Hīt in 39/659, in the wake of Sufyān ibn ʿAwf's raid. Text and context in Balād-hurī, *Ansāb*, 2:473–476. Hīt is a town in northern Iraq on the Euphrates River toward Syria.

2   "You opened the gates," lit., "you became a bridge."

3   From Kufa to Egypt in 38/658. § 2.62.1 is cited by Thaqafī (*Ghārāt*, 1:303–305) as part of a letter ʿAlī wrote to be read out to his followers there after Muḥammad ibn Abī Bakr was killed. Related letters are § 2.38 and § 2.53. "So-and-So" is Abū Bakr, the first Sunni caliph. The apostasy reference is to the so-called Wars of Apostasy (*ḥurūb al-riddah*), where several tribes renounced Islam and/or refused to accept Medina's overlordship, soon after Muḥammad's death.

مُنحّوه عنّي من بعده فما راعني إلّا آنثيال الناس على فلان يبايعونه. فأمسكت يدي حتّى رأيت راجعة الناس قد رجعت عن الإسلام يدعون إلى مَحق دين محمّد صلّى الله عليه وآله فخشيت إن لم أنصر الإسلام وأهله أن أرى فيه ثَلَمًا أو هَدَمًا تكون المصيبة به علَيّ أعظم من فوت وِلايتكم التي إنّما هي متاع أيّام قلائل يزول منها ما كان كما يزول السراب أو كما يتقشّع السحاب فنهضت في تلك الأحداث حتّى زاحَ الباطل وزهق وٱطمأنّ الدين وتنهنه.

2.62.2 ومن هذا الكِّاب

إنّي والله لو لقيتهم واحدًا وهم طِلاع الأرض كلّها ما باليتُ ولا ٱستوحشت وإنّي من ضلالهم الذي هم فيه والهدى الذي أنا عليه لعلى بصيرة من نفسي ويقين من ربّي وإنّي إلى لقاء الله لمشتاق١ ولحسن ثوابه لمنتظر راج ولكنّي آسى أن يلي هذه الأمّة سفهاؤها وفجّارها فيتّخذوا مال الله دُوَلًا وعباده خَوَلًا والصالحين حربًا والفاسقين حزبًا فإنّ منهم الذي شرب فيكم الحرام وجُلد حدًّا في الإسلام وإنّ منهم من لم يسلم حتّى رضخت له على الإسلام الرضائخ فلولا ذلك ما أكثرت تأليبكم وتأنيبكم وجمعكم وتحريضكم ولتركتكم إذ أبيتم ووَنيتم. ألا ترون إلى أطرافكم قد ٱنتقصت وإلى أمصاركم قد ٱفتتحت وإلى ممالككم تُروى وإلى بلادكم تُغزى انفروا رحمكم الله إلى قتال عدوّكم ولا تَثّاقلوا إلى الأرض فتقرّوا بالخَسف وتبوءوا بالذلّ ويكون نصيبكم الأخَسّ. إنّ أخا الحرب الأرِقُ ومن نام لم يُنَم عنه. والسلام.

١م، ي، ه، ومصحّحة في ش و ن: كذا. أصل ش، ن: ﴿لمحتاج﴾.

that they would seize it from me, and I was stunned when people rushed to So-and-So to pledge allegiance. I held back my hand, I withheld my pledge, until I saw that large numbers had apostatized from Islam and were calling for the eradication of Muḥammad's religion. I feared then that if I did not show public support for Islam and its people, I would see it breached or destroyed. That calamity would be far greater than losing my right to rule, a rule whose wares last for a few, short days, then cease to be, as a mirage evaporates or as clouds disperse. I rose to confront those challenges until falsehood ceased and disappeared and religion became calm and still.

2.62.2 From the same epistle:
By God, if I were to face them alone while their legions filled the length of the earth, I would still not feel uneasy or afraid. I know that I am righteous, and my certainty is bequeathed by my Lord. I know that they stray while I walk the path of guidance. I long to meet God, I anticipate and expect his beautiful reward. What grieves me is the thought that this community could be ruled by the rash and depraved who take what belongs to God as their own property, treat his servants like slaves, view the pious as enemies to be struck down and the wicked as allies, whose numbers include men who drank prohibited drinks, who were whipped under the aegis of Islam as punishment for their blatant crime, as well as those who did not accept Islam until they were bought for a paltry sum.[1] If not, I would never go to the trouble to rouse, reprehend, gather, or goad you, but would consign you to your refusal and your tepid response. Do you not see that your borders shrink, your cities are conquered, your territories are seized, and your lands are attacked? March to fight your enemy, may God have mercy on you! Do not sink to the earth in languor, else you acknowledge your shame and accept dishonor, and your share will be the vilest and ugliest of all. The true warrior is ever wakeful. If you sleep, be aware that your enemy does not. Go in peace.

---

1 "Those who drank" refers to Walīd ibn ʿUqbah ibn Abī Muʿīṭ, ʿUthmān's stepbrother and his governor in Kufa (Ḥ 17:227–245—lengthy narrative, after Abū al-Faraj al-Isfahānī and Ibn ʿAbd al-Barr; B 919; F 393), and/or al-Mughīrah ibn Shuʿbah (F 393 again; R 3:226–227). "Those who did not accept Islam until they were bought" by gifts from the Prophet after the Conquest of Mecca, refers to Muʿāwiyah and his father, Abū Sufyān (B 919), also several members of Muʿāwiyah's Umayyad clan (Ḥ 17:226), and/or ʿAmr ibn al-ʿĀṣ (F 393; R 3:227; B 919).

٢٦٣.٢ ومن كتاب له عليه السلام إلى أبي موسى الأشعريّ وهو عامله على الكوفة وقد بلغه عنه تثبيطه الناس عن الخروج إليه لمّا ندبهم لحرب أصحاب الجمل من عبد الله أمير المؤمنين إلى عبد الله بن قيس. أمّا بعد.

فقد بلغني عنك قول هو لك وعليك فإذا قدم عليك رسولي فأرفع ذَيلك وأشدد مِئْزَرَك وأخرج من جُحرك وأندُب من معك. فإن حقّقتَ١ فأنفذ وإن تفشّلت فأبعد وأيم الله لتؤتينّ حيث أنت ولا تُترك حتّى يُخلَط زُبدُك بخاثرك وذائبُك بجامدك وحتّى تُعجَل عن قِعدتك وتُحذَر من أمامك كحذرك من خلفك. وما هي بالهُوَينا التي ترجو ولكنّها الداهية الكبرى يُركب جملها ويُذَلّ صعبها ويسهل جبلها. فأعقل عقلك وأملك أمرك وخذ نصيبك وحظّك فإن كرهت فتنحّ إلى غير رُحب ولا في نَجاة فبالحَرَى لتُكفَينّ وأنت نائم حتّى لا يقال أين فلان والله إنّه لحقّ مع مُحِقّ وما نبالي ما صنع الملحدون. والسلام.

٢٦٤.٢ ومن كتاب له عليه السلام إلى معاوية جواباً عن كتاب منه أمّا بعد. فإنّا كنّا نحن وأنتم على ما ذكرت من الألفة والجماعة ففرّق بيننا وبينكم أمس أنّا آمنّا وكفرتم واليوم أنّا استقمنا وفُتنتم وما أسلم مسلمكم إلّا كرهاً وبعد أن كان أنف

١م، ي، ومصحّحة في ش، ه: كذا. ن، وأصل ش، ه: ﴿خففت﴾.

2.63 From ʿAlī's letter to Abū Mūsā al-Ashʿarī, his governor in Kufa. ʿAlī had sent word to the Kufans soliciting their support against his opponents at the Battle of the Camel, and he learned that Abū Mūsā was actively dissuading them:[1]

From God's servant, Commander of the Faithful, to ʿAbdallāh ibn Qays.

I am told that you have spoken words that go both for you and against you. When my messenger arrives, roll up your sleeves, gird your loins, emerge from your hideout, and urge your townspeople to fight. If you are capable, get going. If you are a coward, stand down. By God, you will be seized wherever you go and pounded until you are creamed and crushed,[2] you will be thrown from your seat, fearing what comes at you from the front and from behind. You are not looking at a trivial protest here but at a grave calamity—its camel stallions must be ridden, its restive beasts must be tamed, its threatening heights must be levelled. Return to your senses, man, regain your command, and take your due share and portion. Or, if you find this repugnant, then step aside and leave, taking with you neither greeting nor safe-conduct—we are better off without you! Sleep on. No one will even ask, "Where is So-and-So?" We are righteous, by God, and on the path of right. We care nothing for what the heretics do. Go in peace.

2.64 From ʿAlī's reply to Muʿāwiyah:[3]

Yes, my clan and yours were on terms of affection and unity, as you say, but what divided us yesterday was our belief and your unbelief, and what divides us today is our right and your wrong. Those of you who accepted Islam did so only because they were forced to, after the foremost Arabians had joined God's Messenger and formed the vanguard of Islam.[4] You claim that I killed Ṭalḥah and Zubayr, threatened ʿĀʾishah, and set up a military base between the two

---

1   From his camp in Dhū Qār to Kufa in 36/656, in the lead-up to the Battle of the Camel, addressing Abū Mūsā by his given name and patronymic, ʿAbdallāh ibn Qays. In response to ʿAlī's earlier message instructing him to recruit, Abū Mūsā had given a speech in which, though acknowledging ʿAlī's caliphate, he cautioned the Kufans against answering ʿAlī's call to fight; he said he had heard the Prophet say there would come a time when it was better to sit back than to fight, and this was that time, because it was not permitted to Muslims to fight their fellow Muslims. ʿAlī sent his letter with his son Ḥasan to Abū Mūsā in Kufa. Ḥasan dismissed Abū Mūsā from his post and recruited the Kufans to join ʿAlī. B 920; Ḥ 17:246.

2   Lit. "… until your cream mixes with your whey, your liquids with your solids."

3   Presumably sent from Kufa to Damascus in 37/657, in the lead-up to the Battle of Ṣiffīn (contains lines similar to § 2.10). See Muʿāwiyah's letter that prompted ʿAlī's response in Ḥ 17:251–256.

4   After having fought the Muslims in the early years, Muʿāwiyah's father, Abū Sufyān, and most of his clan accepted Islam only after the Conquest of Mecca, when a large part of the Arabian Peninsula had come under Muḥammad's control. Abū Sufyān's story in R 3:231–232; B 922.

الإسلام كلّه لرسول الله صلّى الله عليه وآله حزبًا. وذكرت أنّي قتلت طلحة والزبير وشرّدت بعائشة ونزلت بين المِصرَين وذلك أمرٌ غِبتَ عنه فلا عليك ولا العذر فيه إليك. وذكرت أنّك زائري في المهاجرين والأنصار وقد اَنقطعت الهجرة يوم أُسِر أخوك فإن كان فيك عجل فاَستَرِفْهْ فإنّي إن أزرك فذلك جدير أن يكون الله إنّما بعثني للنقمة منك وإن تزرني فكما قال أخو بني أسد[1]

مُسْتَقْبِلِينَ رِيَاحَ الصَّيْفِ تَضْرِبُهُمْ   بِحَاصِبٍ بَيْنَ أَغْـوَارٍ وَجَلْمُودِ

وعندي السيف الذي أعضضته بجدّك وخالك وأخيك في مقام واحد. وإنّك والله ما علمتُ الأغلفُ القلبِ المقاربُ العقلِ والأولى أن يقال لك إنّك رقيت سُلّمًا أطلعك مطلع سوء عليك لا لك لإنّك نشدت غير ضالّتك ورَعَيْت غير سائمتك وطلبت أمرًا لست من أهله ولا في معدنه فما أبعد قولك من فعلك وقريبٌ ما أشبهت من أعمام وأخوال حملتهم الشقاوة وتمنّي الباطل على الجحود بمحمّد صلّى الله عليه فصُرِعوا مصارعهم حيث علمت لم يدفعوا عظيمًا ولم يمنعوا حريمًا بوقع سيوف ما خلا منها الوغى ولم تُماشِها

---

garrison towns.[1] This was an event at which you were not present. Even if an infraction were committed, it was not committed against you, and you are owed no explanation. You threaten to attack me with a group of Emigrants and Allies—in fact, Emigration ended with the battle in which your brother was taken captive.[2] Don't bother to make haste, but get some rest—when I attack you, it will be over. God has sent me to visit his punishment on you. If you attack me now, then it will be as the Asadī tribesman has said:[3]

> They advance into the burning winds of high summer
> As they enter the lowlands,
> it blows dust, and pebbles, and rocks in their faces.

I have the same sword with me now with which I severed the heads of your grandfather, your uncle, and your brother in a single battle,[4] while you, by God—for as long as I have known you—have had a hardened heart,[5] and a deficient mind. Someone should tell you that you have climbed the ladder to a height that shows you an evil time ahead, which will go against you, not for you. You seek another's camels and pasture another's goats, you pursue a thing to which you have no right, that lies in a different quarry than yours. How far your words from your deeds! How close your resemblance to paternal and maternal uncles, who were prompted by their wretched views and unholy desires to challenge Muḥammad! They were killed in battle, as you know only too well, unable to defend themselves against the great calamity that befell them, or to protect their sanctuary from the clash of swords. No battle is empty of sword-thrusts,

---

1 The "two garrison towns" are Kufa and Basra.

2 Lit. "You say you will visit me." The subtext is that there are no Emigrants or Allies among Muʿāwiyah's supporters; that, in fact, Muʿāwiyah, and his associates are all enemies of Islam. The Emigrants, mainly from Mecca, who left their homes and emigrated with Muḥammad to Medina, together with the Allies of Medina, are revered for their early and sincere service to Islam. "The battle" is the Conquest of Mecca, following which Muḥammad said that the chapter of Emigration was now closed; "your brother" is Yazīd ibn Abī Sufyān, who was taken captive in a skirmish just ahead of the Conquest. Ḥ 17:256; F 394. A different and more convoluted explanation is that the "brother" is ʿAmr ibn Abī Sufyān, who was taken captive (by ʿAlī) during the Battle of Badr earlier, and that the "end of Emigration" is not meant literally but denotes Muʿāwiyah's family's enmity for Islam. B 922. A variant reading here (also B 922) is "your father"—i.e., Abū Sufyān—instead of "your brother," and "taken captive" denotes Abū Sufyān's defeat rather than actual capture.

3 Verse attributed to the pre-Islamic poet Bishr ibn Abī Khāzim al-Asadī. Ḥ 18:19.

4 ʿAlī killed Muʿāwiyah's maternal grandfather, ʿUtbah ibn Rabīʿah, his maternal uncle Walīd ibn ʿUtbah, and his brother Ḥanẓalah ibn Abī Sufyān at the Battle of Badr. Ḥ 19:19; B 792/923; R 3:31/234; F 369/394.

5 Reference to Qurʾan, Baqarah 2:88.

الهُوَينا. وقد أكثرت في قتلة عثمان فأدخل فيما دخل فيه الناس ثمّ حاكم القوم إليّ أحملك وإيّاهم على كتاب الله. وأمّا تلك التي تريد فإنّها خُدعة الصبيّ عن اللبن في أوّل الفصال. والسلام لأهله.

2.65 ومن كتاب له عليه السلام إليه أيضًا

أمّا بعد. فقد آن لك أن تنتفع باللَّمح الباصر من عيان الأمور فقد سلكت مدارج أسلافك بادّعائك الأباطيل وإقحامك غرور المَين والأكاذيب وبانتحالك ما قد علا عنك وابتزازك لما اختزُن دونك فرارًا من الحقّ وجحودًا لما هو ألزم لك من لحمك ودمك ممّا قد وعاه سمعك ومُلئ به صدرك. ﴿فَمَاذَا بَعْدَ الْحَقِّ إِلَّا الضَّلَالُ﴾ وبعد البيان إلّا اللَّبس. فاحذر الشبهة واشتمالها على لَبستها فإنّ الفتنة طالما أغدفت جلابيبها وأعشت[1] الأبصار ظلمتها. وقد أتاني كتاب منك ذو أفانين من القول ضعفت قُواها عن السِّلْم وأساطير لم يَحُكها منك علم ولا حلم. أصبحت منها كالخائض في الدَّهاس والخابط في الدَّيماس وترقّيت إلى مَرقَبة بعيدة المَرام نازحة الأعلام تقصر دونها الأنوق ويحاذى بها العَيوق. وحَاشَ لله أن تلي للمسلمين بعدي صَدَرًا أو ورِدًا أو أجري لك على أحد منهم عقدًا أو عهدًا فمن الآن فتدارك نفسك وانظر لها فإنّك إن فرّطت حتّى ينهد إليك عباد الله أُرتِجتْ عليك الأمور ومُنعتَ أمرًا هو منك اليوم مقبول.

<hr>

١ م، ن، ه: كذا. ش: ﴿وأغشت﴾. ي: معًا.

and you will not find these slow in coming! You go on and on about 'Uthmān's killers—enter the fold that all the people have entered, then raise to me your plaint against that group, and I shall settle the matter between them and you according to God's Book. As for your other demand, it is but a toy one gives to an infant to distract him from milk while being weaned.[1] Peace to those who deserve it.

2.65 From another letter sent by 'Alī to Mu'āwiyah:[2]
This is the time for you to understand fully the affairs swiftly unfolding before your eyes and take heed. You walked in the path of your forebears by making false allegations, rushing headlong into the paths of deception and dishonesty, claiming what is above your reach, and plundering what is not meant for you. You fled from the truth and denied something that is closer unto you than your own flesh and blood—words your own ears have heard, and your own breast enfolds.[3] «But what is there after truth save error»,[4] and after clarity save confusion? Beware of suspicion and the doubts that it brings along! Long has sedition spread its cloak and, with its darkness, robbed eyes of sight! I have received a strange letter from you, filled with contradictory utterances, whose supposedly potent points are too weak to forge any kind of peace;[5] in fact, it is stuffed with nonsensical myths that you have clearly not fashioned with any knowledge or maturity. With these proposals, you are like a man sinking into a swamp or stumbling about in a cavern. You attempt to climb a tower that rises beyond your reach, that gives you no waymarks, a tower that is too high even for the soaring kite, as lofty as twinkling Capella. God forbid that after me you should have charge of taking the Muslims to and from their waterhole, or that I should grant you authority now to oversee a single contract or covenant for even one of them![6] Save your soul and look directly to its welfare. If you continue to transgress until God's servants attack you, all your pathways will be blocked. At that time, you will be denied the chance to offer me what I am willing to accept from you today.

---

1 Soon after the Battle of the Camel, Mu'āwiyah demanded that 'Alī confirm him as governor of Damascus, else he would not pledge allegiance. 'Alī characterizes the demand as a cheap ruse. Ḥ 19:21; R 3:235; B 923.

2 Response to Mu'āwiyah's letter (not transcribed in the commentaries) after the Battle of Nahrawān in 38/658, proposing that 'Alī appoint him successor, whereupon he would cease hostilities and pledge allegiance (see also § 2.73). Ḥ 19:27; B 924–925.

3 Refers to the Prophet's numerous hadiths in praise of 'Alī, including the proclamation at Ghadīr Khumm, which made obeying 'Alī incumbent on Mu'āwiyah. Ḥ 19:24–25; B 925.

4 Qur'an, Yūnus 10:32.

5 I translate *silm* as "peace" (following B 924; R 3:243). If we translate *silm* as "being Muslim" (following Ḥ 19:25–26), the line reads: "too weak to have come from a Muslim."

6 The translation is based on B 925; R 3:245.

2.66 ومن كتاب له عليه السلام إلى عبد الله بن العبّاس رحمه الله وقد مضى هذا الكتاب فيما تقدّم بخلاف هذه الرواية

أمّا بعد. فإنّ العبد لَيَفرَح بالشيء الذي لم يكن لِيفوته ويحزن على الشيء الذي لم يكن ليصيبه فلا يكن أفضل ما نِلتَ في نفسك من دنياك بلوغُ لَذّة أو شفاء غَيظ ولكن إطفاء باطل أو إحياء حقّ.١

2.67 ومن كتاب كتبه عليه السلام إلى قُثَم بن العبّاس رحمه الله وهو عامله على مكّة

أمّا بعد. فأقم للناس الحجّ وذكِّرهم بأيّام الله وآجلس لهم العصرَين فأفْتِ المستفتي وعلِّم الجاهل وذاكِر العالم. ولا يكن لك إلى الناس سفير إلّا لسانك ولا حاجب إلّا وجهك ولا تحجبنّ ذا حاجة عن لقائك بها فإنّها إن ذِيدَت عن أبوابك في أوّل وِردها لم تُحمد فيما بعد على قضائها. وآنظر إلى ما آجتمع عندك من مال الله فآصرفه إلى من قِبَلَك من ذي العيال والمَجاعة مصيباً به مواضع المَفاقر والخَلَّات وما فضل عن ذلك فآحمله إلينا لنقسمه فيمن قِبَلَنا. ومُرْ أهل مكّة ألّا يأخذوا من ساكن أجرًا فإنّ الله سبحانه يقول ﴿سَوَاءً الْعَاكِفُ فِيهِ وَالْبَادِ﴾ فالعاكف المقيم به والبادي الذي يحُجّ إليه من غير أهله. وفّقنا الله وإيّاكم لمَحابّه. والسلام.

2.68 ومن كتاب له عليه السلام إلى سلمان الفارسيّ رحمه الله قبل أيّام خلافته صلوات الله عليه

أمّا بعد. فإنّ مَثَل الدنيا مَثَل الحَيّة لَيّن مَسُّها قاتل سَمُّها فأعرِض عمّا يعجبك فيها لقلّة ما يصحبك منها وضع عنك همومها لما أيقنت به من فراقها وكُن آنَس ما تكون بها أحذر ما تكون منها فإنّ صاحبها كلّما آطمأنّ فيها إلى سرور أشخصته عنه إلى محذور.٢

―――――――――

١م، ش، ن، ه: كذا. ي: كذا، ونسخة في هامش ه: أضيفت ﴿وليكن سرورك بما قدّمت وأسفك على ما خلّفت وهمّك فيما بعد الموت﴾. ٢ن، م، ش: كذا. ي: كذا، ه، وزيادة في هامش ش، م: أضيفت ﴿وإلى إيناس أزاله عنه إيحاش﴾.

2.66 From 'Alī's letter to 'Abdallāh ibn al-'Abbās (this letter was recorded earlier with slightly different wording):[1]
A man is overjoyed by gaining a thing he was not going to lose and grieved by the loss of a thing he was not going to gain. The choicest thing your soul takes from your life in this world should not be a pleasure indulged or a revenge achieved, but the obliteration of a wrong or the restoration of a right.

2.67 From a letter sent by 'Alī to Qutham ibn al-'Abbās, his governor in Mecca:[2]
Lead the hajj among the people and remind them to revere these, God's special days. Hold audience every morning and evening, and explain legal rulings to the inquirer, teach the ignorant, and discourse with the knowledgeable. Your tongue should be your only ambassador, your face your only chamberlain. Do not conceal yourself from any petitioner who wants to present his petition—if a petitioner is driven away from your door when he first approaches, you will not be thanked for a subsequent response. Keep an eye on goods belonging to God that have accumulated in your jurisdiction—disburse them among the destitute and the starving in your land, those who are beset with poverty and need; whatever remains, send it to me so that I may distribute it among the people here. Forbid the people of Mecca from charging rent to pilgrims, for God has said, «its resident and the foreigner are equal»[3]—a resident is one who lives there permanently, and a foreigner is someone who has come for the pilgrimage. May God direct you and me both to perform the deeds that he loves. Go in peace.

2.68 From 'Alī's letter to Salmān al-Fārisī, before the time of his caliphate:[4]
This world is like a snake—it is soft to the touch, but its venom is lethal. Turn away from its attractions, for it will be with you only a short while. Shrug off its cares, for you know you will soon depart. Beware of it most when you are most comfortable in it. For each time the dweller finds himself happy in a joyful event, it hurls him toward something he had feared.

---

1 § 2.22, see note there.
2 From Kufa to Mecca in 38/659, when 'Alī deputed Qutham to lead the pilgrimage. Ṭabarī, *Tārīkh*, 5:132.
3 Qurʾan, Ḥajj 22:25.
4 'Umar appointed Salmān as governor of Madāʾin, near present-day Baghdad; he died there around the end of 'Uthmān's reign in 35/655. Hārūnī (*Taysīr*, 506) says 'Alī's letter was in response to Salmān's letter asking him, "I fear that I may lean toward worldliness, so counsel me!"

2.69   ومن كتاب له عليه السلام إلى الحارث الهمدانيّ

وتمسّك بحبل القرآن واستنصحه وأحِلَّ حلاله وحرّم حرامه.

وصدّق بما سلف من الحقّ واعتبر بما مضى من الدنيا ما بقي منها فإنّ بعضها يشبه بعضًا وآخرها لاحق بأوّلها وكلّها حائل مفارق.

وعَظِّم اسمَ الله أن تذكره إلّا على حقّ.

وأكْثِر ذكر الموت وما بعد الموت ولا تَتَمَنَّ الموت إلّا بشرط وثيق.

واحذر كلّ عمل يرضاه صاحبه لنفسه ويكره لعامّة المسلمين واحذر كلّ عمل يُعمل به في السرّ ويُستحيى منه في العلانية واحذر كلّ عمل إذا سئل عنه صاحبه أنكره أو اعتذر منه.

ولا تجعل عِرضك غرضًا لنبال القول.

ولا تحدّث الناس بكلّ ما سمعت فكفى بذلك كذبًا ولا تردّ على الناس كلّ ما حدّثوك به فكفى بذلك جهلًا

واكظِم الغَيْظ واحلُم عند الغضب وتجاوز عند القدرة واصفح مع الدولة تكن لك العاقبة.

واستصلح كلّ نعمة أنعمها الله عليك ولا تُضيعنّ نعمة من نعم الله عندك ولْيُرَ عليك أثرُ ما أنعم الله به عليك.

واعلم أنّ أفضل المؤمنين أفضلهم تَقدِمةً من نفسه وأهله وماله وأنّك ما تقدّم من خير يَبقَ لك ذخره وما تؤخّريكن لغيرك خيره.

واحذر صحابة من يَفِيل رأيه وينكر عمله فإنّ الصاحب مُعتبَر بصاحبه.

واسكن الأمصار العظام فإنّها جماع المسلمين واحذر منازل الغفلة والجفاء وقلّة الأعوان على طاعة الله.

واقْصُرْ رأيَك على ما يَعنيك. وإيّاك ومَقاعد الأسواق فإنّها محاضرُ١ الشيطان ومَعاريض الفتن.

<hr>

١ م، ش، ي، هـ: كذا. ن: ‹محاصر›.

2.69 From a letter sent by ʿAlī to al-Ḥārith al-Hamdānī:
Hold fast to the Qurʾan and embrace its counsel. Deem licit what it deems licit and deem illicit what it deems illicit.

Believe in the true messages brought in bygone times,[1] and apply the lessons you learn from the past to what is yet to come. One time resembles another, and the last will catch up with the first—then all of it will end and be gone.

Exalt the name of God, do not invoke it save in truth.[2]

Contemplate death and what comes after death. Don't wish for death without surety.[3]

Beware of every deed that a man finds pleasing when he does it, but hateful when other Muslims do it. Beware of every deed that a man does in private and is ashamed of in public. Beware of every deed that a man denies when asked about it or for which he offers excuses.

Don't let your honor become a target for the arrows of scandal.

It is a sufficient mark of falsehood that you pass on everything you hear, a sufficient mark of ignorance that you dispute everything you are told. Don't venture there!

Swallow your rage, be patient in times of anger, forgive when you could punish, and pardon when you have power.[4] Do this, and the outcome will be good.

Be grateful for each blessing God has bestowed. Don't squander any of God's blessings. Let the marks of God's blessings be manifest on your person.[5]

Know that the most generous of believers is the most generous in presenting his life, his family, and his property to God. The treasury of deeds you present will remain in safekeeping for you, the benefits of deeds you hold back will accrue to others.

Beware of keeping company with those of unsound judgment and evil deeds—a man is judged by the company he keeps.

Live in large towns, for that is where Muslims gather. Beware of camps where rashness and vulgarity prevail, where there are few allies in obedience to God.

Confine your opinions to things that concern you.

Beware of loitering in the marketplace—it is Satan's home and the place where seditions shoot their arrows.

---

1 I.e., the missions of past prophets. B 927; Ḥ 18:43.
2 Reference to Qurʾan, Baqarah 2:224.
3 I.e., don't wish for death unless you are sure your deeds will gain you entry to paradise. Ḥ 18:44; B 928. Reference to Qurʾan, Jumʿah 62:6–7.
4 Reference to Qurʾan, Āl ʿImrān 3:134.
5 Reference to Qurʾan, Ḍuḥā 93:11.

وأكثرْ أن تنظرَ إلى من فُضّلتَ عليه فإنّ ذلك من أبواب الشكر.

ولا تسافرْ في يوم جمعة حتّى تشهد الصلاة إلّا فاصلًا في سبيل الله أو في أمرٍ تُعذر به.

وأطع الله في جُمَل أمورك فإنّ طاعة الله فاضلة على ما سواها.

وخادِعْ نفسك في العبادة وأرفُقْ بها ولا تقهرها وخذ عَفْوها ونشاطها إلّا ما كان مكتوبًا عليك من الفريضة فإنّه لا بدّ من قضائها وتعاهدها عند محلّها.

وإيّاك أن ينزل بك الموت وأنت آبق من ربّك في طلب الدنيا.

وإيّاك ومُصاحبة الفُسّاق فإنّ الشرّ بالشرّ مُلحَق.

ووَقِّر الله وأحبب أحبّاءه.

واحذر الغضب فإنّه جند عظيم من جنود إبليس.

والسلام.

2.70   ومن كتاب له عليه السلام إلى سَهل بن حُنَيف الأنصاريّ وهو عامله على المدينة في معنى قوم من أهلها لحقوا بمعاوية

أمّا بعد. فقد بلغني أنّ رجالًا ممّن قِبَلَك يتسلّلون إلى معاوية فلا تأسف على ما يفوتك من عددهم ويذهب عنك من مَددهم فكفى لهم غَيًّا ولك منهم شافيًا فِرارهم من الهدى والحقّ وإيضاعهم إلى العمى والجهل. وإنّما هم أهل دنيا مقبلون عليها ومُهطعون إليها قد عرفوا العدل ورأوه وسمعوه ووَعوه وعلموا أنّ الناس عندنا في الحقّ إِسْوَة فهربوا إلى الأَثَرَة فبُعْدًا لهم وسُحقًا. إنّهم والله لم ينفروا من جور ولم يلحقوا بعدل. وإنّا لنطمع في هذا الأمر أن يذلّل الله لنا صعبه ويسهّل لنا حَزنه إن شاء الله. والسلام عليك.

2.71   ومن كتاب له عليه السلام إلى المُنذِر بن الجارود العبديّ وقد خان في بعض ما ولّاه من أعماله

Always think about those who have less—that door leads to gratitude.

Do not commence a journey on Friday until after the prayer, unless it is to fight in God's path, or for another urgent matter.

Obey God in all that you do, for that is more important than anything else.

Coax your heart to worship God but be gentle and do not force its compliance—take advantage of it when it first awakens and enjoys its moments of fresh vigor. The exception is the case of mandated acts—these must be performed with regularity at the prescribed times.

Beware lest death seize you while you are fleeing from your Lord in pursuit of the world.

Beware of keeping company with the depraved—vice is drawn to vice.

Extol God, and love those whom he loves.

Beware of anger, for it is one of Iblīs's most powerful battalions.

Go in peace.

2.70 From a letter sent by ʿAlī to Sahl ibn Ḥunayf al-Anṣārī, his governor in Medina, about a group of Medinans who had defected to join Muʿāwiyah:[1]
I have learned that men from your town are stealing out to join Muʿāwiyah. Do not grieve over the loss of their numbers or supplies! Their flight from true guidance, their haste toward blind ignorance, proves their waywardness and shows that you are well rid of them. They are worldly people, stretching their necks toward wealth and power. They personally experienced my justice—they saw it, heard it, understood it, and realized that all are equal before me in claiming their rights—and they fled from this toward nepotism! Let them go far away and yet farther! By God, they did not leave to escape from injustice or to arrive at justice! I beseech God to make the recalcitrant camel docile and the rough ground smooth. God willing, it will happen. Go in peace.

2.71 From ʿAlī's letter to al-Mundhir ibn al-Jārūd al-ʿAbdī, whom he had appointed tax collector in a certain district, after Mundhir had embezzled treasury funds:[2]

---

1 Sahl was ʿAlī's governor in Medina for a short while in 36/656, before the Battle of the Camel, and if the letter is addressed to him, then it was sent from Iraq at that time; it is possible that some people left Medina for Damascus immediately after ʿAlī left for Iraq, in the lead-up to the Battle of the Camel, and the references to witnessing ʿAlī's fairness fit well with the steps he took to level stipends immediately upon assuming the caliphate. Or, if there is an error in naming Sahl as the recipient, the letter could be from after the Battle of Ṣiffīn in 37/657.

2 Presumably sent from Kufa to Iṣṭakhr, in Fars, where Mundhir was tax collector or governor sometime during ʿAlī's caliphate, 35–40/656–661. Text and context in Balādhurī, *Ansāb*, 2:163–164. The follow-up lines about Mundhir were spoken by ʿAlī to Ṣaʿṣaʿah ibn Ṣūḥān in Kufa. Yaʿqūbī, *Tārīkh*, 2:204.

أمّا بعد. فإنّ صلاح أبيك غرّني منك وظننت أنّك تتبع هَدْيه وتسلك سبيله فإذا أنت فيما رُقّي إليّ عنك لا تدع لهواك اَنقيادًا ولا تُبقي لآخرتك عَتادًا تعمر دنياك بخراب آخرتك وتصل عشيرتك بقطيعة دينك. ولئن كان ما بلغني عنك حقًّا لَجمَلُ أهلِك وشِسعُ نَعلِك خير منك ومن كان بصفتك فليس بأهل أن يُسَدَّ به ثغر أو ينفذ به أمر أو يعلى له قدر أو يشرك في أمانة أو يؤمن على خيانة. فأقبِل إليّ حين يصل إليك كتابي هذا إن شاء الله.

والمنذر هذا هو الذي قال فيه أمير المؤمنين عليه السلام
إنّه لَنظّارٌ في عِطفَيه مختال في بُردَيه تَفّال في شِراكَيه.

2.72 ومن كتاب له عليه السلام إلى عبد الله بن العبّاس رحمه الله
أمّا بعد. فإنّك لست بسابق أجلك ولا مرزوق ما ليس لك. واعلم بأنّ الدهر يومان يوم لك ويوم عليك وأنّ الدنيا دارُ دُوَل فما كان منها لك أتاك على ضعفك وما كان منها عليك لم تدفعه بقوّتك.

2.73 ومن كتاب له عليه السلام إلى معاوية
أمّا بعد. فإنّي على التردّد في جوابك والاستماع إلى كتابك لَموهَّنٌ رأيي ومخُطَّئ فِراستي وإنّك إذ تحاولني الأمور وتراجعني السطور كالمستثقل النائم تكذبه أحلامه أو المتحيّر القائم يبهَظه مقامه لا يدري ألَهُ ما يأتي أم عليه ولست بك غير أنّه بك شبيه. وأقسم بالله

I was deceived about you by your father's piety—I thought you would follow his guidance and walk his path. According to what I have learned, however, you neither pull against passion's halter, nor put aside provisions for the next world—you adorn your abode in this world by demolishing your home in the hereafter, you strengthen bonds of gift-giving with kin by severing the bonds of your faith. If what I am told about you is true, your family's mangy pack-camel and your sandal's frayed thong are more valuable than you! Someone with your immoral character cannot be expected to fill a breach or carry out a command, he cannot be raised in station, given partnership in matters of responsibility, or trusted not to embezzle. Come to me when my letter, God willing, reaches you.

Raḍī: Mundhir is the one about whom the Commander of the Faithful also said: He looks at himself in glee, preens in his pretty robes, and shines his sandal straps with his spittle.

2.72   From ʿAlī's letter to ʿAbdallāh ibn al-ʿAbbās:[1]
You will not exceed your lifespan or be granted sustenance that is not yours. Know that life alternates between two days—one day is for you, another day is against you. The world is an abode of change—whatever is decreed for you will come despite your weakness, whatever is decreed against you cannot be repelled by your strength.

2.73   From ʿAlī's letter to Muʿāwiyah:[2]
I attribute to weak judgment and flawed acumen the fact that I exchanged letters with you in the first place and listened to your epistles at all! When you make such demands of me and repeat such lines, you are like a man deep in slumber who dreams false dreams, or like one who stands perplexed, not knowing whether the future will be for or against him! If you are not that man, then that man certainly resembles you! I swear this by God: If I did not have good reasons to hold my tongue, you would have received evidence from it damning

---

1   Possibly part of the same letter sent from Kufa to Mecca in 40/661, parts recorded as §2.22 (see note there), §2.41, and §2.66.

2   Presumably from Kufa to Damascus after the arbitration in 37/658, in the context of Muʿāwiyah's demand that ʿAlī make him successor (similar themes in §2.65). "Listened (*istimāʿ*) to your epistles" signals the practice of official epistles being read out in a public setting; see also §2.1.

لولا بعض الاستبقاء لوصلت إليك منّي نوازع١ تَقرع العَظم وتَهلِس٢ اللحم. واعلم أنّ الشيطان قد ثبّطك عن أن تراجع أحسن أمورك وتأذن لمقال نصيحك.٣ والسلام.

٢٫٧٤ ومن حِلف كتبه عليه السلام بين اليمن وربيعة نُقل من خطّ هشام بن الكلبيّ

هذا ما اجتمع عليه أهل اليمن حاضرها وباديها وربيعة حاضرها وباديها أنّهم على كتاب الله يدعون إليه ويأمرون به ويجيبون من دعا إليه وأمر به لا يشترون به ثمنًا ولا يرضون به بدلًا وأنّهم يد واحدة على من خالف ذلك وتركه أنصار بعضهم لبعض دعوتهم٬ واحدة. لا ينقضون عهدهم لمَعتبة عاتب ولا لغضب غاضب ولا لاستذلال قوم قومًا ولا لمَسبّة قوم قومًا. على ذلك شاهدهم وغائبهم وحليمهم وجاهلهم. ثمّ إنّ عليهم بذلك عهد الله وميثاقه .

وكتب عليّ بن أبي طالب.

٢٫٧٥ ومن كتاب له عليه السلام إلى معاوية من المدينة في أوّل ما بويع له وذكره الواقديّ في كتاب الجمل

من عبد الله عليّ أمير المؤمنين إلى معاوية بن أبي سفيان. أمّا بعد. فقد علمت إعذاري فيكم

١ش، ن، ي، هـ: كذا. م، ونسخة في هـ: ﴿قوارع﴾.   ٢م، ي، ومصحّحة في هـ: كذا. ن، وأصل هـ، ومصحّحة في ش، ونسخة في ي: ﴿تلهس﴾. نسخة ثالثة في ي، هـ: ﴿تنهس﴾.   ٣ش، هـ: كذا. م، ي: ﴿نصيحتك﴾. ن: ﴿فصيحك﴾.   ٤م، ي، ونسخة في ش، هـ: كذا. ن، وأصل ش، هـ، ونسخة في ي: ﴿دعوة﴾.

enough to crush bones and consume flesh![1] But know this: It is Satan who prevents you from returning to a better way, or from listening to the words of a sincere counselor. Go in peace.

2.74 From a treaty of alliance that ʿAlī concluded between the people of Yemen and the tribe of Rabīʿah (copied here from a script in the hand of Hishām Ibn al-Kalbī):[2] This is what the people of Yemen, both its townspeople and its countrydwellers, and the tribe of Rabīʿah, both its townspeople and its countrydwellers, have agreed upon: They will follow God's Book—they will call to it and command by it, and answer those who call to it and command by it; they will not betray it for a price or accept another in its place; they will act as one hand against all who oppose or abandon it. They will support one another—their mission will be one. They will not break their pledge, even if one tribesman hurls rebuke, rage, humiliation, or abuse at another. This agreement has hereby been accepted by all present as well as those absent, mature elders as well as impetuous youths. They are bound to it through God's pledge, to which all are accountable.[3]

Written by ʿAlī ibn Abī Ṭālib.

2.75 From ʿAlī's letter to Muʿāwiyah from Medina, when allegiance was first pledged to him as caliph. (It is recorded by Wāqidī in the Book of the Camel, *Kitāb al-Jamal*):[4] From God's servant, ʿAlī, Commander of the Faithful, to Muʿāwiyah ibn Abī Sufyān.

You know that I was justified both in my efforts for your clan and in turning away from them, until that which was going to happen, that which could not be repelled, came to pass.[5] The story is long and there is much to be said, but

---

1   Ibn Abī al-Ḥadīd (Ḥ 17:65) explains that ʿAlī had witnesses to the fact that the Prophet had cursed Muʿāwiyah as a hypocrite destined for hellfire, and that he chose not to make this information public for fear of Muʿāwiyah's false retaliation.

2   Rabīʿah and Yemen signify North and South Arabia respectively. Hishām ibn Muḥammad ibn al-Sāʾib al-Kalbī (= Ibn al-Kalbī) (d. 206/821) is the famous genealogist, whose grandfather, Sāʾib fought alongside ʿAlī in the Battles of the Camel and Ṣiffīn. Ibn al-Kalbī is the compiler of a lost book titled *Khuṭab ʿAlī* (Orations of ʿAlī, Ibn al-Nadīm, *al-Fihrist*, 125). The treaty would have been concluded some time in ʿAlī's caliphate in Kufa, 35–40/656–661.

3   Reference to Qurʾan, Isrāʾ 17:34.

4   In 35/656.

5   The reference is to ʿAlī's efforts to negotiate between ʿUthmān, who was from Muʿāwiyah's Umayyad clan, and the group of Muslims who had come to Medina demanding his resignation and who eventually killed him (Ḥ 18:67; B 932). Another, to me less convincing, reading (R 3:258) is that the reference is to ʿAlī's efforts to appease Muʿāwiyah when ʿAlī first became caliph.

وإعراضي عنكم حتّى كان ما لا بدّ منه ولا دفع له والحديث طويل والكلام كثير وقد أدبر ما أدبر وأقبل ما أقبل. فبايع مَن قِبلَك وأقبل إليّ في وَفد من أصحابك. والسلام.

2.76 ومن وصيّته عليه السلام لعبد الله بن العبّاس عند ٱستخلافه إيّاه على البصرة

سَع[1] الناس بوجهك ومجلسك وحكمك. وإيّاك والغضب فإنّه طِيَرَةٌ من الشيطان. وٱعلم أنّ ما قرّبك من الله يباعدك من النار وما باعدك من الله يقرّبك من النار.

2.77 ومن وصيّته له عليه السلام لمّا بعثه للاحتجاج على الخوارج

لا تخاصمهم بالقرآن فإنّ القرآن حَمّالٌ ذو وجوه تقول ويقولون ولكن حاجّهم[2] بالسنّة فإنّهم لن يجدوا عنها مَحيصًا.

2.78 ومن كتاب له عليه السلام إلى أبي موسى الأشعريّ جوابًا في أمر الحَكَمين ذكره سعيد ٱبن يحيى الأمويّ في المغازي

فإنّ الناس قد تغيّر كثير منهم عن كثير من حظّهم فمالوا مع الدنيا ونطقوا بالهوى. وإنّي نزلت من هذا الأمر منزلًا مُعجبًا ٱجتمع به أقوام أعجبتهم أنفسهم فأنا أداوي منهم قَرْحًا أخاف أن يعود[3] عَلَقًا. وليس رجل فأعلم أحرص على جماعة أمّة محمّد وألفتها منّي أبتغي بذلك حسن الثواب وكرم المآب وسأفي بالذي وأيت على نفسي وإن تغيّرتَ عن صالح

‏‏١ن، ش، ي، ه، ونسخة في م: كذا. وأصل م: ﴿مَتِّع﴾.   ‏٢ش، م، ي، ه: كذا. ن: ﴿خاصِمهم﴾.   ‏٣م، ي، ومصحّحة في ش: كذا. ن، ه، وأصل ش: ﴿يكون﴾.

what has passed has passed, and what is coming is coming. Take the pledge of allegiance for me, then, from your townspeople, and come to me here with a delegation of your associates. Go in peace.

2.76 From 'Alī's counsel to 'Abdallāh ibn al-'Abbās when 'Alī departed from Basra, and appointed Ibn al-'Abbās to remain there as governor:[1]
Be generous with your attention, your audiences, and your judgment. Beware of anger, for it is a surge of rashness prompted by Satan. Know that whatever takes you closer to God takes you away from the Fire, and whatever takes you away from God takes you closer to the Fire.

2.77 From 'Alī's counsel to 'Abdallāh ibn al-'Abbās when he sent him to debate the Kharijites:[2]
Don't argue with them on the basis of the Qur'an, for the Qur'an can be interpreted in many ways—you will say something, and they will say something else. Debate with them instead with the Sunnah, for there they will find no escape.

2.78 From 'Alī's letter to Abū Mūsā al-Ash'arī, replying to him in the matter of the arbitrators (recorded by Sa'īd ibn Yaḥyā al-Umawī in his book The Expeditions, *al-Maghāzī*):[3]
The state of the people is such that many have bartered away most of their allotted share,[4] they sway with the world's swaying and speak from sheer caprice. In the matter at hand, I am astonished that my camp has become a gathering place for the conceited and the disobedient. I treat the wound they have inflicted,[5] but fear that it might suddenly spurt blood again. There is no man—and you should know this—who is more concerned than I am to maintain unity and affection among Muḥammad's community. I seek only God's

---

1　In 36/656, after the Battle of the Camel. Mufīd, *Jamal*, 223–224, after Wāqidī.

2　Soon after the Battle of Ṣiffīn in 37/657, when the Kharijites faulted 'Alī for accepting the arbitration and encamped at Ḥarūrāʾ. Context in Ṭabarī, *Tārīkh*, 5:73.

3　In the lead-up to arbitration at Dūmat al-Jandal in 37/657–658. Abū Mūsā al-Ash'arī was the arbitrator from 'Alī's side, and 'Amr ibn al-'Āṣ from Mu'āwiyah's. This letter signals 'Alī's distrust of Abū Mūsā. Ḥ 18:75.

4　I.e., of religion and the hereafter.

5　Refers to both the arbitration with Mu'āwiyah, which a group of 'Alī's own army forced him to accept, even though they were on the verge of victory, and the choice of Abū Mūsā as the arbitrator from their side, who was not loyal to 'Alī. See also § 2.63.

ما فارقتني عليه فإنّ الشقيّ مَن حُرِم نفع ما أوتي من العقل والتجربة. وإنّي لَأَعْبُدُ[1] أن أقول قائلٌ بباطل وأن أُفسد أمرًا قد أصلحه الله. فدَع ما لا تعرف فإنّ شِرار الناس طائرون إليك بأقاويل السوء.

زيادة على الأصل[2]

2.79   ومن كتاب له عليه السلام لمّا استخلف إلى أمراء الأجناد

أمّا بعد. فإنّما أهلك من كان قبلكم أنّهم منعوا الناس الحقّ فاشترَوه وأخذوهم بالباطل فاقتدَوه.

---

[1] م، ي، ه: كذا. ن، ش: ﴿لَأَعِيد﴾.   [2] أضيفت هنا في جميع المخطوطات زيادة على الأصل، وهي عبارة عن كتاب آخر لعليّ مسبوق في مخطوطة ه ومخطوطة ل بسطر يشير الى أنّه زيادة على أصل الرضيّ: ﴿زيادة من نسخة كتبت على عهد المصنّف﴾. والكتاب ساقط عن متن مخطوطة م، وأضيفت في الهامش. وهو مثبت في متون مخطوطة ي، ش، ن من غير إشارة إلى أنّها زائدة.

pleasing reward and an honorable return to him, and I shall remain true to my pledge, even if you move away from the position that you held when you left here. The true wretch is the person who is deprived from using his own intelligence and experience, and I refuse to let anyone speak what is wrong or to blight a matter that God has resolved. Don't heed false suspicions—the foulest of men are racing to you now, carrying wicked rumors.

Additional Letter[1]

2.79   From a missive 'Alī wrote to governors of the garrison towns when he became caliph:

Governors before you were destroyed by this: They denied the people their rights, so the people were forced to purchase them. They ruled the people unjustly, and the people emulated their injustice.

---

1   An additional letter—perhaps added by Raḍī, or by others—is transcribed in all our primary and secondary *Nahj al-Balāghah* manuscripts (further details in the Edition's footnotes, and in Note on the Edition and Translation).

باب المختار من حكم أمير المؤمنين عليه السلام ومواعظه
ويدخل في ذلك المختار من أجوبة مسائله والكلام القصير الخارج في سائر أغراضه

3.1 قال عليه السلام: كن في الفتنة كابن اللَّبُون لا ظهرٌ فيُركب ولا ضَرعٌ فيُحلَب.

3.2 وقال عليه السلام
أزرى بنفسه من استشعر الطَّمَع ورضي بالذلّ من كشف ضرّه وهانت عليه نفسه من أمّر عليها لسانه.

والبخل عارٌ والجبن مَنقصة والفقر يُخرس الفَطِن عن حجّته والمُقِلّ غريب في بلدته.

والعجز آفة والصبر شجاعة والزهد ثروة والورع جُنّة ونعم القرين الرضى.

والعلم وراثة كريمة والآداب حُلَل مُجدّدة والفكر مِرآة صافية.

وصدر العاقل صُندوق سرّه.

والبَشاشة حِبالة المودّة والاحتمال قبر العيوب.

وروي أنّه عليه السلام قال في العبارة عن هذا المعنى أيضًا: المُسالَمَة خَبء العيوب.

ومن رضي عن نفسه كثر الساخط عليه.

والصدقة دواء مُنجِح.

وأعمال العباد في عاجلهم نَصْبَ أعينِهم في آجلهم.

3

Sayings

Chapter containing selections from the Commander of the Faithful's wise sayings and words of counsel, including selections from his answers to questions and short texts from all genres of his literary production

3.1 In times of sedition, be like a young camel buck—no back to be ridden, no udders to be milked.[1]

3.2 To wear the robe of greed is to degrade yourself. To reveal your troubles to others is to humiliate yourself. To let your tongue control you is to demean yourself.[2]

Stinginess is a vice, cowardice is a defect, poverty strikes a clever man dumb, and a pauper is an exile in his hometown.

Incapacity is a calamity, forbearance is a form of courage, renunciation is a treasure, restraint is a shield, and acceptance of God's will is the best companion.

Knowledge is a noble legacy, refined behavior is like new clothing, and thought is a polished mirror.

A wise man's heart is a vault for his secrets.

Cheerfulness is a snare for friendship, forbearance is a tomb for shortcomings.

Raḍī: It is also narrated that ʿAlī said similarly: Conciliation is a tomb for flaws.

The smug invite detractors.

Almsgiving is powerful medicine.

Believers' deeds in this world will be placed before them in the hereafter.

---

1 Ar. *ibn al-labūn*, lit. "the son of a lactating camel mare," referring to a buck that has just reached two years of age—his mother has had another foal and is again producing milk—he has no udders because he's male and his back is weak because he's young. ʿAlī advises his followers to be shrewd in times of conflict, so that despotic rulers are not able to harness their support for evil acts or bully them (Ḥ 18:82; B 935; R 3:267; F 397). From ʿAlī's counsel to his son Ḥasan (Majlisī, *Biḥār*, 74:234).

2 The sayings in § 3.2 are from ʿAlī's counsel to Ashtar. Ḥarrānī, *Tuḥaf*, 201–202.

3.3 وقال عليه السلام: اِعجَبوا لهذا الإنسان ينظر بشَحم ويتكلّم بلَحم ويسمع بعَظم ويتنفّس من خُرم.

3.4 وقال عليه السلام: إذا أقبلت الدنيا على أحد أعارته محاسن غيره وإذا أدبرت عنه سلبته محاسن نفسه.

3.5 وقال عليه السلام: خالِطوا الناس مُخالَطة إن مُتّم معها بكَوا عليكم وإن عِشتم¹ حَنّوا إليكم.

3.6 وقال عليه السلام: إذا قدرت على عدوّك فاًجعل العفو عنه شكرًا للقدرة عليه.

3.7 وقال عليه السلام: أعجز الناس من عجز عن اًكتساب الإخوان وأعجز منه من ضيّع من ظفر به منهم.

3.8 وقال عليه السلام في الذين اًعتزلوا القتال معه خذلوا الحقّ ولم ينصروا الباطل.

3.9 وقال عليه السلام: إذا وصلت إليكم أطراف النعم فلا تنفّروا أقصاها بقلّة الشكر.

3.10 وقال عليه السلام: من ضيّعه الأقرب أُتيح له الأبعد.

3.11 وقال عليه السلام: ما كُلّ مفتون يُعاتَب.

---

¹م، ي، ه، ومصحّحة في ش: كذا. ن، وأصل ش: ﴿غبتم﴾.

3.3 Behold the wonder of the human! He sees with a bit of fat, speaks with a piece of flesh, hears with a shard of bone, and breathes through a tiny hole!

3.4 When the world smiles at a person, it lends him the good qualities of others. When it turns away from him, it snatches from him his own.[1]

3.5 Associate with people in such a manner that they cherish your company while you live and weep for your loss when you die.[2]

3.6 If you succeed in subduing your enemy, thank God by forgiving the man.

3.7 The most incapable person in the world is the one who is incapable of making friends. Even more incapable than he, though, is the person who loses the friends he has made.

3.8 ʿAlī said this about the men who sat out the battles during his reign:[3]
They abandoned right, while not aiding wrong.

3.9 If the harbingers of God's blessings reach you, don't drive away the favors yet to come with a lack of gratitude.

3.10 A man who is shunned by those close to him will find help from distant strangers.

3.11 Not every deluded person can be chastised.[4]

---

1   I.e., when a person's luck is in, people attribute to him qualities he doesn't have, but when his luck is out, they don't give him credit for the qualities he does have.

2   Or, per the variant reading in MSS N and Sh, "they long for you when you are absent (*ghibtum*, vs. *ʿishtum*), and weep for your loss when you die." From ʿAlī's deathbed counsel to his children (Sibṭ, *Tadhkirah*, 142; Ṭūsī, *Amālī*, 209). I have switched the two phrases around in the translation for more idiomatic English.

3   These were the prominent Medinans ʿAbdallāh ibn ʿUmar, Saʿd ibn Abī Waqqāṣ, Saʿīd ibn Zayd, Usāmah ibn Zayd, Muḥammad ibn Maslamah, and Anas ibn Mālik (Ḥ 18:115; text and context in Ṭūsī, *Amālī*, 83). According to some commentators, they also include the Kufans Abū Mūsā al-Ashʿarī and Aḥnaf ibn Qays (B 939; F 402).

4   Interpreted as (1) a reference to the prominent Medinans who refused to support ʿAlī against the associates of the Camel (Ḥ 18:119; Mufīd, *Jamal*, 46; names in note to § 3.8), or (2) a general observation on human nature (F 401; B 938).

3.12 وقال عليه السلام: تَذِلّ الأمور للمقادير حتّى يكون الحَتف في التدبير.

3.13 وسئل عليه السلام عن قول النبيّ صلّى الله عليه وآله ﴿غَيِّروا الشَّيب ولا تشبّهوا باليهود﴾.
فقال عليه السلام
إنّما قال صلّى الله عليه وآله ذلك والدين قُلٌّ فأمّا الآن وقد اتّسع نِطاقه وضرب بِجِرانه
فآمرؤٌ وما اختار.

3.14 وقال عليه السلام: من جرى في عِنان أمله عَثر بأجله.

3.15 وقال عليه السلام: أقيلوا ذوي المُروّات عثراتهم فما يعثر منهم عاثرٌ إلّا ويده بيد الله
يرفعه.

3.16 وقال عليه السلام: قُرنت الهيبة بالخيبة والحياء بالحرمان.
والفرصة تمُرّ مَرّ السحاب فآنتهزوا فُرص الخير.

3.17 وقال عليه السلام: لنا حقّ فإن أُعطيناه وإلّا ركبنا أعجاز الإبل وإن طال السُّرى.

وهذا من لطيف الكلام وفصيحه ومعناه أنّا إن لم نُعطَ حقّنا كّا أذلّاء وذلك أنّ الرديف يركب
عَجُز البعير كالعبد والأسير ومن يجري مجراهما.

3.18 وقال عليه السلام: من أبطأ به عمله لم يسرع به حسبه.

3.19 وقال عليه السلام: من كفّارات الذنوب العظام إغاثة الملهوف والتنفيس عن
المكروب.

3.12   Affairs bow to the fates—sometimes planning leads to death.[1]

3.13   ʿAlī was asked about the Prophet's words, ⟨Dye your white hair and don't emulate the Jews⟩, to which he answered:[2]
The Prophet said this when Muslims were few. Now that Islam has loosened its halter and laid its withers flat on the ground, let every man decide for himself.

3.14   Whoever gallops forward, giving the rein to his hopes, will be hurled into the pit of death.

3.15   Forgive good people their mistakes—when one of them slips, God takes his hand and helps him to rise.

3.16   The timid will falter, the meek will lose their share.
   Opportunity passes like a cloud, so seize every opportunity for good.

3.17   We have a right. If it is given to us, good. If not, we will ride the camel's rump through the long night.[3]

Raḍī: This statement is among the most refined and eloquent of expressions, and it means that when we are not given our due, we are being dishonored; that is because a pillion rider rides on the camel's rump, as does a slave, or captive, or another person of lowly status.

3.18   If your deeds are slow, your lineage will not take you far.[4]

3.19   To console the heartbroken and comfort the grieving is to atone for the gravest sins.

---

1   In an address to the Persian emperor's daughter Shāh Zanān (= Shahr Banū) after her capture, ca. 17/638 (Mufīd, *Irshād*, 1:302). Similar to §3.426.

2   The hadith is cited by, e.g., Ibn Ḥanbal, *Musnad*, §1415. The command is for men to dye white hair black in battle and pertains to the importance of appearing young and strong in order to instill fear in the enemy (Ḥ 18:122; B 939; R 3:269; F 402). The metaphor of the camel relaxing indicates Islam's expansion and firm establishment.

3   The sources place these words by ʿAlī in Medina, either (1) immediately after the death of the Prophet, in 11/632, when Abū Bakr was sworn in as caliph (Ḥ 18:133, citing the Twelver Shiʿa interpretation); or (2) in ʿAlī's oration to the Shūrā Election Council, following the death of ʿUmar, in 23/644 (Ṭabarī, *Tārīkh*, 4:236; Māmaṭīrī, *Nuzhah*, 327–328; full text in both; Ḥ 18:133).

4   The line is attributed to the Prophet in Ibn Ḥanbal, *Musnad* 2:252; Ibn ʿAbd Rabbih, *ʿIqd*, 2:148; Rāzī, *Mafātīḥ*, 3:573.

3.20 وقال عليه السلام: يا ٱبن آدم إذا رأيت ربّك سبحانه يتابع عليك نعمه فاَحذره.

3.21 وقال عليه السلام: ما أضمر أحد شيئًا إلّا ظهر في فَلَتات لسانه وصفحات وجهه.

3.22 وقال عليه السلام: اِمشِ بِدائك ما مشى بك.

3.23 وقال عليه السلام: أفضل الزهد إخفاء الزهد.

3.24 وقال عليه السلام: إذا كنت في إدبار والموت في إقبال فما أسرع المُلتقى.

3.25 وقال عليه السلام: الحذرَ الحذرَ فوالله لقد ستر حتّى كأنّه قد غفر.

3.26 وسئل عليه السلام عن الإيمان فقال

الإيمان على أربع دعائم على الصبر واليقين والعدل والجهاد. فالصبر منها على أربع شُعَب
على الشوق والشَّفَق والزهد والترقُّب فمن ٱشتاق إلى الجنّة سلا عن الشهوات ومن أشفق
من النار ٱجتنب المحرّمات ومن زهد في الدنيا ٱستهان بالمصيبات ومن ٱرتقب الموت
سارع إلى الخيرات. واليقين منها على أربع شعب على تبصرة الفطنة وتأوُّل الحكمة
وموعظة العبرة وسنّة الأوّلين فمن تبصّر في الفطنة تبيّنت له الحكمة ومن تبيّنت له الحكمة
عرَف العبرة ومن عرَف العبرة فكأنّما كان في الأوّلين. والعدل منها على أربع شعب على
غائص الفهم وغَور العلم وزَهرة الحُكم ورَساخة الحلم فمن فهم علم غور العلم ومن علم غور

3.20 Son of Adam! When your Lord's blessings keep coming, be on guard![1]

3.21 When a person conceals something in his heart, it shows in the slips of his tongue and the planes of his face.

3.22 If you fall ill, get on with your life as best as you can.

3.23 Rejection of worldliness is best done in secret.

3.24 How soon the meeting when you retreat and death presses forward!

3.25 Fear God and beware! I swear he has concealed for so long you think he has forgiven!

3.26 ʿAlī was asked about faith, and he expounded:[2]
Faith stands on four pillars: forbearance, conviction, justice, and struggle against evil. Forbearance has four branches: longing, fear, rejection of worldliness, and patient expectation. Whoever longs for paradise is diverted from indulging passions, whoever fears hellfire retreats from forbidden things, whoever rejects worldliness makes light of calamities, and whoever awaits death hastens to do good. Conviction also has four branches: sagacious perceptivity, interpreting divine wisdom, heeding the counsel offered by history's lessons, and following the practice of those who went before. Whoever perceives with sagacity recognizes divine wisdom, whoever recognizes divine wisdom heeds history's lessons, and whoever heeds history's lessons has lived with those who went before. Justice, in its turn, has four branches: deep understanding, profound knowledge, blossoms of wisdom, and deep-rooted restraint. Whoever understands gains profound knowledge, whoever gains profound knowledge

---

1 I.e., if you continue to be ungrateful and disobey God while still enjoying his blessings, beware his retribution, which will surely come (F 403). Some later MSS and commentaries (Ḥ 18:136 and B 940) make this subtext explicit by adding to the text, "while you continue to disobey him" (*wa-anta taʿṣīhi*).

2 Excerpt from oration delivered in his home, either in Medina or Kufa, additional parts recorded as §1.69, §1.103 (further details in note there), §3.259. Alternatively, the text is cited as an answer given during an oration in the mosque in Basra, a few days after the Battle of the Camel in 36/656 (Māmaṭīrī, *Nuzhah*, 225–227), where the questioner is named as ʿAbbād ibn Qays (another version, which conforms more directly to the version here, is also recorded in ibid., 198–199). Other parts of the same oration (ibid., 221–233) are listed in note to §1.23. On this text, see Qutbuddin, "Piety and Virtue in Early Islam: Two Sermons by Imam Ali."

العلم صدر عن شرائع الحكم ومن حلم لم يفرط في أمره وعاش في الناس حميدًا. والجهاد منها على أربع شعب على الأمر بالمعروف والنهي عن المنكر والصدق في المواطن وشنآن الفاسقين فمن أمر بالمعروف شدّ ظهور المؤمنين ومن نهى عن المنكر أرغم أنوف المنافقين ومن صدق في المواطن قضى ما عليه ومن شَنِئ الفاسقين وغضب لله غضب الله له وأرضاه يوم القيامة.

والكفر على أربع دعائم على التعمّق والتنازع والزيغ والشقاق فمن تعمّق لم يُنِب إلى الحقّ ومن كثر نزاعه بالجهل دام عماه عن الحقّ ومن زاغ ساءت عنده الحسنة وحسنت عنده السيّئة وسَكِرَ سُكرَ الضلالة ومن شاقّ وَعُرت عليه طرقه وأعضل عليه أمره وضاق مخرجه. والشكّ على أربع شعب على التماري والهَول والتردّد والاستسلام فمن جعل المِراء دَيْدَنًا لم يصبح ليله ومن هاله ما بين يديه نكص على عقبيه ومن تردّد في الريب وطئته سَنابِك الشياطين ومن اَستسلم لهلكة الدنيا والآخرة هلك فيهما.

وبعد هذا كلام تركتُ ذكره خوف الإطالة والخروج عن الغرض المقصود في هذا الكّاب.

3.27   وقال عليه السلام: فاعل الخير خير منه وفاعل الشرّ شرّ منه.

3.28   وقال عليه السلام: كن سَمْحًا ولا تكن مُبذِّرًا وكن مُقدِّرًا ولا تكن مُقتِّرًا.

3.29   وقال عليه السلام: أشرف الغنى ترك المُنى.

3.30   وقال عليه السلام: من أسرع إلى الناس بما يكرهون قالوا فيه ما لا يعلمون.

3.31   وقال عليه السلام: من أطال الأمل أساء العمل.

advances on the path of wisdom, and whoever possesses restraint shuns extremes in his affairs and lives among people loved and respected. Struggle against evil similarly has four branches: commanding good, forbidding evil, valor in battle, and abhorring the corrupt. Whoever commands good strengthens the believers' backs, whoever forbids evil cuts off the hypocrites' noses, whoever shows valor in battle has discharged his duty, and whoever abhors the corrupt and is roused to anger for the sake of God, so too will God be roused to anger on his behalf, and, on the day of resurrection, will make him truly happy.

Unbelief stands on four pillars: overthinking, fractiousness, deviation, and rebellion. Whoever overthinks misses what is right, whoever constantly disputes remains blind to the truth, whoever deviates deems good to be evil and evil to be good until he becomes intoxicated by his errant ways, and whoever rebels finds his way rugged, his affairs straitened, and his escape blocked. Doubt also has four branches: skepticism, dread, vacillation, and surrender. Whoever makes skepticism his practice finds that his night never brightens into day, whoever dreads what is ahead turns back on his heels, whoever is suspicious and vacillates is trampled by devils' hooves, and whoever surrenders to the perishing forces of this world and the next perishes in both.

Raḍī: There is text after this that I have omitted, for fear of being prolix or going beyond the book's goals.

3.27 The doer of a good deed is better than the deed itself. The doer of an evil deed is worse than the deed itself.

3.28 Be generous without being extravagant. Be thrifty without being stingy.

3.29 The most honorable wealth is abandoned desire.[1]

3.30 If you are quick to say bad things about people, they will make up things about you.

3.31 Long hopes, foul deeds.

---

1   Identical line in § 3.195.

3.32   وقال عليه السلام وقد لقيه عند مسيره إلى الشام دَهاقين الأنبار فترجّلوا له وَاشتدّوا بين يديه ما هذا الذي صنعتموه فقالوا خُلُق منّا نُعظِّم به أمراءنا فقال عليه السلام والله ما ينتفع بهذا أمراؤكم وإنّكم لَتُشُقّون به على أنفسكم وتَشقَون به في آخرتكم وما أخسر المشقّة وراءها العقاب وأربح الدعة معها الأمان من النار.

3.33   وقال لأبنه الحسن عليهما السلام

يا بُنَيّ احفظ عنّي أربعًا وأربعًا لا يضرّك ما عملتَ معهنّ إنّ أغنى الغنى العقل وأكبر الفقر الحُمق وأوحش الوحشة العُجب وأكرم الحسب حسن الخلق. يا بُنَيّ إيّاك ومُصادقةَ الأحمق فإنّه يريد أن ينفعك فيضرّك وإيّاك ومصادقة البخيل فإنّه يَقعُد عنك أَحْوَج ما تكون إليه وإيّاك ومصادقة الفاجر¹ فإنّه يبيعك بالتافه وإيّاك ومصادقة الكذّاب فإنّه كالسَّراب يقرّب عليك البعيد ويُبعد عليك القريب.

3.34   وقال عليه السلام: لا قربة بالنوافل إذا أضرّت بالفرائض.

3.35   وقال عليه السلام

لسان العاقل وراء قلبه وقلب الأحمق وراء لسانه.

وهذا من المعاني العجيبة الشريفة والمراد به أنّ العاقل لا يطلق لسانه إلّا بعد مُشاورة الرويّة ومؤامرة الفكرة والأحمق تَسبق خَذَفات لسانه وفَلَتات كلامه مراجعة فكره ومماخضة رأيه. فكأنّ لسان العاقل تابع لقلبه وكأنّ قلب الأحمق تابع للسانه. وقد روي عنه عليه السلام هذا المعنى بلفظ آخر وهو قوله ﴿قلب الأحمق في فيه ولسان العاقل في قلبه﴾ ومعناهما واحد.

---

¹ م، ي، ه، ومصحّحة في ش: كذا. ن، وأصل ش: ﴿العاجز﴾.

3.32 At Anbar, during 'Alī's march to Syria, its landowners and merchants came out to meet him, and when they reached him, they dismounted and began to run ahead of his mount on foot. He asked, "What is it you are doing?" and they answered, "This is our custom—it is our way of showing respect to our rulers." 'Alī responded:[1]

By God, this behavior does not benefit your rulers at all! All you are doing is causing suffering to yourself while earning wretchedness for the hereafter. O how great the loss when suffering is followed by punishment! How great the profit when ease is followed by freedom from hellfire!

3.33 'Alī said to his son Ḥasan:[2]

My dear son, remember four things from me, and four things more—nothing will harm you as long as you follow them. The best wealth is intelligence, the greatest poverty is foolishness, the loneliest alienation comes from conceit, and the noblest lineage is good character. My dear son, beware of befriending a fool—he wants to help you but will harm you. Beware of befriending a miser—he will hold back from helping you when you need him most. Beware of befriending a wanton—he will sell you out for a trifle. Beware of befriending a liar—he is like a mirage that makes near what is distant and makes distant what is near.

3.34 Supplementary acts of worship bring no reward if they cause you to neglect mandatory ones.[3]

3.35 'Alī said:

A sage's tongue is located behind his heart, a fool's heart is located behind his tongue.

Raḍī: This is among the most wondrous and noblest of concepts. The point is that an intelligent man doesn't allow his tongue free rein until after consulting with his mind and conferring with his reason, while the pebbles flung by the fool's tongue and the blunders of his speech race out of his mouth without being reviewed by his reason or assessed by his thought. The intelligent man's tongue follows his heart, while the fool's heart follows his tongue. The aphorism has also been narrated from 'Alī in a variant rendering, thus: ⟨A fool's heart is located in his mouth, a sage's tongue is located in his heart.⟩ The meaning of both versions is the same.

---

1   In 36/656, during the march toward Ṣiffīn. Anbar is in northern Iraq, and the merchant family is named as the Banū Khushnūshak (Persian name). Text and context in Minqarī, *Waqʿat Ṣiffīn*, 143–144.

2   This text is among 'Alī's deathbed counsels to Ḥasan. Māmaṭīrī, *Nuzhah*, 182–183, Hārūnī, *Taysīr*, 563, Quḍāʿī, *Dustūr*, 100–101, Ibn ʿAsākir, *Tārīkh*, 42:561.

3   Similar to § 3.271.

٣٦.٣ وقال عليه السلام لبعض أصحابه في علّة اعتلّها

جعل الله ما كان من شكواك حَطًّا لسيّئاتك. فإنّ المرض لا أجر فيه ولكنّه يُحُطُّ السيّئات ويَحُتّها حَتَّ الأوراق وإنّما الأجر في القول باللسان والعمل بالأيدي والأقدام. وإنّ الله سبحانه يُدخل بصدق النيّة والسريرة الصالحة من يشاء من عباده الجنّة.

وأقول صدق عليه السلام إنّ المرض لا أجر فيه لأنّه من قَبيل ما يُستحقّ عليه العِوض لأنّ العوض يستحقّ على ما كان في مقابلة فعل الله تعالى بالعبد من الآلام والأمراض وما يجري مجرى ذلك. والأجر والثواب يُستَحَقّان على ما كان في مقابلة فعل العبد. فبينهما فرق قد بيّنه عليه السلام كما يقتضيه علمه الثاقب ورأيه الصائب.

٣٧.٣ وقال عليه السلام في ذكر خَبّاب بن الأَرَتّ رحمه الله

يرحم الله خبّابًا فلقد أسلم راغبًا وهاجر طائعًا وعاش مجاهدًا. طوبى لمن ذكر المعاد وعمل للحساب وقنِع بالكَفاف ورضي عن الله.

٣٨.٣ وقال عليه السلام: لو ضربتُ خَيشوم المؤمن بسيفي هذا على أن يُبغِضني ما أبغضني ولو صببت الدنيا بجَمّاتها على المنافق على أن يحبّني ما أحبّني وذلك أنّه قُضِي فأنقضى على لسان النبيّ الأمّيّ أنّه قال ﴿لا يبغضك مؤمن ولا يحبّك منافق﴾.

3.36 'Alī said to an associate who had been taken ill:[1]
May it please God to make your suffering decrease your burden of sin! Illness, while it does not earn you reward, decreases your sins, making them fall off like leaves in the Fall. Reward, on the other hand, is earned through words spoken by tongues, and actions performed by hands and feet. Nevertheless, God willingly admits into paradise all his servants who possess true intentions and pious hearts.

Raḍī: 'Alī is absolutely correct when he says that illness earns no reward, for it belongs to the category of things that are requited, and requital operates in cases of God's actions toward his servant, such as suffering, illness, and their like. Reward and recompense, on the other hand, operate in cases of God's servant's actions. There is clearly a difference between the two categories, which 'Alī explains with penetrating knowledge and precise judgment.

3.37 'Alī prayed for Khabbāb ibn al-Aratt:[2]
May God have mercy on Khabbāb! He accepted Islam with joy, emigrated in obedience to his Lord, and lived his life fighting for the truth. Blessed is he who contemplates the return to God, does good in anticipation of judgment, contents himself with basic rations, and accepts God's will.

3.38 Were I to strike a believer on the bridge of his nose with my sword, an action that should cause him to hate me, he will not hate me. Were I to shower the riches of the world on a hypocrite, an action that should prompt him to love me, he will not love me. This is because it was proclaimed, and thus decreed, on the tongue of our Meccan Prophet, who said, ⟨No believer will hate you, 'Alī, and no hypocrite will love you⟩.[3]

---

1 In 37/657, on the return from Ṣiffīn, within view of Kufa. The addressee was an old man named Ṣāliḥ ibn Sulaym from the tribe of Salāmān ibn Ṭayy, a follower of 'Alī, who apologized that his illness had kept him from accompanying 'Alī to battle—note the last line comforting Ṣāliḥ, reassuring him that his good intention had earned him paradise. Text and context in Minqarī, *Waqʿat Ṣiffīn*, 528–529.

2 Also in 37/657, on the return from Ṣiffīn, just outside Kufa. 'Alī enquired about the graves he saw there and was told that one was the grave of Khabbāb, a venerable Companion of the Prophet and 'Alī's supporter, who had died after 'Alī left for Ṣiffīn. Text and context in Minqarī, *Waqʿat Ṣiffīn*, 530–531; Ṭabarī, *Tārīkh*, 5:61–62. 'Alī's address to the people of those graves in §3.119.

3 From an oration in Kufa, after the Battle of Nahrawān, around 39–40/659–661, attempting to mobilize the Kufans to fight Muʿāwiyah. Text and context in Ḥ 2:195–196 (within their commentary on §1.34 of present volume; see my note there). "The Meccan Prophet," lit. "the *ummī* Prophet," see note at §1.151.2.

3.39 وقال عليه السلام: سيّئة تسوءك خير عند الله من حسنة تعجبك.

3.40 وقال عليه السلام: قدر الرجل على قدر همّته وصدقه على قدر مُروّته وشجاعته على قدر أَنَفته وعِفّته على قدر غَيرته.

3.41 وقال عليه السلام: الظفر بالحزم والحزم بإجالة الرأي والرأي بتحصين الأسرار.

3.42 وقال عليه السلام: احذروا صَولة الكريم إذا جاعَ واللئيم إذا شَبِع.

3.43 وقال عليه السلام: قلوب الرجال وحشيّة فمن تألّفها أقبلت عليه.

3.44 وقال عليه السلام: عيبك مستور ما أسعدك جَدُّك.

3.45 وقال عليه السلام: أَولى الناس بالعفو أقدرهم على العقوبة.

3.46 وقال عليه السلام: السخاء ما كان ابتداءً فأمّا ما كان عن مسألة فحياء وتذمُّم.

3.47 وقال عليه السلام: لا غنى كالعقل ولا فقر كالجهل ولا ميراث كالأدب ولا ظهير كالمُشاورة.

3.48 وقال عليه السلام: الصبر صبران صبرٌ على ما تَكرَه وصبر عمّا تحبّ.

3.49 وقال عليه السلام: الغنى في الغُربة وطن والفقر في الوطن غربة.

3.50 وقال عليه السلام: القناعة مال لا يَنفَد.

3.51 وقال عليه السلام: المال مادّة الشهوات.

3.39 A shameful act about which you are sorry is better in God's eyes than a virtuous act of which you are proud.

3.40 The measure of a man is in accord with the measure of his resolution, the measure of his truthfulness is in accord with the measure of his chivalry, the measure of his valor is in accord with the measure of his self-respect, and the measure of his chastity is in accord with the measure of his jealous sense of honor.

3.41 Victory is reached through resolution, resolution is reached through reflection, and reflection is reached through guarding your secrets.

3.42 Beware the peer's attack when he's hungry, and the churl's when he's sated.

3.43 Men's hearts are wild beasts, but they soften toward those they love.

3.44 Your flaws will remain concealed as long as your luck holds.

3.45 Those who hold the most power to punish should be the foremost in forgiving.

3.46 True generosity is spontaneous. Giving when solicited is merely to avoid shame and blame.

3.47 There is no wealth like intelligence, no poverty like ignorance, no bequest like refinement, and no shield like consultation.

3.48 Patience is of two kinds: patience in the face of adversity and patience in the absence of privilege.

3.49 The rich man is at home in a foreign land, the pauper is a stranger in his hometown.

3.50 Contentment is wealth that never runs out.

3.51 Wealth fuels passions.

3.52 وقال عليه السلام: من حذّرك كمن بشّرك.

3.53 وقال عليه السلام: اللسان سَبُعٌ إن خُلّي عنه عَقَر.

3.54 وقال عليه السلام: المرأة عقرب حُلوة اللَّسبة.

3.55 وقال عليه السلام: الشفيع جناح الطالب.

3.56 وقال عليه السلام: أهل الدنيا كرَكب يُسار بهم وهم نِيام.

3.57 وقال عليه السلام: فَقدُ الأحبّة غُربة.

3.58 وقال عليه السلام: فوت الحاجة أهون من طلبها إلى غير أهلها.

3.59 وقال عليه السلام: لا تستحي من إعطاء القليل فإنّ الحرمان أقلّ منه.

3.60 وقال عليه السلام: العَفاف زينة الفقر.

3.61 وقال عليه السلام: إذا لم يكن ما تريد فلا تُبَل كيف كنت.

3.62 وقال عليه السلام: لا ترى الجاهل إلّا مُفرِطًا أو مُفرِّطًا.

3.63 وقال عليه السلام: إذا تَمّ العقل نقص الكلام.

3.64 وقال عليه السلام: الدهر يُخلِق الأبدان ويُجدِّد الآمال ويقرّب المنيّة ويباعد الأُمنيّة من ظفر به نَصِب ومن فاتَه تَعِب.

3.65 وقال عليه السلام: من نصب نفسه للناس إمامًا فعليه أن يبدأ بتعليم نفسه قبل تعليم غيره وليكن تأديبه بسيرته قبل تأديبه بلسانه ومُعلِّم نفسه ومؤدِّبها أحقّ بالإجلال من معلّم الناس ومؤدّبهم.

3.52 One who brings dire warnings is like one who gives glad tidings.

3.53 The tongue is a wild beast—let loose, it attacks.[1]

3.54 A woman is a scorpion with a sweet sting.

3.55 The intercessor is the suppliant's wing.

3.56 People in this world are a company of travelers who are carried along while they sleep.

3.57 Living without loved ones is like living in a strange land.

3.58 Not getting what you want is better than asking those you shouldn't.

3.59 Don't be embarrassed to give a little—not giving is even less.

3.60 Temperance adorns poverty.[2]

3.61 If what you wanted didn't happen, don't bewail your lot—in fact, don't bewail anything at all!

3.62 An ignoramus is either stingy or extravagant.

3.63 Where intelligence abounds, words are few.

3.64 Time wears out bodies, renews hopes, draws death close, and makes goals distant. It wearies those who win a share and grieves those who don't.

3.65 A man who would lead should teach himself before teaching others, he should discipline with his behavior ahead of his tongue—a man who teaches and disciplines himself is worthier of reverence than a man who teaches and disciplines others.

---

1 From ʿAlī's counsel to Muḥammad ibn al-Ḥanafiyyah. Mufīd, *Ikhtiṣāṣ*, 229.
2 From ʿAlī's oration titled *Wasīlah* (Ḥarrānī, *Tuḥaf*, 90). This saying is similar to the first half of §3.325.

3.66 وقال عليه السلام: نفَس المرء خُطاه إلى أجله.

3.67 وقال عليه السلام: كل معدود مُنقَضٍ وكل متوقَّعٍ آتٍ.

3.68 وقال عليه السلام: إنّ الأمور إذا اَشتَبهت اَعتُبر آخِرها بأوّلها.

3.69 ومن خبر ضِرار بن ضَمرة الضِّبابيّ عند دخوله على معاوية ومسألته عن أمير المؤمنين عليه السلام. قال فأشهد لقد رأيته في بعض مواقفه وقد أرخى الليل سُدوله وهو قائم في محرابه قابض على لِحيته يَتململ تملمُل السَّليم ويبكي بكاء الحزين ويقول

يا دنيا يا دنيا إليك عنّي أبي تعرّضتِ أم إليّ تشوّفت[1] لا حانَ حَينُك هَيهاتَ غُرّي غيري لا حاجة لي فيك قد طلّقتك ثلاثًا لا رجعة فيها فعيشك قصير وخطَرك يسير وأملك حقير. آهِ من قلّة الزاد وطول الطريق وبعد السفر وعظيم المَورِد.

3.70 ومن كلام له عليه السلام للشاميّ لمّا سأله أكان مسيره إلى الشام بقضاء من الله وقدر بعد كلام طويل هذا مختاره

وَيحَك لعلّك ظننت قضاء لازمًا وقدَرًا حاتمًا. ولو كان كذلك لبطل الثواب والعقاب وسقط الوعد والوعيد. إنّ الله سبحانه أمر عباده تخييرًا ونهاهم تحذيرًا وكلّف يسيرًا ولم يكلّف عسيرًا وأعطى على القليل كثيرًا. ولم يُعصَ مغلوبًا ولم يُطَع مكرِهًا ولم يرسل الأنبياء لَعبًا ولم ينزل الكتب للعباد عبثًا ولا خلق السماوات ﴿وَالْأَرْضَ وَمَا بَيْنَهُمَا بَاطِلًا ذَٰلِكَ ظَنُّ الَّذِينَ كَفَرُوا فَوَيْلٌ لِلَّذِينَ كَفَرُوا مِنَ النَّارِ﴾.

---

[1] م، ي، ومصحّحة في ش، ن: كذا. وأصل ش، ن، ونسخة في م، ﻫ: ﴿تشوّقت﴾.

3.66 Each breath is another step toward death.

3.67 Everything you can tally will run out. Everything you can anticipate will happen.

3.68 When affairs grow murky, predicate endings on beginnings.[1]

3.69 From a report relating Ḍirār ibn Ḍamrah al-Ḍibābī's visit to Muʿāwiyah, who asked him to describe the Commander of the Faithful. Ḍirār declared: I testify that I saw ʿAlī as he prayed when night had lowered its curtain. Standing in his prayer niche, hand upon his beard, writhing as though bitten by a snake and weeping grievously, he exclaimed:[2]
World, O world, get away from me! Is it me you try to tempt, is it for me you adorn yourself? May your time never arrive, go deceive another, for I have no need of you—I have divorced you thrice and there can be no reversal![3] Your life is short, your worth is little, all hopes placed in you are of no consequence. Alas, how scarce my provisions, how long the road, how distant the journey, and how momentous the arrival at the watering hole!

3.70 From ʿAlī's words to the Syrian who asked whether the march on Syria was decreed by God. ʿAlī gave a lengthy answer from which the following is a selection:[4]
Woe! Perhaps you think destiny is final and fate absolute! If that were the case, God's reward and punishment would be invalid, and God's promise and threat would have no meaning. God has commanded his servants to do certain things, while giving them free choice, and forbidden them from doing other things, while giving them fair warning. He has imposed on them easy, not harsh tasks, and has promised great rewards for small efforts. When he is disobeyed, it is not because he is overpowered. When he is obeyed, it is not because he coerced. He has not sent prophets in play, or revealed scriptures on a whim, or created the skies «and the earth in vain. That is the claim of those who do not believe—woe and hellfire to unbelievers!»[5]

---

1 From ʿAlī's oration on the last night of fighting, The Night of Clamor, at the Battle of Ṣiffīn in 37/657. Minqarī, *Waqʿat Ṣiffīn*, 476.
2 Presumably in Kufa, during the final years of his caliphate, around 39–40/660–661.
3 In most schools of Islamic law, a man is permitted to remarry his divorced wife up to a total of three times.
4 According to Ṣadūq (*Tawḥīd*, 380), the man who asked the question was not a Syrian, but one of ʿAlī's Iraqi followers.
5 Qurʾan, Ṣād 38:27.

3.71 وقال عليه السلام: خذ الحكمة أنّى١ كانت فإنّ الحكمة تكون في صدر المنافق فتَلَجلَجُ في صدره حتّى تَخرج فتسكن إلى صواحبها في صدر المؤمن.

وقال عليه السلام في مثل ذلك

الحكمة ضالّة المؤمن نخذ الحكمة ولو من أهل النفاق.

3.72 وقال عليه السلام: قيمة كلّ آمرئ ما يحسن.٢

وهذه الكلمة التي لا تصاب لها قيمة ولا توزن بها حكمة ولا تقرن إليها كلمة.

3.73 وقال عليه السلام: أوصيكم بخمس لو ضربتم إليها آباط الإبل لكانت لذلك أهلًا لا يَرجُوَنّ أحد منكم إلّا ربّه ولا يَخَافنّ إلّا ذنبه ولا يَستحيينّ أحد إذا سُئل عمّا لا يعلم أن يقول لا أعلم ولا يستحيينّ أحد إذا لم يعلم الشيء أن يتعلّمه وبالصبر٣ فإنّ الصبر من الإيمان كالرأس من الجسد لا خير في جسد لا رأس معه ولا في إيمان لا صبر معه.

3.74 وقال عليه السلام لرجل أفرط في الثناء عليه وكان له مُتّهِمًا أنا دون ما تقول وفوق ما في نفسك.

3.75 وقال عليه السلام: بقيّة السيف أبقى عددًا وأكثر ولدًا.

3.76 وقال عليه السلام: من ترك قول لا أدري أصيبت مَقاتله.

3.77 وقال عليه السلام: رأي الشيخ أحبّ إليّ من جَلَد الغلام.

١ن، ش، ي، ه: كذا. م: وفي ش في نسخة ⟨أين⟩.   ٢ن، ي، ه، ش: كذا. م: وفي ش في نسخة ⟨يحسنه⟩.   ٣ن، ش، م، ه: كذا. ي: وفي هامش ه: أضيفت قبلها ⟨عليكم⟩. مصحّحة في ش أضيفت قبلها ⟨عليك⟩.

3.71 Seize wisdom wherever you find it. A wise maxim may reside in the breast of a hypocrite, and it quivers and trembles there until it settles next to its kin, in the breast of a believer.

'Alī also said in a similar vein:
Believers, wisdom is your own lost camel—seize it, then, even from hypocrites!

3.72 The measure of a man is the good he does.[1]

Raḍī: This maxim is priceless. No adage can be equated with it, no maxim can be compared to it.

3.73 I counsel you to five traits so precious it is only right that you should whip your camels to reach them: Place your hopes in no one save your Lord. Fear nothing save your sins. When asked about something you don't know, don't be ashamed to say, "I don't know." If you don't know something, don't be ashamed to learn. And be patient in adversity, for patience is to faith as the head is to the body—what good is a body without a head, or faith without patience?[2]

3.74 'Alī said to a secret calumniator who praised him effusively to his face:[3]
I am less than you say but more than you think.

3.75 Survivors of the sword multiply in number and their descendants proliferate.[4]

3.76 The moment you stop saying, "I don't know," you will be struck the death-blow.

3.77 An elder's advice is worth more to me than a youth's muscle.[5]

---

1 Listed among 'Alī's "signature replies" (*tawqīʿāt*), inscribed on the letter to his associate Ṣaʿṣaʿah ibn Ṣūḥān (Ibn ʿAbd Rabbih, *ʿIqd*, 4:288). The line could also be translated as, "The measure of a man is what he does well"—i.e., does well in terms of professional skill (B 954), or knowledge and worship (F 408).

2 Part of a sermon in the mosque (Māmaṭīrī, *Nuzhah*, 154–157), presumably in Kufa; other parts are § 3.81, § 3.100.

3 The calumniator was al-Ashʿath ibn Qays, and the exchange presumably happened in Kufa during 'Alī's caliphate, 35–40/656–661. Abū ʿUbayd al-Bakrī, *Faṣl al-Maqāl*, 33.

4 Among 'Alī's signature replies (*tawqīʿāt*), inscribed on his letter to his associate Ḥuṣayn (or Ḥuḍayn) ibn al-Mundhir. Ibn ʿAbd Rabbih, *ʿIqd*, 4:288.

5 Among 'Alī's "signature replies" (*tawqīʿāt*), inscribed on his letter to his son Ḥasan. Ibn ʿAbd Rabbih, *ʿIqd*, 4:288.

وروي ﴿من مشهد الغلام﴾.

3.78 وقال عليه السلام: عجبت لمن يَقنَط ومعه الاستغفار.

3.79 وحكى عنه أبو جعفر محمّد بن عليّ الباقر عليهم السلام أنّه قال
كان في الأرض أمانان من عذاب الله سبحانه فرُفع أحدهما فدُونكم الآخَر فتمسّكوا به.
أمّا الأمان الذي رفع فهو رسول الله صلّى الله عليه وآله. وأمّا الأمان الباقي فالاستغفار
قال الله عزّ من قائل ﴿وَمَا كَانَ ٱللّٰهُ لِيُعَذِّبَهُمْ وَأَنتَ فِيهِمْ وَمَا كَانَ ٱللّٰهُ مُعَذِّبَهُمْ وَهُمْ
يَسْتَغْفِرُونَ﴾.

وهذا من محاسن الاستخراج ولطائف الاستنباط.

3.80 وقال عليه السلام: من أصلح ما بينه وبين الله أصلح الله ما بينه وبين الناس ومن
أصلح أمر آخرته أصلح الله له أمر دنياه ومن كان له من نفسه واعظ كان عليه من الله
حافظ.

3.81 وقال عليه السلام: الفقيه كلُّ الفقيه من لم يُقنِط الناس من رحمة الله ولم يؤيسهم
من رَوح الله ولم يؤمنهم من مكر الله.

3.82 وقال عليه السلام: أوضعُ العلم ما وقف على اللسان وأرفعه ما ظهر في الجوارح
والأركان.

3.83 وقال عليه السلام: إنّ هذه القلوب تَمَلّ كما تمَلّ الأبدان فابتغوا لها طرائف الحكمة.

3.84 وقال عليه السلام: لا يقولنّ أحدكم اَللّهم إنّي أعوذ بك من الفتنة لأنّه ليس
أحد إلّا وهو مشتمل على فتنة ولكن من اَستعاذ فليستعذ من مُضِلّات الفتن فإنّ الله
سبحانه يقول ﴿وَٱعْلَمُوٓا أَنَّمَا أَمْوَالُكُمْ وَأَوْلَادُكُمْ فِتْنَةٌ﴾. ومعنى ذلك أنّه سبحانه يختبرهم

Raḍī: The saying is also narrated as "a youth's martyrdom."

3.78 I marvel at one who despairs when he could ask forgiveness!

3.79 Abū Jaʿfar Muḥammad ibn ʿAlī, al-Bāqir, reported these words by ʿAlī:
Of the two refuges from God's punishment, one is taken away, but the other
remains—so hold fast! The refuge that is taken away is God's Messenger, the
one that remains is repentance—the Almighty said to the Prophet, «God will
not punish them while you are among them, and he will not punish them if
they repent.»[1]

Raḍī: This is one of the most beautiful of interpretations and the most sublime of infer-
ences.

3.80 Whoever puts right what is between him and God, God puts right what is
between him and others. Whoever puts right affairs of the hereafter, God puts
right for him affairs of the world. Whoever has himself as counsellor has God
as protector.

3.81 A true sage teaches people never to despair of God's mercy, and never
to lose hope in God's compassion, yet, at the same time, never to stop fearing
God's retribution.[2]

3.82 The lowest form of knowledge stops at the tongue. The highest form of
knowledge manifests in limbs and appendages.

3.83 Minds tire just as bodies tire, so seek for them wondrous novelties of wis-
dom![3]

3.84 Never say, "God, protect me from trial!" for no one is free from exposure
to trial. If you wish to seek God's protection, seek it against the inducements to
stray that occur during times of trial. God has said, «Know that the riches you
own and the children you beget are nothing but trials!»[4] This means that the
Almighty tests people through wealth and children to see who is unhappy with
his lot and who accepts his share with equanimity. The Almighty knows what

---

1   Qurʾan, Anfāl 8:33.
2   Part of a sermon in the mosque (Māmaṭīrī, *Nuzhah*, 154–157), presumably in Kufa; other parts
     are § 3.73, § 3.100.
3   Nearly identical to § 3.181.
4   Qurʾan, Anfāl 8:28.

بالأموال والأولاد ليتبيّن الساخط لرزقه بقِسمه والراضي وإن كان سبحانه أعلم بهم من أنفسهم ولكن لتظهر الأفعال التي بها يُستحَقّ الثواب والعقاب لأنّ بعضهم يحبّ الذُّكور ويكره الإناث وبعضهم يحبّ تثمير المال ويكره ٱنثلام الحال.

وهذا من غريب ما سمع منه عليه السلام في التفسير.

3.85 وسئل عليه السلام عن الخير ما هو فقال

ليس الخير أن يكثر مالك وولدك ولكنّ الخير أن يكثر علمك وأن يعظم حلمك وأن تُباهي الناس بعبادة ربّك فإن أحسنتَ حمدتَ الله وإن أسأت ٱستغفرت الله. ولا خير في الدنيا إلّا لرجلين رجل أذنب ذنوباً فهو يتداركها بالتوبة ورجل يسارع في الخيرات. ولا يقلّ عمل مع التقوى وكيف يَقلّ ما يُتقبَّل.

3.86 وقال عليه السلام: إنّ أولى الناس بالأنبياء أعلمهم بما جاءوا به ثمّ تلى عليه السلام ﴿إِنَّ أَوْلَى النَّاسِ بِإِبْرَاهِيمَ لَلَّذِينَ ٱتَّبَعُوهُ وَهَٰذَا النَّبِيُّ وَالَّذِينَ آمَنُوا وَاللَّهُ وَلِيُّ الْمُؤْمِنِينَ﴾ ثم قال عليه السلام إنّ وليّ محمّد من أطاع الله وإن بعدت لُحمته وإنّ عدوّ محمّد من عصى الله وإن قربت قرابته.

3.87 وقال عليه السلام: وقد سمع رجلاً من الحَروريّة يتهجّد ويقرأ

نوم على يقين خير من صلاة في شكّ.

3.88 وقال عليه السلام: اِعقِلوا الخبر إذا سمعتموه عقل رعاية لا عقل رواية فإنّ رواة العلم كثير ورعاته قليل.

3.89 وقال عليه السلام: وقد سمع رجلاً يقول ﴿إِنَّا لِلَّهِ وَإِنَّا إِلَيْهِ رَاجِعُونَ﴾

is in their hearts more than they do, but the trials prompt them to actions by which they earn either reward or punishment. Some prefer male children and dislike girls. Others are obsessed with amassing wealth and lose patience when their robes fray.

Raḍī: This is among the wondrous commentaries on the Qurʾan heard from ʿAlī.

3.85 ʿAlī was asked, "What constitutes distinction?" and he replied:
Possessing great wealth and having many children are not marks of distinction—distinction is obtained through vast knowledge and abundant kindness, and by vying to worship the Lord. If you do good, praise God, if you do ill, beg his forgiveness. Distinction in this world is reserved for two kinds of men: one who commits a sin but atones for it by repenting, and one who hastens to perform good deeds. No deed is too small if performed with piety—how can something that God accepts ever be small?

3.86 ʿAlī said: Closest to prophets are those who discern their message best. Then he recited, «Closest to Abraham are those who followed him, as is this Prophet, and those who profess belief—God is close to believers.»[1] Then he continued: One who obeys God is Muḥammad's kinsman, however distant he may be in bloodline. One who disobeys God is Muḥammad's enemy, however close he may be in kinship.

3.87 ʿAlī heard a Ḥarūrī Kharijite praying late in the night and reciting the Qurʾan, and he said:[2]
Sleep accompanied by certainty is better than prayer accompanied by doubt.

3.88 Study any hadith you hear with mindful attention, not by rote learning.[3] Narrators of knowledge are many, its true custodians few.

3.89 ʿAlī heard a man intone, «To God we belong and to him we shall return!» and he said:[4]

---

1 Qurʾan, Āl ʿImrān 3:68.
2 Presumably in Kufa, soon after the Kharijites' secession in 37/658. The Ḥarūriyyah were the first Kharijites—Ḥarūraʾ was the place near Kufa where they initially gathered to protest against ʿAlī.
3 Ar. *khabar*, lit. "report," translated here as "hadith." The last lines of §1.236 are similar.
4 Qurʾan, Baqarah 2:156. The man is al-Ashʿath ibn Qays, to whom ʿAlī was offering condolences at the death of his brother, ʿAbd al-Raḥmān (Ḥarrānī, *Tuḥaf*, 209). See also ʿAlī's condolence to Ashʿath on his son's death in §3.277, and for an unnamed relative in §3.385.

إنّ قولنا ﴿إِنَّا لِلّهِ﴾ إقرار على أنفسنا بالمُلك. وقولنا ﴿وَإِنَّا إِلَيْهِ رَاجِعُوْن﴾ إقرار على أنفسنا بالهُلك.

3.90 وقال عليه السلام وقد مدحه قوم في وجهه

اللّهمّ إنّك أعلم بي من نفسي وأنا أعلم بنفسي منهم اللّهمّ اجعلنا خيرًا ممّا يظنّون واغفر لنا ما لا يعلمون.

3.91 وقال عليه السلام: لا يستقيم قضاء الحوائج إلّا بثلاث باستصغارها لتعظم وباستكتامها لتظهر وبتعجيلها لتهنأ.

3.92 وقال عليه السلام: يأتي على الناس زمان لا يُقرَّب فيه إلّا الماحل ولا يُظرَّف فيه إلّا الفاجر ولا يضعَّف فيه إلّا المنصف. يعُدّون الصدقة فيه غُرمًا وصلة الرحم مَنًّا والعبادة استطالة على الناس. فعند ذلك يكون السلطان بمشورة الإماء وإمارة الصبيان وتدبير الخصيان.[١]

3.93 ورُؤّي عليه إزارُ خَلِقٍ مرقوع فقيل له في ذلك فقال يخشع له القلب وتذلّ به النفس ويقتدي به المؤمنون.

3.94 وقال عليه السلام: إنّ الدنيا والآخرة عدوّان متفاوتان وسبيلان مختلفان فمن أحبّ الدنيا وتولّاها أبغض الآخرة وعاداها وهما بمنزلة المشرق والمغرب وماشٍ بينهما كلّما قرب من واحد بعد من الآخر وهما بعدُ ضَرّتان.

3.95 وعن نَوف البِكاليّ قال رأيت أمير المؤمنين عليه السلام ذات ليلة وقد خرج من فراشه فنظر إلى النجوم فقال يا نوف أراقد أنت أم رامق قلت بل رامق يا أمير المؤمنين فقال

____

[١] ن، ش، ي، ه، وأضيفت في م: كذا. أصل م: سقطت ﴿وتدبير الخصيان﴾.

When we say, «To God we belong,» we acknowledge our subjugation. When we say, «To him we shall return,» we acknowledge our mortality.

3.90 Lord, you know me better than I know myself, and I know myself better than others know me. Lord, make me more virtuous than they think, and forgive those of my actions they don't know.[1]

3.91 Your benefaction becomes perfect only when you add three more actions: when you deem your favors small, they become great, when you conceal them, they become clear, and when you expedite them, they are received with joy.

3.92 An age is coming to the world in which none but the schemer will be granted intimacy, none but the debauched will be considered witty, and none but the just will be deemed weak. People will regard charity a tax, gifts to relatives a favor, and God's worship a means to self-glorification. At that time, power will be wielded through the counsel of concubines, the command of boys, and the governance of eunuchs.

3.93 ʿAlī was seen wearing a worn and patched garment, and when someone remarked on this, he explained:
The heart bows to him and the soul prostrates before him—true believers will follow my practice.

3.94 This world and the hereafter are mutual enemies and divergent paths— to love and follow this world is to hate and reject the hereafter. The two are like East and West for the person who walks between them—the nearer he draws to one, the further he moves from the other. They are like two wives married to one man.

3.95 Nawf al-Bikālī narrated this report, and he said: I saw the Commander of the Faithful one night as he rose from his bed, gazed at the stars, then said to me, "Nawf, are you asleep or awake?" "I'm awake, Commander of the Faithful," I replied. ʿAlī then said to me:[2]

---

1 Presumably in Kufa during ʿAlī's caliphate, 35–40/656–661. Response when he was praised to his face (Māmaṭīrī, *Nuzhah*, 243–244). Similar final line in §1.191.3 (see note on context there).
2 Presumably in Kufa during ʿAlī's caliphate, 35–40/656–661. The words in parentheses within ʿAlī's text are Raḍī's explanatory insertions.

يا نوف طوبى للزاهدين في الدنيا الراغبين في الآخرة أولئك قوم آتّخذوا الأرض بساطًا وترابها فراشًا وماءها طيبًا والقرآن شعارًا والدعاء دثارًا ثمّ قرضوا الدنيا قرضًا على منهاج المسيح. يا نوف إنّ داود عليه السلام قام في مثل هذه الساعة من الليل فقال ﴿إنّها ساعة لا يدعو فيها عبد إلّا آستجيب له إلّا أن يكون عَشّارًا أو عَريفًا أو شُرطيًّا أو صاحب عَرطبة (وهي الطُّنبور) أو صاحب كوبة (وهي الطَّبل)﴾.

وقد قيل أيضًا إنّ العرطبة الطبل والكوبة الطنبور.

3.96 وقال عليه السلام: إنّ الله آقترض عليكم الفرائض فلا تُضيّعوها وحدّ لكم حدودًا فلا تعتدّوها ونهاكم عن أشياء فلا تنتهكوها وسكت لكم عن أشياء ولم يدعها نسيانًا فلا تتكلّفوها.

3.97 وقال عليه السلام: لا يترك الناس شيئًا من دينهم لآستصلاح دنياهم إلّا فتح الله عليهم ما هو أضرّ منه.

3.98 وقال عليه السلام: رُبَّ عالم قتله جهله وعلمه معه لا ينفعه.

3.99 وقال عليه السلام: لقد عُلّق بنياط هذا الإنسان بَضعة هي أعجب ما فيه وذلك القلب وله مَوادُّ من الحكمة وأضداد من خلافها. فإن سَنح له الرجاء أذلّه الطمع وإن هاج به الطمع أهلكه الحرص وإن ملكه اليأس قتله الأسف وإن عَرض له الغضب آشتدّ به الغَيظ وإن أسعده الرضى نسي التحفّظ وإن عالَه[١] الخوف شغله الحذر وإن آتّسع له الأمن آستلبته الغِرّة[٢] وإن أصابته مصيبة فضحه الجزع وإن أفاد مالًا أطغاه الغنى وإن عضّته الفاقة شغله البلاء وإن جَهده الجوع قعد به الضعف وإن أفرط به الشّبَع كظّته البِطنة. فكلّ تقصير به مُضِرّ وكلّ إفراط له مفسد.

____

[١] م، ي، ونسخة في ش، ن: كذا. أصل ش، ن، ونسخة في م: ﴿ناله﴾. ه، ونسخة في ي: ﴿غاله﴾.
[٢] م، ي: كذا. ش، ن، ه: ﴿عزّة﴾.

Nawf, blessed are those who reject worldliness and focus their desire on the hereafter! They take God's earth for a carpet, its dust for a bed, its water for perfume, the Qur'an as their garment, and prayer as their robe. They cut their bonds with the world as the Messiah did. Nawf, the Prophet David stepped outside at just such an hour, and said, ⟨This is an hour when the prayer of any who prays will be answered, unless he is a tax collector, an appraiser, an enforcer, an oud player (that is, a lute player), or a percussionist (that is, a drummer).⟩

Raḍī: Alternatively, it is said that ʿarṭabah, the first word of the last pair, means drum, and kūbah, the second word, means lute.

3.96 God has mandated certain things for you—don't squander them. He has laid down certain limits for you—don't transgress them. He has forbidden you certain actions—don't violate them. He has stayed silent about certain things deliberately and not because he had forgotten—don't burden yourself with them.[1]

3.97 When people forego a religious duty to rally their worldly affairs, God opens for them a door that leads to more harm.

3.98 A learned man is sometimes killed by ignorance, and his learning fails to come to his aid.[2]

3.99 There is a piece of flesh attached to the jugular vein that is the human's most wondrous organ—the heart. It has elements of wisdom, and others that are quite the opposite. If it is lifted by hope, ambition debases it, and if ambition boils over, greed destroys it, but if disappointment takes hold, regret kills it. If aggravated, its rage runs rampant, but if made happy, it forgets to be circumspect. If overwhelmed by fear, caution preoccupies it, but if safety is secured, heedlessness strips it away, and if calamity strikes, it panics. If it gains property, wealth makes it a tyrant, but if poverty bites, distress preoccupies it. If hunger enfeebles it, weakness prevents it from rising, but if satiety is excessive, surfeit oppresses it. Every deficiency does it harm, and every excess injures it.[3]

---

1 Hārūnī (*Taysīr*, 272) cites this excerpt as part of §1.50, an oration ʿAlī delivered in Medina six days after he became caliph, in 35/656.

2 The line—which refers to Ṭalḥah and Zubayr—is from ʿAlī's oration in Medina in 36/656, when news arrived that the two had set out for Basra with ʿĀʾishah to raise an army against him. Ḥ 1:233 (in commentary on §1.8), after Abū Mikhnaf, *Jamal*.

3 From an aphoristic oration titled *Wasīlah* (Ḥarrānī, *Tuḥaf*, 92–100).

3.100 وقال عليه السلام: نحن النُّمرُقة الوسطى بها يلحق التالي وإليها يرجع الغالي.

3.101 وقال عليه السلام: لا يقيم أمر الله سبحانه إلّا من لا يصانع ولا يضارع ولا يتبع المَطامع.

3.102 وقال عليه السلام وقد توفّي سَهل بن حُنيف الأنصاريّ رحمه الله بالكوفة مَرجِعَه معه من صفّين وكان من أحبّ الناس إليه
لو أحبّني جبلٌ لَتَهَافَت.

ومعنى ذلك أنّ المحنة تغلظ عليه فتسرع المصائب إليه ولا يُفعَل ذلك إلّا بالأتقياء الأبرار والمصطفين الأخيار. وهذا مثل قوله عليه السلام
مَن أحبّنا أهلَ البيت فليستعدّ للفقر جِلباباً.

وقد تُؤَوِّل ذلك على معنى آخر ليس هذا موضع ذكره.

3.103 وقال عليه السلام: لا مال أعود من العقل ولا وحدة أوحش من العُجب ولا عقل كالتدبير ولا كرم كالتقوى ولا قرين كحسن الخلق ولا ميراث كالأدب ولا قائد كالتوفيق ولا تجارة كالعمل الصالح ولا رِبح كالثواب ولا ورع كالوقوف عند الشبهة

3.100 We are the saddle-pad in the middle—those who lag must catch up, while those who exceed bounds must return to it.[1]

3.101 God's faith is established only by a man who never blandishes, or succumbs, or follows the path of greed.

3.102 When Sahl ibn Ḥunayf, one of the people ʿAlī loved dearly, died in Kufa soon after returning with him from Ṣiffīn, he exclaimed:[2]
Were a mountain to love me, it would crumble!

Raḍī: The expression means that troubles bear down on such a man and calamities rush to strike him, and that this happens only to pious savants and virtuous saints. It resembles another saying by ʿAlī, in which he said:
Whoever loves us, the family of the Prophet, should prepare to wear the robe of poverty.

Raḍī: This saying has also been interpreted differently, but this is not the place for those details.

3.103 There is no wealth more profitable than intelligence, no solitude more desolate than vanity, no intelligence like prudent planning, no honor like god-fearing piety, no companion like a beautiful character, no legacy like mannered refinement, no leader like divine direction, no trade like good deeds, no profit like heavenly reward, no restraint like pausing when in doubt, no renunciation

---

1 "We" refers to the Prophet's family according to all the commentators, but the enigmatic image of the "saddle-pad in the middle" (*al-numruqah al-wusṭā*) is interpreted variously as: (1) the true and just Imams, embodiment of the middle way between two extremes, presumably those who deem ʿAlī the fourth caliph and those who believe in his divinity; this explanation focuses on "in the middle," while "saddle-pad" is not explained (B 961; F 419); (2) the virtuous mean between the vices, because the "saddle-pad" is placed higher than everything else on the camel's back, and, being the place where the rider sits, it is akin to a person's theological position (Ḥ 18:273); (3) the intermediate position of authority held by the family of the Prophet, where the Prophet is the "greatest saddle-pad," and other Muslim authorities are the "lesser saddle-pad" (R 3:302–303); (4) comfort-givers, like the saddle-pad that supports and cushions the body (ʿA 713). The text's context is also given variously as: (1) part of ʿAlī's address to Ḥārith al-Hamdānī (ʿImād al-Dīn al-Ṭabarī, *Bishārah*, 21); (2) Part of a sermon in the mosque, presumably in Kufa; other parts are §3.73, §3.81 (Māmaṭīrī, *Nuzhah*, 154–157, where the first line is, "Follow the middle path," while the rest is the same as here); (3) ʿAlī's address to a group from "the West" (presumably, Syria), in praise of the truly pious (Yaʿqūbī, *Tārīkh*, 2:210).

2 In 37/657 or 38/658.

ولا زهد كالزهد في الحرام ولا علم كالتفكّر ولا عبادة كأداء الفرائض ولا إيمان كالحياء والصبر ولا حسب كالتواضع ولا شرف كالعلم ولا مُظاهرة أوثق من مُشاورة.

3.104 وقال عليه السلام: إذا اُستولى الصلاح على الزمان وأهله ثمّ أساء رجل الظنّ برجل لم تَظهر منه خِزية فقد ظلم وإذا اُستولى الفساد على الزمان وأهله فأحسن رجل الظنّ برجل فقد غرّر.

3.105 وقيل له عليه السلام كيف تجدك يا أمير المؤمنين فقال كيف يكون من يفنى ببقائه ويَسقَم بصحّته ويؤتى من مأمنه.

3.106 وقال عليه السلام كم من مُستدرَج بالإحسان إليه ومغرور بالستر عليه ومَفتون بحسن القول فيه وما اُبتلى الله أحدًا بمثل الإملاء له.

3.107 وقال عليه السلام: هلك فيّ رجلان محبّ غالٍ ومبغض قالٍ.

3.108 وقال عليه السلام: إضاعة الفرصة غُصّة.

3.109 وقال عليه السلام: مَثَل الدنيا كمثل الحيّة لَيّنٌ مَسُّها والسَّمّ الناقع في جَوفها يهوي إليها الغِرّ الجاهل ويحذرها ذو اللُّبّ العاقل.

3.110 وقال عليه السلام وقد سئل عن قريش أمّا بنو مخزوم فريحانة قريش تحبّ حديث رجالهم والنكاح في نسائهم وأمّا بنو عبد شمس فأبعدها رأيًا وأمنعها لما وراء ظهورها وأمّا نحن فأبذل لما في أيدينا وأسمح عند الموت بنفوسنا. وهم أكثر وأمكر وأنكر ونحن أفصح وأنصح وأصبح.

like renouncing the forbidden, no knowledge like contemplation, no worship like the mandated rites, no faith like modesty and endurance, no lineage like humility, no nobility like knowledge, and no support surer than consultation.[1]

3.104 Among a people and at a time when integrity prevails, you are being unjust if you entertain suspicions about a man who has never performed an act of villainy. Among a people and at a time when corruption prevails, you are rushing into peril if you trust any man.

3.105 ʿAlī was asked, "How do you fare, Commander of the Faithful?" and he replied:[2] How fares he who is led to death by his life, carried to sickness by his health, and about to be attacked in his place of safety?

3.106 ʿAlī said:
How many are made complacent by continued favors, deceived by concealment of sins, and duped by people's praise! The most severe of God's tests is time and a slack rein.

3.107 Two kinds of men are damned because of how they feel about me: one is excessive in his love, the other is extreme in his hatred.[3]

3.108 Missed opportunities produce regret.

3.109 This world is like a snake—soft to the touch but filled with deadly poison. The foolish lad reaches out for it, but the intelligent man is wary.[4]

3.110 ʿAlī was asked to describe the clans of the Quraysh, and he said:
Makhzūm are the sweet blossoms of Quraysh, you enjoy the conversation of their men and delight in marrying their women. ʿAbd Shams are the most farsighted and the most valiant in protecting their own. We, Hāshim, are the most openhanded in giving and have the biggest hearts when facing death. They are more numerous, more cunning, and more repugnant. We are more eloquent, more sincere, and fairer of countenance.

---

1   Part of an oration ʿAlī delivered nine days after Muḥammad's death, in Medina in 11/632 (Ṣadūq, *Amālī*, 399). Also included in *Wasīlah* (Ḥarrānī, *Tuḥaf*, 94).
2   The man who asked is ʿAlī's nephew ʿAbdallāh ibn Jaʿfar, who had come to visit ʿAlī, who was ill. Ṭūsī, *Amālī*, 631.
3   Similar to §1.125, addressed to the Kharijites in Kufa, 37/658.
4   Similar to § 2.68, written to Salmān al-Fārisī, who was appointed governor of Madāʾin, near present-day Baghdad, by ʿUmar, and died there around the end of ʿUthmān's reign in 35/655.

3.111 وقال عليه السلام: شَتَّانَ بين عملين عمل تذهب لذّته وتبقى تَبِعته وعمل تذهب مَؤونته ويبقى أجره.

3.112 وتبع جنازة فسمع رجلًا يضحك فقال عليه السلام كأنّ الموت فيها على غيرنا كُتِب وكأنّ الحقّ فيها على غيرنا وَجَب وكأنّ الذي نرى من الأموات سَفْرُ عمّا قليل إلينا راجعون نُبوّئهم أجداثهم ونأكل تراثهم قد نَسِينا كل واعظة ورَمَينا بكلّ جائحة. طوبى لمن ذلّ في نفسه وطاب كسبه وصلحت سريرته وحسنت خليقته وأنفق الفضل من ماله وأمسك الفضل من لسانه وعزل عن الناس شرّه ووسعته السنّة ولم ينسب إلى بدعة.

ومن الناس من ينسب هذا الكلام إلى رسول الله صلّى الله عليه وآله.

3.113 وقال عليه السلام: غَيرة المرأة كفر وغيرة الرجل إيمان.

3.114 وقال عليه السلام: لَأَنْسُبَنَّ الإسلام نسبة لم يَنسُبها أحد قبلي الإسلام هو التسليم والتسليم هو اليقين واليقين هو التصديق والتصديق هو الإقرار والإقرار هو الأداء والأداء هو العمل.

3.115 وقال عليه السلام: عجبت للبخيل يستعجل الفقر الذي منه هرب ويفوته الغنى الذي إيّاه طلب فيعيش في الدنيا عيش الفقراء ويحاسَب في الآخرة حساب الأغنياء وعجبت للمتكبّر الذي كان بالأمس نطفة ويكون غدًا جيفة وعجبت لمن شكّ في الله وهو يرى خَلق الله وعجبت لمن نسي الموت وهو يرى من يموت وعجبت لمن أنكر النشأة الأخرى وهو يرى النشأة الأولى وعجبت لعامر دار الفناء وتارك دار البقاء.

3.111 How different these two actions! An action whose pleasure passes but whose punishment remains, and an action whose suffering passes but whose reward remains.

3.112 ʿAlī was following a bier in a funeral procession when he heard a man laugh. He exclaimed:

We behave as though death were decreed for everyone other than ourselves, as though duties were incumbent upon everyone other than ourselves, as if those who die before our eyes are travelers who will soon return! We consign their bodies to the grave and consume their wealth, forgetting every counselor and shrugging off every tragedy. Blessed is he whose soul is humble, whose earnings are pure, whose heart is sincere, whose character is good, who shares his surplus wealth, who restrains his tongue from gratuitous utterances, who spares people his evil, who finds sufficient room within the accepted practice, and to whom no heretical innovation can be ascribed!

Raḍī: Some people attribute these words to God's Messenger.[1]

3.113 Woman's jealousy is heresy, man's jealousy is faith.[2]

3.114 I shall trace the pedigree of Islam as no one has done before: Islam means submission, submission means certainty, certainty means belief, belief means acknowledgment, acknowledgment means discharge of duties, and discharge of duties means action.[3]

3.115 I am amazed by the miser who hastens to bring on himself the very poverty he flees and fails to enjoy the very wealth he seeks—he spends his life in this world among the destitute, yet is held to account in the hereafter with the wealthy. I am amazed by the conceited bighead who was but yesterday a droplet of sperm and who will tomorrow be a rotting corpse. I am amazed by one who doubts God when he can see God's creation. I am amazed by one who forgets death when he can see the dead. I am amazed by one who denies the afterlife when he can observe this life. I am amazed by one who furnishes the abode of transience and ignores the abode of eternity.

---

1 Within an oration the Prophet delivered "from the back of his camel" upon his return to Medina from the Last Pilgrimage in 10/632. Yaʿqūbī, *Tārīkh*, 2:100; Kulaynī, *Kāfī*, 8:168.

2 Islamic law allows a man to marry up to four co-wives, while a woman may only marry one man at a time. B 966; R 3:315; F 421–422, citing Qurʾan, Nisāʾ 4:3.

3 "Submission" (*taslīm*) derives from the same root ("S-L-M") as "Islam," whose lexical purview includes submission, commitment, peace, and wellbeing.

3.116 وقال عليه السلام: من قصّر في العمل ٱبتُلي بالهمّ ولا حاجة لله فيمن ليس لله في نفسه وماله نصيب.

3.117 وقال عليه السلام: تَوَقَّوا البرد في أوّله وتلقَّوه في آخره فإنّه يفعل في الأبدان كفعله في الأشجار أوّله يُحرق وآخره يورق.

3.118 وقال عليه السلام: عِظَمُ الخالق عندك يصغّر المخلوق في عينك.

3.119 وقال عليه السلام: وقد رجع من صفّين فأشرف على القبور بظاهر الكوفة يا أهل الديار الموحشة والمحالّ المُقفرة والقبور المُظلمة يا أهل التربة يا أهل الغربة يا أهل الوحدة يا أهل الوحشة أنتم لنا فَرَطٌ سابق ونحن لكم تبَعٌ لاحق أمّا الدُّورَ فقد سُكنت وأمّا الأزواج فقد نكحت وأمّا الأموال فقد قسمت. هذا خبر ما عندنا فما خبر ما عندكم.

ثمّ ٱلتفت إلى أصحابه فقال
أما لو أُذن لهم في الكلام لأخبروكم أنّ ﴿خَيْرَ الزَّادِ التَّقْوَى﴾.

3.120 وقال عليه السلام: وقد سمع رجلًا يذمّ الدنيا

3.116 If you fall short in deeds, you will be afflicted with anxiety. God has no need of someone who offers him no share of his life or wealth.

3.117 Protect yourself against the cold when the wintry weather begins, and expose yourself to it as it ends, for its action on bodies is the same as its action on trees: the first cold burns, while the last prompts leaves to sprout.

3.118 The majesty of the Creator in your heart should make his creatures insignificant in your eyes.[1]

3.119 When ʿAlī reached the cemetery outside Kufa upon his return from Ṣiffīn, he intoned:[2]
O people of desolate abodes, ruined quarters, and dark tombs! O people of dust, O people of exile, O people of isolation, O people of desolation! You preceded us, and we shall follow. As for your homes—others have occupied them. As for your wives—others have bedded them. As for your properties—others have divided them. This is our news—what is yours?

Then he turned to his companions and said:
If they were permitted to answer, they would say, «The best provision is piety.»[3]

3.120 ʿAlī retorted to a man whom he overheard criticizing this world:[4]

---

1   From ʿAlī's Hammām Oration describing the pious, § 1.191.2.
2   According to Ḥarrānī (*Tuḥaf*, 186–188), this is the second part of an oration ʿAlī delivered late in the night immediately following the Battle of the Camel, outside Basra in 36/656, to a group of men from his own army, of which the first part is recorded with some variants as § 3.120 (the next text here). Alternatively, the first line is recorded by Minqarī (*Waqʿat Ṣiffīn*, 531) and Ṭabarī (*Tārīkh*, 5:61–62) as part of a longer address ʿAlī intoned just outside Kufa in 37/657, on his return from Ṣiffīn, when he saw the graves of his companion Khabbāb ibn al-Aratt and others; he prayed for them (§ 3.37), then addressed them thus. The line could have been used more than once by ʿAlī, and both contexts could be correct.
3   Qurʾan, Baqarah 2:197.
4   Ḥarrānī (*Tuḥaf*, 186–188) says ʿAlī delivered this oration late in the night outside Basra, immediately following the Battle of the Camel in 36/656, to a group of men from ʿAlī's own army, who were presumably blaming the world for the inexplicable failings of Ṭalḥah, Zubayr, and ʿĀʾishah. ʿAlī reminds them that the world is not responsible for the fate of its inhabitants. It is followed in this source and some others by § 3.119. Ibn al-ʿAsākir (*Tārīkh*, 42:499) places this oration in the Grand Mosque in Kufa, in response to a man whom ʿAlī heard chastising the world. Muwaffaq bi'llāh (*Iʿtibār*, 51) narrates it from Aṣbagh ibn Nubātah, who says ʿAlī spoke these words in response to a man who complained about the state of the world. See further analysis of § 3.119–20 in Qutbuddin, "ʿAlī's Contemplations on this World and the Hereafter," 345–348.

أيّها الذامّ للدنيا أتغترّ بالدنيا' ثمّ تذمّها أنت المتجرّم عليها أم هي المتجرّمة عليك. متى
استهوتك أم متى غرّتك أبمصارع آبائك من البِلى أم بمضاجع أمّهاتك تحت الثرى. كم
علّلت بكفّيك وكم مرّضت بيديك تبغي لهم الشفاء وتستوصف لهم الأطبّاء لم ينفع
أحدهم إشفاقك ولم تُسعَف فيه بطَلِبتك ولم تدفع عنه بقوّتك. قد مثّلت لك به الدنيا
نفسك وبمصرعه مصرعك. إنّ الدنيا دار صدق لمن صَدَقها ودار عافية لمن فهم عنها
ودار غنى لمن تزوّد منها ودار موعظة لمن اتّعظ بها. مسجدُ أحبّاء الله ومُصلّى ملائكة
الله ومَهبِط وحي الله ومَتجَر أولياء الله اكتسبوا فيها الرحمة ورَبِحوا فيها الجنّة. فمن ذا يذمّها
وقد آذَنَت ببينها ونادت بفراقها ونعَتْ نفسها وأهلها فمثّلت لهم ببلائها البلاء وشوّقتهم
بسرورها إلى السرور. راحت بعافية وابتكرت بفجيعة ترغيبًا وترهيبًا وتخويفًا وتحذيرًا
فذمّها رجال غداة الندامة وحمدها آخرون يوم القيامة ذكّرتهم الدنيا فذكروا وحدّثتهم
فصدّقوا ووعظتهم فاتّعظوا.

3.121 وقال عليه السلام: إنّ لله ملكًا ينادي في كلّ يوم لِدُوا للموت واجمعوا للفناء وابنوا
للخراب.

3.122 وقال عليه السلام: الدنيا دار ممرّ إلى دار مقرّ والناس فيها رجلان رجل باعَ نفسه
فأوبقها ورجل ابتاع نفسه فأعتقها.

' ش، ن، هـ: كذا. م: ⟨المغترّ بغرورها⟩. ي: ⟨المغترّ بغرورها بِمَ تذمّها أتغترّ بالدنيا⟩.

You who reproach this world—do you choose to be deceived by her yet censure her? Should you be accusing her, or should she be accusing you? When did she lure or deceive you? Was it by her destruction of your father and grandfather and great-grandfather through decay? Or by her consigning your mother and grandmother and great-grandmother to the earth?[1] How carefully did your hands tend them! How tenderly did your fingers nurse them! All the while you were hoping against hope for a cure, begging physician after physician for a treatment. Your apprehension did not benefit any one of them, your appeal remained unanswered, and you could not keep death away from them, even though you applied all your strength. In this way, the world warned you of your own approaching end. By their death, she illustrated your own. Indeed, this world is a house of truth for all who stay true to her, a house of wellbeing for all who understand her, a house of riches for all who gather her provisions, a house of counsel for all who take her advice. She is a mosque for God's loved ones, a place where God's angels pray, where God's revelation alights, where God's saints transact, earning his mercy and gaining paradise. Who would blame her, when she has declared her imminent separation, proclaimed her impending departure, and announced her and her people's impending destruction? By her trials she has illustrated the greatest trial, and by her delights awakened a desire for the truest delight. In the evening she leaves you healthy and happy, only to turn up the next morning with a terrible calamity. All this, to awaken your desire and your alarm, to stir up your fear and your vigilance. Some will blame her on the morning of regret. Others will praise her on the day of resurrection. For she reminded them, and they took heed. She told them about herself, and they believed. She counseled them, and they were mindful.

3.121 An angel has been assigned by God to call out every day: "Give birth for death! Gather for annihilation! Build for destruction!"[2]

3.122 The world is a course through which we must pass, not a permanent home. Its people are of two kinds: those who sell their souls and destroy them, and those who ransom their souls and set them free.

---

1   Lit. "your fathers" (*ābāʾika*) and "your mothers" (*ummahātika*), meaning parents and forebears.
2   This saying is echoed in the verse of the Abbasid poet Abū al-ʿAtāhiyah (*Dīwān*, 46), "Give birth for death and build for destruction, for each of you walks the path of death."

لدوا للموت وأبنوا للخراب   فكلّكم تصير إلى تباب

3.123 وقال عليه السلام: لا يكون الصديق صديقًا حتّى يحفظ أخاه في ثلاث في نكبته وغيبته ووفاته.

3.124 وقال عليه السلام: من أُعطي أربعًا لم يُحرَم أربعًا من أعطي الدعاء لم يحرم الإجابة ومن أعطي التوبة لم يحرم القبول ومن أعطي الاستغفار لم يحرم المغفرة ومن أعطي الشكر لم يحرم الزيادة.

وتصديق ذلك في كتاب الله سبحانه قال الله عزّ وجلّ في الدعاء ﴿ادْعُونِي أَسْتَجِبْ لَكُمْ﴾ وقال في الاستغفار ﴿وَمَن يَعْمَلْ سُوءًا أَوْ يَظْلِمْ نَفْسَهُ ثُمَّ يَسْتَغْفِرِ اللّهَ يَجِدِ اللّهَ غَفُورًا رَحِيمًا﴾ وقال في الشكر ﴿لَئِن شَكَرْتُمْ لَأَزِيدَنَّكُمْ﴾ وقال في التوبة ﴿إِنَّمَا التَّوْبَةُ عَلَى اللّهِ لِلَّذِينَ يَعْمَلُونَ السُّوءَ بِجَهَالَةٍ ثُمَّ يَتُوبُونَ مِن قَرِيبٍ فَأُولَئِكَ يَتُوبُ اللّهُ عَلَيْهِمْ وَكَانَ اللّهُ عَلِيمًا حَكِيمًا﴾.

3.125 وقال عليه السلام: الصلاة قربان كلّ تقيّ.

والحجّ جهاد كلّ ضعيف.

ولكلّ شيء زكاة وزكاة البدن الصيام.

وجهاد المرأة حسن التبعُّل.

3.126 وقال عليه السلام: استنزلوا الرزق بالصدقة ومن أيقن بالخلف جادَ بالعطيّة.

3.127 وقال عليه السلام: تنزل المعونة على قدر المؤونة.

3.123 A friend is not true unless he protects his brother in three circumstances: in his misfortune, during his absence, and after his death.

3.124 Whoever is granted four gifts will not be refused four others: Whoever is granted the gift of prayer will not be refused an answer. Whoever is granted the gift of repentance will not be refused acceptance. Whoever is granted the gift of seeking forgiveness will not be refused forgiveness. And whoever is granted the gift of gratitude will not be refused further blessings.[1]

Verification is provided by the Book of God:[2] About prayer, he has said, «Pray to me and I will answer.»[3] About seeking forgiveness, he has said, «Whoever does wrong or oppresses his soul, but then seeks forgiveness from God, will find that God is forgiving and merciful.»[4] About gratitude, he has said, «If you give thanks, you will be given more.»[5] About repentance, he has said, «God accepts the repentance of those who do wrong in ignorance then repent soon thereafter; they are the ones whose repentance God accepts; God is knowing and wise.»[6]

3.125 The pious draw near to God through the ritual prayer.[7]
Hajj is the jihad of the frail.
There is a levy on all things—the body's is fasting.
Being a good wife is a woman's jihad.

3.126 Draw down God's sustenance by giving alms. Those who are certain about the hereafter give generously.[8]

3.127 Assistance is sent in accordance with need.[9]

---

1 Similar to §3.407.
2 Both paragraphs of §3.124 are attributed to ʿAlī in Sibṭ, *Tadhkirah*, 133, which is how I have presented it here, whereas Ibn Abī al-Ḥadīd (H 18:331) reads the second paragraph as Raḍī's commentary, Baḥrānī (B 970) does not clarify his position, and the manuscripts of Rāwandī's commentary (R 3:309) differ between the two positions. Both paragraphs are attributed to Imam Jaʿfar al-Ṣādiq in Ṣadūq, *Khiṣāl*, 202.
3 Qurʾan, Ghāfir 40:60.
4 Qurʾan, Nisāʾ 4:110.
5 Qurʾan, Ibrāhīm 14:7.
6 Qurʾan, Nisāʾ 4:17.
7 This set of sayings, §3.125, is attributed to the Prophet in Quḍāʿī, *Shihāb*, §1.205, 1.72, 1.176, 1.73.
8 Second line attributed to the Prophet in Quḍāʿī, *Shihāb*, §2.31.
9 Similar line attributed to the Prophet in Quḍāʿī, *Shihāb*, §7.21.

3.128   وقال عليه السلام: ما عالَ امرؤٌ اقتصد.

3.129   وقال عليه السلام: قلّة العِيال أحد اليسارين.

والتودُّد نصف العقل.

والهمّ نصف الهَرم.

3.130   وقال عليه السلام: ينزل الصبر على قدر المصيبة ومن ضرب يده على نخَذِه عند مصيبته حَبِط أجره.

3.131   وقال عليه السلام: كم من صائم ليس له من صيامه إلّا الظماا وكم من قائم ليس له من قيامه إلّا العنا. حَبّذا نوم الأكياس وإفطارهم.

3.132   وقال عليه السلام: سوسوا إيمانكم بالصدقة وحصّنوا أموالكم بالزكاة وأدفعوا أمواج البلاء بالدعاء.

3.133   كلامه عليه السلام لكُميل بن زياد النَّخَعيّ. قال كميل بن زياد أخذ بيدي أمير المؤمنين عليّ بن أبي طالب صلوات الله عليه فأخرجني إلى الجبّان فلمّا أصْحَر تنفَّس الصُّعداء ثمّ قال يا كميل بن زياد إنّ هذه القلوب أوعية نخيرها أوعاها فاحفظ عنّي ما أقول لك. الناس ثلاثة فعالم رَبّانيّ ومتعلّم على سبيل النجاة وهَمجٌ رَعاعٌ أتباع كلّ ناعق يميلون مع كلّ ريح لم يستضيئوا بنور العلم ولم يلجؤوا إلى ركن وثيق. يا كميل العلم خير من المال العلم يحرسك وأنت تحرس المال والمال تنقصه النفقة والعلم يزكو على الإنفاق وصنيع المال يزول بزواله. يا كميل بن زياد معرفة العلم دينٌ يُدانُ به يَكسِب الإنسانُ الطاعة في حياته وجميل الأحدوثة بعد وفاته والعلم حاكم والمال محكوم عليه. يا كميل بن زياد هلك خزّان الأموال وهم أحياء والعلماء باقون ما بقي الدهر أعيانهم مفقودة وأمثالهم في القلوب

―――――――

ا م، ش، ن، هـ: كذا. ي: كذا. هـ: كذا، وزيادة في م، ش، وفي هامش هـ: أضيفت ﴿والجوع﴾.

3.128 Practice moderation and need nothing.[1]

3.129 Having a small family is one way to affluence.[2]
Affection is one half of discernment.
Worry is one half of aging.

3.130 Patience is rewarded in proportion to the affliction. Those who strike their hand on their thigh when afflicted lose their reward.

3.131 Many who fast gain nothing but thirst. Many who pray gain nothing but fatigue. O how excellent the sleep and the food of the wise!

3.132 Foster your faith through charity. Fortify your wealth by paying the alms-levy.[3] Ward off the gales of calamity by supplicating God.

3.133 These are ʿAlī's words to Kumayl ibn Ziyād al-Nakhaʿī, who narrated: The Commander of the Faithful, ʿAlī ibn Abī Ṭālib, took my hand and led me toward the cemetery. When he reached the desert, he sighed deeply, and said to me:[4]
Kumayl, these hearts are like vessels, and the best are those that best receive and store. Take heed of what I am about to tell you. There are three types of people: those with divine learning, apprentices who walk the path of salvation, and the ignorant rabble, followers of any bleating fool, who sway with every wind, seeking neither illumination from the light of knowledge, nor support from a sturdy column. Kumayl, knowledge is better than wealth: knowledge protects you, whereas you must protect wealth, wealth decreases with spending, whereas knowledge increases when you distribute it, and the benefits of wealth cease with its ceasing. Kumayl, knowledge is a faith to be followed: it earns a man obedience during his lifetime,[5] and leaves a beautiful legacy of remembrance after his death—and knowledge rules, whereas wealth is ruled over. Kumayl, those who hoard wealth are dead even as they live, whereas the learned remain for as long as the world remains—their persons may be lost, but their teachings live on in the hearts of men. Truly, abundant knowledge is housed here (signaling to his breast), if only I could find bearers for it! But no! I

---

1 Similar line attributed to the Prophet Muḥammad in Quḍāʿī, *Shihāb*, § 5.1.
2 Similar lines to § 3.129, attributed to the Prophet in Quḍāʿī, *Shihāb*, § 1.23, 1.21, 1.22.
3 Ar. *zakāh*. The line is attributed to the Prophet in Quḍāʿī, *Shihāb*, § 4.56.
4 Presumably in Kufa during ʿAlī's caliphate, 35–40/656–661. The Arabic word *jabbān*, an uncommon word for "cemetery," frequently refers in the sources to the cemetery outside Kufa.
5 Translation based on B 973. Or, "It helps you practice obedience to your Lord in your lifetime," based on Ḥ 18:349, citing Qurʾan, Fāṭir 35:28.

موجودة. ها إنّ هاهنا لعلمًا جمًّا (وأشار إلى صدره) لو أصبت له حملة بَلى أُصيب لَقِنًا غير مأمون عليه مستعملًا آلة الدين للدنيا ومستظهِرًا بنعم الله على عباده وبحججه على أوليائه أو مُنقادًا لحملة الحقّ لا بصيرة له في أحنائه ينقدح الشكّ في قلبه لأوّل عارض من شبهة ألا لا ذا ولا ذاك أو منهومًا باللذة سَلِس القياد للشهوة أو مُغرَمًا بالجمع والادّخار ليسا من رعاة الدين في شيء أقرب شيء شَبَهًا بهما الأنعام السائمة. كذلك يموت العلم بموت حامليه. اللّهمّ بلى لا تخلو الأرض من قائم لله بحجّة إمّا ظاهرًا مشهورًا أو خائفًا مغمورًا لئلّا تبطل حجج الله وبيّناته وكم ذا وأين أولئك أولئك والله الأقلّون عددًا والأعظمون قدرًا يحفظ الله حججه وبيّناته بهم حتّى يودعوها نظراءهم ويزرعوها في قلوب أشباههم هجم بهم العلم على حقيقة البصيرة وباشروا روح اليقين واستلانوا ما استوعره المُتَرَفون وأَنِسوا بما استوحش منه الجاهلون وصحبوا الدنيا بأبدان أرواحها مُعلَّقة بالمحلّ الأعلى أولئك خلفاء الله في أرضه والدعاة إلى دينه. آه آه شوقًا إلى رؤيتهم. انصرف إذا شئت.

3.134 وقال عليه السلام: المرء مخبوء تحت لسانه.

3.135 وقال عليه السلام: هلك امرؤ لم يعرف قَدْره.

3.136 وقال عليه السلام لرجل سأله أن يعظه

لا تكن ممّن يرجو الآخرة بغير العمل ويُرجّي[1] التوبة بطول الأمل يقول في الدنيا بقول الزاهدين ويعمل فيها بعمل الراغبين إن أعطي منها لم يشبع وإن منع منها لم يقنع يعجز عن شكر ما أوتي ويبتغي الزيادة فيما بقي ولا ينتهي ويأمر بما لا يأتي يحبّ الصالحين ولا يعمل عملهم ويبغض المذنبين وهو أحدهم يكره الموت لكثرة ذنوبه ويقيم على ما يكره الموت له إن سقم ظلّ نادمًا وإن صحّ أمن لاهيًا يُعجَب بنفسه إذا عوفي ويقنط إذا ابتلي إن أصابه بلاء دعا مضطرًّا وإن ناله رخاء أعرض مُغترًّا تغلبه

---

[1] ن، ش، ه: كذا. ي، ونسخة في ه: ﴿يرجئ﴾.

encounter clever students who are not trustworthy, who use the instrument of religion for worldly benefit, who attempt to use God's favors to attack his servants, and his proofs to gain victory over his select. I encounter others who have been guided to the bearers of truth but have no real perception—doubt is kindled in their hearts by the first appearance of misgivings. Hark, neither is to be countenanced! There is a third type, enamored of carnal pleasures, easily led to passions, or yet another, in thrall to hoarding and collecting. Neither is mindful of religion. In fact, they are closest to grazing cattle. This is how knowledge dies, through the death of its bearers. But no, by God! There will always be a person on earth who upholds God's proof—whether visible and known or fearful and concealed—for God's proof can never be overthrown. How many are they, and where? By God, they are few in number, but great in stature! Through them God protects his proof, until they entrust it to others like them, sowing it in the hearts of their peers. Knowledge has led them to real perception, enabling them to touch the spirit of certainty, to deem easy what the dissolute find difficult, and take comfort in what the ignorant find miserable. In this world they live in bodies whose spirits are linked to the highest abode. They are God's vicegerents on his earth, who call to his religion. Ah! Would that I could see them!

You may take your leave now.

3.134 A man is concealed behind his tongue.

3.135 The man who does not recognize his own worth will perish.

3.136 ʿAlī said to a man who asked him for counsel:[1]
Do not be one of those who expect the hereafter without work or who postpone repentance through complacent hopes of a long life. They talk of rejecting the world but reveal their desire for it in their conduct. When they are given of its stocks, they are not satisfied, when those are withheld from them, they are angry. Incapable of gratitude for God's gifts, they want more. They forbid others from evil but do not desist, they command others to do good but do not perform. They love good people but do not behave like them, they detest the wicked but resemble them. They fear death because of their many sins yet continue to do the very things that make them fearful. If they fall ill, they repent, but once healthy, they feel secure and resume their frolics. When fit, they are full of themselves, but when tested, they despair. When afflicted with poverty, they supplicate God and beg him, but when they regain affluence, they turn

---

1 Part of an oration delivered on the pulpit in the Grand Mosque of Kufa, following the Battle of Nahrawān in 38/658. Muttaqī-Hindī, *Kanz*, 16:205.

نفسه على ما يظنّ ولا يغلبها على ما يستيقن يخاف على غيره بأدنى من ذنبه ويرجو لنفسه بأكثر من عمله إن ٱستغنى بَطِر وفُتِن وإن ٱفتقر قَنَط ووَهَن يقصّر إذا عمل ويبالغ إذا سأل إن عرضت له شهوة أسلف المعصية وسوّف التوبة وإن عَرَته محنة ٱنفرج عن شرائط الملّة يصف العبرة ولا يعتبر ويبالغ في الموعظة ولا يتّعظ فهو بالقول مُدِلّ ومن العمل مُقِلّ ينافس فيما يفنى ويسامح فيما يبقى يرى الغُنْم مَغْرَمًا والغرم مَغْنَمًا يخشى الموت ولا يبادر الفوت يستعظم من معصية غيره ما يستقلّ أكثر منه من نفسه ويستكثر من طاعته ما يحقره من طاعة غيره فهو على الناس طاعن ولنفسه مُداهِن اللهو مع الأغنياء أحبّ إليه من الذكر مع الفقراء يحكم على غيره لنفسه ولا يحكم عليها لغيره ويرشد غيره ويغوي نفسه فهو يُطاع ويَعصي ويَستوفي ولا يُوفي ويخشى الخلق في غير ربّه ولا يخشى ربّه في خلقه.

ولو لم يكن في هذا الكتاب إلّا هذا الكلام لكفى به موعظة ناجعة وحكمة بالغة وبصيرة لمبصر وعبرة لناظر مفكّر.

3.137 وقال عليه السلام: لكلّ ٱمرئٍ[1] عاقبة حلوة أو مرّة.

3.138 وقال عليه السلام: لكلّ مقبل إدبار وما أدبر كأن لم يكن.

3.139 وقال عليه السلام: لا يعدم الصبور الظفر وإن طال به الزمان.

3.140 وقال عليه السلام: الراضي بفعل قوم كالداخل معهم فيه وعلى كلّ داخل في باطل إثمان إثم العمل به وإثم الرضى به.

---

١ ن، ي، ه: كذا. ش: ‹أمرٍ›.

away in prideful delusion. Their ego compels them to follow its inclinations, they do not compel it to follow the path of certainty. For others, they expect punishment for sins lesser than their own, for themselves, they expect greater reward than their deeds have earned. If they acquire wealth, they turn insolent and are seduced, if they become poor, they despair and grow weak. They fall short in their deeds yet make grand requests. If passions tempt them, they go ahead and sin, postponing repentance for later. If tribulation strikes them, they cast off the curbs of religion. They describe the world's lessons to others but do not themselves learn. They deliver pretentious sermons but do not take them to heart. Their words are bold, but their deeds are few. They compete for what perishes but are generous in giving away what endures. They see gain as loss and loss as gain. They fear death yet do nothing in its anticipation. They consider others' sins momentous yet deem insignificant their own numerous transgressions. They glorify their own acts of obedience yet think the same acts contemptible when others do them. They calumniate others and flatter themselves. Idle talk with the rich is dearer to them than worshipping God with the poor. They judge others but not themselves. They counsel others but delude themselves. They expect others to obey them, yet they disobey. They expect full measure but do not pay a fair price. When facing their Lord, they fear his creatures. When facing his creatures, they do not fear their Lord.

Raḍī: If this book contained just these words and nothing else, it would contain enough effective counsel, far-reaching wisdom, discernment for those who discern, and lessons for those who see and think!

3.137 Every man faces an outcome, whether sweet or bitter.[1]

3.138 Everything that moves forward turns back, and everything that turns back is as if it never were.

3.139 Success comes to those who are patient, even if the wait is long.

3.140 Anyone who agrees with other people's deeds is a doer himself, and anyone who does wrong commits two sins: the sin of committing the deed and the sin of agreeing with those who committed it.

---

1   Ar. *kullu -mri'in*. Or, based on the variant reading in MS Sh, "Everything (*kullu amrin*) has a consequence, whether sweet or bitter."

3.141　وقال عليه السلام: اعتصموا بالذمم في أوتادها.

3.142　وقال عليه السلام: عليكم بطاعة من لا تُعذرون بجهالته.

3.143　وقال عليه السلام: قد بُصّرتم إن أبصرتم وقد هُديتم إن آهتديتم.

3.144　وقال عليه السلام: عاتِب أخاك بالإحسان إليه وآردد شرّه بالإنعام عليه.

3.145　وقال عليه السلام: من وضع نفسه مواضع التُّهمة فلا يلومنّ من أساء به الظنّ.

3.146　وقال عليه السلام: من ملك آستأثر ومن آستبدّ برأيه هلك ومن شاور الرجال شاركها في عقولها ومن كتم سرّه كانت الخِيَرة بيده.

3.147　وقال عليه السلام: الفقر الموت الأكبر.

3.148　وقال عليه السلام: من قضى حقّ من لا يقضي حقّه فقد عبده.

3.149　وقال عليه السلام: لا طاعة لمخلوق في معصية الخالق.

3.141 Protect your covenants and secure their fastenings.[1]

3.142 Obey the one you are required to obey—your failure to recognize him will not be pardoned.[2]

3.143 Truly, you have been given the capacity to see if you would but look, to be guided if you would but follow.[3]

3.144 Chastise your brother by being good to him. Deflect his malice by being generous to him.

3.145 A person who frequents places of ill repute should not blame those who suspect him of wrongdoing.

3.146 One who gains power usurps. One who clings to his own opinion perishes. One who consults mature men partakes of the fruit of their minds. One who conceals his secret retains his options.

3.147 Poverty is the ultimate death.

3.148 If you offer dues to a man who does not offer you yours in return, you have offered him servile worship.

3.149 Do not obey humans if it means that you will disobey God.[4]

---

1 From a lengthy address by ʿAlī when Marwān ibn al-Ḥakam and several of the Freedmen of Quraysh came to offer him allegiance after they were taken captive by ʿAlī's forces at the Battle of the Camel in 36/656. ʿAlī is reported to have exclaimed, "Did you not pledge allegiance to me yesterday?" i.e., in Medina after ʿUthmān's death (similar lines in §1.70). Ḥ 18:372. "Fastenings," lit. "pegs" (*awtād*) refers to "commitments," after R 3:336; or to "trustworthy persons," thus translating as: "Protect your compacts with trustworthy persons," and do not rely on compacts offered by disbelievers and rebels, after Ḥ 18:372, citing Qurʾan, Tawbah 9:10–12.

2 Included in a deathbed testament of counsel ʿAlī wrote for his children and followers, thus in Kufa in 40/661 (Nuʿmān, *Daʿāʾim*, 2:353). According to all the commentators, "the one you must obey" refers to ʿAlī himself. Ibn Abī al-Ḥadīd (Ḥ 18:373) explains: ʿAlī is an Imam, obedience to whom is mandatory according to all Muslims, through the community's pledge, according to Sunnis, and through the Prophet's appointment, according to the Shiʿa; and whoever fails to recognize his imamate will burn in hellfire; no excuse will be deemed acceptable.

3 Included in §1.20.

4 Attributed to the Prophet in Quḍāʿī, *Shihāb*, §6.34.

3.150 وقال عليه السلام: لا يُعاب المرء بتأخير حقّه إنّما يعاب من أخذ ما ليس له.

3.151 وقال عليه السلام: الإعجاب يمنع من الازدياد.

3.152 وقال عليه السلام: الأمر قريب والاصطحاب قليل.

3.153 وقال عليه السلام: قد أضاء الصبح لذي عينين.

3.154 وقال عليه السلام: ترك الذنب أهون من طلب التوبة.

3.155 وقال عليه السلام: كم من أَكْلة منعت أَكَلات.

3.156 وقال عليه السلام: الناس أعداء ما جهلوا.

3.157 وقال عليه السلام: من اُستقبل وجوه الآراء عرف مواقع الخطأ.

3.158 وقال عليه السلام: من أحدّ سِنان الغضب لله قوي على قتل أشدّاء الباطل.

3.159 وقال عليه السلام: إذا هِبْتَ أمرًا فقَعْ فيه فإنّ شدّة تَوَقّيه أعظم ممّا تخاف منه.

3.160 وقال عليه السلام: آلة الرياسة سعة الصدر.

3.161 وقال عليه السلام: ازجر المسيء بثواب المحسن.

3.162 وقال عليه السلام: احصد الشرّ من صدر غيرك بقلعه من صدرك.

3.163 وقال عليه السلام: اللَّجَاجة تَسُلّ الرأي.

3.164 وقال عليه السلام: الطمع رِقّ مُؤبّد.

3.150 Don't condemn the man who delays in securing what belongs to him. It's the man who takes what does not belong to him who deserves your condemnation.

3.151 Vanity impedes growth.

3.152 The end is near, and the fellowship is short.

3.153 The morning is bright for those who have eyes.

3.154 Not sinning is easier than seeking pardon.

3.155 How many a morsel has prevented a full meal![1]

3.156 People hate the unfamiliar.[2]

3.157 Those who seek others' opinions recognize potential pitfalls.[3]

3.158 Those who sharpen spears of righteous anger have the strength to strike down champions of evil.

3.159 If you fear something, jump right into it. The strain of avoiding is worse than the thing you fear.

3.160 Broad-mindedness is the instrument of leadership.[4]

3.161 Repay malice with kindness and you will have rebuked.

3.162 Cut away malice from others' hearts by uprooting it from your own.

3.163 Hostility robs one of judgment.[5]

3.164 Greed is perpetual bondage.

---

1 Repurposed by Ḥarīrī (*Maqāmāt*, 24), in his Kufa Maqāmah, § 5.
2 Identical to § 3.409.
3 Part of ʿAlī's testament of counsel to his son Ḥusayn. Ḥarrānī, *Tuḥaf*, 90.
4 Ar. *saʿat al-ṣadr*, lit. "An expansive chest is the instrument of leadership."
5 The translation follows B 979. Or it could be translated more specifically as "[Your] hostility steals [the opportunity to implement my, i.e., ʿAlī's] good strategy," after Ḥ 18:412.

٣،١٦٥ وقال عليه السلام: ثمرة التفريط الندامة وثمرة الحزم السلامة.

٣،١٦٦ وقال عليه السلام: لا خير في الصمت عن الحكم كما أنّه لا خير في القول بالجهل.

٣،١٦٧ وقال عليه السلام: ما اختلفت دعوتان إلّا كانت إحداهما ضلالة.

٣،١٦٨ وقال عليه السلام: ما شككتُ في الحقّ مذ أُريته.

٣،١٦٩ وقال عليه السلام: ما كَذبتُ ولا كُذبت ولا ضَللت ولا ضُلَّ بي.

٣،١٧٠ وقال عليه السلام: للظالم البادي غدًا بكفّه عَضّة.

٣،١٧١ وقال عليه السلام: الرحيل وشيك.

٣،١٧٢ وقال عليه السلام: من أبدى صفحته للحقّ هلك.

٣،١٧٣ وقال عليه السلام: من لم يُنجِه الصبر أهلكه الجزع.

3.165 Extravagance yields regret, prudence yields wellbeing.

3.166 There is no virtue in holding back wisdom, just as there is no virtue in ignorant speech.

3.167 When two missions differ, one is wrong.

3.168 I have never doubted the truth ever since it was shown to me.[1]

3.169 I have never lied, nor have I been lied to.[2] I have never strayed, nor have I been led to stray.

3.170 One who instigates violence will bite his knuckles on the morrow.[3]

3.171 The time for departure draws nigh.

3.172 Those who challenge the truth perish.[4]

3.173 Those who are not saved by patience are slain by panic.

---

1   From oration §1.4, delivered after the Battle of the Camel in 36/656, addressing Ṭalḥah and Zubayr posthumously, as well as their defeated followers. R 136 (after Miskawayh); Ḥ 1:209; B 164.

2   "Nor have I been lied to," means I have never been lied to by the Prophet in what he informed me would happen (B 980). This line is placed by the sources within several orations by ʿAlī, and may have been spoken by him on various occasions: (1) At the Battle of the Camel, outside Basra in 36/656, responding to a man who chastised him for fighting Muslims (Ḥ 1:265, after Abū Mikhnaf); (2) in the Kufa mosque, addressing a man from Basra (Māmaṭīrī, *Nuzhah*, 178); (3) at Ṣiffīn in 37/657, addressing his followers (Minqarī, *Waqʿat Ṣiffīn*, 315); and (4) at the Battle of Nahrawān, in 38/658 either before the battle, or afterward, while instructing people to look for Dhū al-Thudayyah among the Kharijites' corpses (Ṭabarī, *Tārīkh*, 5:88; Nuʿmān, *Manāqib*, 214; Ḥ 6:129, 18:368).

3   I.e., in remorse. Reference to Qurʾan, Furqān 25:27.

4   Included in §1.16, ʿAlī's first oration after the pledge of allegiance to him as caliph in Medina in 35/656. Translation follows Ḥ 18:371; R 3:337. Following B 980 and F 436, the line may alternatively be translated as, "Whoever exposes his face for the sake of truth will be killed [by the ignorant masses]"—the inserted final phrase is stated explicitly in §1.16.

٣،١٧٤ وقال عليه السلام: واعِجباه أتكون الخلافة بالصحابة ولا تكون بالصحابة والقرابة.

وروي له شعر في هذا المعنى وهو¹

فَكَيْفَ بِهَـٰذَا وَالمُشِيرُونَ غُيَّبْ	فَإِنْ كُنْتَ بِالشُّورى مَلَكْتَ أُمُورَهُمْ
فَغَيْرُكَ أَوْلـى بِالنَّبِـيِّ وَأَقْرَبْ	وَإِنْ كُنْتَ بِالقُرْبى حَجَجْتَ خَصِيمَهُمْ

٣،١٧٥ وقال عليه السلام: إنّما المرء في الدنيا غَرَض تَنتضل فيه المنايا ونَهْب تبادره المصائب ومع كلّ جُرعة شَرَقٌ وفي كلّ أُكلة غَصَص. ولا ينال العبد نعمة إلّا بفراق أخرى ولا يستقبل يوماً من عمره إلّا بفراق آخر من أجله. فنحن أعوان المَنون وأنفسنا نَصْبُ الحُتوف فمن أين نرجو البقاء وهذا الليل والنهار لم يرفعا من شيء شرفاً إلّا أسرعا الكرَّة في هدم ما بَنَيا وتفريق ما جمعا.

٣،١٧٦ وقال عليه السلام: يا ابن آدم ما كسبت فوق قوتك فأنت فيه خازن لغيرك.

٣،١٧٧ وقال عليه السلام: إنّ للقلوب شهوة وإقبالًا وإدبارًا فأتوها من قِبَل شهوتها وإقبالها فإنّ القلب إذا أُكره عَمِي.

٣،١٧٨ وكان عليه السلام يقول

متى أشفي غيظي إذا غضبت أحين أعجز عن الانتقام فيقال لي لو صبرت أم حين أقدر عليه فيقال لي لو عفوت.²

<hr>

١ البحر: الطويل.   ٢ ش، ن، ونسخة في ه: كذا. ي، ه، ونسخة في ش، ن: ⟨غفرت⟩.

3.174 How sad, how strange! So, the caliphate can be justified through the Prophet's companionship, but not through companionship and kinship together![1]

The following verses are attributed to ʿAlī in the same vein:

> If you became their ruler through consultation,
> How is this valid when the counsellors were absent?
> If you argued against your opponent through kinship,
> Then another, closer than you to the Prophet, is worthier!

3.175 Every man in this world is a target at which fate shoots its arrows, he is booty for calamity to plunder. With every sip he chokes, with every bite he gags. He obtains no blessing without relinquishing another, greets no new day except after bidding farewell to one from his allotted share. We are all death's assistants, and our human forms are quarries of doom—how can we hope to survive? Night and Day erect nothing without swerving back to destroy what they have built, to scatter what they have brought together![2]

3.176 Son of Adam, whatever you earn above your needs, you keep in store for another.

3.177 Hearts have passions, there are times when they are receptive and others when they are withdrawn. Approach them by way of their passions, then, and at times when they are receptive, for a heart turns blind when coerced.[3]

3.178 When should I satisfy my rage? Should it be when I have no power to demand vengeance and am admonished, "You should forbear!" or when I have the power to exact retribution and am advised, "You should forgive"?

---

1 Immediately after the death of the Prophet in Medina in 11/632, when Abū Bakr was sworn in as caliph. As explained in my Note on the Edition and Translation: Previous Editions (p. 48), this is the original text (واعجباه أتكون الخلافة بالصحابة ولا تكون بالصحابة والقرابة), transcribed thus in all early manuscripts I used and all medieval commentaries I looked at. (See also lines to this effect in ʿAlī's letter to Muʿāwiyah, §2.28.2.) In the modern print editions, it has been corrupted to: (واعجباه أتكون الخلافة بالصحابة والقرابة): "How strange that the caliphate is justified through companionship and kinship!"
2 Related with some variants in §1.143.1. Ḥarrānī (*Tuḥaf*, 98) transcribes it within the aphoristic oration titled *Wasīlah*.
3 First lines similar to §3.298.

3.179 وقال عليه السلام وقد مرّ بقذر على مَزبلة

هذا ما بخل به الباخلون.

ورُوي أنّه قال عليه السلام

هذا ما كنتم تتنافسون فيه بالأمس.

3.180 وقال عليه السلام: لم يذهب من مالك ما وعظك.

3.181 وقال عليه السلام: إنّ القلوب تَمَلّ كما تملّ الأبدان فابتغوا لها طرائف الحكمة.

3.182 وقال عليه السلام لمّا سمع قول الخوارج ﴿لا حكم إلا لله﴾

كلمة حقّ يُراد بها باطل.

3.183 وقال عليه السلام في صفة الغَوغاء

هم الذين إذا اجتمعوا غَلبوا وإذا تفرّقوا لم يُعرفوا.

وقيل بل قال

هم الذين إذا اجتمعوا ضَرّوا وإذا تفرّقوا نفعوا.

فقيل قد علمنا مَضَرّة اجتماعهم فما منفعة افتراقهم فقال

يرجع أصحاب المِهَن إلى مِهنهم فينتفع الناس بهم كرجوع البَنّاء إلى بنائه والنَّسّاج إلى مَنسجه والخَبّاز إلى مَخبزه.

3.184 وقال عليه السلام وقد أُتي بجانٍ ومعه غَوغاء

لا مرحبًا بوجوه لا تُرى إلّا عند كلّ سَوءة.

3.185 وقال عليه السلام: إنّ مع كلّ إنسان ملكَين يحفظانه فإذا جاء القدر خَلّيا بينه وبينه وإنّ الأجل جُنّة حصينة.

3.179 Walking past refuse on a rubbish dump, 'Alī exclaimed:
This is what the misers hoarded!

Raḍī: It is alternatively narrated that 'Alī exclaimed:
This is what you were brawling over yesterday!

3.180 Wealth is not lost if losing it teaches you a lesson.

3.181 Minds tire, just as bodies tire, so seek for them wondrous novelties of wisdom.[1]

3.182 Hearing the Kharijites' slogan, ⟨No rule save God's!⟩ 'Alī remarked:[2]
The statement is true, but the intent is false.

3.183 Describing the rabble among people, 'Alī said:[3]
When they unite, they overpower. When they disperse, they can't be recognized.

Raḍī: It is alternatively narrated that what he said was this:
When they unite, they harm. When they disperse, they benefit.

Raḍī: He was asked, "We know of the harm they cause when they unite, but what is the benefit they offer when they disperse?" and he replied:
Workers return to their work, and everyone benefits. The builder returns to building, the weaver returns to weaving, and the baker returns to baking.

3.184 A felon, with a crowd behind him, was brought before 'Alī, who exclaimed:[4]
How contemptible these faces seen only at the site of someone's shame!

3.185 Each person has two angels assigned to protect him, until, when his ordained fate approaches, they let it in. In truth, your allotted span is a powerful shield.[5]

---

1 Nearly identical to §3.83.
2 In Kufa, after the arbitration in 37/658. Yaʿqūbī, *Tārīkh*, 2:191; Ṭabarī, *Tārīkh* 5:72–73. See also §1.40 and §1.182 and the accompanying notes.
3 Presumably in Kufa, during 'Alī's caliphate, 35–40/656–661.
4 Presumably in Kufa, during 'Alī's caliphate, 35–40/656–661. Lit. "No welcome to these faces" (*lā marḥaban bi-wujūhin*).
5 A little before 'Alī was killed in Kufa in 40/661, when a man from the Murād tribe came to him to warn him of his tribesmen Ibn Muljam al-Murādī's intent to kill him. Ibn Saʿd, *Ṭabaqāt*, 3:43.

3.186   وقال عليه السلام وقد قال له طلحة والزبير نبايعك على أنّا شركاؤك في هذا الأمر لا ولكنّكما شريكان في القوّة والاستعانة وعونان على العجز والأَوَد.

3.187   وقال عليه السلام: أيّها الناس اتّقوا الله الذي إن قلتم سمع وإن أضمرتم علم وبادروا الموت الذي إن هربتم أدرككم وإن أقمتم أخذكم وإن نسيتموه ذكركم.

3.188   وقال عليه السلام: لا يُزهدنّك في المعروف من لا يشكره لك فقد يشكرك عليه من لا يستمتع بشيء منه وقد تُدرك من شكر الشاكر أكثر ممّا أضاع الكافر ﴿وَٱللَّهُ يُحِبُّ ٱلْمُحْسِنِينَ﴾.

3.189   وقال عليه السلام: كلّ وِعاء يضيق بما جُعل فيه إلّا وعاء العلم فإنّه يتّسع.

3.190   وقال عليه السلام: أوّل عِوَض الحليم من حلمه أنّ الناس أنصاره على الجاهل.

3.191   وقال عليه السلام: إن لم تكن حليمًا فتحلّم فإنّه قَلَّ مَن تشبّه بقوم إلّا أوشك أن يكون منهم.

3.192   وقال عليه السلام: مَن حاسَبَ نفسه رَبِح ومن غفل عنها خسر ومن خاف أمن ومن اعتبر أبصر ومن أبصر فهم ومن فهم علم.

3.186 Ṭalḥah and Zubayr said to ʿAlī, "We will pledge allegiance to you if you make us partners in your caliphate," and he replied:[1]
No, but you are partners in strength and victory, and advisors in distress and adversity.

3.187 People, fear God, for he hears what you say and knows what you conceal. Hasten to prepare for death, for death will seize you even when you stay still and remember you even if you forget.

3.188 Don't let a recipient's ingratitude stop you from doing good—the one who reaps no benefit from your generosity thanks you, and you may well find more gratitude there than the ingrate withheld! «God loves those who do good.»[2]

3.189 Every vessel constricts as it fills up, except the vessel of knowledge, which expands.

3.190 The first reward of a man who shows restraint is that people side with him against his boorish challenger.

3.191 If you are not a patient man, then mimic those who are—rarely does someone mimic people without becoming at least a little bit like them.

3.192 Whoever takes himself to task profits, whoever neglects his soul loses, and whoever fears God secures safety. Whoever heeds lessons discerns, whoever discerns understands, and whoever understands realizes the truth.

---

1 Presumably in Medina in 35 or 36/656, soon after the pledge of allegiance to ʿAlī as caliph. "Victory" (*istiʿānah*, after Ḥ 19:22, who explains it as *al-fawz wa-l-ẓafar*) is an unusual denotation for *istiʿānah*, which is more commonly used to denote "seeking aid." As Ibn Abī al-Ḥadīd explains, though, here it is derived from the proverb, *qad jarā bnā ʿinān* (⟨The two 'sons' of *ʿinān*⟩—i.e., two lines drawn in the earth to frighten off birds—⟨have made their run⟩), said of one who draws the winning arrow in a pre-Islamic game of chance; *istaʿāna al-insān* ("A person performed *istiʿānah*", with the xth form verb of the same root, "ʿ-W-N") is said of someone who utters this proverb. On Ṭalḥah's and Zubayr's pledge to ʿAlī and their subsequent breaking of it, see Ḥ 11:10–20. See also §1.203.
2 Qurʾan, Āl ʿImrān 3:134,148, Māʾidah 5:93.

3.193   وقال عليه السلام: لَتَعْطِفَنَّ الدنيا علينا بعد شِماسِها عطف الضَّروس على ولدها. وتلا عقيب ذلك ﴿وَنُرِيدُ أَن نَّمُنَّ عَلَى ٱلَّذِينَ ٱسْتُضْعِفُواْ فِي ٱلْأَرْضِ وَنَجْعَلَهُمْ أَئِمَّةً وَنَجْعَلَهُمُ ٱلْوَارِثِينَ﴾ .

3.194   وقال عليه السلام: اتّقوا الله تقيّة من شمّر تجريدًا وجدَّ تشميرًا وأَكْمَش في مَهَل وبادر عن وجل ونظر في كَرّة المَوئِل وعاقبة المَصدَر ومَغبّة المَرجِع.

3.195   وقال عليه السلام

الجود حارس الأعراض.

والحلم فِدام السَّفيه.

والعفو زكاة الظفر.

والسُّلوّ عِوَضك ممّن غدر.

والاستشارة عين الهداية وقد خاطر من ٱستغنى برأيه.

والصبر يناضل الحِدْثان والجزع من أعوان الزمان.

وأشرف الغنى ترك المُنى.

وكَم من عقل أسير تحت هوًى أمير.

ومن التوفيق حفظ التجربة.

والمودّة قرابة مُستفادة.

ولا تأمنّ مَلولًا.

3.196   وقال عليه السلام: عُجْب المرء بنفسه أحد حُسّاد عقله.

3.197   وقال عليه السلام: أَغْضِ على القَذى وإلّا لم تَرضَ أبدًا.

3.198   وقال عليه السلام: مَن لانَ عُوده كَثُف أغصانه.

3.199   وقال عليه السلام: الخلاف يهدم الرأي.

3.193 ʿAlī said: The world will bend for us after refusing us its back, just as an irascible camel mare bends toward its young. He then recited the Qurʾanic verse: «We intend to bless those rendered weak on earth with abundant favors. We shall make them Imams. We shall make them inherit.»[1]

3.194 Fear God, people! Gird your loins and sprint, roll your sleeves and strive, race ahead during this brief reprieve, act quickly against the danger that looms! Remember the final return, the inexorable outcome, and the ultimate end!

3.195 Generosity protects reputations.
Forbearance muzzles the fool.
The tax due on victory is pardon.
Solace serves as recompense for betrayal.
Consultation is the essence of direction—whoever disdains advice faces danger.
Patience shoots down calamities. Panic is an ally of fate.
The most honorable wealth is abandoned desire.[2]
Many minds lie captive under passion's rule.
Learning from experience is evidence of God's direction.
Affection is a valuable form of kinship.
Don't trust the discontent.

3.196 A man's vanity is his intellect's jealous foe.

3.197 Forget about the speck in your eye, else you will never be happy.

3.198 If your trunk is pliant, your branches will be thick.[3]

3.199 Resistance ruins strategy.

---

1 Qurʾan, Qaṣaṣ 28:5.
2 Exact line in § 3.29.
3 I.e., if you are humble, you will have many supporters (B 985; Ḥ 19:35). Or, "One who is too soft is disrespected by his subordinates" (Waṭwāṭ, *Maṭlūb*, 44).

3.200 وقال عليه السلام: من نالَ استطال.

3.201 وقال عليه السلام: في تقلُّب الأحوال علمُ جواهر الرجال.

3.202 وقال عليه السلام: حسد الصديق من سُقم المودّة.

3.203 وقال عليه السلام: أكثر مصارع العقول تحت بُروق المطامع.

3.204 وقال عليه السلام: ليس من العدل القضاء على الثقة بالظنّ.

3.205 وقال عليه السلام: بِئسَ الزادُ إلى المعاد العُدوان على العباد.

3.206 وقال عليه السلام: من أشرف أفعال الكريم غفلته عمّا يعلم.

3.207 وقال عليه السلام: مَن كَساه الحياءُ ثوبه لم يَرَ الناس عيبه.

3.208 وقال عليه السلام: بكثرة الصمت تكون الهَيبة وبالنَّصَفة يكثر الواصلون وبالإفضال تعظم الأقدار وبالتواضع تتمّ النعمة وباحتمال المُؤَن يجب السودد وبالسيرة العادلة يُقهر المُناوي وبالحلم عن السَّفيه تكثر الأنصار عليه.

3.209 وقال عليه السلام: العَجَبُ لغفلة الحُسّاد عن سلامة الأجساد.

3.210 وقال عليه السلام: الطامع في وَثاق الذلّ.

3.211 وقال عليه السلام وقد سئل عن الإيمان
الإيمان معرفة بالقلب وإقرار باللسان وعمل بالأركان.

3.200 One who gets what he wants waxes arrogant.

3.201 Capricious conditions reveal the mettle of men.

3.202 Envying a friend poisons affection.

3.203 Most shattered minds are felled by the lightning bolt of greed.

3.204 When suspicions dictate judgment, justice fails.

3.205 Aggression toward God's servants is your worst provision for the return to him.

3.206 The noblest deed of the generous is to overlook.

3.207 Wear the robe of modesty and conceal your flaws.

3.208 Silence generates awe, justice multiplies friends, generosity elevates stature, humility completes blessings, providing for others brings glory, upright behavior vanquishes the enemy, and forbearance in the face of a fool increases your helpers against him.

3.209 I wonder at the envier's disregard for the harm he brings to his own health!

3.210 The greedy are tethered to shame.

3.211 ʿAlī was asked about faith, and he said:
To believe is to recognize with your heart, acknowledge with your tongue, and act with your limbs.

3.212 وقال عليه السلام

من أصبح على الدنيا حزينًا فقد أصبح لقضاء الله ساخطًا ومن أصبح يشكو مصيبة نزلت به فقد أصبح يشكو ربّه ومن أتى غنيًّا فتواضع لغناه ذهب ثُلثا دينه ومن قرأ القرآن فمات فدخل النار فهو ممّن كان يتّخذ آيات الله هُزُوًا ومن لَهِج قلبه بحبّ الدنيا ٱلتاط منها بثلاثٍ همّ لا يُغبّه وحرص لا يتركه وأمل لا يدركه.

3.213 وقال عليه السلام: كفى بالقناعة مُلكًا وبحسن الخلق نعيمًا.

3.214 وسئل عليه السلام: عن قوله تعالى ﴿فَلَنُحْيِيَنَّهُ حَيَاةً طَيِّبَةً﴾ فقال هي القناعة.

3.215 وقال عليه السلام: شارِكوا الذي قد أقبل عليه الرزق فإنّه أخلق للغنى وأجدر بإقبال الحظّ.

3.216 وقال عليه السلام في قول الله تعالى ﴿إِنَّ ٱللَّهَ يَأْمُرُ بِٱلْعَدْلِ وَٱلْإِحْسَانِ﴾ العدل الإنصاف والإحسان التفضّل.

3.217 وقال عليه السلام: مَن يُعطِ باليد القصيرة يُعطَ باليد الطويلة.

ومعنى ذلك أنّ ما ينفقه المرء من ماله في سبيل الخير والبرّ وإن كان يسيرًا فإنّ الله تعالى يجعل الجزاء عليه عظيمًا كثيرًا. واليدان هاهنا عبارتان عن النعمتين ففرّق بين نعمة العبد ونعمة الربّ فجعل تلك قصيرة وهذه طويلة لأنّ نعم الله سبحانه أبدًا تُضعَف على نعم المخلوقين أضعافًا كثيرة إذ كانت نعمه تعالى أصل النعم كلّها فكلّ نعمة إليها ترجع ومنها تنزَع.

3.218 وقال لٱبنه الحسن عليهما السلام

لا تَدعُوَنَّ إلى مُبارزة وإن دُعيت إليها فأجب فإنّ الداعي باغٍ والباغي مصروع.

3.212 'Alī said:

Whoever laments the world is discontent with God's providence, whoever complains about an affliction complains about his Lord, whoever humbles himself before a rich man because he is rich forfeits two thirds of his religion, any Qur'an reciter who dies and enters hellfire was one of those who mocked God's signs,[1] and any heart that accustoms itself to loving the world will receive three gifts in return: worries that will not quit him, greed that will not forsake him, and aspirations he will never attain.

3.213 Contentment is kingdom enough. Character is blessing enough.

3.214 'Alī was asked about the meaning of God's words, «We shall grant him a good life»,[2] and he said:

A good life is a life of contentment.

3.215 Partner with the prosperous and win a share of his riches and luck.

3.216 'Alī explained the meaning of God's words, «God commands justice and goodness»:[3]

Justice means balanced behavior. Goodness means bountiful giving.

3.217 Whoever gives with a constrained hand will be recompensed by an open one.

Raḍī: The meaning of this saying is that God will recompense whatever a man spends in the way of charity and benevolence, no matter how little, with a great and abundant reward. "Hands" refers to "gifts," and 'Alī differentiates between gifts given by God's servant and gifts given by the Lord, making one constrained (lit. short) and the other open (lit. long). God's gifts are always many times more than the gifts of his creatures. God's gifts are the source of all gifts—all gifts may be traced back to God's gifts and originate from them.

3.218 'Alī said to his son, Ḥasan:

Don't challenge someone to a duel,[4] but if you are challenged, respond, for a challenger is a traitor, and a traitor will be felled.

---

1 Reference to Qur'an, Jāthiyah 45:9, Baqarah 2:231.
2 Qur'an, Naḥl 16:97.
3 Qur'an, Naḥl 16:90.
4 I.e., for frivolous issues. In contrast, and in a grave situation, 'Alī himself challenged Muʿāwiyah to a duel at Ṣiffīn. Minqarī, *Waqʿat Ṣiffīn*, 387.

3.219 وقال عليه السلام: خيار خصال النساء شرار خصال الرجال الزَّهْو والجبن والبخل فإذا كانت المرأة مَزهُوَّة لم تمكِّن من نفسها وإذا كانت بخيلة حفظت مالها ومال بَعْلها وإذا كانت جبانة فَرِقت من كلّ شيء يعرض لها.

3.220 وقيل له عليه السلام صف لنا العاقل فقال

هو الذي يضع الشيء مواضعه.

قيل فصف لنا الجاهل قال قد فعلت.

يعني أنّ الجاهل هو الذي لا يضع الشيء مواضعه فكان ترك صفته صفة له إذا كان بخلاف وصف العاقل.

3.221 وقال عليه السلام: والله لدنياكم هذه أهون في عيني من عِراق خنزير في يد مجذوم.

3.222 وقال عليه السلام: إنّ قومًا عبدوا الله رغبة فتلك عبادة التجّار وإنّ قومًا عبدوا الله رهبة فتلك عبادة العبيد وإنّ قومًا عبدوا الله شكرًا فتلك عبادة الأحرار.

3.223 وقال عليه السلام: المرأة شرٌّ كلّها وشرُّ ما فيها أنّه لا بدّ منها.

3.224 وقال عليه السلام: مَن أطاع التواني ضَيّع الحقوق ومن أطاع الواشي ضيّع الصديق.

3.225 وقال عليه السلام: الحجر الغَصْب في الدار رَهْن على خرابها.

ويروى هذا الكلام للنبيّ صلّى الله عليه وآله ولا عجب أن يشبه الكلامان فإنّ مُستَقاهما من قَليب ومَفرغهما من ذَنوب.

3.219 The best traits of women are the worst traits of men: pride, cowardice, and stinginess. If a woman is proud, she will not allow a strange man to touch her. If she is stingy, she will safeguard her property as well as her husband's. If she is a coward, she will draw back from dubious invitations.

3.220 People asked ʿAlī, "Describe for us a man of reason," and he said:
One who puts things in their rightful place.

They then asked him, "Describe for us a man of ignorance," and he replied, "I have already done so."
Raḍī: He means that the ignorant man is one who does not put things in their rightful place, describing him without actually describing him, for the description of an ignorant man is the reverse of the description of a man of reason.

3.221 By God, this world of yours is worth less in my eyes than the bones of a pig in the hand of a leper.[1]

3.222 Some worship God out of desire for his reward—that is the worship of merchants. Others worship God from fear of his punishment—that is the worship of slaves. A third group worship God to give thanks for his favors—that is the worship of the free!

3.223 Woman is utterly evil, and the evilest thing about her is that there is no doing without her!

3.224 Whoever bows to languor squanders rights. Whoever listens to slander squanders friends.

3.225 One stolen brick guarantees a home's destruction.[2]

Raḍī: This saying is also attributed to the Prophet—it is no surprise that the two sayings should resemble each other, for they are drawn from the same well and poured from the same bucket.

---

1 Ṣadūq (*Amālī*, 370) includes the line as part of the oration in which ʿAlī also exclaims, "This world of yours is worth less to me than a leaf being chomped in the mouth of a locust," §1.221.3, which was reportedly delivered in Kufa after the arbitration in 37/658 (see note at §1.221).
2 Lit. "one stolen stone (*ḥajar*)."

3.226 وقال عليه السلام: يوم المظلوم على الظالم أشدّ من يوم الظالم على المظلوم.

3.227 وقال عليه السلام: اتقِ الله بعضَ التقى وإن قَلَّ وٱجعل بينك وبين الله سِترًا وإن رَقَّ.

3.228 وقال عليه السلام: إذا ٱزدحم الجواب خفي الصواب.

3.229 وقال عليه السلام: إنّ لله في كلّ نعمة حقًّا فمن أدّاه زاده منها ومن قصّر عنه خاطر بزوال نعمته.

3.230 وقال عليه السلام: إذا كثرت المقدرة قلّت الشهوة.

3.231 وقال عليه السلام: احذروا نِفار النِّعم فما كلّ شارد بمردود.

3.232 وقال عليه السلام: الكرم أعطف من الرَّحِم.

3.233 وقال عليه السلام: من ظنّ بك خيرًا فصَدِّق ظنّه.

3.234 وقال عليه السلام: أفضل الأعمال ما أكرهت نفسك عليه.

3.235 وقال عليه السلام: عرفتُ الله سبحانه بفَسْخ العزائم وحَلّ العقود.

3.236 وقال عليه السلام: مَرارة الدنيا حلاوة الآخرة وحلاوة الدنيا مرارة الآخرة.

3.237 وقال عليه السلام: فرض الله الإيمان تطهيرًا من الشرك والصلاة تنزيهًا عن الكبر والزكاة تسبيبًا للرزق والصيام ٱبتلاء لإخلاص الخلق والحجّ تقوية للدين والجهاد عزًّا للإسلام والأمر بالمعروف مَصْلَحة للعوامّ والنهي عن المنكر رَدْعًا للسفهاء وصلة

۱ش، ي، ه، ونسخة في ن: كذا. أصل ن: ⟨حقّ⟩.

3.226 The day of the oppressed over the oppressor will be harsher than the day of the oppressor over the oppressed.[1]

3.227 Fear God, even if just a smidgen. Draw a curtain between you and God, even if almost sheer.

3.228 Too many answers obscure the answer.

3.229 God is due a share from your every blessing. If you render it to him, you are rewarded with more. If you fall short, you risk losing the original one.

3.230 When opportunity increases, desire decreases.

3.231 Beware lest blessings abscond, for not every runaway camel can be recovered.

3.232 Generosity produces more affection than kinship does.

3.233 If someone thinks you are good, prove them right![2]

3.234 The most virtuous deeds are those you force yourself to do.

3.235 I recognized the hand of God through broken resolves and dissolved compacts!

3.236 Bitterness in this world leads to sweetness in the next, sweetness in this world leads to bitterness in the next.

3.237 God has mandated belief to purify you from polytheism, the ritual prayer to repulse pride, the alms-levy to draw in sustenance, fasting to test people's sincerity, the hajj to strengthen faith, jihad to fortify Islam, the commanding of good for the public's benefit, the forbidding of evil to restrain fools, and the fostering of relatives to increase numbers. He has mandated fair retribution to prevent bloodshed, criminal penalties to emphasize the gravity of his prohibitions, abstention from wine-drinking to preserve reason, desisting from thievery to promote temperance, refraining from fornication to safeguard lineage,

---

1 § 3.326 is similar.

2 From ʿAlī's lengthy testament of counsel for Ḥasan (§ 2.31), written in Ḥāḍirīn after leaving Ṣiffīn in 37/657.

الرحم مَنْماة للعدد والقصاص حَقْنًا للدماء وإقامة الحدود إعظامًا للمحارم وترك شرب
الخمر تحصينًا للعقل ومجانبة السرقة إيجابًا للعفّة وترك الزنا تحصينًا للنسب وترك اللّواط
تكثيرًا للنسل والشهادات اّستظهارًا على المُجاحدات وترك الكَذب تشريفًا للصدق
والسلام أمانًا من المخَاوف والإمامة١ نظامًا للأمّة والطاعة تعظيمًا للإمامة.

3.238 وكان عليه السلام يقول
أَحْلِفوا الظالم إذا أردتم يمينه بأنّه ﴿بريءٌ من حول الله وقوّته﴾ فإنّه إذا حلف بها كاذبًا
عوجِل وإذا حلف بـ﴿الله الذي لا إلٰه إلّا هو﴾ لم يعاجَل لأنّه قد وَحّده سبحانه.

3.239 وقال عليه السلام: يا اّبن آدم كن وصيّ نفسك واّعمل في مالك ما تؤثر أن يُعمَل
فيه مِن بعدك.

3.240 وقال عليه السلام: الحِدّة ضرب من الجنُون لأنّ صاحبها يندم فإن لم يندم فجنونه
مُستحكِم.

3.241 وقال عليه السلام: صحّة الجسد من قلّة الحسد.

3.242 وقال عليه السلام لكُمَيل بن زياد النَّخَعيّ
يا كُميل مُر أهلك أن يَروحوا٢ في كَسْب المكارم ويُدلجوا في حاجة من هو نائم فوالذي
وسع سمعه للأصوات ما من أحد أودع قلبًا سرورًا إلّا وخلق الله له من ذلك السرور
لطفًا فإذا نزلت به نائبة جرى إليها كالماء في اّنحداره حتّى يَطرُدها عنه كما تُطرد غريبة
الإبل.

١ش، ن، ي، هـ، (أي جميع المخطوطات الرئيسيّة ما عدام التي تفقد هذه الصفحة)، ل، ز، ق،
آ، ت، لك: كذا. س، ج، ومصحّحة في ش، ق: ﴿الأمانة﴾، ويبدو أنها غُيّرت في زمنٍ ما عمداً.
٢ش، هـ، ومصحّحة في ن، ونسخة في ي: كذا. أصل ي، ويبدو وأصل ن: ﴿يرجوا﴾.

refraining from sodomy to ensure an abundance of offspring, and the giving of testimony to curb false denials. He has mandated refraining from untruth to honor truth, and a plainly voiced peace-greeting to protect against fear. He has mandated the Imamate as a system of governance for the community,[1] and obedience to the Imam to show the Imamate's lofty status.

3.238 When a criminal takes the oath at his testimony, have him swear that if he lies, he will be cut loose from God's strength and power. Then, if he lies, God will punish him soon. Whereas if he swears by God, there is no god but He, his punishment will be delayed because he has acknowledged the oneness of the Almighty.

3.239 Son of Adam, execute your own will. Do with your property now what you wish to be done with it after you are gone.

3.240 Rage is a kind of madness, and the perpetrator repents. If he does not repent, his madness still rages.

3.241 Health increases when envy decreases.

3.242 ʿAlī said to Kumayl ibn Ziyād al-Nakhaʿī:
Kumayl, teach your children to venture out every morning to perform noble deeds, and to go out every night to ease people's travails while they sleep. I swear by the one whose hearing encompasses all sounds, that if anyone puts a bit of joy in another's heart, God creates a grace from that joy—then, if ever a calamity descends upon him, that grace flows to him like streaming water, driving away the calamity like a herdsman driving away trespassing camels.

---

1 Thus in all my primary manuscripts. The word "Imamate (*imāmah*)" is substituted in later manuscripts with the word "trust (*amānah*)," which could be a deliberate corruption. See details in my Note on the Edition and Translation: Previous Editions (p. 48).

3.243 وقال عليه السلام: إذا أملقتم فتاجِروا الله بالصدقة.

3.244 وقال عليه السلام: الوفاء لأهل الغدر غدر عند الله والغدر بأهل الغدر وفاء عند الله.

3.243 If ever you fall into penury, make a deal with God by offering alms to the poor.

3.244 Loyalty toward people of deception counts with God as deception. Deception toward people of deception counts with God as loyalty.

فصل

نذكر فيه شيئًا من اختيار غريب كلامه المحتاج إلى التفسير

3.245 في حديثه عليه السلام

فإذا كان ذلك ضَرب يَعسوبُ الدين بذنَبه فيجتمعون إليه كما يجتمع قَزَع الخريف.

‹يعسوب الدين› السيّد العظيم المالك لأمور الناس يومئذ و‹القزع› قِطَع الغَيم التي لا ماء فيها.

3.246 في حديثه عليه السلام
هذا الخطيب الشَّحْشَح.

يريد الماهر بالخطبة الماضي فيها وكلّ ماضٍ في كلام أو سير فهو ‹شحشح›. والشحشح في غير هذا الموضع البخيل الممسك.

3.247 في حديثه عليه السلام
إنّ للخصومة قُحَمًا.

يريد بـ‹القحم› المَهالك لأنّها تُقحم أصحابها في المَهالك والمَتالف في الأكثر. ومن ذلك قُحْمة الأَعراب وهو أن تصيبهم السَّنة فتتعرَّق أموالهم فذلك تقحّمها فيهم. وقيل فيه وجه آخر وهو أنّها تُقحمهم بلادَ الرّيف أي تُحوِجهم إلى دخول الحَضَر عند مُحول البَدو.

3.248 في حديثه عليه السلام
إذا بلغ النساء نَصّ الحقائق فالعصبة أولى.

ويروى ‹نصّ الحِقاق›. و‹النصّ› منتهى الأشياء ومبلغ أقصاها كالنصّ في السير لأنه أقصى ما تقدر عليه الدابّة وتقول ‹نَصَصْتُ الرجلَ عن الأمر› إذا استقصيت مسألته عنه لتستخرج ما

Section on Rare Words
A selection from ʿAlī's sayings that need lexical explanations

3.245 When that happens, religion's queen bee will rest its abdomen on the ground, and people will gather around it like puffs of cloud gathering rapidly in autumn.[1]

Raḍī: "Religion's queen bee (*yaʿsūb al-dīn*)" denotes the great leader who will rule people's affairs on that day. "Puffs (*quzaʿ*)" are wisps of waterless clouds.

3.246 This swift-tongued orator.[2]

Raḍī: ʿAlī means someone who is skilled and adept in oratory. A man who is adept in speech or travel is called "swift (*shahshah*)." *Shahshah* in other contexts can also mean stingy and tight-fisted.

3.247 Quarrels are bucking steeds that hurl their riders into perils.[3]

Raḍī: By "hurling into perils (*quham*)," ʿAlī means into pits of death, because quarrels often fling their riders into pits of death and perdition. The similar phrase, "the peril into which the Bedouin are hurled (*quhmat al-aʿrāb*)," denotes a year when drought strikes the Bedouin and emaciates their herds; that is what drought's bucking with them means. The latter phrase is alternatively explained as the desert's hurling the Bedouin into farmlands, meaning that it forces them to enter settled locales when their nomadic pastures dry up.

3.248 When a girl enters the life-phase of a three-year-old camel, her paternal relatives have greater right over her guardianship.

Raḍī: The phrase is also narrated as *naṣṣ al-ḥiqāq*, instead of *naṣṣ al-ḥaqāʾiq*. *Naṣṣ* means the limit of things and their ultimate reach, like the limit in traveling, because that is the farthest a camel can go. You say "I pressed the man to the limit about that matter"

---

1 Explained as a prophecy about the Messiah (*Mahdī*) coming at the end of time. "Resting its abdomen on the ground" refers to the establishment of his rule. R 3:362–363; Ḥ 19:104–105.
2 ʿAlī is praising (1) Ṣaʿṣaʿah ibn Ṣūḥān (Ḥ 19:106); or (2), an unnamed young orator from the tribe of Qays, just before the Battle of the Camel outside Basra in 36/656 (Ṭabarī, *Tārīkh* 4:492).
3 When appointing his nephew ʿAbdallāh ibn Jaʿfar as his deputy in resolving a dispute. Ḥ 19:107.

عنده فيه فـ﴿نصّ الحِقاق﴾ يريد به الإدراك لأنّه منتهى الصِّغَر والوقت الذي يخرج منه الصغير إلى حدّ الكبير وهو من أفصح الكنايات عن هذا الأمر وأغرِبها يقول فإذا بلغ ذلك النساء فالعصبة أولى بالمرأة من أمّها إذا كانوا مَحرَمًا مثل الإخوة والأعمام وبتزويجها إن أرادوا ذلك. و﴿الحِقاق﴾ مُحاقّة الأمّ للعصبة في المرأة وهو الجدال والخصومة وقول كلّ واحد منهما للآخر أنا أحقّ منك بهذا ويقال منه ﴿حاققته حِقاقًا﴾ مثل جادلته جدالًا. وقد قيل إنّ ﴿نصّ الحِقاق﴾ بلوغ العقل وهو الإدراك لأنّه عليه السلام أراد منتهى الأمر الذي يجب به الحقوق والأحكام. ومن رواه ﴿نصّ الحقائق﴾ فإنّما أراد جمع ﴿حقيقة﴾. هذا معنى ما ذكره أبو عُبيد القاسم بن سلّام. والذي عندي أنّ المراد بـ﴿نصّ الحِقاق﴾ هاهنا بلوغ المرأة إلى الحدّ الذي يجوز فيه تزويجها وتصرّفها في حقوقها تشبيهًا بالحِقاق من الإبل وهي جمع حِقّة وحِقّ وهو الذي اُستكمل ثلاث سنين ودخل في الرابعة وعند ذلك يبلغ إلى الحدّ الذي يتمكّن فيه من ركوب ظهره ونصّه في السير. و﴿الحقائق﴾ أيضًا جمع حِقّة. فالروايتان جميعًا ترجعان إلى معنى واحد وهذا أشبه بطريقة العرب من المعنى المذكور أوّلًا.

3.249 في حديثه عليه السلام

إنّ الإيمان يبدو لُمْظَةً في القلب كلّما اّزداد الإيمان اّزدادت اللُّمْظة.

﴿اللمظة﴾ مثل النكتة أو نحوها من البياض. ومنه قيل ﴿فرس أَلْمَظ﴾ إذا كان بجَحفَلته شيء من البياض.

if you pushed him on a question to extract all the information that he had about it. *Naṣṣ al-ḥiqāq* means reaching physical maturity, because that is the limit of childhood, the point at which a child becomes an adult. This is among the most eloquent and marvelous of expressions that connote this transformation. 'Alī is saying: When a girl reaches that stage, her paternal relatives—close blood relatives such as brothers and uncles—have a greater right to her than her mother does, and they have a right to contract the girl's marriage if they choose to do so. *Ḥiqāq* is the dispute (*muḥāqqah*) in which the mother engages against the girl's paternal relatives, i.e., the clash and the quarrel, each of the two parties saying to the other, "I have more right (*anā aḥaqq*) in this matter than you." From this comes the phrase, "I contested with him for a right (*ḥāqaqtuhu ḥiqāqan*)," which is similar to, "I disputed with him (*jādaltuhu jidālan*)." It is also said that *naṣṣ al-ḥiqāq* refers to the development of the mind, and that is what is meant by maturity, because 'Alī meant the final stage of mental development, after which an individual can be trusted to look after her own rights and obligations. As for those who narrate the phrase with the variant *naṣṣ al-ḥaqā'iq*, they take *ḥaqā'iq* to be the plural of *ḥaqīqah* (a reality). The above paragraph constitutes Abū 'Ubayd al-Qāsim ibn Sallām's explanation of the phrase.[1] In my view, what is meant here by the phrase *naṣṣ al-ḥiqāq* is a woman's reaching the stage at which she can be married and when she can be allowed to administer her own rights. 'Alī compares young women at that stage to *ḥiqāq*, the plural of *ḥiqqah* and of *ḥiqq*, namely, a camel that has ended three years and begun its fourth. At this age, its back is strong enough to ride, and it can be pushed hard on a journey. The word in the variant narration, *ḥaqā'iq*, is also a plural of *ḥiqqah*, and thus, both variants in the narration have the same meaning. This explanation conforms better with the ways of the Arabs than the first one given by Abū 'Ubayd.[2]

3.249 Faith begins as a shining spot in the heart. As faith increases, the light expands.

Raḍī: "A shining spot (*lumẓah*)" is a fleck of white or something like a fleck. From this comes the phrase "a horse with a shining spot (*farasun almaẓ*)," when it has a fleck of white on its lip.

---

1   Abū 'Ubayd, *Gharīb al-ḥadīth*, s.v. "Ḥ-Q-Q."
2   Ibn Abī al-Ḥadīd (Ḥ 19:109–110) also finds problems with Abū 'Ubayd's grammatical and lexical parsing. He prefers Raḍī's explanations overall, but corrects the last part, saying that the Arabic word *ḥaqā'iq* is the "plural of the plural" (*jamʿ al-jamʿ*) of *ḥiqqah*, the plural being *ḥiqāq*.

3.250 في حديثه عليه السلام

إنّ الرجل إذا كان له الدَّين الظَّنون يجب عليه أن يُزكّيه لِما مضى إذا قبضه.

ف⟨الظنون⟩ الذي لا يعلم صاحبه أيقبضه من الذي هو عليه أم لا فكأنّه الذي يظنّ به فمرّة يرجوه ومرّة لا يرجوه. وهو من أفصح الكلام. وكذلك كلّ أمر تطالبه ولا تدري على أيّ شيء أنت منه فهو ⟨ظنون⟩. ومن ذلك قول الأعشى[1]

مَا يَجْعَلُ الجُدُّ الظَّنُونُ الَّذِي   جُنِّبَ صَوْبَ اللَّجِبِ المَاطِرِ

مِثْلَ الفُرَاتِيِّ إِذَا مَا طَمَا   يَقْـذِفُ بِالبُوصِيِّ وَالمَاهِرِ

و⟨الجدّ⟩ البئر و⟨الظنون⟩ التي لا يُدرى هل فيها ماء أم لا.

3.251 في حديثه عليه السلام أنّه شيّع جيشًا يغزيه فقال

أَعذِبوا عن النساء ما استطعتم.

ومعناه اصدفوا عن ذكر النساء وشغل القلب بهنّ وامتنعوا من المُقاربة لهنّ لأنّ ذلك يَفُتّ في عضد الحميّة ويقدح في مَعاقد العزيمة ويكسر عن العَدْو ويلَفِت عن الإبعاد في الغَزو. وكلّ من امتنع من شيء فقد أعذب عنه والعاذب والعَذوب الممتنع من الأكل والشرب.

3.252 في حديثه عليه السلام

كالياسِر الفالِج يَنتظر أوّلَ فوزة من قِداحه.

<hr>

[1] البحر: السريع.

3.250 If a man recovers a dubious debt, he should pay any past levies due on it.

Raḍī: A "dubious (ẓanūn)" debt is one whose owner is not sure whether he will recover it from the borrower or not. He vacillates, at one point hopeful, and at another losing heart. This is among the most eloquent of expressions. Similarly, everything you seek but do not know where you stand regarding it is "dubious." Aʿshā's verses are relevant to this explanation:[1]

> The dubious well
> That the thunder clouds pass by
> Is not the surging Euphrates
> Which tosses ship and captain.

"Well (*judd*)" means a borehole, and "dubious (*ẓanūn*)" describes a well which one cannot be certain contains water.

3.251 As ʿAlī bade farewell to a military contingent he was sending on a raid, he said to them:
Abstain as much as possible from the sweetness of women.

Raḍī: This means desist from brooding over your women and occupying your hearts with thoughts about them; do not have intimacy with them either. These things dampen zeal, undo the knots of resolve, delay expeditious travel, and distract from committed fighting. A person who refrains from something has "desisted from it (*aʿdhaba ʿanhu*)."[2] "A person who desists (*ʿādhib* or *ʿadhūb*)" is one who refrains from eating and drinking.

3.252 Like the successful gambler who awaits his first winning arrow.[3]

---

1   Aʿshā, *Dīwān*, 141, verses 19–20.
2   Ibn Abī al-Ḥadīd (Ḥ 19:114) agrees with Raḍī's explanation overall, but he says the verb in this explanatory phrase should be in Form I (*ʿadhaba*), not Form IV (*aʿdhaba*).
3   Part of oration §1.23 (see context and note on drawing arrows to divide camel meat there).

⟨الياسرون⟩ هم الذين يتضاربون بالقداح على الجَزور. و⟨الفالج⟩ القاهر الغالب يقال ⟨قد فَلَجَ
عليهم وفَلَجَهم⟩ وقال الراجز ⟨لَمَّا رَأَيْتُ فالِجًا قَدْ فَلَجا⟩.

3.253 في حديثه عليه السلام

كَنّا إذا اَحمرَّ البأس اَتّقينا برسول الله صلّى الله عليه وآله فلم يكن منّا أقرب إلى العدوّ منه.

ومعنى ذلك أنّه إذا عظم الخوف من العدوّ واَشتدّ عِضاض الحرب فزع المسلمون إلى قتال
رسول الله بنفسه فيُنزِل الله تعالى النصر عليهم ويأمنون ممّا كانوا يخافونه بمكانه. وقوله عليه
السلام ⟨إذا اَحمرَّ البأس⟩ كناية عن اَشتداد الأمر. وقد قيل في ذلك أقوال أحسنها أنّه شبّه
حَمْيَ الحرب بالنار التي تجمع الحرارة والحُمرة بفعلها ولونها. وممّا يقوّي ذلك قول النبيّ صلّى الله
عليه وآله وقد رأى مُجتَلَد الناس يوم حُنين وهي حرب هَوازِن ⟨الآنَ حَمِيَ الوَطِيس⟩ والوطيس
مُستوقَد النار فشبّه صلّى الله عليه وآله ما اَستحرّ من جِلاد القوم باَحتدام النار وشدّة اَلتهابها.

انقضى هذا الفصل ورجعنا إلى سَنن الغرض الأوّل في هذا الباب.

Raḍī: "Gamblers (*yāsirūn*)" are those who draw arrows to divide a slaughtered camel's meat. A "successful (*fālij*)" person is one who conquers and is victorious. It is said, "He was victorious over them (*falaja ʿalayhim*)" or "He successfully overpowered them (*falajahum*)." A *rajaz*-poet has said, ⟨When I saw a successful man who was victorious (*fālijan qad falajā*).⟩[1]

3.253 When the fighting raged red-hot, we would seek help from the Messenger, and when that happened, no one engaged the enemy more closely than he did.

Raḍī: This means that when fear of the enemy was greatest and the battle sank its teeth into us, the Muslims beseeched help from God's Messenger, who then entered the fray in person. When that happened, God sent them victory and they were secured against what they had feared, because of the Messenger's closeness to God. ʿAlī's words, "When the fighting raged red-hot (*idhā ḥmarra l-baʾs*)," connotes the severity of the battle. Many explanations have been given for this metaphor, and the best of them holds that ʿAlī compared the heat of battle to fire because it combines burning and redness, thus, action and color. This explanation is supported by some words the Prophet spoke when he observed the impassioned fighting against the Hawāzin in the Battle of Ḥunayn: ⟨Now the furnace burns (*al-āna ḥamiya l-waṭīs*)!⟩[2] A furnace is the place where fire is stoked, and the Prophet compared the heat of the fighting to the flames of a fire and its intense blaze.

The section on rare words ends here. We return now to the chapter's original thread.

---

1 *Rajaz* is a poetic meter used, in pre-Islamic and early Islamic times, for spontaneous verse recited in battle or otherwise, in the form *mustafʿilun mustafʿilun mustafʿilun*. The line is grammatically incomplete, and the second hemistich is not recorded in the commentaries. I have not been able to identify the poet: the line is not in the published *Dīwāns* of the famous Umayyad *rajaz* poets ʿAjjāj (d. ca. 90/715) or his son Ruʾbah (d. 145/762).
2 Hadith cited by Suyūṭī, *Jāmiʿ*, § 3012.

٣.٢٥٤ وقال عليه السلام لمّا بلغه إغارة أصحاب معاوية على الأنبار نخرج بنفسه ماشياً حتّى أتى النُّخَيلة فأدركه الناس وقالوا يا أمير المؤمنين نحن نكفيكهم فقال عليه السلام والله ما تكفونني أنفسكم فكيف تكفونني غيركم إن كانت الرعايا قبلي لتشكو حَيف رُعاتها فإنّي اليوم لأشكو حَيف رعيّتي كأنّي المَقود وهم القادة أو الموزوع وهم الوَزَعة.

فلمّا قال هذا القول في كلام طويل قد ذكرنا مختاره في جملة الخطب تقدّم إليه رجلان من أصحابه فقال أحدهما ﴿إِنِّي لا أَمْلِكُ إِلاَّ نَفْسِي وَأَخِي﴾ فمُرنا بأمرك يا أمير المؤمنين نَنفُذ له فقال عليه السلام وأين تقعان ممّا أريد.

٣.٢٥٥ وقيل إنّ الحارث بن حَوط أتاه عليه السلام فقال أتُراني أظنّ أصحاب الجمل كانوا على ضلالة فقال عليه السلام

3.254 When news reached ʿAlī that Muʿāwiyah's militia had raided Anbar, he stormed from the town and walked all the way to Nukhaylah. People caught up with him there and entreated him, "Stay back, Commander of the Faithful, let us take care of them for you!" He exclaimed:[1]

By God, you are not even able to protect me against yourselves, how will you protect me against others? In the past, people used to complain of the injustice of their rulers. I complain of the injustice wrought by my subjects! I seem to be the one being led, they the leaders. I seem to be the one under command, they the commanders.

Raḍī: When ʿAlī spoke these lines—followed by a long oration (of which a selection is included in our chapter on orations)[2]—two men from among his supporters stepped forward, and one of them declared, "«I have jurisdiction only over myself and my brother»[3] so give us your command, Commander of the Faithful, and we shall execute it forthwith." ʿAlī replied, "What can the two of you accomplish? You are far short of what I need!"

3.255 It is narrated that al-Ḥārith ibn Ḥawṭ came to ʿAlī and challenged him, "Are you asking me to believe that the people who fought you at the Battle of the Camel were misguided?" ʿAlī replied:[4]

---

1 In 39/660, led by Sufyān ibn ʿAwf al-Ghāmidī, in which he killed ʿAlī's governor, Ḥassān al-Bakrī. After the event described in our text, ʿAlī set up camp at Nukhaylah, preparing to march against Muʿāwiyah, but when evening came, most people returned to Kufa and ʿAlī was left with only his family and a handful of his staunch supporters, and he was forced to return to Kufa (F 443). ʿAlī's oration at Nukhaylah is recorded in § 1.27.

2 § 1.27, § 1.94.1.

3 Qurʾan, Māʾidah 5:25.

4 Ḥārith ibn Ḥawṭ challenged ʿAlī thus while orating on the pulpit, presumably in Kufa, before marching to Ṣiffīn in 36/356. Jāḥiẓ, *Bayān*, 3:211. There are various speculations about Ḥārith's father's name, which indicate that Ḥārith was not well known. Most likely the name is "Ḥawṭ," following MSS Sh and N, and the commentaries R 3:374, and Ḥ 19:147, 148, as well as Jāḥiẓ, *Bayān*, 3:211, who adds "al-Laythī." R 3:368 and Ḥ 19:148 also record the variant "Khūṭ," and state that Raḍī wrote the name thus in his own hand, "with the letter 'Kh', dotted, and vocalized as 'ū' (*khāʾ muʿjamah maḍmūmah*)." MS Y says the same, but adds that the correct spelling according to the hadith scholars, however, is "Ḥawṭ." Other variants of the name are "Ḥawt" and "Ḥūt" (B 993).

يا حارِ إنّك نظرت تحتك ولم تنظر فوقك فَحِرْتَ إنّك لم تعرف الحقّ فتعرف من أباه[1] ولم تعرف الباطل فتعرف من أتاه.

فقال الحارث فإنّي أعتزل مع سعد بن مالك وعبد الله بن عمر فقال عليه السلام إنّ سعدًا وعبد الله بن عمر لم ينصرا الحقّ ولم يخذلا الباطل.

3.256 وقال عليه السلام: صاحب السلطان كراكب الأسد يُغبَط بموقعه وهو أعلم بموضعه.

3.257 وقال عليه السلام: أحسنوا في عَقِب غيركم تُحفَظوا في عقبكم.

3.258 وقال عليه السلام: إنّ كلام الحكماء إذا كان صوابًا كان دواء وإذا كان خطأ كان داء.

3.259 وسأله عليه السلام رجل أن يعرّفه ما الإيمان فقال إذا كان غَدُ فأتني حتّى أُخبرك على أسماع الناس فإن نسيت مقالتي حفظها عليك غيرك فإنّ الكلام كالشاردة يَثقَفها هذا ويُخطئها هذا.

وقد ذكرنا ما أجابه به عليه السلام فيما تقدّم من هذا الباب وهو قوله ﴿الإيمان على أربع شعب﴾.

3.260 وقال عليه السلام: يا ابن آدم لا تَحمل همّ يومك الذي لم يأتك على يومك الذي أتاك فإنّه إن يكُ من عمرك يأت الله فيه برزقك.

---

[1] ش، ن، ه: كذا. ي، وتبدو مصحّحة في ش: ﴿فتعرف أهله﴾.

Ḥārith, you have looked below you and not above you, which is why you have strayed.[1] You haven't recognized right, else you would have recognized its deniers, and you haven't recognized wrong, else you would have recognized its perpetrators.

Raḍī: Ḥārith responded, "I will sit out the fighting, alongside Saʿd ibn Mālik and ʿAbdallāh ibn ʿUmar,"[2] and ʿAlī exclaimed:
But Saʿd and ʿAbdallāh ibn ʿUmar refused to aid right or fight wrong!

3.256 A ruler rides a lion. People envy his status, but he knows his situation.

3.257 Be kind to orphans, and others will care for yours.[3]

3.258 When the learned speak truth, their words heal. When they speak falsehoods, they cause disease.

3.259 A man asked ʿAlī to define faith for him, and ʿAlī directed him:[4]
Come back tomorrow and I will inform you when others are present to hear me. Then, if you forget my words, others will remember them. Words are like runaway camels—this person catches them, another person loses them.

Raḍī: I have recorded the answer ʿAlī gave to this man in a text earlier in this chapter, which begins, "Faith has four branches."[5]

3.260 Son of Adam, add not the worries of a day that has yet to arrive to the burdens of the day that is here! If your lifespan extends to tomorrow, God will provide sustenance.[6]

---

1 The line is interpreted as follows: (1) You have followed those who broke the pledge of allegiance at the Battle of the Camel and not followed your rightful Imam (B 993); or, (2) you have followed the Syrians and Muʿāwiyah and not the majority of the Prophet's Companions (F 443). *Yā Ḥāri* (O Ḥārith), with the final letter "Th" dropped, is the apocopated (*murakhkham*) form of the vocative, *Yā Ḥārith*.
2 Saʿd ibn Mālik is better known as Saʿd ibn Abī Waqqāṣ.
3 Ibn ʿAsākir (*Tārīkh*, 42:497–498) places this line within oration §1.63, that ʿAlī delivered in Ṣiffīn, in 37/657.
4 Excerpt from oration that ʿAlī delivered in his home, either in Medina or Kufa, additional parts of which are as §1.69, §1.103 (details in note), §3.26.
5 §3.26.
6 Similar lines in §3.358.

3.261 وقال عليه السلام: أَحبِب حبيبك هَونًا ما عسى أن يكون بَغيضك يومًا ما وأبغض بغيضك هونًا ما عسى أن يكون حبيبك يومًا ما.

3.262 وقال عليه السلام: الناس في الدنيا عاملان عامل في الدنيا للدنيا قد شغلته دنياه عن آخرته يَخشى على من يُخَلِّف الفقر ويأمَنه على نفسه فيُفني عمره في منفعة غيره. وعامل عمل في الدنيا لما بعدها بجاءه الذي له من الدنيا بغير عمل فأحرز الحَظَّين معًا وملك الدارين جميعًا فأصبح وَجيهًا عند الله لا يسأل الله حاجة فيمنعه.

3.263 ورُوي أنّه ذُكر عند عمر بن الخطّاب في أيّامه حُلِيّ الكعبة وكثرته فقال قوم لو أخذتَه فجَهّزتَ به جيوش المسلمين كان أعظم للأجر وما تصنع الكعبة بالحَلِيّ فهَمّ عمر بذلك وسأل عنه أميرَ المؤمنين عليه السلام فقال إنّ القرآن أُنزل على النبيّ عليه السلام والأموالُ أربعة أموال المسلمين فقسمها بين الورثة في الفرائض والفَيء فقسمه على مستحقّيه والخُمْس فوضعه الله حيث وضعه والصدقات بجعلها الله حيث جعلها. وكان حلِيّ الكعبة فيها يومئذ فتركه الله على حاله ولم يتركه نِسيانًا ولم يَخْفَ عليه مكانًا فأقِرّه حيث أقرّه الله ورسوله.

فقال عمر لولاك لأَفتضحنا وترك الحلِيّ بحاله.

3.264 ورُوي أنّه عليه السلام رُفع إليه رجلان سرقا من مال الله أحدهما عبدٌ من مال الله والآخَر مِن عُرْض الناس فقال عليه السلام أمّا هذا فهو من مال الله ولا حدّ عليه مال الله أكل بعضُه بعضًا وأمّا الآخَر فعليه الحدّ.

3.261 Love your friend but hold back some—someday he could be your foe. Hate your foe but hold back some—someday he could be your friend.[1]

3.262 Those who labor in this world are of two kinds. The first is a man who labors in this world for this world. This world has distracted him from the hereafter. He fears leaving his family without means but thinks himself safe from want, and he uses his life only to provide profit to others. The second is a man who labors in this world for the hereafter and this world's benefits come to him without effort. He wins both fortunes and secures both abodes. He has earned a place of honor in God's eyes—whatever he asks for, God grants him.

3.263 It has been narrated that the many precious objects inside the Kaʿbah were brought to ʿUmar ibn al-Khaṭṭāb's attention, and someone suggested to him, "Why don't you sell these ornaments to equip the Muslim armies? That would win you greater reward from God, for what does the Kaʿbah want with jewels!" The idea appealed to ʿUmar, and he asked the Commander of the Faithful for his opinion—ʿAlī replied:[2]

At the time when the Qurʾan was revealed to the Prophet, there were four kinds of property: property that belonged to Muslims that the Prophet distributed among their heirs according to the mandated shares; war gains that he distributed to whomever they accrued; the fifth share that God assigned where he did; and the alms-levy that he allocated where he did. These precious objects were present then inside the Kaʿbah, and God left them as they were. It was not that he forgot to legislate about them, nor was their presence unknown to him—you too must keep them where God and his Prophet kept them.

ʿUmar exclaimed, "But for you, I would have been disgraced!" and he left the precious objects as they were.

3.264 It is narrated that two men who had stolen from the public treasury were brought before ʿAlī. One was a slave, himself belonging to the public treasury, and the other was a member of the public. ʿAlī pronounced:[3]

As for this one, he comes from God's treasury and no corporal punishment accrues to him. In his case, part of God's property consumed another part of God's property. The other, however, is warranted the criminal penalty.

---

1 Reportedly spoken on the day that ʿUthmān was killed, in Medina in 35/656. Balādhurī, *Ansāb*, 5:588.

2 Presumably in Medina, sometime during ʿUmar's caliphate, 13–23/634–644.

3 Presumably in Kufa, sometime during ʿAlī's caliphate, 35–40/656–661.

فقطع يده.

3.265 وقال عليه السلام: لو قد اُستوت قدماي من هذه المَداحِض لغَيَّرتُ أشياء.

3.266 وقال عليه السلام: اعلموا علمًا يقينًا أنّ الله لم يجعل للعبد وإن عظمت حيلته واشتدّت طَلِبته وقَوِيَت مكيدته أكثر ممّا سُمّي له في الذكر الحكيم ولم يحل بين العبد في ضعفه وقلّة حيلته وبين أن يبلغ ما سمّي له في الذكر الحكيم والعارف لهذا العامل به أعظم الناس راحة في منفعة والتارك له الشاكّ فيه أعظم الناس شغلًا في مَضَرّة وربَّ مُنعِمٍ عليه مَستدرَج بالنعمى وربَّ مُبتلى مصنوع له بالبلوى فزِدْ أيّها المستمع في شكرك وقصّر من عَجَلَتِك وقِف عند منتهى رزقك.

3.267 وقال عليه السلام: لا تجعلوا علمكم جهلًا ويقينكم شكًّا إذا علمتم فاعملوا وإذا تيقّنتم فأقدِموا.

3.268 وقال عليه السلام: إنّ الطمع مُورد غير مُصدِر وضامن غير وَفيّ. وربّما شَرِقَ شارب الماء قبل رِيِّه وكلّما عظم قدر الشيء المتنافَس فيه عظمت الرزيّة لفقده والأمانيّ تُعمي أعين البصائر والحظّ يأتي مَن لا يأتيه.

3.269 وقال عليه السلام: اللّهمّ إنّي أعوذ بك أن تَحسُن في لامعة العيون علانيتي وتَقبَح فيما أُبطِنُ لك سريرتي محافظًا على رياء الناس من نفسي بجميع ما أنت مُطَّلِــع عليه منّي فأُبدي للناس حسن ظاهري وأفضي إليك بسوء عملي تقرّبًا إلى عبادك وتباعُدًا من مَرضاتك.

Accordingly, he ordered the second thief's hand to be cut off.

3.265 If my feet had gained a foothold on this slippery path, I would have changed many things.

3.266 People, know with full certainty that God never gives to any of his servants—no matter how great his intrigues, how intense his passions, or how strong his maneuvers—more than what is ordained for him in the Wise Remembrance.[1] God also never withholds from any of his servants—no matter how weak his form, or how paltry his wiles—what is ordained for him in the Wise Remembrance. The person who recognizes this truth and acts on it enjoys the greatest comfort and the most abundant gains. The person who rejects and doubts it is beset with the greatest preoccupations and much harm. Some who have been given many blessings are deceived by their blessings. Others who are burdened with many afflictions are given much good through their trials. So multiply your thanks, O listener, and lessen your haste. Do not stretch your hand beyond your share of sustenance.

3.267 Don't exchange knowledge for ignorance or certainty for doubt. If you have knowledge, then act. If you are certain, go forward.

3.268 Greed drives people to the pools of death, from which there is no return, and it promises success but breaks its pledge—a man drinking water could choke before his thirst is quenched. Moreover, the greater the value of a thing, the greater the grief over its loss. Desire blinds the eyes of the discerning, while fortune comes to those who don't chase after it.

3.269 God, I seek refuge in you! Let me not present a beautiful appearance to people's eyes, while concealing from you an ugly heart. Let me not try to save face before them, when you know everything about me. Let me not show a beautiful form to them, while approaching you with wicked deeds. Let me not seek closeness to your servants, while distancing myself from your pleasure.[2]

---

1 The Wise Remembrance (*al-Dhikr al-ḥakīm*) is the Qurʾan, believed by Muslims to contain knowledge of all things.

2 Ibn ʿAbd Rabbih (*ʿIqd*, 3:174) ascribes this supplication to ʿAlī's grandson ʿAlī Zayn al-ʿĀbidīn. Ibn Abī al-Ḥadīd (H 6:178–187) explains—with examples, including the famous Eid supplication—that Zayn al-ʿĀbidīn often recited his grandfather's supplications, and some of them became part of the latter's collection of supplications, *al-Ṣaḥīfah al-Sajjādiyyah*.

3.270 وقال عليه السلام: لا والذي أمسينا منه في غُبَّر ليلة دَهْماء تكثِر عن يوم أغرّ ما كان كذا وكذا.

3.271 وقال عليه السلام

قليل تدوم عليه أرجى من كثير مملول منه.

إذا أضرّت النوافل بالفرائض فٱرفضوها.

من تذكّر بعد السفر ٱستعدّ.

ليست الرؤية مع الأبصار فقد تكذب العيون أهلها ولا يَغِشّ العقل من ٱستنصحه.

بينكم وبين الموعظة حجاب من الغِرّة.

جاهلكم مُزدادُ مُسوّف.

قطَعَ العلمُ عذر المتعلّمين.

كلّ مُعاجِل يسأل الإنظار وكلّ مُؤجَّل يتعلّل بالتسويف.

3.272 وقال عليه السلام: ما قال الناس لشيء طوبى له إلّا وقد خَبأ له الدهر يوم سَوء.

3.273 قال عليه السلام وقد سئل عن القَدَر

طريقٌ مُظلِم فلا تسلكوه وبحر عميق فلا تَلِجوه وسرّ الله فلا تتكلّفوه.

3.274 وقال عليه السلام: إذا أرذل الله عبدًا حظر عليه العلم.

3.275 وقال عليه السلام: كان لي فيما مضى أخٌ في الله وكان يُعظّمه في عيني صِغَر الدنيا في عينه وكان خارجًا من سلطان بطنه فلا يشتهي ما لا يجد ولا يُكثِر إذا وجد وكان أكثر دهره صامتًا فإن قال بَذَّ القائلين ونَقَع غليل السائلين وكان ضعيفًا مُستضعَفًا

3.270 No, I swear by the one in whose protection we spent the black night, a night that smiled to reveal the brightness of day—that such-and-such a thing never happened!

3.271 Doing a little often is better than tiring of a lot.[1]

If supplemental deeds of worship cause you to neglect mandatory ones, stop doing them.[2]

One who ponders the journey's length will be prepared.

True sight is not just seeing with your eyes. Eyes can lie, but the intellect never deceives those who seek its counsel.

Negligence veils you from counsel.

The ignorant among you do more of this and put off that.[3]

Knowledge severs excuses.

Those who are summoned early ask for more time. Those who are given time indulge and procrastinate.

3.272 Never have people exclaimed, "What joy!" without fate setting up their secret day of doom.

3.273 ʿAlī was asked about destiny, and he warned:
It's a dark road, don't tread it. It's a deep sea, don't enter it. It's God's mystery, don't torment yourself trying to understand it.

3.274 When God wants to debase a man, he denies him knowledge.

3.275 In a time now past, I had a brother whom I loved in God's name.[4] What made him great in my eyes was the smallness of the world in his. He was not controlled by his stomach—he neither craved what he could not have, nor indulged in what he had obtained. Mostly, he was silent. When he spoke, he quietened all who spoke and quenched the thirst of any who sought. He was frail, and people considered him weak, but when battle approached, he was a

---

1 Similar to § 3.414.

2 Similar to § 3.34.

3 I.e., they continue to sin and delay repentance. Ḥ 19:175; B 998.

4 Lit. "brother in God" (*akhun fī-llāh*). The reference could be to the Prophet Muḥammad, or Abū Dharr al-Ghifārī, or Miqdād ibn al-Aswad, or ʿUthmān ibn Maẓʿūn; or to an ideal, rather than real, brother (Ḥ 19:184; B 999). The text has also been attributed to ʿAlī's son Ḥasan. (B 999 and R 3:385, after Ibn al-Muqaffaʿ; Ḥarrānī, *Tuḥaf*, 234–235, and others); it is presented in the edition of Ibn al-Muqaffaʿ's *al-Adab al-kabīr*, 314, without attribution, perhaps a copyist error.

فإن جاء الجِدّ فهو لَيث غَاب وصِلُّ وادٍ لا يُدلي بحجّة حتّى يأتي قاضياً وكان لا يلوم أحدًا على ما يجد العذر في مثله حتّى يسمع اعتذاره وكان لا يشكو وَجَعًا إلّا عند بُرئه وكان يقول ما يفعل ولا يقول ما لا يفعل وكان إن غُلب على الكلام لم يُغلَب على السكوت وكان على ما يسمع أحرص منه على أن يتكلّم وكان إذا بَدَهه أمران نظر أيّهما أقرب إلى الهوى نخالفه. فعليكم بهذه الخلائق فالزموها وتنافسوا فيها فإن لم تستطيعوها فاعلموا أنّ أخذ القليل خير من ترك الكثير.

3.276 وقال عليه السلام: لو لم يَتوعّد الله على معصية لكان يجب أن لا يُعصى شكرًا لنعمه.

3.277 وقال عليه السلام وقد عزّى الأشعث بن قيس عن ابن له
يا أشعث إن تحزن على ابنك فقد استحقّت ذلك منك الرَّحِم وإن تصبر ففي الله من كلّ مصيبة خَلَف يا أشعث إن صبرت جرى عليك القَدَر وأنت مأجور وإن جَزِعت جرى عليك القدر وأنت مأزور. سَرَّك وهو بلاء وفتنة وحزنك وهو ثواب ورحمة.

3.278 وقال عليه السلام على قبر رسول الله صلّى الله عليه وآله ساعة دُفن
إنّ الصبر لجميل إلّا عنك وإنّ الجزع لقبيح إلّا عليك وإنّ المُصاب بك لجليل وإنّه قبلك وبعدك لَجَلَل.

3.279 وقال عليه السلام: لا تصحب المائق فإنّه يُزيّن لك فعله ويَوَدّ أن تكون مثله.

lion of the thicket, a viper of the ravine. He never presented an argument unless it was decisive. He never censured anyone for what might be excused until he had heard them out. He never complained of an ailment until he had recovered. He preached only what he practiced, and never what he did not. He may have been overcome in words, but he was never overcome in silence—he was more eager to listen than to speak. If two options presented themselves to him, he would look to see which appealed to his passions and do the opposite. You, too, should emulate these character traits. Stay with them, race to acquire them. If you cannot do them all, then know that doing a little is better than renouncing a lot.

3.276 Even if disobedience were not subject to punishment, you should never disobey God, in gratitude for his many blessings.

3.277 Offering condolences to al-Ashʿath ibn Qays on the death of his son, ʿAlī said:[1] Ashʿath, it is fitting that you mourn your son—his relationship to you makes it right that you should mourn. But if you can bear his loss with fortitude, know this: you can find consolation for every loss in God. Ashʿath, if you bear your affliction with fortitude, fate will have assailed you, yes, but you will be rewarded, whereas if you break down in shock, fate will have assailed you anyway, and you will be punished. Your son's life made you happy, but he was a trial for you then and a test.[2] His death has caused you grief, but it is a means for you now to earn God's mercy and reward.

3.278 ʿAlī spoke these lines at the Messenger of God's grave, just after burying him:[3] Patience is beautiful except in our loss of you. Shock is loathsome except in our loss of you. The calamity brought by your death is enormous, while deaths before and after you mean nothing.

3.279 Don't spend time with a fool. He will lure you to his ways and try to turn you into him.

---

1 See also ʿAlī's expressions of condolence to Ashʿath on the death of his brother in § 3.89, and to an unnamed relative, in § 3.385. Abū al-ʿAtāhiyah paraphrased this theme in a line of condolence, "You will no doubt be subject to the flow of destiny, and either you will be rewarded for your response or a sinner" (ولا بدّ من جريان القضاء—إمّا مثابا وإمّا أثيما). Ḥ 19:192; not in the published *Dīwān*.

2 Reference to Qurʾan, Taghābun 64:15.

3 In Medina, 11/632.

3.280　وقال عليه السلام وقد سئل عن مسافة ما بين المشرق والمغرب

مَسيرة يوم للشمس.

3.281　وقال عليه السلام: أصدقاؤك ثلاثة وأعداؤك ثلاثة فأصدقاؤك صديقك

وصديق صديقك وعدوّ عدوّك وأعداؤك عدوّك وعدوّ صديقك وصديق عدوّك.

3.282　وقال عليه السلام لرجل رآه يسعى على عدوّه بما فيه إضرار بنفسه

إنّما أنت كالطاعن نفسَه ليقتل رِدْفَه.

3.283　وقال عليه السلام: ما أكثر العِبَر وأقلّ الاعتبار.

3.284　وقال عليه السلام: مَن بالَغ في الخصومة أثِم ومن قصّر فيها ظُلِم ولا يستطيع أن

يتّقي الله من خاصم.

3.285　وقال عليه السلام: ما أهمّني ذنب أُمهِلت بعده حتّى أصلّي ركعتين.

3.286　وسئل عليه السلام: كيف يحاسب الله الخلق على كثرتهم فقال

كما يرزقهم على كثرتهم.

فقيل كيف يحاسبهم ولا يَرونه قال

كما يرزقهم ولا يرونه.

3.287　وقال عليه السلام: رسولك تَرجُمان عقلك وكتابك أبلغ من[1] ينطق عنك.

3.288　وقال عليه السلام: ما المبتلى الذي قد اشتدّ به البلاء بأحوج إلى الدعاء من

المعافى الذي لا يأمن البلاء.

ي، ه، ونسخة في ش: كذا. أصل ش: ﴿ما﴾. ن: معًا.

3.280 ʿAlī was asked, "What is the distance between East and West?" and he answered:
The sun's day-long trek.

3.281 You have three friends and three enemies. Your friends are your friend, the friend of your friend, and the enemy of your enemy. Your enemies are your enemy, the enemy of your friend, and the friend of your enemy.

3.282 A man bore down on an enemy, putting himself in harm's way. Seeing this, ʿAlī said to him:[1]
You are like one who pierces himself with a spear to kill the man riding pillion behind.

3.283 How many lessons and how few heeded!

3.284 To argue too much is to sin, and to argue too little is to lose, but it is impossible for a man who argues all the time to remain godfearing.

3.285 As long as I can pray for forgiveness, I don't fear punishment for past sins.

3.286 ʿAlī was asked, "How will God judge people when there are so many?" and he replied:[2]
Just as he feeds them though there are so many!

He was then asked, "How will he judge them when they cannot see him?" and he replied:
Just as he feeds them though they cannot see him!

3.287 Your envoy is your intellect's interpreter, your letter your most effective spokesman.

3.288 A man who is afflicted, whose hardship is severe, is not more in need of prayer than a man who has been spared but has no guarantee of safety.

---

1 Ṭabarī (*Tārīkh*, 4:277) narrates a version of this line as ʿAlī's words to a group of people in Medina who were criticizing ʿUthmān in the affair of his governor in Kufa, Walīd ibn ʿUqbah, in 30/651.
2 The man who asked is reported to be Salmān al-Fārisī, presumably in Medina, before Salmān left for Iraq in ʿUmar's caliphate (r. 13-23/634–644). Ibn ʿAbd Rabbih, *ʿIqd*, 4:288.

٣٫٢٨٩ وقال عليه السلام: الناس أبناء الدنيا ولا يُلام الرجل على حبّ أُمّه.

٣٫٢٩٠ وقال عليه السلام: إنّ المسكين رسول الله فمن منعه فقد منع الله ومن أعطاه
فقد أعطى الله.

٣٫٢٩١ وقال عليه السلام: ما زَنَى غَيور قطّ.

٣٫٢٩٢ وقال عليه السلام: كفى بالأجل حارسًا.

٣٫٢٩٣ وقال عليه السلام: ينام الرجل على الثُّكْل ولا ينام على الحَرَب .

ومعنى ذلك أنّه يصبر على قتل الأولاد ولا يصبر على سلب الأموال.

٣٫٢٩٤ وقال عليه السلام: مودّة الآباء قرابة¹ الأبناء والقرابة إلى المودّة أحوج من المودّة
إلى القرابة.

٣٫٢٩٥ وقال عليه السلام: اتّقوا ظُنون المؤمنين فإنّ الله تعالى جعل الحقّ على ألسنتهم.

٣٫٢٩٦ وقال عليه السلام: لا يصدق إيمان عبد حتّى يكون بما في يد الله سبحانه أوثق
منه بما في يده.

---

١ ن، ش: كذا. ي، ه، ومصحّحة في ش: أضيفت ﴿بين﴾.

3.289 People are children of the world, and a man can't be blamed for loving his mother.

3.290 A beggar is God's messenger, whoever refuses him, refuses God, whoever gives to him, gives to God.[1]

3.291 A man with a jealous sense of honor never fornicates.

3.292 My allotted lifespan is protection enough![2]

3.293 A man may sleep when bereaved, but he can't find sleep when looted.

Raḍī: This means that a man might endure if his sons are killed, but he cannot endure when his wealth is plundered.

3.294 Affection among fathers produces kinship among their sons. Kinship needs affection more than affection needs kinship.

3.295 Beware lest you arouse suspicions in believers' hearts, for God has placed truth on their tongues!

3.296 A person's faith is not sincere until he trusts God's gifts more than his own possessions.[3]

---

1 Narrated by ʿAlī from the Prophet in Nuʿmān, *Daʿāʾim*, 1:243.
2 Spoken at Ṣiffīn when ʿAlī's associates asked him to be wary of Muʿāwiyah's assassins. Ṣadūq, *Tawḥīd*, 368.
3 Masʿūdī (*Murūj*, 2:417–418) reports that a suppliant came to ʿAlī's door, and ʿAlī instructed his son Ḥasan to fetch a dirham from his mother, Fāṭimah (this would presumably be shortly before Fāṭimah died, in 11/632, when Ḥasan was a young child). Ḥasan came back with her caution that they had only six dirhams, which were needed to buy flour. ʿAlī responded with the line at hand, and told Ḥasan to bring all six dirhams, which he proceeded to give to the beggar. The next morning, ʿAlī bought a camel on credit for 140 dirhams, which he then resold for 200, thus coming home with a profit of 60 dirhams, and he said to Fāṭimah that this was a fulfilment of God's promise, ﴿مَن جَاءَ بِالْحَسَنَةِ فَلَهُ عَشْرُ أَمْثَالِهَا﴾ «Whoever brings one good deed shall be rewarded with ten of its kind» (Qurʾan, Anʿām 6:160). A similar line is attributed to the Prophet in Quḍāʿī, *Shihāb*, §2.34.

3.297 وقال عليه السلام لأَنَس بن مالك وقد كان بعثه إلى طلحة والزبير لمّا جاء إلى البصرة يذكّرهما شيئًا سمعه من رسول الله صلّى الله عليه وآله في معناهما فلُوِي عن ذلك فرجع إليه فقال إنّي أُنسيت ذلك الأمر فقال عليه السلام

إن كنت كاذبًا فضربك الله بها بيضاء لامعة لا تُواريها العِمامة.

يعني البَرَص. فأصاب أنسًا هذا الداء فيما بعد في وجهه وكان لا يرى إلّا مُتَبَرقِعًا.

3.298 وقال عليه السلام: إنّ للقلوب إقبالًا وإدبارًا فإذا أقبلت فاحملوها على النوافل وإذا أدبرت فاقتصروا بها على الفرائض.

3.299 وقال عليه السلام: في القرآن نبأ ما قبلكم وخبر ما بعدكم وحكم ما بينكم.

3.300 وقال عليه السلام: رُدَّ الحجر من حيث جاء فإنّ الشرّ لا يدفعه إلّا الشرّ.

3.297 When Ṭalḥah and Zubayr marched on Basra, ʿAlī sent Anas ibn Mālik to remind them of something he, Anas, had heard about the two of them from God's Messenger. Anas wanted to evade this task, and he came back to ʿAlī, saying, "I forgot what it was I had heard." ʿAlī exclaimed:[1]

If you are lying, may God mar your face with a bright white patch that your turban cannot conceal!

Raḍī: He meant vitiligo (*baraṣ*). Shortly thereafter, Anas contracted this disease, and was never seen thereafter without a veil on his face.

3.298 Hearts are sometimes receptive and sometimes withdrawn. When they are receptive, urge them to the supplementary rites of worship. When they are withdrawn, let them stay with the mandatory rites.[2]

3.299 The Qurʾan contains reports about what happened before you, prophecies about what will come after you, and laws about what is present among you.[3]

3.300 Cast back the stone to whence it came. Only evil repels evil.

---

1 Some commentators (R 3:390; B 1000) say that this line, with Raḍī's contextualization, refers to ʿAlī's sending Anas to Ṭalḥah and Zubayr before the Battle of the Camel outside Basra in 36/656, to remind them of Muḥammad's prophetic warning, ⟨You will fight ʿAlī in battle, and you will be in the wrong.⟩ Disagreeing with the etymology, Ibn Abī al-Ḥadīd (19:217–218, citing Ibn Qutaybah, *Maʿārif*, chapter on vitiligo, *baraṣ*) says the histories do not report that ʿAlī ever sent Anas to speak with Ṭalḥah and Zubayr. Rather, they report that ʿAlī once called out to people in the gathering space of Kufa (sometime during his caliphate between 36/656 and 40/661), and said, "Whoever has heard God's Messenger say about me, while he was returning from the Farewell Pilgrimage, ⟨For whomsoever I am master, ʿAlī is his master; God, love those who love him, and hate those who hate him⟩, I ask him in God's name to step forward and testify!" Some men stepped forward and testified that they had been present and heard. ʿAlī said to Anas, "You were there too! What is the matter with you?" Anas replied, "Commander of the Faithful, I have grown old, and what I have forgotten is more than what I remember." It was then that ʿAlī spoke the lines in the text above.
2 Similar to § 3.177.
3 Masʿūdī (*Murūj*, 3:106) reports that Ḥārith al-Hamdānī complained to ʿAlī that people had forsaken the Qurʾan and were following specious hadith. ʿAlī replied that the Prophet had informed him about upcoming seditions and instructed that people should cleave in such times to the Qurʾan, and the saying at hand is from the Prophet's words that ʿAlī quoted.

3.301 وقال عليه السلام لكاتبه عبيد الله بن أبي رافع
أَلِقْ دَواتك وأَطِلْ جِلْفة قلمك وفَرِّج بين السطور وقَرمِط بين الحروف فإنّ ذلك أجدر بصباحة الخطّ.

3.302 وقال عليه السلام: أنا يَعسوب المؤمنين والمال يعسوب الفجّار.

ومعنى ذلك أنّ المؤمنين يتبعونني والفجّار يتبعون المال كما يتبع النحل يعسوبها وهو رئيسها.

3.303 وقال له بعض اليهود ما دفنتم نبيّكم حتّى اختلفتم فقال له
إنّما اختلفنا عنه لا فيه ولكنّكم ما جَفّت أرجلكم من البحر حتّى قلتم لنبيّكم ﴿اجْعَلْ لَّنَآ إِلَـٰهًا كَمَا لَهُمْ آلِهَةٌ قَالَ إِنَّكُمْ قَوْمٌ تَجْهَلُونَ﴾.

3.304 وقيل له بأيّ شيء غلبتَ الأقرانَ فقال عليه السلام
ما لَقيتُ رجلًا إلّا أعانني على نفسه.

يؤمئ بذلك إلى تمكّن هيبته في القلوب.

3.305 وقال عليه السلام لابنه محمّد رحمه الله
يا بُنَيَّ إنّي أخاف عليك الفقر فاستعذ بالله منه فإنّ الفقر مَنقَصة للدِّين مَدهَشة للعقل داعية للمَقْت.

3.306 وقال عليه السلام لسائل سأله عن مُعضِلة
سَلْ تفقُّهًا ولا تسأل تعنّتًا. فإنّ الجاهل المتعلّم شبيه بالعالم وإنّ العالم المتعسّف شبيه بالجاهل.[1]

---

[1] ش، ي، ه: كذا. ن: أضيفت ﴿المتعنّت﴾.

3.301 'Alī instructed his scribe, 'Ubaydallāh ibn Abī Rāfi', as follows:
Thicken the ink in your inkpot, lengthen the nib of your reed-pen, keep spaces
between the lines, and bring the letters close together. Your lettering will then
be beautiful.

3.302 I am the queen bee of the believers.[1] Money is the queen bee of the
depraved.

Raḍī: This means that while the depraved follow money, believers follow me, just as
honeybees follow the queen. The "queen bee (*ya'sūb*)" is the leader of the honeybees.

3.303 A Jew taunted 'Alī, "Hardly had you buried your Prophet, when you fell into dis-
agreement!" and 'Alī retorted:
We disagreed after him, not about him. But your feet had not dried from the
sea when you demanded of your Prophet, «"Make for us a god like their gods!"
whereby he castigated you saying, "you are an ignorant people!"»[2]

3.304 'Alī was asked, "What force did you use to overthrow your adversaries?" and he
replied:
I never met a man who didn't help me against himself!

Raḍī: 'Alī is alluding to the terror he would strike deep into their hearts.

3.305 'Alī counseled his son Muḥammad ibn al-Ḥanafiyyah:
My dear son, I fear for you if you ever fall into poverty, so ask God to protect
you from it. Poverty harms the faith, bewilders the mind, and incites to malice.

3.306 'Alī replied thus to a man who asked him about a complicated matter:[3]
Ask to understand, not to challenge. An ignorant man who seeks knowledge
is almost like the learned, whereas a learned man who is overly aggressive is
almost an ignoramus.

---

1 'Izz al-Dīn Ibn al-Athīr (*Usd*, 5:287) states that the Prophet made this statement about 'Alī.
2 Qur'an, A'rāf 7:138.
3 In Kufa, to a man named Ibn al-Kawwā', who later became one of the leaders of the Kharijites.
   Māmaṭīrī, *Nuzhah*, 146; Jurjānī, *I'tibār*, 587.

3.307   وقال عليه السلام لعبد الله بن العبّاس وقد أشار عليه في شيء لم يوافق رأيه

لك أن تشير عليّ وأرى فإن عصيتك فأطعني.

3.308   ورُوي أنّه عليه السلام لمّا ورد الكوفة قادمًا من صفّين مرّ بالشِّباميّين فسمع بكاء

النساء على قتلى صفّين وخرج إليه حَرْب ابن شُرَحْبيل الشبامي وكان من وجوه قومه فقال له

أيغلبكم نساؤكم على ما أسمع ألا تَنهونهنّ عن هذا الرّنين.

وأقبل يمشي معه وهو عليه السلام راكب فقال له

ارجع فإنّ مَشْي مثلك مع مثلي فتنة للوالي ومَذَلّة للمؤمن.

3.309   وقال عليه السلام وقد مرّ بقتلى الخوارج يوم النهر

بُؤسًا لكم لقد ضرّكم من غرّكم.

فقيل له من غرّهم يا أمير المؤمنين فقال

الشيطان المُضِلّ والأنفس الأمّارة بالسوء غرّتهم بالأماني وفَسحت لهم في المعاصي

ووعدتهم الإظهار فاقتحمت بهم النار.

3.310   وقال عليه السلام: اتّقوا معاصي الله في الخَلَوات فإنّ الشاهد هو الحاكم.

3.307 ʿAbdallāh ibn al-ʿAbbās offered ʿAlī counsel in a certain matter. ʿAlī, who had a different opinion, replied:[1]
You have the right to offer counsel, and I shall give it thought. But if I decide against it, then you will need to obey.

3.308 It is related that when ʿAlī arrived in Kufa from Ṣiffīn, he passed by the lodgings of the Shibām clan and heard women weeping loudly over their fallen warriors. One of their leaders, Ḥarb ibn Shuraḥbīl al-Shibāmī, came out to greet ʿAlī, who said to him:[2]
Do your women rule you? What is this I hear—can't you stop their wailing?

Ḥarb then began to walk alongside ʿAlī, who was on horseback, and ʿAlī said to him:
Go back inside! A man like you, walking beside a man like me, bodes nothing but sedition for the ruler and shame for the believer.[3]

3.309 Following the Battle of Nahrawān, ʿAlī walked out among the Kharijites' corpses, and he addressed them as follows:[4]
What misfortune you have earned! The one who deceived you is the one who injured you.

Asked, "Who deceived them, Commander of the Faithful?" he answered:
Satan the great deceiver and their own evil-inciting passions. The two together deceived them with false hopes, opened their path to sin, promised them conquest and victory, and then pitched them into hellfire.

3.310 Beware of disobeying God in private, for the witness is himself the judge.

---

1 When the Muslims had pledged allegiance to ʿAlī in 35/656 in Medina, ʿAbdallāh ibn al-ʿAbbās advised him to appoint Ṭalḥah as governor of Basra and Zubayr as governor of Kufa. Ibn al-ʿAbbās also advised ʿAlī to reaffirm Muʿāwiyah as governor of Damascus, and then, when Muʿāwiyah had pledged allegiance, to affirm him if he continued to obey, and replace him if he stirred up dissent. ʿAlī exclaimed, "Great God! Should I corrupt my faith with another's worldliness!" then spoke the lines in our text. F 452; B 1004; Ṭabarī, *Tārīkh* 4:441.

2 In 37/657. Details in Ṭabarī, *Tārīkh*, 5:62; Minqarī, *Waqʿat Ṣiffīn*, 531 (with this text).

3 I.e., it puffs up the ruler and humiliates the believer, because his chest and face are close to the mounted rider's feet. Ḥ 19:234.

4 In 38/658. Details and text in Ṭabarī, *Tārīkh*, 5:88.

3.311 وقال عليه السلام لمّا بلغه قتل محمّد بن أبي بكر

إنّ حزننا عليه على قدر سرورهم به إلّا أنّهم نُقِصوا بَغيضًا ونُقِصنا حبيبًا.

3.312 وقال عليه السلام: العمر الذي أعذر الله فيه إلى اَبن آدم ستّون سنة.

3.313 وقال عليه السلام: ما ظَفِر مَن ظفر الإثم به والغالب بالشرّ مغلوب.

3.314 وقال عليه السلام: إنّ الله سبحانه فرض في أموال الأغنياء أقوات الفقراء فما جاعَ فقير إلّا بما منع غنيّ والله تعالى سائلهم عن ذلك.

3.315 وقال عليه السلام: الاستغناء عن العذر أعزّ من الصدق به.

3.316 وقال عليه السلام: أقلّ ما يَلزمكم لله أن لا تَستعينوا بنعمه على معاصيه.

3.317 وقال عليه السلام: إنّ الله سبحانه جعل الطاعة غنيمة الأكْياس عند تفريط العَجزة.

3.318 وقال عليه السلام: السلطان وَزَعة الله في أرضه.

3.319 وقال عليه السلام في صفة المؤمن

المؤمن بِشْرُه في وجهه وحزنه في قلبه أوسع شيء صدرًا وأذلّ شيء نفسًا يكره الرفعة ويَشنأ السُّمعة. طويلٌ غمُّه بعيد همّه كثير صمته مشغول وقته شكور صبور مغمور بفكرته ضَنين بخُلّته سهل الخليقة لَيِّن العَريكة نفسه أصلب من الصَّلْد وهو أذلّ من العبد.

3.311 When the report of Muḥammad ibn Abī Bakr's slaying reached ʿAlī, he exclaimed:[1]

Our grief for him equals their joy at his death! They have dispatched an enemy and we have lost someone we loved!

3.312 Anyone to whom God has granted sixty years of life has no excuse left.[2]

3.313 A person who is conquered by sin can never win. A person who prevails through evil will be crushed.

3.314 God has mandated food for the poor from the wealth of the rich. Whenever a poor man goes hungry, it is because a rich man has refused to give, and God will surely hold him accountable.

3.315 Not needing to give an excuse is even better than giving a genuine one.

3.316 The least you owe God is not to use his gifts to sin against him.

3.317 God has made obedience to him a prize for the wise at a time when the weak are remiss.

3.318 The ruler is God's custodian on earth.[3]

3.319 Describing the believer, ʿAlī said:[4]

A believer shows his joy in his face and hides his sorrow in his heart. His generosity is vast, his humility is deep. He dislikes fame and detests praise. His grief is long lasting, his aspirations reach far. He stays mostly silent and spends his time well. He always gives thanks and is patient in adversity. He remains immersed in thought and is cautious when making friends. His temperament is mild and his nature is easygoing. He is stronger than a rock yet humbler than a slave.

---

1 In Kufa, 38/658. Muḥammad ibn Abī Bakr, ʿAlī's ward and his governor in Egypt, was tortured and killed by ʿAmr ibn al-ʿĀṣ. Text and details of the news reaching ʿAlī from Egypt of Muḥammad's death and from Syria of the Syrian's rejoicing, in Ṭabarī, *Tārīkh*, 5:108.

2 Similar saying attributed to the Prophet in Quḍāʿī, *Shihāb*, § 2.66.

3 Narrated within ʿAlī's epistle to commanders, presumably sent from Kufa at the beginning of his caliphate in 36/656. Minqarī, *Waqʿat Ṣiffīn*, 125–126.

4 Kulaynī (*Kāfī*, 2:226–230) presents this saying as part of the Hammām Oration (§ 1.191) in which ʿAlī describes the pious.

3.320 وقال عليه السلام: لو رأى العبد الأجل ومصيره لأبغض الأمل وغروره.

3.321 وقال عليه السلام: لكلّ آمرئ في ماله شريكان الوارث والحوادث.

3.322 وقال عليه السلام: الداعي بلا عمل كالرامي بلا وَتَر.

3.323 وقال عليه السلام: العلم علمان مطبوع ومسموع ولا ينفع المسموع إذا لم يكن المطبوع.

3.324 وقال عليه السلام: صواب الرأي بالدُّوَل يُقبل بإقبالها ويذهب بذهابها.

3.325 وقال عليه السلام: العفاف زينة الفقر والشكر زينة الغنى.

3.326 وقال عليه السلام: يوم العدل على الظالم أشدّ من يوم الجَور على المظلوم.

3.327 وقال عليه السلام: الأقاويل محفوظة والسرائر مبلوّة و﴿كُلُّ نَفْسٍ بِمَا كَسَبَتْ رَهِينَةٌ﴾ والناس منقوصون مدخولون إلّا من عصم الله سائلهم مُتعنّت ومجيبهم متكلّف يكاد أفضلهم رأيًا يردّه عن فضل رأيه الرضى والسخط ويكاد أصلبهم عودًا تنكأه اللحظة وتستحيله الكلمة الواحدة. معاشر الناس اتّقوا الله فكم من مؤمّل ما لا يبلغه وبان ما لا يسكنه وجامع ما سوف يتركه ولعلّه من باطل جمعه ومن حقّ منعه أصابه حرامًا واحتمل به آثامًا فباء بوزره وقدم على ربّه آسفًا لا هفًا قد ﴿خَسِرَ الدُّنْيَا وَٱلْآخِرَةَ ذَلِكَ هُوَ ٱلْخُسْرَانُ ٱلْمُبِينُ﴾.

3.328 وقال عليه السلام: من العصمة تعذُّر المعاصي.

3.320 If a man saw his end and his final destination, he would scorn all desires and their deadly deception.

3.321 Every man's wealth is shared by two partners: heirs and accidents.

3.322 A person who prays without deeds is like an archer who shoots with an unstrung bow.

3.323 Knowledge is of two kinds, innate and acquired—the acquired gives no benefit in the absence of the innate.

3.324 Good judgment turns on preordained revolutions of power. It comes when they come, and leaves when they leave.

3.325 Temperance adorns poverty, gratitude adorns wealth.[1]

3.326 Justice's day against the oppressor will be harsher than tyranny's day against the oppressed.[2]

3.327 Words are remembered, intentions are tested, and «every soul is mortgaged to what it has earned.»[3] Most people—except those whom God has protected—are flawed and weak-minded. The one who asks questions asks only to object, the one who answers pretends to know the answer. Even the person who possesses judgment is in danger of being subverted by desire or annoyance. Even the person who has inner strength is in danger of being injured by a look or altered by a word. O people, remain conscious of God! How many a person hopes for what he will not attain! How many a person builds what he will not inhabit! How many a person amasses what he will soon abandon! And perhaps he amassed it from illicit sources or by denying someone's rights. Perhaps he seized it unlawfully and loaded his back with a burden of sin. He then returns to the hereafter with his heavy load and arrives before his Lord filled with guilt and pain, «having lost this world and the hereafter—that is the most catastrophic loss!»[4]

3.328 One way to protect from sinning is to deny access to its means.

---

1   From ʿAlī's oration titled *Wasīlah* (Ḥarrānī, *Tuḥaf*, 90). The first half of this saying is similar to §3.60.
2   §3.226 is similar.
3   Qurʾan, Muddaththir 74:38.
4   Qurʾan, Ḥajj 22:11.

3.329 وقال عليه السلام: ماء وجهك جامد يُقطره السؤال فآنظر عند من تقطره.

3.330 وقال عليه السلام: الثناء بأكثر من الاستحقاق مَلَق والتقصير عن الاستحقاق عِيّ أو حسد.

3.331 وقال عليه السلام: أشدّ الذنوب ما آستهان به صاحبه.

3.332 وقال عليه السلام
من نظر في عيب نفسه آشتغل عن عيب غيره.
ومن رضي برزق الله لم يحزن على ما فاته.
ومن سَلّ سيف البغي قُتل به.
ومن كابَدَ الأمور عَطِب.
ومن آقتحم اللُّجَج غَرِق.
ومن دخل مَداخل السَّوء اتُّهِم.
ومن كثر كلامه كثر خطاؤه ومن كثر خطاؤه قلّ حياؤه ومن قلّ حياؤه قلّ ورعه ومن قلّ ورعه مات قلبه ومن مات قلبه دخل النار.
ومن نظر في عيوب الناس فأنكرها ثمّ رضيها لنفسه فذلك الأحمق بعينه.
القناعة مال لا ينفد.
ومن أكثر من ذكر الموت رضي من الدنيا باليسير.
ومن علم أنّ كلامه من عمله قلّ كلامه إلّا فيما يَعنيه.

3.333 وقال عليه السلام: للظالم من الرجال ثلاث علامات يظلم من فوقه بالمعصية ومن دونه بالغلَبة ويُظاهر القوم الظلَمَة.

3.334 وقال عليه السلام: عند تناهي الشدّة تكون الفُرجة وعند تضايُق حَلَق البلاء يكون الرخاء.

3.329 Think of the dignity of your countenance as water frozen in place until melted away by solicitation—to whom will you offer its droplets?

3.330 Praise beyond a person's worth is flattery. Praise below a person's worth is impotence or envy.

3.331 The worst sin is one its perpetrator thinks inconsequential.

3.332 Those who perceive their own faults are too preoccupied to notice the faults of others.

Those who are happy with the sustenance God has given them are not saddened by what they don't have.

Those who draw the sword of treachery are slain by it.

Those who pitch themselves against fate perish.

Those who rush blindly into the deep sea drown.

Those who enter places of vice invite suspicion.

When words multiply, errors multiply; when errors multiply, modesty decreases; when modesty decreases, restraint decreases; when restraint decreases, the heart dies—and whoever's heart has died enters the Fire.

If you remark on the faults of others while tolerating your own, you are the epitome of the fool.

Contentment is wealth that never runs out.[1]

Contemplate death, and you will want little from this world.

If you realize that words are deeds, you will speak only when it benefits you.

3.333 An oppressor is identified in three ways: he oppresses those above him by his disobedience, he oppresses those below him by his brutality, and he supports the faction of oppressors.

3.334 When suffering becomes intense, deliverance will arrive. When an ordeal's noose tightens, its grip will slacken.

---

1 § 3.50 is identical.

3.335 وقال عليه السلام لبعض أصحابه

لا تجعلنّ أكثر شغلك بأهلك وولدك فإن يكن أهلك وولدك أولياء الله فإنّ الله لا يُضيّع أولياءه وإن يكونوا أعداء الله فما همُّك وشغلك بأعداء الله.

3.336 وقال عليه السلام: أكبر العيب أن تَعيب ما فيك مثله.

3.337 وهنّأ بحضرته رجل رجلًا بغلام ولد له فقال له ⟨لِيَهْنِكَ الفارسُ⟩ فقال عليه السلام لا تقل ذاك ولكن قل شَكرتَ الواهب وبورك لك في الموهوب وبلغ أشدَّه ورُزِقتَ برَّه.

3.338 وبنى رجل من عمّاله بناء نَفْمًا فقال

أطلعَت الوَرِقُ رؤوسها إنّ البناء ليصف لك الغنى.

3.339 وقيل له عليه السلام لو سُدّ على رجل باب بيت وتُرك فيه من أين يأتيه رزقه فقال من حيث يأتيه أجله.

3.340 وعزّى عليه السلام قومًا عن ميّت فقال

إنّ هذا الأمر ليس بكم بدأ ولا إليكم انتهى وقد كان صاحبكم هذا يسافر فعُدّوه في بعض أسفاره فإن قدم عليكم وإلّا قدمتم عليه.

3.341 وقال عليه السلام: أيّها الناس لِيَرَكم اللهُ من النعمة وَجِلين كما يراكم من النقمة فَرِقين إنّه من وُسّع عليه في ذات يده فلم ير ذلك استدراجًا فقد أمن مخوفًا ومن ضُيّق عليه في ذات يده فلم ير ذلك اختبارًا فقد ضيّع مأمولًا.

3.342 وقال عليه السلام: يا أسرى الرغبة أقصِروا فإنّ المُعرّج على الدنيا لا يروعه منها إلّا صريف أنياب الحِدثان. أيّها الناس تولّوا من أنفسكم تأديبها واعدلوا بها عن ضَراية[1] عاداتها.

<hr>

[1] ش، ن، ي، ونسخة في ه: كذا. أصل ه، ومصحَّحة في ش، ونسخة في ن، ي: ⟨ضَراوة⟩.

3.335 ʿAlī said to one of his associates:
Don't devote the major part of your life to your spouses and children. If they are God's devotees, God will take care of them. And if they are God's enemies, well then, why should you occupy yourself with caring for God's enemies?

3.336 Your biggest fault is faulting others for a fault you too possess.

3.337 A man congratulated another on the birth of a son in ʿAlī's presence, saying, ⟨May the warrior bring you joy!⟩[1] ʿAlī rebuked him:[2]
Don't say that! Say instead: May you thank your divine benefactor, may his heavenly grace encompass this child who is his gift, may the child grow to full strength, and may you be blessed with his devotion!

3.338 One of ʿAlī governors built a grand mansion, and ʿAlī said to him in rebuke:
Here are silver dirhams displaying their faces! The mansion speaks loudly of your wealth.

3.339 Asked, "If a man's door is locked with him inside, from where does his sustenance enter?" ʿAlī replied:
The same place from where his death will enter.

3.340 Offering condolences to some persons upon the death of a loved one, ʿAlī said:
This matter has not begun with you and will not end with you. Your friend used to travel, so think of him as being away on one of his journeys. If he does not come back to you, you will go forward to meet him.

3.341 People! Let God see you vigilant in times of ease, just as he sees you wary in times of hardship. Whoever fails to see the test when his hands fill with blessings is complacent about the impending terror. Whoever fails to see the trial when his hands straiten, squanders the reward he could have received.

3.342 Prisoners of craving, desist! Anyone who fixes his hopes on the world fails to take warning until calamity, gnashing her teeth, approaches. People, restrain yourselves, turn away from your rapacious ways!

---

1   Preferred felicitation used in the pre-Islamic period at the birth of a son. Ḥ 19:270; R 3:403.

2   Māmaṭīrī (*Nuzhah*, 394) records ʿAlī's line (without the rebuke) as having been addressed to ʿAbdallāh ibn al-ʿAbbās, congratulating him on the birth of a son, upon whom ʿAlī then proceeded to bestow, at ʿAbdallāh's request for a name, the name ʿAlī and the patronymic Abū al-Ḥasan, after his own.

3.343 وقال عليه السلام: لا تظنّنّ بكلمة خرجت من أحد سُوءًا وأنت تجد لها في الخير محتَمَلًا.

3.344 وقال عليه السلام إذا كانت لك إلى الله سبحانه حاجة فابدأ بمسألة الصلاة على النبيّ صلّى الله عليه وآله ثم سَل حاجتك فإنّ الله أكرم من أن يسأل حاجتين فيقضي إحداهما ويمنع الأخرى.

3.345 وقال عليه السلام: من ضَنّ بعِرضه فليدع المِراء.

3.346 وقال عليه السلام: من الخُرْق المعاجلة قبل الإمكان والأناة بعد الفرصة.

3.347 وقال عليه السلام: لا تَسَل عمّا لا يكون ففي الذي قد كان لك شغل.

3.348 وقال عليه السلام
الفكر مِرآة صافية.
والاعتبار منذر ناصح.
وكفى أدبًا لنفسك تجنُّبك ما كرهته لغيرك.

3.349 وقال عليه السلام: العلم مقرون بالعمل فَمن علِم عَمِل والعلم يَهْتِف بالعمل فإن أجابه وإلّا ارتحل.

3.350 وقال عليه السلام: يا أيّها الناس مَتاع الدنيا حُطام موبئ فتجنّبوا مَرعاه قُلعتها أحظى من طمأنينتها وبُلغتها أزكى من ثروتها حُكِم على مُكثِريها بالفاقة وأُعين مَن غَني عنها بالراحة ومَن راقه زِبرِجها أعقبت ناظِريه كَمَهًا ومن اَستشعر الشغَف بها ملأت ضميره أشجانًا لهنّ رقصٌ على سُويداء قلبه همّ يشغله وهمّ يحزنه. كذلك حتى يؤخذ بكَظْمه فيُلقى بالفضاء منقطعًا أبْهَراه هَيِّنًا على الله فناؤه وعلى الإخوان إلقاؤه. وإنّما ينظر المؤمن إلى الدنيا بعين الاعتبار ويقتات منها ببطن الاضطرار ويسمع فيها بأذن المقت والإبغاض إن قيل أثرى قيل أكدى وإن فُرح له بالبقاء حُزِن له بالفناء. هذا ولم يأتِهم

3.343 Don't regard a statement as spiteful if you can find a way to interpret it as good.

3.344 If you wish to ask God for something, begin by asking him to bless the Prophet, then put forward your petition. When God is asked for two things, he is too generous to grant the one and deny the other.

3.345 Anyone who wishes to preserve his dignity should not quarrel.

3.346 The one who rushes in before the time is right and the one who hesitates when the opportunity arrives are both fools.

3.347 Don't ask about what is not going to happen. You have enough to preoccupy you in dealing with what has happened.[1]

3.348 Thought is a polished mirror.
  A lesson learned counsels best.
  To shun doing what you dislike in others is discipline enough![2]

3.349 Knowledge is linked with action—whoever knows should act. In fact, knowledge calls out to action—if action steps forward, good, otherwise, knowledge will depart.

3.350 People! The stuff of this world is like rotten grass, so stay away from its pastures! Leaving it is better than residing in it, obtaining basic rations here is more wholesome than finding great wealth. He who covets its riches is destined for poverty, while he who is content is at peace, and he who is drawn to its glitter finds both his eyes blinded. In fact, he who is enamored of it finds his heart crowded with sorrows that dance inside its dusky core, one sorrow giving him worry, another causing him pain, continuing in this manner until his breathing stops, his arteries puncture, and he is thrown into an empty strip of earth. God feels no compunction in taking his life, and his brothers feel no guilt in tossing him into the grave. Beware! A true believer looks at the world with eyes that reflect on it, swallows a bit of its food into a belly compelled to consume it, and hears its sounds with ears that hate and abhor their frivolity. A man may get

---

1 Or, "Don't yearn for forbidden things, for what you have is enough to stop you from withholding acts of obedience to God" (R 3:408). Or, "Don't yearn for more and more worldly things—what you have should be enough to satisfy you" (B 1011).
2 § 3.385 is similar.

يوم فيه يُبلِسون إنّ الله سبحانه وضع الثواب على طاعته والعقاب على معصيته زِيادة لعباده عن نقمته وحِياشة لهم إلى جنّته.‏¹

3.351 ورُوي أنّه عليه السلام قلّما اعتدل به المنبر إلّا قال أمام خطبته

أيّها الناس اتّقوا الله فما خُلِق امرؤ عبثًا فيلهو ولا تُرك سدًى فيَلغو وما دنياه الّتي تحسّنت له بخلَف من الآخرة الّتي قبّحها سوء النظر عنده وما المغرور الذي ظفر من الدنيا بأعلى همّته كالآخر الذي ظفر من الآخرة بأدنى سُهمته.

3.352 وقال عليه السلام

لا شرف أعلى من الإسلام.

ولا عزّ أعزّ من التقوى.

ولا مَعْقِل أحصن من الورع.

ولا شفيع أنجح من التوبة.

ولا كنز أغنى من القناعة.

ولا مال أذهب للفاقة من الرضى بالقوت.

ومن اقتصر على بُلغة الكفاف فقد انتظم الراحة وتبوّأ خفض الدعة.

والرغبة مفتاح النصب ومطيّة التعب.

والحرص والكبر والحسد دواعٍ إلى التقحُّم في الذنوب.

والشَّرَه² جامعٌ مساوئ العيوب.

---

¹ ش، ن، ومصحّحة في ه: كذا. ي، وأصل ه: أُضيفت كلمة ⟨وقال يأتي على الناس زمان لا يبقى فيهم من القرآن إلّا رسمه ومن الإسلام إلّا اسمه مساجدهم يومئذ عامرة من البُنى خراب من الهدى سكّانها وعمّارها شرّ أهل الأرض منهم تخرج الفتنة واليهم تأوي الخطيئة يردّون من شذّ عنها فيها ويسوقون من تأخّر عنها إليها يقول الله في حلفتُ لأبعثنّ إلى اولئك فتنة أترك الحليم فيها حيران وقد فعل ونحن نستقيل الله عثرة الغفلة⟩. ¹² الحرّاني في تحف العقول: كذا. مخطوطات النهج الرئيسيّة (ما عدا م، حيث هذه الحكمة ساقطة عنها) وأكثر الشروح: ⟨الشرّ⟩. ونسخة في هامش ه: ⟨البخل⟩.

rich in this world, but then he is reduced to penury; people may rejoice at his living, but soon they must grieve at his death; and this is but little, for the day of despair is yet to come![1] God has promised reward for those who obey him and punishment for those who disobey him, in order to caution them against his Fire and tempt them toward his Garden.

3.351 It is said that ʿAlī rarely ascended the pulpit to deliver an oration without opening with these lines:[2]

People, be conscious of God at all times! Humans are not created in vain[3]—don't waste your lives in the pursuit of pleasure! You are not given an indefinite reprieve[4]—don't squander your time in idle chatter! This world that you find so pleasing is no substitute for the hereafter that you find so distasteful. Indeed, the fool who wins the largest share of this world falls far short of the man who wins the smallest part of the hereafter.

3.352 There is no honor more exalted than Islam.[5]

There is no might more powerful than piety.

There is no refuge more shielding than restraint.

There is no intercessor more effective than repentance.

There is no treasure more precious than contentment.

No wealth alleviates poverty faster than satisfaction with one's basic rations.

If you content yourself with basic rations, you will attain tranquility and peace of mind.

Desire is the key to fatigue and the steed of exhaustion.

Greed, pride, and envy invite you to rush blindly into sin.

Gluttony combines all the worst faults.[6]

---

1   Reference to Qurʾan, Muʾminūn 23:77, Rūm 30:12.

2   Presumably in Medina and Kufa throughout his caliphate, 35–40/656–661.

3   Reference to Qurʾan, Muʾminūn 23:115.

4   Reference to Qurʾan, Qiyāmah 75:36.

5   These sayings are from ʿAlī's oration titled *Wasīlah*. Ḥarrānī, *Tuḥaf*, 93.

6   Ar. *sharah*, after Ḥarrānī, *Tuḥaf*, 93, thus similar to § 3.357: "Stinginess (*bukhl*) combines all the worst faults." My *Nahj al-Balāghah* primary manuscripts all have "*sharr*," lit. "evil," thus, "Evil combines all the worst faults," which appears to be a tautology, and thus a mistranscription from *sharah*.

3.353 وقال عليه السلام[1]

قِوام الدنيا بأربعة عالِم مُستعمِل عِلمه وجاهل لا يَستنكف أن يتعلّم وجَواد لا يبخل بمعروفه وفقير لا يَبيع آخرته بدنياه. فإذا ضيّع العالِم عِلمه اْستنكف الجاهل أن يتعلّم وإذا بخل الغنيّ بمعروفه باعَ الفقير آخرته بدنياه. من كثرت نِعم الله عليه كثرت حوائج الناس إليه فمن قام لله فيها بما يجب عرّضها للدوام والبقاء ومن لم يقم لله فيها بما يجب عرّضها للزوال والفناء.

3.354

3.354.1 أيّها المؤمنون[2] إنّه من رأى عُدوانًا يُعمَل به ومُنكَرًا يُدعى إليه فأنكره بقلبه فقد سَلِم وبرِئ ومن أنكره بلسانه فقد أُجر وهو أفضل من صاحبه ومن أنكره بالسيف لتكون ﴿كَلِمَةُ ٱللهِ هِيَ ٱلْعُلْيَا﴾ و﴿كَلِمَةَ﴾ الظالمين ﴿ٱلسُّفْلَى﴾ فذلك الذي أصاب سبيل الهدى وقام على الطريق ونوّر في قلبه اليقين.

3.354.2 وقد قال عليه السلام في كلام آخر غير هذا يجري هذا المجرى

فمنهم المنكِر للمنكَر بيده ولسانه وقلبه فذلك المستكمِل لخصال الخير ومنهم المنكِر بلسانه وقلبه والتارك بيده فذلك متمسّك بخصلتين من خصال الخير ومضيّع خصلة ومنهم المنكِر بقلبه والتارك بيده ولسانه فذلك الذي ضيّع أشرف الخصلتين من الثلاث وتمسّك بواحدة ومنهم تارك لإنكار المنكَر بلسانه وقلبه ويده فذلك ميّت الأحياء. وما أعمال البرّ

---

[1] ش، ن: كذا. ي، ه: ﴿وقال لجابر بن عبد الله الأنصاريّ يا جابر﴾.   [2] ش، ن: كذا. ي، ه ﴿وفي هامش ه: ﴿وفي نسخة الرضيّ ...﴾﴾: أضيفت قبلها ﴿وروى اْبن جرير الطبريّ في تاريخه عن عبد الرحمن بن أبي ليلى الفقيه وكان ممّن خرِج لقتال الحجّاج مع اْبن الأشعث أنّه قال فيما كان يُحضّض به الناس على الجهاد إني سمعت عليًّا رفع الله درجته في الصالحين وأثابه ثواب الشهداء والصدّيقين يقول يوم لقينا أهل الشام﴾. تاريخ الطبريّ ٣٥٧:٦.

3.353 The world is sustained by four types of people: the learned who act according to their knowledge, the ignorant who are not reluctant to learn, the generous who are not stingy with acts of charity, and the poor who don't trade in their share of the hereafter for worldly chattels. But if the learned squander their knowledge, the ignorant will be reluctant to learn, and if the wealthy are stingy with their charity, the poor will trade in their share of the hereafter for worldly chattels. Know that when God's blessings increase for a person, people's petitions to him also increase. The one who shares his blessings as he ought to do for the sake of God earns their continuance and perpetuity. The one who does not share them as he ought to do for the sake of God exposes them to cessation and termination.[1]

3.354

3.354.1 Believers, whoever sees wrong enacted and evil propagated and condemns them with his heart is cleared and absolved. Whoever also condemns them with his tongue earns greater reward. Whoever also condemns them with his sword in order that «God's word may be the most lofty» and the oppressors' «word the most lowly»[2] has walked the way of guidance, stayed true to the path, and illuminated his heart with certainty.[3]

3.354.2 'Alī spoke similar words in another address:[4]
One of them condemns evil with his hand, his tongue, and his heart—this man has perfected all the traits of virtue. Another condemns evil with his tongue and his heart, but not with his hand—this man has grasped two aspects of virtue but has squandered the third. A third condemns evil with his heart, but not with his hand or his tongue—this man has squandered the two noblest aspects while still holding on to one. Finally, there is the man who fails to condemn evil at all, be it with tongue, heart, or hand—that man is the living dead. Know this:

---

1   Reportedly addressed to (1) Jābir ibn 'Abdallāh al-Anṣārī, when he went to visit 'Alī during an illness (Māmaṭīrī, *Nuzhah*, 173; Khwārazmī, *Manāqib*, 368; MSS Y and H); and/or (2) Jarīr ibn 'Abdallāh al-Bajalī (Sibṭ, *Tadhkirah*, 168).

2   Reference to Qur'an, Tawbah 9:40.

3   § 3.354.1 is said to be part of an oration by 'Alī at Ṣiffīn in 37/657, cited by 'Abd al-Raḥmān ibn Abī Laylā to rouse the Qur'an reciters in his army in the fight against Ḥajjāj and the Umayyads at Dayr al-Jamājim, in central Iraq in 83/702. Ṭabarī, *Tārīkh*, 6:357.

4   § 3.354.2 is cited as an answer given during an oration in the mosque in Basra, a few days after the Battle of the Camel (Māmaṭīrī, *Nuzhah*, 228). Other parts of the same oration as cited in ibid., 221–233 are listed in note to § 1.23.

كلّها والجهاد في سبيل الله عند الأمر بالمعروف والنهي عن المنكر إلّا كنَفْثَة ﴿فِي بَحْرٍ لُجِّيّ﴾ وإنّ الأمر بالمعروف والنهي عن المنكر لا يقرّبان من أجل ولا يَنْقُصان من رزق وأفضلُ ذلك كلمة عدل عند إمام جائر.

3.354.3 وعن أبي بُحَيْفة قال سمعت أمير المؤمنين عليه السلام يقول إنّ أوّل ما تُغلبون عليه من الجهاد الجهاد بأيديكم ثمّ بألسنتكم ثمّ بقلوبكم فمن لم يعرف بقلبه معروفًا ولم ينكر منكرًا قُلِب فجُعل أعلاه أسفله.

3.355 وقال عليه السلام: إنّ الحقّ ثقيل مَرِيّ وإنّ الباطل خفيف وبيّ.

3.356 وقال عليه السلام: لا تأمننّ على خير هذه الأمّة عذاب الله لقول الله سبحانه ﴿فَلَا يَأْمَنُ مَكْرَ ٱللَّهِ إِلَّا ٱلْقَوْمُ ٱلْخَٰسِرُونَ﴾ ولا تَيأسَنّ لشرّ هذه الأمّة من روح الله لقوله سبحانه ﴿إِنَّهُ لَا يَايْـَسُ مِن رَّوْحِ ٱللَّهِ إِلَّا ٱلْقَوْمُ ٱلْكَٰفِرُونَ﴾.

3.357 وقال عليه السلام: البخل جامع لمساوئ العيوب وهو زمام يُقاد به إلى كلّ سوء.

3.358 وقال عليه السلام: الرزق رزقان رزق تطلبه ورزق يطلبك فإن لم تأته أتاك فلا تحمل همّ سنتك على همّ يومك كفاك كلّ يوم ما فيه فإن تكن السنة من عمرك فإنّ الله تعالى سيؤتيك في كلّ غد جديد ما قَسَم لك وإن لم تكن السنة من عمرك فما تصنع بالهمّ لما ليس لك ولن يسبقك إلى رزقك طالب ولن يغلبك عليه غالب ولن يبطئ عنك ما قد قُدّر لك.

Compared to fighting in the path of God, compared to commanding good and forbidding evil, all other deeds together are like ephemeral foam «upon the deep ocean».[1] Commanding good and forbidding evil never bring your death closer, nor do they cause your sustenance to lessen. Best of all is a just word spoken in the face of a tyrannical ruler.

3.354.3 Abū Juḥayfah related: I heard the Commander of the Faithful say: In the fight against evil, the first thing to be overcome is the hand, then the tongue, then the heart. Once the heart stops recognizing good or condemning evil, it is upended and turned topsy-turvy.

3.355 Right is heavy but wholesome. Wrong is light but pestilent.[2]

3.356 Don't suppose even the best of this community secure against God's punishment, for the Almighty says, «Only losers feel secure against God's reckoning».[3] Don't suppose that even the worst of this community is without hope of receiving God's grace, for the Almighty says, «Only unbelievers despair of God's grace».[4]

3.357 Stinginess combines all the worst faults—its halter is used to lead people to evil acts.

3.358 Sustenance is of two types: one that seeks and one that is sought.[5] If you don't find it, it will find you. Don't add the worries of the coming year to the burdens of the present day—the present day has worries enough of its own. If your life extends to the rest of the year, God will provide you with his ordained sustenance in each new day, but your life may not extend to the rest of the year, in which case, why worry about a time when you may not be alive? Know this: No seeker can outrace you to your sustenance, no oppressor can seize your share, and nothing ordained for you will be slow in coming.

---

1 Qur'an, Nūr 24:40. Note that "fighting in God's path (*jihād*)" is equated with "commanding good and forbidding evil" twice in the subsequent lines.
2 To ʿUthmān, who had lost control of the populace and summoned his governors to strategize. Balādhurī, *Ansāb*, 5:533; Ibn Aʿtham, *Futūḥ*, 2:395.
3 Qur'an, Aʿrāf 7:99.
4 Qur'an, Yūsuf 12:87.
5 This first line identical to § 3.402. The next few lines are similar to § 3.260.

وقد مضى هذا الكلام فيما تقدّم من هذا الباب إلّا أنّه هاهنا أوضح وأشرح فلذلك كرّرناه على القاعدة المقرّرة في أوّل هذا الكتاب.

3.359   وقال عليه السلام: رُبَّ مُستقبِل يومًا ليس بمُستدبِره ومَغبوط في أوّل ليلة قامت بَواكيه في آخره.

3.360   وقال عليه السلام: الكلام في وَثاقك ما لم تتكلّم به فإذا تكلّمت به صرت في وثاقه فأخزُن لسانك كما تخزن ذهبك ووَرِقَك فرُبَّ كلمة سلبت نعمة.

3.361   وقال عليه السلام: لا تقل ما لا تعلم فإنّ الله سبحانه قد فرض على جوارحك كلّها فرائض يَحتجّ بها عليك يوم القيامة.

3.362   وقال عليه السلام: احذر أن يراك الله عند معصيته ويَفقدك عند طاعته فتكون من الخاسرين وإذا قَويت فاقوَ على طاعة الله وإذا ضعفت فاضعف عن معصية الله.

3.363   وقال عليه السلام: الركون إلى الدنيا مع ما تُعايِن منها جهل والتقصير في حسن العمل إذا وَثِقتَ بالثواب عليه غَبْن والطمأنينة إلى كلّ أحد قبل الاختبار عجز.

3.364   وقال عليه السلام: من هوان الدنيا على الله أنّه لا يعصى إلّا فيها ولا يُنال ما عنده إلّا بتركها.

3.365   وقال عليه السلام: من طلب شيئًا نالَه أو بعضه.

Raḍī: This text was recorded above, but this version is clearer and more detailed. That is why I have replicated it here, following the method I outlined in the book's Introduction.[1]

3.359 Many begin a day they will not survive. Many enter a night joyful and end it dead and mourned.[2]

3.360 Words are in your control until you let them go. Once you let them go, you are bound by their tether. Guard your tongue as you guard your gold and silver, for many a careless word has caused the loss of a great blessing!

3.361 Don't say things that you don't know to be true. God has assigned duties to each of your limbs, and he will hold you accountable on the day of resurrection.[3]

3.362 Beware lest God see you where he is disobeyed and not find you where he is obeyed, else you will be one of the losers. Be strong in your obedience to God. Be weak in your transgression of his prohibitions.

3.363 To depend on this world despite everything you see of her is reckless. To fall short in doing good when you are certain of God's reward is stupid. To trust everyone before putting them to the test is naive.

3.364 The world's low worth in God's eyes is clear from the fact that it is only in her that he is disobeyed, and only by forsaking her that his are blessings obtained.

3.365 Whoever seeks something obtains it or at least a part of it.

---

1 §3.358 was transcribed in a variant version earlier in §3.260. Raḍī explained in his Introduction §0.7 that he would record variant renderings of text if their language or content adds something new or noteworthy.

2 From ʿAlī's testament of counsel to his son Muḥammad ibn al-Ḥanafiyyah (Ṣadūq, *Man lā yahḍuruhu*, 4:386). A similar line is attributed to the Prophet in Quḍāʿī, *Shihāb*, §3.18.

3 From ʿAlī's testament of counsel to his son Muḥammad ibn al-Ḥanafiyyah. Ṣadūq, *Man lā yahḍuruhu*, 2:626.

3.366 وقال عليه السلام: ما خير بخير بعده النار وما شرّ بشرّ بعده الجنّة وكلّ نعيم دون الجنّة محقور وكلّ بلاء دون النار عافية. ألا وإنّ من البلاء الفاقة وأشدّ من الفاقة مرض البدن وأشدّ من مرض البدن مرض القلب. ألا وإنّ من النعم سعة المال وأفضل من سعة المال صحّة البدن وأفضل من صحّة البدن تقوى القلب.

3.367 وقال عليه السلام: للمؤمن ثلاث ساعات فساعة يناجي فيها ربّه وساعة يُرمّ معاشه وساعة يخلّي بين نفسه وبين لذّتها فيما يحلّ ويجمُل. وليس للعاقل أن يكون شاخصًا إلّا في ثلاثٍ مَرَمَّةً لمعاش أو خُطوةً في معاد أو لذّةً في غير محرَم.

3.368 وقال عليه السلام: ازهَد في الدنيا يُبصِرك الله عوراتها ولا تغفل فلست بمغفول عنك.

3.369 وقال عليه السلام: تكلّموا تُعرَفوا فإنّ المرء مخبوّ تحت لسانه.

3.370 وقال عليه السلام: خذ من الدنيا ما أتاك وتَوَلَّ عمّا تولّى عنك فإن أنت لم تفعل فأجمِل في الطلب.

3.371 وقال عليه السلام: رُبَّ قول أنفذ من صَول.

3.372 وقال عليه السلام: كلّ مُقتصَرٍ عليه كافٍ.

3.373 وقال عليه السلام: المنيّة ولا الدنيّة والتقلُّل ولا التوسُّل ومن لم يُعطَ قاعدًا لم يعط قائمًا والدهر يومان يوم لك ويوم عليك فإذا كان لك فلا تَبطَر وإذا كان عليك فاصبر.

3.366 How can a thing be good if it leads you into the Fire? How can a thing be bad if it leads you into the Garden? Compared to the Garden, every blessing is contemptible. Compared to the Fire, every trial is a comfort. Hark! A trial may come in the form of poverty—but worse than poverty is disease of the body, and worse than disease of the body is disease of the heart. Hark! A blessing may come in the form of abundant wealth—but better than abundant wealth is soundness of the body, and better than soundness of the body is piety of the heart.

3.367 The believer divides his time into three parts: in one part, he communes with his Lord, in another, he seeks his livelihood, and in the third, he allows himself to enjoy pleasures that are licit and good. The man of reason sets out for no purpose other than these three: to seek his livelihood, to take a step forward on the path of return to God, or to enjoy pleasures that are not forbidden.[1]

3.368 Renounce the world and God will show you her flaws. Don't remain heedless for you go not unheeded.

3.369 Speak and you will be known—a man is concealed behind his tongue.

3.370 Take what comes to you of this world and turn away from what turns away. If you can't bring yourself to do so, be moderate in your ventures.

3.371 Many a word pierces deeper than a sword.

3.372 What you are content with is enough.

3.373 Death, not shame! Poverty, not begging! Someone who doesn't receive while sitting will not receive when standing. Life consists of two days: one day is for you, another day is against you. When things are working in your favor, don't swagger. When things are going against you, be patient.

---

1 From ʿAlī's testament of counsel to his son Ḥasan. Barqī, *Maḥāsin*, 2:345.

3.374 وقال عليه السلام: مُقَارَبة الناس في أخلاقهم أمنٌ من غَوائلهم.[1]

3.375 وقال عليه السلام: من أومأ إلى مُتفاوِتٍ خذلته الحِيل.

3.376 وقال عليه السلام وقد سُئل عن معنى قولهم ﴿لا حول ولا قوّة إلّا بالله﴾ إنّا لا نملك مع الله شيئًا ولا نملك إلّا ما مَلَّكَنا فمتى ملَّكَنا ما هو منّا كَلَّفنا ومتى أخذه منّا وضع تكليفه عنّا.

3.377 وقال عليه السلام لعَمّار بن ياسر رحمه الله وقد سمعه يراجع المُغيرة بن شُعْبة كلامًا دَعْهُ يا عمّار فإنّه لم يأخذ من الدين إلّا ما قاربته الدنيا وعلى عَمدٍ لَبّس على نفسه ليجعل الشبهات عاذرًا لسقطاته.

3.378 وقال عليه السلام: ما أحسن تواضع الأغنياء للفقراء طلبًا لما عند الله وأحسن منه تِيهُ الفقراء على الأغنياء اتّكالًا على الله.

3.379 وقال عليه السلام: ما اُستودع الله امرأً عقلًا إلّا اُستنقذه به يومًا ما.

3.380 وقال عليه السلام: من صارعَ الحقَّ صَرعه.

3.381 وقال عليه السلام: القلب مُصحَف البصر.

3.382 وقال عليه السلام: التقى رئيس الأخلاق.

---

[1] ن، ش، م: كذا. ي، هـ، وزيادة في هامش م: أضيفت كلمة ﴿وقال عليه السلام لبعض مخاطبيه وقد تكلّم بكلمة يستصغر مثله عن قول مثلها لقد طرت شَكيرًا وهدرت سَقْبًا﴾. و﴿الشكير﴾ ههنا أوّل ما ينبت من ريش الطائر قبل أن يقوى ويستحصف. و﴿السقب﴾ الصغير من الإبل ولا يهدر إلّا بعد أن يستفحل.

3.374 Coming closer to people's ways protects you from their malice.[1]

3.375 One who seeks contradictory goals will not find a way to achieve them.

3.376 'Alī was asked about the meaning of the creed, ⟨There is no power or strength save from God⟩, and he replied:
We are not masters of anything in partnership with God, nor are we masters of anything without him having made us its master. When he makes us master over his possessions, he gives us a burden to carry, and when he takes it from us, he relieves us of the burden.

3.377 Hearing 'Ammār ibn Yāsir arguing with al-Mughīrah ibn Shu'bah, 'Alī said:[2]
Leave him, 'Ammār! Mughīrah has never accepted any aspect of religion that didn't bring him worldly benefit. He deliberately creates doubts for himself so he can use them to excuse his blunders.

3.378 How wonderful when the rich, seeking God's reward, are humble before the poor! How even more wonderful when the poor, placing their trust in God, are dignified before the rich!

3.379 If God has bestowed a man with reason, he will use it to save him someday.

3.380 If you wrestle with truth, you will be felled by it.

3.381 The heart is the register of the eye.

3.382 Consciousness of God is the chief of all virtues.

---

1 MSS Y, H, and M (in margin) add another saying here, with accompanying commentary, thus: Rebuking a person who said something that was not his place to say, 'Alī exclaimed: "You fly when you still have a fledgling's down, and bellow when you are but a calf!" Raḍī: "A fledgling's down (*shakīr*)" are the first feathers just appearing on a bird before they have strengthened and toughened. A "calf (*saqb*)" is the young of a camel, and it does not bellow until it has become a stallion.
2 In Medina, soon after 'Alī became caliph in 35/656, when 'Ammār urged Mughīrah to pledge allegiance to 'Alī and Mughīrah refused, saying he would wait until the confusion about 'Uthmān's death cleared. Ibn 'Asākir, *Tārīkh*, 60:44; Ibn Qutaybah, *Imāmah*, 1:69.

٣.٣٨٣ وقال عليه السلام: لا تجعلنّ ذَرَب لسانك على من أنطقك وبلاغة قولك على من سدّدك.

٣.٣٨٤ وقال عليه السلام: كفاك أدبًا لنفسك اجتناب ما تكرهه من غيرك.

٣.٣٨٥ وقال عليه السلام: من صَبَّرَ صَبْرَ الأحرار وإلّا سَلا سُلوّ الأغمار.

وقال للأشعث بن قَيس مُعَزِّيًا
إن صبرت صبر الأكارم وإلّا سلوت سلوّ البهائم.

٣.٣٨٦ وقال عليه السلام في صفة الدنيا
الدنيا تغرّ وتضُرّ وتمُرّ إنّ الله تعالى لم يَرضَها ثوابًا لأوليائه ولا عقابًا لأعدائه وإنّ أهل الدنيا كرَكبٍ بَيناهم حَلُّوا إذ صاحَ بهم سائقهم فارتحلوا.

٣.٣٨٧ وقال لابنه الحسن عليهما السلام
يا بُنَيّ لا تُخَلِّفَنّ وراءك شيئًا من الدنيا فإنّك تُخَلِّفه لأحد رجلين إمّا رجل عمل فيه بطاعة الله فسعد بما شقيت به وإمّا رجل عمل فيه بمعصية الله فكنت عونًا له على معصيته وليس أحد هذين حَقيقًا أن تؤثره على نفسك.

3.383 Don't use the sharpness of your tongue against the one who gave you speech, nor the eloquence of your words against the one who gave you direction.

3.384 To avoid doing what you dislike in others is discipline enough.[1]

3.385 Endure with the free or grow fat with the heedless.

Another report states that ʿAlī, offering his condolences, said the following to al-Ashʿath ibn Qays:
You can endure like the noble or grow fat like sheep.[2]

3.386 Describing the world, ʿAlī said:
The world betrays, and harms, and passes—God has rejected her both as reward for his devotees and as punishment for his enemies. People in the world are like a band of travelers—no sooner do they set up camp than the cameleer gives the call to depart.

3.387 ʿAlī said to his son Ḥasan:[3]
My dear son, do not leave your wealth for others to inherit, for your heir will be one of two men: a man who will use it to obey God, in which case he will earn happiness where you earned only misery, or a man who uses it to disobey God, in which case you will have aided him in his disobedience. Neither deserves more consideration from you than you give to yourself.

———

1   § 3.348 is similar.

2   From ʿAlī's expressions of condolence to al-Ashʿath ibn Qays on the death of his son (Ibn ʿAbd Rabbih, *ʿIqd*, 3:255). See also ʿAlī's expressions of condolence to Ashʿath on the death of his brother in § 3.89, and of his son in § 3.277. "To be fat like sheep (*istalā*)" is said of one who does not take a lesson from seeing death and prepare more diligently for the hereafter. Another translation is "to be forgetful like sheep." The commentators note that the Abbasid poet Abū Tammām echoed this saying explicitly citing ʿAlī in his verse: "ʿAlī said to Ashʿath in condolence, fearing that he may otherwise sin: Will you take solace and endure this trial—and if you do, you shall be rewarded—or will you be heedless and grow fat like sheep"

وقال عليّ في التعازي لأشعث   وخاف عليه بعض تلك المآثم
أتصبر للبلوى عـزاء وحسبـة   فتؤجـر أم تَسلـو سلـوّ البهائـم

H 19:50; F 455; Ibn ʿAbd Rabbih, *ʿIqd*, 3:255; Abū Tammām, *Dīwān*, 3:258–259.

3   Kulaynī (*Kāfī*, 8:72) cites part of this text in a letter from ʿAlī to his freedman, who, dissatisfied with ʿAlī's offer to help him financially from his personal stipend, went to Muʿāwiyah to ask for money. Similar line in § 3.400.

ويروى هذا الكلام على وجه آخر وهو

أمّا بعد. فإنّ الذي في يديك من الدنيا قد كان له أهل قبلك وهو صائر إلى أهل

بعدك وإنّما أنت جامع لأحد رجلين رجل عمل فيما جمعته بطاعة الله فسعد بما شقيت

به أو رجل عمل فيه بمعصية الله فشقي بما جمعت له وليس أحد هذين أهلًا أن

تؤثره على نفسك وتحمل له على ظهرك فأرجُ لمن مضى رحمة الله ولمن بقي رزق الله.

3.388 وقال عليه السلام لقائل قال بحضرته ﴿أستغفر الله﴾

ثَكِلَتْكَ أُمُّكَ أتدري ما الاستغفار إنّ الاستغفار درجة العِلّيّين[١] وهو اسم واقع على ستّة

معانٍ أوّلها الندم على ما مضى والثاني العزم على ترك العود إليه أبدًا والثالث أن تؤدّي إلى

المخلوقين حقوقهم حتّى تلقى الله أملَس ليس عليك تَبِعة والرابع أن تَعمِد إلى كلّ فريضة

عليك ضيعتها فتؤدّي حقّها والخامس أن تعمد إلى اللحم[٢] الذي نبت على السُّحت فتُذيبه

بالأحزان حتّى يَلصَق الجِلد بالعظم وينشأ بينهما لحم جديد. والسادس أن تُذيق الجسم

ألم الطاعة كما أذقته حلاوة المعصية فعند ذلك تقول أستغفر الله.

3.389 وقال عليه السلام: الحِلم عشيرة.

3.390 وقال عليه السلام: مسكينٌ ابن آدم مكتوم الأجل مكنون العلل محفوظ العمل

تؤلمه البَقّة وتقتله الشَّرقة وتُنتِنه العَرقة.

3.391 وروي أنّه عليه السلام كان جالسًا في أصحابه فمرّت بهم امرأة جميلة فرمَقها القوم

بأبصارهم فقال عليه السلام

إنّ أبصار هذه الفُحول طَوامح وإنّ ذلك سبب هِبابها فإذا نظر أحدكم إلى امرأة تعجبه

فَلْيُلامِس أهله فإنّما هي امرأة كامرأة.

This text is also narrated in the following variant rendering:
All the worldly riches your hands possess have had other masters before you and will pass to other masters after you. You gather riches for one of two men: a man who will use it to obey God, in which case he will earn happiness where you earned only misery, or a man who will use it to disobey God, in which case you will have aided him in his disobedience. Neither deserves more consideration from you than you give to yourself. Neither is worth your carrying their sins on your back. Instead, beseech God's mercy for those who have passed, and solicit God's sustenance for those who remain.

3.388 A man uttered the dictum, ⟨I beg God's forgiveness!⟩ in ʿAlī's presence, and ʿAlī rebuked him, saying:
May your mother be bereaved! Do you know what it means to beg God's forgiveness? That is the lofty state of the angels, and it requires six actions: The first is to regret what you have done. The second is to resolve never to do it again. The third is to give back to all God's creatures what you owe them, so that you can meet God with a smooth and unburdened back. The fourth is to make up for every mandated act that you have squandered and give it its full due. The fifth is to target the unlawfully nourished flesh in your body and melt it away by grieving, until, after your skin touches your bones, new flesh grows and fills it out. The sixth is to force your body to taste the pain of good deeds, just as you let it taste the sweetness of sin. Then you can truthfully say: I beg God's forgiveness!

3.389 Clemency generates kinship.

3.390 How wretched is the son of Adam! Lifespan unknown, ailments concealed, actions recorded; he hurts from the sting of a gnat, chokes from a sip of water, and stinks from a drop of sweat.

3.391 It is related that ʿAlī was sitting among his associates when a beautiful woman passed. The men's eyes followed her, and ʿAlī exclaimed:[1]
O how covetous the eyes of these virile stallions—they stare and they throb! If your eyes fall on an attractive woman, people, go home and embrace your wife, for a woman is a woman!

---

1   Presumably in Kufa, between the emergence of the Kharijites—who are mentioned here—in 37/657 and the Battle of Nahrawān in 38/658 when they were killed.

فقال رجل من الخوارج قاتله الله كافرًا ما أَفْقَهه فوثب القوم ليقتلوه فقال عليه السلام رُوَيدًا إنّما هو سَبّ بسبّ أو عفو عن ذنب.

3.392 وقال عليه السلام: كفاك من عقلك ما أوضح لك سبيل غَيّك من رشدك.

3.393 وقال عليه السلام: افعلوا الخير ولا تحقروا منه شيئًا فإنّ صغيره كبير وقليله كثير ولا يقولنّ أحدكم إنّ أحدًا أولى بفعل الخير منّي فيكون والله كذلك إنّ للخير والشرّ أهلًا فما تركتموه منهما كفاكموه أهله.

3.394 وقال عليه السلام: من أصلح سريرته أصلح الله له علانيته ومن عمل لدينه كفاه الله أمر دنياه ومن أحسن فيما بينه وبين الله كفاه الله ما بينه وبين الناس.

3.395 وقال عليه السلام: الحلم غطاء ساتر والعقل حسام قاطع فاستر خَلَل خُلُقك بحلمك وقاتِل هواك بعقلك.

3.396 وقال عليه السلام: إنّ لله عبادًا يختصّهم بالنعم لمنافع العباد فيُقِرّها في أيديهم ما بذلوها فإذا منعوها نزعها منهم ثمّ حوّلها إلى غيرهم.

3.397 وقال عليه السلام: لا ينبغي للعبد أن يثق بخصلتين العافية والغنى بينا تراه مُعافًى إذ سَقِمَ وبينا تراه غنيًّا إذ افتقر.

3.398 وقال عليه السلام: مَن شكا الحاجة إلى مؤمن فكأنّما شكاها إلى الله ومن شكاها إلى كافر فكأنّما شكا الله.

3.399 وقال عليه السلام في بعض الأعياد
إنّما هو عيدٌ لمن قبل الله صيامه وشكر قيامه وكلّ يوم لا يُعصى الله فيه فهو يوم عيد.

A Kharijite muttered, "May God fight this heretic, how well he understands!" People jumped on him to slay him, and ʿAlī held them back, saying:
Slow down! You can either return his curse with another curse or pardon his offence.

3.392 Your intellect gives you enough guidance if it distinguishes error from direction.

3.393 Do good and don't think any deed too humble, for a small deed is large in value and though little it counts for a lot. No one among you should say that so-and-so is better able to do good than I, else, by God, it will be so. Both good and evil have their adherents—whatever you leave off doing, others will step forward to do.

3.394 If someone sets right his thoughts, God sets right his behavior. If someone strives for his religion, God takes care of his needs. If someone steps forward to serve God, God helps him in his dealings with people.

3.395 Forbearance is a curtain that conceals, and intelligence is a keen blade— veil your flaws by exercising forbearance and fight your passions by using your intelligence.

3.396 God has singled out some servants for particular blessings to use for the benefit of all—he leaves them in their hands as long as they do. If they don't, he takes them back and entrusts them to others.

3.397 There are two things no one should take for granted: health and wealth. You see a man healthy one day and suddenly he is taken ill. You see a man wealthy one day and suddenly he loses all his money.

3.398 To complain to a believer is to complain to God. To complain to an unbeliever is to complain about God.

3.399 On a certain feast day, ʿAlī declared:
The blessing of Eid is for those whose fast God accepts and whose worship he rewards. In fact, every day in which God is not disobeyed is Eid.

3.400 وقال عليه السلام: إنّ أعظم الحسرات يوم القيامة حسرة رجل كسب مالًا في غير طاعة الله فورّثه رجلًا فأنفقه في طاعة الله فدخل به الجنّة ودخل به الأوّل النار.

3.401 وقال عليه السلام: إنّ أخسر الناس صَفقةً وأخيبَهم سعيًا رجل أخلقَ بدنه في طلب آماله ولم تساعده المقادير على إرادته نخرج من الدنيا بحسرته وقدم على الآخرة بتَبِعَته.

3.402 وقال عليه السلام: الرزق رزقان طالب ومطلوب فمن طلب الدنيا طلبه الموت حتّى يُخرجه عنها ومن طلب الآخرة طلبته الدنيا حتّى يستوفي رزقه منها.

3.403 وقال عليه السلام: إنّ أولياء الله هم الذين نظروا إلى باطن الدنيا إذا نظر الناس إلى ظاهرها وَاشتغلوا بآجِلها إذا اشتغل الناس بعاجلها فأماتوا منها ما خشوا أن يميتهم وتركوا منها ما علموا أنّه سيتركهم ورأوا استكثار غيرهم منها استقلالًا ودرَكَهم لها فَوتًا أعداء ما سالمَ الناسُ وسلمُ ما عادى الناس بهم عِلم الكِّاب وبه علموا وبهم قام الكِّاب وبه قاموا لا يرون مَرجوًّا فوق ما يرجون ولا مخوفًا فوق ما يخافون.

3.404 وقال عليه السلام: اذكروا انقطاع اللذّات وبقاء التَّبِعات.

3.405 وقال عليه السلام: أُخبرْ تَقْلِهْ.

ومن الناس من يروي هذا لرسول الله صلّى الله عليه وآله وممّا يقوّي أنّه من كلام أمير المؤمنين عليه السلام ما حكاه ثَعْلَب عن ابن الأعرابيّ قال المأمون لولا أنّ عليًّا قال ‹أخبر تقله› لقلت ‹أقلِهْ تَخْبُرْ›.

3.400 The greatest remorse on judgment day will be felt by a man who earned his wealth through God's disobedience and bequeathed it to an heir who spent it in his obedience—the heir will enter the Garden, the man will enter the Fire.[1]

3.401 The biggest loser, the worst failure, is a man who wears down his body to satisfy his desires, but destiny does not side with him—he leaves the world with only remorse and arrives in the hereafter with a burden of sin.

3.402 Sustenance is of two types: one that seeks and one that is sought. Seekers of the world are sought by death, and death will expel them from her. Seekers of the hereafter are sought by the world, and she will give them her full share.[2]

3.403 God's special devotees are those who perceive the world's reality when others are deceived by her appearance. They occupy themselves with what is coming when others occupy themselves with the present. They kill desires they fear will kill them and reject pleasures they know will reject them. They find wealth of meager benefit, and other men's gain as loss. They deem the world an enemy when others deem it an ally. They deem the hereafter an ally when others deem it an enemy. God's Book is recognized through them, and they are recognized through God's Book. God's Book is established through them, and they are established through God's Book. They see nothing more desirable than what they desire and nothing more terrifying than what they fear.[3]

3.404 Remember that pleasures pass, and consequences remain.

3.405 Put people to the test and you will come to hate them.

Raḍī: Some people attribute these lines to God's Messenger, but what supports its attribution to the Commander of the Faithful is Thaʿlab's narration on the authority of Ibn al-Aʿrābī, who reported: Maʾmūn stated: If ʿAlī had not said "Put people to the test and you will come to hate them (*ukhbur taqlih*)," I would have said, "Hate people and you will have an incentive to test them (*aqlih takhbur*)."[4]

---

1   Similar line in §3.387.
2   First line identical in §3.358.
3   This text is attributed to Jesus in Abū Nuʿaym, *Ḥilyat*, 1:10.
4   §3.405 is attributed to the Prophet in Quḍāʿī, *Shihāb*, §4.8. Thaʿlab and Ibn al-Aʿrābī were grammarians. Maʾmūn was an Abbasid caliph.

3.406 وقال عليه السلام: ما كان الله ليفتح على عبد باب الشكر ويغلق عنه باب الزيادة ولا ليفتح على عبد باب الدعاء ويغلق عنه باب الإجابة ولا ليفتح على عبد باب التوبة ويغلق عنه باب المغفرة.

3.407 وسئل عليه السلام أيّما أفضل العدل أو الجود فقال العدل يضع الأمور مواضعها والجود يخرجها عن جهتها والعدل سائس عامّ والجود عارض خاصّ فالعدل أشرفهما وأفضلهما.

3.408 وقال عليه السلام: الناس أعداء ما جهلوا.

3.409 وقال عليه السلام: الزهد كلّه بين كلمتين من القرآن قال الله عزوجلّ ﴿لِّكَيْلَا تَأْسَوْا۟ عَلَىٰ مَا فَاتَكُمْ وَلَا تَفْرَحُوا۟ بِمَآ آتَىٰكُمْ﴾ ومن لم يأسَ على الماضي ولم يفرح بالآتي فقد أخذ الزهد بطرَفَيه.

3.410 وقال عليه السلام: الوِلايات مَضامير الرجال.

3.411 وقال عليه السلام: ما أنقض النوم لعزائم اليوم.

3.412 وقال عليه السلام: ليس بلد بأحقّ بك من بلد خير البلاد ما حملك.

3.413 وقال عليه السلام وقد جاءه نَعْي الأشتر رحمه الله مَالكُ وما مَالكُ لو كان جبلًا لكان فِنْدًا لا يرتقيه الحافر ولا يوفي عليه الطائر.

﴿الفند﴾ المنفرد من الجبال.

3.414 وقال عليه السلام: قليلٌ مَدوم عليه خير من كثير مملول منه.

3.406 When God has opened the door of gratitude for you, he will not close the door of increase. When he has opened the door of prayer for you, he will not close the door of fulfillment. When he has opened the door of repentance for you, he will not close the door of forgiveness.[1]

3.407 ʿAlī was asked, "Which is better, justice or generosity?" and he replied: Justice puts things in their rightful place, while generosity takes things out of their proper sphere. Justice is a universal motivator, while generosity is a particular aspect. Justice is thus the nobler and better of the two.

3.408 People hate the unfamiliar.[2]

3.409 The whole of renunciation is encompassed in two injunctions from the Qurʾan: «Do not weep over what you have lost, and do not exult over what you have gained.»[3] Those who don't weep over the past or exult over what they have gained have grasped renunciation from both sides.

3.410 Rulership is the racecourse where men show their mettle.

3.411 How completely does sleep crush the resolutions of the day![4]

3.412 No land is better for you than another—the best land is one that sustains you.

3.413 When news arrived of Mālik al-Ashtar's death, ʿAlī exclaimed:[5] Mālik, O Mālik, O what a man! If he were a mountain, he would be a towering peak that no hoof could ascend, no bird fly over.

Raḍī: "A towering peak (*find*)" is a mountain that soars above all others.

3.414 A little done often is better than a lot you tire of.[6]

---

1 Similar to §3.407. Reference to Qurʾan, Nisāʾ 4:60, 110, Ibrāhīm 14:7.

2 §3.156 is identical.

3 Qurʾan, Ḥadīd 57:23.

4 From ʿAlī's oration §1.237 (one of the early additions to Raḍī's original *Nahj a-balāghah*), presumably delivered in Kufa, after the arbitration in 37/658.

5 In Kufa, 38/658. ʿAlī had sent Ashtar to replace Muḥammad ibn Abī Bakr as governor of Egypt and he was poisoned en route by Muʿāwiyah's agent. Māmaṭīrī, *Nuzhah*, 282–283.

6 §3.271 is similar.

3.415 وقال عليه السلام: إذا كان في الرجل خُلّة رائعة فأنتظروا أخواتها.

3.416 وقال عليه السلام لغالب بن صَعصعة أبي الفرزدق في كلام دار بينهما
ما فعلت إبلك الكثيرة.

قال ذَعْذَعَتْها الحقوق يا أمير المؤمنين فقال صلوات الله عليه
ذلك أحمدُ سبلها.[1]

3.417 وقال عليه السلام: من عظّم صغار المصائب أبتلاه الله بكبارها.

3.418 وقال عليه السلام: من كرمت عليه نفسه هانت عليه شهوته.

3.419 وقال عليه السلام: ما مَزَح رجل[2] مَزْحة إلّا مَجّ من عقله مَجّة.

3.420 وقال عليه السلام: زهدك في راغب فيك نقصان حظّ ورغبتك في زاهد فيك
ذلّ نفس.

3.421 وقال عليه السلام: ما لأبن آدم والفخر أوّله نطفة وآخره جيفة لا يرزق نفسه
ولا يدفع حتفه.

3.422 وقال عليه السلام: الغنى والفقر بعد العرض على الله.

3.423 وسئل عليه السلام عن أشعر الشعراء فقال
إنّ القوم لم يجروا في حَلْبة تعرف الغاية عند قَصَبتها فإن كان ولا بدّ فالمَلِك الضِّلّيل.

يريد آمرأ القيس.

---

[1] ن، م، ش، ه: كذا. ي: كذا. وزيادة في هامش م، ش: أضيفت كلمة: وقال عليه السلام ﴿من آتّجر
بغير فقهٍ أرتطم في الربا﴾.   [2] ش، ن، ي، ه: كذا. م: ﴿أمرؤ﴾.

3.415 If a man possesses one brilliant quality, expect to see others.

3.416 ʿAlī said to Ghālib ibn Ṣaʿṣaʿah, Farazdaq's father, during a longer conversation:[1]
What happened to your large herd of camels?

Ghālib replied, "The winds of duty have scattered them, Commander of the Faithful," and ʿAlī responded:
That is the most admirable path they could have taken.[2]

3.417 If someone makes much ado about small trials, God will afflict him with large ones.

3.418 The self-respecting don't follow their passions.

3.419 Each time a man spurts out a joke, he spits out a bit of his brain.

3.420 If you spurn a person who wants you, you reduce your designated share. If you want a person who spurns you, you humiliate yourself.

3.421 How, O son of Adam, are you entitled to conceit? You began as a drop of semen and will end as a rotting corpse. You cannot sustain your life, nor can you fight off your death.[3]

3.422 Who is wealthy and who is poor will be known after God's accounting.

3.423 Asked who was the best poet, ʿAlī replied:
Poets don't all race on the same track, so we can't speak about who reached the goalpost first. But if you insist on an answer, I choose the Wandering King.

Raḍī: He meant Imruʾ al-Qays.

---

1 In Kufa, sometime during ʿAlī's caliphate, 35–40/656–661 (Ḥ 20:96). Farazdaq is the famous poet.
2 MS Y adds another saying here: "Whoever trades without knowing the law becomes mired in usury."
3 Mubarrad, *Kāmil*, 2:11: Abū al-ʿAtāhiyah (*Dīwān*, 178) paraphrased this saying in four verses:

ما أحمق الإنسان في نخْره   وهو غدًا في حفرة يقبر

ما بال من أوّله نطفة   وجيفة آخره يفخر

أصبح لا يملك تقديم ما   يرجو ولا تأخير ما يحذر

وأصبح الأمر إلى غيره   في كلّ ما يقضى وما يقدر

٣.٤٢٤ وقال عليه السلام: ألا حُرٌّ يدع هذه اللُّماظة لأهلها إنّه ليس لأنفسكم ثمن إلّا الجنّة فلا تبيعوها إلّا بها.

٣.٤٢٥ وقال عليه السلام: علامة الإيمان أن تؤثر الصدق حيث يضرّك على الكذب حيث ينفعك وألّا يكون في حديثك فضلٌ عن عملك وأن تتّقي الله في حديث غيرك.

٣.٤٢٦ وقال عليه السلام: يغلب المِقدار على التقدير حتّى تكون الآفة في التدبير.

وقد مضى هذا المعنى فيما تقدّم برواية تخالف بعض هذه الألفاظ.

٣.٤٢٧ وقال عليه السلام: الحلم والأناة تَوأمان يُنتجهما علوّ الهمّة.

٣.٤٢٨ وقال عليه السلام: الغيبة جهد العاجز.

٣.٤٢٩ وقال عليه السلام: رُبَّ مفتون بحسن القول فيه.

3.424 Is there no free man who will leave these chewed-up scraps for the gluttons? There is no price high enough for your souls except paradise—don't sell them for anything less.

3.425 True belief is this: to prefer a truth that hurts you over a falsehood that benefits you, to ensure that your words don't outpace your deeds, and to fear God when speaking about others.

3.426 The fates vanquish all—sometimes too much planning can lead to pain.

Raḍī: This saying was recorded earlier with some variant words.[1]

3.427 Clemency and patience are twins born of lofty aspirations.[2]

3.428 Slander is the enterprise of the weak.

3.429 Many are seduced by praise.

---

1 §3.12.
2 In praise of the Persian emperor Anūshīrwān. Māmaṭīrī, *Nuzhah*, 380; Muwaffaq biʾllāh, *Iʿtibār*, 576.

3.430 وقال عليه السلام: الدنيا خُلِقَت لغيرها ولم تخلق لنفسها.

3.431 وقال عليه السلام: إنّ لبني أميّة مِرْوَدًا يجرون فيه ولو قد اختلفوا فيما بينهم ثمّ كادتهم الضباع لغلبتهم.

والمرود هنا مفعل من الإرواد وهو الإمهال والإنظار وهذا من أفصح الكلام وأغربه فكأنّه عليه السلام شبّه المهلة التي هم فيها بالمضمار الّذي يجرون فيه إلى الغاية فإذا بلغوا منقطعها انتقض نظامهم بعدها.

3.432 وقال عليه السلام في مدح الأنصار: هم والله ربّوا الإسلام كما يُرَبّى الفُلُوّ مع غنائهم بأيديهم السِّباط وألسنتهم السِّلاط.

---

[1] أضيفت في بعض المخطوطات قبل الخاتمة أو بعدها زيادة على الأصل قديمة، وهي عبارة عن سبع عشرة كلمة لعليّ، مسبوقة في أقدم المخطوطات بسطر يشير إلى أنها زائدة على الأصل: ش: ⟨زيادة من نسخة كتبت في عهد المصنّف⟩ (ملاحظة عن ش: ثبتت الزيادات من ١§ إلى وسط ٤§، حيث فقدت بعدها صفحة من المخطوطة). ن: ⟨زيادة كتبت من نسخة سريّة عراقيّة⟩. ي: ⟨زيادة من نسخة كتبت على عهد المصنّف رحمه الله⟩. والزيادة لم تثبت في م، أو في شرح ابن الفندق المؤلّف سنة ٥٥٢ هجريّة وهو من أقدم الشروح. وأثبتت الزيادة بلا فاصلة أو تنبيه في أكثر المخطوطات التالية في الزمن، وكذلك في بعض الشروح مثل شرح الراونديّ. والرضيّ كان قد ترك فراغات لإثبات زيادات في نهاية كلّ من الأبواب الثلاثة للكتاب، وذكر هذا الأمر في خاتمته للكتاب. وقيل إن الزيادة التي بين أيدينا أثبتت في حياة الرضيّ وبإمضائه: قال ابن أبي الحديد (٢٠:١٨٠): ⟨ثمّ وجدنا نسخًا كثيرة فيها زيادات بعد هذا الكلام قيل إنّها وجدت في نسخة كتبت في حياة الرضيّ رحمه الله وقرئت عليه فأمضاها وأذن في إلحاقها بالكتاب ونحن نذكرها⟩. وقال البحرانيّ (١٠٢٩): ⟨أقول إنّه رضوان الله عليه بلغ في اختيار كلامه عليه السلام إلى هذه الغاية وقطعه عليها ثمّ كتبت على عهده زيادة من محاسن الكلمات إمّا باختياره هو أو بعض من كان يحضره من أهل العلم وتلك الزيادة تارة توجد خارجة عن المتن وتارة موضوعة فيه ملحقة بمنقطع اختياره. وروي أنّها قرئت عليه وأمر بإلحاقها بالمتن⟩.

Additional Sayings[1]

3.430 The world was created not for herself but for another.

3.431 The Umayyads have a short stretch in which to race ahead. Once they quarrel,
the hyenas will strike.
Raḍī: "Reprieve (*mirwad*)" is the *mifʿal* form derived from the verbal noun *irwād*, which
means "delay (*imhāl*)" and "respite (*inẓār*)." This is among the most eloquent of usages
and the most wondrous. ʿAlī compared the reprieve they have been given to a race-
course in which they race toward the goal; once they reach it, their government will
collapse.

3.432 ʿAlī said in praise of the Allies: By God, they nurtured Islam as one would a prize
colt, with generous hands and eloquent tongues.

---

1 An additional seventeen sayings—perhaps added by Raḍī, or by others—are transcribed in
   some of our primary and secondary manuscripts and commentaries (details in footnote to
   the present edition, and in the Note on the Edition and Translation)

3.433 وقال عليه السلام: العين وِكاءُ السَّه.

وهذه من الاستعارات العجيبة كأنّه شبّه السه بالوعاء والعين بالوكاء فإذا أطلق الوكاء لم ينضبط الوعاء وهذا القول في الأشهر الأظهر من كلام النبيّ صلّى الله عليه وآله وقد رواه قوم لأمير المؤمنين عليه السلام وذكر ذلك المبرّد في كتاب المقتضب في باب اللفظ بالحروف وقد تكلّمنا على هذه الاستعارة في كتابنا الموسوم بمجازات الآثار النبويّة.

3.434 وقال عليه السلام في كلام له: ووليهم والٍ فأقام وأستقام حتّى ضرب الدين بجِرانه.

3.435 وقال عليه السلام: يأتي على الناس زمان عَضوض يَعَضّ المُوسِر فيه على ما في يديه ولم يؤمر بذلك قال الله سبحانه ﴿وَلَا تَنْسَوُا الْفَضْلَ بَيْنَكُمْ﴾. يَنْهَد فيه الأشرار ويُستَذَلّ فيه الأخيار ويُبايَع المضطرّون وقد نهى رسول الله صلّى الله عليه وآله عن بيع المضطرّين.

3.436 وقال عليه السلام: يَهلِك فيَّ رجلان مُحبّ مُطْرٍ وباهِتٌ مفتَرٍ.

وهذا مثل قوله عليه السلام: هلك فيَّ رجلان محبّ غالٍ ومبغض قالٍ.

3.437 وسئل عليه السلام عن التوحيد والعدل فقال: التوحيد أن لا تتوهّمه والعدل أن لا تتّهمه.

3.438 وقال عليه السلام: إنّه لا خير في الصمت عن الحُكم كما أنّه لا خير في القول بالجهل.

3.433 The eye is a leather strap fastening the buttocks.

Raḍī: This is among the most wondrous of metaphors, as though he likened the buttocks to a vessel and the eye to a leather strap—if the strap is loosened (i.e., if the eye is closed in sleep), the vessel is not held fast (i.e., it can emit involuntary secretions). In most narrations, this saying is attributed to the Prophet, but some have attributed it to the Commander of the Faithful, such as Mubarrad, in his Book of Extemporaneous Discourse (*Kitāb al-Muqtaḍab*), in the chapter on speech with single syllables. I have also discussed this metaphor in my book, Figurative Language of Prophetic Hadith (*Majāzāt al-āthār al-nabawiyyah*).

3.434 ʿAlī said in an oration: Then a certain ruler came to rule them. He stood them upright and he himself stayed upright, until religion, like a docile camel, laid its neck flat on the earth.

3.435 A time like a gnashing camel will come upon the people, when the rich will grip onto their wealth by their teeth, even though they have been commanded otherwise, for God has said, «Do not forget to be generous to one another».[1] At this time, the wicked will rise, while the virtuous will be humiliated, and the helpless will be forced to sell their goods for a pittance, despite the prohibition by God's Messenger.

3.436 Two kinds of men are damned because of how they feel about me: one who praises too lavishly, and one who slanders and lies.

Raḍī: This is similar to his saying: Two kinds of men are damned because of how they feel about me: one is excessive in his love, the other is extreme in his hatred.[2]

3.437 ʿAlī was asked about God's oneness and justice, and he replied: Declaring God's oneness means not imagining him, and declaring his justice means never accusing him.

3.438 There is no benefit in keeping silent when you can offer wisdom, just as there is no benefit in speaking words of ignorance.[3]

---

1   Qurʾan, Baqarah 2:237.
2   § 3.107.
3   Similar to § 3.166.

٣٩‏.٣ وقال عليه السلام في دعاء آستسقى به: اللّهمّ آسقنا ذُلُل السحائب دون صِعابها.
وهذا من الكلام العجيب الفصاحة وذلك أنّه عليه السلام شبّه السحائب ذوات الرعود
والبوارق والرياح والصواعق بالإبل الصعاب التي تَقَمَّص برحالها وتتوقّص بركبانها وشبّه
السحاب الحالية من تلك الروائع بالإبل الذلل التي تُحتلَب طَيِّعة وتُقتعَد مُسمِحة.

٤٤٠‏.٣ وقيل له عليه السلام: لو غيّرت شيبك يا أمير المؤمنين فقال: الخِضاب زينة ونحن قوم
في مصيبة.
يريد برسول الله صلّى الله عليه وآله.

٤٤١‏.٣ وقال عليه السلام: القناعة مال لا ينفد.
وقد روى بعضهم هذا الكلام عن النبيّ صلّى الله عليه وآله.

٤٤٢‏.٣ وقال عليه السلام لزياد بن أبيه وقد آستخلفه لعبد الله بن العبّاس على فارس وأعمالها
في كلام طويل كان بينهما نهاه فيه عن تقدُّم الخراج: استعمل العدل وآحذر العَسف والحَيف
فإنّ العسف يعود بالجَلاء والحيف يدعو إلى السيف.

٤٤٣‏.٣ وقال عليه السلام: أشدّ الذنوب ما آستخفّ به صاحبه.

٤٤٤‏.٣ وقال عليه السلام: ما أخذ الله على أهل الجهل أن يتعلّموا حتّى أخذ على أهل العلم أن
يُعلِّموا.

٤٤٥‏.٣ وقال عليه السلام: شرّ الإخوان مَن تُكُلِّف له.

٤٤٦‏.٣ وقال عليه السلام: إذا آحتشم المؤمن أخاه فقد فارقه.

3.439 ʿAlī intoned in a prayer for rain: God, send us docile rainclouds, not unruly ones that bolt.

Raḍī: This is an amazingly eloquent saying. He likened rainclouds that have thunder, lightning, and hail with unruly camels that hurl off their saddles and throw off their riders. He likened clouds that do not bring these frightening phenomena to docile camels that are easy to milk and pleasant to ride.

3.440 Someone asked ʿAlī, Commander of the Faithful, why don't you dye your white hair? (meaning in battle), and he replied: Dyeing your hair is a form of adornment, and we are a people in mourning.

Raḍī: He means after the death of God's Messenger.

3.441 Contentment is wealth that never runs out.[1]

Raḍī: Some people attribute this saying to the Prophet.

3.442 When ʿAlī replaced ʿAbdallāh ibn al-ʿAbbās with Ziyād ibn Abīhi as governor of Fars and its environs, he had a lengthy conversation with Ziyād in which he forbade him from collecting the land tax before it came due, and he warned: Practice justice and beware violence or misappropriation, for violence leads to people fleeing en masse, and misappropriation calls people to arms.

3.443 The worst sin is one its perpetrator thinks insignificant.[2]

3.444 God has not required the ignorant to learn without first requiring the learned to teach.

3.445 The worst friend is one in whose company you feel constrained.

3.446 If a believer shames his brother, he has disowned him.

---

1 Identical to § 3.50 and § 3.332.
2 Similar to § 3.331.

وهذا حين أنتهى الغاية بنا إلى قطع المختار من كلام أمير المؤمنين صلوات الله عليه حامدين لله سبحانه على ما مَنّ به من توفيقنا لضمّ ما أنتشر من أطرافه وتقريب ما بعد من أقطاره ومقرّرين العزم كما شرطنا أوّلًا على تفضيل أوراق من البياض في آخر كلّ باب من الأبواب ليكون لأقتناص الشارد وأستلحاق الوارد وما عساه أن يظهر لنا بعد الغموض ويقع إلينا بعد الشُّذوذ.

وما توفيقنا إلّا بالله عليه توكّلنا وهو حسبنا ونعم الوكيل

وذلك في رجب من سنة أربعمائة.[1]

<hr>

[1] ن: كذا. م: كذا، وسقط التاريخ. ي: كذا، وأضيفت ⟨والحمد لله وصلواته على رسوله محمّد وآله الطاهرين⟩. ش: فقدت صفحة تشمل بداية الخاتمة، وثبتت في الصفحة التالية: ⟨ويقع إلينا الشذوذ ... أربعمائة⟩.

Raḍī's Conclusion

I come here to the end of my selection from the words of the Commander of the Faithful. I praise Almighty God who, by his immense grace, has guided me to gather from these words what was scattered here and there, and to collect what was dispersed far and wide. I have carried out my resolve—as I had stated in the beginning—to leave blank pages at the end of each chapter, so that I may capture therein any strays and add any additional discoveries, including anything that becomes clear to me after having been obscure or falls into my hands after being out of sight.

> I seek my direction from God. In him I place my trust. He is my refuge, and he is the best trustee.
>
> I write this in the month of Rajab, in the year four hundred [1010 AD].

Glossary of Names, Places, and Terms

This alphabetical list provides dates and brief biographies for all individuals mentioned in the text of the present volume, all unnamed interlocutors identified in the notes, and individuals important to understanding the text who are mentioned in my Introduction. Also glossed are groups, places, battles, and key terms.[1]

Aaron (*Ar. Hārūn*) (fl. 14th c. BC), a prophet in Islam, Moses' brother, whom he appointed over the Israelites.

al-'Abbās ibn 'Abd al-Muṭṭalib ibn Hāshim (d. ca. 32/653), from the Hāshim clan of Quraysh, paternal uncle of Muḥammad and 'Alī and eponym of the Abbasid dynasty.

al-'Abbās ibn Mirdās al-Sulamī (d. between 18/639 and 35/656), of the Sulaym tribe, pagan poet and warrior who converted to Islam after Muḥammad's conquest of Mecca.

Abbasids caliphal dynasty that came to power in 132/750 after defeating the Umayyads and ended in 656/1258 with the sack of their capital, Baghdad, by the Mongols.

'Abdallāh ibn al-'Abbās (d. 68/686), 'Alī's cousin, governor, and staunch supporter, who fought in all his battles, a prolific hadith narrator and esteemed scholar.

'Abdallāh ibn Awfah al-Yashkurī See *Ibn al-Kawwā'*

'Abdallāh ibn al-Ḥaḍramī (d. ca. 38/658), stepbrother of Ṭalḥah ibn 'Ubaydallāh and the agent Mu'āwiyah sent to recruit in Basra after the Battle of Ṣiffīn. Ibn al-Ḥaḍramī was killed by 'Alī's agent, Jāriyah ibn Qudāmah al-Sa'dī. (See further: Ḥ 4:34–53.)

'Abdallāh ibn Ja'far (d. after 80/699), from the Hāshim clan of Quraysh, son of Ja'far al-Ṭayyār, who was killed in the Battle of Mu'tah. 'Abdallāh was 'Alī's nephew, son-in-law, and staunch supporter.

'Abdallāh ibn Mālik ibn Dajnah (or Dujunnah, or Diḥyah, lived during 'Alī's r. 35–40/656–661), one of 'Alī's followers who narrated his words. Not much is said about him in the sources, as evidenced also by the confusion about his name. (See further: Ḥ 13:18; B 680.)

---

1 This information has been culled from multiple sources, including *EI*[2], *EI*[3], *EIr*, 'Abd al-Zahrā''s *Maṣādir Nahj al-balāghah*, medieval biographical dictionaries, and a variety of online sources. Some *Nahj al-Balāghah* commentators, especially Ibn Abī al-Ḥadīd, Baḥrānī, and Rāwandī, and also Ibn Funduq and Mughniyyah, offer detailed biographies and event narratives, and their commentaries are referenced in parentheses.

'Abdallāh ibn Mas'ūd   (d. ca. 32/653), early Companion of Muḥammad and prolific transmitter of hadith, famed also for his knowledge of the Qur'an. He opposed 'Uthmān's standardization of the holy book. He settled in Kufa, where he taught, and 'Alī reportedly encouraged the Kufans to respect Ibn Mas'ūd's teachings.

'Abdallāh ibn Qays   see *Abū Mūsā al-Ash'arī*

'Abdallāh ibn Ṣafwān   (d. 73/692), from the Jumaḥ clan of Quraysh, who fought with Ṭalḥah and Zubayr at the Battle of the Camel against 'Alī and escaped from the battlefield. Later, he became a follower of Ibn al-Zubayr and was killed with him. (See further: B 652; Ḥ 11:125.)

'Abdallāh ibn 'Umar   (d. 73/693), son of the second caliph, 'Umar, brother-in-law of Muḥammad, and prolific transmitter of hadith. Ibn 'Umar was among the handful of prominent Companions who refused to pledge allegiance to 'Alī and sat out his battles.

'Abdallāh ibn Zama'ah ibn al-Aswad ibn 'Abd al-Muṭṭalib   (d. after 40/661), from the Asad clan of Quraysh, one of 'Alī's followers, even though 'Alī had slain his father, uncle, and brother at the Battle of Badr. Brother of Muḥammad's wife Sawdah bint Zama'ah, 'Abdallāh married a daughter of another of Muḥammad's wives, Umm Salamah, from her previous marriage. (See further: B 678; Ḥ 13:10.)

'Abdallāh ibn al-Zubayr   (d. 73/692), son of the prominent Companion al-Zubayr ibn al-'Awwām, who fought with his father against 'Alī in the Battle of the Camel. During Umayyad rule, Ibn al-Zubayr laid claim to the caliphate and exercised control over the Ḥijāz and Iraq for almost a decade before being killed by Umayyad forces.

'Abd al-'Azīz ibn Marwān   (d. 86/705), son of the Umayyad caliph Marwān I and half-brother of the Umayyad caliph 'Abd al-Malik. He served under both as governor of Egypt.

'Abd al-Malik ibn Marwān   (r. 65–86/685–705), Umayyad caliph.

'Abd Manāf ibn Quṣayy ibn Kilāb   (fl. 6th c. AD), chieftain of Quraysh, whose son Hāshim was Muḥammad's and 'Alī's great-grandfather. His other son, 'Abd Shams, was the Umayyads' progenitor.

'Abd al-Muṭṭalib ibn Hāshim   (d. ca. 579 AD), patriarch of the Hāshim clan of Quraysh, Muḥammad's and 'Alī's paternal grandfather. 'Abd al-Muṭṭalib raised Muḥammad in the first eight years of his life, after the death of his parents.

'Abd al-Raḥmān ibn 'Attāb ibn Asīd   (d. 36/656), from the Umayyad clan, killed fighting against 'Alī during the Battle of the Camel. (See further: B 651; Ḥ 11:123–124.)

'Abd al-Raḥmān ibn 'Awf   (d. ca. 31/652), early Muslim convert from the Zuhrah clan of Quraysh, key supporter of Abū Bakr's nomination to the caliphate and presiding member of the Shūrā Council that elected 'Uthmān.

'Abd al-Raḥmān ibn Ṣafwān   (d. after 36/656), from the Jumaḥ clan of Quraysh, fought against 'Alī at the Battle of the Camel.

'Abd Shams ibn 'Abd Manāf ibn Quṣayy   (fl. 6th c. AD), chieftain of the Quraysh tribe
  of Mecca, father of Umayyah, and great-grandfather of Mu'āwiyah. 'Abd Shams and
  Hāshim were twins whose foreheads were reportedly separated by a sword strike,
  taken as an omen for enmity among their descendants.

'Abduh, Muḥammad   (d. 1905), Grand Mufti of Egypt and Shaykh al-Azhar, author of
  a brief word-list commentary on *Nahj al-Balāghah*, with an important introduction.

Abel (*Ar. Hābīl*)   see *Cain and Abel*

Abraham (*Ar. Ibrāhīm*)   a prophet in Islam, originator of the Ka'bah rites. Abraham is
  the progenitor of the Arabs and the Jews through his sons Ishmael and Isaac respec-
  tively.

Abū al-A'war al-Sulamī   (fl. 1st/7th c.), son of 'Amr ibn Sufyān ibn 'Abd Shams, com-
  mander who led Mu'āwiyah's vanguard in the Battle of Ṣiffīn and served as 'Amr ibn
  al-'Āṣ's aide when he took Egypt for Mu'āwiyah. Abū al-A'war's mother was Christian,
  while his father had fought against Muḥammad at Uḥud. During the early Muslim
  conquests, Abū al-A'war served under various Umayyad commanders in Syria and
  later remained attached to them.

Abū Ayyūb al-Anṣārī   (d. ca. 52/672), Companion of Muḥammad and supporter of 'Alī
  who participated in his battles. Abū Ayyūb had taken part in the Muslim conquest
  of Egypt and later participated in the Umayyad expedition against Constantinople,
  where he died and is buried. (See further: Ḥ 10:111–112; B 591–592.)

Abū Bakr ibn Abī Quḥāfah   (r. 11–13/632–634), of the Taym clan of Quraysh, promi-
  nent Companion of Muḥammad and first of the four Sunni caliphs. He was the
  father of Muḥammad's wife 'Ā'ishah.

Abū Dharr al-Ghifārī   (d. 32/652), Muḥammad's Companion, 'Alī's strong supporter,
  and pious preacher, exiled by 'Uthmān to Rabadhah for his support of 'Alī and his
  criticism of Umayyad impiety. (See further: Ḥ 8:252–262; B 473–474.)

Abū Dhu'ayb al-Hudhalī   (d. ca. 28/649), famous pre-Islamic poet of the Hudhayl
  tribe, who probably embraced Islam together with his tribe in 9/630.

Abū Hurayrah al-Dawsī al-Yamānī   (d. 59/679), Companion of Muḥammad and pro-
  lific transmitter of hadith. Although there are some contrary reports, it appears
  that Abū Hurayrah leaned to the Umayyads. He is said to have been with 'Uthmān
  when he was killed, held back from pledging allegiance to 'Alī, and later supported
  Mu'āwiyah.

Abū Jahl 'Amr ibn Hishām   (d. 2/624), from the Makhzūm clan of Quraysh, fierce
  enemy of Muḥammad, polemically called Abū Jahl: Father of Ignorance. Abū Jahl
  was killed fighting against Muḥammad at the Battle of Badr. (See further: B 776; Ḥ
  13:214; F 365.)

Abū Juḥayfah Wahb ibn 'Abdallāh al-Suwā'ī   (d. 74/694), from the 'Āmir ibn Ṣa'ṣa'ah
  clan of the Suwā' tribe, who settled in Kufa. Abū Juḥayfah served as chief of 'Alī's
  police force and would stand at the foot of the pulpit when 'Alī orated. He narrated
  hadith from the Prophet and from 'Alī.

Abū Jundub al-Hudhalī   (fl. 6th c. AD), son of Murrah ibn ʿAmr from the Hudhayl
tribe, pre-Islamic poet known as al-Mashʾūm (the Inauspicious One).

Abū Lahab ʿAbd al-ʿUzzā ibn ʿAbd al-Muṭṭalib   (d. 2/624), Muḥammad's and ʿAlī's
paternal uncle and fierce enemy, assigned by the Qurʾan with his wife to hellfire
(Qurʾan, Masad 111:1–5).

Abū Mūsā al-Ashʿarī, ʿAbdallāh ibn Qays   (d. ca. 48/668), ostensibly one of ʿAlī's sup-
porters but one who caused him great harm. Abū Mūsā was an early convert to Islam
who took part in the conquest of Iraq, served as governor of Basra under ʿUmar and
ʿUthmān and as the locally appointed governor of Kufa at the chaotic end of ʿUth-
mān's reign. When ʿAlī instructed him to rally the Kufans in the lead-up to the Battle
of the Camel, Abū Mūsā refused and ʿAlī dismissed him. He was later imposed on
ʿAlī as his representative in the post-Ṣiffīn arbitration, where he ruled against his
master.

Abū Muslim al-Khawlānī   (d. ca. 62/682), Yemeni convert to Islam of ascetic bent,
who settled in Syria, an associate of Muʿāwiyah, sent as emissary to ʿAlī in the lead-
up to the Battle of Ṣiffīn.

Abū Sufyān ibn al-Ḥarb   (d. 32/653), of the Umayyad clan of the Quraysh tribe of
Mecca, Muʿāwiyah's father, and leader of the Meccan opposition against Muḥam-
mad. Abū Sufyān converted to Islam when the Muslims conquered Mecca and later
participated in the Syrian conquests. (See further: B 776; Ḥ 13:214; F 365.)

Abū Ṭālib ibn ʿAbd al-Muṭṭalib ibn Hāshim   (d. 620 AD), patriarch of the Hāshim clan
of Quraysh, ʿAlī's father, and Muḥammad's paternal uncle and foster-father, who
offered him the clan's protection.

Abū Tharwān   (d. after 37/657), ʿAlī's scribe in Kufa. Not much else is known about
him.

Abū ʿUbayd al-Qāsim ibn Sallām al-Harawī   (d. 224/838), prolific philologist from
Khurasan who authored works on lexicography, jurisprudence, Qurʾanic sciences,
and hadith. His book titled *Gharīb al-ḥadīth* (Rare words in the hadith) became an
instant classic. Cited by Raḍī in *Nahj al-Balāghah*.

Abū Umāmah al-Bāhilī   (d. 86/705), early convert to Islam and transmitter of hadith.
Abū Umāmah served as intermediary between ʿAlī and Muʿāwiyah during and after
the Battle of Ṣiffīn, but the reports are contradictory about where his loyalties
lay.

Adam (*Ar. Ādam*)   a prophet in Islam and the first human.

ʿAfīf ibn Qays   (d. after 38/658), from the tribe of Kindah, remonstrated with ʿAlī about
marching to Syria, brother of the notorious al-Ashʿath ibn Qays. (See further: R 1:315;
B 308.)

Age of Ignorance (*Ar. Jāhiliyyah*)   the pre-Islamic period in which inhabitants of the
Arabian Peninsula worshipped idols. Ignorance here is specifically meant as igno-
rance of the one true God.

Ahl al-bayt   (lit. "people of the house"), Muḥammad's family, according to the Shiʿa, his daughter Fāṭimah, her husband ʿAlī, and their descendants.

ʿahd   covenant, testament, or document of appointment.

ahl al-dhimmah   see *protected peoples*

Aḥmad ibn Qutaybah al-Hamdānī   (fl. late 2nd/8th c.), mentioned as narrator of oration §1.231, likely from the generation after Jaʿfar al-Ṣādiq (d. 148/765) or the next one, among the leaders and narrators of the Shiʿa. (See further: Ḥ 13:18; B 680.)

al-Aḥnaf ibn Qays   (d. 72/691), chieftain of the Tamīm tribe and resident of Basra, who had a reputation for sagacity and was instrumental in persuading his tribe to accept Islam. Aḥnaf sat out the Battle of the Camel but fought on ʿAlī's side at Ṣiffīn. He later allied with the Umayyads to fight against the Kharijites and Shiʿites. (See further: B 470; Gh 2:253.)

Ahwaz (*Ar. Ahwāz*)   city in the Khuzistan province of southwestern Iran on the Dujayl River, conquered by the Muslims in 17/638.

Aḥzāb   see *Confederates*

ʿĀʾishah bint Abī Bakr   (d. 58/678), daughter of the first caliph, Abū Bakr, and one of Muḥammad's wives. She, with Ṭalḥah and Zubayr, led an army against ʿAlī at the Battle of the Camel.

ʿAlāʾ ibn Ziyād al-Ḥārithī   (n.d.), who features in oration §1.207, is an otherwise unknown individual not mentioned in the sources. Ibn Abī al-Ḥadīd (Ḥ 11:37) states that the man was actually named al-Rabīʿ ibn Ziyād al-Ḥārithī and that the name ʿAlāʾ is an error in Raḍī's transcription.

ʿAlī ibn Abī Ṭālib   (r. 35–40/656–661), Muḥammad's cousin and ward, who married his daughter Fāṭimah. ʿAlī is the first Shiʿi Imam and the fourth Sunni caliph. (See details of ʿAlī's biography in Introduction.)

ʿAlī ibn al-Ḥusayn al-Sajjād Zayn al-ʿĀbidīn   (d. 95/713), Shiʿi Imam following his father, martyr of Karbala, al-Ḥusayn ibn ʿAlī. Zayn al-ʿĀbidīn was present with Ḥusayn at the Battle of Karbala but fell ill and did not take part in the fighting. He later composed a set of supplications, famously known as *al-Ṣaḥīfah al-Sajjādiyyah*.

ʿAlī ibn Muḥammad al-Zanjī   (d. 270/883), Chief of the Zanj, who led a fifteen-year rebellion of East African slaves, from 255/869 to 270/883, against the Abbasids, which ravaged southern Iraq.

Allies (*Ar. Anṣār, sing. Anṣārī*)   also translated as Helpers, the people of Medina from the tribes of Aws and Khazraj who supported Muḥammad when he migrated there from Mecca.

Amalekites (*Ar. ʿamālīq, sing. ʿimlāq*)   ancient pre-Islamic people, reportedly among the first speakers of Arabic and residents of Mecca. (See further: Ḥ 10:93–94; B 588; R 2:190; F 304.)

Amīr al-Muʾminīn   see *Commander of the Faithful*

ʿAmmār ibn Yāsir   (d. 37/657), eminent Companion of the Prophet and staunch supporter of ʿAlī who was killed in the Battle of Ṣiffīn. Muḥammad had prophesied that ʿAmmār would be killed by the "treacherous party," and the Shiʿa see his death at Ṣiffīn as proof of Muʿāwiyah's iniquity. (See further: Ḥ 10:102–107; B 590.)

ʿAmr ibn ʿAbd Wadd   (d. 5/626), of the ʿĀmir ibn Luʾayy tribe, famous pagan warrior whom ʿAlī slew in single combat at the Battle of the Confederates. (See further: B 776; Ḥ 13:214; F 365.)

ʿAmr ibn Abī Sufyān   (fl. 1st/7th c.), Muʿāwiyah's brother, from the Umayyad clan of Quraysh, taken captive at the Battle of Badr by ʿAlī.

ʿAmr ibn al-ʿĀṣ   (d. 43/664), Muʿāwiyah's chief advisor at the Battle of Ṣiffīn, proverbial for his cunning. Earlier commander of the Muslim armies that conquered Egypt during the reign of ʿUmar, ʿAmr was dismissed by ʿUmar for corruption, but was later governor there for the Umayyads. Before he accepted Islam, ʿAmr had been one of Muḥammad's fiercest enemies. (See further: Ḥ 6:281–326.)

ʿAmr ibn al-Ḥamiq al-Khuzāʿī   (d. ca. 50/670), Companion of Muḥammad and a supporter of ʿAlī. He commanded a battalion in ʿAlī's army at the battles of the Camel and Ṣiffīn.

ʿAmr ibn Salamah al-Hamdānī al-Arḥabī   (d. 85/704), resident of Kufa, poet, and a leader of the Hamdān tribe who participated in the Muslim conquest of Persia. ʿAmr was ʿAlī's staunch follower, who fought in all his battles and served as his governor in Isfahan. He was also a follower of ʿAlī's son Ḥasan.

amṣār (sing. *miṣr*)   garrison cities in the early Islamic period. In ʿAlī's time, the major garrison cities were Kufa and Basra in Iraq, and Fusṭāṭ in Egypt. Initially set up to serve the early conquests, by his time they had become permanent and important settled towns in the region. Other towns in Iran and Central Asia are also identified in ʿAlī's time as housing permanent garrisons, and as such may be included under this appellation.

Anas ibn Mālik al-Anṣārī   (d. 93/712), resident of Medina, Muḥammad's servant from the age of ten, and prolific narrator of hadith, although Shiʿa sources accuse him of widespread forgery. Anas was among the handful of prominent Companions who refused to pledge allegiance to ʿAlī and sat out his battles, and who also refused when ʿAlī entreated all those who had heard Muḥammad's words about him at Ghadīr Khumm to testify to what they had heard.

Anbar (*Ar. Anbār*)   pre-Sasanian town on the Euphrates, in western Iraq, conquered by the Muslims in 12/634, whose ruins are situated 5 kilometers northwest of present-day Falluja. Lying on a cultivable plain near the first navigable canal between the two great rivers, Anbar controlled an important crossing in early Islamic times. It was also strategically important as the head of the irrigation system of arable lands in Iraq.

Antichrist   see *Dajjāl*

'Aqīl ibn Abī Ṭālib   (d. ca. 50/670), 'Alī's brother, who was vocal in his support for him but for a brief period accepted funds from Mu'āwiyah. He later rejected Mu'āwiyah's sponsorship and returned to Medina. (See further: Ḥ 11:250–254.)

Arabian Peninsula (*Ar. Jazīrat al-'Arab*)   Arabia to the ancients, land mass that projects southwards from the main body of the Middle East, surrounded on three sides by sea. Important to Muslims as the birthplace of Islam and its Prophet Muḥammad and site of the Holy Mosques of Mecca and Medina, Arabia was the seat of the Muslim empire for a brief two decades after Muḥammad.

arbitration (*Ar. taḥkīm*)   post-Ṣiffīn adjudication at Dūmat al-Jandal in Ramaḍān 37/February 658, with Abū Mūsā al-Ash'arī and 'Amr ibn al-'Āṣ representing 'Alī and Mu'āwiyah respectively. The arbitration ended with Abū Mūsā ruling against his master, 'Alī, and 'Amr ruling for his master, Mu'āwiyah. 'Alī rejected the outcome of the arbitration, declaring it contrary to the Qur'an.

Ardashīr-khurrah   city in the Fars province of Iran, near Shiraz, surrounded by fertile countryside, built by the Persian emperor Ardashīr (r. 226–240 AD) at the site of the ancient Achaemenid city of Gūr. Conquered by the Muslims in the early 1st/7th century, Ardashīr-khurrah was renamed Firuzabad in the 4th/10th century. The site of the ancient city is located three kilometers east of the new city also named Firuzabad.

'Araj   caravan stop near Ṭā'if, between Mecca and Medina (See further: Ḥ 13:303.)

Asad   tribe in northern Arabia, whose people led a mainly nomadic life in pre-Islamic times. In the Muslim wars of conquest, the Asad served in Iraq and Persia. Most settled in Kufa, where they evolved from warriors to men of learning, including many who handed down the Shi'a tradition. Smaller groups were incorporated into the Syrian army and settled near Aleppo.

A'shā Maymūn   (d. ca. 7/629), pre-Islamic poet, one of the composers of the famous set of long poems known as the Hanging Odes.

al-Aṣbagh ibn Nubātah   (d. early 2nd/7th c.), a close companion of 'Alī and a prolific transmitter of his words, including the famous testament to Mālik al-Ashtar. An account of the killing of Ḥusayn at Karbala is also attributed to him. He belonged to the tribe of Tamīm, was a resident of Kufa, and fought alongside 'Alī at Ṣiffīn.

al-Ash'ath ibn Qays   (d. 40/661), Kufan noble of the Kindah tribe who revolted at Muḥammad's death. He later repented and fought for the Muslims at the Battle of Yarmūk, and he served as governor of Azerbaijan during 'Alī's reign. Despite fighting on 'Alī's side at the Battle of Ṣiffīn, Ash'ath was instrumental in forcing 'Alī to accept arbitration and to appoint Abū Mūsā as arbiter.

'Āṣim ibn Ziyād al-Ḥārithī   (d. after 36/656), Basran ascetic, brother of 'Alī's supporter 'Alā' or Rabī'.

Ashras ibn Ḥassān al-Bakrī al-Balawī   see *Ḥassān ibn Ḥassān al-Bakrī al-Balawī*

Ashtar   see *Mālik ibn al-Ḥārith al-Ashtar*

Associates of the Camel (*Ar. aṣḥāb al-jamal*)   see *Camel*

al-Aswad ibn Quṭbah   (or al-Aswad ibn Quṭnah, or al-Aswad ibn Zayd ibn Quṭbah;
  fl. 1st/6th c.), commander of the Ḥulwān garrison during ʿAlī's caliphate, named in
  § 2.59 (see note there re the confusion about his genealogy).

ʿAyn al-Tamr   lit. wellspring of dates, so called because of its abundant palms, a small
  town in Iraq west of the Euphrates, on the frontier between Syria and Iraq. In early
  Islamic times, ʿAyn al-Tamr commanded the military approaches from the western
  desert to Kufa; it was attacked by Muʿāwiyah's commander al-Nuʿmān ibn Bashīr al-
  Anṣārī in 39/659. Today the town is called Shithāthah and lies 128 kilometers west
  of Karbala.

Azerbaijan (*Ar. Ādharbāyjān or Adhrabījān*)   Sasanian town in northwest Iran con-
  quered by the Muslims in 22/643 under the command of Ḥudhayfah ibn al-Yamān,
  an early Companion of Muḥammad and close associate of ʿAlī. Al-Ashʿath ibn Qays
  was governor of Azerbaijan during the caliphates of ʿUthmān and ʿAlī.

Badr   site of the first pitched battle between the Muslims and the Meccans, in 2/624,
  the year after Muḥammad's migration to Medina. Badr is located 160 kilometers
  southwest of Medina and 50 kilometers inland from the Red Sea.

Bahrain (*Ar. Baḥrayn*)   archipelago in the Persian/Arabian Gulf consisting of 33 is-
  lands offshore from present-day eastern Saudi Arabia, site of the ancient town of
  Tylos. Emperor Ardashīr conquered it in the first half of the third century AD, and
  Sasanian control lasted until ca. 6/628, when the population voluntarily converted
  to Islam. Also used in the sources to describe the eastern seaboard of the Arabian
  Peninsula.

Baḥrānī, Maytham   (d. 679/1280), early Twelver Shiʿi commentator of *Nahj al-Bal-
  āghah*, philosopher and theologian active in Bahrain, famous for his commentaries
  on the works of Avicenna.

Baghdad (*Ar. Baghdād*)   capital of the Abbasid caliphate from its founding in 145/762
  until the fall of the dynasty in 656/1258, with a small interregnum when the capi-
  tal was in adjacent Sāmarrāʾ. Located at the confluence of the Tigris and Euphrates
  Rivers, Baghdad was a major hub for political and intellectual activity. Raḍī, com-
  piler of the present volume, lived his entire life in this city.

Basra (*Ar. Baṣrah*)   garrison city founded in 17/638, during the Islamic conquests of
  southern Iraq, located near the Shaṭṭ al-ʿArab, the river formed by the confluence of
  the Tigris and Euphrates. The Battle of the Camel was fought just outside Basra early
  in ʿAlī's caliphate.

Baṭḥāʾ (*The Flatland*)   see *Mecca*

Battle of Badr   see *Badr*

Battle of the Camel   see *Camel*

Battle of the Confederates   see *Confederates*

Battle of Ḥunayn   see *Ḥunayn*

Battle of Khaybar   see *Khaybar*

Battle of Muʾtah   see *Muʾtah*

Battle of Nahāwand   see *Nahāwand*

Battle of Nahrawān   see *Nahrawān*

Battle of Qādisiyyah   see *Qādisiyyah*

Battle of Ṣiffīn   see *Ṣiffīn*

Battle of Uḥud   see *Uḥud*

Bayhaqī   see *Ibn Funduq al-Bayhaqī*

Bedouins (*Ar. aʿrāb*)   pastoral nomads or semi-nomads of the Arabian Peninsula.

Book   see *Qurʾan*

Bishr ibn Abī Khāzim al-Asadī   (d. after 575 AD), pre-Islamic poet of the Asad ibn Khuzaymah tribe, predecessor of the Umayyad poet Farazdaq. Bishr's poems were collected by the anthologists Aṣmaʿī and Ibn al-Sikkīt, and the philologist Abū ʿUbaydah wrote a commentary.

Bishr ibn Marwān   (d. 74/693), son of the Umayyad caliph Marwān I and half-brother of the Umayyad caliph ʿAbd al-Malik, under whom he served as governor of Iraq.

Burak ibn ʿAbdallāh al-Tamīmī   (d. 40/661), sometimes called Ḥajjāj, from the Ṣuraym clan of Tamīm, first to utter the Kharijite slogan, ⟨No rule save God's!⟩ (*lā ḥukma illā li-llāh*). Burak was one of three Kharijites who conspired to assassinate ʿAlī, Muʿāwiyah, and ʿAmr ibn al-ʿĀṣ in the same night. He undertook to kill Muʿāwiyah but was captured and executed.

Burj ibn Musʾhir al-Ṭāʾī   (fl. 1st/7th c.), identified by Raḍī as a Kharijite who called out in ʿAlī's hearing their slogan, ⟨No rule save God's!⟩ (§1.182). The commentators identify him with the drunkard pagan poet b. 595 AD who migrated to Syria and converted to Christianity (See further: Ḥ 10:130; B 597).

Busr ibn Abī Arṭāt   (d. 70/689), of the ʿĀmir ibn Luʾayy tribe, one of Muʿāwiyah's particularly brutal commanders, who fought with him at Ṣiffīn. Earlier, Busr took part in the Muslim conquest of Syria and probably of Egypt under ʿAmr ibn al-ʿĀṣ. Muʿāwiyah sent Busr in 37/658 to attack Medina, Mecca, and Yemen, where he killed or forced out ʿAlī's commanders and terrorized the locals. (See further: Ḥ 1:340.)

Byzantium (*Ar. Rūm*)   refers to the eastern half of the Roman empire, with its capital in Constantinople, which survived for a thousand years after the western Roman empire crumbled. Constantinople was conquered in 1453 AD by the Ottoman Turks, who named it Istanbul.

Cain and Abel (*Ar. Qābīl and Hābīl*)   two sons of the Prophet Adam.

Camel (*Ar. Jamal*)   name of a battle fought outside Basra in Jumādā II 36/ November–December 656 between the Caliph ʿAlī on one side, and Muḥammad's widow ʿĀʾishah bint Abī Bakr and two Quraysh Emigrants, Ṭalḥah ibn ʿUbaydallāh and al-

Zubayr ibn al-ʿAwwām, on the other. The battle is named for the camel that ʿĀʾishah rode onto the battlefield and is a metaphor for the rider herself. The rebel leaders and their Basran supporters are referred to in the sources as "associates of the Camel" (*aṣḥāb al-Jamal*).

colocynth (*Ar. ḥanẓal*)   bitter desert plant used for medicinal purposes. Swallowing or peeling colocynth was a metaphor in early Arabic for bitter grief.

Commander of the Faithful (*Ar. Amīr al-Muʾminīn*)   caliphal title in Islam, according to the Shiʿa associated primarily with ʿAlī. The title was also used by the caliph-imams of the Fatimid dynasty.

Companions of the Prophet (*Ar. aṣḥāb and ṣaḥābah, sing. m. ṣaḥābī, f. ṣaḥābiyyah*) individuals who had sustained personal contact with Muḥammad and are revered for their sincere service to Islam in its nascent stage. Key figures in the early history of Islam, Muḥammad's Companions are also the first transmitters of his statements and deeds.

Confederates (*Ar. Aḥzāb*)   name of a battle in 5/627 fought by the Meccan Quraysh, joined by several other tribes, to form a force of 10,000 men with 600 cavalry against the Muslims. Muḥammad foiled their attempt to storm Medina by digging a protective trench, and the battle is also known as the Battle of the Trench (*al-Khandaq*). Unable to enter, the confederates besieged Medina, but their confederacy broke up after a fortnight, and the siege was abandoned. Its failure strengthened Muḥammad's position. ʿAlī played a major role by slaying the enemy champion ʿAmr ibn ʿAbd Wadd in single combat.

covenant, people with   see *protected peoples*

al-Ḍaḥḥāk ibn Qays al-Fihrī   (d. 64/684), Muʿāwiyah's commander, active at the Battle of Ṣiffīn and in its aftermath. (See further: Ḥ 2:113–117; B 225).

Dajjāl   the Antichrist. According to Islamic tradition, he is an evil man who will appear at the end of time, signaling the approach of judgment day.

Damascus (*Ar. Dimashq, Dimashq al-Shām, or Shām*)   largest city in Syria, earlier under Byzantine rule, conquered by the Muslims in 14/635. Muʿāwiyah was governor of Damascus during the reigns of ʿUmar and ʿUthmān, and after ʿUthmān's death he fought ʿAlī. After ʿAlī's death in 40/661, Muʿāwiyah became caliph and Damascus remained the Umayyad seat of government of the Muslim empire until the Abbasids defeated them in 132/750 and set up their capital in Baghdad.

Dārī   attributive of Dārīn, an island near Qaṭīf, on the east coast of present-day Saudi Arabia. In pre-Islamic and early Islamic times, Dārīn was the main port of Bahrain, through which musk was imported from India, which is why Dārī musk is famous. (See further: B 549; Ḥ 9:268.)

David (*Ar. Dāʾūd*)   (fl. 10th c. BC), the biblical King David, a prophet in the Islamic tradition, mentioned in the Qurʾan as someone granted prophecy, kingship, wisdom, and justice, as well as being the recipient of the Psalms. Muḥammad's hadith and ʿAlī's orations emphasize David's fervent prayer and fasting.

Dhakwān   (fl. 1st/7th c.), an individual who is said to have memorized and narrated
   ʿAlī's words to Abū Dharr al-Ghifārī (§ 1.128). There is some confusion about his iden-
   tity: Ibn Abī al-Ḥadīd identifies him as a freedman of ʿAlī's sister Umm Hānī bint Abī
   Ṭālib (Ḥ 8:253). More often, the sources name Umm Hānī's freedman as Bādhām (full
   name: Abū Ṣāliḥ Bādhām), adding that he narrated hadith. Elsewhere, they speak of
   a freedman of Muḥammad's wife Juwayriyah, named Dhakwān (full name: Abū Ṣāliḥ
   al-Sammān Dhakwān ibn ʿAbdallāh), who likewise narrated hadith. Yet elsewhere,
   they speak of another Dhakwān, freedman of the Hāshim clan or of al-Ḥusayn ibn
   ʿAlī.

Dhiʿlib al-Yamānī   (fl. 1st/7th c.), individual from Yemen who asked ʿAlī to describe
   God (§ 1.177), identified by the sources as among the leaders and narrators of the
   Shiʿa. (See further: Ḥ 13:18; B 680.)

Dhū Qār   caravan stop east of Kufa in the direction of Wāsiṭ, where ʿAlī camped
   enroute to Basra, where he fought the Battle of the Camel. Dhū Qār was also the
   site of a major early 7th-century AD battle between the Arabs and the Sasanian Per-
   sians. (See further: Ḥ 2:187–188.)

Dhū al-Rummah, Abū al-Ḥārith Ghaylān ibn ʿUqbah   (d. 117/735), important Bedou-
   in poet of the Umayyad era.

Dhū al-Shahādatayn (*The-Twice-Martyred*)   see *Khuzaymah ibn al-Thābit*

Dhū al-Thudayyah (*The Man with the Breast*)   (d. 38/658), Kharijite killed at Nah-
   rawān, called thus because of a lump of flesh on his shoulder. Some sources identify
   Dhū al-Thudayyah as Ḥurqūṣ ibn Zuhayr al-Saʿdī, a leader of the Bajīlah tribe, who
   was killed fighting ʿAlī at Nahrawān. Ḥurqūṣ is in turn identified as ʿAmr Dhū al-
   Khuwayṣirah al-Tamīmī, who was insolent to Muḥammad regarding the distribution
   of war spoils. (See further: Ḥ 13:183–184; B 771–772; F 364–365.)

Ḍirār ibn Ḍamrah al-Ḍibābī   (d. after 40/661), of the clan of Fihr from the Quraysh
   tribe, a loyal associate of ʿAlī, reported in several early sources to have spoken elo-
   quently of his late master's virtues at the court of ʿAlī's archenemy, Muʿāwiyah. (See
   further: Ḥ 18:225–226, R 3:294–295).

duʿāʾ   supplication.

Durayd ibn al-Ṣimmah   (d. 8/630), of the Hawāzin tribe, famous poet and warrior
   who lived mostly in the pre-Islamic period. Durayd was reportedly killed at the age
   of one hundred, fighting against Muḥammad in the Battle of Ḥunayn.

Dūmat al-Jandal   site of the post-Ṣiffīn arbitration in 37/658, with Abū Mūsā al-
   Ashʿarī and ʿAmr ibn al-ʿĀṣ representing ʿAlī and Muʿāwiyah respectively. It was an
   oasis on the route between Medina and Damascus in early Islamic times, and part
   of Syria. It is located today in the Jawf province of Saudi Arabia, southwest of the
   provincial capital, Sakākah.

Egypt (*Ar. Miṣr*)   refers in the early Islamic period both to the province and to its capi-
   tal city, Fusṭāṭ. Egypt was conquered by the Muslims in 22/643, under the command

of 'Amr ibn al-'Āṣ. At the onset of 'Alī's caliphate, in 35/656, the province pledged allegiance to him, but following the arbitration in 37/658, 'Amr, now Mu'āwiyah's chief advisor and governor-designate, killed 'Alī's governor, Muḥammad ibn Abī Bakr, and took over Egypt.

Emigrants (*Ar. Muhājirūn*)   those who migrated with Muḥammad from Mecca to Medina, and those who migrated from elsewhere to be with him. Along with the Allies, they are revered by later Muslims for their sincere service to Islam in its difficult early years and are considered among Muḥammad's closest Companions.

Euphrates (*Ar. Furāt*)   together with the Tigris, one of the two defining rivers of Mesopotamia. Originating in Turkey, it flows through Syria and Iraq to join the Tigris and empties into the Arabian/Persian Gulf. The major cities of early Islamic Iraq—Kufa, Basra, and later Baghdad—were all built along or near the Euphrates.

Fadak   village near Khaybar, with abundant dates and grain, a three-day journey from Medina in early Islamic times. After Muḥammad's death, his daughter Fāṭimah claimed ownership of Fadak as her inherited right, a right denied her by Abū Bakr. The Umayyad caliph 'Umar II (r. 99–101/717–720) returned Fadak to Fāṭimah's heirs.

faith-leavers (*Ar. māriqūn*)   appellation applied to the Kharijites. (See further: Ḥ 13:183–184; B 771–772; F 364–365.)

Family of the Prophet   see *Ahl al-bayt*

Farazdaq, Abū Firās Hammām ibn Ghālib   (d. 114/732), Umayyad-era poet who composed eulogies for the Umayyad caliphs, also famous for a lengthy poem in praise of the Shiʻi Imam Zayn al-'Ābidīn. When Farazdaq was young, his father reportedly brought him to Iraq to visit 'Alī.

Fars (*Ar. al-Fāris*)   Arabicized form of Pārs, English Persia, province in southwestern Iran, with Shiraz as its main city. Earlier center of the Achaemenid and Sasanian dynasties, the Muslims conquered Fars in 28/648, and it became a major province of the Islamic empire.

Fāṭimah al-Zahrāʾ bint Muḥammad   (d. 11/632), 'Alī's wife and Muḥammad's youngest daughter, about whom he said, ⟨May my life be ransom for yours, Fāṭimah, you are the queen of the women of paradise.⟩ She died young, just two months after her father. Fāṭimah had four children with 'Alī: Ḥasan, Ḥusayn, Zaynab, and Umm Kulthūm, all of whom played key roles in the political and religious life of early Islam.

fifth (*Ar. khums*)   one-fifth share mandated by the Qurʾan of the spoils of war and other specified forms of income, set aside for the Prophet and other designated beneficiaries (Qurʾan, Anfāl 8:41).

Firās ibn Ghanam   tribe descended from Kinānah and Muḍar, residing in the area north of Mecca in Wādī Qadīd, famous for its members' courage and loyalty. (See further: R 1:203; B 211.)

Followers-in-Virtue (*Ar. al-tābiʿūna bi-iḥsān*)   or Successors, appellation applied to the second generation of Muslims, directly following Muḥammad's Companions.

Freedmen (*Ar. ṭulaqāʾ*)   derogatory term referring to those members of the Quraysh, including Muʿāwiyah's father, Abū Sufyān, who remained Muḥammad's committed enemies until forced to capitulate upon his conquest of Mecca. On that day, instead of forcing them into captivity as per the standard practice, Muḥammad pardoned them, saying, "You are freedmen."

Fusṭāṭ   originally a military encampment on the Nile alongside the Byzantine fortress of Babylon, built in the wake of the Muslim conquest of Egypt in 22/643, and thence capital of the province of Egypt. It was replaced in 358/969 as the capital by the conquering Fatimids' newly built city of Cairo.

Gabriel (*Ar. Jibrīl*)   archangel in Islamic tradition, who served as God's messenger in bringing revelation to the prophets, including Muḥammad.

Ghadīr Khumm (*Pool of Khumm*)   oasis located 5 kilometers from Juḥfah, on the caravan route between Mecca and Medina, where Muḥammad delivered an important oration to a large gathering of Muslims following his farewell pilgrimage, and declared, "For whomsoever I am Mawlā, ʿAlī is henceforth his Mawlā." The Shiʿa interpret the word Mawlā here to mean "master" and deem it proof of Muḥammad's designation of ʿAlī as his successor. Sunnis interpret the word to mean "kinsman," and state that the Prophet said what he said to protect ʿAlī from those who wished him harm, but the words did not signify an appointment of succession. Ghadīr Khumm is also used to denote the day and the event.

Ghālib ibn Ṣaʿṣaʿah   (d. ca. 40/666), Tamīmī chieftain famed for his generosity, father of the renowned Umayyad-era poet Farazdaq. A contemporary of Muḥammad, Ghālib is also said to have visited ʿAlī in Iraq and introduced Farazdaq to him; ʿAlī advised Ghālib to teach his son the Qurʾan. (See further: Ḥ 19:96; R 3:441–442.)

Ghāmidī   see *Sufyān ibn ʿAwf al-Ghāmidī*

gharīb   rare words in Muḥammad's hadith, ʿAlī's sayings, and elsewhere in the Arabic literary corpus, that medieval critics deemed in need of explication. A section of 9 wisdom sayings in the present volume contains *gharīb* words.

Golden Calf (*Ar. ʿijl*)   calf-shaped idol worshipped by the Israelites under the direction of the Samaritan (Ar. Sāmirī), while Moses was on the mountain communing with God.

Ḥāḍirīn   place in northern Syria where ʿAlī reportedly wrote a testament for his son Ḥasan on the way back from Ṣiffīn. Ḥāḍirīn does not appear to be mentioned anywhere in the sources; perhaps it is a mistranscription for some form of *ḥāḍir*, meaning urban space or town. (See further: Ḥ 16:52.)

hadith (*Ar. ḥadīth*)   often translated as Traditions, these are reports of Muḥammad's words, deeds, and gestures. The hadith hold a special position of authority and guidance for Muslims, complementing the Qurʾan.

Hajar   town near Bahrain proverbial for its dates. (See further: Ḥ 15:188; B 819; F 372.)

hajj (*Ar. ḥajj*)   pilgrimage to the Kaʿbah in Mecca mandated once in a lifetime for every Muslim, combining rituals performed by Abraham and Muḥammad. The hajj is performed in the month named for it, Dhū al-Ḥijjah, the final month in the Islamic lunar calendar.

al-Ḥajjāj ibn Yūsuf al-Thaqafī   (d. 95/714), Umayyad governor of Iraq famed for his eloquence and notorious for his harsh rule.

Ḥakīm ibn Jabalah al-ʿAbdī   (d. 35/656), early Muslim, contemporary of Muḥammad, known for his piety and valor. Ḥakīm was killed combating the forces of Ṭalḥah and Zubayr, who were attempting to remove ʿAlī's governor in Basra in the lead-up to the Battle of the Camel. (See further: Ḥ 9:110.)

Ḥamal ibn Badr   (d. late 6th c. AD), pre-Islamic warrior from the clan of Fazārah of the Dhubyān tribe, who was killed in the Battle of Dāḥis, a decades-long conflict between the tribes of Dhubyān and ʿAbs, during the latter half of the 6th century AD. (See further: F 374; R 3:82; B 824.)

Ḥamal ibn Saʿd al-ʿAshīrah   (fl. 6th c. AD), pre-Islamic warrior from the clan of Saʿd al-ʿAshīrah of the Madhḥij tribe.

Ḥammām   (d. ca. 36/656), devout associate of ʿAlī who reportedly passed away upon hearing ʿAlī's oration describing the truly pious, named after him as The Oration to Hammām (§ 1.191). Some commentators give his full name as Hammām ibn Shurayḥ ibn Yazīd, while others identify him as Hammām ibn ʿUbādah ibn Khuthaym. (See further: Ḥ 10:134; B 599.)

Ḥamzah ibn ʿAbd al-Muṭṭalib ibn Hāshim   (d. 3/624), known as King of Martyrs and God's Lion, paternal uncle of Muḥammad and ʿAlī, who fought valiantly at the Battle of Badr and killed several Meccan warriors in single combat. He was slain by treachery the following year at the Battle of Uḥud by a man who was incited by Muʿāwiyah's mother, Hind. Muḥammad grieved deeply for Ḥamzah and recited the funeral prayer for him 70 times, placing Ḥamzah's bier in front of the bier of each martyr as he prayed for them one by one.

Ḥanẓalah ibn Abī Sufyān   (d. 2/624), Muʿāwiyah's brother from the Umayyah clan of Quraysh, killed by ʿAlī in the fighting against Muḥammad at the Battle of Badr. (See further: B 792; R 3:31; F 369.)

Ḥarb ibn Shuraḥbīl al-Shibāmī   (d. after 37/657), chieftain of the clan of Shibām from the Yemeni tribe of Hamdān, who settled in Kufa. Ḥarb was a follower of ʿAlī and fought with him at Ṣiffīn.

Ḥarb ibn Umayyah ibn ʿAbd Shams   (d. ca. 607 AD), Muʿāwiyah's grandfather, from the clan of Umayyah of Quraysh, father of Abu Sufyān and father-in-law of Abū Lahab, both fierce enemies of Muḥammad. Ḥarb was one of the leading chieftains of Mecca in his day.

al-Ḥārith (al-Aʿwar) al-Hamdānī   (d. 65/685), resident of Kufa and a learned man, staunch supporter of 'Alī who participated in his battles. Ḥārith belonged to the Ḥūth clan of the Hamdān tribe of Yemen, and his full name is al-Ḥārith ibn 'Abdallāh ibn Ka'b al-Hamdānī. A famous set of verses addressing him by name is attributed to 'Alī. He appears in several reports in the present volume. (See further: Ḥ 17:42–43.)

al-Ḥārith ibn Ḥawṭ al-Laythī (or Khuṭ, or less likely Ḥawt or Ḥūt)   (d. after 36/656), a man who challenged 'Alī after the Battle of the Camel over the rightfulness of fighting 'Ā'ishah, Ṭalḥah, and Zubayr. Nothing else is found in the sources about Ḥārith, except discussions regarding the spelling of his father's name, an additional indication that he was not well known.

Harlot   see *Nābighah*

Ḥarūriyyah (*sing. Ḥarūrī*)   twelve thousand men who gathered in Ḥarūrā' near Kufa in 37/657 to protest 'Alī's decision to accept arbitration in his dispute with Mu'āwiyah over the caliphate. The Ḥarūriyyah are considered the first Kharijites. (See further: B 958.).

al-Ḥasan ibn 'Alī   (d. 49/669), eldest son of 'Alī and Fāṭimah, grandson of Muḥammad, and Shi'a Imam after his father. The Prophet said, ⟨Hasan and Husayn are the leaders of the youth of paradise.⟩ After 'Alī's death in 40/661, Hasan received the pledge of the caliphate in Kufa. He abdicated six months later and returned to Medina, where he was reportedly poisoned on Mu'āwiyah's orders ten years later. (See further: Ḥ 16:9–52.)

Hāshim   Muḥammad's and 'Alī's clan within Quraysh, named after their great-grandfather, Hāshim ibn 'Abd Manāf.

Hāshim ibn 'Abd Manāf   (d. ca. 497 AD), Muḥammad's and 'Alī's paternal great-grandfather and custodian of the sanctuary in Mecca. Hāshim used to travel to Syria to trade and he married and set up a second home in Gaza. He died and is buried there in a shrine within the mosque complex named for him.

Hāshim ibn 'Utbah al-Mirqāl   (d. 37/656), tribal chieftain of Kufa, nephew of Muḥammad's Companion Sa'd ibn Abī Waqqāṣ, and one of 'Alī's staunch supporters. Hāshim was killed at the Battle of Ṣiffīn. (See further: Ḥ 6:55–56.)

Ḥassān (or Ashras) ibn Ḥassān al-Bakrī al-Balawī   (d. 38/658), 'Alī's governor in Anbar, who was killed by a cavalry troop led by Mu'āwiyah's commander, Sufyān ibn 'Awf al-Ghāmidī. (See further: R 1:214–215; B 215–216; Ḥ 2:75–76, 85–90.)

Ḥassān ibn Thābit al-Anṣārī   (d. ca. 40/659 or 50/669 or 54/673), of the Khazraj tribe of Medina, the best-known of several poets associated with the rise of Islam. Ḥassān was among the handful of prominent Companions who refused to pledge allegiance to 'Alī.

Ḥātim al-Ṭā'ī   (fl. second half of 6th century AD), pre-Islamic poet of the tribe of Ṭayy, proverbial for his generosity.

Hawāzin   north Arabian tribal federation, including the tribes of Thaqīf and Sa'd ibn Bakr, who fought the Muslims at the Battle of Ḥunayn in 8/630.

Ḥijāz   western part of the Arabian Peninsula, where the cities of Mecca and Medina are located. The province runs along the Red Sea coast and is bordered to the east by the Sarāt Mountains.

Hijrah (*Migration*)   Muḥammad's migration from Mecca to Medina in 622 AD. The Islamic calendar begins from this year, which is considered the first "Hijri" year.

ḥikmah   wisdom, or wisdom saying, or aphorism.

Ḥirā'   mountain located northeast of Mecca, where Muḥammad is said to have spent a month every year immersed in God's worship. It is here that he is said to have received his first Qur'anic revelation.

Hishām ibn 'Abd al-Malik   (r. 105–125/724–743), Umayyad caliph.

Hishām ibn Muḥammad ibn al-Sā'ib al-Kalbī   (d. 206/821), famous Kufan genealogist and scholar, whose grandfather Sā'ib fought with 'Alī in the Battles of the Camel and Ṣiffīn. Ibn al-Kalbī is also the compiler of a lost book titled *Khuṭab 'Alī* (Orations of 'Alī). (See further: Ḥ 18:66.)

Hīt   town in northern Iraq on the Euphrates River toward Syria, site of a raid by Mu'āwiyah's commander, Sufyān ibn 'Awf al-Ghāmidī, in 39/659. (See further F 392; R:219.)

House of God   see *Ka'bah*

Ḥudaybiyyah (*or Ḥudaybiyah*)   village just outside Mecca, site of a peace treaty concluded in 6/628 between Muḥammad and the Quraysh.

Ḥujr ibn 'Adī   (d. 52/672), Kufan chieftain of the Kindah tribe of Yemen, staunch supporter of 'Alī who fought with him at the Battle of the Camel and at Ṣiffīn. During Mu'āwiyah's caliphate, Ḥujr challenged the Umayyads' cursing of 'Alī, and he, along with several other Shi'is, was tortured and beheaded by Mu'āwiyah's governor Ziyād.

Ḥulwān   ancient town situated near the entrance to the Paytak pass through the Zagros range, identified with the present-day village of Sar-i Pul, 33 kilometers east of Qaṣr-i Shīrīn, in the Kermanshah province of Iran. Ḥulwān was a town of note in early Islamic times, and a garrison was stationed there during 'Alī's caliphate.

Ḥunayn   site of the Battle of Ḥunayn, fought between the Muslims and the Hawāzin tribal confederation in 8/630, following the conquest of Mecca, which ended in a decisive victory for the Muslims. Ḥunayn is a deep valley situated a day's journey from Mecca on the road to Ṭā'if.

Ḥurayth (*or Ḥarīth*)   Kharijite leader who fled from Iraq to Ramhormoz, against whom 'Alī sent a battalion under Ma'qil ibn Qays in 38/658. (See further: F 369–370.)

al-Ḥusayn ibn 'Alī   (d. 61/680), second son of 'Alī and Fāṭimah, grandson of Muḥammad, and Shi'a Imam after his older brother, Ḥasan. Muḥammad said, ⟨Ḥasan and Ḥusayn are the leaders of the youth of paradise.⟩ Ḥusayn was killed by the Umayyads with his family and a handful of supporters at Karbala and is famous in Shi'i lore as King of Martyrs (*sayyid al-shuhadā'*).

al-Ḥusayn (*or al-Ḥuḍayn*) *ibn al-Mundhir al-Raqāshī, Abū Sāsān*   (d. ca. 100/718), notable and poet of Basra, among the leading members of the second generation of Muslims, a follower of ʿAlī, who carried the banner of Rabīʿah at Ṣiffīn. Later one of the associates of Jaʿfar al-Ṣādiq.

Iblīs   (*Eng. Lucifer*), archdevil condemned in the Qurʾan. Originally a jinni or angel, he refused to bow down before Adam when God commanded him and was expelled from heaven for his disobedience. He vowed to lead the sons of Adam astray in every age.

Ibn al-ʿAbbās   see *ʿAbdallāh ibn al-ʿAbbās*

Ibn Abī al-Ḥadīd, ʿIzz al-Dīn ʿAbd al-Ḥamīd ibn Hibatallāh   (d. ca. 656/1258), Sunni-Muʿtazilī theologian, "*tafḍīlī*" (one who gave precedence to ʿAlī over the three earlier Sunni caliphs), and a poet, historian, and literary theorist, best known for his twenty-volume commentary on *Nahj al-Balāghah*. An official in the Abbasid state, he held various administrative posts in the capital, Baghdad, just before the Mongol sack.

Ibn Abī Rāfiʿ   see *ʿUbaydallāh ibn Abī Rāfiʿ*

Ibn al-Aʿrābī   (d. 231/846), prominent philologist of the Kufan school.

Ibn Funduq al-Bayhaqī   (d. 565/1170), early Sunni commentator of *Nahj al-Balāghah* from Khurasan, who relied on the lost, possibly the first, *Nahj al-Balāghah* commentary, by Aḥmad ibn Muḥammad al-Wabrī (fl. early 6th/12th c.), from Khwārazm. Ibn Funduq is the author of more than 70 works in Arabic and Persian on history and an encyclopedic range of subjects.

Ibn al-Ḥaḍramī   see *ʿAbdallāh ibn al-Ḥaḍramī*

Ibn al-Ḥanafiyyah   see *Muḥammad ibn ʿAlī ibn Abī Ṭālib*

Ibn Ḥunayf   see *ʿUthmān ibn Ḥunayf al-Anṣārī*

Ibn al-Kawwāʾ   (d. after 44/664), whose given name was ʿAbdallāh ibn Awfah al-Yashkurī, a Kharijite leader who fought against ʿAlī at Nahrawān and escaped. He visited Muʿāwiyah in 44/664.

Ibn al-Tayyihān Abū al-Haytham al-Anṣārī   (d. 37/657), early convert to Islam from the Medinan tribe of Aws and one of the Allies who fought for Muḥammad in the earliest battles of Badr and Uḥud. Ibn al-Tayyihān was killed fighting for ʿAlī at the Battle of Ṣiffīn. (See further: Ḥ 10:107–108; B 590–591.)

Ibn Masʿūd   see *ʿAbdallāh ibn Masʿūd*

Ibn Muljam (or Ibn Muljim) al-Murādī   (d. 40/661), of the Kindah tribe of Yemen, the Kharijite who assassinated ʿAlī. He was executed by ʿAlī's son and successor, Ḥasan.

Ibn Nubātah al-Saʿdī al-Khaṭīb   (d. 374/985), famous Aleppan preacher who memorized a large number of ʿAlī's orations and drew on them for his own.

Ibn al-Sikkīt   (d. 244/858), scholar of Arabic lexicography, poetry, and grammar, author of about twenty books.

Ibn ʿUmar   see *ʿAbdallāh ibn ʿUmar*

Ibn al-Zubayr   see *ʿAbdallāh ibn al-Zubayr*

ʿĪd al-Aḍḥā   Eid of Sacrifice, major feast day following the hajj, on 10th Dhū al-Ḥijjah.

ʿĪd al-Fiṭr   Eid of Breaking-the-Fast, major feast day following the fasting month of Ramaḍān, on 1st Shawwāl.

ʿIkrimah ibn Abī Jahl   (d. 13/634 or 15/636), from the Makhzūm clan, son of Muḥammad's fierce enemy and a leader of the Quraysh in their battles against Muḥammad. ʿIkrimah fled to Yemen near the time of the Muslim conquest of Mecca in 10/632 but was later pardoned. Abū Bakr appointed him to command Muslim expeditions in Yemen and Syria; he was likely killed fighting the Byzantines in the Battle of Ajnādayn in Palestine in 13/634. (See further: B 776; Ḥ 13:214; F 365.)

imam (*Ar. imām*)   lit. leader, refers either to the supreme leader of the Muslim community or to an exemplary scholar or prayer-leader. In Shia doctrine, the term denotes the Prophet Muḥammad, his legatee, ʿAlī, and their descendants, one in each age, who inherit their role of spiritual and temporal leadership, who are divinely guided and sole legitimate leaders of the Muslim community. The concept is rendered as Imamate (Ar. *imāmah*).

ʿImrān ibn al-Ḥuṣayn al-Khuzāʿī   (d. 52/672), converted to Islam in 7/628 and settled in Basra soon after the conquest of Iraq. He was among the handful of early Muslims who refused to pledge allegiance to ʿAlī, and he actively attempted to dissuade the Iraqis from supporting ʿAlī. ʿImrān fell ill soon thereafter and lived with chronic illness for nearly two decades until his death. (See further: Ḥ 17:132.)

Imruʾ al-Qays ibn Ḥujr al-Kindī   (d. ca. 550 AD), ranked by medieval critics—and by ʿAlī—as the best pre-Islamic poet, one of the composers of the celebrated Hanging Odes. Princely descendant of the Kindah, Imruʾ al-Qays is often called the Wandering King.

Iraq (*Ar. ʿIrāq*)   important province in the early Islamic empire, conquered 14–17/635–638. Its major cities in ʿAlī's reign were Basra and Kufa, the seat of his caliphate.

Isaac (*Ar. Isḥāq*)   a prophet in Islam, son of the Prophet Abraham and ancestor of the Jews.

Ishmael (*Ar. Ismāʿīl*)   a prophet in Islam, son of the Prophet Abraham, and ancestor of the Arabs. Muḥammad and ʿAlī reportedly descend from his line.

Iskāfī, Abū Jaʿfar Muḥammad ibn ʿAbdallāh   (d. 240/854), Baghdadi Muʿtazilī who lived to a great age, and "*tafḍīlī*" Sunni, who maintained ʿAlī's superiority to all other Companions of Muḥammad. Among Iskāfī's lost works is *Kitāb al-Maqāmāt fī tafḍīl ʿAlī* (Book of exhortations, on ʿAlī's superiority). (See further: Ḥ 17:132–133; B 913.)

Iṣṭakhr   town in the Fars district of Iran, an hour's journey north of the ancient Achaemenid capital Persepolis, religious center of the Sasanian kingdom. The Muslims conquered it in 23/643 and it remained a fairly important place during the early centuries of Islam.

Jābir ibn ʿAbdallāh al-Anṣārī   (d. ca. 78/697), early Companion and one of the Allies,

resident of Medina from the tribe of Khazraj. He pledged allegiance to Muḥammad
at ʿAqabah before the Emigration and remained a staunch supporter of ʿAlī, fighting
in all his battles. He died in Madāʾin, near present-day Baghdad, in his nineties. Jābir
was a prolific narrator of Muḥammad's hadith and ʿAlī's words.

Jaʿdah ibn Hubayrah al-Makhzūmī   (d. after 40/661), ʿAlī's nephew, son of his sister
Umm Hānī, a brave warrior and a learned man. Jaʿdah was close to ʿAlī and served
as his governor in Khurasan. (See further: Ḥ 10:77–78; B 585; Ḥ 13:130; B 679.)

Jaʿfar ibn Abī Ṭālib   (d. 8/629), ʿAlī's older brother, commander of Muḥammad's
forces at the Battle of Muʾtah, killed with his arms cut off in the battle. Muḥam-
mad bestowed on him the epithets *Ṭayyār*, "He-Who-Soars-in-Paradise," and *Dhū
al-Janāḥayn*, "He-of-the-Two-Wings." He is buried in Muʾtah, in the south of present-
day Jordan.

Jaʿfar al-Ṣādiq ibn Muḥammad al-Bāqir, Abū ʿAbdallāh   (d. 148/765), great-grandson
of the Prophet's grandson Ḥusayn, recognized by the Ismaʿili and Twelver Shiʿa as
the Imam succeeding his father, Muḥammad al-Bāqir. He spent most of his life in
Medina and died there. Known as al-Ṣādiq, The Truthful, he, like his father, is the
source of many oral reports in Shiʿi tradition. Jaʿfar al-Ṣādiq is also reported to be
the teacher of two eponymous founders of Sunni legal schools, Abū Ḥanīfah and
Mālik.

Jāḥiẓ, ʿAmr ibn Baḥr   (d. 255/868), prolific author who wrote some 240 books and
essays on diverse topics, of which 75 survive whole or in part. Among his most
famous full-length books is the 4-volume *al-Bayān wa-l-tabyīn* (Eloquence and expo-
sition), mentioned by Raḍī. He cites and praises ʿAlī's words frequently in his books,
and a compilation of ʿAlī's sayings titled *Miʾat kalimah* (One Hundred Proverbs) is
also attributed to him.

Jarīr ibn ʿAbdallāh al-Bajalī   (d. after 55/675), of the Bajīlah tribe, converted to Islam
shortly before Muḥammad's death and settled in Kufa, later becoming ʿUthmān's
governor in Hamadhān. Dismissed by ʿAlī, he came to Kufa and pledged allegiance,
then served as ʿAlī's emissary to Muʿāwiyah in the lead-up to Ṣiffīn and later as
his governor in Hamadhān. According to the sources Jarīr remained secretly pro-
Umayyad. (See further: Ḥ 3:70–74.)

Jāriyah ibn Qudāmah al-Saʿdī   (d. before 67/686), from the tribe of Tamīm, was a
Companion of the Prophet and staunch supporter of ʿAlī. He died in Basra.

al-Jārūd al-ʿAbdī, Bishr ibn Khunays ibn al-Muʿallā   (d. 21/642), chieftain of ʿAbd al-
Qays who came with a delegation from his tribe to Muḥammad in Medina ca. 9/630
and converted to Islam. Jārūd dissuaded the ʿAbd al-Qays from apostatizing after
Muḥammad's death. He was killed fighting with the Muslims during their conquest
of Persia. (See further: Ḥ 18:55–57.)

Jesus (*Ar. ʿĪsā*)   a prophet in Islam. In the Qurʾan, he is called the Son of Mary, the
Messiah (*masīḥ*), the Word (*kalimah*), and the Spirit (*rūḥ*).

jihad (*Ar. jihād*)   righteous struggle against the forces of evil. Jihad can refer equally to battle with outside enemies or combat with one's own base instincts.

jinn   category of beings created from fire, non-corporeal spirits, believed to possess powers for evil and good.

Jisr al-Nahrawān (*The Bridge of Nahrawān*)   see *Nahrawān*

Jumaḥ   clan of the Quraysh.

Jumayḥ ibn al-Sharīd al-Taghlibī   (d. ca. 570 AD), pre-Islamic warrior and poet cited as a source of proverbial verses. Jumayḥ is sometimes said to be the sobriquet of Munqidh ibn al-Ṭammāḥ al-Asadī.

Kaʿbah   cuboid in Mecca, the holiest sanctuary of Islam, reportedly built by the Prophet Abraham, also called The House of God (*Bayt Allāh*). Muslim worshippers throughout the world face the Kaʿbah in their daily prayer, and hundreds of thousands of pilgrims circumambulate it every year during the hajj and *ʿumrah* pilgrimages.

Kalb   Arabian lineage group of the Quḍāʿah tribal federation. Predominantly camel-breeding pastoralists, the Kalb comprised powerful clans in the deserts between Syria and Iraq in pre-Islamic times and later were allies of the Umayyads.

Khabbāb ibn al-Aratt   (d. 37/63), one of the earliest converts to Islam and an eminent Companion of Muḥammad. As a freed slave of Nabataean origin, he suffered cruel torture at the hands of the Quraysh in Mecca because of his conversion. A strong supporter of ʿAlī, he died in Kufa soon after ʿAlī left for Ṣiffīn. (See further: Ḥ 18:171–172; B 947.)

Khadījah bint Khuwaylid   (d. 619 AD), Muḥammad's first wife, the first Muslim, mother of all but one (Ibrāhīm, son of Māriyah the Copt) of Muḥammad's children: daughters Fāṭimah, Zaynab, Ruqayyah, and Umm Kulthūm, and two sons, Qāsim and ʿAbdallāh, both of whom died in infancy.

Khālid ibn al-Walīd   (d. 21/642), from the Makhzūm clan of Meccan Quraysh, lauded by Sunnis for his prominent role as military commander in the conquests of Iraq and Syria and condemned by the Shiʿis for his antagonism toward ʿAlī.

Kharijites (*Ar. Khawārij, sing. Khārijī, Eng. Seceders*)   strongly militarist group of Muslims who seceded from ʿAlī's following subsequent to the post-Ṣiffīn arbitration. With the anti-ʿAlī dictum, ⟨No rule save God's!⟩ (*lā ḥukma illā li-llāh*), they killed any who disagreed. ʿAlī fought and defeated them at the Battle of Nahrawān in 38/658. Most Kharijite factions eventually died out; they survive today as the milder Ibāḍī denomination in Oman and North Africa. (See further: Ḥ 4:132–278.)

Khaybar   oasis 150 kilometers north of Medina, famous for its abundance of date palms, with a large Jewish population in pre-Islamic times. Khaybar was the site of a major battle between Muḥammad and the Jews in 7/628. ʿAlī played a major role in the Muslim victory when he slew the Jewish champion Marḥab in single combat.

al-Khirrīt ibn Rāshid al-Nājī   (d. 38/658), chieftain of the Nājiyah tribe, which had converted to Islam and who, under his leadership, deserted from ʿAlī's army after the post-Ṣiffīn arbitration and reverted to Christianity. ʿAlī sent troops under Maʿqil ibn Qays al-Riyāḥī to fight them, and Khirrīt was killed in the ensuing battle. (See further: Ḥ 3:120–151.)

Khurasan (*Ar. Khurāsān*)   region comprising present-day northeastern Iran, Afghanistan, and parts of Central Asia. In Sasanian times, Khurasan was one of the four great provincial governorates. The Muslims conquered it ca. 30/651, and it remained one of the richest provinces of the early Islamic period.

Khushnūshak   Persian merchant clan, which ʿAlī encountered in Anbar, in northern Iraq, in 36/656, on the march toward the Battle of Ṣiffīn.

khuṭbah (*oration*)   official discourse serving various religious, political, legislative, military, and other purposes, and containing diverse themes of piety, policy, exhortation to battle, and law. In modern usage, the term almost exclusively denotes the ritual Friday sermon.

Khuzaymah ibn Thābit al-Anṣārī   (d. 37/657), famous as *Dhū al-Shahādatayn*, The Twice-Martyred, from Muḥammad's hadith stating that his martyrdom had a twofold worth. Dhū al-Shahādatayn was an early convert to Islam from the Medinan tribe of Aws and one of the Allies who fought for Muḥammad at Badr and Uḥud. He was killed fighting for ʿAlī at the Battle of Ṣiffīn. (See further: Ḥ 10:107–108; B 591; n. 3 of R 2:192.)

Kirman (*or Kerman, Ar. Kirmān*)   province in the southwest of present-day Iran, adjacent to the province of Fars, conquered by the Muslims in ca. 17/638.

kitab   letter or book. The Book (Ar. *Kitāb*) is the Qurʾan.

Kufa   garrison city founded in 17/638, during the Muslim conquests along the Euphrates, on the alluvial plains of Iraq. The city served as ʿAlī's capital and remained a center for Shiʿi Islam for centuries afterward. Today it is a suburb of Najaf, the city that houses ʿAlī's shrine, and a place of pilgrimage.

Kulayb al-Jarmī   (d. after 61/680), son of Shihāb ibn al-Majnūn, a Basran (also identified as Kufan, perhaps having moved there during ʿAlī's caliphate) who is said to have been an associate of ʿAlī, his sons Ḥasan and Ḥusayn, and his grandson ʿAlī Zayn al-ʿĀbidīn.

Kumayl ibn Ziyād al-Nakhaʿī   (d. 82/701), close companion of ʿAlī who fought at Ṣiffīn and served as governor of Hīt, a frontier town in the north of Iraq. He narrated ʿAlī's words and the famous Kumayl's Prayer is one he is said to have learned from ʿAlī. Kumayl, alongside other staunch and vocal supporters of ʿAlī, was executed by the Umayyad governor Ḥajjāj. (See further: Ḥ 17:149–150.)

Laylā bint Masʿūd ibn Khālid al-Nahshaliyyah   (d. ca. 61/681), ʿAlī's wife whom he married during the early part of his caliphate in Basra. She bore him three sons: two died fighting for Ḥusayn in Karbala. In some reports, Laylā also accompanied Ḥusayn to Karbala. She died soon thereafter in Medina. (See further: F 271–272.)

Lucifer   see *Iblīs*

Madā'in   lit. The Cities, metropolis of several adjacent cities on the Tigris River, 32 kilometers southeast of Abbasid Baghdad; one of them, Ctesiphon, was the Sasanian capital. At the time of the Muslim conquest in 16/637, Ctesiphon was the residence of the Jewish Exilarch and the Nestorian Catholicos. It was home to a population of around 130,000, with diverse faiths including Jews, Christians, and Zoroastrians, and varied ethnicities, including Aramaeans, Greeks, Persians, and Syrians.

Madhḥij   large tribal group in the southern Arabian Peninsula and Yemen. Madhḥij played an important role in the early Muslim conquests, especially of Egypt. They fought with ʿAlī at Ṣiffīn, under the leadership of Mālik al-Ashtar.

Mahdī   lit. The Rightly Guided One, the Messiah who will come at the end of time and institute an era of justice and peace. The Mahdī is a descendant of Muḥammad.

Makhzūm   prominent clan of Quraysh. (See further: B 964.)

Mālik   angel who guards the gates of hell.

Mālik ibn al-Ḥārith al-Ashtar al-Nakhaʿī   (d. ca. 37/658), tribal chieftain of the Madhḥij tribe of Kufa, one of the foremost warriors of the early Muslim conquests and one of ʿAlī's strongest supporters. ʿAlī sent Ashtar as governor to Egypt, where he was reportedly poisoned at Muʿāwiyah's behest. Earlier, he had been among the group who called for ʿUthmān's resignation. (See further: Ḥ 15:98–102; B 888.)

Maʾmūn   (r. 198–218/813–833), Abbasid caliph.

Maʿqil ibn Qays al-Riyāḥī   (d. 43/663), chieftain of the Tamīm tribe of Kufa, loyal supporter of ʿAlī. Maʿqil commanded battalions at the Battle of the Camel and Ṣiffīn and led troops against renegade groups during ʿAlī's caliphate. Later, he was killed fighting the Kharijites. (See further: Ḥ 3:120–151, 15:92; B 794; F 369–370.)

Maʾrib (or Mārib)   site of a great dam and capital of the Sabaean realm in southwest Arabia, ruled in classical antiquity by the legendary Bilqīs, Queen of Sheba (Sabaʾ, or Sabā), whose story is recounted together with the story of Solomon in the Qurʾan (Q Naml 27:20–44). The Qurʾan also speaks of a devastating flood that submerged the gardens of Sheba and brought drought (Q Sabaʾ 34:15–17). Present-day Maʾrib is the main town of the district of the same name, 135 kilometers east of Sanaa.

māriqūn   see *faith-leavers*

Marwān ibn al-Ḥakam   (r. 64–65/684–685), first caliph of the Marwānid branch of the Umayyads, earlier exiled along with his father from Medina by Muḥammad. Marwān returned to become a key supporter of his cousin ʿUthmān. He fought against ʿAlī in the Battle of the Camel but reluctantly pledged allegiance to him when defeated. (See further: Ḥ 6:148–165.)

Mary (Ar. Maryam)   holy woman in Islam, mother of the Prophet Jesus. An entire chapter of the Qurʾan is named for her, which relates there and elsewhere the story

of her upbringing by Zachariah, her receiving food directly from God, her miracu-
lous conception and birth of Jesus.

Mas'adah ibn Ṣadaqah al-'Abdī   (fl. 2nd/8th c.), one of the associates of the Shi'i
Imams Muḥammad al-Bāqir and Ja'far al-Ṣādiq, who narrated their words. Mas'adah
is the author of a lost book titled *Khuṭab Amīr al-Mu'minīn* (Orations of the Com-
mander of the Faithful).

Mashrafī sword   an excellent type of blade, so called in relation to Mashārif, a town
in Yemen, or to certain towns called the Mashārif of Syria.

Maṣqalah ibn Hubayrah al-Shaybānī   (d. 50/670), of the Bakr tribe, 'Alī's governor in
Ardashīr-khurrah. Maṣqalah is noted for purchasing the freedom of the Nājiyah war
captives from 'Alī's commander Ma'qil ibn Qays, then fleeing to Mu'āwiyah with-
out paying. After 'Alī's death, he remained in Mu'āwiyah's service and participated
in the killing of 'Alī's supporter Ḥujr ibn 'Adī. Mu'āwiyah sent Maṣqalah to conquer
Ṭabaristān, where he was killed. (See further: Ḥ 3:120–151.)

maysir   pre-Islamic game of chance that involved drawing arrows to determine the
division of a slaughtered camel's meat; the man who drew the longest arrow won the
choicest part. The Qur'an condemns the practice as Satan's handiwork (Q Baqarah
2:219; Mā'idah 5:90–91.)

Mecca (*Ar. Makkah*)   holiest city of Islam, birthplace of Muḥammad and 'Alī, home to
the Ka'bah and locus of worship for Muslims worldwide. In pre-Islamic times, Mecca
was the abode of the Quraysh tribe and a site of pilgrimage. Muḥammad spent his
youth and the first thirteen years of his mission there. Mecca is also known as Umm
al-Qurā (Mother of all Cities), Baṭḥā' (The Flatland), and Bakkah.

Medina (*Ar. Madīnah*)   second holiest city of Islam, Muḥammad's home for his final
ten years, after he had migrated from Mecca, and capital of the Islamic polity during
the first three caliphates. It is located 160 kilometers from the Red Sea and 350 kilo-
meters north of Mecca, in the Ḥijāz province of present-day Saudi Arabia. Medina is
short for *Madīnat al-Nabī*, City of the Prophet. It is also known as Ṭaybah (The Pure
City) and Dār al-Hijrah (Home of Migration). In pre-Islamic times, it was a flourish-
ing and fertile settlement named Yathrib, populated by the pagan tribes of Aws and
Khazraj, and the Jewish tribes of Naḍīr, Qaynuqā', and Qurayẓah, who collectively
invited Muḥammad to settle there as its chief.

Messiah (*Ar. Masīḥ*)   an epithet of Jesus, a prophet in Islam.

Michael (*Ar. Mīkā'īl*)   an archangel of Islamic tradition, mentioned in the Qur'an and
paired with Gabriel.

Migration   see *Hijrah*

Mīkā'īl   see *Michael.*

Mikhnaf ibn Sulaym al-Azdī   (d. 65/684), embraced Islam, along with his tribal del-
egation, at Muḥammad's hands. Afterward, he fought at the Battle of Qādisiyyah in
Iraq and settled in Kufa. Mikhnaf was a strong supporter of 'Alī. He commanded the

Azdī battalion in ʿAlī's battles and served as ʿAlī's governor in Isfahan. Later, after
ʿAlī's son Ḥusayn was martyred at Karbala, Mikhnaf joined the Tawwābūn (Peni-
tents), who sought revenge for Ḥusayn's death, and was killed in the ensuing Battle of
ʿAyn al-Wardah. Mikhnaf's grandson, the important historian Abū Mikhnaf Lūṭ ibn
Yaḥyā (d. 157/774), relates much of his material on ʿAlī and Ḥusayn from his grand-
father.

al-Miqdād ibn ʿAmr al-Baḥrāʾī   (d. 33/653), also known as al-Miqdād ibn al-Aswad,
staunch supporter of ʿAlī, Companion of Muḥammad, and one of the first Muslims.
Earlier, after an altercation in his homeland of Kindah, in Yemen, Miqdād fled to
Mecca, where he was adopted by al-Aswad ibn ʿAbd Yaghūth al-Zuhrī. He fought in
all Muḥammad's battles and was given command in several. Later, he took part in
the Muslim conquest of Syria.

Moses (*Ar. Mūsā*)   prophet in Islam

Mosul (*Ar. Mawṣil*)   fortress city in north Iraq, important in early Islamic times,
located on the Tigris River, opposite ancient Nineveh. After the Muslim conquest
of Nineveh in 20/641, Mosul was set up nearby as a military camp city.

Muʿāwiyah ibn Abī Sufyān   (d. 60/680), major enemy of ʿAlī and the first Umay-
yad caliph. Muʿāwiyah was ʿUthmān's cousin and had served as governor of Syria
under him and earlier under ʿUmar. He refused to accept ʿAlī as caliph and fought
him, with the support of the people of Syria, at the Battle of Ṣiffīn, in 37/657.
After ʿAlī's death in 40/661, ʿAlī's son Ḥasan concluded a peace agreement and
Muʿāwiyah became caliph. He ruled from Damascus for 20 years. (See further: Ḥ
6:334–340.)

Muḍar   one of the two largest tribal federations in ancient north Arabia (the other
is Rabīʿah). The federation is named for Muḍar ibn Nizār ibn Maʿadd ibn ʿAdnān,
eponymous ancestor of Muḥammad's and ʿAlī's tribe of Quraysh. (See further: B 772;
Ḥ 13:198.)

al-Mughīrah ibn Shuʿbah al-Thaqafī   (d. ca. 50/670), late Emigrant notorious for the
laxness of his faith and for his political cunning. Mughīrah was appointed governor
of Basra by ʿUmar, then dismissed for indecency. He returned to Iraq to serve as
ʿUthmān's governor in Kufa, and again after ʿAlī's death under Muʿāwiyah, at which
time he openly cursed ʿAlī on the pulpit. He had been among those who refused to
pledge allegiance to ʿAlī after ʿUthmān's death. (See further: Ḥ 20:8–10.)

al-Mughīrah ibn al-Akhnas ibn Shurayq al-Thaqafī   (d. 35/656), poet from the Tha-
qīf tribe, close associate of ʿUthmān (he was killed alongside him), and keen enemy
of ʿAlī. Mughīrah's brother Abū al-Ḥakam had been among the Meccans ʿAlī had
slain at the Battle of Uḥud. Mughīrah's father, Akhnas, Muḥammad's fierce enemy,
had accepted Islam reluctantly following the conquest of Mecca; presumably,
Mughīrah also converted then. (See further: Ḥ 8:301–303.)

Muḥammad al-Bāqir ibn ʿAlī Zayn al-ʿĀbidīn, Abū Jaʿfar   (d. ca. 114/732), grandson
of the Prophet's grandson Ḥusayn, recognized by the Ismaʿili and Twelver Shiʿa as

the Imam after his father, Zayn al-ʿĀbidīn. He was a child when he accompanied his father and grandfather to Karbala. Known as *al-Bāqir* or *Bāqir al-ʿilm*, "the one who possesses full knowledge," he is the source of many oral reports in Shiʿi tradition. He spent his life in Medina and died there.

Muḥammad ibn ʿAbdallāh (d. 11/632), Prophet of Islam and Messenger of God (*Rasūl Allāh*).

Muḥammad ibn Abī Bakr (d. 38/658), ʿAlī's ward and staunch supporter. His father, the first caliph, Abū Bakr, died when he was a child, and ʿAlī, who married his widowed mother, Asmāʾ bint ʿUmays, raised him. Muḥammad fought alongside ʿAlī at the Battle of the Camel, against his sister ʿĀʾishah. Serving for a short time as ʿAlī's governor in Egypt, he was tortured and killed by Muʿāwiyah's commander ʿAmr ibn al-ʿĀṣ when ʿAmr captured Egypt after the arbitration. (See further: Ḥ 6:53–54, 16:142–143; B 861; R 1:295.)

Muḥammad ibn ʿAlī ibn Abī Ṭālib (d. 81/700), also known as Muḥammad ibn al-Ḥanafiyyah and Ibn al-Ḥanafiyyah, ʿAlī's son, Ḥasan's and Ḥusayn's half-brother, who was active in his father's service, especially at Ṣiffīn. In Umayyad times, the Kufan chieftain al-Mukhtār al-Thaqafī led a major rebellion in Iraq in Ibn al-Ḥanafiyyah's name.

Muḥammad ibn Marwān (d. 101/719), son of the Umayyad caliph Marwān I and half-brother of the Umayyad caliph ʿAbd al-Malik, Muḥammad served as governor of Armenia under ʿAbd al-Malik and as the commander of military expeditions.

Muḥammad ibn Maslamah al-Anṣārī (d. 43/663 or 45/666), of the Aws tribe of Medina, an early convert to Islam who later participated in the conquest of Egypt. He was among a handful of Companions who refused to pledge allegiance to ʿAlī and sat out his battles.

al-Mundhir ibn al-Jārūd al-ʿAbdī (d. 61/681), recalcitrant Kufan chieftain who initially fought alongside ʿAlī at the Battle of the Camel, but later, when appointed governor of Fars, stole from the treasury and was dismissed. In 61/681, two decades after ʿAlī's death, when al-Ḥusayn ibn ʿAlī sent a messenger to Mundhir asking for help, he turned the messenger over to the Umayyad governor Ibn Ziyād for execution. As a reward, Ibn Ziyād appointed Mundhir governor of Sind, where he died almost immediately. (See further: Ḥ 17:55–57.)

Muʾtah a town two hours south of Karak, in present-day Jordan, site of a battle between the Muslims and the Byzantines in 8/629, in which three Muslim commanders were killed, one following the other, including ʿAlī's brother Jaʿfar al-Ṭayyār. Three years later, the Muslims returned, under the command of Usāmah ibn Zayd, to defeat the Byzantines.

Muʿtazilah (sing. Muʿtazilī) rationalist school of Islamic theology, which used the dialectics of Greek philosophy. Its subscribers called themselves "people of unity and justice" (*ahl al-tawḥīd wa-l-'adl*), meaning that they were strictly non-anthropomorphic proponents of God's oneness and advocates for his justice and thus of human free will.

Nābighah   (fl. 1st/7th c.), "The Harlot," lit. "the woman who shows herself," infamous appellation of 'Amr ibn al-'Āṣ's mother in pre-Islamic times. Her given name is not mentioned in the sources. (See further: Ḥ 6:283; B 335; M 1:415.)

Nahāwand (or Nihāwand or Nahāvand or Nihāvand)   town in the Zagros Mountains of western Iran, 80 kilometers south of the city of Hamadhān, site of a battle in 21/642 between the Muslims and the Persian Sasanians, in which the Muslims won a decisive victory.

Nahrawān (present-day Sifwah)   also called Jisr al-Nahrawān, a town in the lower Diyālā region east of the Tigris River in Iraq, location of a battle between 'Alī and the Kharijite defectors from his Ṣiffīn army under 'Abdallāh ibn Wahb, on 9 Safar 38/17 July 658. Persuaded by 'Alī's speech, over a thousand Kharijite fighters left without fighting. Of the 2,800 men remaining, a handful fled during the battle, the 400 wounded were pardoned by 'Alī, and the rest were killed. (See further: Ḥ 2:265–283; B 245–246.)

Nājiyah   Christian tribe in pre-Islamic times of contested origins (Nājiyah is their eponymous mother), many of whom had converted to Islam. The Nājiyah tribe served in 'Alī's army in the Battle of Ṣiffīn, then deserted under the leadership of al-Khirrīt ibn Rāshid and reverted to Christianity. (See further: Ḥ 3:120–151.)

nākithūn   see *pledge-breakers*

Naṣībīn   classical Nasibis or Nisibis or Nesbin, Nusaybin in modern Turkey, where it is now located, earlier in northern Iraq. An ancient, fortified, frontier city on the Hirmās River, conquered by the Muslims in 18/639.

Nawf ibn Faḍālah al-Bikālī   (fl. 1st/7th c.), member of the Bikāl clan of the Ḥimyar tribe of Yemen, an associate of 'Alī. (See further: B 585; Ḥ 10:76–77, 18:265–266.)

Night of Clamor (*Ar. laylat al-harīr*)   Thursday-Friday 7–8 Ṣafar 37/27–28 July 658, the final, bloody night of the two-month Battle of Ṣiffīn, between the forces of 'Alī and Mu'āwiyah. (See further: B 289.)

nock (*Ar. fūq*)   notch at the end of an arrow into which the bowstring fits, *fūq* also indicates a broken nock.

Nukhaylah   town in Iraq near Kufa, on the road to Syria, where 'Alī stopped enroute to Ṣiffīn. It is said to correspond to present-day Khān Ibn Nukhaylah, located between Karbala and Kufa.

al-Nu'mān ibn 'Ajlān al-Zuraqī   (d. after 40/661), from the Zurayq clan of the Khazraj tribe, one of the leaders of Muḥammad's Allies in Medina, and a poet. Outspoken in supporting 'Alī's right to the caliphate over Abū Bakr, Nu'mān was also one of the thirty witnesses who testified to Muḥammad's appointment of 'Alī at Ghadīr Khumm, when 'Alī called on them in Kufa. He participated in Ṣiffīn and served as 'Alī's governor in Bahrain. (See further: Ḥ 16:174; B 869.)

al-Nuʿmān ibn Bashīr al-Anṣārī   (d. 65/684), among the handful of Medinans who refused to pledge allegiance to ʿAlī after ʿUthmān's death and the only person from the Allies who became Muʿāwiyah's staunch supporter. According to some reports, Nuʿmān brought ʿUthmān's bloodstained shirt to Damascus, and Muʿāwiyah then exhibited it in the mosque. He fought with Muʿāwiyah against ʿAlī in the Battle of Ṣiffīn, and he undertook an expedition against ʿAyn al-Tamr on ʿAlī's frontier in 39/659 but was forced to retreat. (Ḥ 1:301–306.)

oath of allegiance (*bayʿah*)   formal profession of loyalty and obedience rendered, with an oath, to the Prophet and the Caliphs by each of their subjects.

Pharaoh (*Ar. Firʿawn*)   title of the ancient rulers of Egypt in the Qurʾan, Pharaoh is condemned as an evil ruler who refused to obey God and his messenger, Moses.

Persia   see *Fars*

Persian empire (*Ar. Furs*)   ruled by the Sasanian dynasty, defeated by the Muslims in the Battle of Qādisiyyah in Iraq (bet. 14–17/635–638) and the Battle of Nahāwand in Iran (21/642).

pilgrimage   see *hajj and ʿumrah*

pledge of allegiance   see *oath of allegiance*

pledge-breakers (*Ar. nākithūn*)   appellation of those who fought ʿAlī at the Battle of the Camel. (See further: Ḥ 13:183–184; B 771–772; F 364–365.)

protected peoples (*Ar. ahl al-dhimmah*)   also called "people with a covenant," members of revealed religions, to whom the early Islamic state provided protected status.

Psalms (*Ar. Zabūr, pl. Zubur*)   David's book of hymns, to which reference is made in the Qurʾan.

Qādisiyyah   small town south of present-day Najaf in Iraq, site of a major Muslim victory over the Sasanians in ca. 16/637, which opened Iraq and Persia to further conquest.

Qarqīsiyā (Latin: Circesium)   Roman fortress city near the junction of the Euphrates and Khābūr rivers at the empire's eastern frontier, corresponding to the present-day village of Buṣayrah. Conquered by the Muslims in 18/638, Qarqīsiyā continued to be contested by competing Muslim states due to its strategic location between Syria and Iraq.

Qaṣīr ibn Saʿd al-Lakhmī   (fl. 3rd c. AD), proverbial counsellor to the pre-Islamic Iraqi Azdī king Jadhīmah ibn Mālik ibn Naṣr. Jadhīmah was killed by Zenobia (Ar. Zabbāʾ), Queen of Palmyra, whose father he had killed, and whom he had set out to wed against Qaṣīr's advice.

qāsiṭūn   see *wrongdoers*

Qays ibn Saʿd   (d. ca. 59/678), son of Muḥammad's Companion Saʿd ibn ʿUbādah al-Anṣārī, Qays was ʿAlī's first governor in Egypt and one of his commanders at the Battle of Ṣiffīn. (See further: Ḥ 10:112; B 591.)

Qiblah   direction of the Kaʿbah in Mecca, which all Muslims face in ritual prayer. People of the Qiblah refers to Muslims.

Qurʾan (*Ar. Qurʾān*)   holy book of the Muslims, revealed by God to Muḥammad, also called The Book (Ar. *Kitāb*) and The Wise Remembrance (Ar. *al-Dhikr al-ḥakīm*).

Quraysh   Muḥammad's tribe. They lived in Mecca and were initially his bitter enemies, fighting him in the Battles of Badr, Uḥud, and The Confederates. When Muḥammad conquered Mecca in 8/630, they reluctantly accepted Islam en masse.

Qutham ibn al-ʿAbbās   (d. 56/676), cousin of Muḥammad and ʿAlī, brother of ʿAbdallāh ibn al-ʿAbbās, served as ʿAlī's governor in charge of Mecca, Medina, and Ṭāʾif. (See further: Ḥ 16:140–141.)

Rabadhah   early Muslim settlement in the foothills of the Ḥijāz mountains, 200 kilometers to the northeast of Medina, now an archaeological site marked by the cistern of Abū Salīm. In early Islamic times it lay on the main pilgrimage route from Kufa to Mecca.

al-Rabīʿ ibn Ziyād al-Ḥārithī   (d. ca. 48/668), participated in the Muslim conquest of Khurasan and served as governor of Bahrain during ʿUmar's caliphate, and of Khurasan during Muʿāwiyah's. (See further: Ḥ 11:37.)

Rabīʿah   one of the two largest tribal federations in ancient north Arabia (the other is Muḍar), named for Rabīʿat al-Faras ibn Nizār ibn Maʿadd ibn ʿAdnān, eponymous ancestor of the tribes of Bakr and Taghlib. Rabīʿah was divided among ʿAlī and his opponents during the Battle of the Camel and Ṣiffīn. (See further: B 772; Ḥ 13:198.)

Raḍī, Sharīf, Muḥammad ibn al-Ḥusayn   (d. 406/1015) descendant of Muḥammad who lived in Abbasid Baghdad, distinguished scholar and poet, compiler of *Nahj al-Balāghah*.

Ramhormoz (*Ar. Rāmahurmuz*)   town in the Khuzistan province of southwestern Iran, conquered by the Muslims in 17/638, reportedly the ancestral homeland of Salman al-Fārisī.

Raqqah   town in northwest Syria on the Euphrates, conquered by the Muslims in ca. 18/639. In 36/656, ʿAlī crossed the Euphrates at Raqqah on his way to Ṣiffīn. Located close by, the burials of ʿAlī's followers remain venerated places of Shiʿi pilgrimage.

rare words   see *gharīb*

Rass   lit. well. The "people of Rass" (*aṣḥāb al-Rass*) are mentioned in the Qurʾan, alongside ʿĀd and Thamūd, as unbelieving peoples of ancient times, destroyed for their impiety (Q Furqān 25:38). (See further: Ḥ 10:94–95; B 589; R 2:191; F 303–304.)

Rāwandī, Quṭb al-Dīn   (d. 573/1177), early Twelver Shiʿi commentator on *Nahj al-Balāghah*, a jurist, exegete, theologian, and hadith scholar, student of Ṭabrisī, author of around 60 books. He died in Qum and is buried there.

risālah   letter, treatise, or message.

Sabā   (rendered into English as Sheba; fl. before 7th c. AD), proverbial pre-Islamic

individual from Yemen. In the proverb, "They dispersed like the hands of Sabā,"
Sabā's hands are a metaphor for his sons. Warned by a sybil of the Maʾrib dam's
imminent rupture, they dispersed across Arabia. (See further: Ḥ 7:74–75; B 403;
R 1:432.)

Sacred House   see *Kaʿbah*

Saʿd ibn (Muḥammad) Abī Waqqāṣ   (d. between 50/670 and 58/677), among the first
Muslims, commander of the Arab armies during the conquest of Iraq, and mem-
ber of the Shūrā Council that elected ʿUthmān. Saʿd was among the handful of
prominent Companions who refused to pledge allegiance to ʿAlī and sat out his bat-
tles.

Saʿdān   plant growing in the arid wastes of Arabia, prized for camel pasturing, with a
head of prickles that wound human feet.

Ṣafiyyah bint ʿAbd al-Muṭṭalib   (d. ca. 20/640), from the Hāshim clan of Quraysh,
paternal aunt of Muḥammad and ʿAlī, and mother of al-Zubayr ibn al-ʿAwwām.
Ṣafiyyah was one of the earliest converts to Islam and migrated with Muḥammad
to Medina.

Ṣafwān ibn Umayyah al-Jumaḥī   (d. ca. 41/661), one of the leaders of Quraysh who
spearheaded the Battle of the Confederates against Muḥammad. His father, Umay-
yah ibn Khalaf, was also Muḥammad's inveterate opponent. Ṣafwān converted to
Islam after the Battle of Ḥunayn, in 8/630. (See further: B 776; Ḥ 13:214; F 365.)

Sahl ibn Ḥunayf al-Anṣārī   (d. 38/658), of the Medinan Aws tribe, was an early Com-
panion and narrator of hadith. ʿAlī's staunch supporter, Sahl reportedly debated with
Abū Bakr about ʿAlī's rightful succession to Muḥammad. During ʿAlī's caliphate, he
served as governor in Medina, Basra, and Fars, and he fought in the Battle of Ṣiffīn.
He died in Kufa, soon after returning from Ṣiffīn.

Saʿīd ibn al-ʿĀṣ   (d. 59/678), from the Umayyad clan of Quraysh, ʿUthmān's governor
of Kufa 29–34/649–655, and later, Muʿāwiyah's governor of Medina.

Saʿīd ibn Nimrān al-Hamdānī   (d. ca. 70/689), participated in the battles of Yarmūk
and Qādisiyyah during the Muslim conquests. A loyal follower of ʿAlī, Saʿīd served as
his scribe, and as his governor in Yemen. Later imprisoned by the Umayyad governor
Ziyād for denouncing the Umayyads' cursing of ʿAlī, alongside ʿAlī's supporter Ḥujr
ibn ʿAdī. Saʿīd was released, while Ḥujr was executed.

Saʿīd ibn Yaḥyā al-Umawī   (d. 249/863), author of *Maghāzī* (Expeditions), a recen-
sion of the Book of Expeditions composed by his father, Abū Ayyūb Yaḥyā ibn Saʿīd
al-Umawī (d. 194/809). His father was a native of Kufa who settled in Baghdad and
had studied with Ibn Isḥāq (d. ca. 151/768), author of one of the earliest Expedi-
tions.

Saʿīd ibn Zayd   (d. 50 or 51/670–671), from Quraysh, cousin and brother-in-law of
ʿUmar, and one of the earliest Muslims. Saʿīd was among the handful of prominent
Medinans who refused to support ʿAlī during his caliphate.

Salāmān ibn Ṭayy   clan of the ancient Yemeni tribe of Ṭayy (or Ṭayyiʾ) who migrated
in the 2nd century AD to Syria, to what is known as Jabal Ṭayy (later Jabal Sham-
mār).

Ṣāliḥ   ancient Arabian prophet sent to the tribe of Thamūd. The focus of his story is
that God sent him with a camel mare as a divine sign; his tribe killed the camel mare,
and God destroyed them in retribution.

Ṣāliḥ ibn Sulaym   (d. after 37/658), from the tribe of Salāmān ibn Ṭayy in Kufa, fol-
lower of ʿAlī, who was ill and unable to accompany him to Ṣiffīn.

Salmān al-Fārisī   (d. 35/655), prominent early Companion of Muḥammad who came
from Persia. Muḥammad said, "Salmān is one of us, People of the House." Salmān
was also a close companion and staunch supporter of ʿAlī. Governor of Madāʾin in
ʿUmar's reign, he died and was buried there. (See further: Ḥ 19:34–39.)

Saqīfah (Portico)   estate in Medina belonging to the Sāʿidah clan, where, immediately
after Muḥammad's death, some of his Companions gathered and pledged allegiance
to Abū Bakr as caliph. (See further: B 292–293.)

Ṣaʿṣaʿah ibn Ṣūḥān al-ʿAbdī   (d. ca. 56/676), poet, orator, and chieftain of his tribe of
ʿAbd al-Qays, devoted supporter of ʿAlī who fought in all his battles and attempted to
persuade the Kharijites to return to the fold in the lead-up to the Battle of Nahrawān.
After ʿAlī's death, at Muʿāwiyah's court, Ṣaʿṣaʿah discoursed eloquently on ʿAlī's mer-
its. In some reports, Muʿāwiyah exiled him to Bahrain, where he died. In other
reports, Ṣaʿṣaʿah paid homage to Zayn al-ʿĀbidīn when the latter returned from Kar-
bala after Ḥusayn was killed.

Shariʿah (*Ar. sharīʿah*)   lit. wide path to the watering hole, term indicating the Law
laid down by each of God's six major prophets: Adam, Noah, Abraham, Moses, Jesus,
and Muḥammad.

al-Sharīf al-Raḍī   see *Raḍī.*

Shaybah ibn Rabīʿah ibn ʿAbd Shams   (d. 2/624), chieftain of the ʿAbd Shams clan of
the Meccan Quraysh, slain by Muḥammad's uncle Ḥamzah in single combat at the
Battle of Badr. (See further: B 776; Ḥ 13:214; F 365.)

Shiʿa   lit. followers, shortened from *Shīʿat ʿAlī* (followers of ʿAlī), Muslims who believe
that Muḥammad appointed ʿAlī through divine revelation to lead the Muslim com-
munity after him as Imam, and, therefore, that ʿAlī was his rightful successor in
both his temporal and spiritual roles. Over time, three major branches of the Shiʿa
evolved: Twelver, Ismāʿīlī, and Zaydī.

Shibām (*or Shabām*)   clan of the large Yemeni tribe of Hamdan, most of whom fought
for ʿAlī at the Battle of Ṣiffīn. The clan is unusually named after the mountain that is
their ancestral homeland, Shibām Kawkabān, northwest of Sanaa, and not after an
eponymous ancestor.

Shūrā (*consultation*)   electoral council set up by ʿUmar to choose one of their mem-
bers as the next caliph. The six members consisted of ʿUthmān ibn ʿAffān, who was

elected caliph by the council, ʿAlī ibn Abī Ṭālib, who opposed the election, and ʿAbd al-Raḥmān ibn ʿAwf, who presided, as well as al-Zubayr ibn al-ʿAwwām, Saʿd ibn Abī Waqqāṣ, and Ṭalḥah ibn ʿUbaydallāh.

Shurayḥ ibn al-Ḥārith (d. ca. 80/699), of Yemeni birth and Persian ethnicity, jurist, hadith scholar, and litterateur, served as judge in Kufa during the caliphates of ʿUmar, ʿUthmān, ʿAlī, and Muʿāwiyah. (See further: Ḥ 14:28–29.)

Shurayḥ ibn Hānī al-Ḥārithī (d. 78/697), ʿAlī's loyal follower and one of his commanders at the Battle of Ṣiffīn, who lived to an old age. Shurayḥ challenged Muʿāwiyah's execution of ʿAlī's follower Ḥujr ibn ʿAdī, and was forced to flee to Sijistān, where he was killed. (See further: Ḥ 17:138.)

Ṣiffīn site of the major Battle of Ṣiffīn fought between ʿAlī and Muʿāwiyah in 37/657, which ended in arbitration. Ṣiffīn was then an abandoned Byzantine village near Raqqah, in north-central Syria, on the Euphrates River; it is identified in the present day with the village named Abū Hurayrah. The main extant source for the battle is Minqarī's Battle of Ṣiffīn (*Waqʿat Ṣiffīn*).

signature reply (*Ar. tawqīʿ, pl. tawqīʿāt*) signature or seal placed on a decree.

Solomon (*Ar. Sulaymān*) (fl. 10th c. BC), biblical king of Israel, son and successor of King David, revered alongside his father as a prophet in Islam. Solomon is frequently mentioned in the Qurʾan, particularly in connection with his knowledge of the language of the birds, and his command over the jinn and the winds.

Sufyān ibn ʿAwf al-Ghāmidī (d. ca. 54/674), from the Ghāmid clan of the Azd Sarāt tribe of western Arabia, who fought in the Muslim conquests of Syria and became attached to the Umayyads. Sufyān served as Muʿāwiyah's commander in his conflict with ʿAlī and led a notoriously brutal raid against Anbar. Later, he commanded a large Umayyad force against the Byzantines and was killed in the battle.

Sufyānī lit. the man from the Sufyān clan, whose harm is prophesied in §1.136.3. The commentators state that it refers to the Umayyad caliph ʿAbd al-Malik. (Ḥ 9:47; B 486.)

Suhayl ibn ʿAmr ibn ʿAbd Shams (d. 18/639), of the Umayyad clan of Quraysh, a leader in the Battle of the Confederates in 5/627 against the Muslims, an eloquent orator and one of Muḥammad's fiercest enemies. Suhayl converted to Islam when Muḥammad conquered Mecca and later participated with the Muslims in the Battle of Yarmūk. (See further: B 776; Ḥ 13:214; F 365.)

Sulaym ibn Qays al-Hilālī al-ʿĀmirī (d. 76/695), loyal follower of ʿAlī, who supported him before his caliphate, and who, during his caliphate, participated in all his battles. Later, Sulaym remained a follower of ʿAlī's sons Ḥasan and Ḥusayn and of Ḥusayn's son Zayn al-ʿĀbidīn. He is said to be the author of a compilation of ʿAlī's sayings and sayings of the early Shiʿi Imams, known as *Kitāb Sulaym* (Sulaym's Book).

Sulaymān ibn ʿAbd al-Malik (r. 96–99/715–717), Umayyad caliph.

Sumayyah (*or Asmā'*) *bint al-A'war*   (fl. 1st/7th c.), from the 'Abd Shams clan of the Zayd Manāt tribe of Tamīm, slave, mother of the Umayyad governor Ziyād. Married to Muḥammad ibn 'Abdallāh al-Azraqī, Sumayyah is characterized in the sources as promiscuous. Among the stories of Ziyād's parentage, one story recounts that Mu'āwiyah's father, Abū Sufyān, boasted that he, Abū Sufyān, had "placed Ziyād inside Sumayyah's womb."

Sunnah, lit. "well-trodden path to a waterhole,"   refers to the accepted practice of the pious forbears, and when used without qualifiers, specifically to Muḥammad's.

Sunni, lit. "emulator of the Prophet's practice,"   someone belonging to the denomination of Muslims who believe that Muḥammad died without appointing an heir, and who revere the first four leaders of the community—Abū Bakr, 'Umar, 'Uthmān, and 'Alī—as Rightly Guided Caliphs. The term Sunni emerged from the earlier political appellation, "people adhering to the sunnah and majority."

Surah (*Ar. sūrah*)   one of the 114 chapters in the Qur'an.

Syria (*Ar. Shām*)   the Levant. Syria in early Islam included the present-day nation states of Israel-Palestine, Jordan, Syria, Lebanon, and southeastern Turkey. Then, too, the capital was Damascus.

Syrians (*Ar. ahl al-Shām*)   refers, in the context of 'Alī's caliphate, to Mu'āwiyah and his supporters.

Ṭalḥah ibn Abī Ṭalḥah al-'Abdarī   (d. 3/624), of the clan of 'Abd al-Dār of the Quraysh tribe, part of the Meccan opposition against Muḥammad. Ṭalḥah was the Meccans' standard-bearer during the Battle of Uḥud, where he was slain by Muḥammad's uncle Ḥamzah, or by 'Alī, and where his two brothers and four sons were also killed.

Ṭalḥah ibn 'Ubaydallāh   (d. 36/656), of the Taym clan of the Meccan Quraysh tribe, Muḥammad's Companion who later took part in the Muslim conquest of Syria and Egypt and was a member of the Shūrā Council that elected 'Uthmān. Ṭalḥah was killed leading the fight against 'Alī in the Battle of the Camel, outside Basra.

Tamīm   large tribe in central and eastern Arabia. Their pedigree is Tamīm ibn Murr ibn Udd ibn Ṭābikhah ibn Ilyās ibn Muḍar ibn Nizār ibn Ma'add ibn 'Adnān. In the early Islamic period, both Basra and Kufa were extensions of Tamīm's territories. Tamīmīs in Basra were further divided into the clans of Sa'd, Ḥanẓalah, and 'Amr; the Sa'd sat out the Battle of the Camel, but they fought for 'Alī at Ṣiffīn. (See further: Ḥ 15:126–136.)

Ṭaybah   see *Medina*

Taym   clan of the Quraysh tribe of Mecca, whose pedigree is Taym ibn Murrah ibn Ka'b ibn Lu'ayy ibn Ghālib ibn Fihr. Abū Bakr and Ṭalḥah were from this clan.

Tha'lab, Abū al-'Abbās Aḥmad ibn Yaḥyā   (d. 291/904), leading scholar of the Kufan school of Arabic grammar, cited by Raḍī in *Nahj al-Balāghah*.

Tha'labiyyah   caravan stop in Najd, on the Kufa-to-Mecca pilgrimage route, in what is now the northeastern corner of Saudi Arabia toward the Iraqi border. Ḥusayn ibn ʿAlī also stopped there en route to Karbala.

Thamūd   ancient Arabian tribe that disappeared before the rise of Islam. They are mentioned in the Qurʾan as an impious people who disobeyed the Prophet Ṣāliḥ, slaughtered God's camel mare, and were destroyed by an exemplary divine punishment. Legend associates the cliff dwellings around the northern Ḥijāzī town of Madāʾin Ṣāliḥ with the Thamūd.

Thaqīf   north Arabian tribe of the Hawāzin federation who controlled the walled town of Ṭāʾif in pre-Islamic times and were among Muḥammad's staunchest enemies, until they converted to Islam after their defeat at the Battle of Ḥunayn. The Thaqīf were a major trading partner with Quraysh, and they intermarried extensively. Later the Umayyads appointed several of their governors from Thaqīf.

Tigris (*Ar. Dijlah*)   along with the Euphrates, one the two great rivers of Iraq. The Tigris flows south from the mountains of the Armenian highlands through the Syrian and Arabian deserts and empties into the Arabian/Persian Gulf.

Turks   refers in the present volume to the Mongols who attacked the Muslim heartlands in the 7th/13th century under Chingiz Khan and his grandson Hülegü Khan.

ʿUbaydah ibn al-Ḥārith ibn ʿAbd al-Muṭṭalib   (d. 2/624), of the Hāshim clan of Quraysh, Muḥammad's and ʿAlī's cousin, one of the earliest converts to Islam, killed fighting for Muḥammad at the Battle of Badr.

ʿUbaydallāh ibn al-ʿAbbās ibn ʿAbd al-Muṭṭalib   (d. 58/677), of the Hāshim clan of Quraysh, Muḥammad's and ʿAlī's cousin, and ʿAlī's governor in Yemen. (See further: Ḥ 1:341–343.)

ʿUbaydallāh ibn Abī Rāfiʿ   (d. after 40/661), whose father, Abū Rāfiʿ, was one of the first Muslims and Muḥammad's freedman, was ʿAlī's loyal follower, who participated in all his battles and served as his scribe in Kufa. (See further: B 1003; R 3:391.)

Uḥud   mountain 5 kilometers north of Medina, site of the second major battle between the Muslims and the Meccans, in 3/625, in which the Muslims suffered heavy losses and Muḥammad's uncle Ḥamzah was killed.

ʿUmar ibn Abī Salamah al-Makhzūmī   (d. 83/702), Muḥammad's stepson and ward, son of his wife Umm Salamah from her previous husband. ʿUmar served as ʿAlī's governor in Bahrain in the lead-up to the Battle of Ṣiffīn. (See further: Ḥ 16:173–174; B 869.)

ʿUmar ibn al-Khaṭṭāb   (r. 13–23/634–644), of the ʿAdī clan of Quraysh, prominent Companion of Muḥammad and father of his wife Ḥafṣah. ʿUmar was the second Sunni caliph of the Muslim community, during whose rule the Muslim polity underwent rapid expansion into Syria, Egypt, Iraq, and Iran.

Umayyads (*Ar. Banū Umayyah*)   clan of the Quraysh tribe of Mecca and the first dynasty to rule the Islamic world, beginning with Muʿāwiyah, who became caliph following ʿAlī's death in 40/661. From their seat in Damascus, the Umayyads ruled until 132/750, when they were overthrown by the Abbasids. The third Sunni caliph, ʿUthmān, was also from this clan.

Umayyah ibn ʿAbd Shams ibn ʿAbd Manāf   (d. 2/624), ancestor of the Umayyad clan of Quraysh, a leader of the Meccan opposition against Muḥammad, killed at the Battle of Badr. (See further: B 776; Ḥ 13:214; F 365.)

Umm Hānī (Fākhitah) bint Abī Ṭālib   (d. after 40/661), a learned woman from the Hāshim clan of Quraysh, ʿAlī's sister and Muḥammad's cousin, and close to both. Umm Hānī was one of the earliest Muslims, and although her husband Hubayrah was not, Muḥammad spent many nights in Mecca at their home. Muḥammad's Ascension (Ar. *Miʿrāj*) to the heavens is reported to have taken place on one such night.

ummī   epithet used to describe Muḥammad in the Qurʾan (Q Aʿrāf 7:157), variously interpreted as: "Meccan," an attributive adjective formed from Umm al-Qurā, one of the names of Mecca; or "unlettered"; or "of the community (*ummah*)"; or "affiliated to previous scriptural communities."

Umm Jamīl (Arwā) bint Ḥarb   (fl. 1st/7th c.), Muʿāwiyah's paternal aunt, from the Umayyad clan of the Quraysh tribe, married to Muḥammad's paternal uncle and fierce foe, Abū Lahab. Umm Jamīl actively sought to torment Muḥammad while he lived in Mecca, and in the Surah that curses Abū Lahab, she is characterized as "The Woman-Who-Carries-Firewood-to-Hell" (Ar. *ḥammālat al-ḥaṭab*), (Q Masad 111:1–4). (See further: Ḥ 15:197; B 822; R 3:77; F 374; ʿA 681.)

Umm al-Qurā   see *Mecca*

ʿumrah   the lesser pilgrimage to the Kaʿbah in Mecca, mandated, along with the hajj, once in a lifetime for every Muslim, combining rituals performed by Abraham and Muḥammad. Unlike the hajj, the *ʿumrah* may be performed at any time in the year.

Usāmah ibn Zayd   (d. ca. 54/674), son of Muḥammad's Abyssinian freedwoman Barakah Umm Ayman and Muḥammad's adopted son Zayd ibn al-Ḥārithah, born in Mecca in the early years of Islam. In 11/632, Muḥammad put Usāmah in command of an expedition to fight the Byzantines at Muʾtah, but the group turned back just before Muḥammad died. Later, Usāmah was among the handful of prominent Companions who refused to pledge allegiance to ʿAlī and sat out his battles.

ʿUtbah ibn Rabīʿah ibn ʿAbd Shams   (d. 2/624), of the Quraysh tribe, a leader of the Meccan opposition against Muḥammad, killed at the Battle of Badr. (See further: B 776; Ḥ 13:214; F 365.)

ʿUthmān ibn ʿAffān   (r. 23–35/644–656), of the Umayyad clan of Quraysh, third Sunni caliph of the Muslim community. ʿUthmān married two of Muḥammad's daughters in succession, Ruqayyah and Umm Kulthūm. Major Muslim conquests in Central Asia took place during his reign. Later, he was accused of nepotism and corruption and killed in Medina by a group of Muslims.

'Uthmān ibn Ḥunayf al-Anṣārī   (d. after 40/661), of the Aws tribe of Medina, Companion of Muḥammad who served as 'Umar's tax collector in Iraq and 'Alī's first governor in Basra. After the Battle of the Camel, 'Alī replaced Ibn Ḥunayf with 'Abdallāh ibn al-'Abbās as governor of Basra, and Ibn Ḥunayf left with 'Alī for Kufa, where he settled. (See further: Ḥ 16:205–206.)

'Uthmān ibn Maẓ'ūn   (d. 3/624), of the Jumaḥ clan of Quraysh, one of Muḥammad's earliest Companions, who took part in the first Muslim migration to Abyssinia, returned soon thereafter, then migrated with Muḥammad to Medina.

al-Walīd ibn 'Abd al-Malik   (r. 86–96/715–705), Umayyad caliph.

al-Walīd ibn al-Mughīrah   (d. 2/624), of the Makhzūm clan of Quraysh, persecutor of Muḥammad's followers in Mecca and a leader of the Meccan opposition against the Muslims at Medina, killed fighting against Muḥammad at the Battle of Badr. (See further: B 776; Ḥ 13:214; F 365.)

al-Walīd ibn 'Uqbah ibn Abī Mu'īṭ   (d. 61/680), of the Umayyad clan of Mecca's Quraysh tribe, whose father, 'Uqbah, was killed fighting against Muḥammad at Badr. Walīd converted to Islam after the conquest of Mecca, in 8/630. He was half-brother to 'Uthmān, who appointed him governor of Kufa, then removed him from office because of his wine-drinking. Later, Walīd supported Mu'āwiyah and fought against 'Alī. (See further: Ḥ 17:227–245.)

al-Walīd ibn 'Utbah ibn Rabī'ah   (d. 2/624), chieftain of the 'Abd Shams clan of Quraysh, Mu'āwiyah's maternal grandfather, slain by 'Alī in single combat at the Battle of Badr. (See further: B 792; R 3:31; F 369; Ḥ 4:34.)

Wāqidī   (d. 207/822), preeminent historian from Medina, also jurist and judge, who settled in Baghdad. Wāqidī authored many books, and only a portion of one book, *Kitāb al-Maghāzī* (Expeditions), is extant. Names of his lost works, including *Kitāb al-Jamal* (The Battle of the Camel), and copious quotations from them survive in the historical literature.

waṣiyyah   testament, including but not limited to a deathbed testament, containing moral advice and/or instructions for distribution of property.

Wise Remembrance   see *Qur'an*

wrongdoers (*Ar. qāsiṭūn*)   appellation applied to Mu'āwiyah and the Syrians who fought 'Alī at the Battle of Ṣiffīn. (See further: Ḥ 13:183–184; B 771–772; F 364–365.)

Yamāmah   early Islamic town in the Najd region of Arabia near Kharj, 70 kilometers southeast of the present-day Saudi Arabian capital of Riyadh.

al-Yamānī   lit. the Yemeni, the otherwise unidentified individual who narrated oration §1.231 from one Aḥmad ibn Qutaybah, identified by some commentators as the equally mysterious Dhi'lib al-Yamānī, one of 'Alī's interlocutors in the present volume.

Yanbu' al-Nakhl   oasis with wellsprings and date groves, 120 kilometers east of Medina (different from the coastal town of Yanbu' or Yenbo, formerly called Yanbu' al-

Baḥr). In pre-Islamic times, Yanbu' al-Nakhl was a worship center for a deity called Suwā'. Muḥammad conquered Yanbu' al-Nakhl and reportedly built a mosque there. 'Alī owned an estate there. (See further: Ḥ 13:296.)

Yazīd (II) ibn 'Abd al-Malik   (r. 101–105/720–724), Umayyad caliph.

Yazīd ibn Abī Sufyān   (d. 18/639), from the Umayyad clan of the Quraysh tribe, and Mu'āwiyah's brother. Yazīd was one of the Meccans who fought against Muḥammad, and after the conquest of Mecca in 8/630 converted to Islam. Afterward, he fought in the Muslim army under 'Amr ibn al-'Āṣ against the Byzantines. When 'Amr left for Egypt, he appointed Yazīd in charge of Syria, where he died in the Plague of Emmaus. (See further: Ḥ 17:256–257.)

Yemen   well-known region in the southwest of the Arabian Peninsula. Muḥammad sent 'Alī to Yemen in 10/632 to call its people to Islam. Yemen and Yemenis feature in several texts in the present volume.

Zanj   black slaves from East Africa brought into early Abbasid Iraq in large numbers to work in the saltpeter mines near Basra. The Zanj rebelled three times within a space of two centuries, including a violent, lengthy rebellion under 'Alī ibn Muḥammad al-Zanjī, which ravaged Basra from 255/869 to 270/883, causing immeasurable material damage and killing tens of thousands of people. (See further: Ḥ 8:126–214.)

Zayd ibn Thābit al-Anṣārī   (d. ca. 55/674), of the Khazraj tribe of Medina, one of Muḥammad's Companions, who served as his scribe and recorded passages of the Qur'an.

Zayn al-'Ābidīn   see *'Alī ibn al-Ḥusayn al-Sajjād Zayn al-'Ābidīn.*

Zaynab bint Jaḥsh al-Asadiyyah   (d. 20/641), Muḥammad's wife, whom he married in 4/626, after her divorce from his freedman and adopted son Zayd ibn Ḥārithah (Q Aḥzāb 33:37). (See further: Ḥ 9:242.)

Ziyād ibn Abīhi   (d. 53/673), also known as Ziyād ibn Abī Sufyān, deputy for 'Alī's governor 'Abdallāh ibn al-'Abbās in Basra. Born out of wedlock to a slave named Sumayyah, Ziyād was later declared his half-brother by Mu'āwiyah and made governor of Iraq. (See further: Ḥ 16:179–204.)

Ziyād ibn al-Naḍr al-Ḥārithī   (d. after 37/658), of the Madhḥij tribe, fought for 'Alī as a subcommander under his tribesman Mālik al-Ashtar at Ṣiffīn and Nahrawān.

al-Zubayr ibn al-'Awwām   (d. 35/656), of the Quraysh, son of Muḥammad's and 'Alī's paternal aunt Ṣafiyyah, one of the earliest Muslims, later a member of the Shūrā Council that elected 'Uthmān. Zubayr was one of the leaders at the Battle of the Camel against 'Alī. He left the battlefield after the fighting began but was killed by a personal enemy as he was leaving.

Appendix of Sources for the Texts of *Nahj al-Balāghah*

This chronological list enumerates all primary medieval sources I was able to locate for each of the texts of *Nahj al-Balāghah*, before and after the time of Raḍī's compilation in 400/1010. The list not only provides evidence for the early spread of these texts, but it also offers a guide to a better understanding of their historical context. A large number of texts are found in the earliest extant works of the Arabic-Islamic corpus: books from the early 3rd/9th century by well-known authors, such as Minqarī (d. 212/827), Abū ʿUbayd (d. 224/838), Ibn Saʿd (d. 230/845), Iskāfī (d. 240/854), and Ibn Aʿtham (died early 3rd/9th c.), not to mention copious transcriptions by late 3rd/9th-century and early 4th/10th-century historians such as Balādhurī (d. 279/892), Yaʿqūbī (d. 284/897), Ṭabarī (d. 310/ 923), and Māmaṭīrī (d. ca. 360/971). Several scholars have compiled print books and online websites that list sources of *Nahj al-Balāghah* texts, ʿAbd al-Zahrāʾ's 4-volume *Maṣādir Nahj al-balāghah wa-asānīduhu* being one of the most important. The present Appendix makes use of earlier inventories, but it also goes beyond them to catalog sources they do not mention—it is possibly the most complete list to date.[1] My hope is that yet more sources will be tracked—and compared and analyzed—by future researchers.

1　　Logistics

- **Numbering**: The numbering of texts in this Appendix corresponds to the numbering in the present volume, including sub-numbers for longer texts.
- **Sequence**: Within the list of citations for each text, the sequence of authors is chronological, based on the author's death date.
- **Names**: For the sake of concision, authors with a single book listed in the Bibliography are noted only by name. For authors with more than one book listed in the Bibliography, a truncated title is also provided. For multiple authors with the same name, either their first name is also given, or their

---

1　My thanks to Tynan Kelly for his dedicated and expert assistance in researching this Appendix of Sources.

© TAHERA QUTBUDDIN, 2024 | DOI:10.1163/9789004682603_007

book title is listed alongside their name of fame. The definite particle (al-) is omitted from names and titles.

- **Versions:** Since the materials are attributed to ʿAlī's time, when production and transmission were predominantly oral, and the materials were initially transmitted in different oral recensions, versions recorded in the written sources vary both in length and language. Many are excerpts from larger texts.
- **Raḍī's stated sources:** These are mentioned at the relevant place in the Appendix, and they include four lost books, one extant book, and several oral transmitters (also listed in the Introduction). Among books of earlier authors, Raḍī's version is closest to the versions of Minqarī, Ḥarrānī, and Māmaṭīrī, and also close to the versions of Sulaym, Ibn Aʿtham, Iskāfī, Barqī, Ibn Qutaybah, Balādhurī, Yaʿqūbī, Ṭabarī, Abū al-Faraj, and Ṣadūq. The rare words section follows Abū ʿUbayd's sequence.
- **Commentaries:** *Nahj al-Balāghah* commentaries are not listed as sources for the obvious reason that they copy from it directly; instances are listed in which Ibn Abī al-Ḥadīd provides additional sources.
- **Attributions to other speakers:** A handful of texts are attributed in other sources to other early figures, especially the Prophet Muḥammad; these are flagged below.

Chapter 1: Orations

Text no.	References
1.1.1	Thaqafī 1:170–176; Kulaynī 1:134–136; Ḥarrānī 61; Qudāʿī, *Dustūr* 170; Ṭabrisī, *Iḥtijāj* 1:294, 2:174 (attrib. ʿAlī al-Riḍā); Ḥātim, *Tuḥfah* 22; Ibn Ṭalḥah 154.
1.1.2	Zamakhsharī, *Rabīʿ* 1:97–98; Ṭabrisī, *Iḥtijāj* 1:297–298; Rāzī, *Mafātīḥ* 2:388; Majd al-Dīn Ibn al-Athīr s.v. "J-W-Y"; Ibn Ṭalḥah 155; Ibn Manẓūr s.v. "J-W-Y."
1.1.3	Ibn Ṭalḥah 156.
1.1.4–5	Zamakhsharī, *Rabīʿ* 1:326, 367; Shahrastānī, *Mafātīḥ* 2:327; Muʾayyad, *Ṭirāz* 2:137.
1.1.6–7	Muʾayyad, *Ṭirāz* 2:137.
1.1.8	None
1.2.1	Muʾaddib 543; Ibn Ṭalḥah 285–286.
1.2.2	Ṭabarī-Āmulī 399; Āmidī 331, 354; Muḥammad ibn Ṭāhir 187.

(*cont.*)

Text no.	References
1.3	Shiqshiqiyyah Oration: Ibn Abī al-Ḥadīd (Ḥ 1:205–206, cites the now lost works of Abū al-Qāsim al-Balkhī, d. 319/931, chief of the Basran Muʿtazilites, for a large portion of this oration). Ibn Mardawayh 134–135; Ābī 1:186–187; Ṭūsī, *Talkhīṣ al-Shāfī* 3:53–57; Ibn Hibat Allāh 484; Rāzī, *Mafātīḥ* 2:388; Ḥumayd 1:111–112; Sibṭ 124–125.
1.3.1	as in §1.3 above, and Ṣadūq, *ʿIlal* 1:150; Ṣadūq, *Maʿānī* 360–361; Mufīd, *Jamal* 62, 92; Mufīd, *Irshād* 1:287; Abū al-Ṣalāḥ 329; Ṭūsī, *Amālī* 372; Ṭabrisī, *Iḥtijāj* 1:282; Ibn Shahrāshūb 2:48; Majd al-Dīn Ibn al-Athīr s.v. "J-Dh-Dh"; Sibṭ 124; Qāsimī 249; Ibn Ṭāwūs, *Ṭarāʾif* 2:418.
1.3.2	as in §1.3 above, and Ibn Ḥanbal, *Faḍāʾil* 1:151; Ṣadūq, *ʿIlal* 1:151; Ṣadūq, *Maʿānī* 361; Mufīd, *Irshād* 1:288; Murtaḍā, *Rasāʾil* 2:109–110; Karājikī, *Taʿajjub* 99; ʿĀṣimī 1:257; Ṭūsī, *Amālī* 373; Muʾayyad al-Shīrāzī vol. 4 majlis 83; Ṭabrisī, *Iḥtijāj* 1:284; Ibn Shahrāshūb 2:48; Ibn Ṭāwūs, *Ṭarāʾif* 2:418.
1.3.3	as in §1.3 above, and Ṣadūq, *ʿIlal* 1:151; Mufīd, *Irshād* 1:288; 286; Murtaḍā, *Rasāʾil* 2:109–110; Ṭūsī, *Amālī* 373; Ṭabrisī, *Iḥtijāj* 1:225; Ibn Shahrāshūb 2:48; Majd al-Dīn Ibn al-Athīr s.v. "Kh-Ḍ-M"; "Sh-N-Q"; Ibn Ṭāwūs, *Ṭarāʾif* 2:418.
1.3.4	as in §1.3 above, and Māmaṭīrī 255; Ṣadūq, *Maʿānī* 362; Ṣadūq, *ʿIlal* 1:152; Mufīd, *Ifṣāḥ* 46; Mufīd, *Irshād* 1:289; Ābī 1:274; Abū al-Ṣalāḥ 240; Ṭūsī, *Amālī* 374; Muʾaddib 507; Ṭabrisī, *Iḥtijāj* 1:287; Ibn Shahrāshūb 2:48; Majd al-Dīn Ibn al-Athīr s.v. "Ḥ-L-Y," "Z-B-R-J," "ʿ-N-Z"; Ibn Ṭāwūs, *Ṭarāʾif* 2:418.
1.3.5	as in §1.3 above, and Māmaṭīrī 256; Ṣadūq, *ʿIlal* 1:153; Ṣadūq, *Maʿānī* 362; Murtaḍā, *Rasāʾil* 2:113; Ṭūsī, *Amālī* 374; Ṭabrisī, *Iḥtijāj* 1:288; Maydānī, 1:369; Ibn Shahrāshūb 2:49; Majd al-Dīn Ibn al-Athīr s.v. "Sh-Q-Sh-Q"; Ibn Ṭāwūs, *Ṭarāʾif* 2:419; Ibn Manẓūr s.v. "Sh-Q-Sh-Q."
1.4	Ṭabarī-Āmulī 408; Mufīd, *Irshād* 1:253; Muʾaddib 196.
1.5	Ḥulwānī 56; Muʾaddib 298; Ṭabrisī, *Iḥtijāj* 1:127; Majd al-Dīn Ibn al-Athīr s.v. "D-M-J"; Sibṭ 137; Ibn Ṭalḥah 287; Ibn Manẓūr s.v. "D-M-J."
1.6	Ibn Abī Shaybah 7:487 (§ 37371); Ibn Shabbah 4:1257; Ṭabarī, *Tārīkh* 4:456, 458; Ṭabarī-Āmulī 403; Ṭūsī, *Amālī* 52.
1.7	Muʾaddib 223; Zamakhsharī, *Rabīʿ* 1:323; Majd al-Dīn Ibn al-Athīr s.v. "Kh-Ṭ-L"; Ibn Manẓūr s.v. "Kh-Ṭ-L."
1.8	Mufīd, *Jamal* 175; Majd al-Dīn Ibn al-Athīr s.v. "W-L-J"; Ibn Manẓūr s.v. "W-L-J."

(*cont.*)

Text no.	References
1.9	Mufīd, *Jamal* 177.
1.10	Mufīd, *Irshād* 1:251; Muʾaddib 110.
1.11	Zamakhsharī, *Rabīʿ* 4:102; Ibn Shahrāshūb 2:341.
1.12	Barqī 1:262.
1.13	Ibn Qutaybah, *ʿUyūn* 1:316; Abū Ḥanīfah al-Dīnawarī 151; Qummī 2:339; Ibn ʿAbd Rabbih 4:170, 5:76; Masʿūdī, *Murūj* 2:364; Mufīd, *Jamal* 217; Ṭūsī, *Amālī* 702–703; Ṭabrisī, *Iḥtijāj* 1:250; Muwaffaq Khwārazmī 189; Ibn Shahrāshūb 2:110; Yāqūt 1:436, s.v. "al-Baṣrah"; Majd al-Dīn Ibn al-Athīr s.v. "J-ʾ-J-ʾ"; Sibṭ 79; Ibn Manẓūr s.v. "J-ʾ-J-ʾ."
1.14	Ibn Qutaybah, *ʿUyūn* 1:317; Abū Ḥanīfah al-Dīnawarī 151; Mufīd, *Jamal* 218; Muʾaddib 243.
1.15	Yaʿqūbī 2:179; Masʿūdī, *Ithbāt* 120; Nuʿmān, *Sharḥ* 1:373; Nuʿmān, *Daʿāʾim* 1:396; Ibn Shahrāshūb 1:377; Ibn Abī al-Ḥadīd 1:269 (cites Ibn al-Kalbī).
1.16	Iskāfī, *Miʿyār* 289; Jāḥiẓ, *Bayān* 2:50–51; Jāḥiẓ, *Miʾat* 222, 230; Ibn Qutaybah, *Gharīb* 1:360; Ibn Qutaybah, *ʿUyūn* 2:260; Yaʿqūbī 2:211; Kulaynī 1:369, 8:96; Ibn ʿAbd Rabbih 4:157; Māmaṭīrī 317–319; Nuʿmān, *Ikhtilāf* 174; Nuʿmān, *Daʿāʾim* 1:97; Mufīd, *Irshād* 1:231; Hārūnī 258, 270; Muwaffaq biʾllāh 554; Quḍāʿī, *Dustūr* 140; Ṭūsī, *Amālī* 235; Muʾaddib 255; Warrām 2:103; Majd al-Dīn Ibn al-Athīr s.v. "W-Sh-M"; Ibn Ṭalḥah 156.
1.17	Iskāfī, *Miʿyār* 289; Ibn Qutaybah, *Gharīb* 1:360; Ibn Qutaybah, *ʿUyūn* 1:99; Yaʿqūbī 2:211; Kulaynī 1:55; Māmaṭīrī 318–319; Makkī 1:246; Harawī s.v. "Kh-B-Ṭ"; Mufīd, *Irshād* 1:231; Hārūnī 259; Muwaffaq biʾllāh 554–555; Quḍāʿī, *Dustūr* 160; Ṭūsī, *Amālī* 235; Muʾaddib 112, 153; Ṭabrisī, *Iḥtijāj* 1:390; Majd al-Dīn Ibn al-Athīr s.v. "Kh-B-Ṭ"; Ibn Ṭalḥah 247.
1.18	Ṭabrisī, *Iḥtijāj* 1:389; Ibn Ṭalḥah 248.
1.19	Abū al-Faraj, *Aghānī* 20:10; Khaṭīb, *Riḥlah* 131; Ibn ʿAsākir 46:38.
1.20	Kulaynī 1:405.
1.21	Ṭabarī, *Tārīkh* 4:436; Raḍī, *Khaṣāʾiṣ* 87; Muʾaddib 203; Fattāl 490.
1.22	Kulaynī 5:53; Mufīd, *Jamal* 144; Mufīd, *Irshād* 1:251; Hārūnī 291–292; Ṭūsī, *Amālī* 169; Muʾaddib 110, 407; Majd al-Dīn Ibn al-Athīr s.v. "Dh-M-R," "H-B-L," "N-Ṣ-F"; ʿIzz al-Dīn Ibn al-Athīr, *Usd* 3:21; Ibn Abī al-Ḥadīd 1:305 (cites Abū Mikhnaf); Ibn Manẓūr s.v. "Dh-M-R."
1.23	Minqarī 10; Abū ʿUbayd, *Gharīb* 4:360; Ibn Qutaybah, *Imāmah* 1:70; Thaqafī 80; Yaʿqūbī 2:207; Kulaynī 2:154, 5:57; Ibn ʿAbd Rabbih 2:208;

(cont.)

Text no.	References
	Makkī 2:13; Māmaṭīrī 228–229; Qummī 2:36; ʿAbdallāh al-Ḥimyarī 38; Kūfī 106; Zamakhsharī, *Fāʾiq* s.v. "Y-S-R"; Zamakhsharī, *Rabīʿ* 4:267; Ibn ʿAsākir 42:502; Majd al-Dīn Ibn al-Athīr s.v. "Gh-F-R," "F-L-J"; Ibn Kathīr, *Bidāyah* 8:8.
1.24	Majd al-Dīn Ibn al-Athīr s.v. "ʿ-Ṣ-B"; Ibn Manẓūr s.v. "ʿ-Ṣ-B."
1.25	Ibn Saʿd 5:93; Balādhurī 2:383; Thaqafī 2:636; Ibn ʿAbd Rabbih 3:293; Masʿūdī, *Murūj* 3:150; Ibn Ḥibbān 2:301; Ṭabrisī, *Iḥtijāj* 1:257; Ibn ʿAsākir 42:535; Majd al-Dīn Ibn al-Athīr s.v. "F-R-W"; Ibn Manẓūr s.v. "F-R-W."
1.26.1	Ibn Qutaybah, *Imāmah* 1:157; Thaqafī 1:303; Ṭabarī-Āmulī 408; Ibn Ṭāwūs, *Kashf* 174.
1.26.2	Ibn Qutaybah, *Imāmah* 1:176; Thaqafī 1:307; Ṭabarī-Āmulī 416; Ibn Shahrāshūb 2:47.
1.26.3	Thaqafī 1:317–318.
1.27	Ibn Aʿtham 4:236–238; Jāḥiẓ, *Bayān* 2:53; Ibn Qutaybah, *ʿUyūn* 2:261; Ibn Qutaybah, *Gharīb* 2:137; Ibn Qutaybah, *ʿUyūn* 2:261; Balādhurī 2:442; Abū Ḥanīfah al-Dīnawarī 211; Thaqafī 2:474; Mubarrad, *Kāmil* 1:20; Kulaynī 5:4; Ibn ʿAbd Rabbih 4:160; Abū al-Faraj, *Aghānī* 16:286; Abū al-Faraj, *Maqātil* 47; Māmaṭīrī 291–293; Nuʿmān, *Daʿāʾim* 1:390; Nuʿmān, *Sharḥ* 2:75; Ṣadūq, *Maʿānī* 309–310; Ābī 1:297; Hārūnī 266–268; Ṭūsī, *Tahdhīb*, 6:123; Fattāl 363.
1.28	Ibn al-Mubārak 1:86; Minqarī 3–4; Ibn Abī Shaybah 7:100; Ibn Ḥanbal, *Faḍāʾil* 1:530; Ibn Abī al-Dunyā, *Qiṣar* 1:26, 50; Ibn Abī ʿĀṣim, *Zuhd* 1:130; Iskāfī, *Miʿyār* 283; Jāḥiẓ, *Bayān* 2:52; Ibn Qutaybah, *ʿUyūn* 2:259; Ibn Qutaybah, *Imāmah* 1:70; Thaqafī 2:633–635; Yaʿqūbī 2:208–209; Naḥḥās 280; Ḥarrānī 153; Ibn ʿAbd Rabbih 4:159; Masʿūdī, *Murūj* 2:418; Ibn ʿAdī 6:316, 6:454, 9:33 (attrib. Prophet); Māmaṭīrī 211 (attrib. Prophet via ʿAlī), 421; Ṣadūq, *Faqīh* 1:516; Ṣadūq, *Khiṣāl* 51; Bāqillānī 145; Mufīd, *Irshād* 1:235; Ābī 1:323; Hārūnī 270, 565 (attrib. Prophet via ʿAlī); Muwaffaq biʾllāh 554, 584; Quḍāʿī, *Dustūr* 44; Ibn Ḥamdūn 1:63; Bayhaqī, *Shuʿab* 13:172 (§ 10129); Muwaffaq Khwārazmī 363; Ibn ʿAsākir 1:268; Warrām 2:103; Ibn Kathīr, *Bidāyah* 8:7; Suyūṭī 3:219.
1.29	Ibn Aʿtham 4:257–259; Iskāfī, *Miʿyār* 98; Jāḥiẓ, *Bayān* 2:56; Ibn Qutaybah, *Imāmah* 1:171; Balādhurī 2:380; Thaqafī 2:482; Ibn ʿAbd Rabbih 1:105, 4:161; Nuʿmān, *Daʿāʾim* 1:391; Nuʿmān, *Sharḥ* 2:73; Mufīd, *Irshād* 1:273; Ṭūsī, *Amālī* 180; Ibn Abī al-Ḥadīd 2:117 (cites Kulaynī); Ibn ʿAsākir 1:320; Majd al-Dīn Ibn al-Athīr s.v. "N-Ṣ-N-Ṣ"; Ibn Manẓūr s.v. "Ḥ-Y-D," "F-W-Q."

(cont.)

Text no.	References
1.30	Abū al-Faraj, *Aghānī* 16:248; Ṭabarī-Āmulī 418; Muʾaddib 403; Ibn ʿAsākir 5:177; Ibn Ṭāwūs, *Kashf* 180 (cites Kulaynī).
1.31	Jāḥiẓ, *Bayān* 3:221; Ibn Qutaybah, *ʿUyūn* 1:291; Mufaḍḍal 301; Ibn ʿAbd Rabbih 5:64; Māmaṭīrī 398–399, 430; Mufīd, *Jamal*, 180; Zamakhsharī, *Fāʾiq* s.v. "ʿ-D-W"; Ibn ʿAsākir 18:405; Majd al-Dīn Ibn al-Athīr s.v. "ʿ-D-W"; Ibn Manẓūr s.v. "ʿ-D-W"; Ibn Abī al-Ḥadīd 2:169 (cites Ibn Bakkār); Ibn Khallikān 5:8.
1.32	Jāḥiẓ, *Bayān* 2:59; Ibn Qutaybah, *ʿUyūn* 2:261 (attrib. Muʿāwiyah); Ibn ʿAbd Rabbih 4:176 (attrib. Muʿāwiyah); Bāqillānī 148 (attrib. Muʿāwiyah); Warrām 2:102; Majd al-Dīn Ibn al-Athīr s.v. "K-ʿ-M"; Ibn Ṭalḥah 176; Ibn Manẓūr s.v. "K-ʿ-M."
1.33	Mufīd, *Irshād* 1:247–248.
1.34	Sulaym 2:213; Ibn Aʿtham 4:260–261; Ibn Qutaybah, *Imāmah* 1:172; Balādhurī 2:477; Thaqafī 1:36; Ṭabarī, *Tārīkh* 5:90–91; Mufīd, *Amālī* 146–147; Majd al-Dīn Ibn al-Athīr s.v. "Ḥ-M-S"; Ibn Ṭalḥah 290; Sibṭ 106; Ibn Manẓūr s.v. "Ḥ-M-S."
1.35	Ibn Qutaybah, *Imāmah* 1:163; Balādhurī 2:477–478; Ṭabarī, *Tārīkh* 5:77; Masʿūdī, *Murūj* 2:297; Abū al-Faraj, *Aghānī* 10:12; Ābī 1:319; ʿIzz al-Dīn Ibn al-Athīr, *Kāmil* 2:688; Ibn Ṭalḥah 290; Sibṭ 103; Ibn Abī al-Ḥadīd 2:259 (cites Minqarī); Nuwayrī 20:169; Ibn Kathīr, *Bidāyah* 7:317.
1.36	Ibn Bakkār 122; Ibn Qutaybah, *Imāmah* 1:168; Ṭabarī, *Tārīkh* 5:84; Majd al-Dīn Ibn al-Athīr s.v. "B-J-R," "H-Ḍ-M"; Sibṭ 100; Ibn Abī al-Ḥadīd (cites Muḥammad ibn Ḥabīb), 2:283; Ibn Manẓūr s.v. "B-J-R," "H-Ḍ-M."
1.37	Kulaynī 1:455 (attrib. anon. addressing ʿAlī); Ibn ʿAbd Rabbih 5:53; Ṣadūq, *Amālī* 313; Ṣadūq, *Man* 2:593.
1.38.1	Ibn Aʿtham 2:539; Āmidī 98; Muʾaddib 179.
1.38.2	Minqarī 95 (attrib. Ashtar); Iskāfī, *Miʿyār* 126 (attrib. Ashtar); Abū Ḥanīfah al-Dīnawarī 164 (attrib. Ashtar).
1.39	Balādhurī 2:404; Thaqafī 1:297, 2:453; Ṭabarī, *Tārīkh* 5:107; Ibn ʿAsākir 34:432; Majd al-Dīn Ibn al-Athīr s.v. "Dh-ʾ-B"; Ibn Manẓūr s.v. "Dh-ʾ-B."
1.40	Ibn Abī Shaybah 7:562 (§ 37930); Minqarī 489; Shāfiʿī 4:229; Ibn Shādhān 474; Balādhurī 2:352, 355; Yaʿqūbī 2:191; Mubarrad, *Kāmil* 3:152; Ṭabarī, *Tārīkh* 5:72–73; Ibn ʿAbd Rabbih 2:232; Nuʿmān, *Daʿāʾim* 1:393; Nuʿmān, *Sharḥ* 2:9; Makkī 1:434; Miskawayh 1:557; Raḍī, *Khaṣāʾiṣ* 113; Quṭb al-Dīn Rāwandī, *Fiqh* 1:375; Ibn Shahrāshūb 2:369.

(*cont.*)

Text no.	References
1.41	Iskāfī, *Mi'yār* 96; Raḍī, *Khaṣā'iṣ* 98; Mu'addib 27, 152; Warrām 3:43; Ibn Ṭalḥah 209.
1.42	Sulaym 2:261; Minqarī 3–4; Ibn Abī Shaybah 7:100 (§ 34495); Ibn A'tham 2:490–491; Barqī 1:211; Ibn Qutaybah, *'Uyūn* 2:381; Balādhurī 2:114; Ibn Abī al-Dunyā, *Qiṣar*, 50; Ya'qūbī 2:208–209; Kulaynī 2:335, 8:58, Mas'ūdī, *Murūj* 2:418; Māmaṭīrī 211 (attrib. Prophet via 'Alī), 421; Ibn 'Adī 6:316 (attrib. Prophet); Ḥarrānī 204; 8:58; Ṣadūq, *Khiṣāl* 51; Mufīd, *Amālī* 345; Mufīd, *Irshād* 1:236; Abū Nu'aym 1:76; Ābī 1:324; Hārūnī 224; Muwaffaq bi'llāh 554; Bayhaqī, *Shu'ab* 13:172 (§ 10129); Quḍā'ī, *Dustūr* 44; Muwaffaq Khwārazmī 363; Ibn 'Asākir 1:268; Ibn al-Jawzī, *Tabṣirah* 1:156; Warrām 1:253, 2:75; Sibṭ 122–123; Ibn Kathīr, *Bidāyah* 8:6.
1.43	Minqarī 55; Ibn A'tham 2:510; Ibn Qutaybah, *Imāmah* 1:114; Abū Ḥanīfah al-Dīnawarī 163; Ibn 'Asākir 59:130.
1.44	Balādhurī 2:417; Thaqafī 1:366, 2:770; Ṭabarī, *Tārīkh* 5:130; Mas'ūdī, *Murūj* 3:402; 'Izz al-Dīn Ibn al-Athīr, *Kāmil* 2:719.
1.45	Ṣadūq, *Man* 1:514; Muwaffaq bi'llāh 583–584; Fattāl 440; Mu'addib 148.
1.46	Minqarī 132–133; Ibn A'tham 2:461; Muslim, *Ṣaḥīḥ* 2:979 (§ 1343) (attrib. Prophet); Nu'mān, *Da'ā'im* 1:347; Ṣadūq, *Man* 2:526; Ḥarbī, *Gharīb* s.v. W-'-Th (attrib. Prophet); Zamakhsharī, *Fā'iq* s.v. "W-'-Th" (attrib. Prophet); Warrām 1:134.
1.47	Ibn al-Faqīh 201–202; Zamakhsharī, *Rabī'* 1:252–253.
1.48	Minqarī 131–132; Ibn A'tham 2:551; Iskāfī, *Mi'yār* 131; Majd al-Dīn Ibn al-Athīr s.v. "L-Ṭ-L-Ṭ"; Ibn Manẓūr s.v. "L-Ṭ-L-Ṭ."
1.49	Nu'mān, *Sharḥ* 2:311; Mu'addib 413.
1.50	Sulaym 2:262; Iskāfī, *Mi'yār* 291; Barqī 1:208, 218; Ya'qūbī 2:191; Kulaynī 1:54, 8:58; Tawḥīdī, *Baṣā'ir* 1:36; Hārūnī 270, 272; Quḍā'ī, *Dustūr* 153.
1.51	Majd al-Dīn Ibn al-Athīr s.v. "'-M-S"; Ibn Manẓūr s.v. "'-M-S."
1.52.1	Ṣadūq, *Man* 1:518; Mufīd, *Amālī* 159; Ṭūsī, *Miṣbāḥ* 663; Mu'addib 108; Majd al-Dīn Ibn al-Athīr s.v. "M-Q-L"; Ibn Manẓūr s.v. "M-Q-L."
1.52.2	Ṣadūq, *Man* 1:519; Mufīd, *Amālī* 159; Abū Nu'aym 1:77; Ṭūsī, *Miṣbāḥ* 663.
1.52.3	Ṣadūq, *Man* 1:520; Ṭūsī, *Miṣbāḥ* 664.
1.53	Abū 'Ubayd, *Gharīb* 2:240 (attrib. a Bedouin); Ibn Qutaybah, *Imāmah* 1:176; Thaqafī 1:310; Kulaynī 2:123; Ibn 'Abd Rabbih 4:162; Ṭabarī-Āmulī 417; Mufīd, *Irshād* 1:244–245; Mufīd, *Jamal* 144; Ṣadūq, *'Ilal* 1:222 (attrib. "'arab"); Raḍī, *Majāzāt* 251; Ibn Abī al-Ḥadīd 1:340 (cites Abū Mikhnaf); Majd al-Dīn Ibn al-Athīr s.v. "D-K-K"; Ibn Ṭāwūs, *Kashf* 181.

(*cont.*)

Text no.	References
1.54	Mubarrad, *Kāmil* 1:167; Ibn ʿAbd Rabbih 1:94; Māmaṭīrī 376; Abū al-Faraj, *Maqātil* 48.
1.55	Sulaym 2:244; Minqarī 520–521; Iskāfī, *Miʿyār* 184–185; Mufīd, *Irshād* 1:268; Zamakhsharī, *Rabīʿ* 4:103; Ibn Abī al-Ḥadīd 1:348 (cites Wāqidī).
1.56	Nuʿaym 1:164; Balādhurī 2:119; Kūfī 2:64, 417; Kulaynī 2:219; Ṣadūq, *ʿUyūn* 1:69; Mufīd, *Irshād* 1:322; Ṭūsī, *Amālī* 210; Muʾaddib 174; Quṭb al-Dīn Rāwandī, *Kharāʾij* 1:202; Ibn Shahrāshūb 2:107; Majd al-Dīn Ibn al-Athīr s.v. "D-Ḥ-Q"; Ibn Manẓūr s.v. "D-Ḥ-Q."
1.57	Iskāfī, *Miʿyār* 186; Ibn Aʿtham 4:257; Ibn Qutaybah, *Imāmah* 1:168; Balādhurī 2:369; Abū Ḥanīfah al-Dīnawarī 208; Thaqafī 2:492; Yaʿqūbī 2:193; Ṭabarī, *Tārīkh* 5:84; Nuʿmān, *Daʿāʾim* 1:391; Ṭabarī-Āmulī 672; Ṭūsī, *Amālī* 180–181; Ibn ʿAsākir 1:321; Ibn Shahrāshūb 2:107; Majd al-Dīn Ibn al-Athīr s.v. "ʾ-B-R"; Ibn Ṭalhah 293; Sibṭ 100; Ibn Manẓūr s.v. "ʾ-B-R."
1.58.1	Mubarrad, *Kāmil* 3:139; Dāraquṭnī 4:151.
1.58.2	Mubarrad, *Kāmil* 3:139.
1.58.3	Masʿūdī, *Murūj* 2:401; Ṣadūq, *ʿIlal* 1:218; Ṣadūq, *Kamāl* 120.
1.59	Āmidī 89; Zamakhsharī, *Rabīʿ* 4:102–103; Ibn ʿAsākir 42:552; Ibn Kathīr, *Bidāyah* 8:13 (cites Ibn Dāʾūd).
1.60	Fattāl 440; Āmidī 10, 88, 199; Muʾaddib 108, 148.
1.61.1	Ḥarrānī 274; Mufīd, *Irshād* 1:234; Muʾaddib 152, 191, 202, 396; Sibṭ 145; Ibn ʿAsākir 33:300.
1.61.2	Iskāfī, *Miʿyār* 270; Āmidī 104–105, 154, 246; Ibn ʿAsākir 33:300; Ibn Ṭalhah 289.
1.61.3	Ibn ʿAsākir 33:300.
1.62.1	Āmidī 238; Muʾaddib 375.
1.62.2	Ibn ʿAbd Rabbih 4:164; Ṣadūq, *Tawḥīd* 43.
1.63	Minqarī 235; Jāḥiẓ, *Bayān* 2:285; Ibn Qutaybah, *ʿUyūn* 1:171; Ibn Qutaybah, *Gharīb* 1:363; anon. 3rd/9th c. author, *Akhbār al-dawlah al-ʿAbbāsiyyah*, 119; Bayhaqī, *Maḥāsin* 45; Masʿūdī, *Murūj* 2:377; Furāt 431; Māmaṭīrī 416–417; Raḍī, *Khaṣāʾiṣ* 75; Ābī 1:269; Muwaffaq biʾllāh 580–581; Muʾaddib 341; Quḍāʿī, *Dustūr* 142; Zamakhsharī, *Fāʾiq* s.v. "Z-N-N"; Ibn Ṭalhah, *Maṭālib* 291; Ibn ʿAsākir 42:460.
1.64	Raḍī, *Khaṣāʾiṣ* 86.
1.65	Balādhurī 2:404; Thaqafī 1:301; Yaʿqūbī 2:194; Ṭabarī, *Tārīkh* 5:110; Māmaṭīrī 287; Ibn Abī l-Ḥadīd (after Madāʾinī) 6:94.

(*cont.*)

Text no.	References
1.66	Balādhurī 2:437; Thaqafī 2:451; Yaʿqūbī 2:195–196; Ṭabarī, *Tārīkh* 5:134; Majd al-Dīn Ibn al-Athīr s.v. "ʾ-M-D," "F-W-Q," "N-S-M," "W-J-R."
1.67	Ibn Saʿd 3:36; Muḥammad ibn Ḥabīb 121; Balādhurī 2:495; Ibn Qutaybah, *Imāmah* 1:180; Nuʿmān, *Sharḥ* 2:432; Qālī, *Dhayl* 190; Abū al-Faraj, *Maqātil* 53; Ibn ʿAbd al-Barr, *Istīʿāb* 3:1127; Zamakhsharī, *Fāʾiq* s.v. "ʾ-W-D"; Majd al-Dīn Ibn al-Athīr s.v. "L-D-D"; ʿIzz al-Dīn Ibn al-Athīr, *Kāmil* 2:738; ʿIzz al-Dīn Ibn al-Athīr, *Usd* 4:37.
1.68	Mufīd, *Ikhtiṣāṣ* 154; Mufīd, *Irshād* 1:278; Ṭabrisī, *Iḥtijāj* 1:254; Zamakhsharī, *Fāʾiq* s.v. "W-Y-L"; Majd al-Dīn Ibn al-Athīr s.v. "M-L-Ṣ," "W-Y-L."
1.69	Ibn Abī Shaybah 6:66 (§ 29520); Iskāfī, *Miʿyār* 272; Ibn Qutaybah, *Gharīb* 1:373; Thaqafī 1:160; Ḥarbī 2:569; Qālī, *Dhayl* 173; Ṭabarānī, *Muʿjam awsaṭ* 9:43; Quḍāʿī, *Dustūr* 138; Ḥātim, *Tuḥfah* 54–55; Zamakhsharī, *Fāʾiq* s.v. "D-Ḥ-Q"; Sibṭ 127.
1.70	Balādhurī 2:263; Zamakhsharī, *Rabīʿ* 5:192; Majd al-Dīn Ibn al-Athīr s.v. "ʾ-M-R"; Sibṭ 78.
1.71	None
1.72	Majd al-Dīn Ibn al-Athīr s.v. "Q-R-F"; Ibn Manẓūr s.v. "Q-R-F."
1.73	Iskāfī, *Miʿyār* 278; Ḥulwānī 50; Ḥarrānī 213; Māmaṭīrī 208; Raḍī, *Khaṣāʾiṣ* 111; Tawḥīdī, *Baṣāʾir* 3:27; Muwaffaq biʾllāh 535; Ḥuṣrī 1:79; Karājikī, *Kanz* 162; Muʾaddib 261, 314; Quḍāʿī, *Dustūr* 42; Ibn Ṭalḥah 292.
1.74	Ibn Abī Shaybah 7:469 (§ 37304); Abū ʿUbayd, *Gharīb* 4:329; Ibn Ḥanbal, *ʿIlal* 2:163; Abū al-Faraj, *Aghānī* 12:169; Azharī 15:22 s.v. "W-Dh-M"; Abū Hilāl, *Jamharah* 1:165; Jawharī s.v. "W-Dh-M"; Harawī s.v. "W-Dh-M"; Majd al-Dīn Ibn al-Athīr s.v. "T-R-B," "W-Dh-M"; Ibn Manẓūr s.v. "T-R-B," "Q-Ṣ-B," "W-Dh-F," "W-Dh-M."
1.75	Jāḥiẓ, *Miʾat* 232; Kulaynī 4:432–433; Muwaffaq Khwārazmī 376.
1.76	Ṭabarī, *Tārīkh* 5:83; Ṣadūq, *Amālī* 500; Māmaṭīrī 347–349; Ṭabrisī, *Iḥtijāj* 1:357; Sibṭ 158; Ibn Abī al-Ḥadīd 2:269 (cites Ibrāhīm ibn Aḥmad Ibn Dayzīl's *Kitāb Ṣiffīn*); Ibn Ṭāwūs, *Faraj* 57; Qurṭubī 19:29.
1.77	Kulaynī 5:517 (attrib. Prophet); Ṣadūq, *Amālī* 380; Ṣadūq, *Khiṣāl* 14; Ṣadūq, *Maʿānī* 251; Mufīd, *Ikhtiṣāṣ* 226; Ṭabarī-Āmulī 418; Fattāl 434; Ṭabrisī, *Mishkāt* 208; Sibṭ 79; Ibn Ṭāwūs, *Kashf* 181 (cites Kulaynī).
1.78	Ibn Abī Shaybah 7:240 (§ 35683, attrib. Sufyān [al-Thawrī?]); Ḥarrānī 58; Kulaynī 5:71; Māmaṭīrī 365; Ṣadūq, *Khiṣāl* 14; Ṣadūq, *Maʿānī* 251; Ibn ʿAbd al-Barr, *Jāmiʿ* 2:16, 387 (attrib. Jaʿfar al-Ṣādiq); Muʾaddib 148; Muwaffaq biʾllāh 47; Quḍāʿī, *Dustūr* 15; Fattāl 434; Āmidī 119; Ṭabrisī, *Mishkāt* 208.

(cont.)

Text no.	References
1.79	Ḥulwānī 66; Ibn Abī al-Dunyā, *Dhāmm* 21; Mubarrad, *Kāmil* 1:125; Ibn Durayd, *Mujtanā* 19; Qālī, *Amālī* 2:120; Ḥarrānī 201; Masʿūdī, *Murūj* 2:415; Ibn ʿAbd Rabbih 3:119; Raḍī, *Khaṣāʾiṣ* 118; Hārūnī 505; Muwaffaq biʾllāh 536; Murtaḍā, *Amālī* 1:153; Quḍāʿī, *Dustūr* 46; Karājikī, *Kanz* 160; Quḍāʿī, *Dustūr* 43; Fattāl 445; Āmidī 86; Ṭabrisī, *Mishkāt* 469; Muwaffaq Khwārazmī 364; Warrām 1:272, 2:104; Majd al-Dīn Ibn al-Athīr s.v. "S-ʿ-Y"; Sibṭ 136.
1.80	Gharrāʾ Oration
1.80.1	Ibn ʿAbd Rabbih 4:163; Muʾayyad, *Ṭirāz* 3:18.
1.80.2	Hārūnī 275; Abū Nuʿaym 1:78; Muʾaddib 144; Quḍāʿī, *Dustūr* 70; Muʾayyad, *Ṭirāz* 3:18.
1.80.3	Hārūnī 275; Quḍāʿī, *Dustūr* 64; Muʾayyad, *Ṭirāz* 3:18.
1.80.4	Muʾayyad, *Ṭirāz* 3:23.
1.80.5	Ḥarrānī 210; Māmaṭīrī 209; Muwaffaq biʾllāh 535–536; Quḍāʿī, *Dustūr* 66; Muʾaddib 340.
1.80.6	Ḥarrānī 210; Abū Nuʿaym 1:78–79; Quḍāʿī, *Dustūr* 66; Muʾaddib 59, 359–360.
1.80.7	Ḥarrānī 210; Māmaṭīrī 209–210; Abū Nuʿaym 1:78; Quḍāʿī, *Dustūr* 66; Muʾaddib 512; Majd al-Dīn Ibn al-Athīr s.v. "J-R-Sh," "B-Ḍ-Ḍ"; Ibn Manẓūr s.v. "B-Ḍ-Ḍ."
1.80.8	Quḍāʿī, *Dustūr* 70; Majd al-Dīn Ibn al-Athīr s.v. "N-Ḥ-B"; Ibn Manẓūr s.v. "N-Ḥ-B."
1.80.9	Ḥarrānī 211; Māmaṭīrī 210; Abū Nuʿaym 1:79; Muʾaddib 260, 359; Quḍāʿī, *Dustūr* 72.
1.80.10–11	Muʾaddib 507, 542.
1.80.12	None
1.80.13	Ḥulwānī 49; Ḥarrānī 202; Muʾaddib 109, 191, 512.
1.81	Ibn Qutaybah, *ʿUyūn* 1:251; Balādhurī 2:127, 145, 151; Thaqafī 2:513–515; Ibn ʿAbd Rabbih 5:88; Nuʿmān, *Manāqib* 273; Tawḥīdī, *Imtāʿ* 390; Bayhaqī, *Maḥāsin* 54; Ṭūsī, *Amālī* 132–133; Ṭabrisī, *Iḥtijāj* 1:268; Majd al-Dīn Ibn al-Athīr s.v. "ʾ-L-L," "T-L-ʿ-B," "R-Ḍ-K-h"; Ibn Manẓūr s.v. "ʾ-L-L."
1.82.1	None
1.82.2	Hārūnī 275; Abū Nuʿaym 1:78; Muʾaddib 438; Sibṭ 131.
1.82.3	Ibn Ṭalḥah 246.
1.83.1–2	None
1.83.3	Minqarī 10; Abū Ḥanīfah al-Dīnawarī 153; Muʾaddib 314, 368.

(*cont.*)

Text no.	References
1.83.4	Iskāfī, *Miʿyār* 284; Jāḥiẓ, *Miʾat* 228; Ḥarrānī 150; Barqī 1:289; Kulaynī 1:45; Mufīd, *Amālī* 206; Abū Hilāl 1:74; Ṭabrisī, *Mishkāt* 244; Muʾaddib 47, 112, 142, 526; Ibn Kathīr, *Bidāyah* 7:341.
1.84.1	Ibn Durayd, *Mujtanā* 1:21; Quḍāʿī, *Dustūr* 72, 162; Āmidī 290.
1.84.2	Hārūnī 258.
1.84.3	None
1.85	Kulaynī 8:64; Mufīd, *Irshād* 1:291; Majd al-Dīn Ibn al-Athīr s.v. "ʾ-Z-L"; Muʾaddib 361.
1.86	Qummī 1:2–3; Kulaynī 1:60; Muʾayyad, *Ṭirāz* 2:179.
1.87	Āmidī 285; Muwaffaq biʾllāh 72; Majd al-Dīn Ibn al-Athīr s.v. "S-J-Y."
1.88	Ashbāḥ Oration
1.88.1	Ṣadūq, *Tawḥīd* 48–49; Hārūnī 287.
1.88.2	Ibn ʿAbd Rabbih 4:164; Ṣadūq, *Tawḥīd* 50, 51, 55; Hārūnī 288.
1.88.3	Ṣadūq, *Tawḥīd* 53; Muʾayyad, *Ṭirāz* 2:135.
1.88.4	Ṣadūq, *Tawḥīd* 54, 55.
1.88.5	Majd al-Dīn Ibn al-Athīr s.v. "W-Sh-J"; Ibn Manẓūr s.v. "W-Sh-J"; Ibn Ṭāwūs, *Faraj* 56.
1.88.6	Zamakhsharī, *Rabīʿ* 1:310.
1.88.7	Āmidī 329; Majd al-Dīn Ibn al-Athīr s.v. "ʾ-S-L"; Ibn Manẓūr s.v. "ʾ-S-L."
1.88.8	Majd al-Dīn Ibn al-Athīr s.v. "Z-ʿ-R," "S-H-B," "H-M-D"; Ibn Manẓūr s.v. "S-H-B," "H-M-D," "Z-ʿ-R."
1.88.9	None
1.88.10	Majd al-Dīn Ibn al-Athīr s.v. "D-Y-J-R"; Ibn Manẓūr s.v. "D-Y-J-R."
1.88.11	Muʾaddib 401.
1.89	Ṭabarī, *Tārīkh* 4:434; Miskawayh 1:458; Ibn Shahrāshūb 1:378; ʿIzz al-Dīn Ibn al-Athīr, *Kāmil* 2:556.
1.90.1	Sulaym 2:256; Ibn Abī Shaybah 7:528 (§ 37734); Thaqafī 1:3; Yaʿqūbī 2:193; Nuʿmān, *Sharḥ* 2:38, 286; Abū Nuʿaym 1:68.
1.90.2	Ibn Abī Shaybah 7:528 (§ 37734); Thaqafī 1:7; Yaʿqūbī 2:193; Nuʿmān, *Sharḥ* 2:39, 231, 311; Nuʿmān, *Manāqib* 261; Ibn Shahrāshūb 1:318.
1.90.3	Sulaym 2:256; Ibn Abī Shaybah 7:528 (§ 37734); Thaqafī 1:8; Majd al-Dīn Ibn al-Athīr s.v. "Ḥ-Z-B."
1.90.4	Sulaym 2:256; Ibn Abī Shaybah 7:528 (§ 37734); Thaqafī 1:10; Majd al-Dīn Ibn al-Athīr s.v. "ʾ-Dh-M"; Ibn Manẓūr s.v. "ʾ-Dh-M."
1.90.5	Sulaym 2:258; Thaqafī 1:12.
1.91.1	Iskāfī, *Miʿyār* 255; Thaqafī 1:172; Kulaynī 1:134; Ṣadūq, *Tawḥīd* 42.

(*cont.*)

Text no.	References
1.91.2	Ibn ʿAbd Rabbih 4:165; Ṣadūq, *Tawḥīd* 72.
1.91.3	Kulaynī 1:135; Muʾaddib 192.
1.92–93	None
1.94.1	Sulaym 2:213; Mufīd, *Amālī* 146; Mufīd, *Irshād* 1:277; Ṭabrisī, *Iḥtijāj* 1:254; Muʾaddib 506; Warrām 2:104.
1.94.2	Ibn ʿAbd Rabbih 4:161; Mufīd, *Irshād* 1:280; Ṭabrisī, *Iḥtijāj* 1:255.
1.94.3	Sulaym 2:213; Ibn Qutaybah, *Imāmah* 1:172; Thaqafī 2:451–453, 494; Mufīd, *Irshād* 1:282; Ṭabrisī, *Iḥtijāj* 1:257; Ibn ʿAsākir 42:492.
1.94.4	Iskāfī, *Miʿyār* 241; Kulaynī 2:236; Mufīd, *Irshād* 1:237; Warrām 1:575; Sibṭ 137; Ibn Kathīr, *Bidāyah* 8:6.
1.95	Ibn Qutaybah, *Imāmah* 1:174; Thaqafī 2:487–488; Ḥarrānī 185; Ṭabarānī, *Muʿjam kabīr* 3:102; Ibn ʿAsākir 14:178.
1.96	Iskāfī, *Miʿyār* 271; Ṣadūq, *Amālī* 478; Ṣadūq, *Maʿānī* 198; Ṣadūq, *Man* 1:429; Māmaṭīrī 235; Quḍāʿī, *Dustūr* 58; Ṭūsī, *Miṣbāḥ* 381; Muʾaddib 88; Ṭabrisī, *Mishkāt* 209; Warrām 2:506.
1.97–98–99	None
1.100.1	Kulaynī 8:17; Ḥarrānī 202; Hārūnī 508; Quḍāʿī, *Dustūr* 56–58; Muʾaddib 90–92; Ibn Ṭalḥah 258–259.
1.100.2	Muʾaddib 29, 163; Quḍāʿī, *Dustūr* 160.
1.100.3	Khalīl s.v. "N-W-M"; Abū ʿUbayd, *Gharīb* 4:356; Nuʿaym 1:259; Dārimī 1:318; Ibn Qutaybah, *Gharīb* 1:110; Ibn Qutaybah, *Taʾwīl* 424; Ibn Qutaybah, *ʿUyūn* 2:380; Ibn Durayd, *Jamharah* 2:992; Māmaṭīrī 322; Makkī 1:276, 333; Mufīd, *Irshād* 1:248; Ibn Khālawayh 313; Zamakhsharī, *Fāʾiq* s.v. "N-W-M"; Zamakhsharī, *Rabīʿ* 2:129; Majd al-Dīn Ibn al-Athīr s.v. "N-W-M"; Ibn Manẓūr s.v. "N-W-M"; Ibn Kathīr, *Bidāyah* 8:6.
1.101	Mufīd, *Irshād* 1:248.
1.102.1	Iskāfī, *Miʿyār* 277; Qummī 1:384; Ḥarrānī 238; Mufīd, *Irshād* 1:276; Majd al-Dīn Ibn al-Athīr s.v. "Kh-Ḍ-Ḍ"; Ibn Manẓūr s.v. "Kh-Ḍ-Ḍ."
1.102.2	Iskāfī, *Miʿyār* 278; Ṭabarī-Āmulī 403; Majd al-Dīn Ibn al-Athīr s.v. "Ṣ-W-Ḥ."
1.103.1	Sulaym 2:179; Iskāfī, *Miʿyār* 260; Thaqafī 1:138; Kulaynī 2:49; Ḥarrānī 162; Māmaṭīrī 224; Mufīd, *Amālī* 275; Ṭūsī, *Amālī* 37; Muʾaddib 513; Quḍāʿī, *Dustūr* 132.
1.103.2	Ibn Abī Shaybah 6:66 (§ 29520); Iskāfī, *Miʿyār* 276; Ibn Qutaybah, *Gharīb* 1:373; Thaqafī 1:160; Quḍāʿī, *Dustūr* 138; Zamakhsharī, *Fāʾiq* s.v. "D-Ḥ-W."

(cont.)

Text no.	References
1.103.3	Iskāfī, *Miʿyār* 276–277.
1.104	Minqarī 256; Iskāfī, *Miʿyār* 149; Ṭabarī, *Tārīkh* 5:25; Kulaynī 5:40; Ibn ʿAbd Rabbih 4:162; Majd al-Dīn Ibn al-Athīr s.v. "Ḥ-S-S," "H-M-M," "Y-ʾ-F-Kh."
1.105.1	Muʾaddib 242.
1.105.2	Āmidī 85, 209; Muʾaddib 319; Zamakhsharī, *Rabīʿ* 1:445; Ibn Shahrāshūb 1:136 (from *Nahj al-Balāghah*).
1.105.3	Muʾaddib 79.
1.106.1	Ibn ʿAbd Rabbih 4:166.
1.106.2	Ibn ʿAbd Rabbih 4:167; Zamakhsharī, *Rabīʿ* 1:313.
1.106.3	Iskāfī, *Miʿyār* 284–285; Ibn ʿAbd Rabbih 4:168.
1.106.4	Iskāfī, *Miʿyār* 288; Muʾaddib 544.
1.106.5	Muʾaddib 161, 499; Ṭabrisī, *Makārim* 10.
1.107	Iskāfī, *Miʿyār* 281; Barqī 1:289; Yaʿqūbī 2:96 (attrib. Prophet); Ahwāzī, *Zuhd* 13; Ḥarrānī 149; Ṣadūq, *ʿIlal* 1:247; Ṣadūq, *Man* 1:205; Ṭūsī, *Amālī* 216.
1.108.1	Iskāfī, *Miʿyār* 264–265; Jāḥiẓ, *Bayān* 2:126 (attrib. Qaṭarī ibn al-Fujāʾah); Kulaynī 8:256; Ibn ʿAbd Rabbih 4:178 (attrib. Yazīd ibn Muʿāwiyah); Ḥarrānī 180–181; Hārūnī 261; Quḍāʿī, *Dustūr* 60; Muʾaddib 233; Majd al-Dīn Ibn al-Athīr s.v. "ʾ-B-H," "ʾ-J-J"; Ibn Ṭalḥah 252; Ibn Abī al-Ḥadīd 2:242 (cites Marzubānī).
1.108.2	Iskāfī, *Miʿyār* 265–267; Ḥarrānī 182; Hārūnī 262; Quḍāʿī, *Dustūr* 60; Ibn Ṭalḥah 253; Nuwayrī 7:252.
1.108.3	Iskāfī, *Miʿyār* 267–268; Ḥarrānī 182; Hārūnī 262; Majd al-Dīn Ibn al-Athīr s.v. "J-N-N"; Ibn Manẓūr s.v. "J-N-N."
1.109	None
1.110	Āmidī 86, 189; Muʾaddib 145; Zamakhsharī, *Rabīʿ* 1:63; Warrām 1:247; Ibn Ṭalḥah 176.
1.111.1	Naḥḥās 352.
1.111.2	Ḥarrānī 219; Naḥḥās 353 (attrib. Zayd ibn ʿAlī); Ṭūsī, *Amālī* 443; Muʾaddib 147, 157; Quḍāʿī, *Dustūr* 42; Warrām 2:494; Ibn Ṭalḥah 260.
1.111.3	Muʾaddib 370; Zamakhsharī, *Rabīʿ* 2:10.
1.112	Ṣadūq, *Man* 1:535; Ṭūsī, *Miṣbāḥ* 527; Ṭūsī, *Tahdhīb* 3:154; Zamakhsharī, *Rabīʿ* 1:128–129; Majd al-Dīn Ibn al-Athīr s.v. "Ḥ-D-R," "Dh-H-B," "Sh-F-W"; Ibn Manẓūr s.v. "Ḥ-D-R."
1.113.1	Ṣadūq, *Man* 1:428; Ṭūsī, *Miṣbāḥ* 381; Ibn Shahrāshūb 1:136 (from *Nahj al-Balāghah*).

(*cont.*)

Text no.	References
1.113.2	Ḥarbī 2:451; Ibn al-Faqīh 223; Masʿūdī, *Murūj* 3:150; Azharī s.v. "Kh-Ḍ-R"; Zamakhsharī, *Fāʾiq* s.v. "F-R-W"; Ibn ʿAsākir 12:226; Majd al-Dīn Ibn al-Athīr s.v. "Kh-Ḍ-R," "F-R-W," "W-Dh-Kh."
1.114	None
1.115	Ibn Qutaybah, *Imāmah* 1:165; Ṭabarī, *Tārīkh* 5:79; Ibn Abī al-Ḥadīd 2:259 (cites Wāqidī and Madāʾinī).
1.116	Thaqafī 2:626; Majd al-Dīn Ibn al-Athīr s.v. "Th-F-L."
1.117	Sulaym 2:142; Ḥarrānī 152; Āmidī 81–83; Muʾaddib 104; Ibn Kathīr, *Bidāyah* 8:78.
1.118	Iskāfī, *Miʿyār* 241; Ibn ʿAbd Rabbih 4:163; Mufīd, *Ikhtiṣāṣ* 155; Zamakhsharī, *Rabīʿ* 2:178; Ṭabrisī, *Iḥtijāj* 1:273; Majd al-Dīn Ibn al-Athīr s.v. "M-R-H."
1.119	Ṭabrisī, *Iḥtijāj* 1:274.
1.120	Yaʿqūbī 2:209; Kulaynī 5:53; Ibn ʿAbd Rabbih 5:86; Mufīd, *Jamal* 190–191 (cites Wāqidī); Mufīd, *Irshād* 1:253; Ṭūsī, *Amālī* 169; Muwaffaq Khwārazmī 185.
1.121	Minqarī 235; Ibn Qutaybah, *Imāmah* 1:172; Thaqafī 2:512; Kulaynī 5:39; Majd al-Dīn Ibn al-Athīr s.v. "K-Sh-Sh"; Ibn Manẓūr s.v. "K-Sh-Sh."
1.122.1	Minqarī 235, 295; Ibn Aʿtham 3:49; Ṭabarī, *Tārīkh* 5:16; Kulaynī 5:39; Mufīd, *Irshād* 1:266; Raḍī, *Khaṣāʾiṣ* 75; Muʾaddib 341, 370; ʿIzz al-Dīn Ibn al-Athīr, *Kāmil* 2:648; Ibn Kathīr, *Bidāyah* 7:292.
1.122.2	Minqarī 236, 392; Ṭabarī, *Tārīkh* 5:17; Kulaynī 5:39; Mufīd, *Irshād* 1:266; Muʾaddib 507; ʿIzz al-Dīn Ibn al-Athīr, *Kāmil* 2:656.
1.123	Minqarī 542; Iskāfī, *Miʿyār* 199; Thaqafī 1:34–35; Ṭabarī, *Tārīkh* 5:66; Mufīd, *Irshād* 1:271; Hārūnī 281; Ṭabrisī, *Iḥtijāj* 1:275; Majd al-Dīn Ibn al-Athīr s.v. "K-Ẓ-M."
1.124	Ibn Qutaybah, *Imāmah* 1:174; Thaqafī 1:75; Kulaynī 4:31; Ḥarrānī 185; Mufīd, *Amālī* 176; Ṭūsī, *Amālī* 195; Muʾaddib 108; Majd al-Dīn Ibn al-Athīr, s.v. "Kh-D-N"; Ibn Manẓūr s.v. "Kh-D-N"; Ibn Abī al-Ḥadīd 1:182 (cites Madāʾinī).
1.125	Ṭabarī, *Tārīkh* 5:85; Ibn ʿAbd Rabbih 2:211, 4:162; Masʿūdī, *Murūj* 2:398; Majd al-Dīn Ibn al-Athīr s.v. "B-J-R"; Qurṭubī 2:154.
1.126	Balādhurī 2:369; Bayhaqī, *Maḥāsin* 41; Karākijī, *Maʿdin* 226; Āmidī 329; Ṭabrisī, *Tafsīr* 5:353; Ibn Shahrāshūb 2:107.
1.127	Āmidī 320; Zamakhsharī, *Rabīʿ* 1:456.
1.128	Kulaynī 8:207; Ṣadūq, *Man* 2:275; Quḍāʿī, *Dustūr* 120; Ibn ʿAbd al-Barr, *Istīʿāb* 1:357; Muʾaddib 416, 553; Ibn Abī al-Ḥadīd 2:375 (cites Jawharī).

(cont.)

Text no.	References
1.129	Iskāfī, *Miʿyār* 277; Nuʿmān, *Daʿāʾim* 2:531; Majd al-Dīn Ibn al-Athīr s.v. "Ẓ-ʾ-R," "W-ʿ-Y"; Sibṭ 120; Ibn Manẓūr s.v. "Ẓ-ʾ-R."
1.130.1	None
1.130.2	Āmidī 282; Majd al-Dīn Ibn al-Athīr s.v. "W-F-Z," "H-B-L."
1.131.1, 5	None
1.131.2	Muwaffaq Khwārazmī 7.
1.131.3	Ibn ʿAbd Rabbih 4:159; Āmidī 88; Ibn Shahrāshūb 1:136.
1.131.4	Muʾaddib 147.
1.132	Majd al-Dīn Ibn al-Athīr s.v. "K-N-F."
1.133	Ibn Aʿtham 2:380; Muʾayyad al-Shīrāzī vol. 4, majlis 56.
1.134	Iskāfī, *Miʿyār* 105; Mufīd, *Irshād* 1:243; Majd al-Dīn Ibn al-Athīr s.v. "F-L-T."
1.135.1	Mufīd, *Jamal* 144; Mufīd, *Irshād* 1:251; Ibn ʿAbd al-Barr, *Istīʿāb* 2:499, 767; Muʾaddib 110; ʿIzz al-Dīn Ibn al-Athīr, *Usd* 2:60–61; Majd al-Dīn Ibn al-Athīr s.v. "N-Ṣ-F."
1.135.2	Ibn ʿAbd Rabbih 4:162; Majd al-Dīn Ibn al-Athīr s.v. "ʿ-W-Dh."
1.136.1	Muʾaddib 554; Āmidī 296; Ṭabrisī, *Iḥtijāj* 1:290.
1.136.2–3	None
1.137	Ṭabarī, *Tārīkh* 4:236–237.
1.138	Muʾaddib 179; Āmidī 135, 359.
1.139	Thaqafī 1:188; Ṣadūq, *Khiṣāl* 236; Quḍāʿī, *Dustūr* 158.
1.140	Minqarī 235; Thaqafī 1:76; Kulaynī 4:32, 5:39; Ḥarrānī 186; Ṭūsī, *Amālī* 195.
1.141.1	None
1.141.2	Majd al-Dīn Ibn al-Athīr s.v. "B-Ṭ-N."
1.142.1	Ṭabarī-Āmūlī, *Dalāʾil al-imāmah* 20; Ibn al-Maghāzilī 78.
1.142.2	Majd al-Dīn Ibn al-Athīr s.v. "T-Y-R."
1.143.1	Qālī, *Amālī* 2:54, 100 (attrib. ʿUmar ibn ʿAbd al-ʿAzīz); Ḥarrānī 98, 299 (attrib. Muḥammad al-Bāqir); Mufīd, *Irshād* 1:238; Hārūnī 261; Ṭūsī, *Amālī* 216; Zamakhsharī, *Rabīʿ* 1:48; Warrām 2:186; Ibn Kathīr, *Bidāyah* 9:311.
1.143.2	Iskāfī, *Miʿyār* 282; Majd al-Dīn Ibn al-Athīr s.v. "M-H-Y-ʿ"; Ibn Kathīr, *Bidāyah* 7:341.
1.144	Ibn Aʿtham 1:291; Abū Ḥanīfah al-Dīnawarī 134; Ṭabarī, *Tārīkh* 4:124; Mufīd, *Irshād* 1:209; Ibn Kathīr, *Bidāyah* 7:122.
1.145.1	Kulaynī 8:386; Ḥarrānī 227.

(*cont.*)

Text no.	References
1.145.2–3	Kulaynī 8:388, 391.
1.146	Majd al-Dīn Ibn al-Athīr s.v. "Ḍ-B-B"; Ibn Abī al-Ḥadīd 1:78 (cites Abū Mikhnaf).
1.147	Ibn Abī al-Dunyā, *Maqtal* 55; Kulaynī 1:299; Qummī 2:367; Masʿūdī, *Ithbāt* 103; Masʿūdī, *Murūj* 2:418; Ṭabarānī, *Muʿjam kabīr* 1:96; Raḍī, *Khaṣāʾiṣ* 108; Hārūnī 269–270; Majd al-Dīn Ibn al-Athīr s.v. "Kh-L-W"; Ibn ʿAsākir 42:562.
1.148.1	Muʾaddib 521.
1.148.2	None
1.148.3	Ṭabarī-Āmulī 401.
1.149.1, 4	None
1.149.2	Muʾayyad, *Ṭirāz* 1:170.
1.149.3	Muʾayyad, *Ṭirāz* 1:169.
150.1	Kulaynī 1:139; Āmidī 232; Warrām 1:549.
150.2	Karājikī, *Kanz* 114; Muʾaddib 179, 366.
151.1	Kulaynī 5:86; Ḥarrānī 154; Muʾaddib 513.
151.2	Ḥarrānī 154; Muʾaddib 77.
151.3	Ḥarrānī 154; Muʾaddib 49, 142.
152.1	Muʾaddib 498; Āmidī 324.
152.2	Muʾaddib 155, 359, 401; Āmidī 331, 252; Muʾayyad, *Ṭirāz* 1:113.
153.1	Muʾayyad, *Ṭirāz* 1:170.
153.2	None
1.154.1	Māmaṭīrī 223; Ṭūsī, *Talkhīṣ* 1/2:274–275; Ṭabrisī, *Iḥtijāj* 1:247.
1.154.2	Sulaym 2:180; Iskāfī, *Miʿyār* 261; Thaqafī 1:140; Kulaynī 2:50; Ḥarrānī 164; Furāt 615; Māmaṭīrī 225; Mufīd, *Amālī* 277; Ṭūsī, *Amālī* 37.
1.154.3	Warrām 2:394.
1.154.4	Ṭabarānī, *Muʿjam kabīr* 11:295; Māmaṭīrī 230.
1.155.1	Ḥarrānī 223; Māmaṭīrī 233; Majd al-Dīn Ibn al-Athīr s.v. "Sh-W-L," "R-B-K."
1.155.2	Māmaṭīrī 233–235; Āmidī 97; Muʾaddib 202.
1.156.1	Ibn ʿAbd Rabbih 2:340 (attrib. Prophet); Kulaynī 1:60; Qummī 1:2; Majd al-Dīn Ibn al-Athīr s.v. "ʿ-Dh-R."
1.156.2	Qummī 1:384; Majd al-Dīn Ibn al-Athīr s.v. "M-Q-R," "N-Kh-M."
1.157	None
1.158.1	Iskāfī, *Miʿyār* 257; Qummī 2:138; Ibn ʿAbd Rabbih 4:167.
1.158.2	Ṭabrisī, *Makārim* 8.

(*cont.*)

Text no.	References
1.158.3	Zamakhsharī, *Rabīʿ* 5:342; Ṭabrisī, *Makārim* 9; Quḍāʿī, *Dustūr* 50; Ghazālī, *Iḥyāʾ* 3:212–213.
1.158.4	Ṣadūq, *Amālī* 718; Zamakhsharī, *Rabīʿ* 5:342–343; Ṭabrisī, *Makārim* 9; Ibn Shahrāshūb 1:370.
1.159	None
1.160	Māmaṭīrī 427; Ṣadūq, *Amālī* 716–717; Ṣadūq, *ʿIlal* 1:146; Ābī 1:287; Khazzāz 213; Ṭabarī-Āmulī 371; Mufīd, *Irshād* 1:294; Murtaḍā, *Fuṣūl* 77; Samʿānī, *Tafsīr* 2:455; Ibn Shahrāshūb 3:15; Majd al-Dīn Ibn al-Athīr s.v. "W-Ḍ-N."
1.161.1	Ṣadūq, *Tawḥīd* 78–79; Abū Nuʿaym 1:72; Zamakhsharī, *Rabīʿ* 1:326.
1.161.2	Zamakhsharī, *Rabīʿ* 1:327; Warrām 1:233.
1.162.1	Balādhurī 2:549 (§ 1411); Ṭabarī, *Tārīkh* 4:337; Ibn ʿAbd Rabbih 5:58; Mufīd, *Jamal* 100; Majd al-Dīn Ibn al-Athīr s.v. "S-F-Ḥ"; Ibn Manẓūr s.v. "S-F-Ḥ."
1.162.2	Ṭabarī, *Tārīkh* 4:337; Ibn ʿAbd Rabbih 5:58.
1.162.3	ʿIzz al-Dīn Ibn al-Athīr, *Kāmil* 2:539.
1.163	Peacock Oration
1.163.1	Majd al-Dīn Ibn al-Athīr s.v. "D-W-R," "ʿ-N-J," "ʿ-Q-L-ʿ," "N-W-T."
1.163.2	Majd al-Dīn Ibn al-Athīr s.v. "ʾ-R-R."
1.163.3	Zamakhsharī, *Rabīʿ* 1:239; Warrām 1:226; Majd al-Dīn Ibn al-Athīr s.v. "ʾ-S-L-J."
1.164.1	Majd al-Dīn Ibn al-Athīr s.v. "Q-Y-Ḍ."
1.164.2	Kulaynī 8:65.
1.164.3	Mufīd, *Irshād* 1:290.
1.165	Ṭabarī, *Tārīkh* 4:436; ʿIzz al-Dīn Ibn al-Athīr, *Kāmil* 2:557; Ibn Kathīr, *Bidāyah* 7:254; Qalqashandī 1:258.
1.166	Ṭabarī, *Tārīkh* 4:437; ʿIzz al-Dīn Ibn al-Athīr, *Kāmil* 2:558.
1.167	Ṭabarī, *Tārīkh* 4:445.
1.168	Ṭabarī, *Tārīkh* 4:491; Mufīd, *Jamal* 156 (cites Wāqidī); Zamakhsharī, *Rabīʿ* 2:80.
1.169	Minqarī 232; Ṭabarī, *Tārīkh* 5:14–15; Ibn Ṭāwūs, *Muhaj* 133 (cites Ahwāzī); Ibn Kathīr, *Bidāyah* 7:291.
1.170.1	None
1.170.2	Ibn Qutaybah, *Imāmah* 1:176; Thaqafī 1:308; Ṭabarī-Āmulī 416; Ibn Shahrāshūb 2:19.
1.170.3	Ibn Qutaybah, *Imāmah* 1:176; Thaqafī 1:308; Ṭabarī-Āmulī 416; Mufīd, *Jamal* 92.

(*cont.*)

Text no.	References
1.170.4	Ibn Qutaybah, *Imāmah* 1:176; Māmaṭīrī 228.
1.171.1	ʿImād al-Dīn al-Ṭabarī 3.
1.171.2	Minqarī 10; Abū Ḥanīfah al-Dīnawarī 153; Nuʿmān, *Sharḥ* 1:369; Ibn Shahrāshūb 1:222.
1.171.3	Iskāfī, *Miʿyār* 111; Ḥarrānī 184.
1.172	Kulaynī 5:53; Ṭūsī, *Amālī* 169; Muwaffaq Khwārazmī 184; Muʾaddib 406; Majd al-Dīn Ibn al-Athīr s.v. "J-L-B," "Dh-M-R," "N-Ṣ-F," "H-B-L"; Ibn Ṭalḥah 213.
1.173	Āmidī 191.
1.174.1	Muʾaddib 151.
1.174.2	Zamakhsharī, *Rabīʿ* 2:258; Muʾaddib 143.
1.174.3	Muʾaddib 152.
1.174.4, 6	None
1.174.5	Zamakhsharī, *Rabīʿ* 2:130; Muʾaddib 511.
1.174.7	Muʾaddib 513.
1.174.8	Barqī 1:7; Ḥarrānī 293; Qummī 2:70; Kulaynī 2:331, 443; ʿAyyāshī 2:352 (attrib. Muḥammad al-Bāqir); Ṣadūq, *Amālī* 325–326 (attrib. Jaʿfar al-Ṣādiq); Ṣadūq, *Khiṣāl* 118–119 (attrib. Jaʿfar al-Ṣādiq); Muʾaddib 109; Fattāl 466 (attrib. Muḥammad al-Bāqir).
1.174.9	Ṭabrisī, *Mishkāt* 159; Quḍāʿī, *Shihāb* § 3.35 (attrib. Prophet).
1.175	Ṭabarī, *Tārīkh* 5:85.
1.176.1	Majd al-Dīn Ibn al-Athīr s.v. "ʿ-Q-L."
1.176.2	Ibn ʿAbd Rabbih 4:157; Ḥarrānī 114; Ṣadūq, *Khiṣāl* 624; Karājikī, *Kanz* 271; Zamakhsharī, *Rabīʿ* 1:463.
1.177	Kulaynī 1:98, 138; Ṣadūq, *Amālī* 423; Ṣadūq, *Tawḥīd* 109, 205, 308; Mufīd, *Ikhtiṣāṣ* 236; Mufīd, *Irshād* 1:225; Muʾaddib 543; Sibṭ 157.
1.178	Thaqafī 1:291; Ṭabarī, *Tārīkh* 5:107; Majd al-Dīn Ibn al-Athīr s.v. "T-R-K."
1.179	Thaqafī 1:336; Ṭabarī, *Tārīkh* 5:115.
1.180	Nawf al-Bikālī transmitter (Raḍī names him).
1.180.1, 4–5	None
1.180.2	Majd al-Dīn Ibn al-Athīr s.v. "D-H-M."
1.180.3	Majd al-Dīn Ibn al-Athīr s.v. "R-J-Ḥ."
1.180.6	Muʾaddib 107; Zamakhsharī, *Rabīʿ* 5:192.
1.180.7	Ibn Shahrāshūb 2:373.
1.181.1–2	None
1.181.3	Zamakhsharī, *Rabīʿ* 1:163; Majd al-Dīn Ibn al-Athīr s.v. "Y-F-N."

(cont.)

Text no.	References
1.182	Abū Hilāl, *Ṣinā'atayn* 277.
1.183.1	Hārūnī 273, 282; Ṭabrisī, *Iḥtijāj* 1:305.
1.183.2	Zamakhsharī, *Rabī'* 5:444; Ṭabrisī, *Iḥtijāj* 1:305.
1.183.3–4	Ṭabrisī, *Iḥtijāj* 1:306.
1.184.1	Kulaynī 1:138; Ḥarrānī 64; Ṣadūq, *'Uyūn* 2:136–137; Ṣadūq, *Tawḥīd* 35, 37, 38, 40, 308; Mufīd, *Amālī* 254, 256; Ṭūsī, *Amālī* 22; Ṭabrisī, *Iḥtijāj* 1:177, 219, 299.
1.184.2–4	Ṭabrisī, *Iḥtijāj* 1:302–303.
1.184.5	Thaqafī 1:173–174; Ḥarrānī 63.
1.185	Mu'addib 526, 566; Zamakhsharī, *Rabī'* 5:90; Ibn Abī al-Ḥadīd 2:49 (cites Madā'inī).
1.186	Iskāfī, *Mi'yār* 111; Ḥarrānī 184; Tha'ālibī, *I'jāz* 40–41; Mu'addib 360; Warrām 1:230.
1.187	Sulaym 2:256; 'Ayyāshī 2:305; Ṣaffār 48–49 (attrib. Ja'far al-Ṣādiq), 497; Ṣadūq, *Amālī* 196, 423–425; Tha'ālibī, *I'jāz* 41–42; Mufīd, *Ikhtiṣāṣ* 236; Ṣadūq, *'Uyūn* 1:73; Mu'ayyad al-Shīrāzī vol. 1 majlis 45, vol. 4 majlis 56; Mu'addib 360; Āmidī 80, 140; Muḥammad ibn Ṭāhir 378; Ibn Ṭāwūs, *Yaqīn* 489.
1.188	Mu'addib 158, 349, 474; Āmidī 50, 108; Ibn Abī al-Ḥadīd 3:220 (cites Ibn Nubātah).
1.189	Mu'addib 153, 518; Āmidī 87, 180, 245.
1.190	Qāṣi'ah Oration
1.190.1	Zamakhsharī, *Rabī'* 1:332; Ibn Ṭāwūs, *Yaqīn* 414, 504.
1.190.2	Thaqafī 2:396; Mu'addib 104.
1.190.3	Mu'addib 521.
1.190.4	Kulaynī 4:198; Mu'addib 88.
1.190.5	Kulaynī 4:199; Iskāfī, *Tamḥīṣ* 5; Mu'addib 19, 358.
1.190.6, 9–10	None
1.190.7–8	Mu'addib 204, 200.
1.190.11	Ṭūsī, *Talkhīṣ* 1/2:264
1.190.12	Māwardī, *A'lām* 144; Mu'addib 167; Ibn Shahrāshūb 2:28.
1.191	Oration to Hammām Sulaym 2:371–375; Ibn Qutaybah, *'Uyūn* 2:380–381; Kulaynī 2:226; Iskāfī, *Tamḥīṣ* 70–73; Ḥarrānī 159–162; Māmaṭīrī 425–427; Ṣadūq, *Amālī* 665–669; Ṣadūq, *Ṣifāt* 61; Ḥarrānī 159–161; Muwaffaq bi'llāh 71–72, 532–534;

(cont.)

Text no.	References
	Abū Nuʿaym 1:76 (attrib. ʿAlī), 2:151 (attrib. al-Ḥasan al-Baṣrī); Karājikī, *Kanz* 31–33; Fattāl 439; Ibn ʿAsākir 42:493; Warrām 2:254; Ibn Ṭalḥah 269–271; Qurṭubī 18:94; Ibn Kathīr, *Bidāyah* 8:6–7.
1.192	Muʾaddib 498; Āmidī 54, 269; Muʾayyad, *Ṭirāz* 2:160.
1.193	None
1.194	Muwaffaq biʾllāh 534; Muʾaddib 109, 146, 556; Āmidī 87.
1.195	Minqarī 224; Ṣadūq, *Man* 4:420; Mufīd, *Amālī* 234–235; Mufīd, *Kāfiyah* 24; Ṭūsī, *Amālī* 10–11; Muʾaddib 506; Āmidī 243.
1.196.1–2	Majd al-Dīn Ibn al-Athīr s.v. "A-W-R," "N-W-N"; Ibn Manẓūr s.v. "A-W-R," "N-W-N."
1.196.3–4	None
1.197	Kulaynī 5:36–38.
1.198	Iskāfī, *Miʿyār* 166; Kulaynī 2:336, 338; Nuʿmān, *Manāqib* 267.
1.199	Barqī 1:262; Thaqafī 2:584; Ibn Abī Zaynab 37; Ṭabarī-Āmulī 407; Mufīd, *Irshād* 1:276; Mufīd, *Amālī* 137; Ibn Abī Zaynab, *Ghaybah* 1:33.
1.200	Kulaynī 1:458; Mufīd, *Amālī* 281; Ṭūsī, *Amālī* 109; Fattāl 152; Irbilī 2:147; Ibn Shahrāshūb 3:139; Sibṭ 319.
1.201	Ṣadūq, *Amālī* 172; Ṣadūq, *ʿUyūn* 2:267; Mufīd, *Irshād* 1:295–296; Fattāl 442; Ṭabrisī, *Mishkāt* 468; Muʾaddib 147; Warrām 66; Sibṭ 132.
1.202	Iskāfī, *Miʿyār* 270; Māmaṭīrī 236, 420; Ṣadūq, *Amālī* 587; Tawḥīdī, *Baṣāʾir* 2:63; Mufīd, *Amālī* 198–199; Mufīd, *Irshād* 1:234; Raḍī, *Khaṣāʾiṣ* 98; Ābī 1:213; Quḍāʿī, *Dustūr* 104; Ṭabrisī, *Mishkāt* 524.
1.203	Iskāfī, *Miʿyār* 114; Ṭūsī, *Amālī* 732.
1.204	Minqarī 103; Iskāfī, *Miʿyār* 137; Abū Ḥanīfah al-Dīnawarī 165; Sibṭ 154.
1.205	Minqarī 530; Iskāfī, *Miʿyār* 151; Ṭabarī, *Tārīkh* 5:61, 7:169 (attrib. ʿAbdallāh ibn Ḥasan).
1.206	Ibn Aʿtham 3:186; Minqarī 484; Iskāfī, *Miʿyār* 175; Ibn Qutaybah, *Imāmah* 1:139; Masʿūdī, *Murūj* 2:387.
1.207.1	Iskāfī, *Miʿyār* 243; Ibn ʿAbd Rabbih 2:214; Zamakhsharī, *Rabīʿ* 1:277; Rāwandī, *Daʿawāt* 230.
1.207.2	Kulaynī 1:410; Māmaṭīrī 384; Ibn ʿAbd Rabbih 7:250.
1.208	Sulaym 2:181; Iskāfī, *Miʿyār* 301–302; Kulaynī 1:62, 2:62; Ḥarrānī 193; Ibn Abī Zaynab 76; Māmaṭīrī 229; Ṣadūq, *Khiṣāl* 255; Ṭabarī-Āmulī 231; Ṭabrisī, *Iḥtijāj* 1:393; Sibṭ 142.
1.209	Zamakhsharī, *Rabīʿ* 1:98; Majd al-Dīn Ibn al-Athīr s.v. "ʾ-Z-R."
1.210	Iskāfī, *Miʿyār* 279.

(*cont.*)

Text no.	References
1.211	None
1.212	Mu'addib 313; Ibn Ṭāwūs, *Kashf* 192.
1.213	None
1.214.1–2	Kulaynī 8:352–355.
1.215.1	Ibn Qutaybah, *Imāmah* 1:134; Thaqafī 1:308, 2:570; Mufīd, *Jamal* 92; Ṭabarī-Āmulī 416; Ibn Shahrāshūb 2:48; Ibn Ṭāwūs, *Kashf* 180.
1.215.2	Thaqafī 1:311.
1.216	Balādhurī 2:261; Mubarrad, *Kāmil* 1:174; Abū al-Faraj, *Aghānī* 18:331; Ibn 'Abd Rabbih 5:70; Bayhaqī, *Maḥāsin* 371; Māmaṭīrī 391; Sam'ānī, *Tafsīr* 3:186; Ibn 'Asākir 25:114; Majd al-Dīn Ibn al-Athīr s.v. "T-L-'"; Ibn Manẓūr s.v. "T-L-'."
1.217	Mu'addib 366; Āmidī 233.
1.218.1	Mu'ayyad, *Ṭirāz* 2:45; Muhallabī 1:141.
1.218.2, 4	None
1.218.3	Majd al-Dīn Ibn al-Athīr s.v. "S-M-J."
1.219.1	Mu'addib 157; Āmidī 81; Majd al-Dīn Ibn al-Athīr s.v. "W-Q-R"; Ibn Manẓūr s.v. "W-Q-R."
1.219.2	Mu'ayyad, *Ṭirāz* 2:159.
1.220.1	Mu'addib 203, 392, 483; Āmidī 232; Mu'ayyad, *Ṭirāz* 2:143.
1.220.2	Mu'addib 203.
1.221.1	Kulaynī 5:39; Mu'addib 506; Ṣadūq, *Amālī* 719; Zamakhsharī, *Rabī'* 3:319; Ibn Ḥamdūn 1:97; Warrām 1:197; Sibṭ 155.
1.221.2	Nu'mān, *Sharḥ* 3:241; Ibn Shahrāshūb 1:376–377; Warrām 1:157.
1.221.3	Ṣadūq, *Amālī* 722; Warrām 1:197.
1.222	Zamakhsharī, *Rabī'* 2:374; Quṭb al-Dīn Rāwandī, *Da'awāt* 133; Mu'ayyad, *Ṭirāz* 1:65.
1.223	Abū Bakr al-Dīnawarī 5:281; Abū Nu'aym 6:206 (attrib. Faḍl ibn 'Īsā al-Raqqāshī); Quḍā'ī, *Dustūr* 46; Ghazālī, *Iḥyā'* 3:212–213; Mu'addib 91, 251; Muwaffaq Khwārazmī 370; Ibn 'Asākir 42:500; Ibn al-Jawzī, *Ṣifat* 1:121; Sibṭ 122; Nuwayrī 5:253; Suyūṭī 18:103.
1.224	Ṭūsī, *Miṣbāḥ* 355–356.
1.225	Ṭabarī, *Tārīkh* 4:218; Majd al-Dīn Ibn al-Athīr s.v. "'-M-D"; Ibn Manẓūr, s.v. "'-M-D."
1.226	Mufīd, *Jamal* 144 (cites Wāqidī); Ṭabarī-Āmulī 418; Ṭabrisī, *Iḥtijāj* 1:236; Ibn Ṭāwūs, *Kashf* 181; Ibn Manẓūr s.v. "H-D-J."
1.227.1	Thaqafī 2:238–239; Mu'addib 154, 318; Āmidī 112, 113, 148; Majd al-Dīn Ibn al-Athīr s.v. "Ḥ-D-M," "Kh-L-S," "D-J-Y," "'-B-L"; Sibṭ 131–132.

(*cont.*)

Text no.	References
1.227.2	Muʾaddib 146, 334; Āmidī 213.
1.227.3	Zamakhsharī, *Rabīʿ* 5:145.
1.228	Ibn ʿAbd Rabbih 4:162; Mufīd, *Jamal* 143–144; Mufīd, *Irshād* 1:244; Ṭabrisī, *Iḥtijāj* 1:236; Ibn Abī al-Ḥadīd 1:102 (cites Abū Mikhnaf).
1.229	Ibn Shahrāshūb 1:377; Āmidī 69.
1.230	Muʾaddib 108, 173; Āmidī 82, 132; Zamakhsharī, *Rabīʿ* 1:80; Warrām 1:251, 2:74.
1.231	Dhiʿlib al-Yamānī, transmitter, through Aḥmad ibn Qutaybah, through ʿAbdallāh ibn Mālik ibn Dajnah (Raḍī names them). Zamakhsharī, *Rabīʿ* 1:326.
1.232	Zajjājī 174; Mufīd, *Amālī* 103; Ibn ʿAbd al-Barr, *Tamhīd* 2:162; Ibn Abī al-Ḥadīd 3:194 (cites Muḥammad ibn Ḥabīb).

Additional Orations:
1.233 Majd al-Dīn Ibn al-Athīr s.v. "W-Ṭ-ʾ"; Ibn Manẓūr s.v. "W-Ṭ-ʾ."
1.234 Ibn Qutaybah, *Imāmah* 1:135; Thaqafī 1:312.
1.235 Kulaynī 8:386; Ḥarrānī 227; Muʾaddib 514.
1.236 Āmidī 54; Muʾaddib 91.
1.237 Āmidī 308, 346.
1.238 Ibn ʿAbd Rabbih 5:59.

Chapter 2: Letters

Text no.	References
2.1	Ibn Qutaybah, *Imāmah* 1:86; Mufīd, *Jamal* 131–132; Ṭūsī, *Amālī* 718; Zamakhsharī, *Rabīʿ* 3:372; Ibn Shahrāshūb 2:337.
2.2	Mufīd, *Jamal* 215–216 (cites Wāqidī); Mufīd, *Kāfiyah* 28.
2.3	Māmaṭīrī 350–352; Ṣadūq, *Amālī* 388; Muwaffaq bi'llāh 557–558; Quḍāʿī, *Dustūr* 154; Fattāl 446; Sibṭ 149; Zarandī 169–171.
2.4	Sibṭ 66, 129, 157.
2.5	Minqarī 20; Ibn Qutaybah, *Imāmah* 1:111; Ibn ʿAbd Rabbih 5:78.
2.6	Sulaym 2:305; Ibn Aʿtham 2:506, 4:494; Minqarī 29; Ibn Qutaybah, *Imāmah* 1:121; Abū Ḥanīfah al-Dīnawarī 163; Ibn ʿAbd Rabbih 5:80.
2.7	Ibn Aʿtham 2:534; Minqarī 57–58; Ibn Qutaybah, *Imāmah* 1:122;

(*cont.*)

Text no.	References
	Mubarrad, *Kāmil* 1:261; Māmaṭīrī 302; Muwaffaq bi'llāh 614; Muwaffaq Khwārazmī 204.
2.8	Ibn A'tham 2:516; Minqarī 55; Ibn Qutaybah, *Imāmah* 1:116; Ibn 'Abd Rabbih 5:80.
2.9	Minqarī 85; Balādhurī 2:281; Abū Ḥanīfah al-Dīnawarī 163; Ibn 'Abd Rabbih 5:84; Muwaffaq Khwārazmī 252.
2.10	Ibn A'tham 2:536; Minqarī 109; Ibn 'Asākir 59:133; Mu'ayyad, *Ṭirāz* 1:116, 1:171, 2:153.
2.11	Minqarī 123; Iskāfī, *Mi'yār* 142; Abū Ḥanīfah al-Dīnawarī 166; Ḥarrānī 191; Majd al-Dīn Ibn al-Athīr s.v. "K-F-F"; Ibn Manẓūr s.v. "K-F-F."
2.12	Minqarī 148–149; Ibn Abī Shaybah 7:100 (§ 34499); Muwaffaq Khwārazmī 368; Mu'addib 82.
2.13	Minqarī 154; Ṭabarī, *Tārīkh* 4:567.
2.14	Ibn A'tham 3:32; Minqarī 203; Ṭabarī, *Tārīkh* 4:492, 5:10–11; Kulaynī 5:38; Mas'ūdī, *Murūj* 2:359.
2.15	Minqarī 230, 477; Mufīd, *Jamal* 182.
2.16	Minqarī 215; Kulaynī 5:41; Nu'mān, *Sharḥ* 2:155, 531; Mu'addib 505, 530.
2.17	Sulaym 2:337; Ibn A'tham 3:154–155; Minqarī 150, 471; Ibn Qutaybah, *Imāmah* 1:104; Abū Ḥanīfah al-Dīnawarī 187; Mas'ūdī, *Murūj* 3:23; Māmaṭīrī 259; Karājikī, *Kanz* 201; Bayhaqī, *Maḥāsin* 53; Muwaffaq Khwārazmī 256; Ibn Shahrāshūb 2:361.
2.18	Māmaṭīrī 352–353; Bāqillānī 68; Mu'ayyad, *Ṭirāz* 1:114, 210, 416.
2.19	Balādhurī 2:161; Ya'qūbī 2:203; Māmaṭīrī 258.
2.20	Balādhurī 2:162; Ya'qūbī 2:204; Bayhaqī, *Maḥāsin* 449; Mu'ayyad, *Ṭirāz* 1:197.
2.21	Balādhurī 2:164–165; Mu'addib 359.
2.22	Minqarī 107; Balādhurī 2:116–117; Ya'qūbī 2:205; Tha'lab 155; Kulaynī 8:240; Ibn Durayd, *Amālī* 149; Ibn 'Abd Rabbih 3:84; Naḥḥās 377; Ḥarrānī 200; Qālī, *Amālī* 2:94; Māmaṭīrī 220; Makkī 1:138; Bāqillānī 146; Raḍī, *Khaṣā'iṣ* 95; Quḍā'ī, *Dustūr* 106; Mu'addib 155, 525; Rāghib, *Muḥāḍarāt* 2:416; Ghazālī, *Iḥyā'* 4:402; Ibn 'Asākir 42:503; Ḍiyā' Ibn al-Athīr 1:275; Sibṭ 150; Ibn Ṭalḥah 272; Muwaffaq Khwārazmī 374; Mu'ayyad, *Ṭirāz* 2:192.
2.23	Ibn Abī al-Dunyā, *Maqtal* 56; Kulaynī 1:299; Mas'ūdī, *Ithbāt* 103; Mas'ūdī, *Murūj* 2:418; Ṭabarānī, *Mu'jam kabīr* 1:96; Raḍī, *Khaṣā'iṣ* 108; Ibn 'Asākir 42:562.

(*cont.*)

Text no.	References
2.24	Ibn Shabbah 1:226; Kulaynī 7:49–52; Nuʿmān, *Daʿāʾim* 2:342; Ṭūsī, *Tahdhīb* 9:148.
2.25.1	Thaqafī 1:125; Kulaynī 3:536; Mufīd, *Muqniʿah* 255; Thaʿālibī, *Shakwā* 115; Zamakhsharī, *Rabīʿ* 3:395; Quṭb al-Dīn Rāwandī, *Fiqh* 1:235.
2.25.2	Mufīd, *Muqniʿah* 255; Quṭb al-Dīn Rāwandī, *Fiqh* 1:235,
2.25.3	Thaqafī 1:129–130; Ṭūsī, *Tahdhīb* 4:97.
2.26.1	Muʾaddib 440.
2.26.2	Nuʿmān, *Daʿāʾim* 1:252.
2.27.1	Ḥarrānī 177; Māmaṭīrī 268; Muwaffaq bi'llāh 562; Warrām 1:80.
2.27.2	Thaqafī 1:235; Māmaṭīrī 269; Mufīd, *Amālī* 263; Muwaffaq bi'llāh 563–564; Ṭūsī, *Amālī* 26; Warrām 1:80.
2.27.3	Thaqafī 2:238–239; Māmaṭīrī 270–271; Mufīd, *Amālī* 266; Hārūnī 265; Muwaffaq bi'llāh 564–565; Ibn Ḥamdūn 1:81; Ṭūsī, *Amālī* 29; Muʾaddib 174.
2.27.4	Māmaṭīrī 275; Mufīd, *Amālī* 266; Muwaffaq bi'llāh 568; Ṭūsī, *Amālī* 29.
2.27.5	Thaqafī 1:248; Muwaffaq bi'llāh 570.
2.28.1	Ibn Aʿtham 2:560; Nuwayrī 7:233.
2.28.2	Ṭabrisī, *Iḥtijāj* 1:258–259; Nuwayrī 7:233; Qalqashandī 1:275.
2.28.3	Abū al-Ṣalāḥ 23; Nuwayrī 7:236; Qalqashandī 1:276.
2.28.4	Ṭabrisī, *Iḥtijāj* 1:262; Nuwayrī 7:236; Qalqashandī 1:276.
2.28.5	Ibn Aʿtham 2:561; Ibn Shahrāshūb 2:351; Nuwayrī 7:236; Qalqashandī 1:276–277.
2.29	Thaqafī 2:403.
2.30	Muʾayyad, *Ṭirāz* 2:66.
2.31	Testament of Counsel for al-Ḥasan
2.31.1	Ibn ʿAbd Rabbih 3:100; Ḥarrānī 68; Māmaṭīrī 201; Raḍī, *Khaṣāʾiṣ* 118; Hārūnī 130; Muwaffaq bi'llāh 540; Muʾaddib 505; Ibn Ṭāwūs, *Kashf* 159 (cites Kulaynī and Abū Hilāl).
2.31.2	Ḥarrānī 68; Ibn ʿAbd Rabbih 3:100; Māmaṭīrī 201–202; Hārūnī 130–131; Muwaffaq bi'llāh 541; Ibn Ṭāwūs, *Kashf* 160.
2.31.3	Ibn ʿAbd Rabbih 3:100; Ḥarrānī 69; Māmaṭīrī 202–203; Hārūnī 131; Muwaffaq bi'llāh 541; Muʾaddib 79; Ibn Ṭāwūs, *Kashf* 160.
2.31.4	Ḥulwānī 58; Ibn ʿAbd Rabbih 4:166; Ḥarrānī 70; Raḍī, *Khaṣāʾiṣ* 116; Ibn Ṭāwūs, *Kashf* 161.
2.31.5–6	Ḥarrānī 70–71; Ibn Ṭāwūs, *Kashf* 161–162.
2.31.7	Ḥarrānī 72.

(cont.)

Text no.	References
2.31.8	Ḥarrānī 71.
2.31.9	Ḥarrānī 72; Muʾaddib 416.
2.31.10	Ḥarrānī 73; Ibn Ṭāwūs, *Kashf* 163.
2.31.11	Ḥarrānī 74; Māmaṭīrī 211; Quḍāʿī, *Dustūr* 22; Muʾaddib 79, 136.
2.31.12	Ḥarrānī 74; Ṣadūq, *Man* 4:389; Māmaṭīrī 203; Raḍī, *Khaṣāʾiṣ* 116; Hārūnī 131; Muwaffaq biʾllāh 542–543; Muʾaddib 137, 331; Quṭb al-Dīn Rāwandī, *Daʿawāt* 238; Ibn ʿAṭiyyah 5:12 (attrib. Prophet); Gharnāṭī 9:300 (attrib. Prophet).
2.31.13	Māmaṭīrī 203–204; Hārūnī 133; Muwaffaq biʾllāh 543; Ibn Ṭāwūs, *Kashf* 165.
2.31.14	Ḥarrānī 76; Māmaṭīrī 204; Hārūnī 133; Muwaffaq biʾllāh 544; Warrām 2:346; Ibn Ṭāwūs, *Kashf* 165.
2.31.15	Ḥarrānī 76; Māmaṭīrī 204; Hārūnī 133; Muwaffaq biʾllāh 544–545; Muʾaddib 155; Warrām 1:246; Ibn Ṭāwūs, *Kashf* 166.
2.31.16	Ḥarrānī 77; Māmaṭīrī 204; Muwaffaq biʾllāh 545–546; Quḍāʿī, *Dustūr* 26; Muʾaddib 80, 171, 526; Ibn ʿAsākir 66:347; Ibn Ṭāwūs, *Kashf* 166.
2.31.17	Ḥulwānī 59; Jāḥiẓ, *Miʾat* 226, 228; ʿIjlī 2:43 (attrib. anon., quoted by Ibn al-ʿAbbās); Kulaynī 8:24; Ḥarrānī 79; Māmaṭīrī 205; Raḍī, *Khaṣāʾiṣ* 117; Hārūnī 132; Muwaffaq biʾllāh 546–547; Quḍāʿī, *Dustūr* 8, 12, 18, 22, 32, 38, 76, 86; Muʾaddib 30, 34, 50, 59, 69, 95, 96, 136, 143, 191, 193, 233, 275, 284, 285, 369, 323, 402, 472, 486, 538; Ibn Ṭāwūs, *Kashf* 167, 172.
2.31.18	Ḥulwānī 59; Ibn ʿAbd Rabbih 3:160; Ḥarrānī 81, 205; Māmaṭīrī 205–206; Ṣadūq, *Man* 4:390, 392; Raḍī, *Khaṣāʾiṣ* 117; Muwaffaq biʾllāh 548; Karājikī, *Kanz* 34, 57; Quḍāʿī, *Dustūr* 83, 85; Ṭabrisī, *Mishkāt* 188 (attrib. Mūsā Kāẓim); Muʾaddib 79, 162, 242, 419, 524, 525, 526; Ibn ʿAsākir 29:180 (attrib. ʿAbdallāh ibn Ṣāliḥ, governor of the frontier towns under Rashīd); Warrām 1:187, 2:348; Ibn Ṭalḥah 276; Ibn Ṭāwūs, *Kashf* 167, 169; Dhahabī, *Tārīkh* 12:210 (attrib. ʿAbdallāh ibn Ṣāliḥ).
2.31.19	Ḥulwānī 59; Kulaynī 8:24; Ḥarrānī 83, 86, 98; Māmaṭīrī 206; Makkī 2:26; Ṣadūq, *Hidāyah* 314; Ṣadūq, *Man* 4:386, 390, 391; Ṣadūq, *Tawḥīd* 372; Raḍī, *Khaṣāʾiṣ* 117; al-Hārūnī 131–132; Muwaffaq biʾllāh 548–550; Karājikī, *Kanz* 88, 283; Quḍāʿī, *Dustūr* 8, 9, 20–22, 30, 31, 34, 40; Muʾaddib 45, 50, 69, 79, 84, 115, 266, 284, 367, 372, 441, 444, 462; 525, 555; Warrām 2:349; Ibn Ṭāwūs, *Kashf* 169.

(*cont.*)

Text no.	References
2.31.20	Ḥulwānī 60; Kulaynī 5:338, 510; Ḥarrānī 86; Muwaffaq bi'llāh 550; Quḍāʿī, *Dustūr* 86; Muʾaddib 100; Ibn Ṭāwūs, *Kashf* 171; Ibn Manẓūr s.v. "ʾ-F-N."
2.31.21	Ḥarrānī 87; Muwaffaq bi'llāh 550; Ibn Ṭāwūs, *Kashf* 173.
2.31.22	Ḥarrānī 88; Muwaffaq bi'llāh 551.
2.32	Iskāfī, *Miʿyār* 138.
2.33	Thaqafī 2:509; Ibn Aʿtham 4:222.
2.34	Balādhurī 2:400; Thaqafī 1:269, 2:368; Ṭabarī, *Tārīkh* 5:96–97; Māmaṭīrī 286; Muʾayyad, *Ṭirāz* 2:154.
2.35	Thaqafī 1:299; Ṭabarī, *Tārīkh* 5:109; ʿIzz al-Dīn Ibn al-Athīr, *Kāmil* 2:710.
2.36	Iskāfī, *Miʿyār* 180; Ibn Qutaybah, *Imāmah* 1:75; Thaqafī 2:432; Abū al-Faraj, *Aghānī* 16:289; Māmaṭīrī 296–297; Hārūnī 104–105.
2.37	Ṭabrisī, *Iḥtijāj* 1:264
2.38	Thaqafī 1:267–269; Yaʿqūbī 2:194; Ṭabarī, *Tārīkh* 5:96; Māmaṭīrī 283; Mufīd, *Amālī* 81; Mufīd, *Ikhtiṣāṣ* 80; Najāshī 203; Ibn ʿAsākir 56:390.
2.39	Ṭabrisī, *Iḥtijāj* 1:267–268; Ibn Abī al-Ḥadīd 4:61 (cites Minqarī).
2.40	Balādhurī 2:170; Ibn ʿAbd Rabbih 5:103.
2.41	Balādhurī 2:174; Ibn Qutaybah, *Gharīb* 1:376; Ibn Qutaybah, *ʿUyūn* 1:94; Ibn ʿAbd Rabbih 5:106; Māmaṭīrī 299; Kashshī 58; Maydānī 2:101; Sibṭ 151.
2.42	Balādhurī 2:158; Yaʿqūbī 2:201.
2.43	Balādhurī 2:170; Yaʿqūbī 2:201.
2.44	Zamakhsharī, *Rabīʿ* 4:281.
2.45.1–2	Zamakhsharī, *Rabīʿ* 3:241; Warrām 2:506.
2.45.3	None
2.45.4	Ṣadūq, *Amālī* 604; Fattāl 127; Ibn Shahrāshūb 1:355.
2.45.5	Warrām 2:172; Muʾayyad al-Shīrāzī vol. 4 majlis 99.
2.46	Balādhurī 2:398; Thaqafī 1:257–258; Ṭabarī, *Tārīkh* 5:95; Māmaṭīrī 282; Mufīd, *Amālī* 80.
2.47.1	Sulaym 2:446; Iskāfī, *Miʿyār* 245; Ṭabarī, *Tārīkh* 5:147; Kulaynī 7:51; Nuʿmān, *Sharḥ* 2:447; Ḥarrānī 198; Zajjājī 112; Masʿūdī, *Murūj* 2:408; Abū al-Faraj, *Maqātil* 51–52; Ṭabarānī, *Muʿjam kabīr* 1:101; Māmaṭīrī 375; Ṣadūq, *Man* 4:190; Hārūnī 126, 128–129; Muwaffaq bi'llāh 315–316, 5-572 73; Fattāl 136; Muwaffaq Khwārazmī 384; ʿIzz al-Dīn Ibn al-Athīr, *Kāmil* 2:741.
2.47.2	Iskāfī, *Miʿyār* 246; Kulaynī 7:51; Nuʿmān, *Sharḥ* 2:449; Ḥarrānī 198; Abū

(*cont.*)

Text no.	References
	al-Faraj, *Maqātil* 48; Ṭabarānī, *Muʿjam kabīr* 1:101; Ṣadūq, *Man* 4:191; Muwaffaq Khwārazmī 386; Fattāl 136; Ibn Shahrāshūb 3:95; ʿIzz al-Dīn Ibn al-Athīr, *Kāmil* 2:740.
2.48	Ibn Aʿtham 3:191; Minqarī 493.
2.49	Ibn Aʿtham 3:192; Minqarī 110, 498; Iskāfī, *Miʿyār* 103; Abū Ḥanīfah al-Dīnawarī 163, 191; Warrām 2:172.
2.50	Minqarī 107; Iskāfī, *Miʿyār* 103; Ṭūsī, *Amālī* 217.
2.51	Minqarī 108, 132; Iskāfī, *Miʿyār* 122.
2.52	Thaʿālibī, *Iʿjāz* 42.
2.53	The Testament of Ashtar Ḥarrānī 126–148; Nuʿmān, *Daʿāʾim* 1:353–367 (attrib. either ʿAlī or Prophet, Ashtar not mentioned; omits §2.53.15–19, 21–24); Ibn Ḥamdūn 1:316–327; Nuwayrī 6:19–32; and:
2.53.3	as in §2.53 above, and Muʾaddib 137.
2.53.5	as in §2.53 above, Warrām 1:215, 2:125; and Ibn Manẓūr s.v. "Gh-B-Y."
2.53.7	as in §2.53 above, and Quḍāʿī, *Dustūr* 166.
2.53.16–18	as in §2.53 above, and Raḍī, *Khaṣāʾiṣ* 122, 123.
2.53.17	as in §2.53 above, and Raḍī, *Khaṣāʾiṣ* 122; Ibn ʿAsākir 42:516; Ibn Kathīr, *Bidāyah* 8:8.
2.54	Ibn Aʿtham 2:465; Iskāfī, *Maqāmāt*, lost (Raḍī's stated source); Ibn Qutaybah, *Imāmah* 1:66; Muʾayyad, *Ṭirāz* 2:154.
2.55	Ibn Aʿtham 4:225; Iskāfī, *Miʿyār* 137–138; Āmidī 56, 119; Muʾaddib 148; Muʾayyad, *Ṭirāz* 2:153.
2.56	Minqarī 121; Iskāfī, *Miʿyār* 140; Ḥarrānī 191; Muʾaddib 393.
2.57	Ṭabarī, *Tārīkh* 4:500.
2.58	None
2.59	Minqarī 106; Muʾayyad, *Ṭirāz* 1:89.
2.60	Minqarī 125; Māmaṭīrī 298; Muwaffaq biʾllāh 613; Majd al-Dīn Ibn al-Athīr s.v. "Sh-Dh-Y"; Ibn Manẓūr s.v. "Sh-Dh-Y."
2.61	Balādhurī 2:473; Muʾayyad, *Ṭirāz* 1:89.
2.62.1	Ibn Qutaybah, *Imāmah* 1:133; Thaqafī 1:303–305; Ṭabarī-Āmulī 411.
2.62.2	None
2.63	None
2.64	Ibn Aʿtham 2:506; Minqarī 29; Ibn Qutaybah, *Imāmah* 1:100–101; Ṭabrisī, *Iḥtijāj* 1:263–264; Ibn ʿAsākir 59:128.
2.65	None

(*cont.*)

Text no.	References
2.66	This epistle is similar to epistle § 2.22. See sources there.
2.67	Ṭabarī, *Tārīkh* 5:132; Quṭb al-Dīn Rāwandī, *Fiqh* 1:327.
2.68	Ḥulwānī 55; Kulaynī 2:136; Ḥarrānī 396; Raḍī, *Khaṣāʾiṣ* 101; Hārūnī 506; Muwaffaq biʾllāh 537; Mufīd, *Irshād* 1:233; Quḍāʿī, *Dustūr* 46; Ghazālī, *Iḥyāʾ* 3:212–213; Fattāl 441; Warrām 2:562.
2.69	Muʾaddib 84, 85, 96, 98, 99 203, 504, 528.
2.70	Balādhurī 2:157; Yaʿqūbī 2:203; Raḍī, *Khaṣāʾiṣ* 113.
2.71	Balādhurī 2:163; Yaʿqūbī 2:203–204.
2.72	Karājikī, *Kanz* 16; Muʾaddib 21.
2.73	Muʾayyad, *Ṭirāz* 2:154.
2.74	Ibn al-Kalbī's transcribed document, lost (Raḍī's stated source).
2.75	Wāqidī, *Jamal*, lost (Raḍī's stated source).
2.76	Ibn Qutaybah, *Imāmah* 1:105; Mufīd, *Jamal* 223–224; Muʾayyad, *Ṭirāz* 2:153; Warrām 2:171.
2.77	Majd al-Dīn Ibn al-Athīr s.v. "Ḥ-M-M."
2.78	Saʿīd ibn Yaḥyā al-Umawī, *Maghāzī*, from his father, after Ibn Isḥāq, lost (Raḍī's stated source).

Additional Letter

2.79	Ibn ʿAbd al-Barr, *Bahjah* 583.

Chapter 3: Sayings

Text no.	References
3.1	Jāḥiẓ, *Bayān* 2:97 (attrib. Ḥudhayfah [ibn al-Yamān?]); Tawḥīdī, *Imtāʿ* 179; Āmidī 246.
3.2	Ḥarrānī 201–202; Ḥuṣrī 1:80; Muʾaddib 449; Warrām 1:128.
3.3	Muʾaddib 88; Āmidī 70.
3.4	Masʿūdī 3:416; Quḍāʿī, *Dustūr* 29; Āmidī 142.
3.5	Ṣadūq, *Man* 4:387; Ṭūsī, *Amālī* 595; Muʾaddib 242; Sibṭ 142.
3.6	Jāḥiẓ, *Miʾat* 232; Māmaṭīrī 212; Muwaffaq biʾllāh 535; Ḥuṣrī 1:81; Rāghib, *Muḥāḍarāt* 1:282; Ibn Munqidh 335; Nuwayrī 3:258.

(*cont.*)

Text no.	References
3.7	Qālī, *Dhayl* 110.
3.8	Iskāfī, *Miʿyār* 52; Minqarī 449 (attrib. al-Nuʿmān ibn Bashīr); Ibn Qutaybah, *Imāmah* 1:130 (attrib. al-Nuʿmān ibn Bashīr); Muʾaddib 243; Ibn ʿAbd al-Barr, *Istīʿāb* 2:610, 3:1121.
3.9	Jāḥiẓ, *Miʾat* 232; Quḍāʿī, *Dustūr* 26; Fattāl 483; Āmidī 141; Zamakhsharī, *Rabīʿ* 5:276; Ibn al-ʿArabī 1:318.
3.10	Maydānī 2:318, 453.
3.11	Mufīd, *Jamal* 46 (cites Abū Mikhnaf); Muʾaddib 476; Āmidī 307.
3.12	Ḥarrānī 223; Mufīd, *Irshād* 1:302; Quḍāʿī, *Dustūr* 16; Muʾaddib 202.
3.13	Ibn al-Muʿtazz 77; Ḥarrānī 13; Bāqillānī 68, 91; Zamakhsharī, *Rabīʿ* 4:419.
3.14	Jāḥiẓ, *Miʾat* 232; Quḍāʿī, *Dustūr* 34; Muʾaddib 436; Fattāl 490.
3.15	Ibn Qutaybah, *ʿUyūn* 2:518 (attrib. Prophet); Bayhaqī, *Sunan* 8:279, 465, 579, 580 (attrib. Prophet); Muʾaddib 87; Āmidī 70.
3.16	Ḥulwānī 42; Ibn Qutaybah, *ʿUyūn* 2:148; Balādhurī 2:115; Ibn ʿAbd Rabbih 1:42, 90, 2:254; Qālī, *Amālī* 2:94; Māmaṭīrī 325; Quḍāʿī, *Dustūr* 16; Ibn ʿAbd al-Barr, *Jāmiʿ* 1:383; Ḥarrānī 201; Muʾaddib 371; Ibn ʿAsākir 51:264.
3.17	Ibn Aʿtham 2:332; Ibn Qutaybah, *Gharīb al-ḥadīth* 1:138; Ṭabarī, *Tārīkh* 4:236; Māmaṭīrī 327; Azharī s.v. "ʿ-J-Z"; Harawī s.v. "ʿ-J-Z"; Muʾaddib 42; Zamakhsharī, *Fāʾiq* s.v. "ʿ-J-Z"; Ibn ʿAsākir 42:431; Majd al-Dīn Ibn al-Athīr s.v. "ʿ-J-Z."
3.18	Ibn Ḥanbal, *Musnad* 2:252 (attrib. Prophet); Ibn ʿAbd Rabbih 2:148 (attrib. Prophet); Āmidī 272; Rāzī, *Mafātīḥ* 3:573 (attrib. Prophet).
3.19	Tawḥīdī, *Baṣāʾir* 1:117; Quḍāʿī, *Dustūr* 29; Muʾaddib 469; Warrām 1:235; Sibṭ 132.
3.20	Muʾaddib 550; Fattāl 473; Āmidī 139; Ṭabrisī, *Majmaʿ* 4:55; Sibṭ 132; Dhahabī, *Tārīkh* 8:443.
3.21	Jāḥiẓ, *Miʾat* 323; Quḍāʿī, *Dustūr* 26, 222; Khaṭīb, *Tārīkh* 11:246 (attrib. Abbasid caliph Manṣūr); Ibn Kathīr, *Bidāyah* 10:76 (attrib. Abbasid caliph Manṣūr).
3.22	Muʾaddib 75; Āmidī 62.
3.23	Quḍāʿī, *Dustūr* 20; Muʾaddib 119; Sibṭ 136.
3.24	Quḍāʿī, *Dustūr* 22; Muʾaddib 132; Fattāl 490; Āmidī 142; Sibṭ 132.
3.25	Fattāl 490.
3.26	Sulaym 2:176; ʿAdanī 118; Thaqafī 1:135–138; Yaʿqūbī 2:207; Ḥarrānī 126; Kulaynī 2:50, 391; Māmaṭīrī 198–199, 225–227; Muwaffaq biʾllāh 48 (attrib. Prophet), 71; Makkī 1:418; Ṣadūq, *Khiṣāl* 231; Mufīd, *Amālī* 275;

(*cont.*)

Text no.	References
	Abū Nuʿaym 1:74; Quḍāʿī, *Dustūr* 134; Fattāl 43; Ṭabrisī, *Mishkāt* 43, 84; Muwaffaq Khwārazmī 372; Ibn ʿAsākir 3:288; Suyūṭī (after Ibn Abī al-Dunyā and others), *Jamʿ* 17:616–619, 18:109–110, 213–214, 385.
3.27	Ḥarrānī 57; Muʾaddib 358.
3.28	Muʾaddib 393; Fattāl 384; Ṭabrisī, *Mishkāt* 408.
3.29	Kulaynī 8:23; Ḥarrānī 97; Ṣadūq, *Man* 4:389; Muʾaddib 114.
3.30	Ḥarrānī 97; Muʾaddib 435; Ibn ʿAsākir 24:337; Muḥammad al-Waṭwāṭ 134; Dhahabī, *Siyar* 4:93.
3.31	Kulaynī 3:259; Ḥarrānī 211; Kūfī 81; Ṣadūq, *Khiṣāl* 15; Muʾaddib 479; Muwaffaq Khwārazmī 377; Maydānī 2:455; Rāwandī, *Daʿawāt* 236; Ṭabrisī, *Mishkāt* 525; Sibṭ 132; Warrām 78.
3.32	Minqarī 144.
3.33	Jāḥiẓ, *Miʾat* 230; Māmaṭīrī 182–183; Hārūnī 563; Muwaffaq biʾllāh 551–552; Quḍāʿī, *Dustūr* 86; Zamakhsharī, *Rabīʿ* 1:405; Ibn ʿAsākir 42:561.
3.34	Muʾaddib 533; Āmidī 345; Ṭabrisī, *Iḥtijāj* 3:53.
3.35	Jāḥiẓ, *Miʾat* 230, 232; Muʾaddib 419; Muwaffaq Khwārazmī 377.
3.36	Minqarī 529; Iskāfī, *Miʿyār* 193; Ṭabarī, *Tārīkh* 5:60; ʿAyyāshī 2:104; Abū Hilāl, *Furūq* 18; Ṭūsī, *Amālī* 602; ʿIzz al-Dīn Ibn al-Athīr, *Kāmil* 2:674.
3.37	Minqarī 530; Ṭabarī, *Tārīkh* 5:61; Ibn ʿAbd Rabbih 3:195; Ṭabarānī, *Muʿjam kabīr* 4:56.
3.38	Thaqafī 1:43; Kulaynī, *Kāfī* 8:268; Furāt 482; ʿImād al-Dīn al-Ṭabarī 130, 172; Ṭūsī, *Amālī* 206; Ṭabrisī, *Mishkāt* 151; Fattāl 295.
3.39	Ibn ʿAbd Rabbih 3:167 (unattrib.); Ṭabrisī, *Mishkāt* 539; Sibṭ 132.
3.40	Āmidī 199, 202, 235; Maydānī 2:455; Ṭarṭūshī 199; Ibn Ṭalḥah 281.
3.41	Muʾaddib 36; Shahrastānī, *Milal* 2:140; Nuwayrī 6:82.
3.42	Jāḥiẓ, *Bayān* 3:169 (attrib. Ardashīr); Ibn ʿAbd Rabbih 2:200 (attrib. Kisrā).
3.43	Muʾaddib 372; Zamakhsharī, *Rabīʿ* 1:397; Ṭarṭūshī 203.
3.44	Muʾaddib 339; Zamakhsharī, *Rabīʿ* 1:432.
3.45	Ṣadūq, *Amālī* 73; Ṣadūq, *Maʿānī* 196; Ṣadūq, *Man* 4:396; Ibn ʿAbd al-Barr, *Adab* 117; Muʾaddib 120; Ibn ʿAsākir 16:114 (attrib. Khālid ibn Ṣafwān); Nuwayrī 3:258.
3.46	Māwardī, *Adab* 188; Zamakhsharī, *Rabīʿ* 4:380; Ibn ʿAsākir 42:517.
3.47	Fattāl 4; Ṭabrisī, *Mishkāt* 437.
3:48	Kulaynī 2:90; Ḥarrānī 216; Ṣadūq, *Man* 1:187; Āmidī 51; Ṭabrisī, *Mishkāt* 58; Warrām 1:93.

(cont.)

Text no.	References
3.49	Mu'addib 28; Fattāl, *'Uyūn* 454; Āmidī 33; Ṭabrisī, *Mishkāt* 228.
3.50	Ḥarrānī 100; Raḍī, *Khaṣā'iṣ* 152; Fattāl 454 (attrib. Prophet); Ṭabrisī, *Mishkāt* 228 (attrib. 'Alī), 233 (attrib. Prophet).
3.51	Mu'addib 25; Maydānī 2:455; Ibn al-'Arabī 1:293; Ibn Ṭalḥah 281.
3.52	Mu'addib 430; Āmidī 269; Ṭarṭūshī 203.
3.53	Ṣadūq, *Man* 4:388; Mufīd, *Ikhtiṣāṣ* 229; Mu'addib 46.
3.54	Ābī 1:222.
3.55	Jāḥiẓ, *Mi'at* 224; Mu'addib 28; Muwaffaq Khwārazmī 375 (cites Jāḥiẓ).
3.56	Mu'addib 71, 127; Ḥuṣrī 3:826 (attrib. Ibn al-Mu'tazz).
3.57	Mu'addib 358; Maydānī 2:83 (attrib. anon); Dhahabī, *Siyar* 4:396 (attrib. 'Alī ibn al-Ḥusayn); Ibn Kathīr, *Bidāyah* 9:132 (attrib. 'Alī ibn al-Ḥusayn).
3.58	Ḥarrānī 359; Āmidī 228.
3.59	Ṭabrisī, *Mishkāt* 408; Āmidī 234; Zamakhsharī, *Rabī'* 4:369; Nuwayrī 3:204 (attrib. Ja'far al-Ṣādiq).
3.60	Ḥarrānī 90; Mufīd, *Irshād* 1:300; Quḍā'ī, *Dustūr* 14; Mu'addib 69; Ibn Ṭalḥah 280.
3.61	Mu'addib 135; Āmidī 140.
3.62	Āmidī 40; Majd al-Dīn Ibn al-Athīr s.v. "F-R-Ṭ"; Ibn al-'Arabī 1:86.
3.63	Jāḥiẓ, *Mi'at* 226; Mu'addib 1:134; Zamakhsharī, *Rabī'* 2:122; Maydānī 2:454; Ibn Ṭalḥah 281.
3.64	Mu'addib 22; Āmidī 42; Sibṭ 133.
3.65	Zamakhsharī, *Rabī'* 4:21.
3.66	Mu'addib 497; Warrām 2:370.
3.67	Mu'addib 376; Āmidī 322.
3.68	Sulaym 2:335; Ibn A'tham 3:171; Minqarī 476; Mu'addib 141.
3.69	Nu'mān, *Sharḥ* 2:391; Mas'ūdī, *Murūj* 3:415; Ṣadūq, *Amālī* 724; Kūfī 2:52; Abū Nu'aym 1:85; Karājikī, *Kanz* 270; Ḥuṣrī 1:78; Ibn 'Abd al-Barr, *Istī'āb* 3:1108; Mu'ayyad al-Shīrāzī vol. 1 majlis 40; Mu'addib 556; Fattāl 441; Ṭabrisī, *Mishkāt* 467; Ibn 'Asākir 24:402; Warrām 1:253, 2:75; Sibṭ 119; Irbilī 1:72.
3.70	Ibn A'tham 4:217; Kulaynī 1:155; Ḥarrānī 467; Ṣadūq, *Tawḥīd* 380; Ṣadūq, *'Uyūn* 2:127; Mufīd, *Irshād* 1:225; Karājikī, *Kanz* 169; Ṭabrisī, *Iḥtijāj* 1:310.
3.71	Ḥulwānī 42; Jāḥiẓ, *Bayān* 2:285; Jāḥiẓ, *Mi'at* 228; Ibn Qutaybah, *Gharīb* 1:376; Ibn Qutaybah, *'Uyūn* 2:148; Ḥarrānī 201; Ibn 'Abd Rabbih 2:116; Mas'ūdī, *Murūj* 4:77; Qālī, *Amālī* 1:194 (attrib. Mu'āwiyah); Māmaṭīrī 325–326; Ṭūsī, *Amālī* 625; Raḍī, *Khaṣā'iṣ* 94; Muwaffaq bi'llāh 45;

(cont.)

Text no.	References

	Warrām 1:256; Majd al-Dīn Ibn al-Athīr s.v. "L-J-L-J"; Muḥammad al-Waṭwāṭ 57.
3.72	Jāḥiẓ, *Bayān* 1:83, 2:77; Jāḥiẓ, *Mi'at* 222; Ibn Qutaybah, *'Uyūn* 2:144; Balādhurī, *Ansāb* 2:115; Ya'qūbī 2:206; Mubarrad, *Fāḍil* 2; Ibn 'Abd Rabbih 2:79, 128, 3:14, 4:288; Abū Hilāl, *Dīwān* 1:146; Māmaṭīrī 151; Ṣadūq, *Amālī* 532; Ṣadūq, *Khiṣāl* 420; Ṣadūq, *'Uyūn* 1:58; Ḥarrānī 201; Bāqillānī 68; Raḍī, *Khaṣā'iṣ* 95; Mufīd, *Irshād* 1:300; Tha'ālibī, *Tafsīr* 1:533; Muwaffaq bi'llāh 297; Karājikī, *Kanz* 147; Fattāl 109; Muwaffaq Khwārazmī 375; Ibn Shahrāshūb 1:326.
3.73	Ḥulwānī 51; Jāḥiẓ, *Bayān* 2:77; Barqī 1:229; Ibn Qutaybah, *'Uyūn* 2:143; Ya'qūbī 2:206; Kulaynī 2:89; Ibn 'Abd Rabbih 3:90, 4:169; Māmaṭīrī 154–157; Nu'mān, *Da'ā'im*, 1:80; Ḥarrānī 218; Ṣadūq, *Khiṣāl* 315; Ṣadūq, *'Uyūn* 1:48; Raḍī, *Khaṣā'iṣ* 94; Mufīd, *Irshād* 1:297; Hārūnī 211; Ṭūsī, *Tibyān* 6:470; Abū Nu'aym 1:75; Māwardī, *Adab* 58; Fattāl 422; Muwaffaq Khwārazmī 374; Ibn 'Asākir 41:198; Sibṭ 140.
3.74	Jāḥiẓ, *Bayān* 2:77, 200; Ibn Qutaybah, *'Uyūn* 1:396; Balādhurī 2:188; 'Alī al-Ḥimyarī 64; Māmaṭīrī 244; Muwaffaq bi'llāh 587; Murtaḍā, *Amālī* 1:274; Rāghib, *Muḥāḍarāt* 1:453; Maydānī 1:53; Rāzī, *Mafātīḥ* 2:364. Muḥammad al-Waṭwāṭ 57; Ibn Kathīr, *Bidāyah* 8:7; Ibn Rifā'ah 1:70.
3.75	Jāḥiẓ, *Bayān* 2:316; Ibn Qutaybah, *'Uyūn* 1:201; Ibn 'Abd Rabbih 1:94, 4:288; Raḍī, *Khaṣā'iṣ* 95; Mu'addib 196.
3.76	Jāḥiẓ, *Bayān* 1:398, 2:90 (attrib. Ibn 'Abbās); Ibn 'Abd Rabbih 2:85 (attrib. Mālik ibn Anas); Makkī 1:172 (attrib. anon. scholar); Ibn 'Abd al-Barr, *Jāmi'* 2:838 (attrib. Ibn 'Abbās).
3.77	Abū 'Ubayd, *Amthāl* 108; Jāḥiẓ, *Bayān* 2:14; Jāḥiẓ, *Rasā'il* 1:273; Ibn 'Abd Rabbih, 1:59, 2:104, 4:288; Abū Hilāl, *Jamharah* 1:502; Raḍī, *Khaṣā'iṣ* 95; Bayhaqī, *Sunan* 10:193; Maydānī 1:292; Ibn Rifā'ah 1:140.
3.78	Ibn Qutaybah, *'Uyūn* 2:401; Mubarrad, *Kāmil* 1:240; Ibn 'Abd Rabbih 3:130; Abū Bakr al-Dīnawarī 4:49 (§ 1207); Māmaṭīrī 395; Ṭūsī, *Amālī* 88; Mu'addib 331; Rāghib, *Muḥāḍarāt* 2:419; Ghazālī, *Iḥyā'* 1:313; Ṭabrisī, *Makārim* 313.
3.79	Muḥammad al-Bāqir, transmitter (Raḍī names him); Fattāl 2:478; Ṭabrisī, *Majma'* 4:461; Rāzī, *Mafātīḥ* 15:480 (attrib. Ibn 'Abbās); Ibn al-'Arabī 1:279.
3.80	Barqī 1:29; Kulaynī 8:307; Ṣadūq, *Amālī* 87; Ṣadūq, *Khiṣāl* 129; Ṣadūq, *Man* 4:396.

(*cont.*)

Text no.	References
3:81	Abū Khaythamah 33; Dārimī 1:338; Kulaynī 1:32; Ibn ʿAbd Rabbih 4:170; Ḥarrānī 204; Ṣadūq, *Maʿānī* 226; Māmaṭīrī 156, 398; Makkī 1:370; Ibn Baṭṭah 16, 27; Abū Nuʿaym 1:77, 7:298; Ibn ʿAbd al-Barr, *Jāmiʿ* 2:811; Muʾaddib 55; Ghazālī, *Iḥyāʾ* 1:32; Ibn Munqidh 293; Ibn ʿAsākir 42:510; Ibn Ṭalḥah 245; Dhahabī, *Tadhkirah* 1:15.
3.82	Āmidī 91; Zamakhsharī, *Rabīʿ* 4:40.
3.83	Jāḥiẓ, *Rasāʾil* 289 (attrib. Shaʿbī); Balādhurī 2:135; Ibn Abī al-Dunyā, *ʿAql* 71; Kulaynī 1:48; Ibn ʿAbd Rabbih, 8:90; Māmaṭīrī 153; Thaʿālibī, *Tamthīl* 30; Māwardī, *Amthāl* 1:9; Ḥuṣrī 1:202 (attrib. Ibn Masʿūd); Quḍāʿī, *Dustūr* 26; Ibn ʿAbd al-Barr, *Adab* 107; Ibn ʿAbd al-Barr, *Bahjah* 115; Ibn ʿAbd al-Barr, *ʿIlm* 1:126; Ibn ʿAbd al-Barr, *Jāmiʿ* 2:984; Muʾaddib 152; Fattāl 414; Zamakhsharī, *Rabīʿ* 1:23; Suyūṭī 2:715.
3:84	Ṭūsī, *Tafsīr* 5:107 (attrib. Ibn Masʿūd); Ṭabrisī, *Majmaʿ* 4:456; Warrām 2:255; Ibn al-Qayyim, *Ighāthah* 2:160 (attrib. Ibn Masʿūd).
3.85	Ibn Abī Shaybah 7:100 (§ 34499); Iskāfī, *Miʿyār* 250; Barqī 1:224; Ḥarrānī 174; Māmaṭīrī 185; Dāraquṭnī, *Muʾtalif* 2:1062; Muwaffaq biʾllāh 617; Makkī 1:357; Abū Nuʿaym 1:75, 212 (attrib. Abū al-Dardāʾ), 10:388; Quḍāʿī, *Dustūr* 38, 158; Āmidī 258; Zamakhsharī, *Rabīʿ* 2:155; Ibn ʿAsākir 47:159 (attrib. Abū al-Dardāʾ); Warrām 1:110, 355, 2:539.
3.86	Muʾaddib 142; Āmidī 90; Zamakhsharī, *Rabīʿ* 4:281; Ṭabrisī, *Majmaʿ* 2:318; Warrām 1:111.
3.87	Tawḥīdī, *Baṣāʾir* 2:25; Hārūnī 213; Āmidī 322; Maydānī 2:455; Ibn Ṭalḥah 281; Sibṭ 105 (attrib. Ibn ʿAbbās); Warrām 1:111.
3:88	Kulaynī 8:391; Muʾaddib 92; Rāghib, *Muḥāḍarāt* 1:53; Fattāl 4; Ṭabrisī, *Mishkāt* 437.
3:89	Ḥarrānī 209; Ṭabrisī, *Majmaʿ* 1:441.
3.90	Sulaym 2:373; Balādhurī 2:188; Ḥarrānī 160; Ṣadūq, *Amālī* 668; Māmaṭīrī 244–245; Muwaffaq biʾllāh 587; Mufīd, *Ṣifāt* 22; Murtaḍā, *Amālī* 1:198; Raḍī, *Khaṣāʾiṣ* 96; Karājikī, *Kanz* 32; Āmidī 57; Zamakhsharī, *Rabīʿ* 5:97; ʿIzz al-Dīn Ibn al-Athīr, *Usd* 3:217; Ibn Ṭalḥah 264; Muḥammad al-Waṭwāṭ 52.
3.91	Ḥulwānī 50; Yaʿqūbī 2:210; Raḍī, *Khaṣāʾiṣ* 96; Muʾaddib 543; Āmidī 57; Zamakhsharī, *Rabīʿ* 1:56.
3.92	Yaʿqūbī 2:209; Mubarrad, *Kāmil* 1:241; Māmaṭīrī 409; Samarqandī 1:587 (attrib. Prophet); Raḍī, *Khaṣāʾiṣ* 96; Ābī 1:277; Muʾaddib 554; Rāghib, *Muḥāḍarāt* 1:230; Āmidī 363; Warrām 2:200; Muʾaddib 144.

(*cont.*)

Text no.	References
3.93	Balādhurī 2:129; Nuʿmān, *Daʿāʾim* 2:159; Ṭabrisī, *Makārim* 113.
3.94	Ibn Saʿd 3:28; Ḥarrānī 212; Raḍī, *Khaṣāʾiṣ* 96; Nuʿmān, *Sharḥ* 1:233; Warrām 2:143; Ibn Ṭalḥah 183.
3.95	Nawf al-Bikālī, transmitter (Raḍī names him); Iskāfī, *Miʿyār* 263; Ibn Abī al-Dunyā, *Tawāḍuʿ* 51; Masʿūdī, *Murūj* 4:195; Māmaṭīrī 346–347; Ṣadūq, *Khiṣāl* 337; Kūfī 2:476; Hārūnī 496; Muwaffaq biʾllāh 52; Mufīd, *Amālī* 133; Abū Nuʿaym 1:79, 6:52; Karājikī, *Kanz* 30; Quḍāʿī, *Dustūr* 44; Khaṭīb, *Tārīkh* 8:42; Āmidī 209; Ibn ʿAsākir 62:305; Ibn Kathīr, *Bidāyah* 8:6.
3.96	Mufīd, *Amālī* 159; Ṭūsī, *Amālī* 510–511; Raḍī, *Khaṣāʾiṣ* 97; Hārūnī 272; Muʾaddib 156; Ibn al-Athīr, *Usd* 5:155.
3.97	Raḍī, *Khaṣāʾiṣ* 97; Āmidī 351.
3.98	Iskāfī, *Miʿyār* 54; Mufīd, *Irshād* 1:247; Āmidī 183.
3.99	Mubarrad, *Fāḍil* 2; Ḥarrānī 95; Masʿūdī, *Murūj* 2:415; Ṣadūq, *ʿIlal* 1:109; Mufīd, *Irshād* 1:301; Ḥuṣrī 2:540; Quḍāʿī, *Dustūr* 149; Muʾaddib 420; Āmidī 225; Ibn ʿAsākir 42:513.
3.100	Khalīl 7:442; Ibn Qutaybah, *ʿUyūn* 1:463; Yaʿqūbī 2:210; Ḥarrānī 116; Māmaṭīrī 154–157 (156); Raḍī, *Khaṣāʾiṣ* 98; Muʾaddib 499; ʿImād al-Dīn al-Ṭabarī 21; Muḥammad ibn Ṭāhir 187; Rāzī, *Maḥṣūl* 4:70 (attrib. Prophet); Qurṭubī 2:154; Ibn al-ʿArabī 1:140.
3.101	ʿAbd al-Razzāq 8:299 (attrib. ʿUmar); Muʾaddib 431; Āmidī 351.
3.102	Abū ʿUbayd, *Gharīb* 4:359; Ibn Qutaybah, *Iṣlāḥ* 117; Ṣaffār 410; Māmaṭīrī 237; Ṣadūq, *Maʿānī* 182; Muwaffaq biʾllāh 588–589; Ahwāzī, *Muʾmin* 16; Ḥarrānī 343; Mufīd, *Ikhtiṣāṣ* 311; Murtaḍā, *Amālī 1:13*; Zamakhsharī, *Rabīʿ* 1:379.
3.103	Jāḥiẓ, *Miʾat* 224; Barqī 1:17; Kulaynī 8:20; Ibn ʿAbd Rabbih 2:115; Ṭabarānī, *Muʿjam kabīr* 3:69; Ṣadūq, *Amālī* 399; Ṣadūq, *Tawḥīd* 376 (few lines attrib. Prophet, speaking to ʿAlī); Ḥarrānī 94; Tawḥīdī, *Baṣāʾir* 1:11 (attrib. Prophet); Mufīd, *Ikhtiṣāṣ* 246; Muʾaddib 543; Fattāl 4; Ṭabrisī, *Mishkāt* 400, 538.
3.104	Muʾaddib 131; Āmidī 143; Zamakhsharī, *Rabīʿ* 3:297.
3.105	Ṭūsī, *Amālī* 641; Muʾaddib 384; Rāwandī, *Daʿawāt* 121.
3.106	Yaʿqūbī 2:206; Ḥarrānī 203; Kulaynī 8:112; Ṭūsī, *Amālī* 443; Ibn ʿAṭiyyah 5:353 (attrib. al-Ḥasan [al-Ḥasan al-Baṣrī/al-Ḥasan ibn ʿAlī?]); Warrām 2:495; Sibṭ 133.
3.107	ʿAbd al-Razzāq 11:319; Ibn Ḥanbal, *Musnad* 2:468; Balādhurī 2:119; Thaqafī 2:588; Ibn Abī ʿĀṣim, Sunnah 476; Nuʿmān, *Sharḥ* 1:160; Ṣadūq,

(*cont.*)

Text no.	References

	Amālī 709; Ṣadūq, *ʿUyūn* 1:217; Kūfī 2:284; Raḍī, *Khaṣāʾiṣ* 124; Ābī 1:296; Kārākijī, *Maʿdin* 26; Bayhaqī, *Maḥāsin* 41; Muʾaddib 511; Āmidī 329.
3.108	Muʾaddib 70, 127, 132; Āmidī 24.
3.109	Kulaynī 2:136; Ḥarrānī 396; Naḥḥās 320; Thaʿālibī, *Yatīmah* 5:30; Muʾaddib 487; Warrām 1:405, 2:562.
3.110	Zamakhsharī, *Rabīʿ* 4:217.
3.111	Raḍī, *Khaṣāʾiṣ* 99; Murtaḍā, *Amālī* 1:153; Āmidī 199; Zamakhsharī, *Rabīʿ* 4:217; Warrām 1:108.
3.112	Yaʿqūbī 2:100 (attrib. Prophet); Qummī 2:70; Kulaynī 8:168 (attrib. Prophet); Makkī 1:139 (attrib. Prophet); Raḍī, *Khaṣāʾiṣ* 99; Abū Nuʿaym 3:203; Karājikī, *Kanz* 178 (attrib. Prophet); Bayhaqī, *Sunan* 4:306 (attrib. Prophet); Muʾaddib 315; Fattāl 490; Ibn ʿAsākir 58:353 (attrib. Prophet); Dhahabī, *Siyar* 13:557 (attrib. Prophet); Dhahabī, *Mīzān* 3:68, 658, 4:263 (attrib. Prophet).
3.113	Nuʿmān, *Majālis* 305; Abū Bakr al-Khwārazmī 132; Raḍī, *Khaṣāʾiṣ* 100; Muʾaddib 347; Āmidī 223; Zamakhsharī, *Rabīʿ* 1:345; Muḥammad ibn Ṭāhir 378–379.
3.114	Ḥulwānī 53; Barqī 1:222; Kulaynī 2:45; Qummī 1:100; Ṣadūq, *Amālī* 432; Ṣadūq, *Maʿānī* 185; Fattāl 43.
3.115	Muʾaddib 330; Zamakhsharī, *Rabīʿ* 3:422; Warrām 1:211.
3.116	Raḍī, *Khaṣāʾiṣ* 101; Muʾaddib 426; Āmidī 295; Warrām 1:148.
3.117	Ḥulwānī 65; Raḍī, *Khaṣāʾiṣ* 101; Muʾaddib 204; Nuwayrī 1:176.
3.118	Raḍī, *Khaṣāʾiṣ* 101; Ibn al-ʿArabī 1:80.
3.119	Minqarī 531; Jāḥiẓ, *Bayān* 3:148; Ḥarrānī 186–188; Ṭabarī, *Tārīkh* 5:61–62; Ibn ʿAbd Rabbih 3:193; Ibn Ḥibbān 9:235; Bayhaqī, *Maḥāsin* 358; Ṣadūq, *Amālī* 169; Ṣadūq, *Man* 1:179; Māmaṭīrī 241; Raḍī, *Khaṣāʾiṣ* 102; Tawḥīdī 5:227; Fattāl 493; Ibn ʿAsākir 42:498–499, 58:79–80.
3.120	Iskāfī, *Miʿyār* 268; Ḥulwānī 66; Jāḥiẓ, *Bayān* 2:190; Jāḥiẓ, *Maḥāsin* 132; Ibn Qutaybah, *ʿUyūn* 2:358; Ibn Abī al-Dunyā, *Dhamm* 77; Ibn Abī al-Dunyā, *Iṣlāḥ al-māl* 1:50; Yaʿqūbī 2:208; Ahwāzī, *Zuhd* 47; Ḥarrānī 188; Abū Bakr al-Dīnawarī 4:51; Masʿūdī, *Murūj* 2:398; Māmaṭīrī 240; Nuʿmān, *Sharḥ* 2:224; Kūfī 47; Raḍī, *Khaṣāʾiṣ* 102; Ḥuṣrī 1:80; Tawḥīdī 5:227; Mufīd, *Irshād* 1:296; Ābī 1:185–186; Hārūnī 506–507; Muwaffaq biʾllāh 63; Māwardī, *Adab* 131; Bayhaqī, *Maḥāsin* 358; Ṭūsī, *Amālī* 594; Khaṭīb, *Tārīkh* 7:297; Rāghib, *Muḥāḍarāt* 2:403; Fattāl 441; Zamakhsharī,

(*cont.*)

Text no.	References
	Rabīʿ 1:64; Ibn Ḥamdūn 1:73; Ibn ʿAsākir 42:499, 58:79–80; Warrām 1:272; Sibṭ 153; Ibn Ṭalḥah 215–216; Ibn Abī al-Iṣbaʿ 277–279; Ṣafadī 18:7; Ibn Kathīr, *Bidāyah* 8:7; Suyūṭī 18:99.
3.121	Kulaynī 2:132; Mufīd, *Ikhtiṣāṣ* 234; Raḍī, *Khaṣāʾiṣ* 103; Muʾaddib 160.
3.122	Ibn Durayd, *Jamharah* 1:125; Māmaṭīrī 209; Raḍī, *Khaṣāʾiṣ* 103; Mufīd, *Irshād* 1:298; Ābī 1:296; Muwaffaq biʾllāh 535; Quḍāʿī, *Dustūr* 46; Ḥulwānī 67; Ibn ʿAbd al-Barr, *Bahjah* 2:281; Zamakhsharī, *Rabīʿ* 1:48; Warrām 1:243, 3:22; Nuwayrī 7:96.
3.123	Ḥarrānī 219; Raḍī, *Khaṣāʾiṣ* 103; Muwaffaq biʾllāh 586; Zamakhsharī, *Rabīʿ* 1:355; Muḥammad al-Waṭwāṭ 540.
3.124	Ṣadūq, *Khiṣāl* 202 (attrib. Jaʿfar al-Ṣādiq); Sibṭ 133.
3.125	Kulaynī 5:9; Ḥarrānī 110, 221; Ṣadūq, *Hidāyah* 60; Ṣadūq, *Khiṣāl* 620; Ṣadūq, *Man* 1:210, 3:439, 4:416; Raḍī, *Khaṣāʾiṣ* 103; Quḍāʿī, *Musnad* 1:95, 181 (attrib. Prophet); Muʾaddib 223; Ibn ʿAbd al-Barr, *Tamhīd* 21:21; Ṭabrisī, *Makārim* 215; Majd al-Dīn Ibn al-Athīr s.v. "Q-R-B" (attrib. Prophet); Ibn Manẓūr s.v. "Q-R-B" (attrib. Prophet); Dhahabī, *Siyar* 6:262 (attrib. Jaʿfar al-Ṣādiq).
3.126	Kulaynī 4:10; Ḥarrānī 111, 221, 403; Ṣadūq, *Amālī* 532; Ṣadūq, *Khiṣāl* 619, 621; Ṣadūq, *Man* 4:381, 416; Ṣadūq, *ʿUyūn* 1:59; Raḍī, *Khaṣāʾiṣ* 104; Thaʿālibī, *Tafsīr* 5:446 (attrib. Prophet); Ḥuṣrī 1:81; Quḍāʿī, *Musnad* 1:233 (attrib. Prophet); Muʾaddib 89; Ṭabrisī, *Mishkāt* 138; Faḍlallāh al-Rāwandī 86; Dhahabī, *Mīzān* 1:452 (attrib. Prophet).
3.127	Raḍī, *Khaṣāʾiṣ* 104; Āmidī 152; Ibn al-ʿArabī 1:102.
3.128	Ḥarrānī 60, 214; Ṣadūq, *Khiṣāl* 620; Ṣadūq, *Man* 2:64; Ibn ʿAbd al-Barr, *Tamhīd* 21:20 (attrib. Prophet through ʿAlī).
3.129	Ḥulwānī 49; Jāḥiẓ, *Bayān* 1:85; Jāḥiẓ, *ʿUthmāniyyah* 36; Ṣūlī 74; Raḍī, *Khaṣāʾiṣ* 104; Ḥarrānī 111, 214, 221, 403; Ṣadūq, *Amālī* 532; Ṣadūq, *Khiṣāl* 620; Ṣadūq, *ʿUyūn* 1:59; Ṣadūq, *Man* 4:416; Karājikī, *Kanz* 287; Bayhaqī, *Maḥāsin* 232 (attrib. Luqmān al-Ḥakīm); Zamakhsharī, *Rabīʿ* 4:160; Dhahabī, *Mīzān* 1:626, 2:481.
3.130	Ḥarrānī 221; Ṣadūq, *Man* 4:416 (attrib. Jaʿfar al-Ṣādiq); Raḍī, *Khaṣāʾiṣ* 104; Zamakhsharī, *Rabīʿ* 5:145; Dhahabī, *Siyar* 6:262 (attrib. Jaʿfar al-Ṣādiq).
3.131	Raḍī, *Khaṣāʾiṣ* 104; Muwaffaq biʾllāh 51; Muʾaddib 380; Fattāl 350; Zamakhsharī, *Rabīʿ* 2:283.
3.132	Raḍī, *Khaṣāʾiṣ* 105; Muʾaddib 284.
3.133	Kumayl ibn Ziyād transmitter (Raḍī names him); Ḥulwānī 57; Iskāfī,

(*cont.*)

Text no.	References

	Miʿyār 79; Ibn Qutaybah, *Gharīb* 2:108; Ibn Qutaybah, *ʿUyūn* 2:129, 358; Thaqafī 1:148–154; Yaʿqūbī 2:205–206; Ibn al-Anbārī 1:178; Nuʿmān, *Asās* 62; Nuʿmān, *Sharḥ* 2:370; Ibn ʿAbd Rabbih 2:81–82; Abū Bakr al-Dīnawarī 2:148; Ḥarrānī 169; Ṣadūq, *Kamāl* 290; Ṣadūq, *Khiṣāl* 186; Māmaṭīrī 147–150; Makkī 1:246; Azharī s.v. "H-M-J"; Abū Hilāl, *Dīwān* 1:146; Kūfī 2:95; Raḍī, *Khaṣāʾiṣ* 105; Mufīd, *Amālī* 247; Mufīd, *Irshād* 1:227; Abū Nuʿaym 1:131; Hārūnī 202–203; Muwaffaq biʾllāh 145–147; Quḍāʿī, *Dustūr* 92; Bayhaqī, *Maḥāsin* 400; Ṭūsī, *Amālī* 20; Khaṭīb, *Tārīkh* 7:408; Ibn ʿAbd al-Barr, *Jāmiʿ* 2:984; Muʾayyad al-Shīrāzī vol. 2 majlis 1, majlis 60; Jurjānī 81–82; Muʾaddib 150; Fattāl 10; ʿImād al-Dīn al-Ṭabarī 52; Muwaffaq Khwārazmī 365–366; Ṭabrisī, *Majmaʿ* 10:308; Ibn ʿAsākir 5:252; Rāzī, *Mafātīḥ* 2:410; ʿAlī ibn Muḥammad, *Tāj* 126; Sibṭ 141; Qurṭubī 18:94–95; Mizzī 24:220; Ibn al-Qayyim, *Iʿlām* 2:135; Ibn al-Qayyim, *Miftāḥ* 1:123; Ibn al-Kathīr, *Bidāyah* 9:57; Dhahabī, *Tadhkirah* 1:15; Ibn Abī al-ʿIzz 85.
3.134	Jāḥiẓ, *Miʾat* 222; Mubarrad, *Fāḍil* 6; Ṣadūq, *Amālī* 532; Ṣadūq, *ʿUyūn* 1:58–59; Raḍī, *Khaṣāʾiṣ* 106; Muwaffaq biʾllāh 295; Mufīd, *Irshād* 1:300; Thaʿālibī, *Iʿjāz* 34; Karājikī, *Maʿdin* 67; Ṭūsī, *Amālī* 494; Ḥuṣrī 1:77; Ibn ʿAbd al-Barr, *Adab* 44; Muʾaddib 18, 201; Fattāl 109; Ibn ʿAṭiyyah 3:255 (unattrib.); Muwaffaq Khwārazmī 375; Ibn Munqidh 330 (attrib. Prophet); Rāzī, *Mafātīḥ* 22:42 (attrib. Prophet).
3.135	Jāḥiẓ, *Miʾat* 222; Ṣadūq, *Khiṣāl* 420; Raḍī, *Khaṣāʾiṣ* 106; Muwaffaq biʾllāh 297.
3.136	Jāḥiẓ, *Bayān* 2:101; Ibn Abī al-Dunyā, *Tawbah* 55; Mubarrad, *Fāḍil* 94–95; Ibn ʿAbd Rabbih 3:134; Ḥarrānī 157; Māmaṭīrī 385–386; Abū Hilāl, *Jamharah* 1:272; Raḍī, *Khaṣāʾiṣ* 109; Mufīd, *Amālī* 330; Ābī 1:277; Muwaffaq biʾllāh 552; Ḥuṣrī 1:77; Quḍāʿī, *Dustūr* 88; Māwardī, *Ḥāwī* 16:212; Ṭūsī, *Amālī* 111; Muʾaddib 550; Ṭarṭūshī 109; Ibn Ḥamdūn 1:75; Ḍiyāʾ Ibn al-Athīr 1:275; Sibṭ 134; Muʾayyad, *Ṭirāz* 2:192; Ibn Rajab 344; Muttaqī-Hindī 16:205.
3.137	Quḍāʿī, *Dustūr* 8; Muʾaddib 402.
3.138	Raḍī, *Khaṣāʾiṣ* 106; Quḍāʿī, *Dustūr* 8.
3.139	Zamakhsharī, *Rabīʿ* 3:102; Muʾaddib 543; Muʾayyad, *Ṭirāz* 2:69.
3.140	Muʾaddib 64, 98; Āmidī 54.
3.141	Āmidī 46.
3.142	Nuʿmān, *Daʿāʾim* 1:98, 2:353; Raḍī, *Khaṣāʾiṣ* 107; Mufīd, *Irshād* 1:232; Muʾayyad, *Ṭirāz* 2:66.

(cont.)

Text no.	References
3.143	Raḍī, *Khaṣāʾiṣ* 107.
3.144	Muʾaddib 339; Zamakhsharī, *Rabīʿ* 2:7; Muḥammad al-Waṭwāṭ 283.
3.145	Kulaynī 8:152; Ḥarrānī 220; Ṣadūq, *Amālī* 380 (attrib. Jaʿfar); Mufīd, *Ikhtiṣāṣ* 226.
3.146	Ḥarrānī 7, 220, 368; Ṣadūq, *Amālī* 380; Raḍī, *Khaṣāʾiṣ* 108; Mufīd, *Ikhtiṣāṣ* 226; Muʾaddib 69, 443; Āmidī 264–266; Zamakhsharī, *Rabīʿ* 3:455; Ibn ʿAsākir 44:359 (attrib. ʿUmar).
3.147	Ḥarrānī 214; ʿAyyāshī 1:139; Ṣadūq, *Khiṣāl* 620; Zamakhsharī, *Rabīʿ* 5:90; Ṭabrisī, *Mishkāt* 228.
3.148	Mufīd, *Ikhtiṣāṣ* 243; Āmidī 196.
3.149	Sulaym 2:405; Ibn Ḥanbal, *Musnad* 6:432 (attrib. Prophet); Nuʿmān, *Daʿāʾim* 1:350; Jaṣṣāṣ 1:84, 2:243, 3:590 (attrib. Prophet); Ṣadūq, *Khiṣāl* 568; Majd al-Dīn Ibn al-Athīr s.v. "Ṭ-W-ʿ" (attrib. Prophet).
3.150	Ṭūsī, *Amālī* 567; Muʾaddib 542; Ibn Ṭāwūs, *Kashf* 180.
3.151	Muʾaddib 40; Āmidī 21; Zamakhsharī 4:186; Warrām 1:252.
3.152	Muʾaddib 37, 512; Āmidī 13–14.
3.153	Ibn Aʿtham 4:260; Thaqafī 1:317; Quḍāʿī, *Dustūr* 26; Muʾaddib 367; Ibn al-ʿArabī 1:106 (unattrib.); Ibn Ṭalḥah 295.
3.154	Kulaynī 2:451, 8:385; Ḥarrānī 208; Raḍī, *Khaṣāʾiṣ* 110.
3.155	Jāḥiẓ, *Bukhalāʾ* 148 (attrib. anon); Raḍī, *Khaṣāʾiṣ* 110; Muʾaddib 103, 380; Āmidī 236.
3.156	Raḍī, *Khaṣāʾiṣ* 110; Mufīd, *Ikhtiṣāṣ* 245; Thaʿālibī, *Iʿjāz* 34; Muwaffaq biʾllāh 297; Muʾaddib 61; Ghazālī, *Iḥyāʾ* 1:41 (attrib. anon).
3.157	Kulaynī 8:22; Ḥarrānī 90; Ṣadūq, *Man* 4:388; Raḍī, *Khaṣāʾiṣ* 110; Quḍāʿī, *Dustūr* 34; Muʾaddib 436; Āmidī 289.
3.158	Raḍī, *Khaṣāʾiṣ* 110; Muʾaddib 438; Āmidī 286; Zamakhsharī, *Rabīʿ* 1:335; Muʾayyad, *Ṭirāz* 1:88, 2:69; Warrām 1:234.
3.159	Raḍī, *Khaṣāʾiṣ* 110; Muʾaddib 132; Āmidī 142; Zamakhsharī, *Rabīʿ* 5:311; Muʾayyad, *Ṭirāz* 1:168.
3.160	Āmidī 27; Muʾayyad, *Ṭirāz* 1:88, 2:69.
3.161	Raḍī, *Khaṣāʾiṣ* 110; Zamakhsharī, *Rabīʿ* 2:7.
3.162	Muʾaddib 82; Āmidī 61; Ṭarṭūshī 203; Zamakhsharī, *Rabīʿ* 3:75; Warrām 34.
3.163	Raḍī, *Khaṣāʾiṣ* 110.
3.164	Āmidī 20; Zamakhsharī, *Rabīʿ* 3:270; Muʾayyad, *Ṭirāz* 1:88, 2:69.
3.165	Āmidī 158; Muʾayyad, *Ṭirāz* 1:88, 2:69.

(*cont.*)

Text no.	References
3.166	Balādhurī 2:114; Kulaynī 8:20; Ḥarrānī 94; Māmaṭīrī 354; Raḍī, *Khaṣāʾiṣ* 112, 124; Muwaffaq biʾllāh 155; Muʾaddib 542; Warrām 2:183, 3:113; Rāzī, *Mafātīḥ* 2:401.
3.167	Raḍī, *Khaṣāʾiṣ* 107; Muʾaddib 377; Āmidī 310.
3.168	Mufīd, *Irshād* 1:254.
3.169	Minqarī 315; Iskāfī, *Miʿyār* 61; Ibn Abī Shaybah 6:333 (§ 31840), 7:555 (§ 37898), 7:559 (§ 37915); Mubarrad, *Kāmil* 3:139, 163; Abū Yaʿlā, *Musnad* 1:397; Ṭabarī, *Tārīkh* 5:88; Masʿūdī, *Murūj* 2:408; Māmaṭīrī 178; Nuʿmān, *Sharḥ* 2:293, 321; Nuʿmān, *Manāqib* 214, 225; Ṣadūq, *Amālī* 491; Raḍī, *Khaṣāʾiṣ* 107; Mufīd, *Irshād* 1:16, 317; Murtaḍā, *Tanzīh* 200; Ṭūsī, *Amālī* 261; Ṭūsī, *Talkhīṣ* v. 1 pt. 2 pp. 263–264; Khaṭīb, *Tārīkh* 8:160; Ibn ʿAbd al-Barr, *Tamhīd* 23:332; Muʾaddib 480; Fattāl 136; Ibn ʿAsākir 42:396, 534; Ibn Shahrāshūb 2:182, 372; ʿIzz al-Dīn Ibn al-Athīr, *Kāmil* 2:694; Ibn Kathīr, *Bidāyah* 7:323, 327.
3.170	Qummī 2:287; Raḍī, *Khaṣāʾiṣ* 107; Muʾaddib 404.
3.171	Raḍī, *Khaṣāʾiṣ* 107.
3.172	Jāḥiẓ, *Bayān* 2:50; Jāḥiẓ, *Miʾat* 230; Iskāfī, *Miʿyār* 292; Ibn Qutaybah, *ʿUyūn* 2:260; Yaʿqūbī 2:212; Kulaynī 8:67; Ibn ʿAbd Rabbih 4:157; Nuʿmān, *Sharḥ* 1:373; Raḍī, *Khaṣāʾiṣ* 107; Mufīd, *Irshād* 1:240; Muwaffaq Khwārazmī 376.
3.173	Raḍī, *Khaṣāʾiṣ* 111; Muʾaddib 444; Āmidī 274.
3.174	Raḍī, *Khaṣāʾiṣ* 111; Karājikī, *Taʿajjub* 54; Āmidī 326.
3.175	Qālī, *Amālī* 2:54, 2:100 (attrib. ʿUmar ibn ʿAbd al-ʿAzīz); Hārūnī 261; Muʾaddib 179; Warrām 1:243.
3.176	Balādhurī 2:115; Masʿūdī, *Murūj* 4:262; Ṣadūq, *Khiṣāl* 16; Tanūkhī 1:158; Raḍī, *Khaṣāʾiṣ* 112; al-Mufīd, *Irshād* 1:234; Muwaffaq biʾllāh 587; Fattāl 427; Zamakhsharī, *Rabīʿ* 5:90.
3.177	Ḥulwānī 47; Jāḥiẓ, *Miʾat* 228; Balādhurī 2:115; Mubarrad, *Kāmil* 2:211; Māmaṭīrī 153; Raḍī, *Khaṣāʾiṣ* 112; Āmidī 113.
3.178	Ibn Qutaybah, *ʿUyūn* 1:415 (attrib. ʿUmar ibn ʿAbd al-ʿAzīz); Balādhurī 122; Raḍī, *Khaṣāʾiṣ* 112; Muʾaddib 489; Āmidī 318; Ṭarṭūshī 86 (attrib. anonymous sages); Zamakhsharī, *Rabīʿ* 2:217.
3.179	Balādhurī 2:134; Raḍī, *Khaṣāʾiṣ* 112; Muʾaddib 512; Zamakhsharī, *Rabīʿ* 4:393; Ibn Shahrāshūb 1:370.
3.180	Jāḥiẓ, *Bukhalāʾ* 248 (unattrib.); Balādhurī 2:135; Mubarrad, *Kāmil* 1:166 (attrib. "proverbs of the Arabs"); Raḍī, *Khaṣāʾiṣ* 113; Āmidī 256.

(*cont.*)

Text no.	References
3.181	Nearly identical to § 3.83. See sources there.
3.182	'Abd al-Razzāq 10:150; Minqarī 489; Iskāfī, *Mi'yār* 170; Ibn Abī Shaybah 7:562 (§ 37930); Shāfi'ī 4:229; Ibn Shādhān 474; Muslim 2:749 (§ 1066); Balādhurī 2:352; Ya'qūbī 2:191; Ibn Abī 'Āṣim 2:453; Ṭabarī, *Tārīkh* 5:72–73; Ibn Durayd, *Ishtiqāq* 219–220; Ibn 'Abd Rabbih 2:232; Nu'mān, *Da'ā'im* 1:393; Makkī 1:434; Jaṣṣāṣ 2:45, 3:533; Kūfī 341; Raḍī, *Khaṣā'iṣ* 113; Hārūnī 118; Ibn Barrāj 1:322; Ibn Shahrāshūb 2:369.
3.183	Jāḥiẓ, *Rasā'il* 1:283; Balādhurī 2:115; Ibn 'Abd Rabbih 2:152 (attrib. Ibn al-'Abbās); Raḍī, *Khaṣā'iṣ* 113; Zamakhsharī, *Rabī'* 2:345; Sam'ānī, *Tafsīr* 2:424;
3.184	Balādhurī 2:115; Ya'qūbī 2:209–210: Ibn 'Abd Rabbih 2:152 (attrib. 'Umar); Ṭūsī, *Tahdhīb* 10:150; Rāghib, *Muḥāḍarāt* 1:376; Mu'addib 544; Āmidī 354; Zamakhsharī, *Rabī'* 5:313.
3.185	Minqarī 250; Ibn Sa'd 3:43; Ibn Qutaybah, *Imāmah* 1:183; Balādhurī 2:500; Ṭabarī, *Tafsīr* 13:156; Raḍī, *Khaṣā'iṣ* 114; Tha'labī 5:276. Mu'addib 152; Ibn Kathīr, *Bidāyah* 1:53.
3.186	Ibn Qutaybah, *Imāmah* 1:71; Ya'qūbī 2:180; Raḍī, *Khaṣā'iṣ* 114; Ibn Abī al-Ḥadīd 2:173 (cites Iskāfī).
3.187	Mubarrad, *Kāmil* 1:298; Mu'addib 87; Fattāl 437; Ṭabrisī, *Mishkāt* 523.
3.188	Mubarrad, *Fāḍil* 94; Abū Hilāl, *Dīwān* 1:154; Raḍī, *Khaṣā'iṣ* 115; Māwardī, *Adab* 202; Bayhaqī, *Maḥāsin* 124; Āmidī 340; Ibn Munqidh 335; Nuwayrī 3:248.
3.189	Māmaṭīrī 153; Raḍī, *Khaṣā'iṣ* 115; Mu'addib 376; Āmidī 239; Mu'ayyad, *Ṭirāz* 1:88.
3.190	Ibn Qutaybah, *'Uyūn* 1:408; Ibn 'Abd Rabbih 2:140; Māmaṭīrī 243; Raḍī, *Khaṣā'iṣ* 115; Muwaffaq bi'llāh 588; Karājikī, *Kanz* 147; Quḍā'ī, *Dustūr* 29; Mu'addib 55; Ghazālī, *Iḥyā'* 3:178; Zamakhsharī, *Rabī'* 2:238; Mu'ayyad, *Ṭirāz* 1:88; Warrām 1:355.
3.191	Ḥulwānī 53; Kulaynī 2:112; Mu'addib 162; Daylamī 296.
3.192	Ḥulwānī 51; Ibn 'Abd Rabbih 3:96; Ḥarrānī 89; Raḍī, *Khaṣā'iṣ* 118; Karājikī, *Kanz* 225; Āmidī 265.
3.193	Furāt 314; Raḍī, *Khaṣā'iṣ* 70; Mu'addib 405; Zamakhsharī, *Rabī'* 1:463; Ṭabrisī, *Majma'* 7:414.
3.194	Ḥarrānī 211; Māmaṭīrī 210; Quḍā'ī, *Dustūr* 72; Mu'addib 360.
3.195	Ibn Abī al-Dunyā, *Ikhwān* 128; Kulaynī 8:16; Ḥarrānī 97, 98, 381; Ṣadūq, *Man* 4:389; Karājikī, *Kanz* 34, 163; Māwardī, *Adab* 185, 342 (anon);

(*cont.*)

Text no.	References
	Quḍāʿī, *Dustūr* 10; Muʾaddib 23, 38–39, 61, 114, 355, 524; Samʿānī, *Ansāb* 6:213 (attrib. Abū ʿAbdallāh al-Ḥusayn ibn Aḥmad al-Rīḥānī); Majd al-Dīn Ibn al-Athīr s.v. "F-D-M"; Ibn al-Jawzī, *Zād* 2:47; Ibn Ṭalḥah 277; Daylamī 178; Ibn Manẓūr s.v. "F-D-M"; Nuwayrī 29:182.
3.196	Ḥarrānī 90, 214; Abū Hilāl, *Dīwān* 2:94; Tawḥīdī, *Imtāʿ* 260; Rāghib, *Muḥāḍarāt* 1:324; Zamakhsharī, *Rabīʿ* 4:186; Ṭabrisi, *Mishkāt* 539; Ibn Ṭalḥah 274.
3.197	Ḥuṣrī 4:1056; Āmidī 62; Muʾayyad, *Ṭirāz* 2:69.
3.198	Jāḥiẓ, *Miʾat* 230; Thaʿālibī, *Iʿjāz* 39; Muʾaddib 448; Zamakhsharī, *Rabīʿ* 2:217; Muwaffaq Khwārazmī 376.
3.199	Ibn ʿAbd al-Barr, *Adab* 111; Ṭarṭūshī 203.
3.200	Kulaynī 8:23; Ḥarrānī 98; Abū Hilāl, *Dīwān* 2:94; Tawḥīdī, *Imtāʿ* 260; Muʾaddib 451.
3.201	Kulaynī 8:23; Ḥarrānī 97; Ṣadūq, *Man* 4:388; Tawḥīdī, *Imtāʿ* 260; Karājikī, *Kanz* 34; Karājikī, *Maʿdin* 22; Quḍāʿī, *Dustūr* 36; Muʾaddib 18, 354; Ṭarṭūshī 203; Warrām 2:185; Daylamī 178.
3.202	Muʾaddib 234; Āmidī 170; Zamakhsharī, *Rabīʿ* 1:365.
3.203	Ḥulwānī 63; Jāḥiẓ, *Miʾat* 230; Thaʿālibī, *Iʿjāz* 39; Muwaffaq Khwārazmī 376; Muʾaddib 13, 125; Rāghib, *Muḥāḍarāt* 1:608 (attrib. anon); Maydānī 2:162; Zamakhsharī, *Rabīʿ* 3:269; Muʾayyad, *Ṭirāz* 1:88; Warrām 1:180.
3.204	Ṣadūq, *Man* 4:390; Muʾaddib 411; Zamakhsharī, *Rabīʿ* 3:297.
3.205	Ḥarrānī 91; Ṣadūq, *Amālī* 531; Ṣadūq, *Man* 4:389; Ṣadūq, *ʿUyūn* 1:58; Karājikī, *Kanz* 57; Fattāl 466; Āmidī 150; Muʾaddib 193; Zamakhsharī, *Rabīʿ* 3:322 (attrib. al-Ḥasan ibn ʿAlī); Ibn ʿAsākir 51:411 (attrib. Faḍl ibn ʿIyāḍ); Ibn Kathīr, *Ṭabaqāt* 1:32 (attrib. Shāfiʿī); Dhahabī, *Siyar* 10:41 (attrib. Shāfiʿī); Dhahabī, *Tārīkh* 14:326 (attrib. Shāfiʿī).
3.206	Muʾaddib 121, 467.
3.207	Ḥarrānī 98, 215; Kulaynī 8:23; Ṣadūq, *Man* 4:391; Ḥuṣrī 4:1054; Fattāl 360; Muʾaddib 450; Zamakhsharī, *Rabīʿ* 2:119.
3.208	Ḥulwānī 47; Ibn ʿAbd Rabbih 2:138; Āmidī 145; Ṭarṭūshī 108; Zamakhsharī, *Rabīʿ* 2:136.
3.209	Muʾaddib 54; Āmidī 219; Zamakhsharī, *Rabīʿ* 3:136.
3.210	Jāḥiẓ, *Miʾat* 230; Zamakhsharī, *Rabīʿ* 3:273; Ibn al-Ṣabbāgh 1:546.
3.211	Ḥulwānī 17; Ibn Mājah 1:26; Ḥarrānī 422 (unattrib.); Ṭabarānī, *Muʿjam awsaṭ* 6:226 (attrib. Prophet); Ṣadūq, *Khiṣāl* 179 (attrib. Prophet), 609

(*cont.*)

Text no.	References
	(unattrib.); Ṣadūq, *Maʿānī* 186 (attrib. ʿAlī al-Riḍā); Ṣadūq, *ʿUyūn* 1:31 (attrib. Prophet), 1:133, 2:205 (attrib. Prophet); Raḍī, *Khaṣāʾiṣ* 100; Thaʿlabī 1:146; Ṭūsī, *Amālī* 369, 448; Ibn al-Jawzī, *Mawḍūʿāt* 1:128 (attrib. Prophet); Daylamī 134; Ibn al-Jazarī 75.
3.212	Ḥarrānī 8, 217; ʿAyyāshī 1:120; Mufīd, *Amālī* 188 (attrib. Jaʿfar al-Ṣādiq); Karājikī, *Kanz* 160; Ṭūsī, *Amālī* 229; Sibṭ 134.
3.213	Muʾaddib 386; Āmidī 242; Zamakhsharī, *Rabīʿ* 5:327; Nuwayrī 3:247.
3.214	Ṭabarī, *Tafsīr* 14:223; Qummī 2:390; Muwaffaq biʾllāh 81; Zamakhsharī, *Kashshāf* 2:366; Qurṭubī 10:174.
3.215	Muʾaddib 298; Zamakhsharī, *Rabīʿ* 1:432.
3.216	Ibn Qutaybah, *ʿUyūn* 2:429; ʿAyyāshī 2:289; Ṣadūq, *Maʿānī* 257; Muʾaddib 34; Qurṭubī 10:165.
3.217	Muʾaddib 432; Raḍī, *Majāzāt* 67; Āmidī 271; Zamakhsharī, *Rabīʿ* 2:7; Ibn ʿAsākir 50:163.
3.218	Ibn Qutaybah, *ʿUyūn* 1:197; Mubarrad, *Kāmil* 1:167; Ibn ʿAbd Rabbih 1:94; Māmaṭīrī 376; Muwaffaq biʾllāh 573; Muʾaddib 527; Rāghib, *Muḥāḍarāt* 2:147; Ibn Munqidh 222.
3.219	Makkī 2:422; Fattāl 372; Zamakhsharī, *Rabīʿ* 5:252.
3.220	Āmidī 48; Zamakhsharī, *Rabīʿ* 446.
3.221	Ṣadūq, *Amālī* 722; Muʾaddib 145, 404; Āmidī 116; Muḥammad al-Waṭwāṭ 138; Warrām 1:249.
3.222	Ḥulwānī 99; Ḥarrānī 246; Kulaynī 2:84, 5:35; Ṣadūq, *Khiṣāl* 188 (attrib. Jaʿfar al-Ṣādiq); Muʾaddib 158; Āmidī 111; Zamakhsharī, *Rabīʿ* 2:299; Ibn ʿAsākir 41:410; Ibn Kathīr, *Bidāyah* 9:123 (attrib. ʿAlī Zayn al-ʿĀbidīn).
3.223	Āmidī 47; Ṭabrisī, *Majmaʿ* 2:252.
3.224	Āmidī 279; Zamakhsharī, *Rabīʿ* 3:399; Warrām 1:206.
3.225	Ḥuṣrī 1:80; Muʾaddib 53; Āmidī 42; Ṭarṭūshī 203.
3.226	Zamakhsharī, *Rabīʿ* 3:312; Muḥammad al-Waṭwāṭ 81; Warrām 2:531.
3.227	Ḥarrānī 361; Muʾaddib 84; Āmidī 63; Rāghib, *Muḥāḍarāt* 2:416 (attrib. Jaʿfar al-Ṣādiq); Zamakhsharī, *Rabīʿ* 2:171.
3.228	Ḥuṣrī 2:430; Āmidī 139; Ṭarṭūshī 197; Zamakhsharī, *Rabīʿ* 2:85.
3.229	Ḥarrānī 206; Muʾaddib 155; Āmidī 108.
3.230	Ibn Qutaybah, *ʿUyūn* 3:119 (attrib. anon); Makkī 2:316 3:119 (attrib. anon); Āmidī 139.
3.231	Jāḥiẓ, *Bukhalāʾ* 245 (attrib. anon); Jāḥiẓ, *Miʾat* 230; Thaʿālibī, *Iʿjāz* 39; Muwaffaq Khwārazmī 376; Fattāl 473; Zamakhsharī, *Rabīʿ* 5:276.

(cont.)

Text no.	References
3.232	Muʾaddib 28.
3.233	Ḥarrānī 82; Zamakhsharī, *Rabīʿ* 3:297.
3.234	Jāḥiẓ, *Miʾat* 230; Muʾaddib 120; Ghazālī, *Iḥyāʾ* 4:288 (attrib. Prophet); Āmidī 90; Zamakhsharī, *Rabīʿ* 3:459; Warrām 1:215; Sibṭ 135; Ibn Rajab 40 (unattrib.)
3.235	Ṣadūq, *Khiṣāl* 33; Ṣadūq, *Tawḥīd* 288; Muʾaddib 339; Fattāl 30.
3.236	Muʾaddib 479; Fattāl 441; Āmidī 168; Ibn Kathīr, *Bidāyah* 2:105 (attrib. Jesus); Ibn Kathīr, *Qiṣaṣ* 2:441 (attrib. Jesus).
3.237	Ḥulwānī 46; Āmidī 230; Muḥammad ibn Ṭāhir 323–324; Nuwayrī, 8:182; Ibn Ṭalḥah 301.
3.238	Kulaynī 6:445; Masʿūdī, *Murūj* 3:353 (attrib. Prophet by way of ʿAlī); Abū al-Faraj, *Maqātil* 317; Muʾaddib 93.
3.239	Muʾaddib 392; Āmidī 246.
3.240	Muʾaddib 62; Āmidī 52.
3.241	Zamakhsharī, *Rabīʿ* 3:163.
3.242	Kumayl ibn Ziyād transmitter (Raḍī names him); Bāʿūnī 2:140.
3.443	Muwaffaq Khwārazmī 376 (cites Jāḥiẓ); Muʾaddib 135.
3.244	Zamakhsharī, *Rabīʿ* 4:143.
3.245	Abū ʿUbayd, *Gharīb* 1:235; Jāḥiẓ, *Ḥayawān* 3:329; Nuʿmān, *Sharḥ* 3:361; Azharī s.v. "Q-Z-ʿ"; Harawī s.v. "Dh-N-B"; Zamakhsharī, *Fāʾiq* s.v. "ʿ-S-B"; Majd al-Dīn Ibn al-Athīr s.v. "ʿ-S-B."
3.246	Abū ʿUbayd, *Gharīb* 4:331; Ibn Ḥanbal, *Musnad* 2:411; Jāḥiẓ, *Bayān* 2:274; Ṭabarī, *Tārīkh* 4:492; Harawī s.v. "Sh-Ḥ-Ḥ"; Azharī s.v. "Sh-Ḥ-Ḥ"; Zamakhsharī, *Fāʾiq* s.v. "Sh-Ḥ-Ḥ"; Ibn ʿAsākir 29:8, 30:293, 44:219; Majd al-Dīn Ibn al-Athīr s.v. "Sh-Ḥ-Ḥ"; Ibn Manẓūr s.v. "Sh-Ḥ-Ḥ."
3.247	Khalīl s.v. "Q-Ḥ-M"; Abū ʿUbayd, *Gharīb* 4:342; Shāfiʿī 3:237, 7:127; Ibn Fāris 5:61 s.v. "Q-Ḥ-M"; Jawharī s.v. "Q-Ḥ-M"; Harawī s.v. "Q-Ḥ-M"; Ṭūsī, *Mabsūṭ* 2:360; Majd al-Dīn Ibn al-Athīr s.v. "Q-Ḥ-M"; Ibn Manẓūr s.v. "Q-Ḥ-M."
3.248	Abū ʿUbayd, *Gharīb* 4:349; Jawharī s.v. "N-Ṣ-Ṣ"; Harawī s.v. "Ḥ-Q-Q"; Zamakhsharī, *Fāʾiq* s.v. "N-Ṣ-Ṣ"; Majd al-Dīn Ibn al-Athīr s.v. "Ḥ-Q-Q," "N-Ṣ-Ṣ"; Ibn Manẓūr s.v. "N-Ṣ-Ṣ."
3.249	Abū ʿUbayd, *Gharīb* 4:353; Harawī s.v. "lumẓah"; Thaʿlabī 5:113; Thaʿālibī, *Tafsīr* 1:53, 5:113; Zamakhsharī, *Fāʾiq* s.v. "L-M-Ẓ"; Ibn Manẓūr s.v. "N-Ṣ-Ṣ."
3.250	Abū ʿUbayd, *Gharīb* 4:357; Bayhaqī, *Sunan* 4:252 (cites Abū ʿUbayd); Zamakhsharī, *Fāʾiq* s.v. "Ẓ-N-N" (attrib. ʿUthmān); Qurṭubī 19:242; Ibn Manẓūr s.v. "Ẓ-N-N."

(*cont.*)

Text no.	References
3.251	Abū ʿUbayd, *Gharīb* 4:359; Harawī s.v. "ʿ-Dh-B."
3.252	Abū ʿUbayd, *Gharīb* 4:361; Yaʿqūbī 2:207; Harawī s.v. "Y-S-R"; Ibn ʿAsākir 42:502.
3.253	Minqarī 90; Abū ʿUbayd, *Gharīb* 4:371; Ibn Ḥanbal, *Musnad* 2:453; Abū Yaʿlā, *Musnad* 1:258; Ibn Fāris 2:101 s.v. "Ḥ-M-R"; Jawharī s.v. "Ḥ-M-R"; Harawī s.v. "Ḥ-M-R"; Thaʿlabī 2:53; Thaʿālibī, *Tafsīr* 2:126; Baghawī 1:206; Ṭabrisī, *Majmaʿ* 1:488; Samʿānī, *Tafsīr* 1:42 (attrib. anon.); Ibn ʿAsākir 4:13; Majd al-Dīn Ibn al-Athīr s.v. "B-ʾ-S," "T-Q-Y," "Ḥ-M-R," "W-Q-Y"; ʿIzz al-Dīn Ibn al-Athīr, *Usd* 1:29; Qurṭubī 1:227; Ibn Manẓūr s.v. "Ḥ-M-R"; Gharnāṭī 3:386 (attrib. Salamah).
3.254	Muʾaddib 164.
3.255	Jāḥiẓ, *Bayān* 3:211; Balādhurī 2:238, 274; Yaʿqūbī 2:210; Ṭūsī, *Amālī* 134.
3.256	Ḥuṣrī 3:730; Muʾaddib 304; Ṭarṭūshī 120 (attrib. "a wise man").
3.257	Fattāl 372; Quṭb al-Dīn Rāwandī, *Daʿawāt* 293; Ibn ʿAsākir 42:498.
3.258–259	None
3.260	This saying is part of § 3.358. See sources there.
3.261	Balādhurī 5:588; Ibn Abī Shaybah 7:259 (§ 35876); Ḥarbī 3:1059; Ḥarrānī 201; Qālī, *Amālī* 2:204; Makkī 2:362; Abū Hilāl, *Jamharah* 1:184.
3.262	Ḥulwānī 53; Raḍī, *Khaṣāʾiṣ* 98; Muʾaddib 66.
3.263	Ibn Mājah 2:269; Zamakhsharī, *Rabīʿ* 4:440; Ibn Shahrāshūb 2:189.
3.264	Kulaynī 7:264; Ibn Shahrāshūb 2:202.
3.265	Muʾaddib 414.
3.266	Ḥarrānī 155; Kulaynī 5:82.
3.267	Āmidī 337; Ibn ʿAsākir 42:493.
3.268	Muʾaddib 160; Maydānī 2:455; Ibn Ṭalḥah 281; Nuwayrī 3:376.
3.269	Ibn ʿAbd Rabbih 3:174 (attrib. Zayn al-ʿĀbidīn); Ghazālī, *Iḥyāʾ* 3:332; Zamakhsharī, *Rabīʿ* 2:389.
3.270	None
3.271	Ḥarrānī 236; Muʾaddib 135; Āmidī 234–235.
3.272	Āmidī 310; Zamakhsharī, *Rabīʿ* 1:451; Sibṭ 156; Muḥammad al-Waṭwāṭ 104.
3.273	Māmaṭīrī 329; Ṣadūq, *Tawḥīd* 365; Thaʿlabī 2:225; Muʾaddib 319; Fattāl 40; Ibn ʿAsākir 42:512, 51:182; Burrī 2:251; Sibṭ 156.
3.274	Ibn Qutaybah, *ʿUyūn* 2:144; Muʾaddib 132.
3.275	Ibn Qutaybah, *ʿUyūn* 2:385; Kulaynī 2:237; Ḥarrānī 234; Khaṭīb, *Tārīkh* 14:265; Muʾaddib 398; Ṭabrisī, *Mishkāt* 421; Ibn ʿAsākir 13:254; Ibn Kathīr, *Bidāyah* 8:43.

(cont.)

Text no.	References
3.276	Fattāl 420; Āmidī 262.
3.277	Yaʿqūbī 2:209; Ibn ʿAbd Rabbih 3:255; Kulaynī 3:261; Ḥarrānī 209; Māmaṭīrī 289–290; Fattāl 423; Muʾaddib 161–162; Āmidī 121; Ṭabrisī, *Mishkāt* 489; Ibn ʿAsākir 9:131; Nuwayrī 5:167.
3.278	Quḍāʿī, *Dustūr* 212; Āmidī 103; Nuwayrī 5:196.
3.279	Ibn Qutaybah, *ʿUyūn* 2:494; Ḥarrānī 205; Muʾaddib 523.
3.280	Jāḥiẓ, *Bayān* 3:275; Ibn Qutaybah, *ʿUyūn* 2:227; Thaqafī 1:180; Yaʿqūbī 2:209; Ibn ʿAbd Rabbih 2:128; Ṣadūq, *Khiṣāl* 441; Tawḥīdī, *Baṣāʾir* 5:225; Quḍāʿī, *Dustūr* 128; Fattāl 46; Rāghib, *Muḥāḍarāt* 2:559; Ṭabrisī, *Iḥtijāj* 1:400; Quṭb al-Dīn Rāwandī, *Kharāʾij* 2:572; Zamakhsharī, *Rabīʿ* 2:48; Ibn Shahrāshūb 2:203.
3.281	Ibn ʿAbd Rabbih 2:227 (rendered into verse); Zamakhsharī, *Rabīʿ* 1:405.
3.282	Ṭabarī, *Tārīkh* 4:277; Ibn ʿAsākir 63:246.
3.283	Muʾaddib 476; Āmidī 309; Sibṭ 135.
3.284	Mufīd, *Ikhtiṣāṣ* 239; Mufīd, *Irshād* 1:298; Maydānī 2:453; Nuwayrī 3:6; Warrām 2:369.
3.285	Āmidī 313; Muʾaddib 64; Ṭarṭūshī 197; Irbilī 3:139.
3.286	Ibn ʿAbd Rabbih 4:288; Murtaḍā, *Amālī* 1:149.
3.287	Quḍāʿī, *Dustūr* 14; Āmidī 187; Maydānī 2:454; Ṭarṭūshī 203; Ibn Ṭalḥah 280.
3.288	Quḍāʿī, *Dustūr* 28; Muʾaddib 478; Āmidī 313; Zamakhsharī, *Rabīʿ* 3:163; Quṭb al-Dīn Rāwandī, *Daʿawāt* 21.
3.289	Māmaṭīrī 239; Ābī 1:284; Muwaffaq biʾllāh 586; Rāghib, *Muḥāḍarāt* 2:405.
3.290	Nuʿmān, *Daʿāʾim* 1:243; Āmidī 107.
3.291	Abū ʿUbayd, *Amthāl* 110 (attrib. "an Arab sage"); Muʾaddib 476; Āmidī 307; Maydānī 2:292 (attrib. anon. Bedouin sage).
3.292	Ḥarrānī 224; Ṣadūq, *Tawḥīd* 368; Abū Nuʿaym 1:75; Muʾaddib 386; Irbilī 3:142.
3.293	Mubarrad, *Kāmil* 1:70; Mufīd, *Irshād* 2:185; Fattāl 209; Āmidī 361; Zamakhsharī, *Rabīʿ* 5:292; Maydānī 2:454; Ibn Shahrāshūb 3:357; Irbilī 2:383.
3.294	Ibn Ṭalḥah 279.
3.295	Āmidī 68; Zamakhsharī, *Rabīʿ* 3:297; Warrām 1:187.
3.296	Masʿūdī, *Murūj* 2:418; Hārūnī 506.
3.297	Ibn Qutaybah, *Maʿārif* 1:580; Ṭabarī-Āmulī 674; Abū Nuʿaym 5:26; Rāghib, *Muḥāḍarāt* 1:490.

(cont.)

Text no.	References
3.298	Ḥulwānī 129; Kulaynī 3:454; Muʾaddib 158; Fattāl 414; Āmidī 113; Zamakhsharī, *Rabīʿ* 2:279.
3.299	Dārimī 4:2098; Tirmidhī 5:172 (attrib. Prophet); Kulaynī 1:61; Ibn ʿAbd Rabbih 2:103; Kūfī 2:30; Masʿūdī, *Murūj* 3:106. Rāzī, *Mafātīḥ* 2:251.
3.300	Zamakhsharī, *Rabīʿ* 2:7; Maydānī 1:306; Nuwayrī 6:65 (attrib. anon).
3.301	Rāghib, *Muḥāḍarāt* 1:133.
3.302	Iskāfī, *Miʿyār* 251; Nuʿmān, *Manāqib* 216 (attrib. Prophet re. ʿAlī); Ṣadūq, *Khiṣāl* 633; Ṣadūq, *Maʿānī* 314; Ibn ʿAbd al-Barr, *Istīʿāb* 4:1744; Muʾaddib 32, 165; Majd al-Dīn Ibn al-Athīr s.v. "Y-ʿ-S-B"; ʿIzz al-Dīn Ibn al-Athīr, *Usd* 5:287 (attrib. Prophet re ʿAlī).
3.303	Murtaḍā, *Amālī* 1:274; Zamakhsharī, *Rabīʿ* 2:47; Sibṭ 162; Nuwayrī 8:169.
3.304	Tawḥīdī, *Baṣāʾir* 1:117.
3.305	Āmidī 102; Zamakhsharī, *Rabīʿ* 5:91.
3.306	Isḥāq 179; Thaqafī 1:179; Kulaynī 6:381; Ibn ʿAbd Rabbih 2:91; Māmaṭīrī 146; Muwaffaq biʾllāh 589; Ṣadūq, *Khiṣāl* 209; Ṣadūq, *ʿIlal* 2:593; Ṣadūq, *ʿUyūn* 2:218; Muʾaddib 132; Maydānī 2:454.
3.307	Ṭabarī, *Tārīkh* 4:441; Masʿūdī, *Murūj* 2:353.
3.308	Minqarī 531; Iskāfī, *Miʿyār* 193; Ṭabarī, *Tārīkh* 5:62; ʿIzz al-Dīn Ibn al-Athīr, *Kāmil* 2:575.
3.309	Ṭabarī, *Tārīkh* 5:88; Masʿūdī, *Murūj* 2:402; ʿIzz al-Dīn Ibn al-Athīr, *Kāmil* 2:697; Ibn Kathīr, *Bidāyah* 7:320.
3.310	Muʾaddib 90; Zamakhsharī, *Rabīʿ* 2:171; Warrām 2:460.
3.311	Thaqafī 1:295; Ṭabarī, *Tārīkh* 5:108; Ibn ʿAsākir 34:431; Nuwayrī 20:252.
3.312	Ṭabarī, *Tārīkh* 5:552; Ṭabarī, *Tafsīr* 23:170; Baghawī 3:698.
3.313	Ḥuṣrī 1:80; Āmidī 202, 308.
3.314	Nuʿmān, *Daʿāʾim* 1:245; Fattāl 454; Āmidī 108; Ṭabrisī, *Mishkāt* 228.
3.315	Muʾaddib 59.
3.316	Āmidī 97; Zamakhsharī, *Rabīʿ* 5:278.
3.317	Āmidī 20, 106; Zamakhsharī, *Rabīʿ* 3:291.
3.318	Minqarī 126; Jāḥiẓ, *Rasāʾil* 106; Harawī s.v. "Ẓ-L-L"; Majd al-Dīn Ibn al-Athīr s.v. "Ẓ-L-L."
3.319	Kulaynī 2:226; Maydānī 2:454; Zamakhsharī, *Rabīʿ* 2:157; Ibn ʿAsākir 17:419 (attrib. Dhū al-Nūn al-Miṣrī); Sibṭ 138; Dhahabī, *Tārīkh* 21:277.
3.320	Kūfī 81; Kulaynī 3:259; Ṣadūq, *ʿUyūn* 1:43; Mufīd, *Amālī* 309.
3.321	Dajājī 11.
3.322	Ḥarrānī 112; Ṣadūq, *Khiṣāl* 621.

(*cont.*)

Text no.	References
3.323	Makkī 2:272 (attrib. anon.); Muʾaddib 64; Ghazālī, *Iḥyāʾ* 1:86 (rendered in *rajaz* verse); Irbilī 3:139.
3.324	Āmidī 292; Maydānī 2:454.
3.325	Ḥarrānī 90; Karājikī, *Kanz* 138; Quḍāʿī, *Dustūr* 14; Muʾaddib 69; Maydānī 2:454; Zamakhsharī, *Rabīʿ* 3:407; Warrām 1:208; Ibn Ṭalḥah 280; Irbilī 3:139.
3.326	Āmidī 221; Muḥammad al-Waṭwāṭ 81.
3.327	Muʾaddib 66, 472; Āmidī 57; Sibṭ 135.
3.328	Muʾaddib 472; Āmidī 101, 224.
3.329	Zamakhsharī, *Rabīʿ* 3:194.
3.330	Thaʿālibī, *Iʿjāz* 85 (attrib. Maʾmūn); Rāghib, *Muḥāḍarāt* 1:449; Ṭarṭushī 204; Zamakhsharī, *Rabīʿ* 5:104.
3.331	Zamakhsharī, *Rabīʿ* 2:108.
3.332	Ḥarrānī 88; Kulaynī 8:19; Quḍāʿī 36; Maydānī 2:454; Zamakhsharī, *Rabīʿ* 2:328; Warrām 2:182.
3.333	Yaʿqūbī 2:207; Kulaynī 1:37; Ḥarrānī 10, 21; Karājikī, *Maʿdin* 33; Muʾaddib 404; Fattāl 466; Warrām 2:378.
3.334	Tanūkhī 1:177; Āmidī 416.
3.335	Fattāl 429; Āmidī 340; Zamakhsharī, *Rabīʿ* 4:282; Ṭabrisī, *Mishkāt* 159.
3.336	Āmidī 68; Ḥarrānī 203.
3.337	Kulaynī 6:17; Māmaṭīrī 394.
3.338	Zamakhsharī, *Rabīʿ* 1:300.
3.339	Zamakhsharī, *Rabīʿ* 5:342.
3.340	Muʾaddib 151; Āmidī 77.
3.341	Iskāfī, *Tamḥīṣ* 48; Ḥarrānī 206.
3.342	Muʾaddib 556; Āmidī 154, 359; Warrām 3:215; Majd al-Dīn Ibn al-Athīr s.v. "Ṣ-R-F"; Ibn Manẓūr s.v. "Ṣ-R-F."
3.343	Kulaynī 2:362; Ṣadūq, *Amālī* 380; Mufīd, *Ikhtiṣāṣ* 226; Warrām 3:210.
3.344	Ḥulwānī 48; Āmidī 43.
3.345	Ḥulwānī 48.
3.346	Ḥulwānī 48; Maydānī 2:454.
3.347	Ḥulwānī 48; Āmidī 250.
3.348	Ḥarrānī 202; Mufīd, *Amālī* 336; Karājikī, *Kanz* 225; Quḍāʿī, *Dustūr* 10; Ṭūsī, *Amālī* 115; Muʾaddib 31; Āmidī 243; Fattāl 10.
3.349	Kulaynī 1:44 (attrib. Jaʿfar al-Ṣādiq); Māmaṭīrī 153; Āmidī 49; Ṭabrisī, *Mishkāt* 243; Ibn al-ʿArabī 2:159.

(*cont.*)

Text no.	References
3.350	Ḥarrānī 221.
3.351	Bāqillānī 146; Quḍāʿī, *Dustūr* 56; Muʾaddib 90; Zamakhsharī, *Rabīʿ* 1:88; Warrām 2:74.
3.352	Jāḥiẓ, *Miʾat* 224; Kulaynī 8:19; Ḥarrānī 90–93; Ṣadūq, *Amālī* 399; Ṣadūq, *Man* 3:573; Ṣadūq, *Tawḥīd* 73; Karājikī, *Kanz* 128; Quḍāʿī, *Dustūr* 224; Warrām 2:181–182.
3.353	Ḥarrānī 222; Māmaṭīrī 173; Ṣadūq, *Khiṣāl* 197; Hārūnī 207; Muwaffaq bi'llāh 551; Ibn al-Ṭuyūrī 2:538; Fattāl 1:6; Maydānī 2:454; Ṭabrisī, *Mishkāt* 241; Muwaffaq Khwārazmī 368; Sibṭ 159; Ḥammūʾī 1:403; Ḥasan al-ʿAskarī, 402–403.
3.354.1	Ṭabarī, *Tārīkh* 6:357; Fattāl 364; Ṭabrisī, *Mishkāt* 100; ʿIzz al-Dīn Ibn al-Athīr, *Kāmil* 3:501.
3.354.2	Māmaṭīrī 227–228.
3.354.3	Nuʿaym 1:69; Qummī 1:213; Muʾaddib 153; Āmidī 11, 152; Ghazālī, *Iḥyāʾ* 2:311.
3.355	Ibn Aʿtham 2:395; Balādhurī 5:533.
3.356	Ibn ʿAbd Rabbih 4:170; Fattāl 502; Ibn Munqidh 90, 393.
3.357	Jāḥiẓ, *Miʾat* 228; Ḥarrānī 66; Fattāl 385; Ṭarṭūshī 204.
3.358	Ḥulwānī 52; Ibn Qutaybah, *ʿUyūn* 2:400; Mubarrad, *Kāmil* 1:130; Ḥarrānī 86; Ibn ʿAbd Rabbih 3:102, 160; Makkī 1:138, 2:26; Māmaṭīrī 243; Ṣadūq, *Hidāyah* 314; Ṣadūq, *Man* 4:386; Mufīd, *Muqniʿah* 361; Tanūkhī 1:158; Muwaffaq bi'llāh 587; Karājikī, *Kanz* 290–291; Raḍī, *Khaṣāʾiṣ* 115.
3.359	Ṣadūq, *Man* 4:386; Sibṭ 135.
3.360	Ṣadūq, *Man* 4:388; Muʾaddib 63; Fattāl 469; Muḥammad ibn Ṭāhir 318.
3.361	Ḥarrānī 74; Ṣadūq, *Man* 2:626; Mufīd, *Ikhtiṣāṣ* 231; Quḍāʿī, *Dustūr* 80; Muʾaddib 530, 526.
3.362	Ḥarrānī 409; Ṣadūq, *Man* 2:628; Āmidī 77.
3.363	Muʾaddib 59, 62; Maydānī 2:454; Ibn Ṭalḥah 280.
3.364	Āmidī 304.
3.365	Quḍāʿī, *Dustūr* 34; Maydānī 2:454; Muʾaddib 456; Ibn Ṭalḥah 280.
3.366	Ḥulwānī 61; Kulaynī 8:24; Ḥarrānī 99; Ṣadūq, *Amālī* 400; Ṣadūq, *Man* 4:392; Ṣadūq, *Tawḥīd* 74; Rāghib, *Mufradāt* 300; Warrām 2:186–187.
3.367	Barqī 2:345; Ḥarrānī 203; Ṭūsī, *Amālī* 147; Maydānī 2:260 (attrib. Prophet David); Irbilī 2:11.
3.368	Muʾaddib 84; Warrām 3:215.

(cont.)

Text no.	References
3.369	(See 3.134; second part is the same; no citations for first part).
3.370	Ḥarrānī 78; Muwaffaq bi'llāh 545; Āmidī 117.
3.371	Mu'addib 266; Āmidī 133; Maydānī 1:290 (unattrib.).
3.372	Maydānī 2:454.
3.373	Kulaynī 8:21; Ḥarrānī 95, 207; Maydānī 2:303 (attrib. Aws ibn al-Ḥārith); Warrām 2:298, 3:215.
3.374	Āmidī 171; Ṭarṭūshī 204.
3.375	Ḥarrānī 202.
3.376	Ḥarrānī 345; Quḍā'ī, *Dustūr* 126.
3.377	Ibn Shādhān 505; Ibn Qutaybah, *Imāmah* 1:69; Ibn 'Asākir 14:105, 60:44.
3.378	Mas'ūdī, *Murūj* 4:261; Makkī 2:88; Tha'labī 2:261; Muwaffaq bi'llāh 584; Khaṭīb, *Tārīkh* 11:81, 13:87; Maydānī 2:454.
3.379	Āmidī 232.
3.380	Mufīd, *Irshād* 1:300; Quḍā'ī, *Dustūr* 32; Maydānī 2:454; Zamakhsharī, *Rabī'* 3:148; Ibn Ṭalḥah 280.
3.381	Maydānī 2:454.
3.382	Zamakhsharī, *Rabī'* 2:238.
3.383	Mu'addib 524; Āmidī 253.
3.384	Ḥulwānī 144; Kulaynī 8:22; Ḥarrānī 97.
3.385	Ibn 'Abd Rabbih 3:255 (in verse); Māmaṭīrī 291; Māwardī, *Adab* 264; Mu'addib 162; Āmidī 121.
3.386	Māwardī, *Adab* 264; Mu'addib 42; Rāghib, *Muḥāḍarāt* 2:401; Fattāl 441; Āmidī 32; Maydānī 2:454; Ṭabrisī, *Mishkāt* 468; Ibn Ṭalḥah 279.
3.387	Kulaynī 8:72; Ṣadūq, *Khiṣāl* 139; Mu'addib 519; Āmidī 257; Ibn 'Asākir 42:508; Ibn Shahrāshūb 1:378.
3.388	Ḥarrānī 197; Tha'labī 8:315; Rāzī, *Mafātīḥ* 3:471 (attrib. Abū Idrīs).
3.389	Mu'addib 38.
3.390	Mufīd, *Ikhtiṣāṣ* 342; Murtaḍā, *Amālī* 1:156; Mu'addib 488; Āmidī 236; Zamakhsharī, *Rabī'* 2:342; Muwaffaq Khwārazmī 377.
3.391	Ḥarrānī 89; Ṣadūq, *Khiṣāl* 637; Ibn Shahrāshūb 1:380.
3.392	Āmidī 177.
3.393	Āmidī 253.
3.394	Kulaynī 8:307; Ṣadūq, *Amālī* 87; Ṣadūq, *Khiṣāl* 129; Ṣadūq, *Man* 4:396; Fattāl 442.
3.395	Kulaynī 1:20.
3.396	Ibn Abī al-Dunyā, *Qaḍā'* 23 (attrib. Prophet); Ṭabarānī, *Mu'jam awsaṭ*

(cont.)

Text no.	References
	5:228; Muʾaddib 141; Āmidī 76; Ṭabrisī, *Mishkāt* 546 (attrib. Prophet); Muḥammad ibn Ṭāhir 321.
3.397	None
3.398	Āmidī 212; Ṭabrisī, *Mishkāt* 369.
3.399	Fattāl 354.
3.400	Māmaṭīrī 355; Fattāl 498; Muwaffaq biʾllāh 580; Warrām 2:322.
3.401	Āmidī 82.
3.402	Ḥarrānī 82; Āmidī 150.
3.403	Abū Nuʿaym 1:10 (attrib. Jesus); Muʾaddib 160.
3.404	Āmidī 48.
3.405	Thaʿlab (Raḍī's stated source).
3.406	Muʾaddib 482; Āmidī 230.
3.407	Fattāl 466.
3.408	Mufīd, *Ikhtiṣāṣ* 245; Thaʿālibī, *Iʿjāz* 34; Ḥuṣrī 1:80; Maydānī 2:454; Zamakhsharī, *Rabīʿ* 2:23.
3.409	Muʾaddib 459; Fattāl 434; Zamakhsharī, *Rabīʿ* 2:171; Ṭabrisī, *Mishkāt* 208.
3.410	Maydānī 2:453; Ibn Ṭalḥah 279.
3.411	Muʾaddib 481.
3.412	Ibn Ṭalḥah 279.
3.413	Thaqafī 1:65; Māmaṭīrī 268; Mufīd, *Ikhtiṣāṣ* 81; Muʾaddib 416; Āmidī 262; Zamakhsharī, *Rabīʿ* 1:182; Majd al-Dīn Ibn al-Athīr s.v. "F-N-D"; Ibn Manẓūr s.v. "F-N-D."
3.414	Zamakhsharī, *Rabīʿ* 3:459.
3.415	Maydānī 2:454; Ibn Ṭalḥah 279.
3.416	Zamakhsharī, *Rabīʿ* 2:256; Zamakhsharī, *Fāʾiq* 2:10, s.v. "Dh-ʿ-Dh-ʿ"; Majd al-Dīn Ibn al-Athīr s.v. "Dh-ʿ-Dh-ʿ."
3.417	Muʾaddib 437; Maydānī 2:453; Ibn Ṭalḥah 279.
3.418	Ibn ʿAbd Rabbih 3:121 (attrib. Ibn al-Ḥanafiyyah); Muʾaddib 437; Maydānī 2:453; Ibn Ṭalḥah 279.
3.419	Muʾaddib 480; Āmidī 232; Zamakhsharī, *Rabīʿ* 5:111.
3.420	Āmidī 135.
3.421	Mubarrad, *Kāmil* 2:11; Māmaṭīrī 408; Ṣadūq, *ʿIlal* 1:276; Ābī 1:299; Muwaffaq biʾllāh 577; Muʾaddib 479; Fattāl, *Rawḍah* 412; Maydānī 2:454; Ibn Ṭalḥah 279.
3.422	Āmidī 23.
3.423	Zamakhsharī, *Rabīʿ* 5:224.

(*cont.*)

Text no.	References
3.424	Ḥarrānī 391; Muʾaddib 108; Āmidī 59; Maydānī 2:453; Zamakhsharī, *Rabīʿ* 1:239; Warrām 1:226.
3.425	Ibn Abī al-Dunyā, *Makārim* 51; Jarīrī 261; Quḍāʿī, *Dustūr* 28; Ibn ʿAsākir 9:216; Ibn al-ʿAdīm 7:389; Nuwayrī 3:237.
3.426	Ḥarrānī 223.
3.427	Ibn al-Muʿtazz 21; Ibn ʿAbd Rabbih 2:143; Māmaṭīrī 380; Bāqillānī 68; Muwaffaq bi'llāh 576; Ṭarṭūshī 83, 87.
3.428	Maydānī 2:454; Zamakhsharī, *Rabīʿ* 2:332; Ibn Ṭalḥah 279.
3.429	Yaʿqūbī 2:206; Ḥarrānī 203, 281; Ṭūsī, *Amālī* 443; Muʾaddib 268; Ibn Abī Zaynab 37; Maydānī 2:454.

Bibliography

Primary Sources

ʿAbd al-Bāqī Tabrīzī Dānishmand (d. after 1039/1630) (comm.). *Minhāj al-walāyah: Fī Sharḥ Nahj al-balāghah.* Edited by Ḥabīballāh ʿAẓīmī. 2 vols. Tehran: Intishārāt-i Daftar-i Mīrāth-i Maktūb, 1378/1959.

ʿAbd al-Jabbār ibn Aḥmad, al-Qāḍī al-Asadābādī (d. 415/1025). *Firaq wa-ṭabaqāt al-Muʿtazilah.* Edited by ʿAlī Sāmī al-Nashshār and ʿIṣām al-Dīn Muḥammad ʿAlī. Cairo: Dār al-Maṭbūʿāt al-Jāmiʿiyyah, 1972.

ʿAbd al-Jabbār ibn Aḥmad, al-Qāḍī al-Asadābādī (d. 415/1025). *Al-Mughnī fī abwāb al-tawḥīd wa-l-ʿadl.* General editor Ṭāhā Ḥusayn. 20 vols. Vol. 20 edited by ʿAbd al-Ḥalīm Maḥmūd and Sulaymān al-Dunyā. Cairo: al-Dār al-Miṣriyyah, 1961.

ʿAbd al-Razzāq, Abū Bakr al-Ṣanʿānī (d. 211/827) (comp.). *Muṣannaf ʿAbd al-Razzāq.* Edited by Ḥabīb al-Raḥmān al-Aʿẓamī. Beirut: al-Maktab al-Islāmī, 1403/1983.

al-Ābī, Manṣūr ibn al-Ḥasan (d. 421/1030). *Nathr al-durr.* 7 vols. Edited by Muḥammad ʿAlī Qurnah. Cairo: al-Hayʾah al-Miṣriyyah al-ʿĀmmah li-l-Kitāb, 1980.

Abu al ʿAtāhiyah (d. ca. 198/813). *Dīwān.* Beirut: Dār Bayrūt, 1986.

Abū Dhuʾayb al-Hudhalī (d. ca. 28/649). Poems in *Dīwān al-Hudhaliyyīn.* Edited by Muḥammad Maḥmūd al-Shinqīṭī. 3 vols. Cairo: al-Dār al-Qawmiyyah, 1965.

Abū al-Faraj al-Iṣfahānī (d. 356/976). *Kitāb al-Aghānī.* 27 vols. in 15. Edited by ʿAbd al-Amīr ʿAlī Muhannā and Samīr Jābir. Beirut: Dār al-Kutub al-ʿIlmiyyah, 1422/2002.

Abū al-Faraj al-Iṣfahānī (d. 356/976). *Maqātil al-Ṭālibiyyīn.* Edited by Kāẓim al-Muẓaffar. Najaf: al-Maktabah al-Ḥaydariyyah, 1385/1965.

Abū Hilāl al-ʿAskarī (d. 395/1005). *Dīwān al-maʿānī.* Beirut: Dār al-Jīl, 1980–1995.

Abū Hilāl al-ʿAskarī (d. 395/1005). *Jamharat al-amthāl.* 2 vols. Beirut: Dār al-Fikr, 1988.

Abū Hilāl al-ʿAskarī (d. 395/1005). *Al-Furūq al-lughawiyyah.* Qum: Muʾassasat al-Nashr al-Islāmī, 1992.

Abū Hilāl al-ʿAskarī (d. 395/1005). *Kitāb al-Ṣināʿatayn.* Cairo: ʿĪsā al-Bābī al-Ḥalabī, 1971.

Abū Khaythamah Zuhayr ibn Ḥarb al-Nasāʾī (d. 243/857). *Kitāb al-ʿIlm.* Edited by Muḥammad Nāṣir al-Dīn al-Albānī. Beirut: al-Maktab al-Islāmī, 1983.

Abū Nuʿaym al-Iṣfahānī (d. 430/1038). *Ḥilyat al-awliyāʾ wa-ṭabaqāt al-aṣfiyāʾ.* 8 vols. Cairo: Maṭbaʿat al-Saʿādah, 1416/1996.

Abū al-Saʿādāt al-Isfahānī (d. 634/1237) (comp.). *Maṭlaʿ al-ṣabāḥatayn wa-majmaʿ al-faṣāḥatayn.* Tehran: Pazhūhishgāh-i ʿUlūm-i Insānī va Muṭālāʿāt-i Farhangī, 1965.

Abū al-Ṣalāḥ al-Ḥalabī, Taqī al-Dīn (d. 447/1055). *Taqrīb al-maʿārif.* Edited by Fāris Tabrīziyyān al-Ḥassūn. Tehran: Fāris Tabrīziyān al-Ḥassūn, 1996.

Abū Tammām (d. ca. 232/845) and al-Khaṭīb al-Tabrīzī (d. 502/1109) (comm.). *Sharḥ Dīwān Abī Tammām.* Edited by Muḥammad ʿAbduh ʿAzzām. 3 vols. Cairo: Dār al-Maʿārif, 1964.

Abū ʿUbayd al-Qāsim ibn Sallām al-Harawī (d. 224/838). *Kitāb al-Amthāl*. Cairo: Dār al-Maʾmūn, 1400/1980.

Abū ʿUbayd al-Qāsim ibn Sallām al-Harawī (d. 224/838). *Gharīb al-ḥadīth*. Edited by Ḥusayn Muḥammad Sharaf. Cairo: al-Hayʾah al-ʿĀmmah li-Shuʾūn al-Maṭābiʿ al-Amīriyyah, 1404/1984.

Abū Yaʿlā (d. 307/919) (comp.). *Musnad Abī Yaʿlā*. Edited by Ḥusayn Salīm Asad. Damascus: Dār al-Maʾmūn, 1404/1984.

al-ʿAdanī, Muḥammad ibn Yaḥyā (d. 243/858). *Al-Īmān*. Edited by Ḥamad ibn Ḥamdī al-Jābirī. Kuwait: Al-Dār al-Salafiyyah, 1407/1986.

al-Ahwāzī al-Kūfī, al-Ḥusayn ibn Saʿīd (active 300/913). *Kitāb al-Zuhd*. Edited by Ghulām Riḍā ʿIrfāniyyān. Qum: al-Maṭbaʿah al-ʿIlmiyyah, 1361/1979.

al-Ahwāzī al-Kūfī, al-Ḥusayn ibn Saʿīd (active 300/913). *Kitāb al-Muʾmin*. Qum: Madrasat al-Imām al-Mahdī, 1993.

ʿAlī ibn Abī Ṭālib (d. 40/661), attrib. Medieval compilations of orations, aphorisms, epistles, testaments, prayers, and poetry are listed under the compiler's name: Āmidī, Ḥarrānī, Ḥātim, Jāḥiẓ, Kaydarī, Nuʿmān, Raḍī, Quḍāʿī, Sulaym, and Ṭabrisī, as are modern compilations by Ḥaydar, Jindī, Kāshif al-Ghiṭāʾ, Maḥmūdī, Mīr-Jahānī, Qubānchī, and Shams al-Dīn.

ʿAlī ibn Abī Ṭālib (d. 40/661) attrib. *Al-Ṣaḥīfah al-ʿAlawiyyah al-mubārakah*. Beirut: n.p., 1979. Excerpt translated by William Chittick as *Supplications (Duʿa) of Amir al-muʾminin ʿAli ibn Abi Talib*. London: Muhammadi Trust, 1986.

ʿAlī ibn Muḥammad ibn al-Walīd (d. 612/1215). *Dāmigh al-bāṭil wa-ḥatf al-munāḍil*. Edited by Muṣṭafā Ghālib. 2 vols. Beirut: Muʾassasat ʿIzz al-Dīn, 1982.

ʿAlī ibn Muḥammad ibn al-Walīd (d. 612/1215) *Tāj al-ʿaqāʾid wa-maʿdin al-fawāʾid*. Edited by ʿĀrif Tāmir. Beirut: Muʾassasat ʿIzz al-Dīn, 1982.

al-Āmidī (d. 510/1155) (comp.). *Ghurar al-ḥikam wa-durar al-kalim*. Edited by Aḥmad Shawqī Amīn. Najaf: Dār al-Thaqāfah, 1960s.

Anon. (3rd/9th c.), *Akhbār al-dawlah al-ʿAbbāsiyyah*. Edited by ʿAbd al-ʿAzīz al-Dūrī and ʿAbd al-Jabbār al-Muṭṭalibī. Beirut: Dār al-Ṭalīʿah, 1971.

al-Aʿshā, Maymūn ibn Qays (d. ca. 7/629). *Dīwān al-Aʿshā al-kabīr*. Edited by Muḥammad Ḥusayn. Cairo: Maktabat al-Ādāb, 1950.

al-ʿĀṣimī, Aḥmad ibn Muḥammad (d. 450/1058). *Al-ʿAsal al-muṣaffā min tahdhīb Zayn al-fatā fī sharḥ Surat Hal Atā*. Edited by Muḥammad Bāqir Maḥmūdī. 2 vols. Qum: Majmaʿ Iḥyāʾ al-Thaqāfah al-Islāmiyyah, 1997.

al-ʿAyyāshī, Muḥammad ibn Masʿūd (d. 329/941) (comm.). *Tafsīr al-ʿAyyāshī*. Edited by Hāshim Rasūlī-Maḥallātī. Beirut: Muʾassasat al-Aʿlamī, 1991.

al-Azharī (d. 370/980). *Tahdhīb al-lughah*. Edited by Muḥammad ʿAwaḍ Murʿib. 8 vols. Beirut: Dār Iḥyāʾ al-Turāth al-ʿArabī, 2001.

al-Baghawī (d. ca. 516/1122) (comm.). *Maʿālim al-tanzīl fī tafsīr al-Qurʾān*. Edited by ʿAbd al-Razzāq al-Mahdī. Beirut: Dār Iḥyāʾ al-Turāth, 1420/2000.

al-Baḥrānī, Kamāl al-Dīn Ibn Maytham (d. 679/1280) (comm.). *Sharḥ Nahj al-balāghah.* 5 parts in 1 vol. Manama, Bahrain: Maktabat Fakhrāwī, 2007.

al-Bakrī, Abū ʿUbayd (d. 487/1094) (comm.). *Kitāb Faṣl al-maqāl: Fī Sharḥ Kitāb al-Amthāl.* Edited by Iḥsān ʿAbbās and ʿAbd al-Majīd ʿĀbidīn. Beirut: Muʾassasat al-Risālah, 1971.

al-Balādhurī (d. 279/892). *Ansāb al-ashrāf.* Edited by Muḥammad Bāqir al-Maḥmūdī. 2 vols. Beirut: Muʾassasat al-Aʿlamī, 1394/1974.

al-Bāqillānī (d. 403/1013). *Iʿjāz al-Qurʾān.* Edited by Aḥmad Ṣaqr. Cairo: Dār al-Maʿārif, 1997.

al-Barqī (d. 274/887). *Kitāb al-Maḥāsin.* Edited by Jalāl al-Dīn al-Ḥusaynī al-Muḥaddith. Tehran: Dār al-Kutub al-Islāmiyyah, 1327/1950.

al-Bāʿūnī, Shams al-Dīn Muḥammad (d. 877/1472). *Jawāhir al-maṭālib fī manāqib ʿAlī ibn Abī Ṭālib.* Edited by Muḥammad Bāqir al-Maḥmūdī. Qum: Majmaʿ Iḥyāʾ al-Thaqāfah al-Islāmiyyah, 1995.

al-Bayhaqī, Abū Bakr (d. 458/1066) (comp.). *Al-Iʿtiqād wa-l-hidāyah ilā sabīl al-rashād ʿalā madhhab al-salaf wa-aṣḥāb al-ḥadīth.* Edited by Aḥmad ʿIṣām al-Kātib. Beirut: Dār al-Āfāq al-Jadīdah, 1981.

al-Bayhaqī, Abū Bakr (d. 458/1066) (comp.). *Shuʿab al-īmān.* Edited by ʿAbd al-ʿAlī ʿAbd al-Ḥamīd Ḥāmid. 14 vols. Riyadh: Maktabat al-Rushd, 2003.

al-Bayhaqī, Abū Bakr (d. 458/1066) (comp.). *Al-Sunan al-kubrā.* Edited by Muḥammad ʿAbd al-Qādir ʿAṭā. 11 vols. Beirut: Dār al-Kutub al-ʿIlmiyyah, 2003.

al-Bayhaqī, Ibrāhīm ibn Muḥammad (fl. ca. 320/932). *Al-Maḥāsin wa-l-masāwiʾ.* Beirut: Dār Ṣādir, 1380/1960.

al-Burrī, Muḥammad ibn Abī Bakr al-Tilimsānī (d. after 644/1246). *Al-Jawharah fī nasab al-nabī wa-aṣḥābihi al-ʿashrah.* Edited by Muḥammad al-Tūnjī. 2 vols. Riyadh: Dār al-Rifāʿī, 1983.

al-Dajājī, Ibn Naṣr (d. 564/1168). *Safaṭ al-mulaḥ wa-zawḥ al-taraḥ.* Edited by Khālid Aḥmad al-Mullā al-Suwaydī. Damascus: Muʾassasat Bayn al-Nahrayn, 1426/2007.

al-Damīrī, Muḥammad ibn Mūsā (d. 808/1405). *Hayāt al-ḥayawān al-kubrā.* Translated by A.S.G. Jayakar as *ad-Damîrî's Hayāt al-ḥayawān: A Zoological Lexicon.* 2 vols. London: Luzac, 1906–1908.

al-Dāraquṭnī (d. 385/995) (comp.). *Al-Muʾtalif wa-l-mukhtalif.* Edited by Muwaffaq ibn ʿAbdallāh ibn ʿAbd al-Qādir. Beirut: Dār al-Gharb al-Islāmī, 1406/1986.

al-Dāraquṭnī (d. 385/995). *Sunan al-Dāraquṭnī.* Edited by Shuʿayb al-Arnāʾūṭ et al. Beirut: Muʾassasat al-Risālah, 1424/2004.

al-Dārimī (d. 255/869) (comp.). *Sunan al-Dārimī.* Edited by Ḥusayn Asad. 4 vols. Riyadh: Dār al-Mughnī, 1421/2000.

al-Daylamī (d. 673/1274). *Aʿlām al-dīn fī ṣifāt al-muʾminīn.* Qum: Muʾassasat Āl al-Bayt li-Iḥyāʾ al-Turāth, 1408/1988.

al-Dhahabī (d. 748/1348). *Mīzān al-iʿtidāl fī naqd al-rijāl*. Edited by ʿAlī Muḥammad Bajāwī. 4 vols. Beirut: Dār al-Maʿrifah, 1382/1963.

al-Dhahabī (d. 748/1348). *Siyar aʿlām al-nubalāʾ*. Edited by Shuʿayb al-Arnāʾūṭ et al. 25 vols. Beirut: Muʾassasat al-Risālah, 1405/1985.

al-Dhahabī (d. 748/1348). *Tadhkirat al-ḥuffāẓ*. 4 vols. Beirut: Dār al-Kutub al-ʿIlmiyyah, 1998.

al-Dhahabī (d. 748/1348). *Tārīkh al-Islām*. Edited by ʿUmar Tadmurī. Beirut: Dār al-Kitāb al-ʿArabī, 1413/1993.

al-Dīnawarī, Abū Bakr Aḥmad ibn Marwān (d. 333/945). *Al-Mujālasah wa-jawāhir al-ʿilm*. Edited by Abū ʿUbaydah Mashhūr ibn Ḥasan Āl Salmān. 10 vols. Beirut: Dār Ibn Ḥazm, 1419/1998.

al-Dīnawarī, Abū Ḥanīfah Aḥmad ibn Dāʾūd (d. 282/896). *Al-Akhbār al-ṭiwāl*. Edited by ʿAbd al-Munʿim ʿĀmir. Cairo: Dār Iḥyāʾ al-Kutub al-ʿArabī, 1960.

Durayd ibn al-Ṣimmah (d. 8/630). *Dīwān*. Edited by ʿUmar ʿAbd al-Rasūl. Cairo: Dār al-Maʿārif, 1985.

al-Farazdaq (d. 114/732). *Dīwān*. Edited by ʿAlī Fāʿūr. Beirut: Dār al-Kutub al-ʿIlmiyyah, 1987.

al-Fattāl (d. 508/1114). *Rawḍat al-wāʿiẓīn*. Edited by Muḥammad Mahdī. Najaf: al-Maktabah al-Ḥaydariyyah, 1966.

Furāt ibn Ibrāhīm al-Kūfī (fl. 3–4th/9th–10th c.) (comm.). *Tafsīr Furāt*. Edited by Muḥammad al-Kāẓim. Tehran: Wizārat al-Thaqāfah wa-l-Irshād al-Īrāniyyah, 1410/1990.

al-Gharnāṭī, Abū Ḥayyān (d. 745/1344) (comm.). *Al-Baḥr al-muḥīṭ fī l-tafsīr*. Edited by Ṣidqī Muḥammad Jamīl. Beirut: Dār al-Fikr, 1420/2000.

al-Ghazālī (d. 505/1111). *Iḥyāʾ ʿulūm al-dīn*. Beirut: Dār al-Maʿrifah, 1404/1984.

al-Ghazālī (d. 505/1111). *Sirr al-ʿālamayn wa-kashf mā fī l-dārayn*. Edited by Muḥammad Ḥasan Ismāʿīl and Aḥmad Farīd al-Mazyadī. Beirut: Dār al-Kutub al-ʿIlmiyyah, 2003.

al-Ḥammūʾī al-Juwaynī, Ṣadr al-Dīn Ibrāhīm ibn Muḥammad (d. 722/1322). *Farāʾid al-simṭayn fī faḍāʾil al-Murtaḍā wa-l-Batūl wa-Sibṭayn wa-l-aʾimmah min dhurriyyatihim ʿalayhim al-salām*. Edited by Muḥammad Bāqir Maḥmūdī. 2 vols. Beirut: Muʾassasat al-Maḥmūdī, 1978.

al-Harawī, Abū ʿUbayd Aḥmad ibn Muḥammad (d. 401/1011). *Kitāb al-Gharībayn fī l-Qurʾān wa-l-ḥadīth*. Edited by Aḥmad Farīdī al-Mazyadī. 6 vols. Mecca: Maktabat Nizār Muṣṭafā al-Bāz, 1419/1999.

al-Ḥarbī, Ibrāhīm ibn Isḥāq (d. 285/898). *Gharīb al-ḥadīth*. Edited by Sulaymān al-ʿĀyid. 3 vols. Mecca: Jāmiʿat Umm al-Qurā, 1405/1985.

al-Ḥarīrī (d. 516/1122). *Maqāmāt Abī Zayd al-Sarūjī*. Edited by Michael Cooperson. New York: New York University Press, *Library of Arabic Literature* series, 2020.

al-Ḥarrānī, Ibn Shuʿbah (fl. 4th/10th c.) (comp.). *Tuḥaf al-ʿuqūl ʿan āl al-rasūl*. Edited by ʿAlī Akbar al-Ghaffārī. Qum: Muʾassasat al-Nashr al-Islāmī, 1404/1983.

Hārūnī, Abū Ṭālib Yaḥyā ibn al-Ḥusayn al-Zaydī (d. 424/1033), thematic edition by Jaʿfar

ibn Aḥmad al-Buhlūlī (d. 573/1177). *Taysīr al-maṭālib fī Amālī Abī Ṭālib.* Edited by
'Abdallāh ibn Ḥammūd al-ʿIzzī. Sanaa: Maktabat al-Imām Zayd ibn ʿAlī, 2002.

al-Ḥasan al-ʿAskarī (attrib.). *Tafsīr al-Imām al-ʿAskarī.* Edited by Muḥammad Bāqir Najl
al-Murtaḍā. Qum: Madrasat al-Imām al-Mahdī, 1409/1989.

Ḥātim ibn Ibrāhīm al-Ḥāmidī Muḥyī al-Dīn (d. 596/1199). *Al-Majālis al-Ḥātimiyyah.* MS.
Mumbai: Ṭayyibī Daʿwah Libraries.

Ḥātim ibn Ibrāhīm al-Ḥāmidī Muḥyī al-Dīn (d. 596/1199). *Tuḥfat al-qulūb wa-furjat al-
makrūb,* or: *Tuḥfat al-qulūb fī tartīb al-hudāt wa-l-duʿāt fī jazīrat al-Yaman.* Edited by
Abbas Hamdani. London: Dār al-Sāqī, 2012.

al-Ḥillī, al-Ḥasan ibn Sulaymān (died after 802/1399). *Mukhtaṣar al-Baṣāʾir.* Edited by
Mushtāq Muẓaffar. Qum: Muʾassasat al-Nashr al-Islāmī, 1959.

al-Ḥimyarī, ʿAbdallāh ibn Jaʿfar (d. ca. 309/922). *Qurb al-isnād.* Beirut: al-Kutub al-
Islāmiyyah, 1992.

al-Ḥimyarī, ʿAlī ibn Muḥammad (d. 323/935). *Juzʾ ʿAlī ibn Muḥammad al-Ḥimyarī.*
Edited by ʿAbd al-ʿAzīz ibn Sulaymān al-Buʿaymī. Riyadh: Maktabat al-Rushd,
1998.

al-Ḥulwānī, al-Ḥusayn ibn Muḥammad (d. 241/856). *Nuzhat al-nāẓir fī tanbīh al-khāṭir.*
Edited by Muḥammad Bāqir ibn al-Murtaḍā et al. Qum: Muʾassasat al-Imām al-
Mahdī, 1408/1987.

Ḥumayd ibn Ahmad al-Muḥallī, al-Qāḍī al-Shahīd (d. 652/1255). *Al-Ḥadāʾiq al-wardiy-
yah fī manāqib aʾimmat al-Zaydiyyah.* Edited by Murtaḍā ibn Zayd al-Maḥaṭwarī.
Sanaa: Maktabat Markaz Badr al-ʿIlmī wa-l-Thaqāfī, 2002.

al-Ḥuṣrī, Abū Isḥāq Ibrāhīm ibn ʿAlī (d. 453/1061). *Zahr al-ādāb wa-thamar al-ālbāb.*
Edited by Muḥammad Muḥyī al-Dīn ʿAbd al-Ḥamīd and Zakī Mubārak. 4 vols. Beirut:
Dār al-Jīl, 1980s.

Ibn ʿAbd al-Barr (463/1070). *Adab al-mujālasah wa-ḥamd al-lisān.* Edited by Samīr Ḥal-
abī. Tanta, Egypt: Dār al-Ṣaḥābah li-l-Turāth, 1409/1989.

Ibn ʿAbd al-Barr (463/1070). *Bahjat al-majālis wa-uns al-mujālis.* Edited by Muḥammad
Mursī al-Khawlī. 2 vols. Beirut: Dār al-Kutub al-ʿIlmiyyah, 1982.

Ibn ʿAbd al-Barr (463/1070). *Al-Istīʿāb fī maʿrifat al-aṣḥāb.* Edited by ʿAlī Muḥammad
al-Bajāwī. Beirut: Dār al-Jīl, 1412/1992.

Ibn ʿAbd al-Barr (463/1070). *Jāmiʿ bayān al-ʿilm wa-faḍluhu.* Edited by ʿAbd al-Hādī
Munīr and Muṣṭafā Āl Ibrāhīm. Cairo: Idārat al-Ṭibāʿah al-Munīriyyah, 1398/1978.

Ibn ʿAbd al-Barr (463/1070). *Al-Tamhīd li-mā fī l-Muwaṭṭā min al-maʿānī wa-l-asānīd.*
Edited by Muṣṭafā ibn Aḥmad al-ʿAlawī and Muḥammad ʿAbd al-Karīm al-Bakrī.
26 vols. Morocco: Wizārat ʿUmūm al-Awqāf wa-l-Shuʾūn al-Islāmiyyah, 1387/1968.

Ibn ʿAbd Rabbih (328/940). *Al-ʿIqd al-farīd.* 8 vols. Beirut: Dār al-Kutub al-ʿIlmiyyah,
1404/1983.

Ibn Abī ʿĀṣim al-Ḍaḥḥāk, Abū Bakr (d. 287/900) (comp.). *Sunnah.* Edited by Muḥam-
mad Nāṣir al-Dīn al-Albānī. Beirut: al-Maktab al-Islāmī, 1400/1980.

Ibn Abī ʿĀṣim al-Ḍaḥḥāk, Abū Bakr (d. 287/900). *Kitāb al-Zuhd.* Edited by ʿAbd al-ʿAlī ʿAbd al-Ḥamīd al-Aʿẓamī. Beirut: Dār al-Kutub al-ʿIlmiyyah, 1985.

Ibn Abī al-Dunyā (d. 281/894). *Al-ʿAql wa-faḍluhu.* Edited by Luṭfī Muḥammad al-Ṣaghīr and Najm ʿAbd al-Raḥmān Khalaf. Riyadh: Dār al-Rāyah, 1989.

Ibn Abī al-Dunyā (d. 281/894). *Kitāb Dhamm al-dunyā.* Edited by Muḥammad ʿAbd al-Qādir ʿAṭā. Beirut: Muʾassasat al-Kutub al-Thaqāfiyyah, 1993.

Ibn Abī al-Dunyā (d. 281/894). *Kitāb al-Ikhwān.* Edited by Muṣṭafā ʿAbd al-Qādir ʿAṭā. Beirut: Dār al-Kutub al-ʿIlmiyyah, 1409/1988.

Ibn Abī al-Dunyā (d. 281/894). *Iṣlāḥ al-māl.* Edited by Muḥammad ʿAbd al-Qādir ʿAṭā. Beirut: Muʾassasat al-Kutub al-Thaqāfiyyah, 1414/1993.

Ibn Abī al-Dunyā (d. 281/894). *Makārim al-akhlāq.* Edited by Magdī Sayyid Ibrāhīm. Cairo: Maktabat al-Qurʾān, 1411/1990.

Ibn Abī al-Dunyā (d. 281/894). *Maqtal al-Imām Amīr al-muʾminīn.* Mashhad: Muʾassasat al-Ṭabʿ wa-l-Nashr, 1411/1991.

Ibn Abī al-Dunyā (d. 281/894). *Qaḍāʾ al-ḥawāʾij.* Edited by Magdī al-Sayyid Ibrāhīm. Cairo: Maktabat al-Qurʾān, 1986.

Ibn Abī al-Dunyā (d. 281/894). *Qiṣar al-amal.* Edited by Muḥammad Khayr Ramaḍān Yūsuf. Beirut: Dār Ibn Ḥazm, 1997.

Ibn Abī al-Dunyā (d. 281/894). *Al-Tawāḍuʿ wa-l-khumūl.* Beirut: Dār al-Kutub al-ʿIlmiyyah, 1409/1989.

Ibn Abī al-Dunyā (d. 281/894). *Kitāb al-Tawbah.* Edited by Magdī al-Sayyid Ibrāhīm. Cairo: Maktabat al-Qurʾan, 1991.

Ibn Abī al-Ḥadīd (d. 655/1257) (comm.). *Sharḥ Nahj al-balāghah.* Edited by Muḥammad Abū al-Faḍl Ibrāhīm. 20 vols. Cairo: Dār Iḥyāʾ al-Kutub al-ʿArabiyyah, 1965.

Ibn Abī al-ʿIzz al-Ḥanafī (d. 792/1390). *Kitāb al-Atbāʿ.* Edited by Muḥammad ʿAṭāʾallāh Ḥanīf. Beirut: ʿĀlam al-Kutub, 1405/1985.

Ibn Abī al-Iṣbaʿ (d. 654/1256). *Taḥrīr al-taḥbīr fī ṣināʿat al-shiʿr wa-l-nathr.* Edited by Ḥifnī Muḥammad Sharaf. Cairo: Al-Majlis al-Aʿlā li-l-Shuʾūn al-Islāmiyyah Lajnat Iḥyāʾ al-Turāth al-Islāmī, 1383/1963.

Ibn Abī Shaybah (d. 235/849) (comp.). *Al-Muṣannaf fī l-aḥādīth wa-l-āthār.* Edited by Kamāl Yūsuf al-Ḥūt. 7 vols. Riyadh: Dār ʿĀlam al-Kutub, 1409/1988.

Ibn Abī Zaynab, Muḥammad ibn Ibrāhīm al-Nuʿmānī (fl. early 4th/10th c.). *Al-Ghaybah.* Qum: Manshūrāt Anwār al-Hudā, 1422/2002.

Ibn ʿAdī al-Jurjānī (d. 365/976). *Al-Kāmil fī ḍuʿafāʾ al-rijāl.* Edited by ʿĀdil Aḥmad ʿAbd al-Mawjūd. 9 vols. Beirut: Dār al-Kutub al-ʿIlmiyyah, 1997.

Ibn al-ʿAdīm, Kamāl al-Dīn ʿUmar (d. 660/1261). *Bughyat al-ṭalab fī tārīkh Ḥalab.* Edited by al-Mahdī ʿĪd al-Rawāḍiyyah. London: Muʾassasat al-Furqān, 1437/2016.

Ibn al-Anbārī, Abū Bakr (d. 328/940) *Al-Zāhir fī maʿānī kalimāt al-nās.* Edited by Ḥātim Ṣāliḥ. 2 vols. Beirut: Muʾassasat al-Risālah, 1992.

Ibn al-ʿArabī, Muḥyī al-Dīn (d. 638/1240) (comm.). *Tafsīr Ibn al-ʿArabī.* Edited by ʿAbd al-Wārith Muḥammad ʿAlī. Beirut: Dār al-Kutub al-ʿIlmiyyah, 2010.

Ibn ʿAsākir (d. 571/1176). *Tārīkh Madīnat Dimashq*, or *Tārīkh Dimashq*. Edited by ʿAmr ibn Gharāmah al-ʿAmrawī. 80 vols. Beirut: Dār al-Fikr, 1995–2000.

Ibn Aʿtham al-Kūfī (died early 3rd/9th c.). *Kitāb al-Futūḥ*. Edited by ʿAlī Shīrī. 8 vols. Beirut: Dār al-Aḍwāʾ, 1411/1991.

Ibn al-Athīr, Ḍiyāʾ al-Dīn (d. 637/1239). *Al-Mathal al-sāʾir fī adab al-kātib wa-l-shāʿir*. Edited by Aḥmad al-Ḥūfī and Badawī Ṭabānah. Cairo: Maktabat Nahḍat Miṣr, 1959–1962.

Ibn al-Athīr, ʿIzz al-Dīn (d. 630/1233). *Al-Kāmil fī l-tārīkh*. Edited by ʿUmar ʿAbd al-Salām Tadmurī. 10 vols. Beirut: Dār al-Kutub al-ʿArabī, 1417/1997.

Ibn al-Athīr, ʿIzz al-Dīn (d. 630/1233). *Usd al-ghābah*. Beirut: Dār Ibn Ḥazm, 1433/2012.

Ibn al-Athīr, Majd al-Dīn (d. 606/1210). *Al-Nihāyah fī gharīb al-ḥadīth wa-l-āthār*. Edited by Ṭāhir Aḥmad al-Zāwī and Maḥmūd Muḥammad al-Ṭanāḥī. 5 vols. Beirut: al-Maktabah al-ʿIlmiyyah, 1399/1979.

Ibn ʿAṭiyyah (d. ca. 541/1147) (comm.). *Al-Muḥarrir al-wajīz fī tafsīr al-Kitāb al-ʿazīz*. Edited by ʿAbd al-Salām ʿAbd al-Shāfī Muḥammad. Beirut: Dar al-Kutub al-ʿIlmiyyah, 2002.

Ibn Bakkār, Zubayr (d. 256/870). *Al-Akhbār al-muwaffaqiyyāt*. Edited by Sāmī Makkī al-ʿĀnī. Beirut: Maṭbaʿat al-ʿĀnī, 1416/1996.

Ibn Barrāj (d. ca. 480/1088). *Al-Muhadhdhab*. Edited by Jaʿfar al-Subḥānī. Qum: Muʾassasat al-Nashr al-Islāmī, 1406/1986.

Ibn Baṭṭah (d. 387/997). *Ibṭāl al-ḥiyal*. Edited by Zuhayr al-Shāwīsh. Beirut: al-Maktab al-Islāmī, 1403/1983.

Ibn Durayd (d. 321/933). *Al-Amālī: Taʿlīq min Amālī Ibn Durayd*. Edited by Muṣṭafā al-Sanūsī. Kuwait: al-Majlis al-Waṭanī li-l-Thaqāfah wa-l-Funūn wa-l-Ādāb, Qism al-Turāth al-ʿArabī, 1984.

Ibn Durayd (d. 321/933). *Al-Ishtiqāq*. Beirut: Dār al-Jīl, 1411/1991.

Ibn Durayd (d. 321/933). *Jamharat al-lughah*. Edited by Ramzī Baʿlabakkī. Beirut: Dār al-ʿIlm li-l-Malāyīn, 1987.

Ibn Durayd (d. 321/933). *Al-Mujtanā*. Hyderabad: Dāʾirat al-Maʿārif al-ʿUthmāniyyah, 1963.

Ibn al-Faqīh al-Hamadhānī (fl. 290/903). *Kitāb al-Buldān*. Edited by Yūsuf al-Hādī. Beirut: ʿĀlam al-Kutub, 1416/1996.

Ibn Fāris al-Qazwīnī (d. 395/1004). *Muʿjam Maqāyīs al-lughah*. Edited by ʿAbd al-Salām Muḥammad Hārūn. Beirut: Dār al-Fikr, 1399/1979.

Ibn Funduq al-Bayhaqī, ʿAlī ibn Zayd Farīd-Khurāsān (d. 565/1170) (comm.). *Maʿārij Nahj al-balāghah*. Edited by Muḥammad Taqī Dānishpazhūh. Qum: Maktabat Āyatallāh al-ʿUẓmā al-Marʿashī al-Najafī, 1409/1988.

Ibn Ḥajar al-ʿAsqalānī (d. 852/1449). *Lisān al-mīzān*. Edited by ʿAbd al-Fattāḥ Abū Ghadda. 10 vols. Beirut: Maktab al-Maṭbūʿāt al-Islāmiyyah, 1423/2002.

Ibn Ḥamdūn (d. 562/1166). *Al-Tadhkirah al-Ḥamdūniyyah*. Edited by Iḥsān ʿAbbās. 10 vols. Beirut: Dār Ṣādir, 1996.

Ibn Ḥanbal (d. 240/855). *Faḍāʾil al-ṣaḥābah*. Edited by Waṣiyyallāh Muḥammad ʿAbbās. 2 vols. Beirut: Muʾassasat al-Risālah, 1403/1983.

Ibn Ḥanbal (d. 240/855). *Al-ʿIlal wa maʿrifat al-rijāl*. Edited by Waṣiyyallāh ʿAbbās. Beirut: Al-Maktab al-Islāmī, 1408/1988.

Ibn Ḥanbal (d. 240/855) (comp.). *Musnad Aḥmad*. Edited by Shuʿayb al-Arnāʾūṭ et al. Beirut: Muʾassasat al-Risālah, 1421/2001.

Ibn Hibatallāh al-Afṭasī, Muḥammad ibn Muḥammad (d. after 515/1121). *Al-Majmūʿ al-laṭīf: Mukhtārāt turāthiyyah fī l-adab wa-l-fikr wa-l-ḥaḍārah*. Edited by Yaḥyā Wahīb al-Jubūrī. Beirut: Dār al-Gharb al-Islāmī, 2005.

Ibn Ḥibbān (d. 354/965). *Al-Thiqāt*. 9 vols. Beirut: Muʾassasat al-Kutub al-Thaqāfiyyah, 1393/1973.

Ibn Hishām (d. 218/833) from Ibn Isḥāq (d. 151/768). *Al-Sīrah al-nabawiyyah*. Edited by Aḥmad Ḥijāzī al-Saqqā. 4 parts in 2 vols. Cairo: Dār al-Turāth al-ʿArabī, n.d. Translated by Alfred Guillaume as *The Life of Muhammad: A Translation of Isḥāqʾs Sīrat Rasūl Allāh*. Oxford: Oxford University Press, 1955.

Ibn al-Jawzī (d. 597/1201). *Al-Mawḍūʿāt*. Edited by ʿAbd al-Raḥmān Muḥammad ʿUthmān. Medina: al-Maktabah al-Salafiyyah, 1386/1966.

Ibn al-Jawzī (d. 597/1201). *Ṣifat al-ṣifwah*. Edited by Aḥmad ibn ʿAlī. 2 vols. Cairo: Dār al-Ḥadīth, 2000.

Ibn al-Jawzī (d. 597/1201). *Al-Tabṣirah*. Edited by Muṣṭafā ʿAbd al-Wāḥid. Beirut and Cairo: Dār al-Kitāb al-Lubnānī, 1970.

Ibn al-Jawzī (d. 597/1201). *Zād al-masīr fī ʿilm al-tafsīr*. Edited by ʿAbd al-Razzāq al-Mahdī. Beirut: Dār al-Kitāb al-ʿArabī, 1422/2002.

Ibn al-Jazarī, Shams al-Dīn Abū al-Khayr (d. 833/1429). *Manāqib al-asad al-ghālib ʿAlī ibn Abī Ṭālib*. Edited by Ṭāriq al-Ṭanṭāwī. Cairo: Maktabat al-Qurʾān, 1994.

Ibn Kathīr (d. 774/1373). *Al-Bidāyah wa-l-nihāyah*. Edited by ʿAlī Shīrī. Beirut: Dār Iḥyāʾ al-Turāth al-ʿArabī, 1408/1988.

Ibn Kathīr (d. 774/1373). *Qiṣaṣ al-anbiyāʾ*. Edited by Muṣṭafā ʿAbd al-Wāḥid. Cairo: Dār al-Taʾlīf, 1388/1968.

Ibn Kathīr (d. 774/1373). *Ṭabaqāt al-Shāfiʿiyyīn*. Cairo: Maktabat al-Thaqāfah al-Dīniyyah, 1413/1993.

Ibn Khālawayh (d. 370/980). *Laysa fī kalām al-ʿArab*. Edited by Aḥmad ʿAbd al-Ghafūr ʿAṭṭār. Mecca: n.p., 1399/1979.

Ibn Khallikān (d. 681/1282). *Wafayāt al-aʿyān wa-anbāʾ abnāʾ al-zamān*. Edited by Iḥsān ʿAbbās. 7 vols. Beirut: Dār Ṣādir, 1994.

Ibn al-Maghāzilī (d. 483/1090). *Manāqib al-Imām ʿAlī ibn Abī Ṭālib*. Edited by Jaʿfar Hādī al-Dajīlī. Beirut: Dār al-Aḍwāʾ, 1412/1992

Ibn Mājah (d. 273/887) (comp.). *Sunan Ibn Mājah*. 2 vols. Edited by Muḥammad Fuʾād ʿAbd al-Bāqī. Cairo: Dār Iḥyāʾ al-Kutub al-ʿArabiyyah, 1952–1953.

Ibn Mākūlā (d. 474/1082). *Al-Ikmāl fī rafʿ al-irtiyāb ʿan al-muʾtalif wa-l-mukhtalif fī l-*

asmā' wa-l-kunā wa-l-ansāb. Edited by Nāyif al-ʿAbbās. 6 vols. Cairo: Dār al-Kitāb al-Islāmī, n.d.

Ibn Manẓūr (d. 711/1311). *Lisān al-ʿArab*. Edited by ʿAbdallāh ʿAlī al-Kabīr et al. 2 vols. Cairo: Dār al-Maʿārif, 1981.

Ibn Mardawayh, Aḥmad ibn Mūsā (d. 410/1019). *Manāqib ʿAlī ibn Abī Ṭālib wa-mā nazala min al-Qurʾān fī ʿAlī*. Edited by ʿAbd al-Razzāq Muḥammad Ḥusayn Ḥirz al-Dīn. Qum: Dār al-Ḥadīth, 1422/2001.

Ibn al-Mubārak (d. 181/797). *Kitāb al-Zuhd*. Edited by Ḥabīb al-Raḥmān al-Aʿzamī. Beirut: Dār al-Kutub al-ʿIlmiyyah, 1970.

Ibn Munqidh (d. 584/1188). *Lubāb al-ādāb*. Edited by Aḥmad Shākir. Cairo: Maktabat al-Sunnah, 1407/1987.

Ibn al-Muʿtazz (d. 296/908). *Al-Badīʿ fī l-badīʿ*. Beirut: Dār al-Jīl, 1410/1990.

Ibn al-Nadīm (d. 380/990). *Al-Fihrist*. Beirut: Dār al-Maʿrifah, 1970s.

Ibn al-Qayyim al-Jawziyyah (d. 751/1350). *Ighāthat al-lahfān min maṣāyid al-shayṭān*. Edited by Muḥammad Ḥāmid al-Faqī. Riyadh: Maktabat al-Maʿārif, 1395/1975.

Ibn al-Qayyim al-Jawziyyah (d. 751/1350). *Iʿlām al-muwaqqiʿīn ʿan rabb al-ʿālamīn*. Edited by Muḥammad ʿAbd al-Salām Ibrāhīm. Beirut: Dār al-Kutub al-ʿIlmiyyah, 1991.

Ibn al-Qayyim al-Jawziyyah (d. 751/1350). *Miftāḥ dār al-saʿādah wa-manshūr walāyat al-ʿilm wa-l-irādah*. 2 vols. Beirut: Dār al-Kutub al-ʿIlmiyyah, 2005.

Ibn Qutaybah (d. 276/889). *Gharīb al-ḥadīth*. 3 vols. Edited by ʿAbdallāh al-Jubūrī. Beirut: Dār al-Kutub al-ʿIlmiyyah, 1408/1988.

Ibn Qutaybah (d. 276/889) (attrib.). *Al-Imāmah wa-l-siyāsah*. Edited by ʿAlī al-Shīrī. Qum: Manshūrāt al-Sharīf al-Raḍī, 1413/1992.

Ibn Qutaybah (d. 276/889). *Iṣlāḥ ghalaṭ Abī ʿUbayd fī Gharīb al-ḥadīth*. Edited by ʿAbdallāh al-Jubūrī. Beirut: Dār al-Gharb al-Islāmī, 1983.

Ibn Qutaybah (d. 276/889). *Taʾwīl mukhtalif al-ḥadīth*. Beirut: al-Maktab al-Islāmī, 1419/1999.

Ibn Qutaybah (d. 276/889). *ʿUyūn al-akhbār*. Edited by Mundhir Muḥammad Saʿīd Abū Shaʿr. Beirut: al-Maktab al-Islāmī, 1429/2008.

Ibn Rajab (d. 795/1393). *Laṭāʾif al-maʿārif fī-mā li-mawāsim al-ʿām min al-waẓāʾif*. Beirut: Dār Ibn Ḥazm, 1424/2004.

Ibn Rifāʿah (d. 932/1526). *Kitāb al-Amthāl*. Edited by ʿAlī Ibrāhīm Kurdī. Damascus: Dār Saʿd al-Dīn, 2003.

Ibn al-Ṣabbāgh (d. ca. 854/1451). *Al-Fuṣūl al-muhimmah fī maʿrifat al-aʾimmah*. Edited by Sāmī al-Gharīrī. Qum: Dār al-Ḥadīth, 1422/2002.

Ibn Saʿd (d. 230/845). *Al-Ṭabaqāt al-kubrā*. Edited by Iḥsān ʿAbbās. 8 vols. Beirut: Dār Ṣādir, 1968.

Ibn Shabbah, ʿUmar (d. 262/876). *Tārīkh al-Madīnah al-munawwarah*. 4 vols. Beirut: Dār al-Fikr, 1410/1989.

Ibn Shādhān, al-Faḍl (d. 260/873). *Al-Īḍāḥ*. Edited by Jalāl al-Dīn al-Ḥusaynī Muḥaddith. Tehran: Mu'assasah-i Intishārāt va Chāp-i Dānishgāh-i Tihrān, 1363/1944.

Ibn Shahrāshūb (d. 588/1192). *Manāqib Āl Abī Ṭālib*. Najaf: al-Maktabah al-Ḥaydariyyah, 1956.

Ibn Taghrībirdī (d. 874/1470). *Al-Nujūm al-zāhirah: Fī Mulūk Miṣr wa-l-Qāhirah*. Edited by Muḥammad Ḥusayn Shams al-Dīn. 16 vols. Beirut: Dār al-Kutub al-ʿIlmiyyah, 1992.

Ibn Ṭalḥah, Muḥammad (d. 652/1255). *Maṭālib al-saʾūl fī āl al-rasūl*. Edited by Mājid ʿAṭiyyah. Beirut: Muʾassasat Umm al-Qurā, 1420/2000.

Ibn Ṭāwūs al-Ḥillī (d. 664/1266). *Kashf al-maḥajjah li-thamarat al-muhjah*. Najaf: al-Maṭbaʿah al-Ḥaydariyyah, 1370/1950.

Ibn Ṭāwūs al-Ḥillī (d. 664/1266). *Faraj al-mahmūm fī tārīkh ʿulamāʾ al-nujūm*. Qum: Dār al-Dhakhāʾir, 1368/1949.

Ibn Ṭāwūs al-Ḥillī (d. 664/1266). *Muhaj al-daʿawāt wa-manhaj al-ʿibādāt*. Beirut: Muʾassasat al-Aʿlamī, 1414/1994.

Ibn Ṭāwūs al-Ḥillī (d. 664/1266). *Al-Ṭarāʾif fī maʿrifat madhāhib al-ṭawāʾif*. Edited by ʿAlī ʿĀshūr. 2 vols. Qum: Khayām, 1400/1980.

Ibn Ṭāwūs al-Ḥillī (d. 664/1266). *Al-Yaqīn bi-khtiṣāṣ mawlānā ʿAlī bi-imārat al-muʾminīn*. Qum: Dār al-Kitāb al-Jazāʾirī, 1413/1992.

Ibn Taymiyyah (d. 728/1328). *Minhāj al-sunnah al-nabawiyyah: Fī Naqḍ kalām al-shīʿah al-qadariyyah*. Edited by Muḥammad Rashād Sālim. 9 vols. Riyadh: Jāmiʿat al-Imām Muḥammad ibn Saʿūd al-Islāmiyyah, 1986.

Ibn al-Ṭuyūrī (d. 500/1106), abridged by Abū Ṭāhir al-Silafī (d. 576/1180). *Al-Ṭuyūriyyāt*. Edited by Dasmān Yaḥyā Maʿālī and ʿAbbās Ṣakhr al-Ḥasan. 4 vols. Riyadh: Maktabat Aḍwāʾ al-Salaf, 2004.

Ibn al-Ẓāhir, al-Irbilī (d. 677/1278). *Mukhtaṣar Amthāl al-Sharīf al-Raḍī*. Edited by Nūrī al-Qaysī and Hilāl Nājī. Baghdad: Dār al-Shuʾūn al-Thaqāfiyyah al-ʿĀmmah, 1986.

Idrīs ʿImād al-Dīn (d. 872/1468). *ʿUyūn al-akhbār wa-funūn al-āthār fī dhikr al-nabī al-muṣṭafā l-mukhtār wa-waṣiyyihi ʿAlī ibn Abī Ṭālib qātil al-kuffār wa-ālihimā l-aʾimmah al-aṭhār ʿalayhim ṣalawāt Allāh al-ʿazīz al-ghaffār*. Edited by Ahmad Chleilat et al. 7 vols. London and Damascus: Institut français du Proche-Orient, and The Institute of Ismaili Studies, 2007–2010.

al-ʿIjlī, Aḥmad ibn ʿAbdallāh al-Kūfī (d. 261/875). *Maʿrifat al-thiqāt min rijāl ahl al-ʿilm wa-l-ḥadīth wa-min al-ḍuʿafāʾ wa-dhikr madhāhibihim wa-akhbārihim*. Edited by ʿAbd al-ʿAlīm ʿAbd al-ʿAẓīm al-Bastawī. 2 vols. Medina: Maktabat al-Dār, 1405/1985.

Ilāhī-Ardabīlī, Ḥusayn ibn ʿAbd al-Ḥaqq (fl. ca. 9th/15th c.) (comm.). *Manhaj al-faṣāḥah: Fī Sharḥ Nahj al-balāghah*. Edited by Ilāhah Rūḥī Dil. Mashhad: Bunyād-i Pizhushhā-yi Islāmī Āstān-i Quds-i Riḍawī, 1972.

Imruʾ al-Qays (d. ca. 550 AD). *Dīwān*. Edited by ʿAbd al-Raḥmān al-Musṭāwī. Beirut: Dār al-Maʿrifah, 2004.

al-Irbilī, Bahāʾ al-Dīn ʿAlī ibn ʿĪsā (d. 692/1293). *Kashf al-ghummah fī maʿrifat al-aʾimmah*. Beirut: Dār al-Aḍwāʾ, 1405/1985.

Isḥāq ibn Ibrāhīm al-Kātib (fl. 4th/10th c.). *Al-Burhān fī wujūh al-bayān*. Cairo: Maktabat al-Shabāb, 1979.

al-Iskāfī, Muḥammad ibn ʿAbdallāh (d. 240/854). *Al-Miʿyār wa-l-muwāzanah: Fī Faḍāʾil al-Imām Amīr al-muʾminīn ʿAlī ibn Abī Ṭālib wa-bayān afḍaliyyatihi ʿalā jamīʿ al-ʿālamīn baʿd al-anbiyāʾ wa-l-mursalīn*. Edited by Muḥammad Bāqir al-Maḥmūdī. Beirut: Dār Maḥmūdī, 1981.

al-Iskāfī, Muḥammad ibn Hammām (d. 336/947). *Kitāb al-Tamḥīṣ*. Qum: Madrasat al-Imām al-Mahdī, n.d.

al-Jāḥiẓ (d. 255/869). *Al-Bayān wa-l-tabyīn*. Edited by ʿAbd al-Salām Muḥammad Hārūn. 4 parts in 2 vols. Cairo: Maktabat al-Khānjī, 1985.

al-Jāḥiẓ (d. 255/869). *Kitāb al-Bukhalāʾ*. Beirut: Dār wa-Maktabat al-Hilāl, 1419/1999.

al-Jāḥiẓ (d. 255/869). *Kitāb al-Ḥayawān*. Edited by ʿAbd al-Salām Muḥammad Hārūn. Beirut: Dār al-Jīl, 1996.

al-Jāḥiẓ (d. 255/869). *Kitāb al-Maḥāsin wa-l-aḍdād*. Beirut: Dār wa-Maktabat al-Hilāl, 1423/2003.

al-Jāḥiẓ (d. 255/869) (comp.). *Miʾat kalimah*. In al-Quḍāʿī, *A Treasury of Virtues: Sayings, Sermons, and Teachings of ʿAlī with the One Hundred Proverbs Attributed to al-Jāḥiẓ*. Edited and translated by Tahera Qutbuddin. New York: New York University Press, 2013, pp. 219–233.

al-Jāḥiẓ (d. 255/869). *Al-ʿUthmāniyyah*. Edited by ʿAbd al-Salām Muḥammad Hārūn. Beirut: Dār al-Jīl, 1411/1991.

al-Jahshiyārī, Muḥammad ibn ʿAbdūs (d. 331/942). *Kitāb al-Wuzarāʾ wa-l-kuttāb*. Edited by Muṣṭafā al-Saqqā et al. Cairo: Muṣṭafā al-Bābī al-Ḥalabī, 1980.

al-Jarīrī, al-Muʿāfā ibn Zakariyyā (d. 390/1000). *Al-Jalīs al-ṣāliḥ al-kāfī wa-l-anīs al-nāṣiḥ al-shāfī*. Edited by ʿAbd al-Karīm Sāmī al-Jundī. Beirut: Dār al-Kutub al-ʿIlmiyyah, 1426/2005.

al-Jaṣṣāṣ, Aḥmad ibn ʿAlī al-Rāzī (d. 370/981). *Aḥkām al-Qurʾān*. Edited by ʿAbd al-Salām Muḥammad ʿAlī Shāhīn. 3 vols. Beirut: Dār al-Kutub al-ʿIlmiyyah, 1415/1994.

al-Jawharī (d. between 393/1003 and 400/1010). *Al-Ṣiḥāḥ: Tāj al-lughah wa-ṣiḥāḥ al-ʿarabiyyah*. Edited by Aḥmad ʿAbd al-Ghafūr ʿAṭṭār. 6 vols. Beirut: Dār al-ʿIlm li-l-Malāyīn, 1407/1987.

al-Jīlānī, Niẓām al-Dīn (d. 1053/1643) (comm.). *Anwār al-faṣāḥah wa-asrār al-barāʿah: Sharḥ Nahj al-balāghah*. MS. Dubai, Juma al-Majid Center for Culture and Heritage, catalog no. MS 339694.

al-Jurjānī, ʿAbd al-Qāhir (d. ca. 474/1081). *Asrār al-balāghah*. Edited by Maḥmūd Muḥammad Shākir. Cairo and Jeddah: Dār al-Madanī, 1991.

al-Karājikī, Muḥammad ibn ʿAlī (d. 449/1058). *Kanz al-fawāʾid*. Qum: Maktabat al-Muṣṭafawī, 1369/1949.

al-Karājikī, Muḥammad ibn ʿAlī (d. 449/1058). *Maʿdin al-jawāhir wa-riyāḍat al-khawā-ṭir.* Edited by Aḥmad al-Ḥusaynī. Tehran: al-Maktabah al-Murtaḍawiyyah, 1394/1973.

al-Karājikī, Muḥammad ibn ʿAlī (d. 449/1058). *Al-Taʿajjub min aghlāṭ al-ʿāmmah fī masʾalat al-imāmah.* Edited by Fāris Ḥassūn Karīm. Qum: Dār al-Ghadīr, 2000.

al-Kashshī, Muḥammad ibn ʿUmar (d. 340/952). *Rijāl al-Kashshī.* Abridged by al-Ṭūsī (d. 460/1067) as *Ikhtiyār maʿrifat al-rijāl.* Qum: Muʾassasat Āl al-Bayt, 1404/1984.

al-Kaydarī, Quṭb al-Dīn al-Bayhaqī (d. after 576/1180) (comp.). *Dīwān al-Imām ʿAlī,* or *Anwār al-ʿuqūl min ashʿār waṣī al-rasūl.* Edited by Kāmil Salmān al-Jubūrī. Beirut: Dār al-Maḥajjah al-Bayḍāʾ, 1999.

al-Kaydarī, Quṭb al-Dīn al-Bayhaqī (d. after 576/1180) (comm.). *Ḥadāʾiq al-ḥaqāʾiq: Fī Sharḥ Nahj al-balāghah.* 2 vols. Edited by ʿAzīzallāh al-ʿUṭāridī. Tehran: Muʾassasat Nahj al-Balāghah, 1996.

al-Khalīl ibn Aḥmad al-Farāhīdī (d. ca. 160/776). *Kitāb al-ʿAyn.* Edited by Mahdī al-Makhzūmī and Ibrāhīm al-Sāmarrāʾī. 8 vols. Cairo: Dār wa-Maktabat al-Hilāl, n.d.

al-Khaṭīb al-Baghdādī (d. 463/1071). *Al-Riḥlah fī ṭalab al-ḥadīth.* Edited by Nūr al-Dīn ʿItr. Beirut: Dār al-Kutub al-ʿIlmiyyah, 1395/1975.

al-Khaṭīb al-Baghdādī (d. 463/1071). *Tārīkh Baghdād.* Edited by Bashshār ʿAwwād Maʿrūf. Beirut: Dār al-Gharb al-Islāmī, 1422/2002.

al-Khazzāz, ʿAlī ibn Muḥammad al-Qummī (fl. 4th/10th c.). *Kifāyat al-athar fī l-nuṣūṣ ʿalā l-aʾimmah al-ithnay ʿashar.* Qum: Intishārāt-i Bīdār, 1410/1990.

al-Khwārazmī, Abū Bakr (d. 383/993). *Al-Amthāl al-muwalladah.* Abu Dhabi: al-Majmaʿ al-Thaqāfī, 1424/2004.

al-Khwārazmī, al-Muwaffaq ibn Aḥmad al-Bakrī (d. 568/1173). *Al-Manāqib.* Edited by Mālik al-Maḥmūdī. Qum: Muʾassasat al-Nashr al-Islāmī, 1414/1993.

al-Kūfī, Muḥammad ibn Sulaymān (fl. 4th/10th c.). *Manāqib al-Imām Amīr al-muʾminīn ʿAlī ibn Abī Ṭālib.* Edited by Muḥammad Bāqir al-Maḥmūdī. Qum: Majmaʿ Iḥyāʾ al-Thaqāfah al-Islāmiyyah, 1412/1991.

al-Kulaynī (d. 329/941). *Al-Kāfī.* Edited by ʿAlī Akbar al-Ghaffārī. 8 vols. Tehran: Dār al-Kutub al-Islāmiyyah, 1377–1381/1957–1961.

al-Majlisī, Muḥammad Bāqir (d. 1110/1699). *Biḥār al-anwār.* 110 vols. Beirut: Dār Iḥyāʾ al-Turāth al-ʿArabī, 1987.

al-Makkī, Abū Ṭālib Muḥammad (d. 386/996). *Qūt al-qulūb fī muʿāmalat al-maḥbūb wa-waṣf ṭarīq al-murīd ilā maqam al-tawḥīd.* Edited by ʿĀṣim Ibrāhīm al-Kayyālī. 2 vols. Beirut: Dār al-Kutub al-ʿIlmiyyah, 1426/2005.

al-Māmaṭīrī, Abū al-Ḥasan ʿAlī ibn Mahdī al-Ṭabarī (d. ca. 360/971). *Nuzhat al-abṣār wa-maḥāsin al-āthār.* Edited by Muḥammad Bāqir al-Maḥmūdī. Tehran: Markaz al-Taḥqīqāt wa-l-Dirāsāt al-ʿIlmiyyah, 2009.

al-Masʿūdī (d. 345/956). *Ithbāt al-waṣiyyah li-Imam ʿAlī ibn Abī Ṭālib.* Najaf: al-Maṭbaʿah al-Ḥaydariyyah, 1955.

al-Masʿūdī (d. 345/956). *Murūj al-dhahab wa-maʿādin al-jawhar*. Edited by Saʿīd al-Laḥḥām. 5 vols. Beirut: Dār al-Fikr, 2000.

al-Māwardī (d. 450/1058). *Adab al-dunyā wa-l-dīn*. Beirut: Dār Maktabat al-Ḥayāt, 1986.

al-Māwardī (d. 450/1058). *Aʿlām al-nubuwwah*. Beirut: Dār wa-Maktabat al-Hilāl, 1409/ 1989.

al-Māwardī (d. 450/1058). *Al-Amthāl*. Edited by Fuʾād ʿAbd al-Munʿim Aḥmad. Riyadh: Dār al-Waṭan, 1420/1999.

al-Māwardī (d. 450/1058). *Al-Ḥāwī al-kabīr fī fiqh madhhab al-Imām al-Shāfiʿī wa-huwa Sharḥ Mukhtaṣar al-Muzanī*. Edited by ʿAlī Muḥammad Muʿawwaḍ. 19 vols. Beirut: Dār al-Kutub al-ʿIlmiyyah, 1999.

al-Maydānī (d. 518/1124). *Majmaʿ al-amthāl*. Edited by Muḥammad Muḥyī al-Dīn ʿAbd al-Ḥamīd. 2 vols. Cairo: al-Maktabah al-Tijāriyyah al-Kubrā, 1379/1959.

al-Minqarī, Naṣr ibn Muzāḥim (d. 212/827). *Waqʿat Ṣiffīn*. Edited by ʿAbd al-Salām Muḥammad Hārūn. Cairo: Maktabat al-Khānjī, 1981.

Miskawayh, ʿAlī ibn Muḥammad (d. 421/1030). *Tajārib al-umam wa-taʿāqub al-himam*. Edited by Abū al-Qāsim Imāmī. 7 vols. Tehran: Dār Surūsh, 2000.

al-Mizzī, Yūsuf ibn ʿAbd al-Raḥmān Jamāl al-Dīn (d. 742/1341). *Tahdhīb al-Kamāl fī asmāʾ al-rijāl*. Edited by Bashshār ʿAwwād Maʿrūf. 35 vols. Beirut: Muʾassasat al-Risālah, 1980–1992.

al-Muʾaddib, ʿAlī ibn Muḥammad (fl. 5th/11th c.). *ʿUyūn al-ḥikam wa-l-mawāʿiẓ*. Edited by Ḥusayn al-Ḥasanī al-Bīrjandī. Qum: Dār al-Ḥadīth, 1418/1997.

al-Muʾayyad bi-llāh Yaḥyâ ibn Ḥamzah (d. ca. 749/1348) (comm.). *Al-Dībāj al-waḍī fī l-kashf ʿan asrār al-waṣī: Sharḥ Nahj al-balāghah*. Edited by Khālid Qāsim al-Mutawakkil. 6 vols. Sanaa: Muʾassasat al-Imām Zayd ibn ʿAlī al-Thaqāfiyyah, 2003.

al-Muʾayyad bi-llāh Yaḥyā ibn Ḥamzah (d. ca. 749/1348). *Al-Ṭirāz li-asrār al-balāghah wa-ʿulūm ḥaqāʾiq al-iʿjāz*. 3 vols. Beirut: al-Maktabah al-ʿUnṣuriyyah, 1423/2003.

al-Muʾayyad fī l-Dīn al-Shīrāzī (d. 470/1078). *Al-Majālis al-Muʾayyadiyya*. 8 vols. Vols. 1–4 edited by Ḥātim Ḥamīd al-Dīn. Bombay and Oxford: Oxford Printers. 1975–2011.

al-Mubarrad (d. 286/899). *Al-Fāḍil*. Cairo: Dār al-Kutub al-Miṣriyyah, 1421/2001.

al-Mubarrad (d. 286/899). *Al-Kāmil fī l-lughah wa-l-adab*. Edited by Muḥammad Abū al-Faḍl Ibrāhīm. 4 vols. Beirut: Dār al-Fikr, 1417/1997.

Mufaḍḍal ibn Salamah al-Kūfī (d. after 290/903), *Al-Fākhir fī l-amthāl*. Edited by ʿAbd al-ʿAlīm al-Ṭaḥāwī. Cairo: Dār Iḥyāʾ al-Kutub al-ʿArabiyyah ʿĪsā al-Bābī al-Ḥalabī, 1380/1960.

al-Mufīd (d. 413/1023). *Amālī al-Mufīd*. Edited by ʿAlī Akbar al-Ghaffārī. Qum: Manshū-rāt Jamāʿat al-Mudarrisīn fī l-Ḥawzah al-ʿIlmiyyah, 1982.

al-Mufīd (d. 413/1023). *Al-Ifṣāḥ fī l-imāmah*. Qum: Muʾassasat al-Biʿthah, n.d.

al-Mufīd (d. 413/1023). *Al-Ikhtiṣāṣ*. Qum: Manshūrāt Jamāʿat al-Mudarrisīn fī l-Ḥawzah al-ʿIlmiyyah, 1980.

al-Mufīd (d. 413/1023). *Al-Irshād fī maʿrifat ḥujaj Allāh ʿalā l-ʿibād*. Mashhad: Muʾassasat Āl al-Bayt li-Iḥyāʾ al-Turāth, n.d.

al-Mufīd (d. 413/1023). *Kitāb al-Jamal*. Najaf: al-Maṭbaʿah al-Ḥaydariyyah, 1983.

al-Mufīd (d. 413/1023). *Al-Kāfiyah fī ibṭāl tawbat al-khāṭiyah*. Edited by ʿAlī Akbar Za mānī Nizād. Qum: al-Muʾtamar al-ʿĀlamī li-Alfiyyat al-Shaykh al-Mufīd, 1413/1993.

al-Mufīd (d. 413/1023). *Al-Muqniʿah*. Qum: Dār al-Nashr al-Islāmī, 1410/1990.

al-Muhallabī, Aḥmad ibn ʿAlī (d. 644/1246). *Al-Maʾākhidh ʿalā shurrāḥ Dīwān Abī al-Ṭayyib al-Mutanabbī*. Edited by ʿAbd al-ʿAzīz ibn Nāṣir al-Māniʿ. Riyadh: Markaz al-Malik Fayṣal li-l-Buḥūth wa-al-Dirāsāt al-Islāmiyyah, 1424/2003.

Muḥammad, Prophet of Islam (d. 11/632), attrib. Medieval compilations of hadith listed under the compiler's name: ʿAbd al-Razzāq, Abū ʿUbayd, Abū Yaʿlā, Abū Bakr al-Bayhaqī, Dāraquṭnī, Dārimī, Harawī, Ibn Abī ʿĀṣim, Ibn Abī Shaybah, Majd Ibn al-Athīr, Ibn Ḥanbal, Ibn Mājah, Ibn Qutaybah, Muslim, Nasāʾī, Nuʿmān, Quḍāʿī, Raḍī, ʿImād al-Ṭabarī, and Tirmidhī.

Muḥammad ibn Ḥabīb (d. 245/860). *Asmāʾ al-mughtālīn min al-ashrāf fī l-jāhiliyyah wa-l-Islām*. Edited by Kasrawī Ḥasan. Beirut: Dār al-Kutub al-ʿIlmiyyah, 1422/2001.

Muḥammad ibn Ṭāhir al-Ḥārithī (d. 584/1188). *Majmūʿ al-tarbiyah*. Edited by Ḥusām Khaddūr. Salamiyya, Syria: Dār al-Ghadīr, 2019.

al-Murtaḍā, al-Sharīf (436/1044). *Al-Amālī*. Edited by Muḥammad Abū al-Faḍl Ibrāhīm. 2 vols. Cairo: Dār Iḥyāʾ al-Kutub al-ʿArabiyyah, 1373/1954.

al-Murtaḍā, al-Sharīf (436/1044). *Rasāʾil*. Edited by Mahdī al-Rajāʾī. Beirut: Muʾassasat al-Nūr, 1405/1984.

al-Murtaḍā, al-Sharīf (436/1044). *Tanzīh al-anbiyāʾ*. Beirut: Dār al-Aḍwāʾ, 1409/1989.

Muslim ibn Ḥajjāj (d. 261/875) (comp.). *Al-Musnad al-ṣaḥīḥ*. Edited by Muḥammad Fuʾād ʿAbd al-Bāqī. 5 vols. Beirut: Dār Iḥyāʾ al-Turāth al-ʿArabī, 1970.

al-Muttaqī al-Hindī, ʿAlī ibn ʿAbd al-Malik (d. 975/1567). *Kanz al-ʿummāl fī sunan al-aqwāl wa-l-afʿāl*. 18 vols. Beirut: Muʾassasat al-Risālah, 1989.

al-Muwaffaq biʾllāh, al-Ḥusayn ibn Ismāʿīl al-Zaydī al-Jurjānī (d. ca. 430/1038). *Al-Iʿtibār wa-sulwat al-ʿārifīn*. Edited by ʿAbd al-Salām ʿAbbās al-Wajīh. Sanaa: Muʾassasat al-Imām Zayd ibn ʿAlī al-Thaqāfiyyah, 2008.

al-Naḥḥās, Abū Jaʿfar (d. 338/950). *ʿUmdat al-kātib*. Edited by Bassām ʿAbd al-Wahhāb Jābī. Beirut: Dār Ibn Ḥazm, 1425/2005.

al-Najāshī (d. after 463/1071). *Rijāl al-Najāshī*. Edited by Mūsā al-Shubayrī al-Zanjānī. Qum: Muʾassasat al-Nashr al-Islāmī al-Tābiʿah li-Jamāʿat al-Mudarrisīn, 1986.

Naṣīr al-Dīn al-Ṭūsī (d. 672/1274). *Rawḍah-yi taslīm*. Edited and translated by Jalal Hosseini Badakhchani as *Paradise of Submission. A Medieval Treatise on Ismaili Thought*. London: I.B. Tauris, 2005.

Naṣīr al-Dīn al-Ṭūsī (d. 672/1274). *Tawallā wa-tabarrā, Maṭlūb al-muʾminīn*, and *Āghāz wa-anjām*. Edited and translated by Jalal Hosseini Badakhchani as *Shīʿī Interpretations of Islam. Three Treatises on Theology and Eschatology*. London: I.B. Tauris, 2010.

Nuʿaym ibn Ḥammād al-Khuzāʿī al-Marwazī (d. 228/843). *Kitāb al-Fitan.* Edited by Samīr Amīn al-Zuhayrī. 2 vols. Cairo: Maktabat al-Tawḥīd, 1414/1992.

al-Nuʿmān, al-Qāḍī (d. 363/974). *Asās al-taʾwīl.* Edited by ʿĀrif Tāmir. Beirut: Dār al-Thaqāfah, 1960.

al-Nuʿmān, al-Qāḍī (d. 363/974). *Daʿāʾim al-Islām wa-dhikr al-ḥalāl wa-l-ḥarām wa-l-qaḍāyā wa-l-aḥkām ʿan ahl bayt Rasūl Allāh.* Edited by Asaf Fyzee. 2 vols. Cairo: Dār al-Maʿārif, 1951–1961. Translated by Asaf Fyzee and Ismail Poonawala as *The Pillars of Islam.* 2 vols. Oxford and New Delhi: Oxford University Press, 2002.

al-Nuʿmān, al-Qāḍī (d. 363/974). *Ikhtilāf uṣūl al-madhāhib.* Edited and translated by Devin J. Stewart as *Disagreements of the Jurists: A Manual of Islamic Legal Theory.* New York: New York University Press, 2015.

al-Nuʿmān, al-Qāḍī (d. 363/974). *Al-Majālis wa-l-musāyarāt.* Edited by Ḥabīb al-Faqī, Ibrāhīm Shabbūḥ, and Muḥammad Yaʿlāwī. Beirut: Dar al-Muntaẓar, 1996.

al-Nuʿmān, al-Qāḍī (d. 363/974). *Al-Manāqib wa-l-mathālib.* Edited by Mājid ibn Aḥmad al-ʿAṭiyyah. Beirut: Muʾassasat al-Aʿlamī, 2002.

al-Nuʿmān, al-Qāḍī (d. 363/974). *Sharḥ al-akhbār.* 16 parts in 4 vols. Qum: Muʾassasat al-Nashr al-Islāmī, 1991.

al-Nuʿmān, al-Qāḍī (d. 363/974) (comp. and comm.). *Kitāb al-Tawḥīd min khuṭab amīr al-muʾminīn ʿAlī ibn Abī Ṭālib.* Edited by ʿAbd al-Razzāq Muḥammad, in *Al-Kalām al-Ismāʿīlī: Khamsat kutub Ismāʿīliyyah fī l-tawḥīd wa-l-bāṭin wa-mukāsarat al-aḍdād.* Cairo: Markaz Iḥyāʾ li-l-Buḥūth wa-l-Dirāsāt, 2021, 36–212.

al-Nuwayrī (d. 733/1333). *Nihāyat al-arab fī funūn al-adab.* Edited by Saʿīd ʿĀshūr. 33 vols. Cairo: Dār al-Kutub wa-l-Wathāʾiq al-Qawmiyyah, 1423/2002

al-Qālī (d. 356/967). *Al-Amālī.* Edited by Muḥammad ʿAbd al-Jawād al-Aṣmaʿī. Cairo: Dār al-Kutub al-Miṣriyyah, 1344/1926.

al-Qālī (d. 356/967). *Dhayl al-Amālī wa-l-nawādir.* Cairo: Dār al-Kutub al-Miṣriyyah, 1344/1926.

al-Qalqashandī (d. 821/1418). *Ṣubḥ al-aʿshā fī ṣināʿat al-inshā.* 15 vols. Beirut: Dār al-Kutub al-ʿIlmiyyah, 2012.

al-Qāsimī, Ḥumaydān ibn Yaḥyā (d. 656/1258). *Majmūʿ Rasāʾil fī uṣūl al-tafsīr wa-uṣūl al-fiqh.* Saada, Yemen: Markaz Ahl al-Bayt li-l-Dirāsāt al-Islāmiyyah, 2003.

al-Quḍāʿī, al-Qāḍī Muḥammad ibn Salāmah (d. 454/1062) (comp.). *Dustūr maʿālim al-ḥikam wa-maʾthūr makārim al-shiyam.* Edited and translated by Tahera Qutbuddin as *A Treasury of Virtues: Sayings, Sermons, and Teachings of ʿAlī with the One Hundred Proverbs Attributed to al-Jāḥiẓ.* New York: New York University Press, *Library of Arabic Literature* series, 2013.

al-Quḍāʿī, al-Qāḍī Muḥammad ibn Salāmah (d. 454/1062) (comp.). *Kitāb al-Shihāb.* Edited and translated by Tahera Qutbuddin as *Light in the Heavens: Sayings of the Prophet Muhammad.* New York: New York University Press, *Library of Arabic Literature* series, 2016.

al-Quḍāʿī, al-Qāḍī Muḥammad ibn Salāmah (d. 454/1062). *Musnad al-Shihāb*. Edited by Ḥamdī al-Salafī. 2 vols. Beirut: Muʾassasat al-Risālah, 1407/1986.

al-Qummī, ʿAlī ibn Ibrāhīm (d. after 307/919) (comm.). *Tafsīr al-Qummī*. 2 vols. Edited by Ṭayyib al-Jazāʾirī. Qum: Muʾassasat Dār al-Kitāb, 1404/1984.

al-Qurṭubī, Muḥammad (d. 671/1212) (comm.). *Al-Jāmiʿ li-aḥkām al-Qurʾān*, or *Tafsīr al-Qurṭubī*. 20 vols. Edited by Aḥmad ʿAbd al-ʿAlīm al-Bardūnī. Beirut: Dār Iḥyāʾ al-Turāth al-ʿArabī, 1405/1985.

al-Raḍī, al-Sharīf (d. 406/1015). *Dīwān*. Edited by Muḥammad Muḥyī al-Dīn ʿAbd al-Ḥamīd as *Sharḥ Dīwān al-Sharīf al-Raḍī*. 2 vols. Cairo: Dār Iḥyāʾ al-Kutub al-ʿArabiyyah, 1949.

al-Raḍī, al-Sharīf (d. 406/1015) (comm.). *Ḥaqāʾiq al-taʾwīl fī mutashābih al-tanzīl*. Vol. 5 edited by Muḥammad al-Riḍā Āl Kāshif al-Ghiṭāʾ. Beirut: Dār al-Muhājir, 1960s.

al-Raḍī, al-Sharīf (d. 406/1015). *Khaṣāʾiṣ Amīr al-muʾminīn ʿAlī ibn Abī Ṭālib*. Beirut: Muʾassasat al-Aʿlamī, 1986.

al-Raḍī, al-Sharīf (d. 406/1015). *Al-Majāzāt al-nabawiyyah*. Edited by Ṭāhā Muḥammad al-Zaytī. Cairo: Muʾassasat al-Ḥalabī, 1387/1967. Abridged in Persian by Muḥammad Mahdī Jaʿfarī as *Āfarīnish-hā-yi hunarī dar guftār-i nabawī*. Tehran: Mīrāthbān, 2007.

al-Raḍī, al-Sharīf (d. 406/1015) (comp.). *Nahj al-balāghah*. Present volume. Edited earlier by Muḥammad Ḥusayn al-Jalālī. 2 vols., n.p., 1422/2002. Edited by Qays Bahjat ʿAṭṭār. Qum: Muʾassasat al-Rāfid, 2010. Edited by Hāshim Mīlānī. Najaf: al-ʿAtabah al-ʿAlawiyyah al-Muqaddasah, 2009. Translated into Persian by Mullā Fatḥallāh Kāshānī (d. 988/1580) as *Tanbīh al-ghāfilīn wa-tadhkirat al-ʿārifīn fī l-sharḥ al-Fārisī li-Nahj al-balāghah*. Tehran: n.p., 1888. Extant medieval commentaries by Sarakhsī, Ibn Funduq, Rāwandī, Kaydarī, Ibn Abī al-Ḥadīd, Baḥrānī, al-Muʾayyad bi-llāh, Ilāhī-Ardabīlī, ʿAbd al-Bāqī, and Jīlānī are listed under the compiler's name, as are modern commentaries by ʿAbd al-Ḥamīd, ʿAbduh, Jalālī, Lāhījānī, Mughniyyah, al-Marṣafī, Naqavī, Ṭāliqānī, and Tustarī, and index volumes by Baydūn, Muḥammad, and Muḥammadī and Dashtī. Translated into Persian by ʿAlī Naqī Fayḍ al-Islām as *Tarjamah va sharḥ Nahj al-balāghah*. Tehran: n.p., 1946. Translated into Turkish by Abdülbâki Gölpınarlı as *Nehc'ül Belâga: Hz. Alî'nin hutbeleri, vasiyyetleri, emirleri, mektupları, hikmet ve vecizeleri: metnin terceme ve şerhi*. Istanbul: Neşriyat Yurdu, 1972. Translated into Persian by Muḥammad Taqī-Jaʿfarī as *Tarjamah va tafsīr-i Nahj al-balāghah*. Tehran: Farhang-i Islāmī, 1978. Translated into French by Attia Abul Naga as *La voie de l'éloquence*. Beirut: Dār al-Kutub al-Islāmiyyah, 1986. Cairo: Dār al-Kitāb al-Miṣrī, 1986. Translated into Spanish by Mohammed ʿAlí Anzaldúa-Morales as *La cumbre de la elocuencia: Sermones, cartas y dichos de Imam Alí ibn Abi Talib*, Elmhurst, NY: Tahrike Tarsile Quran, 1988. Sayings section partially translated into English by Thomas Cleary as *Living and Dying with Grace. Counsels of Ḥaḍrat ʾAlī*. Boston: Shambhala, 1996. Translated into Urdu by Dhīshān Ḥaydar Jawādī as *Nahj al-balāghah*. Karachi: Maḥfūẓ Book Agency, 1999. Translated into French by Leila

Sourani as *Sagesses de l'Imam 'Ali: Tirées de Nahj al Balaghat*. Beirut: Albouraq, 2001. Translated into Chinese by Zhihua Zhang as *Ci zhang zhi dao: Yimamuali Ben Aibi Talibo yan lun ji*. Beijing: Zong jiao wen hua chu ban she, 2003. Translated into Urdu by Mufti Ja'far Ḥusayn as *Nahj al-balāghah*. Lahore: al-Mi'rāj Company, 2003. Translated into German by Fatima Özoguz as *Nahdsch-ul-Balagha. Pfad der Eloquenz: Aussagen und Reden Imam Alis*. 2 vols. Bremen: M-haditec, 2007. Translated into Russian by Abdulkarim Taras Cherniyenko as *Put' krasnorechiya*. Moscow: Vostochnaya Literatura, 2008. (Among several other translations into various languages).[1]

al-Raḍī, al-Sharīf (d. 406/1015). *Talkhīṣ al-bayān fī majāzāt al-Qur'ān*. Edited by Muḥammad al-Mishkāt, Tehran 1953. Translated into Persian by Muḥammad Bāqir Sabzavārī. Tehran: Chāpkhānah-i Dānishgāh, 1951.

al-Raḍī, al-Sharīf (d. 406/1015) and Hilāl al-Ṣābī (d. 448/1056). *Rasā'il al-Ṣābī wa-l-Sharīf al-Raḍī*. Edited by Muḥammad Yūsuf Najm. Kuwait: Dā'irat al-Maṭbū'āt wa-l-Nashr, 1961.

al-Rāghib al-Iṣfahānī (d. early 5th/11th c.). *Kitāb Mufradāt fī gharīb al-Qur'ān*. Edited by Ṣafwān 'Adnān al-Dā'ūdī. Damascus: Dār al-Qalam, 1412/1992.

al-Rāghib al-Iṣfahānī (d. early 5th/11th c.). *Muḥāḍarāt al-udabā' wa-muḥāwarāt al-shu'arā' wa-l-bulaghā'*. 2 vols. Edited by 'Umar Ṭabbā'. Beirut: Dār al-Arqam, 1420/2000.

al-Rāwandī, Faḍlallāh ibn 'Alī (d. 571/1175). *Kitāb al-Nawādir*. Edited by Sa'īd 'Askarī. Qum: Dār al-Ḥadīth, 1956.

al-Rāwandī, Quṭb al-Dīn (d. 573/1177). *Al-Da'awāt*, or *Salwat al-ḥazīn*. Qum: Madrasat al-Imām al-Mahdī, 1987.

al-Rāwandī, Quṭb al-Dīn (d. 573/1177). *Fiqh al-Qur'ān*. Edited by Aḥmad al-Ḥusaynī. Qum: Maktabat Āyatallāh al-'Uẓmā al-Mar'ashī al-Najafī, 1404/1984.

al-Rāwandī, Quṭb al-Dīn (d. 573/1177). *Al-Kharā'ij wa-l-jarā'iḥ*. Edited by Muḥammad Bāqir al-Muwaḥḥid al-Abṭaḥī. Qum: Mu'assasat al-Imām al-Mahdī, 1409/1989.

al-Rāwandī, Quṭb al-Dīn (d. 573/1177) (comm.). *Minhāj al-barā'ah: Fī Sharḥ Nahj al-balāghah*. Edited by 'Abd Laṭīf al-Kūhkamarī. 3 vols. Qum: Maktabat Āyatallāh al-Mar'ashī al-'Āmmah, 1986.

al-Rāzī, Fakhr al-Dīn (d. 606/1210) (comm.). *Mafātīḥ al-ghayb*, or *Tafsīr al-Rāzī*. 32 vols. Beirut: Dār Iḥyā' al-Turāth al-'Arabī, 1420/2000.

al-Rāzī, Fakhr al-Dīn (d. 606/1210). *Al-Maḥṣūl*. Edited by Ṭāhā Jābir Fayyāḍ al-'Alwānī. Beirut: Mu'assasat al-Risālah, 1418/1997.

al-Ṣadūq al-Qummī, Ibn Bābawayh (d. 381/991). *Al-Amālī*. Qum: Mu'assasat al-Bi'thah, 1417/1997.

1　For a fuller list of *Nahj al-balāghah* translations, see Esḥāqī, "Manba'-shināsī," *passim*.

al-Ṣadūq al-Qummī, Ibn Bābawayh (d. 381/991). *Al-Hidāyah*. Qum: Muʾassasat al-Imām al-Hādī, 1418/1998.

al-Ṣadūq al-Qummī, Ibn Bābawayh (d. 381/991). *ʿIlal al-sharāʾiʿ*. Edited by Muḥammad Ṣādiq Baḥr al-ʿUlūm. Najaf: al-Maktabah al-Ḥaydariyyah, 1385/1966.

al-Ṣadūq al-Qummī, Ibn Bābawayh (d. 381/991). *Kamāl al-dīn wa-tamām al-niʿmah*. Qum: Muʾassasat al-Nashr al-Islāmī, 1405/1985.

al-Ṣadūq al-Qummī, Ibn Bābawayh (d. 381/991). *Al-Khiṣāl*. Edited by ʿAlī Akbar al-Ghaffārī. Qum: Muʾassasat al-Nashr al-Islāmī, 1403/1982.

al-Ṣadūq al-Qummī, Ibn Bābawayh (d. 381/991). *Maʿānī al-akhbār*. Edited by ʿAlī Akbar al-Ghaffārī. Najaf: Maṭbaʿat al-Ḥaydarī, 1379/1960.

al-Ṣadūq al-Qummī, Ibn Bābawayh (d. 381/991). *Man lā yaḥḍuruhu al-faqīh*. Edited by ʿAlī Akbar al-Ghaffārī. 4 vols. Manshūrāt Jamāʿat al-Mudarrisīn fī l-Ḥawzah al-ʿIlmiyyah, 1404/1983.

al-Ṣadūq al-Qummī, Ibn Bābawayh (d. 381/991). *Ṣifāt al-shīʿah wa-faḍāʾil al-shīʿah*. Tehran: Kānūn-i Intishārāt-i ʿĀbidī, 1970.

al-Ṣadūq al-Qummī, Ibn Bābawayh (d. 381/991). *Al-Tawḥīd*. Edited by Hāshim al-Ḥusaynī al-Ṭihrānī. Qum: Manshūrāt Jamāʿat al-Mudarrisīn fī l-Ḥawzah al-ʿIlmiyyah, 1363/1943.

al-Ṣadūq al-Qummī, Ibn Bābawayh (d. 381/991). *ʿUyūn akhbār al-Riḍā*. Edited by Ḥusayn al-Aʿlamī. Beirut: Muʾassasat al-Aʿlamī, 1404/1983.

al-Ṣafadī (d. 764/1362). *Al-Wāfī bi-l-Wafayāt*. Edited by Aḥmad al-Arnāʾūṭ and Turkī Muṣṭafā. Beirut: Dār Iḥyāʾ al-Turāth, 2000.

al-Ṣaffār, Muḥammad ibn al-Ḥasan al-Qummī (d. 290/902). *Baṣāʾir al-darajāt fī faḍāʾil Āl Muḥammad*. Edited by Muḥsin Kūchahʾbāghī. Qum: Maktabat Āyatallāh al-ʿUẓmā al-Marʿashī al-Najafī, 1983.

al-Samʿānī, ʿAbd al-Karīm ibn Muḥammad (d. 562/1166). *Kitāb al-Ansāb*. Edited by ʿAbd al-Raḥmān ibn Yaḥyā al-Muʿallimī al-Yamānī. Hyderabad: Dāʾirat al-Maʿārif al-ʿUthmāniyyah, 1382/1962.

al-Samʿānī, ʿAbd al-Karīm ibn Muḥammad (d. 562/1166) (comm.). *Tafsīr al-Qurʾān*. Edited by Yāsir ibn Ibrāhīm and Ghanīm ibn ʿAbbās ibn Ghanīm. Riyadh: Dār al-Waṭan, 1418/1997.

al-Samarqandī, Abū al-Layth Naṣr ibn Muḥammad (d. 375/985) (comm.). *Baḥr al-ʿulūm*, or *Tafsīr al-Samarqandī*. Edited by ʿAlī Muḥammad Muʿawwaḍ et al. 3 vols. Beirut: Dār al-Kutub al-ʿIlmiyyah, 1993.

al-Sarakhsī, ʿAlī ibn Nāṣir (fl. 6th/12th c.) (comm.). *Aʿlām Nahj al-balāghah*. Edited by ʿAbd ʿAzīz al-ʿUṭāridī. Qum: Muʾassasat al-Ṭibāʿah wa-l-Nashr Wizārat al-Thaqāfah wa-l-Irshād al-Islāmī Dār ʿUṭārid, 1996.

al-Shāfiʿī (d. 204/820). *Kitāb al-Umm*. 8 vols. Beirut: Dār al-Maʿrifah, 1410/1990.

al-Shahrastānī (d. 548/1153). *Mafātīḥ al-asrār wa-maṣābīḥ al-abrār*, or *Tafsīr al-Shahrastānī*, Edited by Muḥammad ʿAlī Ādharshab. 2 vols. Tehran: Markaz al-Buḥūth wa-l-Dirāsāt li-l-Turāth al-Makhṭūṭ, 2008.

al-Shahrastānī (d. 548/1153). *Al-Milal wa-l-niḥal.* Edited by Muḥammad Gīlānī. Beirut: Dār al-Maʿrifah, 1414/1993.

Sibṭ Ibn al-Jawzī (d. 654/1256). *Tadhkirat al-khawāṣṣ.* Edited by Muḥammad Ṣādiq Baḥr al-ʿUlūm. Najaf: al-Maṭbaʿah al-Ḥaydariyyah, 1383/1964.

al-Sukkarī (d. 275/888) (comm.). *Sharḥ Ashʿār al-Hudhaliyyīn.* Edited by ʿAbd al-Sattār Farrāj with Maḥmūd Muḥammad Shākir. Cairo: Maktabat Dār al-ʿUrūbah, 1965.

Sulaym ibn Qays (d. 76/695), attrib., most likely an early 2nd/8th c. text, *Kitāb Sulaym ibn Qays al-Hilālī.* Edited by Muḥammad Bāqir al-Anṣārī. 3 vols. Qum: Maṭbaʿat al-Hādī, 2000.

al-Ṣūlī, Abū Bakr Muḥammad ibn Yaḥyā (d. 335/946). *Adab al-kuttāb.* Edited by Muḥammad Bahjat al-Atharī. Baghdad: al-Maktabah al-ʿArabiyyah, 1922.

al-Suyūṭī (d. 911/1505) (comp.). *Jāmʿ al-jawāmiʿ,* or *al-Jāmiʿ al-kabīr.* Edited by Mukhtār Ibrāhīm al-Hāʾij et al. 25 vols. Cairo: al-Azhar al-Sharīf, 2005.

al-Ṭabarānī, Abū al-Qāsim Sulaymān (d. 360/971). *Al-Muʿjam al-awsaṭ.* Edited by Ṭāriq ibn ʿAwaḍallāh and ʿAbd al-Muḥsin ibn Ibrāhīm al-Ḥusaynī. Cairo: Dār al-Ḥaramayn, 1995.

al-Ṭabarānī, Abū al-Qāsim Sulaymān (d. 360/971). *Al-Muʿjam al-kabīr.* Edited by Ḥamdī ibn ʿAbd al-Majīd al-Salafī. 25 vols. Cairo: Maktabat Ibn Taymiyyah, 1415/1994.

al-Ṭabarī al-Āmulī, Muḥammad ibn Jarīr ibn Rustam (d. 411/1021). *Dalāʾil al-imāmah.* Qum: Muʾassasat al-Biʿthah, 1413/1992.

al-Ṭabarī al-Āmulī, Muḥammad ibn Jarīr ibn Rustam (d. 411/1021). *Al-Mustarshid fī imāmat Amīr al-muʾminīn ʿAlī ibn Abī Ṭālib.* Edited by Aḥmad al-Maḥmūdī. Tehran: Muʾassasat al-Thaqāfah al-Islāmiyyah li-Kūshānbūr, 1415/1994.

al-Ṭabarī, Muḥammad ibn Abī al-Qāsim ʿImād al-Dīn (d. 525/1131). *Bishārat al-Muṣṭafā li-shīʿat al-Murtaḍā.* Edited by Jawād al-Qayyūmī al-Iṣfahānī. Qum: Muʾassasat al-Nashr al-Islāmī, 1420/2000.

al-Ṭabarī, Muḥammad ibn Jarīr ibn Yazīd (d. 310/923) (comm.). *Jāmiʿ al-bayān fī taʾwīl al-Qurʾān.* Edited by Aḥmad Muḥammad Shākir. 24 vols. Cairo: Muʾassasat al-Risālah, 1420/2000.

al-Ṭabarī, Muḥammad ibn Jarīr ibn Yazīd (d. 310/923). *Tārīkh al-rusul wa-l-mulūk.* Edited by Muḥammad ʿAbd al-Ḥamīd Ibrāhīm. 10 vols. Cairo: Dār al-Maʿārif, 1960–1969. Translated by Franz Rosenthal et al. as *The History of al-Tabari.* Edited by Ehsan Yarshater. 39 vols. + index. Albany: State University of New York Press, 1989–2007.

al-Ṭabrisī, ʿAlī ibn al-Ḥasan (fl. late 6th/12th c.). *Mishkāt al-anwār fī ghurar al-akhbār.* Edited by Mahdī Hūshmand. Qum: Dār al-Ḥadīth, 1418/1998.

al-Ṭabrisī, al-Faḍl ibn al-Ḥasan (d. 548/1153) (comm.). *Majmaʿ al-bayān fī tafsīr al-Qurʾān.* Beirut: Muʾassasat al-Aʿlamī li-l-Maṭbūʿāt, 1415/1995.

al-Ṭabrisī, al-Faḍl ibn al-Ḥasan (d. 548/1153) (comp.). *Nathr al-laʾālī.* Edited and translated into Latin by Jacob Golius as *Proverbia quaedam Alis, imperatoris Muslimici, et Carmen Tograi, nec non Dissertatio quædam Aben Sinæ.* Leiden: Ex Officina Bonaventura et Abr. Elzevir, 1629.

al-Ṭabrisī, al-Faḍl ibn al-Ḥasan (d. 548/1153) or Aḥmad ibn ʿAlī al-Ṭabrisī (d. 588/1192). *Al-Iḥtijāj*. Edited by Muḥammad Bāqir al-Khurāsānī. Najaf: Dār al-Nuʿmān, 1386/1966.

al-Ṭabrisī, al-Ḥasan ibn al-Faḍl (fl. mid- 6th/12th c.). *Makārim al-akhlāq*. Edited by Muḥammad Ḥusayn Sulaymān. Beirut: Muʾassasat al-Aʿlamī, 1972.

al-Tanūkhī (d. 384/994). *Al-Faraj baʿd al-shiddah*. Edited by ʿAbbūd al-Shāljī. 5 vols. Beirut: Dār Ṣādir, 1398/1978.

al-Ṭarṭūshī (d. 520/1126). *Sirāj al-mulūk*. Cairo: al-Maktabah al-Azhariyyah al-Miṣriyyah, 1289/1872.

Taşköprüzāde, Ahmad Efendi (d. 968/1561) (comm.). *Şerhu'l-Ahlaki'l-Adudiyye Ahlak-ı Adudiyye Şerhi*. Edited by Mustakim Arıcı and Elzem İçöz. Translated into Turkish by Mustakim Arıcı. Istanbul: Türkiye Yazma Eserler, 2014.

al-Tawḥīdī, Abū Ḥayyān (d. 414/1023). *Al-Baṣāʾir wa-l-dhakhāʾir*. Edited by Wadād al-Qāḍī. 10 vols. Beirut: Dār Ṣādir, 1408/1988.

al-Tawḥīdī, Abū Ḥayyān (d. 414/1023). *Al-Imtāʿ wa-l-muʾānasah*. Beirut: al-Maktabah al-ʿUnṣuriyyah, 1424/2004.

al-Thaʿālibī (d. 429/1038). *Al-Iʿjāz wa-l-ījāz*. Edited by Muḥammad Ibrāhīm Salīm. Cairo: Maktabat al-Qurʾān, n.d.

al-Thaʿālibī (d. 429/1038) (comm.). *Al-Jawāhir al-ḥisān fī tafsīr al-Qurʾān*, or *Tafsīr al-Thaʿālibī*. Edited by Muḥammad ʿAlī Muʿawwaḍ and ʿĀdil Aḥmad ʿAbd al-Mawjūd. Beirut: Dār Iḥyāʾ al-Turāth al-ʿArabī, 1998.

al-Thaʿālibī (d. 429/1038). *Laṭāʾif al-maʿārif*. Beirut: Dār al-Manāhil, 1992.

al-Thaʿālibī (d. 429/1038). *Al-Shakwā wa-l-ʿitāb*. Edited by Ilhām ʿAbd al-Wahhāb al-Muftī. Kuwait: Al-Majlis al-Waṭanī li-l-Thaqāfah wa-l-Funūn wa-l-Ādāb, 1421/2000.

al-Thaʿālibī (d. 429/1038). *Al-Tamthīl wa-l-muḥāḍarah*. Edited by ʿAbd al-Fattāḥ Muḥammad al-Ḥulw. Cairo: Al-Dār al-ʿArabiyyah li-l-Kitāb, 1401/1981.

al-Thaʿālibī (d. 429/1038). *Thimār al-qulūb fī l-muḍāf wa-l-mansūb*. Edited by Muḥammad Abū al-Faḍl Ibrāhīm. Sidon and Beirut: al-Maktabah al-ʿAṣriyyah, 2003.

al-Thaʿālibī (d. 429/1038). *Yatīmat al-dahr fī maḥāsin ahl al-ʿaṣr*. Beirut: Dār al-Kutub al-ʿIlmiyyah, 1403/1983.

Thaʿlab (d. 291/904). *Majālis Thaʿlab*. Edited by ʿAbd al-Salām Muḥammad Hārūn. Cairo: Dār al-Maʿārif, 1950.

al-Thaʿlabī (d. 427/1035) (comm.). *Al-Kashf wa-l-bayān ʿan tafsīr al-Qurʾān* or *Tafsīr al-Thaʿlabī*. Edited by Abū Muḥammad ibn ʿĀshūr. Beirut: Dār Iḥyāʾ al-Turāth al-ʿArabī, 1422/2002.

al-Thaqafī, Ibrāhīm ibn Muḥammad (d. 283/896). *Al-Ghārāt*. Edited by Jalāl al-Dīn Ḥusaynī Muḥaddith. Tehran: Anjuman-i Āthār-i Millī, 1976.

al-Tirmidhī (d. 279/892) (comp.). *Sunan al-Tirmidhī*. Edited by Aḥmad Shākir et al. Cairo: Maktabat Muṣṭafā al-Bābī al-Ḥalabī, 1395/1975.

al-Ṭūfī, Najm al-Dīn Sulaymān ibn ʿAbd al-Qawī (d. 716/1316). *Mawāʾid al-ḥays fī fawāʾid Imriʾ al-Qays*. Edited by Muṣṭafā ʿAliyyān. Kuwait: Wizārat al-Awqāf wa-l-Shuʾūn al-Islāmiyyah Qiṭāʿ al-Shuʾūn al-Thaqāfiyyah, 1435/2014, 168–173.

al-Tushtarī (d. after 533/1139). *Maʿrifat-i Khudāy taʿālā*. Edited and translated by Shafique N. Virani as "Early Nizari Ismailism. A Critical Edition and Annotated Translation of Khwajah Qasim Tushtari's Recognizing God." *Iran: Journal of the British Institute of Persian Studies* 57/2 (2019), 245–266.

al-Ṭūsī, Shaykh al-Ṭāʾifah (d. 460/1067). *Al-Amālī*. Qum: Muʾassasat al-Biʿthah, 1414/1994.

al-Ṭūsī, Shaykh al-Ṭāʾifah (d. 460/1067). *Al-Fihrist*. Edited by Muḥammad Ṣādiq Baḥr al-ʿUlūm. Najaf: al-Maktabah al-Murtaḍawiyyah, 1937.

al-Ṭūsī, Shaykh al-Ṭāʾifah (d. 460/1067). *Al-Istibṣār fīmā ʾkhtalafa min al-akhbār*. Edited by Ḥasan al-Mūsawī al-Kharsān. Qum: Muʾassasat al-Nashr al-Islāmī, 1363/1943.

al-Ṭūsī, Shaykh al-Ṭāʾifah (d. 460/1067). *Al-Mabsūṭ fī fiqh al-Imāmiyyah*. Edited by Muḥammad Taqī al-Kashfī. Tehran: Al-Maktabah al-Murtaḍawiyyah, 1387/1967.

al-Ṭūsī, Shaykh al-Ṭāʾifah (d. 460/1067). *Miṣbāḥ al-mujtahid*. Beirut: Muʾassasat Fiqh al-Shīʿah, 1991.

al-Ṭūsī, Shaykh al-Ṭāʾifah (d. 460/1067). *Tahdhīb al-aḥkām*. Edited by Ḥasan al-Mūsawī al-Kharsān. Tehran: Dār al-Kutub al-Islamiyyah, 1365/1945.

al-Ṭūsī, Shaykh al-Ṭāʾifah (d. 460/1067). *Tafsīr al-tibyān al-jāmiʿ li-ʿulūm al-Qurʾān*. Edited by Aḥmad Ḥabīb Quṣayr al-ʿĀmilī. Beirut: Dār Iḥyāʾ al-Turāth al-ʿArabī, 1409/1989.

al-Ṭūsī, Shaykh al-Ṭāʾifah (d. 460/1067) (comm.). *Talkhīṣ al-Shāfī li-l-Sharīf al-Murtaḍā*. Edited Ḥusayn Baḥr al-ʿUlūm. 3 parts in 4 vols. Najaf: Maktabat al-ʿAlamayn al-Ṭūsī wa-Baḥr al-ʿUlūm, 1963.

Warrām al-Ḥillī, Ibn Abī Fāris (d. 605/1208). *Majmūʿat Warrām: Tanbīh al-khawāṭir wa-nuzhat al-nawāẓir*. 3 vols. Edited by Bāsim Muḥammad Mālallāh al-Asadī. Karbala: Al-ʿAtabah al-Ḥusayniyyah al-Muqaddasah, 1434/2013.

al-Waṭwāṭ, Muḥammad ibn Ibrāhīm (d. 718/1318). *Ghurar al-khaṣāʾiṣ al-wāḍiḥah*. Edited by Ibrāhīm Shams al-Dīn. Beirut: Dār al-Kutub al-ʿIlmiyyah, 1429/2008.

al-Waṭwāṭ, al-Rashīd (d. 578/1182) (comm.). *Maṭlūb kull ṭālib min kalām ʿAlī ibn Abī Ṭālib: Sharḥ Miʾat kalimah li-l-Jāḥiẓ*. (Persian). Edited by Jalāl al-Dīn Ḥusaynī Armawī Muḥaddith. Tehran: Kitābkhānah-yi Markazī Dānishgāh-i Tihrān, 1382/1962.

al-Yaʿqūbī, Ibn Wāḍiḥ (d. 284/897). *Tārīkh al-Yaʿqūbī*. 2 vols. Beirut: Dār Ṣādir, 1379/1960.

Yāqūt al-Ḥamawī (d. 626/1229). *Muʿjam al-Buldān*. 8 parts in 4 vols. Beirut: Dār Iḥyāʾ al-Turāth al-ʿArabī, 1997.

al-Zajjājī (d. ca. 337/948). *Amālī al-Zajjājī*. Edited by ʿAbd al-Salām Hārūn. Beirut: Dār al-Jīl, 1407/1987.

al-Zamakhsharī (d. 538/1144). *Al-Fāʾiq fī gharīb al-ḥadīth*. Edited by ʿAlī Muḥammad al-Bajāwī and Muḥammad Abū al-Faḍl Ibrāhīm. 4 vols. Beirut: Dār al-Maʿrifah, n.d.

al-Zamakhsharī (d. 538/1144) (comm.). *Al-Kashshāf ʿan ḥaqāʾiq ghawāmiḍ al-tanzīl*, or *Tafsīr al-Zamakhsharī*. Beirut: Dār al-Kitāb al-ʿArabī, 1407/1987.

al-Zamakhsharī (d. 538/1144). *Rabīʿ al-abrār*. Edited by ʿAbd al-Amīr ʿAlī Muhannā. 5 vols. Beirut: Muʾassasat al-Aʿlamī, 1412/1991.

al-Zarandī al-Ḥanafī, Muḥammad ibn Yūsuf (d. 750/1349). *Naẓm Durar al-simṭayn fī faḍāʾil al-Muṣṭafā wa-l-Murtaḍā wa-l-Batūl wa-l-Sibṭayn*. Najaf: Maṭbaʿat al-Qaḍāʾ, 1958.

Secondary Sources

Abbas, Hassan. *The Prophet's Heir: The Life of ʿAlī ibn Abī Ṭālib*. New Haven, Conn.: Yale University Press, 2021.

ʿAbbās, Iḥsān. *Al-Sharīf al-Raḍī*. Beirut: Dār Bayrūt, 1959.

ʿAbd al-Muṭṭalib, Rifʿat Fawzī (comp.). *Ṣaḥīfat ʿAlī ibn Abī Ṭālib ʿan Rasūl Allāh SA: Dirāsah tawthīqiyyah fiqhiyyah*. Cairo: Dār al-Salām, 1986.

ʿAbd al-Zahrāʾ, al-Sayyid al-Ḥusaynī al-Khaṭīb. *Maṣādir Nahj al-balāghah wa-asānīduhu*. 4 vols. Beirut: Muʾassasat al-Aʿlamī, 1975.

ʿAbd al-Zahrāʾ, al-Sayyid al-Ḥusaynī al-Khaṭīb. *Miʾat shāhid wa-shāhid min maʿānī kalām al-Imām ʿAlī ʿalayhi l-salām fī shiʿr Abī al-Ṭayyib al-Mutanabbī*. Beirut: Dār al-Aḍwāʾ, 1985.

ʿAbduh, Muḥammad (comm.). *Nahj al-balāghah: Wa-huwa majmūʿ mā ʾkhtārahu al-Sharīf al-Raḍī min kalām sayyidinā Amīr al-muʾminīn ʿAlī ibn Abī Ṭālib ʿalayhi al-salām*. Beirut: al-Maṭbaʿah al-Adabiyyah, 1885. Expanded commentary by Muḥammad Muḥyī al-Dīn ʿAbd al-Ḥamīd as *Nahj al-balāghah*. Cairo: Al-Maktabah al-Tijāriyyah al-Kubrā, 1965.

Afsaruddin, Asma. "Abū Dharr al-Ghifārī." *EI*[3].

Ali, Aun Hasan. "The Canonization of *Nahj al-Balāgha* between Najaf and Ḥilla: Sistani and the Iconic Authority of the Marājiʿ." *Journal of the Contemporary Study of Islam* 2:1 (2021), 2–23.

al-ʿĀmilī, Ḥusayn Jumʿah. *Shurūḥ Nahj al-balāghah*. Beirut: Maṭbaʿat wa-Zinkūghrāf al-Fikr, 1983.

Amīn, Aḥmad. *Fajr al-Islām: Yabḥathu ʿan al-ḥayāh al-ʿaqliyyah fī ṣadr al-Islām ilā ākhir al-dawlah al-Umawiyyah*. Beirut: Dār al-Kitāb al-ʿArabī, 1929.

al-Amīnī, ʿAbd al-Ḥusayn (comp.). *Al-Ghadīr fī l-kitāb wa-l-sunnah wa-l-adab*. 11 vols. Qum: Al-Ghadir Centre for Islamic Studies, 1995.

Amir-Moezzi, Mohammad Ali. *Ali, le secret bien gardé: Figures du premier Maître en spiritualité shiʿite*. Paris: CNRS Éditions, 2020. Translated into English by Fransisco José Luis and Anthony Gledhill as *Ali, the Well-Guarded Secret: Figures of the First Master in Shiʿi Spirituality*. Leiden: Brill, 2023.

Anṣārī, Ḥasan (= Hassan Ansari). "Riwāyat wa-nuskhah-ī jadīd az ʿahdnāmah-yi Mālik-i Ashtar." Online: https://ansari.kateban.com/post/3149. Accessed February 10, 2022.

Anṣārī, Ḥasan (= Hassan Ansari). "Majmūʿah-yi dīgar az nuskhah-hā-yi khaṭṭī Ambrosiana." Online: https://ansari.kateban.com/post/3494. Accessed February 13, 2022.

Anṣārī, Ḥasan (= Hassan Ansari). "Tāzah-hā-yi darbārah-yi riwāyat Nahj al-balāghah." Online: https://ansari.kateban.com/post/1617. Accessed February 10, 2022.

Ansari, Hassan, and Sabine Schmidtke. "The Literary-Religious Tradition among Seventh/Thirteenth-Century Yemeni Zaydīs (II), The Case of ʿAbd Allāh b. Zayd al-ʿAnsī. (Appendix II)." In *Studies in Medieval Islamic Intellectual Traditions*, edited by Sabine Schmidtke and Hassan Ansari. Atlanta, Georgia: Lockwood Press, *Resources in Arabic and Islamic Studies* series, 2017, 193–230.

ʿArshī, Imtiyāz ʿAlī Khān. *Istinād Nahj al-balāghah* (Urdu). Lucknow: Aḥbāb Publishers, 1972. Translated into Arabic by ʿAzīzallah ʿUṭāridī as *Istinād Nahj al-balāghah*. Tehran: Maṭbaʿat al-Ḥaydarī, 1979. Translated into Persian by Murtaḍā Āyatallāhzādah Shīrāzī as *Istinād-i Nahj al-balāghah*. Tehran: Amīr Kabīr, 1984.

Asad, Muhammad (trans. and comm.). *The Message of the Qurʾān*. Gibraltar: Dar al-Andalus, 1980.

Asatryan, Mushegh. *Controversies in Formative Shīʿī Islam: The Ghulāt Muslims and Their Beliefs*. London: I.B. Tauris, 2017.

Bayḍūn, Labīb Wajīh. *Taṣnīf Nahj al-balāghah: Min Kalām Amīr al-muʾminīn ʿAlī ibn Abī Ṭālib*. Damascus and Beirut: Dār al-Qalam, 1978.

Bernheimer, Teresa. "Rulers as Authors: ʿAlī b. Abī Ṭālib and the Other Twelver Imams." In *Rulers as Authors in the Islamic World: Knowledge, Authority and Legitimacy*. Edited by Maribel Fierro, Sonja Brentjes, and Tilman Seidensticker. Leiden: Brill, 2024, 9–29.

Biran, Michal. "Chinggis Khān." *EI*[3].

Dashtī, Muḥammad. *Ravish-i taḥqīq dar asnād va madārik-i Nahj al-balāghah*. Qum: Nashr-i Imām ʿAlī ʿalayhi al-salām, 1409/1989.

Djebli, Moktar. *Encore à propos de l'authenticité du Nahj al-Balagha*. Paris: Maisonneuve-Larose, 1992.

Djebli, Moktar. "Nahdj al-Balagha." *EI*[2].

EIr = *Encyclopedia Iranica*. Edited by Ehsan Yarshater et al. London and Boston: Routledge and Kegan Paul, 1982–. Online: http://www.iranicaonline.org/. Accessed February 19, 2022.

EI[2] = *Encyclopaedia of Islam*. 2nd ed. Edited by P.J. Bearman, Th. Bianquis, C.E. Bosworth, E. van Donzel, and W.P. Heinrichs. Brill: Leiden, 1960–2011, online 2012. Accessed February 19, 2022.

EI[3] = *Encyclopaedia of Islam, THREE*. Edited by K. Fleet, G. Krämer, D. Matringe, J. Nawas, E. Rowson, and D. Stewart. Brill: Leiden, print and online, 2007–. Accessed February 19, 2022.

Esḥāqī, Peymān (= Peyman Eshaghi). "Manbaʿ-shināsī-yi tarjamah-hā-yi Nahj al-balāghah be-barkhī zabān-hā-i ghayr-i ʿArabī." *Falsafah wa-kalām* 4 (2011), 337–360. Online: https://www.noormags.ir/view/fa/articlepage/837967/-منبع-شناسی-ترجمه-های منبع-شناسی-ترجمه-های نهج-البلاغه-به-برخی-زبان-های-غیر-عربی. Accessed February 10, 2022.

Fierro, Maribel. *Historia de los Autores y Transmisores Andalusíes (HATA)*. Online database: https://www.eea.csic.es/red/hata/index.html. Accessed February 10, 2022.

Gleave, Robert M. "ʿAlī b. Abī Ṭālib." *EI³*.

Halm, Heinz. *Die islamische Gnosis: Die extreme Schia und die ʿAlawiten*. Munich: Artemis Verlag, 1982.

Halm, Heinz. "Ğolāt." *EIr*.

al-Hansawī, Sibṭ al-Ḥasan. *Minhāj Nahj al-balāghah*. Lucknow: Dār al-Nashr li-l-Maʿārif al-Islāmiyyah, 1951.

Hassan, Syed Mohammad Waris. *A Critical Study of Nahj al-balāgha*. Ph.D. diss., University of Edinburgh, 1979.

Hawting, G.R. "Muḥammad b. Abī Bakr." *EI²*.

Ḥaydar, Kāmil (comp.). *Rasāʾil al-Imām ʿAlī*. Beirut: Dār al-Fikr al-Lubnānī, 1995.

Husayn, Nebil. *Opposing the Imām: The Legacy of the* Nawāṣib *in Islamic Literature*. Cambridge: Cambridge University Press, 2021.

al-Ḥusaynī, Ibrāhīm Khalīl Dhahab Maḥmūd. *Al-Imām ʿAlī ibn Abī Ṭālib fī kutub al-Qāḍī al-Nuʿmān al-Maghribī (d. 363 AH/974 AD)*. PhD diss., University of Karbala, 2019.

Inloes, Amina. "Was Imam ʿAli a Misogynist? The Portrayal of Women in Nahj al-Balaghah and Kitab Sulaym ibn Qays." *Journal of Shīʿa Islamic Studies* 8/3 (2015), 325–365.

Jackson, Peter. "Hülegü b. Toluy b. Chinggis Khān." *EI³*.

al-Jalālī, Muḥammad Ḥusayn. *Dirāsah ḥawl Nahj al-balāghah*. Beirut: Muʾassasat al-Aʿlamī li-l-Maṭbūʿāt, 1421/2001.

al-Jalālī, Muḥammad Ḥusayn. *Sharḥ Nahj al-balāghah li-l-Imām ʿAlī ibn Abī Ṭālib*. 5 vols. Qum: n.p., 1422/2002.

al-Jindī, ʿAlī, Muḥammad Abū al-Faḍl Ibrāhīm, and Muḥammad Yūsuf Maḥjūb (comp.). *Sajʿ al-ḥamām: Fī Ḥikam al-Imām Amīr al-muʾminīn ʿAlī ibn Abī Ṭālib*. Cairo: Maktabat al-Anjlū-Miṣriyyah, 1967.

Jiwa, Shainool. "The Baghdad Manifesto (402/1011). A Re-Examination of Fatimid-Abbasid Rivalry." In *The Fatimid Caliphate: Diversity of Traditions*, edited by Farhad Daftary and Shainool Jiwa. London: I.B. Tauris, 2018, 22–79.

Jurdāq, Jurj. *Rawāʾiʿ Nahj al-balāghah*. Beirut: al-Sharikah al-Sharqiyyah, 1973.

Kara, Seyfeddin. *In Search of Ali Ibn Abi Talib's Codex: History and Traditions of the Earliest Copy of the Qurʾan*. Berlin: Gerlach Press, 2018.

Kāshif al-Ghiṭāʾ, al-Hādī (comp.). *Mustadrak Nahj al-balāghah*. Beirut: Manshūrāt Maktabat al-Andalus, 1970.

Kaur, Kuldip. *Madrasa Education in India: A Study of its Past and Present.* Chandigarh, India: Centre for Research in Rural & Industrial Development, 1990.

Kawar, Irfan. "Djadhīma al-Abrash or al-Waḍḍāḥ." *EI²*.

Kazmi, Latif Hussain. "An Essay on the Place of Tolerance in Islam." *Journal of Shīʿa Islamic Studies* 2/1 (2009), 27–51.

Keizoghani, S.M., and A. Moulavi Nafchi. "The Greatness of *Nahj Al-Balagha* and the Words of Imam Ali from the Perspective of Modern Christian Figures." *International Letters of Social and Humanistic Sciences* 69 (2016), 5–14.

Khulūṣī, Ṣafāʾ. "The Authenticity of Nahj al-Balagha." *Islamic Review* 38 (1950), 31–350.

Kohlberg, Etan. "ʿAlī b. Abī Ṭāleb." *EIr.*

Lāhījānī (or: al-Lāhījī), Mīrzā Muḥammad-Bāqir Nawwāb (d. ca. 1824) (comm.). *Sharḥ Nahj al-balāghah* (Persian). 2 vols. Edited by Muḥammad Mahdī Jaʿfarī and Muḥammad Yūsuf Nayyirī. Tehran: Mīrāth-i Maktūb 2000.

Lane, Edward William. *An Arabic-English Lexicon: Derived from the Best and the Most Copious Eastern Sources.* London and Edinburgh: Williams and Norgate, 1863–1893.

Lanham, Richard. *Analyzing Prose.* New York: Charles Scribner, 1983.

Lecomte, G. "Al-Saḳīfa." *EI².*

Madelung, Wilferd. "Shīʿa." *EI².*

Madelung, Wilferd. *The Succession to Muhammad: A Study of the Early Caliphate.* Cambridge: Cambridge University Press, 1997.

al-Maḥmūdī, Muḥammad Bāqir (comp.). *Nahj al-saʿādah fī mustadrak Nahj al-balāghah.* 13 vols. Tehran: Muʾassasat al-Ṭibāʿah wa-l-Nashr Wizārat al-Thaqāfah wa-l-Irshād al-Islāmī, 2002.

Manouchehri, Faramarz, Reza Shah-Kazemi, Ali Bahramian, Ahmad Pakatchi, Daryoush Poor, Masoud Tareh, Mohammad Jozi, Sadeq Sajjadi, Ali Bulookbashi, Mahbanoo Alizadeh, and Yadollah Gholami. "ʿAlī b. Abī Ṭālib." In *Encyclopaedia Islamica*, edited by Wilferd Madelung and Farhad Daftary. First published online: 2015. Online: http://dx.doi.org.proxy.uchicago.edu/10.1163/1875-9831_isla_COM_0252. Accessed February 22, 2022.

al-Marṣafī, Muḥammad Ḥasan Nāʾil (comm.). *Kitāb Nahj al-balāghah: Al-Jāmiʿ li-khuṭab wa-rasāʾil mawlānā Amīr al-muʾminīn ʿAlī ibn Abī Ṭālib ṣalawāt Allāh ʿalayhi.* 2 vols. Cairo: Dār al-Kutub al-ʿArabiyyah al-Kubrā, 1910.

Matthiesen, Toby. "Sectarian Orientalism: How Orientalists (mostly) adopted the Sunni Narrative of Islamic History, and then helped institutionalise sectarian difference." In *The I.B. Tauris Handbook to Rethinking Islamic Studies: Explorations in Interactions, Ambiguities and Peripheries.* Edited by Seyfeddin Kara and Suleyman Dost. Bloomsbury/I.B. Tauris forthcoming 2024.

Mīr-Jahānī, Ḥasan (comp.). *Miṣbāḥ al-balāghah,* or *Mustadrakāt Nahj al-balāghah.* 3 vols. Beirut: Muʾassasat al-Tārīkh al-ʿArabī, 2008.

Morgan, David. "Mongols." *EI².*

Morony, M. "Al-Nahrawān." *EI².*

Morrow, John Andrew. *Shi'ism in the Maghrib and Al-Andalus.* Vol. 2: *Traditions.* Newcastle upon Tyne: Cambridge Scholars Publishing, 2020.

Mourad, Suleiman. *Early Islam between Myth and History: Al-Ḥasan al-Baṣrī (d. 110 H/ 728 CE) and the Formation of his Legacy in Classical Islamic Scholarship.* Leiden: Brill, 2006.

Mughniyyah, Muḥammad Jawād (comm.). *Fī Ẓilāl Nahj al-balāghah: Muḥāwalah li-fahm jadīd.* 4 vols. Beirut: Dār al-'Ilm li-l-Malāyīn, 1972–1973.

Muḥammad, Uways Karīm. *Al-Mu'jam al-mawḍū'ī li-Nahj al-balāghah.* Mashhad: Mu'assasat al-Ṭab' wa-l-Nashr fī l-Āsitānah al-Raḍawiyyah al-Muqaddasah, 1988.

Muḥammadī, Kāẓim and Muḥammad Dashtī. *Al-Mu'jam al-mufahras li-alfāẓ Nahj al-balāghah.* Beirut: Dār al-Aḍwā', 1986.

Muntaẓirī, Ḥusayn 'Alī. *Dars-hā-yi az Nahj al-balāghah.* 11 vols. Qum: Daftar-e Entesharat-e Eslami, 1983.

Musil, Alois. *The Middle Euphrates: A Topographical Itinerary.* New York: American Geographical Society, 1927.

Muṭahharī, Murtaḍā. *Sayr-ī dar Nahj al-balāghah,* Qum 1975. Translated into English by Ali Quli Qara'i as *Glimpses of Nahjul-Balagha.* Online: https://www.al-islam.org/ glimpses-nahjul-balagha-murtadha-mutahhari. Accessed February 10, 2022.

Muttaqī, Ḥusayn. *"Iṭlālah 'alā makhṭūṭāt Nahj al-balāghah fī l-maktabāt al-'ālamiyyah* [Overview of *Nahj al-balāghah* manuscripts in libraries across the world]." *Paygāh-i Khabarī-yi Nusakh-i Khaṭṭī.* Last modified Tīr 5, 1395 [June 25, 2016]. Online: http://manuscripts.ir/fa/90/اطلاعات-بانک/news/ ‏-في-البلاغة-نهج-مخطوطات-على-إطلالة‎ ‏العالمية-المكتبات-3835/مقالات‎. Accessed May 17, 2023.

Muttaqī, Ḥusayn. *Mu'jam al-āthār al-makhṭūṭah fī al-Imām 'Alī 'alayhi al-salām (Lexicon of Ancient Manuscripts on Imam Ali, PBUH).* Karbala: Maktabat wa-Dār Makhṭūṭāt al-'Atabah al-'Abbāsiyyah al-Muqaddasah, 2019.

al-Najaf Ābādī, al-Durrī. "La conception du gouvernement islamique dans Nahj al balāghah." *Aux Sources de la Sagesse* 1/2 (1994), 95–114.

Naqavī, Muḥammad Taqī (comm.). *Miftāḥ al-sa'ādah: Fī Sharḥ Nahj al-balāghah.* 18 vols. Tehran: Qā'in, 2005–2007.

Ong, Walter J. *Orality and Literacy: The Technologizing of the Word.* London: Methuen, 1982.

Osborne, Hannah. "Hyena Burger? Saudi Taste for Wild Meat Threatens Species Extinction," *International Business Times,* June 21, 2013. Online at https://www.ibtimes.co .uk/hyena-meat-extinction-saudi-arabia-consumption-halal-481755.

Paul, Jürgen. "Dihqān." *EI³*.

Pellat, Charles. "Al-Khirrīt," *EI².*

Popovic, Alexandre. "Al-Zandj, 2. The Zandj revolts in 'Irāḳ." *EI².*

al-Qāḍī, Wadād (= Wadad Kadi). "An Early Fāṭimid Political Document." *Studia Islamica* 48 (1978), 71–108.

Qubānchī, Ḥasan, with Ṭāhir Sallāmī (comp.). *Musnad al-Imām ʿAlī ʿalayhi al-salām.* 10 vols, Tehran: Muʾassasat al-Aʿlamī, 1999.

Qutbuddin, Tahera. "ʿAli ibn Abi Talib." In *Dictionary of Literary Biography.* Vol. 311: *Arabic Literary Culture, 500–925.* Edited by Michael Cooperson and Shawkat Toorawa. Farmington Hills, Michigan: Thomson Gale, 2005, 68–76.

Qutbuddin, Tahera. *"Khuṭba:* The Evolution of Early Arabic Oration." In *Classical Arabic Humanities in their Own Terms: Festschrift for Wolfhart Heinrichs on His 65th Birthday Presented by His Students and Colleagues.* Edited by Beatrice Gruendler with Michael Cooperson. Leiden: Brill, 2008, 176–273.

Qutbuddin, Tahera. "The Sermons of ʿAlī ibn Abī Ṭālib: At the Confluence of the Core Islamic Teachings of the Qurʾan and the Oral, Nature-Based Cultural Ethos of Seventh Century Arabia." *Anuario de Estudios Medievales* 42:1 (2012), 201–228.

Qutbuddin, Tahera. "Khoṭba." In *Encyclopaedia Iranica.* Edited by Ehsan Yarshater. Online edition, 2013.

Qutbuddin, Tahera. "ʿAlī's Contemplations on this World and the Hereafter in the Context of His Life and Times." In *Essays in Islamic Philology, History, and Philosophy,* edited by A. Korangy, W. Thackston, R. Mottahedeh, and W. Granara. Berlin and Boston: De Gruyter, 2016, 333–353.

Qutbuddin, Tahera. "Qurʾan Citation in Early Arabic Oration (*khuṭba*): Mnemonic, Liturgical and Testimonial Functions." In *The Qurʾan and* Adab: *The Shaping of Literary Traditions in Classical Islam.* Edited by Nuha Alshaar. Oxford: Oxford University Press, 2017, 315–340.

Qutbuddin, Tahera. "A Sermon on Piety by Imam ʿAlī ibn Abī Ṭālib: How the Rhythm of the Classical Arabic Oration Tacitly Persuaded." In *Religion and Aesthetic Experience: Drama—Sermons—Literature.* Edited by Jan Scholz, Max Stille, Sabine Dorpmüller, and Ines Weinrich. Heidelberg: Heidelberg University Press, *Heidelberg Studies on Transculturality* series, 2018, 109–124.

Qutbuddin, Tahera. "Piety and Virtue in Early Islam: Two Sermons by Imam Ali." In *Self-Transcendence and Virtue: Perspectives from Philosophy, Psychology, and Theology.* Edited by Jennifer Frey and Candace Vogler. London and New York: Routledge, *Studies in Ethics and Moral Theory* series, 2018, 125–153.

Qutbuddin, Tahera. "Ibn Abī l-Ḥadīd." *EI*^{3}. 2018-2, 78–81.

Qutbuddin, Tahera. "Orations of Zaynab and Umm Kulthūm in the Aftermath of Ḥusayn's Martyrdom at Karbala: Speaking Truth to Power." In *The Other Martyrs: Women and the Poetics of Sexuality, Sacrifice, and Death in World Literatures.* Edited by Alireza Korangy and Leila Rouhi. Wiesbaden: Harrassowitz Verlag, 2019, 103–132.

Qutbuddin, Tahera. *Arabic Oration: Art and Function.* Leiden: Brill, 2019.

Qutbuddin, Tahera. "Books on Arabic Philology and Literature: A Teaching Collection Focused on Religious Learning and the State Chancery." In *Treasures of Knowledge: An Inventory of the Ottoman Palace Library (1502/3–1503/4),* 2 vols. Edited by G. Necipoglu, C. Kefadar, and C. Fleischer. *Muqarnas Supplements* 14 (2019), 1:607–634.

Qutbuddin, Tahera. "Nahj al-balāgha," *EI³*, 2023-1, 99–107.

Qutbuddin, Tahera. "Al-Sharīf al-Raḍī." *EI³*, 2023-1, 147–151.

Qutbuddin, Tahera. "Classical Islamic Oration's Art, Function, and Life-Altering Power of Persuasion: The Ultimate Response by Hammam to Ali's Sermon on Piety, and by Hurr to Husayn's Battle Oration in Karbala." *Medieval Sermon Studies* 67:1 (2023), 74–87. Special volume edited by Linda G. Jones and Jussi Hanska.

Qutbuddin, Tahera. "Arabic Oration in Early Islam: Religion, Ritual, and Rhetoric." In *Speaking to God and the World: Ritual and Social Dynamics of Religious Speech.* Edited by Ruth Conrad and Matthias Mader, London: Bloomsbury, 2024, 156–172.

Qutbuddin, Tahera. "Just Leadership in Early Islam: The Teachings and Practice of Imam Ali." In *The Arts of Leading: Perspectives from the Humanities and the Liberal Arts.* Edited by Edward Brooks and Michael Lamb. Washington, D.C.: Georgetown University Press, 2024, 78–92.

Qutbuddin, Tahera. "Is Oration Literature? Establishing the *Khuṭbah* of the Pre- and Early Islamic Oral Period as the Foundational Genre of Classical Arabic Prose," *Journal of Arabic Literature*, 55:2–3 (2024), 213–237.

Qutbuddin, Tahera. "Orality as Driver of Qur'anic Aesthetics: Mnemonic and Metonymic Techniques of Pulsating Rhythm, Vivid Imagery, Agonistic Engagement, and Context Evocation." In *The Edinburgh Companion to Qur'anic Literary Studies.* Edited by Shawkat Toorawa. Edinburgh: Edinburgh University Press, forthcoming 2026.

Qutbuddin, Tahera. "Is *Nahj al-balāghah* a Shiʿi Book? Insidious Labels and Academia's Myth of Objectivity." In *The I.B. Tauris Handbook to Rethinking Islamic Studies: Explorations in Interactions, Ambiguities and Peripheries.* Edited by Seyfeddin Kara and Suleyman Dost. Bloomsbury/I.B. Tauris, forthcoming 2026.

Rahim, Habibeh. "ʿAli ibn Abi Talib." In *The Encyclopedia of Religion.* Edited by Mircea Eliade et al. New York: Macmillan, 1987, 1:204–210.

al-Rayshahri, Muḥammad. *Mawsūʿat al-Imam ʿAlī ibn Abī Ṭālib fī l-kitāb wa-l-sunnah wa-l-tārīkh.* 12 volumes. Beirut: Dār Iḥyāʾ al-Turāth al-ʿArabī, 2000.

Sayf al-Dīn, Ṭāhir. *Al-Risālah al-Ramaḍāniyyah: Ḍawʾ nūr al-ḥaqq al-mubīn.* Mumbai: Ṭayyibī Daʿwa Publications, 1335/1917.

Sayf al-Dīn, Ṭāhir. *Al-Risālah al-Ramaḍāniyyah: Zubdat al-burhān al-ṣidq al-wāḍih.* Mumbai: Ṭayyibī Daʿwa Publications, 1347/1929.

Sayf al-Dīn, Ṭāhir. *Al-Risālah al-Ramaḍāniyyah: Masarrāt al-fatḥ al-mubīn,* Mumbai: Ṭayyibī Daʿwa Publications, 1353/1934.

Sayf al-Dīn, Ṭāhir. *Al-Risālah al-Ramaḍāniyyah: Dalw ghadīr ḥaqq.* Mumbai: Ṭayyibī Daʿwa Publications, 1362/1943.

Schoeler, Gregor. *The Genesis of Literature in Islam: From the Aural to the Read.* Translated by Shawkat M. Toorawa. Edinburgh: Edinburgh University Press, 2009.

Shahīd, Irfan. "Al-Zabbāʾ." *EI².*

Shah-Kazemi, Reza. *Justice and Remembrance. Introducing the Spirituality of Imam Ali.* London: I.B. Tauris, 2006.

Shams al-Dīn, Ibrāhīm (comp.). *Khuṭab Amīr al-muʾminīn ʿAlī ibn Abī Ṭālib: Yaḥtawī ʿalā 230 khuṭbah fī l-dīn wa-l-siyāsah wa-l-targhīb wa-l-tarhīb wa-l-waʿẓ wa-l-tadhkīr wa-l-zuhd wa-ghayr dhālik.* Beirut: Dār al-Kutub al-ʿIlmiyyah, 2007.

Silsilah fī riḥāb Nahj al-balāghah. Series published by Imam Ali Shrine, Najaf 2018. Online: https://www.haydarya.com/?id=132. Accessed February 10, 2022.

Stetkevych, Suzanne. "Al-Sharīf al-Raḍī and *Nahj al-balāghah.* Rhetoric, Dispossession, and the Lyric." *Journal of Arabic Literature* 50 (2019), 211–250.

Stillman, N.A. "Yahūd." *EI².*

Sultan, Jamil. *Étude sur Nahj al-Balâgha.* Paris: Adrien-Maisonneuve, 1940.

al-Ṭabāṭabāʾī, ʿAbd al-ʿAzīz. "Al-Mutabaqqī min makhṭūṭāt Nahj al-balāghah ḥattā l-qarn al-thāmin al-hijrī," *Turāthunā* 5 (1406/1986), pp. 25–102. Online: https://books .rafed.net/view.php?type=c_fbook&b_id=2621. Accessed February 10, 2022.

al-Ṭabāṭabāʾī, ʿAbd al-ʿAzīz. "Ma tabaqqā min makhṭūṭāt Nahj al-balāghah," *Turāthunā* 7/8 (1407/1987), pp. 13–36. Online: https://arabic.balaghah.net/content/%D9%85 %D8%A7-%D8%AA%D8%A8%D9%82%D9%89-%D9%85%D9%86-%D9%85% D8%AE%D8%B7%D9%88%D8%B7%D8%A7%D8%AA-%D9%86%D9%87%D8 %AC-%%D8%A7%D9%84%D8%A8%D9%84%D8%A7%D8%BA%D8%A9. Accessed January 31, 2024.

al-Ṭabāṭabāʾī, ʿAbd al-ʿAzīz. "Fī Riḥāb Nahj al-Balāghah. Makhṭūṭātuhu, ṭabʿātuhu, muntakhabātuhu, tarjamātuhu ilā shattā l-lughāt, shurūḥu, mā qīla fīhi min naẓm wa-nathr," Part 1–3: *Turāthunā* 29 (1412/1992), pp. 7–89. Online: https://books.rafed .net/view.php?type=c_fbook&b_id=2769&page=7. Accessed February 10, 2022.

al-Ṭabāṭabāʾī, Muḥammad Ḥusayn (comp.), and William Chittick, trans., with introduction by Hossein Nasr. *A Shiʿite Anthology.* Albany, NY: SUNY, 1981.

Ṭāliqānī, Maḥmūd (trans. and comm.). *Tarjumah va sharḥ-i Nahj al-balāghah.* Tehran: Kitābfurūshī-i Bīnish, 1970.

Thaver, Tehseen. *Beyond Sectarianism: Ambiguity, Hermeneutics, and the Formations of Religious Identity in Islam.* University of Pennsylvania Press, forthcoming 2024.

al-Tihrānī, Āghā Buzurg. *Al-Dharīʿah ilā taṣānif al-shīʿah.* 25 vols. + 3 index vols. Beirut: Dār al-Aḍwāʾ, 1983.

Tijani, Smaoui Mohamed. *Les méthodes d'analyse et de pensée dans le Nahj-al-Balagha de l'imam Ali Ibn Abi Taleb.* Ph.D. diss., University of Paris I (Sorbonne), 1984.

al-Tustarī, Muḥammad Taqī (comm.). *Bahj al-ṣabāghah: Fī Sharḥ Nahj al-balāghah.* 14 vols. Tehran: Dār Amīr Kabīr li-l-Nashr, 1997.

Veccia Vaglieri, L. "ʿAlī b. Abī Ṭālib." *EI².*

Veccia Vaglieri, L. "Observations sur le Nahdj al-balāgha," in *Proceedings. of the 24th Congress of Orientalists,* Munich 1957, 318–319.

Veccia Vaglieri, L. "Sul *Nahǧ al-balāǧa* e sul suo compilatore al-Raḍī." *Annali dell'Istituto Universitario Orientale di Napoli,* new series 8 (1958), 1–46.

Viré, F. "Ḍabuʿ." *EI².*

Waseem, Shah-Mohammad, and S. Ali Mohammad Naqavi, eds. *Nahjul Balagha and Inter-religious Understanding*. Delhi: Renaissance Publishing House, 1997.

Zetterstéen, K.V. "al-Nuʿmān ibn Bashīr." *EI*[2].

Online Resources for *Nahj al-balāghah*

All accessed January 1, 2024.

Aviny.com (*Nahj al-balāghah*), website affiliated with the office of the late Sayyed Morteza Aviny, includes sections on "sources, contents, commentaries, and misconceptions" regarding *Nahj al-balāghah*, in English.

Balaghah.net (*Fī Riḥāb Nahj al-balāghah*), website supervised by the office of Ayatollah Sistani, begun 2004, aims to edit and publish all materials related to *Nahj al-balāghah*.

Haydarya.com (*al-Maktabah al-mukhtaṣṣah bi-l-Imām Amīr al-muʾminīn. Shurūḥ Nahj al-balāghah*), online access to all *Nahj al-balāghah* commentaries and other relevant works in Arabic.

Hadith.net (Shiʿa Ḥadīth Web Site), text, translation, sources, *Encyclopedia of Imam Ali*.

Al-Islam.org (*Nahj al-balāghah*), text, translation, sources, studies.

Imamalinet.net (*Pāyigāh-i Imām ʿAlī*), text, translation, studies.

Nahjalbalaghah.org, text, translation, manuscripts, commentaries, studies (under construction).

Shiaonlinelibrary.com (*al-Maktabah al-Shīʿiyyah*), text, commentaries, studies.

Index of Names and Places

This Index lists names and places from the Detailed Contents and Translation (and from the footnotes in parentheses)

Aaron (Ar. Hārūn)   447
al-ʿAbbās ibn ʿAbd al-Muṭṭalib   56, 125
al-ʿAbbās ibn Mirdās al-Sulamī   (601*n*2)
Abbasids   (99*n*1, 245*n*3, 521*n*5, 717*n*2, 805*n*2, 811*n*4)
ʿAbd al-ʿAzīz ibn Marwān   (197*n*4)
ʿAbd al-Malik ibn Marwān   (197*n*4, 257*n*2, 321*n*4)
ʿAbd al-Muṭṭalib ibn Hāshim   547, 571, 619
ʿAbd al-Raḥmān ibn ʿAttāb ibn Asīd   78, 501
ʿAbd al-Raḥmān ibn ʿAwf   (121*n*2)
ʿAbd al-Raḥmān ibn Ṣafwān   (501*n*2)
ʿAbd Manāf ibn Quṣayy   501, 547
ʿAbd Shams   711
ʿAbdallāh ibn al-ʿAbbās   59, 82, 84–85, 88–89, 123, 153, 157, 527, 549, 551, 599, 665, 671, 675, 781, 825, (187*n*3, 605*nn*1–2, 789*n*2)
ʿAbdallāh ibn Awfah al-Yashkurī   *See* Ibn al-Kawwāʾ
ʿAbdallāh ibn al-Ḥaḍramī   (179*n*1)
ʿAbdallāh ibn Jaʿfar   (711*n*2, 753*n*3)
ʿAbdallāh ibn Mālik ibn Dajnah   523
ʿAbdallāh ibn Masʿūd   (153*n*3)
ʿAbdallāh ibn Qays   *See* Abū Mūsā al-Ashʿarī
ʿAbdallāh ibn Ṣafwān   (501*n*2)
ʿAbdallāh ibn ʿUmar   763, (319*n*1, 681*n*3)
ʿAbdallāh ibn Zamaʿah   79, 521
ʿAbdallāh ibn al-Zubayr   (127*n*2)
ʿAbduh, Muḥammad (Abbr. "A", *passim*)
Abel (Ar. Hābīl)   *See* Cain and Abel
Abraham (Ar. Ibrāhīm)   567, 703
Abū al-Aʿwar al-Sulamī   (545*n*1)
Abū Ayyūb al-Anṣārī   413
Abū Bakr   80, 537, (119*n*1, 125*n*2, 145*n*3, 189*n*2, 191*n*2, 319*n*2, 367*n*1, 371*n*3, 471*n*1, 563*n*4, 569*n*1, 613*n*1, 655*n*3, 683*n*3, 733*n*1)
Abū Dharr al-Ghifārī   311, (317*n*2, 487*n*1, 769*n*4)
Abū Dhuʾayb al-Hudhalī   (569*n*2)
Abū Firās Hammām ibn Ghālib   *See* Farazdaq

Abū Hurayrah al-Dawsī al-Yamānī   (649*n*2)
Abū Jahl ʿAmr ibn Hishām   (459*n*3, 567*n*2)
Abū Juḥayfah Wahb ibn ʿAbdallāh al-Suwāʾī   797
Abū Jundub al-Hudhalī   (145*n*1)
Abū Lahab   (215*n*1, 567*n*5)
Abū Mūsā al-Ashʿarī   88–89, 525, 659, 675, (159*n*2, 401*n*3, 483*n*1, 681*n*3)
Abū Muslim al-Khawlānī   (539*n*2)
Abū Sufyān   56, 125, 369, 547, 605, 611, (215*n*1, 459*n*3, 567*nn*2–3, 603*n*3, 609*n*2, 657*n*1, 659*n*4, 661*n*2)
Abū Ṭālib   125, 149, 159, 251, 299, 389, 547, 613
Abū Tharwān   (653*n*3)
Abū ʿUbayd al-Harawī   755
Abū Umāmah al-Bāhilī   (563*n*2)
Adam (Ar. Ādam)   56, 75, 107, 111, 239, 241, 441, 447, 451
    son(s) of   399, 685, 733, 749, 763, 807, 815
ʿAfīf ibn Qays   (201*n*2)
Aḥmad ibn Qutaybah al-Hamdānī   523
al-Aḥnaf ibn Qays   69, 307, (681*n*3)
Ahwaz   551
ʿĀʾishah bint Abī Bakr   64, 72, 80, 531, (129*n*4, 139*n*2, 157*n*2, 203*n*1, 335*n*1, 345*n*3, 347*n*5, 353*n*2, 389*n*3, 481*n*3, 535*n*2, 595*n*1, 619*n*3, 661, 707*n*2, 715*n*4)
ʿAlāʾ ibn Ziyād al-Ḥārithī   485
ʿAlī ibn Abī Ṭālib *passim*
ʿAlī ibn al-Ḥusayn al-Sajjād Zayn al-ʿĀbidīn   (101*n*1, 767*n*2)
ʿAlī ibn Muḥammad al-Zanjī   (307*n*4)
Allies (Ar. Anṣār)   189, 531, 569, 819. *See also* Emigrants and Allies
Amalekites (Ar. ʿamāliq)   411
ʿAmmār ibn Yāsir   413, 803, (265*n*1, 317*n*2, 531*n*1, 651*n*2)
ʿAmr ibn ʿAbd Wadd   (179*n*3, 459*n*3)
ʿAmr ibn Abī Sufyān   (661*n*2)
ʿAmr ibn al-ʿĀṣ   59, 64, 74, 84, 86, 147, 215, 525, 603, 783, (145*n*2, 159*n*2, 165*n*1, 165*n*3, 191*n*1, 401*n*3, 405*n*1, 405*n*4,

'Amr ibn al-'Āṣ (*cont.*) 471*n*1, 483*n*1, 499*n*2,
 565*n*7, 599*n*1, 621*n*1, 649*n*2, 657*n*1,
 675*n*3)
'Amr ibn al-Ḥamiq al-Khuzā'ī (483*n*1)
'Amr ibn Salamah al-Hamdānī al-Arḥabī
 82, (533*n*2, 549*n*3)
Anas ibn Mālik 777, (681*n*3)
Anbar 59, 147, 689, 761
Antichrist. *See Dajjāl*
'Aqīl ibn Abī Ṭālib 79, 84, 513, 599
Arabs 59, 66, 125, 145, 157, 261, 267, 291, 301,
 323, 331, 341, 385, 457, 467, 531, 547, 615,
 655, 755
Ardashīr-khurrah 85, 609, (169*n*3, 407*n*1,
 605*n*1)
'Arj 525
Asad 72, 367, (501*n*2, 567*n*3)
al-Aṣbagh ibn Nubātah (153*n*2, 325*n*1, 715*n*4)
A'shā Maymūn 757, (119*n*2)
al-Ash'ath ibn Qays 58, 79–80, 91, 137, 535,
 771, 805, (201*n*2, 513*nn*3–4, 699*n*3,
 703*n*4)
Ashtar *See* Mālik ibn al-Ḥārith al-Ashtar
'Āṣim ibn Ziyād al-Ḥārithī 77, 487
al-Aswad ibn Quṭbah 87, 653
'Ayn al-Tamr 60, 63, (165*n*1, 191*n*3)
Azerbaijan 80, 535

Badr, Battle of Badr 539, 541, 571, (179*n*2,
 459*n*3, 567*n*2, 567*n*4, 661*n*2, 661*n*4)
Baghdad (309*n*1, 665*n*4)
Bahrain 85, 607, (375*n*1, 485*n*3, 563*n*3)
Bahrānī, Maytham (abbr. "B", *passim*)
Basra 57, 60, 69, 72, 78, 80, 82–83, 85,
 87, 89, 129, 157, 195, 259, 307, 319,
 335, 353, 385, 389, 485, 501, 521, 531,
 533, 549, 551, 571, 611, 651, 675, 777,
 (127*n*4, 139*n*2, 139*n*4, 153*n*4, 179*n*1,
 203*n*1, 253*n*4, 255*n*4, 257*n*3, 261*n*3,
 265*n*1, 279*n*1, 293*n*3, 321*n*1, 331*n*3,
 345*n*3, 355*n*3, 387*n*1, 393*n*1, 439*n*4,
 481*n*1, 487*n*1, 517*n*4, 535*n*2, 599*n*1,
 605*n*1, 647*n*2, 661*n*1, 685*n*2, 707*n*2,
 715*n*2, 715*n*4, 731*n*2, 753*n*2, 781*n*1,
 795*n*4)
 Basran 5, 64, 73, 385, (571*n*6)
Baṭḥā' *See* Mecca
Bishr ibn Abī Khāzim al-Asadī (661*n*3)
Bishr ibn Marwān (197*n*4)

(The) Book (Ar. *al-Kitāb*) 113, 135, 199, 217,
 221, 229, 299, 303, 315, 321, 333, 335, 385,
 405, 475, 577, 673, 719. *See also* Qur'an,
 Wise Remembrance
Boys-of-Hellfire 567
Burak ibn 'Abdallāh al-Tamīmī (165*n*3)
Burj ibn Mus'hir al-Ṭā'ī 74, 419
Busr ibn Abī Arṭāt 143
Byzantium (Ar. Rūm) 453

Caesar (Ar. Qayṣar) 535
Cain (Ar. Qābīl) and Abel (443*n*2)
Camel (Ar. Jamal), Battle of the Camel 56–
 60, 63–64, 68, 70–73, 78–80, 82, 87–89,
 129, 153, 195, 203, 385, 501, 521, 573, 659,
 761, (123*n*2, 125*n*4, 127*nn*1–4, 131*n*1,
 139*n*2, 139*n*4, 157*n*2, 167*n*2, 169*n*1,
 243*n*3, 253*n*4, 255*n*4, 257*n*3, 265*n*1,
 279*n*1, 293*n*3, 299*n*2, 307*n*3, 319*n*3,
 321*n*1, 331*n*3, 335*n*1, 335*n*4, 345*n*3,
 353*nn*1–2, 355*n*3, 373*n*1, 387*n*1, 389,
 391*n*1, 393*n*1, 457*n*1, 457*n*3, 481*n*1, 481*n*3,
 485*n*3, 487*n*1, 515*n*2, 517*n*4, 533*nn*1–2,
 535*nn*2–3, 537*n*1, 539*n*1, 549*n*1, 595*n*1,
 611*n*1, 619*n*3, 647*n*2, 651*n*2, 663*n*1,
 669*n*1, 673*n*2, 675*n*1, 681*n*4, 685*n*2,
 715*n*2, 715*n*4, 727*n*1, 731*nn*1–2, 753*n*2,
 763*n*1, 777*n*1, 795*n*4)
Chiefs-of-the-Youth-of-Paradise 567. *See
 also* al-Ḥasan ibn 'Alī; al-Ḥusayn ibn
 'Alī
Chosroes (Ar. Kisrā) 535
Confederates (Ar. Aḥzāb), Battle of the Con-
 federates 459

al-Ḍaḥḥāk ibn Qays al-Fihrī 59, 84, 599,
 (151*n*2)
Dajjāl, the Antichrist (257*n*2)
Damascus (169*n*1, 369*n*1, 537*n*1, 537*n*3,
 539*n*1, 601*n*3, 603*n*3, 619*n*1, 649*n*1,
 659*n*3, 663*n*1, 669*n*1, 671*n*2, 781*n*1)
Dārī 375, 379
David (Ar. Dā'ūd) 72, 90, 363, 411, 707
Dhakwān (311*n*2)
Dhi'lib al-Yamānī 74, 403, (431*n*3, 523*n*3)
Dhū al-Rummah 291
Dhū al-Shahādatayn *See* Khuzaymah ibn
 al-Thābit
Dhū al-Thudayyah (457*n*2, 731*n*2)

Dhū Qār   59, 79, 87, 157, 521, (125*n*4, 127*n*4,
    319*n*3, 331*n*3, 387*n*1, 517*n*4, 651*n*2,
    659*n*1)
Ḍirār ibn Ḍamrah al-Ḍibābī   90, 697
Dūmat al-Jandal   (129*n*2, 675*n*3)
Durayd ibn al-Ṣimmah   (161*n*3)

Egypt   62, 83–87, 191, 559, 561, 597, 599, 603,
    625, 655, (145*n*2, 165*n*1, 169*n*2, 197*n*4,
    405*n*1, 499*n*2, 571*n*6, 617*n*1, 651*n*3,
    783*n*1, 813*n*5)
Emigrants (Ar. *Muhājirūn*)   531, 547, 549,
    565, 569, 649
    and Allies   455, 525, 537, 571, 661. *See also*
    Allies
Euphrates (Ar. Furāt)   173, 175, 757, (165*n*1,
    655*n*1)

Fadak   85, 613, (125*n*2)
Family of the Prophet   *See* Muḥammad,
    Family of
Farazdaq   101, 815
Fars   551, 825 (605*n*1, 609*nn*1–2, 669*n*2). *See
    also* Persia
Fāṭimah al-Zahrāʾ   76, 479, 555, (125*n*2,
    354*n*2, 567*nn*4–5, 613*n*1, 775*n*3)
Firās ibn Ghanam   145
Followers-in-Virtue (Ar. *al-tābiʿūna bi-iḥsān*)
    88–89, 113, 247, 411, 571
Freedmen (Ar. *ṭulaqāʾ*)   547, 563, 565, (311*n*2,
    551*n*2, 727*n*1, 805*n*3)
Fusṭāṭ   (651*n*3)

Gabriel (Ar. Jibrīl)   409, 455
Ghadīr Khumm   (99*n*2, 663*n*3)
Ghālib ibn Ṣaʿṣaʿah   815
Ghāmidī   *See* Sufyān ibn ʿAwf al-Ghāmidī
God, Lord *passim*
    assigning partners/peers to   82, 219, 285,
        315, 337, 347, 401, 553
    (no) attributes of   105, 107, 109, 229, 371,
        427, 445, 467, 489, 581
    blessings of   63, 75, 99, 113, 141, 173, 195,
        205, 209, 255, 267, 273, 285, 287, 289,
        309, 325, 327, 355, 393, 407, 431, 433,
        437, 453, 461, 465, 467, 469, 473, 495,
        497, 545, 565, 573, 579, 621, 627, 645,
        647, 667, 681, 685, 719, 733, 741, 747, 767,
        771, 789, 795, 799, 801, 809
    bounty of   75, 185, 187, 205, 227, 267, 279,
        291, 355, 403, 407, 417, 421, 423, 431, 453,
        469, 495, 561, 563, 621
    consciousness of   54, 62, 75, 79, 83, 86–
        87, 185, 205, 207, 209, 211, 285, 289, 311,
        367, 391, 411, 415, 431, 435, 437, 445, 467,
        469, 471, 473, 519, 555, 559, 575, 579, 617,
        625, 651, 785, 793, 803. *See also* God,
        fear of
    decree of   109, 113, 163, 187, 273, 409, 445,
        495, 517
    direction of   105, 185, 217, 231, 333, 395,
        469, 579, 739
    Emissary of   195, 267, 411
    favors of   56, 66–67, 99, 107, 113, 115, 117,
        171, 173, 177, 203, 205, 209, 225, 227, 241,
        253, 255, 267, 273, 285, 295, 347, 365,
        407, 431, 437, 445, 455, 469, 473, 497,
        511, 533, 585, 617, 623, 647, 681, 723, 745
    fear of   81, 83, 121, 123, 141, 143, 207, 209,
        217, 235, 263, 273, 287, 327, 347, 357, 361,
        373, 383, 399, 417, 423, 435, 443, 449,
        453, 463, 489, 517, 527, 543, 561, 573,
        579, 581, 595, 597, 607, 617, 619, 639,
        645, 649, 653, 685, 701, 709, 737, 739,
        745, 747, 773, 817. *See also* God, con-
        sciousness of
    grace of   64, 66, 82, 205, 255, 289, 327,
        429, 497, 549, 631, 749, 789, 797, 825
    kingdom of   229, 233, 273, 351, 435, 447,
        581, 627
    mercy of   60, 107, 111, 129, 171, 225, 241,
        261, 267, 277, 289, 327, 355, 359, 379,
        391, 395, 431, 435, 449, 465, 469, 471,
        473, 583, 585, 625, 641, 645, 647, 657,
        701, 717, 771, 807
    messenger(s) of   *See* messengers (in
        Index of Terms)
    obedience to   76, 185, 231, 235, 273, 311,
        329, 333, 343, 351, 385, 393, 395, 401,
        409, 431, 447, 453, 467, 473, 493, 497,
        517, 527, 559, 569, 573, 625, 641, 667,
        691, 783, 799, 811
    oneness of, unity of   75, 105, 107, 233, 241,
        297, 369, 375, 383, 407, 423, 449, 749, 825
    power of   77, 107, 113, 115, 207, 229, 233,
        273, 275, 279, 331, 333, 335, 343, 361, 371,
        375, 413, 419, 421, 427, 429, 475, 489,
        499, 577, 581, 627, 647, 749, 803

praise of   56, 59–61, 64–67, 69, 71–76, 78,
    99, 107, 109, 115, 133, 161, 171, 173, 205,
    227, 233, 241, 243, 249, 253, 255, 265,
    269, 285, 287, 289, 313, 343, 351, 355,
    359, 361, 369, 389, 405, 407, 409, 413,
    415, 419, 433, 437, 439, 461, 467, 491,
    495, 539, 545, 703, 825
proof of   74, 91, 113, 139, 203, 217, 229, 239,
    269, 327, 365, 395, 397, 407, 411, 415,
    433, 601, 723
prophets of   *See* prophets (in Index of
    terms)
punishment of   115, 129, 141, 177, 207, 213,
    221, 225, 251, 261, 279, 327, 329, 333, 341,
    355, 391, 431, 435, 441, 445, 451, 463,
    477, 479, 497, 535, 551, 573, 581, 623,
    627, 645, 653, 661, 689, 697, 701, 703,
    725, 745, 749, 765, 771, 773, 793, 797,
    805
return to   147, 151, 155, 167, 213, 271, 273,
    287, 301, 311, 343, 407, 413, 415, 429, 471,
    479, 517, 579, 595, 607, 615, 647, 677,
    691, 703, 705, 739, 741, 801
servants of *passim*
signs of   113, 173, 229, 231, 233, 265, 269,
    327, 355, 403, 409, 415, 493, 743
threat of   697
throne of   109, 115, 235, 361, 409, 415
unity of   *See* God, oneness of

Ḥāḍirīn   573, (747*n*2)
Hajar   563
al-Ḥajjāj ibn Yūsuf al-Thaqafī   293, (179*n*5,
    795*n*3)
Ḥakīm ibn Jabalah al-ʿAbdī   (335*n*4)
Ḥamal ibn Badr   571
Ḥamal ibn Saʿd al-ʿAshīrah   (571*n*3)
Hammām   75, 461, 465, (715*n*1, 783*n*4)
Ḥamzah ibn ʿAbd al-Muṭṭalib   539, (179*n*2,
    565*n*4, 567*n*3)
Ḥanẓalah ibn Abī Sufyān   (541*n*3, 571*n*4,
    661*n*4)
Ḥarb ibn Shuraḥbīl al-Shibāmī   781
Ḥarb ibn Umayyah ibn ʿAbd Shams   547
al-Ḥārith (al-Aʿwar) al-Hamdānī   88, 667,
    (709*n*1, 777*n*3)
al-Ḥārith ibn Ḥawṭ al-Laythī   761, 763
(The) Harlot (Ar. al-Nābighah)   215, (405*n*4)
Ḥarūriyyah (sing. Ḥarūrī), Ḥarūrāʾ   703

al-Ḥasan ibn ʿAlī   77, 83, 86, 90, 121, 195,
    485, 555, 573, 607, 617, 689, 743,
    805, (125*n*4, 153*n*2, 193*n*1, 381*n*3,
    531*n*1, 567*n*4, 609*n*2, 651*n*2, 659*n*1,
    679*n*1, 699*n*5, 747*n*2, 769*n*4, 775*n*3,
    801*n*1)
Hāshim ibn ʿAbd Manāf   547
    Banū   90, 329, 571, 711 (501*n*2, 565*n*4,
        567*n*1, 567*n*6)
Hāshim ibn ʿUtbah al-Mirqāl   62, 191
Ḥassān (or Ashras) ibn Ḥassān al-Bakrī al-
    Balawī   147, (761*n*1)
Ḥassān ibn Thābit al-Anṣārī   (319*n*1)
Ḥātim al-Ṭāʾī   (613*n*2)
Hawāzin   161, 759
He-of-the-Two-Wings   565. *See also* Jaʿfar
    ibn Abī Ṭālib
He-who-Soars-in-Paradise   565. *See also*
    Jaʿfar ibn Abī Ṭālib
Ḥijāz   613, (607*n*1)
Ḥimyar   535
Ḥirāʾ   457
Hishām ibn ʿAbd al-Malik   (197*n*4)
Hishām ibn Muḥammad ibn al-Sāʾib al-Kalbī
    673
Hīt   87, 655
House of God   *See* Kaʿbah
Ḥudaybiyyah   (471*n*1)
Ḥujr ibn ʿAdī   84, (483*n*1, 599*n*3)
Ḥulwān   87, 653
Ḥunayn, Battle of Ḥunayn   759, (161*n*3)
Ḥurayth   81, 88
al-Ḥuṣayn (or al-Ḥuḍayn) ibn al-Mundhir
    al-Raqāshī   (699*n*4)
al-Ḥusayn ibn ʿAlī   86, 121, 195, 413, 485, 555,
    607, 617, (153*n*2, 567*n*4, 729*n*3)

Iblīs (Eng. Lucifer)   75, 82, 111, 439, 441, 443,
    445, 449, 451, 549, 669
Ibn Abī al-Ḥadīd (Abbr. "Ḥ", *passim*)
Ibn Abī Rāfiʿ   *See* ʿUbaydallāh ibn Abī Rāfiʿ
Ibn al-ʿAbbās   *See* ʿAbdallāh ibn al-ʿAbbās
Ibn al-Aʿrābī   811
Ibn al-Ḥaḍramī   *See* ʿAbdallāh ibn al-
    Ḥaḍramī
Ibn al-Ḥanafiyyah   *See* Muḥammad ibn ʿAlī
    ibn Abī Ṭālib
Ibn al-Kawwāʾ   (265*n*1, 779*n*4)
Ibn al-Sikkīt   123

Ibn al-Ṭayyihān Abū al-Haytham al-Anṣārī
    413
Ibn al-Zubayr   *See* ʿAbdallāh ibn al-Zubayr
Ibn Funduq al-Bayhaqī (Abbr. "F", *passim*)
Ibn Ḥunayf   *See* ʿUthmān ibn Ḥunayf al-
    Anṣārī
Ibn Masʿūd   *See* ʿAbdallāh ibn Masʿūd
Ibn Muljam (or Ibn Muljim) al-Murādī   62,
    413, 553, 617, (165n3, 183n4, 735n5)
Ibn Nubātah al-Saʿdī al-Khaṭīb   (433n6)
Ibn ʿUmar   *See* ʿAbdallāh ibn ʿUmar
ʿIkrimah ibn Abī Jahl   (459n3)
ʿImrān ibn al-Ḥusayn al-Khuzāʿī   647
Imruʾ al-Qays   815, (369n1)
Iraq   70, 80, 84, 153, 169, 545, 547, (125n4,
    161n4, 165n1, 183n1, 197n4, 215n1, 259n1,
    293n1, 307n4, 385n2, 543n4, 609n2,
    617n1, 651n3, 653n2, 655n1, 669n1,
    689n1, 773n2, 795n3)
Isaac (Ar. Isḥāq)   453
Ishmael (Ar. Ismāʿīl)   453
Iskāfī, Abū Jaʿfar   647
Israelites, children of Israel   381, 453
Isṭakhr   88, (669n2)

Jābir ibn ʿAbdallāh al-Anṣārī   92, 119, (795n1)
Jaʿdah ibn Hubayrah al-Makhzūmī   407,
    (521n5)
Jaʿfar al-Ṣādiq   227, (131n3, 719n2)
Jaʿfar ibn Abī Ṭālib   539, (565n5)
Jāḥiẓ   157
Jarīr (Umayyad poet)   101
Jarīr ibn ʿAbdallāh al-Bajalī   60, 80–81, 169,
    539, (537n1, 537n3, 541n1, 795n1)
Jāriyah ibn Qudāmah al-Saʿdī   83, (571n6)
al-Jārūd al-ʿAbdī   669
Jesus (Ar. ʿĪsā)   72, 90, 363, (201n1, 811n3)
Jibrīl   *See* Gabriel
Jumaḥ   501
Jumayḥ ibn al-Sharīd al-Taghlibī   (365n1)

Kaʿbah   91, 611, 765, (115n1, 201n1, 391n3,
    567n3)
Kalb   309
Khabbāb ibn al-Aratt   691, (715n2)
Khadījah bint Khuwaylid   459
Khālid ibn al-Walīd   137
Kharijites   60, 62, 64, 68–69, 74, 81, 89, 165,
    181, 183, 201, 299, 303, 305, 407, 419,
    675, 703, 735, 781, 809, (137n1, 159n1,
    161n4, 163n1, 297n1, 307n1, 401n3,
    433n6, 457nn1–2, 711n3, 731n2, 779n4,
    807n1)
Khaybar, Battle of Khaybar   (613n1)
al-Khirrīt ibn Rāshid al-Nājī   (407n1)
Khurasan   (485n3)
Khushnūshak   (689n1)
al-Khuṭbah/Khuṭbat
    al-Ashbāḥ (Ethereal Forms)   65, 227
    al-Gharrāʾ (The Radiant Oration)   64,
        205, 213 (187n1, 419n3)
    al-Qāṣiʿah (The Crushing Oration)   75,
        439 (571n6)
    al-Shiqshiqiyyah (The Camel-Stallion's
        Roar)   56, 119 (319n6, 517n4)
    al-Wasīlah (The Intercessor) (329n4,
        695n2, 707n3, 711n1, 733n2, 785n1,
        793n5)
Khuzaymah ibn Thābit al-Anṣārī   (413n1)
King of Martyrs   565. *See also* Ḥamzah ibn
        ʿAbd al-Muṭṭalib
Kirman (or Kerman)   551
Kitāb
    al-Bayān wa-l-tabyīn (by Jāḥiẓ)   157
        (131n3, 761n4)
    Gharīb al-ḥadīth (by Abū ʿUbayd)
        (755n1)
    Iṣlāḥ al-manṭiq (by Ibn Sikkīt)   123
    al-Jamal (by Wāqidī)   673
    al-Khaṣāʾiṣ (by Raḍī)   139 (99nn1–2)
    al-Maghāzī (by Saʿīd ibn Yaḥyā al-Umawī)
        675
    Majāzāt al-āthār al-nabawiyyah (by Raḍī)
        821
    al-Maqāmāt (by Abū Jaʿfar al-Iskāfī)   647
    al-Muqtaḍab (by Mubarrad)   821
Kufa, Kufan   58, 61, 63, 74, 80–81, 87–88, 91,
        137, 143, 171, 227, 251, 257, 323, 407, 531,
        533, 651, 659, 709, 715, 781 (and *passim*
        in footnotes)
Kulayb al-Jarmī   387
Kumayl ibn Ziyād al-Nakhaʿī   87, 91, 655, 721,
        749

Laylā bint Masʿūd   (367n3)
Lion-
    of-God   7, 567. See also Ḥamzah ibn
        ʿAbd al-Muṭṭalib

of-the-Alliances   567
Lucifer   *See* Iblīs

Madāʾin   (201*n*2, 543*n*4, 665*n*4, 711*n*4)
Madhḥij   603
Mahdī   (337*n*3, 753*n*1)
Makhzūm   90, 711
Mālik (angel who guards the gates of Hell)
     417
Mālik ibn al-Ḥārith al-Ashtar al-Nakhaʿī   81,
     86, 545, 603, 625, 655, 813, (163*n*4, 617*n*1)
Maʾmūn   811
Maʿqil ibn Qays al-Riyāḥī   81, 543, (169*n*3,
     407*n*1)
Maʾrib   (249*n*3, 381*n*4)
Marwān ibn al-Ḥakam   63, 195, 373, (131*n*2,
     153*n*3, 197*n*n*3–4, 501*n*2, 567*n*4, 649*n*2,
     727*n*1)
Masʿadah ibn Ṣadaqah al-ʿAbdī   227
Maṣqalah ibn Hubayrah al-Shaybānī   60, 85,
     169, (407*n*1, 605*n*1, 609, 609*n*n*1–2)
Mecca   3, 13, 82, 84–85, 88–89, 279, 365, 597,
     607, 665
Medina   57, 58, 65, 66, 71, 73, 74, 80, 84,
     88, 89, 131, 153, 375, 525, 531, 649, 669,
     673
Messiah   707, (321*n*1, 337*n*3, 753*n*1)
Michael (Ar. Mīkāʾīl)   409, 455
Mīkāʾīl   *See* Michael
Mikhnaf ibn Sulaym al-Azdī   83, (559*n*1)
al-Miqdād ibn ʿAmr (al-Aswad) al-Bahrāʾī
     (487*n*1, 769*n*4)
Miracle of the Tree   (459*n*1)
Moses (Ar. Mūsā)   72, 75, 125, 363, 409, 445,
     (197*n*5, 327*n*3)
Most-Virtuous-Woman-of-all-People   567.
     See also Fāṭimah al-Zahrāʾ
Mosul   (543*n*4)
Muʿāwiyah   59–61, 74, 76–77, 80–86, 88–89,
     143, 147, 157, 169, 175, 183, 215, 251, 405,
     479, 537, 539, 541, 547, 549, 563, 573,
     595, 601, 609, 611, 619, 649, 659, 663,
     669, 671, 673, 697, 761 (and *passim* in
     footnotes)
Muḍar   457
al-Mughīrah ibn al-Akhnas al-Thaqafī   69,
     317
al-Mughīrah ibn Shuʿbah al-Thaqafī   803,
     (179*n*5, 649*n*2, 657*n*1)

Muḥammad, the Prophet, Messenger of God
     56, 59–63, 65–67, 69–76, 78–81, 83, 87,
     91, 99, 113, 115, 117, 125, 127, 131, 135, 139,
     145, 157, 161, 163, 171, 177, 179, 189, 191,
     193, 195, 199, 205, 217, 221, 225, 227, 229,
     239, 245, 247, 249, 251, 255, 257, 261,
     263, 265, 269, 277, 279, 285, 291, 295,
     299, 303, 305, 309, 313, 315, 323, 333,
     337, 339, 341, 347, 353, 355, 359, 361,
     363, 365, 367, 373, 383, 385, 389, 391,
     395, 399, 403, 415, 419, 433, 435, 437,
     455, 457, 459, 461, 467, 469, 471, 475,
     477, 479, 483, 485, 487, 489, 491, 493,
     513, 521, 523, 525, 527, 539, 547, 551, 553,
     555, 559, 563, 565, 567, 569, 581, 601,
     613, 617, 619, 631, 633, 639, 641, 647, 651,
     655, 657, 659, 661, 675, 683, 691, 701,
     703, 713, 733, 745, 759, 765, 771, 777, 779,
     791, 811, 821, 825 (and *passim* in foot-
     notes)
     Family of (Ar. *Āl Muḥammad, Ahl al-bayt*)
     56, 64, 71, 79–80, 83, 117, 221, 247, 251,
     297, 339, 523, 527, 533, 709 (131*n*3,
     171*n*4, 189*n*2, 329*n*3, 337*n*3, 551*n*3)
Muḥammad al-Bāqir   701
Muḥammad ibn Abī Bakr   62, 83–84, 177,
     191, 195, 405, 559, 561, 597, 599, 625,
     783, (145*n*2, 153*n*2, 165*n*1, 189*n*2, 499*n*2,
     603*n*1, 617*n*1, 655*n*3, 813*n*5)
Muḥammad ibn ʿAlī ibn Abī Ṭālib (Muḥam-
     mad ibn al-Ḥanafiyyah, Ibn al-Ḥanafiy-
     yah)   129, 779, (573*n*2, 695*n*1, 799*n*n*2–3)
Muḥammad ibn Marwān   (197*n*4)
Muḥammad ibn Maslamah al-Anṣārī
     (319*n*1, 681*n*3)
al-Mundhir ibn al-Jārūd al-ʿAbdī   88, 669,
     671
Muʾtah   539, (565*n*5)

Nahāwand, Battle of Nahāwand   (331*n*1)
Nahrawān, Battle of Nahrawān   59–60, 62,
     88, 91, 781, (107*n*1, 127*n*1, 137*n*1, 159*n*2,
     161*n*4, 163*n*1, 165*n*3, 183*n*1, 183*n*3, 201*n*2,
     295*n*1, 299*n*1, 429*n*1, 439*n*4, 663*n*2,
     691*n*3, 723*n*1, 731*n*2, 807*n*1)
Nājiyah, Banū   60, 169, (407*n*1)
Naṣībīn   85, (617*n*1)
Nawf ibn Faḍālah al-Bikālī   90, 407, 413, 705,
     707

Night of Clamor (Ar. *laylat al-ḥarīr*)   (187*n*3, 697*n*1)
Nukhaylah   81, 86, 761, (159*n*1, 173*n*1, 249*n*1, 543*n*3, 621*n*n*1–3, 651*n*1, 653*n*3)
al-Nuʿmān ibn ʿAjlān al-Zuraqī   607
al-Nuʿmān ibn Bashīr al-Anṣārī   (165*n*1, 191*n*3)

Palestine   (317*n*1)
Persia, Persian(s)   71, 331, 453. *See also* Fars
Pharaoh (Ar. Firʿawn)   339, 411, 447, 453, 535
Psalms (Ar. *Zabūr*)   363

Qādisiyyah   (331*n*1)
Qarqīsiyā (Latin: Circesium)   655
Qaṣīr ibn Saʿd al-Lakhmī   161
Qaṭīf   (375*n*1)
Qays ibn Saʿd   413
Qurʾan   68–69, 74, 76, 86, 88–89, 91, 135, 199, 201, 221, 229, 279, 297, 299, 303, 307, 317, 321, 333, 359, 397, 399, 401, 413, 415, 461, 463, 543, 617, 619, 649, 667, 675, 703, 707, 765, 777, 813. *See also* Book, Wise Remembrance
   reader, reciter   523, 743
Quraysh   78, 84, 90, 149, 157, 189, 245, 329, 389, 459, 499, 501, 539, 601, 711
Qutham ibn al-ʿAbbās   84, 88, 597, 665

Rabadhah   69, 311, (125*n*4, 157*n*2, 317*n*2, 531*n*1)
al-Rabīʿ ibn Ziyād al-Ḥārithī   (485*n*3)
Rabīʿah   89, 457, 673
Raḍī, Sharīf   123, 133, 137, 139, 143, 145, 151, 153, 155, 165, 171, 173, 181, 183, 193, 199, 205, 213, 261, 267, 291, 293, 303, 307, 379, 413, 465, 481, 485, 487, 499, 525, 553, 555, 611, 671, 679, 683, 687, 689, 691, 699, 701, 703, 707, 709, 713, 725, 735, 743, 745, 753, 755, 757, 759, 761, 763, 775, 777, 779, 799, 811, 813, 815, 817, 821, 825 (and *passim* in footnotes)
Ramaḍān   279
Ramhormoz   81
Raqqah   (543*n*4)
Rass   411
Rāwandī (Abbr. "R" *passim*)

Sabā (Sheba)   249, (381*n*4)
Sacred House   75, 447, 449. *See also* Kaʿbah
Saʿd ibn Abī Waqqāṣ   (121*n*1, 319*n*1, 681*n*3, 763*n*2)
Ṣafiyyah bint ʿAbd al-Muṭṭalib   (153*n*4)
Ṣafwān ibn Umayyah al-Jumaḥī   (459*n*3)
Sahl ibn Ḥunayf al-Anṣārī   88, 669, 709, (611*n*1)
Saʿīd ibn al-ʿĀṣ   63, (199*n*2)
Saʿīd ibn Nimrān al-Hamdānī   143
Saʿīd ibn Yaḥyā al-Umawī   675
Saʿīd ibn Zayd   (681*n*3)
Salāmān ibn Ṭayy   (691*n*1)
Ṣāliḥ (Arabian prophet)   (407*n*2)
Ṣāliḥ ibn Sulaym   (691*n*1)
Salmān al-Fārisī   88, 665, (487*n*1, 711*n*4, 773*n*2)
Saqīfah (Portico)   62, 189, (569*n*1)
Ṣaʿṣaʿah ibn Ṣūḥān al-ʿAbdī   (669*n*2, 699*n*1, 753*n*2)
Shaybah ibn Rabīʿah ibn ʿAbd Shams   (179*n*2, 459*n*3)
Shibām (or Shabām)   781
Shūrā (Electoral) Council   63, 70, 80–81, 87, 197, 323, 537, 693, 711, 733, 739, (119*n*1, 367*n*1, 369*n*1, 389*n*1, 499*n*2, 683*n*3)
Shurayḥ ibn al-Ḥārith   80, 533
Shurayḥ ibn Hānī al-Ḥārithī   81, 87, 651, (543*n*3, 545*n*1)
Ṣiffīn, Battle of Ṣiffīn   61, 73, 81–84, 87–88, 187, 267, 485, (127*n*1, 159*n*2, 163*n*4, 165*n*3, 215*n*2, 243*n*3, 297*n*1, 299*n*2, 301*n*n*1–2, 369*n*1, 387*n*2, 413*n*1, 483*n*1, 539*n*n*1–2, 543*n*2, 547*n*4, 551*n*2, 563*n*2, 573*n*1, 595*n*2, 607*n*5, 619*n*2, 649*n*1, 659*n*3, 669*n*1, 675*n*2, 697*n*1)
Solomon (Ar. Sulaymān)   411
Sufyān ibn ʿAwf al-Ghāmidī   59, 87, (147*n*2, 655*n*1, 761*n*1)
Sufyānī   (321*n*4)
Suhayl ibn ʿAmr ibn ʿAbd Shams   459
Sulaym ibn Qays al-Hilālī al-ʿĀmirī   (203*n*1, 487*n*1)
Sulaymān ibn ʿAbd al-Malik   (197*n*4)
Sumayyah (or Asmāʾ) bint al-Aʿwar   609
Syria (Ar. Shām), Syrians   60–61, 64, 68, 77, 81–82, 84–87, 89–90, 159, 169, 171, 173, 179, 191, 215, 251, 257, 267, 299, 303, 323, 483, 525, 543, 547, 609, 649, 651,

Syria (Ar. Shām), Syrians (*cont.*)   689, 697,
     (165*n*1, 177*n*2, 177*n*4, 249*n*2, 291*n*1,
     295*n*1, 457*n*1, 471*n*1, 491*n*2, 545*n*1,
     573*n*2, 597, 621*n*1, 655*n*1, 709*n*1, 763*n*1,
     783*n*1)

Ṭalḥah ibn Abī Ṭalḥah al-ʿAbdarī   (179*n*3)
Ṭalḥah ibn ʿUbaydallāh   57, 59, 70–71, 73,
     77–78, 80, 87, 123*n*2, 125, 153, 319, 321,
     393, 481, 501, 531, 647, 659, 737, 777,
     (127*n*3, 139*n*2, 157*n*2, 177*n*2, 335*n*1,
     335*n*4, 345*n*3, 387*n*1, 389*n*3, 391*n*1,
     431*n*1, 535*n*2, 619*n*3, 707*n*2, 715*n*4, 731*n*1,
     781*n*1)
Tamīm   82, 549, (101*n*1, 439*n*4)
Ṭaybah   365. *See also* Medina
Taym   (501*n*2)
Thaʿlab   811
Thaʿlabiyyah   59, (151*n*2)
Thamūd   74, 76, 407, 479
Thaqīf   293
Tigris (Ar. Dijlah)   173, (161*n*4, 183*n*1)
Tubbaʿ   535
Turks   309

ʿUbaydah ibn al-Ḥārith ibn ʿAbd al-Muṭṭalib
     539
ʿUbaydallāh ibn al-ʿAbbās ibn ʿAbd al-
     Muṭṭalib   143, (551*n*3)
ʿUbaydallāh ibn Abī Rāfiʿ   779
Uḥud, Battle of Uḥud   355, 539, (317*n*2,
     565*n*4)
ʿUkāẓ   61, 171
ʿUmar ibn Abī Salamah al-Makhzūmī   85,
     607
ʿUmar ibn al-Khaṭṭāb   69, 71, 80, 331, 611,
     765, (119*n*1, 179*n*2, 197*n*5, 215*n*1, 317,
     319*n*2, 367*n*1, 371*n*3, 471*n*1, 485*n*3, 517*n*3,
     537, 563*n*4, 603*n*3, 683*n*3)
Umayyads   62–63, 65–66, 72–73, 87, 191, 197,
     199, 223, 245, 263, 359, 381, 819, (119*n*1,
     181*n*1, 249*n*2, 253*n*n*1–2, 307*n*1, 311*n*2,
     373*n*1, 521*n*5, 567*n*3, 567*n*6, 795*n*3)
Umayyah ibn ʿAbd Shams   547, (459*n*3)
Umm Hānī bint Abī Ṭālib   (311*n*2)
Umm Jamīl bint Ḥarb   (567*n*5)
Usāmah ibn Zayd   (319*n*1, 681*n*3)

ʿUtbah ibn Rabīʿah ibn ʿAbd Shams   (459*n*3,
     541*n*3, 567*n*3, 571*n*4, 661*n*4)
ʿUthmān ibn ʿAffān   57–59, 63, 65, 69–70,
     72–73, 80, 84, 131, 153, 243, 197, 317,
     371, 373, 383, 385, 393, 529, 531, 537,
     539, 543, 569, 601, 649, 651, 661, (119*n*1,
     169*n*n*1–2, 175*n*2, 177*n*2, 199*n*2, 311*n*2,
     319*n*6, 323*n*2, 367*n*1, 389*n*1, 391*n*4,
     403*n*1, 471*n*1, 499*n*2, 565*n*7, 603*n*2,
     619*n*n*2–3, 635*n*1, 657*n*1, 665*n*4, 673*n*5,
     711*n*4, 727*n*1, 765*n*1, 773*n*n*1–2, 797*n*2,
     803*n*2)
ʿUthmān ibn Ḥunayf al-Anṣārī   611, (389*n*3,
     535*n*2)
ʿUthmān ibn Maẓʿūn   (769*n*4)

al-Walīd ibn ʿAbd al-Malik   (197*n*4)
al-Walīd ibn al-Mughīrah   (459*n*3)
al-Walīd ibn ʿUqbah   (657*n*1, 773*n*1)
al-Walīd ibn ʿUtbah   (179*n*3, 541*n*3, 571*n*4,
     661*n*4)
Wāqidī   521
Woman-who-Carries-Firewood-to-Hell   567
Wise Remembrance (Ar. *al-Dhikr al-ḥakīm*)
     347, 767. See also Book, Qurʾan

Yamāmah   137, 613
al-Yamānī   523
Yanbuʿ al-Nakhl   529
Yazīd ibn ʿAbd al-Malik   (197*n*4)
Yazīd ibn Abī Sufyān   (661*n*2)
Yemen, Yemeni   89, 143, 377, 641, 673,
     (249*n*3, 369*n*4, 381*n*4)

Zanj   69, 307, (259*n*1)
Zayd ibn Thābit al-Anṣārī   (317*n*2)
Zaynab bint Jaḥsh   (367*n*3)
Ziyād ibn Abīhi   82, 85, 551, 609, 611, 825,
     (179*n*5, 571*n*6)
Ziyād ibn al-Naḍr al-Ḥārithī   81, (543*n*3,
     545*n*1, 651*n*1)
al-Zubayr ibn al-ʿAwwām   57, 59, 70–71, 77,
     80, 87, 125, 127, 153, 319, 321, 481, 531,
     647, 661, 737, 777, (123*n*2, 139*n*2, 157*n*2,
     177*n*2, 335*n*1, 345*n*3, 387*n*1, 389*n*3,
     391*n*1, 393*n*1, 431*n*1, 501*n*2, 535*n*2, 619*n*3,
     707*n*2, 715*n*4, 731*n*1, 781*n*1)

Index of Terms

This Index lists terms from the Detailed Contents and Translation (not footnotes).

abrogation, abrogated act   113, 489
act(s), action(s) *passim*
adder   145
adornments   197, 283, 347, 363, 825
adultery   271. *See also* fornication
advice   81, 247, 249, 265, 317, 331, 351, 483,
    537, 581, 591, 595, 699, 717, 739. *See also*
    counsel
affection   88, 141, 271, 285, 455, 493, 503,
    629, 659, 675, 721, 739, 741, 747,
    775
afterlife   195, 275, 283, 285, 713. *See also* here-
    after
Age of Ignorance (Ar. Jāhiliyyah)   245, 261,
    381, 385, 443, 445, 455, 545, 549
alms, almsgiving, alms levy (Ar. ṣadaqāt)
    76, 277, 279, 449, 451, 477, 513, 559, 679,
    719, 721, 747, 751, 765
ambition   251, 443, 497, 587, 707
ancestors   101, 253, 267, 415, 443, 445
angel(s)   56, 65, 67, 109, 111, 115, 177, 233, 235,
    237, 273, 277, 283, 387, 397, 409, 415,
    417, 441, 457, 471, 481, 509, 527, 717, 735,
    807
    of death   67, 283
anger   69, 159, 227, 267, 285, 297, 311, 367,
    393, 417, 443, 451, 469, 499, 533, 603,
    647, 667, 669, 675, 687, 729. *See also*
    rage
animals   61, 73, 83, 177, 199, 289, 421, 447,
    557, 565, 607, 613. *See also* bat, beast,
    bull, camel, carnivore, cattle, dog, goat,
    horse, hyena, lamb, pig, ram, sacrificial
    animal, sheep, wolf
anklets   147
annihilation   175, 207, 411, 419, 427, 429, 575,
    585, 717
ants   75, 241, 379, 403, 409, 421, 515
apostasy   355
arbitration (Ar. taḥkīm)   59, 61, 65, 68, 77,
    85–86, 89, 159, 161, 297, 299, 303, 307,
    485
    arbitrators   74, 307, 401, 525, 675
archer   131, 325, 785. *See also* hunter

arguments   78, 203, 205, 389, 419, 451, 509,
    511, 569, 601, 627, 771. *See also* proofs
armies   61, 64, 77, 81–82, 84, 87, 155, 175, 241,
    259, 281, 295, 303, 307, 309, 331, 389,
    391, 407, 411, 433, 437, 443, 445, 477,
    535, 541, 543, 545, 559, 571, 599, 627,
    639, 651, 655, 765. *See also* battalions,
    cavalry, forces
arrogance   117, 211, 247, 317, 347, 439, 441,
    443, 447, 459, 461, 465. *See also* pride
artisan   421, 425, 437, 631, 639
aspirations   59, 65, 109, 151, 219, 235, 247,
    281, 287, 441, 523, 527, 579, 633, 743, 783,
    817
assayer   157
atone   209, 683, 703. *See also* expiation
autumn   381, 753

baker   735
balance   337
banner(s)   117, 191, 221, 235, 257, 269, 323,
    329, 355, 373, 419, 467, 509
barley   363, 513
Barzakh   507
bat(s)   351
battalions   157, 245, 261, 295, 303, 543, 669
battle   56–57, 60, 66, 73, 103, 107, 139, 147,
    151, 159, 169, 177, 179, 183, 215, 225, 243,
    251, 267, 299, 321, 347, 393, 455, 473, 521,
    533, 539, 543, 545.547, 573, 599, 609,
    639, 649, 661, 681, 687, 759, 769, 825.
    See also fighting, war
beacon   99, 219, 221, 233, 239, 245, 265, 329,
    343, 419, 461, 469, 473, 475, 587
beads   331
beard   413, 697
beauty, beauties   133, 205, 239, 253, 259, 505,
    541, 585
Bedouins (Ar. aʿrāb)   267, 331, 343, 383, 455,
    489, 609, 753
beetle   293
beggars   449, 559, 607, 639, 775
belief   75, 91, 107, 115, 179, 201, 209, 233, 269,
    277, 311, 339, 343, 399, 405, 421, 433,

belief (*cont.*)   455, 461, 463, 467, 475, 563, 567, 651, 659, 703, 713, 747, 817. *See also* faith, unbelief

  believer   92, 119, 165, 261, 271, 347, 349, 395, 399, 407, 429, 431, 443, 445, 447, 451, 477, 537, 539, 547, 563, 565, 567, 607, 613, 633, 641, 667, 679, 687, 691, 699, 703, 705, 775, 779, 781, 783, 791, 795, 801, 809, 825. *See also* disbeliever, unbeliever

benedictions   227

betrayal   167, 739

bigots   441. *See also* zeal, zealotry

birds   72, 119, 129, 207, 241, 271, 375, 423, 427, 447, 459, 813. *See also* cockerel, crow, dove, eagle, ostrich, peacock, pigeon

blade   85, 139, 155, 187, 301, 269, 603, 609, 647, 809. *See also* sword

blind, blindness   67, 117, 119, 133, 135, 163, 187, 203, 209, 217, 219, 221, 245, 251, 269, 315, 329, 373, 397, 399, 403, 405, 407, 429, 471, 475, 499, 503, 507, 579, 587, 593, 597, 669, 687, 733

blood   86, 103, 135, 139, 145, 147, 175, 177, 179, 241, 319, 343, 393, 399, 411, 417, 439, 483, 503, 519, 537, 541, 543, 553, 609, 619, 645, 651, 663, 675

  -clot   211

blossoms   90, 239, 685, 711. *See also* flowers

boatman   375, 379

bondage, bondsman   339, 417, 495, 499, 525, 555, 729. *See also* slave

booty   305, 609, 733. *See also* war gains

bracelets   147, 447

brain   815

bread   363, 611, 613, 615

brick   253, 359, 745

bridle, bridle-strap   207, 257, 259, 343, 527

brigands   183

brother(s), brethren   68, 70, 73, 91, 165, 179, 209, 213, 225, 249, 251, 271, 283, 285, 293, 297, 299, 301, 303, 323, 325, 383, 411, 413, 441, 483, 559, 569, 571, 589, 591, 621, 625, 629, 661, 719, 727, 755, 761, 769, 791, 825

build, builder   287, 365, 411, 421, 575, 629, 717, 735, 785

bull   59, 153

burn, burning   159, 209, 235, 249, 267, 329, 417, 475, 509, 519, 613, 623, 651, 653, 661, 715, 759

butcher   199

calamities   59, 113, 125, 141, 147, 155, 161, 171, 179, 205, 213, 215, 221, 223, 225, 233, 239, 245, 269, 273, 279, 281, 299, 333, 341, 353, 369, 403, 429, 439, 445, 465, 479, 481, 493, 505, 507n3, 511, 517, 533, 573, 575, 597, 615, 627, 649, 657, 659, 661, 679, 685, 707, 709, 717, 721, 733, 739, 749, 771, 789. *See also* hardships, troubles

caliph   57–58, 61, 63, 79, 81, 83, 197, 481, 517, 531, 557, 569, 673

caliphate   56, 63, 65–66, 70–71, 73–74, 88–89, 121, 197, 303, 331, 335, 359, 383, 389, 483, 521, 529, 649, 655, 665, 733, 737

camel   57, 61, 63, 90, 121, 123, 129, 139, 145, 159, 165, 177, 185, 191, 199, 207, 211, 221, 223, 233, 243, 245, 251, 267, 269, 289, 291, 295, 297, 301, 315, 339, 355, 359, 373, 379, 403, 411, 443, 447, 467, 515, 519, 529, 531, 543, 557, 569, 579, 587, 589, 595, 601, 607n2, 615, 661, 669, 671, 683, 699, 747, 749, 753, 755, 759, 763, 821, 825

  buck   89, 679

  calf   199, 457

  herd of   121, 815

  herders   159, 177, 453

  mare   76, 123, 175, 321, 323, 469, 479, 739

  stallion   56, 119, 123, 237, 271, 407, 659

cameleer   805

camp   81, 155, 221, 303, 395, 413, 543, 667, 675, 805

caprice, capricious opinions   58, 121, 133, 135, 223, 263, 321, 341, 635, 675

caravan   137, 313, 357, 405, 513

carcass   245, 273, 341, 615

carnivore   271

cattle   115, 239, 269, 327, 347, 383, 387, 427, 593, 615, 723

cauldron   131, 353, 435, 533, 547

cavalry   57, 127, 147, 155, 303, 441, 443, 609

cemetery   715, 721

certainty   111, 117, 163, 207, 219, 235, 239, 285, 343, 357, 403, 407, 463, 467, 517, 547, 569, 575, 587, 657, 703, 713, 723, 725, 767, 795. *See also* conviction

chameleon   467

chamomile   377

character   63, 90, 129, 141, 199, 223, 263, 323,
    329, 457, 493, 577, 635, 637, 671, 689,
    709, 713, 743, 771

charity, charitable   88, 279, 469, 513, 551, 643,
    705, 721, 743, 795

chastisement   65, 68–69, 73, 75, 88, 217, 259,
    455

chastity, chaste   247, 271, 463, 465, 693

chickpeas   611

chieftains   169, 301, 445, 451, 501

child(ren)   63, 119, 141, 149, 167, 171, 175,
    193, 209, 211, 213, 227, 241, 257, 263,
    327, 337, 349, 367, 435, 447, 451,
    453, 477, 487, 513, 519, 535, 555,
    571, 617, 631, 701, 703, 749, 755, 775,
    789

Christian   86, 147, 623

clay   80, 99, 111, 371, 441, 451, 523

clemency   359, 437, 807, 817

cloud(s)   145, 235, 237, 239, 241, 263, 289, 291,
    327, 337, 381, 409, 423, 439, 491, 519,
    657, 683, 753, 757, 825

cockerel   375, 377

colocynth (Ar. ḥanẓal)   145, 359, 499

colt   819

column(s)   117, 159, 409, 445, 453, 473, 475,
    491, 721

command
    good and forbid evil   311, 353, 415, 455,
        507, 575, 619, 687, 747, 797
    (s) and prohibitions   167, 217, 233

commander(s)   81, 83, 86, 87, 143, 169, 189,
    251, 281, 365, 413, 473, 485, 535, 545, 621,
    633, 651, 653
    Commander of the Faithful (Ar. Amīr al-
        Muʾminīn)   56, 80, 82, 86, 89, 99, 101,
        107, 123, 137, 155, 157, 189, 195, 201, 227,
        295, 309, 353, 403, 407, 461, 465, 481n1,
        487, 523, 531, 533, 553, 603, 619, 621, 625,
        655, 659, 671, 673, 679, 697, 705, 711,
        721, 761, 765, 781, 797, 811, 815, 821, 823,
        825

community   83, 99, 113, 117, 121, 133, 165, 169,
    193, 223, 249, 277, 303, 305, 313, 317, 343,
    355, 373, 401, 433, 475, 515, 541, 547, 557,
    559, 563, 571, 605, 607, 623, 627, 629,
    651, 657, 675, 749, 797

companion(s), companionship   76, 80, 103,
    111, 141, 171, 193, 259, 291, 333, 335, 337,
    349, 367, 415, 417, 445, 461, 471, 531, 553,
    573, 679, 709, 715, 733
    Companions of the Prophet   61, 65, 79,
        251, 383, 389, 487, 489, 539, 563

compassion   70, 83, 86, 141, 323, 327, 405,
    487, 509, 511, 549, 617, 625, 627, 631, 637,
    641, 701

complain, complaint   68, 82, 135, 263, 305,
    327, 371, 487, 547, 549, 635, 643, 655,
    743, 761, 771, 809

conceit   219, 449, 461, 583, 675, 689, 713, 815.
    See also vanity

consequence(s)   109, 463, 589, 629, 635, 645,
    697, 811

consultation   537, 693, 711, 733, 739

contemplation   103, 711

contentment   92, 155, 447, 535, 693, 743, 787,
    793, 825

conviction   90, 117, 127, 233, 287, 319, 593,
    685. See also certainty

cooking pot   271

coral   227

corpse   60, 78, 161, 275, 337, 501, 503, 713, 781,
    815

corrupt, corruption   59, 69, 121, 143, 155, 253,
    307, 311, 313, 333, 401, 461, 471, 491, 497,
    603, 605, 687, 711, 749, 781

counsel, counselor   59–69, 71–77, 83, 85–87,
    89–92, 99, 101, 103, 151, 155, 159, 161, 207,
    215, 227, 243, 247, 249, 251, 263, 275,
    293, 297, 309, 315, 333, 365, 391, 395,
    397, 399, 411, 431, 435, 445, 465, 493,
    499, 511, 569, 573, 575, 589, 593, 623,
    629, 667, 673, 675, 679, 685, 701, 705,
    713, 717, 723, 725, 733, 769, 781. See also
    advice

courage   61, 179, 189, 211, 299, 301, 303, 471,
    501, 631, 679

course   68, 207, 251, 295, 297, 299, 357, 369,
    385, 387, 393, 409, 435, 443, 469, 475,
    511, 517, 633, 637, 643, 653, 717. See also
    path, way

covenant (Ar. ʿahd)   111, 455, 539, 631, 643,
    645, 663, 727. See also testament

coward, cowardice   57, 127, 157, 159, 261, 407,
    629, 659, 679, 745

cowrie shell   271. See also seashells

craft, crafting, craftsman, craftsmanship 77, 133, 343, 351, 375, 425, 427, 429, 489

creation, creator, creatures 56, 58, 65–67, 71–72, 74–75, 78, 105, 107, 111, 113, 133, 173, 187, 195, 211, 225, 227, 229, 231, 233, 235, 239, 241, 255, 269, 273, 275, 283, 289, 343, 345, 351, 359, 361, 371, 371, 375, 377, 379, 387, 397, 403, 407, 409, 413, 415, 419, 421, 423, 425, 427, 429, 437, 441, 451, 463, 467, 473, 491, 495, 501, 515, 517, 561, 579, 587, 597, 625, 641, 647, 713, 715, 725, 743, 807

crimes, criminal, criminal penalties 78, 211, 265, 323, 347, 369, 389, 441, 443, 569, 571, 585, 607, 629, 657, 747, 749, 765

crop 397, 423, 503

crow 377, 423

cunning 167, 299, 465, 479, 637, 711

cure 105, 139, 153, 251, 279, 297, 329, 353, 355, 359, 397, 407, 427, 463, 471, 475, 493, 509, 511, 589, 717. *See also* heal

curse 69, 77, 137, 181, 311, 317, 341, 413, 483, 809

custodian 195, 331, 389, 501, 557, 703, 783

custom 129, 181, 689

damn, damnation 455, 507, 509, 571, 671, 711, 821

darkness. *See* light and darkness

date(s) 355, 563
    palms 181, 555

daughter 76, 479

deaf, deafen 123, 187, 207, 233, 251, 269, 273, 309, 315, 399, 435, 503, 507, 597

death, the dead *passim*
    pools of 767

debt 141, 275, 757
    debtor 151, 309, 325, 559, 573

decay 209, 253, 275, 281, 425, 505, 513, 515, 717

deceit, deception 79, 84, 111, 193, 205, 219, 225, 279, 283, 293, 299, 479, 483, 515, 541, 559, 573, 581, 603, 645, 663, 751, 785

deed(s) *passim. See also* act
    bad, evil, hateful, mis-, vile, wicked 275, 339, 357, 417, 431, 445, 495, 511, 667, 767
    good and bad 451, 567, 585, 687

good, noble, pious, virtuous 62, 74, 141, 155, 167, 185, 199, 265, 329, 409, 435, 447, 523, 619, 625, 631, 633, 645, 649, 703, 709, 741, 747, 749, 807

deliverance 213, 367, 787

demons 157, 233

dens 191, 207

desert 291, 449, 469, 479, 565, 573, 721, 753

desires 105, 151, 167, 195, 199, 209, 219, 235, 273, 345, 367, 393, 395, 401, 447, 453, 463, 591, 605, 661, 687, 707, 717, 717, 723, 739, 745, 747, 767, 785, 793, 811

despots 67, 181, 359, 535, 609

destined 165, 353, 405, 619, 791. *See also* fates, ordained

destitution, destitute 239, 243, 289, 313, 429, 447, 451, 513, 559, 637, 639, 665, 713. *See also* indigence, poverty

deviation, deviate 209, 237, 267, 297, 299, 353, 383, 403, 437, 439, 573, 593, 621, 687

devil(s) 111, 235, 357, 417, 513, 687. *See also* Iblīs (in Index of Names), Satan

devotees 59, 92, 147, 225, 353, 361, 789, 805, 811

dignity 515, 557, 787, 791

Dihqān (landowner or merchant) 82, 549

dinar 251, 533

dirham 251, 429, 533, 789

dirt 155, 199, 251, 281, 445, 505, 515, 615

discernment, discern 64, 157, 167, 179, 203, 205, 209, 217, 219, 223, 249, 259, 275, 345, 349, 361, 365, 475, 595, 597, 703, 721, 725, 737, 767

discipline 411, 525, 695, 791, 805

dispatch(es) 80, 84, 87, 109, 111, 173, 195, 267, 317, 413, 437, 531, 533, 535, 537, 543, 597, 599, 655, 783

disposition 133, 195, 231, 269, 577

dispute 199, 319, 633, 667, 687, 755

dissolute, dissolution 219, 587, 723

dog 197, 341, 585, 603, 619

doubt(s) 60, 90, 103, 105, 111, 115, 121, 131, 133, 163, 187, 207, 221, 223, 233, 235, 285, 287, 293, 299, 335, 393, 439, 449, 493, 507, 547, 555, 579, 595, 633, 641, 663, 687, 703, 709, 723, 767, 803. *See also* suspicion doves   115, 175

(strong) drink   159, 287, 429, 591, 657, 747.
     See also wine

drought   281, 289, 291, 327, 345, 387, 473, 581,
     635, 753. *See also* famine

duel   563, 743

dunes   241, 379

eagle   307, 423

earrings   147

earth *passim*

East and West   363, 705, 773

easygoing   783

eggs   127, 377, 381

Eid (Ar. ʿĪd)
     blessing of   809
     sermon   59, 60, 61, 177

elite   627, 631

embezzlement   559

emerald   377, 379, 449

endurance   179, 397, 479, 711. *See also* for-
     bearance, patience

enemy *passim*

envy, envier   81, 83, 141, 219, 235, 275, 287, 311,
     385, 443, 445, 467, 569, 741, 749, 763,
     787, 793

epistle   81, 86, 101, 529, 537, 621, 625, 637, 651,
     653, 655, 657, 671

error   71, 103, 127, 131, 135, 143, 151, 163, 195,
     201, 221, 223, 267, 269, 303, 305, 333,
     335, 337, 341, 345, 397, 407, 415, 445,
     473, 483, 493, 499, 503, 545, 573, 575,
     579, 601, 613, 625, 633, 663, 787, 809. *See
     also* sin, transgression

eternity, eternal   177, 225, 273, 277, 281,
     283, 301, 343, 357, 367, 369, 371,
     411, 415, 419, 423, 425, 435, 443,
     713

ethics   397

evil *passim*
     struggle against   90, 685, 687, 797

excuse(s)   61, 119, 151, 179, 333, 357, 469, 509,
     511, 537, 599, 623, 645, 647, 653, 667,
     769, 783

exile   69, 78, 213, 283, 311, 333, 357, 411, 501,
     593, 679, 715

expiation   477. *See also* atone

extravagance   82, 551, 731

factionalism, factions   68, 74–75, 249, 319,
     335, 405, 439, 441, 443, 445, 453, 455,
     467, 543, 787

faith   64, 68–70, 76, 84, 86, 90, 99, 113, 115,
     117, 121, 129, 139, 141, 163, 177, 179, 199,
     203, 215, 217, 219, 221, 223, 235, 237, 253,
     265, 269, 281, 293, 299, 317, 325, 331,
     339, 343, 353, 365, 373, 393, 397, 419,
     457, 463, 465, 467, 479, 487, 495, 559,
     569, 585, 589, 595, 603, 619, 625, 637,
     671, 685, 699, 709, 711, 713, 721, 741, 747,
     755, 763, 775, 779. *See also* belief

falsehood   127, 131, 143, 151, 157, 173, 191, 261,
     271, 311, 319, 325, 357, 511, 517, 643, 657,
     667, 763, 817. *See also* lie

family, families   56, 64, 66–67, 70–71, 75,
     79–80, 82–83, 85–86, 107, 117, 141, 145,
     171, 247, 251, 275, 283, 305, 329*n*3, 337,
     339, 365, 387, 437, 477, 499, 505, 523,
     527, 531, 533, 539, 541, 579, 591, 605,
     607, 617, 619, 627, 631, 633, 635, 645,
     655, 667, 671, 709, 721, 765. *See also*
     brother, daughter, father, grandfather,
     grandmother, kin, mother, offspring,
     son

famine   289. *See also* drought

farmlands, farmers   423, 637, 753

fasting   203, 279, 297, 449, 719, 747

fat, fat-tail, fatty   143, 293, 381, 517, 527, 557,
     681, 805

fate(s)   70, 99, 155, 161, 175, 179, 185, 209,
     211, 215, 273, 281, 287, 313, 329, 343,
     543, 569, 573, 575, 589, 601, 613, 649,
     683, 697, 733, 735, 739, 769, 771, 787,
     817

father   61, 69, 75, 80, 83, 88, 113, 143, 161, 165,
     179, 195, 207, 209, 211, 225, 299, 307, 317,
     405, 429, 481, 523, 525, 573, 577, 607,
     671, 717, 775, 815

feast   85, 527, 611, 809

feelings   64, 217, 275

female   291, 309, 375, 379, 409

fetus   211, 283, 341, 371

(the) fifth (share, Ar. *khums*)   765

fight, fighting   57–60, 61, 63, 69–70, 77, 84,
     87, 129, 143, 153, 169, 179, 181, 251, 255,
     299, 307, 309, 317, 321, 351, 387, 433,
     443, 491, 545, 601, 691, 697, 731, 757, 759,
     763, 797

fire, the Fire   111, 113, 131, 137, 201, 219, 277, 295, 329, 381, 395, 417, 421, 435, 441, 443, 449, 451, 463, 473, 475, 477, 493, 513, 547, 561, 603, 607, 651, 675, 759, 787, 793, 801, 811. *See also* flame(s), hell

fish   471. *See also* whale

flame(s)   249, 417, 455, 473, 475, 513, 649, 759. *See also* fire

flattery   78, 499, 515, 645, 787

flaws   361, 365, 679, 693, 741, 801, 809

flint   151, 161, 247, 269

flock   257, 323, 411, 557. *See also* herd

flowers, flowerbeds   239, 377, 449, 595. *See also* blossoms, chamomile, rose

fodder   121, 613, 615

follower   58–60, 63, 65, 67–69, 73–74, 76, 113, 131, 139, 143, 159, 165, 173, 179, 187, 231, 301, 317, 323, 341, 395475, 479, 501, 511, 521, 611, 721

food   145, 225, 227, 239, 273, 287, 327, 351, 359, 363, 401, 409, 413, 421, 423, 457, 487, 581, 589, 611, 613, 721, 783, 791. *See also* grain, fruit

fool, foolishness   64, 161, 175, 215, 323, 327, 451, 497, 589, 593, 603, 645, 655, 689, 711, 721, 739, 741, 747, 771, 787, 791, 793

forbearance   72, 90, 119, 199, 463, 527, 679, 685, 739, 741, 809. *See also* endurance, patience

forces   195, 261, 301, 423, 655

forest   76, 227, 471

forgiveness   92, 111, 113, 115, 171, 175, 201, 241, 285, 327, 435, 449, 471, 493, 511, 517, 553, 625, 627, 649, 701, 703, 719, 773, 807, 813

fornication, fornicator   305, 493, 747. *See also* adultery

fortifications   147, 345, 493

fortress   321, 357, 439, 441, 455, 469, 475, 593, 631

free   169, 195, 251, 325, 339, 359, 417, 463, 555, 587, 701, 717, 745, 805, 817

Friday sermon   66 (139*n*4, 151*n*2, 153*n*2, 217*n*2, 253*n*4, 255*n*1, 291*n*1, 391*n*1)

friend(s), friendship, befriend   90, 99, 101, 107, 209, 219, 271, 283, 305, 311, 329, 333, 451, 453, 503, 573, 581, 589, 591, 593, 601, 617, 679, 681, 689, 719, 741, 745, 765, 773, 783, 789, 825

frivolity   215, 791

frolic   127, 215, 505, 575, 613, 723

fruits   99, 191, 225, 241, 247, 273, 289, 315, 325, 327, 349, 363, 365, 379, 397, 449, 451, 555. *See also* dates

fur   271

future   62, 219, 269, 289, 359, 415, 671. *See also* past, present

gallop   131, 205, 211, 237, 443, 531, 601, 683

gambler   757, 759

Garden   99, 109, 353, 367, 379, 381, 437, 441, 447, 449, 553, 793, 801, 811. *See also* paradise

garments, undergarments   155, 191, 207, 223, 225, 239, 245, 277, 291, 345, 359, 363, 377, 407, 441, 463, 471, 517, 549, 599, 605, 611, 623, 705, 707. *See also* loincloth, robes, shirt

gemstones   377. *See also* coral, emerald, pearl, ruby

generosity   143, 195, 227, 229, 243, 267, 281, 413, 445, 449, 451, 453, 469, 473, 495, 509, 511, 595, 629, 631, 643, 693, 737, 739, 741, 747, 783, 813

gentle, gentleness   123, 141, 189, 195, 235, 463, 465, 509, 557, 617, 669

gift(s)   63, 70, 79, 91, 115, 171, 173, 185, 195, 205, 213, 227, 241, 255, 267, 325, 355, 361, 407, 409, 437, 453, 455, 469, 471, 507, 511, 513, 585, 627, 671, 705, 719, 723, 743, 775, 783, 789

girls   519, 703, 753, 755

    baby-   453

    slave-   131, 267, 389, 393, 607

glad tidings   66, 277, 695

glutton, gluttony   271, 613, 629, 790

gnat   241, 379, 409, 427, 807

goal(s)   78, 99, 101, 149, 151, 201, 207, 211, 231, 253, 261, 265, 317, 349, 357, 379, 397, 503, 517, 543, 579, 643, 687, 695, 803, 819

goat   86, 121, 251, 253, 311, 359, 419, 557, 607, 623, 661

gold   155, 225, 357, 377, 447, 557, 611, 799

good *passim*

good and evil   383, 809. *See also* deeds

governing, governance, governor, governorate   62–63, 65, 80, 82–89, 143, 191, 241, 321,

governing, governance, governor, governorate
  (*cont.*)   389, 481, 483, 489, 501, 531, 535,
    535, 535*n2*, 549, 551, 597, 599, 603, 605,
    607, 609, 611, 617, 623, 625, 629, 631,
    635, 635*n1*, 637, 647, 655, 659, 665, 669,
    675, 705, 749, 789, 825
grace   82, 195, 505, 549, 749. See also God,
    grace of (in Index of Names)
grain   271, 273, 331, 449, 493, 513, 547, 609,
    615, 639. *See also* barley, wheat
grandchildren   209
grandfather   541, 571, 617, 661, 717
grandmother   717
grass   92, 121, 293, 387, 503, 557, 587, 613, 615,
    791
gratitude, grateful, ingrate, ingratitude,
    ungrateful   239, 297, 305, 309, 323, 355,
    359, 437, 439, 627, 667, 669, 681, 719,
    723, 737, 771, 785, 813. *See also* thanks
graves   78, 90, 207, 209, 275, 281, 313, 347,
    353, 379, 431, 435, 471, 473, 479, 501, 503,
    505, 507, 515, 517, 533, 591, 613, 615, 713,
    771, 791
greed, greedy   121, 131, 153, 235, 309, 313, 363,
    463, 467, 549, 621, 629, 633, 635, 679,
    707, 709, 729, 741, 743, 767, 793. *See also*
    gluttony
grief   137, 147, 171, 185, 209, 219, 259, 283, 307,
    327, 359, 367, 465, 479, 487, 499, 503,
    505, 525, 573, 581, 585, 597, 767, 771,
    783. *See also* sorrow
guest(s)   219, 281, 325, 485
guidance, guide, guided, misguidance *passim*
gum   271

hadith   77, 135, 487, 527, 703, 821
hajj   56, 84, 88, 279, 597, 623, 665, 719, 747
halter   209, 213, 263, 527, 595, 649, 671, 683,
    797
handmill   261
happiness, happy   159, 259, 279, 355, 367,
    403, 465, 511, 625, 631, 647, 665, 687,
    707, 717, 739, 771, 787, 805, 807. *See also*
    joy
hardships   61, 171, 205, 299, 353, 397, 429,
    449, 453, 463, 467, 473, 539, 577, 583,
    613, 655, 773, 789. *See also* calamities,
    troubles
harmony   375, 451, 629

harvest   141, 215, 225, 315, 453, 521
hate, hatred   193, 219, 281, 307, 443, 711, 821
heal   67, 183, 207, 243, 269, 279, 287, 345, 357,
    359, 365, 403, 437, 467, 471, 475, 517,
    561, 763. *See also* cure
health, healthy   78, 141, 209, 213, 247, 281,
    287, 335, 365, 413, 417, 435, 445, 495,
    505, 557, 585, 595, 711, 717, 723, 741, 749,
    809
hearts *passim*
heaven(s)   59, 75, 109, 147, 157, 305, 379, 409,
    429, 433, 441, 509, 523
heir   245, 255, 297, 313, 409, 519, 573, 765,
    785, 805, 811. *See also* inherit
hell, hellfire   131, 149, 151, 167, 185, 189, 211,
    213, 225, 309, 329, 345, 357, 413, 433, 435,
    463, 467, 477, 487, 489, 513, 561, 567, 583,
    607, 685, 689, 697, 743, 781. *See also* fire
herd   83, 121, 207, 243, 341, 349, 395, 477, 753,
    815. *See also* flock
hereafter *passim. See also* afterlife, (this)
    world and the hereafter
heresy, heresies, heretical, heretical innova-
    tions   70, 133, 139, 173, 221, 263, 331, 343,
    347, 349, 365, 373, 385, 397, 399, 413, 713
hermits   175
Hijrah (Migration)   75, 365, 433, 455, 525
honest, honesty   60, 79, 167, 275, 309, 635,
    637, 649
honey, honeybees   379, 421, 613, 779
honor   99, 111, 151, 165, 195, 219, 247, 249, 255,
    267, 293, 301, 317, 325, 345, 355, 365, 373,
    387, 399, 405, 415, 433, 475, 493, 503,
    509, 541, 545, 547, 555, 587, 595, 621, 631,
    635, 667, 693, 709, 749, 765, 775, 793
hope   72, 131, 149, 175, 177, 179, 197, 207, 215,
    235, 241, 251, 255, 289, 293, 295, 313, 333,
    361, 395, 407, 415, 429, 431, 453, 467,
    471, 485, 503, 519, 539, 553, 561, 577, 579,
    587, 589, 593, 613, 633, 643, 645, 647,
    653, 683, 687, 695, 697, 699, 701, 707,
    717, 723, 789, 797, 863
  false   151, 185, 209, 219, 279, 283, 287, 535,
    541, 615, 781
horn   59, 153, 177, 183, 257, 419, 457, 469, 543
horses, horsemen   147, 235, 259, 265, 303,
    307, 441, 467, 541, 623, 755. *See also*
    cavalry, colt, mount, stallion, steed
hot spring   477

(the) hour, last/final hour   58, 63, 137, 185,
     193, 243, 261, 269, 275, 309, 355, 357,
     365, 383, 427, 435, 439, 561, 599, 603
human   67, 72, 78, 111, 133, 137, 211, 221,
     239, 289, 387, 409, 411, 413, 441, 447,
     469, 477, 509, 511, 513, 581, 597, 643,
     681, 707, 727, 733, 793. *See also* mor-
     tal
humble, humility   75, 163, 187, 211, 225, 233,
     235, 261, 271, 273, 281, 335, 347, 409, 435,
     441, 443, 445, 447, 449, 463, 465, 467,
     473, 497, 533, 547, 551, 575, 579, 583, 591,
     601, 617, 633, 639, 641, 711, 713, 741, 743,
     783, 803, 809
humiliation   159, 181, 207, 245, 385, 443, 453,
     559, 673
hump   63, 123, 191, 301
hunger, hungry   259, 277, 331, 363, 365, 423,
     445, 479, 613, 655, 693, 707, 783
hunter   125. *See also* archer
hyena   57, 121, 125, 191, 335, 819
hypocrisy, hypocrite   64, 76, 117, 129, 137, 397,
     399, 467, 487, 489, 523, 563, 687, 691,
     699

idols   71, 145, 231, 333, 453
ignorance, ignoramus, ignorant   113, 117, 125,
     133, 135, 159, 167, 217, 221, 225, 245, 247,
     259, 261, 263, 271, 279, 303, 313, 325, 327,
     333, 335, 337, 341, 373, 381, 385, 403,
     405, 429, 435, 443, 445, 451, 453, 455,
     477, 483, 503, 509, 527, 545, 549, 567,
     573, 579, 637, 647, 649, 665, 667, 669,
     693, 695, 707, 719, 721, 723, 731, 745, 767,
     769, 779, 795, 825
illness, ill   211, 213, 273, 277, 281, 287, 359, 413,
     417, 463, 467, 475, 485, 513, 519, 641, 685,
     691, 723, 809. *See also* sickness
illumine, illumination   163, 219, 233, 265,
     269, 329, 357, 373, 491, 611, 721. *See also*
     light
imagination   109, 229, 231, 351, 369, 379, 409,
     419, 425, 505
imam (Ar. *imām*)   99, 229, 329, 333, 337, 345,
     559, 563, 597, 605, 609, 623, 631, 739, 749
     imamate   329, 391, 749
indigence   327, 463. *See also* destitution,
     poverty
indigo   513

inherit, inheritance, inheritors   63, 92, 117,
     119, 135, 193, 199, 203, 225, 305, 341, 411,
     505, 519, 521, 583, 607, 611, 617, 739, 805.
     See also heirs
ink, inkpot   247, 519, 779
innovations   70, 133, 331, 349, 373, 385, 399,
     713. *See also* heresy
insects   387, 403. *See also* ant, beetle, gnat,
     honeybee, locust, maggot, mite
intellect, intelligence, intelligent   71, 78, 113,
     167, 173, 185, 207, 229, 231, 247, 295, 317,
     343, 349, 351, 361, 367, 375, 377, 379,
     409, 425, 467, 501, 505, 507, 515, 535,
     573, 593, 607, 677, 689, 693, 695, 709,
     711, 739, 769, 773, 809
intentions   92, 155, 249, 283, 319, 403, 437,
     447, 539, 541, 577, 641, 691, 785
intercessor   397, 469, 695, 793
interpret, interpretation, misinterpretation
     69, 145, 221, 299, 303, 339, 445, 489, 579,
     619, 645, 649, 675, 685, 701, 709, 773, 791
intoxicated, intoxication   339, 341, 347, 429,
     687
Islam   59–60, 66, 68, 76, 115, 137, 169, 179,
     199, 261, 265, 271, 277, 297, 299, 305, 313,
     331, 343, 345, 355, 365, 385, 397, 405,
     411, 419, 455, 457, 459, 473, 475, 477,
     799, 527, 547, 549, 567, 577, 623, 631,
     635, 651, 657, 659, 683, 691, 713, 747, 793,
     819

jealousy   595, 713
Jew, Jewish   86, 197, 623, 683, 779
jewels, jewelry   99, 349, 377, 439, 615, 765.
     See also anklet, bracelet, earring, neck-
     lace
jihad   59, 74, 147, 277, 413, 527, 619, 719, 747
jinn   409, 411, 413, 469, 513
joke, joker   215, 593, 815
journey   151, 171, 235, 277, 281, 283, 285, 315,
     379, 395, 411, 447, 493, 511, 545, 581, 593,
     669, 697, 755, 769, 789. *See also* travel
joy   92, 239, 279, 355, 367, 465, 561, 581, 637,
     691, 705, 749, 769, 783, 789. *See also*
     happiness
judge, judgment   58, 66, 72, 80, 89, 133, 135,
     153, 157, 187, 189, 195, 207, 223, 227, 247,
     257, 263, 267, 307, 323, 335, 357, 359,
     369, 373, 397, 419, 441, 455, 475, 479, 493,

judge, judgment (*cont.*)   533, 535, 543, 565,
  583, 613, 619, 621, 627, 631, 633, 645, 649,
  655, 667, 671, 675, 691, 725, 729, 741, 773,
  781, 785, 811
jug   175, 377
jugular vein   90, 707
justice, injustice   78, 86, 90, 105, 131, 133, 135,
  147, 151, 197, 221, 223, 241, 247, 261, 267,
  295, 307, 311, 319, 321, 367, 385, 401, 451,
  475, 493, 497, 507, 511, 517, 523, 555, 561,
  607, 617, 623, 627, 631, 635, 637, 639,
  641, 643, 647, 651, 683, 669, 685, 741,
  743, 761, 785, 813, 825

kin, kinship, kinsman   58, 78, 137, 141, 143,
  145, 215, 271, 279, 299, 321, 323, 325, 339,
  343, 367, 373, 383, 389, 453, 457, 467,
  469, 485, 499, 519, 521, 539, 549, 555,
  569, 571, 589, 593, 595, 601, 617, 671,
  699, 703, 733, 739, 747, 775, 807. *See
  also* family, relatives
kindling   219, 539, 613
kindness   82–83, 243, 321, 323, 511, 515, 549,
  589, 621, 625, 631, 633, 703, 729
kingdom   229, 233, 273, 281, 351, 411, 429, 435,
  447, 581, 627, 743
knife   401, 499
knowledge   63, 75–76, 78, 91, 101, 103, 107,
  115, 117, 125, 133, 135, 139, 149, 155, 187,
  195, 199, 201, 213, 225, 227, 229, 237, 241,
  265, 269, 277, 285, 309, 315, 329, 335,
  337, 345, 349, 353, 359, 371, 373, 395,
  423, 427, 429, 437, 449, 463, 475, 477,
  491, 493, 511, 527, 531, 533, 577, 611, 663,
  679, 685, 691, 701, 703, 711, 721, 723, 737,
  767, 769, 779, 785, 791, 795
kohl   117, 323, 505

lambs   405
lamp   99, 219, 221, 233, 247, 261, 263, 265,
  269, 329, 337, 345, 351, 353, 363, 369,
  467, 473, 475, 507, 509
language(s)   421, 499, 517, 523, 625, 641, 821
laugh   283, 309, 369, 377, 465, 571, 713
lawful, unlawful   203, 263, 283, 287, 341, 343,
  383, 391, 533. *See also* licit
leader(s)   66, 135, 143, 151, 169, 193, 221, 223,
  247, 249, 255, 263, 269, 271, 291, 323,
  345, 373, 391, 405, 411, 453, 441, 487, 489,

  537, 545, 557, 581, 597, 611, 629, 709, 753,
  761, 779, 781
  leadership   313, 391, 535, 631, 729
learned, learning   66, 117, 121, 133, 161, 187,
  221, 259, 279, 449, 467, 475, 491, 527,
  579, 589, 597, 649, 703, 707, 721, 739,
  763, 779, 795, 825
leather   61, 171, 271
  strap   821
legatee   223, 411
leisure   217
leper   745
lesson(s)   75, 103, 113, 131, 137, 159, 207, 209,
  215, 223, 265, 275, 281, 287, 337, 345, 357,
  411, 413, 435, 441, 445, 453, 491, 503, 553,
  621, 637, 667, 685, 725, 735, 737, 773, 791,
  805
letter   80–81, 83, 89, 99, 101, 529, 531, 537,
  539, 541, 547, 551, 563, 571, 573, 595, 597,
  599, 601, 603, 605, 611, 617, 619, 621, 647,
  649, 651, 653, 655, 659, 663, 665, 667,
  669, 671, 673, 675, 773. *See also* epis-
  tle
  lettering   779
levies   559, 719, 757. *See also* alms levy, taxes
licit, illicit   74, 113, 203, 223, 275, 383, 399, 413,
  429, 463, 487, 507, 555, 577, 607, 625,
  635, 667, 785, 801. *See also* lawful
lie   76, 86, 131, 199, 215, 219, 257, 271, 299, 313,
  333, 349, 361, 479, 489, 575, 619, 821. *See
  also* falsehood, truth
life   67, 69, 72, 103, 111, 115, 119, 125, 133, 171,
  175, 179, 181, 199, 207, 237, 253, 263, 275,
  279, 281, 283, 287, 291, 315, 335, 337, 353,
  373, 403, 411, 431, 453, 455, 461, 471, 481,
  503, 505, 515, 527, 539, 541, 559, 577,
  579, 585, 609, 613, 615, 627, 631, 649,
  665, 667, 685, 691, 697, 711, 713, 715, 721,
  723, 743, 753, 765, 771, 783, 789, 791, 797,
  801, 815
  span   89, 107, 113, 185, 205, 209, 217, 239,
  277, 301, 313, 333, 361, 415, 427, 435, 463,
  465, 475, 519, 587, 645, 671, 763, 775, 807
light   72, 109, 115, 123, 163, 179, 195, 205, 219,
  225, 229, 233, 265, 269, 279, 283, 285,
  295, 303, 341, 347, 351, 353, 359, 365,
  369, 411, 419, 433, 441, 449, 459, 461, 493,
  615, 645, 721, 755. *See also* illumination
  and darkness   415, 423, 425, 471, 475, 491

lightning   237, 257, 289, 501, 511
   bolt   343, 409, 741
   and thunder   343, 825
limbs   111, 117, 159, 231, 239, 283, 337, 351,
      357, 367, 369, 379, 409, 421, 425, 439,
      449, 469, 477, 505, 583, 661, 701, 741,
      799
lineage   367, 443, 445, 609, 611, 631, 683, 689,
      711, 747
lion   303, 311, 603, 625, 763, 771
lizard   68, 191, 301, 335, 351
loan   225, 417, 433, 479, 583, 637
locust   75, 423, 515
loincloth   245
loins   57, 129, 183, 225, 241, 247, 273, 585, 659,
      739
longbow   191, 441
love   67, 227, 235, 273, 279, 307, 363, 397, 453,
      473, 597, 625, 645, 711, 821
loyalty   60, 76, 129, 167, 281, 305, 493, 751
luck   693, 743
lute player   707

madness   243, 605, 749
maggots   209
magician   201, 459, 461
male   309, 377, 703
maledictions   193
malice   235, 271, 277, 299, 317, 335, 353, 451,
      463, 547, 645, 727, 729, 779, 803
mansion(s)   225, 789
march   61, 64, 69, 71, 81, 84–87, 90, 157, 171,
      297, 307, 525, 543, 689, 697
marshland   387
martyr(s), martyrdom   74, 84, 141, 295, 355,
      387, 437, 539, 565, 599, 647, 701
master   57, 127, 143, 185, 187, 245, 249, 253,
      285, 343, 399, 517, 567, 579, 587, 803,
      807
meadows   239, 291, 475, 573
merchandise   639
messenger(s)   70, 73, 75, 111, 113, 115, 137, 161,
      181, 195, 205, 233, 237, 255, 267, 277,
      285, 313, 315, 327, 341, 349, 403, 413, 415,
      417, 433, 437, 447, 453, 459, 467, 471,
      581, 659, 775. *See also* Muḥammad (in
      Index of Names), prophet
metaphor   151, 183, 759, 821
meteors   233. *See also* stars

might   64, 75, 109, 115, 159, 205, 207, 229, 237,
      249, 253, 271, 273, 367, 381, 409, 413, 419,
      427, 429, 439, 447, 451, 453, 455, 475,
      477, 491, 503, 535, 567, 601, 631, 645,
      793. *See also* strength
migration   75, 365, 433, 455, 525. *See also*
      Hijrah
military   599, 621, 661, 757
milk   119, 207, 223, 361, 663
mimic   737
mind(s)   85, 107, 109, 111, 131, 147, 149, 159,
      177, 203, 207, 215, 219, 223, 229, 243, 247,
      251, 273, 277, 295n3, 311, 329, 339n1, 361,
      365, 377, 419, 421, 427, 433, 441, 445, 451,
      471, 495, 503, 507, 517, 523, 537, 545,
      577, 579, 583, 597, 605, 609, 655, 661,
      689, 701, 727, 735, 739, 741, 755, 779, 793
mindful   199, 211, 399, 527, 703, 717, 723
mine(s)   247, 277
mirage   469, 657, 689
mirror   377, 679, 791
miser, miserliness   309, 313, 629, 689, 713,
      735
mission   65–66, 69, 71, 76, 151, 245, 305, 453,
      673, 731
mites   241
moderation   82, 551, 721. *See also* temper-
      ance
modesty   443, 595, 635, 711, 741, 787
money   57, 79, 131, 199, 305, 521, 533, 605,
      607, 779, 809
moon   409, 423. *See also* sun and moon
morals   399, 405
morning   78, 87, 99, 153, 251, 279, 339, 345,
      351, 365, 395, 415, 465, 479, 495, 501,
      503, 587, 651, 665, 717, 729, 749
mortal, mortality   187, 323, 705. *See also*
      human
mortgage   503, 573
mosque   129, 227, 717
mother   75, 80, 125, 167, 199, 283, 289, 339,
      351, 371, 429, 457, 523, 607, 717, 755,
      775
mount   72, 131, 281, 309, 363, 449, 457, 543,
      569, 573, 611, 689. *See also* horse, steed
mountain   57, 67, 103, 109, 129, 163, 221, 227,
      235, 237, 239, 241, 253, 275, 289, 291, 375,
      387, 409, 421, 447, 473, 477, 491, 539,
      541, 543, 639, 709, 813

mourn, mourner   91, 123, 139, 213, 241, 281,
    307, 335, 477, 513, 771, 799, 825
murder, murderer   305, 313, 347
musical instruments. *See* lute, oud, drum
musk   379
Muslim(s)   62, 75, 84, 86, 101, 137, 141, 147,
    187, 197, 305, 313, 331, 383, 385, 389, 391,
    399, 405, 443, 483, 487, 489, 521, 531,
    539, 551, 555, 557, 563, 569, 599, 609,
    619, 623, 627, 639, 645, 655, 663, 667,
    683, 759, 765
mutiny   133, 195, 225. *See also* rebel
mysteries   61, 117, 125, 173, 223, 229, 241, 269,
    273, 285, 291, 309, 337, 351, 361, 395,
    507, 769

necklace   147, 239
need(s)   92, 115, 197, 207, 209, 235, 243, 269,
    287, 303, 363, 371, 377, 379, 405, 419,
    429, 433, 437, 461, 463, 465, 483, 485,
    497, 581, 583, 591, 623, 627, 631, 633,
    639, 665, 697, 715, 719, 733, 773, 809
neighbors   117, 175, 267, 281, 337, 417, 451,
    465, 503, 515, 561, 593, 617, 623
night and day   387, 421, 425, 641, 733
nomadic   753
noose   205, 787
novelties   103, 701, 735

oath   113, 179, 245, 321, 343, 415, 429, 615, 649,
    749. *See also* pledge
    of allegiance (Ar. *bay'ah*)   70, 163, 319, 387
obedience, disobedience   65, 69, 74, 76, 80,
    83, 117, 149, 153, 163, 185, 231, 235, 273,
    293, 311, 329, 333, 343, 345, 351, 385, 389,
    393, 395, 401, 409, 431, 447, 453, 461,
    467, 473, 493, 497, 501, 517, 523, 527,
    535, 559, 569, 573, 621, 625, 641, 667,
    691, 721, 725, 749, 771, 783, 787, 799, 805,
    807, 811
ocean   77, 101, 471, 489, 491, 797. *See also* sea
offspring   241, 441, 445, 749. *See also* chil-
    dren
opportunity   167, 169, 191, 333, 383, 583, 589,
    593, 605, 615, 645, 683, 711, 747, 791
oppress, oppressed, oppression, oppressor
    68, 87, 131, 135, 139, 155, 245, 279, 305,
    307, 313, 319, 343, 359, 393, 443, 449,
    465, 495, 497, 513, 557, 569, 583, 589,

    591, 601, 617, 627, 635, 651, 707, 719, 747,
    785, 787, 795, 797
oration(s) *passim*
    oratory, orate, orator   101, 105, 407, 487,
    753
orbit   233, 387
ordained   74, 205, 233, 239, 275, 297, 339, 371,
    405, 437, 489, 543, 631, 735, 767, 797.
    See also destined
ordeal   209, 213, 449, 787
organ   209, 343, 425, 443, 505, 707
ornament   91, 121, 231, 233, 277, 297, 363, 365,
    631, 675
orphan   607, 617, 639, 763
ostrich   129, 307, 423
oud player   707
overthinking   687

palace   195, 267, 273, 515
palm-fronds   143, 407
parables   113, 205, 207, 399
paradise   64, 72, 111, 131, 149, 151, 185, 203*n*1,
    211, 217, 239, 265, 267, 277, 285, 301, 309,
    311, 329, 345, 357, 363, 365, 379, 383, 387,
    395, 397, 413, 435, 461, 463, 477, 561,
    565, 567, 583, 685, 691, 717, 817. *See also*
    Garden
pardon   189, 337, 359, 437, 509, 571, 585, 625,
    627, 631, 639, 667, 727, 729, 739, 809
partner   57, 64, 82, 111, 127, 135, 139, 187, 215,
    219, 231, 285, 319, 337, 347, 401, 409, 421,
    429, 549, 553, 555, 559, 581, 629, 737,
    743, 785
passion(s)   64, 70, 84, 87, 185, 199, 201, 209,
    211, 219, 221, 223, 227, 235, 247, 255, 267,
    273, 317, 321, 341, 345, 355, 367, 395, 397,
    419, 495, 497, 519, 533, 535, 537, 561, 573,
    575, 577, 587, 593, 601, 613, 625, 627,
    635, 647, 651, 653, 671, 685, 693, 723,
    725, 733, 739, 767, 771, 781, 809, 815
past   66, 74–75, 91, 207, 235, 253, 281, 289,
    331, 335, 359, 403, 435, 437, 443, 451,
    505, 517, 519, 575, 621, 629, 637, 645,
    667, 735, 757, 761, 769, 773, 813. *See also*
    future, present
pastures   265, 283, 289, 303, 345, 395, 427,
    449, 453, 503, 559, 581, 607, 613, 661,
    753, 791
path *passim. See also* course, road, way

patient, patience 239, 253, 385, 393, 437, 463, 465, 465, 479, 483, 505, 525, 575, 593, 601, 623, 627, 633, 641, 643, 645, 667, 685, 693, 699, 703, 721, 725, 731, 737, 739, 771, 783, 801, 817. *See also* endurance, forbearance

peace 133, 233, 405, 463, 475, 535, 537, 539, 541, 545, 549, 551, 557, 595, 601, 605, 609, 617, 621, 643, 647, 649, 657, 659, 663, 665, 669, 673, 675, 791
of mind 793

peacock 72, 375, 377

pearl 229, 379

pebble 57, 125, 175, 335, 545, 661, 689

percussionist 707. *See also* drummer

perdition 117, 151, 209, 219, 325, 365, 385, 563, 653, 753

physician 67, 269, 297, 505, 717

piety 75–76, 83, 88, 131, 147, 153, 199, 269, 279, 285, 313, 329, 357, 399, 415, 437, 469, 481, 509, 613, 671, 703, 709, 715, 793, 801. See also God, consciousness of (in Index of Names)

pig 745

pigeon 423

pilgrims, pilgrimage 3, 17, 13, 59, 88, 115, 279, 623, 665. *See also* hajj and 'umrah

pillars 90, 109, 117, 143, 189, 315, 337, 343, 427, 445, 449, 467, 473, 493, 527, 553, 555, 599, 609, 685, 687

pitch 189, 277, 557, 585, 587, 595, 615, 781, 787

planets 387

plantation 555

plants 125, 239, 265, 289, 291, 349, 363, 421, 613. *See also* aloes, colocynth, dates, date-palm, fruits, grass, gum, indigo, palm-fronds, trees, vegetation

pleasure(s) 82, 151, 195, 211, 225, 233, 255, 287, 311, 367, 379, 393, 395, 415, 445, 467, 497, 505, 515, 519, 553, 555, 561, 581, 587, 665, 713, 723, 767, 793, 801, 811

pledge, pledgee, pledger 57–58, 61, 63, 73, 79, 80, 89, 111, 113, 121, 125, 127, 131, 147, 159, 163, 195, 197, 209, 215, 225, 243, 283, 295, 307, 321, 323, 331, 335, 379, 383, 387, 389, 391, 401, 413, 415, 451, 457, 477, 501, 517, 519, 531, 537, 539, 543, 569, 573,

601, 615, 643, 645, 647, 649, 657, 673, 675, 677, 737, 767. *See also* oath of allegiance

ploughshare 479, 503

plunder 181, 235, 259, 281, 357, 439, 453, 609, 663, 733, 775

poet(s), poetry 145, 161, 613, 759, 815

poison 281, 449, 711, 741

polytheism 91, 549, 747

pools 241, 327, 409, 473, 475, 557. *See also* death, pools of

possessions 141, 229, 253, 313, 357, 469, 487, 521, 555, 775, 803

poverty 239, 279, 429, 445, 513, 515, 629, 665, 679, 689, 693, 695, 707, 407, 713, 727, 779, 785, 791, 793, 801. *See also* destitution, indigence

power, powerful 83, 109, 125, 155, 187, 205, 213, 215, 243, 281, 313, 327, 383, 385, 443, 455, 459, 493, 495, 511, 513, 515, 547, 561, 573, 607, 617, 645, 651, 667, 669, 679, 693, 705, 727, 733, 735, 785, 793. *See also* God, power of (in Index of Names)

praise 56, 66–68, 70, 72, 75, 78, 92, 99, 141, 229, 241, 243, 265, 269, 277, 285, 325, 359, 365, 437, 451, 463, 467, 491, 497, 499, 507, 509, 521, 565, 569, 629, 633, 637, 647, 699, 711, 717, 783, 787, 817, 821. *See also* God, praise of (in Index of Names)

prayer 83, 65, 86, 115, 203, 209, 235, 251, 283, 285, 313, 387, 457, 461, 477, 561, 615, 619, 623, 641, 669, 703, 707, 719, 773, 813, 825
niche 697
ritual 76, 86, 227, 277, 449, 477, 563, 617, 623, 641, 719, 747

precious objects 765

predators 271, 347, 585

pregnant 63, 193, 443, 445, 555

prejudice 451, 641

present 211, 219, 285, 329, 355, 481, 777, 797, 811. *See also* future, past

pride 75, 101, 111, 121, 125, 237, 347, 439, 441, 443, 445, 449, 451, 459, 497, 503, 617, 627, 629, 641, 745, 747, 793. *See also* arrogance

prisoner(s) 195, 573, 635, 789

profit 74, 115, 133, 269, 287, 311, 395, 407, 437, 561, 639, 689, 709, 737, 765 prohibition(s)   113, 623, 747, 799, 821. *See also* commands and prohibitions

promise   113, 201, 207, 215, 279, 361, 385, 397, 419, 479, 509, 621, 641, 645, 697

proof(s)   74, 91, 113, 115, 127, 139, 161, 203, 217, 229, 239, 251, 265, 269, 327, 345, 361, 365, 375, 395, 397, 399, 405, 407, 411, 415, 421, 433, 475, 545, 601, 723. *See also* arguments

property, properties   82, 86, 91, 121, 171, 175, 275, 287, 291, 313, 399, 513, 535, 553, 555, 557, 559, 587, 589, 607, 623, 647, 657, 667, 707, 715, 745, 749, 765

distribution of   82, 305, 553

prophet(s), prophecy   56, 61–62, 65–66, 70, 72, 75, 111, 113, 115, 133, 141, 157, 223, 225, 239, 247, 261, 269, 277, 309, 315, 359, 391, 411, 445, 447, 459, 461, 523, 541, 547, 697, 703, 777. *See also* Muḥammad (in Index of Names), messenger

prostration   115, 251, 297, 441

protected peoples (Ar. *ahl al-dhimmah*)   631

providence   585, 591, 743

provisions   86, 151, 171, 185, 199, 207, 211, 217, 279, 281, 283, 285, 295, 315, 357, 395, 415, 417, 421, 481, 511, 519, 527, 541, 561, 583, 585, 589, 615, 623, 671, 697, 715, 717, 741

prudence   575, 643, 651, 731

pulpit   58, 137, 143, 145, 155, 227, 793

punishment   75, 113, 115, 129, 141, 177, 211, 213, 221, 225, 251, 261, 279, 287, 327, 329, 333, 341, 355, 357, 365, 367, 391, 421, 431, 435, 441, 445, 451, 463, 477, 479, 495, 497, 551, 561, 573, 581, 623, 627, 635, 645, 653, 657, 661, 689, 701, 713, 725, 745, 749, 765, 771, 773, 793, 797, 805. *See also* reward and punishment

pure, purity   111, 139, 181, 199, 207, 223, 237, 263, 283, 293, 299, 329, 349, 363, 377, 379, 403, 409, 425, 445, 447, 493, 577, 579, 613, 713

Qiblah (direction of prayer)   391

quarrel   315, 329, 589, 655, 753, 755, 791, 819

queen bee   91, 753, 779

rabble   141, 219, 267, 525, 721, 735

race   149, 151, 207, 209, 527

-course   265, 813, 819

rage   277, 331, 347, 465, 591, 667, 673, 707, 733, 749. *See also* anger

raid   68, 84, 147, 149, 451651, 757, 761

rain, raindrops   58, 67, 70, 73, 107, 127, 141, 241, 271, 281, 289, 291, 309, 317, 325, 327, 345, 387, 409, 423, 473, 511, 613, 635, 825

ram   197

rare words (Ar. *gharīb*)   91, 291, 379, 753, 759

reason   265, 317, 323, 335, 361, 451, 689, 689, 745, 747, 801, 803

rebel, rebellion   56, 121, 125, 161, 177, 309, 391, 445, 457, 617, 687. *See also* mutiny

reckoning   167, 205, 207, 233, 241, 309, 333, 353, 357, 371, 441, 509, 535, 541, 607, 645, 797

reconciliation   60, 169

reed-pen   779

refinement   449, 577, 693, 709

refuge   99, 157, 213, 261, 271, 299, 317, 357, 387, 435, 437, 445, 455, 495, 517, 541, 579, 583, 701, 767, 793, 825

regret   111, 123, 149, 161, 179, 185, 275, 281, 295, 299, 407, 439, 477, 479, 599, 619, 627, 653, 707, 711, 717, 731, 807

reins   69, 121, 123, 131, 163, 221, 225, 239, 315, 375, 423, 433, 437, 445, 465, 467, 475, 517, 537, 569, 589, 615, 619, 625, 683, 689, 711. *See also* halters

relatives   141, 193, 209, 467, 519, 643, 705, 747, 753, 755. *See also* family, kin

religion *passim*

renunciant, renunciation   79, 85, 103, 105, 155, 157, 209, 283, 521, 575, 679, 709, 813

repent, repentance   149, 185, 207, 213, 239, 247, 313, 327, 333, 415, 509, 519, 527, 585, 627, 701, 703, 719, 723, 725, 749, 793, 813

reptiles. *See* adder, chameleon, lizard, snake, viper

repute, reputation   297, 637, 639, 727, 739

resolution(s)   239, 301, 347, 447, 453, 527, 693, 813

restraint   86, 549, 587, 611, 629, 679, 685, 687, 709, 737, 787, 793

resurrection   155, 167, 207, 265, 353, 369, 373,
     435, 443, 509, 511, 513, 559, 583, 645,
     653, 687, 717, 799
retribution   73, 245, 313, 327, 383, 401, 407,
     441, 455, 701, 733, 747
revelation   70, 73–74, 109, 111, 145, 195, 233,
     261, 315, 327, 359, 391, 395, 459, 471, 717
revenue   295
reward *passim*
   and punishment   207, 347, 535, 697, 703
ribs   159
riches, rich man   241, 429, 447, 451, 495, 611,
     691, 693, 701, 717, 743, 783, 791, 807. *See
     also* wealth
rider   123, 131, 225*n*1, 259, 343, 449, 547*n*1,
     601, 611, 683, 753, 825
right(s) *passim*
river   60, 161, 183, 237, 355, 379, 449, 453, 475,
     543
road *passim. See also* course, path, way
robes   75, 81, 123, 147, 219, 225, 277, 309, 377,
     439, 441, 471, 541, 571, 671, 679, 703, 707,
     709, 741. *See also* garments
rocks, rocky   107, 151, 237, 269, 363, 381, 403,
     407, 421, 447, 453, 455, 469, 491, 515,
     661, 783
rope(s)   61, 83, 109, 117, 121, 125, 175, 177, 219,
     221, 223, 231, 239, 267, 281, 293, 297, 303,
     321, 335, 343, 399, 419, 435, 455, 467,
     469, 475, 493, 503, 513, 571, 575, 587,
     593, 595, 613, 627
rose   377
ruby   449
ruler   87, 165, 245, 249, 251, 271, 321, 455, 495,
     497, 503, 533, 535, 541, 593, 625, 627,
     629, 637, 639, 641, 643, 653, 689, 733,
     761, 763, 781, 783, 797, 821
ruling(s)   86, 263, 307, 313, 401, 415, 453, 483,
     489, 665

sacrifice, sacrificial animal   61, 177
saddle, saddle-pad   119, 447, 449, 611, 709,
     825
safety   211, 247, 265, 313, 315, 321, 345, 351,
     359, 413, 455, 501, 707, 711, 737, 773. *See
     also* protection
sage   209, 629, 689, 701
sail   375, 379
salutations   76, 479

salvation   56, 125, 199, 219, 265, 353, 367, 507,
     511, 581, 721
sand   161, 241, 381, 417, 447
   storms   62, 181
sandal   157, 363, 407, 519, 671
Satan   57–58, 71, 115, 117, 127, 139, 173, 185, 189,
     219, 229, 297, 305, 307, 309, 323, 329,
     333, 341, 343, 407, 443, 445, 449, 459,
     465, 467, 533, 541, 549, 595, 609, 611,
     619, 645, 649, 667, 673, 675, 781. *See also*
     Iblīs (in Index of Names), devils
   of the Stony Hollow   457
sated   127, 319, 693
scales   99, 115, 273, 285, 403, 609, 639
scorpion   319, 357, 467, 505, 695
scribe(s)   631, 637, 641
scripture(s)   59, 66, 113, 115, 117, 133, 157, 261,
     697
sea   57, 129, 131, 155, 201, 219, 225, 237, 257,
     349, 379, 421, 449, 469, 475, 491, 541,
     595, 639, 769, 779, 787. *See also* ocean
seashells   227, 241. *See also* cowrie shell
seasons   84, 217, 225, 421, 427, 597
secrets   101, 151, 211, 225, 239, 271, 273, 279,
     327, 341, 395, 441, 481, 517, 621, 679, 685,
     693, 727
sedition (Ar. *fitnah*)   66, 71–72, 75, 89, 117,
     245, 247, 257, 259, 267, 271, 339, 341,
     343, 353, 355, 373, 387, 415, 431, 433, 445,
     517, 525, 549, 623, 663, 667, 679, 781
self-respect   693, 815
semen   211, 241, 815 *See also* sperm
separation   209, 213, 275, 281, 297, 367, 369,
     435, 479, 507, 581, 621, 717
shadow   86, 173, 185, 205, 207, 271, 337, 351,
     561, 623
shame   60, 147, 169, 207, 273, 279, 301, 387,
     415, 429, 431, 439, 455, 467, 475, 503,
     545, 551, 559, 569, 575, 585, 627, 649,
     657, 693, 735, 741, 781, 801
Shari‘ah   91
shears   155
sheep   289, 291, 293, 307, 395, 413, 447, 615,
     805
sheikh(s)   649
shepherd   349, 413, 587
shield   62, 147, 167, 183, 265, 279, 293, 309,
     411, 473, 475, 477, 539, 541, 545, 605,
     679, 693, 735

shining spot   755

sick, sickness   105, 209, 305, 335, 471, 519,
     595, 711. *See also* illness

sight, eyesight   179, 247, 269, 275, 315, 351,
     363, 365, 373, 421, 471, 493, 499, 663,
     769, 821

signs   113, 115, 123, 173, 209, 215, 229, 231, 233,
     261, 265, 269, 327, 331, 337, 403, 409,
     415, 425, 475, 493, 503, 743. *See also*
     waymarks

silk and brocade   309

silver   227, 377, 533, 557, 623, 789, 799

sincere, sincerity   61, 107, 115, 141, 155, 159,
     221, 247, 277, 285, 293, 347, 403, 407,
     409, 447, 449, 467, 557, 559, 573, 577,
     591, 597, 599, 603, 633, 637, 641, 673, 711,
     713, 747, 775

sins   64, 70, 113, 131, 133, 145, 149, 175, 179, 201,
     211, 213, 221, 233, 239, 275, 279, 289, 301,
     305, 313, 323, 327, 347, 339, 343, 359,
     381, 383, 399, 401, 403, 437, 471, 477,
     509, 511, 549, 615, 683, 691, 699, 703, 711,
     723, 725, 773, 783, 787, 807, 825. *See also*
     errors, transgressions

sky *passim*

slander, slanderer   253, 261, 443, 603, 627,
     635, 745, 817, 821

slaughterhouse   177

slave   131, 169, 187, 245, 253, 267, 275, 383, 389,
     393, 499, 573, 587, 591, 607, 623, 657,
     683, 745, 765, 783. *See also* bondage

smoke   233

snake(s)   88, 513, 665, 697, 711

snare(s)   161, 205, 211, 221, 341, 449, 519, 615,
     651, 679

sodomy   749

soldiers   155, 631, 641. *See also* warriors

son(s)   64, 69, 91, 113, 125, 137, 179, 207, 213,
     271, 299, 317, 363, 399, 405, 425, 445,
     453, 547, 555, 563, 571, 573, 599, 613, 619,
     685, 733, 749, 771, 775, 789, 807
     my dear son   90, 92, 575, 577, 579, 581,
          583, 585, 591, 689, 779, 805

soothsayer   201

sorrow   92, 149, 239, 253, 505, 519, 573, 585,
     783, 791. *See also* grief

soul   69, 86, 92, 141, 149, 151, 155, 185, 191, 209,
     211, 215, 217, 221, 269, 275, 279, 281, 283,
     299, 311, 313, 337, 355, 357, 367, 373, 379,

     415, 417, 449, 463, 465, 467, 471, 495,
     497, 509, 511, 517, 535, 547, 549, 559, 573,
     577, 583, 585, 609, 613, 623, 641, 649,
     651, 653, 663, 665, 705, 713, 717, 719, 737,
     785, 817

  appetitive   395

  sentient   78, 501, 527, 625

spear   68, 139, 187, 269, 299, 301, 407, 443,
     455, 539, 543, 547, 729, 773

species   111, 231, 421, 423, 427

sperm   273, 713. *See also* semen

spouses   273, 367, 789

spring, springtime   121, 279, 377, 399, 475

stallions   123, 179, 237, 271, 407, 659, 807

stars   99, 109, 173, 201, 233, 247, 255, 267, 305,
     403, 409, 501, 549, 705

stealing, stolen   88, 239, 669, 745, 765

steed(s)   117, 131, 135, 185, 199, 225, 253, 271,
     309, 445, 455, 475, 503, 511, 517, 573, 587,
     753, 793. *See also* mount

stinginess   679, 745, 797

stomach   199, 297, 343, 347, 363, 421, 613, 615,
     769

stoning   341

strangers   137, 175, 489, 513, 681, 693

stray   73, 75, 103, 123, 133, 181, 221, 233, 239,
     251, 255, 259, 295, 303, 307, 325, 341,
     349, 381, 385, 401, 439, 441, 467, 479,
     495, 507, 517, 537, 565, 573, 579, 595,
     657, 701, 731, 763, 825

strength   129, 141, 153, 159, 173, 259, 271, 303,
     331, 361, 447, 451, 453, 463, 477, 479,
     509, 511, 517, 545, 551, 623, 627, 631, 637,
     645, 671, 717, 729, 737, 749, 785, 789,
     803. *See also* might

students   105, 187, 723

subjects   78, 83, 86, 151, 241, 249, 495, 497,
     503, 535, 559, 617, 621, 623, 625, 627,
     629, 631, 633, 635, 639, 641, 643, 645,
     653, 761

suffering   113, 377, 449, 451, 453, 469, 473,
     577, 639, 689, 691, 713, 787

summer   145, 149, 241, 377, 623, 661

sun   86, 211, 221, 351, 371, 377, 509, 599, 623,
     773
     and moon   109, 225, 233, 363, 387, 421

Sunnah   113, 133, 229, 265, 279, 303, 313, 321,
     337, 373, 385, 413, 477, 483, 497, 553,
     559, 633, 675

supplication(s) (Ar. *du'ā'*) 61, 64, 67, 70, 78–
79, 81, 171, 201, 229, 469, 493, 515, 517,
519, 545, 565, 721
  suppliant 409, 509, 639, 695
support 61, 66, 85, 109, 117, 125, 141, 143, 145,
153, 155, 159, 179, 205, 265, 331, 355, 365,
385, 397, 399, 409, 419, 423, 427, 475,
491, 569, 575, 599, 609, 617, 627, 629,
633, 637, 639, 657, 659, 711, 721
suspicion 233, 241, 281, 319, 355, 525, 571,
643, 663, 677, 711, 741, 775, 787. *See also*
doubt
sustenance 89, 92, 141, 209, 225, 227, 239,
271, 287, 289, 327, 351, 353, 421, 423, 461,
515, 587, 671, 719, 747, 763, 767, 787, 789,
797, 807, 811
swear 70, 82, 121, 129, 131, 143, 153, 179, 225,
243, 249, 257, 359, 395, 429, 459, 471,
547, 551, 607, 609, 649, 671, 685, 749,
769
sword *passim*
  Mashrafī 159

talons 215
tax(es) 83, 165, 623, 631, 635, 637, 705, 739
  collectors 80, 83, 86, 531, 555, 559, 631,
637, 655, 669, 707
  land- 621, 625, 631, 635, 635, 825
  poll- 631
  See also levy
tear, teardrop 117, 155, 279, 375, 377, 435,
463, 467, 509, 525, 615
teeth 129, 135, 187, 299, 301, 321, 399, 423,
759, 789, 821
temperance 463, 467, 695, 747, 785. *See also*
moderation
tenants 225, 259, 469
tent 157, 253, 359, 557
test(s) 60, 92, 131, 165, 185, 205, 239, 251, 253,
261, 295, 301, 313, 325, 329, 355, 417, 433,
439, 441, 445, 447, 449, 451, 481, 581,
627, 629, 635, 649, 701, 711, 723, 747, 771,
785, 789, 799, 811. *See also* trial
testament (Ar. *waṣiyyah, 'ahd*) 80, 82–83,
117, 277, 337, 409, 531, 553, 555, 559,
563, 575, 577, 579, 617, 625, 647. *See also*
covenant
testify, testimony 78, 107, 115, 161, 181, 185,
203, 217, 285, 299, 313, 375, 377, 403, 419,
433, 459, 465, 467, 471, 493, 533, 611,
635, 697, 749
thanks 67, 75, 203, 285, 407, 415, 431, 433,
437, 621, 719, 737, 745, 767, 783. *See also*
gratitude
thieves 183, 305, 349, 635, 767. *See also*
stealing
thought(s) 64, 107, 209, 215, 217, 231, 235,
239, 257, 269, 277, 291, 311, 313, 327, 421,
423, 451, 467, 491, 505, 517, 525, 579,
649, 655, 657, 679, 689, 757, 781, 783,
791, 809
tongue(s) *passim*
torch 207, 267
torture 211, 213, 277, 333, 417, 453, 463, 619
trade, trader 69, 78, 185, 245, 251, 355, 467,
477, 507, 589, 709, 795
traitor 137, 537, 743
tranquility 351, 793
transgress, transgression 113, 189, 209, 213,
231, 279, 305, 307, 323, 397, 401, 465,
509, 511, 593, 643, 645, 647, 649, 663,
707, 725, 799. *See also* errors, sins
transience 67, 69, 72, 367, 481, 713
travel, traveler(s) 61, 171, 185, 253, 261, 291,
365, 379, 417, 473, 475, 581, 587, 593,
603, 695, 713, 753, 757, 805. *See also*
journey
treachery 86, 127, 193, 291, 339, 387, 389, 443,
449, 451, 457, 501, 619, 623, 639, 645,
651, 787
treasure 115, 195, 199, 207, 221, 229, 235, 241,
321, 327, 349, 409, 417, 447, 519, 583,
585, 623, 625, 679, 793
treasury 57, 68, 79, 80, 82–83, 85, 88, 131,
265, 295, 305, 389, 483, 501, 513, 551,
585, 639, 667, 669, 765
tree(s) 99, 191, 239, 241, 247, 251, 269, 271,
277, 289, 315, 317, 327, 331, 337, 365, 379,
381, 421, 449, 459, 459, 461, 473, 549,
595, 613, 715. *See also* date-palm, for-
est
  forbidden 239
  lote 263
trial(s) 79, 99, 111, 205, 223, 245, 251, 261, 285,
323, 327, 353, 369, 399, 437, 441, 445,
447, 449, 451, 453, 515, 521, 627, 653, 701,
703, 717, 767, 771, 789, 801, 815. *See also*
test

tribe(s), tribal, tribesmen   72, 75, 81–82, 89,
      111, 137, 145, 149, 173, 303, 309, 367, 387,
      439, 451, 467, 539, 547, 549, 557, 601,
      603, 609, 661, 673
troops   61–62, 68–69, 71, 81, 87, 177, 207, 307,
      331, 411, 413, 623, 633, 643, 655
troubles   473, 789, 541, 657, 679, 709. *See also*
      calamities, hardships
trust   76, 111, 139, 153, 159, 205, 217, 225, 241,
      253, 255, 265, 281, 303, 311, 367, 395,
      407, 413, 431, 433, 465, 477, 495, 517,
      535, 555, 559, 571, 593, 605, 607, 633,
      635, 639, 641, 647, 651, 671, 711, 739, 775,
      799, 803
   trustee(s)   73, 145, 195, 247, 267, 391, 419,
      623, 825
   trustworthy, untrustworthy   155, 251, 437,
      595, 629, 637, 723
truth, untruth *passim*. See also falsehood, lie
turban   307, 377, 649, 777
tyranny, tyrant   65, 121, 171, 217, 223, 245, 249,
      253, 267, 271, 303, 313, 341, 359, 411, 477,
      499, 603, 607, 627, 629, 707, 785

udder(s)   119, 179, 321, 519, 597, 679
'umrah   279
unbelief   90, 137, 181, 231, 397, 405, 479, 547,
      563, 573, 659, 687. *See also* belief
   unbeliever, disbeliever   137, 157, 165, 201,
      305, 341, 455, 539, 545, 563, 697, 797,
      809. *See also* believer
usurp   381, 513, 607, 727

valley   369, 381, 409, 427, 447, 449, 453, 475,
      587
vanity   235, 441, 629, 709, 729, 739. *See also*
      conceit
vegetation   237, 279, 289. *See also* plants
veil, veiled   109, 137, 155, 173, 185, 225, 229,
      233, 239, 269, 343, 351, 357, 361, 369, 371,
      377, 389, 395, 409, 413, 419, 441, 469,
      481, 505, 509, 511, 519, 583, 595, 647,
      769, 777, 809
vessel   91, 117, 167, 193, 261, 499, 721, 737, 821
victim   309, 343, 391, 393, 365, 371
victory   57, 63, 68, 71, 80, 129, 143, 179, 211,
      245, 305, 317, 331, 387, 393, 419, 469, 473,
      475, 499, 533, 565, 591, 605, 693, 723
vinegar   359

violence   153, 257, 423, 355, 631, 731, 825
viper   381, 771
virtue(s), virtuous   64–65, 68, 75, 83, 91, 99,
      101, 103, 113, 143, 167, 207, 223, 249, 309,
      325, 331, 341, 363, 443, 451, 457, 459, 461,
      463, 467, 497, 553, 565, 567, 571, 573,
      577, 631, 635, 637, 645, 647, 693, 705,
      709, 731, 747, 795, 803, 821
vitiligo (Ar. *baraṣ*)   777
vows   211

wailing women   209
war, warfare   61, 77, 147, 149, 159, 175, 177,
      191, 245, 251, 257, 305, 313, 321, 331, 339,
      387, 391, 453, 455, 485, 521, 539, 541, 547,
      605, 609, 621, 627, 653, 765. *See also*
      battle
   gains   313, 605, 765. *See also* booty
warriors   103, 145, 179, 295, 301, 317, 565, 571,
      607, 613, 657, 781, 789
warnings   60, 67, 71, 82–86, 90, 137, 151, 161,
      205, 207, 215, 217, 239, 275, 277, 333, 335,
      347, 357, 569, 595, 437, 463, 505, 507,
      511, 541, 575, 585, 695, 697, 789
water   61–62, 109, 111, 115, 123, 125, 129, 133,
      145, 173, 175, 183, 205, 219, 221, 223, 225,
      237, 239, 241, 261, 263, 279, 281, 289, 297,
      315, 327, 339, 349, 361, 369, 377, 387,
      395, 403, 413, 421, 445, 447, 471, 473,
      475, 479, 491, 503, 529, 557, 565, 573,
      601, 613, 621, 643, 707, 749, 757, 767, 787,
      807
   carriers   473
   hole   61, 117, 127, 135, 137, 177, 205, 215,
      219, 221, 265, 267, 269, 289, 301, 319, 355,
      359, 397, 473, 475, 493, 503, 519, 553,
      557, 587, 609, 615, 663, 697
waves   56, 109, 125, 237, 241, 257, 373, 437,
      449, 467, 469, 473, 537, 595, 615
way *passim*. *See also* course, path, road
   waymarks   76, 195, 221, 225, 247, 261, 313,
      343, 409, 469, 473, 475, 497, 573, 643,
      663. *See also* signs
wealth, wealthy *passim*. *See also* riches
weapons   147, 423, 623. *See also* arrows,
      blades, bow, longbow, shields, spears,
      swords
weaver   137, 735
wedding banquet   611

weep, weeper, weeping   253, 275, 283, 291,
     297, 369, 401, 439, 503, 509, 511, 521,
     525, 681, 697, 781, 813
well   125, 211, 297, 745, 757
     -spring   101, 229, 269, 271, 369, 399, 427,
        455, 473, 475, 631
     (The) Well   459. See also Badr (in Index
        of Names)
whale   379
wheat   449, 513, 613
wicked, wickedness   165, 167, 257, 271, 325,
     359, 361, 399, 465, 487, 511, 541, 571, 575,
     603, 607, 619, 629, 635, 657, 677, 723,
     767, 821
widow   193, 551, 607
wife, wives   313, 363, 389, 487, 595, 705, 715,
     719, 807
wilderness   221, 291, 507, 613
will   82, 231, 239, 383, 393, 535, 649
wind   107, 109, 135, 143, 163, 165, 197, 239, 241,
     245, 257, 279, 289, 291, 295, 337, 403,
     409, 421, 453, 469, 471, 491, 661, 721, 815
wine   355, 379, 747. See also drink
wings   109, 233, 237, 307, 351, 361, 375, 377,
     445, 453, 459, 565, 595, 641, 653
winter   145, 149, 241, 363, 381, 623
wisdom   56, 63, 72, 99, 117, 139, 199, 209, 229,
     247, 249, 269, 277, 295, 315, 339, 341,
     345, 359, 399, 411, 437, 463, 475, 527,
     575, 685, 687, 699, 701, 707, 725, 731,
     735, 825
witness   57, 64, 66–67, 77, 129, 173, 195, 205,
     215, 217, 231, 255, 257, 263, 265, 267, 285,
     287, 291, 325, 335, 337, 341, 343, 371, 397,
     403, 437, 455, 475, 477, 491, 505, 507,
     533, 535, 559, 655, 781
wolf, wolves   165, 271, 307, 413, 607
wombs   129, 183, 211, 225, 247, 273, 283, 309,
     371, 567, 609n2

woman, women   57, 63–64, 129, 131, 139, 147,
     149, 183, 193, 203, 209, 211, 241, 251, 305,
     347, 353, 379, 389, 425, 479, 513, 531n4,
     545, 567, 595, 607, 695, 711, 713, 719, 745,
     755, 757, 781, 807
worker   639, 735
(this) world, worldly passim
     and the hereafter   69, 315, 595, 705, 785.
        See also afterlife, hereafter
worldliness   561
     rejection of   64, 90, 203, 685, 707
worry   575, 721, 791
worship, worshipper   67, 71, 103, 111, 115, 157,
     171, 229, 235, 237, 273, 281, 287, 333, 347,
     387, 397, 403, 441, 447, 449, 453, 459,
     461, 463, 473, 511, 559, 579, 669, 703,
     705, 711, 725, 727, 745, 777, 809
     mandatory acts of   641
     supplemental deeds of   689, 769
worth   133, 157, 259, 305, 307, 333, 337, 363,
     429, 515, 587, 637, 697, 699, 723, 745,
     787, 799, 807
wound   119, 183, 287, 299, 301, 341, 443, 499,
     675
wrong(s)   77, 111, 125, 139, 149, 153, 183, 203,
     217, 223, 303, 307, 333, 359, 371, 373, 381,
     391, 401, 419, 437, 445, 467, 471, 483,
     487, 527, 569, 581, 597, 625, 643, 651,
     655, 659, 665, 677, 681, 719, 725, 731,
     763, 795, 797

yearnings   151, 167, 229, 235, 251, 463, 613
youth   99, 209, 211, 281, 293, 523, 567, 673,
     699, 701

zeal, zealotry   387, 441, 443, 451, 655, 757. See
     also bigots

Index of Qur'an, Hadith, Poetry, and Proverbs

Qur'an (direct quotes)

Surah number	Surah name	Verse number	Verse text	Verse translation	Text number	Page number
2	Baqarah	20, 109, 148	إِنَّ اللهَ عَلَى كُلِّ شَيْءٍ قَدِير	Truly, God is powerful over all things.	1.190.12	458–459
2	Baqarah	34	اسْجُدُواْ لِآدَم فَسَجَدُواْ إِلَّا إِبْلِيس	prostrate before Adam, and they all prostrated except Iblīs.	1.1.5	110–111
2	Baqarah	117	كُنْ فَيَكُون	Be!—and it is.	1.184.2	424–425
2	Baqarah	156	إِنَّا لِلهِ وَإِنَّا إِلَيْهِ رَاجِعُون	We belong to God, and to him we shall return.	1.80.12, 1.127, 1.200, 3.89	212–213, 310–311, 478–479, 702–705
2	Baqarah	197	إِنَّ خَيْرَ الزَّادِ التَّقْوَى	The best provision is piety.	3.119	714–715
3	Āl 'Imrān	7	الرَّاسِخُونَ فِي الْعِلْم	Men rooted in knowledge	1.88.2, 1.142.1	228–229, 328–329
3	Āl 'Imrān	18	الْمُعَوِّقِينَ مِنكُمْ وَالْقَائِلِين لِإِخْوَانِهِمْ هَلُمَّ إِلَيْنَا وَلَا يَأْتُونَ الْبَأْس إِلَّا قَلِيلًا	those among you who impede, who say to their brothers, "Come help us," while they themselves seldom enter the fray.	2.28.4	568–569
3	Āl 'Imrān	68	إِنَّ أَوْلَى النَّاس بِإِبْرَاهِيم لَلَّذِين اتَّبَعُوه وَهَذَا النَّبِي وَالَّذِينَ آمَنُوا وَاللهُ وَلِي الْمُؤْمِنِين	Those who have the most claim on Abraham are the ones who followed him, and this Prophet, and those who profess belief. God is the believers' master.	2.28.2, 3.86	566–567, 702–703
3	Āl 'Imrān	85	مَن يَبْتَغِ غَيْرَ الْإِسْلَام دِينًا	whoever seeks a religion other than Islam	1.159	364–365

(cont.)

Surah number	Surah name	Verse number	Verse text	Verse translation	Text number	Page number
3	Āl 'Imrān	97	وَلِلَّهِ عَلَى ٱلنَّاسِ حِجُّ ٱلْبَيْتِ مَنِ ٱسْتَطَاعَ إِلَيْهِ سَبِيلًا وَمَنْ كَفَرَ فَإِنَّ ٱللَّهَ غَنِيٌّ عَنِ ٱلْعَٰلَمِين	Pilgrimage to the House is compulsory for all who are able to find a path. As for those who disbelieve, they should know that God has need of no one from all the worlds.	1.1.8	114–115
3	Āl 'Imrān	102	ٱتَّقُوا ٱللَّهَ حَقَّ تُقَاتِهِ وَلَا تَمُوتُنَّ إِلَّا وَأَنتُم مُّسْلِمُونَ	be conscious of God as you should, and make sure you die submitting to him	1.111.3	288–289
3	Āl 'Imrān	134, 148	وَٱللَّهُ يُحِبُّ ٱلْمُحْسِنِينَ	God loves those who do good.	3.188	736–737
3	Āl 'Imrān	165	إِنَّ ٱللَّهَ عَلَىٰ كُلِّ شَيْءٍ قَدِيرٌ	Truly, God is powerful over all things.	1.190.12	458–459
3	Āl 'Imrān	198	وَمَا عِندَ ٱللَّهِ خَيْرٌ لِّلْأَبْرَارِ	What God has prepared for people of virtue is the best!	2.23	552–553
4	Nisā'	17	إِنَّمَا ٱلتَّوْبَةُ عَلَى ٱللَّهِ لِلَّذِينَ يَعْمَلُونَ ٱلسُّوءَ بِجَهَالَةٍ ثُمَّ يَتُوبُونَ مِن قَرِيبٍ فَأُولَٰئِكَ يَتُوبُ ٱللَّهُ عَلَيْهِمْ وَكَانَ ٱللَّهُ عَلِيمًا حَكِيمًا	God accepts the repentance of those who do wrong in ignorance then repent soon thereafter; they are the ones whose repentance God accepts; God is knowing and wise.	3.124	718–719
4	Nisā'	48, 116	إِنَّ ٱللَّهَ لَا يَغْفِرُ أَن يُشْرَكَ بِهِ	God does not forgive being assigned partners	1.174.8	400–401
4	Nisā'	58	يَا أَيُّهَا ٱلَّذِينَ آمَنُوا أَطِيعُوا ٱللَّهَ وَأَطِيعُوا ٱلرَّسُولَ وَأُولِي ٱلْأَمْرِ مِنكُمْ فَإِن تَنَازَعْتُمْ فِي شَيْءٍ فَرُدُّوهُ إِلَى ٱللَّهِ وَٱلرَّسُولِ	Believers, obey God, obey the Messenger, and the people in command among you. If you disagree over something, refer it to God and the Messenger.	2.53.8	632–633

(*cont.*)

Surah number	Surah name	Verse number	Verse text	Verse translation	Text number	Page number
4	Nisā'	59	فَإِنْ تَنَازَعْتُمْ فِي شَيْءٍ فَرُدُّوهُ إِلَى اللهِ وَالرَّسُولِ	If you disagree about something, refer it to God and his Messenger.	1.123	302–303
4	Nisā'	82	مَا فَرَّطْنَا فِي الْكِتَابِ مِن شَيْءٍ	If it had come from someone other than God, they would have found it to have many inconsistencies.	1.18	134–135
4	Nisā'	103	كَانَتْ عَلَى الْمُؤْمِنِينَ كِتَابًا مَوْقُوتًا	prescribed for believers at fixed times	1.197	476–477
4	Nisā'	110	وَمَن يَعْمَلْ سُوءًا أَوْ يَظْلِمْ نَفْسَهُ ثُمَّ يَسْتَغْفِرِ اللهَ يَجِدِ اللهَ غَفُورًا رَحِيمًا	Whoever does wrong or oppresses his soul, but then seeks forgiveness from God, will find that God is forgiving and merciful.	3.124	718–719
5	Mā'idah	25	إِنِّي لَا أَمْلِكُ إِلَّا نَفْسِي وَأَخِي	I have jurisdiction only over myself and my brother	3.254	760–761
5	Mā'idah	93	وَاللهُ يُحِبُّ الْمُحْسِنِينَ	God loves those who do good.	3.188	736–737
6	An'ām	38	وَلَوْ كَانَ مِنْ عِندِ غَيْرِ اللهِ لَوَجَدُوا فِيهِ اخْتِلَافًا كَثِيرًا	We have omitted nothing from the Book.	1.18	134–135
6	An'ām	56	قَدْ ضَلَلْتُ إِذًا وَمَا أَنَا مِنَ الْمُهْتَدِينَ	I should stray from the path if so, no longer among the guided	1.57	180–181
6	An'ām	95	فَأَنَّى تُؤْفَكُونَ	how are you deluded	1.80.13 1.84.2 1.105.2	212–213, 220–221, 270–271
7	A'rāf	87	حَتَّى يَحْكُمَ اللهُ بَيْنَنَا وَهُوَ خَيْرُ الْحَاكِمِينَ	until God judges between us—and he is the best of judges	2.55	648–649

(*cont.*)

Surah number	Surah name	Verse number	Verse text	Verse translation	Text number	Page number
7	A'rāf	89	رَبَّنَا افْتَحْ بَيْنَنَا وَبَيْنَ قَوْمِنَا بِالْحَقِّ وَأَنتَ خَيْرُ الْفَاتِحِينَ	Lord, decide between us and our tribesmen with truth, for you are the best conqueror.	2.15	546–547
7	A'rāf	99	فَلَا يَأْمَنُ مَكْرَ اللهِ إِلَّا الْقَوْمُ الْخَاسِرُونَ	Only losers feel secure against God's reckoning	3.356	796–797
7	A'rāf	138	أَجْعَل لَّنَا إِلَهًا كَمَا لَهُمْ آلِهَةٌ قَالَ إِنَّكُمْ قَوْمٌ تَجْهَلُونَ	Make for us a god like their gods! He said, you are an ignorant people!	3.303	778–779
8	Anfāl	6	كَأَنَّمَا يُسَاقُونَ إِلَى الْمَوْتِ وَهُمْ يَنظُرُونَ	as though driven to a death they could see in front of their eyes	1.39	164–165
8	Anfāl	28	وَاعْلَمُوا أَنَّمَا أَمْوَالُكُمْ وَأَوْلَادُكُمْ فِتْنَةٌ	Know that the riches you own and the children you beget are nothing but trials!	3.84	700–701
8	Anfāl	51	وَمَا كَانَ اللهُ لِيُعَذِّبَهُمْ وَأَنتَ فِيهِمْ وَمَا كَانَ اللهُ مُعَذِّبَهُم وَهُمْ يَسْتَغْفِرُونَ	God will not punish them while you are among them, and he will not punish them if they repent.	3.79	700–701
8	Anfāl	51	أَنَّ اللهَ لَيْسَ بِظَلَّامٍ لِّلْعَبِيدِ	God is not unjust to his servants.	1.176.2	402–403
9	Tawbah	109	شَفَا جُرُفٍ هَارٍ	the lip of a crumbling cliff	1.102.2	262–263
10	Yūnus	5	عَدَدَ السِّنِينَ وَالْحِسَابَ	reckoning and calculation of years	1.88.6	232–233

(*cont.*)

Surah number	Surah name	Verse number	Verse text	Verse translation	Text number	Page number
10	Yūnus	30	هُنَالِكَ تَبْلُو كُلُّ نَفْسٍ مَّا أَسْلَفَت وَرُدُّوا إِلَى اللّهِ مَوْلَاهُمُ الْحَقِّ وَضَلَّ عَنْهُم مَّا كَانُوا يَفْتَرُونَ	There, each soul will be tried for what it did in past times, and all creatures will be returned to God, their true master—their falsehoods will no longer avail.	1.223	516–517
10	Yūnus	32	فَمَاذَا بَعْدَ الْحَقِّ إِلَّا الضَّلَالُ	But what is there after truth save error?	2.65	662–663
10	Yūnus	34	فَأَنَّى تُؤْفَكُونَ	how are you deluded?	1.80.13 1.84.2 1.105.2	212–213, 220–221, 270–271
11	Hūd	7	يَبْلُوَكُمْ أَيُّكُمْ أَحْسَنُ عَمَلًا	put you to the test, to see who among you performs the best of deeds.	1.181.3	416–417
11	Hūd	49	إِنَّ الْعَاقِبَةَ لِلْمُتَّقِين	the best outcome is reserved for the pious.	1.95	252–253
11	Hūd	83	وَمَا هِيَ مِنَ الظَّالِمِينَ بِبَعِيدٍ	is never far from the wicked	2.28.5	570–571
11	Hūd	88	إِلَّا الْإِصْلَاحَ مَا اسْتَطَعْتُ وَمَا تَوْفِيقِي إِلَّا بِاللّهِ عَلَيْهِ تَوَكَّلْتُ	only to set things right as much as I can. My direction comes from God. In him I place my trust.	2.28.4	570–571
11	Hūd	89	لَا يَجْرِمَنَّكُمْ شِقَاقِي	Let not your enmity of me drive you to accuse me of lies.	1.98.2	256–257
11	Hūd	95	بُعْدًا ... كَمَا بَعِدَتْ ثَمُودُ	Away with ... as the Thamūd were done away with!	1.179	406–407
12	Yūsuf	53	إِنَّ النَّفْسَ لَأَمَّارَةٌ بِالسُّوءِ إِلَّا مَا رَحِمَ رَبِّي	the sentient soul commands vice unless God shows it mercy.	2.53.1	624–625

(*cont.*)

Surah number	Surah name	Verse number	Verse text	Verse translation	Text number	Page number
12	Yūsuf	87	إِنَّهُ لَا يَايْئَسُ مِن رَّوْحِ ٱللَّهِ إِلَّا ٱلْقَوْمُ ٱلْكَٰفِرُونَ	Only unbelievers despair of God's grace.	3.356	796–797
13	Ra'd	15	مَن فِي ٱلسَّمَاوَاتِ وَٱلْأَرْضِ طَوْعًا وَكَرْهًا	all who are in the skies and the earth, obedient or unwilling	1.183.4	422–423
13	Ra'd	38	لِكُلِّ أَجَلٍ كِتَابٌ	each term is written.	1.105.2 1.181.1	270–271, 414–415
14	Ibrāhīm	4	وَهُوَ ٱلْعَزِيزُ ٱلْحَكِيمُ	and he is mighty and wise.	1.181.3	
14	Ibrāhīm	7	لَئِن شَكَرْتُمْ لَأَزِيدَنَّكُمْ	If you give thanks, you will be given more.	3.124	718–719
14	Ibrāhīm	30	قُل تَمَتَّعُوا فَإِنَّ مَصِيرَكُمْ إِلَى ٱلنَّارِ	Say: Take pleasure if you wish! Your last stop is hellfire.	1.28	150–151
14	Ibrāhīm	42	يَوْمَ تَشْخَصُ فِيهِ ٱلْأَبْصَارُ	the day when eyes stare fixedly in terror	1.193	468–469
15	Ḥijr	37–38	إِنَّكَ مِنَ ٱلْمُنظَرِينَ إِلَىٰ يَوْمِ ٱلْوَقْتِ ٱلْمَعْلُومِ	You have been placed among those who have been granted respite until the day of destiny.	1.1.5	110–111
15	Ḥijr	39	قَالَ رَبِّ بِمَا أَغْوَيْتَنِي لَأُزَيِّنَنَّ لَهُمْ فِي ٱلْأَرْضِ وَلَأُغْوِيَنَّهُمْ أَجْمَعِينَ	He said: My Lord, because you caused me to stray, I shall place temptations before them on earth and lead them all astray.	1.190.2	440–441
16	Naḥl	77	إِنَّ ٱللَّهَ عَلَىٰ كُلِّ شَيْءٍ قَدِيرٌ	Truly, God is powerful over all things.	1.190.12	458–459
16	Naḥl	97	فَلَنُحْيِيَنَّهُ حَيَاةً طَيِّبَةً	we shall grant him a good life.	3.214	742–743
16	Naḥl	125	ٱلْحِكْمَةِ وَٱلْمَوْعِظَةِ	wisdom and counsel	1.92	246–247

(*cont.*)

Surah number	Surah name	Verse number	Verse text	Verse translation	Text number	Page number
16	Naḥl	90	إِنَّ ٱللَّهَ يَأْمُرُ بِٱلْعَدْلِ وَٱلْإِحْسَانِ	God commands justice and goodness	3.216	742–743
16	Naḥl	128	إِنَّ ٱللَّهَ مَعَ ٱلَّذِينَ ٱتَّقَوا وَّٱلَّذِينَ هُم مُّحْسِنُونَ	God is with those who are pious and do good.	1.191	460–461
17	Isrā'	9	لِلَّتِي هِيَ أَقْوَمُ	the path that is straightest	1.145.3	332–333
17	Isrā'	61	ٱسْجُدُوا لِآدَمَ فَسَجَدُوا إِلَّا إِبْلِيسَ	prostrate before Adam, and they all prostrated except Iblīs	1.1.5	110–111
18	Kahf	7	أَيُّهُمْ أَحْسَنُ عَمَلًا	who among them performs the best deeds	1.142.1	328–329
18	Kahf	45	كَمَاءٍ أَنزَلْنَاهُ مِنَ ٱلسَّمَاءِ فَٱخْتَلَطَ بِهِ نَبَاتُ ٱلْأَرْضِ فَأَصْبَحَ هَشِيمًا تَذْرُوهُ ٱلرِّيَاحُ وَكَانَ ٱللَّهُ عَلَى كُلِّ شَيْءٍ مُّقْتَدِرًا	like water that we sent down from the sky: the earth's vegetation drew from it, then became dry straw, and was scattered by the winds. God has power over all things	1.108.1	268–269
20	Ṭāhā	16, 116	ٱسْجُدُوا لِآدَمَ فَسَجَدُوا إِلَّا إِبْلِيسَ	prostrate before Adam, and they all prostrated except Iblīs	1.1.5	110–111
20	Ṭāhā	61	خَابَ مَنِ ٱفْتَرَى	those who lie will fail	1.16	132–133
20	Ṭāhā	132	وَأْمُرْ أَهْلَكَ بِٱلصَّلَاةِ وَٱصْطَبِرْ عَلَيْهَا	command your family to pray, and adhere to it yourself	1.197	476–477
21	Anbiyā'	26–27	بَلْ عِبَادٌ مُّكْرَمُونَ لَا يَسْبِقُونَهُ بِٱلْقَوْلِ وَهُم بِأَمْرِهِ يَعْمَلُونَ	Rather, they are his honored servants, they speak when he has spoken, and act on his command.	1.88.6	232–233

(cont.)

Surah number	Surah name	Verse number	Verse text	Verse translation	Text number	Page number
21	Anbiyā'	101	ٱلَّذِينَ سَبَقَتْ لَهُم مِّنَّا ٱلْحُسْنَى	those for whom blessings have been decreed	1.50	172–173
21	Anbiyā'	104	كَمَا بَدَأْنَا أَوَّلَ خَلْقٍ نُّعِيدُهُ وَعْداً عَلَيْنَا إِنَّا كُنَّا فَاعِلِينَ	As I brought the first creation into being, so I shall bring it forth anew—this is my pledge, and I shall bring it to pass.	1.108.3	282–283
22	Ḥajj	11	خَسِرَ ٱلدُّنْيَا وَٱلْآخِرَةَ ذَلِكَ هُوَ ٱلْخُسْرَانُ ٱلْمُبِينُ	having lost this world and the hereafter—that is the most catastrophic loss!	3.327	784–785
22	Ḥajj	25	سَوَاءً ٱلْعَاكِفُ فِيهِ وَٱلْبَادِ	its resident and the foreigner are equal	2.67	664–665
22	Ḥajj	64	هُوَ ٱلْغَنِيُّ ٱلْحَمِيدُ	He is rich and praised	1.181.3	416–417
23	Mu'minūn	12	مِن سُلَالَةٍ مِّن طِينٍ	an extraction of clay	1.161.2	370–371
23	Mu'minūn	30	إِنَّ فِي ذَلِكَ لَآيَاتٍ وَإِن كُنَّا لَمُبْتَلِينَ	Truly there are signs in that, truly we shall put you to the test.	1.100.3	260–261
23	Mu'minūn	55	أَيَحْسَبُونَ أَنَّمَا نُمِدُّهُم بِهِ مِن مَّالٍ وَبَنِينَ نُسَارِعُ لَهُمْ فِي ٱلْخَيْرَاتِ بَل لَّا يَشْعُرُونَ	Do they think we supply them with wealth and sons in order to increase their comforts? No indeed, they have no idea!	1.190.4	444–445
24	Nūr	22	أَلَا تُحِبُّونَ أَن يَغْفِرَ ٱللَّهُ لَكُمْ	Do you not wish that God should forgive you?	2.23	552–553
24	Nūr	37	رِجَالٌ لَّا تُلْهِيهِمْ تِجَارَةٌ وَلَا بَيْعٌ عَن ذِكْرِ ٱللَّهِ وَإِقَامِ ٱلصَّلَاةِ وَإِيتَاءِ ٱلزَّكَاةِ	men whom neither trade nor commerce divert from remembering God, from performing the prayer, or submitting the alms-levy	1.197 1.219	476–477, 506–507

(cont.)

Surah number	Surah name	Verse number	Verse text	Verse translation	Text number	Page number
24	Nūr	40	فِي بَحْرٍ لُجِّيٍّ	upon the deep ocean	3.354.2	796–797
24	Nūr	45	إِنَّ اللَّهَ عَلَى كُلِّ شَيْءٍ قَدِيرٌ	Truly, God is powerful over all things.	1.190.12	458–459
26	Shu'arā'	97–98	تَاللَّهِ إِن كُنَّا لَفِي ضَلَالٍ مُبِينٍ إِذْ نُسَوِّيكُم بِرَبِّ ٱلْعَالَمِينَ	By God, we were clearly misguided when we equated you with the Lord of the worlds!	1.88.3	230–231
26	Shu'arā'	157	فَعَقَرُوهَا فَأَصْبَحُوا نَادِمِينَ	They slaughtered the mare, and in the morning, they had cause to regret.	1.199	478–479
28	Qaṣaṣ	5	وَنُرِيدُ أَن نَّمُنَّ عَلَى ٱلَّذِينَ ٱسْتُضْعِفُوا۟ فِي ٱلْأَرْضِ وَنَجْعَلَهُمْ أَئِمَّةً وَنَجْعَلَهُمُ ٱلْوَارِثِينَ	We intend to bless those rendered weak on earth with abundant favors. We shall make them Imams. We shall make them inherit.	3.193	738–739
28	Qaṣaṣ	24	رَبِّ إِنِّي لِمَا أَنزَلْتَ إِلَيَّ مِنْ خَيْرٍ فَقِيرٌ	My Lord, I am in dire need of whatever you may bestow!	1.158.3	362–363
28	Qaṣaṣ	83	تِلْكَ ٱلدَّارُ ٱلْآخِرَةُ نَجْعَلُهَا لِلَّذِينَ لَا يُرِيدُونَ عُلُوًّا فِي ٱلْأَرْضِ وَلَا فَسَادًا وَٱلْعَاقِبَةُ لِلْمُتَّقِينَ	We shall reserve the hereafter for those who do not seek to exalt themselves on the earth or spread corruption. The good end is for the god-fearing	1.3.4	120–121
29	'Ankabūt	1–2	الٓمٓ أَحَسِبَ ٱلنَّاسُ أَن يُتْرَكُوا أَن يَقُولُوا آمَنَّا وَهُمْ لَا يُفْتَنُونَ	Alif Lām Mīm. Do people think they can claim, "we believe," without being tested?	1.154.4	354–355
29	'Ankabūt	20	إِنَّ اللَّهَ عَلَى كُلِّ شَيْءٍ قَدِيرٌ	Truly, God is powerful over all things.	1.190.12	458–459

(*cont.*)

Surah number	Surah name	Verse number	Verse text	Verse translation	Text number	Page number
31	Luqmān	34	إِنَّ اللهَ عِنْدَهُ عِلْمُ السَّاعَةِ وَيُنَزِّلُ الْغَيْثَ وَيَعْلَمُ مَا فِي الْأَرْحَامِ وَمَا تَدْرِي نَفْسٌ مَّاذَا تَكْسِبُ غَدًا وَمَا تَدْرِي نَفْسٌ بِأَيِّ أَرْضٍ تَمُوتُ إِنَّ اللهَ عَلِيمٌ خَبِيرٌ	God has knowledge of the coming hour, he sends down rain, and knows what is in wombs. No man knows what he will earn tomorrow, and no man knows the land in which he will die, but God is all-knowing, all-aware.	1.126	308–309
33	Aḥzāb	6	وَأُولُو الْأَرْحَامِ بَعْضُهُمْ أَوْلَىٰ بِبَعْضٍ فِي كِتَابِ اللهِ	Those who are from the same womb have more claim upon each other according to God's Book.	2.28.2	566–567
33	Aḥzāb	72	الْإِنْسَانُ إِنَّهُ كَانَ ظَلُومًا جَهُولًا	the human, for he was a tyrant, an ignoramus.	1.197	476–477
34	Saba'	13	وَقَلِيلٌ مِنْ عِبَادِي الشَّكُورُ	few among my servants are truly grateful	1.189	436–437
34	Saba'	35	نَحْنُ أَكْثَرُ أَمْوَالًا وَأَوْلَادًا وَمَا نَحْنُ بِمُعَذَّبِينَ	We have more wealth and more children; we shall never have to endure suffering.	1.190.7	450–451
35	Fāṭir	1	أُولِي أَجْنِحَةٍ	with sets of wings	1.88.6	232–233
35	Fāṭir	1	إِنَّ اللهَ عَلَىٰ كُلِّ شَيْءٍ قَدِيرٌ	Truly, God is powerful over all things.	1.190.12	458–459
35	Fāṭir	3	فَأَنَّىٰ تُؤْفَكُونَ	How are you deluded?	1.80.13 1.84.2 1.105.2	212–213, 220–221, 270–271

(*cont.*)

Surah number	Surah name	Verse number	Verse text	Verse translation	Text number	Page number
35	Fāṭir	8	فَلَا تَذْهَبْ نَفْسُكَ عَلَيْهِمْ حَسَرَاتٍ إِنَّ اللهَ عَلِيمٌ بِمَا يَصْنَعُونَ	Do not grieve over their actions, for God knows all that they do!	1.160	368–369
35	Fāṭir	14	وَلَا يُنَبِّئُكَ مِثْلُ خَبِيرٍ	No one informs you as well as one who is fully aware	1.151.2	346–347
38	Ṣād	3	وَلَاتَ حِينَ مَنَاصٍ	and it is too late to escape!	1.189 2.41	438–439, 606–607
38	Ṣād	27	وَالْأَرْض وَمَا بَيْنَهُمَا بَاطِلًا ذَلِكَ ظَنُّ الَّذِينَ كَفَرُوا فَوَيْلٌ لِّلَّذِينَ كَفَرُوا مِنَ النَّارِ	and the earth in vain. That is the claim of those who do not believe— woe and hellfire to unbelievers!	3.70	394–395
38	Ṣād	71–74	إِنِّي خَالِقٌ بَشَرًا مِّن طِينٍ فَإِذَا سَوَّيْتُهُ وَنَفَخْتُ فِيهِ مِن رُّوحِي فَقَعُوا لَهُ سَاجِدِينَ فَسَجَدَ الْمَلَائِكَةُ كُلُّهُمْ أَجْمَعُونَ إِلَّا إِبْلِيسَ	I shall create a human out of clay; when I have fashioned him in good proportion and breathed into him my spirit, bow before him in prostration. The angels prostrated, every one of them, except Iblīs	1.190.1	440–441
38	Ṣād	80–81	إِنَّكَ مِنَ الْمُنْظَرِينَ إِلَىٰ يَوْمِ الْوَقْتِ الْمَعْلُومِ	You have been placed among those who have been granted respite until the day of destiny	1.1.5	110–111
38	Ṣād	88	وَلَتَعْلَمُنَّ نَبَأَهُ بَعْدَ حِينٍ	You shall surely learn the truth of its report, but only after a while.	1.68	192–193
39	Zumar	21	يَنَابِيعَ فِي الْأَرْض	flow out in streams	1.164.2	380–381

(*cont.*)

Surah number	Surah name	Verse number	Verse text	Verse translation	Text number	Page number
39	Zumar	73	وَسِيقَ الذينَ اتَّقَوْا رَبَّهُمْ إِلَى الْجَنَّةِ زُمَرًا	Those who were conscious of their Lord will be led in groups into paradise	1.188	434–435
40	Ghāfir	60	أَدْعُونِي أَسْتَجِبْ لَكُمْ	Pray to me and I will answer.	3.124	718–719
40	Ghāfir	62	فَأَنَّى تُؤْفَكُونَ	How are you deluded?	1.80.13 1.84.2 1.105.2	212–213, 220–221, 270–271
40	Ghāfir	78	وَخَسِرَ هُنَالِكَ الْمُبْطِلُونَ	There shall the falsifiers lose everything.	2.3	534–535
41	Fuṣṣilat	15	قَالُوا مَنْ أَشَدُّ مِنَّا قُوَّةً	who said: is anyone mightier than we are?	1.108.3	280–281
41	Fuṣṣilat	30	إِنَّ الذينَ قَالُوا رَبُّنَا الله ثُمَّ اسْتَقَامُوا تَتَنَزَّلُ عَلَيْهِمُ الْمَلَائِكَةُ أَلَّا تَخَافُوا وَلَا تَحْزَنُوا وَأَبْشِرُوا بِالْجَنَّةِ التي كُنتُمْ توعدون	As for those who proclaim that Our Lord is God, and then remain upright, angels come to them, saying, do not fear and do not grieve, but rejoice, for paradise, as promised, is yours!	1.174.4	396–397
44	Dukhān	29	فَمَا بَكَتْ عَلَيْهِمُ السَّمَاءُ وَالْأَرْضُ وَمَا كَانُوا مُنظَرِينَ	Then, neither the sky nor the earth weeps over them, and they are not granted a reprieve.	1.189	438–439
47	Muḥammad	7	إِنْ تَنصُرُوا اللهَ يَنصُرْكُمْ وَيُثَبِّتْ أَقْدَامَكُمْ	If you help God, he will help you and give you a firm foothold.	1.181.3	416–417
47	Muḥammad	35	وَأَنتُمُ الْأَعْلَوْنَ وَاللهُ مَعَكُمْ وَلَن يَتِرَكُمْ أَعْمَالَكُمْ	You shall overcome. God is with you, and he will not let your deeds go to waste	1.63	188–189

(*cont.*)

Surah number	Surah name	Verse number	Verse text	Verse translation	Text number	Page number
48	Fatḥ	7	جُنُودُ السَّمَاوَاتِ وَالْأَرْضِ	the legions of the skies and the earth	1.181.3	416–417
48	Fatḥ	26	وَكَانُوا أَحَقَّ بِهَا وَأَهْلَهَا	and they were worthy of it and deserving	1.188	434–435
50	Qāf	21	كُلُّ نَفْسٍ مَعَهَا سَآئِقٌ وَشَهِيد	Each soul is accompanied by its driver and its witness	1.82.2	214–217
57	Ḥadīd	11	مَن ذَا الذي يُقْرِضُ اللهَ قَرْضًا حَسَنًا فَيُضَاعِفَهُ لَهُ وَلَهُ أَجْرٌ كَرِيمٌ	Who will offer God a beautiful loan of deeds, that he may multiply it for him, and give him a generous recompense?	1.181.3	416–417
57	Ḥadīd	21	ذَلِكَ فَضْلُ اللهِ يُؤْتِيهِ من يَشَاءُ اللهُ ذُو الْفَضْلِ الْعَظِيمِ	That is God's bounty, which he bestows on whom he wills—great is God's bounty!	1.181.3	416–417
57	Ḥadīd	23	لِكَيْلَا تَأْسَوْا عَلَى مَا فَاتَكُمْ وَلَا تَفْرَحُوا بِمَا آتَنكُمْ	Do not weep over what you have lost, and do not exult over what you have gained.	3.409	812–813
58	Mujādalah	19	أُولَئِكَ حِزْبُ الشَّيْطَان أَلَا إنَّ حِزْبَ الشَّيْطَانِ هم الْخَاسِرُونَ	These are Satan's faction. Hark! Satan's faction are losers.	1.192	466–467
61	Ṣaff	3	كَبُرَ مَقْتًا عند اللهِ أَن تَقُولُوا مَا لَا تَفْعَلُونَ	God deems it a great outrage when you say what you do not do.	2.53.21	644–645
62	Jum'ah	4	ذَلِكَ فَضْلُ اللهِ يُؤْتِيهِ من يَشَاءُ اللهُ ذُو الْفَضْلِ الْعَظِيم	That is God's bounty, which he bestows on whom he wills—great is God's bounty!	1.181.3	416–417

(*cont.*)

Surah number	Surah name	Verse number	Verse text	Verse translation	Text number	Page number
63	Munāfiqūn	7	خَزَائِنُ السَّمَاوَاتِ وَالْأَرْضِ	the treasures of the skies and the earth	1.181.3	416–417
65	Ṭalāq	2	مَنْ يَتَّقِ اللهَ يَجْعَلْ لَهُ مَخْرَجًا	God shows the God-conscious a way out	1.181.3	414–415
65	Ṭalāq	3	جَعَلَ اللهُ لِكُلِّ شَيْءٍ قَدْرًا	God has appointed for each thing a measure	1.181.1	
66	Taḥrīm	8	إِنَّكَ عَلَىٰ كُلِّ شَيْءٍ قَدِير	You are powerful over all things	1.88, 1.222	242–243, 514–515
71	Nūḥ	10–12	أَسْتَغْفِرُوا رَبَّكُمْ إِنَّهُ كَانَ غَفَّارًا يُرْسِلِ السَّمَاءَ عَلَيْكُمْ مِدْرَارًا وَيُمْدِدْكُمْ بِأَمْوَالٍ وَبَنِينَ	Ask your Lord for forgiveness, for he is ever forgiving—he will make the sky pour rain and provide you with wealth and children.	1.141.1	326–327
74	Mud-daththir	38	كُلُّ نَفْسٍ بِمَا كَسَبَتْ رَهِينَةٌ	Every soul is mortgaged to what it has earned	3.327	784–785
74	Mud-daththir	42–43	مَا سَلَكَكُمْ فِي سَقَرَ قَالُوا لَمْ نَكُ مِنَ الْمُصَلِّينَ	What led you into the Fire? and they answered, We were not among those who prayed	1.197	476–477
77	Mursalāt	21–22	فِي قَرَارٍ مَكِينٍ إِلَىٰ قَدَرٍ مَعْلُومٍ	a safe abode for a known term	1.161.2	370–371
79	Nāziʿāt	26	إِنَّ فِي ذَٰلِكَ لَعِبْرَةً لِمَنْ يَخْشَىٰ	There is a lesson here for all who venerate God.	1.209	490–491
81	Takwīr	26	فَأَيْنَ تَذْهَبُونَ	So where do you go?	1.84.2	220–221
82	Infiṭār	6	يَا أَيُّهَا الْإِنْسَانُ مَا غَرَّكَ بِرَبِّكَ الْكَرِيمِ	O human, what has deceived you into neglecting your Generous Lord?	1.220	408–409

(*cont.*)

Surah number	Surah name	Verse number	Verse text	Verse translation	Text number	Page number
102	Takāthur	1–2	أَلْهَاكُمُ التَّكَاثُرُ حَتَّى زُرْتُمُ الْمَقَابِرَ	You are obsessed with gathering more and more until you visit your graves	1.218	500–501

Qur'an (references and modified quotes)

Surah Number	Surah Name	Verse Number	Text Number	Page Number
2	Baqarah	24	1.181.3	417
2	Baqarah	35	1.88.9	239
2	Baqarah	88	2.64	661
2	Baqarah	125	1.190.5	449
2	Baqarah	143	1.125	307
2	Baqarah	156	1.27	147
2	Baqarah	163	2.31.9	581
2	Baqarah	189	1.152.2	349
2	Baqarah	224	2.69	667
2	Baqarah	231	3.212	743
2	Baqarah	237	3.435	821
2	Baqarah	255	1.158.1	361
2	Baqarah	264	2.53.21	645
2	Baqarah	265	1.131.1	315
3	Āl 'Imrān	19	1.196.2	473
3	Āl 'Imrān	26	1.88.11	243
3	Āl 'Imrān	103	2.31.3	575
3	Āl 'Imrān	134	2.69	667
3	Āl 'Imrān	139	1.164.3	381
3	Āl 'Imrān	169	1.84.2	221
3	Āl 'Imrān	173	1.181.3	419
4	Nisā'	60	3.406	813
4	Nisā'	69	1.181.3	417
4	Nisā'	97	1.187	433
4	Nisā'	88	2.45.4, 2.58	615, 653
4	Nisā'	110	3.406	719
4	Nisā'	164	1.180.3	409
5	Mā'idah	3	1.83.3, 1.196.2	217, 473
5	Mā'idah	19	1.149.1	341
5	Mā'idah	27–31	1.190.2	443
6	An'ām	57	1.94.3	251

(*cont.*)

Surah Number	Surah Name	Verse Number	Text Number	Page Number
6	An'ām	160	3.296	775
7	A'rāf	17	2.44	609
7	A'rāf	26	1.27	147
7	A'rāf	46–49	1.150.2	347
7	A'rāf	130	1.141.2	327
7	A'rāf	155	1.141.2	327
7	A'rāf	157	1.151.2	347
8	Anfāl	12	1.190.2	443
9	Tawbah	10–12	3.141	727
9	Tawbah	40	3.354.1	795
9	Tawbah	52	1.23	133
9	Tawbah	59	2.53.24	647
9	Tawbah	60	2.26.2	559
11	Hūd	70	1.4	125
12	Yūsuf	53	1.84.1, 1.174.1	219, 395
13	Ra'd	12	1.183.4	423
14	Ibrāhīm	7	1.155, 3.406	355, 813
14	Ibrāhīm	37	1.190.5	449
15	Ḥijr	17–18	1.88.6	233
15	Ḥijr	88	1.190.4	445
15	Ḥijr	94	1.228	521
16	Naḥl	51	2.31.9	581
16	Naḥl	89	1.83.3	217
17	Isrā'	12	1.88.5	233
17	Isrā'	24	2.46	617
17	Isrā'	34	2.74	673
17	Isrā'	64	1.190.2	441
18	Kahf	45	1.17	135
19	Maryam	50	1.23	141
20	Ṭāhā	39	1.196.2	473
20	Ṭāhā	67	1.4	125
21	Anbiyā'	102	1.181.3	415
22	Ḥajj	18	1.131.1	315
22	Ḥajj	36	2.53.14	639
23	Mu'minūn	77	3.350	793
23	Mu'minūn	99–100	1.181.3	417
23	Mu'minūn	115	1.61.1, 1.83.3, 3.351	185, 217, 793
24	Nūr	24	1.197	477
25	Furqān	27	3.170	731
25	Furqān	38	1.180.4	411

(*cont.*)

Surah Number	Surah Name	Verse Number	Text Number	Page Number
26	Shu'arā'	84	1.23	141
28	Qaṣaṣ	4	1.190.4	445
29	'Ankabūt	41	1.17	133
30	Rūm	12	3.350	793
32	Sajdah	12	2.41	607
33	Aḥzāb	45	1.102.1	263
33	Aḥzāb	58	1.72	199
33	Aḥzāb	67	1.190.3	445
34	Saba'	15–16	1.164.2	381
34	Saba'	52	1.218.1	503
35	Fāṭir	10	1.180.2	409
35	Fāṭir	28	3.133	721
35	Fāṭir	35	1.181.3	407
36	Yāsīn	12	1.23	139
36	Yāsīn	80	1.131.1	315
37	Ṣāffāt	6	1.88.6	233
42	Shūrā	20	1.23	141
42	Shūrā	23	1.148.3	339
42	Shūrā	28	1.112	289
43	Zukhruf	13	1.46	171
44	Dukhān	10	1.88.5	233
45	Jāthiyah	9	3.212	743
48	Fatḥ	6	2.58	653
49	Ḥujurāt	12	1.72	199
49	Ḥujurāt	17	1.154.4	355
50	Qāf	12	1.180.4	411
50	Qāf	23	1.181.3	417
55	Raḥmān	41	1.158.1	361
56	Wāqi'ah	28	1.102.1	263
56	Wāqi'ah	93–94	1.80.12	213
62	Jum'ah	6–7	2.69	667
62	Jum'ah	8	1.147	337
64	Taghābun	15	3.277	773
66	Taḥrīm	8	1.69, 1.88.11	195, 243
67	Mulk	22	2.45.4	615
68	Qalam	42	1.149.3	343
73	Muzzammil	11	2.28.2	567
75	Qiyāmah	36	1.61.1, 1.83.3, 3.351	185, 217, 793
78	Naba'	18	1.193	469
81	Takwīr	4	1.193	469
81	Takwīr	8	1.190.10	453

(*cont.*)

Surah Number	Surah Name	Verse Number	Text Number	Page Number
82	Infiṭār	4	1.223	517
82	Infiṭār	10–11	1.181.3	415
83	Muṭaffifūn	14	2.10, 2.58	541, 653
85	Burūj	1	1.87	225
93	Ḍuḥā	11	2.28.2, 2.69	565, 667
111	Masad	4	2.28.2	567
112	Ikhlāṣ	1	2.31.9	581
112	Ikhlāṣ	3	1.180.2, 1.184.2	409

Hadith (direct quotes)

Text	Translation	Text number	Page number
إنّه يموت من مات منّا وليس بميّت ويبلى من بلي منّا وليس ببالٍ.	When one of us dies, he is not dead. When his body disintegrates in the ground, it has not disintegrated.	1.84.2	220–221
إنّ الله يحبّ العبد ويبغض عمله ويحبّ العمل ويبغض بَدَنه.	God can love a servant and yet hate his deeds or love his deeds and yet hate his being.	1.152.2	348–349
إنّ أمّتي سيفتنون من بعدي ... إنّ القوم سيفتنون بأموالهم ويمنّون بدينهم على ربّهم ويتمنّون رحمته ويأمنون سطوته ويستحلّون حرامه بالشبهات الكاذبة والأهواء الساهية فيستحلّون الخمر بالنبيذ والسحت بالهديّة والربا بالبيع.	My community will be thrown into turmoil when I die. ... people will be tested with regard to wealth—thinking their support of Islam a favor to their Lord, they will feel entitled to his mercy and believe themselves secure against his punishment. By raising false suspicions and wayward passions, they will legalize the things he has forbidden—they will drink wine, calling it date juice, take bribes, calling it gift-giving, and practice usury, calling it trade.	1.154.4	354–355
غيّبيه عنّي فإنّي إذا نظرت إليه ذكرت الدنيا وزخارفها.	Remove it from my sight—it reminds me of the world and its ornaments!	1.158.4	362–363

(*cont.*)

Text	Translation	Text number	Page number
يؤتى يوم القيامة بالإمام الجائر وليس معه نصير ولا عاذر فيلقى في جهنّم فيدور فيها كما تدور الرحى ثمّ يرتبط في قعرها.	On the day of resurrection, the unjust leader will be brought for judgment, and he will not have a single person to help him or speak on his behalf. He will be thrown into the Pit of Gehenna and spin there like a millstone, then he will be tethered in its lowest point.	1.162.2	372–373
إنّ الجنّة حُجبت بالمكاره وإنّ النار حُفّت بالشهوات.	Paradise is veiled by torments, while the Fire is surrounded by delights.	1.174.1	394–395
لا يستقيم إيمان عبد حتّى يستقيم قلبه ولا يستقيم قلبه حتّى يستقيم لسانه.	A person's belief is right only when his heart is right, and his heart is right only when his tongue is righteous.	1.174.5	398–399
يا ابْن آدم اعمل الخير ودَع الشرّ فإذا أنت جوادٌ قاصد.	Son of Adam, do good and avoid evil, and you will race ahead like a thoroughbred.	1.174.7	398–399
هذا الشيطان قد أيس من عبادته إنّك تسمع ما أسمع وترى ما أرى إلّا أنّك لست بنبيّ وإنّك لوزير وإنّك لعلى خير.	This is Satan, who now despairs of being worshipped. You see what I see and hear what I hear, 'Alī, though you are not a prophet, but my vizier, and on the path of virtue.	1.190.12	458–459
من كذب عليّ متعمّدًا فليتبوّأ مقعده من النار.	Whoever deliberately misattributes something to me will take possession of a seat in hellfire.	1.208	486–487
إنّي لا أخاف على أمّتي مؤمنًا ولا مشركًا أمّا المؤمن فيمنعه الله بإيمانه وأمّا المشرك فيقمعه الله بشركه ولكنّي أخاف عليكم كلّ منافق الجَنَان عالم اللسان يقول ما تعرفون ويفعل ما تنكرون.	I do not fear harm for my community from either believer or unbeliever. As for the believer, God holds him back because of his belief. As for the unbeliever, God thwarts him because of his unbelief. I fear harm for you from every man whose heart harbors hypocrisy while his tongue spouts knowledge, who says what you know to be good, but does what you know is evil.	2.27.5	562–563
صلاح ذات البين أفضل من عامّة الصلاة والصيام.	To reconcile with kin is even better than to pray and to fast.	2.47.1	616–617

(*cont.*)

Text	Translation	Text number	Page number
لن تُقَدَّس أُمّة لا يؤخذ للضعيف فيها حقّه من القويّ غير متعتع.	A nation in which the weak are not given justice against the strong except by anxiously stammering will never be made holy.	2.53.14	640–641
صَلِّ بهم كصلاة أضعفهم وكن بالمؤمنين رحيمًا.	Pray the prayer of the weakest among them—show compassion to all believers.	2.53.16	640–641
غَيِّروا الشَّيب ولا تشبّهوا باليهود.	Dye your white hair and don't emulate the Jews.	3.13	682–683
لا يبغضك مؤمن ولا يحبّك منافق.	No believer will hate you, and no hypocrite will love you.	3.38	690–691
لا طاعة لمخلوق في معصئة الخالق.	Do not obey humans if it means you will disobey God.	3.149	726–727
الآنَ حَمِيَ الوَطِيس.	Now the furnace burns.	3.253	748–759

Hadith (references)

Text	Translation	Text number	Page number
الإمامة في القريش.	The Imamate is vested in Quraysh.	142.1	329
أنا مدينة العلم وعليّ بابها.	I am the city of knowledge and 'Alī is its gateway.	1.152.2	349
ستقاتل بعدي الناكثين والقاسطين والمارقين	You will battle the pledge-breakers, the wrongdoers, and the faith-leavers after me.	1.190.11	457
لا طاعة لمخلوق في معصية الخالق.	Do not obey humans if it means you will disobey God.	2.33	598

Poetry (direct quotes)

Text	Translation	Poet	Text number	Page number
أُولَئِكَ آبَائِي فَجِئْنِي بِمِثْلِهِمْ إِذَا جَمَعَتْنَا يَا جَرِيرُ الْمَجَامِعُ	These are my ancestors, Jarīr, bring on yours! Who will be your boast in our gatherings?	Farazdaq	0.4	100–101
شَتَّانَ مَا يَوْمِي عَلَى كُورِهَا وَيَوْمُ حَيَّانَ أَخِي جَابِرِ	O how different my days today, always in the saddle, and the days of Jābir's brother, Ḥayyān!	Aʿshā	1.3.2	118–119
لَعَمْرُ أَبِيكَ الْخَيْرِ يَا عَمْرُو إِنَّنِي عَلَى وَضَرٍ مِنْ ذَا الْإِنَاءِ قَلِيلِ	By the life of your virtuous father, I swear My pot has nothing but smudges of fat.	anonymous	1.25	142–143
هُنَالِكَ لَوْ دَعَوْتَ أَتَاكَ مِنْهُمْ رِجَالٌ مِثْلُ أُرْمِيَةِ الْحَمِيمِ	When you call out Their men rush to you Like the hot summer cloud	Abū Jundub al-Hudhalī al-Mashʾūm	1.25	144–145
أَمَرْتُكُمُ أَمْرِي بِمُنْعَرَجِ اللِّوَى فَلَمْ تَسْتَبِينُوا النُّصْحَ إِلَّا ضُحَى الْغَدِ	I gave you my considered opinion At the place of the winding sands But you heeded not my counsel Till forenoon the next day.	Durayd ibn al-Ṣimmah	1.35	160–161
حَدَابِيرُ مَا تَنْفَكُّ إِلَّا مُنَاخَةً عَلَى الْخَسْفِ أَوْ نَرْمِي بِهَا بَلَدًا قَفْرَا	Emaciated camels fodderless in the night when they kneel down to rest, or ridden hard into the desert wastes.	Dhū al-Rummah	1.112	290–291
عِنْدَ الصَّبَاحِ يُحْمَدُ الْقَوْمُ السُّرَى	When morning comes, the night-traveler will be praised.	Jumayḥ ibn al-Sharīd al-Taghlibī	1.158.4	364–365
وَدَعْ عَنْكَ نَهْبًا صِيحَ فِي حَجَرَاتِهِ	forget about the looting that caused screams in the neighborhood	Imruʾ al-Qays	1.160	368–369
وَتِلْكَ شِكَاةٌ ظَاهِرٌ عَنْكَ عَارُهَا	that is a disease whose shame is external to you	Abū Dhuʾayb al-Hudhalī	2.28.3	568–569

(*cont.*)

Text	Translation	Poet	Text number	Page number
وَقَـدْ يَسْتَفِيـدُ الظَّنَّـةَ الْمُتَنَصِّحُ	Sometimes, the only benefit a well-wisher derives is suspicion	anonymous	2.28.4	570–571
لَبِـثْ قَلِيلًا يَلْحَـقِ الْهَيْجَـا حَمَـل	Wait just a little Hamal will soon join the fray!	Ḥamal ibn Badr	2.28.5	570–571
فَـإِنْ تَسْأَلِينِي كَيْـفَ أَنْـتَ فَإِنَّنِي صَبُـورٌ عَلـى رَيْـبِ الزَّمَـانِ صَلِيب يَعِـزُّ عَلَـيَّ أَنْ تُرى بِـي كَآبَـةٌ فَيَشْمَـتَ عَـادٍ أَوْ يُسَـاءُ حَبِيب	If you asked, "How do you fare?" I would answer: I am patient and I am strong in the face of fate's attacks. I do not allow myself to show distress, Lest my enemy gloat, and my friend grieve.	ʿAbbās ibn Mirdās al-Sulamī	2.36	600–601
وَحَسْبُـكَ دَاءً أَنْ تَبِيـتَ بِبِطْنَـة وَحَوْلَـكَ أَكْبَـادٌ تَحِـنُّ إِلَـى الْقِدّ	How sick you are! You sleep with a full belly Surrounded by hearts yearning for a mouthful of dry hide.	Ḥātim al-Ṭāʾī	2.45.3	612–613
مُسْتَقْبِلِيـنَ رِيَـاحَ الصَّيْفِ تَضْرِبُهُـمْ بِحَاصِـبٍ بَيْـنَ أَغْـوَارٍ وجَلْمُود	They advance into the burning winds of high summer As they enter the lowlands it blows dust, and pebbles, and rocks in their faces.	Bishr ibn Abī Khāzim al-Asadī	2.64	660–661
فَإِنْ كُنْتَ بالشُّورى مَلَكْتَ أُمُورَهُـمْ فَكَيْـفَ بِهَـذَا وَالمُشِيـرُونَ غِيَب وَإِنْ كُنْتَ بِالقُرْبى حَجَجْتَ خَصِيمَهُمْ فَغيْـرُكَ أَوْلَـى بِالنَّبِـيِّ وَأَقْرَب	If you became their ruler through consultation, How is this valid when the counsellors were absent? If you argued against your opponent through kinship, Then another, closer than you to the Prophet, is worthier!	ʿAlī	3.174	732–733
مَـا يُجْعَـلُ الجُـدُّ الظَّنُـونُ الَّـذِي جِنِـبَ صَـوْبَ اللَّجِـبِ الْمَاطِر مِثْـلَ الفُرَاتِـيِّ إِذَا مَـا طَمَـا يَقْـذِفُ بِالبُوصِـيِّ وَالمَاهِر	The dubious well, That the thunder clouds pass by, Is not the surging Euphrates, Which tosses ship and captain.	Aʿshā	3.250	756–757

(*cont.*)

Text	Translation	Poet	Text number	Page number
لَمَّا رَأَيْتُ فَالِجًا قَدْ فَلَجَا	When I saw a successful man who was victorious	anonymous	3.252	758–759

Proverbs (direct quotes)

Text	Translation	Text number	Page number
بعد اللتيا والتي	after the small calamity and the large one	1.5	125
لو كان يطاع لقُصيرِ أمرُ	O if only Qaṣīr's command had been obeyed!	1.35	161
متفرّقين أيادَي سَبا	they will disperse like the hands of Sabā	1.94.1	249
ناقش الشوكة بالشوكة	a person who extracts a thorn with a thorn	1.118	297
حاملُ ضَبٍّ	he carries a spiny-tailed lizard	1.145	335
الرائد لا يكذب أهله	The scout does not lie to his people.	1.153.1	349
أخفى من سفاد الغراب	more hidden than the mating of a crow	1.163.2	377
آخِر الداء الكَيّ	Cauterizing is the last resort!	1.166	385
لا تُغمَز لهم قَناة ولا تُقرَع لهم صَفاة	Their spear became hard, their rock uncrushable.	1.190.10	455
كَاقِل التمر إلى هَجَر	like the man who carried dates to sell in Hajar	2.28.1	563
حَنَّ قِدْحٌ لَيْسَ مِنْهَا	An arrow has whirred that does not belong to the quiver!	2.28.1	565
مَنْ مَالَت بِهِ الرَّمِيَّة	one whose arrows pursued an animal that veered to one side	2.28.2	565
إيّاك وما يُعتذَر منه	Beware of an action you must justify!	2.33	597
كلا ولا	Like no and no	2.36	599

(*cont.*)

Text	Translation	Text number	Page number
قلب ظهر المجنّ	Turned the face of his shield	2.41	605
قد جرى أبنا عنان	The two sons of *'inān* have made their run.	3.186	737

فهرس المفاهيم الدينيّة والأخلاقيّة
Index of Religious and Ethical Concepts

This index lists a large selection of ethical and religious concepts from the Arabic text of *Nahj al-Balāghah* (only substantives are listed, not verbs, and the sequence is based on root letters).[1] For names, places, and a wider range of terms, please see the English indexes.[2] You can also search the online version of this volume digitally.

الله. كثير الوقوع

إثم، آثام   144، 178، 232، 358، 442، 628، 724،
782، 784

آخرة. كثير الوقوع

أدب، آداب   410، 576، 592، 678، 692، 708،
790، 804

تأديب، مؤدّب   158، 404، 694، 788

ألفة، تألف   236، 248، 328، 380، 450،
452، 454، 496، 520، 628، 658، 674،
692

إمام، أئمّة. كثير الوقوع

أمر. كثير الوقوع

أمان   358، 514، 688، 700، 748

أمانة   106، 110، 146، 154، 210، 232، 476،
534، 558، 604، 606، 634، 636، 642،
670

أمل   148، 150، 166، 174، 184، 202، 206، 218،
286، 312، 414، 464، 534، 540، 682،
686، 722، 742، 784

إنسان   110، 132، 210، 220، 476، 508، 512،
522، 564، 594، 680، 706، 720،
734

إنابة   366، 584

أناة   168، 206، 230، 790، 816

تأهّب   518

أهل بيت (النبيّ)   250، 436، 538، 654

آية الله، آيات الله   112، 114، 220، 230، 232،
260، 264، 408، 414، 424، 462، 474،
502، 742

بدعة، بدع، مبتدعات   132، 138، 220، 330،
342، 346، 348، 364، 372، 384، 398،
412، 486، 516، 536، 712

بخل   308، 628، 678، 734، 744، 794، 796

بخيل   308، 312، 324، 628، 688، 712، 744،
752

برّ   164، 166، 358، 450، 742، 794

وفاجر   164، 602

---

1   From ʿAlī's texts only, not Raḍī's introduction.
2   For a full print concordance, see Muḥammadī and Dashtī, *al-Muʿjam al-mufahras li-alfāẓ Nahj al-balāghah*. For a thematic index, see Muḥammad, *al-Muʿjam al-mawḍūʿī li-Nahj al-balāghah*, and Bayḍūn, *Taṣnīf Nahj al-balāghah*.

أبرار 110، 244، 248، 378، 460، 462، 496، 552، 596، 708

برزخ 502، 506

بركة، بركات 326، 472، 544

بشاشة 678

بِشر 782

بشرى 210، 354

بصيرة، بصائر 126، 246، 268، 318، 338، 452، 470، 498، 516، 594، 596، 656، 722، 724، 766

تبعّل: حسن ال 718

بغض، بغضاء، بغيض 132، 258، 306، 340، 362، 364، 424، 464، 690، 704، 722، 764، 782، 784

بغي، باغي 248، 290، 318، 328، 334، 386، 442، 448، 450، 456، 464، 618، 622، 650، 742، 786

بقاء 162، 208، 252، 274، 330، 330، 356، 410، 446، 484، 496، 526، 584، 636، 712، 732، 790، 794، 810

بلاء، ابتلاء 146، 222، 244، 246، 250، 278، 316، 338، 398، 428، 436، 442، 446، 448، 450، 452، 462، 466، 498، 510، 514، 562، 578، 614، 626، 632، 706، 716، 720، 722، 770، 772، 786، 800

بهتان 488

بيت الله 114، 446، 448

بيعة 126، 146، 158، 196، 242، 320، 388، 536

ترجمان 302، 772

تقوى. توحيد. توفيق. توكّل. انظر "و"

توبة 132، 184، 212، 238، 246، 332، 414، 492، 518، 526، 582، 584، 702، 718، 722، 724، 728، 792، 812

ثبات 236

ثقة. انظر "و"

جبن، جبان 628، 678، 720، 744

جحيم 212

جِدّ 150، 312، 346، 436، 438، 452، 518، 574، 576، 596، 738، 770

جرأة 322، 508، 510

تجربة، تجارب 108، 230، 398، 576، 588، 634، 676، 738

جرم، جريمة، جرائم، مجرم، متجرّم، متجرّمة 210، 220، 390، 584، 590، 570، 716

جزع 124، 136، 152، 210، 252، 416، 504، 518، 524، 542، 552، 590، 706، 730، 738، 770

جفاء 312، 590، 666

جَلَد 258، 698

جمعة 412، 668

جنّة. كثير الوقوع

جنون 748

جهاد 142، 146، 158، 178، 180، 248، 276، 294، 296، 298، 404، 412، 432، 470، 526، 532، 574، 604، 608، 618، 624، 630، 632، 684، 686، 718، 746، 794، 796

اجتهاد 262، 518

جهل 106، 112، 132، 166، 246، 258، 270، 278، 312، 334، 336، 372، 404، 428، 444، 452، 454، 482، 526، 666، 668، 686، 692، 706، 730، 766، 798، 822

جهالة، جهالات 134، 216، 262، 322، 340،
444، 502، 508، 572، 578، 718، 726

جاهل، جاهلون، جهلاء، جهّال 116، 124،
132، 134، 198، 220، 246، 278، 280،
302، 312، 324، 450، 476، 502، 578،
592، 636، 644، 648، 664، 672، 694،
710، 722، 736، 744، 768، 778، 794

جاهليّة 244، 246، 380، 384، 440، 442،
444، 454، 544، 548، 566

جهنّم 372، 462، 546

جود 226، 228، 254، 412، 738، 812

جور 130، 134، 138، 196، 228، 302، 304،
306، 400، 482، 496، 602، 624، 628،
634، 652، 668، 784

جار، جيران 116، 174، 266، 280، 332، 336،
416، 464، 502، 514، 560، 592، 616

استجارة 516

حبّ، محبّة 226، 234، 272، 284، 304، 316،
362، 396، 452، 472، 492، 496، 624،
644، 774

حبيب، أحبّة 190، 506، 574، 592، 600،
694، 716، 764، 782

حجّ 114

حجّة، حجج 112، 120، 138، 184، 188، 202، 204،
216، 220، 222، 228، 230، 238، 278،
326، 344، 364، 386، 388، 394، 398،
414، 418، 420، 432، 450، 494، 508،
510، 544، 600، 632، 634، 646، 648،
652، 722، 770

احتجاج 674

احتجاب الولاة 642

حجاب (النساء) 594

حِدّة 748

حدود الله 456، 614

حديث (النبيّ) 432، 474، 486

حذر 202، 206، 312، 346، 366، 444، 464،
584، 642، 658، 684، 706

أحرار 250، 302، 308، 744، 804

حرص 124، 462، 496، 620، 628، 648، 706،
742، 792

تحريف 344

حرمة 352، 382، 388، 538، 554

حزم 462، 642، 692، 730

حزن، أحزان، حزين 110، 202، 218، 258، 282،
366، 478، 504، 572، 668، 696، 770،
782، 806

حَسَب 136، 140، 406، 418، 442، 444، 612،
682، 688، 710

محتسب 334، 642

حساب (الله) 166، 188، 202، 206، 232، 256،
352، 356، 534، 540، 604، 606، 690،
712

حسد، تحاسد 218، 236، 310، 384، 442، 466،
740، 748، 786، 792

حسرة 160، 184، 274، 278، 606، 652، 810

حسن 166، 272، 406، 430، 496، 510، 560،
580، 582، 590، 592، 622، 628، 630،
632، 636، 642، 646، 656، 674، 688،
708، 710، 712، 718، 742، 766، 798،
816

إحسان، محسن 114، 132، 154، 188، 254، 406،
446، 460، 468، 496، 548، 570، 590،
628، 644، 650، 710، 726، 728، 736،
742

محشر 154، 216

حقّ ‏106، 114، 116، 122، 126، 132، 134، 136، 146، 150، 152، 158، 162، 166، 188، 194، 214، 220، 228، 262، 266، 268، 272، 282، 288، 290، 292، 298، 300، 304، 306، 308، 318، 322، 326، 334، 338، 344، 350، 356، 366، 368، 386، 388، 390، 392، 394، 396، 404، 406، 412، 418، 436، 458، 464، 472، 474، 476، 482، 492، 510، 516، 522، 554، 556، 568، 572، 574، 590، 592، 602، 608، 616، 618، 620، 626، 628، 630، 632، 638، 640، 644، 650، 652، 658، 662، 664، 666، 668، 670، 682، 686، 712، 722، 726، 728، 730، 746، 774، 784، 802

وباطل ‏110، 124، 130، 138، 142، 148، 156، 164، 172، 182، 190، 248، 260، 302، 310، 324، 332، 372، 380، 400، 414، 444، 466، 470، 486، 496، 526، 596، 606، 642، 680، 734، 762، 796

حقوق ‏216، 254، 294، 312، 324، 380، 382، 384، 432، 484، 494، 496، 498، 546، 558، 744، 754، 806، 814

حقد، أحقاد ‏280، 442، 626

احتكار ‏638

حُكم، أحكام. كثير الوقوع

حكّام ‏452، 454

حكمة، حكم ‏138، 198، 228، 230، 246، 248، 268، 276، 294، 314، 334، 338، 340، 344، 350، 358، 410، 418، 474، 526، 574، 678، 684، 686، 698، 700، 706، 724، 730، 734، 820

حكيم، حكماء ‏340، 346، 416، 436، 628، 718، 762، 766

حلال ‏262، 464، 606

وحرام ‏112، 202، 222، 282، 398، 412، 576، 666

حلم، حِلم، حلماء ‏280، 290، 358، 436، 454، 462، 464، 526، 602، 630، 662، 672، 684، 686، 702، 736، 738، 740، 806، 808، 816

حمق، أحمق ‏688، 786، 815

احتمال ‏452، 678

حميّة ‏110، 164، 440، 442، 646، 756

محاباة ‏634

حاجة ‏196، 228، 268، 350، 370، 428، 432، 590، 630، 640، 664، 696، 714، 748، 764، 790، 810

فوت الـ ‏694

قضاء الـ ‏704

حياء ‏634، 682، 692، 710، 740

حيف ‏560، 616، 642، 760، 820

حياة، حيّ، أحياء. كثير الوقوع

خبيث ‏316، 486

خديعة ‏298، 464، 608

خذلان ‏148، 330

خراج ‏620، 622، 624، 630، 634، 654، 822

خرق ‏232، 238، 268، 510، 588، 640، 790

خزي ‏338، 558

خشوع، تخشيع ‏234، 446، 448، 462

خاشع، خاشعين ‏270، 296، 464

خشية ‏140، 186، 490، 638

خصومة، خصوم، خصام ‏192، 558، 578، 632، 752، 754، 772

خضوع ‏256، 342، 590

خفض الجناح ‏560، 616

خلّة ٢٤٢، ٧٨٢، ٨١٤

إخلاص ١٠٦، ١١٤، ٢٧٦، ٢٨٤، ٣٨٢، ٤٦٦، ٧٤٦

مخالطة ٦٨٠

خلاف، مخالفة ١٣٤، ١٤٢، ١٦٠، ٢٦٠، ٣٧٤، ٣٨٦، ٤٣٦، ٤٨٠، ٥٧٢، ٦٣٦، ٦٦٤، ٧٠٦، ٧٣٨، ٧٤٤

خليفة ١٧٠، ٤١٠، ٥٥٠، ٥٧٢

خَلق، خلقة. كثير الوقوع

خُلق، أخلاق ١٢٨، ٢٢٢، ٣٩٨، ٤٥٠، ٤٥٦، ٤٩٢، ٥١٠، ٥٧٤، ٦٣٤، ٦٣٦، ٦٨٨، ٧٠٨، ٧٤٢، ٨٠٢، ٨٠٨

خُمس ٧٦٤

خوف، مخافة ١٥٤، ١٥٦، ٢٠٨، ٢١٨، ٢٢٤، ٢٣٤، ٢٤٤، ٢٥٠، ٢٧٨، ٢٨٤، ٣٥٨، ٣٦٠، ٣٩٢، ٤٠٤، ٤٠٦، ٤١٢، ٤٢٢، ٤٢٨، ٤٥٢، ٤٦٢، ٤٨٨، ٥٠٢، ٥١٠، ٥٣٨، ٥٤٢، ٥٤٨، ٥٦٠، ٦٠٢، ٦١٢، ٦١٤، ٦٥٠، ٦٨٦، ٧٠٦، ٧٥٨

خائف ١٥٤، ٣٢٦، ٣٣٢، ٣٤٢، ٣٤٦، ٧٢٢

خيبة ١٣٨، ٢٤٠، ٦٨٢

خير ١٣٢، ١٤٠، ١٤٢، ١٥٢، ١٦٨، ١٩٤، ٢٢٠، ٢٤٠، ٢٤٢، ٢٤٦، ٢٤٨، ٢٦٠، ٢٦٢، ٢٦٦، ٢٧٨، ٢٨٤، ٢٨٦، ٢٩٦، ٣٠٦، ٣٢٤، ٣٦٢، ٣٦٤، ٣٩٠، ٤٠٠، ٤٥٨، ٤٩٢، ٥٣٤، ٥٤٦، ٥٥٢، ٥٦٦، ٥٧٤، ٥٧٦، ٥٨٤، ٥٩٠، ٥٩٤، ٦٢٨، ٦٣٦، ٦٣٨، ٦٤٨، ٦٧٠، ٦٨٢، ٦٩٢، ٦٩٨، ٧٠٢، ٧٠٤، ٧١٤، ٧٢٠، ٧٢٦، ٧٣٠، ٧٤٢، ٧٤٦، ٧٧٠، ٧٩٠، ٧٩٤، ٧٩٦، ٨١٢، ٨٢٠

وشرّ ١١٦، ١٤٤، ١٩٢، ٢٨٢، ٣٠٨، ٣٥٦، ٣٨٢، ٣٩٨، ٤٥٠، ٤٦٤، ٥١٦، ٥٤٨، ٥٦٠، ٥٨٦، ٥٨٨، ٥٩٦، ٦٨٦، ٨٠٠، ٨٠٨

استخارة ٥٧٦

خيرات ٣٢٦، ٣٤٤، ٤٤٤، ٦٨٤، ٧٠٢

خُيلاء ٤٤٠، ٤٤٨

خيانة ١٤٠، ١٤٢، ٥٥٨، ٦٠٤، ٦٣٤، ٦٧٠

تدبير ١٨٦، ٢٢٨، ٢٣٠، ٤٠٨، ٤٢٨، ٤٩٠، ٦٨٢، ٧٠٤، ٧٠٨، ٨١٦

دعاء ١٣٢، ١٦٢، ٢٩٦، ٣٧٠، ٤٩٢، ٥٠٦، ٥٠٨، ٥١٤، ٥١٦، ٥١٨، ٥٤٤، ٥٨٢، ٥٨٤، ٧٠٦، ٧١٨، ٧٢٠، ٧٧٢، ٨١٢، ٨٢٢

دعوة ١١٤، ١٥٠، ٢٣٠، ٢٨٢، ٢٩٨، ٣٢٢، ٣٦٤، ٤٥٢، ٥٦٠، ٦٢٠، ٦٧٢، ٧٣٠

داعي ١٣٨، ١٤٠، ٢٠٦، ٢١٠، ٢٧٠، ٢٧٢، ٢٧٤، ٢٨٠، ٢٨٤، ٢٩٠، ٣١٢، ٣٣٦، ٣٤٨، ٣٦٤، ٣٨٢، ٥٦٢، ٦٣٠، ٧٤٢، ٧٧٨، ٧٨٤

دم، دماء ١٣٤، ١٤٦، ١٧٦، ١٧٨، ١٩٦، ٢٤٠، ٢٦٢، ٣١٢، ٣٤٢، ٣٩٢، ٣٩٨، ٤٣٨، ٥٠٢، ٥٣٦، ٥٤٠، ٥٤٢، ٥٥٢، ٦٠٨، ٦١٨، ٦٥٠، ٦٦٢

حقن ال ٤٨٢، ٧٤٨

سفك ال ١٣٨، ١٤٤، ١٧٤، ٣١٨، ٤١٠، ٦٤٤

دنيا. كثير الوقوع

دهر ١٥٤، ١٦٠، ٢٢٢، ٢٢٦، ٢٧٠، ٢٧٤، ٢٨٦، ٣٥٤، ٣٦٨، ٣٩٤، ٤٤٤، ٥٠٤، ٥٣٨، ٥٦٠، ٥٦٢، ٥٧٢، ٥٧٤، ٥٧٦، ٥٨٨، ٦١٢، ٦٢٦، ٦٧٠، ٦٩٤، ٧٢٠، ٧٦٨، ٨٠٠

دواء ٣٥٨، ٤٦٢، ٤٦٦، ٤٧٠، ٤٧٤، ٥٨٦، ٦٧٨، ٧٦٢

دين. كثير الوقوع

ذكر

الله ٢٥٠، ٢٧٨، ٤٧٦، ٥٠٦، ٦٥٠

المعاد ٦٤٦، ٦٩٠

الموت ٢١٤، ٤٣٠، ٥٧٤، ٥٨٤، ٦٦٦، ٧٨٦

ذلّ، ذلّة، مذلّة ١٥٤، ١٧٤، ٢٠٦، ٢٣٦، ٢٤٨، ٣٥٨، ٣٨٤، ٤٤٢، ٤٥٢، ٥٠٢، ٥٠٨، ٦٣٤، ٧٨٠

ذليل، أذلّة   150، 162، 186، 190، 258، 270،
280، 356، 522، 544، 586

تذلّل، تذليل   440، 442، 448

ذمّ، تذمّم   128، 134، 148، 190، 192، 202،
302، 310، 322، 336، 404، 428، 438،
506، 514، 524، 552، 568، 606، 692،
716

الدنيا   360، 714، 716

ذمّة، ذمم   266، 630، 642، 644، 654، 726

ذنب، ذنوب   128، 198، 212، 278، 288، 304،
322، 326، 402، 436، 476، 490، 508،
568، 570، 584، 614، 682، 698، 702،
722، 724، 728، 744، 752، 772، 786،
792، 808، 822

رأي   122، 132، 134، 142، 148، 160، 168، 222،
262، 268، 290، 294، 298، 306، 320،
352، 384، 400، 438، 482، 536، 548،
574، 576، 578، 594، 600، 648، 654،
666، 670، 688، 690، 692، 698، 710،
726، 728، 738، 780، 784

رجاء   208، 234، 236، 250، 288، 294، 360،
428، 466، 502، 588، 706

رحمة   106، 110، 170، 224، 240، 260، 266،
276، 288، 298، 326، 354، 358، 378،
390، 430، 434، 448، 464، 468، 472،
508، 560، 584، 624، 626، 640، 644،
646، 700، 716، 770، 806

ردّ الحجر   776

تردّد   288، 670، 686

رزق، أرزاق   140، 208، 224، 226، 238، 270،
286، 288، 326، 330، 350، 352، 420،
422، 514، 578، 584، 590، 634، 702

718، 742، 746، 762، 766، 786، 788،
796، 806، 810

رسالة، رسول، رسل، مرسلين. كثير الوقوع

رشد   208، 246، 294، 334، 336، 466، 558،
578، 592، 808

رضى، رضاء، راضي   278، 284، 404، 444،
478، 496، 536، 562، 626، 642، 678،
702، 706، 724، 784 792

رعاية، راعي، رعاة   158، 176، 248، 250، 254،
348، 412، 434، 526، 702، 722، 760

رغبة   234، 278، 366، 446، 470، 482، 508،
578، 646، 744، 788، 792، 814

ورهبة   148، 176، 548

رفد   204، 630

رفق   588، 616، 630، 634، 636، 668

ترقّب، تراقب   466، 684

أرامل   604

رهبة   148، 176، 422، 446، 548، 580، 744

رُوح، راحة   212، 508، 700، 796

روح   110، 212، 274، 282، 378، 440، 540،
722

روع   212، 434، 554، 602، 654، 788

رأفة   548

رواية الخبر، رواة   526، 702

رياء، مراء   140، 218، 686، 766، 790

ريب   232، 272، 280، 600

زكاة   180، 276، 448، 450، 476، 512، 718،
720، 738، 746

زمان   128، 144، 166، 186، 216، 224، 260،
270، 332، 402، 408، 426، 474، 496،
506، 522، 572، 592، 600، 604، 704،
710، 724، 738، 820

زنا 748

زهد، زهادة 102، 150، 154، 196، 202، 208، 464، 560، 574، 590، 678، 684، 710، 800، 812، 814

زاهد، زهّاد 102، 104، 156، 258، 282، 520، 706، 722، 814

زهو 628، 744

زاد، تزوّد، متزوّد 150، 170، 184، 198، 206، 210، 216، 280، 282، 284، 314، 356، 416، 480، 518، 560، 582، 588، 614، 696، 714، 716، 740

زور 220، 488، 618

زيغ 236، 298، 686

سَبْق 426، 548

سابق، سبّاقون، سبّاقين 112، 130، 138، 356، 394، 540، 714

سابقة، سابقات 198، 304، 538

سِباق، سبقة 148، 150، 264

ستر 154، 232، 268، 316، 322، 338، 362، 510، 602، 626، 684، 710، 746

سجّد، ساجد 236، 250، 440

مسجد 128، 226، 716

سخط، ساخط 110، 272، 366، 384، 404، 414، 444، 478، 580، 626، 678، 702، 742، 784

سخاء، سخيّ 308، 630، 632

سرّ 116، 146، 150، 154، 238، 248، 256، 268، 270، 272، 278، 312، 442، 480، 516، 558، 588، 590، 598، 620، 634، 666، 678، 768

تحصين ال 692

كتمان ال 726

سرور 110، 258، 286، 366، 504، 518، 552، 664، 716، 748، 782

سريرة، سرائر 206، 216، 268، 284، 294، 312، 336، 516، 540، 558، 690، 712، 766، 784، 808

إسراف 304، 550، 634، 638

سرقة 748

سعادة، سعيد 194، 210، 218، 308، 356، 646

سعير 212، 434، 440

ساعة (الحشر) 136، 184، 242، 260، 268، 308، 354، 356، 364، 382، 434، 440، 470، 706

سلطان 126، 160، 186، 272، 280، 312، 360، 384، 418، 424، 426، 428، 442، 454، 466، 474، 494، 580، 580، 592، 596، 600، 626، 644، 648، 704، 762، 768، 782

سكر 686

سكرة، سكرات 158، 210، 274، 338، 340، 346، 518

سكوت 770

سكون، سكينة، تسكين 186، 232، 336، 424، 448، 502، 504، 508، 556، 650

سلم 218، 220، 264، 300، 320، 380، 382، 392، 422، 430، 474، 534، 538، 638، 656، 662، 794، 810

سلام 478، 748

دار السلام 246

تسليم 178، 298، 712

استسلام 206، 446، 686

مسالمة 678

إسلام، مسلم، مسلمين، مسلمات. كثير الوقوع

سلوّ 738، 804

سفيه، سفهاء   160، 326، 450، 454، 738، 740، 746

سمح، سماحة   638، 630، 686

سمعة   140، 782

سنّة   112، 132، 180، 228، 264، 302، 312، 320، 330، 338، 372، 398، 412، 476، 516، 558، 628، 630، 646، 674، 684، 712، 752

سُنن   122، 278، 322، 334، 348، 380، 460، 496، 624، 628

تسويف   768

سؤال، مسألة   212، 228، 366، 478، 516، 576، 584، 640، 642، 692، 696، 752، 786، 790

سيّئة، سيّئات   174، 210، 312، 326، 332، 510، 584، 686، 690، 692

مسيء   154، 188، 650

شبهة، شبهات   114، 130، 132، 138، 162، 186، 220، 222، 232، 266، 298، 318، 334، 354، 384، 506، 578، 594، 632، 662، 708، 722، 802

شجاعة، شجاع   148، 632، 630، 678، 692

شحّ، شحيح   366، 510، 612، 624، 638

شدّة   120، 224، 298، 376، 434، 462، 548، 550، 594، 602، 604، 616، 728، 758، 786

شرّ   116، 144، 180، 192، 214، 260، 266، 276، 282، 286، 304، 308، 356، 372، 380، 382، 392، 398، 462، 464، 516، 534، 548، 560، 572، 588، 592، 596، 604، 628، 668، 686، 712، 726، 728، 744، 776، 782، 796، 800، 822. انظر أيضًا خير وشرّ

شرائع الدين   264، 294، 364، 472

شرف   138، 218، 266، 304، 324، 366، 474، 504، 540، 632، 710، 732، 792

تشريف   554، 748

شرك   218، 284، 400، 428، 548، 562، 746

مشرك، مشركين، مشركات   544، 562، 644

شَرَه   628، 792

شيطان، شياطين. كثير الوقوع

شفيع، شافع   396، 466، 468، 472، 694، 792

شفق، شفقة، شفيق   160، 206، 210، 234، 236، 366، 510، 578، 556، 576، 580، 622

شفاء   278، 344، 352، 396، 466، 470، 474، 492، 664، 716

شقاق   128، 256، 362، 534، 540، 570، 600، 646

مشقّة   352، 424، 582، 688

شقوة، شقيّ   110، 166، 184، 194، 218، 308، 356، 366، 644، 676، 806

شكّ   154، 178، 232، 284، 286، 392، 448، 546، 686، 702، 712، 722، 766

شكر، شاكر، شكور   202، 226، 238، 284، 304، 322، 354، 358، 406، 414، 432، 436، 464، 526، 532، 626، 668، 680، 718، 722، 736، 744، 766، 770، 782، 784، 812

شَكاة   568، 642

تشمير   510، 738

شنآن   442، 544، 686

شهوة، شهوات   184، 194، 200، 208، 218، 222، 234، 254، 266، 272، 278، 366، 378، 394، 422، 464، 518، 572، 624، 684، 692، 722، 724، 732، 746، 814

مشاورة، مشورة، استشارة   350، 480، 498، 594، 628، 688، 692، 704، 710، 738

شوق، مشتاق ‏378، 462، 656، 684، 722

شيب: تغيير ال ‏682، 822

شيمة ‏262

صبر ‏118، 198، 202، 238، 264، 284، 298، 338، 354، 390، 392، 396، 416، 430، 452، 462، 464، 478، 482، 524، 574، 592، 626، 644، 678، 684، 692، 698، 710، 720، 730، 738، 770، 804

صابر، صبور ‏300، 464، 478، 600، 642، 724، 782

صحّة ‏274، 584، 748، 800

وسقم ‏208، 416

صحبة، صاحب ‏120، 142، 156، 170، 178، 218، 244، 248، 250، 280، 304، 306، 314، 316، 332، 334، 336، 362، 366، 398، 404، 460، 482، 486، 552، 556، 570، 592، 620، 622، 652، 664، 666، 706، 748، 756، 762، 786، 788، 794، 822

صدق ‏122، 140، 166، 178، 206، 220، 250، 302، 326، 332، 356، 402، 522، 628، 634، 640، 686، 690، 716، 748، 782

وكذب ‏270، 486، 574، 642، 816

تصديق ‏106، 264، 358، 446، 460، 626، 650، 712، 718

صادق ‏150، 218، 226، 334، 348، 376، 394، 408، 500، 510، 526، 550

صدقة، صدقات ‏278، 512، 554، 558، 678، 704، 718، 720، 750، 764

صديق ‏580، 588، 590، 592، 718، 740، 744، 772

مصادقة ‏688

صرم ‏588

صفح ‏576، 624

صلاح، استصلاح ‏142، 268، 470، 496، 620، 624، 634، 670، 706، 710

ذات البين ‏616

صلاة ‏192، 202، 226، 276، 312، 476، 562، 564، 616، 622، 640، 702، 718، 746، 790

مصلّى ‏716

صلوات ‏194، 448

صلة، تواصل. انظر "و"

صمت ‏248، 334، 348، 464، 526، 586، 730، 740، 782، 820

أصنام ‏144، 230، 452

صواب ‏462، 582، 636، 746، 762، 784

صوم، صيام ‏202، 276، 296، 448، 616، 718، 720، 746، 808

أضحية ‏176

ضغن، أضغان، ضغائن ‏120، 248، 280، 352، 520، 544

ضلال، ضلالة، ضِلّة، ضالّ ‏112، 124، 132، 134، 148، 162، 178، 230، 268، 270، 304، 322، 332، 334، 340، 344، 396، 406، 444، 472، 482، 488، 492، 498، 502، 516، 536، 574، 578، 600، 612، 656، 662، 686، 730، 760

إطراء ‏496، 628، 632، 644

طعن ‏186، 300، 404، 442، 450، 530، 536، 546

طغيان ‏356

طلب ١٥٤، ١٨٢، ٢٠٦، ٢١٠، ٢٦٢، ٢٨٦، ٣٧٠،
٣٩٢، ٤٦٢، ٤٧٢، ٥١٦، ٥٣٤، ٥٤٠، ٥٤٦،
٥٧٨، ٥٨٠، ٥٨٦، ٦٠٠، ٦٢٢، ٦٣٤، ٦٤٠،
٦٤٢، ٦٤٤، ٦٤٨، ٦٥٢، ٦٦٠، ٦٦٨، ٦٩٤،
٧١٢، ٧٢٨، ٧٩٨، ٨٠٠، ٨٠٢، ٨١٠

طمع، مطامع، طامع ١٥٢، ٣٠٨، ٣٣٠، ٣٦٢،
٤٣٠، ٤٦٢، ٤٦٤، ٤٦٦، ٤٩٦، ٥٨٦، ٥٩٢،
٥٩٨، ٦١٢، ٦٣٢، ٦٣٤، ٦٧٨، ٧٠٦، ٧٠٨،
٧٢٨، ٧٦٦، ٧٤٠

طهر، مطهّر، تطهير ٢٤٦، ٢٦٢، ٣٦٢، ٤٢٤، ٦١٤،
٦٢٦، ٦٤٦

طاعة ١٥٨، ١٨٤، ٢٣٤، ٢٣٦، ٢٧٦، ٢٩٢، ٣٢٨،
٣٣٢، ٣٧٠، ٣٨٨، ٣٩٢، ٤٠٠، ٤٢٢، ٤٣٤،
٤٤٤، ٤٥٤، ٤٧٠، ٤٧٢، ٤٩٢، ٤٩٦، ٥٢٦،
٥٥٨، ٥٦٨، ٥٧٢، ٦٢٠، ٦٦٦، ٦٦٨، ٧٢٠،
٧٢٤، ٧٤٨، ٧٨٢، ٨١٠

وعصيان، معصية ٣٤٢، ٣٩٤، ٤٥٠، ٤٦٠،
٤٦٦، ٥٣٤، ٦٤٨، ٧٢٦، ٧٩٨، ٨٠٤، ٨٠٦

طول، استطالة ٤٠٦، ٦٢٠، ٧٠٤، ٧٤٠

طوبى ٤٠٠، ٤٩٢، ٦١٤، ٦٩٠، ٧٠٦، ٧١٢، ٧٦٨

ظفر ١٢٨، ١٤٦، ٢٠٠، ٢٩٠، ٥٦٤، ٥٩٠، ٦٠٦،
٦٨٠، ٦٩٢، ٦٩٤، ٧٢٤، ٧٣٨، ٧٨٢، ٧٩٢

ظلم، ظالم، مظلوم ١٢٠، ١٥٤، ١٨٠، ٢٤٨، ٢٥٢،
٣١٢، ٣٢٠، ٣١٨، ٣٤٢، ٣٤٤، ٣٥٨، ٣٩٢،
٤٠٠، ٤١٨، ٤٤٨، ٤٦٤، ٤٩٤، ٥١٢، ٥٦٨،
٥٧٠، ٥٨٢، ٥٨٨، ٥٩٠، ٦٠٦، ٦٠٨، ٦١٦،
٦٢٦، ٦٢٨، ٦٤٦، ٦٥٠، ٦٥٤، ٧١٠، ٧٣٠،
٧٤٦، ٧٤٨، ٧٧٢، ٧٨٤، ٧٨٦، ٧٩٤

ظلمة، ظلماء، ظلمات ١٢٢، ١٣٤، ٢١٠، ٢١٦، ٢٢٠،
٢٦٦، ٢٦٨، ٢٨٠، ٣٤٠، ٣٤٤، ٣٥٠، ٣٥٤،
٣٥٦، ٣٥٨، ٣٧٠، ٤٠٢، ٤٣٤، ٤٧٠، ٥٠٦،
٥٩٤، ٦١٢، ٦٦٢. انظر أيضًا نور وظلمة

ظنّ، ظنون ٢٢٢، ٢٣٢، ٢٣٨، ٢٥٢، ٤٤٠، ٤٦٢،
٤٩٦، ٥١٠، ٥١٢، ٥٣٨، ٥٩٠، ٦١٦، ٦٩٦،
٧٤٠، ٧٤٦

حسن، صالح ال ٥٤٨، ٥٦٠، ٦٢٨، ٦٣٠، ٦٣٦،
٦٤٢، ٧١٠

سوء ال ٤٧٨، ٦٢٨، ٦٣٦، ٧١٠، ٧٢٦

عبث ١٨٤، ٢١٦، ٤٦٨، ٦٩٦، ٧٩٢

عبادة ١١٠، ١١٤، ١٧٠، ٢٣٤، ٢٧٢، ٣٣٢، ٣٤٦،
٣٨٦، ٣٩٦، ٤٥٨، ٤٦٢، ٤٧٢، ٥٥٨، ٦٦٨،
٧٠٢، ٧٠٤، ٧١٠، ٧٤٤

عباد الله. كثير الوقوع

عبرة، عبر، اعتبار ١١٢، ١٣٠، ١٣٦، ٢٠٤، ٢٠٨،
٢١٤، ٢٦٤، ٢٧٨، ٢٨٦، ٣٣٦، ٣٤٤، ٣٥٦،
٤١٠، ٤٤٦، ٤٥٢، ٤٩٠، ٥٠٢، ٥٠٤، ٥٥٢،
٦٣٦، ٦٨٤، ٧٢٤، ٧٧٢، ٧٩٠

عثرة، عثرات ٢١٢، ٤١٦، ٤٣٤، ٦٨٢

عُجْب، إعجاب ١١٨، ١٣٢، ١٣٨، ١٤٦، ٢١٤، ٢٢٢،
٢٣٤، ٢٧٠، ٣٦٨، ٤٢٠، ٥٣٨، ٥٦٢، ٥٨٢،
٦٤٤، ٧٢٨، ٧٤٠، ٧٤٤

عجائب ١٣٤، ٢٢٨، ٢٣٠، ٣٤٤، ٣٥٠، ٣٧٤، ٤٦٦،
٤٩٠

عجز، عاجز ١٥٨، ١٨٦، ٢٢٨، ٢٥٠، ٤١٨، ٤٢٦،
٥٨٠، ٦٥٤، ٦٧٨، ٦٨٠، ٧٣٦، ٧٩٨، ٨١٦

عجلة، معاجلة ٦٤٦، ٣٤٦، ٧٦٦، ٧٩٠

استعداد ١٦٨، ٥١٨

عدل ١٣٠، ١٩٤، ٢٢٠، ٢٢٢، ٢٤٠، ٢٤٦، ٢٦٦،
٣٠٦، ٣١٠، ٣١٨، ٣٢٠، ٤٠٠، ٤١٨، ٤٣٦،
٤٧٤، ٤٩٢، ٤٩٤، ٤٩٦، ٤٩٨، ٥١٠، ٥١٦،
٥٥٤، ٥٦٠، ٦١٦، ٦٢٦، ٦٣٠، ٦٣٦، ٦٣٨،
٦٥٢، ٦٦٨، ٦٨٤، ٧٤٠، ٧٤٢، ٧٩٦، ٨١٢،
٨٢٢

وجور ١٣٠، ٣٠٢، ٦٢٤، ٦٥٢، ٦٦٨، ٧٨٤

عدوان 298، 342، 346، 482، 622، 740، 794

عدوّ، أعداء. كثير الوقوع

عذر، إعذار، معذرة 202، 204، 216، 238، 276، 326، 332، 468، 474، 482، 508، 510، 544، 568، 590، 622، 626، 630، 638، 640، 642، 644، 646، 652، 660، 672، 768، 770، 782

معرفة 110، 148، 226، 410، 432، 436، 488، 572، 720، 740

معروف 134، 174، 202، 222، 224، 278، 324، 332، 412، 422، 464، 522، 554، 602، 736، 794

أمر بال 310، 352، 454، 574، 618، 686، 746، 796

عزّ، عزّة 108، 114، 158، 228، 232، 236، 252، 310، 314، 366، 408، 412، 426، 438، 446، 450، 452، 454، 468، 472، 476، 490، 496، 502، 566، 600، 628، 630، 746، 782، 792

وذلّ 158، 248، 270، 428، 438، 452، 474، 496، 534

إعزاز 316، 490، 624

عزم، عزيمة، عزائم 110، 112، 114، 170، 182، 194، 232، 234، 264، 346، 386، 438، 442، 446، 452، 460، 510، 526، 592، 594، 746، 756، 806، 812، 824

عسف، تعسف، متعسف 344، 556، 778، 822

عصبيّة 438، 440، 442، 444، 450

عصمة 322، 352، 384، 786

اعتصام 340، 526

بحبل الله 574

عصيان، معصية 114، 142، 148، 154، 160، 184، 216، 238، 256، 276، 322، 344،

430، 440، 510، 522، 596، 724، 770، 786، 792. انظر أيضًا طاعة وعصيان، معصية

عطف 322، 378، 620، 628، 632، 738، 746

عطاء، إعطاء 226، 240، 304، 404، 468، 514، 576، 584، 626، 646، 694

عفّة، عفاف 270، 586، 692، 694، 748، 784

عفو 448، 510، 516، 552، 624، 626، 668، 680، 692، 738، 808

عافية 208، 212، 222، 252، 320، 450، 504، 514، 716، 800، 808

عقوق 444

عاقبة 132، 396، 448، 588، 590، 618، 640، 666، 724، 738

عواقب 122، 162، 186، 312، 390، 406، 634، 644

العاقبة للمتّقين 120، 252

عقل 218، 228، 264، 272، 274، 348، 360، 364، 366، 434، 476، 494، 500، 504، 508، 514، 522، 526، 534، 536، 588، 626، 658، 660، 676، 692، 694، 702، 708، 720، 738، 748، 754، 768، 772، 778، 802، 808، 814

عاقل 592، 678، 688، 710، 744، 800

علم، علوم 112، 114، 116، 124، 134، 138، 148، 152، 154، 166، 186، 194، 198، 200، 228، 236، 238، 240، 264، 268، 270، 276، 278، 284، 290، 298، 308، 328، 334، 336، 344، 348، 352، 358، 370، 390، 398، 406، 414، 422، 426، 428، 436، 448، 456، 462، 464، 468، 474، 476، 490، 492، 516، 526، 576، 584، 610، 642، 662، 678، 684، 686، 690، 700،

علم، علوم (cont.) ‏702، 706، 710، 720، 722،
736، 740، 766، 768، 784، 790، 794،
810، 822

عالم، علماء ‏108، 116، 120، 132، 134، 160،
186، 190، 220، 258، 269، 302، 312،
342، 440، 446، 448، 456، 462، 474،
490، 522، 562، 628، 648، 664، 706،
720، 778، 794

عليم ‏308، 336، 368

تعليم، تعلّم ‏158، 200، 308، 436، 576، 578،
694

علياء، علوّ ‏120، 122، 172، 268، 380، 420، 458،
578، 816

تعمّق ‏228، 686

عمل ‏120، 140، 148، 150، 154، 166، 198، 204،
208، 216، 222، 246، 258، 274، 284، 286،
302، 308، 312، 314، 320، 328، 348، 360،
372، 384، 396، 400، 406، 408، 416، 436،
440، 460، 464، 476، 494، 496، 498، 518،
522، 526، 534، 562، 594، 596، 616، 618،
624، 628، 634، 640، 642، 646، 648، 652،
666، 682، 686، 690، 702، 708، 712، 714،
722، 724، 740، 764، 766، 784، 786، 790،
798، 806، 816.

عامل. أعمال. كثير الوقوع

عمى ‏216، 218، 220، 328، 372، 396، 402،
406، 428، 470، 498، 586، 592، 668

تعنّت، متعنّت ‏778، 784

عنف ‏226، 244، 630

عناء ‏202، 286، 428، 464، 720

عهد ‏128، 194، 214، 322، 478، 496، 502،
524، 532، 548، 558، 612، 624، 630،
642، 644، 646، 662، 672

استعاذة ‏700، 778

استعانة، معونة ‏200، 232، 280، 304، 330،
350، 404، 428، 480، 578، 596، 622،
626، 628، 630، 632، 654، 718، 736

عار ‏188، 300، 386، 454، 568، 634، 648، 678

عِيّ ‏314، 432، 466، 504، 506، 640، 786

عيب، عيوب، عائب ‏116، 212، 222، 284، 322،
360، 364، 400، 412، 516، 626، 636،
638، 642، 678، 692، 740، 786، 788،
792، 796

غبط، مغبوط ‏218، 274، 286، 762، 798

غدر ‏122، 166، 196، 388، 478، 500، 514، 644،
738، 750

غِرّة، غرور ‏116، 204، 210، 218، 220، 224،
274، 278، 282، 342، 392، 532، 572،
662، 706، 768، 784

غربة، غريب ‏212، 282، 356، 500، 516، 574،
592، 678، 692، 694، 702، 714، 748

غِشّ ‏218، 292، 396، 558، 588، 768

غصب ‏744

غضّ البصر ‏128، 154، 300، 462

غضب ‏416، 442، 468، 512، 530، 630، 646،
666، 668، 672، 674، 686، 706، 728

غفران، مغفرة ‏112، 114، 170، 174، 200، 240،
718، 812

استغفار ‏326، 700، 718، 806

غفلة ‏108، 152، 158، 184، 216، 268، 272، 344،
346، 430، 464، 510، 540، 608، 636،
666، 740

غلبة ‏124، 216، 452، 564، 786، 818

غالب، مغلوب ‏224، 264، 280، 322، 366،
436، 454، 490، 518، 564، 758، 782، 796

غالي ‏116، 708

غمّ ‏366، 434، 464، 498، 782

غنى ‏270، 314، 348، 396، 428، 444، 446، 462، 582، 586، 590، 626، 630، 634، 686، 688، 692، 706، 716، 738، 784، 788، 814

غنيّ، أغنياء ‏308، 450، 460، 712، 724، 742، 782، 802، 808

استغناء ‏782

إغاثة ‏144، 164، 682

غنّي ‏142، 302، 336، 396، 482، 540، 668، 808

غيب ‏308

غِيبة ‏270، 492، 546، 718، 816

غيرة، غيور ‏594، 692، 712، 774

غيظ ‏148، 270، 346، 450، 464، 498، 590، 664، 666، 706، 732

فتنة، فتن ‏114، 116، 124، 132، 140، 172، 184، 194، 202، 210، 224، 242، 244، 246، 256، 258، 326، 338، 340، 342، 348، 352، 354، 372، 386، 414، 430، 432، 444، 516، 524، 532، 548، 576، 662، 666، 678، 700، 724، 770، 780

مفتون ‏116، 156، 266، 680، 710، 816

فجور ‏116، 270، 356، 586

فاجر ‏164، 166، 492، 602، 648، 688، 704

فحش، فاحشة ‏260، 464، 574، 588

فخر، مفاخرة ‏124، 252، 346، 442، 450، 496، 502، 814

فراسة ‏636، 670

فرصة ‏588، 592، 614، 644، 790

إضاعة ال ‏710

انتهاز ال ‏166، 190، 682

فرائض ‏112، 382، 498، 624، 640، 642، 706، 710، 764، 776، 798

ونوافل ‏688، 768

فرط، إفراط، تفريط ‏134، 304، 306، 356، 508، 586، 620، 624، 662، 686، 694، 706، 714، 730، 782

فُرقة، افتراق ‏296، 298، 306، 332، 384، 400، 404، 450، 452، 478

فزع ‏402، 434، 470، 472، 502، 504، 758

فساد، مفسدة، فاسد ‏120، 154، 260، 310، 346، 402، 450، 456، 470، 490، 588، 706، 710

فسوق، فاسق ‏270، 328، 444، 656، 686

فضل، تفضّل ‏194، 196، 204، 240، 242، 254، 266، 298، 326، 340، 354، 406، 416، 426، 434، 442، 444، 448، 450، 464، 494، 508، 510، 546، 548، 550، 558، 564، 572، 590، 602، 620، 628، 636، 644، 664، 712، 742، 784، 816، 820

فضائل ‏112، 324، 462، 564

فضيلة ‏266

فقد ‏106، 340، 366، 504، 694، 766

تفقّد ‏630، 634، 638

فقر ‏278، 308، 428، 446، 450، 486، 512، 628، 678، 688، 692، 694، 708، 712، 726، 764، 778، 784، 814

فقير، فقراء ‏238، 270، 308، 324، 362، 486، 522، 558، 712، 724، 782، 794، 802

فقه، تفقّه ‏380، 524، 574، 778

فقيه، فقهاء ‏474، 700

فكر ‏222، 228، 230، 234، 346، 360، 378، 420، 490، 506، 578، 678، 688، 790

فكرة 422

تفكّر، مفكّر 208، 258، 344، 450، 578، 588، 710، 724

فهم، تفهّم 264، 408، 576، 578، 632، 684

فناء 170، 174، 202، 206، 208، 252، 282، 286، 356، 378، 410، 418، 426، 428، 514، 552، 574، 584، 712، 716، 790، 794

فوز 184، 324

فاقة 114، 206، 234، 238، 242، 396، 462، 508، 558، 582، 706، 790، 792، 800

قبلة 114، 390

قتل، قاتل، قتال. كثير الوقوع

قَدَر، أقدار 130، 230، 232، 370، 396، 564، 568، 648، 696، 734، 740، 768، 770

قدرة 106، 108، 166، 228، 230، 272، 332، 334، 342، 360، 374، 384، 412، 418، 420، 428، 466، 494، 510، 626، 646، 666، 680

قدير 242، 326

قرار 194، 204، 314، 350، 364، 378، 386، 426، 434، 448، 452، 480، 490، 580

قرابة، قرابات 140، 298، 324، 456، 548، 566، 642، 702، 732، 738، 774

قربان 476، 718

قرآن، كتاب الله. كثير الوقوع

قاسطين 456

قسوة 548

قصاص 400، 748

قصد 132، 220، 246، 258، 294، 366، 430، 442، 462، 466، 470، 506، 564، 568، 578، 582، 592، 594، 718

اقتصاد 462

تقصير 234، 240، 398، 706، 786، 798

قطيعة 548، 590، 592، 642، 670

قلب، قلوب. كثير الوقوع

قناعة 154، 446، 534، 692، 742، 786، 792، 822

مقنوط 170

قهر 156، 342، 442، 452

استقامة 396

قوّة 172، 212، 216، 280، 382، 384، 446، 462، 476، 510، 634، 736

لا قوّة إلّا بالله 622، 646، 802

قيامة. كثير الوقوع

كبر، تكبّر، استكبار، متكبّر 210، 258، 346، 360، 418، 440، 442، 444، 448، 450، 460، 464، 496، 550، 560، 712، 746، 792

كبرياء 246، 438، 466، 498

كذب 130، 214، 222، 270، 312، 328، 332، 456، 486، 488، 574، 642، 666، 748، 816

كاذب، كذّاب، مكذّب 218، 348، 354، 360، 438، 458، 460، 486، 510، 526، 566، 598، 688، 748، 776

مكربة، مكروب 210، 682

كرم 204، 246، 322، 630، 674، 708، 746

كريم 264، 416، 508، 602، 642، 692، 740

مكارم 324، 450، 456، 748

اكتساب الإخوان 680

كسل 258

كظم، كظوم 144، 216، 270، 450، 464، 498، 666، 790

كعبة، حلّي ال 764

كفاف 690، 792

كفر 136، 180، 308، 396، 454، 460، 546، 572، 686، 712

كافر، كافرين 136، 156، 200، 230، 538، 542، 736، 808

كفّارة، كفّارات 476، 682

استكانة 206، 446

لجاج، لجاجة، لجج 236، 468، 588، 614، 646، 728، 786

لذّة 262، 514، 540، 560، 664، 712، 722، 800

لعب 214، 312، 504، 512، 574، 696

لطف 428، 496، 500، 510، 588، 624، 630، 632، 748

لهو 212، 504، 612، 670، 724، 792

لواط 748

لوم 460، 574

لئيم 692

تلوّن 120، 400، 466

لين 290، 462، 464، 548، 588، 590، 616، 664، 710، 782

أمثال 112، 198، 204، 206، 398، 412، 452، 454، 580، 652، 720

تمحيص 448، 450، 492

مارقة، مارقين 198، 456

مروّة، مروّات 682، 692

تماري 686

مزحة 814

مسكنة 242، 450، 558، 630

مسكين، مساكين 452، 558، 606، 638، 774، 806

مقت 282، 644، 778، 790

مكر 298، 464، 700، 796

ملول 738

مملول 768، 812

ملق 786

ملائكة 232، 272، 276، 396، 408، 440، 470، 480، 508، 532، 716

منّ، منّة، امتنان 208، 338، 354، 364، 384، 406، 450، 466، 504، 644، 738

مُنى، أمنيّة 194، 210، 214، 254، 278، 540، 588، 686، 694، 738

موت، أموات. كثير الوقوع

مائق 770

مال، أموال. كثير الوقوع

نبوّة، نبيّ، أنبياء. كثير الوقوع

نجاة، منجاة 124، 156، 180، 198، 218، 244، 260، 264، 300، 352، 366، 506، 510، 580، 658، 720

ندم، ندامة 110، 148، 160، 178، 184، 274، 280، 298، 442، 476، 508، 716، 730، 806

نزاع، تنازع 686

نزاهة 464

نصح، نصيحة، تناصح 158، 160، 184، 218، 246، 248، 262، 276، 284، 296، 316، 394، 466، 496، 572، 580، 588، 590، 602، 622، 630، 632، 636، 710

نصر، نصرة، انتصار 116، 128، 142، 152، 164، 178، 190، 208، 244، 252، 304، 316، 330، 380، 392، 404، 416، 454، 472، 490، 568، 600، 622، 624، 656، 680، 758، 762

نَصَفة، إنصاف، نصف 138، 146، 318، 450، 622، 624، 626، 630، 638، 642، 704، 740، 742

نطق، منطق 122، 194، 240، 260، 270، 274، 322، 334، 336، 344، 408، 438، 462، 502، 504، 522، 526، 586

نعمة 110، 114، 116، 170، 184، 194، 266، 308، 320، 326، 328، 340، 392، 402، 420، 428، 430، 450، 452، 454، 472، 496، 510، 532، 562، 564، 572، 584، 586، 590، 620، 626، 644، 646، 666، 732، 740، 742، 746، 788، 798

نعم. كثير الوقوع

نعيم 216، 252، 286، 366، 428، 434، 454، 514، 550، 742، 800

نفس، نفوس، أنفس. كثير الوقوع

نفاق 128، 396، 466، 698

منافق، منافقين 116، 136، 398، 466، 486، 488، 522، 562، 686، 690، 698

منكر 134، 138، 202، 222، 310، 318، 328، 332، 358، 464، 494، 522، 574، 602، 794، 796

نهي عن ال 264، 310، 352، 454، 506، 618، 686، 746، 796

ناكثين 266، 334، 456، 572

نور، أنوار 162، 194، 224، 228، 232، 238، 240، 246، 264، 278، 350، 352، 358، 364، 368، 370، 414، 432، 440، 448، 474، 490، 506، 574، 610، 644، 720، 794

وظلمة 280، 282، 408، 410، 414، 422، 474، 490

نار. كثير الوقوع

نيّة 436، 576، 584، 640

صدق ال 122، 402، 690

هجرة 180، 364، 432، 454، 524، 660

هدى، هداية 132، 148، 218، 220، 224، 228، 244، 250، 260، 320، 328، 332، 396، 402، 406، 414، 464، 466، 474، 478، 492، 494، 498، 508، 516، 562، 568، 586، 656، 668، 738، 794

هادي 204، 364، 382، 384، 396، 518

هرم 208، 556، 720

هزل 438

همّ، هموم 146، 218، 406، 464، 504، 538، 552، 572، 574، 578، 584، 592، 612، 632، 638، 642، 646، 664، 714، 720، 762، 782، 788، 790، 796

همّة، همم 106، 234، 236، 246، 404، 522، 526، 692، 792، 816

هول 206، 434، 686

هوان، استهانة 278، 412، 558، 608، 684، 786، 798

تهاون 454

هوى 198، 210، 218، 220، 306، 320، 394، 400، 436، 482، 496، 532، 534، 536، 546، 576، 592، 626، 634، 646، 652، 674، 738، 770

هيبة 234، 274، 490، 682، 740، 778

ثقة 158، 286، 264، 302، 400، 636، 638، 644، 740

توحيد 106، 232، 242، 382، 422، 820

وحشة 204، 272، 356، 428، 472، 504، 600، 688، 714

وحشيّة 692

وحي 108، 110، 194، 232، 260، 314، 326، 390، 458، 470، 716

ودّ، مودّة، تودّد 140، 270، 304، 336، 338،
678، 720، 738، 740، 774

وراثة، ميراث 116، 304، 518، 606، 678، 692،
708

وارث، ورّاث، وارثين 224، 312، 738، 784

ورع 152، 202، 396، 610، 628، 678، 708،
786، 792

سعة الصدر 728

صلة، تواصل 512، 514، 548، 588، 590، 592،
618

الرحم 278، 322، 704، 746

وصيّ، أوصياء 222، 410

وصية 110، 116، 188، 336، 542، 544، 552،
554، 572، 576، 578، 616، 674

تواضع، متواضع 114، 232، 440، 442، 444،
448، 462، 550، 638، 710، 740،
802

وعظ، موعظة، عظة 216، 246، 248، 262،
364، 398، 472، 510، 536، 574، 592،
684، 716، 724 768

وعد، عدة 110، 112، 278، 282، 330، 360، 396،
434، 696

وعيد 216، 434، 440، 454، 696

توفيق 104، 570، 578، 708، 738، 824

وفاء 158، 166، 200، 450، 556، 634، 642،
644، 750

وقار، وقور 464، 556

تقوى، تقى 130، 132، 146، 198، 204، 210،
278، 284، 312، 328، 356، 366، 390،
398، 410، 414، 430، 434، 436، 466،
468، 470، 472، 480، 518، 554، 558،
574، 578، 612، 616، 624، 702، 708، 714،
746، 792، 800، 802

تقيّ، أتقياء، متّقين 120، 166، 206، 208،
252، 278، 460، 462، 560، 596، 708،
718، 738

توكّل، اتكال 366، 556، 588

وَلاية 116، 482، 492، 494

وليّ 514، 556، 566، 702

أولياء الله 146، 162، 224، 282، 310، 446،
516، 628، 654، 716، 722، 788، 804، 810

أولياء الشيطان 172

وليّ الدم، أولياء المقتول 552، 644

إيمان، مؤمن، مؤمنين. كثير الوقوع

وهن 110، 258، 384، 544، 576، 594، 646

ونى، تواني 236، 258، 744

يأس 288، 454، 466، 586، 592، 706

يتامى، أيتام 604، 606، 616

يعسوب الدين والمؤمنين 752، 778

يقين 110، 116، 138، 162، 218، 230، 232، 238،
284، 286، 342، 356، 402، 462، 546،
568، 574، 586، 592، 656، 684، 702،
712، 722، 766، 794